HOLT McDOUGAL
a division of Houghton Mifflin Harcourt

INDIANA

UNITED STATES HISTORY
GROWTH AND DEVELOPMENT: BEGINNINGS TO 1914

correlated to

Indiana

Academic Standards for Social Studies

CONTENTS

Indiana Program Advisers

Program Consultant
Jill Anne Hahn
Evansville Central High School
Evansville, Indiana

Teacher Reviewers
Christopher G. Cavanaugh
Plainfield High School
Plainfield, Indiana

D. Drew Horvath
Lawrence Central High School
Indianapolis, Indiana

Teacher Advisory Panel
Todd A. Kendrick
Franklin Central High School
Indianapolis, Indiana

Sam Fies
Highland Middle School
Schererville, Indiana

Mary Jane Smith
Warren Central High School
South Greenfield, Indiana

Printed in the United States of America

ISBN-13: 978-0-55-401665-8
ISBN-10: 0-55-401665-6
2 3 0914 10 09

Explanation of Correlation The following document is a correlation of **Holt *United States History: Beginnings to 1914* © 2009** to the Indiana Social Studies Standards (2008). The correlation provides a cross-reference between the skills in the standards and representative page numbers where those skills are taught or assessed. Those references marked with an asterisk represent pages which offer secondary support or where application of the required skill is implied.

The references contained in this correlation reflect the interpretation by Holt McDougal of the Indiana Social Studies Standards.

Key to References

PREFIX	EXPLANATION
SE	*Student's Edition*

Chapter correlation of *Holt McDougal United States History: Beginnings to 1914* to the

Indiana Academic Standards for Social Studies

Chapter	Indiana Academic Standards, Grade 8
Chapter 1 The World before the Opening of the Atlantic	**8.1.1** Identify major Native American Indian groups of eastern North America and describe early conflict and cooperation with European settlers and the influence the two cultures had on each other; **8.3.1** Read maps to interpret symbols and determine the land forms and human features that represent physical and cultural characteristics of areas in the United States; **8.3.3** Identify and locate the major climate regions in the United States and describe the characteristics of these regions.
Chapter 2 New Empires in the Americas	**8.1.1** Identify major Native American Indian groups of eastern North America and describe early conflict and cooperation with European settlers and the influence the two cultures had on each other; **8.1.2** Explain the struggle of the British, French, Spanish and Dutch to gain control of North America during settlement and colonization; **8.1.30** Formulate historical questions by analyzing primary resources and secondary resources about an issue confronting the United States during the period from 1754–1877; **8.3.1** Read maps to interpret symbols and determine the land forms and human features that represent physical and cultural characteristics of areas in the United States; **8.3.7** Using maps identify changes influenced by growth, economic development and human migration in the eighteenth and nineteenth centuries; **8.4.1** Identify economic factors contributing to European exploration and colonization in North America, the American Revolution and the drafting of the Constitution of the United States.

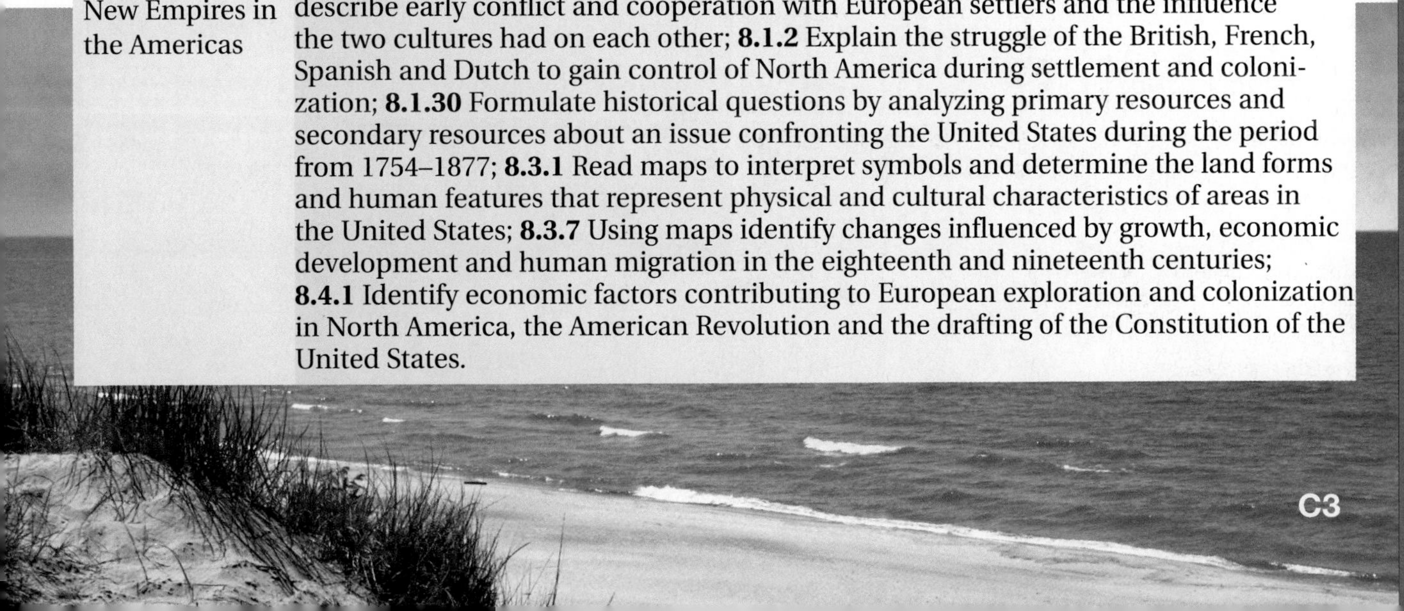

Indiana

The Hoosier State

Chapter 3
The English Colonies

8.1.1 Identify major Native American Indian groups of eastern North America and describe early conflict and cooperation with European settlers and the influence the two cultures had on each other; **8.1.2** Explain the struggle of the British, French, Spanish and Dutch to gain control of North America during settlement and colonization; **8.1.3** Identify and explain the conditions, causes, consequences and significance of the French and Indian War (1754–1763), and the resistance and rebellion against British imperial rule by the thirteen colonies in North America (1761–1775); **8.1.4** Identify fundamental ideas in the Declaration of Independence (1776) and analyze the causes and effects of the Revolutionary War (1775–1783), including enactment of the Articles of Confederation and the Treaty of Paris; **8.1.9** Describe the influence of important individuals on social and political developments of the time such as the Independence movement and the framing of the Constitution; **8.1.29** Differentiate between facts and historical interpretations recognizing that the historian's narrative reflects his or her judgment about the significance of particular facts; **8.1.30** Formulate historical questions by analyzing primary sources and secondary sources about an issue confronting the United States during the period from 1754–1877; **8.2.8** Explain ways that citizens can participate in political parties, campaigns and elections; **8.2.9** Explain how citizens can monitor and influence the development and implementation of public policies at local, state and national levels of government; **8.3.1** Read maps to interpret symbols and determine the land forms and human features that represent physical and cultural characteristics of areas in the United States; **8.3.2** Identify and create maps showing the physical growth and development of the United States from settlement of the original 13 colonies through Reconstruction (1877), including transportation routes used during the period; **8.3.5** Describe the importance of the major mountain ranges and the major river systems in the development of the United States; **8.3.6** Identify the agricultural regions of the United States and be able to give reasons for the type of land use and subsequent land development during different historical periods; **8.3.7** Using maps identify changes influenced by growth, economic development and human migration in the eighteenth and nineteenth centuries; **8.4.1** Identify economic factors contributing to European exploration and colonization in North America, the American Revolution and the drafting of the Constitution of the United States; **8.4.2** Illustrate elements of the three types of economic systems, using cases from United States history; **8.4.9** Explain and evaluate examples of domestic and international interdependence throughout United States history.

Chapter 4 The American Revolution	**8.1.1** Identify major Native American Indian groups of eastern North America and describe early conflict and cooperation with European settlers and the influence the two cultures had on each other; **8.1.3** Identify and explain the conditions, causes, consequences and significance of the French and Indian War (1754–1763), and the resistance and rebellion against British imperial rule by the thirteen colonies in North America (1761–1775); **8.1.4** Identify fundamental ideas in the Declaration of Independence (1776) and analyze the causes and effects of the Revolutionary War (1775–1783), including enactment of the Articles of Confederation and the Treaty of Paris; **8.1.9** Describe the influence of important individuals on social and political developments of the time such as the Independence movement and the framing of the Constitution; **8.1.28** Recognize historical perspective and evaluate alternative courses of action by describing the historical context in which events unfolded and by avoiding evaluation of the past solely in terms of present-day norms; **8.1.29** Differentiate between facts and historical interpretations recognizing that the historian's narrative reflects his or her judgment about the significance of particular facts; **8.1.30** Formulate historical questions by analyzing primary sources and secondary sources about an issue confronting the United States during the period from 1754–1877; **8.2.1** Identify and explain essential ideas of constitutional government, which are expressed in the founding documents of the United States, including the Virginia Declaration of Rights, the Declaration of Independence, the Virginia Statute for Religious Freedom, the Massachusetts Constitution of 1780, the Northwest Ordinance, the 1787 U.S. Constitution, the Bill of Rights, the Federalist and Anti-Federalist Papers, Common Sense, Washington's Farewell Address (1796), and Jefferson's First Inaugural Address (1801); **8.3.2** Identify and create maps showing the physical growth and development of the United States from settlement of the original 13 colonies through Reconstruction (1877), including transportation routes used during the period.

Indiana
The Hoosier State

Chapter 5
Forming a Government

8.1.4 Identify fundamental ideas in the Declaration of Independence (1776) and analyze the causes and effects of the Revolutionary War (1775–1783), including enactment of the Articles of Confederation and the Treaty of Paris; **8.1.5** Identify and explain key events leading to the creation of a strong union among the thirteen original states and in the establishment of the United States as a federal republic; **8.1.9** Describe the influence of important individuals on social and political developments of the time such as the Independence movement and the framing of the Constitution; **8.1.16** Describe the abolition of slavery in the northern states, including the conflicts and compromises associated with westward expansion of slavery; **8.1.28** Recognize historical perspective and evaluate alternative courses of action by describing the historical context in which events unfolded and by avoiding evaluation of the past solely in terms of present-day norms; **8.1.29** Differentiate between facts and historical interpretations recognizing that the historian's narrative reflects his or her judgment about the significance of particular facts; **8.1.30** Formulate historical questions by analyzing primary sources and secondary sources about an issue confronting the United States during the period from 1754–1877; **8.2.1** Identify and explain essential ideas of constitutional government, which are expressed in the founding documents of the United States, including the Virginia Declaration of Rights, the Declaration of Independence, the Virginia Statute for Religious Freedom, the Massachusetts Constitution of 1780, the Northwest Ordinance, the 1787 U.S. Constitution, the Bill of Rights, the Federalist and Anti-Federalist Papers, Common Sense, Washington's Farewell Address (1796), and Jefferson's First Inaugural Address (1801); **8.2.3** Explain how and why legislative, executive and judicial powers are distributed, shared and limited in the constitutional government of the United States; **8.2.5** Compare, and contrast the powers reserved to the federal and state government under the Articles of Confederation and the United States Constitution; **8.2.6** Distinguish among the different functions of national and state government within the federal system by analyzing the United States Constitution and the Indiana Constitution; **8.2.8** Explain ways that citizens can participate in political parties, campaigns and elections; **8.2.9** Explain how citizens can monitor and influence the development and implementation of public policies at local, state and national levels of government; **8.3.1** Read maps to interpret symbols and determine the land forms and human features that represent physical and cultural characteristics of areas in the United States; **8.3.2** Identify and create maps showing the physical growth and development of the United States from settlement of the original 13 colonies through Reconstruction (1877), including transportation routes used during the period; **8.3.7** Using maps identify changes influenced by growth, economic development and human migration in the eighteenth and nineteenth centuries; **8.4.1** Identify economic factors contributing to European exploration and colonization in North America, the American Revolution and the drafting of the Constitution of the United States; **8.4.9** Explain and evaluate examples of domestic and international interdependence throughout United States history.

Chapter 6 Citizenship and the Constitution

8.1.9 Describe the influence of important individuals on social and political developments of the time such as the Independence movement and the framing of the Constitution; **8.1.28** Recognize historical perspective and evaluate alternative courses of action by describing the historical context in which events unfolded and by avoiding evaluation of the past solely in terms of present-day norms; **8.1.29** Differentiate between facts and historical interpretations recognizing that the historian's narrative reflects his or her judgment about the significance of particular facts; **8.1.30** Formulate historical questions by analyzing primary sources and secondary sources about an issue confronting the United States during the period from 1754–1877; **8.2.1** Identify and explain essential ideas of constitutional government, which are expressed in the founding documents of the United States, including the Virginia Declaration of Rights, the Declaration of Independence, the Virginia Statute for Religious Freedom, the Massachusetts Constitution of 1780, the Northwest Ordinance, the 1787 U.S. Constitution, the Bill of Rights, the Federalist and Anti-Federalist Papers, Common Sense, Washington's Farewell Address (1796), and Jefferson's First Inaugural Address (1801); **8.2.2** Identify and explain the relationship between rights and responsibilities of citizenship in the United States; **8.2.3** Explain how and why legislative, executive and judicial powers are distributed, shared and limited in the constitutional government of the United States; **8.2.4** Examine functions of the national government in the lives of people; **8.2.6** Distinguish among the different functions of national and state government within the federal system by analyzing the United States Constitution and the Indiana Constitution; **8.2.7** Explain the importance in a democratic republic of responsible participation by citizens in voluntary civil associations/ nongovernmental organizations that comprise civil society; **8.2.8** Explain ways that citizens can participate in political parties, campaigns and elections; **8.2.9** Explain how citizens can monitor and influence the development and implementation of public policies at local, state and national levels of government; **8.2.10** Research and defend positions on issues in which fundamental values and principles related to the United States Constitution are in conflict, using a variety of information resources.

Chapter 7 Launching the Nation	**8.1.6** Identify the steps in the implementation of the federal government under the United States Constitution, including the First and Second Congresses of the United States (1789–1792); **8.1.7** Describe the origin and development of political parties, the Federalists and the Democratic-Republicans (1793–1801), and examine points of agreement and disagreement between these parties; **8.1.9** Describe the influence of important individuals on social and political developments of the time such as the Independence movement and the framing of the Constitution; **8.1.28** Recognize historical perspective and evaluate alternative courses of action by describing the historical context in which events unfolded and by avoiding evaluation of the past solely in terms of present-day norms; **8.1.29** Differentiate between facts and historical interpretations recognizing that the historian's narrative reflects his or her judgment about the significance of particular facts; **8.1.30** Formulate historical questions by analyzing primary sources and secondary sources about an issue confronting the United States during the period from 1754–1877; **8.2.1** Identify and explain essential ideas of constitutional government, which are expressed in the founding documents of the United States, including the Virginia Declaration of Rights, the Declaration of Independence, the Virginia Statute for Religious Freedom, the Massachusetts Constitution of 1780, the Northwest Ordinance, the 1787 U.S. Constitution, the Bill of Rights, the Federalist and Anti-Federalist Papers, Common Sense, Washington's Farewell Address (1796), and Jefferson's First Inaugural Address (1801); **8.2.4** Examine functions of the national government in the lives of people; **8.2.7** Explain the importance in a democratic republic of responsible participation by citizens in voluntary civil associations/ nongovernmental organizations that comprise civil society; **8.2.10** Research and defend positions on issues in which fundamental values and principles related to the United States Constitution are in conflict, using a variety of information resources; **8.4.4** Explain the basic economic functions of the government in the economy of the United States; **8.4.5** Analyze contributions of entrepreneurs and inventors in the development of the United States economy; **8.4.8** Examine the development of the banking system in the United States.

Chapter 8
The Jefferson Era

8.1.7 Describe the origin and development of political parties, the Federalists and the Democratic-Republicans (1793–1801), and examine points of agreement and disagreement between these parties; **8.1.8** Evaluate the significance of the presidential and congressional election of 1800 and the transfer of political authority and power to the Democratic-Republican Party led by the new president, Thomas Jefferson (1801); **8.1.9** Describe the influence of important individuals on social and political developments of the time such as the Independence movement and the framing of the Constitution; **8.1.11** Explain the events leading up to and the significance of the Louisiana Purchase (1803) and the expedition of Lewis and Clark (1803–1806); **8.1.12** Explain the main issues, decisions and consequences of landmark Supreme Court cases; **8.1.13** Explain the causes and consequences of the War of 1812, including the Rush-Bagot Agreement (1818); **8.1.15** Explain the concept of Manifest Destiny and describe its impact on westward expansion of the United States; **8.1.28** Recognize historical perspective and evaluate alternative courses of action by describing the historical context in which events unfolded and by avoiding evaluation of the past solely in terms of present-day norms; **8.1.30** Formulate historical questions by analyzing primary sources and secondary sources about an issue confronting the United States during the period from 1754–1877; **8.2.1** Identify and explain essential ideas of constitutional government, which are expressed in the founding documents of the United States, including the Virginia Declaration of Rights, the Declaration of Independence, the Virginia Statute for Religious Freedom, the Massachusetts Constitution of 1780, the Northwest Ordinance, the 1787 U.S. Constitution, the Bill of Rights, the Federalist and Anti-Federalist Papers, Common Sense, Washington's Farewell Address (1796), and Jefferson's First Inaugural Address (1801); **8.2.3** Explain how and why legislative, executive and judicial powers are distributed, shared and limited in the constitutional government of the United States; **8.2.4** Examine functions of the national government in the lives of people; **8.3.1** Read maps to interpret symbols and determine the land forms and human features that represent physical and cultural characteristics of areas in the United States; **8.3.2** Identify and create maps showing the physical growth and development of the United States from settlement of the original 13 colonies through Reconstruction (1877), including transportation routes used during the period; **8.3.5** Describe the importance of the major mountain ranges and the major river systems in the development of the United States; **8.3.7** Using maps identify changes influenced by growth, economic development and human migration in the eighteenth and nineteenth centuries; **8.3.9** Analyze human and physical factors that have influenced migration and settlement patterns and relate them to the economic development of the United States; **8.3.10** Create maps, graphs and charts showing the distribution of natural resources—such as forests, water sources and wildlife—in the United States at the beginning of the nineteenth century and give examples of how people exploited these resources as the country became more industrialized and people moved westward.

Indiana
The Hoosier State

Chapter 9 A New National Identity	**8.1.10** Compare differences in ways of life in the northern and southern states, including the growth of towns and cities in the North and the growing dependence on slavery in the South; **8.1.12** Explain the main issues, decisions and consequences of landmark Supreme Court cases; **8.1.14** Examine the international problem that led to the Monroe Doctrine (1823) and assess its consequences; **8.1.15** Explain the concept of Manifest Destiny and describe its impact on westward expansion of the United States; **8.1.16** Describe the abolition of slavery in the northern states, including the conflicts and compromises associated with westward expansion of slavery; **8.1.29** Differentiate between facts and historical interpretations recognizing that the historian's narrative reflects his or her judgment about the significance of particular facts; **8.1.31** Obtain historical data from a variety of sources to compare and contrast examples of art, music and literature during the nineteenth century and explain how these reflect American culture during this time period; **8.2.3** Explain how and why legislative, executive and judicial powers are distributed, shared and limited in the constitutional government of the United States; **8.2.4** Examine functions of the national government in the lives of people; **8.3.1** Read maps to interpret symbols and determine the land forms and human features that represent physical and cultural characteristics of areas in the United States; **8.3.2** Identify and create maps showing the physical growth and development of the United States from settlement of the original 13 colonies through Reconstruction (1877), including transportation routes used during the period; **8.3.5** Describe the importance of the major mountain ranges and the major river systems in the development of the United States; **8.3.7** Using maps identify changes influenced by growth, economic development and human migration in the eighteenth and nineteenth centuries; **8.3.8** Gather information on ways people changed the physical environment of the United States in the nineteenth century using primary sources and secondary sources including digitized photo collections and historic maps; **8.3.9** Analyze human and physical factors that have influenced migration and settlement patterns and relate them to the economic development of the United States; **8.3.10** Create maps, graphs and charts showing the distribution of natural resources—such as forests, water sources and wildlife—in the United States at the beginning of the nineteenth century and give examples of how people exploited these resources as the country became more industrialized and people moved westward; **8.3.11** Identify ways people modified the physical environment as the United States developed and describe the impacts that resulted; **8.4.4** Explain the basic economic functions of the government in the economy of the United States; **8.4.8** Examine the development of the banking system in the United States; **8.4.9** Explain and evaluate examples of domestic and international interdependence throughout United States history.

Chapter 10
The Age of Jackson

8.1.10 Compare differences in ways of life in the northern and southern states, including the growth of towns and cities in the North and the growing dependence on slavery in the South; **8.1.12** Explain the main issues, decisions and consequences of landmark Supreme Court cases; **8.1.15** Explain the concept of Manifest Destiny and describe its impact on westward expansion of the United States; **8.1.17** Identify the key ideas of Jacksonian democracy and explain their influence on political participation, political parties and constitutional government; **8.1.18** Analyze different interests and points of view of individuals and groups involved in the abolitionist, feminist and social reform movements, and in sectional conflicts; **8.1.24** Identify the influence of individuals on political and social events and movements such as the abolition movement, the Dred Scott case, women's rights and Native American Indian removal; **8.1.28** Recognize historical perspective and evaluate alternative courses of action by describing the historical context in which events unfolded and by avoiding evaluation of the past solely in terms of present-day norms; **8.1.29** Differentiate between facts and historical interpretations recognizing that the historian's narrative reflects his or her judgment about the significance of particular facts; **8.1.30** Formulate historical questions by analyzing primary sources and secondary sources about an issue confronting the United States during the period from 1754–1877; **8.2.3** Explain how and why legislative, executive and judicial powers are distributed, shared and limited in the constitutional government of the United States; **8.2.8** Explain ways that citizens can participate in political parties, campaigns and elections; **8.2.10** Research and defend positions on issues in which fundamental values and principles related to the United States Constitution are in conflict, using a variety of information resources; **8.3.1** Read maps to interpret symbols and determine the land forms and human features that represent physical and cultural characteristics of areas in the United States; **8.3.6** Identify the agricultural regions of the United States and be able to give reasons for the type of land use and subsequent land development during different historical periods; **8.4.4** Explain the basic economic functions of the government in the economy of the United States; **8.4.8** Examine the development of the banking system in the United States.

Chapter 11 Expanding West	**8.1.15** Explain the concept of Manifest Destiny and describe its impact on westward expansion of the United States; **8.1.25** Give examples of how immigration affected American culture in the decades before and after the Civil War, including growth of industrial sites in the North; religious differences; tensions between middle-class and working-class people, particularly in the Northeast; and intensification of cultural differences between the North and the South; **8.3.1** Read maps to interpret symbols and determine the land forms and human features that represent physical and cultural characteristics of areas in the United States; **8.3.2** Identify and create maps showing the physical growth and development of the United States from settlement of the original 13 colonies through Reconstruction (1877), including transportation routes used during the period; **8.3.5** Describe the importance of the major mountain ranges and the major river systems in the development of the United States; **8.3.7** Using maps identify changes influenced by growth, economic development and human migration in the eighteenth and nineteenth centuries; **8.3.8** Gather information on ways people changed the physical environment of the United States in the nineteenth century using primary sources and secondary sources including digitized photo collections and historic maps; **8.3.9** Analyze human and physical factors that have influenced migration and settlement patterns and relate them to the economic development of the United States; **8.3.10** Create maps, graphs and charts showing the distribution of natural resources—such as forests, water sources and wildlife—in the United States at the beginning of the nineteenth century and give examples of how people exploited these resources as the country became more industrialized and people moved westward.

Chapter 12
The North

8.1.10 Compare differences in ways of life in the northern and southern states, including the growth of towns and cities in the North and the growing dependence on slavery in the South; **8.1.12** Explain the main issues, decisions and consequences of landmark Supreme Court cases; **8.1.26** Give examples of the changing role of women and minorities in the northern, southern, and western parts of the United States in the mid-nineteenth century, and examine possible causes for these changes; **8.1.27** Give examples of scientific and technological developments that changed cultural life in the nineteenth-century United States, such as the use of photography, growth in the use of the telegraph, the completion of the transcontinental railroad, and the invention of the telephone; **8.1.29** Differentiate between facts and historical interpretations recognizing that the historian's narrative reflects his or her judgment about the significance of particular facts; **8.1.30** Formulate historical questions by analyzing primary sources and secondary sources about an issue confronting the United States during the period from 1754–1877; **8.3.1** Read maps to interpret symbols and determine the land forms and human features that represent physical and cultural characteristics of areas in the United States; **8.3.2** Identify and create maps showing the physical growth and development of the United States from settlement of the original 13 colonies through Reconstruction (1877), including transportation routes used during the period; **8.3.5** Describe the importance of the major mountain ranges and the major river systems in the development of the United States; **8.3.6** Identify the agricultural regions of the United States and be able to give reasons for the type of land use and subsequent land development during different historical periods; **8.3.7** Using maps identify changes influenced by growth, economic development and human migration in the eighteenth and nineteenth centuries; **8.3.8** Gather information on ways people changed the physical environment of the United States in the nineteenth century using primary sources and secondary sources including digitized photo collections and historic maps; **8.3.9** Analyze human and physical factors that have influenced migration and settlement patterns and relate them to the economic development of the United States; **8.3.10** Create maps, graphs and charts showing the distribution of natural resources—such as forests, water sources and wildlife—in the United States at the beginning of the nineteenth century and give examples of how people exploited these resources as the country became more industrialized and people moved westward; **8.3.11** Identify ways people modified the physical environment as the United States developed and describe the impacts that resulted; **8.4.2** Illustrate elements of the three types of economic systems, using cases from United States history; **8.4.3** Evaluate how the characteristics of a market economy have affected the economic and labor development of the United States; **8.4.4** Explain the basic economic functions of the government in the economy of the United States; **8.4.5** Analyze contributions of entrepreneurs and inventors in the development of the United States economy; **8.4.6** Relate technological change and inventions to changes in labor productivity in the United States in the eighteenth and nineteenth centuries; **8.4.9** Explain and evaluate examples of domestic and international interdependence throughout United States history.

Indiana
The Hoosier State

Chapter 13 The South	**8.1.10** Compare differences in ways of life in the northern and southern states, including the growth of towns and cities in the North and the growing dependence on slavery in the South; **8.1.16** Describe the abolition of slavery in the northern states, including the conflicts and compromises associated with westward expansion of slavery; **8.1.18** Analyze different interests and points of view of individuals and groups involved in the abolitionist, feminist and social reform movements, and in sectional conflicts; **8.1.20** Analyze the causes and effects of events leading to the Civil War, including development of sectional conflict over slavery; **8.1.26** Give examples of the changing role of women and minorities in the northern, southern, and western parts of the United States in the mid-nineteenth century, and examine possible causes for these changes; **8.1.28** Recognize historical perspective and evaluate alternative courses of action by describing the historical context in which events unfolded and by avoiding evaluation of the past solely in terms of present-day norms; **8.1.31** Obtain historical data from a variety of sources to compare and contrast examples of art, music and literature during the nineteenth century and explain how these reflect American culture during this time period; **8.3.1** Read maps to interpret symbols and determine the land forms and human features that represent physical and cultural characteristics of areas in the United States; **8.3.6** Identify the agricultural regions of the United States and be able to give reasons for the type of land use and subsequent land development during different historical periods; **8.3.7** Using maps identify changes influenced by growth, economic development and human migration in the eighteenth and nineteenth centuries; **8.3.8** Gather information on ways people changed the physical environment of the United States in the nineteenth century using primary sources and secondary sources including digitized photo collections and historic maps; **8.3.9** Analyze human and physical factors that have influenced migration and settlement patterns and relate them to the economic development of the United States; **8.3.11** Identify ways people modified the physical environment as the United States developed and describe the impacts that resulted; **8.4.3** Evaluate how the characteristics of a market economy have affected the economic and labor development of the United States; **8.4.5** Analyze contributions of entrepreneurs and inventors in the development of the United States economy; **8.4.6** Relate technological change and inventions to changes in labor productivity in the United States in the eighteenth and nineteenth centuries; **8.4.9** Explain and evaluate examples of domestic and international interdependence throughout United States history.

Chapter 14 New Movements in America	**8.1.10** Compare differences in ways of life in the northern and southern states, including the growth of towns and cities in the North and the growing dependence on slavery in the South; **8.1.16** Describe the abolition of slavery in the northern states, including the conflicts and compromises associated with westward expansion of slavery; **8.1.18** Analyze different interests and points of view of individuals and groups involved in the abolitionist, feminist and social reform movements, and in sectional conflicts; **8.1.19** Explain the influence of early individual social reformers and movements; **8.1.20** Analyze the causes and effects of events leading to the Civil War, including development of sectional conflict over slavery; **8.1.24** Identify the influence of individuals on political and social events and movements such as the abolition movement, the Dred Scott case, women's rights and Native American Indian removal; **8.1.25** Give examples of how immigration affected American culture in the decades before and after the Civil War, including growth of industrial sites in the North; religious differences; tensions between middle-class and working-class people, particularly in the Northeast; and intensification of cultural differences between the North and the South; **8.1.26** Give examples of the changing role of women and minorities in the northern, southern, and western parts of the United States in the mid-nineteenth century, and examine possible causes for these changes; **8.1.28** Recognize historical perspective and evaluate alternative courses of action by describing the historical context in which events unfolded and by avoiding evaluation of the past solely in terms of present-day norms; **8.1.29** Differentiate between facts and historical interpretations recognizing that the historian's narrative reflects his or her judgment about the significance of particular facts; **8.1.30** Formulate historical questions by analyzing primary sources and secondary sources about an issue confronting the United States during the period from 1754–1877; **8.1.31** Obtain historical data from a variety of sources to compare and contrast examples of art, music and literature during the nineteenth century and explain how these reflect American culture during this time period; **8.2.7** Explain the importance in a democratic republic of responsible participation by citizens in voluntary civil associations/ nongovernmental organizations that comprise civil society; **8.2.9** Explain how citizens can monitor and influence the development and implementation of public policies at local, state and national levels of government; **8.3.9** Analyze human and physical factors that have influenced migration and settlement patterns and relate them to the economic development of the United States; **8.3.11** Identify ways people modified the physical environment as the United States developed and describe the impacts that resulted.

Chapter 15 A Divided Nation	**8.1.16** Describe the abolition of slavery in the northern states, including the conflicts and compromises associated with westward expansion of slavery; **8.1.18** Analyze different interests and points of view of individuals and groups involved in the abolitionist, feminist and social reform movements, and in sectional conflicts; **8.1.20** Analyze the causes and effects of events leading to the Civil War, including development of sectional conflict over slavery; **8.1.21** Describe the importance of key events and individuals in the Civil War; **8.1.24** Identify the influence of individuals on political and social events and movements such as the abolition movement, the Dred Scott case, women's rights and Native American Indian removal; **8.1.28** Recognize historical perspective and evaluate alternative courses of action by describing the historical context in which events unfolded and by avoiding evaluation of the past solely in terms of present-day norms; **8.1.29** Differentiate between facts and historical interpretations recognizing that the historian's narrative reflects his or her judgment about the significance of particular facts; **8.1.30** Formulate historical questions by analyzing primary sources and secondary sources about an issue confronting the United States during the period from 1754–1877; **8.2.3** Explain how and why legislative, executive and judicial powers are distributed, shared and limited in the constitutional government of the United States; **8.2.7** Explain the importance in a democratic republic of responsible participation by citizens in voluntary civil associations/ nongovernmental organizations that comprise civil society; **8.2.9** Explain how citizens can monitor and influence the development and implementation of public policies at local, state and national levels of government; **8.3.2** Identify and create maps showing the physical growth and development of the United States from settlement of the original 13 colonies through Reconstruction (1877), including transportation routes used during the period; **8.3.7** Using maps identify changes influenced by growth, economic development and human migration in the eighteenth and nineteenth centuries.
Chapter 16 The Civil War	**8.1.21** Describe the importance of key events and individuals in the Civil War; **8.1.24** Identify the influence of individuals on political and social events and movements such as the abolition movement, the Dred Scott case, women's rights and Native American Indian removal; **8.1.26** Give examples of the changing role of women and minorities in the northern, southern, and western parts of the United States in the mid-nineteenth century, and examine possible causes for these changes; **8.1.29** Differentiate between facts and historical interpretations recognizing that the historian's narrative reflects his or her judgment about the significance of particular facts; **8.1.30** Formulate historical questions by analyzing primary sources and secondary sources about an issue confronting the United States during the period from 1754–1877; **8.2.10** Research and defend positions on issues in which fundamental values and principles related to the United States Constitution are in conflict, using a variety of information resources.

Chapter 17 Reconstruction	**8.1.22** Explain and evaluate the policies, practices and consequences of Reconstruction, including the Thirteenth, Fourteenth and Fifteenth Amendments to the Constitution; **8.1.24** Identify the influence of individuals on political and social events and movements such as the abolition movement, the Dred Scott case, women's rights and Native American Indian removal; **8.1.26** Give examples of the changing role of women and minorities in the northern, southern, and western parts of the United States in the mid-nineteenth century, and examine possible causes for these changes; **8.1.28** Recognize historical perspective and evaluate alternative courses of action by describing the historical context in which events unfolded and by avoiding evaluation of the past solely in terms of present-day norms; **8.1.29** Differentiate between facts and historical interpretations recognizing that the historian's narrative reflects his or her judgment about the significance of particular facts; **8.1.30** Formulate historical questions by analyzing primary sources and secondary sources about an issue confronting the United States during the period from 1754–1877; **8.2.3** Explain how and why legislative, executive and judicial powers are distributed, shared and limited in the constitutional government of the United States; **8.2.7** Explain the importance in a democratic republic of responsible participation by citizens in voluntary civil associations/ nongovernmental organizations that comprise civil society; **8.3.6** Identify the agricultural regions of the United States and be able to give reasons for the type of land use and subsequent land development during different historical periods.

Indiana
The Hoosier State

Chapter 18
Americans
Move West

8.1.23 Describe the conflicts between Native American Indians and settlers of the Great Plains; 8.1.24 Identify the influence of individuals on political and social events and movements, such as the abolition movement, the Dred Scott case, women's rights, and Native American Indian removal; **8.1.25** Give examples of how immigration affected American culture in the decades before and after the Civil War, including growth of industrial sites in the North; religious differences; tensions between middle-class and working-class people, particularly in the Northeast; and intensification of cultural differences between the North and the South; **8.1.26** Give examples of the changing role of women and minorities in the northern, southern, and western parts of the United States in the mid-nineteenth century, and examine possible causes for these changes; **8.1.27** Give examples of scientific and technological developments that changed cultural life in the nineteenth-century United States, such as the use of photography, growth in the use of the telegraph, the completion of the transcontinental railroad, and the invention of the telephone; **8.1.30** Formulate historical questions by analyzing primary sources and secondary sources about an issue confronting the United States during the period from 1754–1877; **8.2.3** Explain how and why legislative, executive and judicial powers are distributed, shared and limited in the constitutional government of the United States; **8.2.4** Examine functions of the national government in the lives of people; **8.2.8** Explain ways that citizens can participate in political parties, campaigns and elections; **8.3.1** Read maps to interpret symbols and determine the land forms and human features that represent physical and cultural characteristics of areas in the United States; **8.3.2** Identify and create maps showing the physical growth and development of the United States from settlement of the original 13 colonies through Reconstruction (1877), including transportation routes used during the period; **8.3.6** Identify the agricultural regions of the United States and be able to give reasons for the type of land use and subsequent land development during different historical periods; **8.3.7** Using maps identify changes influenced by growth, economic development and human migration in the eighteenth and nineteenth centuries; **8.3.8** Gather information on ways people changed the physical environment of the United States in the nineteenth century using primary sources and secondary sources including digitized photo collections and historic maps; **8.3.9** Analyze human and physical factors that have influenced migration and settlement patterns and relate them to the economic development of the United States; **8.3.10** Create maps, graphs and charts showing the distribution of natural resources — such as forests, water sources and wildlife — in the United States at the beginning of the nineteenth century and give examples of how people exploited these resources as the country became more industrialized and people moved westward; **8.3.11** Identify ways people modified the physical environment as the United States developed and describe the impacts that resulted; **8.4.4** Explain the basic economic functions of the government in the economy of the United States; **8.4.7** Trace the development of different kinds of money used in the United States and explain how money helps make saving easier; **8.4.8** Examine the development of the banking system in the United States.

Chapter 19 The Industrial Age	**8.1.27** Give examples of scientific and technological developments that changed cultural life in the nineteenth-century United States, such as the use of photography, growth in the use of the telegraph, the completion of the transcontinental railroad, and the invention of the telephone; **8.2.4** Examine functions of the national government in the lives of people; **8.3.1** Read maps to interpret symbols and determine the land forms and human features that represent physical and cultural characteristics of areas in the United States; **8.3.6** Identify the agricultural regions of the United States and be able to give reasons for the type of land use and subsequent land development during different historical periods; **8.3.8** Gather information on ways people changed the physical environment of the United States in the nineteenth century using primary sources and secondary sources including digitized photo collections and historic maps; **8.3.10** Create maps, graphs and charts showing the distribution of natural resources—such as forests, water sources and wildlife—in the United States at the beginning of the nineteenth century and give examples of how people exploited these resources as the country became more industrialized and people moved westward; **8.3.11** Identify ways people modified the physical environment as the United States developed and describe the impacts that resulted; **8.4.2** Illustrate elements of the three types of economic systems, using cases from United States history; **8.4.3** Evaluate how the characteristics of a market economy have affected the economic and labor development of the United States; **8.4.4** Explain the basic economic functions of the government in the economy of the United States; **8.4.5** Analyze contributions of entrepreneurs and inventors in the development of the United States economy; **8.4.6** Relate technological change and inventions to changes in labor productivity in the United States in the eighteenth and nineteenth centuries.

Indiana
The Hoosier State

Chapter 20 Immigrants and Urban Life	**8.1.25** Give examples of how immigration affected American culture in the decades before and after the Civil War, including growth of industrial sites in the North; religious differences; tensions between middle-class and working-class people, particularly in the Northeast; and intensification of cultural differences between the North and the South; **8.3.1** Read maps to interpret symbols and determine the land forms and human features that represent physical and cultural characteristics of areas in the United States; **8.3.5** Describe the importance of the major mountain ranges and the major river systems in the development of the United States; **8.3.6** Identify the agricultural regions of the United States and be able to give reasons for the type of land use and subsequent land development during different historical periods; **8.3.7** Using maps identify changes influenced by growth, economic development and human migration in the eighteenth and nineteenth centuries; **8.3.8** Gather information on ways people changed the physical environment of the United States in the nineteenth century using primary sources and secondary sources including digitized photo collections and historic maps; **8.3.9** Analyze human and physical factors that have influenced migration and settlement patterns and relate them to the economic development of the United States; **8.3.11** Identify ways people modified the physical environment as the United States developed and describe the impacts that resulted; **8.4.5** Analyze contributions of entrepreneurs and inventors in the development of the United States economy.
Chapter 21 The Progressive Spirit of Reform	**8.2.3** Explain how and why legislative, executive and judicial powers are distributed, shared and limited in the constitutional government of the United States; **8.2.4** Examine functions of the national government in the lives of people; **8.2.8** Explain ways that citizens can participate in political parties, campaigns and elections; **8.2.9** Explain how citizens can monitor and influence the development and implementation of public policies at local, state and national levels of government; **8.3.8** Gather information on ways people changed the physical environment of the United States in the nineteenth century using primary sources and secondary sources including digitized photo collections and historic maps; **8.3.10** Create maps, graphs and charts showing the distribution of natural resources—such as forests, water sources and wildlife—in the United States at the beginning of the nineteenth century and give examples of how people exploited these resources as the country became more industrialized and people moved westward; **8.3.11** Identify ways people modified the physical environment as the United States developed and describe the impacts that resulted; **8.4.2** Illustrate elements of the three types of economic systems, using cases from United States history; **8.4.4** Explain the basic economic functions of the government in the economy of the United States; **8.4.5** Analyze contributions of entrepreneurs and inventors in the development of the United States economy.
Chapter 22 America as a World Power	**8.3.6** Identify the agricultural regions of the United States and be able to give reasons for the type of land use and subsequent land development during different historical periods; **8.3.7** Using maps identify changes influenced by growth, economic development and human migration in the eighteenth and nineteenth centuries; **8.3.9** Analyze human and physical factors that have influenced migration and settlement patterns and relate them to the economic development of the United States; **8.4.9** Explain and evaluate examples of domestic and international interdependence throughout United States history.

Detailed correlation of
Holt McDougal United States History: Beginnings to 1914
to the

Indiana Academic Standards for Social Studies

Standard 1 History

Students will examine the relationship and significance of themes, concepts, and movements in the development of United States history, including review of key ideas related to the colonization of America and the revolution and Founding Era. This will be followed by emphasis on social reform, national development and westward expansion, and the Civil War and Reconstruction period.

Historical Knowledge
The American Revolution and Founding of the United States: 1754 to 1801

8.1.1	Identify major Native American Indian groups of eastern North America and describe early conflict and cooperation with European settlers and the influence the two cultures had on each other. (Individuals, Society, and Culture) **Example:** Mohawk, Iroquois, Huron and Ottawa; French and Native American Indian alliances; French and Indian War; British alliances with Native American Indians; settler encroachment on Native American Indian lands; and Native American Indian participation in the Revolutionary War.	**SE**	3, 14, 15, 31, 54, 57, 66, 73, 77, 95, 97, 105–107, 120, 121, 133, 134
8.1.2	Explain the struggle of the British, French, Spanish and Dutch to gain control of North America during settlement and colonization.	**SE**	35, 53–55, 57, 66, 69, 76, 86, 95-97
8.1.3	Identify and explain the conditions, causes, consequences and significance of the French and Indian War (1754–1763), and the resistance and rebellion against British imperial rule by the thirteen colonies in North America (1761–1775).	**SE**	95–97, 98–103, 106, 107, 112–117, 118–125, 126–134, 135–139, 141–143

Indiana
The Hoosier State

The Spread of Cultural, Economic, Social, and Political Ideas: 500 B.C. / (B.C.E. – 1600 A.D./ C.E.			
8.1.4	Identify fundamental ideas in the Declaration of Independence (1776) and analyze the causes and effects of the Revolutionary War (1775–1783), including enactment of the Articles of Confederation and the Treaty of Paris.	SE	95–97, 98–103, 106, 107, 109, 112–114, 116, 118–125, 130, 131, 137, 139, 141–143, 154, 155
8.1.5	Identify and explain key events leading to the creation of a strong union among the thirteen original states and in the establishment of the United States as a federal republic. **Example:** The enactment of state constitutions, the Constitutional Convention, ratifying conventions of the American states, and debate by Federalists versus Anti-Federalists regarding approval or disapproval of the 1787 Constitution (1787–1788).	SE	153, 155, 163–168, 170–173, 175-177
8.1.6	Identify the steps in the implementation of the federal government under the United States Constitution, including the First and Second Congresses of the United States (1789–1792).	SE	234–237, 238–242, 250, 255–257
8.1.7	Describe the origin and development of political parties, the Federalists and the Democratic-Republicans (1793–1801), and examine points of agreement and disagreement between these parties.	SE	250, 251, 253, 256, 257, 266
8.1.8	Evaluate the significance of the presidential and congressional election of 1800 and the transfer of political authority and power to the Democratic-Republican Party led by the new president, Thomas Jefferson (1801).	SE	266–268, 270, 291, 293
8.1.9	Describe the influence of important individuals on social and political developments of the time such as the Independence movement and the framing of the Constitution. (Individuals, Society, and Culture) **Example:** James Otis, Mercy Otis Warren, Samuel Adams, Thomas Paine, George Washington, John Adams, Abigail Adams, Patrick Henry, Thomas Jefferson, James Madison, Alexander Hamilton and Benjamin Banneker.	SE	99, 100, 101, 109, 114, 117, 118–121, 126–134, 136–139, 141–143, 164, 166, 169, 170–172, 187, 234–237, 238–242, 248, 249, 251–253, 255–257, 266–271, 291, 293

8.1.10	Compare differences in ways of life in the northern and southern states, including the growth of towns and cities in the North and the growing dependence on slavery in the South (Individuals, Society, and Culture).	SE	304, 305, 326, 327, 331, 386–389, 400, 401, 408, 409, 414–419, 424, 425, 429, 431, 440–442, 469
8.1.11	Explain the events leading up to and the significance of the Louisiana Purchase (1803) and the expedition of Lewis and Clark (1803–1806).	SE	272–277, 291–293
8.1.12	Explain the main issues, decisions and consequences of landmark Supreme Court cases. **Example:** Marbury v. Madison (1803), McCulloch v. Maryland (1819) and Gibbons v. Ogden (1824).	SE	269, 270, 291, 293, 304, 305, 330, 339, 397, 401
8.1.13	Explain the causes and consequences of the War of 1812, including the Rush-Bagot Agreement (1818).	SE	278–283, 284–287, 292, 293
8.1.14	Examine the international problem that led to the Monroe Doctrine (1823) and assess its consequences.	SE	300, 301, 315–317
8.1.15	Explain the concept of Manifest Destiny and describe its impact on westward expansion of the United States. (Individuals, Society, and Culture) **Example:** Louisiana Purchase (1803), purchase of Florida (1819), Mexican War and the annexation of Texas (1845), acquisition of Oregon Territory (1846), Native American Indian conflicts and removal, and the California gold rush.	SE	273, 274, 277, 288, 289, 291, 293, 299, 301, 317, 332-337, 339–341, 348, 353, 354–363, 364-372, 373–375
8.1.16	Describe the abolition of slavery in the northern states, including the conflicts and compromises associated with westward expansion of slavery. **Example:** Missouri Compromise (1820), the Compromise of 1850, and the Kansas-Nebraska Act (1854)	SE	155, 304, 305, 316, 317, 426, 432, 452, 455–460, 470, 471, 476–481, 484–487, 493, 494, 497, 499–501
8.1.17	Identify the key ideas of Jacksonian democracy and explain their influence on political participation, political parties and constitutional government.	SE	322–325, 327, 339, 341

8.1.18	Analyze different interests and points of view of individuals and groups involved in the abolitionist, feminist and social reform movements, and in sectional conflicts. (Individuals, Society, and Culture) **Example:** Jacksonian Democrats, John Brown, Nat Turner, Frederick Douglass, Harriet Tubman, William Lloyd Garrison, Harriet Beecher Stowe, Sojourner Truth and the Seneca Falls Convention.	**SE**	327–331, 340, 341, 428, 429, 449–453, 454–460, 461–467, 469–471, 476–481, 484–487, 488–492, 493–497, 499–501
8.1.19	Explain the influence of early individual social reformers and movements. (Individuals, Society, and Culture) **Example:** Elizabeth Cady Stanton, Horace Mann, Dorothea Dix, Lucretia Mott, Robert Owen, abolition movement, temperance movement and utopian movements.	**SE**	443–445, 449–453, 454–460, 461–467, 469–471
8.1.20	Analyze the causes and effects of events leading to the Civil War, including development of sectional conflict over slavery. **Example:** The Compromise of 1850, furor over publication of *Uncle Tom's Cabin* (1852), Kansas-Nebraska Act (1854), the Dred Scott Case (1857), the Lincoln-Douglas Debates (1858), and the presidential election of 1860.	**SE**	411, 426, 456, 476–482, 483–487, 488–492, 493–497, 499–501
8.1.21	Describe the importance of key events and individuals in the Civil War **Example:** The battles of Manassas, Antietam, Vicksburg and Gettysburg; and the Emancipation Proclamation and Gettysburg Address (1861–1865); People: Jefferson Davis, Stephen A. Douglas, Abraham Lincoln, Robert E. Lee, Ulysses S. Grant, William T. Sherman and Thaddeus Stevens.	**SE**	497, 516–521, 522–527, 529, 530, 534, 535, 536–543, 545–547
8.1.22	Explain and evaluate the policies, practices and consequences of Reconstruction, including the Thirteenth, Fourteenth and Fifteenth Amendments to the Constitution.	**SE**	554–557, 560–563, 565, 567, 571, 573, 574

8.1.23	Describe the conflicts between Native American Indians and settlers of the Great Plains. (Individuals, Society, and Culture)	**SE**	593–599, 607, 609
8.1.24	Identify the influence of individuals on political and social events and movements such as the abolition movement, the Dred Scott case, women's rights and Native American Indian removal. (Individuals, Society, and Culture) **Examples:** Henry Clay, Harriet Tubman, Harriet Beecher Stowe, Henry Ward Beecher, Roger Taney, Frederick Douglass, John Brown, Clara Barton, Andrew Johnson, Susan B. Anthony, Sitting Bull, Ralph Waldo Emerson and Henry David Thoreau	**SE**	332–337, 340, 341, 443–445, 449–453, 454–460, 461–467, 469–471, 478, 479, 481, 482, 484–487, 488–492, 493–497, 534, 557, 558–563, 573, 595–599, 609
8.1.25	Give examples of how immigration affected American culture in the decades before and after the Civil War, including growth of industrial sites in the North; religious differences; tensions between middle-class and working-class people, particularly in the Northeast; and intensification of cultural differences between the North and the South. (Individuals, Society, and Culture)	**SE**	366, 368, 369, 374, 438–442, 587, 590, 601, 636–641, 642, 643, 645, 648, 651, 653
8.1.26	Give examples of the changing role of women and minorities in the northern, southern, and western parts of the United States in the mid-nineteenth century, and examine possible causes for these changes. (Individuals, Society, and Culture)	**SE**	392–395, 409, 423, 451–453, 461–467, 470, 531, 554–557, 565, 571, 573, 588, 592, 600–602, 608
8.1.27	Give examples of scientific and technological developments that changed cultural life in the nineteenth-century United States, such as the use of photography, growth in the use of the telegraph, the completion of the transcontinental railroad and the invention of the telephone. (Individuals, Society, and Culture)	**SE**	396–401, 402–405, 408, 409, 590–592, 615–618, 629, 630

Chronological Thinking, Historical Comprehension, Analysis and Interpretation, Research, and Issues-Analysis and Decision-Making			
8.1.28	Recognize historical perspective and evaluate alternative courses of action by describing the historical context in which events unfolded and by avoiding evaluation of the past solely in terms of present-day norms. **Example:** Use Internet-based documents and digital archival collections from museums and libraries to compare views of slavery in slave narratives, northern and southern newspapers, and present day accounts of the era.	**SE**	119, 144, 145, 166, 174, 176, 185, 226, 228, 241, 264, 265, 282, 329, 426, 427, 429, 432, 433, 456, 458, 470, 482, 489, 491, 494, 500, 498, 560, 574, 576–579
8.1.29	Differentiate between facts and historical interpretations recognizing that the historian's narrative reflects his or her judgment about the significance of particular facts.	**SE**	101, 121, 140, 173, 174, 176, 226, 232, 233, 296, 297, 320, 321, 329, 406, 408, 436, 437, 470, 471, 474, 475, 492, 498, 500, 508, 509, 521, 550, 551
8.1.30	Formulate historical questions by analyzing primary sources and secondary sources about an issue confronting the United States during the period from 1754–1877. **Example:** ... 786), President ... the First I... the Declaratio... a Falls Conv... ess by Abraham ...	**SE**	64, 66, 101, 119, 132, 140, 156, 166, 172, 188–215, 226, 241, 248, 268, 292, 323, 329, 330, 334, 408, 471, 494, 498, 500, 505, 509, 529, 531, 544, 574, 576, 577, 599, 601, R32–R40
8.1.31	Obtain historical data from a variety of sources to compare and contrast examples of art, music and literature during the nineteenth century and explain how these reflect American culture during this time period. (Individuals, Society, and Culture). **Example:** Art: John James Audubon, Winslow Homer, Hudson River School, Edward Bannister, Edmonia Lewis and Henry Ossawa Tanner; Writers: Louisa May Alcott, Washington Irving, James Fennimore Cooper, Walt Whitman, Frederick Douglass, Paul Dunbar, George Caleb Bingham	**SE**	308–313, 315–317, 427, 443–447, 452, 456, 460

Standard 2 Civics and Government

Students will explain the major principles, values and institutions of constitutional government and citizenship, which are based on the founding documents of the United States and how three branches of government share and check power within our federal system of government.

Foundations of Government

8.2.1	Identify and explain essential ideas of constitutional government, which are expressed in the founding documents of the United States, including the Virginia Declaration of Rights, the Declaration of Independence, the Virginia Statute for Religious Freedom, the Massachusetts Constitution of 1780, the Northwest Ordinance, the 1787 U.S. Constitution, the Bill of Rights, the Federalist and Anti-Federalist Papers, *Common Sense,* Washington's Farewell Address (1796) and Jefferson's First Inaugural Address (1801). **Example:** The essential ideas include limited government; rule of law; due process of law; separated and shared powers; checks and balances; federalism; popular sovereignty; republicanism; representative government; and individual rights to life, liberty, property; and freedom of conscience.	**SE**	118, 119, 121–125, 141, 143, 152–157, 167, 168, 170–173, 175–177, 182–186, 188–215, 216–221, 227–229, 242, 248, 249, 257, 268, 270, 293
8.2.2	Identify and explain the relationship between rights and responsibilities of citizenship in the United States. **Example:** The right to vote and the responsibility to use this right carefully and effectively. The right to free speech and the responsibility not to say or write false statements	**SE**	216–221, 222–225, 228, 229
8.2.3	Explain how and why legislative, executive and judicial powers are distributed, shared and limited in the constitutional government of the United States. **Example:** Examine key Supreme Court cases and describe the role each branch of the government played in each of these cases.	**SE**	167, 168, 183–186, 189–199, 228, 229, 269, 270, 304, 305, 330, 334, 335, 339–341, 489, 490, 492, 500, 568, 569, 603, 674
8.2.4	Examine functions of the national government in the lives of people. **Example:** Purchasing and distributing public goods and services, coining money, financing government through taxation, conducting foreign policy, providing a common defense, and regulating commerce.	**SE**	182, 193, 238–242, 244–247, 249, 255–257, 278–283, 284–287, 292, 293, 298–301, 302–307, 316, 317, 604, 622, 681–683

Functions of Government			
8.2.5	Compare, and contrast the powers reserved to the federal and state government under the Articles of Confederation and the United States Constitution.	**SE**	167, 168, 176, 177
8.2.6	Distinguish among the different functions of national and state government within the federal system by analyzing the United States Constitution and the Indiana Constitution. **Example:** Identify important services provided by state government, such as maintaining state roads and highways, enforcing health and safety laws, and supporting educational institutions. Compare these services to functions of the federal government, such as defense and foreign policy.	**SE**	167, 179, 182, 220, 224
Roles of Citizens			
8.2.7	Explain the importance in a democratic republic of responsible participation by citizens in voluntary civil associations/ non-governmental organizations that comprise civil society. **Example:** Reform movements such as the abolitionist movement, women's suffrage and the Freedman's Bureau	**SE**	224, 225, 228, 229, 250, 251, 253, 256, 449–453, 454–456, 459, 460, 464–468, 470, 480, 556, 557
8.2.8	Explain ways that citizens can participate in political parties, campaigns and elections. **Example:** Local, state, and national elections; referendums; poll work; campaign committees; and voting	**SE**	91, 92, 152, 224, 225, 228, 229, 322–324, 603–605, 666, 667
8.2.9	Explain how citizens can monitor and influence the development and implementation of public policies at local, state and national levels of government. **Example:** Joining action groups, holding leaders accountable through the electoral process, attending town meetings, staying informed by reading newspapers and Web sites, and watching television news broadcasts	**SE**	91, 105, 153, 224, 225, 228, 436, 437, 470, 454–456, 459, 460, 464–468, 470, 480, 666, 667, 675–679, 685, 686
8.2.10	Research and defend positions on issues in which fundamental values and principles related to the United States Constitution are in conflict, using a variety of information resources. **Example:** Powers of federal vs. powers of state government	**SE**	216–221, 242, 253, 256, 327–329, 331, 338, 340, 532, 534

Standard 3 Geography

Students will identify the major geographic characteristics of the United States and its regions. They will name and locate the major physical features of the United States, as well as each of the states, capitals, and major cities, and will use geographic skills and technology to examine the influence of geographic factors on national development.

The World in Spatial Terms			
8.3.1	Read maps to interpret symbols and determine the land forms and human features that represent physical and cultural characteristics of areas in the United States.	**SE**	H19–H21, 7, 60, 88, 89, 91, 154, 273, 277, 289, 303, 306, 307, 337, 362, 370–372, 400, 416, 590, 594, 606, 631, 644
Places and Regions			
8.3.2	Identify and create maps showing the physical growth and development of the United States from settlement of the original 13 colonies through Reconstruction (1877), including transportation routes used during the period.	**SE**	H14–H17, 76, 88, 89, 91, 96, 139, 154, 273, 288, 289, 299, 303, 304, 307, 317, 347, 370–372, 374, 375, 400, 484, 485, 501, 590
8.3.3	Identify and locate the major climate regions in the United States and describe the characteristics of these regions.	**SE**	13
8.3.4	Name and describe processes that build up the land and processes that erode it and identify places these occur. **Example:** The Appalachian Mountains are a formation that has undergone erosion. The Mississippi Delta is made up almost entirely of eroded material.	**SE**	H50
8.3.5	Describe the importance of the major mountain ranges and the major river systems in the development of the United States. **Example:** Locate major U.S. cities during this time period, such as Washington D.C.; New York; Boston; Atlanta; Nashville; Charleston; New Orleans; Philadelphia; and Saint Louis, and suggest reasons for their location and development.	**SE**	88, 97, 272, 273, 275–277, 289, 306, 307, 347, 371, 386, 642–645

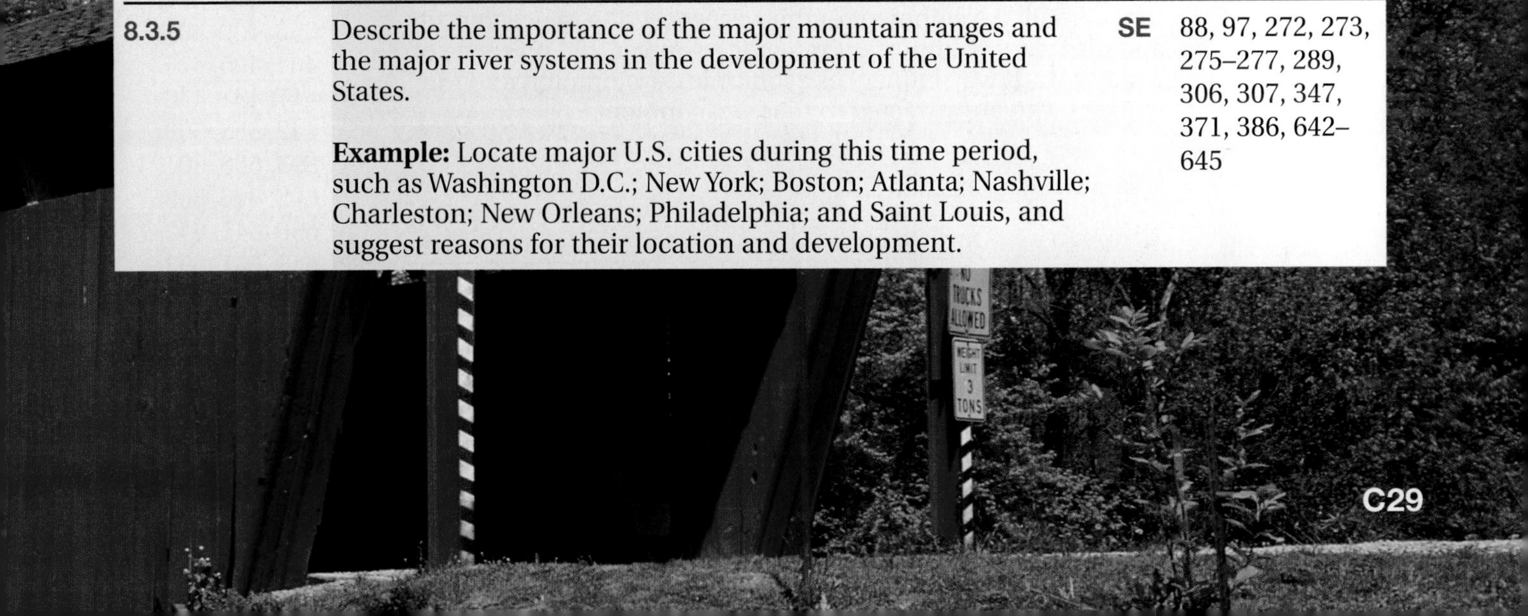

Human Systems

8.3.6	Identify the agricultural regions of the United States and be able to give reasons for the type of land use and subsequent land development during different historical periods. **Example:** Cattle industry in the West and cotton industry in the South.	SE	77, 83, 87, 326, 327, 400, 414–419, 569–571, 586–589, 601, 605, 607, 608, 615, 616, 644, 693, 694
8.3.7	Using maps identify changes influenced by growth, economic development, and human migration in the eighteenth and nineteenth centuries. **Example:** Westward expansion, impact of slavery, Lewis and Clark exploration, new states added to the union and Spanish settlement in California and Texas	SE	50, 56, 60, 88, 89, 154, 273, 288, 289, 299, 303, 304, 307, 317, 347, 352, 362, 370–372, 374, 375, 400, 416, 477, 484, 485, 501, 590, 606, 608, 638, 639, 644, 711
8.3.8	Gather information on ways people changed the physical environment of the United States in the nineteenth century, using primary sources and secondary sources including digitized photo collections and historic maps.	SE	H7, H21, 303, 306, 307, 315, 369, 386, 389, 400, 401, 404, 405, 409, 415, 416, 419, 587, 589, 591, 601, 606, 607, 608, 615, 647, 665, 681
8.3.9	Analyze human and physical factors that have influenced migration and settlement patterns and relate them to the economic development of the United States. **Example:** Growth of communities due to the development of the railroad, development of the west coast due to ocean ports and discovery of important mineral resources; the presence of a major waterway influences economic development and the workers who are attracted to that development	SE	274–277, 288, 289, 303, 306, 307, 346–349, 351, 361–363, 364–371, 374, 386, 400, 401, 404, 405, 416, 417, 431, 438–442, 586–592, 593, 600, 601, 605, 606, 608, 636–641, 642–645, 651, 693, 694, 704–706, 709, 714

Environment and Society			
8.3.10	Create maps, graphs and charts showing the distribution of natural resources—such as forests, water sources and wildlife—in the United States at the beginning of the nineteenth century and give examples of how people exploited these resources as the country became more industrialized and people moved westward.	**SE**	H14–H17, 289, 303, 306, 307, 363, 366, 367, 386, 400, 401, 587, 589, 594, 611, 616, 681
8.3.11	Identify ways people modified the physical environment as the United States developed and describe the impacts that resulted. **Example:** Identify urbanization, deforestation and extinction or near extinction of wildlife species; and development of roads and canals	**SE**	303, 306, 307, 315, 386, 400, 401, 404, 405, 415, 416, 419, 440–442, 469, 587, 589, 591, 598, 601, 607, 608, 615, 616, 642–645, 646–649, 665, 681

Standard 4 Economics

Students will identify, describe and evaluate the influence of economic factors on national development from the founding of the nation to the end of Reconstruction.

8.4.1	Identify economic factors contributing to European exploration and colonization in North America, the American Revolution and the drafting of the Constitution of the United States. **Example:** The search for gold by the Spanish, French fur trade and taxation without representation	**SE**	48–51, 54–57, 66, 72, 76, 77, 89, 99, 100, 102, 106, 160–162, 165, 166, 168, 176
8.4.2	Illustrate elements of the three types of economic systems, using cases from United States history. **Example:** Traditional economy, command economy and market economy.	**SE**	92, 93, 97, 387–389, 390–392, 395, 407, 409, 620–622, 674, 685, 722–725
8.4.3	Evaluate how the characteristics of a market economy have affected the economic and labor development of the United States. **Example:** Characteristics include the role of entrepreneurs, private property, markets, competition and self-interest	**SE**	386-389, 390–395, 397–401, 402–405, 407–409, 415–419, 431–433, 615–618, 619–623, 624–627, 629–631

8.4.4	Explain the basic economic functions of the government in the economy of the United States. **Example:** The government provides a legal framework, promotes competition, provides public goods and services, protects private property, controls the effects of helpful and harmful spillovers, and regulates interstate commerce.	SE	238–242, 247, 249, 255, 257, 302–307, 316, 327–331, 340, 397, 401, 592, 622, 681–683, 686
8.4.5	Analyze contributions of entrepreneurs and inventors in the development of the United States economy. (Individuals, Society, and Culture) **Example:** Benjamin Banneker, George Washington Carver, Eli Whitney, Samuel Gompers, Andrew Carnegie, John D. Rockefeller and Madam C.J. Walker.	SE	240, 386–389, 397–401, 402–405, 402–405, 407–409, 415–419, 431, 615–618, 619-623, 624–627, 629–631, 644, 677
8.4.6	Relate technological change and inventions to changes in labor productivity in the United States in the eighteenth and nineteenth centuries. **Example:** The cotton gin increased labor productivity in the early nineteenth century.	SE	387, 389, 390–395, 407, 409, 415–419, 431–433, 624–627
8.4.7	Trace the development of different kinds of money used in the United States and explain how money helps make saving easier. **Example:** Types of money included wampum, tobacco, gold and silver, state bank notes, greenbacks and Federal Reserve Notes.	SE	604
8.4.8	Examine the development of the banking system in the United States. **Example:** The central bank controversy, the state banking era and the development of a gold standard	SE	241, 242, 255, 257, 302, 329–331, 340, 341, 604
8.4.9	Explain and evaluate examples of domestic and international interdependence throughout United State history. **Example:** Triangular trade routes and regional exchange of resources	SE	92, 93, 97, 159–161, 307, 388, 400, 401, 416–419, 431, 433, 710, 711
8.4.10	Examine the importance of borrowing and lending (the use of credit) in the United States economy and list the advantages and disadvantages of using credit.	SE	722–725
8.4.11	Use a variety of information resources to compare and contrast job skills needed in different time periods in United States history.	SE	H51

Holt McDougal Social Studies Indiana Programs Skills Scope and Sequence

	SKILL	HOLT MCDOUGAL WESTERN WORLD	HOLT MCDOUGAL EASTERN WORLD	HOLT MCDOUGAL UNITED STATES HISTORY, GROWTH AND DEVELOPMENT: BEGINNINGS TO 1914
ACQUIRING INFORMATION	Accepting Social Responsibility			✔
	Acquiring Information	✔	✔	✔
	Analyzing a Bar Graph	✔	✔	✔
	Analyzing a Precipitation Map		✔	
	Analyzing Cause-and-Effect Relationships	✔	✔	✔
	Analyzing Costs and Benefits	✔	✔	✔
	Analyzing Economic Effects	✔	✔	✔
	Analyzing Photographs	✔	✔	✔
	Analyzing Points of View	✔	✔	✔
	Analyzing Primary Sources	✔	✔	✔
	Analyzing Satellite Images		✔	
	Analyzing Secondary Sources	✔	✔	✔
	Analyzing Statistics	✔	✔	✔
	Analyzing Tables	✔	✔	✔

ACQUIRING INFORMATION — SKILL	HOLT MCDOUGAL WESTERN WORLD	HOLT MCDOUGAL EASTERN WORLD	HOLT MCDOUGAL UNITED STATES HISTORY, GROWTH AND DEVELOPMENT: BEGINNINGS TO 1914
Anaylzing Pie Charts	✔	✔	✔
Communicating	✔	✔	✔
Comparing Maps	✔	✔	✔
Comparing Migration Maps			✔
Comparing Time Lines	✔	✔	✔
Comparing Viewpoints of History	✔	✔	✔
Conducting a Debate			✔
Confronting Controversial Issues			✔
Creating Time Lines	✔	✔	✔
Describing Historical Context	✔	✔	✔
Detecting Bias	✔	✔	✔
Determining the Strength of an Argument			✔
Differentiating between Opinion and Fact	✔	✔	✔
Doing Fieldwork and Using Questionnaires		✔	
Drawing on Visual, Literary, and Musical Sources	✔	✔	✔
Evaluating Alternative Courses of Action	✔	✔	✔
Forming Research Questions	✔	✔	✔

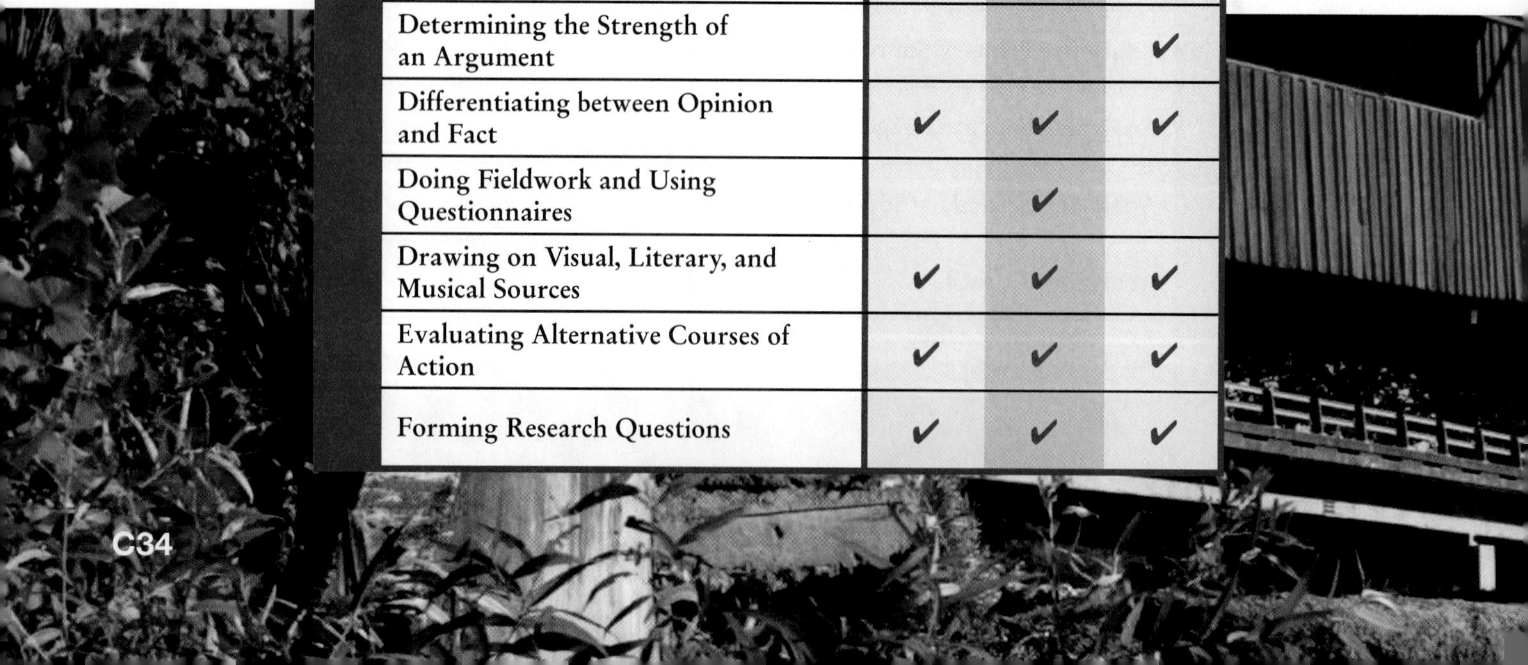

	SKILL	HOLT MCDOUGAL WESTERN WORLD	HOLT MCDOUGAL EASTERN WORLD	HOLT MCDOUGAL UNITED STATES HISTORY, GROWTH AND DEVELOPMENT: BEGINNINGS TO 1914
ACQUIRING INFORMATION	Formulating Historical Questions	✔	✔	✔
	Identifying Historical Context	✔	✔	✔
	Identifying Historical Issues	✔	✔	✔
	Interpreting a Climate Graph		✔	
	Interpreting a Population Map	✔	✔	
	Interpreting a Population Pyramid		✔	
	Interpreting an Elevation Map	✔	✔	
	Interpreting Battle Maps	✔		✔
	Interpreting Cartograms		✔	
	Interpreting Diagrapms	✔	✔	✔
	Interpreting Historical Maps			✔
	Interpreting Movement Maps			✔
	Interpreting Physical Maps	✔	✔	✔
	Interpreting Political Cartoons			✔
	Interpreting Political Maps	✔	✔	✔
	Making Decisions	✔	✔	✔
	Making Group Decisions			✔

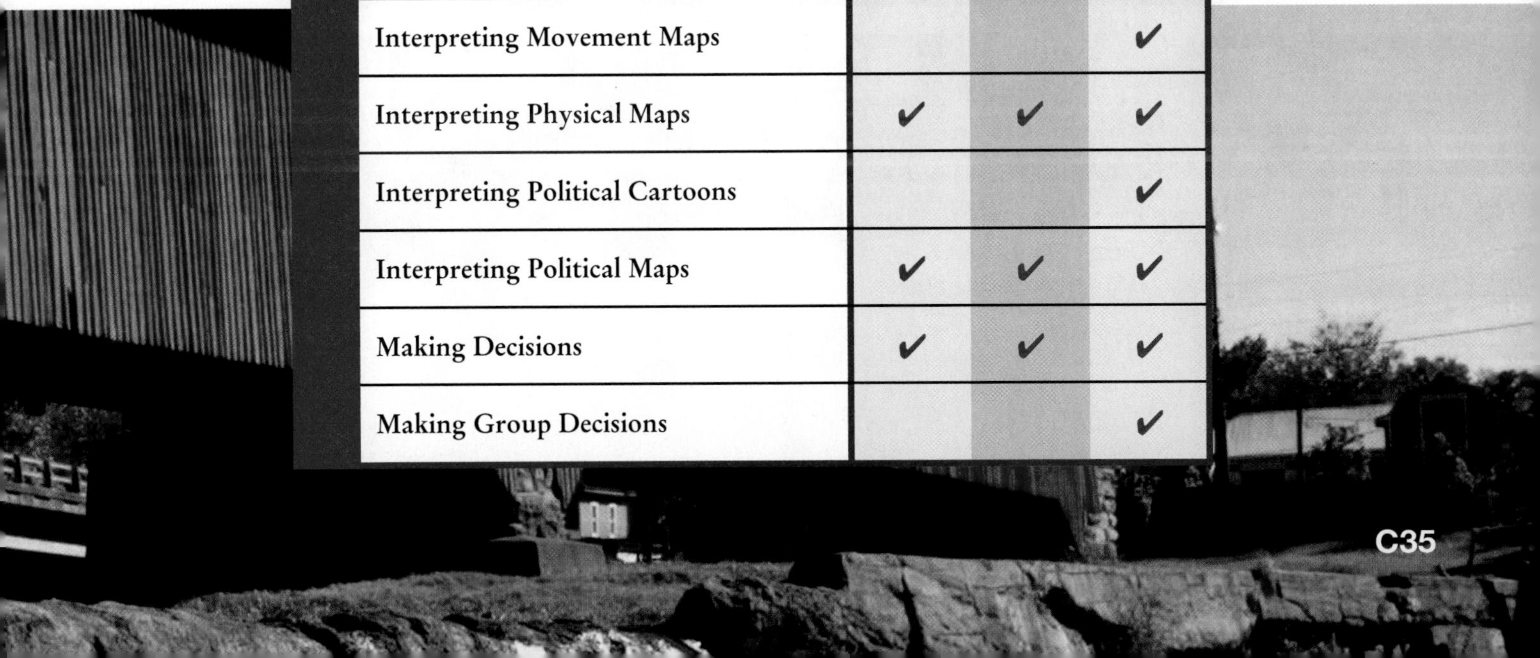

	SKILL	HOLT MCDOUGAL WESTERN WORLD	HOLT MCDOUGAL EASTERN WORLD	HOLT MCDOUGAL UNITED STATES HISTORY, GROWTH AND DEVELOPMENT: BEGINNINGS TO 1914
ACQUIRING INFORMATION	Making Oral Presentations	✔	✔	✔
	Obtaining Historical Data	✔	✔	✔
	Organizing Information	✔	✔	✔
	Reading an Election Map			✔
	Recognizing Historical Perspectives	✔	✔	✔
	Understanding Transportation Maps	✔		✔
	Using a Topographic Map		✔	✔
	Using a Variety of Information Sources	✔	✔	✔
	Using Latitude and Longitude	✔	✔	✔
	Using Scale	✔	✔	✔
	Working in Groups to Solve Issues			✔

Short-Response Questions

Short-response questions are questions that require a short written answer in response to reading literature, a primary source document, or an informational text. You will probably be given blank space in your answer booklet to answer these types of questions. Do not write outside of this space. You should plan to spend about five minutes answering each short-response question.

Read the question carefully, and use the information from the question in your answer. Be sure that you answer the question completely. Write your answer in the answer blank, if one is provided.

Some tips for answering short-response questions are

1. Read the passage in its entirety.
2. Words such as *compare, contrast, interpret, discuss,* and *summarize* often appear in short-response questions. Be sure you have a complete understanding of each of these words.
3. When writing your response, be precise but brief. Be sure to refer to details from the passage in your response.

Short-response questions are scored differently than other types of questions. They are usually given 0, 1, or 2 points. If an answer shows no understanding of the social studies involved in the question, or if a question is left unanswered, that response will receive 0 points. If a response shows understanding, but the final answer is incorrect, then that response will receive 1 point. A response will also receive 1 point if the answer is correct but does not clearly show understanding. A response will receive 2 points if the answer is correct and demonstrates a complete understanding of the social studies concepts involved.

Because of this scoring system, you should always try to answer short-response questions even if you are unsure of the correct answer. If part of your answer is correct, you could receive partial credit.

In short-response questions, you will usually not be penalized for spelling or grammatical mistakes or for leaving off the units in your answer.

Sample Short-Response Question

After reading Edna St. Vincent Millay's poem *Sonnet cxxii* write a short response summarizing Millay's comments about the idea of justice versus the reality of the justice system.

Sample Response

Millay makes the point that justice in theory and justice in practice are two different things. In the line "So have we loved sweet Justice to the last,/ Who now lies here in an unseemly place," Millay is saying that justice has not been served in the Sacco-Vanzetti case. She points out the hypocrisy of people fighting to uphold the idea of justice while settling for injustices such as the death sentence of Sacco and Vanzetti.

Sample Short-Response Question

After reading the primary source "Letter to Father Flye" August 18, 1932, explain what Agee's playing of Beethoven's Ninth Symphony in his office suggest about his ideals.

Sample Response

Agee's playing of Beethoven's Ninth Symphony in his office suggests vulnerability and idealism; it also shows his need to find a refuge, significantly above the "epidemic of despair" he observes in everyday life. Inspired, passionate music and the openness around him remind him of the possibilities for universal love and compassion.

Questions that Analyze and Interpret Visual Information

Many social studies tests include questions that ask you to analyze and interpret visual information such as pictures, charts, graphs, timelines, and cartoons. These questions could require a short written response or a multiple-choice answer.

Here are some **suggestions for answering questions based on visuals:**

- Look at the title and major labels of the visual to figure out the focus or purpose of the visual.
- If the visual is a chart or timeline, for example, read the other headings or labels to find out what data is given and how it is organized.
- If the item includes a map, look at the map's legend or key, which explains symbols, lines, and shadings in the map. Form visual images of maps, and try to draw them from memory. The test will most likely include important maps from the time period and subjects you have been studying. For example, in early U. S. history, be able to see in your mind's eye such things as where the New England, middle, and southern colonies were located, what land the Louisiana Purchase and Mexican Cession covered, and the dividing line for slave and free states.
- Analyze the data in the visual to determine quantities, relationships, intervals of time, directions, sequences, or other patterns.
- When analyzing and interpreting political cartoons, note the objects or people that you see in the cartoon. Are any of the people or objects actually symbols of something else? Look for clues in the cartoon as to the political or social issue that is being presented. It is important that you know this focus. Then look for clues as to the cartoonist's viewpoint on the issue. You must remember this cartoon is the cartoonist's opinion of an issue, so it's important also to know who might agree or disagree with the cartoon and why.
- Adopt an acronym—a word from the first letters of other words—that you will always use for analyzing and interpreting a visual that accompanies a question.

HELPFUL ACRONYM FOR VISUALS: OPTIC

O overview
P parts (labels for details of the visual)
T title
I interrelationships (how the parts work together)
C conclusion (what the visual means)

Sample Question

1. According to the chart below, which type of storm has a wind speed of 120 mph and barometric air pressure less than 28 inches?

A. Category 1
B. Category 2
C. Category 3
D. Category 4

Saffir-Simpson Scale		
Hurricane Type	**Wind Speed HPH**	**Air Pressure MB (inches)**
Category 1	74-95	more than 980 (28.94)
Category 2	96-110	965-979 (28.50-28.91)
Category 3	111-130	945-964 (27.91-28.47)
Category 4	131-155	920-944 (27.17-27.88)
Category 5	more than 155	919 (27.16)

TEACHER'S EDITION

INDIANA

HOLT McDOUGAL
a division of Houghton Mifflin Harcourt

United States History

Growth and Development: Beginnings to 1914

William Deverell
Deborah Gray White

HOLT McDOUGAL
a division of Houghton Mifflin Harcourt

Authors

William Deverell

William Deverell is Professor of History at the University of Southern California. He is the author of *Railroad Crossing: Californians and the Railroad, 1850-1910* and *Whitewashed Adobe: The Rise of Los Angeles and the Remaking of the Mexican Past.* He is the editor of the *Blackwell Companion to the American West.* With Greg Hise, he co-authored *Eden by Design: The 1930 Olmsted-Bartholomew Plan for the Los Angeles Region* and co-edited *Land of Sunshine: The Environmental History of Metropolitan Los Angeles.* He is the former chairman of the California Council for the Humanities.

Deborah Gray White

Deborah Gray White, a former New York City school teacher, is Distinguished Professor of History at Rutgers University in New Brunswick, New Jersey. A specialist in American history and the history of African Americans, she is the author of several books, including: *Ar'n't I A Woman? Female Slaves in the Plantation South; Too Heavy a Load: Black Women in Defense of Themselves, 1894-1994*; and *Let My People Go, African Americans 1804-1860*, Volume 4 in the *Young Oxford History of African Americans.*

For acknowledgments, see page R110, which is an extension of the copyright page.

Printed in the United States of America

ISBN-13: 978-0-55-401665-8
ISBN-10: 0-55-401665-6
2 3 0914 10 09

Program Consultants

Contributing Author

Kylene Beers, Ed.D.
Senior Reading Advisor to Secondary Schools
Teachers College Reading and Writing Project
Columbia University
New York City, New York

A former middle school teacher, Dr. Beers has turned her commitment to helping struggling readers into the major focus of her research, writing, speaking, and teaching. She is the former editor of the National Council of Teachers of English (NCTE) literacy journal *Voices from the Middle*. Currently serving NCTE as vice president, she will assume the presidency in 2008. Her published works include *When Kids Can't Read: What Teachers Can Do* (Heinemann, 2002).

General Editor

Frances Marie Gipson
Secondary Literacy
Los Angeles Unified School District
Los Angeles, California

In her current position, Frances Gipson guides reform work for secondary instruction and supports its implementation. She has designed curriculum at the district, state, and national levels. Her leadership of a coaching collaborative with Subject Matter Projects of the University of California at Los Angeles evolved from her commitment to rigorous instruction and to meeting the needs of diverse learners.

Senior Literature and Writing Specialist

Carol Jago
English Department Chairperson
Santa Monica High School
Santa Monica, California

An English teacher at the middle and high school levels for 26 years, Carol Jago also directs the reading and literature project at UCLA and writes a weekly education column for the Los Angeles Times. She has been published in numerous professional journals and has authored several books, including *Cohesive Writing: Why Concept is Not Enough* (Boynton/Cook, 2002).

Consultants

Martha H. Ball, M.A.
Religion Consultant
Utah 3Rs Project Director
Utah State Office of Education
Salt Lake City, Utah

John Ferguson, M.T.S., J.D.
Senior Religion Consultant
Assistant Professor
Political Science/Criminal Justice
Howard Payne University
Brownwood, Texas

J. Frank Malaret
Senior Consultant
Dean, Downtown and West Sacramento Outreach Centers
Sacramento City College
Sacramento, California

Kimberly A. Plummer, M.A.
Senior Consultant
History-Social Science Educator/Advisor
Holt, Rinehart & Winston

Andrés Reséndez, Ph.D.
Senior Consultant,
Assistant Professor
Department of History
University of California at Davis
Davis, California

Indiana Teacher Advisory Panel

Sam Fies
History and Geography of the Eastern Hemishere
Highland Middle School
Shererville, Indiana

Jill Anne Hahn
Government and Economics
Central High School
Evansville, Indiana

Todd A. Kendrick
U.S. and World History
Franklin Central High School
Indianapolis, Indiana

Mary Jane Smith
Psychology
Warren Central High School
South Greenfield, Indiana

Academic Reviewers

Anne C. Bailey, Ph.D.
Spelman College
Atlanta, Georgia

Albert Camarillo, Ph.D.
Department of History
Stanford University

Larry Conyers, Ph.D.
Department of Anthropology
University of Denver

Willard Gatewood, Ph.D.
Emeritus Alumni Distinguished Professor, Department of History
University of Arkansas

Christopher Hendricks, Ph.D.
Department of History
Armstrong Atlantic State University
Savannah, Georgia

Skip Hyser, Ph.D.
Department of History
James Madison University
Harrisonburg, Virginia

Yasuhide Kawashima
Department of History
University of Texas at El Paso

Brenda E. Stevenson, Ph.D.
Department of History
UCLA
Los Angeles, California

David Switzer, Ph.D.
Department of Social Studies
Plymouth State University
Plymouth, New Hampshire

Jessica Wang, Ph.D.
Department of History
UCLA
Los Angeles, California

Nan Woodruff, Ph.D
Department of History
Pennsylvania State University

Craig Yirush, Ph.D.
Department of History
UCLA
Los Angeles, California

Educational Reviewers

Nelson Acevedo
New York City Alternative Schools and Programs
New York, New York

Henry Assetto
Twin Valley High School
Elverson, Pennsylvania

John Bilsky
Linton Middle School
Penn Hills, Pennsylvania

Julie Chan, Ed.D.
Director, Literacy Instruction
Newport-Mesa Unified School District
Costa Mesa, California

Kermit Cummings
Cockeysville Middle School
Baltimore County Public Schools
Baltimore, Maryland

Katherine A. DeForge
Social Studies Chair
Marcellus Central School
Marcellus, New York

Sandra Eades
Ridgely Middle School
Lutherville, Maryland

Ed Felten
Coopersville Public School District
Coopersville, Michigan

Tim Gearhart
Daniel Lewis Middle School
Paso Robles, California

Stacy Goldman
Lincoln Middle School
Berwyn, Illinois

Joseph P. Macary
Supervisor of Social Studies
Waterbury Public Schools
Waterbury, Connecticut

Carol Eiler Moore
Dundalk Middle School
Dundalk, Maryland

Tina Nelson
Baltimore County Public School District
Baltimore, Maryland

Ann-Jean Paci
Sheepshead Bay High School
Brooklyn, New York

Anthony Powell
Edmund W. Miles Middle School
Amityville, New York

Linda Prior
Floyd T. Binns Middle School
Culpeper County, Virginia

Wendy Schanberger
Hereford Middle School
Monkton, Maryland

Sue A. Shinn
Culpeper Middle School
Culpeper, Virginia

Kathleen Torquata
Lincoln Middle School
Berwyn, Illinois

Teacher's Edition

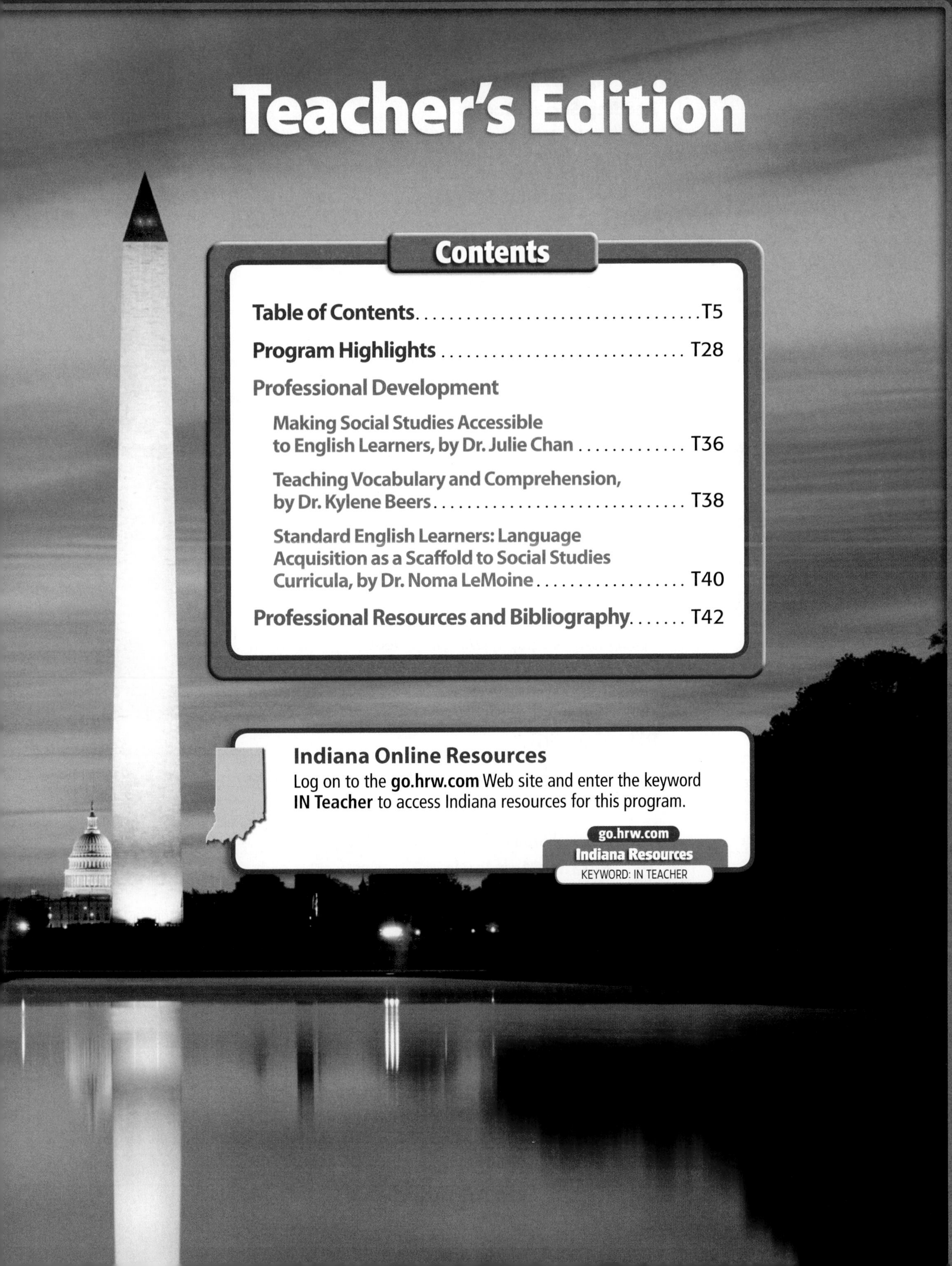

Contents

Indiana Online Resources

Log on to the **go.hrw.com** Web site and enter the keyword **IN Teacher** to access Indiana resources for this program.

go.hrw.com
Indiana Resources
KEYWORD: IN TEACHER

Contents

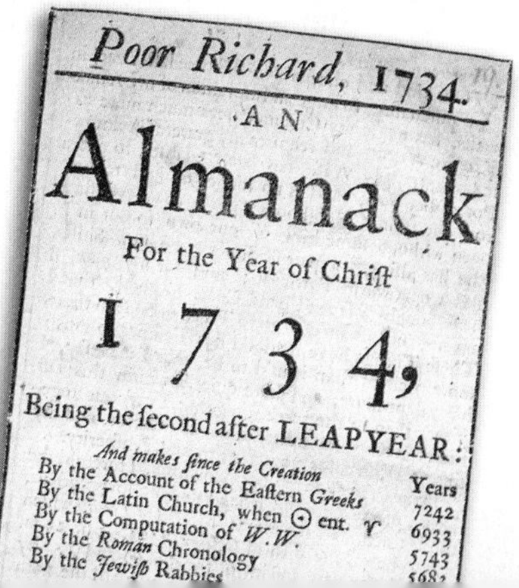
Poor Richard, 1734.
AN
Almanack
For the Year of Chriſt
1734,
Being the ſecond after LEAPYEAR:
And makes ſince the Creation — Years
By the Account of the Eaſtern Greeks — 7242
By the Latin Church, when ☉ ent. ♈ — 6933
By the Computation of W.W. — 5743
By the Roman Chronology
By the Jewiſh Rabbies

UNIT 2 A New Nation (1777–1800)

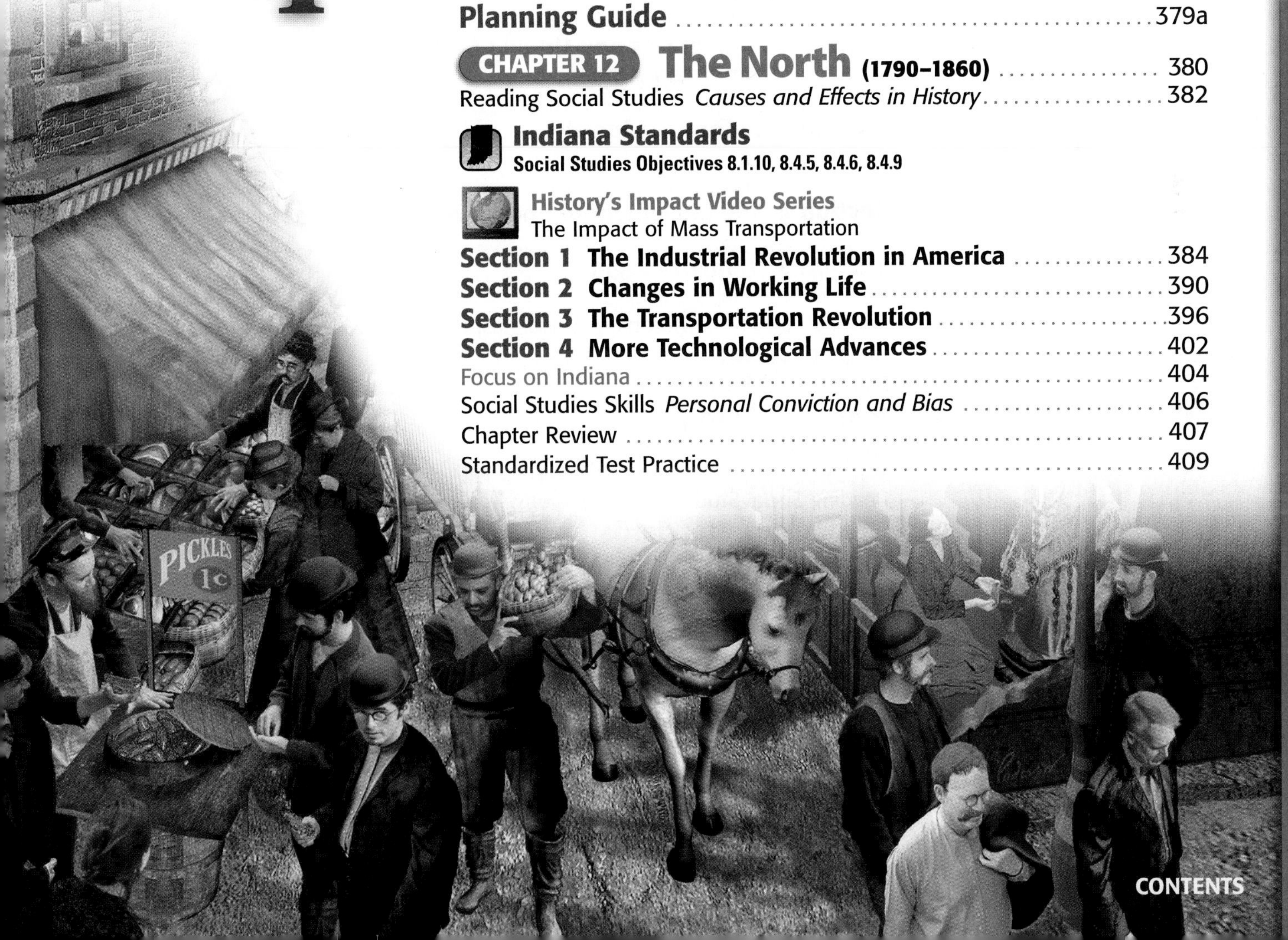
PICKLES
1c

UNIT 5 The Nation Breaks Apart

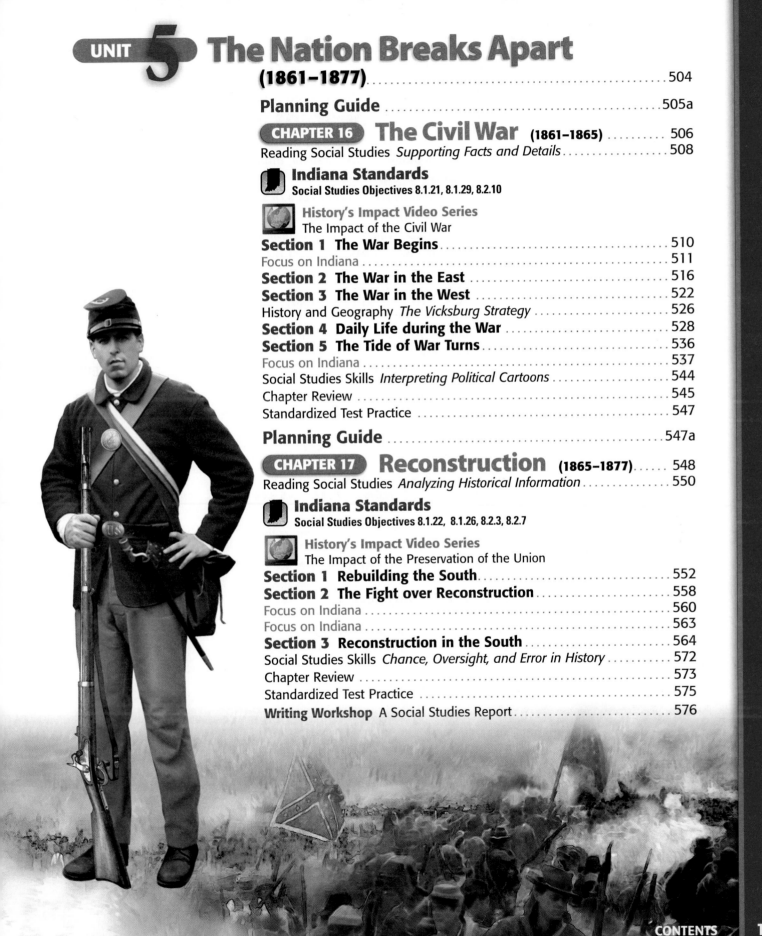

UNIT 6 A Growing America (1850–1914)

JULY
IV
MDCCLXXVI

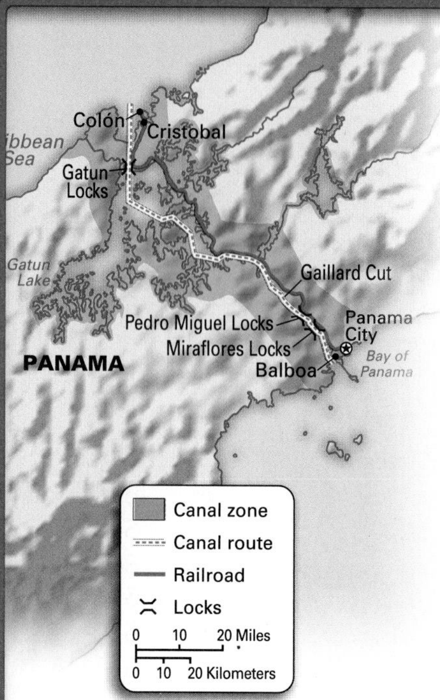

Reference Section

Features

History Close-up

See how people lived and how places looked in the past by taking a close–up view of history.

BIOGRAPHIES

Meet the people who have influenced history and learn about their lives.

History and Geography

Explore the relationships between history and geography.

THE IMPACT TODAY

Understand how events from the past have had an impact on our world today.

LINKING TO TODAY

Link people and events from the past to the world you live in today.

QUICK FACTS

Examine key facts and concepts quickly and easily with graphics.

Charts, Graphs, and Tables

Analyze information presented visually to learn more about history.

CHARTS

INFOGRAPHICS

Analyze and interpret information from graphics.

TIME LINES

See how key events are related in time.

Points of View

See how different people have interpreted historical issues in different ways.

Historic Documents

Examine key documents that have shaped U.S. history.

Literature in History

Learn about the beliefs and experiences of people who lived in other times and places through literature pieces.

Social Studies Skills

Learn, practice, and apply the skills you need to study and analyze history.

Reading Social Studies

Learn and practice skills that will help you read your social studies lesson.

Focus on Writing and Speaking

Use writing and speaking to study and reflect on the events and people who made history.

Writing Workshop

Learn to write about history.

Political Cartoons

Interpret political cartoons to learn about U.S. history.

Supreme Court Decisions

Study the impact of Supreme Court decisions on U.S. history.

Interdisciplinary Connections

Learn history through connections to other disciplines.

Primary Sources

Read and analyze the exact words of important people and documents as related to the study of U.S. history.

Life
HUNDRED PER CENT AMERICAN NUMBER
"THE SPIRIT OF '26"
LIBERTY
PROHIBITION

Tip #2

Read like a Skilled Reader

You will never get better at reading your social studies book—or any book for that matter—unless you spend some time thinking about how to be a better reader.

Skilled readers do the following:

- They preview what they are supposed to read before they actually begin reading. They look for vocabulary words, titles of sections, information in the margin, or maps or charts they should study.
- They divide their notebook paper into two columns. They title one column "Notes from the Chapter" and the other column "Questions or Comments I Have."
- They take notes in both columns as they read.
- They read like **active readers**. The Active Reading list below shows you what that means.
- They use clues in the text to help them figure out where the text is going. The best clues are called signal words.

  Chronological Order Signal Words: *first, second, third, before, after, later, next, following that, earlier, finally*

  Cause and Effect Signal Words: *because of, due to, as a result of, the reason for, therefore, consequently*

  Comparison/Contrast Signal Words: *likewise, also, as well as, similarly, on the other hand*

READING SOCIAL STUDIES

Active Reading

Successful readers are **active readers**. These readers know that it is up to them to figure out what the text means. Here are some steps you can take to become an active, and successful, reader.

Predict what will happen next based on what has already happened. When your predictions don't match what happens in the text, reread the confusing parts.

Question what is happening as you read. Constantly ask yourself why things have happened, what things mean, and what caused certain events.

Summarize what you are reading frequently. Do not try to summarize the entire chapter! Read a bit and then summarize it. Then read on.

Connect what is happening in the part you're reading to what you have already read.

Clarify your understanding. Stop occasionally to ask yourself whether you are confused by anything. You may need to reread to clarify, or you may need to read further and collect more information before you can understand.

Visualize what is happening in the text. Try to see the events or places in your mind by drawing maps, making charts, or jotting down notes about what you are reading.

Tip #3

Pay Attention to Vocabulary

It is no fun to read something when you don't know what the words mean, but you can't learn new words if you only use or read the words you already know. In this book, we know we have probably used some words you don't know. But, we have followed a pattern as we have used more difficult words.

Key Terms and People

At the beginning of each section you will find a list of key terms or people that you will need to know. Be on the lookout for those words as you read through the section.

...men's Bureau
In 1865 Congress established the **Freedmen's Bureau**, an agency providing relief for freed-...ople and certain poor people in the South...

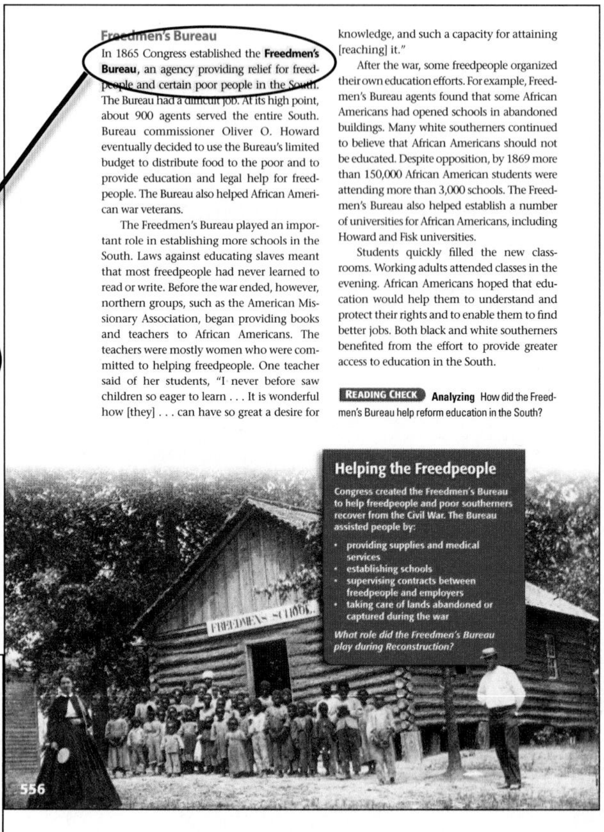

Freedmen's Bureau

In 1865 Congress established the **Freedmen's Bureau**, an agency providing relief for freedpeople and certain poor people in the South. The Bureau had a difficult job. At its high point, about 900 agents served the entire South. Bureau commissioner Oliver O. Howard eventually decided to use the Bureau's limited budget to distribute food to the poor and to provide education and legal help for freedpeople. The Bureau also helped African American war veterans.

The Freedmen's Bureau played an important role in establishing more schools in the South. Laws against educating slaves meant that most freedpeople had never learned to read or write. Before the war ended, however, northern groups, such as the American Missionary Association, began providing books and teachers to African Americans. The teachers were mostly women who were committed to helping freedpeople. One teacher said of her students, "I never before saw children so eager to learn . . . It is wonderful how [they] . . . can have so great a desire for knowledge, and such a capacity for attaining [reaching] it."

After the war, some freedpeople organized their own education efforts. For example, Freedmen's Bureau agents found that some African Americans had opened schools in abandoned buildings. Many white southerners continued to believe that African Americans should not be educated. Despite opposition, by 1869 more than 150,000 African American students were attending more than 3,000 schools. The Freedmen's Bureau also helped establish a number of universities for African Americans, including Howard and Fisk universities.

Students quickly filled the new classrooms. Working adults attended classes in the evening. African Americans hoped that education would help them to understand and protect their rights and to enable them to find better jobs. Both black and white southerners benefited from the effort to provide greater access to education in the South.

READING CHECK **Analyzing** How did the Freedmen's Bureau help reform education in the South?

Helping the Freedpeople
Congress created the Freedmen's Bureau to help freedpeople and poor southerners recover from the Civil War. The Bureau assisted people by:
• providing supplies and medical services
• establishing schools
• supervising contracts between freedpeople and employers
• taking care of lands abandoned or captured during the war
What role did the Freedmen's Bureau play during Reconstruction?
556

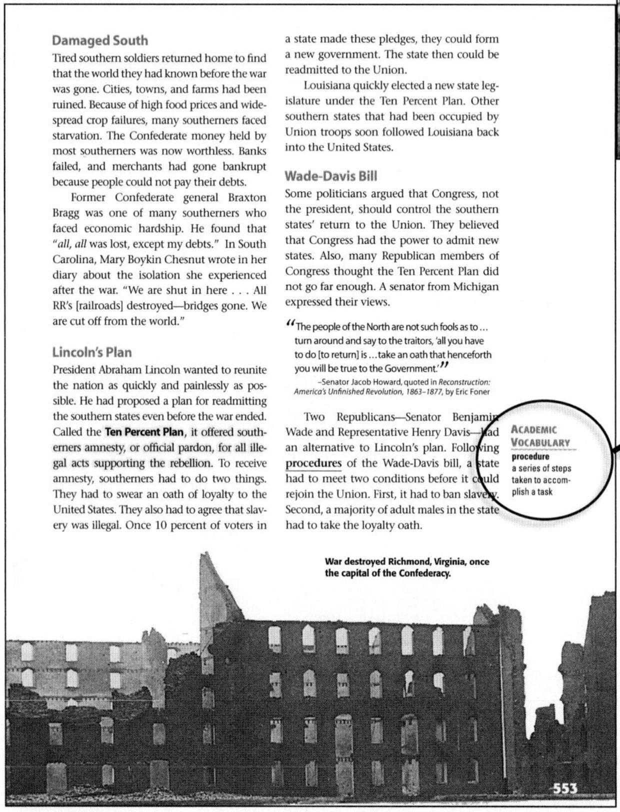

Damaged South

Tired southern soldiers returned home to find that the world they had known before the war was gone. Cities, towns, and farms had been ruined. Because of high food prices and widespread crop failures, many southerners faced starvation. The Confederate money held by most southerners was now worthless. Banks failed, and merchants had gone bankrupt because people could not pay their debts.

Former Confederate general Braxton Bragg was one of many southerners who faced economic hardship. He found that "*all, all* was lost, except my debts." In South Carolina, Mary Boykin Chesnut wrote in her diary about the isolation she experienced after the war. "We are shut in here . . . All RR's [railroads] destroyed—bridges gone. We are cut off from the world."

Lincoln's Plan

President Abraham Lincoln wanted to reunite the nation as quickly and painlessly as possible. He had proposed a plan for readmitting the southern states even before the war ended. Called the **Ten Percent Plan**, it offered southerners amnesty, or official pardon, for all illegal acts supporting the rebellion. To receive amnesty, southerners had to do two things. They had to swear an oath of loyalty to the United States. They also had to agree that slavery was illegal. Once 10 percent of voters in a state made these pledges, they could form a new government. The state then could be readmitted to the Union.

Louisiana quickly elected a new state legislature under the Ten Percent Plan. Other southern states that had been occupied by Union troops soon followed Louisiana back into the United States.

Wade-Davis Bill

Some politicians argued that Congress, not the president, should control the southern states' return to the Union. They believed that Congress had the power to admit new states. Also, many Republican members of Congress thought the Ten Percent Plan did not go far enough. A senator from Michigan expressed their views.

"The people of the North are not such fools as to . . . turn around and say to the traitors, 'all you have to do [to return] is . . . take an oath that henceforth you will be true to the Government.'"
—Senator Jacob Howard, quoted in *Reconstruction: America's Unfinished Revolution, 1863–1877*, by Eric Foner

Two Republicans—Senator Benjamin Wade and Representative Henry Davis—had an alternative to Lincoln's plan. Following procedures of the Wade-Davis bill, a state had to meet two conditions before it could rejoin the Union. First, it had to ban slavery. Second, a majority of adult males in the state had to take the loyalty oath.

ACADEMIC VOCABULARY
procedure a series of steps taken to accomplish a task

War destroyed Richmond, Virginia, once the capital of the Confederacy.

553

ACADEMIC VOCABULARY
procedure
a series of steps taken to accomplish a task

Academic Vocabulary

When we use a word that is important in all classes, not just social studies, we define it in the margin under the heading *Academic Vocabulary.* You will run into these academic words in other textbooks, so you should learn what they mean while reading this book.

Words to Know

As you read this social studies textbook, you will be more successful if you know or learn the meanings of the words on this page. There are two types of words listed here. The first list contains academic words, the words we discussed at the bottom of the previous page. These words are important in all classes, not just social studies. The second list contains words that are special to this particular topic of social studies, U.S. history.

Academic Words

abstract	expressing a quality or idea without reference to an actual thing
acquire	to get
advocate	to plead in favor of
affect	to change or influence
agreement	a decision reached by two or more people or groups
aspects	parts
authority	power, right to rule
cause	the reason something happens
circumstances	surrounding situation
classical	referring to the cultures of ancient Greece or Rome
complex	difficult, not simple
concrete	specific, real
consequences	the effects of a particular event or events
contemporary	existing at the same time
contract	a binding legal agreement
criteria	rules for defining
develop/ development	1. the process of growing or improving 2. Creation
distinct	separate
distribute	to divide among a group of people
effect	the results of an action or decision
efficient/ efficiency	productive and not wasteful
element	part
establish	to set up or create
execute	to perform, carry out
explicit	fully revealed without vagueness
facilitate	to bring about
factor	causes
features	characteristics
function	use or purpose
ideal	ideas or goals that people try to live up to
impact	effect, result
implement	to put in place
implications	effects of a decision
implicit	understood though not clearly put into words
incentive	something that leads people to follow a certain course of action
influence	change or have an effect on
innovation	a new idea or way of doing something
logic/logical	1. reasoned, well thought out 2. well thought out ideas
method	a way of doing something
motive	a reason for doing something
neutral	unbiased, not favoring either side in a conflict
policy	rule, course of action
primary	main, most important
principle	basic belief, rule, or law
procedure	a series of steps taken to accomplish a task
process	a series of steps by which a task is accomplished
purpose	the reason something is done
reaction	a response
rebel	to fight against authority
role	1. a part or function 2. Assigned behavior
strategy	a plan for fighting a battle or war
structure	the way something is set up or organized
traditional	customary, time-honored
values	ideas that people hold dear and try to live by
vary/various	1. To be different 2. of many types

Social Studies Words

AD	refers to dates after Jesus's birth
BC	refers to dates before the birth of Jesus of Nazareth
BCE	refers to "Before Common Era," dates before the birth of Jesus of Nazareth
CE	refers to "Common Era," dates after Jesus's birth
century	a period of 100 years
civilization	the culture of a particular time or place
climate	the weather conditions in a certain area over a long period of time
culture	the knowledge, beliefs, customs, and values of a group of people
custom	a repeated practice; tradition
democracy	governmental rule by the people, usually on a majority rule principle
economy	the system in which people make and exchange goods and services
geography	the study of the earth's physical and cultural features
independence	freedom from forceful rule
monarchy	governmental rule by one person, a king or queen
North	the region of the United States sometimes defined by the states that did not secede from the Union during the Civil War
rebellion	an organized resistance to the established government
society	a group of people who share common traditions
South	the region of the United States sometimes defined by the states that seceded from the Union to form the Confederate States of America

Mapping the Earth

A **globe** is a scale model of the earth. It is useful for showing the entire earth or studying large areas of the earth's surface.

A pattern of lines circles the globe in east-west and north-south directions. It is called a **grid**. The intersection of these imaginary lines helps us find places on the earth.

The east-west lines in the grid are lines of **latitude**. Lines of latitude are called **parallels** because they are always parallel to each other. These imaginary lines measure distance north and south of the **equator**. The equator is an imaginary line that circles the globe halfway between the North and South Poles. Parallels measure distance from the equator in **degrees**. The symbol for degrees is °. Degrees are further divided into **minutes**. The symbol for minutes is ´. There are 60 minutes in a degree. Parallels north of the equator are labeled with an N. Those south of the equator are labeled with an S.

The north-south lines are lines of **longitude**. Lines of longitude are called **meridians**. These imaginary lines pass through the Poles. They measure distance east and west of the **prime meridian**. The prime meridian is an imaginary line that runs through Greenwich, England. It represents 0° longitude.

Lines of latitude range from 0°, for locations on the equator, to 90°N or 90°S, for locations at the Poles. Lines of longitude range from 0° on the prime meridian to 180° on a meridian in the mid-Pacific Ocean. Meridians west of the prime meridian to 180° are labeled with a W. Those east of the prime meridian to 180° are labeled with an E.

Lines of Latitude

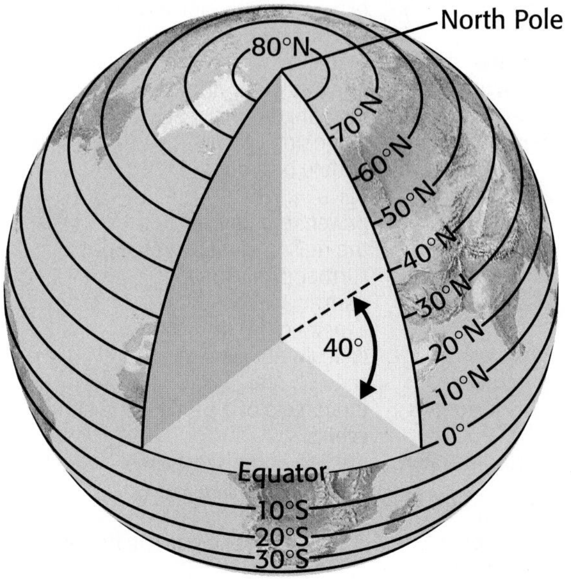

Lines of Longitude

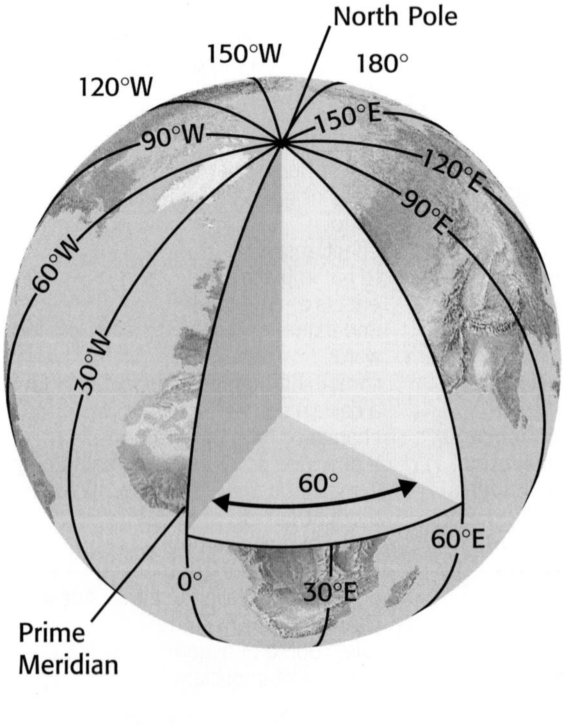

The equator divides the globe into two halves, called **hemispheres**. The half north of the equator is the Northern Hemisphere. The southern half is the Southern Hemisphere. The prime meridian and the 180° meridian divide the world into the Eastern Hemisphere and the Western Hemisphere. However, the prime meridian runs right through Europe and Africa. To avoid dividing these continents between two hemispheres, some mapmakers divide the Eastern and Western hemispheres at 20°W. This places all of Europe and Africa in the Eastern Hemisphere.

Our planet's land surface is divided into seven large landmasses, called **continents**. They are identified in the maps on this page. Landmasses smaller than continents and completely surrounded by water are called **islands**.

Geographers also organize Earth's water surface into parts. The largest is the world ocean. Geographers divide the world ocean into the Pacific Ocean, the Atlantic Ocean, the Indian Ocean, and the Arctic Ocean. Lakes and seas are smaller bodies of water.

Northern Hemisphere

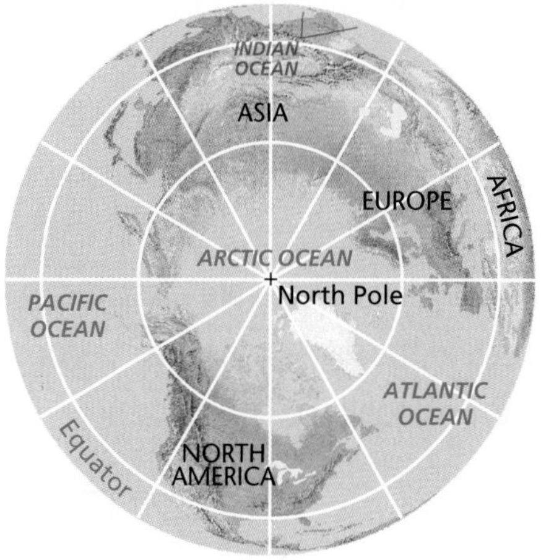

Southern Hemisphere

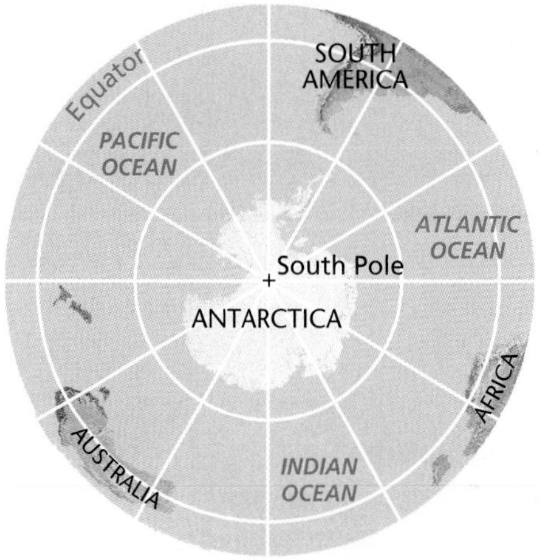

GEOGRAPHY AND MAP SKILLS

Western Hemisphere

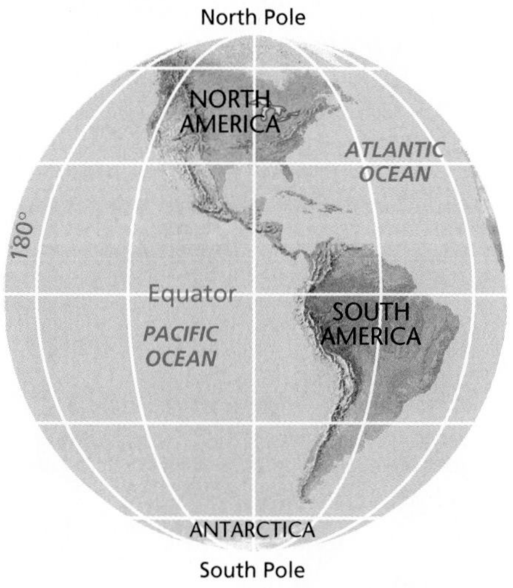

Eastern Hemisphere

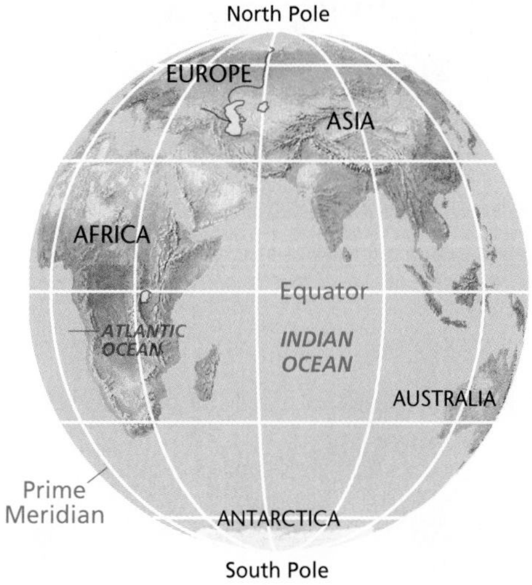

Mapmaking

A **map** is a flat diagram of all or part of the earth's surface. Mapmakers have created different ways of showing our round planet on flat maps. These different ways are called **map projections**. Because the earth is round, there is no way to show it accurately in a flat map. All flat maps are distorted in some way. Mapmakers must choose the type of map projection that is best for their purposes. Many map projections are one of three kinds: cylindrical, conic, or flat-plane.

Cylindrical Projections

Cylindrical projections are based on a cylinder wrapped around the globe. The cylinder touches the globe only at the equator. The meridians are pulled apart and are parallel to each other instead of meeting at the Poles. This causes landmasses near the Poles to appear larger than they really are. The map below is a Mercator projection, one type of cylindrical projection. The Mercator projection is useful for navigators because it shows true direction and shape. However, it distorts the size of land areas near the Poles.

Paper cylinder

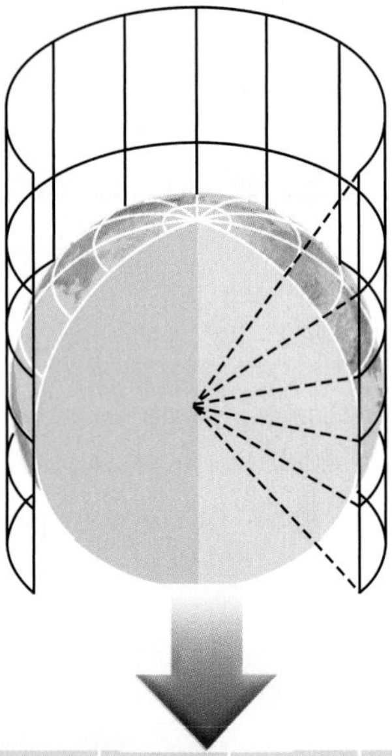

Mercator projection

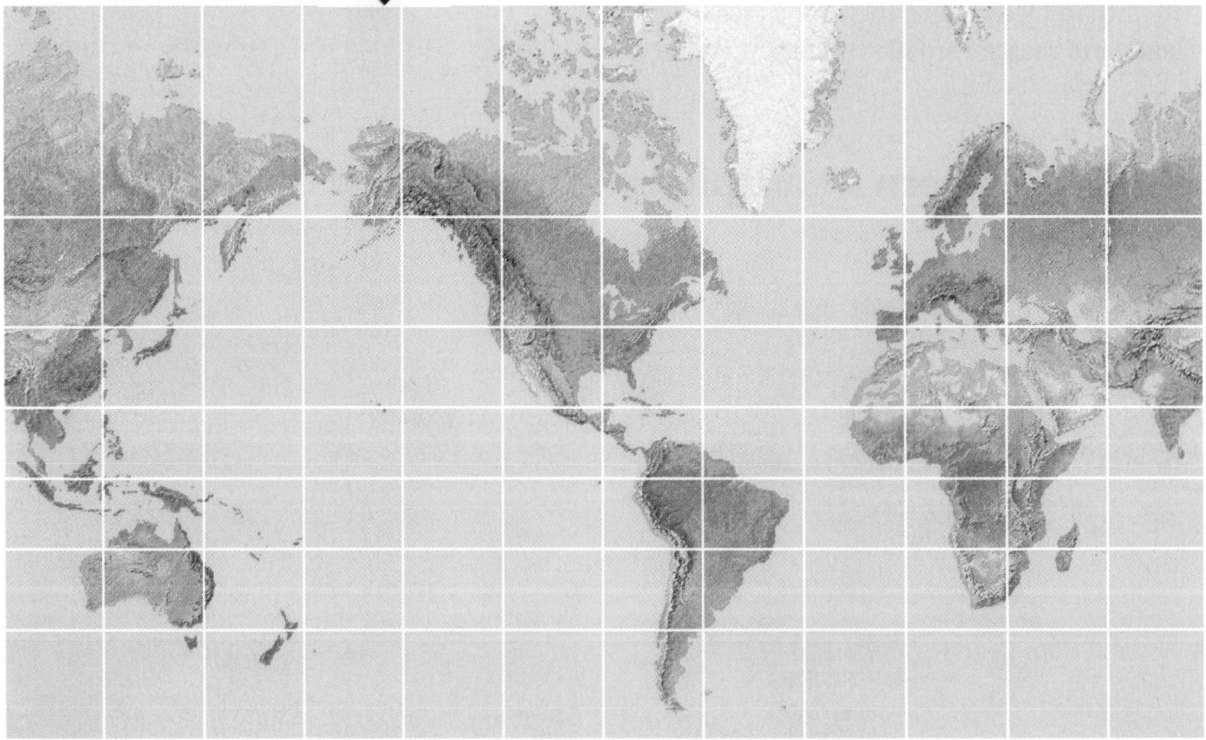

Conic Projections

Conic projections are based on a cone placed over the globe. A conic projection is most accurate along the lines of latitude where it touches the globe. It retains almost true shape and size. Conic projections are most useful for showing areas that have long east-west dimensions, such as the United States.

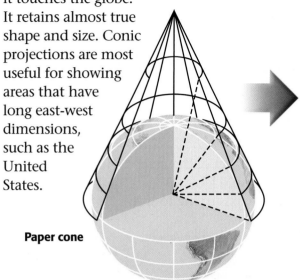

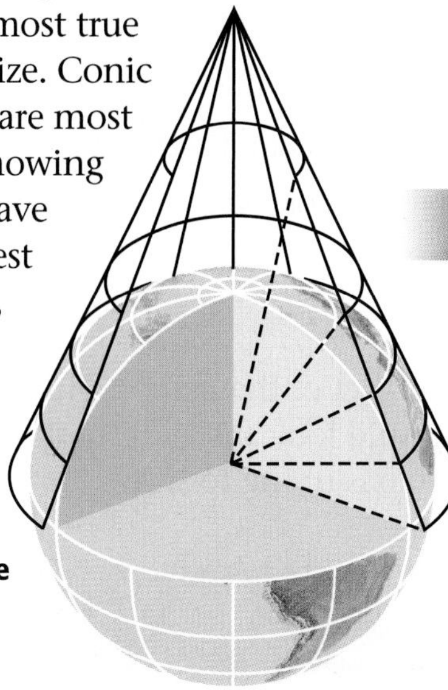

Paper cone

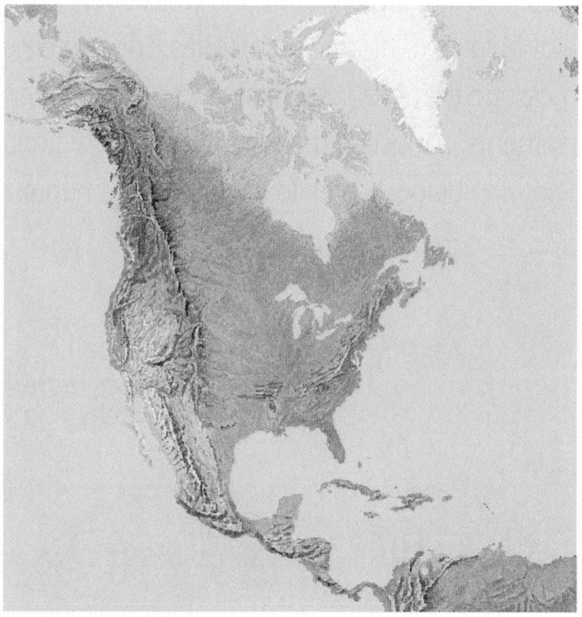

Conic projection

Flat-plane Projections

Flat-plane projections are based on a plane touching the globe at one point, such as at the North Pole or South Pole. A flat-plane projection is useful for showing true direction for airplane pilots and ship navigators. It also shows true area. However, it distorts the true shapes of landmasses.

Flat plane

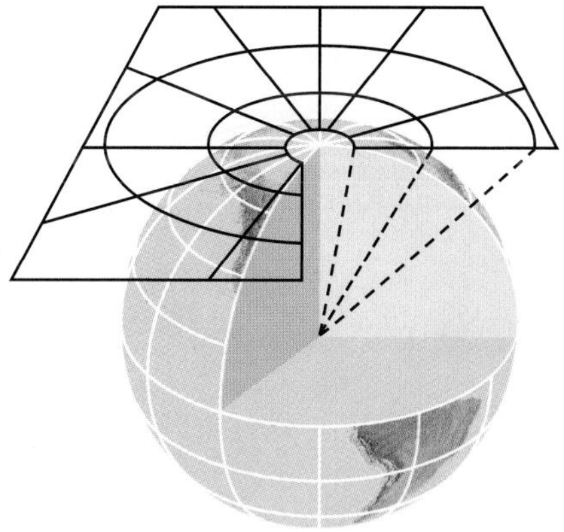

Flat-plane projection

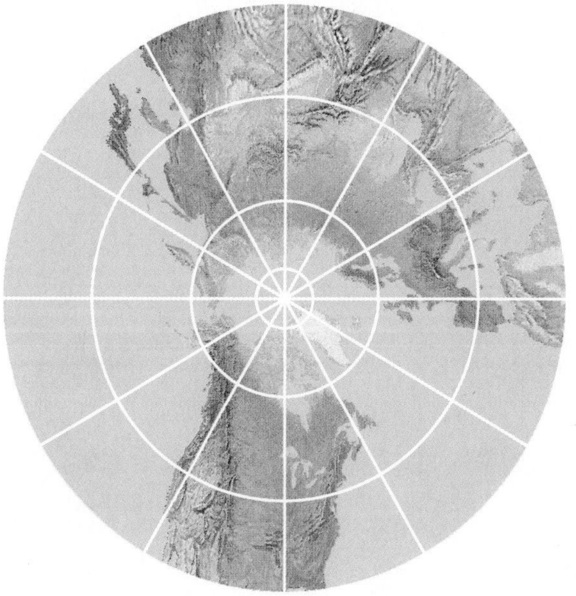

Map Essentials

Maps are like messages sent out in code. Mapmakers provide certain elements that help us translate these codes. These elements help us understand the message they are presenting about a particular part of the world. Of these elements, almost all maps have titles, directional indicators, scales, and legends. The map below has all four of these elements, plus a fifth—a locator map.

❶ Title

A map's **title** shows what the subject of the map is. The map title is usually the first thing you should look at when studying a map, because it tells you what the map is trying to show.

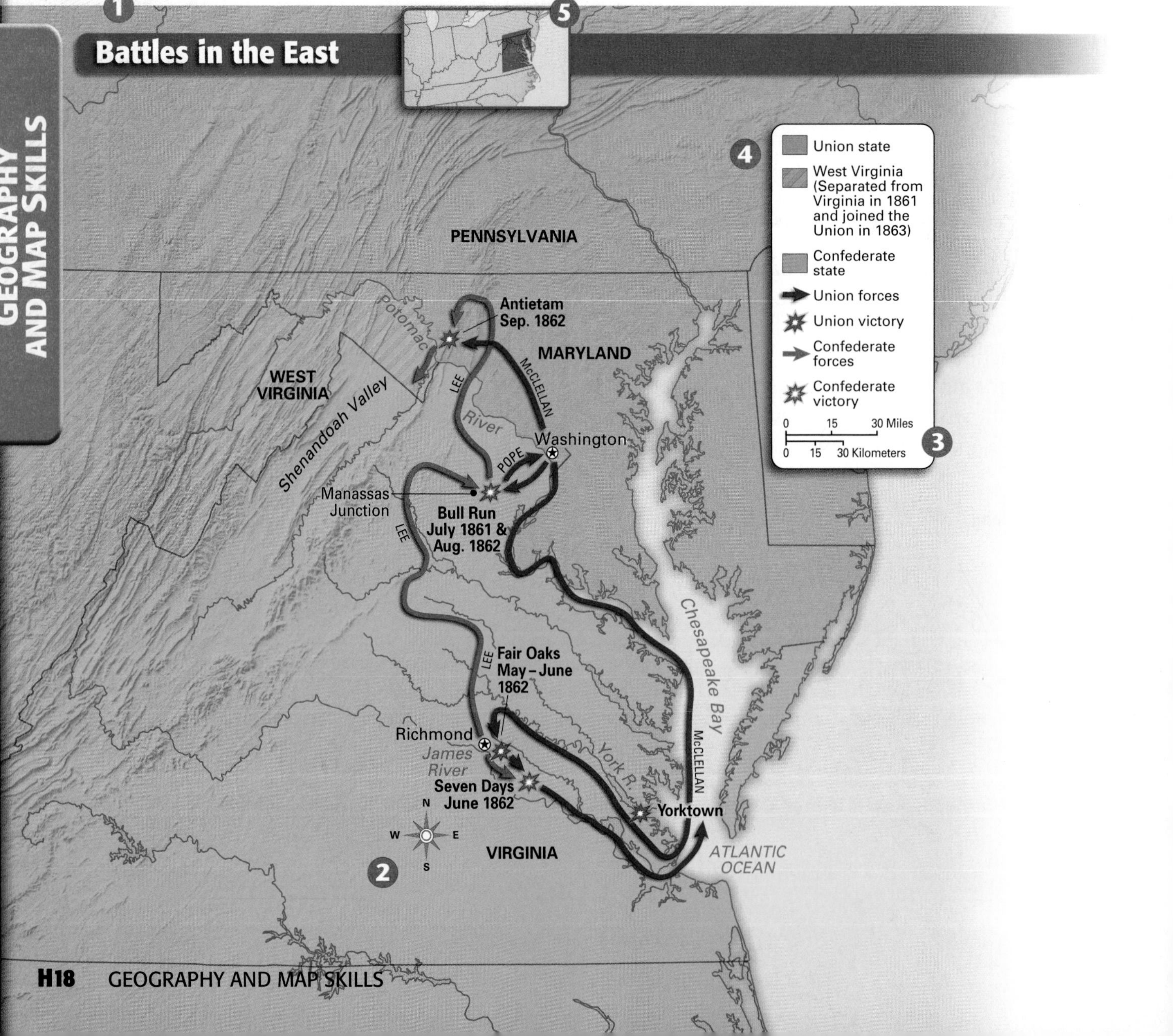

GEOGRAPHY AND MAP SKILLS

❷ Compass Rose

A directional indicator shows which way north, south, east, and west lie on the map. Some mapmakers use a "north arrow," which points toward the North Pole. Remember, "north" is not always at the top of a map. The way a map is drawn and the location of directions on that map depend on the perspective of the mapmaker. Most maps in this textbook indicate direction by using a compass rose. A **compass rose** has arrows that point to all four principal directions, as shown.

❸ Scale

Mapmakers use scales to represent the distances between points on a map. Scales may appear on maps in several different forms. The maps in this textbook provide a bar **scale**. Scales give distances in miles and kilometers.

To find the distance between two points on the map, place a piece of paper so that the edge connects the two points. Mark the location of each point on the paper with a line or dot. Then, compare the distance between the two dots with the map's bar scale. The number on the top of the scale gives the distance in miles. The number on the bottom gives the distance in kilometers. Because the distances are given in large intervals, you may have to approximate the actual distance on the scale.

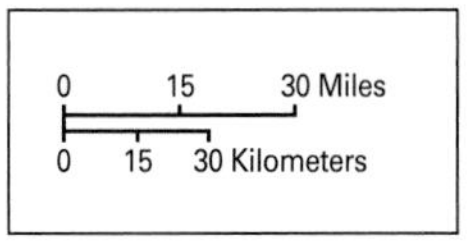

❹ Legend

The **legend**, or key, explains what the symbols on the map represent. Point symbols are used to specify the location of things, such as cities, that do not take up much space on the map. Some legends, such as the one shown here, show colors that represent certain elevations. Other maps might have legends with symbols or colors that represent things such as roads. Legends can also show economic resources, land use, population density, and climate.

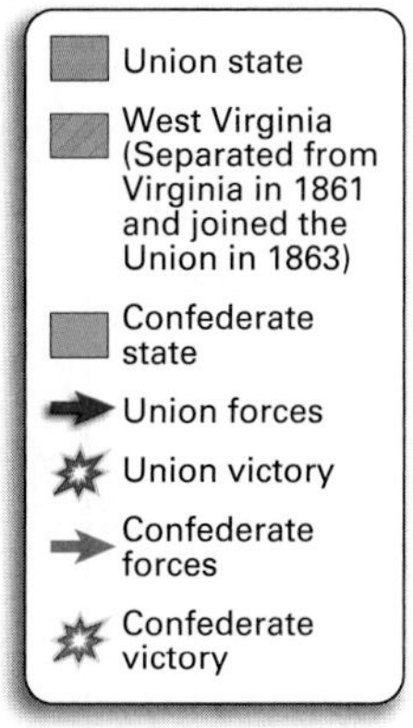

❺ Locator Map

A locator map shows where in the world the area on the map is located. The area shown on the main map is shown in red on the locator map. The locator map also shows surrounding areas so that the map reader can see how the information on the map relates to neighboring lands.

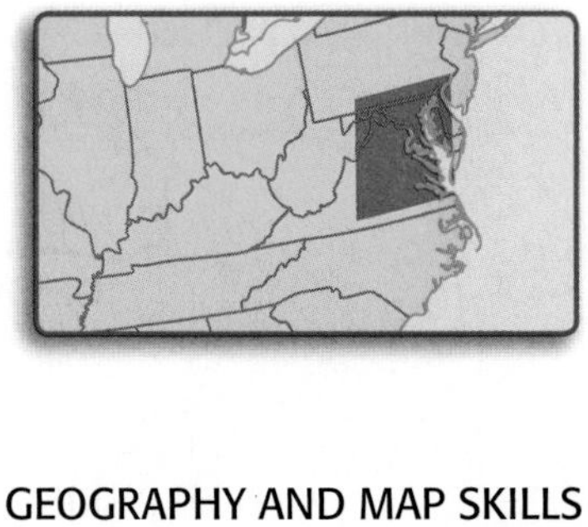

Working with Maps

The Atlas at the back of this textbook includes both physical and political maps. Physical maps, like the one you just saw and the one below, show the major physical features in a region. These features include things like mountain ranges, rivers, islands, and plains. Political maps show the major political features of a region, such as countries and their borders, capitals, and other important cities.

Topographic Maps

Some maps are topographic maps. A topographic map, like this one, shows the shape of the earth's surface using contour lines. Contour lines are imaginary lines connecting points of the same elevation above sea level. The distance between the lines represents the distance between points on the earth's surface. If the lines are close together, the feature is more steep than if the lines are far apart. Symbols on topographic maps represent natural and manmade features such as rivers, mountains, roads, and even buildings. Name five symbols you see on this topographic map.

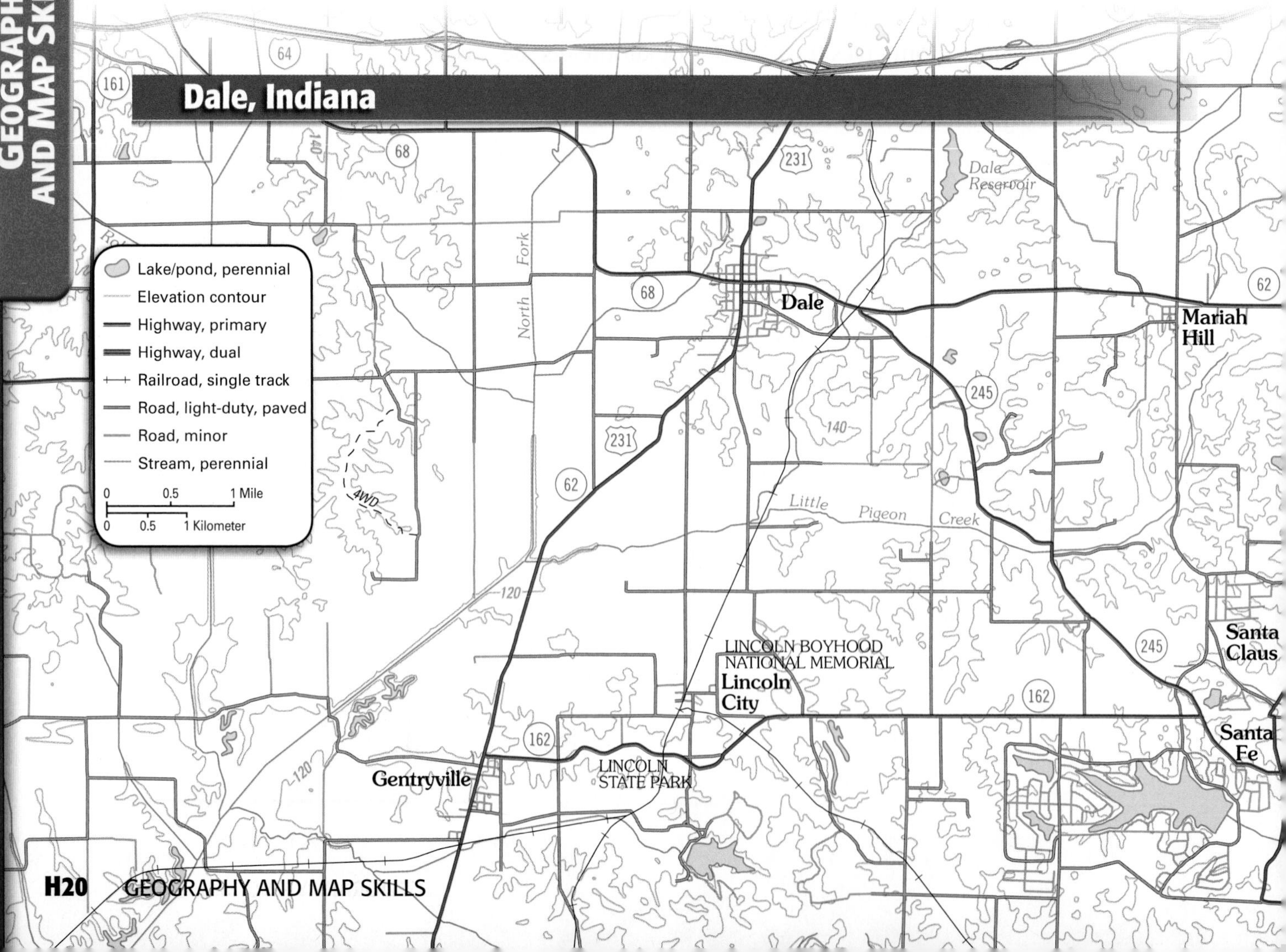

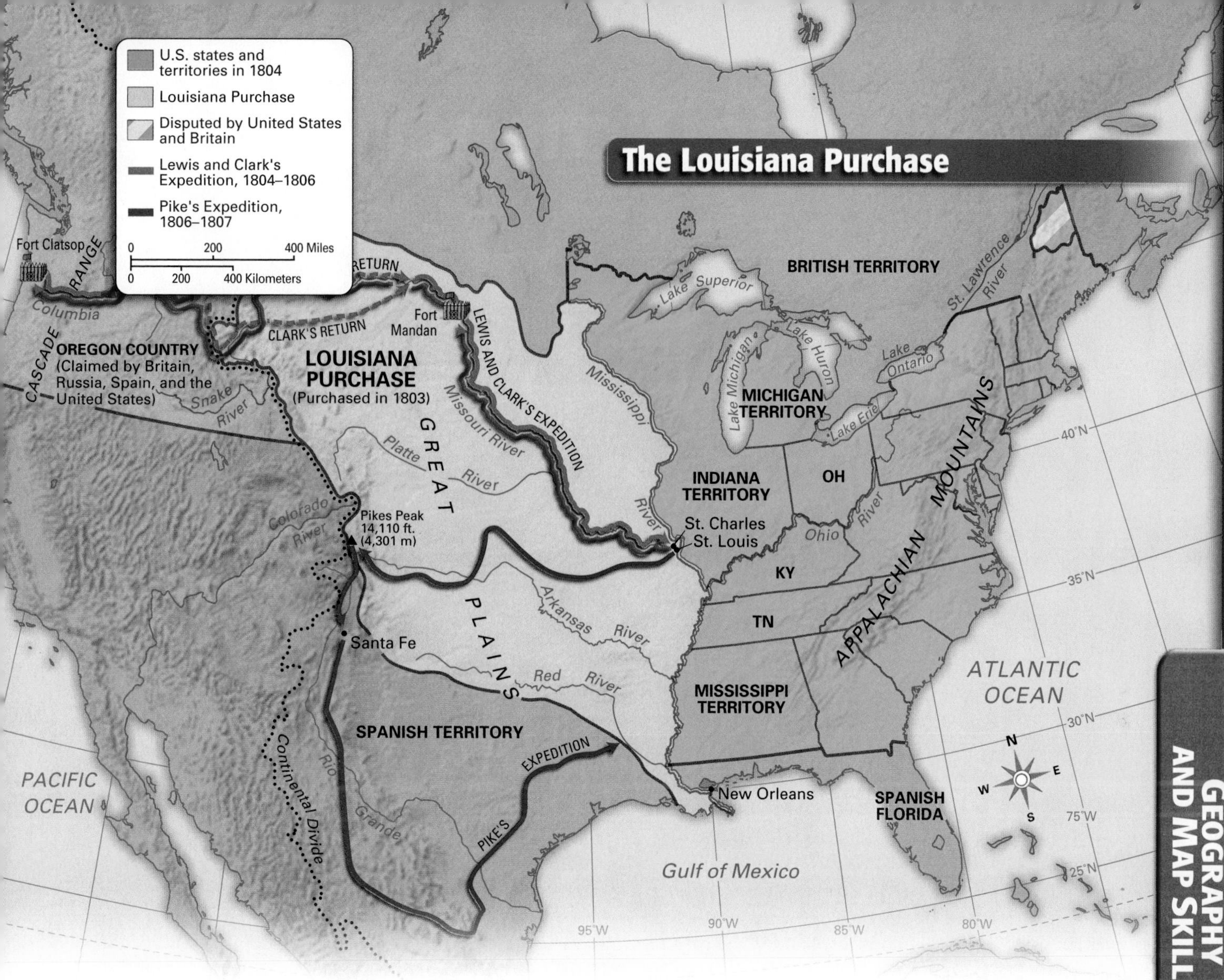

Historical Map

In this textbook, most of the maps you will study are historical maps. Historical maps, such as this one, are maps that show information about the past. This information might be which lands an empire controlled or where a certain group of people lived. Often colors are used to indicate the different things on the map. What does this map show?

Route Map

One special type of historical map is called a route map. A route map, like the one above, shows the route, or path, that someone or something followed. Route maps can show things like trade routes, invasion routes, or the journeys and travels of people. If more than one route is shown, several arrows of different colors may be used. What does this route map show?

The maps in this textbook will help you study and understand history. By working with these maps, you will see where important events happened, where empires rose and fell, and where people moved. In studying these maps, you will learn how geography has influenced history.

Geographic Dictionary

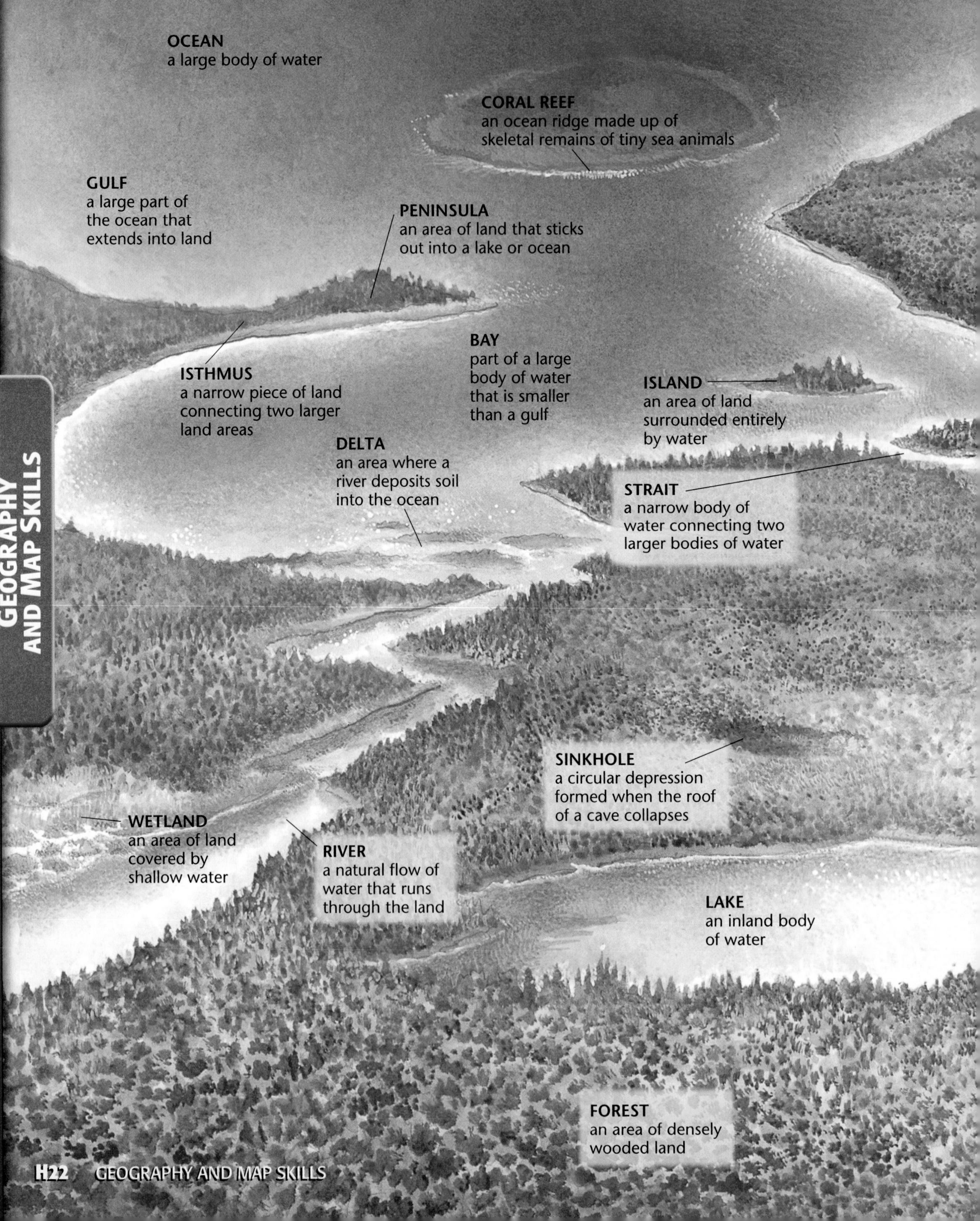
OCEAN
a large body of water
CORAL REEF
an ocean ridge made up of skeletal remains of tiny sea animals
GULF
a large part of the ocean that extends into land
PENINSULA
an area of land that sticks out into a lake or ocean
ISTHMUS
a narrow piece of land connecting two larger land areas
BAY
part of a large body of water that is smaller than a gulf
ISLAND
an area of land surrounded entirely by water
DELTA
an area where a river deposits soil into the ocean
STRAIT
a narrow body of water connecting two larger bodies of water
SINKHOLE
a circular depression formed when the roof of a cave collapses
WETLAND
an area of land covered by shallow water
RIVER
a natural flow of water that runs through the land
LAKE
an inland body of water
FOREST
an area of densely wooded land

COAST
an area of land near the ocean
MOUNTAIN
an area of rugged land that generally rises higher than 2,000 feet
VALLEY
an area of low land between hills or mountains
GLACIER
a large area of slow-moving ice
VOLCANO
an opening in Earth's crust where lava, ash, and gases erupt
CANYON
a deep, narrow valley with steep walls
HILL
a rounded, elevated area of land smaller than a mountain
PLAIN
a nearly flat area
DUNE
a hill of sand shaped by wind
OASIS
an area in the desert with a water source
DESERT
an extremely dry area with little water and few plants
PLATEAU
a large, flat, elevated area of land

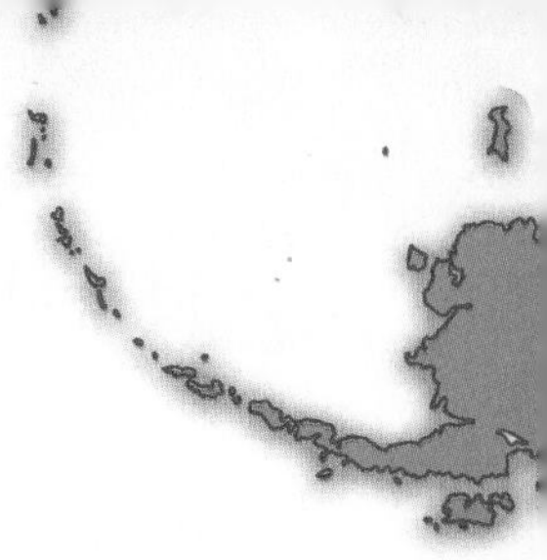

The Five Themes of Geography

Geography is the study of the world's people and places. As you can imagine, studying the entire world is a big job. To make the job easier, geographers have created the Five Themes of Geography. They are: **Location, Place, Human-Environment Interaction, Movement,** and **Region**. You can think of the Five Themes as five windows you can look through to study a place. If you looked at the same place through five different windows, you would have five different perspectives, or viewpoints, of the place. Using the Five Themes in this way will help you better understand the world's people and places.

1 Location The first thing to study about a place is its location. Where is it? Every place has an absolute location—its exact location on Earth. A place also has a relative location—its location in relation to other places. Use the theme of location to ask questions like, "Where is this place located, and how has its location affected it?"

2 Place Every place in the world is unique and has its own personality and character. Some things that can make a place unique include its weather, plants and animals, history, and the people that live there. Use the theme of place to ask questions like, "What are the unique features of this place, and how are they important?"

3 Human-Environment Interaction People interact with their environment in many ways. They use land to grow food and local materials to build houses. At the same time, a place's environment influences how people live. For example, if the weather is cold, people wear warm clothes. Use the theme of human-environment interaction to ask questions like, "What is this place's environment like, and how does it affect the people who live there?"

4 Movement The world is constantly changing, and places are affected by the movement of people, goods, ideas, and physical forces. For example, people come and go, new businesses begin, and rivers change their course. Use the theme of movement to ask questions like, "How is this place changing, and why?"

5 Region A region is an area that has one or more features that make it different from surrounding areas. A desert, a country, and a coastal area are all regions. Geographers use regions to break the world into smaller pieces that are easier to study. Use the theme of region to ask questions like "What common features does this area share, and how is it different from other areas?"

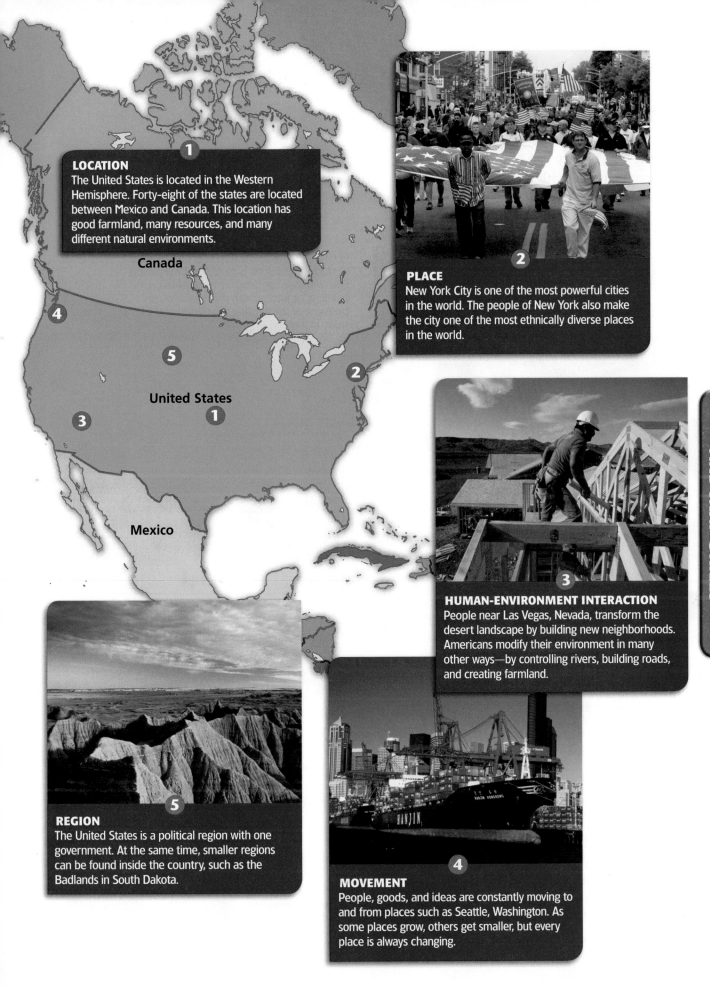

LOCATION
The United States is located in the Western Hemisphere. Forty-eight of the states are located between Mexico and Canada. This location has good farmland, many resources, and many different natural environments.

PLACE
New York City is one of the most powerful cities in the world. The people of New York also make the city one of the most ethnically diverse places in the world.

HUMAN-ENVIRONMENT INTERACTION
People near Las Vegas, Nevada, transform the desert landscape by building new neighborhoods. Americans modify their environment in many other ways—by controlling rivers, building roads, and creating farmland.

MOVEMENT
People, goods, and ideas are constantly moving to and from places such as Seattle, Washington. As some places grow, others get smaller, but every place is always changing.

REGION
The United States is a political region with one government. At the same time, smaller regions can be found inside the country, such as the Badlands in South Dakota.

How to Make This Book Work for You

Studying U.S. history will be easy for you using this textbook. Take a few minutes to become familiar with the easy-to-use structure and special features of this history book. See how this U.S. history textbook will make history come alive for you!

Unit

Each chapter of this textbook is part of a unit of study focusing on a particular time period. Each unit opener provides an illustration, painting, or photograph that gives you an overview of the exciting topics that you will study in the unit.

Chapter

Each chapter begins with a chapter-opener introduction where the sections of the chapter are listed out, and ends with Chapter Review pages and a Standardized Test Practice page.

Reading Social Studies These chapter-level reading lessons teach you skills and provide opportunities for practice to help you read the textbook more successfully. Within each chapter there is a point-of-reference *Focus on Reading* note in the margin to demonstrate the reading skill for the chapter. There are also questions in the Chapter Review activity to make sure that you understand the reading skill.

Social Studies Skills The Social Studies Skills lessons, which appear at the end of each chapter, give you an opportunity to learn and use a skill that you will most likely use again while in school. You will also be given a chance to make sure that you understand each skill by answering related questions in the Chapter Review activity.

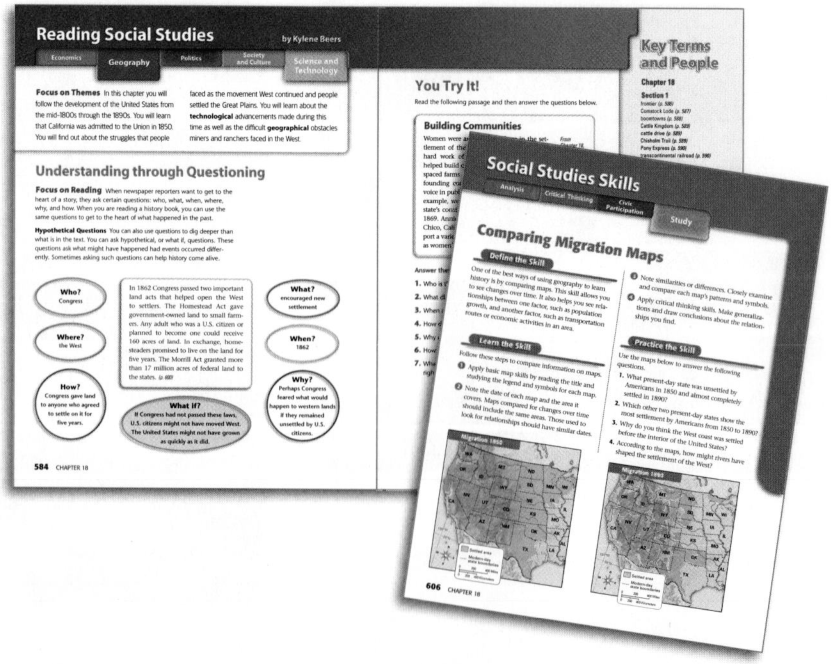

Section

The Section opener pages include: Main Idea statements, an overarching Big Idea statement, and Key Terms and People. In addition, each section includes the following special features.

If You Were There . . . introductions begin each section with a situation for you to respond to, placing you in the time period and in a situation related to the content that you will be studying in the section.

Building Background sections connect what will be covered in this section with what you studied in the previous section.

Short sections of content organize the information in each section into small chunks of text that you should not find too overwhelming.

The **Taking Notes** feature allows you to write down the most important information from the section in a usable format.

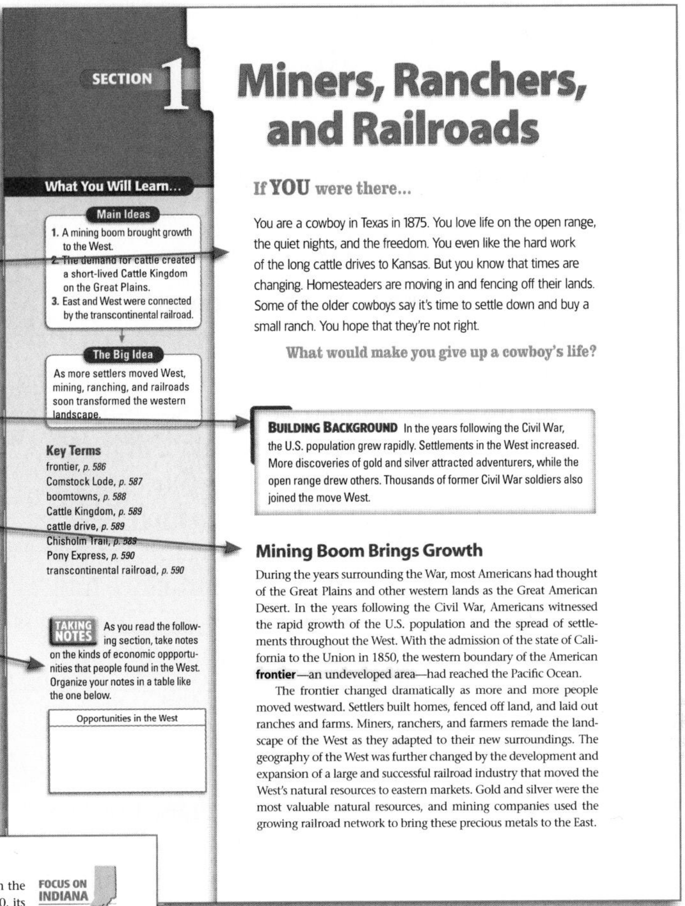

SECTION 1

Miners, Ranchers, and Railroads

What You Will Learn...

Main Ideas

1. A mining boom brought growth to the West.
2. The demand for cattle created a short-lived Cattle Kingdom on the Great Plains.
3. East and West were connected by the transcontinental railroad.

The Big Idea

As more settlers moved West, mining, ranching, and railroads soon transformed the western landscape.

Key Terms

frontier, *p. 586*
Comstock Lode, *p. 587*
boomtowns, *p. 588*
Cattle Kingdom, *p. 589*
cattle drive, *p. 589*
Chisholm Trail, *p. 589*
Pony Express, *p. 590*
transcontinental railroad, *p. 590*

TAKING NOTES As you read the following section, take notes on the kinds of economic oppportunities that people found in the West. Organize your notes in a table like the one below.

Opportunities in the West

If YOU were there...

You are a cowboy in Texas in 1875. You love life on the open range, the quiet nights, and the freedom. You even like the hard work of the long cattle drives to Kansas. But you know that times are changing. Homesteaders are moving in and fencing off their lands. Some of the older cowboys say it's time to settle down and buy a small ranch. You hope that they're not right.

What would make you give up a cowboy's life?

BUILDING BACKGROUND In the years following the Civil War, the U.S. population grew rapidly. Settlements in the West increased. More discoveries of gold and silver attracted adventurers, while the open range drew others. Thousands of former Civil War soldiers also joined the move West.

Mining Boom Brings Growth

During the years surrounding the War, most Americans had thought of the Great Plains and other western lands as the Great American Desert. In the years following the Civil War, Americans witnessed the rapid growth of the U.S. population and the spread of settlements throughout the West. With the admission of the state of California to the Union in 1850, the western boundary of the American **frontier**—an undeveloped area—had reached the Pacific Ocean.

The frontier changed dramatically as more and more people moved westward. Settlers built homes, fenced off land, and laid out ranches and farms. Miners, ranchers, and farmers remade the landscape of the West as they adapted to their new surroundings. The geography of the West was further changed by the development and expansion of a large and successful railroad industry that moved the West's natural resources to eastern markets. Gold and silver were the most valuable natural resources, and mining companies used the growing railroad network to bring these precious metals to the East.

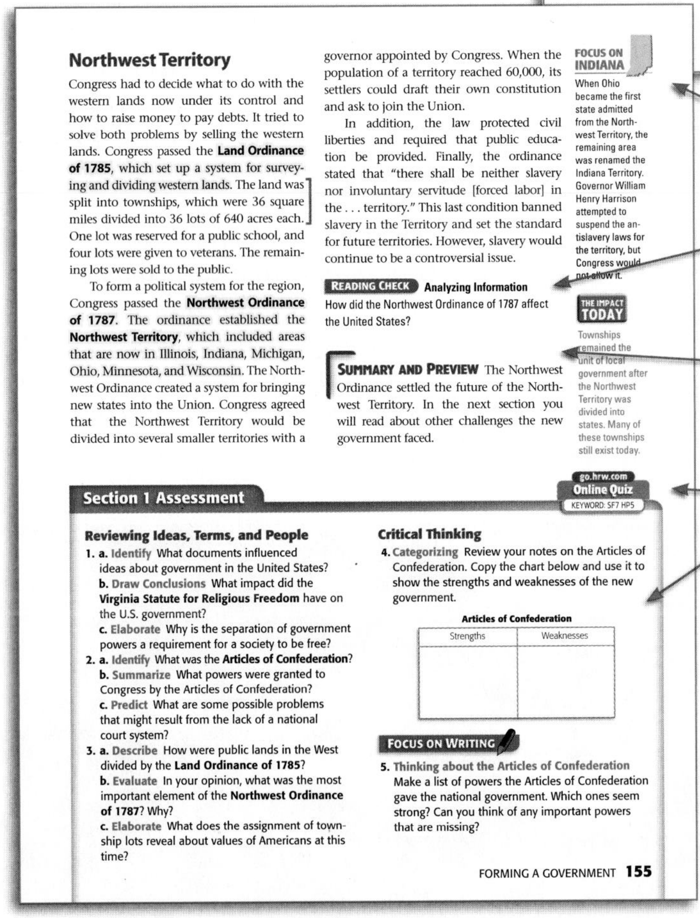

Northwest Territory

Congress had to decide what to do with the western lands now under its control and how to raise money to pay debts. It tried to solve both problems by selling the western lands. Congress passed the **Land Ordinance of 1785**, which set up a system for surveying and dividing western lands. The land was split into townships, which were 36 square miles divided into 36 lots of 640 acres each. One lot was reserved for a public school, and four lots were given to veterans. The remaining lots were sold to the public.

To form a political system for the region, Congress passed the **Northwest Ordinance of 1787**. The ordinance established the **Northwest Territory**, which included areas that are now in Illinois, Indiana, Michigan, Ohio, Minnesota, and Wisconsin. The Northwest Ordinance created a system for bringing new states into the Union. Congress agreed that the Northwest Territory would be divided into several smaller territories with a governor appointed by Congress. When the population of a territory reached 60,000, its settlers could draft their own constitution and ask to join the Union.

In addition, the law protected civil liberties and required that public education be provided. Finally, the ordinance stated that "there shall be neither slavery nor involuntary servitude [forced labor] in the . . . territory." This last condition banned slavery in the Territory and set the standard for future territories. However, slavery would continue to be a controversial issue.

READING CHECK **Analyzing Information** How did the Northwest Ordinance of 1787 affect the United States?

SUMMARY AND PREVIEW The Northwest Ordinance settled the future of the Northwest Territory. In the next section you will read about other challenges the new government faced.

FOCUS ON INDIANA

When Ohio became the first state admitted from the Northwest Territory, the remaining area was renamed the Indiana Territory. Governor William Henry Harrison attempted to suspend the antislavery laws for the territory, but Congress would not allow it.

THE IMPACT TODAY

Townships remained the unit of local government after the Northwest Territory was divided into states. Many of these townships still exist today.

Section 1 Assessment

go.hrw.com
Online Quiz
KEYWORD: SF7 HP5

Reviewing Ideas, Terms, and People

1. a. **Identify** What documents influenced ideas about government in the United States?
   b. **Draw Conclusions** What impact did the **Virginia Statute for Religious Freedom** have on the U.S. government?
   c. **Elaborate** Why is the separation of government powers a requirement for a society to be free?
2. a. **Identify** What was the **Articles of Confederation**?
   b. **Summarize** What powers were granted to Congress by the Articles of Confederation?
   c. **Predict** What are some possible problems that might result from the lack of a national court system?
3. a. **Describe** How were public lands in the West divided by the **Land Ordinance of 1785**?
   b. **Evaluate** In your opinion, what was the most important element of the **Northwest Ordinance of 1787**? Why?
   c. **Elaborate** What does the assignment of township lots reveal about values of Americans at this time?

Critical Thinking

4. **Categorizing** Review your notes on the Articles of Confederation. Copy the chart below and use it to show the strengths and weaknesses of the new government.

Articles of Confederation

Strengths	Weaknesses

FOCUS ON WRITING

5. **Thinking about the Articles of Confederation** Make a list of powers the Articles of Confederation gave the national government. Which ones seem strong? Can you think of any important powers that are missing?

FORMING A GOVERNMENT 155

Focus on Indiana features cover events from Indiana history or point out how information on the page relates to the Indiana Social Studies.

Reading Check questions end each section of content so that you can test whether or not you understand what you have just studied.

Summary and Preview statements connect what you have just studied in the section to what you will study in the next section.

Section Assessment boxes provide an opportunity for you to make sure that you understand the main ideas of the section. We also provide assessment practice online!

Indiana

Indiana Academic Standards

What are the Indiana Academic Standards?

Academic Standards are simply the things you are expected to know, understand, and be able to do as a result of your education. In Indiana, the Academic Standards are organized by subject matter and subdivided into more specific ideas called Performance Indicators. So the Academic Standards and Performance Indicators for your United States history course focus on the knowledge and skills you will need to gain in this class.

In this section you will find the social studies standards and performance indicators that have been approved by the Indiana Board of Education. You will probably notice that some of the subjects in the standards are familiar to you. This course is meant to build on the skills and knowledge you already have. It will also help build a foundation for the more advanced studies you will begin in high school.

How can the Indiana Academic Standards and Performance Indicators help me?

These standards and indicators are helpful because they give you a clear picture of what you will be expected to learn. This can help you to focus on key material. You can think of the standards as a kind of checklist of important subjects and skills. Another advantage of becoming familiar with the standards is that teachers often base lesson plans and tests on these standards. That means that the standards can give you a preview of what to expect in this course.

United States History - Growth and Development
In Grade 8, students focus upon United States history, beginning with a brief review of early history, including the Revolution and Founding Era, and the principles of the United States and Indiana constitutions, as well as other founding documents and their applications to subsequent periods of national history and to civic and political life. Students then study national development, westward expansion, social reform movements, and the Civil War and Reconstruction.

The Indiana's K - 8 academic standards for social studies are organized around four content areas. The content area standards and the types of learning experiences they provide to students in Grade 8 are described below. On the pages that follow, age-appropriate concepts are listed underneath each standard. Skills for thinking, inquiry and participation in a democratic society, including the examination of Individuals, Society and Culture are integrated throughout. Specific terms are defined and examples are provided when necessary.

Standard 1 — History

Students will examine the relationship and significance of themes, concepts, and movements in the development of United States history, including review of key ideas related to the colonization of America and the revolution and Founding Era. This will be followed by emphasis on social reform, national development and westward expansion, and the Civil War and Reconstruction period.

Standard 2 — Civics and Government

Students will explain the major principles, values and institutions of constitutional government and citizenship, which are based on the founding documents of the United States and how three branches of government share and check power within our federal system of government.

Standard 3 — Geography

Students will identify the major geographic characteristics of the United States and its regions. They will name and locate the major physical features of the United States, as well as each of the states, capitals and major cities, and will use geographic skills and technology to examine the influence of geographic factors on national development.

Standard 4 — Economics

Students will identify, describe and evaluate the influence of economic factors on national development from the founding of the nation to the end of Reconstruction.

Suspension bridge, Columbus

Standard 1

History Students will examine the relationship and significance of themes, concepts and movements in the development of United States history, including review of key ideas related to the colonization of America and the revolution and Founding Era. This will be followed by emphasis on social reform, national development and westward expansion, and the Civil War and Reconstruction period.

Historical Knowledge

The American Revolution and Founding of the United States: 1754 to 1801

8.1.1 Identify major Native American Indian groups of eastern North America and describe early conflict and cooperation with European settlers and the influence the two cultures had on each other. (Individuals, Society and Culture)

Example: Mohawk, Iroquois, Huron and Ottawa; French and Native American Indian alliances; French and Indian War; British alliances with Native American Indians; settler encroachment on Native American Indian lands; and Native American Indian participation in the Revolutionary War

8.1.2 Explain the struggle of the British, French, Spanish and Dutch to gain control of North America during settlement and colonization.

8.1.3 Identify and explain the conditions, causes, consequences and significance of the French and Indian War (1754 – 1763), and the resistance and rebellion against British imperial rule by the thirteen colonies in North America (1761 – 1775).

8.1.4 Identify fundamental ideas in the Declaration of Independence (1776) and analyze the causes and effects of the Revolutionary War (1775 – 1783), including enactment of the Articles of Confederation and the Treaty of Paris.

8.1.5 Identify and explain key events leading to the creation of a strong union among the 13 original states and in the establishment of the United States as a federal republic.

Example: The enactment of state constitutions, the Constitutional Conventions, ratifying conventions of the American states, and debate by Federalists versus Anti-Federalists regarding approval or disapproval of the 1787 Constitution (1787 – 1788).

8.1.6 Identify the steps in the implementation of the federal government under the United States Constitution, including the First and Second Congresses of the United States (1789 – 1792).

8.1.7 Describe the origin and development of political parties, the Federalists and the Democratic - Republicans, (1793 – 1801) and examine points of agreement and disagreement between these parties.

8.1.8 **Evaluate the significance of the presidential and congressional election of 1800 and the transfer of political authority and power to the Democratic-Republican Party led by the new president, Thomas Jefferson (1801).**

8.1.9 **Describe the influence of important individuals on social and political developments of the time such as the Independence movement and the framing of the Constitution. (Individuals, Society and Culture)**

Example: James Otis, Mercy Otis Warren, Samuel Adams, Thomas Paine, George Washington, John Adams, Abigail Adams, Patrick Henry, Thomas Jefferson, James Madison, Alexander Hamilton and Benjamin Banneker

8.1.10 **Compare differences in ways of life in the northern and southern states, including the growth of towns and cities in the North and the growing dependence on slavery in the South. (Individuals, Society and Culture)**

National Expansion and Reform: 1801 to 1861

8.1.11 **Explain the events leading up to and the significance of the Louisiana Purchase (1803) and the expedition of Lewis and Clark (1803–1806).**

8.1.12 **Explain the main issues, decisions and consequences of landmark Supreme Court cases.**

Example: Marbury v. Madison (1803), McCulloch v. Maryland (1819) and Gibbons v. Ogden (1824)

8.1.13 **Explain the causes and consequences of the War of 1812, including the Rush-Bagot Agreement (1818).**

8.1.14 **Examine the international problem that led to the Monroe Doctrine (1823) and assess its consequences.**

8.1.15 **Explain the concept of Manifest Destiny and describe its impact on westward expansion of the United States. (Individuals, Society and Culture)**

Example: Louisiana Purchase (1803), purchase of Florida (1819), Mexican War and the annexation of Texas (1845), acquisition of Oregon Territory (1846), Native American Indian conflicts and removal, and the California gold rush

8.1.16 **Describe the abolition of slavery in the northern states, including the conflicts and compromises associated with westward expansion of slavery.**

Example: Missouri Compromise (1820), The Compromise of 1850 and the Kansas-Nebraska Act (1854)

8.1.17 **Identify the key ideas of Jacksonian democracy and explain their influence on political participation, political parties and constitutional government.**

8.1.18 **Analyze different interests and points of view of individuals and groups involved in the abolitionist, feminist and social reform movements, and in sectional conflicts. (Individuals, Society and Culture)**

Example: Jacksonian Democrats, John Brown, Nat Turner, Frederick Douglass, Harriet Tubman, William Lloyd Garrison, Harriet Beecher Stowe, Sojourner Truth and the Seneca Falls Convention.

8.1.19 **Explain the influence of early individual social reformers and movements. (Individuals, Society and Culture)**

Example: Elizabeth Cady Stanton, Horace Mann, Dorothea Dix, Lucretia Mott, Robert Owen, abolition movement, temperance movement and utopian movements

The Civil War and Reconstruction Period: 1850 to 1877

8.1.20 **Analyze the causes and effects of events leading to the Civil War, including development of sectional conflict over slavery.**

Example: The Compromise of 1850, furor over publication of *Uncle Tom's Cabin* (1852), Kansas-Nebraska Act (1854), the Dred Scott Case (1857), the Lincoln-Douglas Debates (1858) and the presidential election of 1860

8.1.21 **Describe the importance of key events and individuals in the Civil War.**

Example: Event: the battles of Manassas, Antietam, Vicksburg and Gettysburg and the Emancipation Proclamation and Gettysburg Address (1861–1865); People: Jefferson Davis, Stephen A. Douglas, Abraham Lincoln, Robert E. Lee, Ulysses S. Grant, William T. Sherman and Thaddeus Stevens

8.1.22 **Explain and evaluate the policies, practices and consequences of Reconstruction, including the Thirteenth, Fourteenth and Fifteenth Amendments to the Constitution.**

8.1.23 **Describe the conflicts between Native American Indians and settlers of the Great Plains. (Individuals, Society and Culture)**

8.1.24 **Identify the influence of individuals on political and social events and movements such as the abolition movement, the Dred Scott case, women rights and Native American Indian removal. (Individuals, Society and Culture)**

Example: Henry Clay, Harriet Tubman, Harriet Beecher Stowe, Henry Ward Beecher, Roger Taney, Frederick Douglass, John Brown, Clara Barton, Andrew Johnson, Susan B. Anthony, Sitting Bull, Ralph Waldo Emerson and Henry David Thoreau

8.1.25 **Give examples of how immigration affected American culture in the decades before and after the Civil War, including growth of industrial sites in the North; religious differences; tensions between middle-class and working-class people, particularly in the Northeast; and intensification of cultural differences between the North and the South. (Individuals, Society and Culture)**

8.1.26 **Give examples of the changing role of women and minorities in the northern, southern and western parts of the United States in the mid-nineteenth century, and examine possible causes for these changes. (Individuals, Society and Culture)**

8.1.27 **Give examples of scientific and technological developments that changed cultural life in the nineteenth-century United States, such as the use of photography, growth in the use of the telegraph, the completion of the transcontinental railroad, and the invention of the telephone. (Individuals, Society and Culture)**

Chronological Thinking, Historical Comprehension, Analysis and Interpretation, Research, and Issues-Analysis and Decision-Making

8.1.28 **Recognize historical perspective and evaluate alternative courses of action by describing the historical context in which events unfolded and by avoiding evaluation of the past solely in terms of present-day norms.**

Example: Use Internet-based documents and digital archival collections from museums and libraries to compare views of slavery in slave narratives, northern and southern newspapers, and present day accounts of the era.

8.1.29 **Differentiate between facts and historical interpretations, recognizing that the historian's narrative reflects his or her judgment about the significance of particular facts.**

8.1.30 **Formulate historical questions by analyzing primary sources* and secondary sources* about an issue confronting the United States during the period from 1754 – 1877.**

Example: The Virginia Statute for Religious Freedom (1786), President George Washington's Farewell Address (1796), the First Inaugural Address by Thomas Jefferson (1801), the Declaration of Sentiments and Resolutions of the Seneca Falls Convention (1848) and the Second Inaugural Address by Abraham Lincoln (1865)

8.1.31 **Obtain historical data from a variety of sources to compare and contrast examples of art, music and literature during the nineteenth century and explain how these reflect American culture during this time period. (Individuals, Society and Culture)**

Example: Art: John James Audubon, Winslow Homer, Hudson River School, Edward Bannister, Edmonia Lewis and Henry Ossawa Tanner; Music: Daniel Decatur Emmett and Stephen Foster; Writers: Louisa May Alcott, Washington Irving, James Fennimore Cooper, Walt Whitman, Frederick Douglass, Paul Dunbar and George Caleb Bingham

* primary source: developed by people who experienced the events being studied (i.e., autobiographies, diaries, letters and government documents)

* secondary source: developed by people who have researched events but did not experience them directly (i.e., articles, biographies, Internet sources and nonfiction books)

Standard 2

Civics and Government **Students will explain the major principles, values and institutions of constitutional government and citizenship, which are based on the founding documents of the United States and how three branches of government share and check power within our federal system of government.**

Foundations of Government

8.2.1 **Identify and explain essential ideas of constitutional government, which are expressed in the founding documents of the United States, including the Virginia Declaration of Rights, the Declaration of Independence, the Virginia Statute for Religious Freedom, the Massachusetts Constitution of 1780, the Northwest Ordinance, the 1787 U.S. Constitution, the Bill of Rights, the Federalist and Anti-Federalist Papers, *Common Sense*, Washington's Farewell Address (1796) and Jefferson's First Inaugural Address (1801).**

Example: The essential ideas include limited government; rule of law; due process of law; separated and shared powers; checks and balances; federalism; popular sovereignty; republicanism; representative government; and individual rights to life, liberty, property; and freedom of conscience

8.2.2 **Identify and explain the relationship between rights and responsibilities of citizenship in the United States.**

Example: The right to vote and the responsibility to use this right carefully and effectively and the right to free speech and the responsibility not to say or write false statements

8.2.3 **Explain how and why legislative, executive and judicial powers are distributed, shared and limited in the constitutional government of the United States.**

Example: Examine key Supreme Court cases and describe the role each branch of the government played in each of these cases.

8.2.4 **Examine functions of the national government in the lives of people.**

Example: Purchasing and distributing public goods and services, coining money, financing government through taxation, conducting foreign policy, providing a common defense, and regulating commerce

Functions of Government

8.2.5 **Compare and contrast the powers reserved to the federal and state government under the Articles of Confederation and the United States Constitution.**

8.2.6 **Distinguish among the different functions of national and state government within the federal system by analyzing the United States Constitution and the Indiana Constitution.**

Example: Identify important services provided by state government, such as maintaining state roads and highways, enforcing health and safety laws, and supporting educational institutions. Compare these services to functions of the federal government, such as defense and foreign policy.

Roles of Citizens

8.2.7 Explain the importance in a democratic republic of responsible participation by citizens in voluntary civil associations/non-governmental organizations that comprise civil society.

Example: Reform movements such as the abolitionist movement, women's suffrage and the Freedman's Bureau

8.2.8 Explain ways that citizens can participate in political parties, campaigns and elections.

Example: Local, state and national elections; referendums; poll work; campaign committees; and voting

8.2.9 Explain how citizens can monitor and influence the development and implementation of public policies at local, state and national levels of government.

Example: Joining action groups, holding leaders accountable through the electoral process, attending town meetings, staying informed by reading newspapers and Web sites, and watching television news broadcasts

8.2.10 Research and defend positions on issues in which fundamental values and principles related to the United States Constitution are in conflict, using a variety of information resources*.

Example: Powers of federal vs. powers of state government

* information resources: print media, such as books, magazines, and newspapers; electronic media, such as radio, television, Web sites, and databases; and community resources, such as individuals and organizations

Standard 3

Geography Students will identify the major geographic characteristics of the United States and its regions. They will name and locate the major physical features of the United States, as well as each of the states, capitals and major cities, and will use geographic skills and technology to examine the influence of geographic factors on national development.

The World in Spatial Terms

8.3.1 Read maps to interpret symbols and determine the land forms and human features that represent physical and cultural characteristics* of areas in the United States.

* cultural characteristics: human features, such as population characteristics, communication and transportation networks, religion and customs, and how people make a living or build homes and other structures

Indianapolis at night

Rocky Hollow, Turkey Run State Park

Places and Regions

8.3.2 Identify and create maps showing the physical growth and development of the United States from settlement of the original 13 colonies through Reconstruction (1877), including transportation routes used during the period.

Physical Systems

8.3.3 Identify and locate the major climate regions in the United States and describe the characteristics of these regions.

8.3.4 Name and describe processes that build* up the land and processes that erode* it and identify places these occur.

Example: The Appalachian Mountains are a formation that has undergone erosion. The Mississippi Delta is made up almost entirely of eroded material.

8.3.5 Describe the importance of the major mountain ranges and the major river systems in the development of the United States.

Example: Locate major U.S. cities during this time period, such as Washington, D.C.; New York; Boston; Atlanta; Nashville; Charleston; New Orleans; Philadelphia; and Saint Louis, and suggest reasons for their location and development.

* building: forces that build up Earth's surface include mountain building and deposit of dirt by water, ice and wind

* erosion: the process by which the products of weathering* are moved from one place to another

* weathering: the breaking down of rocks and other materials on Earth's surface by such processes as rain or wind

Human Systems

8.3.6 Identify the agricultural regions of the United States and be able to give reasons for the type of land use and subsequent land development during different historical periods.

Example: Cattle industry in the West and cotton industry in the South

8.3.7 Using maps identify changes influenced by growth, economic development and human migration in the eighteenth and nineteenth centuries

Example: Westward expansion, impact of slavery, Lewis and Clark exploration, new states added to the union, and Spanish settlement in California and Texas

8.3.8 Gather information on ways people changed the physical environment of the United States in the nineteenth century using primary and secondary sources* including digitized photo collections and historic maps.

8.3.9 Analyze human and physical factors that have influenced migration and settlement patterns and relate them to the economic development of the United States.

Example: Growth of communities due to the development of the railroad, development of the west coast due to ocean ports and discovery of important mineral resources; the presence of a major waterway influences economic development and the workers who are attracted to that development

* primary source: developed by people who experienced the events being studied (i.e., autobiographies, diaries, letters and governmental documents)

* secondary source: developed by people who have researched events but did not experience them directly (i.e., articles, biographies, Internet resources and nonfiction books)

Environment and Society

8.3.10 Create maps, graphs and charts showing the distribution of natural resources — such as forests, water sources, and wildlife — in the United States at the beginning of the nineteenth century and give examples of how people exploited these resources as the country became more industrialized and people moved westward.

8.3.11 Identify ways people modified the physical environment as the United States developed and describe the impacts that resulted.

Examples: Identify urbanization*, deforestation* and extinction* or near extinction of wildlife species; and development of roads and canals

* urbanization: a process in which there is an increase in the percentage of people living/working in urban places as compared to rural places.

* deforestation: the clearing of trees or forests

* extinction: the state in which all members of a group of organisms, such as a species, population, family or class, have disappeared from a given habitat, geographic area or the entire world

Standard 4

Economics Students will identify, describe and evaluate the influence of economic factors on national development from the founding of the nation to the end of Reconstruction.

8.4.1 Identify economic factors contributing to European exploration and colonization in North America, the American Revolution and the drafting of the Constitution of the United States.

Example: The search for gold by the Spanish, French fur trade taxation without representation

8.4.2 Illustrate elements of the three types of economic systems, using cases from United States history

Example: Traditional economy*, command economy* and market economy*

8.4.3 Evaluate how the characteristics of a market economy have affected the economic and labor development of the United States.

Example: Characteristics include the role of entrepreneurs, private property, markets, competition and self-interest

8.4.4 Explain the basic economic functions of the government in the economy of the United States.

Example: The government provides a legal framework, promotes competition, provides public goods* and services, protects private property, controls the effects of helpful and harmful spillovers*, and regulates interstate commerce.

8.4.5 Analyze contributions of entrepreneurs and inventors in the development of the United States economy. (Individuals, Society and Culture)

Example: Benjamin Banneker, George Washington Carver, Eli Whitney, Samuel Gompers, Andrew Carnegie, John d. Rockefeller and Madam C.J. Walker

8.4.6 Relate technological change and inventions to changes in labor productivity in the United States in the eighteenth and nineteenth centuries.

Example: The cotton gin increased labor productivity in the early nineteenth century.

8.4.7 Trace the development of different kinds of money used in the United States and explain how money helps make saving easier.

Example: Types of money included wampum, tobacco, gold and silver, state bank notes, greenbacks and Federal Reserve Notes

8.4.8 Examine the development of the banking system in the United States.

Example: The central bank controversy, the state banking era and the development of a gold standard

8.4.9 Explain and evaluate examples of domestic and international interdependence throughout United States history.

Example: Triangular trade routes and regional exchange of resources

8.4.10 Examine the importance of borrowing and lending (the use of credit) in the United States economy and list the advantages and disadvantages of using credit.

8.4.11 Use a variety of information resources* to compare and contrast job skills needed in different time periods in United States history.

* traditional economy: an economy in which resources are allocated based on custom and tradition

* command economy: an economy in which resources are allocated by the government or other central authority

* market economy: an economy in which resources are allocated by decisions by individuals and businesses

* public goods: goods or services whose benefits can be shared simultaneously by everyone and for which it is generally difficult to exclude people from getting the benefits whether they pay or not

* spillover: the impact of an activity (positive or negative) on the well-being of a third party

* information resources: print media, such as books, magazines and newspapers; electronic media, such as radio, television, Web sites and databases; and community resources , such as individuals and organizations

Civics and Government

In the United States the authority of the government is based on several key documents that express the rights and responsibilities of citizens as well as people in government. The United States and Indiana both have constitutions, or documents that organize the government and assign powers to different parts. Both Indiana and the United States have three branches of government: legislative, executive, and judicial.

Indiana's state constitution was created by a committee of delegates in 1851. It has been amended, or officially changed, several times since then. Although Hoosiers are allowed to have almost any laws that they want, none of their state laws can contradict national laws. This system of power, in which national laws can override state laws, is called federalism. As a result, the national government is often referred to as the federal government.

Just as the state of Indiana cannot have laws that contradict federal laws, local governments in Indiana cannot have laws that contradict state laws. When there is disagreement about what a law means or whether a law is permitted by the constitution, the judicial branch of government decides the matter. Most such court cases begin in local courts, but may also go through state courts and federal courts.

While the government creates and enforces laws, citizens of Indiana can help influence what laws say. Both the United States and Indiana are run by democracies, or governments in which people rule themselves. Citizens of Indiana can vote in local, state, and national elections to choose leaders who will represent them in government and to decide what laws should be passed.

Activity

Research how local, state, and federal governments affect your community. Create a table that shows examples of what each level of government provides for your town or county.

Indiana State House, Indianapolis

Economics

Indiana produces many agricultural and industrial products for export and imports millions of dollars worth of products from other states and countries. This movement of goods is part of the economy of the state. However, many businesses in Indiana do not create products but instead provide services such as medical care or banking. These companies are also a part of the Indiana economy.

During the first years of statehood, Indiana's economy relied heavily on agricultural products such as corn and wheat. By the time of the Civil War, the state was linked by railroads with the rest of the United States, and many factories began producing supplies for the Union troops. The late 1800s and early 1900s saw a dramatic increase in industrial manufacturing in the state. Most recently, Indiana and surrounding areas have been termed the "Rust Belt" to indicate the decline of heavy manufacturing in the area.

Today, the economy of Indiana is still heavily reliant on agriculture. As in the rest of the United States, service industry jobs are increasing as more and more manufacturing is moved to locations overseas. Still, the decline of manufacturing has hurt the state. In the 1990s, unemployment in the state rose. During the early 2000s, the economy of the state grew at a slower pace than that of the United States. Business and political leaders have been challenged to maintain the state's traditionally high standard of living.

Activity

As the economy of Indiana has changed, so have the jobs available to Hoosiers. Choose three of the following periods of Indiana history and research what jobs were available during those periods: early statehood, Civil War, Great Depression, late 1900s, present. Make a chart with lists of skills that would have been needed for a particular job during the periods you have chosen.

Agricultural products are central to Indiana's economy.

Unit Preview

Introduce the Unit

Share the information in the chapter overviews with students.

Chapter 1 Many scholars believe humans migrated to the Americas across a land bridge from Asia during the last Ice Age. Native American societies developed across Mesoamerica and South America, while diverse cultures developed across North America. Increased trade, including slave trade, helped West African kingdoms gain power. A surge in trade and new ideas also had a dramatic impact on Europe.

Chapter 2 The Portuguese ushered in an era of exploration in the 1400s. This was followed by Christopher Columbus's voyages, which paved the way for other explorers to sail to the Americas. As the Spanish established a large empire in the Americas, other European nations challenged Spain's dominance. Between the 1520s and 1860s, about 12 million enslaved Africans were shipped across the Atlantic where Europeans forced them to work in their newly formed colonies.

Chapter 3 In 1607 a group of colonists established the first permanent English settlement in North America. Hoping to gain religious freedom, English colonists began to establish settlements along the Atlantic Coast. Varied ways of life developed in these colonies as settlers adapted to different environments. English settlers *(continued on p. 1)*

UNIT 1 BEGINNINGS TO 1783

Our Colonial Heritage

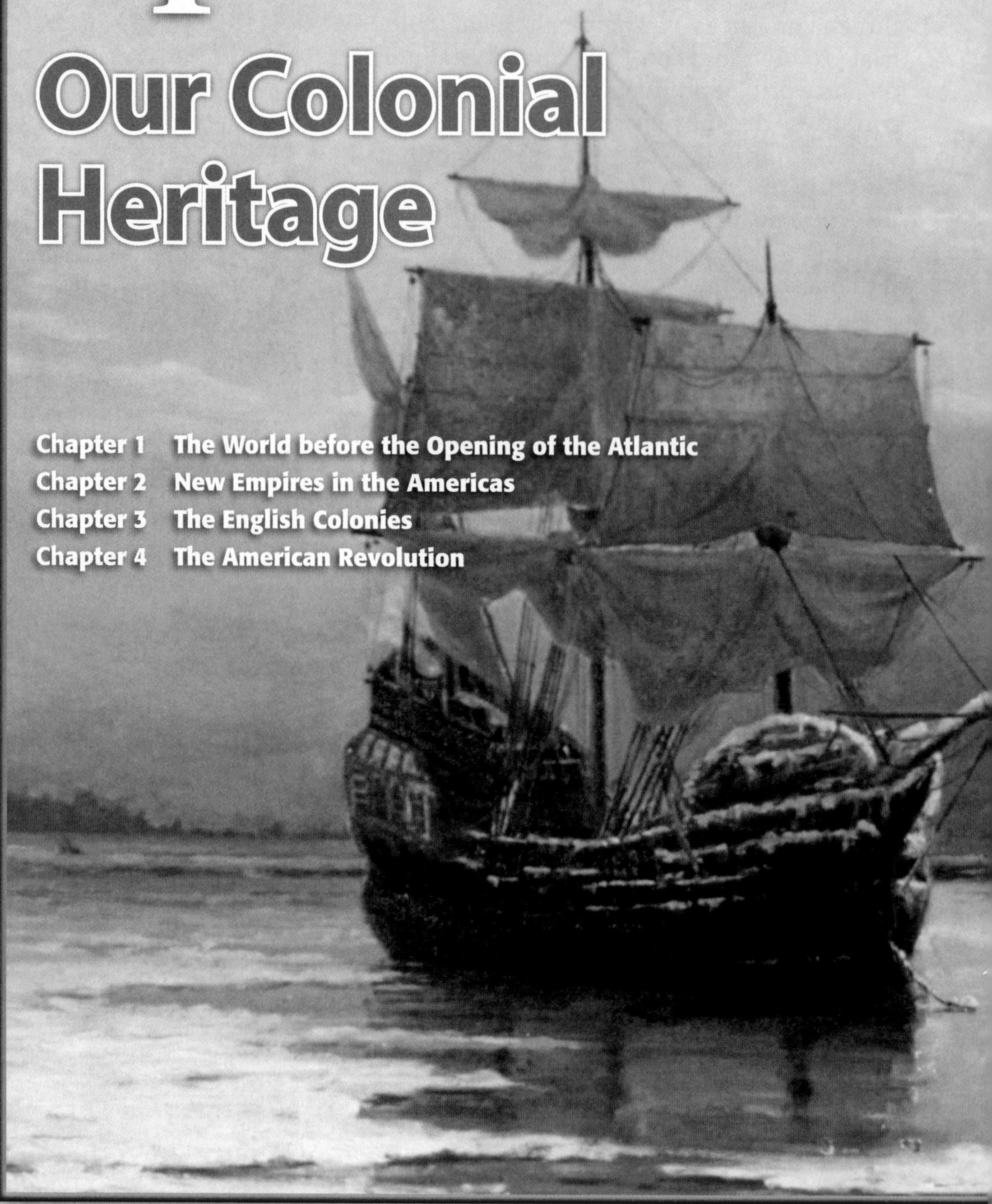

Unit Resources

Planning

- Differentiated Instruction Teacher Management System: Unit Instructional Pacing Guide
- One-Stop Planner CD-ROM with Test Generator: Calendar Planner
- Power Presentations with Video CD-ROM

Differentiating Instruction

- Differentiated Instruction Teacher Management System: Lesson Plans for Differentiated Instruction
- Pre-AP Activities Guide for United States History
- Differentiated Instruction Modified Worksheets and Tests CD-ROM

Enrichment

- **CRF The World before the Opening of the Atlantic:** Economics and History Activity: Mercantilism
- **CRF The World before the Opening of the Atlantic:** Interdisciplinary Project: Food, Clothing, Shelter
- **CRF The World before the Opening of the Atlantic:** Methods of Navigation: Martime Museum Presentation
- Civic Participation Activities
- Primary Source Library CD-ROM

Assessment

- Progress Assessment Support System: Unit 1 Tests, Forms A and B
- OSP ExamView Test Generator: Unit Test
- HOAP Holt Online Assessment Program, in the Premier Online Student Edition
- Alternative Assessment Handbook

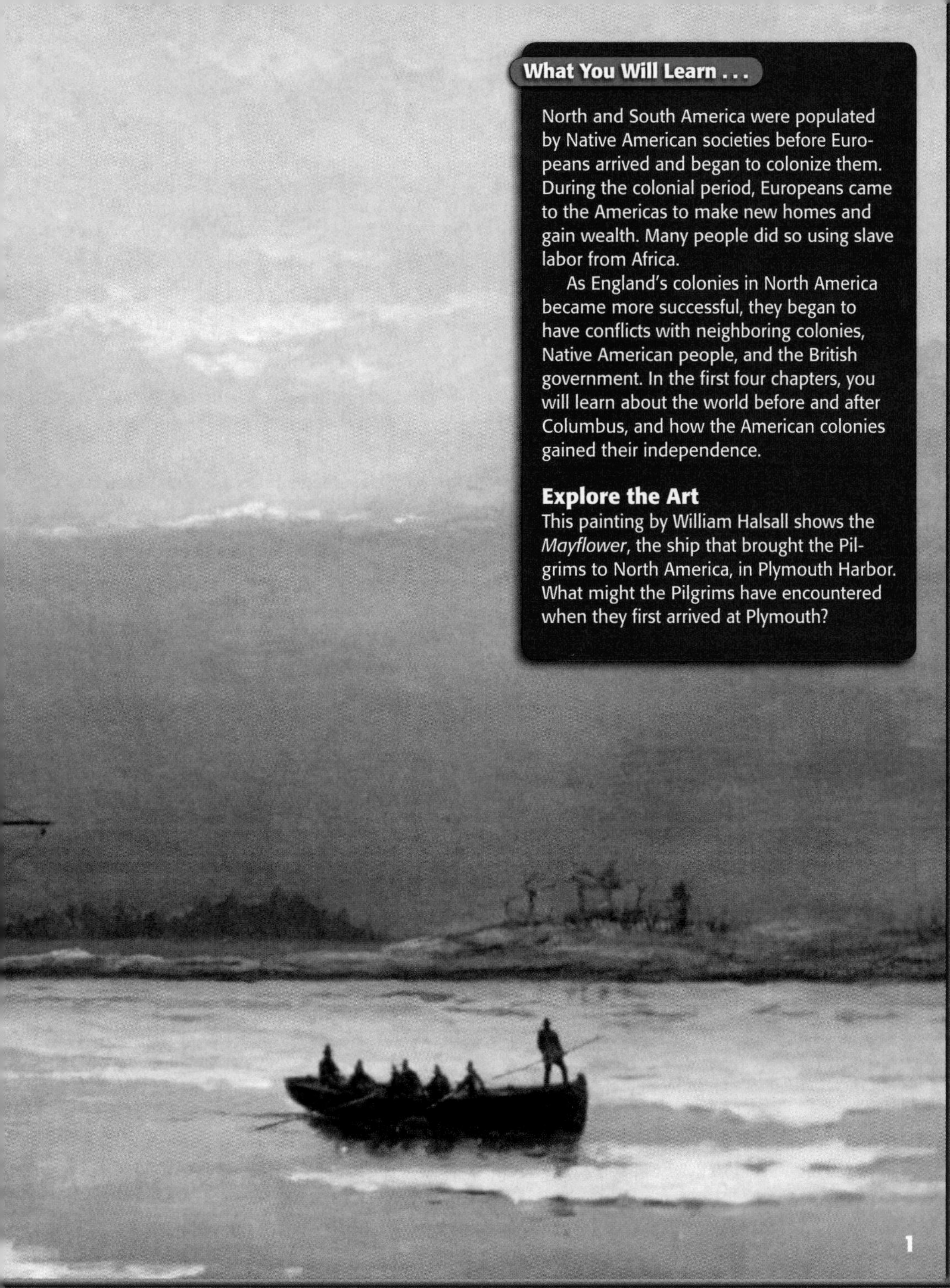

What You Will Learn . . .

North and South America were populated by Native American societies before Europeans arrived and began to colonize them. During the colonial period, Europeans came to the Americas to make new homes and gain wealth. Many people did so using slave labor from Africa.

As England's colonies in North America became more successful, they began to have conflicts with neighboring colonies, Native American people, and the British government. In the first four chapters, you will learn about the world before and after Columbus, and how the American colonies gained their independence.

Explore the Art

This painting by William Halsall shows the *Mayflower*, the ship that brought the Pilgrims to North America, in Plymouth Harbor. What might the Pilgrims have encountered when they first arrived at Plymouth?

1

Unit Preview

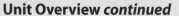

Unit Overview *continued*

came into conflict with Native Americans and the French, causing the French and Indian War, which Great Britain won in 1763. Colonists were angered when they were expected to pay taxes to help pay for the war, and they began to protest British laws.

Chapter 4 Colonial resentment against Britain increased; shots were fired in April of 1775, starting the Revolutionary War. On July 4, 1776, the Declaration of Independence was approved. Though they received help from France and Spain, the Patriots faced obstacles in fighting the British. When the war against Britain spread to the South, Americans defeated British forces and gained their independence.

Connect to the Unit

Activity Simulation Role-Play

Provide students with the following scenario: A multinational space expedition has made contact with a non-hostile civilization on another planet. Communication has been slow but is occurring.

Ask students to predict how life on Earth might change as a result of this new contact. Have students work in pairs or in small groups to create a hypothetical conversation among people on Earth discussing the event and its possible effects. Ask for volunteers to act out their conversations for the class.

LS Interpersonal, Verbal/Linguistic

Explore the Art

The Pilgrims first landed at the tip of Cape Cod and finally arrived in Plymouth Harbor on December 26, 1620. They crossed the Atlantic Ocean on the *Mayflower*, which archaeologists estimate was 90 feet long. The ship was loaded with over 100 settlers, who endured cramped and uncomfortable living quarters. The perilous, stormy journey lasted over two months.

Democracy and Civic Education

At Level

Authority: Reasons for Government Working for Reform

1. Organize students into small groups. Have each group discuss the need for school rules. Each group should create a chart listing the costs and benefits of school rules. How well would the school function without rules? What would happen if students did not obey the school rules or authority figures? Have each group share its chart with the class.
2. Explain that societies, like schools, need governments and laws. Have each group create a second chart listing the costs and benefits of government. The groups should then use their charts to identify what they think the purposes of government should be.
3. Have each group share its findings. Conclude by explaining that the purpose of government in the United States is to protect individual rights and to promote the common good.

LS Interpersonal, Verbal/Linguistic

Alternative Assessment Handbook, Rubrics 7: Charts; and 14: Group Activity

Civic Participation Activities Guide

Answers

Explore the Art *possible answers—unfamiliar territory, meeting Native Americans, lack of housing, limited supplies*

Chapter 1 Planning Guide

The World before the Opening of the Atlantic

Chapter Overview	Reproducible Resources	Technology Resources
CHAPTER 1 pp. 2–33 **Overview: In this chapter, students will learn about the first civilizations in the Americas and will examine trade in West Africa and Europe before transatlantic travel.**	**Differentiated Instruction Teacher Management System:*** • Instructional Pacing Guides • Lesson Plans for Differentiated Instruction **Interactive Reader and Study Guide:** Chapter Summary Graphic Organizer* **Chapter Resource File:*** • Focus on Writing Activity: A Travelogue • Social Studies Skills Activity: Interpreting Diagrams • Chapter Review Activity	**Power Presentations with Video CD-ROM** **Differentiated Instruction Modified Worksheets and Tests CD-ROM** **Primary Source Library CD-ROM for United States History** **Interactive Skills Tutor CD-ROM** **Student Edition on Audio CD Program** **History's Impact: United States History Video Program (VHS/DVD):** The Impact of the Global Economy*
Section 1: **The Earliest Americans** **The Big Idea:** Native American societies developed across Mesoamerica and South America.	**Differentiated Instruction Teacher Management System:** Section 1 Lesson Plan* **Interactive Reader and Study Guide:** Section 1.1 Summary* **Chapter Resource File:*** • Vocabulary Builder Activity, Section 1 • Biography Activity: Huayna Capac	**Daily Bellringer Transparency 1.1*** **Map Transparency 1:** Land Migrations of Early Peoples* **Map Transparency 2:** Aztec and Inca Civilizations* go.hrw.com **Internet Activity:** Need a Push?
Section 2: **Native American Cultures** **The Big Idea:** Many diverse Native American cultures developed across the different geographic regions of North America.	**Differentiated Instruction Teacher Management System:** Section 2 Lesson Plan* **Interactive Reader and Study Guide:** Section 1.2 Summary* **Chapter Resource File:*** • Vocabulary Builder Activity, Section 2	**Daily Bellringer Transparency 1.2*** **Map Transparency 3:** Native American Culture Areas*
Section 3: **Trading Kingdoms of West Africa** **The Big Idea:** Using trade to gain wealth, Ghana, Mali, and Songhai were West Africa's most powerful kingdoms.	**Differentiated Instruction Teacher Management System:** Section 3 Lesson Plan* **Interactive Reader and Study Guide:** Section 1.3 Summary* **Chapter Resource File:*** • Vocabulary Builder Activity, Section 3 • Biography Activity: Askia the Great	**Daily Bellringer Transparency 1.3*** **Map Transparency 4:** Empires of West Africa, 800–1500* go.hrw.com **Internet Activity:** African Traders
Section 4: **Europe before Transatlantic Travel** **The Big Idea:** New ideas and trade changed Europeans' lives.	**Differentiated Instruction Teacher Management System:** Section 4 Lesson Plan* **Interactive Reader and Study Guide:** Section 1.4 Summary* **Chapter Resource File:*** • Vocabulary Builder Activity, Section 4 • Biography Activity: Aristotle • Primary Sources: *The Decameron,* Giovanni Boccacio; the *Mona Lisa,* Leonardo da Vinci	**Daily Bellringer Transparency 1.4*** **Quick Facts Transparency 1:** Democracy and Republic* go.hrw.com **Internet Activity:** Roman Contributions to Government

SE Student Edition | Print Resource | Audio CD

TE Teacher's Edition | Transparency | CD-ROM

go.hrw.com | **LS** Learning Styles | Video

TOS Indiana Teacher One Stop | * also on Indiana Teacher One Stop

Review, Assessment, Intervention

- **Quick Facts Transparency 2:** The World before the Opening of the Atlantic Visual Summary*
- **Spanish Chapter Summaries Audio CD Program**
- **Online Chapter Summaries in Spanish**
- **Quiz Game CD-ROM**
- **Progress Assessment Support System (PASS):** Chapter Tests A and B*
- **Differentiated Instruction Modified Worksheets and Tests CD-ROM:** Modified Chapter Test
- TOS **Indiana Teacher One Stop:** ExamView Test Generator (English/Spanish)
- **Alternative Assessment Handbook**
- HOAP **Holt Online Assessment Program,** in the Holt Premier Online Student Edition

---

- **PASS:** Section Quiz 1.1*
- **Online Quiz:** Section 1.1
- **Alternative Assessment Handbook**

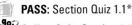

- **PASS:** Section Quiz 1.2*
- **Online Quiz:** Section 1.2
- **Alternative Assessment Handbook**

- **PASS:** Section Quiz 1.3*
- **Online Quiz:** Section 1.3
- **Alternative Assessment Handbook**

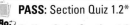

- **PASS:** Section Quiz 1.4*
- **Online Quiz:** Section 1.4
- **Alternative Assessment Handbook**

HOLT

History's Impact

United States History Video Program (VHS/DVD)

The Impact of the Global Economy

Suggested use: as a chapter introduction

Power Presentations with Video CD-ROM

Power Presentations with Video are visual presentations of each chapter's main ideas. Presentations can be customized by including Quick Facts charts, images from the text, and video clips.

DIVISION FOR PUBLIC EDUCATION
AMERICAN BAR ASSOCIATION

Developed by the Division for Public Education of the American Bar Association, these materials are part of the **Democracy and Civic Education Resources.**

- **Constitution Study Guide**
- **Supreme Court Case Studies**

Holt Online Learning

go.hrw.com
Teacher Resources
KEYWORD: SC7 TEACHER

go.hrw.com
Student Resources
KEYWORD: SC7 CH1

- Document-Based Questions
- Interactive Multimedia Activities
- Current Events
- Chapter-based Internet Activities
- and more!

Holt Interactive
Online Student Edition

Complete online support for interactivity, assessment, and reporting

- Interactive Maps and Notebook
- Standardized Test Prep
- Homework Practice and Research Activities Online

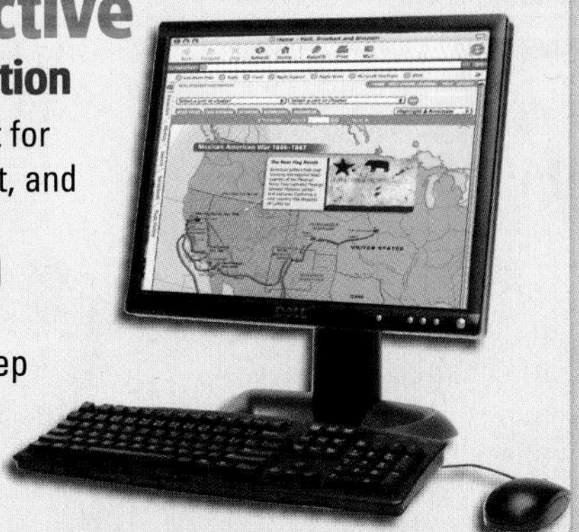

Differentiating Instruction

How do I address the needs of varied learners?

The Target Resource acts as your primary strategy for differentiated instruction.

ENGLISH-LANGUAGE LEARNERS & STRUGGLING READERS

TARGET RESOURCE

English-Language Learner Strategies and Activities

- Build Academic Vocabulary
- Develop Oral and Written Language Structures

Spanish Resources

Spanish Chapter Summaries Audio CD

Spanish Chapter Summaries Online

Teacher's One-Stop Planner:

- ExamView Test Generator, Spanish
- PuzzlePro, Spanish

Additional Resources

Differentiated Instruction Teacher Management System: Lesson Plans for Differentiated Instruction

Chapter Resources:

- Vocabulary Builder Activities
- Social Studies Skills Activity: Interpreting Diagrams

Quick Facts Transparencies:

- Democracy and Republic (TR1)
- The World before the Opening of the Atlantic Visual Summary (TR2)

Student Edition on Audio CD Program

Interactive Skills Tutor CD-ROM

SPECIAL NEEDS LEARNERS

TARGET RESOURCE

Differentiated Instruction Modified Worksheets and Tests CD-ROM

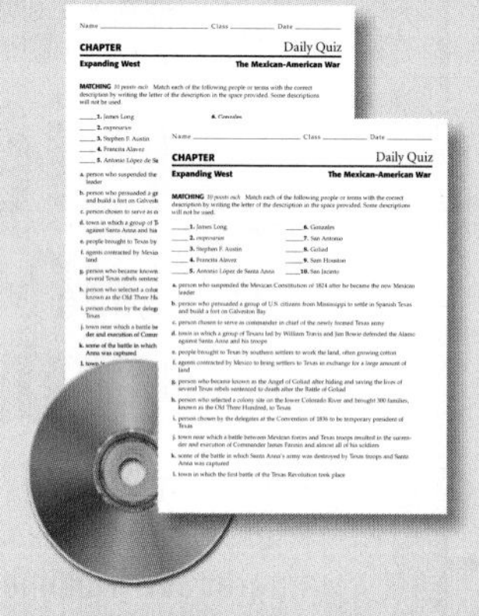

- Vocabulary Flash Cards
- Modified Vocabulary Builder Activities
- Modified Chapter Review Activity
- Modified Chapter Test

Additional Resources

Differentiated Instruction Teacher Management System: Lesson Plans for Differentiated Instruction

Interactive Reader and Study Guide

Social Studies Skills Activity: Interpreting Diagrams

Student Edition on Audio CD Program

Interactive Skills Tutor CD-ROM

ADVANCED/GIFTED-AND-TALENTED STUDENTS

TARGET RESOURCE

Primary Source Library CD-ROM for United States History

The Library contains longer versions of quotations in the text, extra sources, and images. Included are point-of-view articles, journals, diaries, historical fiction, and political documents.

Additional Resources

Differentiated Instruction Teacher Management System: Lesson Plans for Differentiated Instruction

Chapter Resource File:

- Focus on Writing Activity: A Travelogue
- Literature Activity: The *Aeneid*
- Economics and History: Mercantilism
- Interdisciplinary Project: Methods of Navigation

Internet Activities: Chapter Enrichment Links

Differentiated Activities in the Teacher's Edition

- First Americans Maps, p. 7
- Askia the Great's Accomplishments, p. 19
- Black Death Stories, p. 28

Differentiated Activities in the Teacher's Edition

- Mapping Native American Culture Groups, p. 13
- Mapping West Africa's Great Kingdoms, p. 18
- Feudalism Illustrations, p. 24

Differentiated Activities in the Teacher's Edition

- Influence of the Olmecs, p. 8
- Anasazi Presentations, p. 11
- Joining the Iroquois League, p. 14
- Comparing and Contrasting Socrates, Plato, and Aristotle, p. 23
- Analyzing Effects of the Black Death, p. 28

Teacher One Stop™

How can I manage the lesson plans and support materials for differentiated instruction?

With the Indiana Teacher One Stop, you can easily organize and print lesson plans, planning guides, and instructional materials for all learners.
The Indiana Teacher One Stop includes the following materials to help you differentiate instruction:

- Interactive Teacher's Edition
- Calendar Planner and pacing guides
- Editable lesson plans
- All reproducible ancillaries in Adobe Acrobat (PDF) format
- ExamView Test Generator (Eng & Span)
- Transparency and video previews

Professional Development

HOLT Professional Development

What teacher training resources are available to help me grow professionally?

- **In-service and staff development** as part of your Holt Social Studies product purchase
- **Quick Teacher Tutorial Lesson Presentation CD-ROM**
- Intensive tuition-based **Teacher Development Institute**
- **Convenient Holt Speaker Bureau –** face-to-face workshop options
- **PRAXIS™ Test Prep** interactive Web-based content refreshers*
- **Ask A Professional Development Expert** at http://www.hrw.com/prodev/

* PRAXIS is a trademark of Educational Testing Service (ETS).
This publication is not endorsed or approved by ETS.

• Chapter Preview •

Chapter Big Ideas

Section 1 Native American societies developed across Mesoamerica and South America.

Section 2 Many diverse Native American cultures developed across the different geographic regions of North America.

Section 3 Using trade to gain wealth, Ghana, Mali, and Songhai were West Africa's most powerful kingdoms.

Section 4 New ideas and trade changed Europeans' lives.

Focus on Writing

The **Chapter Resource File** provides a Focus on Writing worksheet to help students organize and write their travelogue.

CRF: Focus on Writing Activity: A Travelogue

CHAPTER 1 BEGINNINGS–1500

The World before the Opening of the Atlantic

Indiana Standards

Social Studies Standards

8.1.1 Identify major Native American Indian groups of eastern North America and describe early conflict and cooperation with European settlers and the influence the two cultures had on each other.

8.1.2 Explain the struggle of the British, French, Spanish, and Dutch to gain control of North America during settlement and colonization.

8.3.1 Read maps to interpret symbols and determine the land forms and human features that represent physical and cultural characteristics of areas in the United States.

8.3.3 Identify and locate the major climate regions in the United States and describe the characteristics of these regions.

go.hrw.com
Indiana
KEYWORD: SF10 IN

FOCUS ON WRITING

A Travelogue People who make long trips often write travelogues that describe their journeys. A travelogue allows people who did not make the trip to experience some of the same sights, sounds, and thoughts that the traveler did. In this chapter, you will gather information about different regions of the world and then write a travelogue describing what a place in one of these regions might have been like.

CHAPTER EVENTS

c. 38,000–10,000 BC Paleo-Indians migrate to the Americas.

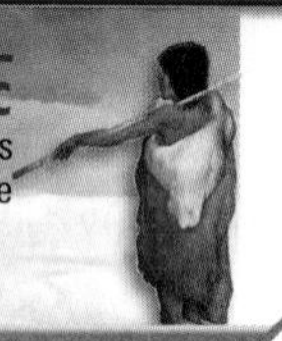

38,000 BC

WORLD EVENTS

Key to Differentiating Instruction

Below Level

Basic-level activities designed for all students encountering new material

At Level

Intermediate-level activities designed for average students

Above Level

Challenging activities designed for honors and gifted and talented students

Standard English Mastery

Activities designed to improve standard English usage

Introduce the Chapter

At Level

The World before the Opening of the Atlantic

1. Tell students that in this chapter they will learn about early civilizations and cultures in the Americas before the arrival of Europeans. Students will also review the conditions in Europe that helped lead to the exploration of the Americas. **LS Verbal/Linguistic**
2. Discuss with students photo albums or scrapbooks they may have created that depict or record special events and achievements in their lives.
3. Have students go through the chapter, noting maps and images, as if it were a scrapbook of the world before 1500.
4. As students look at the images, ask them to create a list of important historical events that occurred before 1500.

Alternative Assessment Handbook, Rubric 11: Discussions

HOLT
History's Impact
▶ **video series**
Watch the video to understand the impact of the global economy.

What You Will Learn...

Buffalo graze on the plains in South Dakota. Millions of these animals used to roam lands from Canada to Texas. In this chapter you will learn about the first peoples in the Americas, some of whom relied on buffalo to survive.

c. 5000 BC Communities in Mexico cultivate corn.

c. 1200 BC Olmec begin their civilization in Mesoamerica.

c. AD 1100 Native Americans of the Mississippian culture begin living in the Angel Mounds settlement in southern Indiana.

1492 Christopher Columbus and his crew reach the Americas on October 12.

5000 BC — 1000 BC — AD 1500

c. 2600 BC The Great Pyramid is built at Giza, Egypt, as the tomb for the pharaoh Khufu.

c. 1350 New ideas begin to spread through Europe during the Renaissance.

3

Chapter Preview

HOLT
History's Impact
▶ **video series**
See the Video Teacher's Guide for strategies for using the chapter video about the impact of the global economy.

Explore the Picture

A Diverse Land Spend a minute looking at the photograph on this page. Notice how the enormous diversity of geography and climate is shown in a single landscape. When the Paleo-Indians began migrating to the Americas over 30,000 years ago, they encountered, and eventually adapted to, a land that encompassed everything from deserts to swamps and from rugged mountains to vast plains flattened by glaciers.

Analyzing Visuals How do you think these earliest Americans might have felt when they saw the landscape in this photograph? *possible answer—They might have thought the foothills and plains would provide good hunting.*

go.hrw.com
Online Resources
Chapter Resources:
KEYWORD SF7 CH1
Teacher Resources:
KEYWORD: SF7 TEACHER

Explore the Time Line

1. Based on this time line, how would you describe Paleo-Indian migration to the Americas? *over a long period of time*
2. How long was it between the initial migration to the Americas and when corn was first cultivated in Mexico? *33,000 years*
3. How long had there been communities in the Americas before Christopher Columbus's arrival in 1492? *over 6,000 years*
4. How long before Columbus's voyage did new ideas spread in Europe? *142 years*

Info to Know

Development of Farming Around 5000 BC groups in what is now Mexico began growing corn. Farming changed life in the Americas. No longer were early Americans dependent on fishing, hunting, and searching for food. Farming enabled early people to settle in one place, to support larger populations, and to focus on things other than finding food. These changes helped in the development of the great Olmec, Maya, Aztec, and Inca civilizations.

Ghana's rulers grew wealthy by controlling trade in salt and gold. Salt came from the north in large slabs, and gold came from the south.

What does the photo to the left suggest about the amount of salt traded in a market?

Ghana was in an ideal position to become a trading center. To the north lay the vast Sahara, the source of much of the salt. Ghana itself was rich in gold. People wanted gold for its beauty, but they needed salt in their diets to survive. Salt, which could be used to preserve food, also made bland food tasty. These qualities made salt very valuable. In fact, Africans sometimes cut up slabs of salt and used the pieces as money.

As trade in gold and salt increased, Ghana's rulers gained power. Eventually, they built up armies equipped with iron weapons that were superior to the weapons of nearby people. Over time, Ghana took control of trade from merchants. Merchants from the north and south then met to exchange goods in Ghana.

By 800 Ghana was firmly in control of West Africa's trade routes. Nearly all trade between northern and southern Africa passed through Ghana. With so many traders passing through their lands, Ghana's rulers looked for ways to make money from them. One way they raised money was by forcing traders to pay taxes. Every trader who entered Ghana had to pay a special tax on the goods he carried. Then he had to pay another tax on any goods he took with him when he left. Ghana's rulers gained incredible wealth from trade, taxes on traders and on the people of Ghana, and their own personal stores of gold. They used their wealth to build an army and an empire.

Islam in Ghana

Extensive trade routes brought the people of Ghana into contact with people of many different cultures and beliefs. As the kingdom of Ghana extended into the Sahara, increased contact with Arab traders from the east brought the religion of Islam to Ghana.

Islam was founded in the 600s by an Arab named Muhammad. Muslims, followers of Islam, believe that God had spoken to Muhammad through an angel and had made him a prophet, someone who tells of God's messages. After Muhammad's death, his followers wrote down his teachings to form the book known as the Qur'an. Islam spread quickly through the Arabian Peninsula.

In the 1060s, a Muslim group called the Almoravids (al-muh-RAH-vuhdz) attacked Ghana in an effort to force its leaders to

Collaborative Learning

At Level

A Ghana Web Page

1. Guide students in a discussion of where various resources, such as salt and gold, were located in relation to Ghana. Encourage students to discuss how these resources increased Ghana's power and wealth.
2. Ask students to imagine that they are creating a Web page to share what they have learned about the ancient empire of Ghana. The page should identify factors that influenced Ghana's rise to power and describe how Ghana's rulers became wealthy.
3. Instruct students to sketch the Web page on their own paper. Students should include images and text that illustrates Ghana's power and wealth. Encourage students to be creative.
4. Ask volunteers to show and explain their Web pages to the class. LS **Verbal/Linguistic, Visual/Spatial**

Alternative Assessment Handbook, Rubrics 3: Artwork; and 40: Writing to Describe

Direct Teach

Main Idea

1 West Africa's Great Kingdoms

West Africa developed three great kingdoms that grew wealthy through their control of trade.

Recall Where was the ancient empire of Ghana located? *in West Africa along the Niger River*

Explain How did Ghana's location lead to wealth and power? *To the north was the Sahara, a source of salt; Ghana itself had gold; trade and control of salt and gold made Ghana powerful and wealthy.*

Summarize How did the religion of Islam reach Ghana? *brought by Arab traders and the Almoravids who attacked Ghana in an attempt to force Ghana's leaders to convert to Islam*

Map Transparency 4: Empires of West Africa, 800–1500

Did you know . . .

The Iron Age took a long time to catch on. Iron was being used in the Middle East by 1000 BC. By around 500 BC, the use of iron had spread throughout most of Europe. When people in Ghana began using iron several hundred years later, they learned how effective it could be. The use of iron tools allowed farmers to grow much more food than before. Soldiers also appreciated their new iron weapons, which made the soldiers far superior to their neighbors without iron.

Info to Know

Camels By the AD 400s, the primary means of transporting goods across the Sahara was on the backs of camels. Camels were introduced to Africa from Arabia, where they were accustomed to desert conditions.

Answers

a large amount of salt was traded

Direct Teach

Main Idea

❶ West Africa's Great Kingdoms

West Africa developed three great kingdoms that grew wealthy through their control of trade.

Recall Why is Sundiata famous? *According to legend, as Mali's ruler, he won back his country's independence and conquered nearby kingdoms.*

Explain Why did Mansa Musa travel to Mecca? *As a Muslim, it was his spiritual duty to make a hajj to Mecca.*

Summarize How did Mansa Musa's belief in Islam affect the country and people of Mali? *Mansa Musa stressed the importance of reading and writing Arabic so that people could read the Qur'an. He sent scholars to study in Morocco, and these scholars later set up schools in Mali. He also brought in artists and architects to build mosques in Mali.*

Map Transparency 4: Empires of West Africa, 800–1500

Biography

Sundiata (c. 1210–c. 1255) Born Mari Diata, Sundiata was the son of the king of the small kingdom of Kangaba. When his father's kingdom was overtaken by King Sumanguru of the Soso Empire, Mari Diata was forced to live in exile. Eventually, he returned to defeat Sumanguru in the Battle of Kirina. After the battle, he took the name Sundiata, which means the "lion prince," and he went on to establish one of the greatest empires in African history.

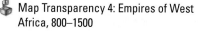

go.hrw.com
Online Resources
KEYWORD: SF7 CH1
ACTIVITY: African Traders

Answers

Interpreting Maps 1. *Niger River*
2. *Mali, Songhai*

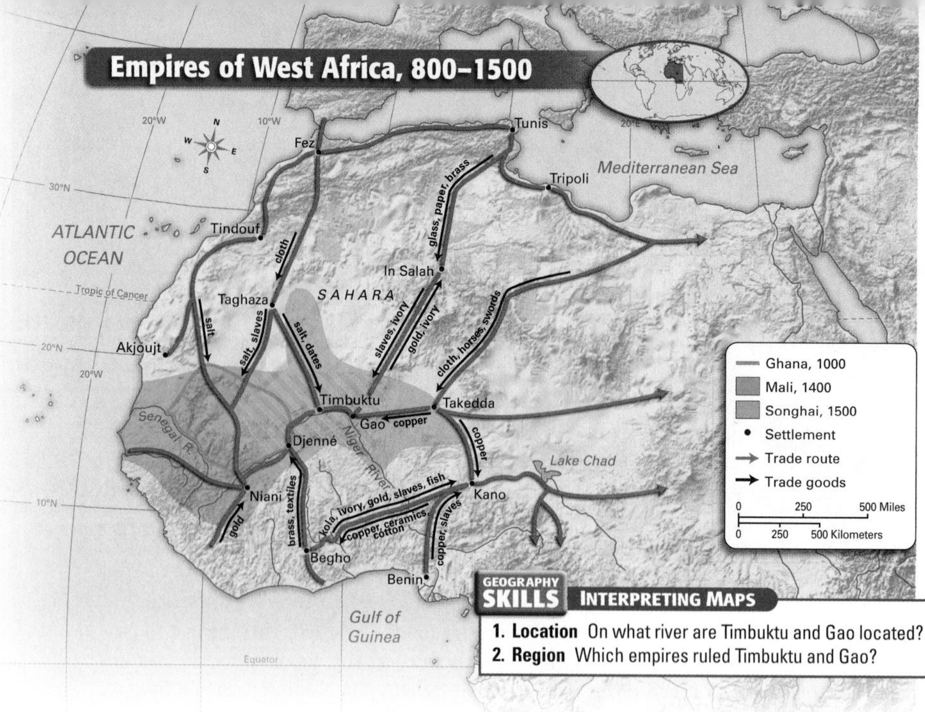

GEOGRAPHY SKILLS INTERPRETING MAPS

1. **Location** On what river are Timbuktu and Gao located?
2. **Region** Which empires ruled Timbuktu and Gao?

convert to Islam. The Almoravids weakened Ghana's empire and cut off many trade routes. Without its trade, Ghana could not support its empire, and the empire eventually fell. The influence of Islam, however, remained strong. By the late 1400s Islam would become the most practiced religion in the region.

Kingdom of Mali

Like Ghana, Mali lay along the upper Niger River. This area's fertile soil helped Mali grow. In addition, Mali's location on the Niger allowed its people to control trade on the river. Through this control of trade, the empire grew rich and powerful. According to legend, Mali's rise to power began under a ruler named Sundiata. Sundiata won back his country's independence and conquered nearby kingdoms, including Ghana.

Mali's most famous ruler, however, was a Muslim king named **Mansa Musa** (MAHN-sah moo-SAH). Under his leadership, Mali reached the height of its wealth, power, and fame.

Mansa Musa ruled Mali for about 25 years, from 1312 to 1337. During that time, Mali added many important trade cities, including Timbuktu (tim-buhk-TOO), Djenné (je-NAY), and Gao (GOW), to its empire. Traders came to Timbuktu from the north and the south to trade for salt, gold, metals, shells, and many other goods.

Religion was also very important to Mansa Musa. In 1324 he left Mali on a **hajj**, or pilgrimage to Mecca. Making this journey once in their lives is the spiritual duty of all Muslims. As he traveled to Mecca, Mansa Musa introduced his empire to the world. The stories of Mali's wealth and religion spread far and wide. Because of Mansa Musa's influence, Islam spread through a large part of West Africa.

Mansa Musa wanted all Muslims to be able to read the Qur'an. Therefore, he stressed the importance of learning to read and write the Arabic language. He sent scholars to study in Morocco. These scholars later set up schools in Mali for studying the Qur'an.

Social Studies Skills Activity: Using Maps

Below Level

Mapping West Africa's Great Kingdoms

Materials: blank outline maps of Africa, colored pencils or markers

1. Using the map on this page, review with students the locations and geography of the Ghana, Mali, and Songhai empires.
2. Give each student a blank outline map. Have students draw the area of each of the three empires on the blank outline map. Remind students to use a different color or pattern for each empire, and to label each empire and the approximate time period it flourished.
3. Instruct students to draw the major trade routes on their maps. They should also draw and label the major bodies of water, including the Niger River, Senegal River, Atlantic Ocean, the Gulf of Guinea, and the Mediterranean Sea. **LS Visual/Spatial**

Alternative Assessment Handbook, Rubric 20: Map Creation

To encourage the spread of Islam in West Africa, Mansa Musa brought back artists and architects from other Muslim countries to build **mosques**, or buildings for Muslim prayer, throughout his lands.

The architectural advances in cities like Timbuktu as well as an organized government, an emphasis on education, and expansion of trade all combined to make Mansa Musa Mali's most successful ruler. Much of Mali's success depended on strong leaders. After Mansa Musa died, poor leadership weakened the empire. By 1500 nearly all of the lands the kingdom once ruled were lost. Only a small area of Mali remained.

Songhai Empire

In the 1300s Mansa Musa had conquered a rival kingdom of people called the Songhai, who also lived along the Niger River. As the Mali Empire weakened in the 1400s, the Songhai grew in strength. They took advantage of Mali's decline, regained their independence, and eventually conquered most of Mali.

One of Songhai's greatest rulers was Muhammad Ture, who chose the title *askia*, a title of military rank. He became known as **Askia the Great**. Like Mansa Musa, Askia the Great was a devout Muslim who supported education and learning. Under his rule, the cities of Gao and Timbuktu flourished. They contained great mosques, universities, schools, and libraries. People came from all parts of West Africa to study mathematics, science, medicine, grammar, and law.

Askia understood that an empire needed effective government. He created a professional army, and to improve the government, he set up five provinces within Songhai. He removed local leaders and appointed new governors who were loyal to him. He also created specialized departments to oversee various tasks, much like modern-day government offices do.

THE IMPACT TODAY

Some of the mosques built by Mansa Musa can still be seen in West Africa today.

LINKING TO TODAY

Music from Senegal to Memphis

Did you know that the music you listen to today may have begun with the griots, musicians from West Africa? From the 1600s to the 1800s, many people from West Africa were brought to America as slaves. In America, these slaves continued to sing the way they had in Africa. They also continued to play traditional instruments such as the kora, shown here being played by Senegalese musician Soriba Kouyaté (far right). Over time, this music developed into a style called the blues, made popular by such artists as B. B. King (near right). In turn, the blues shaped other styles of music, including jazz and rock. So, the next time you hear a Memphis blues song or a cool jazz tune, listen for its ancient African roots.

ANALYSIS SKILL ANALYZING INFORMATION

How did West African music affect modern American music?

Direct Teach

Main Idea

❶ West Africa's Great Kingdoms

West Africa developed three great kingdoms that grew wealthy through their control of trade.

Recall Where did the Songhai people live? *along the Niger River*

Making Inferences Do you think the fact that Askia was a Muslim affected the way that he ruled? Explain your answer. *possible answer—He might have encouraged education so that people could read the Qur'an.*

Activity **Travel Brochure** Have each student create a brochure promoting travel to Timbuktu during this time. Suggest to students that the brochure might feature Timbuktu's great mosques, libraries, and universities.

Map Transparency 4: Empires of West Africa, 800–1500

Did you know . . .

The tomb of Askia the Great was recently added to the list of World Heritage sites kept by the United Nations. The tomb is located in a complex that features two mosques.

Answers

Analyzing Information *Slaves brought to America from West Africa continued their musical traditions, which over time developed into the blues, eventually shaping jazz and rock.*

Differentiating Instruction

Below Level

Struggling Readers

1. To help students understand the contributions of Askia the Great and the significance of his rule, draw the graphic organizer for students to see. Omit the answers.
2. Explain each category to students and ask them to name an example or an accomplishment for each category.
3. Have students copy the graphic organizer and use information in their text to add details about Askia the Great's accomplishments.
4. When students have completed the graphic organizer, review the answers with the class. **LS Visual/Spatial**

Alternative Assessment Handbook, Rubric 13: Graphic Organizers

CRF: Biography: Askia the Great

Accomplishments of Askia the Great

Government	Religion	Education
• *set up five provinces* • *appointed governors loyal to him* • *created departments to oversee tasks*	• *was a devout Muslim* • *built mosques*	• *opened schools and universities* • *encouraged study of mathematics, medicine, science, grammar, law*

Direct Teach

Main Idea

2 West African Slave Trade

Slaves became a valuable trade item in West Africa.

Explain How did slave trading change over time? *At first, black Africans owned slaves who were captured in war, were criminals, or sold to pay debts; gradually Muslim traders began selling black Africans in North Africa; eventually many enslaved Africans were brought to the Americas.*

Review & Assess

Close

Organize students into small groups. Have students discuss the reasons for the rise to power of each of the three West African kingdoms and the major accomplishments of each.

Review

go.hrw.com Online Quiz, Section 1.3

Assess

SE Section 3 Assessment

PASS: Section 1.3 Quiz

Alternative Assessment Handbook

Reteach/Classroom Intervention

Interactive Reader and Study Guide, Section 1.3

Interactive Skills Tutor CD-ROM

Soon after Askia the Great lost power, the empire of Songhai declined. Songhai was invaded by the Moroccans, the kingdom's northern neighbors. The Moroccans wanted to control the Saharan salt mines. They had superior military power and were able to take over Timbuktu and Gao. Changes in trade patterns completed Songhai's fall.

READING CHECK **Comparing** What did Ghana, Mali, and Songhai have in common?

West African Slave Trade

The practice of slavery had existed in Africa and in many parts of the world for centuries. Traditionally, slavery in West Africa mostly involved only black Africans, who were both slaveholders and slaves. This changed in the 600s when Arab Muslims, and later Europeans, became slave traders. Though Europeans had long traded resources with Africa, they became more interested in the growing slave trade.

People who were captured by warring groups during battle could be sold into slavery. In addition, criminals were sometimes sold as slaves. Other enslaved people were captured during raids on villages, and sometimes even the relatives of people who owed money were sold into slavery as payment for debts. Enslaved Africans were often bought to perform menial labor and domestic chores. In some cultures, having slaves raised the status of the slaveholder.

The market for West African slaves increased as Muslim traders bought or seized black Africans to sell in North Africa. West Africa was also home to many enslaved Africans brought to the Americas.

Over time, the slave trade became even more important to the West African economy. Kings traded slaves for valuable goods, such as horses from the Middle East and textiles and weapons from Europe. The trans-Saharan slave trade contributed to the power of Ghana, Mali, and Songhai.

READING CHECK **Drawing Inferences** Why did the slave trade in West Africa continue to grow?

SUMMARY AND PREVIEW Trade was important to the kingdoms of West Africa. In the next section you will learn about European trade.

Section 3 Assessment

go.hrw.com
Online Quiz
KEYWORD: SF7 HP1

Reviewing Ideas, Terms, and People

1. a. **Identify** How did West African kingdoms grow wealthy through trade?
   b. **Describe** How did **Mansa Musa** introduce his empire to the world?
   c. **Elaborate** Why was trade crucial to the survival of Ghana, Mali, and Songhai?
2. a. **Describe** How did some people become slaves in West Africa?
   b. **Analyze** What role did geography play in the development of the slave trade?
   c. **Judge** Why did the value of slaves as an export increase over time?

Critical Thinking

3. **Comparing and Contrasting** Review your chart on African kingdoms and trade. Then copy the diagram below and use it to show the similarities and differences in the fall of each kingdom.

Fall of Ghana, Mali, and Songhai	Similarities	Differences

FOCUS ON WRITING

4. **Gathering Information on Economies** Make a list of things that were important to the economies of the kingdoms of West Africa. Include your ideas about what seems most important to West Africans and things that you did not know about before reading this section.

Section 3 Assessment Answers

1. a. by controlling trade routes and taking traders; by having gold and salt to trade
   b. As a Muslim, he went on a hajj to Mecca.
   c. Trade provided wealth for each kingdom; wealth led to creation of strong governments and strong military. Without the money trade provided, empires could not stay strong.
2. a. captured in battle, criminals were sold as slaves, taken during a raid, sold to pay a debt
   b. Europeans and Arab Muslims became slave traders. Slaves were sold and brought to North Africa and the Americas.
   c. possible answers—Once slaves could be sold in more and more areas, the demand for them grew, causing value to rise.
3. Similarities—trade declined and kingdom lost power; Differences—Ghana's decline brought on by Almoravids; Mali's due to poor leadership; Songhai could not fight off Moroccans who wanted control over salt mines, change in trade patterns
4. Students' lists may include location, valuable natural resources, and control of trade routes.

Answers

Reading Check (left) *strong trading networks that brought wealth to the kingdoms*

Reading Check (right) *Slaves were valuable trade items.*

BIOGRAPHY

Mansa Musa

How could one man's travels become a historic event?

When did he live? the late 1200s and early 1300s

Where did he live? Mali

What did he do? Mansa Musa, the ruler of Mali, was one of the Muslim kings of West Africa. He became a major figure in African and world history largely because of a pilgrimage he made to the city of Mecca.

Why is he important? Mansa Musa's spectacular journey attracted the attention of the Muslim world and of Europe. For the first time, other people's eyes turned to West Africa. During his travels, Mansa Musa gave out huge amounts of gold. His spending made people eager to find the source of such wealth. Within 200 years, European explorers would arrive on the shores of western Africa.

Identifying Points of View How do you think Mansa Musa changed people's views of West Africa?

KEY FACTS

According to chroniclers of the time, Mansa Musa was accompanied on his journey to Mecca by some 60,000 people. Of those people,

- **12,000** were servants to attend to the king.
- **500** were servants to attend to his wife.
- **14,000** were slaves wearing rich fabrics such as silk.
- **500** carried staffs heavily decorated with gold. Historians have estimated that the gold Mansa Musa gave away on his trip would be worth more than $100 million today.

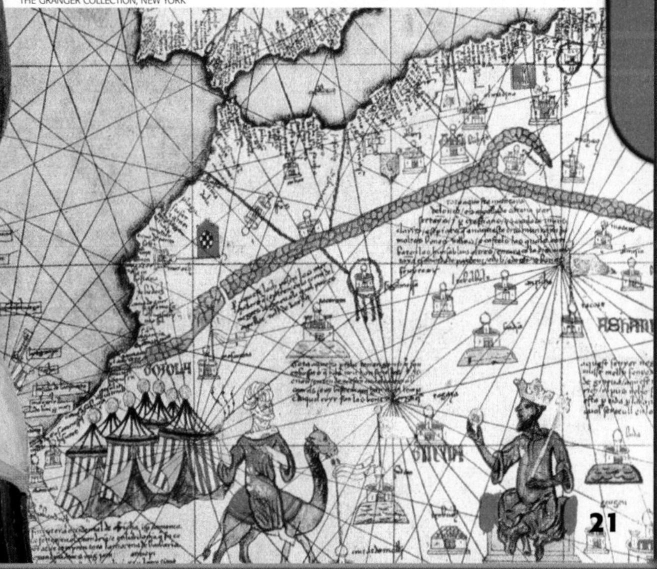

THE GRANGER COLLECTION, NEW YORK

This Spanish map from 1375 shows Mansa Musa sitting on his throne.

21

Biography

Reading Focus Question

Think of different historical figures and how their travels have affected history. Consider what possible effects might result from the travels of one person.

Info to Know

Mansa Musa's Journey On his famous pilgrimage to Mecca, Mansa Musa passed through several kingdoms in North Africa. From his capital of Niani, on the Upper Niger River, Mansa Musa and his entourage of thousands traveled north to Walata, to Tuat in modern-day Algeria, and then to Cairo, Egypt. From Egypt, Mansa Musa traveled to Mecca in Arabia.

Linking to Today

The Hajj The hajj is still an important ritual for Muslims today. Every year, millions of Muslims travel to Mecca for the annual hajj.

During the pilgrimage, which lasts six days, pilgrims perform special rites, including circling the Kaaba, a sacred shrine, seven times. Making the hajj is one of five duties expected of every Muslim who is physically and financially able.

About the Illustration

This illustration of Mansa Musa is an artist's conception based on available sources. However, historians are uncertain exactly what Mansa Musa looked like.

Critical Thinking: Summarizing

At Level

Writing a Eulogy

1. Review with students the biography of Mansa Musa. Tell students that they will write a eulogy that could have been read at Mansa Musa's funeral.
2. Ask students to include details found in this section. Encourage students to include one or two short accounts of interesting events from the life of Mansa Musa. Remind students to consider the purpose of the eulogy and their audience when writing the eulogy.
3. Ask for volunteers to deliver the eulogies to the class. Discuss with students the important contributions or accomplishments of Mansa Musa. LS **Verbal/Linguistic**

Alternative Assessment Handbook, Rubric 41: Writing to Express

Answers

Identifying Points of View *possible answers—spread knowledge of Mali, sparked new trade and even more wealth for Mali*

Preteach

Bellringer

If YOU were there . . . Use the **Daily Bellringer Transparency** for this section to help students answer the question.

Daily Bellringer Transparency 1.4

The World before the Opening of the Atlantic — Daily Bellringer 1.4

Review Section 3

Read the statements below and determine who or what is "speaking."

1. "We ran the trade routes in West Africa for hundreds of years." Who are we?
2. "I am a pilgrimage to Mecca." What am I?
3. "I ruled Mali for 25 years, from 1312 to 1337. I helped Mali gain fame, wealth, and power." Who am I?
4. "We are buildings for Muslim prayer." What are we?

Preview Section 4

If YOU were there ...

You are a peasant in the Middle Ages, living on the land of a noble. Although you and your family work very hard from sunrise to sundown, much of the food you grow goes to the noble. Your house is very small and has a dirt floor. Your parents are tired and weak, and you wish you could do something to improve their lives.

Is there any way you could change your life?

Consider what you CAN change:
- could leave home
- could find new work
- could find different housing

Consider what you CANNOT change:
- the requirement that you give food to noble
- the long hours you have to work
- the health of your parents

Review Answers: 1. Berbers; 2. hajj; 3. Mansa Musa; 4. mosques

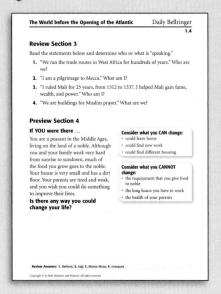

Academic Vocabulary

Review with students the high-use academic term in this section.

classical referring to the cultures of ancient Greece and Rome (p. 23)

CRF: Vocabulary Builder Activity, Section 4

Taking Notes

Have students copy the graphic organizer onto their own paper and then use it to take notes on the section. This activity will prepare students for the Section Assessment, in which they will complete a graphic organizer that builds on the information using a critical-thinking skill.

Section Correlations

IN

8.1.1 Identify major Native American Indian groups of eastern North America and describe early conflict and cooperation with European settlers and the influence the two cultures had on each other. **8.1.2** Explain the struggle of the British, French, Spanish and Dutch to gain control of North America during settlement and colonization.

SECTION 4

Europe before Transatlantic Travel

What You Will Learn...

Main Ideas

1. The Greeks and Romans established new forms of government.
2. During the Middle Ages, society eventually changed from a feudal system to a system with a middle class of artisans and merchants.
3. The Renaissance was a time of rebirth in the arts and in learning.

The Big Idea

New ideas and trade changed Europeans' lives.

Key Terms and People

Socrates, *p. 22*
Plato, *p. 22*
Aristotle, *p. 22*
reason, *p. 22*
democracy, *p. 23*
knights, *p. 24*
Black Death, *p. 25*
Michelangelo, *p. 26*
Leonardo da Vinci, *p. 26*
Johannes Gutenberg, *p. 27*
joint-stock companies, *p. 27*

TAKING NOTES As you read, take notes on the changes in society during the periods listed. Write your notes in a chart like this one.

Period of Time	Major Changes
Ancient Greece	
Roman Republic	
Middle Ages	
Renaissance	

IN **8.1.1, 8.1.2**

If YOU were there...

You are a peasant in the Middle Ages, living on the land of a noble. Although you and your family work very hard from sunrise to sundown, much of the food you grow goes to the noble. Your house is very small and has a dirt floor. Your parents are tired and weak, and you wish you could do something to improve their lives.

Is there any way you could change your life?

BUILDING BACKGROUND Hard work was a constant theme in the lives of peasants in the Middle Ages. Nobles were not free to live as they chose, either. As the Middle Ages ended, the Renaissance brought new ways of thinking, and the growth of cities brought big changes to the way people lived and worked.

Greek and Roman Government

During the Renaissance, European thinkers and artists rediscovered the traditions of Greece and Rome. Ancient Greek and Roman texts were translated, and their ideas began to revolutionize European societies.

Greek Philosophers and Government

Ancient Greeks valued human reason and believed in the power of the human mind to think, explain, and understand life. Three of the greatest Greek thinkers, or philosophers, were **Socrates**, **Plato**, and **Aristotle**. Socrates, a great teacher, wanted to make people think and question their own beliefs. Plato, a philosopher and teacher, wrote a work called *The Republic*. It describes an ideal society based on justice and fairness for everyone. Aristotle taught that people should live lives based on **reason**, or clear and ordered thinking.

Teach the Big Idea

At Level

Europe before Transatlantic Travel

1. **Teach** To teach the main ideas in the section, use the questions in the Direct Teach boxes.
2. **Apply** Create a simple time line for students to see. It should begin with the Greek Classical Period of the 5th and 4th centuries BC and end in the mid-1400s. Give students time to glance through Section 4 to come up with suggestions for events to add to the time line.
3. **Review** Using the time line, ask volunteers to explain the importance of various events. Remind students that the Renaissance ended in the early 1500s.
4. **Practice/Homework** Have students copy the time line developed in class on their own paper. Assign students to illustrate their time lines. **LS Verbal/Linguistic, Visual/Spatial**

Alternative Assessment Handbook, Rubrics 11: Discussions; and 13: Graphic Organizers

Greek scientists and mathematicians also gained fame for their contributions to geometry and for accurately calculating the size of Earth. Doctors studied the human body to understand how it worked. One Greek engineering invention that is still used today is a water screw, which brings water to farm fields.

One of the Greeks' most lasting contributions, however, is their political system. During the time known as the Classical Period, around the fifth and fourth centuries BC, Greece was organized into several hundred independent city-states, which became the foundation for Greek civilization. Athens was the first Greek city-state to establish **democracy**—a form of government in which people rule themselves. All male citizens in Athens had the right to participate in the assembly, a gathering of citizens, to debate and create the city's laws. Because all male citizens in Athens participated directly in government, we call the Greek form of government a direct democracy.

Roman Law and Government

Later, Rome followed Greece's example by establishing a form of democratic government. The Roman Republic was created in 509 BC. Each year Romans elected officials to rule the city. These officials had many powers, but they only stayed in power for one year. This early republic was not a democracy. Later, the Romans changed their government into one with three parts. These three parts were made up of elected representatives who protected the city and its residents.

Roman laws were written and kept on public display so all people could know them. Roman concepts of equality before the law and innocent until proven guilty protected Roman citizens' rights.

The political ideas of Greece and Rome survived to influence governments around the world, including that of the United States. In the U.S. political system, citizens vote for representatives, making the nation a democratic republic.

READING CHECK **Analyzing** How did Roman and Greek governments influence the United States?

Democracy and Republic (QUICK FACTS)

Direct democracies and republics are similar forms of government in which the people rule. There are some slight differences, though.

Direct Democracy	Republic
• Every citizen votes on every issue. • Ideas are debated at an assembly of all citizens.	• Citizens elect representatives to vote on issues. • Ideas are debated at an assembly of representatives.

THE IMPACT TODAY

Many of the geometry rules we learn in school today come straight from the Greek mathematician Euclid. Many doctors recite the Hippocratic Oath, named after the Greek doctor Hippocrates.

ACADEMIC VOCABULARY

classical referring to the cultures of ancient Greece or Rome

The Roman Senate played a principal role in the Roman government.

Differentiating Instruction

Above Level

Advanced/Gifted and Talented

Research Required

1. Have students conduct research to learn more about Socrates, Plato, and Aristotle.
2. Ask each student to write a short paragraph expressing the main ideas of each man's philosophy. Then have students compare and contrast the main ideas of the three philosophers. **LS Verbal/Linguistic**
3. Ask volunteers to share what they have written. Discuss the information with the class, and help students understand the differences among the three philosophers.
4. **Extend** Ask students what issues, such as justice or fairness, would be best explored using the Socratic method.

Alternative Assessment Handbook, Rubrics 9: Comparing and Contrasting; and 11: Discussions

Resources for Differentiating Instruction

See page 1c of the Chapter Planner for additional resources for differentiating instruction.

Direct Teach

Main Idea

1 Greek and Roman Government

The Greeks and Romans established new forms of government.

Define What was the Greek Classical Period? *the time around the 5th and 4th centuries BC when Greece was organized into several hundred city-states that became the foundation for Greek civilization; during this time Athens established a democracy*

Analyze Why was Roman citizenship valued so highly? *Roman laws helped protect the common people; all male citizens could vote or hold office; people were innocent until proven guilty*

Elaborate Do you believe the government of Athens was truly a democracy? Explain your answer. *Possible answers—Women could not vote, and there were restrictions on who could become a citizen.*

Did you know . . .

The assembly in Athens would vote once a year to ostracize or exile citizens from the city. If enough citizens voted in favor of an ostracism, citizens gathered to vote for the person they wanted to see exiled from Athens. The citizen receiving the most votes would be forced to leave the city for up to 10 years.

CRF: Biography Activity: Aristotle

CRF: Literature Activity: The *Aeneid*, by Virgil

Quick Facts Transparency 1: Democracy and Republic

go.hrw.com

Online Resources

KEYWORD: SF7 CH1
ACTIVITY: Roman Government

Answers

Reading Check *The United States has a democratic form of government; it is a republic.*

Direct Teach

Main Idea

❷ Middle Ages

During the Middle Ages, society eventually changed from a feudal system to a system with a middle class of artisans and merchants.

Recall Under the feudal system, what was the relationship between lords and vassals? *Lords divided their land among vassals in exchange for loyalty and military service. Vassals in turn might divide their land among lesser nobles, who were often knights.*

Explain How did the Catholic Church unify Europe during the Middle Ages? *Because nearly everyone in Europe was Christian, life revolved around the church's activities.*

Analyze How did feudalism get its start? *Frankish kings were not able to defend their empire against attacks in the 800s, so Frankish nobles began defending their own land. Nobles became more powerful than kings and began to establish independent territories.*

Info to Know

Magna Carta The signing of Magna Carta by King John in 1215 (on page 25), was an important event. It indicated that he was no longer entirely above the law. This action inspired the English to find even more ways to limit the king's power.

History Humor

When a knight was killed in battle, what did they put on his tombstone? *Rust in peace.*

CRF: Primary Source Activity: The *Mona Lisa,* Leonardo da Vinci

Middle Ages

As the Roman Empire fell, groups from the north and east moved into former Roman lands. By the early 500s Europe was divided into many small kingdoms. This marked the beginning of the Middle Ages, a period that lasted about a thousand years.

Feudalism

In the 480s a powerful group called the Franks conquered Gaul, the region we now call France. The Franks created a huge empire in Europe. When invaders began to attack European settlements in the 800s, the Frankish kings could not defend their empire. Because they could not depend on protection from their kings, nobles had to defend their own lands. As a result, the power of European nobles grew, and kings became less powerful. Although these nobles remained loyal to the king, they ruled their lands as independent territories.

Nobles needed soldiers to defend their lands. Nobles gave **knights**, warriors who fought on horseback, land in exchange for military service. Nobles who gave land to knights so that the knights would defend the land were called lords. A knight who promised to support the noble in battle was called a vassal. This system of promises between lords and vassals is known as feudalism.

Peasants owned no land, so they were not part of the feudal system. They did, however, need to grow food to live. As a result, a new economic system developed. Knights allowed peasants to farm land on their large estates, called manors. In return, the peasants had to give the knights food or other goods as payment.

Because of its structure, feudalism promoted the separation of territories and people. The Catholic Church, however, served as a strong unifying force among the states and people of Europe. During the Middle Ages, nearly everyone in Europe was Christian. Life revolved around the local church with markets, festivals, and religious ceremonies.

The Crusades

In the late 1000s, a long series of wars called the Crusades began between the European Christians and Muslims in Southwest Asia.

Time Line

Key Events in Europe

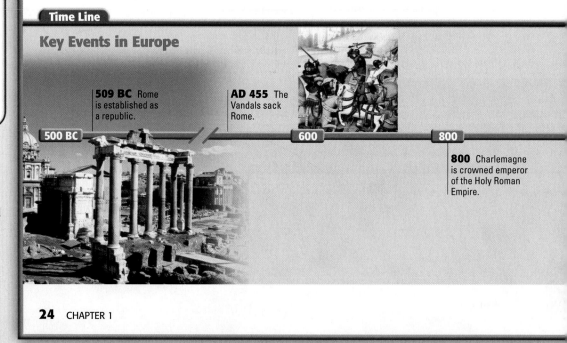

500 BC — **509 BC** Rome is established as a republic.

AD 455 The Vandals sack Rome.

600

800 — **800** Charlemagne is crowned emperor of the Holy Roman Empire.

Differentiating Instruction

Below Level

Special Needs Learners

1. Tell students that the term *feudalism* may sound complicated, but the society was actually organized in a straightforward fashion. Create the following diagram for students to see:

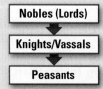

   Nobles (Lords)
   ↓
   Knights/Vassals
   ↓
   Peasants

2. Remind students of each group's role. If necessary, encourage students to reread the section titled Feudalism on this page.
3. Tell students to imagine that they are living during this time and need to explain the feudal system to someone who has just arrived in Europe. Instruct students to create an illustrated page explaining feudalism.

   LS Visual/Spatial

   Alternative Assessment Handbook, Rubric 13: Graphic Organizers

The Turks had captured Palestine, the Holy Land where Jesus had lived. Christians no longer felt safe to travel there on pilgrimages. Christians were called upon to go to war with the Turks to recapture Palestine.

Although the Crusades failed, they changed Europe forever. Trade between Europe and Asia began to grow, introducing Europeans to new products such as apricots, rice, and cotton cloth, as well as the ideas of Muslim thinkers.

Travel, Trade, and Towns

In the Middle Ages, towns were small. After about 1000, this situation began to change. New technology meant farmers could produce larger harvests. As farmers grew more food, the population increased.

Travel became safer as increased protection from stronger rulers kept larger territories secure. Over time, kingdoms became nation-states—organized political units with central governments. This development provided even more protection to merchants.

The rulers of the Mongols made routes like the Silk Road, a caravan route that started in China and ended at the Mediterranean Sea, safe for travelers and traders. Among these traders was Marco Polo. In 1271 he journeyed from Europe to China along part of the old Silk Road. He spent 20 years living and traveling in Asia. When Marco Polo returned to Europe, he brought back stories of spices, coal, and paper money.

Trade routes spread all across Europe. Merchants brought goods from Asia and Africa to sell in European markets. Their ships also brought back rats infected with the plague. The disease, known as the **Black Death**, spread across Europe, killing an estimated 25 million people. The European economy was dramatically affected by the shortage of workers. Peasants and serfs could now demand payment for their labor. They began to move to cities, which began to grow in size.

In time, the growth of trade led to the decline of feudalism and the manor system. A new middle class of artisans and merchants emerged, and trade cities became commercial centers. Trade associations called guilds became an influential part of European life.

READING CHECK **Drawing Conclusions** How did travel and trade affect the feudal system?

1000
1200
1400
1066 England is conquered by the Norman king William the Conqueror.
1215 Nobles force King John to sign Magna Carta.
1347 The Black Death arrives in Europe, eventually killing millions.
c. 1350 The Renaissance begins.
1436 Johannes Gutenberg perfects his invention of the printing press.

ANALYSIS SKILL **READING TIME LINES**

What two factors on the time line most helped spread literacy in Europe?

Direct Teach

Main Idea

❷ Middle Ages

During the Middle Ages, society eventually changed from a feudal system to a system with a middle class of artisans and merchants.

Explain What were the Crusades? *series of holy wars in Palestine between European Christians and Muslim Turks that began in the late 1000s*

Analyze Why were the Crusades significant to the future of Europe? *Trade between Europe and Asia grew; Europeans were exposed to Muslim ideas and products brought back by Crusaders.*

Predict If you grew up on a farm near the end of the Middle Ages, do you think you would stay or move to a city? *possible answer—The opportunity to make money in cities was a strong draw for many people.*

Info to Know

The Holy Land Also known as Palestine, the Holy Land is sacred to three major world religions—Judaism, Islam, and Christianity.

Teaching Tip

The Printing Press Ask students how the invention of the printing press and new ideas worked together and led to major changes in Europe. *The printing press made more ideas available to people.*

Critical Thinking: Drawing Inferences

At Level

Descriptive Letters

1. Remind students that while Marco Polo was in Asia he saw paper money and coal. Europeans had never seen either of these items.
2. Have students choose one of these items and write a descriptive letter about the item to someone who has never seen it. Students should include specific ways that the item can be used. They should also include specifics about the way the item could greatly improve everyday life, and in the case of money, facilitate trade.
3. Have students illustrate their letters with a picture of the item and a picture of the item in use.
4. Ask volunteers to share their letters and their drawings with the class. **LS Verbal/Linguistic**

Alternative Assessment Handbook, Rubric 40: Writing to Describe

Answers

Reading Time Lines *Renaissance, invention of printing press*

Reading Check *As travel became safer and trade developed, people began to move to cities. As they left farms and manors, the feudal system fell into decline.*

Direct Teach

Main Idea

3 Renaissance

The Renaissance was a time of rebirth in the arts and in learning.

Describe How did classical writings that had been in the Byzantine Empire come to Italy? *Scholars fleeing from the Turkish conquest brought the works with them to Italy.*

Contrast How did the studies of Renaissance scholars differ from work done during the Middle Ages? *Renaissance scholars focused on human values, and art, literature, science, political thoughts. People worked to glorify God.*

Make Inferences What does it mean if someone is called a Renaissance man or woman? *interested in learning; have skills and knowledge in a wide range of areas*

Teaching Tip

Pronunciation Many names associated with the Renaissance, such as Leonardo da Vinci and Dante Alighieri, are hard to pronounce. Help students by having the class pronounce the names out loud together.

Biography

Michelangelo (1475–1564)

Michelangelo di Buonarroti Simoni was born in Florence, Italy, but he also worked in Rome and Bologna. He created some of the most famous statues and paintings in world history. One of these paintings is the ceiling of the Sistine Chapel in Rome. Michelangelo continually strove for perfection.

Answers

Trading Centers *Many people are trading.*

Trading Centers

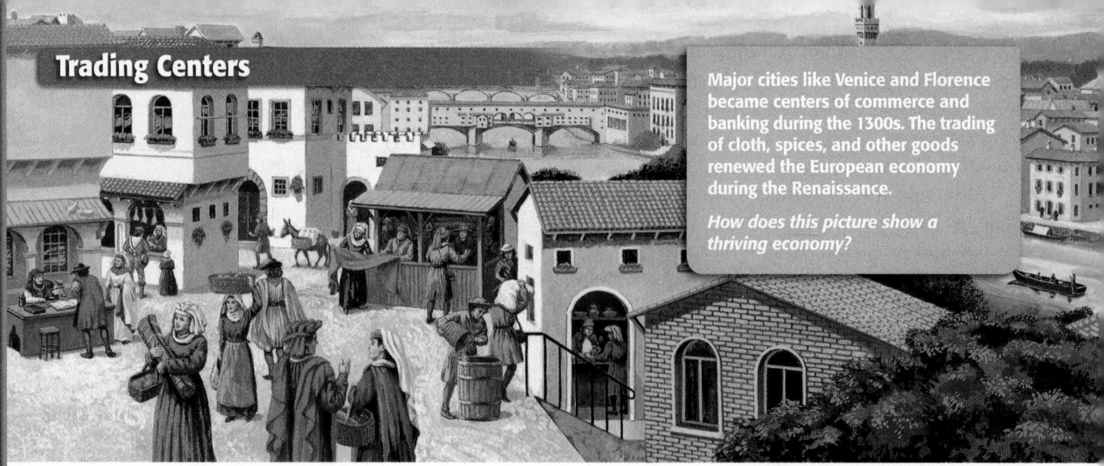

Major cities like Venice and Florence became centers of commerce and banking during the 1300s. The trading of cloth, spices, and other goods renewed the European economy during the Renaissance.

How does this picture show a thriving economy?

Renaissance

The Renaissance period brought new ways of thinking to Europe, weakening the old feudal system even more. The word *Renaissance* means "rebirth" and refers to the period that followed the Middle Ages in Europe. This movement began in Italy and eventually spread to other parts of Europe.

During the Renaissance, European rulers began to increase their power over the nobles in their countries. Fewer invasions from outside forces helped bring a period of order and stability to Europe.

Search for Knowledge

Love of art and education was a key feature of the Renaissance. As Turks conquered much of the Byzantine Empire in the East, scholars fled to Italy. They brought ancient classical writings with them. Some of the works were by Greek thinkers like Plato.

Excited by the discoveries brought by Turkish scholars, European scholars went looking for ancient texts in Latin. They discovered many Latin texts in monasteries, which had preserved works by Roman writers. As Italian scholars read these ancient texts, they rediscovered the glories of Greece and Rome.

The search for knowledge and learning spread to all fields, including art, literature, science, and political thought. The Renaissance emphasized the importance of people rather than focusing on religion. This new focus on human value and the study of humanities was called humanism. People's interest in the humanities led them to respect those who could write, create, or speak well. During the Middle Ages, most people had worked only to glorify God.

Italian artists created some of the most beautiful paintings and sculptures in the world. Their art reflected the basic Renaissance idea—the value of human beings. **Michelangelo** and **Leonardo da Vinci** are two of the greatest Renaissance artists. They are known for their work in painting, sculpture, and architecture. Da Vinci was also an inventor, engineer, and mapmaker.

Italian writers also penned great works of literature. Dante Alighieri was a politician and poet. Before Dante, most authors wrote in Latin, the language of the church. But Dante chose to write in Italian, the common language of the people. This gave ordinary people the opportunity to read Dante's work.

Many texts that Europeans rediscovered in the 1300s dealt with science. After reading these works, Renaissance scholars went on

Critical Thinking: Drawing Conclusions

At Level

Emergence of the Renaissance

1. Ask students to list some events that helped bring about the Renaissance. Write the suggestions for everyone to see. Here are a few ideas:
   - Crusaders returned with new ideas and products.
   - Power of kings increased, leading to more stability.
   - Classical writings were rediscovered.
   - The Black Death led to a large decline in population and a growth in towns and cities.
   - Trading increased along the Silk Road.
2. Organize students into small groups. Have each group rank these events in order of importance.
3. Ask a volunteer from each group to give their rankings. LS **Verbal/Linguistic**

Alternative Assessment Handbook, Rubric 11: Discussions

to make their own scientific advances. They also studied ancient math texts and built on the ideas they read about. For example, they created symbols for the square root and for positive and negative numbers. Astronomers discovered that Earth moves around the sun. Other scientists used measurements and made calculations to create better, more accurate maps.

The development of the printing press was a giant step forward in spreading new ideas. In the mid-1400s, a German man, **Johannes Gutenberg** (GOOT-uhn-berk), developed a printing press that used movable type. This allowed an entire page to be printed at once. For the first time in history, thousands of people could read the same books and share ideas about them.

Economic Changes Affect Trade

The growth in trade and services at the beginning of the Renaissance sparked a commercial revolution. This also brought a rise in mercantilism. Mercantilism is an economic system that unifies and increases the power and wealth of a nation.

Four northern Italian cities, Florence, Genoa, Milan, and Venice, developed into important trading centers. These cities played two major roles in trade. They served as ports along the Mediterranean Sea. They also served as manufacturing centers and specialized in certain crafts. This economic activity made some families in these cities very wealthy.

As trade and commerce grew, the need for banks arose. Bankers in Florence, Italy, kept money for merchants from all over Europe. The bankers also made money by charging interest on funds they loaned to merchants. The greatest bankers in Florence were from the Medici family. Although Florence was already wealthy from trade, banking increased that wealth.

During this time, merchants began to create **joint-stock companies**, or businesses in which a group of people invest together. In a joint-stock company, the investors share in the companies' profits and losses. Forming joint-stock companies allowed investors to take fewer risks.

READING CHECK **Drawing Conclusions** How did the Renaissance lead to trade and a commercial revolution?

THE IMPACT TODAY
The demand for more books led to improvements in printing and binding that have made modern books affordable.

SUMMARY AND PREVIEW Greek and Roman traditions provided new ways for people to govern themselves. In the next chapter you will read about how the Renaissance paved the way for exploration of the Americas.

Section 4 Assessment

go.hrw.com
Online Quiz
KEYWORD: SF7 HP1

Reviewing Ideas, Terms, and People

1. a. **Identify** What is the difference between a direct democracy and a republic?
   b. **Elaborate** What is the importance of having a written law code?
2. a. **Describe** What is the relationship between **knights** and nobles?
   b. **Elaborate** How did the Crusades affect the feudal system?
3. a. **Identify** What does the term *Renaissance* mean?
   b. **Analyze** What is the relationship among trade, banking, and **joint-stock companies**?
   c. **Elaborate** What do you think was the greatest accomplishment of the Renaissance?

Critical Thinking

4. **Supporting a Point of View** Review your notes on the major changes that took place in Europe during the periods discussed in the section. In a chart like the one below, identify which period you think was most important, and explain why.

Most Important	Why

FOCUS ON WRITING

5. **Organizing a Chronology** Make a list of important events in Europe during the time discussed in this section. Reorder them from earliest to most recent.

Direct Teach

Main Idea

3 Renaissance

The Renaissance was a time of rebirth in the arts and in learning.

Identify Which European invented a printing press with movable type? *Johannes Gutenberg*

Summarize Why did banking become an important industry during the Renaissance? *Trade and commerce led to a need for banks to lend and keep money.*

CRF: Economics and History Activity: Mercantilism: Government Control of Trade

Review & Assess

Close

Discuss how Greek and Roman traditions, along with the Middle Ages, led to the resurgence of interest in knowledge and arts during the Renaissance.

Review

Online Quiz, Section 1.4

Assess

SE Section 4 Assessment

PASS: Section 1.4 Quiz

Alternative Assessment Handbook

Reteach/Classroom Intervention

Interactive Reader and Study Guide, Section 1.4

Interactive Skills Tutor CD-ROM

Section 4 Assessment Answers

1. **a.** In a direct democracy, all citizens vote to decide issues and participate in government; in a republic, citizens elect representatives to govern them.
   b. When laws are written, everyone knows what they are, not just those who wrote them.
2. **a.** Knights agreed to protect a noble's lands in exchange for smaller pieces of land.
   b. Trade increased, which led to the decline of the feudal system, and the manor system was weakened.
3. **a.** rebirth
   b. Merchants needed capital to fund their businesses or to expand them; banks loaned money to merchants; joint-stock companies provided ways to raise money for businesses.
   c. possible answers—the art of Michelangelo and Leonardo da Vinci; the printing press
4. possible answer—The Renaissance was the most important because it led to a rebirth in society that spurred new advancements in art, literature, science, and political thought.
5. For possible answers, see the time line in this section.

Answers

Reading Check *Trade, the growth of cities, and new crafts all created an impetus for new economic systems. Banking grew, as did joint-stock companies, which were a means to finance new business ventures.*

History and Geography

Activity **Calculating Percentages** Although estimates of the death toll from the plague vary, many historians agree that Europe's population was reduced by about one third. Use almanacs or other reference works to find population figures for your city. Then calculate how many people in the city would have died from the Black Death if the disease claimed the same percentage of victims. For example, if the population of your city is 100,000, then about 33,000 people would have died.

Did you know . . .

Ships arriving from the East were often greeted at European harbors with enthusiasm—everyone wanted to see what goods they brought. In some cities, once people realized the ships might be carrying disease, ships were not allowed to enter the ports.

Linking to Today

Black Plague Today Figures from the World Health Organization show that today between 1,000 and 3,000 cases of the plague occur annually around the world. Antibiotics are effective against the disease, but treatment must begin very quickly to avoid serious illness or even death.

History and Geography

The Black Death

"And they died by the hundreds," wrote one man who saw the horror, "both day and night." The Black Death had arrived. The Black Death was a series of deadly plagues that hit Europe between 1347 and 1351, killing millions. People didn't know what caused the plague. They also didn't know that geography played a key role in its spread—as people traveled to trade, they unknowingly carried the disease with them to new places.

CENTRAL ASIA
EUROPE
Kaffa
CHINA
AFRICA
The plague probably began in central and eastern Asia. These arrows show how it spread into and through Europe.
This ship has just arrived in Europe from the East with trade goods—and rats with fleas.
The fleas carry the plague and jump onto a man unloading the ship. Soon, he will get sick and die.

28 CHAPTER 1

Differentiating Instruction

Struggling Readers — Below Level

Have students review the feature on these pages. Then ask students to assign names, occupations, and personalities to the people depicted in the illustration. Have students write brief stories about the roles these people are playing in the Black Death. Supply thesauri and dictionaries to help students in choosing words.
LS Visual/Spatial

Advanced/Gifted and Talented — Above Level

Have students imagine that one third of the people in your state have died from the plague. Ask them what would be the short- and long-term economic results. Have students consider such things as loss of labor force, need for skilled workers, and impact on wages. Have students apply their ideas about the present-day results to infer the plague's effects on Europe during the Middle Ages.

Eriksson settled in a coastal area he called Vinland, but the Vikings left after only a few years. Attacks by Native Americans posed a constant threat, and the area may have been too far from other Viking settlements to be supported.

After the Vikings left North America, Europeans did not return to the continent for centuries. In the 1400s, however, a growing interest in discovery and exploration spread across Europe.

READING CHECK **Sequencing** List the stages of exploration that led to the Vikings' landing in North America.

Prince Henry the Navigator

In the early 1400s Portugal became a leader in world exploration. One man in particular, Prince **Henry the Navigator**, was responsible for advances that would make exploration more successful. Although he never set out on a voyage himself, Henry greatly advanced Portugal's exploration efforts.

In the early 1400s Prince Henry built an observatory and founded a school of navigation to teach better methods of sailing. He also financed research by mapmakers and shipbuilders. Finally, he paid for expeditions to explore the west coast of Africa.

Riches in Asia

During the 1400s, Europeans had several reasons to explore the world. First, they wanted Asian spices. They hoped to bypass the merchants who had a monopoly on, or economic control of, the Asian products that reached the Mediterranean. If a sea route to Asia could be found, countries could buy spices and other items directly.

Second, religion played a role in exploration. Christians in Europe wanted to convert more people to their faith. Third, many Europeans had become interested in Asian cultures. Explorer Marco Polo's book about his travels throughout Asia remained popular in Europe long after his death in 1324. Many Europeans wanted to learn more about Asia and its cultures.

History Close-up
The Caravel
A special type of ship called the caravel became the workhorse of many European explorers. Though small, caravels were sturdy. They could sail across huge oceans and up small rivers. Caravels featured important advances in sailing technology.
Triangular sails enabled the caravel to sail into the wind.
The smooth, rounded hull handled high seas well.
The large center rudder made quick turns possible.
ANALYSIS SKILL ANALYZING VISUALS
What features made the caravel an excellent sailing ship?

Direct Teach

Main Idea

❶ Viking Sailors Reach North America

Vikings were skilled sailors, and they were the first Europeans to reach North America.

Explain How did Leif Eriksson and his crew reach North America? *Strong winds blew his ship off course during a voyage from Norway to Greenland.*

Draw Conclusions Why did the Vikings stay in North America for only a few years? *They faced attacks by Native Americans, and other Viking settlements were far away.*

CRF: Literature: Karlsefni Goes to Vinland

Main Idea

❷ Prince Henry the Navigator

Prince Henry the Navigator established a school for sailors and provided financial support that enabled the Portuguese to start exploring the oceans.

Recall What economic reasons made Europeans eager to explore the world? *They wanted Asian spices and hoped to bypass merchants who held a monopoly on Asian products.*

Evaluate How might the establishment of new sea routes help European countries break the monopolies on Asian spices held by merchants? *Sea routes to Asia would allow countries to get spices directly, bypassing merchants who controlled products coming through the Mediterranean Sea.*

Critical Thinking: Making Generalizations

At Level

Adventure Tales

1. Ask students to imagine that they are Prince Henry at the time he was thinking about founding a navigation school.
2. Have students write a persuasive letter inviting people, such as mapmakers and shipbuilders, to move to Portugal to teach. Include the offer of financial assistance to conduct research on their interest in oceanic navigation.
3. In their letters, students should explain why coming to this new school to work with others presents an exciting opportunity for new discovery and groundbreaking research.
4. Ask volunteers to share their letters with the class. LS **Verbal/Linguistic**

Alternative Assessment Handbook, Rubric 43: Writing to Persuade

Answers

Analyzing Visuals *smooth, rounded hull, large center rudder, triangular sails*

Reading Check *longships traveled rough seas; developed trading networks; founded a settlement on Iceland; Erik the Red settled in Greenland; Leif Eriksson was blown off course and landed in northern Canada*

Direct Teach

Main Idea

❸ A Sea Route to Asia

Portuguese sailors sailed around Africa and found a sea route to Asia.

Recall What was the outcome of Bartolomeu Dias's expedition along the African coast? *A storm blew his ships around the southern tip of Africa.*

Make Inferences Do you think the Indians welcomed Vasco da Gama when he reached Calicut? Explain your answer. *The Indians had been trading with Muslim and Italian merchants for many years, so they probably welcomed da Gama as another European trader.*

Evaluate What do you think life was like for enslaved Africans in Portuguese-controlled islands? *poor, because they were forced to work hard, and they endured brutal living conditions*

Quick Facts Transparency 3: Causes and Effects of the Discovery of a Sea Route to Asia

Map Transparency 5: Portuguese Routes and Exploration

Info to Know

Cape of Good Hope The Cape of Good Hope is a headland located near present-day Cape Town, South Africa. It rises about 840 feet above sea level and marks the turning point for ships that are traveling between the Indian and south Atlantic Oceans. Dias named it the Cape of Storms, and later on John II of Portugal renamed it the Cape of Good Hope.

Answers

Focus on Reading *Students should adequately outline the material under the heading, "A Sea Route to Asia."*

Analyzing Information *wanted to gain wealth, convert people to Christianity, learn more about Asia*

Reading Check *Prince Henry built an observatory and a navigation school to teach better methods of navigation. He also financed research by mapmakers and shipbuilders and exploration of Africa's west coast.*

QUICK FACTS

Causes and Effects of the Discovery of a Sea Route to Asia

Several factors led to the discovery of a sea route from Europe to Asia.

Causes

- Financial backing from Prince Henry the Navigator
- New technology (caravel and mariner's astrolabe)
- Seeking trade with Asia and financial gain
- Converting people to Christianity
- Curiosity

Effects

- Discovery of a sea route to Asia
- Face-to-face contact with traders in distant lands
- Awareness of different cultures and ways of life

ANALYSIS SKILL ANALYZING INFORMATION

Why was trade with Asia so important to Europeans?

ACADEMIC VOCABULARY

effect the result of an action or decision

FOCUS ON READING

Make an outline for the heading "A Sea Route to Asia."

Technological Advances

New technology played a major role in advancing world exploration. Sailors began to use tools such as the magnetic compass and the **astrolabe**, a device that enabled navigators to learn their ship's location by charting the position of the stars. Better instruments made it possible for sailors to travel the open seas without landmarks to guide them.

The Portuguese also made advances in shipbuilding. They began designing ships that were smaller, lighter, and easier to steer than the heavy galleons they had used before. These new ships, called **caravels** (ker-uh-velz), used triangular sails that, unlike traditional square sails, allowed ships to sail against the wind. By placing rudders at the back of the ship, the Portuguese also improved the steering of ships.

READING CHECK **Analyzing** How did Henry the Navigator promote exploration?

A Sea Route to Asia

By the 1400s Portugal had several motives, financial support, and the technology necessary for exploration. Portuguese explorers set out to find new lands.

Rounding Africa

Even with new technology, travel on the open seas was dangerous and difficult. One person described the **effect** on sailors of a voyage south from Portugal.

> "Those which survived could hardly be recognized as human. They had lost flesh and hair, the nails had gone from hands and feet . . . They spoke of heat so incredible that it was a marvel that ships and crews were not burnt."
>
> –Sailor, quoted in *World Civilizations*, edited by Edward McNall Burns, et al.

In spite of the dangers, Portuguese explorers continued sailing south, setting up trading posts along the way.

In 1488 Portuguese navigator Bartolomeu Dias led an expedition from Portugal southward along the African coast. A storm blew his ships around the southern tip of Africa. This point became known as the Cape of Good Hope. Dias wanted to continue his voyage, but his men did not. Since supplies were very low, Dias decided to call off the voyage and return to Portugal.

Later, King Manuel of Portugal sent another explorer, Vasco da Gama, on an expedition around the Cape of Good Hope. Da Gama left Lisbon, Portugal, in July 1497 and arrived in southwestern India the next year. Portugal had won the European race for a sea route to Asia.

When da Gama reached the Indian port of Calicut, Muslim traders met him and his men. The Muslims surprised the sailors by speaking to them in Portuguese. Soon da Gama and his crew learned that the people of India had been trading with Muslim and Italian merchants who knew Portuguese. Da Gama made two more trips back to India. He even governed a small colony there.

Differentiating Instruction

Below Level

Struggling Readers

1. Organize students into pairs. Instruct pairs to create a chart of Portuguese explorers. The chart should have three columns labeled *Explorer, Discovery,* and *Outcome.*
2. Review with students the contributions of the Portuguese explorers discussed in this section and the results of their discoveries.
3. Have students work together to fill in each column. *Answers: Bartolomeu Dias, Cape of Good Hope at southern tip of Africa, first Portuguese explorer to travel to the south of Africa, future sailors to West Africa bargained with tribal leaders for gold, ivory, and slaves; Vasco da Gama, traveled around the Cape of Good Hope to Calicut, India, opened direct trade between Portugal and India, governed a small colony in India and gained Portugal more wealth and power*
4. Ask students to share their charts with the class. **LS Interpersonal, Visual/Spatial**

Alternative Assessment Handbook, Rubric 7: Charts

Results of Exploration

Portugal's explorations would have major results, including the start of the Atlantic slave trade. As Portuguese sailors explored the west coast of Africa, they negotiated for gold, ivory, and slaves. The slave trade devastated African communities. It led to increased warfare among kingdoms and broke up many families. The Portuguese sent many enslaved Africans to Europe and to islands in the Atlantic, where they lived and worked under brutal conditions.

The other nations of Europe watched as new trade routes brought increased wealth and power to Portugal. They soon launched voyages of exploration to find their own water routes to Asia.

READING CHECK **Predicting** How would continued exploration affect Africans?

SUMMARY AND PREVIEW In the 1400s, the Portuguese started a new era of exploration. In the next section you will learn how Europeans reached the American continents.

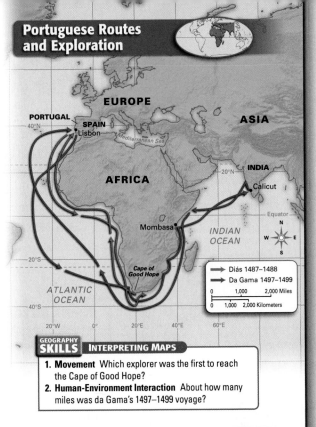

Portuguese Routes and Exploration

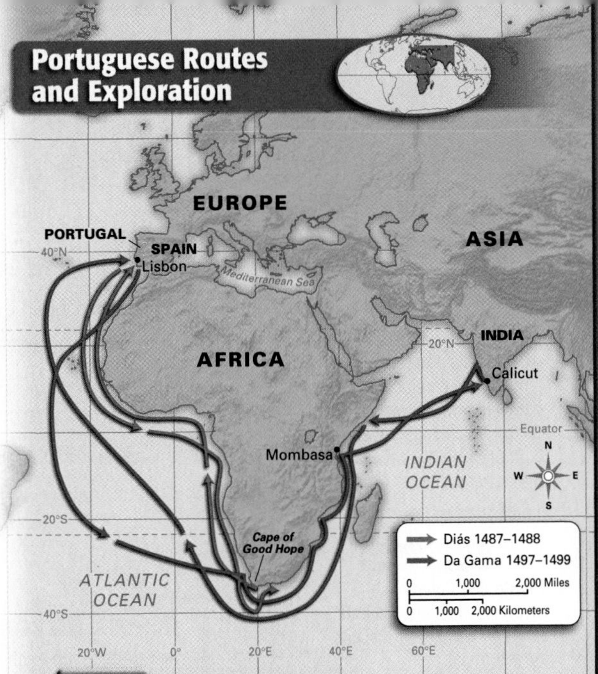

GEOGRAPHY SKILLS **INTERPRETING MAPS**

1. **Movement** Which explorer was the first to reach the Cape of Good Hope?
2. **Human-Environment Interaction** About how many miles was da Gama's 1497–1499 voyage?

Section 1 Assessment

go.hrw.com
Online Quiz
KEYWORD: SF7 HP2

Reviewing Ideas, Terms, and People

1. a. **Identify** Who was Leif Eriksson?
   b. **Summarize** How did the Vikings eventually establish Vinland?
   c. **Draw Inferences** Why do you think the Vikings did not try to colonize the Americas?
2. a. **Identify** Who was Prince **Henry the Navigator**?
   b. **Compare** Why were **caravels** able to sail against the wind while other ships could not?
3. a. **Recall** Who was the first explorer to find a sea route from Europe to Asia?
   b. **Explain** How did Muslims living in India learn Portuguese?
   c. **Draw Conclusions** How did the slave trade affect West Africa?

Critical Thinking

4. **Summarizing** Review your notes on European exploration. Then copy the chart below and use it to explain the reason for the explorations, the technology that made explorations possible, and the results of the explorations.

Reason / Technology	→	Results

FOCUS ON WRITING

5. **Taking Notes on Early Explorers** As you read this section, take notes on groups of explorers. Make sure to note the differences and similarities between the groups, where they traveled, and why.

Direct Teach

Did you know . . .

One of the first West African slaves brought to Europe was a chieftain named Adahu. He told Prince Henry about other African lands to the south and inland.

Review & Assess

Close

Briefly review the development of early European exploration. Remind students of the technological inventions that made lengthy sea voyages possible as well as the impact these innovations had on trade.

Review

go.hrw.com Online Quiz, Section 2.1

Assess

SE Section 1 Assessment

PASS: Section 2.1 Quiz

Alternative Assessment Handbook

Reteach/Classroom Intervention

Interactive Reader and Study Guide, Section 2.1

Interactive Skills Tutor CD-ROM

Section 1 Assessment Answers

1. **a.** first European to sail to North America
   b. sailed south to Newfoundland, settled in a coastal area
   c. discouraged by attacks, other settlements too far away
2. **a.** Portuguese ruler, started a navigation school, encouraged exploration
   b. triangular sails
3. **a.** Vasco da Gama
   b. through trade contacts with other Muslims and Italian merchants
   c. increased warfare among West African countries, broke up families
4. Reasons—desire for cheaper Asian spices, desire to convert people to Christianity, and interest in Asian culture; Technology—observatory, navigation schools, caravels, magnetic compass, astrolabe; Results—sea route to Asia, start of the Atlantic slave trade, other European countries began exploring
5. Vikings—skilled and innovative; explored Iceland, Greenland, and parts of N. America for adventure and trade. Portuguese—skilled and innovative; explored around Africa and to Asia, for adventure, trade, and religion.

Answers

Interpreting Maps **1.** *Dias;* **2.** *over 12,000 miles*

Reading Check *Portuguese sailors bargained with African rulers for gold, ivory, and slaves, establishing the slave trade. The slave trade broke up families and increased warfare among kingdoms.*

Preteach

Bellringer

If YOU were there . . . Use the **Daily Bellringer Transparency** to help students answer the question.

Daily Bellringer Transparency 2.2

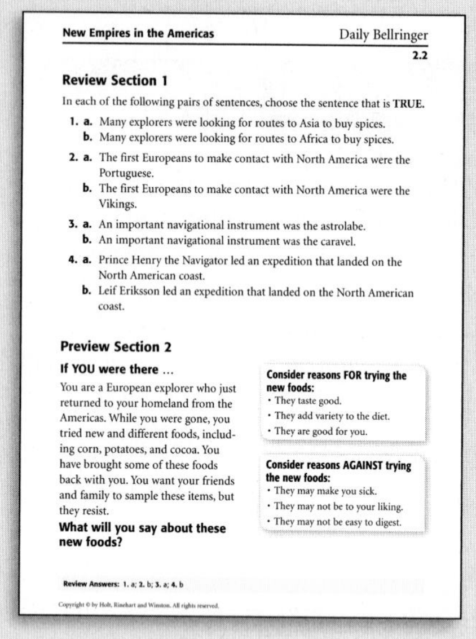

New Empires in the Americas Daily Bellringer **2.2**

Review Section 1

In each of the following pairs of sentences, choose the sentence that is **TRUE.**

1. a. Many explorers were looking for routes to Asia to buy spices.
   b. Many explorers were looking for routes to Africa to buy spices.
2. a. The first Europeans to make contact with North America were the Portuguese.
   b. The first Europeans to make contact with North America were the Vikings.
3. a. An important navigational instrument was the astrolabe.
   b. An important navigational instrument was the caravel.
4. a. Prince Henry the Navigator led an expedition that landed on the North American coast.
   b. Leif Eriksson led an expedition that landed on the North American coast.

Preview Section 2

If YOU were there ...

You are a European explorer who just returned to your homeland from the Americas. While you were gone, you tried new and different foods, including corn, potatoes, and cocoa. You have brought some of these foods back with you. You want your friends and family to sample these items, but they resist.

What will you say about these new foods?

Consider reasons FOR trying the new foods:
- They taste good.
- They add variety to the diet.
- They are good for you.

Consider reasons AGAINST trying the new foods:
- They may make you sick.
- They may not be to your liking.
- They may not be easy to digest.

Review Answers: 1. a; 2. b; 3. a; 4. b

Building Vocabulary

Preteach or review the following terms:

raw materials items found in nature that can be used to manufacture other products (p. 45)

uncharted not previously mapped (p. 43)

CRF: Vocabulary Builder Activity, Section 2

Taking Notes

Have students copy the graphic organizer onto their own paper and then use it to take notes on the section. This activity will prepare students for the Section Assessment, in which they will complete a graphic organizer that builds on the information using a critical-thinking skill.

SECTION 2

Europeans Reach the Americas

What You Will Learn...

Main Ideas

1. Christopher Columbus sailed across the Atlantic Ocean and reached a continent that was previously unknown to him.
2. After Columbus's voyages, other explorers sailed to the Americas.

The Big Idea

Christopher Columbus's voyages led to new exchanges between Europe, Africa, and the Americas.

Key Terms and People

Christopher Columbus, *p. 42*
Line of Demarcation, *p. 44*
Treaty of Tordesillas, *p. 44*
Ferdinand Magellan, *p. 44*
circumnavigate, *p. 44*
Columbian Exchange, *p. 45*

TAKING NOTES As you read, take notes on the explorers, their journeys, and the effects of European voyages to the Americas. Write your notes in a chart like the one below.

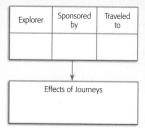

Explorer	Sponsored by	Traveled to

Effects of Journeys

If YOU were there...

You are a European explorer who just returned to your homeland from the Americas. While you were gone, you tried new and different foods, including corn, potatoes, and cocoa. You have brought some of these foods back with you. You want your friends and family to sample these items, but they resist.

What will you say about these new foods?

BUILDING BACKGROUND Europeans, Africans, and Asians had traded with each other for centuries using land and sea routes. Native American groups also knew of each other through trade routes. Although sailors often explored new areas, before 1492 the two worlds had no communication with each other.

Columbus Sails across the Atlantic

Stories of fabulous kingdoms and wealth in Asia captured the imagination of **Christopher Columbus**, a sailor from Genoa, Italy. Columbus was convinced that he could reach Asia by sailing west across the Atlantic Ocean.

The Journey Begins

Columbus asked King Ferdinand and Queen Isabella of Spain to pay for an expedition across the Atlantic. He promised them great riches, new territory, and Catholic converts. It took Columbus several years to convince the king and queen, but they finally agreed to help finance the journey. Ferdinand and Isabella ordered Columbus to bring back any items of value and to claim for Spain any lands he explored.

On August 3, 1492, Columbus's three ships set sail. The *Niña* and the *Pinta* were caravels. Columbus sailed in the larger *Santa María*. The ships carried about 90 sailors and a year's worth of supplies. They made a stop in the Canary Islands, and then on September 6, they resumed their journey. Soon, they passed the limits of Columbus's

Teach the Big Idea

At Level

Europeans Reach the Americas

1. **Teach** To teach the main ideas in the section, use the questions in the Direct Teach boxes.
2. **Apply** Have students create a flow chart to show the impact of Columbus's voyage. Tell students to write *Columbus lands in the Caribbean* in the first block of their charts. Students should draw arrows to link the boxes that will follow. **LS Visual/Spatial**
3. **Review** Tell students to fill in their flow charts with events that occurred as a result of Columbus's voyage. *Students should include land claimed for Spain; conflict between Spain and Portugal; Line of Demarcation; Treaty of Tordesillas; other explorers reach Americas; discovery of the Pacific Ocean; Magellan circumnavigates the planet; Columbian Exchange; triangular trade*
4. **Practice/Homework** Have students illustrate each event in their flow charts.

Alternative Assessment Handbook, Rubric 7: Charts

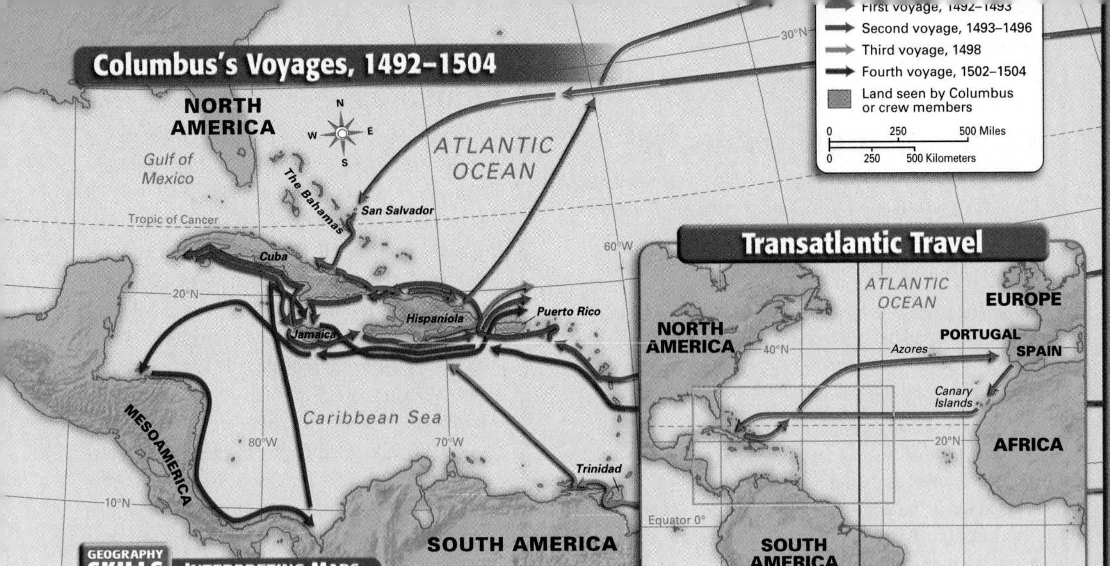

GEOGRAPHY SKILLS INTERPRETING MAPS

1. **Place** Where did Columbus first land?
2. **Human-Environment Interaction** Why do you think Columbus saw only the coastal area of Mesoamerica?

maps and sailed into uncharted seas. After more than a month with no sight of land, the crew grew restless.

Soon the crew saw signs of land—birds and floating tree branches. Columbus promised a reward "to him who first sang out that he saw land." On October 12, 1492, a lookout cried, "Land! Land!" ending the long journey from the Canary Islands.

The ships landed on an island in the Bahamas. Columbus thought he had found a new route to Asia. Instead, he had reached another continent that was unknown to him. Columbus called the island San Salvador, which means "Holy Savior." Columbus also visited another island he called Hispaniola. There he met the Taino (TY-noh). At that time Europeans called Asia the Indies, so Columbus, believing he was in Asia, called these Native American people Indians.

The Taino lived in small farming communities. In his journal, Columbus wrote that the Taino were "so generous . . . that no one would believe it who has not seen it." However, Columbus and his crew were not interested in Taino culture, but in gold. After three months of exploring, looking for gold, and collecting exotic plants and animals, Columbus returned to Spain.

Columbus made three more journeys to the Americas during his lifetime. In 1504 he returned to Spain in poor health. Columbus died two years later, still believing that he had reached Asia.

Impact of Columbus's Voyages

The voyages of Columbus changed the way Europeans thought of the world and their place in it. A new era of interaction between Europe and the Americas had begun.

Columbus's discovery also created conflict between European countries. Both Spain and Portugal wanted to add these lands to their growing empires. In 1493, Pope Alexander VI, originally from Spain, issued a decree that drew a new boundary for Spain and Portugal.

Direct Teach

Main Idea

❶ Columbus Sails across the Atlantic

Christopher Columbus sailed across the Atlantic Ocean and reached a continent that was previously unknown to him.

Recall Who is Christopher Columbus, and why are his voyages of exploration significant? *Italian sailor who led a 1492 voyage; reached the Americas, a continent that was at that time unknown to Europeans*

Summarize What did Columbus hope to find in the new land? What did he take to Spain? *gold and a sea route to Asia; exotic plants and animals*

Evaluate Why was it so difficult for Columbus to convince King Ferdinand and Queen Isabella to finance his voyage? *possible answers—The trip was expensive, there were no guarantees that Columbus would reach Asia, and he was sailing into uncharted waters.*

CRF: Biography Activity: Queen Isabella I

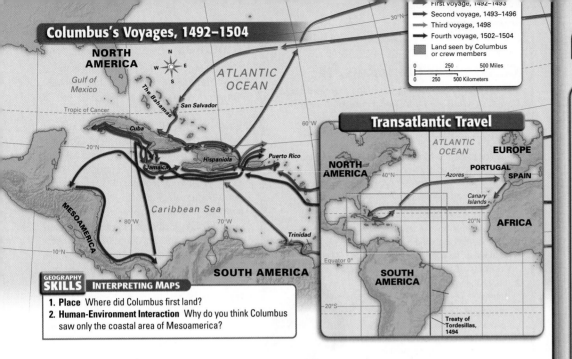

Map Transparency 6: Columbus's Voyages, 1492–1504

Info to Know

The Taino The name *Taino* came from a Native American word meaning "good" or "noble." Columbus described the Taino as gentle and loving, but he did not consider them as "advanced" as Europeans. He pointed out that the Taino had no knowledge of iron or weaponry. They grabbed iron swords by the blade and cut their hands. The Taino used paint to prevent sunburn, but they did not wear as much clothing as the Europeans. Such instances shaped the views of Europeans.

Collaborative Learning

At Level

First Impressions

1. Ask students to imagine what it must have been like for the Taino to meet Columbus and his men. Remind students that this most likely was the first time the Taino had seen large ships. It was undoubtedly the first time the Taino had seen Europeans.
2. Organize students into small groups. Tell the groups that they are to write, direct, and perform a short play describing the meeting of the Taino and Columbus.
3. Remind students that Columbus wrote that the Taino were "so generous . . . that no one would believe it who has not seen it." Also, remind students that Columbus was interested in finding gold. Instruct students that their plays should present both Columbus's and the Taino's reactions to this first meeting.
4. Ask students to perform their plays for the class. **LS Verbal/Linguistic**

Alternative Assessment Handbook, Rubric 33: Skits and Reader's Theater

CRF: Primary Source Activity, The Journal of Christopher Columbus

Answers

Interpreting Maps 1. *an island in the Bahamas he called San Salvador;* **2.** *possible answers—too difficult to explore, fear of Indians*

Direct Teach

Main Idea

❷ Other Explorers Sail to the Americas

After Columbus's voyages, other explorers sailed to the Americas.

Recall How did the Americas get their name? *A mapmaker labeled the continents America in honor of Amerigo Vespucci, who led an expedition to South America and believed that the land was not Asia, but a new continent.*

Summarize How did Magellan's fleet circumnavigate the world? How long did it take to complete the journey? *sailed from Spain down the east coast of South America, into the Pacific, west into the Indian Ocean, then back to Spain; three years*

Make Judgments Which items traded in the Columbian Exchange do you think were most valuable? Why? *possible answers—corn, potatoes, tobacco, and cocoa to Europe; horses, cattle, pigs, wheat, and barley to the Americas*

Did you know . . .

Vasco Núñez de Balboa may have been the first European to see the Pacific Ocean, but it was Ferdinand Magellan who named the body of water. He chose "Pacific" because it described the calm waters.

go.hrw.com
Online Resources
KEYWORD: SF7 CH2
ACTIVITY: The Day Things Changed

Primary Source

LETTER

Christopher Columbus, 1494

Two years after discovering the island of Hispaniola, Columbus wrote a letter to the Spanish king and queen outlining his ideas of its colonization.

Most High and Mighty Sovereigns,

In the first place, as regards the Island of Espanola: Inasmuch as the number of colonists who desire to go thither [there] amounts to two thousand, owing to the land being safer and better for farming and trading . . .

1. That in the said island there shall be founded three or four towns . . .
2. That for the better and more speedy colonization of the said island, no one shall have liberty to collect gold in it except those who have taken out colonists' papers . . .
3. That each town shall have its alcalde [Mayor] . . .
4. That there shall be a church, and parish priests or friars to administer the sacraments, to perform divine worship, and for the conversion of the Indians.

–Christopher Columbus,
letter to the king and queen of Spain, 1494

ANALYSIS SKILL **ANALYZING PRIMARY SOURCES**

What were Columbus's main concerns in founding a colony on Hispaniola?

This imaginary **Line of Demarcation** divided the Atlantic Ocean. Spain could claim all land west of the line.

The Portuguese king believed that this arrangement favored Spain. To prevent war, the leaders of the two nations signed the **Treaty of Tordesillas**, which moved the Line of Demarcation 800 miles further west. This gave Portugal more opportunity to claim lands unexplored by other Europeans.

READING CHECK **Identifying Points of View** Why did Columbus want to sail across the Atlantic?

Other Explorers Sail to the Americas

Columbus's discoveries inspired others to sail across the Atlantic Ocean. In 1501 explorer Amerigo Vespucci (vuh-SPOO-chee) led a Spanish fleet to the coast of present-day South America. He was convinced the land he reached was not Asia. Instead, Vespucci believed he had found a "new world." A German mapmaker labeled the continents across the ocean *America* in honor of Vespucci. Europeans began using the names North America and South America for these lands.

In a Spanish settlement in present-day Panama, another explorer, Vasco Núñez de Balboa (NOON-yays day bahl-BOH-uh), heard stories from local Native Americans about another ocean farther west. Balboa set out to find it. For weeks he and his men struggled through thick jungle and deadly swamps. In 1513 they reached the top of a mountain. From this spot Balboa saw a great blue sea—the Pacific Ocean—stretching out before him.

In 1519, **Ferdinand Magellan** (muh-JEHL-uhn), a Portuguese navigator, set out with a Spanish fleet to sail down the east coast of South America. After sailing around the southern tip of the continent, Magellan continued into the Pacific even though his ships were dangerously low on food and fresh water.

Magellan's fleet sailed across the Pacific Ocean. In the Philippines, Magellan was killed in a battle with native peoples. Down to three ships, the expedition continued sailing west into the Indian Ocean. In 1522 the voyage's only remaining ship returned to Spain. Only 18 members of Magellan's original crew survived. These sailors were the first people to **circumnavigate**, or go all the way around, the globe. Their entire journey was some 40,000 miles long.

European explorers and settlers took plants and animals with them to the Americas. They also brought back a variety of new plants and animals to Europe, Asia, and Africa.

Critical Thinking: Interpreting Maps

At Level

Mapping Voyages of Columbus

Materials: blank outline map of the world, colored pencils

1. Instruct students to reread the information concerning the voyages of Christopher Columbus, Amerigo Vespucci, Vasco Núñez de Balboa, and Ferdinand Magellan. Students should note years and important discoveries.
2. Have students use the blank outline maps and colored pencils to chart the routes of these explorers and to illustrate the Columbian Exchange.
3. On their maps students should note what products traveled from Europe to the Americas, and what products were exported from the Americas to Europe. Students should also map the triangular trade between Europe, Africa, and the Americas.
4. Ask students to share their maps with the class. **LS Interpersonal, Visual/Spatial**

Alternative Assessment Handbook, Rubric 20: Map Creation

Answers

Analyzing Primary Sources *creating towns, controlling the collecting of gold, mayors for towns, priests and a church*

Reading Check *Columbus thought he could reach Asia by sailing west across the Atlantic Ocean from Spain.*

This transfer became known as the **Columbian Exchange** because it started with Columbus's explorations. The Columbian Exchange dramatically changed the world.

European explorers found many plants in the Americas that were unknown to them, including corn, potatoes, tobacco, and cocoa. They brought these items to Europe, where they were highly valued. The explorers also introduced horses, cattle, and pigs to the Americas. Native Americans came to use these animals for food and transportation. They also started to farm European grains such as wheat and barley.

Without intending to do so, the explorers also introduced deadly new diseases to the Americas. Native Americans had no natural resistance to European diseases and often died as a result of their exposure to them.

Over time, a trading pattern involving the exchange of raw materials, manufactured products, and slaves developed among Europe, Africa, and the Americas. Europeans shipped millions of enslaved Africans to work in the colonies in the New World.

READING CHECK **Evaluating** What were the negative aspects of the Columbian Exchange?

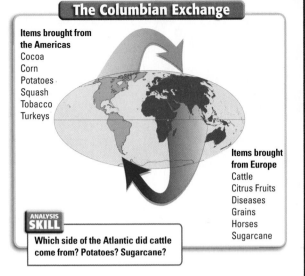

The Columbian Exchange

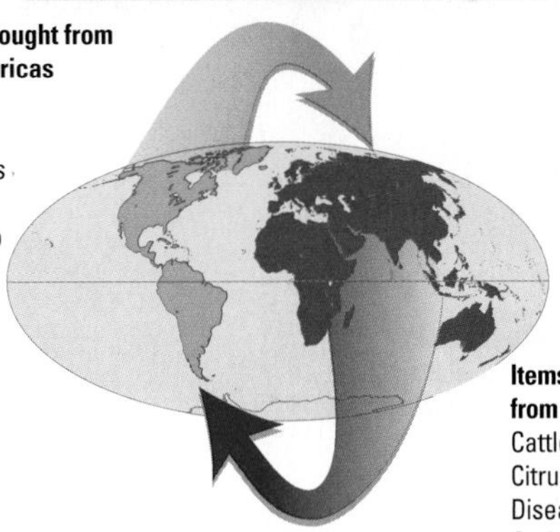

ANALYSIS SKILL Which side of the Atlantic did cattle come from? Potatoes? Sugarcane?

SUMMARY AND PREVIEW Columbus's voyages to America inspired other Europeans to explore the "New World." This led to new exchanges between both sides of the Atlantic. In the next section you will learn about Spain's empire in the Americas.

Section 2 Assessment

go.hrw.com
Online Quiz
KEYWORD: SF7 HP2

Reviewing Ideas, Terms, and People

1. a. **Recall** What agreement did **Christopher Columbus** make with Queen Isabella and King Ferdinand of Spain?
   b. **Explain** Where did Columbus think he had landed when he reached the Bahamas?
   c. **Evaluate** How did Columbus's voyage lead to a dispute between Spain and Portugal?
2. a. **Identify** Who was the first European explorer to see the Pacific Ocean?
   b. **Summarize** What route did **Ferdinand Magellan**'s ships take to **circumnavigate** the globe?
   c. **Draw Conclusions** How did the **Columbian Exchange** and the slave trade affect the economies and the people of Europe, Africa, and the Americas?

Critical Thinking

3. **Supporting a Point of View** Review your notes on European exploration. Then copy the graphic organizer below and use it to rank, in order, the two most important results of European voyages to the Americas. Explain your choices in the "Why" column.

Most Important	Why

FOCUS ON WRITING

4. **Understanding Christopher Columbus** As you read this section, pay attention to what life might have been like for Columbus and his crew as they sailed across the Atlantic. Note ways in which their voyage changed life for many Europeans.

Direct Teach

Linking to Today

A Sweet Find The origins of chocolate date back 4,000 years, and the sweet treat has always been valued—the Aztecs even used the cacao tree beans as currency. When European explorers brought chocolate back with them, the royalty and upper class quickly developed a sweet tooth. Today, Americans eat more than 3 billion pounds of the favorite candy.

Map Transparency 7: The Columbian Exchange

Review & Assess

Close

Briefly review Christopher Columbus's discoveries and how they changed the world, including trade between the Americas and Europe and the expansion of the slave trade.

Review

Online Quiz, Section 2.2

Assess

SE Section 2 Assessment

PASS: Section 2.2 Quiz

Alternative Assessment Handbook

Reteach/Classroom Intervention

Interactive Reader and Study Guide, Section 2.2

Interactive Skills Tutor CD-ROM

Section 2 Assessment Answers

1. **a.** king and queen financed the expedition; Columbus would bring back any items of value and claim territory for Spain
   b. Asia
   c. Both wanted land in the Americas
2. **a.** Vasco Núñez de Balboa
   b. from Spain, to eastern coast of South America, around the southern tip of South America, across the Pacific, west across the Indian Ocean, back to Spain
   c. brought new products to Europe and the Americas, led to slave trade with Africa, introduced deadly new diseases to Native Americans, enriched European nations
3. possible answers—Christopher Columbus's explorations inspired other explorations and resulted in the Columbian Exchange; Ferdinand Magellan's crew circumnavigated the globe and showed the extent of the earth.
4. See answer to Question 2c.

Answers

Analysis Skill *east; west; east*

Reading Check *Europeans introduced diseases to the Native Americans and many died; the triangular trade between Europe, Africa, and the Americas included trading slaves.*

Preteach

Bellringer

If YOU were there . . . Use the **Daily Bellringer Transparency** to help students answer the question.

Daily Bellringer Transparency 2.3

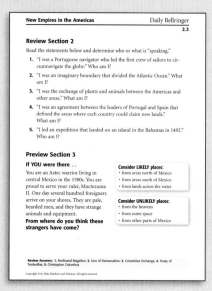

New Empires in the Americas — Daily Bellringer **2.3**

Review Section 2

Read the statements below and determine who or what is "speaking."

1. "I was a Portuguese navigator who led the first crew of sailors to circumnavigate the globe." Who am I?
2. "I was an imaginary boundary that divided the Atlantic Ocean." What am I?
3. "I was the exchange of plants and animals between the Americas and other areas." What am I?
4. "I was an agreement between the leaders of Portugal and Spain that defined the areas where each country could claim new lands." What am I?
5. "I led an expedition that landed on an island in the Bahamas in 1492." Who am I?

Preview Section 3

If YOU were there ...

You are an Aztec warrior living in central Mexico in the 1500s. You are proud to serve your ruler, Moctezuma II. One day several hundred foreigners arrive on your shores. They are pale, bearded men, and they have strange animals and equipment.

From where do you think these strangers have come?

Consider LIKELY places:
- from areas north of Mexico
- from areas south of Mexico
- from lands across the water

Consider UNLIKELY places:
- from the heavens
- from outer space
- from other parts of Mexico

Review Answers: **1.** Ferdinand Magellan; **2.** Line of Demarcation; **3.** Columbian Exchange; **4.** Treaty of Tordesillas; **5.** Christopher Columbus

Building Vocabulary

Preteach or review the following terms:

convert to convince others to change to a different faith or way of thinking (p. 46)

haciendas vast Spanish estates in Central and South America (p. 50)

CRF: Vocabulary Builder Activity, Section 3

Taking Notes

Have students copy the graphic organizer onto their own paper and then use it to take notes on the section. This activity will prepare students for the Section Assessment, in which they will complete a graphic organizer that builds on the information using a critical-thinking skill.

Section Correlations

IN

8.3.7 Using maps identify changes influenced by growth, economic development and human migration in the eighteenth and nineteenth centuries. **8.4.1** Identify economic factors contributing to European exploration and colonization in North America, the American Revolution and the drafting of the Constitution of the United States.

SECTION 3

Spain Builds an Empire

What You Will Learn...

Main Ideas

1. Spanish conquistadors conquered the Aztec and Inca empires.
2. Spanish explorers traveled through the borderlands of New Spain, claiming more land.
3. Spanish settlers treated Native Americans harshly, forcing them to work on plantations and in mines.

The Big Idea

Spain established a large empire in the Americas.

Key Terms and People

conquistadors, *p. 46*
Hernán Cortés, *p. 46*
Moctezuma II, *p. 46*
Francisco Pizarro, *p. 47*
encomienda system, *p. 50*
plantations, *p. 50*
Bartolomé de Las Casas, *p. 51*

TAKING NOTES Create a chart like the one below. As you read, take notes on Spanish conquest and settlement in the Americas.

Spanish Conquest and Settlement	
Aztec Empire	
Inca Empire	
Borderlands–Southeast	
Borderlands–Southwest	

IN 8.3.7, 8.4.1

If YOU were there...

You are an Aztec warrior living in central Mexico in the 1500s. You are proud to serve your ruler, Moctezuma II. One day several hundred foreigners arrive on your shores. They are pale, bearded men, and they have strange animals and equipment.

From where do you think these strangers have come?

BUILDING BACKGROUND Spain sent many expeditions to the Americas. Like explorers from other countries, Spanish explorers claimed the land they found for their country. Much of this land was already filled with Native American communities, however.

Spanish Conquistadors

The Spanish sent **conquistadors** (kahn-kees-tuh-DAWRS), soldiers who led military expeditions in the Americas. Conquistador **Hernán Cortés** left Cuba to sail to present-day Mexico in 1519. Cortés had heard of a wealthy land to the west ruled by a king named **Moctezuma II** (mawk-tay-SOO-mah).

Conquest of the Aztec Empire

Moctezuma ruled the Aztec Empire, which was at the height of its power in the early 1500s. Moctezuma's capital, Tenochtitlán, was built in the middle of Lake Texcoco, near the present-day site of Mexico City. Tenochtitlán was a large city with temples, a palace, and buildings that were built on an island in the middle of the lake. The buildings and riches of the city impressed the Spaniards. They saw the Aztec Empire as a good source of gold and silver. They also wanted to convert the Aztec to Christianity.

The Aztec had thousands of warriors. In contrast, Cortés had only 508 soldiers, about 100 sailors, 16 horses, and some guns. Cortés hoped that his superior weapons would bring him victory. Cortés also sought help from enemies of the Aztec. An Indian woman named Malintzin (mah-LINT-suhn) helped Cortés win allies.

Teach the Big Idea

At Level

Spain Builds an Empire

1. **Teach** To teach the main ideas in the section, use the questions in the Direct Teach boxes.
2. **Apply** Create a 2-column chart for students to see. Label the columns *Cause* and *Effect.* As students read this section, have them look for causes and effects and record their information in the chart. Remind students that not everything they learn in this section needs to be included in the chart, but the information they include should show a logical progression from the conquistadors to the enslavement of Native Americans. **LS Visual/Spatial**
3. **Review** Ask volunteers to share information they have included in their charts.
4. **Practice/Homework** Have students use their charts to write brief descriptions that explain the relationship between the events on their charts.

Alternative Assessment Handbook, Rubric 7: Charts

At first Moctezuma believed Cortés to be a god and welcomed him. Cortés then took Moctezuma prisoner and seized control of Tenochtitlán. Eventually, Tenochtitlán was destroyed and Moctezuma was killed. Smallpox and other diseases brought by the Spanish quickened the fall of the Aztec Empire.

Conquest of the Inca Empire

Another conquistador, **Francisco Pizarro** (puh-ZAHR-oh), heard rumors of the Inca cities in the Andes of South America. The Inca ruled a large territory that stretched along the Pacific coast from present-day Chile to northern Ecuador.

Pizarro had fewer than 400 men in his army. But the Inca, like the Aztec, had no weapons to match the conquistadors' swords and guns. Though outnumbered, Pizarro's troops captured the great Inca capital at Cuzco in present-day Peru and killed the Inca leaders. By 1534 Pizarro and his Native American allies had conquered the entire Inca Empire.

In only a few years, the Spanish had conquered two great American empires. During the conquest, the Spanish and their allies killed thousands of Inca and Aztec and looted their settlements. Moreover, possibly more than three-quarters of the Aztec and Inca populations were killed by the diseases the Europeans brought.

Spanish Settlements

The Spanish began to settle their vast empire, which they called New Spain. Spain's government wanted to control migration to the Americas. Most of the emigrants were Spanish, though a few non-Spanish subjects of the king also migrated. Jews, Muslims, and non-Christians were forbidden to settle in New Spain. At first, most emigrants were men. The government then encouraged families to migrate. Eventually, women comprised one-quarter of the total emigration from Spain.

Spain ruled its large American empire through a system of royal officials. At the top was the Council of the Indies, formed in 1524 to govern the Americas from Spain. The Council appointed two viceroys, or royal governors. The Viceroyalty of Peru governed most of South America. The Viceroyalty of New Spain governed all Spanish territories in

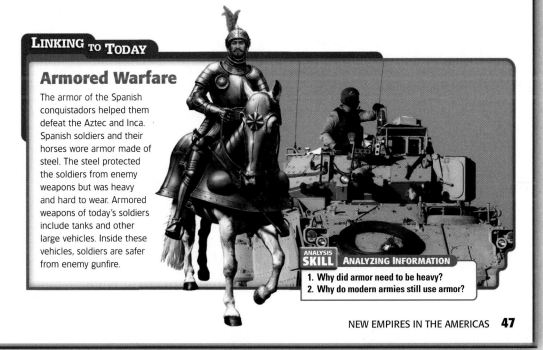

LINKING TO TODAY

Armored Warfare

The armor of the Spanish conquistadors helped them defeat the Aztec and Inca. Spanish soldiers and their horses wore armor made of steel. The steel protected the soldiers from enemy weapons but was heavy and hard to wear. Armored weapons of today's soldiers include tanks and other large vehicles. Inside these vehicles, soldiers are safer from enemy gunfire.

ANALYSIS SKILL **ANALYZING INFORMATION**

1. Why did armor need to be heavy?
2. Why do modern armies still use armor?

Direct Teach

Main Idea

❶ Spanish Conquistadors

Spanish conquistadors conquered the Aztec and Inca empires.

Identify Which Spanish conquistador conquered the Aztec Empire? Which conquistador conquered the Inca Empire? *Hernán Cortés; Francisco Pizarro*

Analyze Why was it fairly easy for Cortés to conquer the Aztec? *The Aztec thought Cortés was a god and welcomed him; Cortés took the Aztec ruler prisoner and used superior weapons to defeat the Aztec.*

Summarize How did Spain rule its empire in the Americas? *through a system of royal officials; two viceroys and royal governors held significant power*

Activity **Explorers' Routes** Give students blank outline maps of the Americas and have students draw the routes of at least three of the explorers discussed in this section.

CRF: Biography Activity: Malintzin

Did you know . . .

When Francisco Pizarro defeated the Inca, it was not his first time in the Americas. Pizarro was with Vasco Núñez de Balboa when Balboa discovered the Pacific Ocean.

Differentiating Instruction

Above Level

Advanced/Gifted and Talented

Research Required

1. Have students imagine they are observers during one of the battles between the Aztec and Hernán Cortés or between the Inca and Francisco Pizarro. Instruct students to write a journal entry describing what they saw.
2. Have students use either print sources or the Internet to conduct research on the conquest they chose. Students may wish to include pictures as part of their journal entries.
3. Remind students that because they are retelling a historical event, they should remain objective and unbiased and not show favor for either the Spanish or the Native Americans.
4. Ask students to read their journal entries aloud to the class. **LS Verbal/Linguistic**

Alternative Assessment Handbook, Rubric 15: Journals

Answers

Analyzing Information 1. *to protect the soldiers and their horses from injury from arrows and spears;* **2.** *to protect soldiers*

Direct Teach

Main Idea

2 Exploring the Borderlands of New Spain

Spanish explorers traveled through the borderlands of New Spain, claiming more land.

Recall What was Juan Ponce de León searching for in Florida? *the Fountain of Youth*

Analyze In what ways did de León succeed and fail in the Americas? *conquered Puerto Rico for Spain, found gold, and founded the city of San Juan; failed to colonize Florida*

Evaluate Why do you think Spain granted de Soto permission to explore such a large area of North America? *possible answers—the quest for gold, land for Spain, to spread Christianity*

Info to Know

Always be Prepared Hernando de Soto's exploration of the southern United States was one of the best-prepared expeditions in the Americas. De Soto gathered 1,000 men not including sailors, 350 horses, 13 hogs, and a number of fighting dogs.

Quick Facts Transparency 4: Reasons for Spanish Victory

Answers

Analyzing Information *Spanish weapons; European diseases*

Reading Check *With their superior weapons, they won battles, but diseases, such as smallpox, also killed thousands of Native Americans.*

Central America, Mexico, and the southern part of what is now the United States.

The Spanish established three kinds of settlements in New Spain. Pueblos served as trading posts and sometimes as centers of government. Priests started missions where they converted local Native Americans to Catholicism. The Spanish also built presidios, or military bases, to protect towns and missions.

To connect some of the scattered communities of New Spain, Spanish settlers built *El Camino Real*, or "the Royal Road." This network of roads ran for hundreds of miles, from Mexico City to Santa Fe. The roads later stretched to settlements in California.

READING CHECK **Analyzing** How did the Spanish conquer the great Aztec and Inca empires?

Reasons for Spanish Victory

QUICK FACTS

Several advantages helped the Spanish defeat the Aztec and Inca.

Causes of the Aztec and Inca Defeat

- Spanish steel armor and weapons
- Spanish horses
- European diseases
- Spanish alliances with Aztec and Inca enemies

Effects

- Reduced Native American population
- Spanish rule of the Americas
- Columbian Exchange

ANALYSIS SKILL **ANALYZING INFORMATION**

Which cause do you think was most important to the Spanish victory?

Exploring the Borderlands of New Spain

Spain's American empire was not limited to lands taken from the conquered Aztec and Inca empires. Many other Spanish explorers came to North America. They explored the borderlands of New Spain and claimed many new lands for the Spanish crown.

Exploring the Southeast

In 1508 explorer Juan Ponce de León landed on the Caribbean island of Puerto Rico. By 1511 he had conquered the island for Spain and founded the city of San Juan. De León also discovered gold on Puerto Rico. Spanish officials appointed him governor of the colony.

In 1512 de León discovered the coast of present-day Florida. The next year he searched Florida for a mythical Fountain of Youth. Though he never found the fabled fountain, Ponce de León acquired royal permission to colonize Florida. However, he failed in his quest to colonize the area.

Two decades later another explorer traveled through Florida. Royal officials gave Hernando de Soto permission to explore the coastal region of the Gulf of Mexico. In 1539 his expedition landed in an area near the present-day city of Tampa Bay, Florida.

De Soto then led his men north through what is now Georgia and the Carolinas. The expedition then turned west and crossed the Appalachian Mountains. De Soto discovered the Mississippi River in 1541. The explorers then traveled west into present-day Oklahoma. De Soto died in 1542 on this journey.

Exploring the Southwest

The Spanish also explored what is now the southwestern United States. In 1528 explorer Álvar Núñez Cabeza de Vaca joined conquistador Pánfilo de Narváez on an expedition to North America. Their group of 300 men first landed on the Florida coast. They faced many severe problems, including a shortage of food.

Critical Thinking: Analyzing

At Level

Settlement Life

Research Required

1. Review with students the three basic types of settlements in New Spain: pueblos, missions, and presidios. Tell students that they will be conducting research on one type of settlement.
2. Have students create a list of questions they want to answer in their research. For example, if researching pueblos, questions might include how pueblos were organized, what goods were traded, and what life was like in the pueblos.
3. Have students conduct research to answer their questions. Each student should then use the answers to create a short report or presentation about their topic. Remind students to evaluate the validity of their research sources.
4. Encourage students to include maps and illustrations in their reports. LS **Verbal/Linguistic**

Alternative Assessment Handbook, Rubrics 29: Presentations; 30: Research; and 42: Writing to Inform

The group built boats, which made it possible for them to travel around the Florida panhandle. The explorers continued along the Gulf Coast and eventually reached the Mississippi River. Severe weather hit this group hard, and many members of the expedition died. De Vaca's boat shipwrecked on what is now Galveston Island in Texas. Only de Vaca and three other men survived. One survivor was a Moroccan-born slave named Estevanico. His Spanish slaveholder also survived.

Each of the four survivors was captured and enslaved by Native American groups living in the area. After six years of captivity, the men finally escaped. They journeyed on foot throughout the North American Southwest, receiving help from Native Americans they met along the way. In 1536, after turning south, the group reached Spanish settlements in Mexico.

Soon after their journey ended, Estevanico's slaveholder sold him to a Spanish viceroy. The viceroy assigned Estevanico to serve as a guide for a new expedition he was sending into the Southwest. Native Americans killed the enslaved African in 1539.

De Vaca eventually returned to Spain, where he called for better treatment of Native Americans. De Vaca later wrote about his experiences in the first European book exclusively devoted to North America. De Vaca's book increased Spanish interest in the New World. His writings fueled the rumors that riches could be found in North America.

> "For two thousand leagues did we travel, on land, and by sea in barges, besides ten months more after our rescue from captivity; untiringly did we walk across the land, ... During all that time we crossed from one ocean to the other, ... We heard that on the shores of the South there are pearls and great wealth, and that the richest and best is near there."
>
> –Cabeza de Vaca, *The Journey of Álvar Núñez Cabeza de Vaca*

De Vaca's account inspired other explorers to travel to North America. In 1540 Francisco Vásquez de Coronado set out to explore the North American Southwest. He wanted to find the legendary Seven Cities of Gold that were rumored to exist there. His expedition went through present-day New Mexico and Arizona, where a group of his men discovered the Grand Canyon. Coronado trekked through Texas

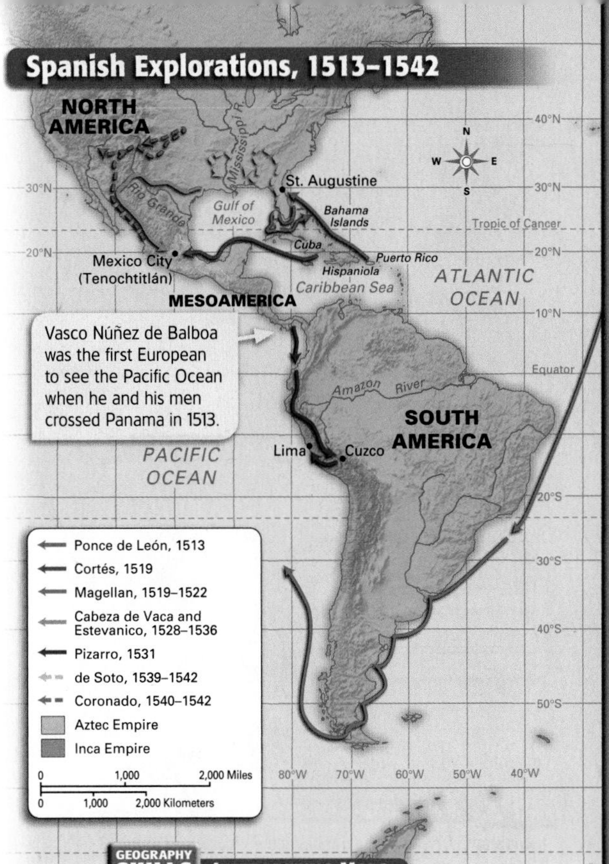

GEOGRAPHY SKILLS **INTERPRETING MAPS**

1. **Movement** Which explorer went the farthest north, according to the map?
2. **Location** What city did Cortés reach in 1519?

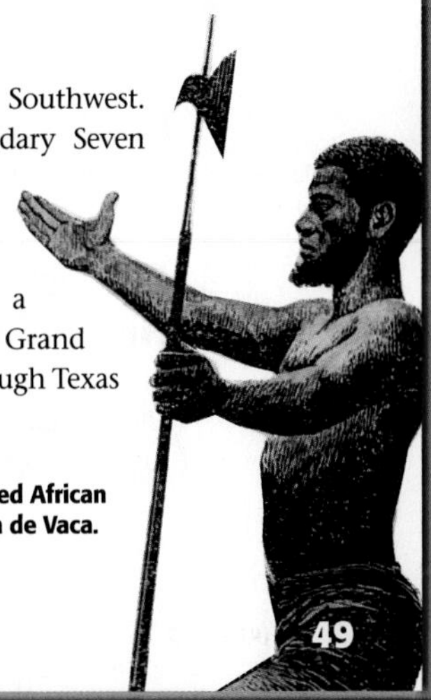

Estevanico was an enslaved African who traveled with Cabeza de Vaca.

Direct Teach

Main Idea

❷ Exploring the Borderlands of New Spain

Spanish explorers traveled through the borderlands of New Spain, claiming more land.

Recall What areas did Álvar Núñez Cabeza de Vaca and his expedition explore? *Florida coast, the Gulf Coast, area along the Mississippi River; they shipwrecked on Galveston Island, Texas*

Summarize What hardships did de Vaca and his men encounter on their expedition? *shortage of food, severe weather, shipwreck; for the survivors, captivity, enslavement, and journey on foot through the North American Southwest*

Make Judgments Why did de Vaca believe the Spanish should treat Native Americans fairly? *possible answer—because de Vaca and his men received assistance from Native Americans during their foot journey through the North American Southwest*

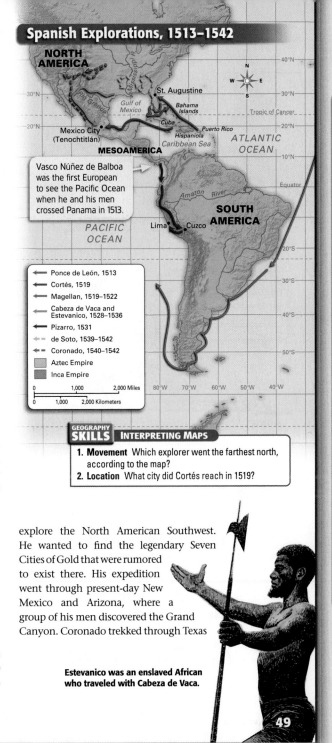

- **CRF:** Biography Activity: Estevanico
- Map Transparency 8: Spanish Explorations, 1513–1542

Answers

Interpreting Maps **1.** *Coronado;* **2.** *Tenochtitlán, now Mexico City*

Differentiating Instruction

Below Level

English-Language Learners

1. Discuss with students that sometimes events have multiple causes. Copy the graphic organizer shown for the class to see.
2. Ask volunteers to list reasons for Spanish exploration into North America. Write these reasons in the ovals. *Reasons may include claiming land for Spain, the search for gold, expanding trade, and spreading Christianity.*
3. Have students list any details related to each reason for exploration. Add these to the circles. *Details may include establishing presidios or military bases, pueblos or trading posts, and missions.*
4. Have students copy the graphic organizer onto their own papers and keep it as a study aid. **LS Interpersonal, Visual/Spatial**

- Alternative Assessment Handbook, Rubric 6: Cause and Effect; and 13: Graphic Organizers

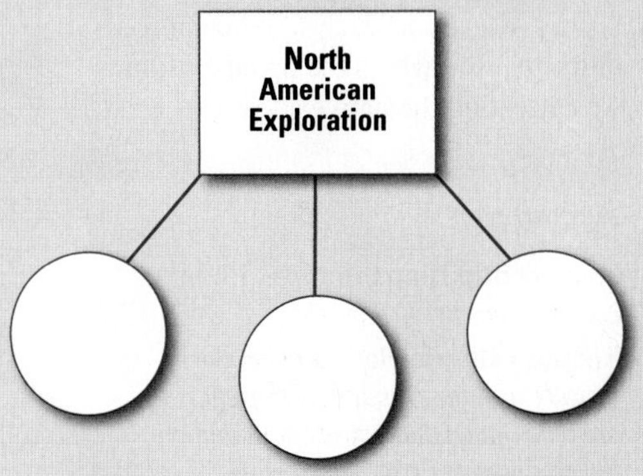

Direct Teach

Main Idea

❸ Spanish Treatment of Native Americans

Spanish settlers treated Native Americans harshly, forcing them to work on plantations and in mines.

Explain What was the relationship between Spanish settlers and Native Americans under the encomienda system? *Settlers could tax Native Americans or make them work; in return settlers were supposed to protect Native Americans and convert them to Christianity.*

Identify Cause and Effect How did the growth of the Spanish Empire affect Native Americans? *Spain mined more gold and silver and needed more food to supply its empire; plantations in the Americas required lots of labor; Native Americans were forced to work in the fields and mines; forced work and harsh treatment killed many Native Americans.*

Evaluate Why didn't the Spanish government enforce the laws that called for the proper treatment of Native Americans? *possible answers—The monarchy was too far away, local governors wanted profit, and there was a huge need for workers.*

Map Transparency 9: Spanish Viceroyalties

Info to Know

More Than Just a Religion The Catholic Church assumed many functions in the Americas. The church operated as a bank, social welfare agency, and center of education. Many times priests would study the natural science and natural history of a region. They also kept records of the ways in which the Spanish culture was affecting the native societies.

Answers

Interpreting Maps 1. *Lima*
2. *New Spain*

Reading Check *Both failed in their search for fabled locations of great promise—the Fountain of Youth and the Seven Cities of Gold.*

Spanish Viceroyalties, c.1650

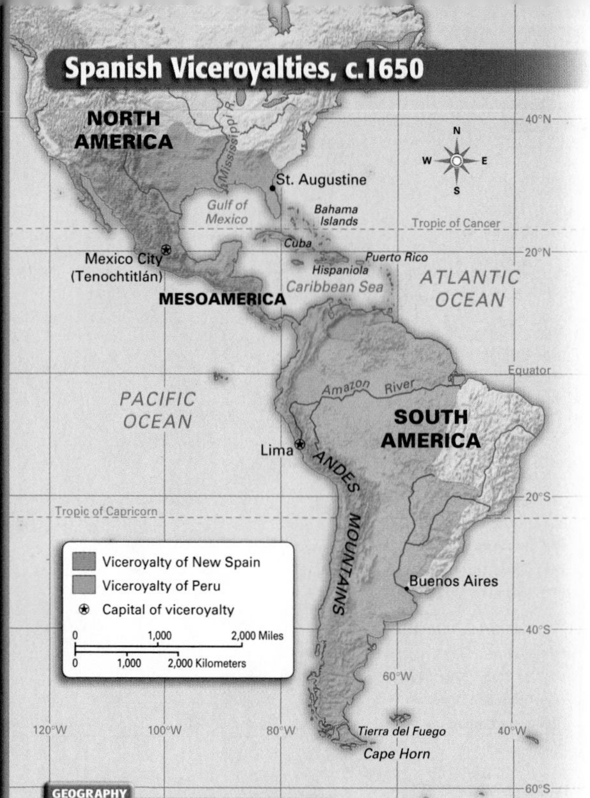

GEOGRAPHY SKILLS — INTERPRETING MAPS

1. **Location** What was the capital of the Viceroyalty of Peru?
2. **Place** Which viceroyalty included modern-day Mexico?

and Oklahoma, going as far north as Kansas before turning around. He never found the fabled cities of gold.

THE IMPACT TODAY Roman Catholicism is still the most commonly practiced religion in Latin America. More than 80 percent of the population is Catholic.

READING CHECK **Comparing** How were the expeditions of Ponce de León and Coronado similar?

Spanish Treatment of Native Americans

The journeys of the Spanish explorers allowed Spain to claim a huge empire in the Americas. Spain's American colonies helped make the country very wealthy. From 1503 to 1660, Spanish fleets loaded with treasure carried 200 tons of gold and 18,600 tons of silver from the former Aztec and Inca empires to Spain. Mexico and Peru also grew food to help support Spain's growing empire. However, these gains came with a price for Native Americans. Native peoples suffered greatly at the hands of the Spanish.

Forced Labor

By 1650 the Spanish Empire in the Americas had grown to some 3 to 4 million people. Native Americans made up about 80 percent of the population. The rest were whites, Africans, and people of mixed racial background. Settlers who came from Spain were called *peninsulares* (pay-neen-soo-LAHR-ays) and usually held the highest government positions. To reward settlers for their service to the Crown, Spain established the **encomienda** (en-koh-mee-EN-duh) **system**. It gave settlers the right to tax local Native Americans or to make them work. In exchange, these settlers were supposed to protect the Native American people and convert them to Christianity. Instead, most Spanish treated the Native Americans as slaves. Native Americans were forced to work in terrible conditions. They faced cruelty and desperate situations on a daily basis.

The Spanish operated many **plantations**, large farms that grew just one kind of crop. Plantations throughout the Caribbean colonies made huge profits for their owners. It took many workers to run a plantation, however, so colonists forced thousands of Native Americans to work in the fields. Indians who were taken to work on haciendas, the vast Spanish estates in Central and South America, had to raise and herd livestock. Other Native Americans were forced to endure the backbreaking work of mining gold and silver. The forced labor and harsh treatment killed many native people in New Spain.

Social Studies Skills Activity: Points of View

At Level

Debating the Treatment of Native Americans

1. Organize students into pairs. Tell the pairs they are to prepare arguments for each side of a debate about how Native Americans should be treated.
2. One student in the pair should take the point of view of Bartolomé de Las Casas, who believed the Spanish should treat Native Americans with gentleness and kindness. The other student should take the side of a plantation owner and explain why Spain established the encomienda system.
3. Instruct students to use logical reasons to support their points of view.
4. Ask students to debate the issue in front of the class. Then ask the class which side presented the most persuasive arguments and to explain why. **LS Interpersonal, Verbal/Linguistic**

Alternative Assessment Handbook, Rubric 43: Writing to Persuade

murder if he killed a slave while punishing him. Enslaved Africans, on the other hand, received harsh penalties for minor offenses, such as breaking a tool. Runaways were often tortured and sometimes killed.

The treatment of enslaved Africans varied. Some slaves reported that their masters treated them kindly. To protect their investment, some slaveholders provided adequate food and clothing for their slaves. However, severe treatment was very common. Whippings, brandings, and even worse torture were all part of American slavery.

READING CHECK **Generalizing** How were enslaved Africans treated in the Americas?

Slave Culture in the Americas

Slaves in the Americas came from many different parts of Africa. They spoke different languages and had different cultural backgrounds. But enslaved Africans also shared many customs and viewpoints. They built upon what they had in common to create a new African American culture.

Families were a vital part of slave culture. Families provided a refuge—a place not fully under the slaveholders' control. However, slave families faced many challenges. Families were often broken apart when a family member was sold to another owner. In Latin America, there were many more enslaved males than females. This made it difficult for slaves there to form stable families.

Religion was a second refuge for slaves. It gave enslaved Africans a form of expression that was partially free from their slaveholders' control. Slave religion was primarily Christian, but it included traditional elements from African religions as well. Religion gave slaves a sense of self worth and a hope for salvation in this life and the next. Spirituals were a common form of religious expression among slaves. Slaves also used songs and folktales to tell their stories of sorrow, hope, agony, and joy.

Many slaves expressed themselves through art and dance. Dances were important social events in slave communities. Like most elements of slave culture, art and dance were heavily influenced by African traditions.

READING CHECK **Identifying Points of View** Why was religion important to slaves in the Americas?

SUMMARY AND PREVIEW After disease wiped out much of the Native American population, colonists turned to slave labor. In the next chapter you will learn about English colonies in the Americas.

Section 5 Assessment

go.hrw.com
Online Quiz
KEYWORD: SF7 HP2

Reviewing Ideas, Terms, and People

1. a. **Recall** Why did so many Native Americans die after coming into contact with Europeans?
   b. **Summarize** Why did plantation owners turn to enslaved Africans as a labor force?
2. a. **Identify** What was the **Middle Passage**?
   b. **Describe** Explain how enslaved Africans were treated after they reached the colonies in the Americas.
3. a. **Explain** What are spirituals?
   b. **Analyze** How did religion and family provide a refuge from the harsh life enslaved Africans were forced to endure?

Critical Thinking

4. **Identifying Cause and Effect** Review your notes on the slave trade. Use a chart like the one below to explain the causes and the effects of the slave trade.

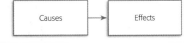

Causes → Effects

FOCUS ON WRITING

5. **Writing about Slavery** Add information about the beginnings of slavery in the Americas to your notes. Include notes about slave culture. What refuges did enslaved people have from their suffering?

Direct Teach

Main Idea

3 Slave Culture in the Americas

Slaves in the Americas created a distinct culture.

Recall What challenges faced slave families? *family members could be sold; in Latin America, more enslaved males than females*

Elaborate Why were African slaves, who came from different cultures and spoke different languages, able to form an African American culture? *They shared many customs and viewpoints; used them to create a new culture.*

CRF: Primary Source Activity: Slave Spirituals

Review & Assess

Close

Briefly review the events that led up to the expansion of slavery in the Americas.

Review

go.hrw.com Online Quiz, Section 2.5

Assess

SE Section 5 Assessment

PASS: Section 2.5 Quiz

Alternative Assessment Handbook

Reteach/Classroom Intervention

Interactive Reader and Study Guide, Section 2.5

Interactive Skills Tutor CD-ROM

Section 5 Assessment Answers

1. **a.** lacked immunity from disease
   b. for cheap labor; already immune to European diseases
2. **a.** voyage of slaves from Africa to the Americas
   b. Some slave owners treated slaves with kindness; most owners provided adequate food and clothing; others forced slaves to endure brutal conditions.
3. **a.** religious songs
   b. Family life provided some stability; religion gave a sense of self worth and hope.
4. Causes—need for labor; Effects—African Diaspora, Middle Passage deaths, treatment of enslaved Africans, African American culture
5. Students will take detailed notes about the beginnings of slavery in the Americas. Refuges included family, religion, songs, folktales, art, and dance.

Answers

Reading Check (left) *treatment varied; some treated kindly, others flogged, whipped, branded, or worse*

Reading Check (right) *form of expression that was partially free from their slaveholders' control*

History and Geography

Activity Chain-of-Events Chart
Ask students to use the map to trace the steps and routes involved in the transatlantic slave trade. Then have students work either individually or in pairs to create chain-of-events charts showing the geographic forces that led to the growth of slavery in the English colonies. A sample chart is shown below.
LS Visual/Spatial

The climate of the southern colonies was suited to certain crops, such as cotton, tobacco, and sugarcane.

↓

These crops required large amounts of labor.

↓

Other sources of labor, such as indentured servants, were not able to fill labor needs.

↓

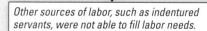

Colonists turned to enslaved Africans to fill labor needs.

Connect to Economics

Social Classes in Colonial America

Colonial America had a variety of socioeconomic classes. Large landowners, wealthy merchants, and professional workers ranked at the top of society. Free wage earners ranked below this group. They ranged from unskilled laborers to skilled workers, such as cabinetmakers or tailors. Farmers with smaller amounts of land were usually considered on the same level as these urban workers. At the bottom were people who were legally not free—white indentured servants and enslaved Africans.

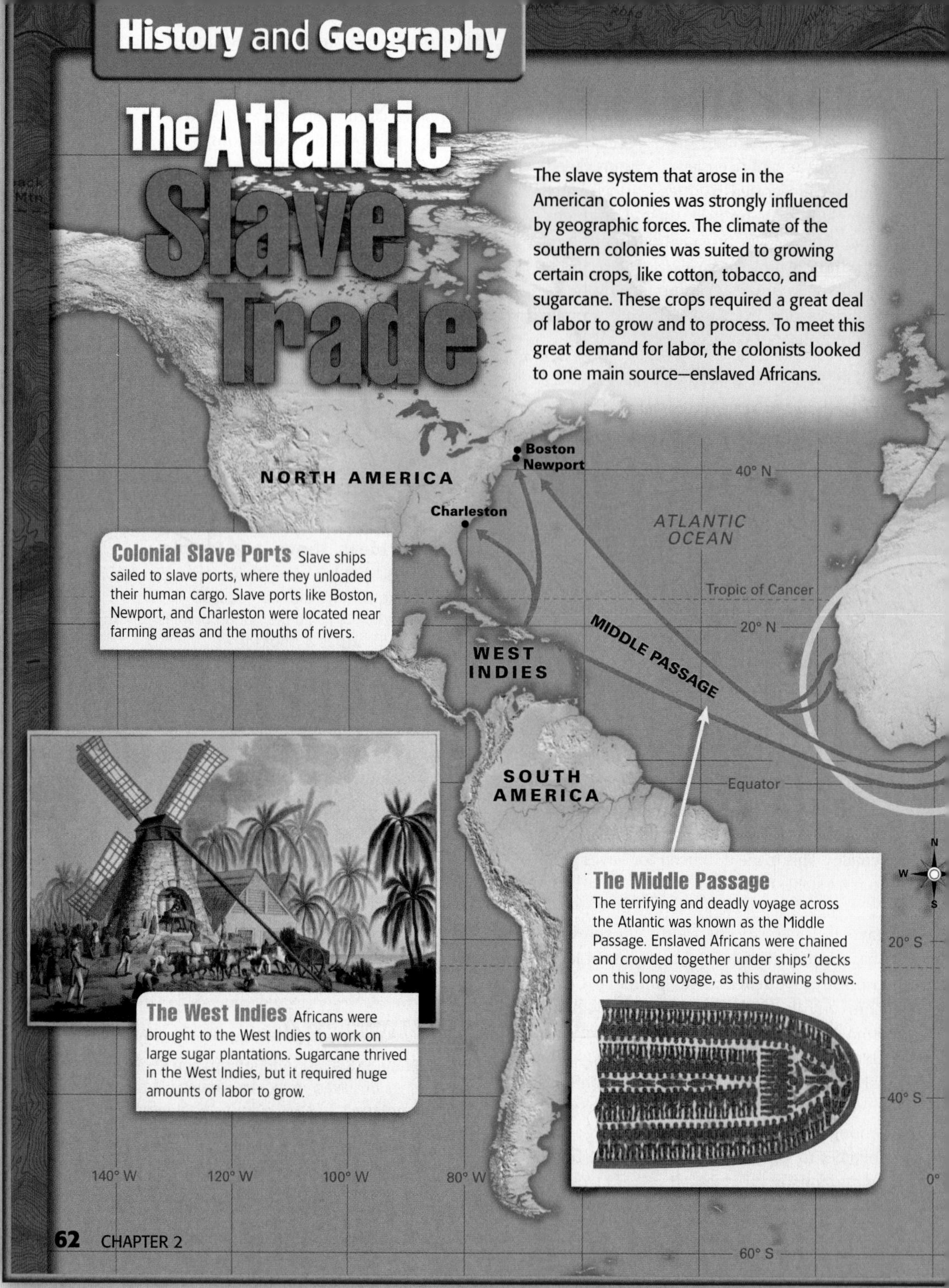

History and Geography
The Atlantic Slave Trade
The slave system that arose in the American colonies was strongly influenced by geographic forces. The climate of the southern colonies was suited to growing certain crops, like cotton, tobacco, and sugarcane. These crops required a great deal of labor to grow and to process. To meet this great demand for labor, the colonists looked to one main source—enslaved Africans.
Boston
Newport
NORTH AMERICA
Charleston
40° N
ATLANTIC OCEAN
Tropic of Cancer
20° N
MIDDLE PASSAGE
WEST INDIES
SOUTH AMERICA
Equator
Colonial Slave Ports Slave ships sailed to slave ports, where they unloaded their human cargo. Slave ports like Boston, Newport, and Charleston were located near farming areas and the mouths of rivers.
The West Indies Africans were brought to the West Indies to work on large sugar plantations. Sugarcane thrived in the West Indies, but it required huge amounts of labor to grow.
The Middle Passage The terrifying and deadly voyage across the Atlantic was known as the Middle Passage. Enslaved Africans were chained and crowded together under ships' decks on this long voyage, as this drawing shows.
N
W
S
20° S
40° S
0°
60° S
140° W
120° W
100° W
80° W
62 CHAPTER 2

Differentiating Instruction

Below Level

Struggling Readers

1. Review inset maps with students. Then have students identify the region shown in the inset map above. Explain that most enslaved Africans came from West Africa. Next, have volunteers read aloud the captions by the slave forts. Then read the primary source to students and have them discuss it.
2. Have a volunteer read aloud the caption about the Middle Passage. Ask students to suggest adjectives to describe the Middle Passage.
3. Ask students to identify the destinations of the Atlantic slave trade. Next, have volunteers read aloud the Colonial Slave Ports and The West Indies captions. Ask students to identify the geographic forces that led to the slave system in the American colonies.
4. Have students interpret the bar graph. Ask students to discuss reasons for the increase in slavery over time. **LS Visual/Spatial**

Alternative Assessment Handbook, Rubric 21: Map Reading

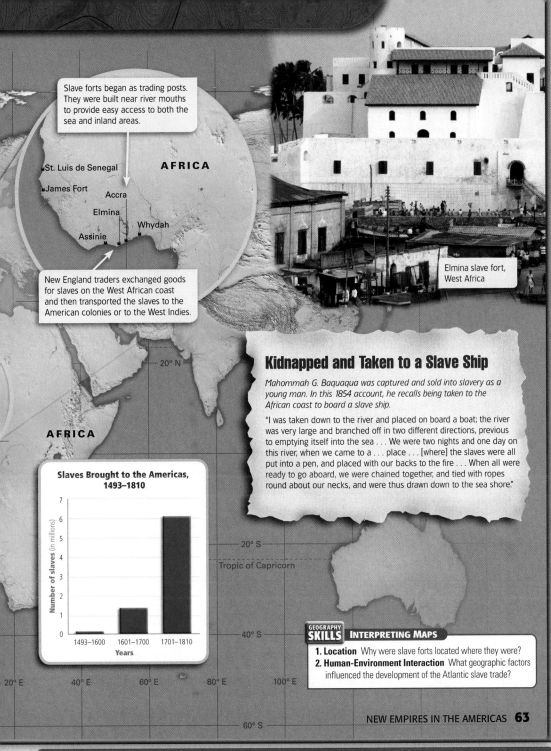

Slave forts began as trading posts. They were built near river mouths to provide easy access to both the sea and inland areas.

New England traders exchanged goods for slaves on the West African coast and then transported the slaves to the American colonies or to the West Indies.

Elmina slave fort, West Africa

Kidnapped and Taken to a Slave Ship

Mahommah G. Baquaqua was captured and sold into slavery as a young man. In this 1854 account, he recalls being taken to the African coast to board a slave ship.

"I was taken down to the river and placed on board a boat; the river was very large and branched off in two different directions, previous to emptying itself into the sea . . . We were two nights and one day on this river, when we came to a . . . place . . . [where] the slaves were all put into a pen, and placed with our backs to the fire . . . When all were ready to go aboard, we were chained together, and tied with ropes round about our necks, and were thus drawn down to the sea shore."

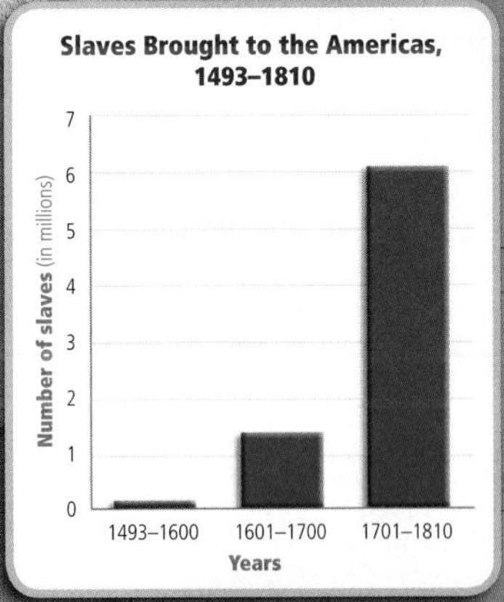

GEOGRAPHY SKILLS INTERPRETING MAPS

1. **Location** Why were slave forts located where they were?
2. **Human-Environment Interaction** What geographic factors influenced the development of the Atlantic slave trade?

History and Geography

Primary Source

Activity **Writing a Poem** Have a volunteer read aloud the primary source at left. Ask students to discuss the thoughts, feelings, and expectations of enslaved Africans sold to European slave traders and put on ships. Then have students work in pairs to write poems in which they express the thoughts and feelings of recently enslaved Africans. **LS Verbal/Linguistic**

World Events

Captives of War About half the Africans sold to traders were captives of war. African kingdoms, like those elsewhere in the world, fought each other for power and wealth. Some of these kingdoms sold war captives into slavery. These kingdoms traded slaves for European goods. As a result of the slave trade, native populations in some parts of Africa greatly decreased. These population losses had disastrous effects on Africa's development.

Info to Know

Slave Languages and Gullah Africans arriving in the Americas often spoke different languages. In time a number of pidgin, or simplified, languages developed based on English, French, Spanish, and Portuguese. One of these that has survived to this day is Gullah. This language is still spoken in parts of Georgia and the Sea Islands of South Carolina.

Differentiating Instruction

English-Language Learners

Below Level

1. Pair students and have partners take turns explaining and summarizing the information above. Students should list and define any words or phrases they do not understand.
2. Read the primary source aloud to students.
3. Then have each student create an image with a caption based on the excerpt.
LS Interpersonal, Visual/Spatial

Alternative Assessment Handbook, Rubrics 3: Artwork; and 21: Map Reading

Advanced/Gifted and Talented

Above Level **Research Required**

1. Have students conduct research on the Middle Passage. Instruct students to take notes on the conditions, perils, and death rates on slave ships.
2. Have students work in pairs to create a script for a voice-over for the opening scenes of a documentary on the Middle Passage.
LS Interpersonal, Verbal/Linguistic

Alternative Assessment Handbook, Rubrics 30: Research; and 37: Writing Assignments

Answers

Interpreting Maps 1. *Slave forts were located on the coast so that captives could be transported by ship to the Americas, and near rivers to provide easy access to inland areas.* **2.** *See the graphic organizer in the side column on the previous page.*

Social Studies Skills

Framing Historical Questions

Activity Evaluating Questions
Ask students to imagine that a friend of theirs has just witnessed a crime taking place. Ask students what sorts of questions they would ask their friend to learn more about the event. Then ask students to imagine that their friend just won an award. What sort of questions might they ask? Write students' suggested questions for the class to see and then evaluate each question. Point out questions that are too broad or that might be biased. Then assign students a topic from the chapter and have students practice the skill by writing five questions that would be effective in helping them conduct research on the topic.
LS Verbal/Linguistic

Alternative Assessment Handbook, Rubric 37: Writing Assignments

CRF: Social Studies Skills Activity: Framing Historical Questions

Social Studies Skills

Analysis | Critical Thinking | Civic Participation | Study

Framing Historical Questions

Define the Skill

One of the most valuable ways that people gain knowledge is by asking effective questions. An effective question is one that obtains the kind of information the person asking the question desires. The ability to frame, or construct, effective questions is an important life skill as well as a key to gaining a better understanding of history. Asking effective historical questions will aid you in studying history and in conducting historical research.

Learn the Skill

Effective questions are specific, straightforward, and directly related to the topic. When we do not obtain the information we want or need, often it is because we have asked the wrong questions. Asking effective questions is not as easy as it seems. It requires thought and preparation. The following guidelines will help you in framing effective questions about history and other topics as well.

1. Determine exactly what you want to know.
2. Decide what questions to ask and write them down. Having written questions is very important. They will help guide your study or research and keep you focused on your topic and goal.
3. Review each of your questions to make sure it is specific, straightforward, and directly related to your topic.
4. Rewrite any questions that are vague, too broad, or biased.

Questions that are vague or too broad are likely to produce information not directly related to what you want to know. For example, if you wanted to know more about trade and the voyages of exploration that are discussed in Chapter 2, "What were the voyages of exploration?" may not be a good question to ask. This question is too broad. Its answer would not give you the information you want.

Asking "Why was trade the most important cause of the voyages of exploration?" would not be an effective question either. This question is biased because it *assumes* trade was the main reason for the voyages, when that might not have been true. Good historical investigation assumes nothing that is not known to be fact. A more effective question, which would get the information you want, is "Were trade and the voyages of exploration connected, and, if so, in what ways?" Do you see now why wording is so important in asking effective questions and why you should write out and review your questions beforehand?

Practice the Skill

Reread the information about Cortés and the Aztec on pages 46–47, then complete the activities below.

1. Suppose you wanted to learn more about Cortés's defeat of the Aztec. Decide whether each of the following would be an effective question to ask about this topic. Explain why or why not.
  a. What happened when the Aztec and the Spanish met?
  b. Why did other Indians betray the Aztec?
  c. What resources did Cortés have that helped him conquer the Aztec?

2. Frame five questions that would be effective in helping you to learn more about this topic.

Answers

Practice the Skill 1. *(a) too broad; (b) biased because of use of word betray; (c) well-framed question;* **2.** *Students' questions will vary but might include some of the following: What events led to conflict between Cortés and the Aztec? What events led up to Cortés's defeat of the Aztec? Where and when did Cortés's defeat of the Aztec take place? How did the weapons and armor of the Aztec compare to those of Cortés and his soldiers? What other resources did Cortés have that helped him defeat the Aztec?*

Social Studies Skills Activity: Historical Questions

At Level

5W-How Questions

1. Write the *5W-How* questions for students to see: *Who? What? When? Where? Why?* and *How?*
2. Explain that these questions can help students frame historical questions to guide their learning and research.
3. Provide students with a topic from the chapter. Write the topic for the class to see. Have students practice as a class in using the *5W-How* questions to frame historical questions about the topic. Provide feedback.
4. Then assign a second topic and have students work independently to use the *5W-How* questions to frame five historical questions about the topic. Have volunteers share their questions with the class. Give other students a chance to evaluate each question. Correct students as needed. **LS Verbal/Linguistic**

Alternative Assessment Handbook, Rubric 37: Writing Assignments

CHAPTER 2

Chapter Review

HOLT
History's Impact
▶ **video series**
Review the video to answer the closing question:
How can protesting and demonstrating help people who feel that their ethnic group is not being treated fairly?

Visual Summary

QUICK FACTS

Use the visual summary below to help you review the main ideas of the chapter.

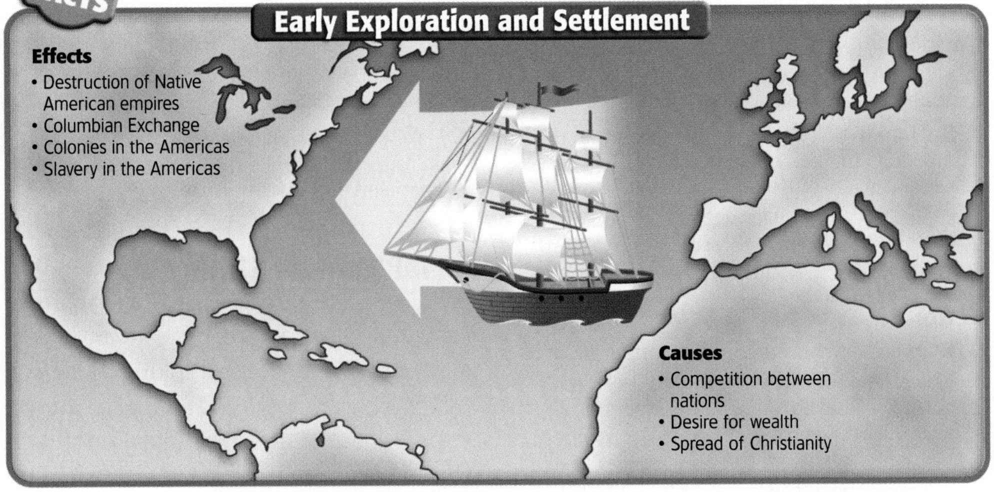

Reviewing Vocabulary, Terms, and People

1. The first Europeans to reach the east coast of North America were the ______________.
2. ______________ established a navigation school and financed expeditions to the west coast of Africa.
3. One of the most important European explorers was ______________, who was the first person to claim lands in the Americas for Spain.
4. The first voyage that sailed completely around the world was headed by ______________.
5. Sir Walter Raleigh founded the colony of Virginia after receiving a ______________, a grant to set up a colony, from the queen of England.
6. Large farms or ______________, that specialize in growing one type of crop for profit, were common in Spanish America.

Comprehension and Critical Thinking

SECTION 1 *(Pages 38–41)*

7. a. **Recall** On which two islands did the Vikings establish settlements before coming to North America?

   b. **Analyze** What factors led Europeans to begin their voyages of exploration?

   c. **Evaluate** What do you think motivated sailors to sign on for voyages of exploration?

SECTION 2 *(Pages 42–45)*

8. a. **Recall** Why was Columbus's first voyage important?

   b. **Summarize** Explain the conflict that emerged between Spain and Portugal over their empires in the Americas and how it was resolved.

   c. **Evaluate** Do you think the Columbian Exchange improved life or made life worse in the Americas? Explain your answer.

Answers

History's Impact

Video Series Protests can draw the public's attention to and help with a problem.

Visual Summary

Review and Inquiry Have students use the illustration to write a summary about European exploration.

Quick Facts Transparency 5: New Empires in the Americas Visual Summary

Reviewing Vocabulary, Terms, and People:

1. Vikings
2. Prince Henry the Navigator
3. Christopher Columbus
4. Ferdinand Magellan
5. charter
6. plantations

Comprehension and Critical Thinking

7. a. Iceland, Greenland

   b. desire to make money by finding safer and faster trade routes, interest in Asian culture, desire to spread Christianity, advances in technology

   c. desire to travel, adventure, riches

8. a. It expanded the European view of the world and began a tide of European exploration and settlement in the Americas.

   b. conflict regarding ownership over new lands in the Americas, pope established the Line of Demarcation in 1493, conflict resolved by the Treaty of Tordesillas in 1494

Review and Assessment Resources

Review and Reinforce

- **SE** Chapter Review
- **CRF:** Chapter Review Activity
- Quick Facts Transparency 5: New Empires in the Americas Visual Summary
- Spanish Chapter Summaries Audio CD Program
- Online Chapter Summaries in Spanish
- **OSP** Holt PuzzlePro, GameTool for ExamView
- Quiz Game CD-ROM

Assess

- **SE** Standardized Test Practice
- PASS: Chapter 2 Tests, Forms A and B
- Alternative Assessment Handbook
- **OSP** ExamView Test Generator, Chapter Test
- Differentiated Instruction Modified Worksheets and Tests CD-ROM: Chapter Test
- **HOAP** Holt Online Assessment Program (in the Premier Online Edition)

Reteach/Intervene

- Interactive Reader and Study Guide
- Differentiated Instruction Teacher Management System: Lesson Plans for Differentiated Instruction
- Differentiated Instruction Modified Worksheets and Tests CD-ROM
- Interactive Skills Tutor CD-ROM

go.hrw.com
Online Resources
Chapter Resources:
KEYWORD: SF7 CH2

Answers

c. Students should recognize that the Columbian Exchange brought new products to both the Americas and to Europe; brought great suffering to Native Americans and led to slavery.

9. a. southern North America, Central America, and much of South America
b. superior weapons and armor, horses, help of some Native Americans, harmful effects of European diseases on Native Americans
c. provided Spanish settlers with a tax system and free labor

10. a. It shocked Spain, weakened their power overseas, and led other countries to challenge Spain.
b. French settlements: located in many areas of North America, mainly outposts for fur trade, treated Native Americans with respect; English settlements: located along the Atlantic Coast, experienced many difficulties building colonies, had problems with Native Americans; Spanish settlements: located in the west and southwest, enslaved the Native American populations, colonies extracted valuable minerals, conversion of Native Americans important, both military outposts and village communities were established
c. Conflicts might arise among them as they vied for land, resources, and power.

11. a. cheap, available in large numbers, could be forced to work, immune to European diseases
b. religion blended Christianity and traditional religions, importance of family, music, and dance
c. loss of young male population, devastation of traditional economy, disintegration of traditional culture

SECTION 3 *(Pages 46–51)*

9. a. Identify What territories in the Americas did Spain control?
b. Analyze What factors enabled the Spanish to defeat the Aztec and the Inca?
c. Elaborate Why was the encomienda system important to Spanish settlers?

SECTION 4 *(Pages 52–57)*

10. a. Describe What were the results of the defeat of the Spanish Armada?
b. Contrast How did French settlements in the Americas differ from the English and Spanish settlements?
c. Predict What problems might arise among the different empires with settlements in North America?

SECTION 5 *(Pages 58–61)*

11. a. Explain Why did the Spanish turn to enslaved Africans as a labor force in the Americas?
b. Analyze In what ways did enslaved Africans create their own unique culture in the Americas?
c. Evaluate What effects do you think slavery had on the populations and cultures of West African countries?

Reviewing Themes

12. Geography What geographic features in North America helped and hindered the exploration and colonization of the continent?

13. Politics In what way were the expansions of empires motivated by the politics among European nations?

Using the Internet

go.hrw.com
KEYWORD: SF7 CH2

14. Activity: Illustrated Map Columbus's successful return from the New World sparked an interest in exploration that resulted in an explosion of explorers. Each explorer mapped his route and the lands that he explored. Our knowledge of the New World increased quickly as explorers made maps and kept detailed logs to catalog what they found. Enter the activity keyword. Then choose a group of explorers and research the routes these sailors took from the country of origin to the place upon which they landed. Present your research in an annotated and illustrated map or log book. Write from the point of view of an explorer and include information about the areas explored.

Reading Skills

Outlining and History *Use the Reading Social Studies Skill taught in this chapter to answer the following question.*

15. Make a short but complete outline of the section on pages 50–51 under the heading "Spanish Treatment of Native Americans."

Social Studies Skills

Framing Historical Questions *Use the Social Studies Skill taught in this chapter to answer the following question.*

16. Write a historical question for each of the five sections of this chapter.

FOCUS ON WRITING

17. Writing Your Letter First, review your notes and decide which group you want to write about. Which details from your notes will your friends and family be most interested in? Which do you find most important? What do you want to tell your family and friends about the Americas?

Reviewing Themes

12. mountains, deserts, wide rivers, forests

13. Many were attempts to gain wealth and power.

Using the Internet

14. Go to the HRW Web site and enter the keyword shown to access a rubric for this activity.

KEYWORD: SF7 CH2

Reading Skills

15. Students will outline section.

Social Studies Skills

16. Students will write five historical questions.

Focus on Writing

17. Students will write detailed letters.

CRF: Focus on Writing Activity: Writing a Letter

CHAPTER 2

Standardized Test Practice

8.1.2, 8.1.30, 8.3.7, 8.4.1

DIRECTIONS: Read each question and write the letter of the best response.

1 Which of the following best illustrates the process known as the Columbian Exchange?

A Christopher Columbus sailed west to reach Asia and encountered the Americas.

B Corn and tomatoes were introduced to Europe from America.

C Asian goods moved long distances along the Silk Road to reach Europe.

D Advances in technology allowed sailors to better navigate on the open seas.

2 The decimation of the native population of the Americas and the need for plantation labor resulted in the

A encomienda system.

B establishment of religious tolerance.

C transatlantic slave trade.

D Columbian Exchange.

3 The desire to convert people to Christianity and the demand for Asian trade goods led to

A increased interest in exploration.

B the Renaissance.

C the conquest of the Americas.

D efforts to end the slave trade.

4 Spain's empire in the Americas included which of the following?

A South America

B Virginia.

C Mexico.

D Florida.

5 Which of the following established colonies in North America?

A the Portuguese.

B the Dutch.

C the English.

D the French.

6 The voyage of enslaved Africans across the Atlantic to the Americas was known as the

A Northwest Passage.

B African Diaspora.

C triangular trade.

D Middle Passage.

7 Examine the following passage from Bernal Díaz del Castillo's account of an Aztec marketplace. Then answer the question below.

> "The bustle and noise caused by this large crowd of people was so great that it could be heard more than four miles away. Some of our men, who had traveled through Italy, said that they never had seen a marketplace that covered so large an area, which was so well regulated, and so crowded with people as this one at Mexico."
>
> —Bernal Díaz del Castillo, adapted from *The Memoirs of the Conquistador Bernal Díaz del Castillo*

Document-Based Question **What is the author's impression of the Aztec marketplace? How can you tell?**

Answers

1. B

Break Down the Question Tell students to consider what they know about the Columbian Exchange to determine the correct answer.

2. C

Break Down the Question This question requires students to identify cause and effect. Refer students who miss the question to the text titled "The Need for a New Labor Force" in Section 5.

3. A

Break Down the Question This question requires students to recall factual information. Refer students who miss the question to coverage of exploration in Section 1.

4. C

Break Down the Question This question requires students to recall factual information. Refer students who miss the question to coverage of Spain's empire in Section 3.

5. B

Break Down the Question After eliminating the two distractor answers, only the Portuguese and the Dutch remain possibilities. The Portuguese did not establish any colonies in North America.

6. D

Break Down the Question This question requires students to recall that information from Section 5.

7. The author is impressed with the marketplace. The author refers to the crowd of people and says that the market is well regulated.

Break Down the Question Students must make inferences from the author's statements.

Intervention Resources

Reproducible

- Interactive Reader and Study Guide
- Differentiated Instruction Teacher Management System: Lesson Plans for Differentiated Instruction

Technology

- Quick Facts Transparency 5: New Empires in the Americas Visual Summary
- Differentiated Instruction Modified Worksheets and Tests CD-ROM
- Interactive Skills Tutor CD-ROM

Tips for Test Taking

Get a Clue! Tell students that when a test item asks for vocabulary knowledge, they should look at the surrounding sentences for clues. Sometimes the context can reveal which definition fits. To identify the best definition of the underlined word as it is used in the **context,** they should consider the surrounding words and phrases.

Chapter 3 Planning Guide

The English Colonies

Chapter Overview	Reproducible Resources	Technology Resources
CHAPTER 3 **pp. 68–107** **Overview: In this chapter, students will learn about the English colonies in North America and the tensions that developed there over British tax policies.**	**Differentiated Instruction Teacher Management System:** Instructional Pacing Guide* **Interactive Reader and Study Guide:** Chapter Summary Graphic Organizer* **Chapter Resource File:*** • Focus on Writing Activity: Writing an Infomercial • Social Studies Skills Activity: Interpreting Time Lines **U.S. History Document-Based Activities:** Activity 4: Patterns of Slavery in the English Colonies	**Power Presentations with Video CD-ROM** **Differentiated Instruction Modified Worksheets and Tests CD-ROM** **Student Edition on Audio CD Program** **History's Impact: United States History Video Program (VHS/DVD):** The Impact of Freedom of Religion*
Section 1: **The Southern Colonies** **The Big Idea:** Despite a difficult beginning, the southern colonies soon flourished.	**Differentiated Instruction Teacher Management System:** Section 1 Lesson Plan* **Interactive Reader and Study Guide:** Section 3.1 Summary* **Chapter Resource File:*** • Vocabulary Builder Activity, Section 1 • Biography Activity: Pocahontas	**Daily Bellringer Transparency 3.1*** **Map Transparency 13:** Jamestown Colony* **Map Transparency 14:** The Southern Colonies* **Internet Activity:** Population Shifts
Section 2: **The New England Colonies** **The Big Idea:** English colonists traveled to New England to gain religious freedom.	**Differentiated Instruction Teacher Management System:** Section 2 Lesson Plan* **Interactive Reader and Study Guide:** Section 3.2 Summary* **Chapter Resource File:*** • Vocabulary Builder Activity, Section 2 • Literature Activity: American Colonial Poetry	**Daily Bellringer Transparency 3.2*** **Quick Facts Transparency 6:** Church and State* **Map Transparency 15:** Plymouth Colony*
Section 3: **The Middle Colonies** **The Big Idea:** People from many nations settled in the middle colonies.	**Differentiated Instruction Teacher Management System:** Section 3 Lesson Plan* **Interactive Reader and Study Guide:** Section 3.3 Summary* **Chapter Resource File:*** • Vocabulary Builder Activity, Section 3	**Daily Bellringer Transparency 3.3*** **Quick Facts Transparency 7:** Characteristics of the Middle Colonies*
Section 4: **Life in the English Colonies** **The Big Idea:** The English colonies continued to grow despite many challenges.	**Differentiated Instruction Teacher Management System:** Section 4 Lesson Plan* **Interactive Reader and Study Guide:** Section 3.4 Summary* **Chapter Resource File:*** • Vocabulary Builder Activity, Section 4 • Primary Source: "Sinners in the Hands of an Angry God"	**Daily Bellringer Transparency 3.4*** **Map Transparencies 16, 17, 18:** The Thirteen Colonies; Triangular Trade; North American Empires before and after the Treaty of Paris* **Internet Activity:** The Pen and Sword
Section 5: **Conflict in the Colonies** **The Big Idea:** Tensions developed as the British government placed tax after tax on the colonies.	**Differentiated Instruction Teacher Management System:** Section 5 Lesson Plan* **Interactive Reader and Study Guide:** Section 3.5 Summary* **Chapter Resource File:*** • Vocabulary Builder Activity, Section 5	**Daily Bellringer Transparency 3.5*** **Quick Facts Transparencies 8, 9:** The Road to Revolution (parts 1 and 2)*

SE Student Edition | Print Resource | Audio CD
TE Teacher's Edition | Transparency | CD-ROM
go.hrw.com | **LS** Learning Styles | Video
TOS Indiana Teacher One Stop | * also on Indiana Teacher One Stop

Review, Assessment, Intervention

- **Quick Facts Transparency 10:** The English Colonies Visual Summary*
- **Progress Assessment Support System (PASS):** Chapter Tests A and B*
- **Differentiated Instruction Modified Worksheets and Tests CD-ROM:** Modified Chapter Test
- TOS **Indiana Teacher One Stop:** ExamView Test Generator
- **Chapter Resource File:** Chapter Review

- **PASS:** Section Quiz 3.1*
- **Online Quiz:** Section 3.1
- **Alternative Assessment Handbook**

- **PASS:** Section Quiz 3.2*
- **Online Quiz:** Section 3.2
- **Alternative Assessment Handbook**

- **PASS:** Section Quiz 3.3*
- **Online Quiz:** Section 3.3
- **Alternative Assessment Handbook**

- **PASS:** Section Quiz 3.4*
- **Online Quiz:** Section 3.4
- **Alternative Assessment Handbook**

- **PASS:** Section Quiz 3.5*
- **Online Quiz:** Section 3.5
- **Alternative Assessment Handbook**

HOLT

History's Impact

United States History Video Program (VHS/DVD)

The Impact of Freedom of Religion

Suggested use: as a chapter introduction

Power Presentations with Video CD-ROM

Power Presentations with Video are visual presentations of each chapter's main ideas. Presentations can be customized by including Quick Facts charts, images from the text, and video clips.

DIVISION FOR PUBLIC EDUCATION
AMERICAN BAR ASSOCIATION

Developed by the Division for Public Education of the American Bar Association, these materials are part of the **Democracy and Civic Education Resources.**

- **Constitution Study Guide**
- **Supreme Court Case Studies**

Holt Online Learning

go.hrw.com
Teacher Resources
KEYWORD: SF7 TEACHER

go.hrw.com
Student Resources
KEYWORD: SF7 CH3

- Document-Based Questions
- Interactive Multimedia Activities
- Current Events
- Chapter-based Internet Activities
- and more!

Holt Interactive

Online Student Edition

Complete online support for interactivity, assessment, and reporting

- Interactive Maps and Notebook
- Standardized Test Prep
- Homework Practice and Research Activities Online

Differentiating Instruction

How do I address the needs of varied learners?

The Target Resource acts as your primary strategy for differentiated instruction.

ENGLISH-LANGUAGE LEARNERS & STRUGGLING READERS

TARGET RESOURCE

English-Language Learner Strategies and Activities

- Build Academic Vocabulary
- Develop Oral and Written Language Structures

Spanish Resources

Spanish Chapter Summaries Audio CD

Spanish Chapter Summaries Online

Teacher's One-Stop Planner:

- ExamView Test Generator, Spanish
- PuzzlePro, Spanish

Additional Resources

Differentiated Instruction Teacher Management System: Lesson Plans for Differentiated Instruction

Chapter Resources:

- Vocabulary Builder Activities
- Social Studies Skills Activity: Interpreting Time Lines

Quick Facts Transparencies:

- Church and State (TR 6)
- Characteristics of the Middle Colonies (TR 7)
- The Road to Revolution (TR 8, TR 9)
- The English Colonies Visual Summary (TR 10)

Student Edition on Audio CD Program

Interactive Skills Tutor CD-ROM

SPECIAL NEEDS LEARNERS

TARGET RESOURCE

Differentiated Instruction Modified Worksheets and Tests CD-ROM

- Vocabulary Flash Cards
- Modified Vocabulary Builder Activities
- Modified Chapter Review Activity
- Modified Chapter Test

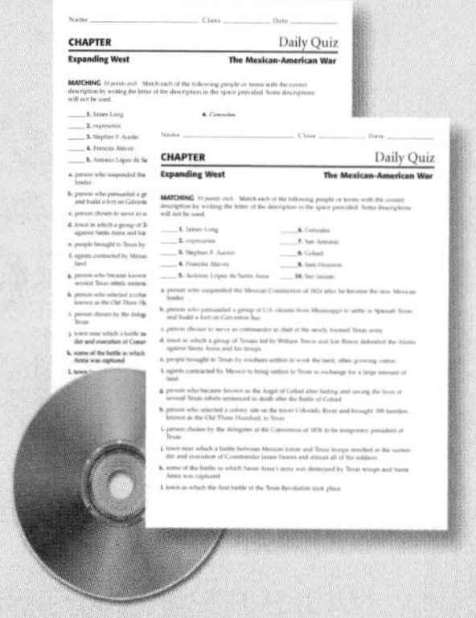

Additional Resources

Differentiated Instruction Teacher Management System: Lesson Plans for Differentiated Instruction

Interactive Reader and Study Guide

Social Studies Skills Activity: Interpreting Time Lines

Student Edition on Audio CD Program

Interactive Skills Tutor CD-ROM

ADVANCED/GIFTED-AND-TALENTED STUDENTS

TARGET RESOURCE

Primary Source Library CD-ROM for United States History

The Library contains longer versions of quotations in the text, extra sources, and images. Included are point-of-view articles, journals, diaries, historical fiction, and political documents.

Additional Resources

Pre-AP Activities Guide for United States History: The English Colonies

Political Cartoons Activities for United States History: Cartoon 1: The Mayflower; Cartoon 2: No Taxation without Representation

United States History Document-Based Activities: Activity 4: Patterns of Slavery in the English Colonies

Chapter Resource File:

- Focus on Writing Activity: Writing an Infomercial
- Literature Activity: American Colonial Poetry

Internet Activities: Chapter Enrichment Links

Differentiated Activities in the Teacher's Edition

- Terms and Definitions, p. 73
- Labor in Virginia Venn Diagram, p. 74
- Map of the Colonies, p. 76
- Guide to Massachusetts Bay, p. 81
- Key Terms of Connecticut and Rhode Island Chart, p. 82
- Colonial Governments Chart, p. 91
- Colonial Trade Posters, p. 93
- Frontier Conflicts Time Line, p. 96

Differentiated Activities in the Teacher's Edition

- Taxation Talk, p. 99

Differentiated Activities in the Teacher's Edition

- Decision-making in the Southern Colonies, p. 75
- Mayflower Compact Simulation, p. 79
- European Influence in the Middle Colonies, p. 86
- Alternative Labor Proposals, p. 93

Teacher One Stop™

How can I manage the lesson plans and support materials for differentiated instruction?

With the Indiana Teacher One Stop, you can easily organize and print lesson plans, planning guides, and instructional materials for all learners.
The Indiana Teacher One Stop includes the following materials to help you differentiate instruction:

- Interactive Teacher's Edition
- Calendar Planner and pacing guides
- Editable lesson plans
- All reproducible ancillaries in Adobe Acrobat (PDF) format
- ExamView Test Generator (Eng & Span)
- Transparency and video previews

Professional Development

HOLT Professional Development

What teacher training resources are available to help me grow professionally?

- **In-service and staff development** as part of your Holt Social Studies product purchase
- **Quick Teacher Tutorial Lesson Presentation CD-ROM**
- Intensive tuition-based **Teacher Development Institute**
- **Convenient Holt Speaker Bureau** – face-to-face workshop options
- **PRAXIS™ Test Prep** interactive Web-based content refreshers*
- **Ask A Professional Development Expert** at http://www.hrw.com/prodev/

* PRAXIS is a trademark of Educational Testing Service (ETS). This publication is not endorsed or approved by ETS.

• Chapter Preview •

Chapter Big Ideas

Section 1 Despite a difficult beginning, the southern colonies soon flourished.

Section 2 English colonists traveled to New England to gain religious freedom.

Section 3 People from many nations settled in the middle colonies.

Section 4 The English colonies continued to grow despite many challenges.

Section 5 Tensions developed as the British government placed tax after tax on the colonies.

Focus on Writing

The **Chapter Resource File** provides a Focus on Writing worksheet to help students write their infomercials.

CRF: Focus on Writing Activity: Writing an Infomercial

Key to Differentiating Instruction

Below Level

Basic-level activities designed for all students encountering new material

At Level

Intermediate-level activities designed for average students

Above Level

Challenging activities designed for honors and gifted and talented students

Standard English Mastery

Activities designed to improve standard English usage

CHAPTER 3 1605–1774

The English Colonies

Indiana Standards

Social Studies Standards

8.1.3 Identify and explain the conditions, causes, consequences, and significance of the French and Indian War (1754–1763), and the resistance and rebellion against British imperial rule by the thirteen colonies in North America (1761–1775).

8.1.4 Identify fundamental ideas in the Declaration of Independence (1776) and analyze the causes and effects of the Revolutionary War (1775–1783), including enactment of the Articles of Confederation and the Treaty of Paris.

8.3.5 Describe the importance ofthe major mountain ranges and the major river systems in the development of the United States.

8.4.9 Explain and evaluate examples of domstic and international interdependence throughout United States history.

go.hrw.com
Indiana
KEYWORD: SF10 IN

FOCUS ON WRITING

Writing an Infomercial What if television had been invented during the time that the English colonies were being founded in North America? Instead of relying on printed flyers and word of mouth to attract settlers, the founders of colonies might have made infomercials. In this chapter you will read about life in the American colonies during different times. You will choose one time period and colony and write an infomercial encouraging English citizens to settle in the colony of your choice.

UNITED STATES

1620 The Pilgrims sign the Mayflower Compact.

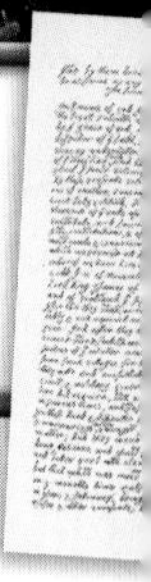

1620

WORLD

1648 Work is finished on India's Taj Mahal.

Mayflower Compact courtesy of the Pilgrim Society, Plymouth, Massachusetts.

68 CHAPTER 3

Introduce the Chapter

At Level

Focus on Reasons for Colonization

1. Write the following scenario for students to see. *The U.S. government has decided to found a colony on another planet. What do you think the government hopes to gain from the colony? What conditions might make you move to this distant colony? What challenges might you and other settlers face at this colony?*
2. Give students time to consider and discuss the scenario and questions. List students' answers for the class to see. Encourage students to explain their reasoning and opinions.
3. Review with students what they learned in the last chapter about European colonies in North America. *(Remind students that England, France, the Netherlands, Spain, and Sweden had all founded American colonies.)* What did these countries hope to gain from their colonies, and what challenges did colonists face?
4. Tell students that in this chapter they will learn about the thirteen colonies that England founded in North America, which would later become the United States. **LS Verbal/Linguistic**

HOLT

History's Impact

▶ **video series**
Watch the video to understand the impact of freedom of religion.

What You Will Learn...

Plymouth Colony thrives again in this highly accurate re-creation. The original colonists came to North America in 1620 in search of religious freedom. By 1627, the year this scene re-creates, the colonists were well established. Their success encouraged others. In this chapter you will learn about English settlements that dotted the east coast of North America.

1670

1681 William Penn establishes the colony of Pennsylvania.

1682 Peter the Great becomes czar of Russia.

1720

1732 Post Vincennes is established by the British.

1763 Pontiac, an American Indian, leads a rebellion on the western frontier.

1768 British explorer James Cook sets sail on his first trip to the South Pacific, meeting people like this Sandwich Islander.

1770

1773 Patriots stage the Boston Tea Party.

• Chapter Preview •

HOLT

History's Impact

▶ **video series**
See the Video Teacher's Guide for strategies for using the chapter video about the impact of freedom of religion.

Explore the Picture

Plymouth Colony The Pilgrims and others on board the *Mayflower* named their colony Plymouth after the last English port the ship stopped at on its journey. Plymouth Colony was built on the site of a former Native American town. Many of the town's inhabitants, the Wampanoag, had died from disease, most likely brought by European fishers and traders. The survivors had moved to other villages.

Analyzing Visuals What can you tell from this picture about the types of homes in the Plymouth Colony? *possible answers—built of wood with thatched roofs; had fireplaces (from chimneys); were small and set close together*

go.hrw.com

Online Resources

Chapter Resources:
KEYWORD: SF7 CH3
Teacher Resources:
KEYWORD: SF7 TEACHER

Explore the Time Line

1. How long after the Pilgrims signed the Mayflower Compact was the Boston Tea Party? *153 years*
2. What colony did William Penn found, and when? *Pennsylvania, in 1681*
3. Based on the time line, what themes are addressed in this chapter? *political and economic themes of colonization and conflict*

Info to Know

English Workers In the early 1600s, English laborers were paid very little. Several able London workers reported that even though they and their families wore themselves out working long, hard hours, they still only earned just enough to keep themselves alive.

Draw Conclusions Why might some English workers at the time have moved to a colony in North America? *in the hope of finding a better life for themselves*

Reading Social Studies

Understanding Themes

The themes of economics and politics are presented in this chapter. Ask students to imagine that their families have decided to move to a foreign country to seek new opportunities. Guide students in a discussion of reasons why their families might have chosen to leave their home countries. Have students identify the difficulties they think their families might face in their new country and how they might try to overcome them. Emphasize issues related to economics and politics, such as trade and government. Write students' responses for everyone to see. Tell students that as they study this chapter, they will learn about the problems early settlers in America faced and how they worked to overcome them.

Vocabulary Clues

Focus on Reading Organize the class into pairs. Then have each pair go through one of their textbooks. Ask students to look for sentences where a word is explained using context clues. Ask students to find five sentences that use vocabulary clues to define a term. Then have students make a list of the different ways in which the meaning of a word is given in the context of the text. Answers might include clue words or punctuation.

Reading Social Studies

by Kylene Beers

Economics | Geography | Politics | Society and Culture | Science and Technology

Focus on Themes In this chapter you will read about the people who settled the early colonies of North America. You will learn about the problems they faced as they felt the tug between their homeland and their new land. You will see how they settled political differences (sometimes peacefully, other times not) and learned how to trade goods and grow crops to establish a thriving economy. You will discover that the **economy** often influenced their **politics**.

Vocabulary Clues

Focus on Reading When you are reading your history textbook, you may often come across a word you do not know. If that word isn't listed as a key term, how do you find out what it means?

Using Context Clues Context means surroundings. Authors often include clues to the meaning of a difficult word in its context. You just have to know how and where to look.

Clue	How It Works	Example	Explanation
Direct Definition	Includes a definition in the same or a nearby sentence	In the late 1600s England, like most western European nations, mercantilism, *a system of creating and maintaining wealth through carefully controlled trade.*	The phrase "a system of creating and maintaining wealth through carefully controlled trade" defines *mercantilism.*
Restatement	Uses different words to say the same thing	The British continued to keep a standing, *or permanent,* army in North America to protect the colonists against Indian attacks.	The word *permanent* is another way to say *standing.*
Comparisons or Contrasts	Compares or contrasts the unfamiliar word with a familiar one	*Unlike legal traders,* smugglers did not have permission to bring goods into the country.	The word *unlike* indicates that smugglers are different from legal traders.

Reading and Skills Resources

Reading Support

- Interactive Reader and Study Guide
- Student Edition on Audio CD Program
- Spanish Chapter Summaries Audio CD Program

Social Studies Skills Support

- Interactive Skills Tutor CD-ROM

Vocabulary Support

- **CRF:** Vocabulary Builder Activities
- **CRF:** Chapter Review Activity
- Differentiated Instruction Modified Worksheets and Tests CD-ROM:
  - Vocabulary Flash Cards
  - Vocabulary Builder Activity
  - Chapter Review Activity

OSP Holt PuzzlePro

You Try It!

The following sentences are from this chapter. Each uses a definition or restatement clue to explain unfamiliar words. See if you can use the context to figure out the meaning of the words in italics.

Context Clues Up Close

From Chapter 3

1. In 1605 a company of English merchants asked King James I for the right to *found*, or establish, a settlement. *(p. 72)*
2. The majority of workers were *indentured servants*. These servants signed a contract to work four to seven years for those who paid for their journey to America. *(p. 74)*
3. In New England, the center of politics was the *town meeting*. In town meetings people talked about and decided on issues of local interest, such as paying for schools. *(p. 91)*

Answer the questions about the sentences you read.

1. In example 1, what does the word *found* mean? What hints did you find in the sentence to figure that out?
2. In example 2, where do you find the meaning of *indentured servants*? What does this phrase mean?
3. In example 3, you learn the definition of *town meeting* in the second sentence. Can you combine these two sentences into one sentence? Try putting a dash after the word *meeting* and replacing "In town meetings" with "a place where . . ."

As you read Chapter 3, look for context clues that can help you figure out the meanings of unfamiliar words or terms.

Key Terms and People

Chapter 3

Section 1
Jamestown *(p. 72)*
John Smith *(p. 73)*
Pocahontas *(p. 73)*
indentured servants *(p. 74)*
Bacon's Rebellion *(p. 74)*
Toleration Act of 1649 *(p. 75)*
Olaudah Equiano *(p. 77)*
slave codes *(p. 77)*

Section 2
Puritans *(p. 78)*
Pilgrims *(p. 78)*
immigrants *(p. 78)*
Mayflower Compact *(p. 79)*
Squanto *(p. 79)*
John Winthrop *(p. 80)*
Anne Hutchinson *(p. 82)*

Section 3
Peter Stuyvesant *(p. 85)*
Quakers *(p. 86)*
William Penn *(p. 86)*
staple crops *(p. 87)*

Section 4
town meeting *(p. 91)*
English Bill of Rights *(p. 91)*
triangular trade *(p. 93)*
Great Awakening *(p. 94)*
Jonathan Edwards *(p. 94)*
Enlightenment *(p. 95)*
Pontiac *(p. 97)*

Section 5
Samuel Adams *(p. 99)*
Committees of Correspondence *(p. 99)*
Stamp Act of 1765 *(p. 100)*
Boston Massacre *(p. 101)*
Tea Act *(p. 102)*
Boston Tea Party *(p. 102)*
Intolerable Acts *(p. 102)*

Academic Vocabulary

In this chapter, you will learn the following academic words:

authority *(p. 73)*
factors *(p. 74)*

Reading Social Studies

Key Terms and People

Challenge students to create a matching game using the key terms and people from this chapter. Organize the class into pairs, then assign each pair a term or person from the list. Have each group write a description or definition for their term on one index card and the word or name on a separate card. Collect all the index cards with descriptions or definitions on them and place them in a basket. Have each student draw a card from the basket. Then have students try to find the person whose word or name matches the description on their card. Challenge the students even more by not allowing any talking while they match terms and descriptions!

LS Interpersonal, Verbal/Linguistic

Focus on Reading

See the **Focus on Reading** questions in this chapter for more practice on this reading social studies skill.

Reading Social Studies Assessment

See the **Chapter Review** at the end of this chapter for student assessment questions related to this reading skill.

Teaching Tip

Point out to students that there are usually hints that indicate when a word is defined in the context of the sentence. One of these hints is the use of punctuation. Commas and dashes often are used to set off phrases from the rest of the sentence. These phrases often define or restate the unfamiliar word. Another hint is the use of signal words and phrases. Phrases are often used to indicate a definition or restatement. Remind students to look for words and phrases such as *which means, which is, in other words, or, called,* and *that is.*

Answers

You Try It! 1. *establish; a restatement of the word was used;* **2.** *in the second sentence; servants who signed a contract to work a number of years for those who paid for their journey to America;* **3.** *In New England, the center of politics was the town meeting—a place where people talked about and decided issues of local interest, such as paying for schools.*

Preteach

Bellringer

If YOU were there . . . Use the **Daily Bellringer Transparency** to help students answer the question.

Daily Bellringer Transparency 3.1

The English Colonies — Daily Bellringer **3.1**

Review the Previous Chapter

List the letters of the events below in the correct order in which the events occurred.

- **a.** Spain establishes an empire in the Americas.
- **b.** Christopher Columbus and his three ships reach the Americas.
- **c.** Paleo-Indians migrate across the Bering Land Bridge to the Americas.
- **d.** The decline of Spain's power enables other countries to establish colonies in North America.
- **e.** European merchants begin searching for sea routes to Africa and Asia.

Preview Section 1

If YOU were there ...

A year ago, in 1609, you moved to the colony of Virginia. But life here has been hard. During the winter many people died of cold or sickness. Food is always scarce. Now it is spring, and a ship has come from England bringing supplies. In a week it will sail home. Some of your neighbors are giving up and returning to England. They ask you to come, too.

Would you take the ship back to England?

Consider reasons to STAY:
- the arrival of spring
- the new supplies
- the time you've invested so far

Consider reasons to GO:
- tired of the hardships
- tired of being hungry
- miss your family and friends

Review Answers: c, e, b, a, d

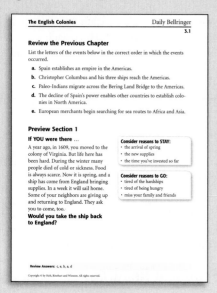

Academic Vocabulary

Review with students the high-use academic terms in this section.

authority power, right to rule (p. 73)

factors causes (p. 74)

CRF: Vocabulary Builder Activity, Section 1

Taking Notes

Have students copy the graphic organizer onto their own paper and then use it to take notes on the section. This activity will prepare students for the Section Assessment, in which they will complete a graphic organizer that builds on the information using a critical-thinking skill.

Section Correlations

IN

8.3.6 Identify the agricultural regions of the United States and be able to give reasons for the type of land use and subsequent land development during different historical periods. **8.4.1** Identify economic factors contributing to European exploration and colonization in North America, the American Revolution and the drafting of the Constitution of the United States.

SECTION 1

The Southern Colonies

What You Will Learn...

Main Ideas

1. Jamestown was the first permanent English settlement in America.
2. Daily life in Virginia was challenging to the colonists.
3. Religious freedom and economic opportunities were motives for founding other southern colonies, including Maryland, the Carolinas, and Georgia.
4. Farming and slavery were important to the economies of the southern colonies.

The Big Idea

Despite a difficult beginning, the southern colonies soon flourished.

Key Terms and People

Jamestown, *p. 72*
John Smith, *p. 73*
Pocahontas, *p. 73*
indentured servants, *p. 74*
Bacon's Rebellion, *p. 74*
Toleration Act of 1649, *p. 75*
Olaudah Equiano, *p. 77*
slave codes, *p. 77*

TAKING NOTES As you read, take notes in a chart like the one below on the founding of the southern colonies.

Colony	Year	Why Founded

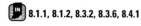

IN 8.1.1, 8.1.2, 8.3.2, 8.3.6, 8.4.1

If YOU were there...

A year ago, in 1609, you moved to the colony of Virginia. Life here has been hard. During the winter many people died of cold or sickness. Food is always scarce. Now it is spring, and a ship has come from England bringing supplies. In a week it will sail home. Some of your neighbors are giving up and returning to England. They ask you to come, too.

Would you take the ship back to England?

BUILDING BACKGROUND Several European nations took part in the race to claim lands in the Americas. Their next step was to establish colonies in the lands that they claimed. The first English colonies were started in the late 1500s but failed. Even in successful colonies, colonists faced hardships and challenges.

Settlement in Jamestown

In 1605 a company of English merchants asked King James I for the right to found, or establish, a settlement. In 1606 the king granted the request of the company to settle in a region called Virginia.

Founding a New Colony

The investors in the new settlement formed a joint-stock company called the London Company. This allowed the group to share the cost and risk of establishing the colony. On April 26, 1607, the first 105 colonists sent by the London Company arrived in America. On May 14, about 40 miles up the James River in Virginia, the colonists founded **Jamestown**, the first permanent English settlement in North America.

A lack of preparation cost a lot of the colonists their lives. Most of the men who came to Jamestown were adventurers with no farming experience or useful skills such as carpentry. Jamestown was surrounded by marshes full of disease-carrying mosquitoes. By the time winter arrived, two-thirds of the original colonists had died.

Teach the Big Idea

At Level

The Southern Colonies

Materials: five blank index cards per student

1. **Teach** To teach the main ideas in the section, use the questions in the Direct Teach boxes.
2. **Apply** Have students create colonial picture postcards. Give each student five blank index cards, one for each of the southern colonies. On the front of the postcards, have students create "I am Here" maps showing the location of the colony, the date it was founded, and its main settlements. On the backs, have students list facts about the colonies. **LS Visual/Spatial**
3. **Review** Have students share some of the facts they listed. Write the list for students to see.
4. **Practice/Homework** Have each student select one southern colony and imagine that he or she has moved there. Each student should write a letter home to England describing the colony, life there, and the challenges that he or she is facing. **LS Verbal/Linguistic**

Alternative Assessment Handbook, Rubric 41: Writing to Express

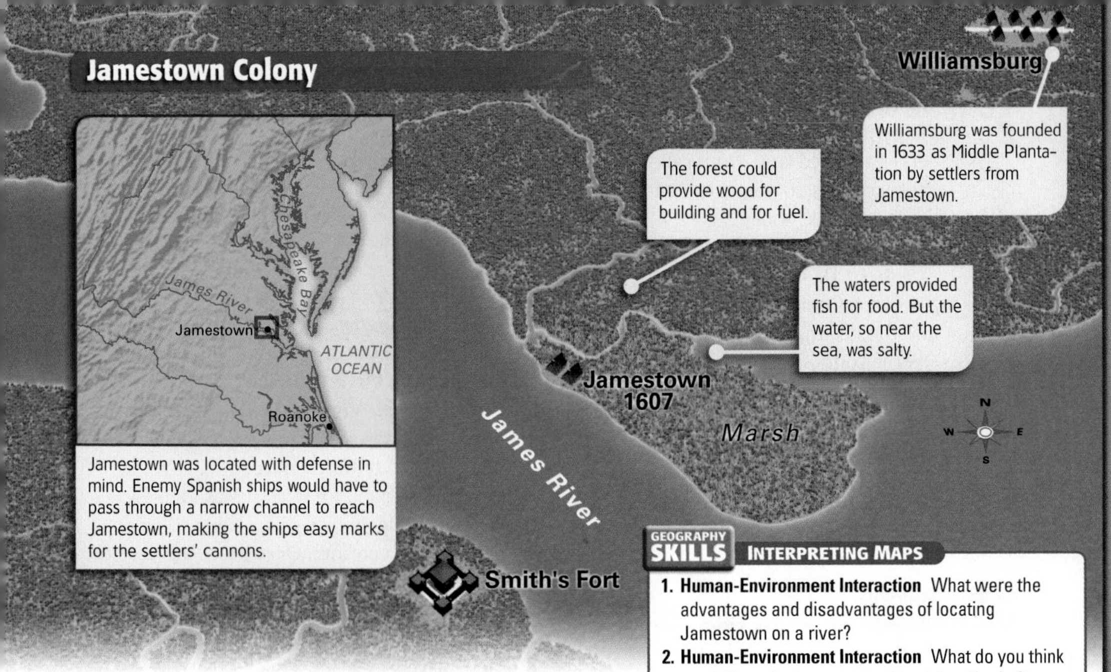

Jamestown Colony
Williamsburg
Williamsburg was founded in 1633 as Middle Plantation by settlers from Jamestown.
The forest could provide wood for building and for fuel.
The waters provided fish for food. But the water, so near the sea, was salty.
Chesapeake Bay
James River
Jamestown
ATLANTIC OCEAN
Roanoke
Jamestown was located with defense in mind. Enemy Spanish ships would have to pass through a narrow channel to reach Jamestown, making the ships easy marks for the settlers' cannons.
Jamestown 1607
Marsh
James River
Smith's Fort
N
W
E
S

GEOGRAPHY SKILLS INTERPRETING MAPS

1. **Human-Environment Interaction** What were the advantages and disadvantages of locating Jamestown on a river?
2. **Human-Environment Interaction** What do you think would have been a commonly used method of transportation for people in this region?

Powhatan Confederacy

Jamestown fared better under **John Smith,** who took control of the colony and built a fort in 1608. He forced the settlers to work harder and to build better housing by creating rules that rewarded harder workers with food. The colonists received help from the powerful Powhatan Confederacy of Native Americans after Smith made an agreement with them. The Powhatan brought food to help the colonists and taught them how to grow corn.

In 1609 some 400 more settlers arrived in Jamestown. That winter, disease and famine once again hit the colony. The colonists called this period the starving time. By the spring of 1610, only 60 colonists were still alive. Jamestown failed to make a profit until colonist John Rolfe introduced a new type of tobacco that sold well in England.

War in Virginia

John Rolfe married **Pocahontas**, daughter of the Powhatan leader, in 1614. Their marriage helped the colonists form more peaceful relations with the Powhatan. However, Pocahontas died three years later in England, which she was visiting with Rolfe.

In 1622, colonists killed a Powhatan leader. The Powhatan responded by attacking the Virginia settlers later that year. Fighting between the colonists and the Powhatan continued for the next 20 years. Because the London Company could not protect its colonists, the English Crown canceled the company's charter in 1624. Virginia became a royal colony and existed under the authority of a governor chosen by the king.

ACADEMIC VOCABULARY
authority power, right to rule

READING CHECK **Finding Main Ideas** What problems did the Jamestown colonists face?

Direct Teach

Main Idea

1 Settlement in Jamestown

Jamestown was the first permanent English settlement in America.

Recall When was Jamestown founded, and where was it located? *1607; on the James River in Virginia*

Summarize Briefly describe the changing nature of the relationship between the Jamestown settlers and the Powhatan Indians. *At first, relations were good, strengthened by a marriage between John Rolfe and Pocahontas, but conflict erupted after settlers murdered a Powhatan leader.*

CRF: Biography Activity: Pocahontas

Map Transparency 13: Jamestown Colony

Info to Know

Smith and Pocahontas Powhatan Indians captured Captain John Smith at one point. Smith wrote in his *Generall Historie of Virginia* that they were preparing to kill him when the 13-year-old Pocahontas threw herself over him, saving his life. Not all historians believe Smith's story, though.

go.hrw.com
Online Resources
KEYWORD: SF7 CH3
ACTIVITY: Population Shifts

Differentiating Instruction

Below Level

English-Language Learners

Standard English Mastery

1. Write the following terms and names for students to see: London Company, joint-stock company, Jamestown, adventurers, mosquitoes, John Smith, Powhatan Confederacy, winter, John Rolfe, tobacco, Pocahontas, peaceful, fighting, and royal colony.
2. Have students work as a class to define each term as it is used in the text on the above pages. Ask volunteers to use each term in a sentence. Help students to improve their use of standard English.
3. Then pair students and have each pair use the list of words to write a summary of the portion of the text titled "Settlement in Jamestown."
4. **Struggling Readers** Write the summary yourself and provide blanks for the words in the list. Have students fill in the blanks.

LS Verbal/Linguistic

Alternative Assessment Handbook, Rubric 37: Writing Assignments

Answers

Interpreting Maps 1. *advantages—fishing, water transportation; disadvantages—mosquitoes in nearby marsh, possible flooding;* **2.** *boats or canoes*

Reading Check *lack of preparation, disease-carrying mosquitoes, famine, conflict with Native Americans*

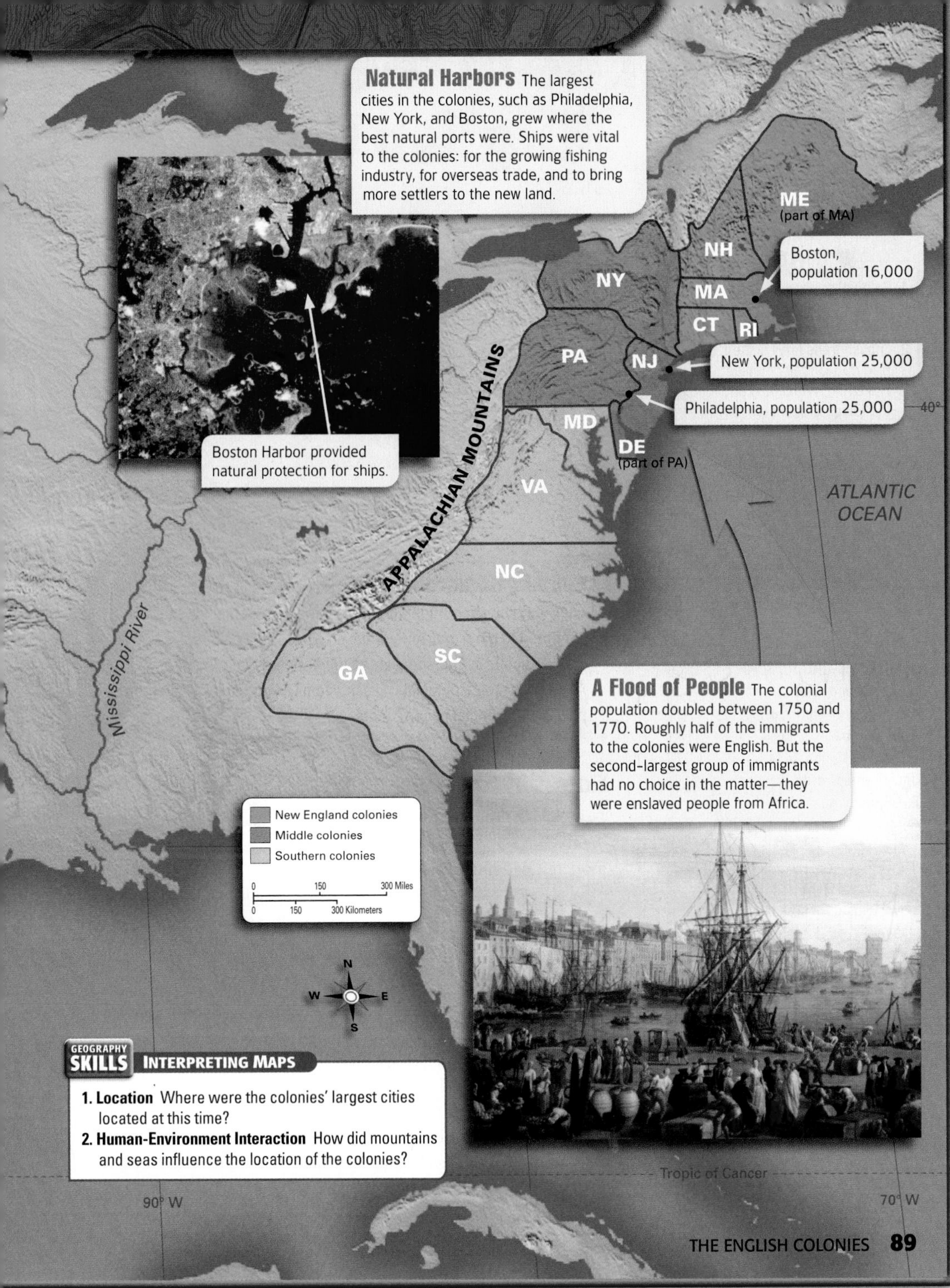

Natural Harbors The largest cities in the colonies, such as Philadelphia, New York, and Boston, grew where the best natural ports were. Ships were vital to the colonies: for the growing fishing industry, for overseas trade, and to bring more settlers to the new land.
Boston Harbor provided natural protection for ships.
ME (part of MA)
NH
MA
NY
CT
RI
PA
NJ
MD
DE (part of PA)
VA
NC
SC
GA
Boston, population 16,000
New York, population 25,000
Philadelphia, population 25,000
40°
APPALACHIAN MOUNTAINS
Mississippi River
ATLANTIC OCEAN
A Flood of People The colonial population doubled between 1750 and 1770. Roughly half of the immigrants to the colonies were English. But the second-largest group of immigrants had no choice in the matter—they were enslaved people from Africa.
New England colonies
Middle colonies
Southern colonies
0 150 300 Miles
0 150 300 Kilometers
N
W
E
S
GEOGRAPHY SKILLS INTERPRETING MAPS
1. Location Where were the colonies' largest cities located at this time?
2. Human-Environment Interaction How did mountains and seas influence the location of the colonies?
Tropic of Cancer
90° W
70° W

History and Geography

Info to Know

Westward Expansion As the map shows, early European colonists settled mainly along the East Coast. West of the Appalachians, fur traders and a few forts were the only signs of Europeans. By the 1750s, however, European pioneers were moving into the Ohio River valley. Pioneers found that the valley provided fertile soil for farming and plenty of wild game. After the French and Indian War, pioneers began crossing the Appalachians in greater numbers. The Proclamation of 1763, which prohibited settlement west of the Appalachians, had little effect. The Proclamation proved difficult to enforce, and pioneers ignored it. The lure of the West proved irresistible.

Linking to Today

New York City As the map shows, New York was one of the largest cities in the English colonies in 1760. Today the city is the nation's largest, with a population of more than 7 million. New York City serves as a cultural and economic center and is one of the most culturally diverse cities in the United States. The city now consists of five boroughs—the Bronx, Brooklyn, Manhattan, Staten Island, and Queens.

Making Inferences Why do you think New York City has remained a major population center? *possible answer—Its strategic location serves as a gateway for incoming immigrants and trade. It has also become a center for many major American industries.*

Critical Thinking: Analyzing Information

At Level

Pioneer Letter

1. Ask students to imagine that they live in the English colonies in 1760. Their families have recently joined a group of pioneers and settled west of the Appalachian Mountains in the Ohio River valley.
2. Have students write letters to relatives or friends in Philadelphia describing why their families have moved west and some of the hardships they faced during the trip. If time allows, have students conduct research to learn more about pioneers and westward expansion in the 1770s.
3. Have volunteers read their letters to the class.
4. **Extend** Have students conduct research on Daniel Boone and his role in westward expansion during this period. Each student should write a biographical sketch of Boone. **LS Verbal/Linguistic**

Alternative Assessment Handbook, Rubrics 4: Biographies; and 25: Personal Letters

Answers

Interpreting Maps 1. *along the mid- and northern Atlantic coast;* **2.** *Immigrants arrived in North America by boat and landed on the East Coast, so many colonists settled along the coast; the Appalachian Mountains formed a barrier to westward movement and settlement.*

Preteach

Bellringer

If YOU were there . . . Use the **Daily Bellringer Transparency** to help students answer the question.

Daily Bellringer Transparency 3.4

The English Colonies Daily Bellringer **3.4**

Review Section 3

In each pair below, select the colony or place that came first.

1. Colony of Pennsylvania **OR** Colony of Delaware
2. New York City **OR** Philadelphia
3. Colony of New Jersey **OR** Colony of Delaware
4. New Amsterdam **OR** New York City

Preview Section 4

If YOU were there ...

Your family migrated to America in the 1700s and started a small farm in western Pennsylvania. Now, more and more people are moving in. You would like to move farther west, into the Ohio River valley. But a new law says you cannot move west of the mountains because it is too dangerous. Still, you are restless and want more land and more freedom.

Why might you decide to break the law and move west?

Consider what you WANT:
- good farmland
- open space

Consider what you THINK:
- about the law
- about English government

Review Answers: 1. Colony of Pennsylvania; 2. New York City; 3. Colony of New Jersey; 4. New Amsterdam

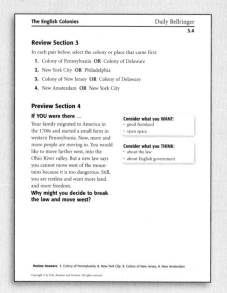

Building Vocabulary

Preteach or review the following terms:

backcountry thinly settled rural area (p. 97)

casualties captured, injured, or killed soldiers (p. 96)

dominion an area governed by a ruler (p. 91)

Privy Council a council or group that advises a ruler (p. 90)

revivals religious gatherings where people came together to hear sermons (p. 94)

CRF: Vocabulary Builder Activity, Section 4

Taking Notes

Have students copy the graphic organizer onto their own paper and then use it to take notes on the section. This activity will prepare students for the Section Assessment, in which they will complete a graphic organizer that builds on the information using a critical-thinking skill.

Section Correlations

IN

8.4.2 Illustrate elements of the three types of economic systems, using cases from United States history. **8.4.9** Explain and evaluate examples of domestic and international interdependence throughout United States history.

SECTION 4

Life in the English Colonies

What You Will Learn...

Main Ideas

1. Colonial governments were influenced by political changes in England.
2. English trade laws limited free trade in the colonies.
3. The Great Awakening and the Enlightenment led to ideas of political equality among many colonists.
4. The French and Indian War gave England control of more land in North America.

The Big Idea

The English colonies continued to grow despite many challenges.

Key Terms and People

town meeting, *p. 91*
English Bill of Rights, *p. 91*
triangular trade, *p. 93*
Great Awakening, *p. 94*
Jonathan Edwards, *p. 94*
Enlightenment, *p. 95*
Pontiac, *p. 97*

TAKING NOTES As you read, take notes on how the following developments affected the growing colonies.

Development	Effects
Establishment of local government	
Political change in England	
Trade laws	
Great Awakening/ Enlightenment	
French and Indian War	

IN **8.1.1, 8.1.2, 8.1.3, 8.1.4, 8.2.8, 8.2.9, 8.3.1, 8.3.2, 8.3.5, 8.4.2, 8.4.9**

If YOU were there...

Your family migrated to America in the 1700s and started a small farm in western Pennsylvania. Now, more and more people are moving in. You would like to move farther west, into the Ohio River valley. But a new law says you cannot move west of the mountains because it is too dangerous. Still, you are restless and want more land and more freedom.

Why might you decide to break the law and move west?

BUILDING BACKGROUND When they moved to America, the English colonists brought their ideas about government. They expected to have the same rights as citizens in England. However, many officials in England wanted tight control over the colonies. As a result, some colonists, like this family, were unhappy with the policies of colonial governments.

Colonial Governments

The English colonies in North America all had their own governments. Each government was given power by a charter. The English monarch had ultimate authority over all of the colonies. A group of royal advisers called the Privy Council set English colonial policies.

Colonial Governors and Legislatures

Each colony had a governor who served as head of the government. Most governors were assisted by an advisory council. In royal colonies the English king or queen selected the governor and the council members. In proprietary colonies, the proprietors chose all of these officials. In a few colonies, such as Connecticut, the people elected the governor.

In some colonies the people also elected representatives to help make laws and set policy. These officials served on assemblies. Each colonial assembly passed laws that had to be approved first by the advisory council and then by the governor.

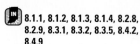

Teach the Big Idea

At Level

Life in the English Colonies

1. **Teach** To teach the main ideas in the section, use the questions in the Direct Teach boxes.
2. **Apply** Organize students into four groups and assign each group one of this section's subsections, indicated by the blue heads. Have each group develop a detailed outline of its subsection. Then ask each group to exchange its outline with another group and write five questions and answers about the information in that outline. **LS Verbal/Linguistic**
3. **Review** Collect students' questions and use them to review the section and quiz the class.
4. **Practice/Homework** Ask students to predict how the British colonists reacted to the Proclamation of 1763. Then have students imagine that they are colonists and write letters to the editor of a colonial newspaper expressing their views on the new law. **LS Verbal/Linguistic**

Alternative Assessment Handbook, Rubrics 37: Writing Assignments; and 41: Writing to Express

Established in 1619, Virginia's assembly was the first colonial legislature in North America. At first it met as a single body, but it was later split into two houses. The first house was known as the Council of State. The governor's advisory council and the London Company selected its members. The House of Burgesses was the assembly's second house. The members were elected by colonists.

In New England the center of politics was the **town meeting**. In town meetings people talked about and decided on issues of local interest, such as paying for schools.

In the southern colonies, people typically lived farther away from one another. Therefore, many decisions were made at the county level. The middle colonies used both county meetings and town meetings to make laws.

Political Change in England

In 1685 James II became king of England. He was determined to take more control over the English government, both in England and in the colonies.

James believed that the colonies were too independent. In 1686 he united the northern colonies under one government called the Dominion of New England. James named Sir Edmund Andros royal governor of the Dominion. The colonists disliked Andros because he used his authority to limit the powers of town meetings.

English Bill of Rights

Parliament replaced the unpopular King James and passed the **English Bill of Rights** in 1689. This act reduced the powers of the English monarch. At the same time, Parliament gained power. As time went on, the colonists valued their own right to elect representatives to decide local issues. Following these changes, the colonies in the Dominion quickly formed new assemblies and charters.

The Thirteen Colonies

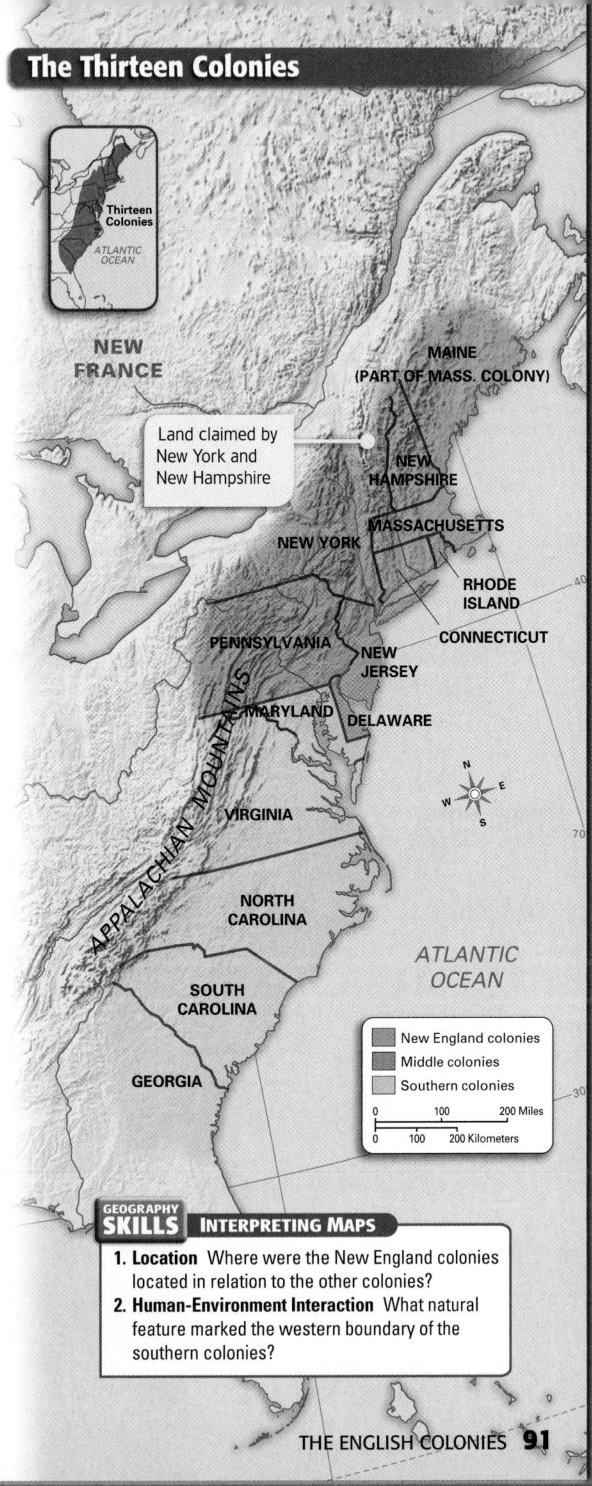

GEOGRAPHY SKILLS **INTERPRETING MAPS**

1. **Location** Where were the New England colonies located in relation to the other colonies?
2. **Human-Environment Interaction** What natural feature marked the western boundary of the southern colonies?

Direct Teach

Main Idea

❶ Colonial Governments

Colonial governments were influenced by political changes in England.

Recall What served as the center of politics in New England? *town meetings, in which people decided local issues*

Analyze What forms of representative government did the English colonists begin to develop? *Some colonies had elected legislative assemblies, such as Virginia's House of Burgesses.*

Draw Conclusions What opinion do you think colonists in New England had of the Dominion of New England? *Most of them probably disliked it because the dominion limited the powers of town meetings.*

Map Transparency 16: The Thirteen Colonies

Answers

Interpreting Maps **1.** *to the north;* **2.** *Appalachian Mountains*

Differentiating Instruction

Below Level

Struggling Readers

1. To help students compare and contrast the different forms of colonial government, draw the graphic organizer. Omit the blue answers.
2. Have students copy and complete the graphic organizer. Review the answers as a class.
3. Then have students discuss how the English Bill of Rights affected colonial government. **LS Verbal/Linguistic, Visual/Spatial**

Alternative Assessment Handbook, Rubric 13: Graphic Organizers

Monarch	*ultimate authority over all English colonies*
Privy Council	*royal advisors; set English colonial policies*
Governors	*appointed by Crown or proprietors, or elected by people; served as head of colonial government; assisted by advisory councils*
Assemblies	*elected representatives; assisted in making laws and setting policies; had to get approval from advisory council and governor*
Town Meetings	*center of politics in New England; decided local issues*
Courts	*provided control over local affairs; protected individual freedoms*

Direct Teach

Main Idea

❷ English Trade Laws

English trade laws limited free trade in the colonies.

Define What is mercantilism? *creating and maintaining wealth by carefully controlling trade and the balance of imports to exports*

Explain How did the Navigation Acts limit colonial trade? *restricted colonial trade to England and imposed duties on some trade goods*

Identify Points of View How did colonists view the trade laws that England set? *Some colonists respected and obeyed the laws, while others considered them too restrictive and smuggled to get around them.*

Make Inferences Why do you think that British officials rarely carried out the Molasses Act? *possible answers—probably was hard to enforce; made the products from the West Indies cheaper for them to buy; did not agree with the law*

Map Transparency 17: Triangular Trade

go.hrw.com
Online Resources

KEYWORD: SF7 CH3
ACTIVITY: The Pen and the Sword

Colonial Courts

Colonial courts made up another important part of colonial governments. Whenever possible, colonists used the courts to control local affairs. In general, the courts reflected the beliefs of their local communities. For example, many laws in Massachusetts enforced the Puritans' religious beliefs. Laws based on the Bible set the standard for the community's conduct.

THE IMPACT TODAY

Like the colonies and Great Britain, nations today are economically interdependent. They rely on one another to buy and sell goods and services to keep their economies healthy. Communications technology has increased this interdependence, as huge sums of money can change hands each day with ease.

Sometimes colonial courts also protected individual freedoms. For example, in 1733 officials arrested John Peter Zenger for printing a false statement that damaged the reputation of the governor of New York. Andrew Hamilton, Zenger's attorney, argued that Zenger could publish whatever he wished as long as it was true. Jury members believed that colonists had a right to voice their ideas openly and found him not guilty.

READING CHECK **Analyzing Information** Why were colonial assemblies and colonial courts created, and what did they do?

English Trade Laws

One of England's main reasons for founding and controlling its American colonies was to earn money from trade. In the late 1600s England, like most western European nations, practiced mercantilism, a system of creating and maintaining wealth through carefully controlled trade. A country gained wealth if it had fewer imports—goods bought from other countries—than exports—goods sold to other countries.

To support this system of mercantilism, between 1650 and 1696 Parliament passed a series of Navigation Acts limiting colonial trade. For example, the Navigation Act of 1660 forbade colonists from trading specific items such as sugar and cotton with any country other than England. The act also required colonists to use English ships to transport goods. Parliament later passed other acts that required all trade goods to pass through English ports, where duties, or import taxes, were added to the items.

Triangular Trade

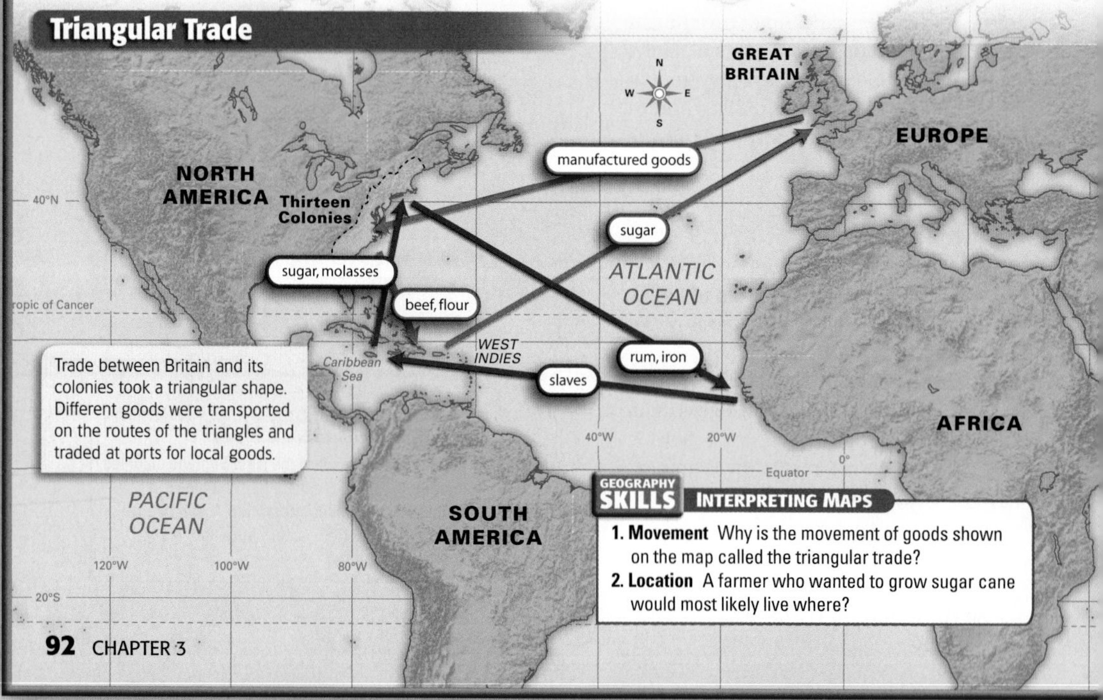

Trade between Britain and its colonies took a triangular shape. Different goods were transported on the routes of the triangles and traded at ports for local goods.

GEOGRAPHY SKILLS **INTERPRETING MAPS**

1. **Movement** Why is the movement of goods shown on the map called the triangular trade?
2. **Location** A farmer who wanted to grow sugar cane would most likely live where?

Cross-Discipline Activity: Government

At Level

Reporting the Zenger Trial

Background On November 5, 1733, John Zenger published his first issue of the *New York Weekly Journal*, in which he criticized New York's colonial governor, John Cosby. As publisher, Zenger was legally responsible for the newspaper's contents. The paper's attacks on Cosby continued for a year, and in November 1734, Zenger was arrested for libel.

1. Provide students with the background of the Zenger trial.
2. Have each student write a headline and a newspaper article about the Zenger trial. In their articles, students should stress the importance of freedom of the press.
3. Have volunteers share their headlines and articles with the class. Have students discuss why freedom of the press continues to be an important right. **LS Verbal/Linguistic**

Alternative Assessment Handbook, Rubric 42: Writing to Inform

Answers

Interpreting Maps **1.** *because trade routes among Africa, Europe, the West Indies, and North America were roughly triangular;* **2.** *West Indies*

Reading Check *to provide colonists with some control over local affairs through setting policies, making laws, and protecting freedoms*

England claimed that the Navigation Acts were good for the colonies. After all, the colonies had a steady market in England for their goods. But not all colonists agreed. Many colonists wanted more freedom to buy or sell goods wherever they could get the best price. Local demand for colonial goods was small compared to foreign demand.

Despite colonial complaints, the trade restrictions continued into the 1700s. Some traders turned to smuggling, or illegal trading. They often smuggled sugar, molasses, and rum into the colonies from non-English islands in the Caribbean. Parliament responded with the Molasses Act of 1733, which placed duties on these items. British officials, however, rarely carried out this law.

By the early 1700s English merchants were trading around the world. Most American merchants traded directly with Great Britain or the West Indies. By importing and exporting goods such as sugar and tobacco, some American merchants became wealthy.

Triangular Trade

Trade between the American colonies and Great Britain was not direct. Rather, it generally took the form of **triangular trade**—a system in which goods and slaves were traded among the Americas, Britain, and Africa. There were several routes of the triangular trade. In one route colonists exchanged goods like beef and flour with plantation owners in the West Indies for sugar, some of which they shipped to Britain. The sugar was then exchanged for manufactured products to be sold in the colonies. Colonial merchants traveled great distances to find the best markets.

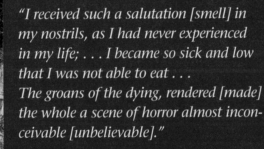

BIOGRAPHY

Olaudah Equiano

1745–1797

Olaudah Equiano claimed to have been born in Africa in present-day Nigeria. His autobiography told the story of his enslavement. According to his autobiography, Equiano survived the Middle Passage, traveling in a slave ship across the Atlantic. After arriving in the colonies, a Virginia planter purchased him and again sold him to a British naval officer. While working as a sailor, Equiano eventually earned enough money to purchase his own freedom in 1766. Equiano later settled in England and devoted himself to ending slavery.

Analyzing Information How did Equiano gain his freedom?

"I received such a salutation [smell] in my nostrils, as I had never experienced in my life; . . . I became so sick and low that I was not able to eat . . . The groans of the dying, rendered [made] the whole a scene of horror almost inconceivable [unbelievable]."

—Olaudah Equiano, from *The Interesting Narrative of the Life of Olaudah Equiano, or Gustavus Vassa, the African*

Direct Teach

Connect to Economics

The Hat Act One of the more unusual restrictive acts that the British government passed was the Hat Act, which prohibited the sale of hats among the colonies and required a seven-year apprenticeship for anyone who wished to become a hat maker. Parliament passed this act in response to pressure from London felt makers who wanted to protect their industry from competition.

Biography

Olaudah Equiano (c. 1745–1797)
After purchasing his freedom, Olaudah Equiano traveled to the Mediterranean, the Arctic, and Central America. However, he was never able to travel to Africa despite strong efforts to do so.

Did you know . . .

The Vermont Constitution of 1777 was the first document in the United States to abolish slavery. The United States, however, did not end slavery until after the Civil War, nearly 100 years later.

Checking for Understanding

Multiple Choice Select the best answer for each of the following:

1. The Zenger case was the first major case establishing
   - **a.** freedom of religion
   - **b.** freedom of assembly
   - **c.** *freedom of the press*
   - **d.** right to trial by jury
2. England controlled trade in the colonies through the practice of
   - **a.** colonialism
   - **b.** *mercantilism*
   - **c.** triangular trade
   - **d.** navigation

Differentiating Instruction

English-Language Learners — Below Level

Colonial Trade Posters Organize students into small groups of mixed ability. Have each group create a poster illustrating the various types of goods traded in the English colonies. Students' posters will vary but should include depictions of common trade items, the triangular trade, and reactions to trade restrictions such as smuggling. **LS Interpersonal, Visual/Spatial**

Advanced/Gifted and Talented — Above Level

Alternative Labor Proposals Have students write a proposal that suggests ways the English colonies could have developed without relying on slave labor. Students' proposals should address the reasons that farming colonies, in particular, participated in the slave trade. Have volunteers share their proposals with the class.
LS Verbal/Linguistic

Answers

Biography *by saving money and purchasing his freedom*

Direct Teach

Main Idea

❸ Great Awakening and Enlightenment

The Great Awakening and the Enlightenment led to ideas of political equality among many colonists.

Define Describe the Great Awakening in your own words. *A religious movement that swept through the colonies in the 1730s and 1740s.*

Draw Conclusions How did John Locke's beliefs influence colonial society? *His ideas about natural rights, such as equality and liberty, began to influence colonial leaders.*

CRF: Primary Source Activity: Sinners in the Hands of an Angry God

Biography

George Whitefield (1714–1770)

George Whitefield was born in Gloucester, England, and educated at Oxford. He experienced a strong religious awakening during his high school and college years, which he called a "new birth." He believed that every truly religious person needs to experience a rebirth in Jesus Christ, and he preached this message throughout America and Great Britain.

The Great Awakening

George Whitefield gives a powerful sermon during the Great Awakening. Ministers like Whitefield emphasized personal religious experiences over official church rules. They also allowed ordinary church members—whatever their race, class, or gender—to play a role in services. The value placed on individuals of all types during the Great Awakening helped shape American political ideas about who should have a say in government.

How do you think religious freedom led to political freedom?

Middle Passage

One version of the triangular trade began with traders exchanging rum for slaves on the West African coast. The traders then sold the enslaved Africans in the West Indies for molasses or brought them to sell in the mainland American colonies.

The slave trade brought millions of Africans across the Atlantic Ocean in a voyage called the Middle Passage. This was a terrifying and deadly journey that could last as long as three months.

Enslaved Africans lived in a space not even three feet high. Slave traders fit as many slaves as possible on board so they could earn greater profits. Thousands of captives died on slave ships during the Middle Passage. In many cases, they died from diseases such as smallpox. As farmers began to use fewer indentured servants, slaves became even more valuable.

READING CHECK **Identifying Cause and Effect** What factors caused the slave trade to grow? How did this affect conditions on the Middle Passage?

Great Awakening and Enlightenment

In the early 1700s revolutions in both religious and nonreligious thought transformed the Western world. These movements began in Europe and affected life in the American colonies.

Great Awakening

After years of population growth, religious leaders wanted to spread religious feeling throughout the colonies. In the late 1730s these ministers began holding revivals, emotional gatherings where people came together to hear sermons.

Many American colonists experienced "a great awakening" in their religious lives. This **Great Awakening**—a religious movement that swept through the colonies in the 1730s and 1740s—changed colonial religion. It also affected social and political life. **Jonathan Edwards** of Massachusetts was one of the most important leaders of the Great Awakening. His dramatic sermons told

Critical Thinking: Finding Main Ideas

At Level

Great Awakening and Enlightenment

1. Discuss with students the significance of the Great Awakening and the Enlightenment.
2. Create a chart with two columns. Label one column *Great Awakening* and the other column *Enlightenment*. Have students copy the chart.
3. In the columns, students should write their own definitions of the movements and identify one or more of their key figures.
4. Next, have students list examples of how each movement affected political and social views in the English colonies.
5. Review students' answers as a class. Conclude by having students discuss the effects of the Great Awakening and the Enlightenment.

LS Verbal/Linguistic

Alternative Assessment Handbook, Rubric 7: Charts

Answers

The Great Awakening *Sermons about spiritual equality led to some demands for more political equality.*

Reading Check *As farmers began to rely less on indentured servants, they needed more slaves to work their farms. Slave traders placed as many slaves on ships as possible to increase profits, which created the terrifying and deadly conditions of the passage.*

SE Student Edition | Print Resource | Audio CD
TE Teacher's Edition | Transparency | CD-ROM
go.hrw.com | **LS** Learning Styles | Video
TOS Indiana Teacher One Stop | * also on Indiana Teacher One Stop

HOLT
History's Impact
United States History Video Program (VHS/DVD)
The Impact of Being Able to Choose Your Own Government
Suggested use: as a chapter introduction

Review, Assessment, Intervention

- **Quick Facts Transparency 11:** The American Revolution Visual Summary*
- **Spanish Chapter Summaries Audio CD Program**
- **Progress Assessment Support System (PASS):** Chapter Tests A and B*
- **Differentiated Instruction Modified Worksheets and Tests CD-ROM:** Modified Chapter Test
- TOS **Indiana Teacher One Stop:** ExamView Test Generator (English/Spanish)

- **PASS:** Section Quiz 4.1*
- **Online Quiz:** Section 4.1
- **Alternative Assessment Handbook**

- **PASS:** Section Quiz 4.2*
- **Online Quiz:** Section 4.2
- **Alternative Assessment Handbook**

- **PASS:** Section Quiz 4.3*
- **Online Quiz:** Section 4.3
- **Alternative Assessment Handbook**

- **PASS:** Section Quiz 4.4*
- **Online Quiz:** Section 4.4
- **Alternative Assessment Handbook**

Power Presentations with Video CD-ROM

Power Presentations with Video are visual presentations of each chapter's main ideas. Presentations can be customized by including Quick Facts charts, images from the text, and video clips.

DIVISION FOR PUBLIC EDUCATION
AMERICAN BAR ASSOCIATION

Developed by the Division for Public Education of the American Bar Association, these materials are part of the **Democracy and Civic Education Resources.**

- **Constitution Study Guide**
- **Supreme Court Case Studies**

Holt Online Learning

go.hrw.com
Teacher Resources
KEYWORD: SF7 TEACHER

go.hrw.com
Student Resources
KEYWORD: SF7 CH4

- Document-Based Questions
- Interactive Multimedia Activities
- Current Events
- Chapter-based Internet Activities
- and more!

Holt Interactive
Online Student Edition

Complete online support for interactivity, assessment, and reporting

- Interactive Maps and Notebook
- Standardized Test Prep
- Homework Practice and Research Activities Online

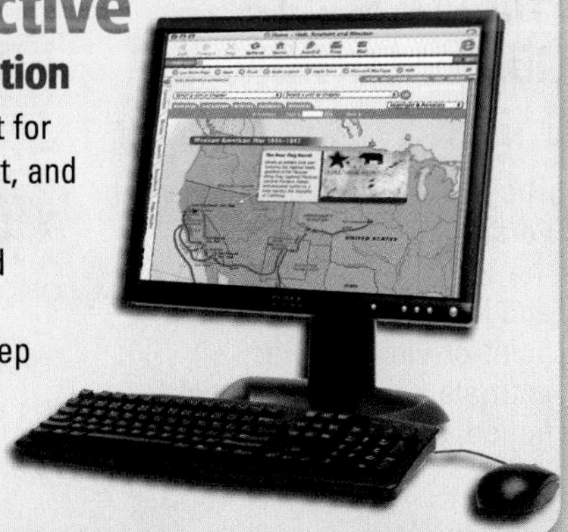

CHAPTER 4 PLANNING GUIDE

How do I address the needs of varied learners?

The Target Resource acts as your primary strategy for differentiated instruction.

ENGLISH-LANGUAGE LEARNERS & STRUGGLING READERS

TARGET RESOURCE

English-Language Learner Strategies and Activities

- Build Academic Vocabulary
- Develop Oral and Written Language Structures

Spanish Resources

Spanish Chapter Summaries Audio CD

Spanish Chapter Summaries Online

Teacher's One-Stop Planner:

- ExamView Test Generator, Spanish
- PuzzlePro, Spanish

Additional Resources

Differentiated Instruction Teacher Management System: Lesson Plans for Differentiated Instruction

Chapter Resource File:

- Vocabulary Builder Activities
- Social Studies Skills Activity: Understanding Historical Interpretation

Quick Facts Transparency 11: The American Revolution Visual Summary

Student Edition on Audio CD Program

Interactive Skills Tutor CD-ROM

SPECIAL NEEDS LEARNERS

TARGET RESOURCE

Differentiated Instruction Modified Worksheets and Tests CD-ROM

- Vocabulary Flash Cards
- Modified Vocabulary Builder Activities
- Modified Chapter Review Activity
- Modified Chapter Test

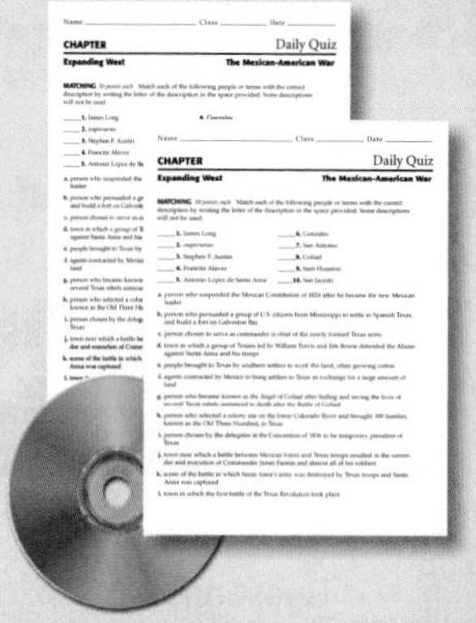

Additional Resources

Differentiated Instruction Teacher Management System: Lesson Plans for Differentiated Instruction

Interactive Reader and Study Guide

Social Studies Skills Activity: Understanding Historical Interpretation

Student Edition on Audio CD Program

Interactive Skills Tutor CD-ROM

ADVANCED/GIFTED-AND-TALENTED STUDENTS

TARGET RESOURCE

Primary Source Library CD-ROM for United States History

The Library contains longer versions of quotations in the text, extra sources, and images. Included are point-of-view articles, journals, diaries, historical fiction, and political documents.

Additional Resources

Differentiated Instruction Teacher Management System: Lesson Plans for Differentiated Instruction

Pre-AP Activities Guide for United States History: The American Revolution

U.S. History Document-Based Activities: Activity 1, The American Revolution

Chapter Resource File:

- Focus on Writing Activity: Giving an Oral Report
- Literature Activity: *The Crisis, No. 1,* by Thomas Paine
- Primary Source Activity: Patrick Henry: The Voice of Freedom

Internet Activities: Chapter Enrichment Links

Differentiated Activities in the Teacher's Edition

- Lexington and Concord Graphic Organizer, p. 114
- Language of the Declaration of Independence, p. 122
- Foreign Aid to Patriots Chart, p. 131

Differentiated Activities in the Teacher's Edition

- *Common Sense* Handbill, p. 119

Differentiated Activities in the Teacher's Edition

- Patriot Battle Maps, p. 129

Teacher One Stop™

How can I manage the lesson plans and support materials for differentiated instruction?

With the Indiana Teacher One Stop, you can easily organize and print lesson plans, planning guides, and instructional materials for all learners. The Indiana Teacher One Stop includes the following materials to help you differentiate instruction:

- Interactive Teacher's Edition
- Calendar Planner and pacing guides
- Editable lesson plans
- All reproducible ancillaries in Adobe Acrobat (PDF) format
- ExamView Test Generator (Eng & Span)
- Transparency and video previews

Professional Development

What teacher training resources are available to help me grow professionally?

- **In-service and staff development** as part of your Holt Social Studies product purchase
- **Quick Teacher Tutorial Lesson Presentation CD-ROM**
- Intensive tuition-based **Teacher Development Institute**
- **Convenient Holt Speaker Bureau –** face-to-face workshop options
- **PRAXIS™ Test Prep** interactive Web-based content refreshers*
- **Ask A Professional Development Expert** at http://www.hrw.com/prodev/

* PRAXIS is a trademark of Educational Testing Service (ETS). This publication is not endorsed or approved by ETS.

Chapter Preview

Chapter Big Ideas

Section 1 The tensions between the colonies and Great Britain led to armed conflict in 1775.

Section 2 The colonies formally declared their independence from Great Britain.

Section 3 Patriot forces faced many obstacles in the war against Britain.

Section 4 The war spread to the southern colonies, where the British were finally defeated.

Focus on Speaking

The **Chapter Resource File** provides a Focus on Speaking worksheet to help students prepare, organize, and present their oral reports.

CRF: Focus on Speaking Activity: Giving an Oral Report

CHAPTER 4

The American Revolution

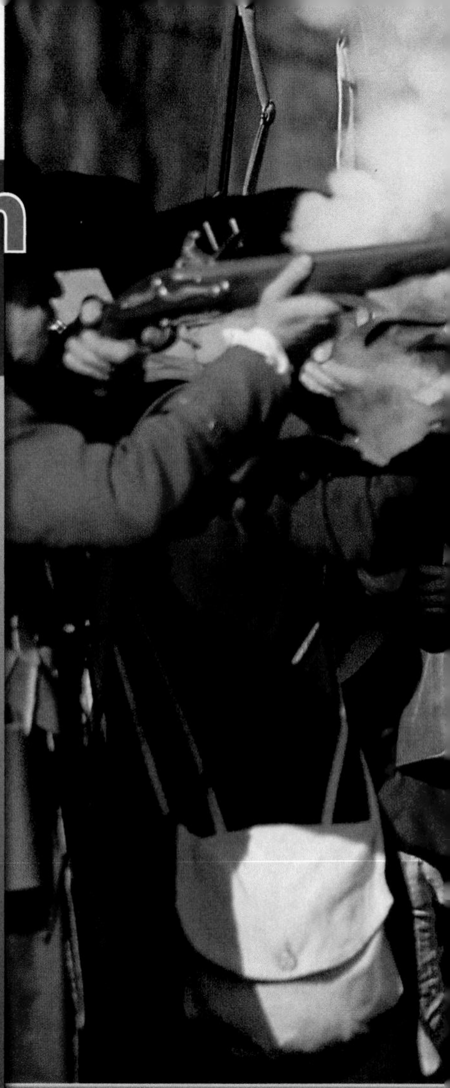

Indiana Standards

Social Studies Standards

8.1.4 Identify fundamental ideas in the Declaration of Independence (1776) and analyze the causes and effects of the Revolutionary War (1775–1783), including enactment of the Articles of Confederation and the Treaty of Paris.

8.1.9 Describe the influence of important individuals on social and political developments of the time such as the Independence movement and the framing of the Constitution.

8.1.28 Recognize historical perspective and evaluate alternative courses of action by describing the historical context in which events unfolded and by avoiding evaluation of the past solely in terms of present-day norms.

8.1.29 Differentiate betweenfacts and historical interpretations recognizing that the historian's narrative reflects his or her judgment about the significance of particular facts.

8.2.1 Identify and explain essential ideas of constitutional government, which are expressed in the founding documents of the United States, including the Virginia Declaration of Rights, the Declaration of Independence, the Virginia Statute for Religious Freedom, the Massachusetts Constitution of 1780, the Northwest Ordinance, the 1787 U.S. Constitution, the Bill of Rights, the Federalist and Anti-Federalist Papers, Common Sense, Washington's Farewell Address (1796), and Jefferson's First Inaugural Address (1801).

go.hrw.com
Indiana
KEYWORD: SF10 IN

FOCUS ON SPEAKING

Giving an Oral Report The Revolutionary War was a very exciting time in our history, a time filled with deeds of courage and daring and ending with an amazing victory for the underdog. As you read this chapter, you will learn about the great events and heroic people of that time. Then you will prepare and give an oral report on the history of the American Revolution.

UNITED STATES

1774 The First Continental Congress meets.

1775 The Revolutionary War begins with the fighting at Lexington and Concord.

1774

WORLD

Key to Differentiating Instruction

Below Level
Basic-level activities designed for all students encountering new material

At Level
Intermediate-level activities designed for average students

Above Level
Challenging activities designed for honors and gifted and talented students

Standard English Mastery
Activities designed to improve standard English usage

Introduce the Chapter

At Level

Considering the Pros and Cons of War

1. Guide students in a discussion about the pros and cons of a nation going to war. To start the discussion, you may wish to ask students to consider the financial and human costs of war and how war might affect a country's relations with other nations.
2. Next, remind students of the problems between the American colonies and Great Britain in the early 1770s. Ask students to imagine that they are colonial leaders debating whether to go to war against Great Britain. Then ask students to suggest some pros and cons for the colonies if they should decide to wage war against Britain. Have students consider the size of the colonies and their lack of a unified economy or military.
3. List responses for students to see. Have students copy the list. Then, as they study the chapter, have students note how accurate their responses were. **LS Verbal/Linguistic**

HOLT

History's Impact

▶ **video series**
Watch the video to understand the impact of being able to choose your own government.

What You Will Learn...

Soldiers fight with single-shot muskets in this re-enactment of the Revolutionary War. The men in the colonial militias did not have regular uniforms like the British soldiers did. They wore their own clothes and often used their own supplies. In this chapter you will learn about the American War for Independence.

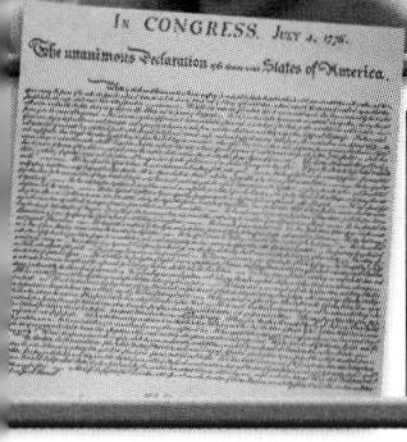

1776 On July 4 the thirteen colonies issue the Declaration of Independence and break away from Great Britain.

1777

1778 France allies with the Americans and joins the war against Great Britain.

1779 George Rogers Clark and his Patriot army capture Fort Sackville for the second time.

1779 Spain declares war against Great Britain.

1780

1781 The British surrender to George Washington at Yorktown.

1783 The Treaty of Paris is signed, ending the war.

1783 Simon Bolívar is born in present-day Venezuela.

• Chapter Preview •

HOLT

History's Impact

▶ **video series**
See the Video Teacher's Guide for strategies for using the chapter video about being able to choose your own government.

Explore the Picture

A Diverse Land At the time of the American Revolution, many colonists used a gun known as a long rifle or Kentucky rifle. A rifle is a type of gun with a grooved barrel. The grooves spin the ball, or bullet, as it is shot. Compared to a musket, a long rifle can shoot a ball farther and with greater accuracy. On the other hand, soldiers could fire and reload muskets faster than rifles. Rifles also lacked bayonets for use in hand-to-hand combat.

Analyzing Visuals What can you tell about the weapons and style of fighting in the Revolutionary War from this picture? *used muskets or rifles, stood in close ranks to shoot, did not always shoot from behind cover*

go.hrw.com
Online Resources

Chapter Resources:
KEYWORD: SF7 CH4
Teacher Resources:
KEYWORD: SF7 TEACHER

Explore the Time Line

1. What year did the American Revolution begin, and what year did it end? *1775; 1783*
2. When did colonial leaders issue the Declaration of Independence? *1776*
3. What other countries fought against Britain during the American Revolution? *France, Spain*
4. Where and when did the British surrender to George Washington? *Yorktown, 1781*

Info to Know

French Aid in the War A turning point in the American Revolution occurred when France joined the colonies in their fight against Britain. The French had remained bitter over the loss of their North American holdings after the French and Indian War. As a result, they were eager to weaken Britain's control in North America. During the American Revolution, the French proved to be a valuable ally, particularly in the colonial victory at the Battle of Yorktown, which ended the war.

Reading Social Studies

Understanding Themes

Two themes are covered in the chapter—geography and politics. These two themes played important roles in the events leading up to the independence of the United States. Ask students to predict how geography might have played a factor in the Revolutionary War. How could geography have helped or hurt the Patriots? Why? Then discuss with students the role politics played in the independence of the United States. How might political views have led the colonists to desire their freedom?

Main Ideas in Social Studies

Focus on Reading Ask students to bring in an article from a newspaper or magazine. Have students read the article and then choose two paragraphs at random. Have students use the steps listed on this page to identify the main idea of each paragraph. Remind students to identify the general topic of the paragraph, highlight important facts and details related to that topic, and then determine the author's point. Have students write out their answers to each step.

Reading Social Studies

by Kylene Beers

Focus on Themes In this chapter you will read about the events of the Revolutionary War, the war by which the United States won its independence. You will learn about some of the major battles that occurred between the American colonists and the British army and how **geography** sometimes affected their outcomes. You will also read the Declaration of Independence, one of the most important **political** documents in all of American history.

Main Ideas in Social Studies

Focus on Reading When you are reading, it is not always necessary to remember every tiny detail of the text. Instead, what you want to remember are the main ideas, the most important concepts around which the text is based.

Identifying Main Ideas Most paragraphs in history books include main ideas. Sometimes the main idea is stated clearly in a single sentence. At other times, the main idea is suggested, not stated. However, that idea still shapes the paragraph's content and the meaning of all of the facts and details in it.

News of the work spread throughout the colonies, eventually selling some 500,000 copies. Paine reached a wide audience by writing as a common person speaking to common people. *Common Sense* changed the way many colonists viewed their king. *(p. 118)*

Topic: The paragraph is about the pamphlet *Common Sense* by Thomas Paine.

+

Facts and Details:
- Many people from different colonies read the pamphlet.
- *Common Sense* eventually sold 500,000 copies.
- Thomas Paine's writing style was easy for the common people to read.

Main Idea: The pamphlet *Common Sense* shaped the way some colonists thought about their rulers.

Steps in Identifying Main Ideas

1. Read the paragraph. Ask yourself, "What is this paragraph mostly about?" This will be the topic of the paragraph.
2. List the important facts and details that relate to that topic.
3. Ask yourself, "What seems to be the most important point the writer is making about the topic?" Or ask, "If the writer could say only one thing about this paragraph, what would it be?" This is the **main idea** of the paragraph.

Reading and Skills Resources

Reading Support

- Interactive Reader and Study Guide
- Student Edition on Audio CD
- Spanish Chapter Summaries Audio CD Program

Social Studies Skills Support

- Interactive Skills Tutor CD-ROM

Vocabulary Support

- **CRF:** Vocabulary Builder Activities
- **CRF:** Chapter Review Activity
- Differentiated Instruction Modified Worksheets and Tests CD-ROM:
  - Vocabulary Flash Cards
  - Vocabulary Builder Activity
  - Chapter Review Activity

OSP Holt PuzzlePro

You Try It!

The following passage is from the chapter you are about to read. Read it and then answer the questions below.

The Treaty of Paris

From Chapter 4, p. 139

After Yorktown, only a few small battles took place. Lacking the money to pay for a new army, Great Britain entered into peace talks with America. Benjamin Franklin had an influential role in the negotiations.

Delegates took more than two years to come to a peace agreement. In the Treaty of Paris of 1783, Great Britain recognized the independence of the United States. The treaty also set America's borders. A separate treaty between Britain and Spain returned Florida to the Spanish. British leaders also accepted American rights to settle and trade west of the original thirteen colonies.

After you have read the passage, answer the following questions.

1. The main idea of the second paragraph is stated in a sentence. Which sentence expresses the main idea?
2. What is the first paragraph about? What facts and details are included in the paragraph? Based on your answers to these questions, what is the main idea of the first paragraph?

As you read Chapter 4, identify the main ideas of the paragraphs you are reading.

Key Terms and People

Chapter 4

Section 1

First Continental Congress *(p. 112)*
Patriots *(p. 113)*
minutemen *(p. 114)*
Redcoats *(p. 114)*
Second Continental Congress *(p. 114)*
Continental Army *(p. 114)*
George Washington *(p. 114)*
Battle of Bunker Hill *(p. 115)*

Section 2

Common Sense *(p. 118)*
Thomas Paine *(p. 118)*
Declaration of Independence *(p. 119)*
Thomas Jefferson *(p. 119)*
Loyalists *(p. 119)*

Section 3

mercenaries *(p. 128)*
Battle of Trenton *(p.129)*
Battle of Saratoga *(p. 130)*
Marquis de Lafayette *(p. 131)*
Baron Friedrich von Steuben *(p. 131)*
Bernardo de Gálvez *(p. 131)*
John Paul Jones *(p. 133)*
George Rogers Clark *(p. 133)*

Section 4

Francis Marion *(p. 136)*
Comte de Rochambeau *(p. 137)*
Battle of Yorktown *(p. 137)*
Treaty of Paris of 1783 *(p. 139)*

Academic Vocabulary

Success in school is related to knowing academic vocabulary—the words that are frequently used in school assignments and discussions. In this chapter, you will learn the following academic words:

reaction *(p. 114)*
strategy *(p. 129)*

Reading Social Studies

Key Terms and People

Preteach the key terms and people for this chapter by reviewing each term with the class. Then instruct students to define or identify each term or person in the list at left. Have students select 10 terms from the list and create a word search using those terms. Have students write the description of each term or person as a clue. When students have finished, have them exchange puzzles with a partner. Then have each student complete their partner's word search by circling the key terms and people identified by the clues. **LS Verbal/Linguistic, Visual/Spatial**

Focus on Reading

See the **Focus on Reading** questions in this chapter for more practice on reading social studies skills.

Reading Social Studies Assessment

See the **Chapter Review** at the end of this chapter for student assessment questions related to this reading skill.

Teaching Tip

Finding the Main Idea Point out to students that writing a main idea statement is not the same thing as summarizing a paragraph. Help students learn how to find the main idea by asking them to identify what point the author is trying to make in a paragraph. Point out to students that not all details in a paragraph may relate to the main idea. Occasionally, other facts and details are used in order to add interest.

Answers

You Try It! 1. *the second sentence;* **2.** *The battle of Yorktown forced Great Britain to begin peace talks with America. Facts—only a few small battles took place; Great Britain couldn't afford a new army and therefore engaged in peace talks with America, Benjamin Franklin had influential role in negotiations; possible main idea—The battle of Yorktown was decisive in the overall outcome of the war because it forced Britain to engage in peace talks with America.*

Preteach

Bellringer

If YOU were there . . . Use the **Daily Bellringer Transparency** for this section to help students answer the question.

Daily Bellringer Transparency 4.1

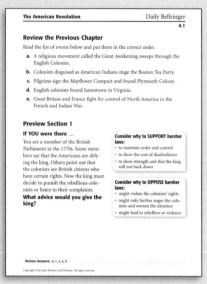

The American Revolution — Daily Bellringer **4.1**

Review the Previous Chapter

Read the list of events below and put them in the correct order.

a. A religious movement called the Great Awakening sweeps through the English Colonies.

b. Colonists disguised as American Indians stage the Boston Tea Party.

c. Pilgrims sign the Mayflower Compact and found Plymouth Colony.

d. English colonists found Jamestown in Virginia.

e. Great Britain and France fight for control of North America in the French and Indian War.

Preview Section 1

If YOU were there ...

You are a member of the British Parliament in the 1770s. Some members say that the Americans are defying the king. Others point out that the colonists are British citizens who have certain rights. Now the king must decide to punish the rebellious colonists or listen to their complaints.

What advice would you give the king?

Consider why to SUPPORT harsher laws:
- to maintain order and control
- to show the cost of disobedience
- to show strength and that the king will not back down

Consider why to OPPOSE harsher laws:
- might violate the colonists' rights
- might only further anger the colonists and worsen the situation
- might lead to rebellion or violence

Review Answers: d, c, a, e, b

Academic Vocabulary

Review with students the high-use academic term in this section.

reaction response (p. 114)

CRF: Vocabulary Builder Activity, Section 1

Taking Notes

Have students copy the graphic organizer onto their own paper and then use it to take notes on the section. This activity will prepare students for the Section Assessment, in which they will complete a graphic organizer that builds on the information using a critical-thinking skill.

Section Correlations

IN

8.1.4 Identify fundamental ideas in the Declaration of Independence (1776) and analyze the causes and effects of the Revolutionary War (1775–1783), including enactment of the Articles of Confederation and the Treaty of Paris. **8.1.9** Describe the influence of important individuals on social and political developments of the time such as the Independence movement and the framing of the Constitution.

SECTION 1

The Revolution Begins

What You Will Learn...

Main Ideas

1. The First Continental Congress demanded certain rights from Great Britain.
2. Armed conflict between British soldiers and colonists broke out with the "shot heard 'round the world."
3. The Second Continental Congress created the Continental Army to fight the British.
4. In two early battles, the army lost control of Boston but then regained it.

The Big Idea

The tensions between the colonies and Great Britain led to armed conflict in 1775.

Key Terms and People

First Continental Congress, *p. 112*
Patriots, *p. 113*
minutemen, *p. 114*
Redcoats, *p. 114*
Second Continental Congress, *p. 114*
Continental Army, *p. 114*
George Washington, *p. 114*
Battle of Bunker Hill, *p. 115*

TAKING NOTES As you read, take notes on the events that occurred in the early days of the American Revolution. Write your notes in a graphic organizer like the one below.

First Continental Congress	Battles	Second Continental Congress

IN 8.1.3, 8.1.4, 8.1.9

If YOU were there...

You are a member of the British Parliament in the 1770s. Some members say that the Americans are defying the king. Others point out that the colonists are British citizens who have certain rights. Now the king must decide to punish the rebellious colonists or listen to their complaints.

What advice would you give the king?

BUILDING BACKGROUND Taxes and harsh new laws led some colonists to protest against the British. In some places, the protests turned violent. The British government refused to listen, ignoring the colonists' demands for more rights. That set the stage for war.

First Continental Congress

To many colonists the closing of Boston Harbor was the final insult in a long list of abuses. In response to the mounting crisis, all the colonies except Georgia sent representatives to a meeting in October 1774. This meeting, known as the **First Continental Congress**, was a gathering of colonial leaders who were deeply troubled about the relationship between Great Britain and its colonies in America. At Carpenters' Hall in Philadelphia, the leaders remained locked in weeks of intense debate. Patrick Henry and others believed that violence was unavoidable. On the other hand, delegates from Pennsylvania and New York had strict orders to seek peace.

Wisely, the delegates compromised. They encouraged colonists to continue boycotting British goods but told colonial militias to prepare for war. Meanwhile, they drafted the Declaration of Rights, a list of 10 resolutions to be presented to King George III. Included was the colonists' right to "life, liberty, and property."

The First Continental Congress did not seek a separation from Britain. Its goal was to state the colonists' concerns and ask the king to correct the problems. But before they left Philadelphia, the delegates agreed to meet in 1775 if the king refused their petition.

Patrick Henry returned from the Congress and reported to his fellow Virginians. To encourage them to support the Patriot cause,

Teach the Big Idea

At Level

The Revolution Begins

1. **Teach** To teach the main ideas in the section, use the questions in the Direct Teach boxes.
2. **Apply** Create a two-column chart for the students to see. Label the columns *British Action* and *American Reaction.* Have students copy the chart and list the British actions—and next to each one, the resulting American reactions—that led to the outbreak of the American Revolution. **LS Verbal/Linguistic**
3. **Review** As you review the section, have students share information from their charts. Use it to complete the master chart you created.
4. **Practice/Homework** Have students choose one of the American reactions and either write a letter to the editor or create a political cartoon in support of the action. **LS Visual/Spatial**

Alternative Assessment Handbook, Rubrics 7: Charts; 27: Political Cartoons; and 43: Writing to Persuade

Battle of Lexington

The Battle of Lexington was the first battle of the Revolutionary War. The map shows the route that Paul Revere used to warn the minutemen of Lexington. He was captured before he could get to Concord. The photo below shows one of the actual candle lanterns used to signal Revere.

Paul Revere's Ride

Henry voiced these famous words:

> "They tell us, Sir, that we are weak; unable to cope with so formidable an adversary. But when will we be stronger? Gentlemen may cry, Peace, Peace—but there is no peace. I know not what course others may take; but as for me, give me liberty or give me death."
>
> —Patrick Henry, quoted in *Eyewitnesses and Others*

In time many colonists came to agree with Henry. They became known as **Patriots**—colonists who chose to fight for independence from Great Britain.

READING CHECK **Identifying Cause and Effect** Why did the delegates attend the First Continental Congress? What were the results?

"Shot Heard 'round the World"

The Continental Congress planned to meet again in 1775. Before it could, the situation in the colonies had changed—for the worse.

The Ride of Paul Revere

British military leaders in the colonies grew uneasy when local militias seemed to be preparing for action. The governor of Massachusetts, Thomas Gage, learned that a stockpile of weapons was stored in Concord, about 20 miles from Boston. In April 1775 he decided to seize the supplies.

Critical Thinking: Identifying Points of View

At Level

Interview with Patrick Henry

1. Discuss with students Patrick Henry's role in the First Continental Congress and his belief that violence was unavoidable.
2. Ask a volunteer to read aloud the quote from Patrick Henry on this page. Have students discuss the quote. Why does Henry think "there is no peace"? Ask students if they agree with his view. What does he mean by "give me liberty or give me death"?
3. Next, ask students to imagine that they are news reporters interviewing Patrick Henry. Have students work in pairs to write three to five questions to ask Henry about the events in this section. Each pair should then write the answers it thinks Henry would have given, based on the text.
4. Have volunteer pairs act out their mock interviews for the class. **LS Verbal/Linguistic**

Alternative Assessment Handbook, Rubric 37: Writing Assignments

CRF: Primary Source Activity: Patrick Henry: The Voice of Freedom

Direct Teach

Main Idea

1 First Continental Congress

The First Continental Congress demanded certain rights from Great Britain.

Describe How did the actions of the First Continental Congress reflect the intense debate of the delegates? *Some delegates believed violence was unavoidable; others had orders to seek peace. Delegates compromised by encouraging colonists to prepare for war, at the same time they drafted the Declaration of Rights.*

Draw Conclusions Why did the First Continental Congress alert the colonial militias to prepare for war? *possible answers—to be prepared in case efforts to resolve problems with Great Britain failed; because relations with Great Britain were deteriorating*

CRF: Primary Source Activity: Patrick Henry: The Voice of Freedom

Main Idea

2 "Shot Heard 'round the World"

Armed conflict between British soldiers and colonists broke out with the "shot heard 'round the world."

Explain Why did a British force march on Concord? *to confiscate colonial militia weapons*

Summarize How did the colonists react to the British advance? *They spread the word and used drums and church bells to call minutemen to prepare to meet the British soldiers.*

CRF: History and Geography Activity: Early Battles around Boston

Map Transparency 19: Paul Revere's Ride

Answers

Reading Check *Delegates sought to voice their concerns to the king about the crisis in the colonies; Declaration of Rights was drafted.*

Direct Teach

Main Idea

❷ "Shot Heard 'round the World"

Armed conflict between British soldiers and colonists broke out with the "shot heard 'round the world."

Identify Cause and Effect How did the minutemen respond to the battle at Lexington? *continued to attack British troops in Concord and as they retreated to Boston*

Evaluate In your opinion, which side won the fighting at Lexington and Concord, and why? *possible answer—minutemen, because the British were forced to retreat*

Did you know . . .

After the battles at Lexington and Concord, some 10,000 colonial civilians moved out of Boston as the town became a base for British troops. By July 1775, some 13,500 British troops occupied the city.

Answers

Reading Check (top) *to cover more ground to ensure the message would still get out even if one were detained*

Reading Check (bottom) *formed the Continental Army and attempted to restore harmony with the Olive Branch Petition*

Gage thought he had kept his plan a secret. However, Boston was full of spies for the Patriot cause. They noticed the British were preparing for action and quickly informed the Patriots. Unsure of how the British would strike, Sons of Liberty member Paul Revere enlisted the aid of Robert Newman. Newman was to climb into the steeple of the Old North Church and watch for British soldiers. If they advanced across land, Newman would display one lantern from the steeple. If they rowed across the Charles River, Newman would display two lanterns.

When Revere and fellow Patriot William Dawes saw two lights shine, they set off on horseback. Using two different routes out of Boston, they sounded the alert. As the riders advanced, drums and church bells called out the local militia, or **minutemen**—who got their name because they were ready to fight at a minute's notice.

Battles at Lexington and Concord

At dawn on April 19, the British troops arrived at the town of Lexington, near Concord, where 70 armed minutemen waited. Patriot captain John Parker yelled to his troops, "Don't fire unless fired upon." Suddenly a shot rang out. To this day, no one knows who fired this "shot heard 'round the world."

The battle at Lexington ended in minutes with only a few volleys fired. When the smoke cleared, 8 of the badly outnumbered minutemen lay dead, and 10 were wounded. The British, with only one soldier wounded, marched on to Concord.

Although Revere had been arrested, the citizens of Concord were warned by another rider, Samuel Prescott. Most of the weapons in Concord had already been hidden, but the few that were left were now concealed. Some of the British troops, frustrated because the stockpile had disappeared, set fire to a few buildings. In reaction the minutemen charged forward.

ACADEMIC VOCABULARY
reaction response

For the skilled colonial marksmen of Concord, the British soldiers made an easy target. They were wearing the British military uniform with its bright red jacket. For some time the colonists had called the British soldiers **Redcoats** because of these jackets. The British were forced to retreat to Boston, suffering many casualties along the way.

READING CHECK **Drawing Inferences** Why did the Patriots need several riders? Why did they take different routes?

Second Continental Congress

King George III had refused to address the concerns listed in the Declaration of Rights. In May 1775, delegates from 12 colonies met again in Philadelphia for the **Second Continental Congress**. This second group of delegates from the colonies was still far from unified, but represented the first attempt at a Republican government in the colonies.

Some of the delegates called for a war, others for peace. Once again they compromised. Although the Congress did not openly revolt, delegates showed their growing dissatisfaction. They sent word to colonial authorities asking for new state constitutions. States set up conventions to write them. They also authorized the Massachusetts militia to become the **Continental Army**. This force would soon include soldiers from all colonies and would carry out the fight against Britain. Congress named a Virginian, **George Washington**, to command the army.

As Washington prepared for war, the Congress pursued peace. On July 5 the delegates signed the Olive Branch Petition as a final attempt to restore harmony. King George refused to read it. Instead, he looked for new ways to punish the colonies.

READING CHECK **Summarizing** What did the Second Continental Congress accomplish?

Differentiating Instruction

Below Level

Struggling Readers

1. Copy the graphic organizer for students to see. Omit the blue sample answers.
2. Have students copy the concept web and complete it by entering key people, dates, and events associated with Lexington and Concord.
3. Then discuss how the outbreak of fighting affected colonial relations with Great Britain. **LS Visual/Spatial**

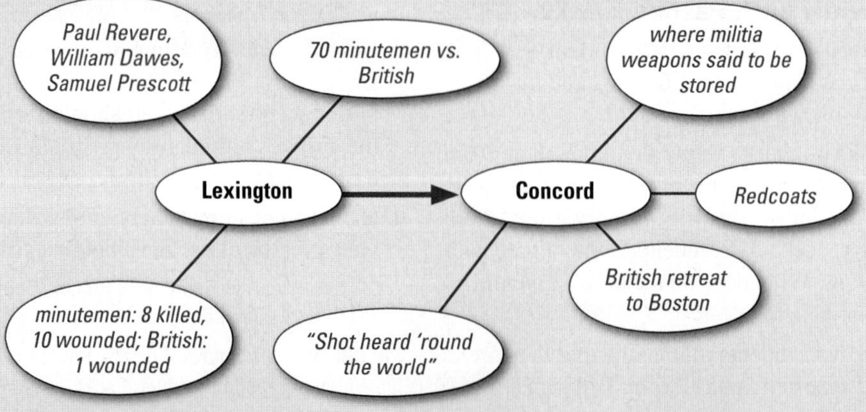

Early Battles

While the Congress discussed peace, the Massachusetts militia began to fight. Boston was a key city in the early days of the war. Both Patriots and the British fought to hold it.

Bunker Hill

Desperate for supplies, leaders in Boston sent Benedict Arnold and a force of 400 men to New York State. Their objective was to attack the British at Fort Ticonderoga. In May 1775, Arnold captured the fort and its large supply of weapons.

Meanwhile, the poorly supplied Patriots kept the British pinned down inside Boston. Although British leaders were trying to form a battle plan, they awoke on June 17 to a stunning sight. The colonial forces had quietly dug in at Breed's Hill, a point overlooking north Boston. The Redcoats would have to cross Boston Harbor and fight their way uphill.

As the British force of 2,400 advanced, 1,600 militia members waited. Low on gunpowder, the commander ordered his troops not to fire "until you see the whites of their eyes." As they climbed the exposed hillside with their heavy packs, the British soldiers were cut down. Twice they retreated. Stepping over the dead and wounded, they returned for a third try. The colonists were now out of ammunition, and eventually they had to retreat.

This famous conflict is now known as the **Battle of Bunker Hill**, although it was actually launched from Breed's Hill. While the Patriots lost, they proved they could take on the Redcoats. For the British, the battle was a tragic victory. To win, they had sacrificed about double the number of Patriot soldiers.

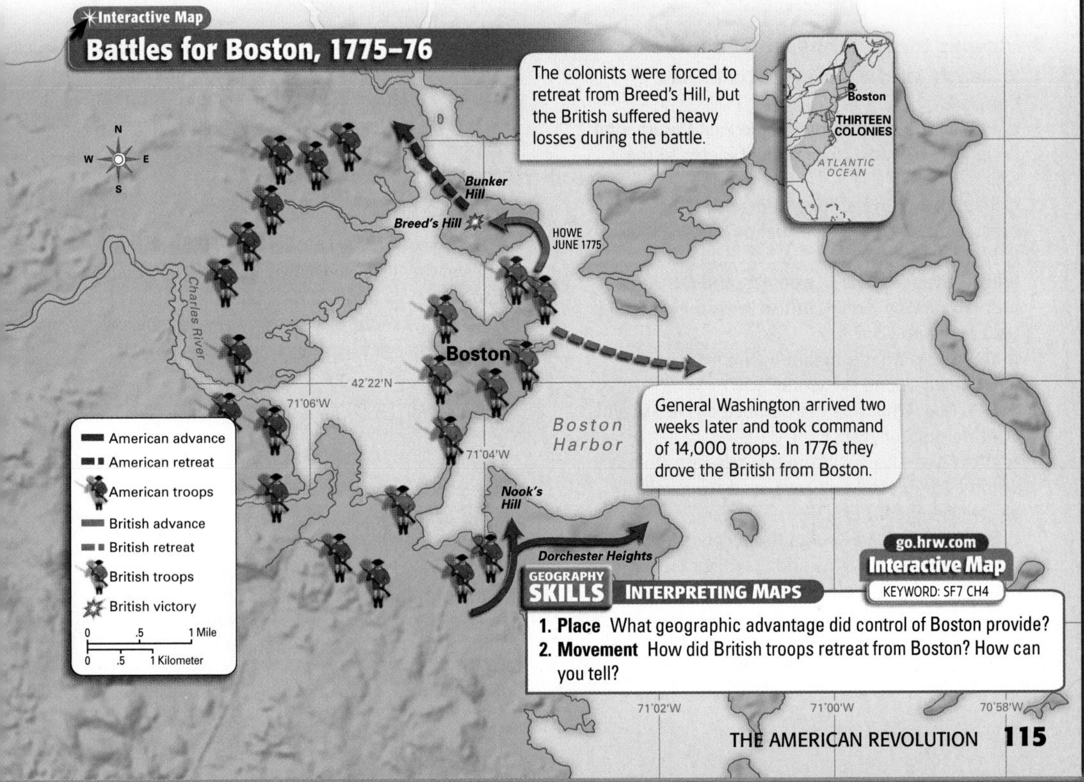

GEOGRAPHY SKILLS INTERPRETING MAPS

1. **Place** What geographic advantage did control of Boston provide?
2. **Movement** How did British troops retreat from Boston? How can you tell?

Direct Teach

Main Idea

3 Second Continental Congress

The Second Continental Congress created the Continental Army to fight the British.

Identify Who was appointed leader of the Continental Army? *George Washington*

Make Judgments Do you think the Second Continental Congress was wise in having Washington prepare for war as it sought peace? Explain your answer. *possible answer—Yes, the colonists needed to be prepared in case Britain attacked or did not accept the Olive Branch Petition.*

Main Idea

4 Early Battles

In two early battles, the army lost control of Boston but then regained it.

Describe Why was the Battle of Bunker Hill considered a tragic victory for the British? *The British suffered heavy losses during the battle.*

Make Inferences Why do you think retaking Boston was important to the Patriots? *Boston was a key city with a harbor, and it was the birthplace of the revolution.*

Map Transparency 20: Battles for Boston, 1775–76

Interactive Map: Battles for Boston, 1775–76

Collaborative Learning

At Level

Continental Congress Newspapers

1. Organize students into small groups. Have half of the groups design the front page of a colonial newspaper that focuses on the actions taken by the First Continental Congress. Have the other half do the same for the Second Continental Congress.
2. Each student should write one headline and the first paragraph of the corresponding article. Tell students to elaborate on the main actions taken by each congress by focusing on the causes and effects.
3. When students have finished, have them design their front page so that the article the group feels is most important is at the top and the least important one is at the bottom.
4. Have each group share its front page with the class. When finished, hold a brief discussion on why groups chose to place their articles in the order they did. **LS Interpersonal, Verbal/Linguistic**

Alternative Assessment Handbook, Rubrics 14: Group Activity; and 23: Newspapers

Answers

Interpreting Maps 1. *Control of Boston meant control of the harbor.*
2. *by ship; because the red dashed line shows they went by sea*

Direct Teach

Connect to Economics

Funding the Revolution When the Second Continental Congress raised the Continental Army, it was reluctant to impose a new tax on the already tax-weary colonists. Thus, the Second Continental Congress printed and issued a new national currency. It was expected that individual colonies would eventually collect an equivalent amount in taxes. Because Congress had no authority to force the colonies to tax their residents, however, its demands went largely ignored. This created a significant national debt. To raise money, Congress then borrowed money from France, sold government bonds, and issued soldiers IOUs in lieu of pay.

Review & Assess

Close

Have students review the section by discussing whether they think war was inevitable or could have been avoided if the colonists had acted differently.

Review

Online Quiz, Section 4.1

Assess

SE Section 1 Assessment

PASS: Section 4.1 Quiz

Alternative Assessment Handbook

Reteach/Classroom Intervention

Interactive Reader and Study Guide, Section 4.1

Interactive Skills Tutor CD-ROM

Dorchester Heights

Shortly after the Battle of Bunker Hill, General Washington arrived in Boston to command the Continental Army. Washington knew that he would need heavier guns to drive the British out of Boston, and he knew where to get them—Fort Ticonderoga. Colonel Henry Knox was assigned to transport the captured cannons from Fort Ticonderoga to Boston. He successfully brought the heavy guns over 300 miles of rough terrain in the middle of winter. When Knox delivered the cannons, Washington was ready to regain control of Boston.

On March 4, 1776, Washington moved his army to Dorchester Heights, an area that overlooked Boston from the south. He stationed the cannons and his troops on Nook's Hill overlooking British general William Howe's position. When Howe awoke the next morning and saw the Patriots' well-positioned artillery, he knew he would have to retreat. "The Rebels have done more in one night than my whole army could do in months," Howe declared. On March 7 Howe retreated from Boston to Canada. The birthplace of the rebellion was now in Patriot hands.

READING CHECK **Drawing Inferences** Why was the geography of the Boston area important in forming a battle plan?

SUMMARY AND PREVIEW Some colonial leaders became convinced that they could not avoid war with Great Britain. In the next section you will read about another step toward war—the writing of the Declaration of Independence.

Section 1 Assessment

go.hrw.com
Online Quiz
KEYWORD: SF7 HP4

Reviewing Ideas, Terms, and People

1. a. **Identify** What was the **First Continental Congress**?
   b. **Make Inferences** Why did the First Continental Congress send the Declaration of Rights to the king?
   c. **Elaborate** Why did King George III refuse to consider the colonists' declaration?
2. a. **Identify** Who warned the colonists of the British advance toward Lexington and Concord?
   b. **Analyze** Why did the British army march on Lexington and Concord?
   c. **Elaborate** What is meant by the expression "shot heard 'round the world"?
3. a. **Describe** What was the purpose of the **Second Continental Congress**?
   b. **Draw Conclusions** Were the delegates to the Second Continental Congress ready to revolt against George III? Explain.
   c. **Evaluate** Defend George III's response to the Declaration of Rights and the Olive Branch Petition.
4. a. **Identify** What leader captured Fort Ticonderoga?
   b. **Draw Conclusions** How was the **Continental Army** able to drive British forces out of Boston?
   c. **Evaluate** How would you evaluate the performance of the Continental Army in the early battles of the war? Explain.

Critical Thinking

5. **Categorizing** Review your notes on the early battles of the Revolution. Then copy the graphic organizer below and use it to categorize events in the early days of the Revolution. Some events will be attempts at peace; others will be movement toward war.

Attempts at Peace	Movement toward War

FOCUS ON SPEAKING

6. **Thinking about the Beginning** You'll have about five minutes for your report and only a minute or two to talk about the beginning of the war. What are the one or two most important things you want to say?

Section 1 Assessment Answers

1. a. a gathering of colonial leaders
   b. to tell him what colonists wanted
   c. possible answer—angry, did not think they had a right to protest
2. a. Revere, Dawes, Prescott
   b. to seize militia weapons stored in Concord
   c. possible answer—The first shot of the Revolution impacted the world.
3. a. created a Continental Army for defense while pursuing peace with Great Britain
   b. See answer to Question 3a.
   c. possible answer—George III was trying to do what he thought was the best for Britain.
4. a. Benedict Arnold
   b. placed cannons overlooking Boston
   c. possible answer—did well for its size and experience, drove the British from Boston
5. Peace—Declaration of Rights, ask king to address problems, Olive Branch Petition; War—militias, boycott goods, create army
6. Despite colonial attempts at peace, fighting broke out.

Answers

Reading Check *possible answer—The city is located on a penninsula making it easy to cut off from the mainland. Knowing this and other geographic features of the area made it possible to design and implement effective military strategy*

George Washington

What would you do if you were asked to lead a new country?

When did he live? 1732–1799

Where did he live? George Washington was a true American, born in the Virginia colony. As president, he lived in New York City and Philadelphia, the nation's first two capitals. When he retired, he returned to his plantation at Mount Vernon.

What did he do? Although Washington was a wealthy farmer, he spent most of his life in the military and in politics. Leading the colonial forces to victory in the Revolutionary War, he then helped shape the new government of the United States. On April 30, 1789, he was sworn in as the first president of the United States.

Why is he so important? George Washington inspired Americans and helped to unite them. One of his great accomplishments as president was to keep the peace with Britain and France. Upon leaving the presidency, he urged Americans to avoid becoming politically divided.

Drawing Conclusions How might Washington's leadership in the Revolutionary War have prepared him for his role as president?

Mount Vernon was Washington's plantation.

KEY EVENTS

- **1775** Serves in Second Continental Congress; selected commander of the Continental Army
- **1789** Inaugurated as president
- **1793** Begins second term as president
- **1796** Publishes his Farewell Address and retires to his plantation at Mount Vernon
- **1799** Dies at Mount Vernon; his will frees his slaves

Biography

Reading Focus Question

Discuss the introductory question. Consider not only the benefits of leadership but also the challenges and disadvantages, such as being attacked in the press. Keep your answers in mind as you read the biography.

Info to Know

Washington's Early Life George Washington spent most of his early childhood on a farm near Fredericksburg, Virginia. He received irregular schooling, first with a local church leader and later with a schoolmaster. His main education came not from books but from hands-on training in outdoor occupations. He mastered tobacco growing and raising livestock, and early in his teens became familiar with surveying.

Linking to Today

Washington's Legacy George Washington may have lived more than 200 years ago, but his legacy remains apparent. He appears on both the U.S. quarter and $1 bill. He is enshrined at the Washington Monument in Washington, D.C. His image is carved in the national memorial at Mount Rushmore, South Dakota, along with those of Thomas Jefferson, Abraham Lincoln, and Theodore Roosevelt. In addition, numerous places, naval ships, and public schools have been named in Washington's honor.

Collaborative Learning

At Level

Washington Time Capsule

1. Present the following scenario: A caretaker at Mount Vernon has discovered a time capsule that George Washington buried on the grounds. Inside were 10 items and a letter from Washington. In the letter, he explains that the items symbolize the major achievements and events in his life. What are the 10 items in the time capsule?
2. Organize students into small groups. Tell each group to list the major achievements and events in Washington's life. Students should then select 10 items to represent these achievements and events. Last, each group should write Washington's letter, listing the 10 items and explaining why each was included.
3. Have each group share some of the items it listed with the class. Then lead students in a brief discussion of Washington's significance in the United States. **LS Interpersonal, Verbal/Linguistic**

Alternative Assessment Handbook, Rubric 14: Group Activity

Answers

Drawing Conclusions *He gained experience as an executive—managing resources, dealing with crises and challenges, overcoming obstacles, making decisions, and working with a diverse group of people under trying circumstances.*

Preteach

Bellringer

If YOU were there. . . Use the **Daily Bellringer Transparency** for this section to help students answer the question.

Daily Bellringer Transparency 4.2

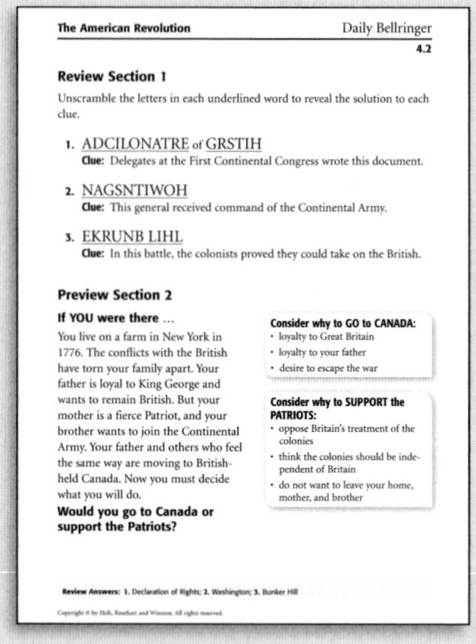
The American Revolution — Daily Bellringer 4.2

Review Section 1

Unscramble the letters in each underlined word to reveal the solution to each clue.

1. ADCILONATRE of GRSTIH
   Clue: Delegates at the First Continental Congress wrote this document.
2. NAGSNTIWOH
   Clue: This general received command of the Continental Army.
3. EKRUNB LIHL
   Clue: In this battle, the colonists proved they could take on the British.

Preview Section 2

If YOU were there …

You live on a farm in New York in 1776. The conflicts with the British have torn your family apart. Your father is loyal to King George and wants to remain British. But your mother is a fierce Patriot, and your brother wants to join the Continental Army. Your father and others who feel the same way are moving to British-held Canada. Now you must decide what you will do.

Would you go to Canada or support the Patriots?

Consider why to GO to CANADA:
- loyalty to Great Britain
- loyalty to your father
- desire to escape the war

Consider why to SUPPORT the PATRIOTS:
- oppose Britain's treatment of the colonies
- think the colonies should be independent of Britain
- do not want to leave your home, mother, and brother

Review Answers: 1. Declaration of Rights; 2. Washington; 3. Bunker Hill

Building Vocabulary

Preteach or review the following terms:

anonymously without giving a name (p. 118)

Enlightenment movement during the 1700s that emphasized the use of reason and logic to improve society (p. 119)

ideal guiding standard or principle (p. 119)

social contract agreement between the people and the government (p. 119)

tyranny abuse of government power (p. 118)

unalienable impossible to take away (p. 119)

CRF: Vocabulary Builder Activity, Section 2

Taking Notes

Have students copy the graphic organizer onto their own paper and then use it to take notes on the section. This activity will prepare students for the Section Assessment, in which they will complete a graphic organizer that builds on the information using a critical-thinking skill.

Section Correlations

IN

8.1.30 Formulate historical questions by analyzing primary sources and secondary sources about an issue confronting the United States during the period from 1754–1877.

SECTION 2

Declaring Independence

What You Will Learn...

Main Ideas

1. Thomas Paine's *Common Sense* led many colonists to support independence.
2. Colonists had to choose sides when independence was declared.
3. The Declaration of Independence did not address the rights of all colonists.

The Big Idea

The colonies formally declared their independence from Great Britain.

Key Terms and People

Common Sense, *p. 118*
Thomas Paine, *p. 118*
Declaration of Independence, *p. 119*
Thomas Jefferson, *p. 119*
Loyalists, *p. 119*

TAKING NOTES As you read, take notes on the Declaration of Independence. Write your notes in a graphic organizer like the one below.

Influence of *Common Sense* on Declaration	Main Ideas of Declaration	People Not Included

IN **8.1.1, 8.1.3, 8.1.4, 8.1.9, 8.1.28, 8.1.29, 8.1.30, 8.2.1**

118 CHAPTER 4

If YOU were there...

You live on a farm in New York in 1776. The conflicts with the British have torn your family apart. Your father is loyal to King George and wants to remain British. But your mother is a fierce Patriot, and your brother wants to join the Continental Army. Your father and others who feel the same way are moving to British-held Canada. Now you must decide what you will do.

Would you go to Canada or support the Patriots?

BUILDING BACKGROUND The outbreak of violence at Lexington, Concord, and Boston took some colonists by surprise. Many, like the father above, opposed independence from Britain. Those who supported freedom began to promote their cause in many ways.

Paine's *Common Sense*

"[There] is something very absurd in supporting a continent to be perpetually [forever] governed by an island." This plainspoken argument against British rule over America appeared in ***Common Sense***, a 47-page pamphlet that was distributed in Philadelphia in January 1776. *Common Sense* was published anonymously—that is, without the author's name. The author, **Thomas Paine**, argued that citizens, not kings and queens, should make laws. At a time when monarchs ruled much of the world, this was a bold idea.

News of the work spread throughout the colonies, eventually selling some 500,000 copies. Paine reached a wide audience by writing as a common person speaking to common people. *Common Sense* changed the way many colonists viewed their king. It made a strong case for economic freedom and for the right to military self-defense. It cried out against tyranny—that is, the abuse of government power. Thomas Paine's words rang out in his time, and they have echoed throughout American history.

READING CHECK **Supporting a Point of View** Would you have agreed with Thomas Paine? Explain.

Teach the Big Idea

At Level

Declaring Independence

Materials: heavy paper or poster board, colored markers

1. **Teach** To teach the main ideas in the section, use the questions in the Direct Teach boxes.
2. **Apply** Have students create their own versions of the Declaration of Independence. Give each student heavy paper and colored markers. Instead of copying the text of the Declaration, have students write the main ideas stated in the document. Encourage students to illustrate the ideas.
3. **Review** As you review the section, ask for volunteers to explain the main ideas and ideals expressed in the Declaration.
4. **Practice/Homework** Have each student create a political cartoon that illustrates some of the reactions to the Declaration of Independence and its failure to recognize the rights of women and enslaved African Americans. **LS Verbal/Linguistic**

Alternative Assessment Handbook, Rubrics 27: Political Cartoons; and 37: Writing Assignments

Independence Is Declared

Many colonial leaders agreed with Paine. In June 1776 the Second Continental Congress formed a committee to write a document declaring the colonies' independence. A committee also created a seal for the new country with the Latin motto *"E pluribus unum"* or "out of many, one." This motto recognized the new union of states.

A New Philosophy of Government

The **Declaration of Independence** formally announced the colonies' break from Great Britain. In doing so, it expressed three main ideas. First, **Thomas Jefferson**, the document's main author, argued that all people possess unalienable rights, including the rights of "life, liberty, and the pursuit of happiness."

Next, Jefferson asserted that King George III had violated the colonists' rights by taxing them without their consent. Jefferson accused the king of passing unfair laws and interfering with colonial governments. He also believed that stationing a large British army within the colonies was a burden.

Third, Jefferson stated that the colonies had the right to break from Britain. Influenced by the Enlightenment ideal of the social contract, he maintained that governments and rulers must protect the rights of citizens. In exchange, the people agree to be governed. Jefferson argued that King George III had broken the social contract.

On July 4, 1776, the Continental Congress approved the Declaration of Independence. This act broke all ties to the British crown. The United States of America was born.

Choosing Sides

The signing of the Declaration made the rebellion a full-scale revolt against Britain. Those who supported it would be considered traitors. Colonists who chose to side with the British were known as **Loyalists**—often called Tories.

FOCUS ON INDIANA

Throughout the colonies, conventions of delegates met to reorganize their governments. In 1776, Virginia delegates issued the Virginia Declaration of Rights, which stated that people had the right to rebel against inadequate government. Parts of the text are still a part of Virginia's state constitution today.

THE IMPACT TODAY

The Continental Congress voted for independence on July 2. However, because the Declaration was not approved until July 4, the fourth is celebrated today as Independence Day.

Primary Source

POINTS OF VIEW

Choosing Sides

When Ben Franklin's son William was a child, he helped his father experiment with lightning. But by the time William had grown and the Revolution started, the two men viewed the conflict differently. They exchanged letters on the subject.

"I am indeed of the opinion, that the parliament has no right to make any law whatever, binding on the colonies . . . I know your sentiments differ from mine on these subjects. You are a thorough government man, which I do not wonder at, nor do I aim at converting you. I only wish you to act uprightly and steadily."

–Benjamin Franklin,
quoted in *The Writings of Benjamin Franklin Vol. III*

"I think that all laws until they are repealed ought to be obeyed and that it is the duty of those who are entrusted with the executive part of government to see that they are so."

–William Franklin,
quoted in *Benjamin and William Franklin* by Sheila L. Skemp

ANALYSIS SKILL ANALYZING PRIMARY SOURCES

How did the two men view the British government differently?

Direct Teach

Main Idea

1 Paine's *Common Sense*

Thomas Paine's *Common Sense* led many colonists to support independence.

Explain What argument did Thomas Paine present in *Common Sense*? *Citizens should make the laws.*

Finding Main Ideas What was the significance of *Common Sense*? *Paine's work reached a wide audience and changed the way many colonists viewed the king.*

Main Idea

2 Independence Is Declared

Colonists had to choose sides when independence was declared.

Identify Who were the members of the committee that was to write a document declaring the colonies' independence? *John Adams, Benjamin Franklin, Thomas Jefferson, Robert R. Livingston, and Roger Sherman*

go.hrw.com
Online Resources
KEYWORD: SF7 CH4
ACTIVITY: Patriots and Loyalists

Focus on Indiana

8.2.1 Identify and explain essential ideas of constitutional government, which are expressed in the founding documents of the United States, including...the 1787 U.S. Constitution...

Make Generalizations How did the Virginia Declaration of Rights reflect revolutionary ideas? *It stated that people had the right to rebel.*

Collaborative Learning

Below Level

Common Sense Handbill

1. Discuss with students how Thomas Paine's *Common Sense* influenced many colonists to support independence from Great Britain.
2. Organize students into pairs and ask them to imagine that they are colonists who were influenced by *Common Sense*. Have each pair create a handbill advertising *Common Sense* and supporting Thomas Paine's ideas. Suggest to students that they address the following ideas: breaking away from Great Britain, the unfairness of the system of monarchy, and the idea that people and not rulers should make the laws.
3. After students have finished, have them share their ads and discuss if Paine's ideas have influenced them. **LS Visual/Spatial, Interpersonal**

Alternative Assessment Handbook, Rubrics 2: Advertisements; and 14: Group Activity

Answers

Reading Check (p. 118) *possible answers—yes, because the king had abused his power and citizens should have the right to self-rule; no, because the monarchy was a good system even if people felt their rights were limited*

Analyzing Primary Sources *William Franklin felt that all laws should be obeyed; Benjamin Franklin felt that the parliament did not have the right to make laws concerning the colonies.*

• Direct Teach •

Main Idea

❷ Independence Is Declared

Colonists had to choose sides when independence was declared.

Recall What was the significance of the Declaration of Independence? *It formally broke all ties between the colonies and Great Britain and created the United States of America.*

Summarize What were the three main arguments in the Declaration of Independence? *All men possess the unalienable rights of "life, liberty, and the pursuit of happiness"; the king had violated colonists' rights by passing unfair laws; the king had broken the social contract with the colonists.*

Make Judgments How would you have reacted if you were a Patriot and your friend was a Loyalist? *Answers should indicate an understanding that differing views over independence divided the colonists.*

CRF: Biography Activity: John Hancock

Info to Know

Reactions to the Declaration of Independence The language of the Declaration of Independence received both criticism and praise throughout the colonies. Some colonial newspapers pointed out the irony of such statements as "all men are created equal" in a slaveholding nation. One newspaper in South Carolina noted that as a clergyman read the Declaration of Independence aloud, a slave held a parasol over the clergyman's head and fanned his face.

Signing the Declaration of Independence

Historians estimate that 40 to 45 percent of Americans were Patriots, while 20 to 30 percent were Loyalists. The rest were neutral.

Because of persecution by Patriots, more than 50,000 Loyalists fled the colonies during the Revolution. Most went to Canada, where Britain allowed them more self-rule after the Revolution. In doing so, they abandoned their homes and property. Divided allegiances tore apart families and friendships—even Benjamin Franklin became separated from his Loyalist son William.

Native Americans were at first encouraged by both sides to remain neutral. By the summer of 1776, however, both Patriots and the British were aggressively recruiting Indian fighters. Most sided with the British. In northern New York, four of the six Iroquois nations fought for the British. However, the Oneida and Tuscarora helped the Patriots, even delivering food to the soldiers at Valley Forge.

READING CHECK **Drawing Conclusions** Why would Native Americans have lost out no matter who won the war?

Unfinished Business

Today we recognize that the Declaration of Independence excluded many colonists. While it declared that "all men are created equal," the document failed to mention women, enslaved Africans, or Native Americans. The rights of these minorities would be subject to the rule of the majority.

Women

Although many women were Patriots, the Declaration did not address their rights. At least one delegate's wife, Abigail Adams, tried to influence her husband, John, to include women's rights in the Declaration. In a failed effort, she expressed her concerns:

> "Remember the Ladies, and be more generous and favorable to them than your ancestors. Do not put such unlimited power into the hands of the Husbands . . . If particular care and attention is not paid to the Ladies we are and will not hold ourselves bound by Laws in which we have no voice, or Representation."
>
> —Abigail Adams, quoted in *Notable American Women*

Critical Thinking: Identifying Points of View — At Level

Letters to the Editor

1. Ask students to imagine that they live in the colonies and have just heard that the Second Continental Congress has approved the Declaration of Independence.
2. Have students write a letter to the editor of a colonial newspaper explaining how they feel about the actions of the congress.
3. Suggest that students write their letters from the perspective of someone living in the colonies such as a Loyalist, Patriot, member of militia, or British officer. Make sure that students explain why they support or do not support the actions of the Second Continental Congress.
4. Ask for volunteers to read their letters to the class. **LS Verbal/Linguistic**

Alternative Assessment Handbook, Rubric 17: Letters to Editors

Answers

Reading Check *possible answer—The British and the United States would have disregarded the rights of Native Americans when the colonies, or states, began growing larger.*

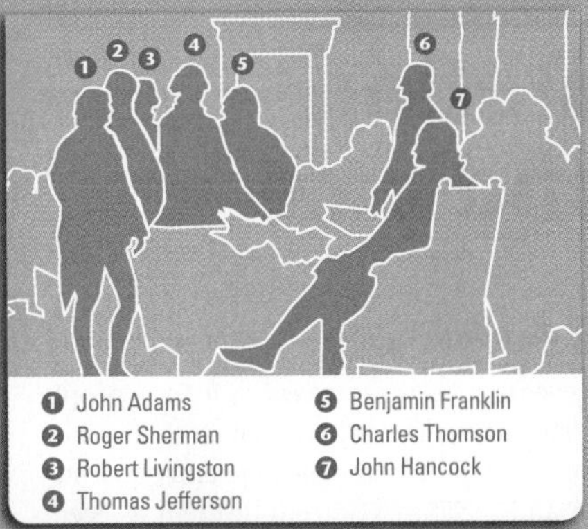

The Declaration of Independence was adopted on July 4, 1776. This painting shows 47 of the 56 signers of the document. The man sitting on the right is John Hancock, who was the president of the Second Continental Congress. He is accepting the Declaration from the committee that wrote it.

How realistic do you think this painting is?

African and Native Americans

The Declaration did not recognize the rights of enslaved Africans, either. The authors had compared life under British rule to living as an enslaved people. The obvious question arose: Why did any form of slavery exist in a land that valued personal freedom? Even Thomas Jefferson, the main author of the Declaration, was a slaveholder.

In July 1776 slavery was legal in all the colonies. By the 1780s the New England colonies were taking steps to end slavery. Even so, the conflict over slavery continued long after the Revolutionary War.

The Declaration of Independence also did not address the rights of Native Americans to life, liberty, or property. Despite the Proclamation of 1763, American colonists had been quietly settling on lands that belonged to Native Americans. This tendency to disregard the rights of Native Americans would develop into a pattern after the colonists won their independence from Great Britain.

READING CHECK **Finding Main Ideas** What groups were unrepresented in the Declaration of Independence?

SUMMARY AND PREVIEW In 1776 the colonists declared their independence. To achieve their goal, however, they would have to win a war against the British army. In the next section you will learn about some of the battles of the Revolutionary War. For a time, it seemed as if the British would defeat the colonists.

Section 2 Assessment

go.hrw.com
Online Quiz
KEYWORD: SF7 HP4

Reviewing Ideas, Terms, and People

1. a. Identify Who was **Thomas Paine**?
b. Make Inferences Why do you think Thomas Paine originally published ***Common Sense*** anonymously?
c. Elaborate Do you think that most colonists would have supported independence from Britain without Thomas Paine's publication of *Common Sense*? Explain.

2. a. Identify What two sides emerged in response to the **Declaration of Independence**? What did each side favor?
b. Explain What arguments did the authors of the Declaration of Independence give for declaring the colonies free from British control?
c. Predict How might some groups use the Declaration of Independence in the future to gain rights?

3. a. Identify Who urged her husband to "remember the ladies"?
b. Making Inferences Why did the authors of the Declaration of Independence fail to address the rights of women, Native Americans, and African Americans in the document?

Critical Thinking

4. Analyzing Review your notes on the Declaration of Independence. Then copy the graphic organizer below and use it to identify three results of the Declaration of Independence.

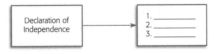

Declaration of Independence → 1. ______ 2. ______ 3. ______

FOCUS ON SPEAKING

5. Gathering Ideas about the Declaration of Independence You are living at the time of the American Revolution. What is new and surprising about the colonists' actions? In one or two minutes, what is the most important thing you can say about the colonies' declaring independence?

Direct Teach

Main Idea

3 Unfinished Business

The Declaration of Independence did not address the rights of all colonists.

Evaluate How are Abigail Adams's concerns about representation similar to the colonists' concerns in Chapter 3? *The colonists were not represented in Parliament. Abigail Adams writes that women are not represented in the Declaration and not bound by it.*

Make Judgments Why do you think the Declaration of Independence did not address the rights of women, enslaved Africans, and Native Americans? *possible answers—Culture and tradition were against extending rights; those groups could not send delegates to the Continental Congress.*

Review & Assess

Close

Discuss whether declaring independence was justified.

Review

go.hrw.com Online Quiz, Section 4.2

Assess

SE Section 2 Assessment

PASS: Section 4.2 Quiz

Alternative Assessment Handbook

Reteach/Classroom Intervention

Interactive Reader and Study Guide, Section 4.2

Interactive Skills Tutor CD-ROM

Section 2 Assessment Answers

1. a. author of *Common Sense*
b. possible answer—fear of punishment
c. possible answers—yes, England was unfair; no, it had a significant impact on public opinion

2. a. Patriots chose to fight for independence; Loyalists remained loyal to Great Britain.
b. All men possess unalienable rights; the king had violated colonists' rights by passing unfair laws; the king had broken the social contract with the colonists.
c. by citing the ideals of equality, freedom, and liberty stated in the document

3. a. Abigail Adams
b. possible answer—These groups had no representation at either Continental Congress.

4. rebellion became a revolt, colonists chose sides, Loyalists fled

5. possible answer—colonial leaders said the British government had denied their rights; they issued the Declaration of Independence, forming the United States of America

Answers

Signing the Declaration of Independence *possible answer—accurate representation of a historic event*

Reading Check *women, enslaved Africans, and Native Americans*

Historical Documents

Primary Source

Reading Like a Historian

Declaration of Independence

- Who wrote and signed the document? What do you know about these people?
- What basic ideas about people and government did the authors and signers hold? Did the people for whom the Declaration was being written hold the same views?
- Why did the authors write the document? What did they hope to achieve?

Activity The Case for Independence Discuss with students the way in which Jefferson and the other authors logically built a case for the right of the colonies to declare independence. Have students, working as a class or in small groups, create graphic organizers that show the logical progression of points in the case for independence. **LS Logical/Mathematical**

Exploring the Document

Top: *The Declaration shows that it is possible for people to change the government in power when it no longer reflects their will.*

Bottom: *Students might point to words such as* absolute despotism, repeated injuries and usurpations, tyranny, refused, forbidden, *and* obstructed *and mention that these words convey a sense of injustice that Jefferson and the other members of the Continental Congress thought the colonists had suffered at the hands of Great Britain.*

The Declaration of Independence

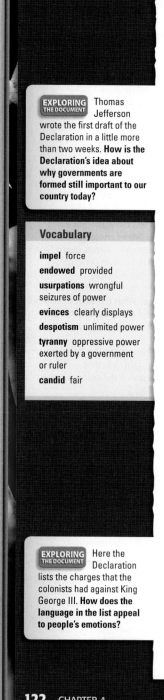

EXPLORING THE DOCUMENT Thomas Jefferson wrote the first draft of the Declaration in a little more than two weeks. **How is the Declaration's idea about why governments are formed still important to our country today?**

Vocabulary

impel force
endowed provided
usurpations wrongful seizures of power
evinces clearly displays
despotism unlimited power
tyranny oppressive power exerted by a government or ruler
candid fair

In Congress, July 4, 1776
The unanimous Declaration of the thirteen united States of America,

When in the Course of human events, it becomes necessary for one people to dissolve the political bands which have connected them with another, and to assume among the Powers of the earth, the separate and equal station to which the Laws of Nature and of Nature's God entitle them, a decent respect to the opinions of mankind requires that they should declare the causes which **impel** them to the separation.

We hold these truths to be self-evident, that all men are created equal, that they are **endowed** by their Creator with certain unalienable Rights, that among these are Life, Liberty, and the pursuit of Happiness. That to secure these rights, Governments are instituted among Men, deriving their just powers from the consent of the governed, That whenever any Form of Government becomes destructive of these ends, it is the Right of the People to alter or to abolish it, and to institute new Government, laying its foundation on such principles and organizing its powers in such form, as to them shall seem most likely to effect their Safety and Happiness. Prudence, indeed, will dictate that Governments long established should not be changed for light and transient causes; and accordingly all experience hath shown, that mankind are more disposed to suffer, while evils are sufferable, than to right themselves by abolishing the forms to which they are accustomed. But when a long train of abuses and **usurpations**, pursuing invariably the same Object **evinces** a design to reduce them under absolute **Despotism**, it is their right, it is their duty, to throw off such Government, and to provide new Guards for their future security.—Such has been the patient sufferance of these Colonies; and such is now the necessity which constrains them to alter their former Systems of Government. The history of the present King of Great Britain is a history of repeated injuries and usurpations, all having in direct object the establishment of an absolute **Tyranny** over these States. To prove this, let Facts be submitted to a **candid** world.

He has refused his Assent to Laws, the most wholesome and necessary for the public good.

He has forbidden his Governors to pass Laws of immediate and pressing importance, unless suspended in their operation till his Assent should be obtained; and when so suspended, he has utterly neglected to attend to them.

EXPLORING THE DOCUMENT Here the Declaration lists the charges that the colonists had against King George III. **How does the language in the list appeal to people's emotions?**

Differentiating Instruction

Below Level

English-Language Learners

Materials: translations of the Declaration of Independence in students' native languages (optional)

1. Help students with vocabulary and phrasing in the Declaration of Independence by writing short, simple summaries of each paragraph.
2. Once students understand the meaning of a portion of the text, help them work through the actual wording. Have students list any words they do not understand. As students work, circulate and help students define the words they listed. If possible, pair English learners with English speakers.
3. **Extend** Provide translations of the Declaration of Independence in students' native languages. Have students use the translations to help them understand the English version. **LS Verbal/Linguistic**

Alternative Assessment Handbook, Rubric 1: Acquiring Information

Independence!

SECTION 4

If YOU were there...

You have grown up on a farm in South Carolina. You know every inch of the woods and marshes around your home. You are too young to join the Continental Army, but you have heard stories about a brave group of soldiers who carry out quick raids on the British, then disappear into the woods. These fighters get no pay and live in constant danger.

Would you consider joining the fighters? Why?

BUILDING BACKGROUND As the war moved to the South, American forces encountered new problems. They suffered several major defeats. But American resistance in the southern colonies was strong. Backwoods fighters confused and frustrated the British army.

War in the South

The war across the ocean was not going the way the British government in London had planned. The northern colonies, with their ragged, scrappy fighters, proved to be tough to tame. So the British switched strategies and set their sights on the South.

The British hoped to find support from the large Loyalist populations living in Georgia, the Carolinas, and Virginia. As they moved across the South, the British also planned to free enslaved Africans and enlist them as British soldiers. Under the leadership of a new commander, General Henry Clinton, the strategy paid off—for a while.

Brutal Fighting

The southern war was particularly brutal. Much more than in the North, this phase of the war pitted Americans—Patriots versus Loyalists—against one another in direct combat. The British also destroyed crops, farm animals, and other property as they marched through the South. One British officer, Banastre Tarleton, sowed fear throughout the South by refusing to take prisoners and killing soldiers who tried to surrender.

What You Will Learn...

Main Ideas

1. Patriot forces faced many problems in the war in the South.
2. The American Patriots finally defeated the British at the Battle of Yorktown.
3. The British and the Americans officially ended the war by signing the Treaty of Paris of 1783.

The Big Idea

The war spread to the southern colonies, where the British were finally defeated.

Key Terms and People

Francis Marion, *p. 136*
Comte de Rochambeau, *p. 137*
Battle of Yorktown, *p. 137*
Treaty of Paris of 1783, *p. 139*

TAKING NOTES As you read, take notes on the major events that led to the British defeat. Write your notes in a graphic organizer like the one below.

1. ________
2. ________
3. ________
→ British Defeat

IN 8.1.1, 8.1.3, 8.1.4, 8.1.9, 8.1.28, 8.1.29, 8.1.30, 8.2.1, 8.3.2

Teach the Big Idea

At Level

Independence!

1. **Teach** To teach the main ideas in the section, use the questions in the Direct Teach boxes.
2. **Apply** Ask students to identify the main events in this section. List the responses for the class to see. Next, have each student write a newspaper headline for each event. **LS Verbal/Linguistic**
3. **Review** As you review the section's main ideas, ask for volunteers to share some of their headlines with the class. List them for students to see. Then help students develop a list of details that might appear in articles accompanying the headlines.
4. **Practice/Homework** Have each student select a headline and write a brief newspaper article to go with it. **LS Visual/Spatial**

Alternative Assessment Handbook, Rubric 37: Writing Assignments

Preteach

Bellringer

If YOU were there. . . Use the **Daily Bellringer Transparency** for this section to help students answer the question.

Daily Bellringer Transparency 4.4

The American Revolution — Daily Bellringer 4.4

Review Section 3

Match the sets of letters to the correct vocabulary term.

1. MARQUIS DE _ _ _ AYETTE — **ENT**
2. VALLEY FO _ _ _ — **ERC**
3. BATTLE OF SARA _ _ _ A — **LAF**
4. M _ _ _ ENARIES — **RGE**
5. BATTLE OF TR _ _ _ ON — **TOG**

Preview Section 4

If YOU were there ...

You have grown up on a farm in South Carolina. You know every inch of the woods and marshes around your home. You are too young to join the Continental Army, but you have heard stories about a brave group of soldiers who carry out quick raids on the British, then disappear into the woods. These fighters get no pay and live in constant danger.

Would you consider joining the fighters? Why?

Consider what you have to GIVE:
- your in-depth knowledge of the area
- your youthful energy
- your loyalty and enthusiasm

Consider what you might RECEIVE:
- excitement and adventure
- pride and self-esteem
- new friendships and experiences

Review Answers: 1. LAF, Marquis de Lafayette; 2. RGE, Valley Forge; 3. TOG, Battle of Saratoga; 4. ERC, mercenaries; 5. ENT, Battle of Trenton

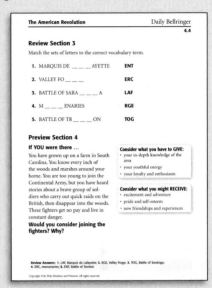

Building Vocabulary

Preteach or review the following terms:

brigade military unit (p. 136)

devastation severe or widespread damage (p. 136)

guerrilla warfare hit-and-run attacks (p. 136)

negotiations talks held to reach an agreement or compromise (p. 139)

pitted set against (p. 135)

CRF: Vocabulary Builder Activity, Section 4

Taking Notes

Have students copy the graphic organizer onto their own paper and then use it to take notes on the section. This activity will prepare students for the Section Assessment, in which they will complete a graphic organizer that builds on the information using a critical-thinking skill.

Section Correlations IN

8.1.9 Describe the influence of important individuals on social and political developments of the time such as the Independence movement and the framing of the Constitution.

Direct Teach

Main Idea

1 War in the South

Patriot forces faced many problems in the war in the South.

Explain Why did the British decide to switch strategies and focus the war in the South? *large Loyalist populations in Georgia, the Carolinas, and Virginia; planned to free slaves and have them fight*

Summarize How did guerrilla colonial fighters help the Continental Army? *by surprising the British with swift hit-and-run attacks to interfere with communication and supply lines*

Draw Conclusions How would you describe the main British strategies in the South? *use Loyalist support, free slaves to fight for British, use harsh tactics to destroy Patriot supplies and morale*

CRF: Primary Source Activity: General Nathanael Greene Writes to His Wife

Info to Know

Native Americans and the War The Revolutionary War was costly to many Native Americans. Some Indian homelands, such as those of the Iroquois and Cherokee, suffered devastation and invasion by both armies. The war also divided some Indian groups and confederacies. For example, the Oneidas and Tuscaroras supported the Patriots. As a result, they were cut off from the rest of the Iroquois League, which supported the British.

Georgia, the last colony to join the Revolution, was the first to fall to the British. A force of 3,500 Redcoats easily took Savannah in 1778 and soon put in place a new colonial government.

Britain's next major target was Charleston, South Carolina. In early 1780 General Clinton landed a force of 14,000 troops around the port city. With a minimal cost of about 250 casualties, the British scored one of their biggest victories of the war. The Patriots surrendered Charleston in May, handing over four ships and some 5,400 prisoners.

A Failed Attack

In August 1780, Patriot forces led by Horatio Gates tried to drive the British out of Camden, South Carolina. The attack was poorly executed, however. Gates had only half as many soldiers as he had planned for, and most were tired and hungry. In the heat of battle, many panicked and ran. The Patriot attack quickly fell apart. Of some 4,000 American troops, only about 700 escaped.

General Nathanael Greene arrived to reorganize the army. As he rode through the southern countryside, he was discouraged by the devastation. He later wrote, "I have never witnessed such scenes."

Guerrilla Warfare

The southern Patriots switched to swift hit-and-run attacks known as guerrilla warfare. No Patriot was better at this style of fighting than **Francis Marion**. He organized Marion's Brigade, a group of guerrilla soldiers.

Marion's Brigade used surprise attacks to disrupt British communication and supply lines. Despite their great efforts, the British could not catch Marion and his men. One frustrated general claimed, "As for this . . . old fox, the devil himself could not catch him." From that point on, Marion was known as the Swamp Fox.

READING CHECK **Sequencing** List the events of the war in the South in chronological order.

Swamp Fox

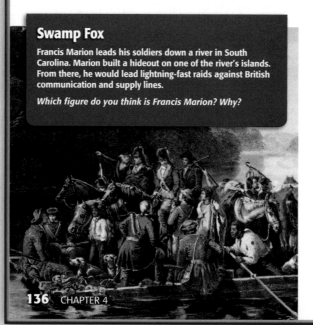

Francis Marion leads his soldiers down a river in South Carolina. Marion built a hideout on one of the river's islands. From there, he would lead lightning-fast raids against British communication and supply lines.

Which figure do you think is Francis Marion? Why?

Battle of Yorktown

In early 1781 the war was going badly for the Patriots. They were low on money to pay soldiers and buy supplies. The help of their foreign allies had not brought the war to a quick end as they had hoped. The British held most of the South, plus Philadelphia and New York City. The Patriots' morale took another blow when Benedict Arnold, one of America's most gifted officers, turned traitor.

Regrouped under Nathanael Greene, the Continental Army began harassing British general Charles Cornwallis in the Carolinas. Hoping to stay in communication with the British naval fleet, Cornwallis moved his force of 7,200 men to Yorktown, Virginia. It was a fatal mistake.

General Washington, in New York, saw a chance to trap Cornwallis at Yorktown. He ordered Lafayette to block Cornwallis's escape by land. Then he combined his 2,500 troops

Collaborative Learning

At Level

War in the South Progress Reports

1. Organize students into four groups. Ask two groups to imagine that they are military leaders stationed in the South during the latter part of the war—one with the Continental Army and the other with the British Army. Ask the other two groups to imagine that they are military leaders stationed near Yorktown in 1781—one with the Continental Army and one with the British Army.
2. Have each group create a report on the progress of the war effort in its area. Encourage students to identify, describe, and explain factors that both hurt or benefited their efforts in the region. Have groups assign each member a role to ensure that all students participate.
3. Ask a representative from each group to present the group's progress report to the class. Then have students discuss the events that led to the war's end. **LS Interpersonal, Verbal/Linguistic**

Alternative Assessment Handbook, Rubrics 14: Group Activity; and 42: Writing to Inform

Answers

Swamp Fox *the man in front on the horse who is looking forward; appears to be leading because of his position on the boat, his mount on horseback, his uniform, and his bearing*

Reading Check *1778: British take Savannah, Georgia; 1780: British take Charleston, South Carolina; Patriots fail to retake Camden, South Carolina*

History Close-up

Battle of Yorktown

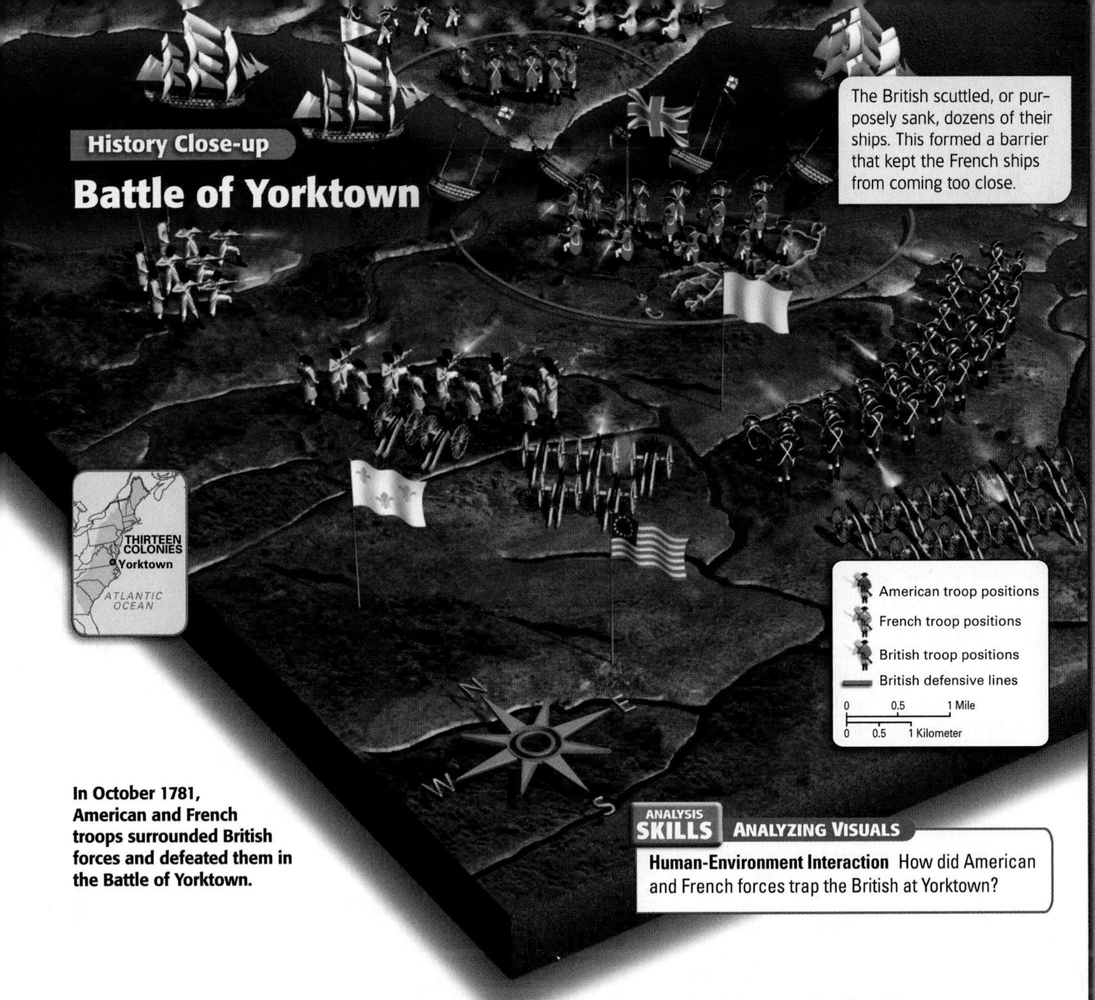

In October 1781, American and French troops surrounded British forces and defeated them in the Battle of Yorktown.

ANALYSIS SKILLS **ANALYZING VISUALS**

Human-Environment Interaction How did American and French forces trap the British at Yorktown?

with 4,000 French troops commanded by the **Comte de Rochambeau** (raw-shahn-BOH). Washington led the French-American force on a swift march to Virginia to cut off the other escape routes. The Patriots surrounded Cornwallis with some 16,000 soldiers. Meanwhile, a French naval fleet seized control of the Chesapeake Bay, preventing British ships from rescuing Cornwallis's stranded army.

The siege began. For weeks, the fighting steadily wore down the British defenses. In early October, Washington prepared for a major attack on the weakened British troops.

Facing near-certain defeat, on October 19, 1781, Cornwallis sent a drummer and a soldier with a white flag of surrender to Washington's camp. The Patriots took some 8,000 British prisoners—the largest British army in America.

The **Battle of Yorktown** was the last major battle of the American Revolution. Prime Minister Lord North received word of the Yorktown surrender in November. In shock he declared, "It is all over!"

READING CHECK **Drawing Conclusions** Why did the victory at Yorktown end the fighting?

Direct Teach

Main Idea

2 Battle of Yorktown

The American Patriots finally defeated the British at the Battle of Yorktown.

Recall Why did the British army move to Yorktown, Virginia? *because of harassment from the Continental Army; to maintain communications with the British naval fleet*

Finding Main Ideas How did Washington and the Patriots defeat the British at Yorktown? *With the aid of the French army and navy, they surrounded and outnumbered Cornwallis, forcing him to surrender.*

Evaluate Do you think the Patriots could have won the Revolutionary War without the help of the French? *possible answers—yes, because they would have continued to fight and eventually have worn down the British; no, because they lacked the troops and supplies needed to win the war*

Map Transparency 24: Battle of Yorktown

go.hrw.com

Online Resources

KEYWORD: SF7 CH4
ACTIVITY: Battlefield Tours

Critical Thinking: Finding Main Ideas

At Level

Revolutionary War Magazine

1. Review with students the major events and people from this chapter.
2. Have each student prepare a table of contents for a historical magazine about the American Revolution. Instruct students to select key people and events to be the subjects of feature articles, spotlights, charts, and maps. Then ask students to create titles for the articles and to describe each article's content.
3. Display students' tables of contents around the classroom and have students view each other's work. LS **Verbal/Linguistic**
4. **Extend** Have students work in groups to create different sections of a historical magazine about the Revolutionary War. LS **Interpersonal, Verbal/Linguistic**

Alternative Assessment Handbook, Rubric 19: Magazines

Answers

Analyzing Visuals *by surrounding them on land and by cutting off British ships so they could not rescue the British army*

Reading Check *British general Cornwallis surrendered his army, the largest British army in America, to the Patriots at Yorktown.*

Direct Teach

Primary Source

Sentiments of an American Woman

Info to Know

Shirts Instead of Cash Esther DeBerdt Reed wanted to donate the money collected by her campaign directly to the troops in the field. George Washington convinced her that distributing the money fairly might be difficult. At Washington's request, the money was used to purchase shirts for his army. Each shirt was embroidered with the name of the woman who made it. In gratitude, Washington awarded the members of the association "an equal place with any who have preceded them in the walk of female patriotism."

Did you know . . .

Esther DeBerdt Reed's effort to organize a large group of women to ask for contributions from women all over the country was the first example of national volunteerism. Reed, the wife of the chief executive of Pennsylvania, received contributions from about 1,645 women.

Linking to Today

Women in Military Service The role of women in military matters has changed greatly since the time *Sentiments of an American Woman* was written. Women who masqueraded as men on the battlefield, lived through the horrors of prisoner of war camps, and died in combat now are honored at the Women in Military Service for America Memorial in Arlington, Virginia. Since its dedication in 1997, about 200,000 people annually have visited the site to learn about women's contributions to military service from the Revolutionary War to today.

Answers

Analyzing Primary Sources

1. *The writers call to mind all the acts of courage, constancy, and patriotism that they have learned about through history.*

2. *with other women in history who have fought for liberty*

Primary Source

PAMPHLET

Sentiments of an American Woman

The Continental Army received aid from female Patriots led by Esther DeBerdt Reed and Sarah Franklin Bache, the daughter of Benjamin Franklin. In 1780 these women organized a campaign that raised $300,000 for soldiers' clothing. The following pamphlet, written by the campaign's leaders, announced the campaign. In it, the authors used images of women helping with war efforts of the past to gain support for their cause.

"On the **commencement** of actual war, the Women of America **manifested** a firm resolution to contribute . . . to the deliverance of their country. Animated by the purest patriotism they are sensible of sorrow at this day, in not offering more than barren wishes for the success of so glorious a Revolution. They aspire to **render** themselves more really useful; and this sentiment is universal from the north to the south of the Thirteen United States. Our ambition is kindled by the fame of those heroines of **antiquity**, who . . . have proved to the universe, that . . . if opinion and manners did not forbid us to march to glory by the same paths as the Men, we should at least equal, and sometimes surpass them in our love for the public good. I glory in all that which my sex has done great and **commendable**. I call to mind with enthusiasm and with admiration, all those acts of courage, of constancy and patriotism, which history has transmitted to us . . ."

"So many famous sieges where the Women have been seen . . . building new walls, digging trenches with their feeble hands, furnishing arms to their defenders, they themselves darting the missile weapons of the enemy, resigning the ornaments of their apparel, and their fortune, to fill the public treasury, and to hasten the deliverance of their country; burying themselves under its ruins; throwing themselves into the flames rather than submit to the disgrace of humiliation before a proud enemy."

"Born for liberty, **disdaining** to bear the irons of a **tyrannic** Government, we associate ourselves . . . [with those rulers] who have extended the empire of liberty, and **contented** to reign by sweetness and justice, have broken the chains of slavery, forged by tyrants."

A female spy passes news to a colonial officer.

1. **commencement**: start 2. **manifested**: presented
3. **render**: make 4. **antiquity**: ancient times
5. **commendable**: praiseworthy 6. **disdaining**: refusing
7. **tyrannic**: unjust 8. **contented**: determined

The women declare that they would fight if they were allowed.

The authors list ways in which women have helped fight wars in the past.

In this phrase, the women link themselves to great women rulers of the past.

ANALYSIS SKILL **ANALYZING PRIMARY SOURCES**

1. **What do the writers "call to mind" in asking women to join the Patriots' cause?**
2. **With whom do the writers associate themselves?**

Collaborative Learning

At Level

Sentiments of an American Woman

1. Discuss with students how *Sentiments* allowed women to contribute to the war effort and why women were prohibited from participating on any other level.
2. Organize students into pairs and ask them to imagine that they are colonists who were influenced by *Sentiments of an American Woman*. Have pairs create pamphlets giving support for the ideas of Reed and Bache. Ask students to propose another idea to benefit Washington's troops.
3. Students' pamphlets should focus on the following idea: In what ways were women able to support the war effort?
4. Have students share their pamphlets with the class. Discuss how Reed's ideas influenced them and brainstorm similar volunteer ideas that might be applicable to show support for today's troops.

Alternative Assessment Handbook, Rubrics 14: Group Activity; and 43: Writing to Persuade

The Treaty of Paris

After Yorktown, only a few small battles took place. Lacking the money to pay for a new army, Great Britain entered into peace talks with America. Benjamin Franklin had a key role in the negotiations.

Delegates took more than two years to come to a peace agreement. In the **Treaty of Paris of 1783**, Great Britain recognized the independence of the United States. The treaty also set America's borders. A separate treaty between Britain and Spain returned Florida to the Spanish. British leaders also accepted American rights to settle and trade west of the original thirteen colonies.

At the war's end, Patriot soldiers returned to their homes and families. The courage of soldiers and civilians had made America's victory possible. As they returned home, George Washington thanked his troops for their devotion. "I . . . wish that your latter days be as prosperous as your former ones have been glorious."

READING CHECK **Summarizing** Explain how the War for Independence finally came to an end.

North America after the Treaty of Paris of 1783

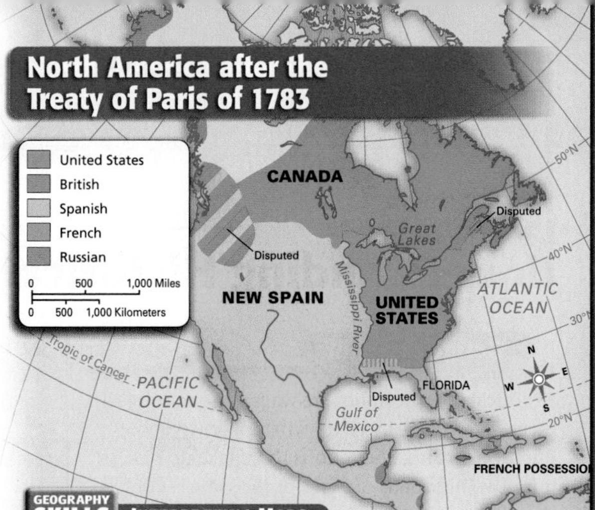

GEOGRAPHY SKILLS **INTERPRETING MAPS**

Region Which three countries disputed the area in the northwest of the continent?

SUMMARY AND PREVIEW Americans won their independence from Great Britain in 1783. In the next chapter you will learn how the new nation formed its first government.

Section 4 Assessment

go.hrw.com **Online Quiz** KEYWORD: SF7 HP4

Reviewing Ideas, Terms, and People

1. a. **Describe** What problems did the Patriots experience in the war in the South?
   b. **Analyze** What advantages did the southern Patriots have over the British in the South?
2. a. **Describe** What was the Patriots' strategy for defeating the British at Yorktown?
   b. **Elaborate** Why do you think General Cornwallis decided to surrender at the **Battle of Yorktown**?
3. a. **Identify** Who helped to negotiate the **Treaty of Paris** for the Americans?
   b. **Predict** How might relations between Great Britain and its former colonies be affected by the war?

Critical Thinking

4. **Evaluating** Review your notes on the events that led to the end of the war. Then copy the graphic organizer below and use it to identify and describe the most important event in turning the war in the Patriots' favor.

Event	Importance to end of war

FOCUS ON SPEAKING

5. **Thinking About the Revolution's End** After reading this section, you have a picture of the whole war. In your talk, what do you want to say about how the war ended? Were there any moments that were especially trying for the colonists?

Direct Teach

Main Idea

❸ The Treaty of Paris

The British and the Americans officially ended the war by signing the Treaty of Paris of 1783.

Define What was the Treaty of Paris? *peace agreement between Great Britain and the United States ending the Revolutionary War*

Summarize What were the terms of the treaty? *recognized United States independence; set U.S. borders; granted American rights to settle and trade west of the original thirteen colonies*

- Political Cartoons Activities for United States History, Cartoon 3: American Independence
- Map Transparency 25: North America after the Treaty of Paris of 1783

Section 4 Assessment Answers

1. a. brutal fighting and devastation, Patriots and Loyalists pitted against each other, several important cities under British control; loss of troops at Camden, South Carolina
   b. knew the land, used guerrilla warfare
2. a. to use the aid of the French army and navy to surround and outnumber the British and cut off their support and retreat by sea
   b. He was surrounded, facing defeat.
3. a. Benjamin Franklin
   b. probably would worsen relations
4. possible answers—Cornwallis moved into Yorktown; Patriot and French troops blocked the British by land and sea; Cornwallis surrendered his army, the largest in the colonies, and Great Britain entered into peace talks with America.
5. See answer to Question 1a.

Review & Assess

Close

Have students discuss the following question: *How is the American Revolution relevant today?*

Review

- Online Quiz, Section 4.4

Assess

- **SE** Section 4 Assessment
- PASS: Section 4.4 Quiz
- Alternative Assessment Handbook

Reteach/Classroom Intervention

- Interactive Reader and Study Guide, Section 4.4
- Interactive Skills Tutor CD-ROM

Answers

Interpreting Maps *Great Britain, Russia, and Spain*

Reading Check *Great Britain could no longer afford to continue fighting, so it entered into peace talks with the Patriots.*

Social Studies Skills

Understanding Historical Interpretation

Activity Chart for Practice the Skill To support the "Practice the Skill" activity, draw a two-column chart for the class to see. Label the columns *Economic Interpretations* and *Political Interpretations.* Have students copy the chart and use it to answer Question 1. Ask for volunteers to share their answers to create a master version of the chart. Then give students time to answer Question 2. Again, ask for volunteers to share their answers with the class. Encourage student discussion and feedback. Remind students to provide reasons to support their positions.

LS Verbal/Linguistic

- Alternative Assessment Handbook, Rubric 16: Judging Information
- **CRF:** Social Studies Skills Activity: Understanding Historical Interpretation

Social Studies Skills

Analysis | Critical Thinking | Civic Participation | Study

Understanding Historical Interpretation

Define the Skill

Historical interpretations are ways of explaining the past. They are based on what is known about the people, ideas, and actions that make up history. Two historians can look at the same set of facts about a person or event of the past and see things in different ways. Their explanations of the person or event, and the conclusions they reach, can be very different. The ability to recognize, understand, and evaluate historical interpretations is a valuable skill in the study of history.

Learn the Skill

When people study the past, they decide which facts are the most important in explaining why something happened. One person may believe certain facts to be important, while other people may believe other facts are more important. Therefore, their explanation of the topic, and the conclusions they draw about it, may not be the same. In addition, if new facts are uncovered about the topic, still more interpretations of it may result.

Asking the following questions will help you to understand and evaluate historical interpretations.

1. What is the main idea in the way the topic is explained? What conclusions are reached? Be aware that these may not be directly stated but only hinted at in the information provided.
2. On what facts has the writer or speaker relied? Do these facts seem to support his or her explanation and conclusions?
3. Is there important information about the topic that the writer or speaker has dismissed or ignored? If so, you should suspect that the interpretation may be inaccurate or deliberately slanted to prove a particular point of view.

Just because interpretations differ, one is not necessarily "right" and others "wrong." As long as a person considers all the evidence and draws conclusions based on a fair evaluation of that evidence, his or her interpretation is probably acceptable.

Remember, however, that trained historians let the facts *lead* them to conclusions. People who *start* with a conclusion, select only facts that support it, and ignore opposing evidence produce interpretations that have little value for understanding history.

Practice the Skill

Two widely accepted interpretations exist of the causes of the American Revolution. One holds that the Revolution was a struggle by freedom-loving Americans to be free from harsh British rule. In this view the colonists were used to self-government and resisted British efforts to take rights they claimed. The other interpretation is that a clash of economic interests caused the Revolution. In this view, the war resulted from a struggle between British and colonial merchants over control of America's economy.

Review Sections 4 and 5 of Chapter 3 and Sections 1 and 2 of Chapter 4. Then answer the following questions.

1. What facts in the textbook support the economic interpretation of the Revolution? What evidence supports the political interpretation?
2. Which interpretation seems more convincing? Explain why.

Answers

Practice and Apply the Skill

1. *economic—one of England's main reasons for founding the colonies was to earn money from trade; British attempts to tax the colonists and crack down on smuggling led to colonial protests, unrest, and eventually violence; political—amount of colonial self-government; reactions to limits on colonial self-government; ideals expressed in the Declaration of Independence;* **2.** *possible answer—the economic interpretation because money and economic power are very tempting and powerful motivators*

Social Studies Skills Activity: Understanding Historical Interpretation

Interpretation of the Battle of Saratoga — At Level

1. Have students review the material in Section 3 under the heading "Saratoga." Based on expert historical interpretation, this passage describes the Battle of Saratoga as "the greatest victory yet for the American forces."
2. Review with students the Revolutionary battles up to and including the Battle of Saratoga. Then have students discuss whether or not they agree with the historical interpretation that the Battle of Saratoga was the greatest American victory up to that point.
3. Then have each student write one to two paragraphs either supporting or refuting this historical interpretation. Students who disagree should indicate which battle they think was the greatest victory yet. Remind students to provide reasons and evidence from the textbook to support their positions.

LS Verbal/Linguistic

- Alternative Assessment Handbook, Rubric 43: Writing to Persuade

CHAPTER 4 Chapter Review

HOLT History's Impact
▶ **video series**
Review the video to answer the closing question:
Why do you think African Americans, women, and young adults under 21 fought for the vote?

Visual Summary

QUICK FACTS

Use the visual summary below to help you review the main ideas of the chapter.

Speeches and protests ignited revolutionary feelings.

Patriots fought Loyalists in the Revolutionary War.

The American colonies gained independence and became the United States.

Reviewing Vocabulary, Terms, and People

1. What were American colonists who remained loyal to Great Britain called?
   - **a.** Whigs
   - **b.** Loyalists
   - **c.** Royalists
   - **d.** Democrats
2. What was the name of the battle in which the Patriots finally defeated the British?
   - **a.** Battle of Saratoga
   - **b.** Battle of New Jersey
   - **c.** Battle of Yorktown
   - **d.** Battle of Valley Forge
3. What was the name for the colonial military force created to fight the British?
   - **a.** mercenaries
   - **b.** Redcoats
   - **c.** Hessians
   - **d.** Continental Army
4. Who was the French nobleman who helped the Patriots fight the British?
   - **a.** Bernardo de Gálvez
   - **b.** Marquis de Lafayette
   - **c.** Baron von Steuben
   - **d.** Lord Dunmore

Comprehension and Critical Thinking

SECTION 1 *(Pages 112–116)*

5. **a. Recall** What actions did the First and Second Continental Congresses take?
   b. Analyze How did the events at Lexington and Concord change the conflict between Great Britain and the colonies?
   c. Elaborate Why do you think that control of Boston early in the Revolutionary War was important?

SECTION 2 *(Pages 118–121)*

6. **a. Identify** Why is July 4, 1776, a significant date?
   b. Draw Conclusions What effect did *Common Sense* have on colonial attitudes toward Great Britain?
   c. Predict How might the content of the Declaration of Independence lead to questions over the issue of slavery?

Answers

History's Impact

Video Series They wanted to elect politicians who would represent minority groups to protect their rights in the future.

Visual Summary

Review and Inquiry Have students provide five to seven supporting details for each panel in the visual summary to explain the main events that led to the independence of the United States.

Quick Facts Transparency 11: The American Revolution Visual Summary

Reviewing Vocabulary, Terms, and People

1. b
2. c
3. d
4. b

Comprehension and Critical Thinking

5. **a.** First—halted all trade with Britain, had colonial militias prepare for war, drafted Declaration of Rights; Second—created Continental Army, appointed George Washington to command the army, sent Olive Branch Petition to Britain
   b. The conflict became violent, and the colonists readied for war.
   c. possible answer—Boston was a major colonial city and port.

Review and Assessment Resources

Review and Reinforce

- **SE** Chapter Review
- **CRF:** Chapter Review Activity
- Quick Facts Transparency 11: The American Revolution Visual Summary
- Spanish Chapter Summaries Audio CD Program
- Online Chapter Summaries in Spanish
- **OSP** Holt PuzzlePro, GameTool for ExamView
- Quiz Game CD-ROM

Assess

- **SE** Standardized Test Practice
- PASS: Unit 1 Tests, Forms A and B; Chapter 4 Tests, Forms A and B
- Alternative Assessment Handbook
- **OSP** ExamView Test Generator, Chapter Test
- Differentiated Instruction Modified Worksheets and Tests CD-ROM: Chapter Test
- **HOAP** Holt Online Assessment Program (in the Premier Online Edition)

Reteach/Intervene

- Interactive Reader and Study Guide
- Differentiated Instruction Teacher Management System: Lesson Plans for Differentiated Instruction
- Differentiated Instruction Modified Worksheets and Tests CD-ROM
- Interactive Skills Tutor CD-ROM

go.hrw.com
Online Resources
Chapter Resources:
KEYWORD: SF7 CH4

Answers

6. a. date on which the Continental Congress approved the Declaration of Independence
b. changed the way many colonists viewed the king, made a strong case for economic freedom and military self-defense
c. It states that "all men are created equal" and have unalienable rights, but at the same time many colonists were slaveholders.

7. a. defeats in Canada, New York
b. with victories at the Battles of Trenton and Saratoga
c. possible answers: No—Foreign aid provided training, money, and military help on sea and land; Yes—the tide had already begun to turn in favor of the Patriots, who would have worn down the British eventually.

8. a. knew there was a large Loyalist population in Georgia, the Carolinas, and Virginia; planned to free enslaved Africans and have them fight
b. possible answer—because of debates over borders, the roles of France and Spain, and whether Americans could settle and trade west of the original thirteen colonies
c. possible answers—victory at Yorktown, because the Patriots captured Britain's largest army in America; French aid, because it enabled the Patriots to surround the British army at Yorktown

Social Studies Skills

9. c
10. possible answer—The Continental Army was no match against the Redcoats.

Reviewing Themes

11. rights to life, liberty, and the pursuit of happiness
12. settlements were scattered, troops had to travel long distances

SECTION 3 *(Pages 126–134)*

7. a. **Describe** What difficulties did the Patriots experience in the early years of the war?
b. **Analyze** How did the Patriots turn the tide of the war?
c. **Elaborate** Could the Patriots have succeeded in the war without foreign help? Explain.

SECTION 4 *(Pages 135–139)*

8. a. **Recall** Why did the British think they might find support in the southern colonies?
b. **Make Inferences** Why did it take more than two years for the British and the Americans to agree to the terms of the Treaty of Paris?
c. **Evaluate** In your opinion, what was the most important reason for the Patriots' defeat of the British?

Social Studies Skills

Understanding Historical Interpretation *Use the Social Studies Skills taught in this chapter to answer the questions about the reading selection below.*

> In a series of battles, Howe pounded the Continental Army, forcing it to retreat farther and farther. The Redcoats captured Patriots as well as supplies. Eventually, the British pushed Washington across the Hudson River into New Jersey. Howe's revenge for his defeat at Boston was complete. (p. 128)

9. Which statement from the passage is an interpretation of historical facts?
a. The Redcoats captured Patriots as well as supplies.
b. Eventually, the British pushed Washington across the Hudson River into New Jersey.
c. Howe's revenge for his defeat at Boston was complete.

10. What might a different interpretation of the facts be?

Reviewing Themes

11. **Politics** What are three important rights listed in the Declaration of Independence?
12. **Geography** What role did geography play in the fighting that took place in the West?

Reading Skills

Main Ideas in Social Studies *Use the Reading Skills taught at the beginning of the chapter to answer the question about the reading selection below.*

> (1) Native Americans were at first encouraged by both sides to remain neutral. (2) By the summer of 1776, however, both Patriots and the British were aggressively recruiting Indian fighters. (3) Most sided with the British. (4) In northern New York, four of the six Iroquois nations fought for the British. (p. 120)

13. Which sentence contains the main idea of the paragraph?
a. Sentence 1
b. Sentence 2
c. Sentence 3
d. Sentence 4

Using the Internet

go.hrw.com
KEYWORD: SF7 CH4

14. **Activity: Researching** The Battle of Saratoga showed the world that the Patriots were capable of defeating the British. This victory gave Benjamin Franklin the chance to use his fame as a scientist and diplomat to convince France to aid the Patriots. Enter the activity keyword and explain how these factors led to a Patriot victory and how the American Revolution affected France.

FOCUS ON SPEAKING

15. **Prepare Your Oral Report** Review your notes and be sure you've identified one or two important ideas, events, or people for each period of the war. Now, start to prepare your oral report by writing a one-sentence introduction to your talk. Then write a sentence or two about each period of the war. Write a concluding sentence that makes a quick connection between the Revolutionary War and our lives today. Practice your talk until you can give it with only a glance or two at your notes.

Reading Skills

13. Sentence 3

Using the Internet

14. Go to the HRW Web site and enter the keyword shown to access a rubric for this activity.

KEYWORD: SF7 CH4

Focus on Speaking

15. **Rubric** Students' oral reports should
- include an introduction, two sentences on each period of the war, and a conclusion.
- discuss the war in chronological order.
- provide vivid descriptions to engage the audience.
- use standard English and proper grammar.

CRF: Focus on Speaking Activity: Giving an Oral Report

CHAPTER 4

Standardized Test Practice

IN 8.1.4, 8.1.9, 8.1.28, 8.1.29, 8.2.1

DIRECTIONS: Read each question and write the letter of the best response.

1 What action would a Loyalist have been likely to take during the Revolution?

A attend the Continental Congress
B support the Olive Branch Petition
C support the Declaration of Independence
D join the Continental Army

2 Which of the following events took place *last*?

A The Declaration of Independence was issued.
B The Second Continental Congress met.
C The battles at Lexington and Concord occurred.
D The Battle of Bunker Hill took place.

3 Why was the victory at the Battle of Saratoga so important to the Patriot cause?

A It allowed the Declaration of Independence to be issued.
B It forced the British army to retreat from Boston.
C It convinced France to aid the colonies in their fight.
D It caused the British government to give up the war.

4 The most brutal and destructive fighting of the war probably occurred

A in the southern colonies.
B at Valley Forge.
C in New England.
D at Lexington and Concord.

5 The Declaration of Independence's claim that people have a right to "life, liberty, and the pursuit of happiness" shows the influence of what Enlightenment thinker from Europe?

A Jonathan Edwards
B John Locke
C King George III
D Thomas Paine

6 In what way was Clark's battle strategy the same as John Paul Jones's strategy?

A They both were badly outnumbered by the British.
B They both knew the colonial midwest region well.
C They both aimed to weaken the British by attacking their supply lines.
D They both survived the winter at Valley Forge.

7 Read the following passage from Thomas Paine's *The Crisis* and use it to answer the question below.

> "These are the times that try men's souls. The summer soldier and the sunshine patriot will, in this crisis, shrink from the service of his country, but he that stands it now, deserves the love and thanks of man and woman. Tyranny . . . is not easily conquered, yet we have this consolation with us, that the harder the conflict, the more glorious the triumph."
>
> —Thomas Paine, *The Crisis,* 1776

Document-Based Question **What point is Paine trying to make in this passage?**

Answers

1. B
Break Down the Question This question asks what a Loyalist would probably have done. Tell students to start by eliminating any actions that Loyalists would not have taken, which leaves only answer B.

2. A
Break Down the Question This question requires students to sequence a series of events. Suggest that students first order the events they are certain about and then try to fill in other events.

3. C
Break Down the Question This question requires students to identify cause and effect. Tell students in such cases to think about what they know about the event in question and what happened after or as a result of the event.

4. A
Break Down the Question Suggest that students first eliminate any choices where fighting did not occur (Valley Forge) and then recall what they know about the remaining options.

5. B
Break Down the Question This question requires students to recall information covered in Grade 7.

6. C
Break Down the Question Suggest that students eliminate any choices that do not involve battle strategy and then recall what they know about the remaining options.

7. Paine is suggesting that a Patriot's satisfaction with self and appreciation by others increases with the difficulty of the struggle.

Break Down the Question Suggest that students go through the reading phrase by phrase and interpret each one in turn. Then have them review the reading to get its full meaning. Here, focus on the phrases "but he that stands it now, deserves the love and thanks of man and woman" and "the harder the conflict, the more glorious the triumph."

Intervention Resources

Reproducible

- Interactive Reader and Study Guide
- Differentiated Instruction Teacher Management System: Lesson Plans for Differentiated Instruction

Technology

- Quick Facts Transparency 11: The American Revolution Visual Summary
- Differentiated Instruction Modified Worksheets and Tests CD-ROM
- Interactive Skills Tutor CD-ROM

Tips for Test Taking

Study the Directions Read the following to students: To follow directions correctly, you have to know what the directions are. Read all test directions as if they contain the key to lifetime happiness and several years of allowance. Then read them again. Next, study the answer sheet. How is it laid out? How are the choices arranged—vertically, horizontally? Be very sure you know exactly what to do and how to do it before you make your first mark.

Preteach

Bellringer

Motivate Ask students to name some of the people they have read about in this unit. Then ask them which of these people's lives would make the most interesting stories. Lead students to discuss what makes a narrative interesting. Tell students they will write a biographical narrative in this workshop.

Direct Teach

Adding Details

Move Beyond Plot Remind students that just telling what happened does not make events come alive. In addition to describing an event, students should tell what the subject thought and felt about what happened. Tell students they want to help their readers experience the events through the subject's eyes.

Using Transitions

Link It Up Model the use of transitions for students. Choose a series of events from the unit. Next, write the events for students to see. Then ask students to help you link each event with an appropriate transition word. When all events are linked, erase the transitions and challenge students to think of a new set of appropriate transition words.

Writing Workshop

A Biographical Narrative

Assignment
Write a biographical narrative about a person who lived in the early Americas before or during the colonial period.

You have been listening to and telling narratives all your life. A biographical narrative, a form of historical writing, is a true story about an event or brief period in a person's life.

1. Prewrite

Getting Started

- Think of all the people you read about in this unit. Which ones interested you most?
- What particular events and situations in these people's lives seem most exciting or significant?

Pick one of these events or situations as the subject of your narrative.

TIP **Asking Questions** Try using the *5W-How?* questions (*Who? What? When? Where? Why? How?*) to help you think of descriptive details. Ask questions such as, **Who** was this person? **What** was he or she doing? Exactly **where** and **when** did the event occur? **How** did the person or other people react to the event?

Creating an Interesting Narrative

Make your narrative lively and interesting by including

- **Physical descriptions** of people, places, and things, using details that appeal to the five senses (sight, hearing, touch, smell, taste)
- **Specific actions** that relate directly to the story you are telling
- **Dialogue** between the people involved or direct **quotations**
- **Background information** about the place, customs, and setting
- **All relevant details and information** needed to relate the events of the story and how they affected the person (and perhaps history)

Organize the events in your narrative in chronological order, the order in which they occurred.

2. Write

You can use this framework to help you draft your narrative.

A Writer's Framework

Introduction	Body	Conclusion
■ Grab your reader's attention with a striking detail or bit of dialogue. ■ Introduce the historical person and setting, using specific details. ■ Set the scene by telling how the event or situation began.	■ Present actions and details in the order in which they occurred. ■ Connect actions with transition words like *first, then, next,* and *finally.* ■ Provide specific details to make the person and the situation come alive.	■ Wrap up the action of the narrative. ■ Tell how the person was affected by what happened. ■ Explain how the event or situation was important in the person's life and how it affected history.

Differentiating Instruction

Advanced/Gifted and Talented — Above Level

1. Challenge students to present their narrative as a historian might by incorporating primary and secondary source quotes.
2. Instruct students to provide a footnote giving the citation, or source, for each quotation. Last, students should create a bibliography of their sources to go with their biographical narrative. **LS Verbal/Linguistic**

English-Language Learners — Below Level

1. Write the sequence words listed in the Tip on the next page for students to see.
2. Have students write each sequence word on a note card and then write the equivalent in their primary language on the card's back.
3. Pair students and have them use the cards to quiz each other. **LS Interpersonal, Verbal/Linguistic**

3. Evaluate and Revise

Evaluating

Read through your completed draft to make sure your narrative is complete, coherent, and clear. Then look for ways to improve it.

Evaluation Questions for a Biographical Narrative

- Does your introduction grab the reader's attention? Do you introduce the historical person and tell how the event or situation began?
- Do you include details to make the person, place, and event seem real?
- Are the actions in the story in the order in which they occurred?
- Have you included all of the actions and details a reader would need to understand what happened?
- Does the conclusion tell how the event or situation affected the person and history?

TIP **Showing Sequence** A clear sense of the sequence of events is important in any narrative. Here is a list of words that show those relationships.

after	next
before	now
finally	soon
first (second, etc.)	still
	then
last	when
later	while

Revising

When you revise your narrative, you may need to add transition words. Transition words help you link ideas between sentences and paragraphs. Notice the words in bold in the following sentences.

> **After** Cabeza de Vaca and the other adventurers left the beach and started inland, they separated into different groups. **Later**, Cabeza de Vaca heard that many of the others had died. **Still**, he never lost faith that he would reach his fellow Spaniards in Mexico.

4. Proofread and Publish

Proofreading

Throughout your narrative, you used transition words to link events. Make sure that you have spelled the words correctly and have not confused them with other words. For example, be sure to use two *l*'s in *finally* and not to mistake the transition word *then* for the comparative word *than*.

Publishing

One good way to share your biographical narrative is to exchange it with one or more classmates who have written about the same person you have. After reading each other's narratives, you can compare and contrast them. How are your stories similar? How do they differ?

5. Practice and Apply

Use the steps and strategies outlined in this workshop to write your biographical narrative.

Reteach

Acting Workshop

Play It Out Encourage students who are having trouble adding thoughts and feelings to their narratives to form small groups and act out each narrative as a play. Then have the student playing the subject describe his or her thoughts and feelings while the other students take notes.

Teaching Tip

Person and Tense
Remind students to use the third person and the past tense throughout their biographical narratives. When students proofread their papers, suggest that they circle all pronouns and underline all verbs to make sure they match.

Practice & Apply

Rubric

Students' biographical narratives should

- start with a striking detail or interesting bit of dialogue.
- clearly identify the subject and the historical setting.
- present actions and details in the order in which they occurred.
- correctly and effectively use transitions to link events.
- provide vivid details and dialogue to bring the person and the story alive.
- wrap up the story and explain how the situation affected the subject.
- use correct grammar, punctuation, spelling, and capitalization.

Special Needs Learners **Below Level**

1. Have special needs learners draw the person and events they have selected as the subject of their biographical narratives.
2. Have a classroom aide or fellow student listen and take notes while the student describes what is happening in the picture.
3. Then have the aide or fellow student use the notes to guide the special needs learners in writing his or her biographical narrative.
4. If the student gets stuck, direct the aide or fellow student to prompt him or her by asking questions about the picture. Questions might include: Who are the people in the picture? What are they doing? Why are they doing these things? What happened next? How do you think the person felt during these events? What sights and sounds did the person see and hear during the events? **LS Visual/Spatial**

OUR COLONIAL HERITAGE 145

Unit Preview

Introduce the Unit

Share the information in the chapter overviews with students.

Chapter 5 American colonists formed state and federal governments based on English laws, Enlightenment ideas, and American models of government. The federal government established by the Articles of Confederation lacked the power to rule effectively, however. To remedy this problem, American leaders wrote a new constitution that created a stronger central government. Eventually, the required nine states ratified the U.S. Constitution.

Chapter 6 The framers of the U.S. Constitution developed a federal system, dividing power between the federal and state governments. A system of checks and balances divides federal power among the legislative, executive, and judicial branches of government. To address concerns about individual rights, the first Congress added 10 amendments, known as the Bill of Rights, to the Constitution. In addition to these rights, all U.S. citizens have certain responsibilities to society.

Chapter 7 With the Constitution ratified, U.S. leaders set about creating a new federal government. These leaders faced numerous challenges, including how to pay off the national debt, how to respond to foreign threats, and how to *(continued on p. 147)*

UNIT 2 1777–1800

A New Nation

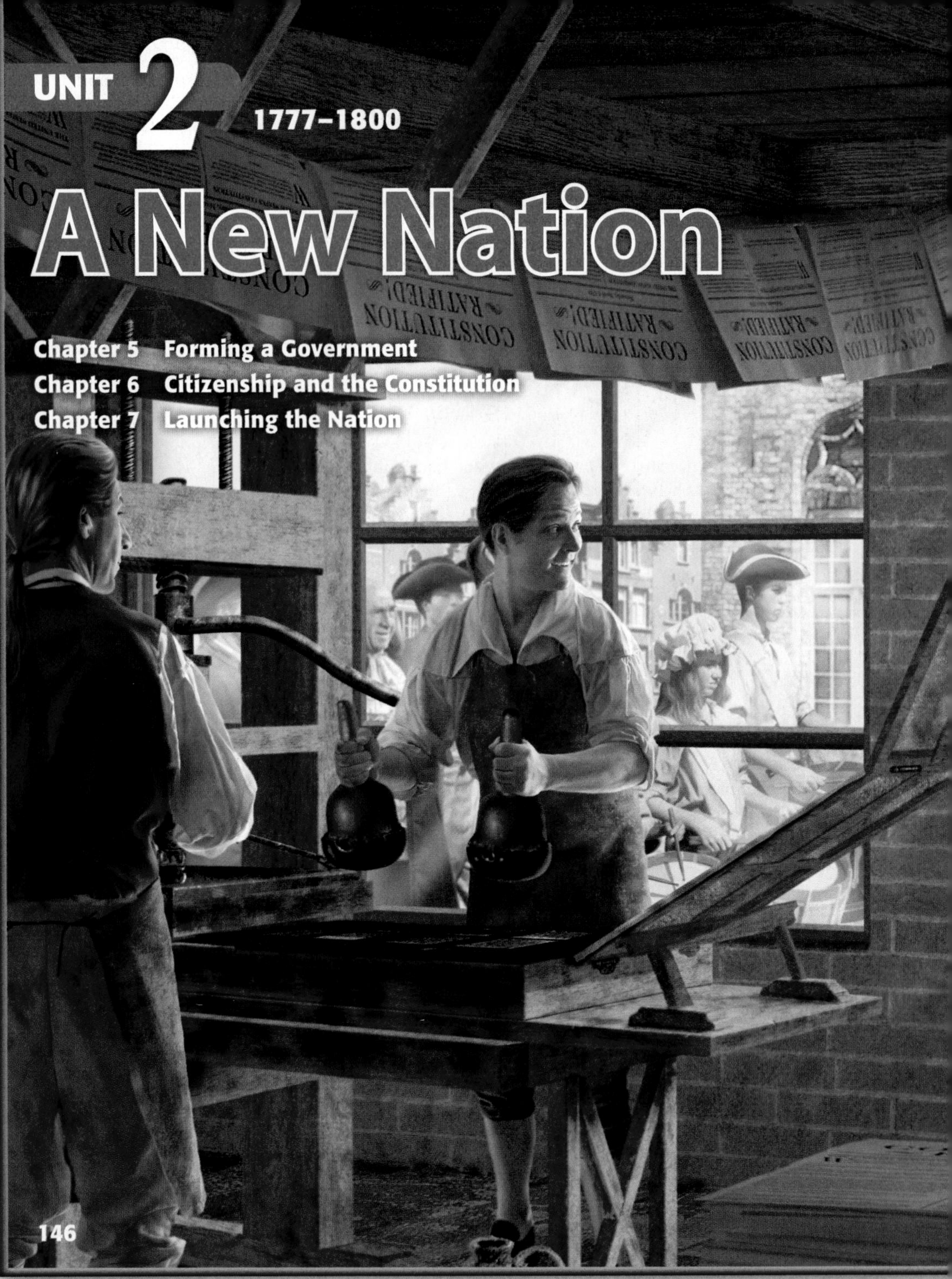

146

Unit Resources

Planning

- Differentiated Instruction Teacher Management System: Unit Instructional Pacing Guide
- One-Stop Planner CD-ROM with Test Generator: Calendar Planner
- Power Presentations with Video CD-ROM

Differentiating Instruction

- Differentiated Instruction Teacher Management System: Lesson Plans for Differentiated Instruction
- Pre-AP Activities Guide for United States History
- Differentiated Instruction Modified Worksheets and Tests CD-ROM

Enrichment

- **CRF Launching the Nation:** Economics and History: The National Debt
- **CRF Launching the Nation:** Interdisciplinary Projects: Planning the New Capital
- Civic Participation Activities
- Primary Source Library CD-ROM

Assessment

- Progress Assessment Support System: Unit 2 Tests, Forms A and B
- OSP ExamView Test Generator: Unit Test
- HOAP Holt Online Assessment Program, in the Premier Online Student Edition
- Alternative Assessment Handbook

The **Differentiated Instruction Teacher Management System** provides a planning and instructional guide for this unit.

Northwest Territory

Congress had to decide what to do with the western lands now under its control and how to raise money to pay debts. It tried to solve both problems by selling the western lands. Congress passed the **Land Ordinance of 1785**, which set up a system for surveying and dividing western lands. The land was split into townships, which were 36 square miles divided into 36 lots of 640 acres each. One lot was reserved for a public school, and four lots were given to veterans. The remaining lots were sold to the public.

To form a political system for the region, Congress passed the **Northwest Ordinance of 1787**. The ordinance established the **Northwest Territory**, which included areas that are now in Illinois, Indiana, Michigan, Ohio, Minnesota, and Wisconsin. The Northwest Ordinance created a system for bringing new states into the Union. Congress agreed that the Northwest Territory would be divided into several smaller territories with a governor appointed by Congress. When the population of a territory reached 60,000, its settlers could draft their own constitution and ask to join the Union.

In addition, the law protected civil liberties and required that public education be provided. Finally, the ordinance stated that "there shall be neither slavery nor involuntary servitude [forced labor] in the . . . territory." This last condition banned slavery in the Territory and set the standard for future territories. However, slavery would continue to be a controversial issue.

READING CHECK **Analyzing Information**
How did the Northwest Ordinance of 1787 affect the United States?

SUMMARY AND PREVIEW The Northwest Ordinance settled the future of the Northwest Territory. In the next section you will read about other challenges the new government faced.

FOCUS ON INDIANA
When Ohio became the first state admitted from the Northwest Territory, the remaining area was renamed the Indiana Territory. Governor William Henry Harrison attempted to suspend the antislavery laws for the territory, but Congress would not allow it.

THE IMPACT TODAY
Townships remained the unit of local government after the Northwest Territory was divided into states. Many of these townships still exist today.

Section 1 Assessment

go.hrw.com
Online Quiz
KEYWORD: SF7 HP5

Reviewing Ideas, Terms, and People

1. a. **Identify** What documents influenced ideas about government in the United States?
   b. **Draw Conclusions** What impact did the **Virginia Statute for Religious Freedom** have on the U.S. government?
   c. **Elaborate** Why is the separation of government powers a requirement for a society to be free?
2. a. **Identify** What was the **Articles of Confederation**?
   b. **Summarize** What powers were granted to Congress by the Articles of Confederation?
   c. **Predict** What are some possible problems that might result from the lack of a national court system?
3. a. **Describe** How were public lands in the West divided by the **Land Ordinance of 1785**?
   b. **Evaluate** In your opinion, what was the most important element of the **Northwest Ordinance of 1787**? Why?
   c. **Elaborate** What does the assignment of township lots reveal about values of Americans at this time?

Critical Thinking

4. **Categorizing** Review your notes on the Articles of Confederation. Copy the chart below and use it to show the strengths and weaknesses of the new government.

Articles of Confederation

Strengths	Weaknesses

FOCUS ON WRITING

5. **Thinking about the Articles of Confederation** Make a list of powers the Articles of Confederation gave the national government. Which ones seem strong? Can you think of any important powers that are missing?

Direct Teach

Main Idea

3 Northwest Territory

The Confederation Congress established the Northwest Territory.

Recall What was the purpose of the Land Ordinance of 1785? *to set up a system for surveying and dividing western public lands*

Summarize What important rights did the Northwest Ordinance of 1787 provide? *civil liberties, public education, freedom from slavery*

CRF: History and Geography Activity: The Northwest Territories

Map Transparency 26: The Land Ordinances of 1785 and 1787

Review & Assess

Close

Have students summarize some of the early actions of the new nation of the United States.

Review

Online Quiz, Section 5.1

Assess

SE Section 1 Assessment

PASS: Section 5.1 Quiz

Alternative Assessment Handbook

Reteach/Classroom Intervention

Interactive Reader and Study Guide, Section 5.1

Interactive Skills Tutor CD-ROM

Section 1 Assessment Answers

1. a. Magna Carta, English Bill of Rights, Mayflower Compact, Declaration of Independence, state constitutions, Virginia Statute for Religious Freedom
   b. established precedent of freedom of religion
   c. limits power, gives citizens a voice
2. a. national constitution for first U.S. government
   b. settle conflicts between states, make coins, borrow money, make treaties, ask states for money and soldiers
   c. possible answers—state courts might interpret laws differently; no federal system of appeal
3. a. into townships; four lots reserved for veterans and one for a public school
   b. established territorial representation and public education; prohibited slavery
   c. valued education and veterans
4. strengths—limited government, Congress could settle conflicts, mint coins, borrow money, negotiate treaties; weaknesses—states could refuse requests from Congress; no president or national court system
5. Answers will vary but should reflect an understanding of the Articles of Confederation.

Focus on Indiana

IN 8.1.4

Identify Why was slavery not allowed in Indiana? *Because it was not allowed in any of the territories making up the Northwest Territory.*

Answers

Reading Check *created a way to incorporate new states, ban slavery, protect civil liberties, and provide public education in the Northwest Territory*

History and Geography

Activity Ship of State Graphic Organizer Draw a simple sailing ship for students to see. Have each student make a large copy of the ship and name it the *US Constitution: The Ship of State*. Then have students label different parts of the ship with the six items listed here that influenced the U.S. Constitution. Each student should write a phrase or sentence explaining the significance of each idea. In addition, encourage students to select parts of the ship that they think represent the idea in some way. Have volunteers share their work with the class. **LS Verbal/Linguistic, Visual/Spatial**

Linking to Today

Parliament Today Parliament, the lawmaking body of Great Britain, is bicameral. That is, it consists of two parts, or houses. Parliament is made up of the House of Lords, appointed by the monarch, and the House of Commons, elected by the people. This system enables each house to check and improve the work of the other house. Today, however, the House of Lords holds little power. The House of Commons is now the only real lawmaking body in Britain. It has complete control of all money bills and most other public legislation.

History and Geography

Origins of the Constitution

The U.S. Constitution created a republican form of government based on the consent of the people. The framers of the Constitution blended ideas and examples from both the American colonies and from England to write this lasting document.

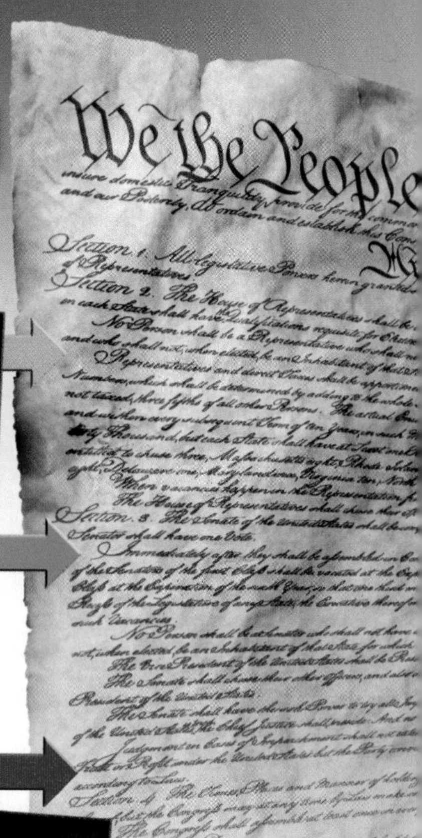

THE MAYFLOWER COMPACT, 1620

The *Mayflower*, shown here in an illustration, sailed to America in 1620. Aboard the ship, 41 men signed the Mayflower Compact, the first document in the colonies to establish guidelines for self-government. The signers agreed that they and their families would combine to form a "civil body politic," or community.

COLONIAL ASSEMBLIES

The British Parliament's two-chamber structure also influenced colonial governments. In Article I, Section 1, of the Constitution, the framers continued the practice of a two-chamber legislature.

"All legislative powers . . . shall be vested in a Congress of the United States, which shall consist of a Senate and House of Representatives."
—Article I, Section 1, U.S. Constitution

VIRGINIA STATUTE FOR RELIGIOUS FREEDOM, 1786

Classical liberal principles such as the written protection of citizens' personal liberties were reflected in the addition of the Bill of Rights. The First Amendment's freedom of religion clauses were based on Thomas Jefferson's Virginia Statute for Religious Freedom. The document, which was accepted by the Virginia legislature in 1786, ensured the separation of church and state in Virginia.

"Congress shall make no law respecting an establishment of religion, or prohibiting the free exercise thereof . . ."
—First Amendment, U.S. Constitution

American colonies

Differentiating Instruction

Below Level

Struggling Readers

Research Required

Materials: blank note cards

1. Organize the class into six groups. Assign each group one of the influences listed above.
2. Have each group use this feature as well as the text in the previous chapter to prepare flash cards that explain the significance of the group's assigned topic and how it influenced the U.S. Constitution.
3. Have volunteers from each group present some of the group's cards to the class. Correct any student misconceptions or errors.
4. Reorganize students into groups that contain one member from each of the previous groups. In these new groups, have each member in turn use his or her flash cards to quiz the other members. **LS Interpersonal, Verbal/Linguistic**

Alternative Assessment Handbook, Rubric 14: Group Activity

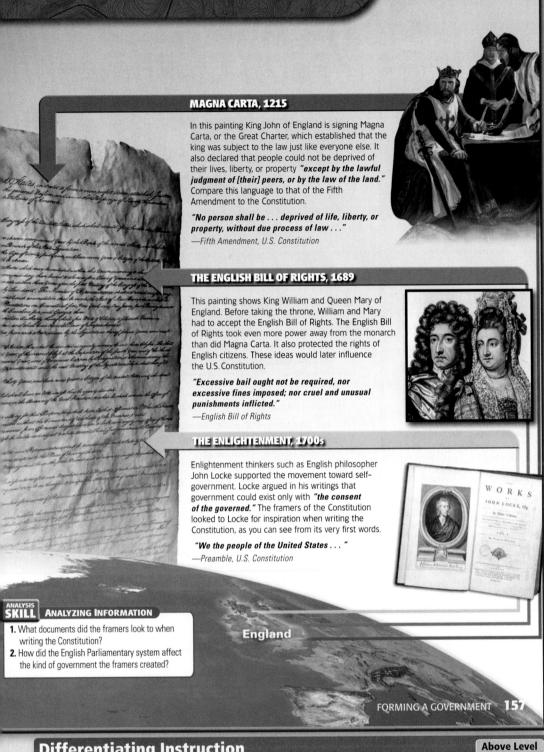

MAGNA CARTA, 1215

In this painting King John of England is signing Magna Carta, or the Great Charter, which established that the king was subject to the law just like everyone else. It also declared that people could not be deprived of their lives, liberty, or property ***"except by the lawful judgment of [their] peers, or by the law of the land."*** Compare this language to that of the Fifth Amendment to the Constitution.

"No person shall be . . . deprived of life, liberty, or property, without due process of law . . ."
—Fifth Amendment, U.S. Constitution

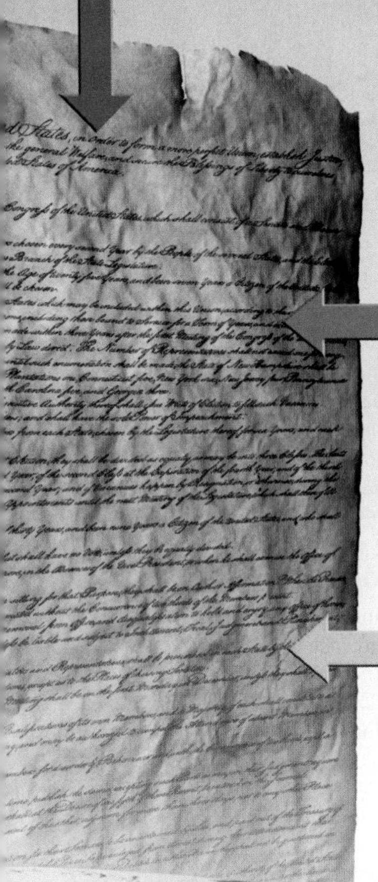

THE ENGLISH BILL OF RIGHTS, 1689

This painting shows King William and Queen Mary of England. Before taking the throne, William and Mary had to accept the English Bill of Rights. The English Bill of Rights took even more power away from the monarch than did Magna Carta. It also protected the rights of English citizens. These ideas would later influence the U.S. Constitution.

"Excessive bail ought not be required, nor excessive fines imposed; nor cruel and unusual punishments inflicted."
—English Bill of Rights

THE ENLIGHTENMENT, 1700s

Enlightenment thinkers such as English philosopher John Locke supported the movement toward self-government. Locke argued in his writings that government could exist only with ***"the consent of the governed."*** The framers of the Constitution looked to Locke for inspiration when writing the Constitution, as you can see from its very first words.

"We the people of the United States . . . "
—Preamble, U.S. Constitution

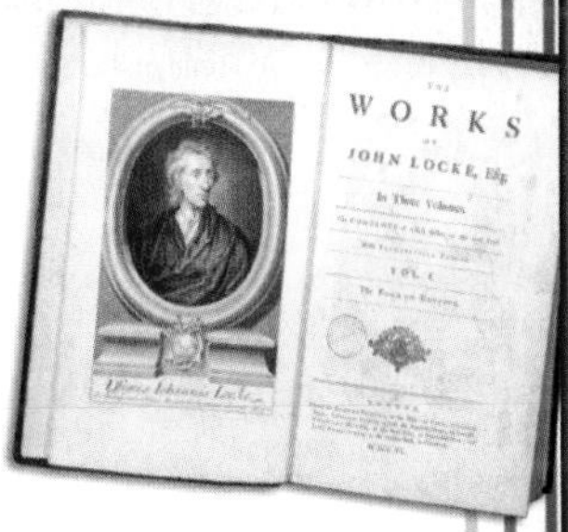

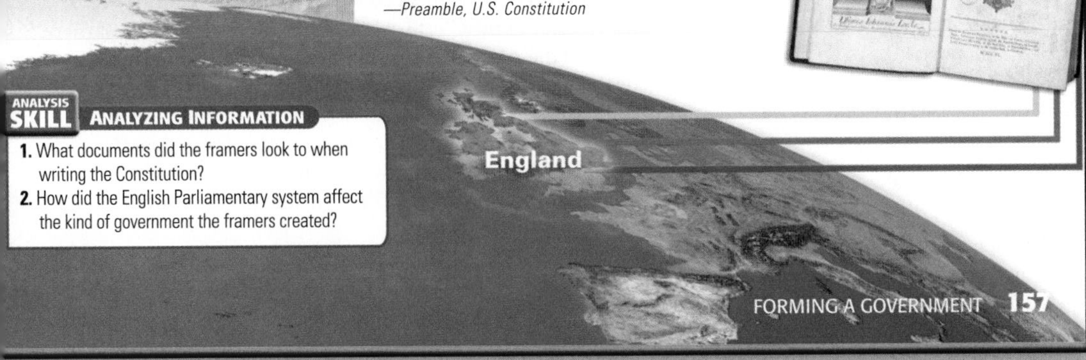

ANALYSIS SKILL ANALYZING INFORMATION

1. What documents did the framers look to when writing the Constitution?
2. How did the English Parliamentary system affect the kind of government the framers created?

History and Geography

World Events

Magna Carta Although Magna Carta became a cornerstone of constitutional government and rule by law, its original purpose was to limit the king's powers and protect the nobles' feudal rights. It included such concepts as church freedom, trial by jury, freedom from taxation without cause and consent, and due process of law. The document's final article empowered English barons to take up arms against the king if he violated its conditions.

Connect to Government

The British Constitution The British Constitution is not a single document. Instead, it consists partly of several great documents. Among them are Magna Carta, the Petition of Rights, the Habeas Corpus Act, the English Bill of Rights, and the Act of Settlement. It also includes acts of Parliament, which can be changed by later Parliaments. Some features of the British government have never even been written down but are based largely on tradition.

Did you know . . .

The College of William and Mary was the second university established in the colonies. Chartered in 1693 and named after King William III and Queen Mary II, it is located in Williamsburg, Virginia.

Differentiating Instruction

Above Level

Advanced/Gifted and Talented

Research Required

Materials: colored markers and pencils

1. Have students discuss the ideas listed above that influenced the U.S. Constitution.
2. Ask students to imagine that they have just opened a new restaurant called Constitutional Cuisine. Have each student create a menu for the restaurant. The menu should list the ideas above as dishes and provide a description of each dish that explains the idea's significance. Encourage students to be creative in their names and descriptions.
3. Students should base the price of each dish on that idea's importance to the Constitution.
4. In addition, students might organize the dishes into categories based on ideas such as rule of law, limited government, consent of the governed, separation of powers, and individual rights. **LS Verbal/Linguistic**

Alternative Assessment Handbook, Rubric 37: Writing Assignments

Answers

Analyzing Information 1. *Mayflower Compact, Virginia Statute for Religious Freedom, Magna Carta, English Bill of Rights;* **2.** *The framers used the same two-chamber structure for Congress that the British Parliament used.*

Preteach

Bellringer

If YOU were there . . . Use the **Daily Bellringer Transparency** to help students answer the question.

Daily Bellringer Transparency 5.2

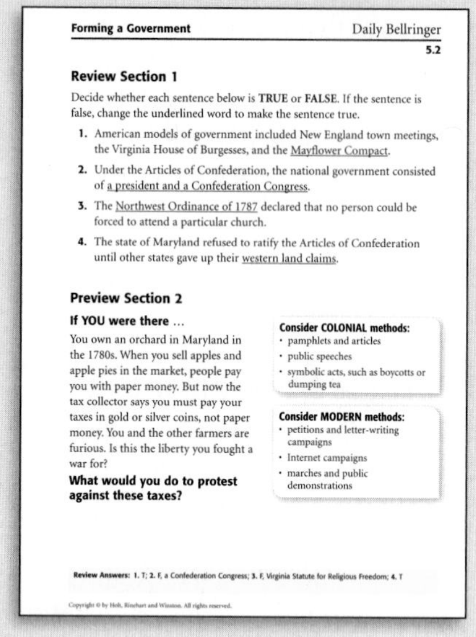
Forming a Government Daily Bellringer 5.2

Review Section 1

Decide whether each sentence below is **TRUE** or **FALSE**. If the sentence is false, change the underlined word to make the sentence true.

1. American models of government included New England town meetings, the Virginia House of Burgesses, and the Mayflower Compact.
2. Under the Articles of Confederation, the national government consisted of a president and a Confederation Congress.
3. The Northwest Ordinance of 1787 declared that no person could be forced to attend a particular church.
4. The state of Maryland refused to ratify the Articles of Confederation until other states gave up their western land claims.

Preview Section 2

If YOU were there ...

You own an orchard in Maryland in the 1780s. When you sell apples and apple pies in the market, people pay you with paper money. But now the tax collector says you must pay your taxes in gold or silver coins, not paper money. You and the other farmers are furious. Is this the liberty you fought a war for?

What would you do to protest against these taxes?

Consider COLONIAL methods:
- pamphlets and articles
- public speeches
- symbolic acts, such as boycotts or dumping tea

Consider MODERN methods:
- petitions and letter-writing campaigns
- Internet campaigns
- marches and public demonstrations

Review Answers: 1. T; 2. F, a Confederation Congress; 3. F, Virginia Statute for Religious Freedom; 4. T

Building Vocabulary

Preteach or review the following terms:

creditors people who lend money (p. 161)

debtors people who owe money (p. 161)

inflation a rise in prices combined with the reduced value of money (p. 161)

CRF: Vocabulary Builder Activity, Section 2

Taking Notes

Have students copy the graphic organizer onto their own paper and then use it to take notes on the section. This activity will prepare students for the Section Assessment, in which they will complete a graphic organizer that builds on the information using a critical-thinking skill.

Section Correlations

IN

8.4.1 Identify economic factors contributing to European exploration and colonization in North America, the American Revolution and the drafting of the Constitution of the United States. **8.4.9** Explain and evaluate examples of domestic and international interdependence throughout United States history.

SECTION 2

The New Nation Faces Challenges

What You Will Learn . . .

Main Ideas

1. The United States had difficulties with other nations.
2. Internal economic problems plagued the new nation.
3. Shays's Rebellion pointed out weaknesses in the Articles of Confederation.
4. Many Americans called for changes in the national government.

The Big Idea

Problems faced by the young nation made it clear that a new constitution was needed.

Key Terms and People

tariffs, *p. 159*
interstate commerce, *p. 160*
inflation, *p. 161*
depression, *p. 161*
Daniel Shays, *p. 161*
Shays's Rebellion, *p. 161*

TAKING NOTES As you read, use a graphic organizer like the one below to identify problems faced by the new nation.

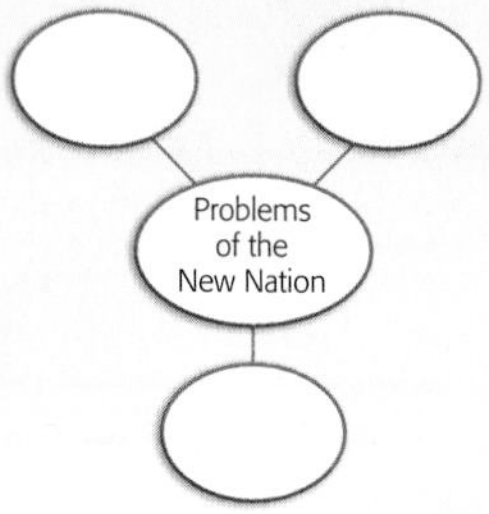

IN 8.4.1, 8.4.9

If YOU were there...

You own an orchard in Maryland in the 1780s. When you sell apples and apple pies in the market, people pay you with paper money. But now the tax collector says you must pay your taxes in gold or silver coins, not paper money. You and the other farmers are furious. Is this the liberty you fought a war for?

What would you do to protest these taxes?

BUILDING BACKGROUND Americans surprised the world by winning their independence from Great Britain. But the 13 new states were far from being a strong nation. Internal problems, especially with taxes and the economy, led to protests and rebellion. The government also had trouble with foreign trade and treaties.

Relations with Other Countries

Under the Articles of Confederation, Congress could not force states to provide soldiers for an army. The Continental Army had disbanded, or dissolved, soon after the signing of the Treaty of Paris of 1783. Without an army, the national government found it difficult to protect its citizens against foreign threats.

Trouble with Britain

It was also difficult to enforce international treaties such as the Treaty of Paris of 1783. The United States found it especially hard to force the British to turn over "with all convenient speed" their forts on the American side of the Great Lakes. The United States wanted to gain control of these forts because they protected valuable land and fur-trade routes. Still, Britain was slow to withdraw from the area. A British official warned against the United States trying to seize the forts by force. He said that any attempt to do so would be opposed by the thousands of British soldiers who had settled in Canada after the Revolution "who are ready to fly to arms at a moment's warning."

Teach the Big Idea

At Level

The New Nation Faces Challenges

1. **Teach** To teach the main ideas in the section, use the questions in the Direct Teach boxes.
2. **Apply** Ask students to imagine that Alexander Hamilton and James Madison have asked each of them to create a large notice to appear in U.S. newspapers announcing the Constitutional Convention. The notice should explain the weaknesses of the Articles of Confederation, the many problems that resulted, and why a Constitutional Convention is needed. The notice should also give the convention's time and place and urge all states to send delegates. **LS Verbal/Linguistic**
3. **Review** As you review the section, have volunteers share their notices with the class.
4. **Practice/Homework** Have each student create a protest sign addressing one problem with the Articles of Confederation. **LS Verbal/Linguistic**

Alternative Assessment Handbook, Rubrics 28: Posters; and 42: Writing to Inform

The United States Faces Trade Barriers

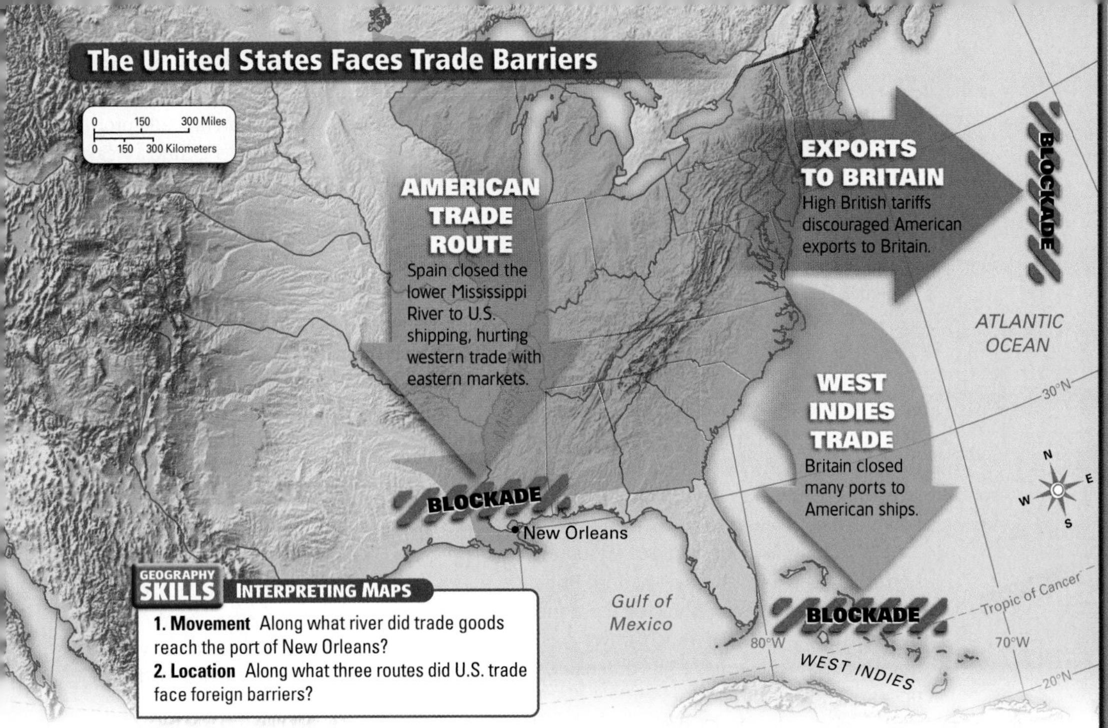

GEOGRAPHY SKILLS INTERPRETING MAPS

1. **Movement** Along what river did trade goods reach the port of New Orleans?
2. **Location** Along what three routes did U.S. trade face foreign barriers?

Trade with Britain

The United States also faced problems trading with Great Britain. After the signing of the Treaty of Paris, Britain closed many of its ports to American ships. Before the Revolutionary War, colonial ships had traded a great deal with the British West Indies and stopped there on their way to other destinations. This travel and trading stopped after 1783.

In addition, Britain forced American merchants to pay high **tariffs**—taxes on imports or exports. The tariffs applied to goods such as rice, tobacco, tar, and oil that were grown or mined in the United States and then sold in Britain. Merchants had to raise prices to cover the tariffs. Ultimately, the costs would be passed on to customers, who had to pay higher prices for the goods. The economic condition of the country was getting worse by the day.

Trade with Spain

In 1784 Spanish officials closed the lower Mississippi River to U.S. shipping. Western farmers and merchants were furious because they used the Mississippi to send goods to eastern and foreign markets. Congress tried to work out an agreement with Spain, but the plan did not receive a majority vote in Congress. The plan could not be passed. As a result, Spain broke off the negotiations.

Many state leaders began to criticize the national government. Rhode Island's representatives wrote, "Our federal government is but a name; a mere shadow without substance [power]." Critics believed that Spain might have continued to negotiate if the United States had possessed a strong military. These leaders believed that the national government needed to be more powerful.

Direct Teach

Main Idea

1 Relations with Other Countries

The United States had difficulties with other nations.

Recall What problems did the United States have with Great Britain? *Britain refused to turn over its forts as the Treaty of Paris required and closed many ports to American ships, which hurt the U.S. economy.*

Identify Cause and Effect How did the weaknesses of the Articles of Confederation affect U.S. relations with other nations? *The United States appeared weak because it had no army to enforce treaties or to give it a position of power in negotiations.*

Map Transparency 27: The United States Faces Trade Barriers

Linking to Today

World Trade Organization International trade has changed a great deal since the 1780s. Today countries are working to make trade easier. In 1993, for example, the United States and 116 other nations expanded an earlier trade agreement to form the World Trade Organization (WTO). Members of the WTO, which went into effect in January 1995, agreed to cut tariffs and eliminate manufacturing quotas.

Critical Thinking: Solving Problems

At Level

International Relations Dialogues

Standard English Mastery

1. Pair students. Assign one student in each pair to be an American official and the other student to be either a British or Spanish official.
2. Have each pair write a dialogue about the problems occurring between their two countries. Students' dialogues should address how each nation views the other, why problems are occurring, and suggestions for solutions.
3. Have each pair write a script for its dialogue. Remind students to use standard English and correct grammar, punctuation, and spelling.
4. Have volunteer pairs present their dialogues to the class. During each presentation, correct any factual errors or problems with students' standard English.
5. Conclude by having the class discuss how weaknesses in the Articles of Confederation led to international problems.

LS Interpersonal, Verbal/Linguistic

Alternative Assessment Handbook, Rubric 37: Writing Assignments

Answers

Interpreting Maps 1. *Mississippi River;* **2.** *route to New Orleans; export route to Britain; route to British West Indies*

Direct Teach

Main Idea

1 Relations with Other Countries

The United States had difficulties with other nations.

Identify Cause and Effect How did closed trade markets affect the U.S. economy? *Exports fell, imports from Britain rose, and British merchants could undersell American merchants, which further hurt the economy.*

Main Idea

2 Economic Problems

Internal economic problems plagued the new nation.

Recall What domestic economic problems did the states experience? *problems with interstate commerce, war debts, and a weak economy*

Analyze How did inflation hurt the economy? *decreased trade and business, which contributed to a depression*

Info to Know

Trade with China In 1785 the ship *Empress of China* returned to New York from China. The ship's owners had traded more than 40 tons of ginseng for tea and other Chinese products. Many Americans hoped that this success at opening trade with China would mean the United States would not have to rely so much on trade with Great Britain.

Impact of Closed Markets

The closing of markets in the British West Indies seriously affected the U.S. economy. James Madison of Virginia wrote about the crisis.

> "The Revolution has robbed us of our trade with the West Indies . . . without opening any other channels to compensate [make up for] it. In every point of view, indeed, the trade of this country is in a deplorable [terrible] condition."
>
> —James Madison, quoted in *Independence on Trial* by Frederick W. Marks III

Farmers could no longer export their goods to the British West Indies. They also had to hire British ships to carry their goods to British markets, which was very expensive. American exports dropped while British goods flowed freely into the United States.

This unequal trade caused serious economic problems for the new nation. British merchants could sell manufactured products in the United States at much lower prices than locally made goods. This difference in prices hurt American businesses.

The Confederation Congress could not correct the problem because it did not have the authority either to pass tariffs or to order the states to pass tariffs. The states could offer little help. If one state passed a tariff, the British could simply sell their goods in another state. Most states did not cooperate in trade matters. Instead, states worked only to increase their own trade rather than working to improve the trade situation for the whole country.

In 1785 the situation led a British magazine to call the new nation the Dis-United States. As a result of the trade problems with Britain, American merchants began looking for other markets such as China, France, and the Netherlands. Despite such attempts, Britain remained the most important trading partner of the United States.

READING CHECK **Analyzing** Why was the Confederation Congress unable to solve America's international trade problems?

Economic Problems

In addition to international trade issues, other challenges soon appeared. Trade problems among the states, war debts, and a weak economy plagued the states.

Trade among States

Because the Confederation Congress had no power to regulate **interstate commerce**—trade between two or more states—states followed their own trade interests. As a result, trade laws differed from state to state. This situation made trade difficult for merchants whose businesses crossed state lines.

Inflation

After the Revolutionary War, most states had a hard time paying off war debts and struggled to collect overdue taxes. To ease this hardship, some states began printing large amounts of paper money. The result was inflation. This money had little

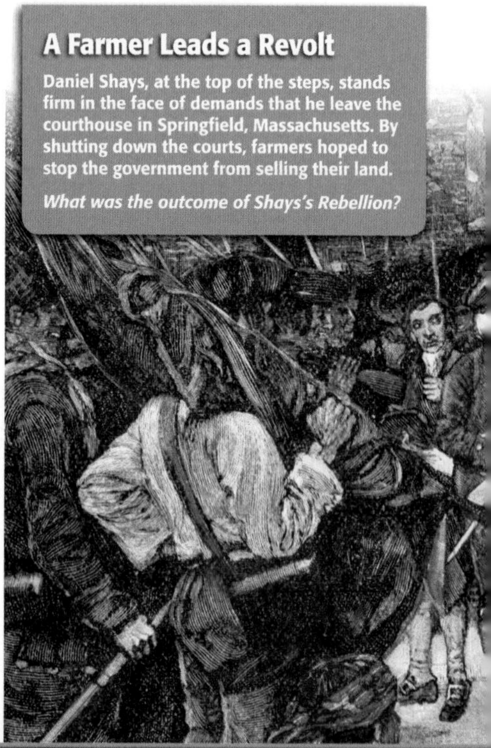

A Farmer Leads a Revolt

Daniel Shays, at the top of the steps, stands firm in the face of demands that he leave the courthouse in Springfield, Massachusetts. By shutting down the courts, farmers hoped to stop the government from selling their land.

What was the outcome of Shays's Rebellion?

Differentiating Instruction

Below Level

Struggling Readers

Materials: poster board, glue or tape

1. Organize the class into small, mixed-level groups. Ask students to imagine that they are newspaper publishers who must determine the headlines for the next issue of their papers.
2. Have each group write a headline and several subheadlines for each of the following topics: problems with Great Britain and Spain; problems associated with tariffs; economic problems that arose under the Articles of Confederation; and the consequences of Shays's Rebellion.
3. Then have each group arrange its headline and subheadlines on a poster board in the way they would appear in a newspaper.

LS Interpersonal, Verbal/Linguistic

Alternative Assessment Handbook, Rubrics 14: Group Activity; and 37: Writing Assignments

Answers

A Farmer Leads a Revolt *The state militia defeated the rebellion and arrested many of those involved, who were later freed. The rebellion convinced many Americans that the Articles of Confederation were too weak.*

Reading Check *The Confederation Congress did not have the authority to pass tariffs or to order the states to do so.*

or no real value, because states did not have gold or silver reserves to back it up. **Inflation** occurs when there are increased prices for goods and services combined with the reduced value of money. Congress had no power to stop states from issuing more paper money and thus stop inflation.

Weak Economy

In Rhode Island the state legislature printed large amounts of paper money worth very little. This made debtors—people who owe money—quite happy. They could pay back their debts with paper money worth less than the coins they had borrowed. However, creditors—people who lend money—were upset. Hundreds of creditors fled Rhode Island to avoid being paid back with worthless money.

The loss of trade with Britain combined with inflation created a **depression**. A depression is a period of low economic activity combined with a rise in unemployment.

READING CHECK **Summarizing** What economic problems did the new nation face?

Shays's Rebellion

Each state handled its economic problems differently. Massachusetts refused to print worthless paper money. It tried to pay its war debts by collecting taxes on land.

Heavy Debts for Farmers

Massachusetts's tax policy hit farmers hard. As landowners, they had to pay the new taxes. However, farmers had trouble paying their debts. The courts began forcing them to sell their property. Some farmers had to serve terms in debtors' prison; others had to sell their labor.

Many government leaders in the state did not care about the problems of poor farmers, however. In some cases, farmers actually owed these leaders money.

Farmers Rebel

In August 1786, farmers in three western counties began a revolt. Bands of angry citizens closed down courts in western Massachusetts. Their reasoning was simple—with the courts shut down, no one's property could be taken. In September a poor farmer and Revolutionary War veteran, **Daniel Shays**, led hundreds of men in a forced shutdown of the Supreme Court in Springfield, Massachusetts. The state government ordered the farmers to stop the revolt under threat of capture and death. These threats only made Shays and his followers more determined. The uprising of farmers to protest high taxes and heavy debt became known as **Shays's Rebellion**.

Shays's Defeat

Shays's forces were defeated by state troops in January 1787. By February many of the rebels were in prison. During their trials, 14 leaders were sentenced to death. However, the state soon freed most of the rebels, including Shays. State officials knew that many citizens of the state agreed with the rebels and their cause.

READING CHECK **Finding Main Ideas** What led to Shays's Rebellion?

Direct Teach

Main Idea

❸ Shays's Rebellion

Shays's Rebellion pointed out weaknesses in the Articles of Confederation.

Recall What was Shays's Rebellion, and why was it significant? *uprising of Massachusetts farmers in 1786; convinced many that the Articles of Confederation were too weak*

Identify Points of View Why do you think Daniel Shays and the other rebels took the actions that they did? *pushed to the breaking point; felt they had nothing to lose*

Make Judgments Do you think the actions of Daniel Shays and the other rebels were justified? Explain your answer. *possible answers—Yes, they were fighting to save their farms; no, they had a right to protest taxes but not in the way that they did.*

Primary Source

Two Views of Shays's Rebellion

Shays's Rebellion greatly upset many American leaders. George Washington exclaimed, "I am mortified [embarrassed] beyond expression." Washington feared that the United States must look "ridiculous in the eyes of all Europe." Not everyone saw the rebellion this way, though. Thomas Jefferson, serving as ambassador to France, responded to the event differently. "A little rebellion, now and then, is a good thing," he said. "The tree of liberty must be refreshed from time to time with the blood of patriots and tyrants."

Critical Thinking: Identifying Points of View

At Level

Economic Problems Journals

1. Assign each student one of the following roles: western merchant who sends items back East, eastern farmer who exports goods to British markets, North Carolina tobacco planter, Rhode Island creditor, or Massachusetts farmer.
2. Have each student write one or more journal entries about the economic problems that he or she faces. Have students refer to the text and to the United States Faces Trade Barriers map.
3. Encourage students to propose solutions to the economic problems they face.
4. **Extend** Have students think about possible solutions to the economic problems caused by the weakness of the Articles of Confederation. Then have each student write a petition to the Confederation Congress asking for specific changes to the Articles and explaining how the changes would improve the economy.

LS Logical/Mathematical, Verbal/Linguistic

Alternative Assessment Handbook, Rubrics 15: Journals; and 35: Solving Problems

Answers

Reading Check (left) *trade problems among the states, war debts, weak economy*

Reading Check (right) *growing anger among Massachusetts farmers over the state's economic policies, which led to rising debts and the risk of losing their farms, having to serve time in debtors' prison, or having to sell their labor*

Direct Teach

Main Idea

4 Calls for Change

Many Americans called for changes in the national government.

Describe How did some states address the problems of the weak national government? *Some states sent delegates to the Annapolis Convention; some delegates called for a Constitutional Convention.*

Evaluate Why do you think some states chose not to send delegates to the Annapolis Convention? *possible answers—fear of losing state power; experienced fewer problems*

Quick Facts Transparency 12: Weaknesses of the Articles of Confederation

Review & Assess

Close

Have students review the strengths and weaknesses of the Articles of Confederation.

Review

Online Quiz, Section 5.2

Assess

SE Section 2 Assessment

PASS: Section 5.2 Quiz

Alternative Assessment Handbook

Reteach/Classroom Intervention

Interactive Reader and Study Guide, Section 5.2

Interactive Skills Tutor CD-ROM

Calls for Change

In the end, Shays's Rebellion showed the weakness of the Confederation government. It led some Americans to admit that the Articles of Confederation had failed to protect the ideals of liberty set forth in the Declaration of Independence.

When Massachusetts had asked the national government to help put down Shays's Rebellion, Congress could offer little help. More Americans began calling for a stronger central government. They wanted leaders who would be able to protect the nation in times of crisis.

Weaknesses of the Articles of Confederation (QUICK FACTS)
• Most power held by states
• One branch of government
• Legislative branch has few powers
• No executive branch
• No judicial system
• No system of checks and balances

Earlier in 1786 the Virginia legislature had called for a national conference. It wanted to talk about economic problems and ways to change the Articles of Confederation. The meeting took place in Annapolis, Maryland, in September 1786.

Nine states decided to send delegates to the Annapolis Convention but some of their delegates were late and missed the meeting. Connecticut, Georgia, Maryland, and South Carolina did not respond to the request at all and sent no delegates.

Because of the poor attendance, the participants, including James Madison and Alexander Hamilton, called on all 13 states to send delegates to a Constitutional Convention in Philadelphia in May 1787. They planned to revise the Articles of Confederation to better meet the needs of the nation.

READING CHECK **Finding Main Ideas** Why did some people believe the national government needed to change?

SUMMARY AND PREVIEW Many Americans believed that Shays's Rebellion was final proof that the national government needed to be changed. In the next section you will read about the Constitutional Convention.

Section 2 Assessment

go.hrw.com
Online Quiz
KEYWORD: SF7 HP5

Reviewing Ideas, Terms, and People

1. a. **Summarize** What problems did the United States experience with Spain and Great Britain?
   b. **Predict** What are some possible results of the growing problems between the United States and Great Britain? Why?
2. a. **Describe** What difficulties were involved with **interstate commerce**?
   b. **Analyze** What was the cause of **inflation** in the new nation, and how could it have been prevented?
3. a. **Explain** How did Massachusetts's tax policy affect farmers?
   b. **Evaluate** Defend the actions of **Daniel Shays** and the other rebels.
4. a. **Recall** Why did Madison and Hamilton call for a Constitutional Convention?
   b. **Analyze** How did **Shays's Rebellion** lead to a call for change in the United States?

Critical Thinking

5. **Categorizing** Review your notes on the problems faced by the new nation. Then identify those problems as either domestic or international in a graphic organizer like the one shown below.

Domestic Problems	International Problems

FOCUS ON WRITING

6. **Identifying Problems** In this section you learned about several problems of the young United States. Were any of those problems made worse by the powers that the Articles of Confederation did or did not give the national government?

Section 2 Assessment Answers

1. a. Great Britain—refused to hand over forts, closed ports to U.S. ships, set high tariffs; Spain—closed Mississippi to U.S. shipping
   b. possible answer—could go to war because of problems stated in previous answer
2. a. Lack of regulation and lack of cooperation between states made trade difficult for some merchants.
   b. Some states began printing large amounts of paper money; little could be done.
3. a. Heavy taxes forced farmers to sell their land or else go into debt and risk imprisonment.
   b. Answers should show an understanding of the rebels' anger over high taxes.
4. a. weaknesses in Articles of Confederation, poor attendance at Annapolis Convention
   b. convinced many Americans that the Articles of Confederation were too weak
5. Domestic—no power to regulate interstate commerce, could not help states keep order, could not stop inflation; International—could not pass tariffs, enforce treaties
6. See answer to Question 5.

Answers

Reading Check *because the weaknesses of the Articles of Confederation caused problems with foreign nations, international trade issues, domestic economic problems, and Shays's Rebellion*

Creating the Constitution

SECTION 3

If YOU were there...

You are a merchant in Connecticut in 1787. You have been a member of your state legislature for several years. This spring, the legislature is choosing delegates to a convention to revise the Articles of Confederation. Delegates will meet in Philadelphia. It means leaving your business in others' hands for most of the summer. Still, you hope to be chosen.

Why would you want to go to the Constitutional Convention?

BUILDING BACKGROUND It did not take long for people to realize that the Articles of Confederation had many weaknesses. By the mid-1780s most political leaders agreed that changes were needed. To make those changes, they called on people with experience in government.

Constitutional Convention

In February 1787 the Confederation Congress invited each state to send delegates to a convention in Philadelphia. The goal of the meeting was to improve the Articles of Confederation.

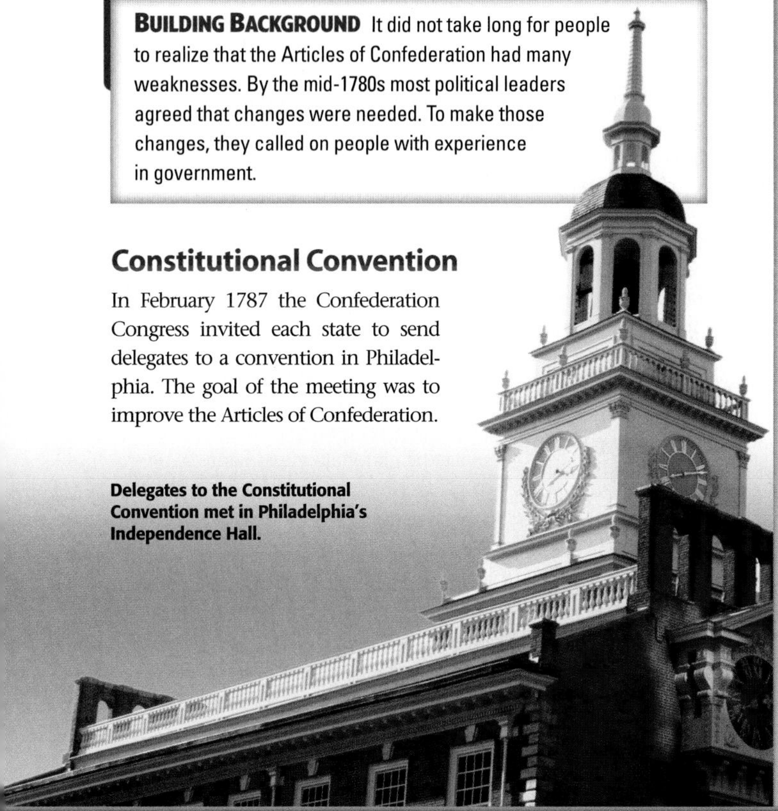

Delegates to the Constitutional Convention met in Philadelphia's Independence Hall.

What You Will Learn . . .

Main Ideas

1. The Constitutional Convention met to improve the government of the United States.
2. The issue of representation led to the Great Compromise.
3. Regional debate over slavery led to the Three-Fifths Compromise.
4. The U.S. Constitution created federalism and a balance of power.

The Big Idea

A new constitution provided a framework for a stronger national government.

Key Terms and People

Constitutional Convention, *p. 164*
James Madison, *p. 164*
Virginia Plan, *p. 164*
New Jersey Plan, *p. 165*
Great Compromise, *p. 165*
Three-Fifths Compromise, *p. 166*
popular sovereignty, *p. 167*
federalism, *p. 167*
legislative branch, *p. 167*
executive branch, *p. 167*
judicial branch, *p. 167*
checks and balances, *p. 167*

TAKING NOTES As you read, take notes on the conflicts that arose during the Constitutional Convention and the compromises reached.

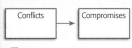

Conflicts → Compromises

IN 8.1.5, 8.1.9, 8.1.28, 8.1.30, 8.2.1, 8.2.3, 8.2.5, 8.2.6, 8.4.1

Teach the Big Idea

At Level

Creating the Constitution

Standard English Mastery

1. **Teach** To teach the main ideas in the section, use the questions in the Direct Teach boxes.
2. **Apply** Have students, working either individually or with a partner, create glossaries for a handbook on the Constitutional Convention. Students' glossaries should include descriptions of key individuals, major proposals and plans, significant compromises, and legal and political terms discussed in the section. Tell students to use standard English when writing their glossaries. **LS Verbal/Linguistic**
3. **Review** Have students share their glossaries. Correct any errors as well as students' use of standard English.
4. **Practice/Homework** Have students make flow charts showing the key plans, debates, and issues that led to the Great Compromise and Three-Fifths Compromise. **LS Visual/Spatial**

Alternative Assessment Handbook, Rubrics 13: Graphic Organizers; and 42: Writing to Inform

Preteach

Bellringer

If YOU were there . . . Use the **Daily Bellringer Transparency** to help students answer the question.

Daily Bellringer Transparency 5.3

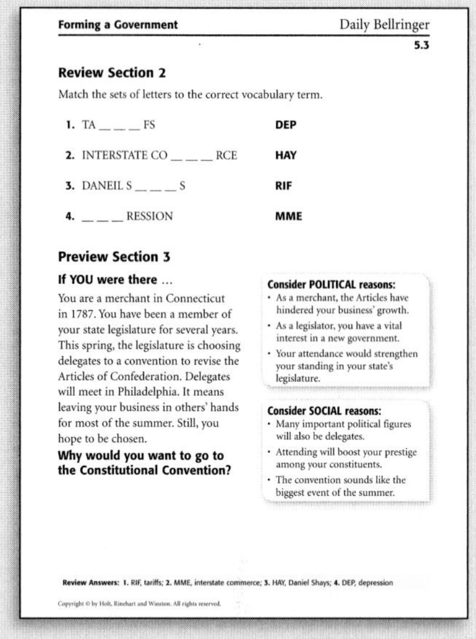

Forming a Government Daily Bellringer 5.3

Review Section 2

Match the sets of letters to the correct vocabulary term.

1.	TA _ _ _ FS	DEP
2.	INTERSTATE CO _ _ _ RCE	HAY
3.	DANEIL S _ _ _ S	RIF
4.	_ _ _ RESSION	MME

Preview Section 3

If YOU were there ...

You are a merchant in Connecticut in 1787. You have been a member of your state legislature for several years. This spring, the legislature is choosing delegates to a convention to revise the Articles of Confederation. Delegates will meet in Philadelphia. It means leaving your business in others' hands for most of the summer. Still, you hope to be chosen.

Why would you want to go to the Constitutional Convention?

Consider POLITICAL reasons:
- As a merchant, the Articles have hindered your business' growth.
- As a legislator, you have a vital interest in a new government.
- Your attendance would strengthen your standing in your state's legislature.

Consider SOCIAL reasons:
- Many important political figures will also be delegates.
- Attending will boost your prestige among your constituents.
- The convention sounds like the biggest event of the summer.

Review Answers: 1. RIF, tariffs; 2. MME, interstate commerce; 3. HAY, Daniel Shays; 4. DEP, depression

Building Vocabulary

Preteach or review the following terms:

bicameral made up of two houses (p. 165)

federalism the sharing of power between a central government and its states (p. 167)

sovereignty supreme power (p. 164)

unicameral made up of one house (p. 165)

CRF: Vocabulary Builder Activity, Section 3

Taking Notes

Have students copy the graphic organizer onto their own paper and then use it to take notes on the section. This activity will prepare students for the Section Assessment, in which they will complete a graphic organizer that builds on the information using a critical-thinking skill.

Section Correlations IN

8.1.5 Identify and explain key events leading to the creation of a strong union among the thirteen original states and in the establishment of the United States as a federal republic. **8.1.9** Describe the influence of important individuals on social and political developments of the time such as the Independence movement and the framing of the Constitution.

Direct Teach

Main Idea

1 Constitutional Convention

The Constitutional Convention met to improve the government of the United States.

Identify Who were some key delegates to the convention, and who served as its president? *Benjamin Franklin, James Madison, George Washington (president)*

Analyze How might the Constitution have been different if African Americans, Native Americans, and women had been able to attend the convention? *possible answer—Issues such as slavery and suffrage might have been addressed differently.*

- **CRF:** Biography Activity: Signers of the Constitution
- **CRF:** Primary Source Activity: Benjamin Franklin Addresses the Constitutional Convention

Info to Know

A Well-Prepared Man James Madison began preparing for the Constitutional Convention in the fall of 1786 by reading works of political history, classical republicanism, and modern political theory. With Thomas Jefferson's help, Madison had acquired a small library of the social and economic philosophies of the Enlightenment, including the 37-volume set of Denis Diderot's *Encyclopédie*.

go.hrw.com
Online Resources
KEYWORD: SF7 CH5
ACTIVITY: Convention Leaders

Roger Sherman James Madison James Wilson

The **Constitutional Convention** was held in May 1787 in Philadelphia's Independence Hall to improve the Articles of Confederation. However, delegates would leave with an entirely new U.S. Constitution. This decision angered some of the participants.

Most delegates were well educated, and many had served in state legislatures or Congress. Benjamin Franklin and **James Madison** were there. Revolutionary War hero George Washington was elected president of the Convention.

Several important voices were absent. John Adams and Thomas Jefferson could not attend. Patrick Henry chose not to attend because he did not want a stronger central government. Women, African Americans, and Native Americans did not take part because they did not yet have the rights of citizens.

READING CHECK **Summarizing** What was the purpose of the Constitutional Convention?

Great Compromise

Several issues divided the delegates to the Constitutional Convention. Some members wanted only small changes to the Articles of Confederation, while others wanted to rewrite the Articles completely.

Those delegates who wanted major changes to the Articles had different goals. For example, small and large states had different ideas about representation, economic concerns such as tariffs, and slavery. In addition, delegates disagreed over how strong to make the national government.

Virginia Plan

After the delegates had met for four days, Edmund Randolph of Virginia presented the **Virginia Plan**. He proposed a new federal constitution that would give sovereignty, or supreme power, to the central government. The legislature would be bicameral—made

Differentiating Instruction

Below Level

Struggling Readers

Materials: paper, art supplies, invitations (optional)

1. Have students identify the purpose of the Constitutional Convention *(to discuss ways to improve the Articles of Confederation)*.
2. Then ask students to identify some characteristics that delegates would need for the convention to succeed *(government experience, education, knowledge of Enlightenment thinkers, charisma, diplomacy, patience, good listening and speaking skills)*. List students' ideas for the class to see.
3. Ask students to imagine that they are creating invitations for the convention. Have each student write a persuasive invitation to send to proposed delegates. (Provide models of invitations, if possible.) The invitations should include the convention's date and location, notable individuals who will attend, and why attendance is vital. **LS Verbal/Linguistic**

- Alternative Assessment Handbook, Rubric 43: Writing to Persuade

Answers

Reading Check *to discuss ways to improve the Articles of Confederation*

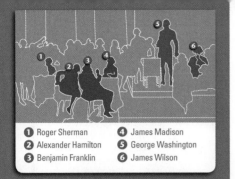

1 Roger Sherman
2 Alexander Hamilton
3 Benjamin Franklin
4 James Madison
5 George Washington
6 James Wilson

This painting shows the signing of the Constitution on September 17, 1787. James Madison, number 4 on the diagram, became known as the "Father of the Constitution" for his ideas about government and his ability to lead the delegates to agreement. ***Which person did the artist choose to make the focus of this painting? Why do you think that is?***

up of two houses, or groups of representatives—and chosen on the basis of state populations. Larger states would thus have more representatives than would smaller states. Delegates from the smaller states believed that it would give too much power to the larger states.

New Jersey Plan

The smaller states came up with a plan to stop the larger states from getting too much power. New Jersey delegate William Paterson presented the small-state or **New Jersey Plan**, which called for a unicameral, or one-house, legislature. The plan gave each state an equal number of votes, and thus an equal voice, in the federal government. The plan gave the federal government the power to tax citizens in all states, and it allowed the government to regulate commerce.

Compromise Is Reached

After a month of debate, the delegates were unable to agree on how states should be represented. The convention reached a deadlock.

Finally, Roger Sherman of Connecticut proposed a compromise plan. The legislative branch would have two houses. Each state, regardless of its size, would have two representatives in the Senate, or upper house. This would give each state an equal voice, pleasing the smaller states. In the House of Representatives, or lower house, the number of representatives for each state would be determined by the state's population. This pleased the larger states. The agreement to create a two-house legislature became known as the **Great Compromise**. James Wilson, a great speaker, saw his dream of a strong national government come true.

THE IMPACT TODAY

All U.S. states but one modeled their legislative branches on the federal one, with a House of Representatives and a Senate. Nebraska has a unicameral legislature.

READING CHECK **Contrasting** How did the Virginia Plan and New Jersey Plan differ?

QUICK FACTS

Virginia Plan
- Gave more power to national government
- Bicameral legislature
- Number in both houses based on population

Great Compromise
- Bicameral legislature
- Number of representatives based on state populations in lower house
- Number of representatives equal from each state in upper house

New Jersey Plan
- Gave more power to state governments
- Unicameral legislature
- Number of representatives equal from each state

Direct Teach

Main Idea

2 Great Compromise

The issue of representation led to the Great Compromise.

Recall What were some issues that divided delegates at the Constitutional Convention? *how much to change the Articles and differing ideas about representation, how strong to make the government, economic concerns such as tariffs, and issues such as slavery*

Summarize How did the Great Compromise combine elements of the Virginia and New Jersey Plans? *bicameral legislature, representation in lower house based on population (Virginia Plan); representation in upper house equal (New Jersey Plan)*

Evaluate Do you think the Great Compromise shared power equally between large and small states? *Answers will vary but should reflect an understanding of the compromise.*

Quick Facts Transparency 13: The Great Compromise

Info to Know

A "Heated" Debate Can you imagine sitting in a hot room wearing a heavy suit and stockings? How about doing so in the middle of summer? That's what the framers of the Constitution did. The weather in Philadelphia during the Constitutional Convention was very hot and humid. Moreover, the delegates kept the windows closed to keep out flies and to prevent passersby from listening.

Critical Thinking: Finding Main Ideas

At Level

Constitutional Convention Notes

Background The delegates to the Constitutional Convention did not allow any outsiders, such as journalists, inside. As a result, historians rely on the careful notes that delegate James Madison took to know what took place during the convention.

1. Ask students to imagine that they are official note takers at the Constitutional Convention.
2. Have students go through the section and make three lists—one list of the main topics of debate, one list of the key decisions made, and one list of the key delegates and their contributions.
3. Have students share the information from their lists. Create master lists for the class to see.
4. **Extend** Ask students to imagine that they have shared their lists with a journalist. Have each student write an article about one aspect of the Convention, such as who attended or one of the major topics of debate. Remind students to address the journalistic questions of "who, what, when, where, and why." **LS Verbal/Linguistic**

Alternative Assessment Handbook, Rubric 37: Writing Assignment

Answers

Signing of the Constitution *Washington, because he served as the president of the convention and later as the first U.S. president*

Reading Check *Virginia Plan—central government sovereign; bicameral legislature based on population; New Jersey Plan—unicameral legislature with equal representation per state; federal government could tax the states and regulate commerce*

Direct Teach

Main Idea

❸ Three-Fifths Compromise

Regional debate over slavery led to the Three-Fifths Compromise.

Explain How did regional differences and the issue of slavery divide the Constitutional Convention? *Southern delegates wanted slaves to be counted as part of state populations, which would give southern states more power; Northerners disagreed, because northern states had fewer slaves.*

Analyze How did the Three-Fifths Compromise resolve the debate? *Delegates agreed to count each slave as three-fifths of a person when determining representation.*

Draw Conclusions Why did the delegates agree to allow the international slave trade to continue for another 20 years? *to appease southern delegates and to give southern economies, which were dependent on the international slave trade, time to adjust to its end*

Primary Source

POINTS OF VIEW

Compromise and the Slave Trade

The issue of slavery highlighted the growing division between the North and the South. Gouverneur Morris of New York spoke with much emotion against the Three-Fifths Compromise. Also, the idea of banning the foreign slave trade prompted southerners such as John Rutledge of South Carolina to defend the practice.

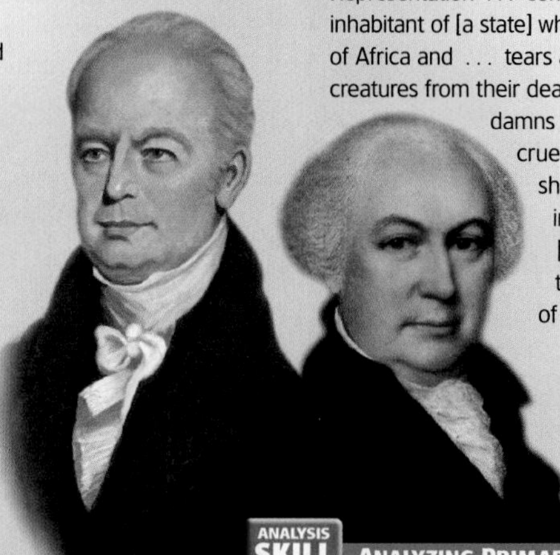

"If the Convention thinks that North Carolina, South Carolina, and Georgia will ever agree to the plan [to prohibit the slave trade], unless their right to import slaves be untouched, the expectation is vain [useless]."

—John Rutledge,
quoted in *The Atlantic Monthly,* February 1891, by Frank Gaylord Cook

"The admission of slaves into the Representation . . . comes to this: that the inhabitant of [a state] who goes to the coast of Africa and . . . tears away his fellow creatures from their dearest connections and damns them to the most cruel bondage [slavery], shall have more votes in a Government [established] for protection of the rights of mankind."

—Gouverneur Morris,
quoted in *Founding the Republic,* edited by John J. Patrick

ANALYSIS SKILL **ANALYZING PRIMARY SOURCES**

Finding Main Ideas How did these two views of slavery differ?

Three-Fifths Compromise

The debate over representation also involved regional differences. Southern delegates wanted enslaved Africans to be counted as part of their state populations. This way they would have more representatives, and more power, in Congress. Northerners disagreed. They wanted the number of slaves to determine taxes but not representation.

To resolve this problem, some delegates thought of a compromise. They wanted to count three-fifths of the slaves in each state as part of that state's population to decide how many representatives a state would have. After much debate, the delegates voted to accept the proposal, called the **Three-Fifths Compromise**. Under this agreement only three-fifths of a state's slave population would count when determining representation.

Another major issue was the foreign slave trade. Some of the delegates believed slavery was wrong and wanted the federal government to ban the slave trade. Others said that the southern states' economies needed the slave trade. Many southern delegates said they would leave the Union if the Constitution immediately ended the slave trade. Also at issue was Congress's ability to tax imports and exports.

Worried delegates reached another compromise. The Commerce Compromises allowed Congress to levy tariffs on imports, but not exports, and allowed the importation of slaves until the end of 1807. The delegates omitted, or left out, the words *slavery* and *slave* in the Constitution. They referred instead to "free Persons" and "all other Persons."

READING CHECK **Summarizing** What compromise was reached over the issue of the slave trade?

Primary Source

Reading Like a Historian

Compromise and the Slave Trade

To help students read the excerpts like historians, ask the following questions:

- What states and regions of the country do Rutledge and Morris represent?
- What regional concerns and biases may have influenced each man's point of view?
- In what context was each statement made? What issues or concerns was each man addressing?

Differentiating Instruction

Advanced/Gifted and Talented **Above Level**

Recipe for Government Have students write a recipe for creating the U.S. government. Tell them that the framers of the Constitution chose political ideas from many sources (the ingredients) to draft the Constitution. Then they decided how to balance these ideas (the measurements) and put them into practice (the directions). LS **Verbal/Linguistic**

Alternative Assessment Handbook, Rubric 39: Writing to Create

English-Language Learners **Below Level**

Visualizing Balanced Government Have each student create a political cartoon or visual diagram illustrating how the U.S. government is balanced under the U.S. Constitution. Students might focus on one aspect, such as federalism or checks and balances, or on the topic in general. LS **Visual/Spatial**

Alternative Assessment Handbook, Rubrics 3: Artwork; and 27: Political Cartoons

Answers

Analyzing Primary Sources *Rutledge is pro-slavery, and Morris is antislavery.*

Reading Check *Delegates agreed to end the international slave trade in 20 years rather than immediately.*

The Living Constitution

Most Convention delegates wanted a strong national government. At the same time, they hoped to protect **popular sovereignty**, the idea that political authority belongs to the people. Americans had boldly declared this idea in the Declaration of Independence.

Federalist Government

The delegates also wanted to balance the power of the central government with the power of the states. Therefore, the delegates created **federalism**. Federalism is the sharing of power between a central government and the states that make up a country. Under the previous confederal system, states were loosely joined together without a strong central government.

Under the Constitution, each state must obey the authority of the federal, or national, government. States have control over government functions not specifically assigned to the federal government. This includes control of local government, education, the chartering of corporations, and the supervision of religious bodies. States also have the power to create and oversee civil and criminal law. States, however, must protect the welfare of their citizens.

Checks and Balances

The Constitution also balances the power among three branches, each responsible for separate tasks. The first is the **legislative branch**, or Congress. Congress is responsible for proposing and passing laws. It is made up of two houses, as created in the Great Compromise. The Senate has two members from each state. In the House of Representatives each state is represented according to its population.

The second branch, the **executive branch**, includes the president and the departments that help run the government. The executive branch makes sure the law is carried out. The third branch is the **judicial branch**. The judicial branch is made up of all the national courts. This branch is responsible for interpreting laws, punishing criminals, and settling disputes between states.

The framers of the Constitution created a system of **checks and balances**, which keeps any branch of government from becoming too powerful. For example, Congress has the power to pass bills into law. The president has the power to veto, or reject, laws that Congress passes. However, Congress can override the president's veto with a two-thirds

FOCUS ON INDIANA

Most states, including Indiana, adopted a similar structure for their governments. Indiana has a governor as executive and a General Assembly as the legislative branch.

LINKING TO TODAY

Legislative Branch

When it first met in 1789, the U.S. House of Representatives had just 65 members. As the nation's population grew, more members were added. Today, the number has been set at 435, to prevent the size of the House from growing unmanageable. Though the numbers of women and minorities in Congress are still unrepresentative of the population as a whole, Congress has become more diverse. Linda and Loretta Sanchez, pictured here, are the first sisters to serve in Congress at the same time.

ANALYSIS SKILL ANALYZING INFORMATION

How is the change in makeup of the legislative branch shown through Linda and Loretta Sanchez?

Direct Teach

Main Idea

4 The Living Constitution

The U.S. Constitution created federalism and a balance of power.

Define What is popular sovereignty? *the idea that political authority belongs to the people*

Identify What is the main responsibility of each branch of government? *legislative—proposing and passing laws; executive—making sure laws are carried out; judicial—interpreting laws*

Analyze How did the framers put into practice the idea of popular sovereignty expressed in the Declaration of Independence? *established a system of federalism, in which government power is shared between the states and the federal government and in which states are required to protect the welfare of citizens*

Quick Facts Transparency 14: The Constitution Strengthens the National Government

Did you know . . .

The word *slavery* did not appear in the U.S. Constitution until the Thirteenth Amendment abolished the practice in 1865. In its sections protecting slavery, the Constitution used indirect wording. For example, the provision that allowed slaveholders the right to pursue runaway slaves read, "No Person held to Service or Labour in one State . . . escaping into another, shall be discharged from such Service or Labour."

Focus on Indiana

IN 8.2.3

Make Inferences Why might Indiana and other states have a government structure similar to the national government? *Because the structure of the national government protects the government from becoming too powerful.*

Collaborative Learning

At Level

Constitutional Convention Web Site

1. Organize the class into groups. Have each group design the home page of a Web site on the Constitutional Convention. Groups can create their designs on poster board or on a computer.
2. Groups' home pages should include a title, general information about the site, and a list of links to supporting pages within the Web site. These pages might provide highlights of the convention, information about key topics or debates, biographies of delegates, primary sources, links to related Web sites, and so on.
3. Groups should assign members roles to ensure that all students participate.
4. Have each group present its design to the class.
LS Interpersonal, Verbal/Linguistic, Visual/Spatial

Alternative Assessment Handbook, Rubric 14: Group Activity

Answers

Analyzing Information *The two sisters are Hispanic women, representing the diversity that has become part of the legislative branch in recent times.*

Direct Teach

Info to Know

Hamilton on Government In the midst of the debates at the Constitutional Convention, Alexander Hamilton gave one of the longest speeches of the proceedings. He was a strong supporter of the British government and urged delegates to create one like it. He suggested that the presidency be a lifetime job and even offered his own plan for the government—one modeled on Britain's. The rest of the delegates appear to have politely listened to Hamilton's suggestions and then ignored them and returned to the discussion at hand.

Review & Assess

Close

Have students summarize how the U.S. Constitution resolved the weaknesses in the Articles of Confederation.

Review

go.hrw.com Online Quiz, Section 5.3

Assess

SE Section 3 Assessment

PASS: Section 5.3 Quiz

Alternative Assessment Handbook

Reteach/Classroom Intervention

Interactive Reader and Study Guide, Section 5.3

Interactive Skills Tutor CD-ROM

go.hrw.com Online Resources

KEYWORD: SF7 CH5
ACTIVITY: The Great Debate

Answers

Reading Check *monarchy—absolute power vested in one individual; federal—dual sovereignty, balance of power between central and local governments; confederal—individual sovereign units in common arrangement, an alliance*

The Constitution Strengthens the National Government (QUICK FACTS)

Strengths of the Constitution	Weaknesses of the Articles of Confederation
✔ most power held by national government	• most power held by states
✔ three branches of government	• one branch of government
✔ legislative branch has many powers	• legislative branch has few powers
✔ executive branch led by president	• no executive branch
✔ judicial branch to review the laws	• no judicial system
✔ firm system of checks and balances	• no system of checks and balances

majority vote. The Supreme Court has the power to review laws passed by Congress and strike down any law that violates the Constitution by declaring it *unconstitutional*.

The final draft of the Constitution was completed in September 1787. Only 3 of the 42 delegates who remained refused to sign. The signed Constitution was sent first to Congress and then to the states for ratification. The delegates knew that the Constitution was not a perfect document, but they believed they had protected the ideas of republicanism.

READING CHECK **Comparing and Contrasting** What are the differences between monarchies, federal systems, and confederal systems?

SUMMARY AND PREVIEW The Constitution balanced power among three branches of the federal government but was only written after many compromises. In the next section you will read about Antifederalist and Federalist views of the Constitution, and the struggle to get it approved by the states.

Section 3 Assessment

go.hrw.com Online Quiz KEYWORD: SF7 HP5

Reviewing Ideas, Terms, and People

1. a. **Recall** Why did the Confederation Congress call for a **Constitutional Convention**?
   b. **Elaborate** Why do you think it was important that most delegates had served in state legislatures?
2. a. **Identify** What was the **Great Compromise**?
   b. **Draw Conclusions** How did state issues lead to debate over structure of the central government?
3. a. **Explain** What was the debate between North and South over counting slave populations?
   b. **Contrast** How did delegates' views differ on the issue of the foreign slave trade?
4. a. **Recall** Why did the framers of the Constitution create a system of **checks and balances**?
   b. **Evaluate** Did the Constitution resolve the weaknesses in the Articles of Confederation? Explain your answer.

Critical Thinking

5. **Identifying Cause and Effect** Review your notes on the Constitutional Convention compromises. Then copy the graphic organizer below and use it to show how the compromises affected the framework of the new government.

Compromise	→	Effect

FOCUS ON WRITING

6. **Thinking about the Constitution** Look back through what you've just read and make a list of important features of the Constitution. Be sure to note important compromises.

Section 3 Assessment Answers

1. a. to improve the Articles of Confederation
   b. needed government experience
2. a. resolved opposing views in the Virginia and New Jersey Plans on how to allot state representation
   b. possible answer—Concerns over state representation led to a bicameral legislature with an upper house based on equal state votes and a lower house based on state population.
3. a. Southern delegates wanted slaves to be counted as part of state populations; Northerners disagreed.
   b. along South-North regional lines
4. a. to limit each branch's power
   b. See Quick Facts chart above.
5. Great Compromise—See the answers to Questions 2a and 2b; Three-Fifths Compromise—resolved opposing southern and northern views on how to count slaves when determining state representation by counting each slave as three-fifths of a person
6. Students should list features of the Constitution and note important compromises.

BIOGRAPHY

Benjamin Franklin

How did one man accomplish so much?

When did he live? 1706–1790

Where did he live? Benjamin Franklin was born in Boston but ran away to Philadelphia at age 17 and made it his home. He also crossed the Atlantic Ocean eight times and visited 10 countries.

What did he do? What *didn't* he do! He was a printer, publisher, creator of the first circulating library, the first president of the University of Pennsylvania, inventor, scientist, philosopher, musician, economist, and the first U.S. Postmaster General. In politics he was a leading revolutionary, signer of the Declaration of Independence, head of an antislavery organization, delegate to the Constitutional Convention, and diplomat.

Why is he important? Benjamin Franklin, son of a candlemaker, became a celebrity in his own time, both in America and in Europe. Few people have mastered so many fields of knowledge and accomplished so much. He invented many useful objects, from bifocal glasses to the lightning rod. One of the oldest founding fathers, Franklin inspired younger revolutionaries such as Thomas Jefferson. Franklin believed strongly that people should volunteer and be in public service.

Finding Main Ideas How did Benjamin Franklin's life reflect his belief in public service?

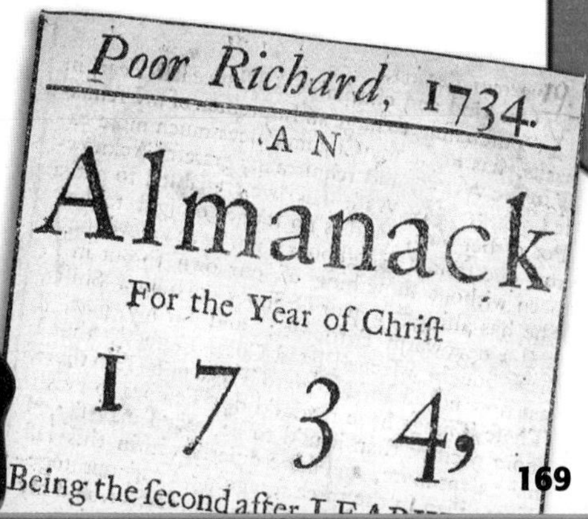
Poor Richard, 1734.
AN
Almanack
For the Year of Chrift
1734,
Being the fecond after

KEY EVENTS

- **1729** Becomes owner and publisher of the *Pennsylvania Gazette*
- **1732–1758** Publishes *Poor Richard: An Almanack*
- **1752** Performs famous experiment using a kite to show that electricity exists in storm clouds
- **1775** Submits the Articles of Confederation
- **1779** Appointed minister to France
- **1782** Helps negotiate the Treaty of Paris with Britain

169

Critical Thinking: Categorizing

Below Level

Accomplishments of Benjamin Franklin

1. Create a chart titled *Accomplishments of Benjamin Franklin.* Ask students to identify Franklin's many accomplishments, based on the biography and time line above. List students' answers for the class to see.
2. Then help students create categories by which to organize Franklin's accomplishments. Categories might include Government Service, Inventions, Community Service, and so on. Add the category labels to your chart.
3. Have students copy the chart and complete it by listing each of Franklin's accomplishments in the correct category.
4. Review the answers as a class. Then summarize for students Franklin's significance in American history.

Alternative Assessment Handbook, Rubric 7: Charts

Biography

Reading Focus Question

Read aloud the introductory question to students. Next, have students read the information under "What did he do?" to see how much Franklin accomplished. Ask students if they can think of any people today who are as accomplished as Franklin was. Then ask students how they think Franklin was able to accomplish so much.

Linking to Today

Daylight Saving Benjamin Franklin is well known for his many inventions that made life better for people. In addition, Franklin also invented daylight saving time. In an essay written in 1784, he first suggested the practice of advancing clocks forward in the summer. During World War I many nations adopted this system to conserve fuel. Today many nations, including the United States, continue the practice of daylight saving time each spring.

Did you know . . .

During the Constitutional Convention, Ben Franklin had an aisle seat. According to some accounts, he enjoyed occasionally tripping delegates as they walked by.

Primary Source

Poor Richard: An Almanack Benjamin Franklin published *Poor Richard: An Almanack* over a period of many decades. Write the following sayings for students to see.

- "He that lies down with dogs, shall rise up with fleas."
- "Great talkers, little doers."
- "Haste makes waste."

Ask students to choose one of the sayings, rewrite it in their own words, and then explain its meaning.

Answers

Finding Main Ideas *Most of his accomplishments and actions benefited others, from his service in government to his many inventions to his support of education and social causes.*

Preteach

Bellringer

If YOU were there . . . Use the **Daily Bellringer Transparency** to help students answer the question.

Daily Bellringer Transparency 5.4

Forming a Government — Daily Bellringer **5.4**

Review Section 3

Read the statements below and determine who or what is "speaking."

1. "I was elected president of the Constitutional Convention. Who am I?"
2. "I prevent any one branch of government from becoming too powerful. What am I?"
3. "I settled the disagreement over representation between the large states and the small states. What am I?"
4. "I am the system of sharing power between a central government and the states that make up a country. What am I?"

Preview Section 4

If YOU were there ...

You are a newspaper editor in Philadelphia. During colonial rule, officials sometimes closed down your newspaper because you had criticized the governor. Now you are one of many Americans who want to be sure the new Constitution will guarantee individual rights. You are writing an editorial in your paper explaining what you want.

What rights would you want the Constitution to protect?

Consider STATES' rights:
- preservation of local self-government
- protection from tyranny
- ability to limit central power

Consider INDIVIDUAL rights:
- life, liberty, and pursuit of happiness
- privacy and security
- religious freedom and tolerance
- freedom of the press

Review Answers: 1. George Washington; 2. checks and balances; 3. the Great Compromise; 4. federalism

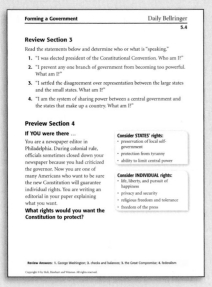

Academic Vocabulary

Review with students the high-use academic term in this section.

advocate to plead in favor of (p. 171)

CRF: Vocabulary Builder Activity, Section 4

Taking Notes

Have students copy the graphic organizer onto their own paper and then use it to take notes on the section. This activity will prepare students for the Section Assessment, in which they will complete a graphic organizer that builds on the information using a critical-thinking skill.

Section Correlations

8.1.5 Identify and explain key events leading to the creation of a strong union among the thirteen original states and in the establishment of the United States as a federal republic. **8.1.9** Describe the influence of important individuals on social and political developments of the time such as the Independence movement and the framing of the Constitution. **8.2.1** Identify and explain essential ideas of constitutional government, which are expressed in the founding documents of the United States, including. . .the 1787 U.S. Constitution, the Bill of Rights, the Federalist and Anti-Federalist Papers. . .

SECTION 4

Ratifying the Constitution

What You Will Learn . . .

Main Ideas

1. Federalists and Antifederalists engaged in debate over the new Constitution.
2. The *Federalist Papers* played an important role in the fight for ratification of the Constitution.
3. Ten amendments were added to the Constitution to provide a Bill of Rights to protect citizens.

The Big Idea

Americans carried on a vigorous debate before ratifying the Constitution.

Key Terms and People

Antifederalists, *p. 170*
George Mason, *p. 170*
Federalists, *p. 170*
Federalist Papers, *p. 171*
amendments, *p. 173*
Bill of Rights, *p. 173*

TAKING NOTES As you read, take notes on the differing views of the U.S. Constitution.

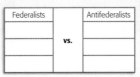

Federalists		Antifederalists
	vs.	

IN 8.1.5, 8.1.9, 8.1.28, 8.1.29, 8.1.30, 8.2.1, 8.2.5, 8.2.6, 8.4.1

If YOU were there...

You are a newspaper editor in Philadelphia. During colonial rule, officials sometimes closed down your newspaper because you had criticized the governor. Now you are one of many Americans who want to be sure the new Constitution will guarantee individual rights. You are writing an editorial in your paper explaining what you want.

What rights would you want the Constitution to protect?

BUILDING BACKGROUND The new Constitution did not make everyone happy. Even its framers knew they had not made a perfect document. Many people were afraid a strong national government would become as tyrannical as the British government had been. Before approving the Constitution, they wanted to be sure that their rights would be protected.

Federalists and Antifederalists

When the Constitution was made public, a huge debate began among many Americans. **Antifederalists**—people who opposed the Constitution—thought that the Constitutional Convention should not have created a new government. Others thought the Constitution gave too much power to the central government. For some Antifederalists, the main problem was that the Constitution did not have a section that guaranteed individual rights. Delegate **George Mason** became an Antifederalist for this reason.

Many Antifederalists were small farmers and debtors. Some Patriots were also strong Antifederalists, including Samuel Adams and Patrick Henry. Antifederalists were challenged by those who believed that the United States needed a stronger central government.

Federalists, supporters of the Constitution, included James Madison, George Washington, Benjamin Franklin, and Alexander Hamilton. Most Federalists believed that the Constitution offered a good balance of power between various political views. Many

Teach the Big Idea

At Level

Ratifying the Constitution

1. **Teach** To teach the main ideas in the section, use the questions in the Direct Teach boxes.
2. **Apply** Have each student create a flow chart for the ratification of the Constitution. Tell students to use the following as the first and last entries.
   - **September 17, 1787:** The Constitutional Convention approves the Constitution.
   - **December 1791:** States ratify the Bill of Rights.

   LS Visual/Spatial
3. **Review** As you review the section, have students share information in their flow charts.
4. **Practice/Homework** Have each student write a newspaper article about one of the events in his or her flow chart.

   LS Verbal/Linguistic

Alternative Assessment Handbook, Rubrics 13: Graphic Organizers; and 37: Writing Assignment

Federalists vs. Antifederalists

QUICK FACTS

Alexander Hamilton
Federalist

- Supported the Constitution as an excellent plan for government
- Defended his views in the *Federalist Papers*

George Mason
Antifederalist

- Opposed the Constitution
- Believed the Constitution needed a section guaranteeing individual rights

Federalists were wealthy planters, farmers, and lawyers. However, others were workers and craftspeople.

Federalists and Antifederalists debated whether the new Constitution should be approved. They made speeches and printed pamphlets **advocating** their views. Mercy Otis Warren, an ardent Patriot during the war, wrote a pamphlet entitled *Observations on the New Constitution*, in which she criticized the lack of individual rights it provided. The Federalists had to convince people a change in the structure of government was needed. To do this, they had to overcome people's fears that the Constitution would make the government too powerful.

READING CHECK **Comparing and Contrasting** Explain the similarities and differences between the Antifederalists and the Federalists.

Federalist Papers

One of the most important defenses of the Constitution appeared in a series of essays that became known as the ***Federalist Papers***. These essays supporting the Constitution were written anonymously under the name Publius. They were actually written by Hamilton, Madison, and Jay.

The authors of the *Federalist Papers* tried to reassure Americans that the new federal government would not overpower the states. In *Federalist Paper* No. 10, Madison argued that the diversity of the United States would prevent any single group from dominating the government.

The *Federalist Papers* were widely reprinted in newspapers around the country as the debate over the Constitution continued. Finally, they were collected and published in book form in 1788.

FOCUS ON READING
Take notes on the chronological order of this section. Which was written first, the *Federalist Papers* or the Bill of Rights?

ACADEMIC VOCABULARY
advocate
to plead in favor of

Direct Teach

Main Idea

1 Federalists and Antifederalists

Federalists and Antifederalists engaged in debate over the new Constitution.

Describe What were the Federalists' main arguments in favor of the Constitution? *that the Constitution offered a good balance of power and was a careful compromise between various political views*

Analyze What were the Antifederalists' main fears regarding the Constitution? *that it would create a government as tyrannical as that of Britain's and fail to protect Americans' individual rights*

Activity **Federalists v. Antifederalists** Have students write a short statement expressing what they think Hamilton and Mason might have said to each other regarding the debate over ratification of the U.S. Constitution.

CRF: Biography Activity: George Mason

Quick Facts Transparency 15: Federalists v. Antifederalists

go.hrw.com
Online Resources
KEYWORD: SF7 CH5
ACTIVITY: Hamilton and Madison

Differentiating Instruction

Above Level

Advanced/Gifted and Talented

1. Organize the class into two groups: one group representing the views of the Federalists and the other group representing the views of the Antifederalists.
2. Have each student make a list of points that support his or her group's assigned position. Ask students to share their lists of points as two students write the lists for the class to see. Correct any student errors or misconceptions.
3. Have each student write a short persuasive essay explaining his or her position and urging other Americans to adopt it. Encourage students to create at least one visual aid, such as a chart or a graph, to support their essays.
4. Ask for volunteers to read their essays to the class. **LS Verbal/Linguistic, Visual/Spatial**

Alternative Assessment Handbook, Rubric 43: Writing to Persuade

Answers

Focus on Reading *the* Federalist Papers

Reading Check *similarities—Many were farmers; most wanted to see the Articles revised in some way; differences—Federalists supported the Constitution and a stronger central government, tended to be wealthier; Antifederalists opposed the Constitution for various reasons; tended to be less affluent.*

Direct Teach

Main Idea

❷ *Federalist Papers*

The *Federalist Papers* played an important role in the fight for ratification of the Constitution.

Identify Who were the main authors of the *Federalist Papers*? *Alexander Hamilton, James Madison, John Jay*

Identify Points of View What fears did the *Federalist Papers* address? *that the federal government would overpower the states; that one group would dominate the government*

- Political Cartoons Activities for United States History, Cartoon 4: Ratifying the Constitution
- **CRF:** History and Geography Activity: Ratifying the Constitution
- **CRF:** Literature Activity: *Federalist Paper* No. 15

Teaching Tip

Reading Historical Documents To help students read difficult historical documents, tell students to scan the material and note any terms or phrases they do not understand. Help students define these terms and phrases. Then have students read the document carefully for its meaning.

Answers

Analyzing Primary Sources *Madison thinks that federalism forms a happy combination, where the great interests belong to the national government and the local interests belong to the state governments.*

Reading Check *Virginia had the largest population in the nation, and New York was an important center for business and trade; political leaders needed the two states' support to maintain national unity and support for the Constitution.*

Primary Source

HISTORIC DOCUMENT

Federalist Paper No. 10

In November 1787, Number 10 in the series called the Federalist Papers *was written in support of the Constitution. In it, James Madison describes the way federalism will overcome disagreements within society.*

"A landed interest, a manufacturing interest, a mercantile [trading] interest, a moneyed interest, with many lesser interests, grow up of necessity in civilized nations, and divide them into different classes, actuated [moved] by different sentiments and views. The regulation of these various and interfering interests [opinions] forms the principal task of modern legislation, and involves the spirit of party and faction [group] in the necessary and ordinary operations of the government . . .

The federal Constitution forms a happy combination . . . the great . . . interests being referred to the national [legislature]; the local and particular to the state legislatures . . . The influence of factious leaders may kindle [start] a flame within their particular states, but will be unable to spread a general conflagration [large fire] through the other states."

—James Madison, quoted in *Living American Documents*, edited by Isidore Starr, et al.

Madison believes that lawmakers are responsible for regulating the many competing concerns that make up society.

The federal government will handle issues affecting the nation as a whole; state and local governments will handle those concerning local issues.

ANALYSIS SKILL ANALYZING PRIMARY SOURCES

Why does Madison think federalism will prevent disagreement?

The Constitution needed only 9 states to pass it. However, to establish and preserve national unity, each state needed to ratify it. Every state except Rhode Island held special state conventions that gave citizens the chance to discuss and vote on the Constitution.

Paul Revere served on a committee supporting ratification. He wrote of the Constitution, "The proposed . . . government, is well calculated [planned] to secure the liberties, protect the property, and guard the rights of the citizens of America." Antifederalists also spoke out in state conventions, and wrote articles and pamphlets that became known as the Antifederalist Papers. In New York, one citizen said, "It appears that the government will fall into the hands of the few and the great."

On December 7, 1787, Delaware became the first state to ratify the Constitution. It went into effect in June 1788 after New Hampshire became the ninth state to ratify it.

Political leaders across America knew the new government needed the support of the large states of Virginia and New York, where debate still raged. Finally, Madison and fellow Virginia Federalists convinced Virginia to ratify it in mid-1788. In New York, riots had occurred when the draft of the Constitution was made public. At the state convention in Poughkeepsie to discuss ratification, Hamilton argued convincingly against the Antifederalists led by DeWitt Clinton. When news arrived of Virginia's ratification, New York ratified it as well. Rhode Island was the last state to ratify the Constitution in May 1790.

READING CHECK **Drawing Conclusions** Why were Virginia and New York important to the ratification of the Constitution?

Collaborative Learning

At Level

Commemorative Stamps

Materials: art supplies

1. Explain to students that the U.S. Post Office occasionally issues special stamps to commemorate an individual or event. Organize students into groups and have each group design and create a series of commemorative stamps celebrating the Constitution and the Bill of Rights.
2. Encourage students to design stamps that represent the following: the Constitutional Convention, the debate over ratification, the *Federalist Papers*, inclusion of a Bill of Rights, and the celebration over ratification.
3. Groups should assign members specific roles or topics to ensure that all students participate.
4. Display the groups' stamps around the classroom. **LS Interpersonal, Visual/Spatial**

- Alternative Assessment Handbook, Rubrics 3: Artwork; and 14: Group Activity

Bill of Rights

Several states ratified the Constitution only after they were promised that a bill protecting individual rights would be added to it. Many Antifederalists did not think that the Constitution would protect personal freedoms.

Some Federalists said that the nation did not need a federal bill of rights because the Constitution itself was a bill of rights. It was, they argued, written to protect the liberty of all U.S. citizens.

James Madison wanted to make a bill of rights one of the new government's first priorities. In Congress's first session, Madison encouraged the legislators to put together a bill of rights. The rights would then be added to the Constitution as **amendments**, or official changes. In Article V of the Constitution, the founders had provided a way to change the document when necessary in order to reflect the will of the people. The process requires that proposed amendments must be approved by a two-thirds majority of both houses of Congress and then ratified by three-fourths of the states before taking effect.

Legislators took ideas from the state ratifying conventions, the Virginia Declaration of Rights, the English Bill of Rights, and the Declaration of Independence to make sure that the abuses listed in the Declaration of Independence would be illegal under the new government. In September 1789 Congress proposed 12 amendments and sent them to the states for ratification. By December 1791 the states had ratified the **Bill of Rights**—10 of the proposed amendments intended to protect citizens' rights.

These 10 amendments set a clear example of how to amend the Constitution to fit the needs of a changing nation. The flexibility of the U.S. Constitution has allowed it to survive for more than 200 years.

THE IMPACT TODAY

In 1789, Madison suggested an amendment limiting Congress's power over its own salary. This amendment was not passed until 1992.

READING CHECK **Summarizing** Why is being able to amend the Constitution important?

SUMMARY AND PREVIEW Early disagreements over individual rights resulted in the Bill of Rights. In the next chapter you will learn about the structure of the Constitution.

Section 4 Assessment

go.hrw.com
Online Quiz
KEYWORD: SF7 HP5

Reviewing Ideas, Terms, and People

1. a. **Identify** Who were the **Federalists** and the **Antifederalists**?
   b. **Draw Conclusions** What was the main argument of the Antifederalists against the Constitution?
   c. **Elaborate** Do you agree with the Antifederalists or the Federalists? Explain your position.
2. a. **Recall** When did the Constitution go into effect?
   b. **Draw Conclusions** Why was it important that all 13 states ratify the Constitution?
   c. **Elaborate** Do you think that the ***Federalist Papers*** played an essential role in the ratification of the Constitution? Explain your answer.
3. a. **Recall** Why did Congress add the **Bill of Rights**?
   b. **Explain** From where did legislators' ideas for the Bill of Rights come?
   c. **Elaborate** Do you think the process for amending the Constitution is too difficult? Explain your position.

Critical Thinking

4. **Analyzing** Review your notes on Federalist and Antifederalist views. Then identify the outcome of the debate in a graphic organizer like the one below. Be sure to mention the Bill of Rights.

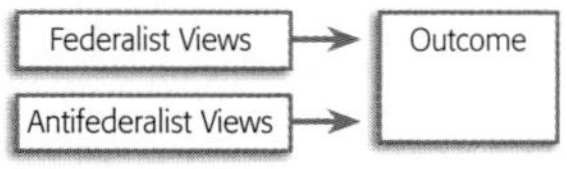

FOCUS ON WRITING

5. **Organizing Your Evidence** In this section you learned how the Bill of Rights was an important addition to the Constitution. You now have all your evidence about the difference between the Articles of Confederation and the Constitution. Choose two or three of the most important points and prepare to defend the Constitution, just like Alexander Hamilton and James Madison did in the *Federalist Papers*.

Direct Teach

Main Idea

❸ Bill of Rights

Ten amendments were added to the Constitution to provide a Bill of Rights to protect citizens.

Identify What did the Bill of Rights protect? *citizens' individual rights*

Summarize How are amendments added to the Constitution? *Proposed amendments must be approved by a two-thirds majority of both houses of Congress and then ratified by three-fourths of the states before taking effect.*

CRF: Biography Activity: Mercy Otis Warren

Review & Assess

Close

Have students discuss why the U.S. Constitution is considered a living document.

Review

Online Quiz, Section 5.4

Assess

SE Section 4 Assessment

PASS: Section 5.4 Quiz

Alternative Assessment Handbook

Reteach/Classroom Intervention

Interactive Reader and Study Guide, Section 5.4

Interactive Skills Tutor CD-ROM

Section 4 Assessment Answers

1. a. Federalists—supported the Constitution and a stronger national government; Antifederalists—opposed the Constitution
   b. gave too much power to the central government; did not contain a bill of rights
   c. Answers should demonstrate an understanding of both Federalist and Antifederalist perspectives.
2. a. June 1788
   b. because of concerns that national unity would be weak if some states did not ratify it
   c. Students should show an understanding of the arguments the *Federalist Papers* used.
3. a. because several states refused to ratify the Constitution unless one was added
   b. state ratifying conventions, Virginia Declaration of Rights, English Bill of Rights, Declaration of Independence
   c. Answers will vary.
4. Outcome: to address concerns of the Antifederalists, a Bill of Rights was added
5. Students should add Federalist arguments presented in the section to their defenses.

Answers

Reading Check *Amendments give political leaders the opportunity to change the Constitution as the nation and Americans' needs change.*

Social Studies Skills

Determining Different Points of View

Activity Analyzing Points of View Ask students to imagine that they attended a basketball game at which their school team lost by a wide margin to a rival school's team. How might their points of view of the game differ from those of the winning team's fans? How might the players' points of view differ from those of the fans, even on the same team? Have students discuss the answers and the factors that might influence each point of view. Then have each student consider a viewpoint that he or she holds about school. Have students free-write for 10 minutes about what factors might shape their points of view. Ask for volunteers to share their answers with the class.
LS Verbal/Linguistic

- Alternative Assessment Handbook, Rubrics 11: Discussions; and 37: Writing Assignments
- Interactive Skills Tutor CD-ROM, Lesson 18: Identify Point of View and Frame of Reference
- **CRF:** Social Studies Skills Activity: Determine Different Points of View

Social Studies Skills

Analysis | Critical Thinking | Civic Participation | Study

Determining Different Points of View

Define the Skill

A *point of view* is a person's outlook or attitude. It is the way that he or she looks at a topic or thing. Each person's point of view is shaped by his or her background. Because people's backgrounds are different, their points of view are too. Since a person's point of view shapes his or her opinions, knowing that point of view helps you understand and evaluate those opinions. Being able to detect differences in point of view is important to understanding differences in people's opinions and actions in history.

Learn the Skill

When you encounter someone's beliefs, opinions, or actions in your study of history, use the following guidelines to determine his or her point of view.

1. Look for information about the person's background.
2. Ask yourself what factors in the person's background might have influenced his or her opinion or action concerning the topic or event.
3. Be aware that sometimes the person's opinions or actions themselves will provide clues to his or her point of view.

Benjamin Lincoln led the troops that put down Shays's Rebellion in Massachusetts. He was also a state politician and a general during the Revolution. Lincoln offered this explanation of Shays's uprising.

> "Among [the main causes] I rank the ease with which … credit was obtained … in the time of [the Revolution] … The moment the day arrived when all discovered that things were fast returning [to normal], … and that the indolent [lazy persons] and improvident [unwise persons] would soon experience the evils of their idleness and sloth, many startled [panicked] … and … complained … of the weight of public taxes … and at the cruelty of … creditors [those to whom money is owed] to call for their just dues [rightful payment] … The disaffected [unhappy people] … attempted … to stop the courts of law, and to suspend the operations of government. This they hoped to do until … an end should thereby be put to public and private debts."

Lincoln's background as a general, state official, and leader against the rebels likely gave him a negative point of view on the revolt. His reference to the rebels as lazy and unwise also provides clues to his attitude. You should weigh such factors when evaluating the accuracy of his statement.

Practice the Skill

The following statement about Shays's Rebellion came from a Massachusetts farmer. Read it and apply the guidelines to answer the questions.

> "I have labored hard … all my days. I have been … obliged to do more than my part in the [Revolution], been loaded with … rates [taxes], … have been … [abused] by sheriffs … and [debt] collectors … I have lost a great deal … [T]he great men are going to get all we have, and I think it is time for us to … put a stop to it."

1. From what point of view is this person commenting on the revolt? What is his opinion of it?
2. How does his view of himself differ from Lincoln's view of people like him?
3. Is this view of the revolt likely to be more accurate than Lincoln's view? Why or why not?

Social Studies Skills Activity: Determine Different Points of View

Federalists Versus Antifederalists — At Level

1. Have students review the material in Section 4 under "Federalists and Antifederalists."
2. Then have each student create a chart contrasting the points of view of the Federalists and Antifederalists. The chart should also list the factors that might have influenced each group's viewpoint.
3. Have students share their answers as you create a master chart. Then have students discuss the factors that contributed to each group's point of view. **LS Verbal/Linguistic, Visual/Spatial**
4. **Extend** Have each student write a short speech that James Madison might have given to explain his point of view on the Bill of Rights. Have volunteers deliver their speeches to the class. **LS Verbal/Linguistic**

- Alternative Assessment Handbook, Rubrics 7: Charts; and 37: Writing Assignments

Answers

Practice the Skill 1. *from the point of view of a farmer who is struggling to pay debts; supports the revolt;* **2.** *sees himself as hardworking, deserving of reward for his part in the Revolution, and abused by officials and used by "great men";* **3.** *The two views are probably equally biased. Together they provide a more complete picture of the perspectives and issues involved in the rebellion.*

CHAPTER 5

Chapter Review

HOLT
History's Impact
▶ **video series**
Review the video to answer the closing question:
Why would adding more U.S. territory have been appealing in the 1700s and 1800s?

Visual Summary

QUICK FACTS

Use the visual summary below to help you review the main ideas of the chapter.

The Articles of Confederation
• first government of United States
• weak union of states
• weaknesses led to Shays's Rebellion
The Constitution
• framework of today's government
• strengthened national government
• three branches
• checks and balances
Bill of Rights
• first 10 amendments
• ensures basic rights

Reviewing Vocabulary, Terms, and People

Match the numbered person or term with the correct lettered definition.

1. Bill of Rights
2. checks and balances
3. constitution
4. Constitutional Convention
5. *Federalist Papers*
6. inflation
7. Northwest Territory
8. George Mason
9. tariffs
10. Three-Fifths Compromise

a. agreement that stated that each slave would be counted as three-fifths of a person when determining representation
b. delegate to the Constitutional Convention who became an Antifederalist
c. increased prices for goods and services combined with the reduced value of money
d. area including present-day Illinois, Indiana, Michigan, Ohio, Wisconsin, and part of Minnesota
e. meetings held in Philadelphia at which delegates from the states attempted to improve the existing government
f. series of essays in support of the Constitution
g. set of basic principles that determines the powers and duties of a government
h. system that prevents any branch of government from becoming too powerful
i. taxes on imports or exports
j. the first 10 amendments to the Constitution

Answers

History's Impact

Video Series More land would provide the United States with additional natural resources and room for population growth.

Visual Summary

Review and Inquiry Have students examine the visual summary.

Quick Facts Transparency 16: Forming a Government Visual Summary

Reviewing Vocabulary, Terms, and People

1. j
2. h
3. g
4. e
5. f
6. c
7. d
8. b
9. i
10. a

Comprehension and Critical Thinking

11. a. could settle conflicts among the states, make coins, borrow money, make treaties with other countries and with Native Americans, and ask the states for money and soldiers
b. passed the Land Ordinance of 1785, which helped systematize the division of territory; passed the Northwest Ordinance of 1787, which established the Northwest Territory
c. Students should show an understanding of the documents and institutions that influenced the development of the nation.

Review and Assessment Resources

Review and Reinforce

SE Chapter Review
CRF: Chapter Review Activity
Quick Facts Transparency 16 : Forming a Government Visual Summary
Spanish Chapter Summaries Audio CD Program
Online Chapter Summaries in Spanish
OSP Holt PuzzlePro; GameTool for ExamView
Quiz Game CD-ROM

Assess

SE Standardized Test Practice
PASS: Chapter 5 Test, Forms A and B
Alternative Assessment Handbook
OSP ExamView Test Generator, Chapter Test
Differentiated Instruction Modified Worksheets and Tests CD-ROM: Chapter Test
HOAP Holt Online Assessment Program (in the Premier Online Edition)

Reteach/Intervene

Interactive Reader and Study Guide
Differentiated Instruction Teacher Management System: Lesson Plans for Differentiated Instruction
Differentiated Instruction Modified Worksheets and Tests CD-ROM
Interactive Skills Tutor CD-ROM

go.hrw.com
Online Resources
Chapter Resources:
KEYWORD: SF7 CH5

Comprehension and Critical Thinking

SECTION 1 *(Pages 152–155)*

11. a. Describe What powers did the Articles of Confederation give the national government?

b. Summarize What did the Confederation Congress do to strengthen the United States?

c. Evaluate Which document or institution do you think had the greatest influence on the development of the United States? Why?

SECTION 2 *(Pages 158–162)*

12. a. Recall What was Shays's Rebellion?

b. Draw Conclusions What was the general attitude of foreign nations toward the new government of the United States? Why?

c. Evaluate Of the problems experienced by the Confederation Congress, which do you think was the most harmful? Why?

SECTION 3 *(Pages 163–168)*

13. a. Describe In what ways did the Constitution strengthen the central government?

b. Explain How did the two compromises reached during the Constitutional Convention satisfy competing groups?

c. Elaborate In your opinion were there any weaknesses in the Constitution? Explain your answer.

SECTION 4 *(Pages 170–173)*

14. a. Recall Why was the Bill of Rights added to the Constitution?

b. Draw Conclusions Why were some Americans opposed to the Constitution?

c. Evaluate Would you have supported the Federalists or the Antifederalists? Explain your answer.

Reviewing Themes

15. Politics What political problems resulted from a weak central government under the Articles of Confederation?

16. Politics How did political disagreements lead to important compromises in the creation of the Constitution?

Reading Skills

Understanding Chronological Order *Use the Reading Skills taught in this chapter to answer the question below.*

17. Organize the following events chronologically according to the chapter.

a. The *Federalist Papers* are published.

b. The Constitution is ratified.

c. The Articles of Confederation are ratified.

d. Shays's Rebellion occurs.

e. The Constitutional Convention meets in Philadelphia.

Social Studies Skills

Determining Different Points of View *Use the Social Studies Skills taught in this chapter to answer the question below.*

18. List three differences between the Virginia Plan and the New Jersey Plan.

FOCUS ON WRITING

19. Writing Your Editorial You should start your editorial with a strong statement of your opinion about the Constitution. Then write two sentences about each of your main points of support—a weakness of the Articles of Confederation and/or a strength of the Constitution. End your editorial with a call to action: Ask the delegates to the Constitutional Convention to ratify the Constitution. Remember that you are trying to convince people to make a very important decision for our country—be persuasive.

Answers

12. a. a revolt by farmers in response to Massachusetts's tax policy

b. Answers may include that foreign nations viewed the United States as weak because its national government had few powers and the nation experienced economic problems.

c. Answers will vary, but students should be familiar with the various trade, economic, domestic, and international problems the nation faced.

13. a. established a system of federalism, created a powerful bicameral legislature, created an executive branch led by a president, created a judicial branch headed by a Supreme Court, balanced power among these three branches, created a system of checks and balances

b. Great Compromise—satisfied small states by creating an upper house with equal state representation, satisfied large states by creating a lower house with representation based on population; Three-Fifths Compromise—satisfied northern and southern states by counting each slave as three-fifths of a person to determine state representation

c. Answers will vary, but students should be aware of the unresolved issues in the Constitution, such as slavery and the lack of a bill of rights.

14. a. to protect individual rights

b. thought it should not have been created, that it gave too much power to the central government, that it needed a bill of rights

c. Answers will vary but should reflect an understanding of each group's views.

Reviewing Themes

15. problems enforcing treaties with foreign nations, limited political authority over the states

16. Political disagreements over state representation, the powers of the national government, how the government should be separated, and slavery led to compromises.

Reading Skills

17. c, d, e, a, b

Social Studies Skills

18. Virginia Plan—proposed by Edmund Randolph, bicameral legislature based on population, larger states had a greater voice in the federal government; New Jersey Plan—proposed by William Paterson, unicameral legislature with equal representation per state, states had an equal voice in the federal government

Focus on Writing

19. Rubric Students' editorials should

- strongly and clearly express the opinion.
- include at least two pieces of evidence to support the opinion.
- end with a call to action.
- be persuasive.
- use correct grammar, punctuation, spelling, and capitalization.

CRF: Focus on Writing Activity: A Newspaper Editorial

CHAPTER 5

Standardized Test Practice

8.1.5, 8.2.3, 8.2.5, 8.4.9

DIRECTIONS: Read each question and write the letter of the best response.

1 Which term would *best* describe the newly independent nation in the 1780s?

A strong
B united
C troubled
D confident

2 Under the Articles of Confederation, the greatest amount of power was in the hands of the

A Congress.
B American people.
C national government.
D states.

3 The structure of the U.S. Congress was created at the Constitutional Convention by the

A Virginia Plan.
B Great Compromise.
C New Jersey Plan.
D Three-Fifths Compromise.

4 The nation's most widespread problems under the Articles of Confederation involved

A trade.
B suffrage.
C slavery.
D rebellion.

5 The main objective of the Northwest Ordinance of 1787 was to

A establish a national government with limited powers.
B create a system for bringing new states into the Union.
C settle border disputes between the United States and Canada.
D regulate interstate commerce and curb inflation.

6 Which of the following documents influenced the system of government established by the U.S. Constitution?

A Bill of Rights
B Mayflower Compact
C Federalist Papers
D Olive Branch Petition

7 Read the following passage from one of the *Federalist Papers* and use it to answer the question below.

> "The powers delegated by the proposed Constitution to the federal government are few and defined. Those which are to remain in the State governments are numerous and . . . will extend to all objects which . . . concern the lives, liberties, and properties of the people . . . The operations of the federal government will be most extensive and important in times of war and danger; those of the State governments in times of peace and security."
>
> —James Madison, *Federalist Paper* No. 45

Document-Based Question **What point was Madison making about the system of government created by the proposed U.S. Constitution?**

Answers

1. C
Break Down the Question: This question requires students to synthesize information in Section 1. Have students think about what they know about the nation under the Articles of Confederation.

2. D
Break Down the Question: This question requires students to recall factual information. Students should use a process of elimination to answer the question.

3. B
Break Down the Question: This question requires students to recall factual information. Students should use the process of elimination to answer the question.

4. A
Break Down the Question: This question requires students to evaluate information. Tell students to consider the types of problems the United States experienced and what most of these problems had in common.

5. B
Break Down the Question: This question requires students to recall factual information. Refer students who have trouble to the text "Northwest Territory" in Section 1.

6. B
Break Down the Question: This question requires students to recall factual information. Encourage students to use the process of elimination to answer this question.

7. Madison says that, unless the country is at war or its citizens are in danger, the states' governments will be more active than the federal government.

Break Down the Question: This questions requires students to interpret information and find the main idea. Suggest that students focus on the phrases, "Those which are to remain in the State governments . . . concern the lives, liberties, and properties of the people," and "those of the State governments in times of peace and security."

Intervention Resources

Reproducible

- Interactive Reader and Study Guide
- Differentiated Instruction Teacher Management System: Lesson Plans for Differentiated Instruction

Technology

- Quick Facts Transparency 16: Forming a Government Visual Summary
- Differentiated Instruction Modified Worksheets and Tests CD-ROM
- Interactive Skills Tutor CD-ROM

Tips for Test Taking

Take It All In When students first start a test, encourage them to briefly preview the test to get a mental map of their tasks:

- Know how many questions they have to complete.
- Know where to stop.
- Set time checkpoints.
- Do the easy sections first; easy questions can be worth just as many points as hard ones.

Chapter 6 Planning Guide

Citizenship and the Constitution

Chapter Overview	Reproducible Resources	Technology Resources
CHAPTER 6 **pp. 178–229** **Overview: In this chapter, students will learn about the Constitution, the Bill of Rights, and what it means to be a U.S. citizen.**	**Differentiated Instruction Teacher Management System:*** • Instructional Pacing Guides • Lesson Plans for Differentiated Instruction **Interactive Reader and Study Guide:** Chapter Summary Graphic Organizer* **Chapter Resource File:*** • Focus on Writing Activity: A Pamphlet • Social Studies Skills Activity: Determining the Context of Statements • Chapter Review Activity **Pre-AP Activities Guide for United States History:** Citizenship and the Constitution*	**Power Presentations with Video CD-ROM** **Differentiated Instruction Modified Worksheets and Tests CD-ROM** **Primary Source Library CD-ROM for United States History** **Interactive Skills Tutor CD-ROM** **Student Edition on Audio CD Program** **History's Impact: United States History Video Program (VHS/DVD):** The Impact of the Bill of Rights* go.hrw.com **Internet Activities:** Checking on Your Legislators; First Ladies
Section 1: **Understanding the Constitution** **The Big Idea:** The U.S. Constitution balances the powers of the federal government among the legislative, executive, and judicial branches.	**Differentiated Instruction Teacher Management System:** Section 1 Lesson Plan* **Interactive Reader and Study Guide:** Section 6.1 Summary* **Chapter Resource File:*** • Vocabulary Builder Activity, Section 1 • Biography Activities: Daniel K. Inouye, John Jay, Sandra Day O'Connor • History and Geography Activity: House Membership, 1990-2000	**Daily Bellringer Transparency 6.1*** **Quick Facts Transparencies 17, 18, 19, 20, 21, 22*** Separation of Powers; Checks and Balances; Federal Office Terms and Requirements; Federal Judicial System; Federalism; Amending the U.S. Constitution* **Map Transparency 28:** The Electoral College* go.hrw.com **Internet Activities:** Supreme Court Case Summa[ries]; Checking on Your Legislators; First Ladies
Section 2: **The Bill of Rights** **The Big Idea:** The Bill of Rights was added to the Constitution to define clearly the rights and freedoms of citizens.	**Differentiated Instruction Teacher Management System:** Section 2 Lesson Plan* **Interactive Reader and Study Guide:** Section 6.2 Summary* **Chapter Resource File:*** • Vocabulary Builder Activity, Section 2 • Primary Source Activity: Hortensius, "An Essay on the Liberty of the Press" **Political Cartoons Activities for United States History,** Cartoon 6: Bill of Rights: "Liberty vs. Order"*	**Daily Bellringer Transparency 6.2***
Section 3: **Rights and Responsibilities of Citizenship** **The Big Idea:** American citizenship involves great privileges and serious responsibilities.	**Differentiated Instruction Teacher Management System:** Section 3 Lesson Plan* **Interactive Reader and Study Guide:** Section 6.3 Summary* **Chapter Resource File:*** • Vocabulary Builder Activity, Section 3 • Primary Source Activity: What It Means to Be an American: Two Views • Literature Activity: *The Free Citizen* **Political Cartoons Activities for United States History,** Cartoon 5: Duties of Citizenship*	**Daily Bellringer Transparency 6.3*** go.hrw.com **Internet Activity:** Tracking U.S. Immigration

SE Student Edition | Print Resource | Audio CD
TE Teacher's Edition | Transparency | CD-ROM
go.hrw.com | **LS** Learning Styles | Video
TOS Indiana Teacher One Stop | * also on Indiana Teacher One Stop

Review, Assessment, Intervention

- **Quick Facts Transparency 23:** Citizenship and the Constitution Visual Summary*
- **Spanish Chapter Summaries Audio CD Program**
- **Online Chapter Summaries in Spanish**
- **Progress Assessment Support System (PASS):** Chapter Tests A and B*
- **Differentiated Instruction Modified Worksheets and Tests CD-ROM:** Modified Chapter Test
- **TOS Indiana Teacher One Stop:** ExamView Test Generator (English/Spanish)
- **HOAP Holt Online Assessment Program,** in the Holt Premier Online Student Edition

---

- **PASS:** Section Quiz 6.1*
- **Online Quiz:** Section 6.1
- **Alternative Assessment Handbook**

- **PASS:** Section Quiz 6.2*
- **Online Quiz:** Section 6.2
- **Alternative Assessment Handbook**

- **PASS:** Section Quiz 6.3*
- **Online Quiz:** Section 6.3
- **Alternative Assessment Handbook**

HOLT

History's Impact

United States History Video Program (VHS/DVD)

The Impact of the Bill of Rights

Suggested use: as a chapter introduction

Power Presentations with Video CD-ROM

Power Presentations with Video are visual presentations of each chapter's main ideas. Presentations can be customized by including Quick Facts charts, images from the text, and video clips.

DIVISION FOR PUBLIC EDUCATION
AMERICAN BAR ASSOCIATION

Developed by the Division for Public Education of the American Bar Association, these materials are part of the **Democracy and Civic Education Resources.**

- **Constitution Study Guide**
- **Supreme Court Case Studies**

Holt Online Learning

go.hrw.com
Teacher Resources
KEYWORD: SF7 TEACHER

go.hrw.com
Student Resources
KEYWORD: SF7 CH6

- Document-Based Questions
- Interactive Multimedia Activities
- Current Events
- Chapter-based Internet Activities
- and more!

Holt Interactive

Online Student Edition

Complete online support for interactivity, assessment, and reporting

- Interactive Maps and Notebook
- Standardized Test Prep
- Homework Practice and Research Activities Online

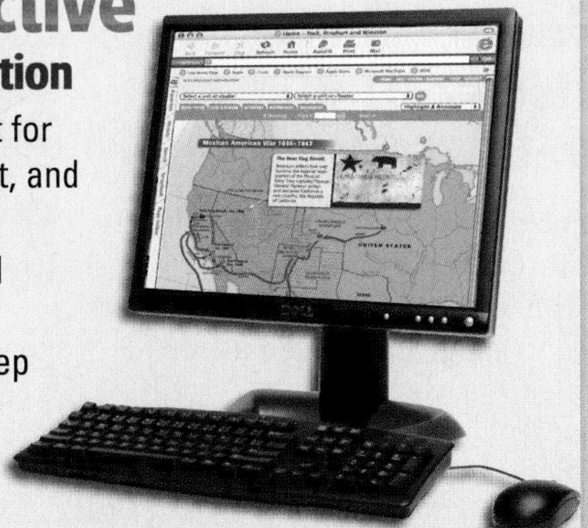

Differentiating Instruction

How do I address the needs of varied learners?

The Target Resource acts as your primary strategy for differentiated instruction.

ENGLISH-LANGUAGE LEARNERS & STRUGGLING READERS

TARGET RESOURCE

English-Language Learner Strategies and Activities

- Build Academic Vocabulary
- Develop Oral and Written Language Structures

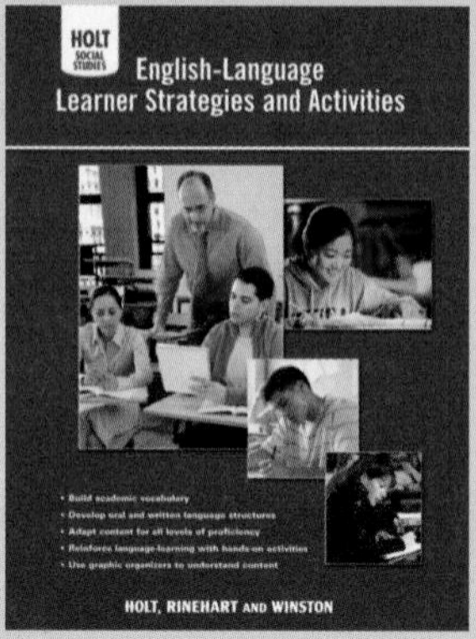

Spanish Resources

Spanish Chapter Summaries Audio CD

Spanish Chapter Summaries Online

Teacher's One-Stop Planner:
- ExamView Test Generator, Spanish
- PuzzlePro, Spanish

Additional Resources

Differentiated Instruction Teacher Management System: Lesson Plans for Differentiated Instruction

Chapter Resources:
- Vocabulary Builder Activities
- Social Studies Skills: Determining the Context

Quick Facts Transparencies:
- Separation of Powers (TR 17)
- Checks and Balances (TR 18)
- Federal Office Terms and Requirements (TR 19)
- Federal Judicial System (TR 20)
- Federalism (TR 21)
- Citizenship and the Constitution Visual Summary (TR 23)

Student Edition on Audio CD Program

SPECIAL NEEDS LEARNERS

TARGET RESOURCE

Differentiated Instruction Modified Worksheets and Tests CD-ROM

- Vocabulary Flash Cards
- Modified Vocabulary Builder Activities
- Modified Chapter Review Activity
- Modified Chapter Test

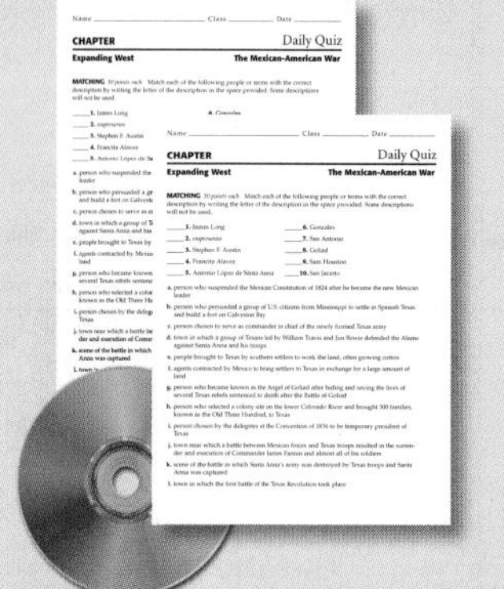

Additional Resources

Differentiated Instruction Teacher Management System: Lesson Plans for Differentiated Instruction

Interactive Reader and Study Guide

Social Studies Skills Activity: Determining the Context of Statements

Student Edition on Audio CD Program

Interactive Skills Tutor CD-ROM

ADVANCED/GIFTED-AND-TALENTED STUDENTS

TARGET RESOURCE

Primary Source Library CD-ROM for United States History

The Library contains longer versions of quotations in the text, extra sources, and images. Included are point-of-view articles, journals, diaries, historical fiction, and political documents.

Additional Resources

Differentiated Instruction Teacher Management System: Lesson Plans for Differentiated Instruction

Pre-AP Activities Guide for United States History: Citizenship and the Constitution

U.S. History Document-Based Activities: Activity 2: Forming the Constitution; Activity 3: Bill of Rights

Chapter Resource File:
- Focus on Writing Activity: A Pamphlet
- Literature Activity: *The Free Citizen*
- Primary Source Activities: Hortensius, "An Essay on the Liberty of the Press"; T. Paine, *The Rights of Man*

Differentiated Activities in the Teacher's Edition

- Separation of Powers Trifold, p. 184
- Illustrated Bill of Rights, p. 220

Teacher One Stop™

How can I manage the lesson plans and support materials for differentiated instruction?

With the Indiana Teacher One Stop, you can easily organize and print lesson plans, planning guides, and instructional materials for all learners.
The Indiana Teacher One Stop includes the following materials to help you differentiate instruction:

- Interactive Teacher's Edition
- Calendar Planner and pacing guides
- Editable lesson plans
- All reproducible ancillaries in Adobe Acrobat (PDF) format
- ExamView Test Generator (Eng & Span)
- Transparency and video previews

Differentiated Activities in the Teacher's Edition

- First Amendment Activity, p. 217

Professional Development

HOLT Professional Development

What teacher training resources are available to help me grow professionally?

- **In-service and staff development** as part of your Holt Social Studies product purchase
- **Quick Teacher Tutorial Lesson Presentation CD-ROM**
- Intensive tuition-based **Teacher Development Institute**
- **Convenient Holt Speaker Bureau** – face-to-face workshop options
- **PRAXIS™ Test Prep** interactive Web-based content refreshers*
- **Ask A Professional Development Expert** at http://www.hrw.com/prodev/

* PRAXIS is a trademark of Educational Testing Service (ETS). This publication is not endorsed or approved by ETS.

Differentiated Activities in the Teacher's Edition

- Analyzing Federalism Skits, p. 183
- Ninth Amendment Discussion, p. 220
- Becoming a U.S. Citizen Poems, p. 223

• Chapter Preview •

Chapter Big Ideas

Section 1 The U.S. Constitution balances the powers of the federal government among the legislative, executive, and judicial branches.

Section 2 The Bill of Rights was added to the Constitution to define clearly the rights and freedoms of citizens.

Section 3 American citizenship involves great privileges and serious responsibilities.

CHAPTER 6 1787–PRESENT

Citizenship and the Constitution

IN Indiana Standards

Social Studies Standards

8.1.9 Describe the influence of important individuals on social and political developments of the time such as the Independence movement and the framing of the Constitution.

8.2.1 Identify and explain essential ideas of constitutional government, which are expressed in the founding documents of the United States, including the Virginia Declaration of Rights, the Declaration of Independence, the Virginia Statute for Religious Freedom, the Massachusetts Constitution of 1780, the Northwest Ordinance, the 1787 U.S. Constitution, the Bill of Rights, the Federalist and Anti-Federalist Papers, Common Sense, Washington's Farewell Address (1796), and Jefferson's First Inaugural Address (1801).

8.2.2 Identify and explain the relationship between rights and responsibilities of citizenship in the United States.

8.2.4 Examine functions of the national government in the lives of people.

8.2.6 Distinguish among the different functions of national and state government within the federal system by analyzing the United States Constitution and the Indiana Constitution.

8.2.8 Explain ways that citizens can participate in political parties, campaigns, and elections.

go.hrw.com
Indiana
KEYWORD: SF10 IN

FOCUS ON WRITING

A Pamphlet Everyone in the United States benefits from our Constitution. However, many people don't know the Constitution as well as they should. In this chapter you will read about the Constitution and the rights and responsibilities it grants to citizens. Then you'll create a four-page pamphlet to share this information with your fellow citizens.

UNITED STATES

1788 The Constitution goes into effect after New Hampshire becomes the ninth state to ratify it.

1787 — 1800

1791 The Bill of Rights becomes part of the Constitution on December 15.

Focus on Writing

The **Chapter Resource File** provides a Focus on Writing worksheet to help students organize and write their pamphlets.

CRF: Focus on Writing Activity: A Pamphlet

Key to Differentiating Instruction

Below Level

Basic-level activities designed for all students encountering new material

At Level

Intermediate-level activities designed for average students

Above Level

Challenging activities designed for honors and gifted and talented students

Standard English Mastery

Activities designed to improve standard English usage

Introduce the Chapter

At Level

Focus on Citizenship

1. Ask students to discuss the concept of citizenship and what it means to them.
2. Ask students if they can identify any rights and responsibilities associated with American citizenship.
3. To help students get started, jot down some rights and responsibilities for the class to see. Rights might include freedom of speech, freedom of religion, freedom of assembly, and the right to trial by jury. Responsibilities might include obeying laws and authority figures, paying taxes, and serving on juries.
4. Explain to students that in this chapter they will learn about two important documents—the U.S. Constitution and the Bill of Rights. Point out that these documents outline many of the rights and responsibilities of American citizens and affect students' lives on a daily basis. **LS Verbal/Linguistic**

HOLT

History's Impact

▶ **video series**

Watch the video to understand the impact of the Bill of Rights.

What You Will Learn...

In this chapter you will learn about the U.S. Constitution, the Bill of Rights, and what it means to be an American citizen. Young citizens like the ones pictured here must be informed in order to fulfill the rights and responsibilities of citizenship.

1851 Indiana voters approve a new constitution, which is still in effect along with its amendments.

1942 The Fair Employment Act bans discrimination in the workplace.

1971 The Twenty-sixth Amendment is ratified, giving the right to vote to all U.S. citizens 18 years or older.

1930 — 1950 — 1970 — 1990

1954 In *Brown* v. *Board of Education*, the Supreme Court declares segregation in public schools to be unconstitutional.

1990 The Americans with Disabilities Act is passed.

Chapter Preview

HOLT

History's Impact

▶ **video series**

See the Video Teacher's Guide for strategies for using the chapter video about the impact of the Bill of Rights.

Explore the Picture

Becoming a U.S. Citizen The process by which foreign citizens become U.S. citizens is called naturalization. Congress established the requirements for naturalization in the Immigration and Nationality Act (INA). Among these requirements are the ability to read, write, and speak English; knowledge and understanding of U.S. history and government; belief in the principles of the U.S. Constitution; and good moral character.

Analyzing Visuals How do you think the young people in the photo feel about becoming old enough to enjoy the full rights and responsibilities of American citizenship? *possible answer—proud, happy, and excited*

Holt's Constitution Study Guide

go.hrw.com

Online Resources

Chapter Resources:
KEYWORD: SF7 CH6

Teacher Resources:
KEYWORD: SF7 TEACHER

Explore the Time Line

1. What year did the U.S. Constitution go into effect? *1788*
2. What became part of the U.S. Constitution on December 15, 1791? *the Bill of Rights*
3. How and when did the Nineteenth Amendment change voting rights? *1920; gave women the right to vote*
4. How and when did the Twenty-sixth Amendment change voting rights? *1971; gave all U.S. citizens 18 years or older the right to vote*

Info to Know

Freedom of Speech Seven years after the Bill of Rights was added to the Constitution, the U.S. Congress passed the Sedition Act of 1798. This act seemed to restrict freedom of speech by making it a crime for a person to say or write anything "false, scandalous and malicious against the government." The U.S. Supreme Court upheld the law's constitutionality, however. Ten people were imprisoned under this law.

Reading Social Studies

Understanding Themes

Introduce the key theme of this chapter—politics—to the class by asking them to briefly explain what they know about our political system in the United States. Write students' ideas for the class to see. Help students to see which ideas are correct and which are incorrect. Have students create a collage that reflects the political ideas that were instituted by the U.S. Constitution.

Summarizing Historical Texts

Focus on Reading Organize the class into pairs. Then assign each pair of students a different amendment from the U.S. Constitution. Have groups use the steps explained at right to create a summary of their amendment. You might want to assign another amendment to groups that finish early. After students have finished, have each group present its summary to the class. Encourage students to write down the key points in each summary.

Reading Social Studies

by Kylene Beers

Economics | Geography | **Politics** | Society and Culture | Science and Technology

Focus on Themes In this chapter you will read about the three branches of government, the Bill of Rights, and the duties and responsibilities of a United States citizen. As you read about each of these topics, you will see the American **political system** at work—not only in the Bill of Rights, but also through the responsibilities U.S. citizens have as they vote for leaders and work to help their communities and nation.

Summarizing Historical Texts

Focus on Reading History books are full of information. Sometimes the sheer amount of information they contain can make processing what you read difficult. In those cases, it may be helpful to stop for a moment and summarize what you've read.

Writing a Summary A summary is a short restatement of the most important ideas in a text. The example below shows three steps used in writing a summary. First underline important details. Then write a short summary of each paragraph. Finally, combine these paragraph summaries into a short summary of the whole passage.

The Constitution

Article II, Section 1

1. The executive Power shall be vested in a President of the United States of America. He shall hold his Office during the Term of four Years, and, together with the Vice President, chosen for the same Term, be elected, as follows:

2. Each State shall appoint, in such Manner as the Legislature thereof may direct, a Number of Electors, equal to the whole Number of Senators and Representatives to which the State may be entitled in the Congress; but no Senator or Representative, or Person holding an Office of Trust or Profit under the United States, shall be appointed an Elector.

Summary of Paragraph 1
The executive branch is headed by a president and vice president, each elected for four-year terms.

Summary of Paragraph 2
The electors who choose the president and vice president are appointed. Each state has the same number of electors as it has members of Congress.

Combined Summary
The president and vice president who run the executive branch are elected every four years by state-appointed electors.

Reading and Skills Resources

Reading Support

- Interactive Reader and Study Guide
- Student Edition on Audio CD Program
- Spanish Chapter Summaries Audio CD Program

Social Studies Skills Support

- Interactive Skills Tutor CD-ROM

Vocabulary Support

- **CRF:** Vocabulary Builder Activities
- **CRF:** Chapter Review Activity
- Differentiated Instruction Modified Worksheets and Tests CD-ROM:
  - Vocabulary Flash Cards
  - Vocabulary Builder Activity
  - Chapter Review Activity
- **OSP** Holt PuzzlePro

You Try It!

The following passage is from the U.S. Constitution. As you read it, decide which facts you would include in a summary of the passage.

The Constitution

Article I, Section 2

1. The House of Representatives shall be composed of Members chosen every second Year by the People of the several States, and the Electors in each State shall have the Qualifications requisite for Electors of the most numerous branch of the State Legislature.

2. No person shall be a Representative who shall not have attained to the Age of twenty five years, and been seven Years a Citizen of the United States, and who shall not, when elected, be an Inhabitant of the State in which he shall be chosen.

After you read the passage, answer the following questions.

1. Which of the following statements best summarizes the first paragraph of this passage?

  a. Congress has a House of Representatives.

  b. Members of the House of Representatives are elected every two years by state electors.

2. Using the steps described on the previous page, write a summary of the second paragraph of this passage.

3. Combine the summary statement you chose in Question 1 with the summary statement you wrote in Question 2 to create a single summary of this entire passage.

Key Terms and People

Chapter 6

Section 1
federal system *(p. 182)*
impeach *(p. 184)*
veto *(p. 184)*
executive orders *(p. 185)*
pardons *(p. 185)*
Thurgood Marshall *(p. 186)*
Sandra Day O'Connor *(p. 186)*

Section 2
James Madison *(p. 216)*
majority rule *(p. 216)*
petition *(p. 217)*
search warrant *(p. 218)*
due process *(p. 218)*
indict *(p. 218)*
double jeopardy *(p. 218)*
eminent domain *(p. 218)*

Section 3
naturalized citizens *(p. 222)*
deport *(p. 222)*
draft *(p. 223)*
political action committees *(p. 224)*
interest groups *(p. 224)*

Academic Vocabulary

Success in school is related to knowing academic vocabulary—the words that are frequently used in school assignments and discussions. In this chapter, you will learn the following academic words:

distinct *(p. 183)*
influence *(p. 224)*

As you read Chapter 6, think about what details you would include in a summary of each paragraph.

Reading Social Studies

Key Terms and People

Read the terms and people to students. Then ask students to choose five to eight terms with which they are unfamiliar. Have students define the terms they selected. Then have each student create a crossword puzzle using the definitions he or she wrote as clues. If time permits, have students exchange their puzzles with a partner and complete the other person's crossword. Then have students check their answers. **LS Verbal/Linguistic, Visual/Spatial**

Focus on Reading

See the **Focus on Reading** questions in this chapter for more practice on this reading social studies skill.

Reading Social Studies Assessment

See the **Chapter Review** at the end of this chapter for student assessment questions related to this reading skill.

Teaching Tip

Summarizing may be a difficult concept for students to grasp. Students may think that every fact is an important detail. Remind students that not every fact is important when writing a summary. One way to help students keep to the important details is to have them identify the main idea of each paragraph in a few words. Then instruct students to identify only those details that support that main idea. Model this strategy for students by summarizing a paragraph or two as a class.

Answers

You Try It! 1. *b;* **2.** *possible answer—Members of the House of Representatives must meet certain age and residency requirements.* **3.** *Members of the House of Representatives are elected every two years and must meet certain age and residency requirements.*

Preteach

Bellringer

If YOU were there . . . Use the **Daily Bellringer Transparency** to help students answer the question.

Daily Bellringer Transparency 6.1

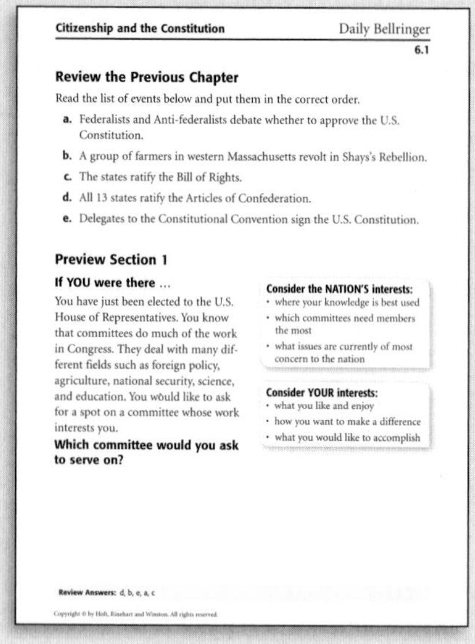

Citizenship and the Constitution — Daily Bellringer 6.1

Review the Previous Chapter

Read the list of events below and put them in the correct order.

a. Federalists and Anti-federalists debate whether to approve the U.S. Constitution.

b. A group of farmers in western Massachusetts revolt in Shays's Rebellion.

c. The states ratify the Bill of Rights.

d. All 13 states ratify the Articles of Confederation.

e. Delegates to the Constitutional Convention sign the U.S. Constitution.

Preview Section 1

If YOU were there ...

You have just been elected to the U.S. House of Representatives. You know that committees do much of the work in Congress. They deal with many different fields such as foreign policy, agriculture, national security, science, and education. You would like to ask for a spot on a committee whose work interests you.

Which committee would you ask to serve on?

Consider the NATION'S interests:
- where your knowledge is best used
- which committees need members the most
- what issues are currently of most concern to the nation

Consider YOUR interests:
- what you like and enjoy
- how you want to make a difference
- what you would like to accomplish

Review Answers: d, b, e, a, c

Academic Vocabulary

Review with students the high-use academic term in this section.

distinct separate (p. 183)

Building Vocabulary

Preteach or review the following term:

apportionment system that keeps total House membership at 435 members (p. 183)

CRF: Vocabulary Builder Activity, Section 1

Taking Notes

Have students copy the graphic organizer onto their own paper and then use it to take notes on the section. This activity will prepare students for the Section Assessment, in which they will complete a graphic organizer that builds on the information using a critical-thinking skill.

Section Correlations

IN

8.2.3 Explain how and why legislative, executive, and judicial powers are distributed, shared and limited in the constitutional government of the United States. **8.2.4** Examine functions of the national government in the lives of people.

SECTION 1

Understanding the Constitution

What You Will Learn...

Main Ideas

1. The framers of the Constitution devised the federal system.
2. The legislative branch makes the nation's laws.
3. The executive branch enforces the nation's laws.
4. The judicial branch determines whether or not laws are constitutional.

The Big Idea

The U.S. Constitution balances the powers of the federal government among the legislative, executive, and judicial branches.

Key Terms and People

federal system, *p. 182*
impeach, *p. 184*
veto, *p. 184*
executive orders, *p. 185*
pardons, *p. 185*
Thurgood Marshall, *p. 186*
Sandra Day O'Connor, *p. 186*

TAKING NOTES As you read, take notes on the structure of each of the branches of government in a chart like the one below.

Branch	Structure
Legislative	
Executive	
Judicial	

IN 8.1.5, 8.1.9, 8.1.28, 8.1.30, 8.2.1, 8.2.3, 8.2.4, 8.2.6

If YOU were there...

You have just been elected to the U.S. House of Representatives. You know that committees do much of the work in Congress. They deal with many different fields such as foreign policy, agriculture, national security, science, and education. You would like to ask for a spot on a committee whose work interests you.

Which committee would you ask to serve on?

BUILDING BACKGROUND When the framers of the Constitution met in Philadelphia in 1787, they created a national government with three branches that balance one another's powers.

The Federal System

The framers of the Constitution wanted to create a government powerful enough to protect the rights of citizens and defend the country against its enemies. To do so, they set up a **federal system** of government, a system that divided powers between the states and the federal government.

The Constitution assigns certain powers to the national government. These are called delegated powers. Among them are the rights to coin money and to regulate trade. Reserved powers are those kept by the states. These powers include creating local governments and holding elections. Concurrent powers are those shared by the federal and state governments. They include taxing, borrowing money, and enforcing laws.

Sometimes, Congress has had to stretch its delegated powers to deal with new or unexpected issues. A clause in the Constitution states that Congress may "make all Laws which shall be necessary and proper" for carrying out its duties. This clause, called the elastic clause—because it can be stretched (like elastic)—provides flexibility for the government. The federal government has used this clause to provide public services such as funding for the arts and humanities.

READING CHECK **Summarizing** How is power divided between the federal and state governments?

Teach the Big Idea

At Level

Understanding the Constitution

1. **Teach** To teach the main ideas in the section, use the questions in the Direct Teach boxes.
2. **Apply** Have students scan the section and the Quick Facts diagrams. Tell students to close their books. List the three branches of government for students to see. Then call out a power of one of the branches. Have students determine to which branch the power belongs. Continue until students have assigned all the powers. **LS Visual/Spatial**
3. **Review** As you review the section's main ideas, have students summarize how the Constitution divides government power.
4. **Practice/Homework** Have each student create a mobile illustrating the division of power between the federal government and state governments and among the three branches of the federal government. **LS Visual/Spatial**

Alternative Assessment Handbook, Rubrics 3: Artwork; and 7: Charts

Separation of Powers — QUICK FACTS

U.S. Constitution

Legislative Branch (Congress)
- Writes the laws
- Confirms presidential appointments
- Approves treaties
- Grants money
- Declares war

Executive Branch (President)
- Proposes laws
- Administers the laws
- Commands armed forces
- Appoints ambassadors and other officials
- Conducts foreign policy
- Makes treaties

Judicial Branch (Supreme Court)
- Interprets the Constitution and other laws
- Reviews lower-court decisions

Legislative Branch

The federal government has three branches, each with **distinct** responsibilities and powers. This separation balances the branches and keeps any one of them from growing too powerful. The first branch of government is the legislative branch, or Congress. It makes the nation's laws. Article I of the Constitution divides Congress into the House of Representatives and the Senate.

With 435 members, the House of Representatives is the larger congressional house. The U.S. Census, a population count made every 10 years, determines how many members represent each state. A system called apportionment keeps total membership at 435. If one state gains a member, another state loses one. Members must be at least 25 years old, live in the state where they were elected, and have been U.S. citizens for seven years. They serve two-year terms.

The Senate has two members, or senators, per state. Senators represent the interests of the whole state, not just a district. They must be at least 30 years old, have been U.S. citizens for nine years, and live in the state they represent. They serve six-year terms. The senior senator of a state is the one who has served the longer of the two. Members of Congress can serve an unlimited number of terms in office.

The political party with more members in each house is the majority party. The one with fewer members is the minority party. The leader of the House of Representatives, or Speaker of the House, is elected by House members from the majority party.

The U.S. vice president serves as president of the Senate. He takes no part in Senate debates but can vote to break ties. If he is absent, the president pro tempore (pro tem for short) leads the Senate. There is no law for how the Senate must choose this position, but it traditionally goes to the majority party's senator who has served the longest.

Congress begins sessions, or meetings, each year in the first week of January. Both houses do most of their work in committees. Each committee studies certain types of bills, or suggested laws. For example, all bills about taxes begin in the House Ways and Means Committee.

ACADEMIC VOCABULARY
distinct separate

READING CHECK **Comparing and Contrasting** What are the similarities in requirements for members of the House of Representatives and the Senate? What are the differences?

Direct Teach

Main Idea

❶ The Federal System

The framers of the Constitution devised the federal system.

Define What is federalism? *a government system that divides powers between the states and the federal government*

Contrast How do delegated, reserved, and concurrent powers differ? *delegated—powers granted to the federal government; reserved—powers kept by the states; concurrent—powers shared by state and federal governments*

Quick Facts Transparency 17: Separation of Powers

Main Idea

❷ Legislative Branch

The legislative branch makes the nation's laws.

Recall Which article of the Constitution defines the legislative branch? *Article I*

Draw Conclusions Why do you think the legislature performs most of its work in committees? *Legislators cannot study every bill, and committees enable legislators to share the work among groups.*

CRF: History and Geography Activity: House Membership, 1990–2000

CRF: Biography Activity: Daniel K. Inouye

Collaborative Learning

Above Level

Analyzing Federalism Skits

1. Explain that one reason the framers of the Constitution delegated some powers to the federal government—rather than reserving them for state governments—was to avoid difficult situations between the states.
2. Organize the class into five small groups. Assign each group one of the following delegated powers: the coining of money, regulating interstate and international trade, providing for national defense, declaring war, and conducting diplomacy.
3. Have each group create a skit highlighting the confusion that might occur if state governments held the delegated power. Each member of the group should participate in the skit in some way.
4. Have each group present its skit. Then lead a class discussion about the importance of the division of powers in the Constitution.

LS Interpersonal, Kinesthetic

Alternative Assessment Handbook, Rubric 33: Skits and Reader's Theater

Answers

Reading Check (left page) *some powers are delegated to the federal government, some reserved to state governments, and others are shared*

Reading Check *similarities—must live in the state they represent and where elected; differences—Representatives must be at least 25 years old and have been U.S. citizens for seven years; senators must be at least 30 and have been U.S. citizens for nine years.*

Direct Teach

Main Idea

❸ Executive Branch

The executive branch enforces the nation's laws.

Describe What are the requirements to serve as president? *native-born U.S. citizen at least 35 years old and a U.S. resident for at least 14 years*

Analyze How does the system of checks and balances make it difficult for Congress to pass a law that the president opposes? *Congress must achieve a two-thirds majority vote to override a presidential veto.*

Quick Facts Transparency 18: Checks and Balances

Connect to Government

Exercising the Veto The president's ability to veto legislation is an important check on Congress's power. Between 1789 and 1990, presidents vetoed 2,492 bills, with 2,433 of these vetoes taking place after 1865. Congress overrode these vetoes only 103 times.

Info to Know

The Nixon Pardon Perhaps the most famous pardon in presidential history took place on September 8, 1974, when President Gerald R. Ford pardoned Richard Nixon, the former president. Nixon had resigned from office after being accused of involvement in illegal actions while president. Ford explained that he granted the pardon because prosecuting a former president would be too disturbing for the nation.

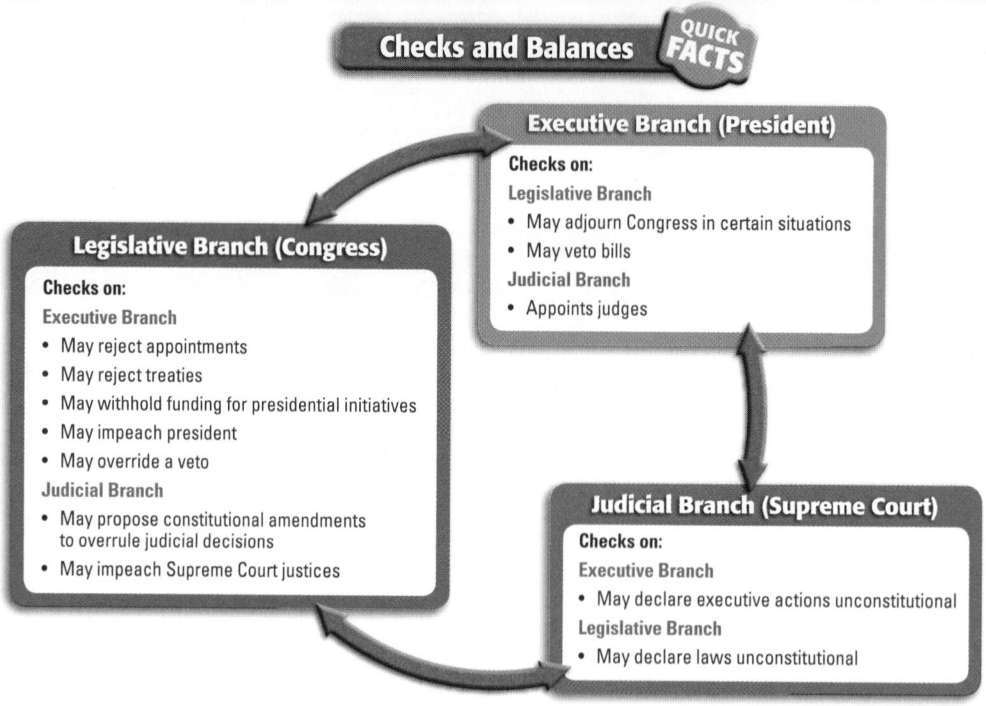

Checks and Balances
QUICK FACTS
Executive Branch (President)
Checks on:
Legislative Branch
• May adjourn Congress in certain situations
• May veto bills
Judicial Branch
• Appoints judges
Legislative Branch (Congress)
Checks on:
Executive Branch
• May reject appointments
• May reject treaties
• May withhold funding for presidential initiatives
• May impeach president
• May override a veto
Judicial Branch
• May propose constitutional amendments to overrule judicial decisions
• May impeach Supreme Court justices
Judicial Branch (Supreme Court)
Checks on:
Executive Branch
• May declare executive actions unconstitutional
Legislative Branch
• May declare laws unconstitutional

Executive Branch

Article II of the Constitution lists the powers of the executive branch. This branch enforces the laws passed by Congress.

President and Vice President

As head of the executive branch, the president is the most powerful elected leader in the United States. To qualify for the presidency or vice presidency, one must be a native-born U.S. citizen at least 35 years old. The president must also have been a U.S. resident for 14 years.

Americans elect a president and vice president every four years. Franklin D. Roosevelt, who won four times, was the only president to serve more than two terms. Now, the Twenty-second Amendment limits presidents to two terms. If a president dies, resigns, or is removed from office, the vice president becomes president for the rest of the term.

The House of Representatives can **impeach**, or vote to bring charges of serious crimes against, a president. Impeachment cases are tried in the Senate. If a president is found guilty, Congress can remove him from office. In 1868 Andrew Johnson was the first president to be impeached. President Bill Clinton was impeached in 1998. However, the Senate found each man not guilty.

Working with Congress

The president and Congress are often on different sides of an issue. However, they must still work together.

Congress passes laws. The president, however, can ask Congress to pass or reject bills. The president also can **veto**, or cancel, laws Congress has passed. Congress can try to override, or undo, the veto. However, this is difficult since it takes a two-thirds

Critical Thinking: Comparing and Contrasting

Below Level

Separation of Powers Trifold

Materials: white construction paper or small poster board

1. Have students fold large pieces of paper into three equal, horizontal sections to create trifolds.
2. Have students label the sections *Legislative Branch, Executive Branch,* and *Judicial Branch.*
3. Ask volunteers to use the Separation of Powers Quick Facts diagram and the text to identify the powers and duties of each branch.

In addition, ask students to identify some government positions in each branch (such as representative, senator, president, and justice) and some requirements and duties of those positions. As volunteers provide information, have students fill in their trifolds.

LS Verbal/Linguistic, Visual/Spatial

Alternative Assessment Handbook, Rubric 7: Charts

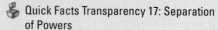

Quick Facts Transparency 17: Separation of Powers

majority vote. To carry out laws affecting the Constitution, treaties, and statutes, the president issues **executive orders**. These commands have the power of law. The president also may grant **pardons**, or freedom from punishment, to persons convicted of federal crimes or facing criminal charges.

The president also commands the armed forces. In emergencies, the president can call on U.S. troops. Only Congress, however, can declare war. Other executive duties include conducting foreign relations and creating treaties. Executive departments do most of the executive branch work. As of 2004 there were 15 such departments. The president chooses department heads, who are called secretaries, and the Senate approves them. The heads make up the cabinet, which advises the president.

READING CHECK **Drawing Conclusions**
What is the president's most important power?

Judicial Branch

The third branch of government, the judicial branch, is made up of a system of federal courts headed by the U.S. Supreme Court. The Constitution created the Supreme Court, but the Judiciary Act of 1789 created the system of lower district and circuit courts.

Article III generally outlines the courts' duties. Federal courts can strike down a state or federal law if the court finds a law unconstitutional. Congress can then try to revise the law to make it constitutional.

District Courts

The president makes appointments to federal courts. In an effort to keep federal judges free of party influence, the judges are given life appointments. The lower federal courts are divided according to cases over which they have jurisdiction, or authority. Each state has at least one of the 94 district courts.

THE IMPACT TODAY
In 2002 the new Department of Homeland Security was given cabinet-level status to protect against terrorism.

Background of the Court
The rest of the Supreme Court decisions you see in this book will highlight important cases of the Court. But in this first one, we'll discuss the history of the Court.

The first Supreme Court met in 1790 at the Royal Exchange in New York City. The ground floor of this building was an open-air market. When the national government moved to Philadelphia, the Court met in basement rooms in Independence Hall. Once in Washington, the Court heard cases in the Capitol building until the present Supreme Court building was completed in 1932.

Circuit Riding
Today the Supreme Court holds court only in Washington, D.C. In the past, however, the justices had to travel through assigned circuits, hearing cases together with a district judge in a practice known as riding circuit.

The justices complained bitterly about the inconvenience of travel, which was often over unpaved roads and in bad weather. This system was not just inconvenient to the justices, however. Some people worried about the fairness of a system that required justices who had heard cases at trial to rule on them again on appeal. Other people, however, thought that the practice helped keep the justices in touch with the needs and feelings of the average citizen. Eventually, circuit riding interfered so much with the increased amount of business of the Supreme Court that Congress passed a law ending the practice in the late 1800s.

Path to the Supreme Court
When a case is decided by a state or federal court, the losing side may have a chance to appeal the decision to a higher court. Under the federal system, this higher court is called the court of appeals. A person who loses in that court may then appeal to the Supreme Court to review the case. But the Supreme Court does not have to accept all appeals. It usually chooses to hear only cases in which there is an important legal principle to be decided or if two federal courts of appeals disagree on how an issue should be decided.

ANALYSIS SKILL **ANALYZING INFORMATION**
1. What are two reasons why the practice of circuit riding ended?
2. Why do you think the Supreme Court does not hear every case that is appealed to it?

Direct Teach

Main Idea

4 Judicial Branch

The judicial branch determines whether or not laws are constitutional.

Explain Why are federal judges appointed for life? *to keep them free of party influence*

Analyze What check does the judicial branch have over the legislative branch? *It can declare a law to be unconstitutional.*

CRF: Biography Activities: John Jay; Sandra Day O'Connor

Did you know . . .

In the nation's early years, the U.S. Supreme Court met in the basement of the Capitol Building. During one year, while the Capitol was under construction, the Court even met in a tavern. The Supreme Court did not gain its own building until 1935.

go.hrw.com
Online Resources
KEYWORD: SF7 CH6
ACTIVITY: Supreme Court Case Summaries

Critical Thinking: Finding Main Ideas

At Level

Promoting American Government

Materials: poster board, art supplies

1. Ask students to imagine that they have been selected to describe the U.S. government to citizens of another country.
2. Have students, working either individually or in small groups, create posters or presentations illustrating how the U.S. Constitution divides power between the federal and state governments and among the three branches of the federal government. In addition, students should illustrate how checks and balances provide a check on abuses of power.
LS Verbal/Linguistic, Visual/Spatial
3. **Extend** Have each student write a speech describing how the United States benefits from its system of government and encouraging other nations to adopt the same form of government. **LS Verbal/Linguistic**

Answers

Analyzing Information **1.** *The travel was inconvenient and interfered with the Supreme Court's increased workload.* **2.** *The Court usually hears only those cases in which an important legal principle is to be decided or where two federal courts of appeals disagree.*

Reading Check *possible answers—enforcing the laws, issuing executive orders, vetoing legislation, commanding the armed forces*

Direct Teach

Biography

Sandra Day O'Connor (b. 1930) Retired Supreme Court justice Sandra Day O'Connor achieved several firsts in her career. By 1965 she was the first female assistant attorney general in Arizona. In the Arizona Senate, she held the position of majority leader for two years—the first woman to hold such a position in the nation. When President Ronald Reagan appointed O'Connor to the Supreme Court, she was yet again the first woman to hold the position.

CRF: Biography Activity: Sandra Day O'Connor

Review & Assess

Close

Have students discuss whether the three branches of government share power equally and, if not, which branch has the most power and why.

Review

Online Quiz, Section 6.1

Holt's Constitution Study Guide

Assess

SE Section 1 Assessment

PASS: Section Quiz 6.1

Alternative Assessment Handbook

Reteach/Classroom Intervention

Interactive Reader and Study Guide, Section 6.1

Interactive Skills Tutor CD-ROM

FOCUS ON READING
Jot down a short summary of the appeals process after reading this paragraph.

Courts of Appeals

If someone convicted of a crime believes the trial was unfair, he or she may take the case to the court of appeals. There are 13 courts of appeals. Each has a panel of judges to decide if cases heard in the lower courts were tried appropriately. If the judges uphold, or accept, the original decision, the original outcome stands. Otherwise, the case may be retried in the lower court.

Supreme Court

THE IMPACT TODAY
Supreme Court rulings can have dramatic effects on the nation, as in *Bush* v. *Gore*, which decided the outcome of the 2000 presidential election.

After a case is decided by the court of appeals, the losing side may appeal the decision to the Supreme Court. Thousands of cases go to the Supreme Court yearly in the hope of a hearing, but the Court has time to hear only about 100. Generally, the cases heard involve important constitutional or public-interest issues. If the Court declines to hear a case, the court of appeals decision is final.

Nine justices sit on the Supreme Court. The chief justice of the United States leads the Court. Unlike the president and members of Congress, there are no specific constitutional requirements for becoming a justice.

In recent decades, the Supreme Court has become more diverse. In 1967 **Thurgood Marshall** became the first African American justice. **Sandra Day O'Connor** became the first female Court justice after her 1981 appointment by President Ronald Reagan.

READING CHECK **Summarizing** Describe the structure and responsibilities of the judicial branch.

SUMMARY AND PREVIEW In this section you learned about the balance between the different branches of the federal government. In the next section you will learn about the Bill of Rights.

Section 1 Assessment

go.hrw.com
Online Quiz
KEYWORD: SF7 HP6

Reviewing Ideas, Terms, and People

1. **a. Describe** What type of government did the Constitution establish for the United States?
   b. Contrast What is the difference between delegated, reserved, and concurrent powers?
2. **a. Recall** What role does the vice president serve in the legislative branch?
   b. Compare and Contrast In what ways are the Senate and the House of Representatives similar and different?
   c. Elaborate Why do you think the requirements for serving in the Senate are stricter than those for serving in the House of Representatives?
3. **a. Describe** What powers are granted to the president?
   b. Make Generalizations Why is it important that the president and Congress work together in resolving governmental issues?
   c. Evaluate What do you think is the most important power granted to the president? Why?
4. **a. Explain** What is the main power of the judicial branch?
   b. Evaluate Which branch of government do you feel is most important? Explain your answer.

Critical Thinking

5. **Categorizing** Review your notes on the branches of government. Then copy the web diagram below and use it to show two powers of each branch of government.

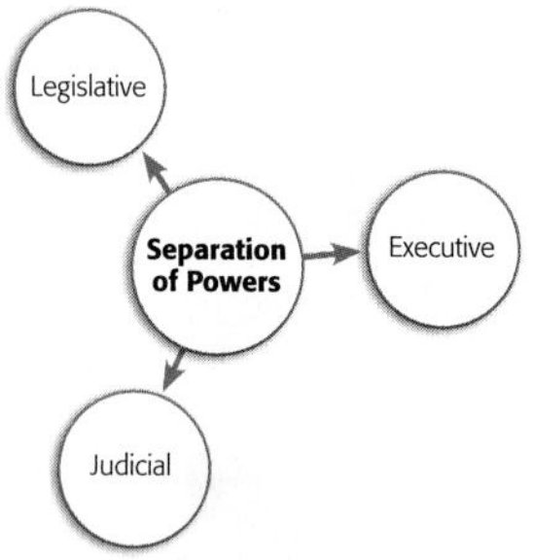

FOCUS ON WRITING

6. **Gathering Information about the Constitution** Look back through what you've just read about the Constitution. Make a list of four or five of the most important features of the Constitution. You'll put that list on the second page of your pamphlet.

Section 1 Assessment Answers

1. **a.** federal system
   b. delegated—powers granted to federal government; reserved—powers kept by states; concurrent—shared powers
2. **a.** serves as president of Senate; can break ties
   b. similar—legislative branch, make laws, meet at same time; different—requirements, size, length of terms, who they represent, leaders
   c. possible answer—because senators serve longer terms, represent a larger area, and are fewer in number than representatives
3. **a.** powers to propose, enforce, and veto laws; command armed forces; appoint ambassadors; conduct foreign policy; make treaties; issue executive orders; grant pardons
   b. to keep the country running smoothly
   c. See answer to Question 3a.
4. **a.** to interpret the U.S. Constitution
   b. Students should support their opinions.
5. See the Separation of Powers Quick Facts.
6. Students might mention federalism, separation of powers, and checks and balances.

Answers

Focus on Reading *A person convicted of a crime may take the case to the courts of appeal, which decides if the lower court heard the case appropriately and, if not, the lower court might retry the case.*

Reading Check *federal court system headed by the Supreme Court and including district courts and courts of appeal; interpret the Constitution; review decisions of lower courts*

BIOGRAPHY

James Madison

What would you do to create a brand-new government?

When did he live? 1751–1836

Where did he live? Like several of the founding fathers, James Madison was a Virginian. He grew up in the town of Montpelier, and he kept a home there for his whole life.

What did he do? Through the persuasive power of his writing, Madison helped create the foundations of the U.S. government.

Why is he important? Madison is known as the Father of the Constitution. A brilliant thinker, he provided many of the basic ideas in the Constitution. He argued tirelessly for a strong national government, for separate branches of government, and for rights such as freedom of religion. He then rallied support for adoption of the Constitution and the Bill of Rights. In 1809 Madison became the fourth president of the United States. As president, he led the country through another war with Britain, the War of 1812. He and his wife, Dolley, were forced to flee Washington temporarily when the British invaded the capital and set fire to the White House.

Summarizing Why is Madison known as the Father of the Constitution?

KEY EVENTS

- **1780** Madison serves in the Continental Congress.
- **1787** Madison keeps a written record of the Constitutional Convention.
- **1787–1788** Madison helps write the *Federalist Papers*, urging support for the Constitution.
- **1801–1809** Madison serves as secretary of state under President Thomas Jefferson.
- **1809–1817** Madison serves two terms as president.

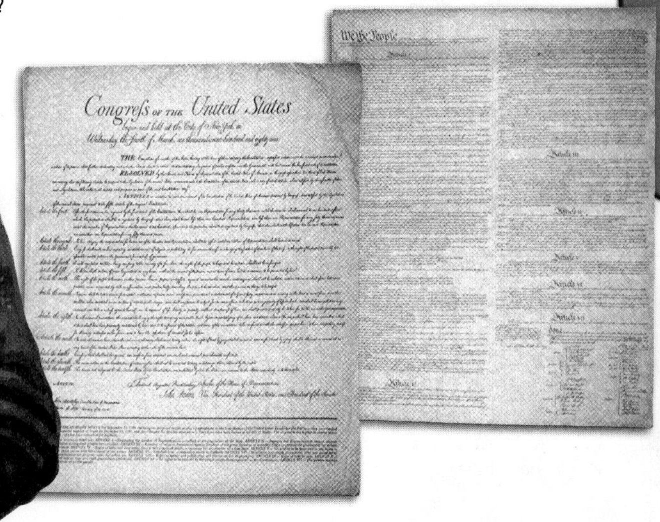

James Madison was an important force in the writing of the Constitution.

Biography

Reading Focus Question

Have students discuss the introductory question. Ask them to consider the actions the founding fathers took to create a new government for the United States. What did the founding fathers think the purpose of government was? *(to serve the people and to promote the common good)* What did they create to serve as the foundation of the government? *(U.S. Constitution)* Tell students to consider Madison's role in creating the U.S. government as they read his biography.

Info to Know

Madison: Supporter for Independence James Madison was an early supporter of colonial independence from Great Britain. While a student at the College of New Jersey (now Princeton University), he participated in demonstrations against British control of the colonies. He was later elected to Virginia's 1776 Revolutionary convention.

Madison: Father of the Constitution During Madison's lifetime, people began calling him the Father of the Constitution. He disliked the nickname, though, and thought it inappropriate. The Constitution was not "the off-spring of a single brain," he explained, but rather "the work of many heads and many hands."

Critical Thinking: Summarizing

At Level

Tribute to Madison

1. Ask students to imagine that they are hosting a tribute to James Madison in his later years.
2. Have each student write a short speech to introduce Madison before he speaks to the audience. The speech should summarize Madison's many accomplishments and explain his significance in the formation of the U.S. government.
3. Ask volunteers to present their Madison introductions to the class. **LS Verbal/Linguistic**
4. **Extend** Have students create the design for a plaque to award to Madison at the tribute. The plaque should focus on Madison's contributions to the writing of the Constitution and as a U.S. president. **LS Verbal/Linguistic, Visual/Spatial**

Alternative Assessment Handbook, Rubrics 3: Artwork; and 37: Writing Assignments

Answers

Summarizing *He provided many of the basic ideas in the Constitution and rallied support for its adoption.*

Historical Documents

Info to Know

The Preamble Although short, the Preamble was hotly debated in the state ratifying conventions. The delegates objected to the Preamble's opening phrase "We the People," because they had been appointed by the states, rather than elected by the people. Patrick Henry challenged this phrase during the ratifying process in Virginia, saying "The people gave them [the delegates to the Constitutional Convention] no power to use their name. That they exceeded their power is perfectly clear."

Interpret What do you think the three opening words of the Preamble to the Constitution mean? *Students might suggest that the words are stating that the American people have the power to create a Constitution and to establish a government.*

CRF: Primary Source Activity: Thomas Paine, *The Rights of Man*

Teaching Tip

Reading Roman Numerals Some students may have trouble reading the Roman numerals that appear in the Constitution. Before starting the document, spend a few minutes going over the Roman numeral system with the class. If possible, provide students with a chart defining Roman numerals through 30.

The Constitution of the United States

Preamble

The short and dignified preamble explains the goals of the new government under the Constitution.

We the People of the United States, in Order to form a more perfect Union, establish Justice, insure domestic Tranquility, provide for the common defense, promote the general Welfare, and secure the Blessings of Liberty to ourselves and our Posterity, do ordain and establish this Constitution for the United States of America.

Note: The parts of the Constitution that have been lined through are no longer in force or no longer apply because of later amendments. The titles of the sections and articles are added for easier reference.

Article I The Legislature

Section 1. Congress

All legislative Powers herein granted shall be vested in a Congress of the United States, which shall consist of a Senate and House of Representatives.

Section 2. The House of Representatives

1. Elections The House of Representatives shall be composed of Members chosen every second Year by the People of the several States, and the Electors in each State shall have the Qualifications requisite for Electors of the most numerous Branch of the State Legislature.

2. Qualifications No Person shall be a Representative who shall not have attained to the Age of twenty five Years, and been seven Years a Citizen of the United States, and who shall not, when elected, be an Inhabitant of that State in which he shall be chosen.

3. Number of Representatives Representatives and direct Taxes shall be apportioned among the several States which may be included within this Union, according to their respective Numbers~~, which shall be determined by adding to the whole Number of free Persons, including **those bound to Service**[1] for a Term of Years, and excluding Indians not taxed, three fifths of **all other Persons**~~.[2] The actual **Enumeration**[3] shall be made within three Years after the first Meeting of the Congress of the United States, and within every subsequent Term of ten Years, in such Manner as they shall by Law direct. The Number of Representatives shall not exceed one for every thirty Thousand, but each State shall have at Least one Representative~~; and until such enumeration shall be made, the State of New Hampshire shall be entitled to choose three, Massachusetts eight, Rhode-Island and Providence Plantations one, Connecticut five, New-York six, New Jersey four, Pennsylvania eight, Delaware one, Maryland six, Virginia ten, North Carolina five, South Carolina five, and Georgia three.~~

4. Vacancies When vacancies happen in the Representation from any State, the Executive Authority thereof shall issue Writs of Election to fill such Vacancies.

5. Officers and Impeachment The House of Representatives shall choose their Speaker and other Officers; and shall have the sole Power of impeachment.

Legislative Branch

Article I explains how the legislative branch, called Congress, is organized. The chief purpose of the legislative branch is to make laws. Congress is made up of the Senate and the House of Representatives.

The House of Representatives

The number of members each state has in the House is based on the population of the individual state. In 1929 Congress permanently fixed the size of the House at 435 members.

Vocabulary

[1] **those bound to Service** indentured servants

[2] **all other Persons** slaves

[3] **Enumeration** census or official population count

Historical Documents

Main Idea

Recall What two groups make up Congress? *the House of Representatives and the Senate*

Identify What information about the House of Representatives is outlined in Article I, Section 2 of the Constitution? *elections, qualifications, number of representatives, vacancies, officers, and impeachment*

Summarize What powers are granted to the House of Representatives? *to make laws, to choose the Speaker of the House and other officers, and to impeach*

Connect to Civics: Justice

The House as a Court The House of Representatives helps make the nation's laws. Sometimes, however, the House becomes a court of law. This situation may occur if a high-ranking federal official disobeys the law. The Constitution gives the House the authority to bring charges against the individual. If the House does so, the Senate conducts the trial.

Did you know . . .

The Union passed the first income tax during the Civil War to pay for maintaining the army.

Historical Documents

Main Idea

Recall How many senators are elected from each state? *two*

Summarize What privileges are outlined in Article I, Section 6? *Senators and representatives are paid for their services out of the U.S. Treasury, and they have a number of other privileges, including immunity from arrest except in cases of treason, felony, and breach of peace.*

Quick Facts Transparency 19: Federal Office Terms and Requirements

Connect to Civics: Responsibility

The Seventeenth Amendment Senators are no longer "chosen by the Legislature thereof," but rather are elected by the people of their state. The Seventeenth Amendment made this change to the Constitution. Before voting, all citizens have the responsibility to learn about the candidates, such as senators and other officials.

Exploring the Document

allows one branch of government to exert power over another branch of government

Section 3. The Senate

1. Number of Senators The Senate of the United States shall be composed of two Senators from each State, ~~chosen by the Legislature thereof,~~ for six Years; and each Senator shall have one Vote.

2. Classifying Terms Immediately after they shall be assembled in Consequence of the first Election, they shall be divided as equally as may be into three Classes. The Seats of the Senators of the first Class shall be vacated at the Expiration of the second Year, of the second Class at the Expiration of the fourth Year, and of the third Class at the Expiration of the sixth Year, so that one third may be chosen every second Year; ~~and if Vacancies happen by Resignation, or otherwise, during the Recess of the Legislature of any State, the Executive thereof may make temporary Appointments until the next Meeting of the Legislature, which shall then fill such Vacancies.~~

3. Qualifications No Person shall be a Senator who shall not have attained to the Age of thirty Years, and been nine Years a Citizen of the United States, and who shall not, when elected, be an Inhabitant of that State for which he shall be chosen.

4. Role of Vice President The Vice President of the United States shall be President of the Senate, but shall have no Vote, unless they be equally divided.

5. Officers The Senate shall choose their other Officers, and also a President **pro tempore**,[4] in the Absence of the Vice President, or when he shall exercise the Office of President of the United States.

6. Impeachment Trials The Senate shall have the sole Power to try all **Impeachments**.[5] When sitting for that Purpose, they shall be on Oath or Affirmation. When the President of the United States is tried, the Chief Justice shall preside: And no Person shall be convicted without the Concurrence of two thirds of the Members present.

7. Punishment for Impeachment Judgment in Cases of Impeachment shall not extend further than to removal from Office, and disqualification to hold and enjoy any Office of honor, Trust or Profit under the United States: but the Party convicted shall nevertheless be liable and subject to Indictment, Trial, Judgment and Punishment, according to Law.

The Vice President

The only duty that the Constitution assigns to the vice president is to preside over meetings of the Senate. Modern presidents have usually given their vice presidents more responsibilities.

EXPLORING THE DOCUMENT If the House of Representatives charges a government official with wrongdoing, the Senate acts as a court to decide if the official is guilty. **How does the power of impeachment represent part of the system of checks and balances?**

Vocabulary

[4] **pro tempore** temporarily

[5] **Impeachments** official accusations of federal wrongdoing

Federal Office Terms and Requirements (QUICK FACTS)

Position	Term	Minimum Age	Residency	Citizenship
President	4 years	35	14 years in the U.S.	natural-born
Vice President	4 years	35	14 years in the U.S.	natural-born
Supreme Court Justice	unlimited	none	none	none
Senator	6 years	30	state in which elected	9 years
Representative	2 years	25	state in which elected	7 years

190 CHAPTER 6

Section 4. Congressional Elections

1. Regulations The Times, Places and Manner of holding Elections for Senators and Representatives, shall be prescribed in each State by the Legislature thereof; but the Congress may at any time by Law make or alter such Regulations, except as to the Places of choosing Senators.

2. Sessions ~~The Congress shall assemble at least once in every Year, and such Meeting shall be on the first Monday in December, unless they shall by Law appoint a different Day.~~

Section 5. Rules/Procedures

1. Quorum Each House shall be the Judge of the Elections, Returns and Qualifications of its own Members, and a Majority of each shall constitute a **Quorum**[6] to do Business; but a smaller Number may **adjourn**[7] from day to day, and may be authorized to compel the Attendance of absent Members, in such Manner, and under such Penalties as each House may provide.

2. Rules and Conduct Each House may determine the Rules of its Proceedings, punish its Members for disorderly Behaviour, and, with the Concurrence of two thirds, expel a Member.

3. Records Each House shall keep a Journal of its Proceedings, and from time to time publish the same, excepting such Parts as may in their Judgment require Secrecy; and the Yeas and Nays of the Members of either House on any question shall, at the Desire of one fifth of those Present, be entered on the Journal.

4. Adjournment Neither House, during the Session of Congress, shall, without the Consent of the other, adjourn for more than three days, nor to any other Place than that in which the two Houses shall be sitting.

Section 6. Payment

1. Salary The Senators and Representatives shall receive a Compensation for their Services, to be ascertained by Law, and paid out of the Treasury of the United States. They shall in all Cases, except Treason, Felony and Breach of the Peace, be privileged from Arrest during their Attendance at the Session of their respective Houses, and in going to and returning from the same; and for any Speech or Debate in either House, they shall not be questioned in any other Place.

2. Restrictions No Senator or Representative shall, during the Time for which he was elected, be appointed to any civil Office under the Authority of the United States, which shall have been created, or the **Emoluments**[8] whereof shall have been increased during such time; and no Person holding any Office under the United States, shall be a Member of either House during his **Continuance**[9] in Office.

Vocabulary

[6] **Quorum** the minimum number of people needed to conduct business

[7] **adjourn** to stop indefinitely

[8] **Emoluments** salary

[9] **Continuance** term

Historical Documents

Info to Know

Senate Firsts Since the Senate's first session in New York City on March 4, 1789, a number of other firsts have taken place in the U.S. Senate.

- September 30, 1788—first two senators elected: Robert Morris and William Maclay, both from Pennsylvania
- November 1816—first former senator to be elected president: James Monroe
- February 1870—first African American to take the oath as U.S. Senator: Hiram R. Revels
- November 1922—first female senator appointed: Rebecca Felton
- January 2001—first presidential First Lady to be elected senator: Hillary Rodham Clinton

Connect to Science and Technology

Availability of Information For many years, the best way for the public to learn about congressional proceedings was to consult the *Congressional Record*, a bulky set of printed volumes. With the increased availability of the Internet, tracking a congressperson's votes has become much easier. The Library of Congress publishes a Web site that covers many aspects of the government. In addition, independent organizations, such as Project Vote Smart, provide links to track congressional votes.

go.hrw.com
Online Resources
KEYWORD: SF7 CH6
ACTIVITY: Checking on Your Legislators

CITIZENSHIP AND THE CONSTITUTION 191

Historical Documents

Main Idea

Describe What bills may a president veto? *any bills passed by both houses and presented to him for approval*

Explain What is required to override a presidential veto? *two-thirds majority vote of Congress*

Analyze Why do you think a larger legislative majority is required to override a presidential veto than to pass a bill? *to balance power between the executive and legislative branches*

Activity **Political Cartoon** Ask students to find out what is meant by a "pocket veto." Then have them create a political cartoon to illustrate the purpose of this legislative maneuver and how it works. **LS Visual/Spatial**

Info to Know

The Line-Item Veto In 1996 Congress passed the line-item veto, which gave the president the power to cancel specific items in spending bills. Supporters of the law hoped that it would help stop wasteful spending by allowing the president to prevent spending that he or she considered unnecessary. However, almost immediately a group of lawmakers challenged the line-item veto on constitutional grounds. In June 1998 the Supreme Court struck down the line-item veto and confirmed a lower court's ruling that it was unconstitutional.

Exploring the Document

top *Officials who are elected more frequently will be held more accountable for raising taxes.*

bottom *to provide the legislative branch with a check on the executive branch; to prevent the president from having too much power*

Vocabulary

[10]**Bills** proposed laws

EXPLORING THE DOCUMENT The framers felt that because members of the House are elected every two years, representatives would listen to the public and seek its approval before passing taxes. **How does Section 7 address the colonial demand of "no taxation without representation"?**

EXPLORING THE DOCUMENT The veto power of the president is one of the important checks and balances in the Constitution. **Why do you think the framers included the ability of Congress to override a veto?**

Section 7. How a Bill Becomes a Law

1. Tax Bills All **Bills**[10] for raising Revenue shall originate in the House of Representatives; but the Senate may propose or concur with Amendments as on other Bills.

2. Lawmaking Every Bill which shall have passed the House of Representatives and the Senate, shall, before it become a Law, be presented to the President of the United States: If he approve he shall sign it, but if not he shall return it, with his Objections to that House in which it shall have originated, who shall enter the Objections at large on their Journal, and proceed to reconsider it. If after such Reconsideration two thirds of that House shall agree to pass the Bill, it shall be sent, together with the Objections, to the other House, by which it shall likewise be reconsidered, and if approved by two thirds of that House, it shall become a Law. But in all such Cases the Votes of both Houses shall be determined by yeas and Nays, and the Names of the Persons voting for and against the Bill shall be entered on the Journal of each House respectively. If any Bill shall not be returned by the President within ten Days (Sundays excepted) after it shall have been presented to him, the Same shall be a Law, in like Manner as if he had signed it, unless the Congress by their Adjournment prevent its Return, in which Case it shall not be a Law.

3. Role of the President Every Order, Resolution, or Vote to which the Concurrence of the Senate and House of Representatives may be necessary (except on a question of Adjournment) shall be presented to the President of the United States; and before the Same shall take Effect, shall be approved by him, or being disapproved by him, shall be repassed by two thirds of the Senate and House of Representatives, according to the Rules and Limitations prescribed in the Case of a Bill.

How a Bill Becomes a Law

1. A member of the House or the Senate introduces a bill and refers it to a committee.
2. The House or Senate Committee may approve, rewrite, or kill the bill.

3. The House or the Senate debates and votes on its version of the bill.
4. House and Senate conference committee members work out the differences between the two versions.
5. Both houses of Congress pass the revised bill.

Section 8.

Powers Granted to Congress

1. Taxation The Congress shall have Power To lay and collect Taxes, **Duties**,[11] **Imposts**[12] and **Excises**,[13] to pay the Debts and provide for the common Defense and general Welfare of the United States; but all Duties, Imposts and Excises shall be uniform throughout the United States;

2. Credit To borrow Money on the credit of the United States;

3. Commerce To regulate Commerce with foreign Nations, and among the several States, and with the Indian Tribes;

4. Naturalization and Bankruptcy To establish an uniform **Rule of Naturalization**,[14] and uniform Laws on the subject of Bankruptcies throughout the United States;

5. Money To coin Money, regulate the Value thereof, and of foreign Coin, and fix the Standard of Weights and Measures;

6. Counterfeiting To provide for the Punishment of counterfeiting the **Securities**[15] and current Coin of the United States;

7. Post Office To establish Post Offices and post Roads;

8. Patents and Copyrights To promote the Progress of Science and useful Arts, by securing for limited Times to Authors and Inventors the exclusive Right to their respective Writings and Discoveries;

9. Courts To constitute Tribunals inferior to the supreme Court;

10. International Law To define and punish Piracies and Felonies committed on the high Seas, and Offences against the Law of Nations;

LINKING TO TODAY

Native Americans and the Commerce Clause

The commerce clause gives Congress the power to "regulate Commerce with . . . the Indian Tribes." The clause has been interpreted to mean that the states cannot tax or interfere with businesses on Indian reservations, but that the federal government can. It also allows American Indian nations to develop their own governments and laws. These laws, however, can be challenged in federal court. Although reservation land usually belongs to the government of the Indian group, it is administered by the U.S. government.

Drawing Conclusions How would you describe the status of American Indian nations under the commerce clause?

Vocabulary

[11] **Duties** tariffs

[12] **Imposts** taxes

[13] **Excises** internal taxes on the manufacture, sale, or consumption of a commodity

[14] **Rule of Naturalization** a law by which a foreign-born person becomes a citizen

[15] **Securities** bonds

6 The president signs or vetoes the bill.

7 Two-thirds majority vote of Congress is needed to approve a vetoed bill. Bill becomes a law.

ANALYSIS SKILL ANALYZING INFORMATION

Why do you think the framers created this complex system for adopting laws?

Historical Documents

Info to Know

The First Postal Service Before the Constitution was ratified, Congress had established a postal service under the Articles of Confederation. Benjamin Franklin served as the postmaster general. The postal service expanded rapidly, with revenue increasing from $37,935 in 1790 to $1,707,000 by 1829. By the early 1800s, the government considered the post office so important that the postmaster general was made into a cabinet member. This distinction ended in 1971, however. Today the postmaster general is no longer part of the cabinet.

Answers

Linking to Today *The status of American Indian nations under the commerce clause is similar to that of the individual states.*

Analyzing Information *to make certain the laws passed represent the will of the people and the good of the nation*

Historical Documents

Main Idea

Describe What do Clauses 11–16 ensure and regulate? *control of the military*

Summarize What Congressional powers are explained in Clause 17? *Congress has the power to make laws for the District of Columbia, the nation's capital. Congress also has the power to regulate use of other property belonging to the national government, such as forts and arsenals.*

Make Inferences Why do you think the framers of the Constitution included a clause prohibiting titles of nobility? *Students might respond that the framers wanted to make sure that no class system or aristocracy would exist in the United States as it did in Great Britain.*

Connect to Civics: Authority

Activity **Elastic Clause Letters** Ask students to conduct research on the minimum wage law or on the creation of military academies as examples of when the elastic clause was used to meet the changing needs of American society. Then have each student write a letter to the framers of the Constitution. In their letters, students should use their research to explain how future government officials have used the elastic clause and their authority responsibly.

Vocabulary

[16] **Letters of Marque and Reprisal** documents issued by governments allowing merchant ships to arm themselves and attack ships of an enemy nation

11. War To declare War, grant **Letters of Marque and Reprisal,**[16] and make Rules concerning Captures on Land and Water;

12. Army To raise and support Armies, but no Appropriation of Money to that Use shall be for a longer Term than two Years;

13. Navy To provide and maintain a Navy;

14. Regulation of the Military To make Rules for the Government and Regulation of the land and naval Forces;

15. Militia To provide for calling forth the Militia to execute the Laws of the Union, suppress Insurrections and repel Invasions;

16. Regulation of the Militia To provide for organizing, arming, and disciplining, the Militia, and for governing such Part of them as may be employed in the Service of the United States, reserving to the States respectively, the Appointment of the Officers, and the Authority of training the Militia according to the discipline prescribed by Congress;

17. District of Columbia To exercise exclusive Legislation in all Cases whatsoever, over such District (not exceeding ten Miles square) as may, by Cession of particular States, and the Acceptance of Congress, become the Seat of the Government of the United States, and to exercise like Authority over all Places purchased by the Consent of the Legislature of the State in which the Same shall be, for the Erection of Forts, Magazines, Arsenals, dock-Yards, and other needful Buildings;—And

The Elastic Clause

The framers of the Constitution wanted a national government that was strong enough to be effective. This section lists the powers given to Congress. The last portion of Section 8 contains the so-called elastic clause.

18. Necessary and Proper Clause To make all Laws which shall be necessary and proper for carrying into Execution the foregoing Powers, and all other Powers vested by this Constitution in the Government of the United States, or in any Department or Officer thereof.

The Elastic Clause
The elastic clause has been stretched (like elastic) to allow Congress to meet changing circumstances.

Section 9. Powers Denied Congress

1. Slave Trade ~~The Migration or Importation of such Persons as any of the States now existing shall think proper to admit, shall not be prohibited by the Congress prior to the Year one thousand eight hundred and eight, but a Tax or duty may be imposed on such Importation, not exceeding ten dollars for each Person.~~

2. Habeas Corpus The Privilege of the **Writ of Habeas Corpus**[17] shall not be suspended, unless when in Cases of Rebellion or Invasion the public Safety may require it.

3. Illegal Punishment No **Bill of Attainder**[18] or **ex post facto Law**[19] shall be passed.

4. Direct Taxes No **Capitation**,[20] or other direct, Tax shall be laid, unless in Proportion to the Census or enumeration herein before directed to be taken.

5. Export Taxes No Tax or Duty shall be laid on Articles exported from any State.

6. No Favorites No Preference shall be given by any Regulation of Commerce or Revenue to the Ports of one State over those of another; nor shall Vessels bound to, or from, one State, be obliged to enter, clear, or pay Duties in another.

7. Public Money No Money shall be drawn from the Treasury, but in Consequence of Appropriations made by Law; and a regular Statement and Account of the Receipts and Expenditures of all public Money shall be published from time to time.

8. Titles of Nobility No Title of Nobility shall be granted by the United States: And no Person holding any Office of Profit or Trust under them, shall, without the Consent of the Congress, accept of any present, Emolument, Office, or Title, of any kind whatever, from any King, Prince, or foreign State.

Section 10. Powers Denied the States

1. Restrictions No State shall enter into any Treaty, Alliance, or Confederation; grant Letters of Marque and Reprisal; coin Money; emit Bills of Credit; make any Thing but gold and silver Coin a Tender in Payment of Debts; pass any Bill of Attainder, ex post facto Law, or Law impairing the Obligation of Contracts, or grant any Title of Nobility.

2. Import and Export Taxes No State shall, without the Consent of the Congress, lay any Imposts or Duties on Imports or Exports, except what may be absolutely necessary for executing it's inspection Laws: and the net Produce of all Duties and Imposts, laid by any State on Imports or Exports, shall be for the Use of the Treasury of the United States; and all such Laws shall be subject to the Revision and Control of the Congress.

3. Peacetime and War Restraints No State shall, without the Consent of Congress, lay any Duty of Tonnage, keep Troops, or Ships of War in time of Peace, enter into any Agreement or Compact with another State, or with a foreign Power, or engage in War, unless actually invaded, or in such imminent Danger as will not admit of delay.

EXPLORING THE DOCUMENT Although Congress has implied powers, there are also limits to its powers. Section 9 lists powers that are denied to the federal government. Several of the clauses protect the people of the United States from unjust treatment. **In what ways does the Constitution limit the powers of the federal government?**

Vocabulary

[17] **Writ of Habeas Corpus** a court order that requires the government to bring a prisoner to court and explain why he or she is being held

[18] **Bill of Attainder** a law declaring that a person is guilty of a particular crime

[19] **ex post facto Law** a law that is made effective prior to the date that it was passed and therefore punishes people for acts that were not illegal at the time

[20] **Capitation** a direct uniform tax imposed on each head, or person

Historical Documents

Info to Know

Writ of Habeas Corpus The term *habeas corpus* derives from medieval Latin and means "you shall have the body." This protection against unlawful imprisonment is the only civil liberty that the framers included in the original text of the Constitution. All other basic rights and liberties guaranteed to American citizens are outlined in the Bill of Rights.

Exploring the Document

The government cannot suspend the writ of habeas corpus or pass bills of attainder or ex post facto laws.

Historical Documents

Main Idea

Identify Which branch of the government is outlined in Article II? *the executive branch*

Make Inferences Why might many of the delegates to the Constitutional Convention have opposed a one-person executive? *Students might suggest that the delegates feared that they might create another monarchy, as in Great Britain.*

Summarize How are the president and vice president elected? *They are chosen by the electoral college—electors chosen by the states according to rules established by the legislatures.*

Map Transparency 28: The Electoral College

Info to Know

The U.S. President Initially, the writers of the Constitution agreed that the president would be chosen by the national legislature for a single, seven-year term. Many delegates opposed a strong executive branch. However, when the Constitution was turned over to the Committee on Style, Gouverneur Morris, who wanted a stronger executive, reworded the article outlining the role of the president. He shortened the length of the president's term, allowed the president to run for more than one term, and altered the method by which the president would be elected. These changes passed with little debate. For one, the delegates were ready to go home. For another, many members thought that George Washington would be the first president and believed that he would not abuse the power of the executive branch.

Executive Branch

The president is the chief of the executive branch. It is the job of the president to enforce the laws. The framers wanted the president's and vice president's terms of office and manner of selection to be different from those of members of Congress. They decided on four-year terms, but they had a difficult time agreeing on how to select the president and vice president. The framers finally set up an electoral system, which varies greatly from our electoral process today.

Presidential Elections

In 1845 Congress set the Tuesday following the first Monday in November of every fourth year as the general election date for selecting presidential electors.

Article II The Executive

Section 1. The Presidency

1. Terms of Office The executive Power shall be vested in a President of the United States of America. He shall hold his Office during the Term of four Years, and, together with the Vice President, chosen for the same Term, be elected, as follows:

2. Electoral College Each State shall appoint, in such Manner as the Legislature thereof may direct, a Number of Electors, equal to the whole Number of Senators and Representatives to which the State may be entitled in the Congress: but no Senator or Representative, or Person holding an Office of Trust or Profit under the United States, shall be appointed an Elector.

3. Former Method of Electing President ~~The Electors shall meet in their respective States, and vote by Ballot for two Persons, of whom one at least shall not be an Inhabitant of the same State with themselves. And they shall make a List of all the Persons voted for, and of the Number of Votes for each; which List they shall sign and certify, and transmit sealed to the Seat of the Government of the United States, directed to the President of the Senate. The President of the Senate shall, in the Presence of the Senate and House of Representatives, open all the Certificates, and the Votes shall~~

The Electoral College

GEOGRAPHY SKILLS INTERPRETING MAPS

Place What two states have the most electors?

Answers

Interpreting Maps *California (55) and Texas (34)*

~~then be counted. The Person having the greatest Number of Votes shall be the President, if such Number be a Majority of the whole Number of Electors appointed; and if there be more than one who have such Majority, and have an equal Number of Votes, then the House of Representatives shall immediately choose by Ballot one of them for President; and if no Person have a Majority, then from the five highest on the List the said House shall in like Manner choose the President. But in choosing the President, the Votes shall be taken by States, the Representation from each State having one Vote; A quorum for this purpose shall consist of a Member or Members from two thirds of the States, and a Majority of all the States shall be necessary to a Choice. In every Case, after the Choice of the President, the Person having the greatest Number of Votes of the Electors shall be the Vice President. But if there should remain two or more who have equal Votes, the Senate shall choose from them by Ballot the Vice President.~~

4. Election Day The Congress may determine the Time of choosing the Electors, and the Day on which they shall give their Votes; which Day shall be the same throughout the United States.

5. Qualifications No Person except a natural born Citizen~~, or a Citizen of the United States, at the time of the Adoption of this Constitution~~, shall be eligible to the Office of President; neither shall any Person be eligible to that Office who shall not have attained to the Age of thirty five Years, and been fourteen Years a Resident within the United States.

6. Succession In Case of the Removal of the President from Office, or of his Death, Resignation, or Inability to discharge the Powers and Duties of the said Office, the Same shall devolve on the Vice President, and the Congress may by Law provide for the Case of Removal, Death, Resignation or Inability, both of the President and Vice President, declaring what Officer shall then act as President, and such Officer shall act accordingly, until the Disability be removed, or a President shall be elected.

7. Salary The President shall, at stated Times, receive for his Services, a Compensation, which shall neither be increased nor diminished during the Period for which he shall have been elected, and he shall not receive within that Period any other Emolument from the United States, or any of them.

8. Oath of Office Before he enter on the Execution of his Office, he shall take the following Oath or Affirmation:—"I do solemnly swear (or affirm) that I will faithfully execute the Office of President of the United States, and will to the best of my Ability, preserve, protect and defend the Constitution of the United States."

EXPLORING THE DOCUMENT The youngest elected president was John F. Kennedy; he was 43 years old when he was inaugurated. (Theodore Roosevelt was 42 when he assumed office after the assassination of McKinley.) **What is the minimum required age for the office of president?**

Presidential Salary

In 1999 Congress voted to set future presidents' salaries at $400,000 per year. The president also receives an annual expense account. The president must pay taxes only on the salary.

Historical Documents

Info to Know

Presidential Qualifications Political concerns of the time determined many of the qualifications for the presidency included in the U.S. Constitution. For example, during the Constitutional Convention, a rumor spread that the delegates intended to invite a foreign king to rule the country. To squelch this rumor, the delegates included a constitutional provision requiring the president to be a natural-born citizen. In addition, the delegates added a 14-year residency requirement for the president to disqualify any Loyalists who had left during the American Revolution and then returned to the United States.

Exploring the Document

35 years old

CITIZENSHIP AND THE CONSTITUTION 197

Historical Documents

Did you know . . .

The term *first lady* became common after the Civil War. Before that time, presidents' wives were referred to as Mrs. President or presidentress. Although first ladies are not mentioned in the Constitution, almost all presidents—even unmarried ones—have found someone to fill that role. For example, Dolley Madison served as first lady for widower Thomas Jefferson, before assuming that role for her own husband. Recent first ladies have done more than serve as their husbands' hostesses, however. Some first ladies—such as Eleanor Roosevelt, Betty Ford, Rosalynn Carter, and Hillary Rodham Clinton—have had highly visible roles.

go.hrw.com
Online Resources
KEYWORD: SF7 CH6
ACTIVITY: First Ladies

Commander in Chief

Today the president is in charge of the army, navy, air force, marines, and coast guard. Only Congress, however, can decide if the United States will declare war.

Appointments

Most of the president's appointments to office must be approved by the Senate.

Vocabulary

[21] **Reprieves** delays of punishment

[22] **Pardons** releases from the legal penalties associated with a crime

The State of the Union

Every year the president presents to Congress a State of the Union message. In this message, the president introduces and explains a legislative plan for the coming year.

Section 2. Powers of Presidency

1. Military Powers The President shall be Commander in Chief of the Army and Navy of the United States, and of the Militia of the several States, when called into the actual Service of the United States; he may require the Opinion, in writing, of the principal Officer in each of the executive Departments, upon any Subject relating to the Duties of their respective Offices, and he shall have Power to grant **Reprieves**[21] and **Pardons**[22] for Offences against the United States, except in Cases of Impeachment.

2. Treaties and Appointments He shall have Power, by and with the Advice and Consent of the Senate, to make Treaties, provided two thirds of the Senators present concur; and he shall nominate, and by and with the Advice and Consent of the Senate, shall appoint Ambassadors, other public Ministers and Consuls, Judges of the supreme Court, and all other Officers of the United States, whose Appointments are not herein otherwise provided for, and which shall be established by Law: but the Congress may by Law vest the Appointment of such inferior Officers, as they think proper, in the President alone, in the Courts of Law, or in the Heads of Departments.

3. Vacancies The President shall have Power to fill up all Vacancies that may happen during the Recess of the Senate, by granting Commissions which shall expire at the End of their next Session.

Section 3. Presidential Duties

He shall from time to time give to the Congress Information of the State of the Union, and recommend to their Consideration such Measures as he shall judge necessary and expedient; he may, on extraordinary Occasions, convene both Houses, or either of them, and in Case of Disagreement between them, with Respect to the Time of Adjournment, he may adjourn them to such Time as he shall think proper; he shall receive Ambassadors and other public Ministers; he shall take Care that the Laws be faithfully executed, and shall Commission all the Officers of the United States.

Section 4. Impeachment

The President, Vice President and all civil Officers of the United States, shall be removed from Office on Impeachment for, and Conviction of, Treason, Bribery, or other high Crimes and Misdemeanors.

198 CHAPTER 6

Article III The Judiciary

Section 1. Federal Courts and Judges

The judicial Power of the United States shall be vested in one supreme Court, and in such inferior Courts as the Congress may from time to time ordain and establish. The Judges, both of the supreme and inferior Courts, shall hold their Offices during good Behavior, and shall, at stated Times, receive for their Services a Compensation, which shall not be diminished during their Continuance in Office.

Section 2. Authority of the Courts

1. General Authority The judicial Power shall extend to all Cases, in Law and Equity, arising under this Constitution, the Laws of the United States, and Treaties made, or which shall be made, under their Authority;—to all Cases affecting Ambassadors, other public Ministers and Consuls;—to all Cases of admiralty and maritime Jurisdiction;—to Controversies to which the United States shall be a Party;—to Controversies between two or more States ~~—between a State and Citizens of another State;~~ —between Citizens of different States;—between Citizens of the same State claiming Lands under Grants of different States~~, and between a State, or the Citizens thereof, and foreign States, Citizens or Subjects.~~

2. Supreme Authority In all Cases affecting Ambassadors, other public Ministers and Consuls, and those in which a State shall be Party, the supreme Court shall have original Jurisdiction. In all the other Cases before mentioned, the supreme Court shall have appellate Jurisdiction, both as to Law and Fact, with such Exceptions, and under such Regulations as the Congress shall make.

Federal Judicial System
QUICK FACTS
Supreme Court
Reviews cases appealed from lower federal courts and highest state courts
Courts of Appeals
Review appeals from district courts
District Courts
Hold trials

Judicial Branch

The Articles of Confederation did not set up a federal court system. One of the first points that the framers of the Constitution agreed upon was to set up a national judiciary. In the Judiciary Act of 1789, Congress provided for the establishment of lower courts, such as district courts, circuit courts of appeals, and various other federal courts. The judicial system provides a check on the legislative branch: it can declare a law unconstitutional.

Historical Documents

Main Idea

Identify What courts does the Constitution include in the judiciary? *Supreme Court and lower federal courts established by Congress*

Explain What power does Article III give to the third branch of government? *the power to interpret the laws of the United States*

Quick Facts Transparency 20: Federal Judicial System

Biography

John Marshall (1755–1835) The U.S. Supreme Court was considered a fairly unimportant institution in its early years. When John Marshall was appointed chief justice in 1801, the Supreme Court did not even have its own building. As chief justice, Marshall established the Supreme Court as the final interpreter of the Constitution and made the Court into an important check on the president and Congress.

Historical Documents

Main Idea

Identify What is the primary subject of Article IV? *relations among states*

Explain What rights are citizens entitled to if they move to or visit another state? *the same privileges and immunities of citizens of that state*

Quick Facts Transparency 21: Federalism

Exploring the Document

allows the people rather than the federal government to determine the laws of each state

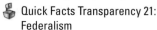

3. Trial by Jury The Trial of all Crimes, except in Cases of Impeachment, shall be by Jury; and such Trial shall be held in the State where the said Crimes shall have been committed; but when not committed within any State, the Trial shall be at such Place or Places as the Congress may by Law have directed.

Section 3. Treason

1. Definition Treason against the United States, shall consist only in levying War against them, or in adhering to their Enemies, giving them Aid and Comfort. No Person shall be convicted of Treason unless on the Testimony of two Witnesses to the same overt Act, or on Confession in open Court.

2. Punishment The Congress shall have Power to declare the Punishment of Treason, but no Attainder of Treason shall work **Corruption of Blood**,[23] or Forfeiture except during the Life of the Person attainted.

Vocabulary

[23] **Corruption of Blood** punishing the family of a person convicted of treason

Article IV Relations among States

Section 1. State Acts and Records

Full Faith and Credit shall be given in each State to the public Acts, Records, and judicial Proceedings of every other State. And the Congress may by general Laws prescribe the Manner in which such Acts, Records and Proceedings shall be proved, and the Effect thereof.

The States

States must honor the laws, records, and court decisions of other states. A person cannot escape a legal obligation by moving from one state to another.

Section 2. Rights of Citizens

1. Citizenship The Citizens of each State shall be entitled to all Privileges and Immunities of Citizens in the several States.

2. Extradition A Person charged in any State with Treason, Felony, or other Crime, who shall flee from Justice, and be found in another State, shall on Demand of the executive Authority of the State from which he fled, be delivered up, to be removed to the State having Jurisdiction of the Crime.

3. Fugitive Slaves ~~No Person held to Service or Labour in one State, under the Laws thereof, escaping into another, shall, in Consequence of any Law or Regulation therein, be discharged from such Service or Labour, but shall be delivered up on Claim of the Party to whom such Service or Labour may be due.~~

EXPLORING THE DOCUMENT The framers wanted to ensure that citizens could determine how state governments would operate. **How does the need to respect the laws of each state support the principle of popular sovereignty?**

200 CHAPTER 6

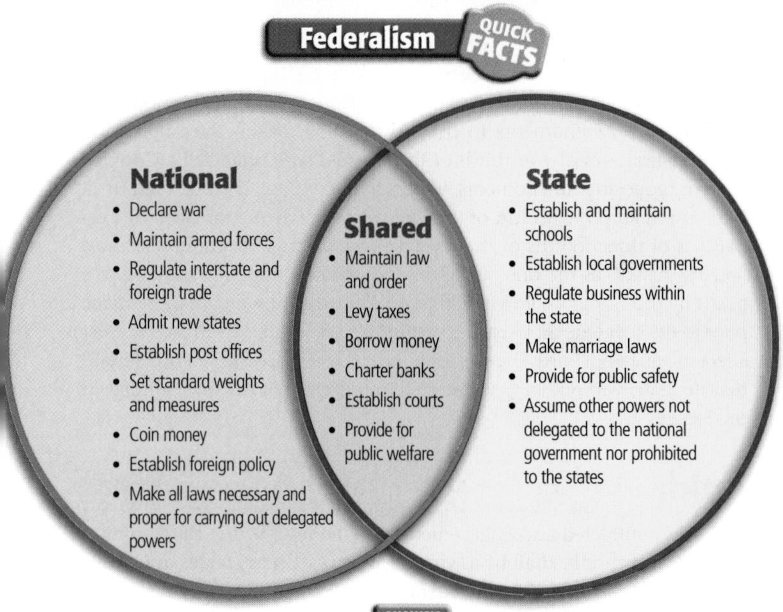

Federalism
QUICK FACTS
National
• Declare war
• Maintain armed forces
• Regulate interstate and foreign trade
• Admit new states
• Establish post offices
• Set standard weights and measures
• Coin money
• Establish foreign policy
• Make all laws necessary and proper for carrying out delegated powers
Shared
• Maintain law and order
• Levy taxes
• Borrow money
• Charter banks
• Establish courts
• Provide for public welfare
State
• Establish and maintain schools
• Establish local governments
• Regulate business within the state
• Make marriage laws
• Provide for public safety
• Assume other powers not delegated to the national government nor prohibited to the states

ANALYSIS SKILL — ANALYZING INFORMATION

Why does the power to declare war belong only to the national government?

Section 3. New States

1. Admission New States may be admitted by the Congress into this Union; but no new State shall be formed or erected within the Jurisdiction of any other State; nor any State be formed by the Junction of two or more States, or Parts of States, without the Consent of the Legislatures of the States concerned as well as of the Congress.

2. Congressional Authority The Congress shall have Power to dispose of and make all needful Rules and Regulations respecting the Territory or other Property belonging to the United States; and nothing in this Constitution shall be so construed as to Prejudice any Claims of the United States, or of any particular State.

Section 4. Guarantees to the States

The United States shall guarantee to every State in this Union a Republican Form of Government, and shall protect each of them against Invasion; and on Application of the Legislature, or of the Executive (when the Legislature cannot be convened), against domestic Violence.

EXPLORING THE DOCUMENT In a republic, voters elect representatives to act in their best interest. **How does Article IV protect the practice of republicanism in the United States?**

Historical Documents

Linking to Today

Admission of New States Although the framers of the Constitution wanted to allow new states to be admitted, many also wanted to preserve the power of the original states. One delegate suggested that the new states' total number of House representatives should never exceed the original states' total number of representatives.

Draw Conclusions If this suggestion had become part of the Constitution, how might it have affected the current U.S. government? *States along the Atlantic coast would have a disproportionate amount of political power.*

Exploring the Document

guarantees that every state will have a representative government

Answers

Analyzing Information *to prevent states from declaring war on one another or on a foreign nation*

Historical Documents

Linking to Today

Amendments to the Constitution Of the thousands of proposals for amendments to the Constitution, only 33 have obtained the required two-thirds vote in Congress. One historic amendment, the Equal Rights Amendment, was first proposed in 1923.

Quick Facts Transparency 22: Amending the U.S. Constitution

Activity Researching the ERA Organize the class into small groups to conduct research on the Equal Rights Amendment. Assign each group one of the following research topics: the text of the Equal Rights Amendment (ERA); Alice Paul, the author of the ERA; the history of the ERA; the current political status of the amendment; and arguments for and against making the ERA part of the Constitution. Have each group present its findings to the class.
LS Interpersonal, Verbal/Linguistic

Exploring the Document

See the chart, Amending the U.S. Constitution, at right; possible answer—changes in American society or culture

EXPLORING THE DOCUMENT America's founders may not have realized how long the Constitution would last, but they did set up a system for changing or adding to it. They did not want to make it easy to change the Constitution. **By what methods may the Constitution be amended? Under what sorts of circumstances do you think an amendment might be necessary?**

Article V Amending the Constitution

The Congress, whenever two thirds of both Houses shall deem it necessary, shall propose Amendments to this Constitution, or, on the Application of the Legislatures of two thirds of the several States, shall call a Convention for proposing Amendments, which, in either Case, shall be valid to all Intents and Purposes, as Part of this Constitution, when ratified by the Legislatures of three fourths of the several States, or by Conventions in three fourths thereof, as the one or the other Mode of Ratification may be proposed by the Congress; Provided that ~~no Amendment which may be made prior to the Year One thousand eight hundred and eight shall in any Manner affect the first and fourth Clauses in the Ninth Section of the first Article; and that no State, without its Consent, shall be deprived of its equal Suffrage in the Senate.~~

National Supremacy

One of the biggest problems facing the delegates to the Constitutional Convention was the question of what would happen if a state law and a federal law conflicted. Which law would be followed? Who would decide? The second clause of Article VI answers those questions. When a federal law and a state law disagree, the federal law overrides the state law. The Constitution and other federal laws are the "supreme Law of the Land." This clause is often called the supremacy clause.

Article VI Supremacy of National Government

All Debts contracted and Engagements entered into, before the Adoption of this Constitution, shall be as valid against the United States under this Constitution, as under the Confederation.

This Constitution, and the Laws of the United States which shall be made in Pursuance thereof; and all Treaties made, or which shall be made, under the Authority of the United States, shall be the supreme Law of the Land; and the Judges in every State shall be bound thereby, any Thing in the Constitution or Laws of any State to the Contrary notwithstanding.

The Senators and Representatives before mentioned, and the Members of the several State Legislatures, and all executive and judicial Officers, both of the United States and of the several States, shall be bound by Oath or Affirmation, to support this Constitution; but no religious Test shall ever be required as a Qualification to any Office or public Trust under the United States.

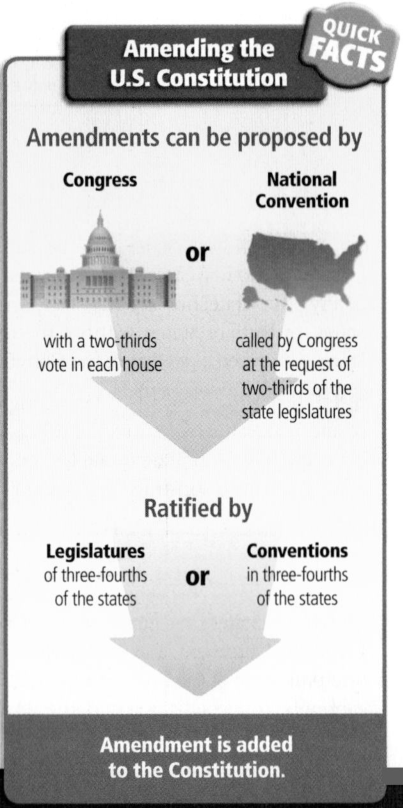

QUICK FACTS
Amending the U.S. Constitution
Amendments can be proposed by
Congress
with a two-thirds vote in each house
or
National Convention
called by Congress at the request of two-thirds of the state legislatures
Ratified by
Legislatures of three-fourths of the states
or
Conventions in three-fourths of the states
Amendment is added to the Constitution.

Article VII **Ratification**

The Ratification of the Conventions of nine States, shall be sufficient for the Establishment of this Constitution between the States so ratifying the Same.

Done in Convention by the Unanimous Consent of the States present the Seventeenth Day of September in the Year of our Lord one thousand seven hundred and Eighty seven and of the Independence of the United States of America the Twelfth In witness whereof We have hereunto subscribed our Names,

George Washington—
President and deputy from Virginia

Delaware
George Read
Gunning Bedford Jr.
John Dickinson
Richard Bassett
Jacob Broom

Maryland
James McHenry
Daniel of St. Thomas Jenifer
Daniel Carroll

Virginia
John Blair
James Madison Jr.

North Carolina
William Blount
Richard Dobbs Spaight
Hugh Williamson

South Carolina
John Rutledge
Charles Cotesworth Pinckney
Charles Pinckney
Pierce Butler

Georgia
William Few
Abraham Baldwin

New Hampshire
John Langdon
Nicholas Gilman

Massachusetts
Nathaniel Gorham
Rufus King

Connecticut
William Samuel Johnson
Roger Sherman

New York
Alexander Hamilton

New Jersey
William Livingston
David Brearley
William Paterson
Jonathan Dayton

Pennsylvania
Benjamin Franklin
Thomas Mifflin
Robert Morris
George Clymer
Thomas FitzSimons
Jared Ingersoll
James Wilson
Gouverneur Morris

Attest:
William Jackson, Secretary

Ratification

The Articles of Confederation called for all 13 states to approve any revision to the Articles. The Constitution required that 9 out of the 13 states would be needed to ratify the Constitution. The first state to ratify was Delaware, on December 7, 1787. Almost two-and-a-half years later, on May 29, 1790, Rhode Island became the last state to ratify the Constitution.

Historical Documents

Info to Know

Signers of the Constitution At 27 years old, Jonathan Dayton was the youngest person to sign the Constitution. At 81, Benjamin Franklin was the oldest. Franklin's signature was particularly important. As one of the most renowned men in America, he lent respectability to the new document.

History Humor

Franklin's Epitaph Benjamin Franklin, well known for his many expressions of wit and wisdom, composed his own tongue-in-cheek epitaph at the age of 22: "The body of Benjamin Franklin, Printer (like the cover of an old book, its contents torn out and stripped of its lettering and gilding), lies here, food for worms; but the work shall not be lost, for it will (as he believed) appear once more in a new and more elegant edition, revised and corrected by the Author."

Historical Documents

Main Idea

Recall What are the first 10 amendments to the Constitution called? *Bill of Rights*

Summarize What fundamental liberties are guaranteed by the First Amendment in the Bill of Rights? *freedom of religion, freedom of speech, freedom of the press, freedom of assembly*

World Events

Jefferson in Paris At the time of the Constitutional Convention, Thomas Jefferson was in Paris as part of a diplomatic mission to France. Jefferson became increasingly convinced of the evils of monarchy as he saw the violations of civil liberties that the French people had to tolerate. For example, the king could issue a *lettre de cachet*, which could order someone exiled or imprisoned without recourse. In addition, the aristocracy could destroy land without having to pay the owner for the damage. In his letters to delegates to the Constitutional Convention, Jefferson strongly urged the inclusion of a bill of rights.

Exploring the Document

possible answer—It is a right on which the United States was founded.

Constitutional Amendments

Note: The first 10 amendments to the Constitution were ratified on December 15, 1791, and form what is known as the Bill of Rights.

Bill of Rights

One of the conditions set by several states for ratifying the Constitution was the inclusion of a bill of rights. Many people feared that a stronger central government might take away basic rights of the people that had been guaranteed in state constitutions.

EXPLORING THE DOCUMENT The First Amendment forbids Congress from making any "law respecting an establishment of religion" or restraining the freedom to practice religion as one chooses. **Why is freedom of religion an important right?**

Rights of the Accused

The Fifth, Sixth, and Seventh Amendments describe the procedures that courts must follow when trying people accused of crimes.

Vocabulary

[24] **quartered** housed

[25] **Warrants** written orders authorizing a person to make an arrest, a seizure, or a search

[26] **infamous** disgraceful

[27] **indictment** the act of charging with a crime

Amendments 1–10. The Bill of Rights

Amendment I

Congress shall make no law respecting an establishment of religion, or prohibiting the free exercise thereof; or abridging the freedom of speech, or of the press; or the right of the people peaceably to assemble, and to petition the Government for a redress of grievances.

Amendment II

A well regulated Militia, being necessary to the security of a free State, the right of the people to keep and bear Arms, shall not be infringed.

Amendment III

No Soldier shall, in time of peace be **quartered**[24] in any house, without the consent of the Owner, nor in time of war, but in a manner to be prescribed by law.

Amendment IV

The right of the people to be secure in their persons, houses, papers, and effects, against unreasonable searches and seizures, shall not be violated, and no **Warrants**[25] shall issue, but upon probable cause, supported by Oath or affirmation, and particularly describing the place to be searched, and the persons or things to be seized.

Amendment V

No person shall be held to answer for a capital, or otherwise **infamous**[26] crime, unless on a presentment or **indictment**[27] of a Grand Jury, except in

Fundamental Liberties

Freedom of Religion

Freedom of Speech

204 CHAPTER 6

cases arising in the land or naval forces, or in the Militia, when in actual service in time of War or public danger; nor shall any person be subject for the same offence to be twice put in jeopardy of life or limb; nor shall be compelled in any criminal case to be a witness against himself, nor be deprived of life, liberty, or property, without due process of law; nor shall private property be taken for public use, without just compensation.

Amendment VI

In all criminal prosecutions, the accused shall enjoy the right to a speedy and public trial, by an impartial jury of the State and district wherein the crime shall have been committed, which district shall have been previously **ascertained**[28] by law, and to be informed of the nature and cause of the accusation; to be confronted with the witnesses against him; to have compulsory process for obtaining witnesses in his favor, and to have the Assistance of Counsel for his defence.

Amendment VII

In suits at common law, where the value in controversy shall exceed twenty dollars, the right of trial by jury shall be preserved, and no fact tried by a jury, shall be otherwise reexamined in any Court of the United States, than according to the rules of the common law.

Amendment VIII

Excessive bail shall not be required, nor excessive fines imposed, nor cruel and unusual punishments inflicted.

Amendment IX

The enumeration in the Constitution, of certain rights, shall not be construed to deny or disparage others retained by the people.

Amendment X

The powers not delegated to the United States by the Constitution, nor prohibited by it to the States, are reserved to the States respectively, or to the people.

Trials

The Sixth Amendment makes several guarantees, including a prompt trial and a trial by a jury chosen from the state and district in which the crime was committed.

Vocabulary

[28] **ascertained** found out

EXPLORING THE DOCUMENT The Ninth and Tenth Amendments were added because not every right of the people or of the states could be listed in the Constitution. **How do the Ninth and Tenth Amendments limit the power of the federal government?**

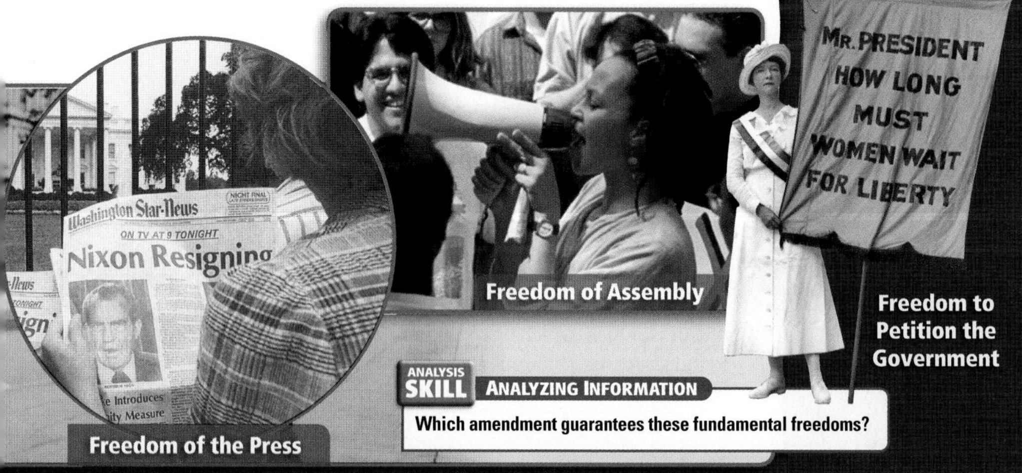

Freedom of the Press

Freedom of Assembly

Freedom to Petition the Government

ANALYSIS SKILL **ANALYZING INFORMATION**

Which amendment guarantees these fundamental freedoms?

Historical Documents

Linking to Today

Speedy and Public Trial

Activity Discussing the Trial Process

Explain to students that some trials attract heavy media attention when celebrities are involved or when the crime is particularly sensational. Ask students to bring to class newspaper and magazine articles about highly publicized criminal cases. Have students use the articles to discuss the concepts of the right to a speedy and public trial by an impartial jury. Ask students to discuss how long certain cases may have been in the news. Then have students describe situations in which impartiality might be difficult to guarantee in highly publicized criminal cases.

Exploring the Document

They extend rights to the people and to the states.

Answers

Analyzing Information
First Amendment

Historical Documents

Main Idea

Explain What does the Eleventh Amendment confirm? *No federal court may try a case in which a state is being sued by a citizen of another state or of a foreign country.*

Summarize How did the Twelfth Amendment change the electoral college? *It changed the procedure for choosing a president. The presidential electors would vote for president and vice president on separate ballots.*

Identify Cause and Effect Which three amendments do you think were a consequence of the Civil War? *Thirteenth, Fourteenth, and Fifteenth Amendments*

Reading Time Lines

Amendments to the U.S. Constitution

Activity **Amendment Collages** Have each student select one amendment on the time line that is of particular interest to him or her. Ask students to conduct research on the amendment's passage and place the amendment in a matrix of events, people, time, and place. Have students use the information to create a collage of words and images that evokes the era in which the amendment was added to the Constitution. **LS Verbal/ Linguistic, Visual/Spatial**

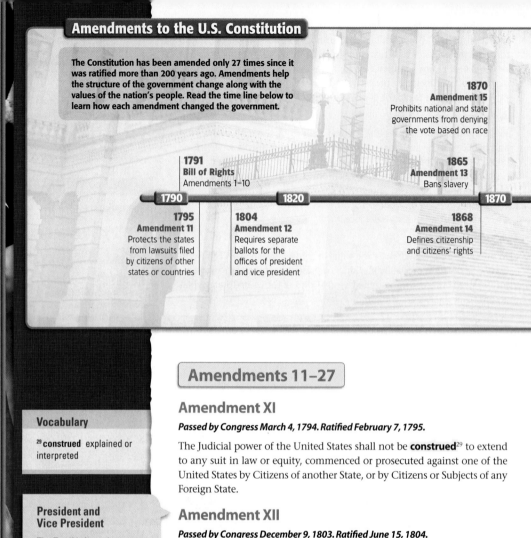

Amendments to the U.S. Constitution

The Constitution has been amended only 27 times since it was ratified more than 200 years ago. Amendments help the structure of the government change along with the values of the nation's people. Read the time line below to learn how each amendment changed the government.

1790 — 1820 — 1870

1791
Bill of Rights
Amendments 1–10

1795
Amendment 11
Protects the states from lawsuits filed by citizens of other states or countries

1804
Amendment 12
Requires separate ballots for the offices of president and vice president

1865
Amendment 13
Bans slavery

1868
Amendment 14
Defines citizenship and citizens' rights

1870
Amendment 15
Prohibits national and state governments from denying the vote based on race

Amendments 11–27

Vocabulary

[29]**construed** explained or interpreted

Amendment XI

Passed by Congress March 4, 1794. Ratified February 7, 1795.

The Judicial power of the United States shall not be **construed**[29] to extend to any suit in law or equity, commenced or prosecuted against one of the United States by Citizens of another State, or by Citizens or Subjects of any Foreign State.

President and Vice President

The Twelfth Amendment changed the election procedure for president and vice president.

Amendment XII

Passed by Congress December 9, 1803. Ratified June 15, 1804.

The Electors shall meet in their respective states and vote by ballot for President and Vice-President, one of whom, at least, shall not be an inhabitant of the same state with themselves; they shall name in their ballots the person voted for as President, and in distinct ballots the person voted for as Vice-President, and they shall make distinct lists of all persons voted for as President, and of all persons voted for as Vice-President, and of the number of votes for each, which lists they shall sign and certify, and transmit sealed to the seat of the government of the United States, directed to the President of the Senate;—the President of the Senate shall, in the presence of the

206 CHAPTER 6

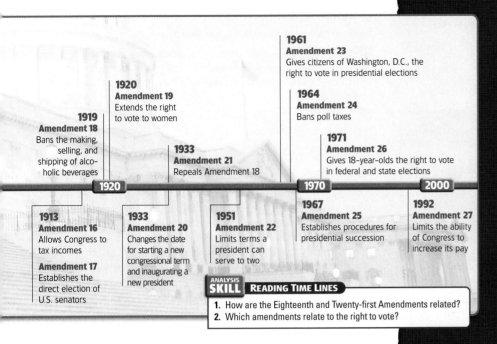

1913
Amendment 16
Allows Congress to tax incomes
Amendment 17
Establishes the direct election of U.S. senators

1919
Amendment 18
Bans the making, selling, and shipping of alcoholic beverages

1920
Amendment 19
Extends the right to vote to women

1933
Amendment 20
Changes the date for starting a new congressional term and inaugurating a new president

1933
Amendment 21
Repeals Amendment 18

1951
Amendment 22
Limits terms a president can serve to two

1961
Amendment 23
Gives citizens of Washington, D.C., the right to vote in presidential elections

1964
Amendment 24
Bans poll taxes

1967
Amendment 25
Establishes procedures for presidential succession

1971
Amendment 26
Gives 18-year-olds the right to vote in federal and state elections

1992
Amendment 27
Limits the ability of Congress to increase its pay

1920 · 1970 · 2000

ANALYSIS SKILL — READING TIME LINES

1. How are the Eighteenth and Twenty-first Amendments related?
2. Which amendments relate to the right to vote?

Senate and House of Representatives, open all the certificates and the votes shall then be counted;—The person having the greatest number of votes for President, shall be the President, if such number be a majority of the whole number of Electors appointed; and if no person have such majority, then from the persons having the highest numbers not exceeding three on the list of those voted for as President, the House of Representatives shall choose immediately, by ballot, the President. But in choosing the President, the votes shall be taken by states, the representation from each state having one vote; a quorum for this purpose shall consist of a member or members from two-thirds of the states, and a majority of all the states shall be necessary to a choice. ~~And if the House of Representatives shall not choose a President whenever the right of choice shall devolve upon them, before the fourth day of March next following, then the Vice-President shall act as President, as in case of the death or other constitutional disability of the President.~~—The person having the greatest number of votes as Vice-President, shall be the Vice-President, if such number be a majority of the whole number of Electors appointed, and if no person have a majority, then from the two highest numbers on the list, the Senate shall choose the Vice-President; a quorum for the purpose shall consist of two-thirds of the whole number of Senators, and a majority of the whole number shall be necessary to a choice. But no person constitutionally ineligible to the office of President shall be eligible to that of Vice-President of the United States.

Info to Know

Postwar Amendments Three amendments—the Thirteenth, Fourteenth, and Fifteenth—were meant initially to respond to changes demanded by the northern victory in the Civil War. When the Fourteenth Amendment was passed, many southerners interpreted it as punishing the South by extending civil rights to African Americans. Scholars have argued that the Fourteenth Amendment remains the most important addition to the Constitution since the Bill of Rights because of its inclusion of due process and equal protection clauses.

Evaluate Why do you think that scholars consider the Fourteenth Amendment so important? *Students might suggest that it redefined citizenship and guaranteed African Americans civil rights. It also made the Bill of Rights apply to state law.*

Answers

Reading Time Lines 1. *Eighteenth Amendment established the ban on alcohol (Prohibition); the Twenty-first Amendment repealed Prohibition.*
2. *Fifteenth, Nineteenth, Twenty-third, Twenty-fourth, and Twenty-sixth Amendments*

Historical Documents

Linking to Today

Civil Liberties Throughout the 1900s, the U.S. Supreme Court extended the coverage of the civil liberties provided in the Bill of Rights. In earlier times, justices had ruled that the Bill of Rights did not override state laws. Although the Fourteenth Amendment stated that the states could not deprive citizens of their constitutional rights, few justices changed their opinions. In the mid-1900s, Justice Hugo Black began to reinterpret the Fourteenth Amendment. He believed that the guarantees in the Bill of Rights were absolute. The Civil Rights Act, passed in 1964, was the most far-reaching civil rights bill in the nation's history. This act forbids discrimination in public accommodations.

Activity Civil Liberties Discussion Have students bring to class newspaper articles related to the exercise of civil liberties. Using these articles as discussion prompts, have students describe what they think are proper and improper limitations of civil liberties.

Abolishing Slavery

Although some slaves had been freed during the Civil War, slavery was not abolished until the Thirteenth Amendment took effect.

Protecting the Rights of Citizens

In 1833 the Supreme Court ruled that the Bill of Rights limited the federal government but not the state governments. This ruling was interpreted to mean that states were able to keep African Americans from becoming state citizens and keep the Bill of Rights from protecting them. The Fourteenth Amendment defines citizenship and prevents states from interfering in the rights of citizens of the United States.

Vocabulary

[30] **involuntary servitude** being forced to work against one's will

Amendment XIII

Passed by Congress January 31, 1865. Ratified December 6, 1865.

1. Slavery Banned Neither slavery nor **involuntary servitude**,[30] except as a punishment for crime whereof the party shall have been duly convicted, shall exist within the United States, or any place subject to their jurisdiction.

2. Enforcement Congress shall have power to enforce this article by appropriate legislation.

Amendment XIV

Passed by Congress June 13, 1866. Ratified July 9, 1868.

1. Citizenship Defined All persons born or naturalized in the United States, and subject to the jurisdiction thereof, are citizens of the United States and of the State wherein they reside. No State shall make or enforce any law which shall abridge the privileges or immunities of citizens of the United States; nor shall any State deprive any person of life, liberty, or property, without due process of law; nor deny to any person within its jurisdiction the equal protection of the laws.

2. Voting Rights Representatives shall be apportioned among the several States according to their respective numbers, counting the whole number of persons in each State, ~~excluding Indians not taxed~~. But when the right to vote at any election for the choice of electors for President and Vice-President of the United States, Representatives in Congress, the Executive and Judicial officers of a State, or the members of the Legislature thereof, is denied to any of the ~~male~~ inhabitants of such State, ~~being twenty-one years of age~~, and citizens of the United States, or in any way abridged, except for participation in rebellion, or other crime, the basis of representation therein shall be reduced in the proportion which the number of such ~~male~~ citizens shall bear to the whole number of ~~male~~ citizens ~~twenty-one years of age~~ in such State.

3. Rebels Banned from Government No person shall be a Senator or Representative in Congress, or elector of President and Vice-President, or hold any office, civil or military, under the United States, or under any State, who, having previously taken an oath, as a member of Congress, or as an officer of the United States, or as a member of any State legislature, or as an executive or judicial officer of any State, to support the Constitution of the United States, shall have engaged in insurrection or rebellion against the same, or given aid or comfort to the enemies thereof. But Congress may by a vote of two-thirds of each House, remove such disability.

4. Payment of Debts The validity of the public debt of the United States, authorized by law, including debts incurred for payment of pensions and

208 CHAPTER 6

The Reconstruction Amendments

The Thirteenth, Fourteenth, and Fifteenth Amendments are often called the Reconstruction Amendments. This is because they arose during Reconstruction, the period of American history following the Civil War. The country was reconstructing itself after that terrible conflict. A key aspect of Reconstruction was extending the rights of citizenship to former slaves.

The Thirteenth Amendment banned slavery. The Fourteenth Amendment required states to respect the freedoms listed in the Bill of Rights, thus preventing states from denying rights to African Americans. The Fifteenth Amendment gave African American men the right to vote.

African Americans participate in an election.

ANALYSIS SKILL ANALYZING INFORMATION

Why was the Thirteenth Amendment needed?

bounties for services in suppressing insurrection or rebellion, shall not be questioned. But neither the United States nor any State shall assume or pay any debt or obligation incurred in aid of insurrection or rebellion against the United States, ~~or any claim for the loss or emancipation of any slave~~; but all such debts, obligations and claims shall be held illegal and void.

5. Enforcement The Congress shall have the power to enforce, by appropriate legislation, the provisions of this article.

Amendment XV

Passed by Congress February 26, 1869. Ratified February 3, 1870.

1. Voting Rights The right of citizens of the United States to vote shall not be denied or abridged by the United States or by any State on account of race, color, or previous condition of servitude.

2. Enforcement The Congress shall have the power to enforce this article by appropriate legislation.

Historical Documents

Main Idea

Analyze Why is the guarantee of the right to vote important in a democracy? *To have equal representation under the law, all people need to have the right to vote.*

Evaluate What might the significance of the passage of the Fifteenth Amendment have been to future suffrage and civil rights movements? *It established the right of citizens to vote—regardless "of race, color, or previous condition of servitude."*

Activity Amendments Storyboard Have students create a three-panel storyboard that illustrates the significance of the Thirteenth, Fourteenth, and Fifteenth Amendments.

Info to Know

African American Vote The passage of the Fourteenth and Fifteenth Amendments dramatically increased African Americans' political participation. Strikes broke out among African American workers throughout the South. The workers staged sit-ins on segregated carriages in Richmond, Virginia. When police tried to stop the protests, angry crowds formed, demanding, "Let's have our rights." Almost every institution of African American life worked to mobilize black voters and to educate new voters. So many African American laborers attended the Republican state convention in Virginia that Richmond's tobacco factories had to close.

Answers

Analyzing Information *to abolish slavery*

Historical Documents

Main Idea

Explain What did the Eighteenth Amendment ban? *the making, sale, and transport of alcohol*

Make Inferences Why do you think the Eighteenth Amendment was repealed? *Students might suggest its impracticality and enormous unpopularity.*

Elaborate What factors do you think contributed to the passage of the Nineteenth Amendment? *Students might suggest the strong leadership and determination of women as well as organized, grassroots suffrage campaigns throughout the country.*

Info to Know

Effects of Prohibition The Eighteenth Amendment may have banned the manufacture, sale, and transportation of liquor, but it also created an underground culture of bootlegging, smuggling, and organized crime. Speakeasies—illegal bars that sold alcoholic beverages—sprang up in large cities. These bars devised elaborate gadgets to hide the illegal evidence in case of police raids. New York City alone had over 30,000 speakeasies, twice the city's number of bars before Prohibition.

Exploring the Document

the principle of direct representation

EXPLORING THE DOCUMENT The Seventeenth Amendment requires that senators be elected directly by the people instead of by the state legislatures. **What principle of our government does the Seventeenth Amendment protect?**

Prohibition

Although many people believed that the Eighteenth Amendment was good for the health and welfare of the American people, it was repealed 14 years later.

Amendment XVI

Passed by Congress July 2, 1909. Ratified February 3, 1913.

The Congress shall have power to lay and collect taxes on incomes, from whatever source derived, without apportionment among the several States, and without regard to any census or enumeration.

Amendment XVII

Passed by Congress May 13, 1912. Ratified April 8, 1913.

1. Senators Elected by Citizens The Senate of the United States shall be composed of two Senators from each State, elected by the people thereof, for six years; and each Senator shall have one vote. The electors in each State shall have the qualifications requisite for electors of the most numerous branch of the State legislatures.

2. Vacancies When vacancies happen in the representation of any State in the Senate, the executive authority of such State shall issue writs of election to fill such vacancies: *Provided,* That the legislature of any State may empower the executive thereof to make temporary appointments until the people fill the vacancies by election as the legislature may direct.

3. Future Elections ~~This amendment shall not be so construed as to affect the election or term of any Senator chosen before it becomes valid as part of the Constitution.~~

Amendment XVIII

Passed by Congress December 18, 1917. Ratified January 16, 1919. Repealed by Amendment XXI.

1. Liquor Banned ~~After one year from the ratification of this article the manufacture, sale, or transportation of intoxicating liquors within, the importation thereof into, or the exportation thereof from the United States and all territory subject to the jurisdiction thereof for beverage purposes is hereby prohibited.~~

2. Enforcement ~~The Congress and the several States shall have concurrent power to enforce this article by appropriate legislation.~~

3. Ratification ~~This article shall be inoperative unless it shall have been ratified as an amendment to the Constitution by the legislatures of the several States, as provided in the Constitution, within seven years from the date of the submission hereof to the States by the Congress.~~

Women Fight for the Vote

To become part of the Constitution, a proposed amendment must be ratified by three-fourths of the states. Here, suffragists witness Kentucky governor Edwin P. Morrow signing the Nineteenth Amendment in January 1920. By June of that year, enough states had ratified the amendment to make it part of the Constitution. American women, after generations of struggle, had finally won the right to vote.

ANALYSIS SKILL ANALYZING INFORMATION

What right did the Nineteenth Amendment grant?

Amendment XIX

Passed by Congress June 4, 1919. Ratified August 18, 1920.

1. Voting Rights The right of citizens of the United States to vote shall not be denied or abridged by the United States or by any State on account of sex.

2. Enforcement Congress shall have power to enforce this article by appropriate legislation.

Amendment XX

Passed by Congress March 2, 1932. Ratified January 23, 1933.

1. Presidential Terms The terms of the President and the Vice President shall end at noon on the 20th day of January, and the terms of Senators and Representatives at noon on the 3d day of January, of the years in which such terms would have ended if this article had not been ratified; and the terms of their successors shall then begin.

Women's Suffrage

Abigail Adams and others were disappointed that the Declaration of Independence and the Constitution did not specifically include women. It took many years and much campaigning before suffrage for women was finally achieved.

Historical Documents

Biography

Elizabeth Cady Stanton (1815–1902) The efforts of Elizabeth Cady Stanton, a tireless crusader for women's rights, contributed to the passage of the Nineteenth Amendment in 1920. At her urging, in 1878 Senator Aaron A. Sargent of California introduced a women's suffrage amendment to the Constitution. This amendment was introduced and defeated repeatedly throughout Stanton's lifetime. She died in 1902, 18 years before the passage of the amendment for which she had worked so hard.

Primary Source

Abigail Adams, "Remember the Ladies"
In 1776, Abigail Adams wrote a letter to John Adams, in which she describes women's determination to be heard and represented. "In the new code of laws which I suppose it will be necessary for you to make I desire you would remember the ladies, and be more generous and favorable to them than your ancestors. Do not put such unlimited power into the hands of the husbands. Remember all men would be tyrants if they could. If particular care and attention is not paid to the ladies we are determined to foment a rebellion, and will not hold ourselves bound by any laws in which we have no voice, or representation."

Answers

Analyzing Information *granted women the right to vote*

Historical Documents

Biography

George W. Norris (1861–1944) During his long congressional career, George W. Norris not only created and worked to pass the Twentieth Amendment but also worked for the introduction of presidential primaries and for the direct election of senators. Though a Republican, Norris rarely voted along party lines. In defense of his independence, he claimed he "would rather be right than regular."

Connect to the Arts and Humanities

Inaugural Poems At the 1961 inauguration of John F. Kennedy, Robert Frost recited his poem "The Gift Outright." To honor Kennedy, Bill Clinton revived the tradition at his 1993 inauguration, during which Maya Angelou read her poem "On the Pulse of Morning."

Activity Interpreting and Reciting Poetry Have students use the library or Internet sources to locate poems read at presidential inaugurations. Ask for volunteers to read the poems aloud. Discuss what these poems convey or evoke about the significance of the moment and the promise of a new presidency.

Taking Office

In the original Constitution, a newly elected president and Congress did not take office until March 4, which was four months after the November election. The officials who were leaving office were called lame ducks because they had little influence during those four months. The Twentieth Amendment changed the date that the new president and Congress take office. Members of Congress now take office during the first week of January, and the president takes office on January 20.

2. Meeting of Congress The Congress shall assemble at least once in every year, and such meeting shall begin at noon on the 3d day of January, unless they shall by law appoint a different day.

3. Succession of Vice President If, at the time fixed for the beginning of the term of the President, the President elect shall have died, the Vice President elect shall become President. If a President shall not have been chosen before the time fixed for the beginning of his term, or if the President elect shall have failed to qualify, then the Vice President elect shall act as President until a President shall have qualified; and the Congress may by law provide for the case wherein neither a President elect nor a Vice President shall have qualified, declaring who shall then act as President, or the manner in which one who is to act shall be selected, and such person shall act accordingly until a President or Vice President shall have qualified.

4. Succession by Vote of Congress The Congress may by law provide for the case of the death of any of the persons from whom the House of Representatives may choose a President whenever the right of choice shall have devolved upon them, and for the case of the death of any of the persons from whom the Senate may choose a Vice President whenever the right of choice shall have devolved upon them.

5. Ratification ~~Sections 1 and 2 shall take effect on the 15th day of October following the ratification of this article.~~

6. Ratification ~~This article shall be inoperative unless it shall have been ratified as an amendment to the Constitution by the legislatures of three-fourths of the several States within seven years from the date of its submission.~~

Amendment XXI

Passed by Congress February 20, 1933. Ratified December 5, 1933.

1. 18th Amendment Repealed The eighteenth article of amendment to the Constitution of the United States is hereby repealed.

2. Liquor Allowed by Law The transportation or importation into any State, Territory, or Possession of the United States for delivery or use therein of intoxicating liquors, in violation of the laws thereof, is hereby prohibited.

3. Ratification ~~This article shall be inoperative unless it shall have been ratified as an amendment to the Constitution by conventions in the several States, as provided in the Constitution, within seven years from the date of the submission hereof to the States by the Congress.~~

Amendment XXII

Passed by Congress March 21, 1947. Ratified February 27, 1951.

1. Term Limits No person shall be elected to the office of the President more than twice, and no person who has held the office of President, or acted as President, for more than two years of a term to which some other person was elected President shall be elected to the office of President more than once. ~~But this Article shall not apply to any person holding the office of President when this Article was proposed by Congress, and shall not prevent any person who may be holding the office of President, or acting as President, during the term within which this Article becomes operative from holding the office of President or acting as President during the remainder of such term.~~

2. Ratification ~~This article shall be inoperative unless it shall have been ratified as an amendment to the Constitution by the legislatures of three-fourths of the several States within seven years from the date of its submission to the States by the Congress.~~

EXPLORING THE DOCUMENT From the time of President George Washington's administration, it was a custom for presidents to serve no more than two terms in office. Franklin D. Roosevelt, however, was elected to four terms. The Twenty-second Amendment restricted presidents to no more than two terms in office. **Why do you think citizens chose to limit the power of the president in this way?**

After Franklin D. Roosevelt was elected to four consecutive terms, limits were placed on the number of terms a president could serve.

Amendment XXIII

Passed by Congress June 16, 1960. Ratified March 29, 1961.

1. District of Columbia Represented The District constituting the seat of Government of the United States shall appoint in such manner as Congress may direct:

A number of electors of President and Vice President equal to the whole number of Senators and Representatives in Congress to which the District would be entitled if it were a State, but in no event more than the least populous State; they shall be in addition to those appointed by the States, but they shall be considered, for the purposes of the election of President and Vice President, to be electors appointed by a State; and they shall meet in the District and perform such duties as provided by the twelfth article of amendment.

2. Enforcement The Congress shall have power to enforce this article by appropriate legislation.

Voting Rights

Until the ratification of the Twenty-third Amendment, the people of Washington, D.C., could not vote in presidential elections.

Historical Documents

Main Idea

Recall What did the Twenty-first Amendment repeal? *prohibition*

Describe What right did the Twenty-third Amendment grant to the people of Washington, D.C.? *right to vote*

Analyze Why were citizens of Washington, D.C., not allowed to vote for president and vice president before the Twenty-third Amendment was adopted? *The District of Columbia is not a state, and the Constitution provided that only states should choose presidential electors.*

Exploring the Document

possible answer—Citizens did not want any one president to gain too much power.

CITIZENSHIP AND THE CONSTITUTION 213

Historical Documents

Info to Know

Poll Taxes Congress started trying to eliminate poll taxes in 1939. These taxes had been instituted in some southern states after Reconstruction and were still in effect in five of those states in 1964. The poll tax was often explicitly adopted to discriminate against African American voters. For example, when a poll tax was passed in Virginia in 1902, one representative said, "Discrimination! Why, that is precisely what we propose."

Twenty-sixth Amendment As of 1970, four states had established a minimum voting age lower than 21. That year, Congress passed a law allowing citizens 18 and older to vote in federal elections. The U.S. Supreme Court found the law constitutional but noted that Congress did not have the power to set the voting age in state elections. To remedy any conflicts between federal and state voting standards, Congress passed the Twenty-sixth Amendment, which established 18 as the minimum voting age in all elections in the United States. The amendment was quickly ratified.

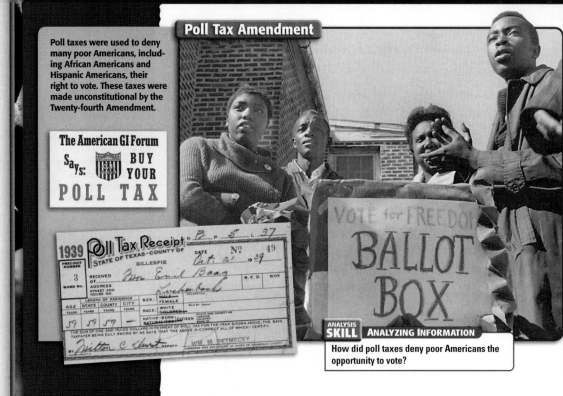

Poll Tax Amendment

Poll taxes were used to deny many poor Americans, including African Americans and Hispanic Americans, their right to vote. These taxes were made unconstitutional by the Twenty-fourth Amendment.

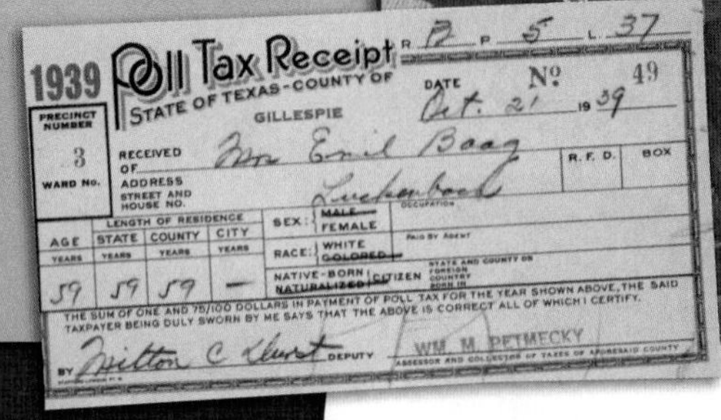

ANALYSIS SKILL ANALYZING INFORMATION

How did poll taxes deny poor Americans the opportunity to vote?

Presidential Disability

The illness of President Eisenhower in the 1950s and the assassination of President Kennedy in 1963 were the events behind the Twenty-fifth Amendment. The Constitution did not provide a clear-cut method for a vice president to take over for a disabled president or upon the death of a president. This amendment provides for filling the office of the vice president if a vacancy occurs, and it provides a way for the vice president—or someone else in the line of succession—to take over if the president is unable to perform the duties of that office.

Amendment XXIV

Passed by Congress August 27, 1962. Ratified January 23, 1964.

1. Voting Rights The right of citizens of the United States to vote in any primary or other election for President or Vice President, for electors for President or Vice President, or for Senator or Representative in Congress, shall not be denied or abridged by the United States or any State by reason of failure to pay poll tax or other tax.

2. Enforcement The Congress shall have power to enforce this article by appropriate legislation.

Amendment XXV

Passed by Congress July 6, 1965. Ratified February 10, 1967.

1. Sucession of Vice President In case of the removal of the President from office or of his death or resignation, the Vice President shall become President.

2. Vacancy of Vice President Whenever there is a vacancy in the office of the Vice President, the President shall nominate a Vice President who shall take office upon confirmation by a majority vote of both Houses of Congress.

Answers

Analyzing Information *by requiring people to pay a tax to vote, which many poor people could not afford*

CHAPTER 7

Chapter Review

HOLT History's Impact
▶ **video series**
Review the video to answer the closing question:
What are the advantages and disadvantages of being a member of a third party?

Visual Summary

QUICK FACTS

Use the visual summary below to help you review the main ideas of the chapter.

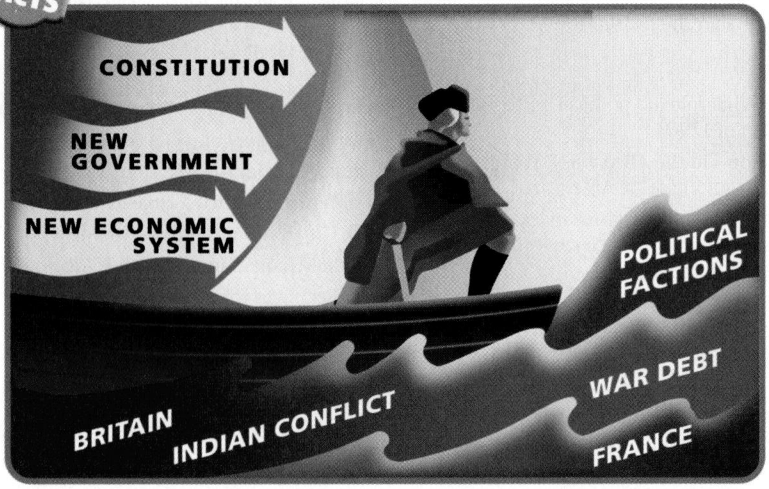

Reviewing Vocabulary, Terms, and People

Complete each sentence by filling in the blank with the correct term or person.

1. The ______________ established the structure of the federal court system and its relationship to state courts.
2. Federalists angered many Republicans when they passed the ______________ to protect the United States from traitors.
3. As president, Washington was able to establish several __________, or decisions that serve as examples for later action.
4. Farmers in western Pennsylvania protested taxes in the ____________.
5. The ______________ was created in order to strengthen the U.S. economy.

Comprehension and Critical Thinking

SECTION 1 *(Pages 234–237)*

6. **a. Recall** What precedents did President Washington and Congress establish for the executive and judicial branches?

   b. Draw Conclusions Why did Americans select George Washington as their first president?

   c. Evaluate Do you think the newly established government met the expectations of its citizens? Why or why not?

SECTION 2 *(Pages 238–242)*

7. **a. Identify** What changes did Alexander Hamilton make to the national economy?

   b. Contrast In what ways did Hamilton and Jefferson disagree on the economy?

   c. Evaluate Which of Hamilton's economic plans do you think was the most important to the new nation? Why?

Answers

History's Impact

Video Series Advantages: concentrate on one main issue and present issues not raised by the two main parties; Disadvantages: not as much support as two main parties

Visual Summary

Review and Inquiry Have volunteers create a cluster diagram of the information in the visual summary for the class to see. Ask students what the visual summary communicates that a cluster diagram cannot. *image of Washington implies his dignity, strength, and influence in leading the country; the sail implies progress; the waves imply danger*

Quick Facts Transparency 25: Launching the Nation Visual Summary

Reviewing Vocabulary, Terms, and People

1. Judiciary Act of 1789
2. Alien and Sedition Acts
3. precedents
4. Whiskey Rebellion
5. Bank of the United States

Comprehension and Critical Thinking

6. **a.** departments and cabinet in the executive branch; Judiciary Act of 1789 to create federal court levels
   b. thought he was honest, patriotic, and a good leader
   c. possible answer—Yes, citizens re-elected Washington so their expectations must have been met.

Review and Assessment Resources

Review and Reinforce

- **SE** Chapter Review
- **CRF:** Chapter Review Activity
- Quick Facts Transparency 25: Launching the Nation Visual Summary
- Spanish Chapter Summaries Audio CD Program
- Online Chapter Summaries in Spanish
- **OSP** Holt PuzzlePro; GameTool for ExamView
- Quiz Game CD-ROM

Assess

- **SE** Standardized Test Practice
- PASS: Chapter 7 Tests, Forms A and B Unit 2 Tests, Forms A and B
- Alternative Assessment Handbook
- **OSP** ExamView Test Generator, Chapter Test
- Differentiated Instruction Modified Worksheets and Tests CD-ROM: Chapter Test
- **HOAP** Holt Online Assessment Program (in the Premier Online Edition)

Reteach/Intervene

- Interactive Reader and Study Guide
- Differentiated Instruction Teacher Management System: Lesson Plans for Differentiated Instruction
- Differentiated Instruction Modified Worksheets and Tests CD-ROM
- Interactive Skills Tutor CD-ROM

go.hrw.com
Online Resources
Chapter Resources:
KEYWORD: SF7 CH7

Answers

7. **a.** had the federal government repay bonds at full value and take on much of the states' war debts, increased tariffs, proposed a national bank and national mint
b. Hamilton—focused on business and manufacturing, wanted higher tariffs and a national bank; Jefferson —focused on farmers, wanted lower tariffs; opposed a national bank
c. possible answers—raised tariffs, protected American manufacturing; National Bank, stabilized the economy

8. **a.** remaining neutral, conflicts with Britain on the high seas and on the frontier, conflict with Spain over access to New Orleans, conflicts with Native Americans in the northwest, Whiskey Rebellion
b. thought neutrality was the safest and most reasonable plan
c. possible answer—successful, nation overcame several challenges and avoided war with Britain

9. **a.** Rivalry between the parties dominated the election and resulted in more than one candidate running for president for the first time.
b. Some Americans supported the acts, while other Americans strongly opposed them, saying they were unconstitutional.
c. possible answers—The two parties would continue to oppose each other and not work together; Congress would be divided; leaders would focus on party goals and not the common good.

Reviewing Themes

10. national debt, including money owed to foreign nations, money owed on Revolutionary War bonds, and states' war debts; Hamilton developed a plan to pay the foreign debt immediately, gradually repay the full value of bonds, raise tariffs to increase revenue, take on much of the states' war debts, and create a national bank and mint.

11. Politics became more divisive and sectionalized, but at the same time offered Americans more of a choice in candidates and views.

SECTION 3 *(Pages 243–249)*

8. **a. Describe** What challenges did the nation face during Washington's presidency?
b. Make Inferences Why did Washington believe that it was important for the United States to remain neutral in foreign conflicts?
c. Evaluate Rate the success of Washington's presidency. Explain the reasons for your rating.

SECTION 4 *(Pages 250–253)*

9. **a. Describe** What role did political parties play in the election of 1796?
b. Analyze How did the Alien and Sedition Acts create division among some Americans?
c. Predict How might the political attacks between the Federalist and Democratic-Republican parties lead to problems in the future?

Reviewing Themes

10. **Economics** What economic problems troubled the nation at the beginning of Washington's presidency? How were they solved?

11. **Politics** How did the creation of political parties change politics in the United States?

Using the Internet

go.hrw.com
KEYWORD: SF7 CH7

12. **Activity: Creating a Poster** In 1798 war with France seemed on the horizon. The Federalist-controlled Congress passed a law that made it a crime to criticize the government in print. In 1971 war raged in Vietnam and the president used a court order to stop publication of information critical of the government's actions in Vietnam. What do these events have in common? Enter the activity keyword. Then research the Alien and Sedition Acts and the Pentagon Papers case during the Vietnam War. Create a poster to display your information and to illustrate the connection between a free press and a democratic society.

Reading Skills

Inferences about History *Use the Reading Skills taught in this chapter to answer the question about the reading selection below.*

> Party differences were based partly on where and how people lived. Businesspeople in the cities tended to support the Federalists. Farmers in more isolated areas generally favored the Democratic-Republicans. *(p. 251)*

13. Which of the following statements can be inferred from the selection?
a. Farmers wanted a large federal government.
b. Urban Americans were usually Republicans.
c. Merchants supported John Adams.
d. People in the cities had different concerns than did the rural population.

Social Studies Skills

Making Group Decisions *Use the Social Studies Skills taught in this chapter to answer the questions below.*

Get together with a group of three or four students and discuss the Alien and Sedition Acts. Answer the following questions individually and as a group.

14. Do you think that limits should have been put on Americans' speeches and printed articles?

15. What other ideas might Congress have considered to resolve the tensions over the issue?

FOCUS ON WRITING

16. **Writing a Nobel Nomination** Now that you've chosen your nominee for the Nobel Prize, you can start to write your nomination. Begin with a sentence that identifies the person you are nominating. Then give at least three reasons for your nomination. Each reason should include a specific achievement or contribution of this person. End your nomination with a sentence that sums up your reasons for nominating this person for the Nobel Prize. Be persuasive. You need to convince the Nobel Prize committee that this person deserves the prize more than anyone else in the world.

Using the Internet

12. Go to the HRW Web site and enter the keyword shown to access a rubric for this activity.

KEYWORD: SF7 CH7

Reading Skills

13. d

Social Studies Skills

14. Answers will vary but students should present their views within the context of the period.

15. possible answers—suggested compromises to address some of each party's concerns; found ways to resolve the issues that were dividing the nation

Focus on Writing

16. **Rubric** Students' Nobel nominations should
- clearly identify the person being nominated.
- provide at least three specific reasons for the nomination.
- be persuasive.
- use correct grammar, punctuation, spelling, and capitalization.

CRF: Focus on Writing: A Nobel Nomination

CHAPTER 7

Standardized Test Practice

IN 8.1.6, 8.1.7, 8.4.5, 8.4.8

DIRECTIONS: Read each question and write the letter of the best response.

1 In the 1790s, most Americans

A lived in the countryside and worked on family farms.

B lived in small towns and worked as laborers or craftspeople.

C lived in cities and worked as laborers, craftspeople, or merchants.

D lived west of the Appalachian Mountains or wanted to move West.

2 In his Farewell Address in 1796, President Washington advised Americans of

A the nation's need for a national bank.

B his fear of a British invasion to end American independence.

C his wish that the office of president be given more power.

D the dangers of ties with foreign nations.

3 President Washington demonstrated the government's power under the new Constitution to enforce federal law in the way he handled the

A Whiskey Rebellion.

B Alien and Sedition Acts.

C XYZ affair.

D Judiciary Act of 1789.

4 The two-party system that exists in American politics today first arose during the election of which president?

A George Washington

B John Adams

C Thomas Jefferson

D James Madison

5 Why did George Washington issue the Neutrality Proclamation?

A He feared that involvement in the war between France and Britain was dangerous.

B He hoped to show the world that the United States was a peaceful nation.

C He wanted to concentrate on internal problems that faced the nation.

D Jefferson persuaded Washington to stay neutral toward France.

6 Which of the following was an issue on which Alexander Hamilton and Thomas Jefferson had differing views?

A protective tariffs

B national bank

C role of the central government

D all of the above

7 Examine the following passage from a description of the Alien Act and then use it to answer the question below.

> "The Alien Law has been bitterly criticized as a direct attack upon our liberties. In fact, it affects only foreigners who are plotting against us, and has nothing to do with American citizens. It gives authority to the President to order out of the country all aliens he judges dangerous to the peace and safety of the United States, or whom he suspects of treason or secret plots against the government."
>
> — Timothy Pickering, adapted from *Life of Timothy Pickering,* Vol. 3

Document-Based Question **What is the author's point of view toward the Alien Law?**

Answers

1. A

Break Down the Question This question requires students to recall factual information. Have students consider where most Americans lived at the time.

2. D

Break Down the Question Tell students who are unsure about the answer to try to think of Washington's various actions in office, such as the Neutrality Proclamation. Students should then look for the option that best aligns with those actions.

3. A

Break Down the Question Tell students first to eliminate any events that did not take place during Washington's administration (B and C). Then have students consider what they know about the remaining two choices.

4. B

Break Down the Question Tell students to consider what they know about Washington's election. *(It was unanimous.)* Students should then eliminate Jefferson and Madison because students have not yet studied their administrations.

5. A

Break Down the Question This question requires students to recall factual information. Refer students to the text titled "The Neutrality Proclamation" in Section 3.

6. D

Break Down the Question This question requires students to recall factual information. Refer students to the text titled "Jefferson Opposes Hamilton" in Section 2.

7. The author believes the law is reasonable and does not infringe on the rights of American citizens.

Break Down the Question Indicate to students that by using the phrase "In fact," the author is setting up a citation of the statement preceding it. That statement being a criticism of the Alien Act, one can infer the author himself approved of it.

Intervention Resources

Reproducible

- Interactive Reader and Study Guide
- Differentiated Instruction Teacher Management System: Lesson Plans for Differentiated Instruction

Technology

- Quick Facts Transparency 25: Launching the Nation Visual Summary
- Differentiated Instruction Modified Worksheets and Tests CD-ROM
- Interactive Skills Tutor CD-ROM

Tips for Test Taking

Jot It Down Quickly Read the following to students: You might have made a special effort to memorize some information for a test. If you are worried you will forget, use this strategy. As soon as the testing period begins, jot the information down on the back of your test or on a piece of scratch paper. You can then stop worrying about forgetting and focus on the test.

Preteach

Bellringer

Motivate Ask volunteers to explain a political process, such as the division of power in Congress. Next, discuss as a class why clear explanations of political processes are important. Lead students to conclude that explanations are important because political participation and awareness is essential in a democracy. Tell students that in this workshop they will write a paper explaining a political process.

Direct Teach

Considering Audience

Adjusting Readability Tell students that when they write something, they should consider whether their audience will understand it. One way to increase comprehension is to adjust readability. Explain that three main factors contribute to a text's readability: difficulty of vocabulary, sentence length, and paragraph length. Select a paragraph from the textbook and have students work as a class to rewrite it at a lower readability level. Help students simplify vocabulary, shorten sentences, and, if appropriate, break up the paragraph. Then have students practice the skill independently on a second paragraph. Remind students to make certain the new version makes sense, is grammatically and factually correct, and includes all the main points in the original.

Explaining a Political Process

Assignment

Write a paper explaining how the federal system balances power among the legislative, executive, and judicial branches of government.

How do you register to vote? What is the difference between a civil court and a federal court? When we want to know about a process or system of our government, we often turn to written explanations.

1. Prewrite

Considering Purpose and Audience

In this assignment, you will be writing for an audience of middle school students. You'll need to

- identify questions they might have about the process or system
- identify factors or details that might confuse them

As you plan your paper, keep your audience in mind.

TIP Using a Graphic Organizer
A chart like the following can help you organize the body of your explanation.

Legislative	Executive	Judicial

Collecting and Organizing the Information

The big idea, or thesis, of your explanation will be that the federal system balances the power among the three branches of government. To collect information about each branch and its powers, you can use a chart like the one on the left. Be sure to note the relationships among the parts. Also, note the important characteristics of each part. When you have completed the chart, you will have the basic organization of your paper.

2. Write

You can use this framework to help you write your first draft.

A Writer's Framework

Introduction
- State the big idea of your paper.
- Explain briefly why this topic is important to the reader.

Body
- Identify the important characteristics of each part of the process or system.
- Explain any relationships between or among the parts.
- Define terms your readers might not know.
- Where appropriate, include graphics to illustrate your explanation.

Conclusion
- Restate your big idea in different words.
- Summarize your main points.

Differentiating Instruction

Struggling Readers — Below Level

1. As students gather information, have them list any terms they do not understand.
2. Tell students to look up each of the terms in a thesaurus to find more familiar synonyms.
3. Then have students replace the difficult terms with the synonyms they found and reread the information. **LS Verbal/Linguistic**

Special Needs Learners — Below Level

1. Have a group of three students role play the three branches of government.
2. Have the student playing the legislative branch write a bill/law on two pieces of paper and give them to the other two students. Each of these students should then explain what his or her branch will do with the bill/law. **LS Interpersonal, Kinesthetic**

3. Evaluate and Revise

Evaluating

Clear, straightforward language is important when explaining how things work. Use the following questions to discover ways to improve your paper.

Evaluation Questions for an Explanation of a Process or System

- Does your big-idea statement accurately reflect your explanation of the process or system?
- Do you discuss each part of the process or system in logical order?
- Do you include details and information to explain each part of the process or system?
- If you used bulleted or numbered lists, are the items parallel—that is, do they have the same grammatical forms or structures?
- Does your conclusion restate your big idea and explain the importance of your topic?

TIP **Using Bulleted Lists** The items in a bulleted list should be in the **same** grammatical forms or structures.

Not the same:

Duties of the judicial branch include
- interpret laws
- overseeing lower courts

The same:

Duties of the judicial branch include
- interpreting laws
- overseeing lower courts

Revising

Sometimes a complex explanation sounds even more complex when you try to explain it in a paragraph. In those cases, a bulleted list of facts or examples may make it easier for your readers to understand the information you are presenting. As you revise your paper, consider whether you have any information you should put in a bulleted list.

4. Proofread and Publish

Proofreading

If you use special formatting in your paper, it is important to make sure that it is consistent. Here are some things to check:

- If you have used boldface or italic type, have you always used it in the same way—for important information, for a heading, for a technical term?
- If you have used a list of items, have you consistently used numbers or bullets?

Publishing

Since you are writing this paper for students, you might find a student in the sixth or seventh grade to read it. Find out whether your explanation seems clear and interesting.

5. Practice and Apply

Use the steps and strategies outlined in this workshop to write your explanation of a process or system.

Reteach

Using Graphics

Making a Flow Chart To help students having trouble understanding the relationships among the branches of government, make a flow chart illustrating the relationships. Use labeled arrows to explain the different relationships among the three branches. Then, for each arrow, have students write a few sentences explaining the relationship represented by that arrow.

Teaching Tip

Avoiding Passive Voice Tell students that they should not use passive voice when writing explanations. Have students exchange papers and circle any passive verbs. Then have students rewrite their papers to eliminate the passive verbs.

Practice & Apply

Rubric

Students' explanations of the federal system should

- begin with a clear statement of the big idea.
- accurately and clearly explain how political power is balanced among the three branches of government.
- indicate an understanding of the system of checks and balances.
- define key terms related to the federal system.
- use a clear and logical organization.
- be written at a middle school level.
- include graphics as visual aids.
- end with a summary and a restatement of the big idea.
- use correct grammar, punctuation, spelling, and capitalization.

Advanced/Gifted and Talented — Above Level

1. Challenge advanced learners to incorporate excerpts from the U.S. Constitution into their papers to support and enhance their explanations of how the federal system balances power among the three branches of government.
2. Alternatively, have advanced students extend their papers by explaining how the separation of powers benefits the American people and promotes the public good. Encourage students to conduct outside research to expand upon the information covered in their papers. **LS Verbal/Linguistic**

Unit Preview

Introduce the Unit

Share the information in the chapter overviews with students.

Chapter 8 Thomas Jefferson's presidency was marked by expansion and conflict. The nation almost doubled in size, and exploration led to new knowledge of the West. Expansionism and impressment caused conflict with Native Americans as well as a war with Britain.

Chapter 9 James Monroe's presidency was marked by the Era of Good Feelings, a time of relative peace, economic growth, and increasing nationalism. The United States asserted itself in foreign affairs and was developing a national identity, but disputes over slavery began to divide the nation.

Chapter 10 The expansion of political rights and Andrew Jackson's election indicated the increased power of the American people. Jackson's presidency was marked by political conflicts, growing sectional differences, economic problems, and the removal of Native Americans from the Southeast.

Chapter 11 Settlers braved difficult trails to reach Oregon and California. In the 1830s, Texas rebelled against Mexican rule and gained independence. In 1846, conflicts with Mexico led to war. Manifest Destiny and land gained from the U.S victory in the war with Mexico resulted in expansion to California, where gold was discovered.

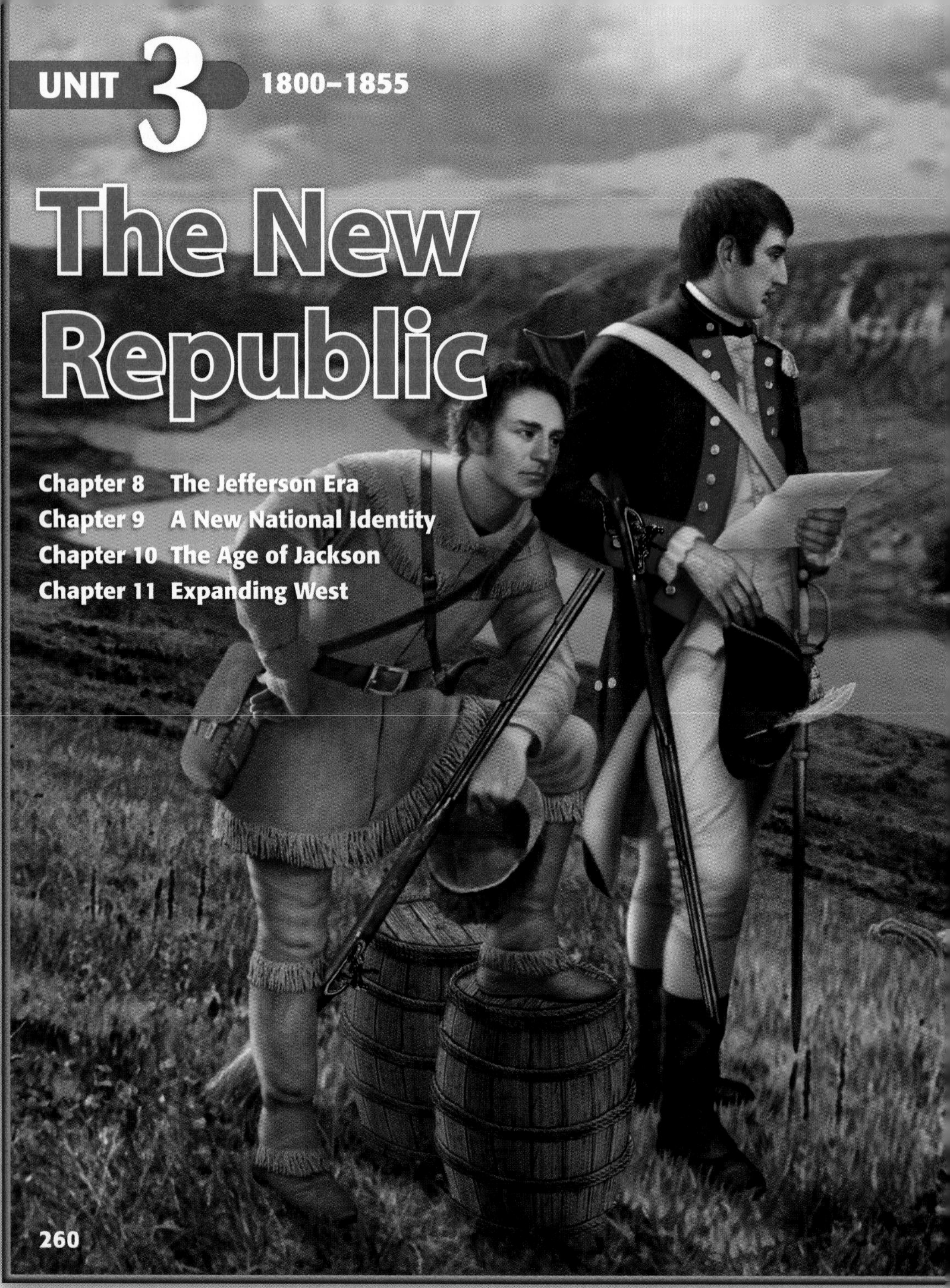

Unit Resources

Planning

- Differentiated Instruction Teacher Management System: Unit Instructional Pacing Guides
- One-Stop Planner CD-ROM with Test Generator: Calendar Planner
- Power Presentations with Video CD-ROM

Differentiating Instruction

- Differentiated Instruction Teacher Management System: Lesson Plans for Differentiated Instruction
- Pre-AP Activities Guide for United States History
- Differentiated Instruction Modified Worksheets and Tests CD-ROM

Enrichment

- **CRF The Age of Jackson:** Economics and History: The Panic of 1837
- **CRF Expanding West:** Interdisciplinary Project: Share the Westward Adventure
- Civic Participation Activities
- Primary Source Library CD-ROM
- Internet Activities: Chapter Enrichment Links

Assessment

- Progress Assessment Support System: Unit 3 Tests, Forms A and B
- OSP ExamView Test Generator: Unit Test
- HOAP Holt Online Assessment Program, in the Premier Online Student Edition
- Alternative Assessment Handbook

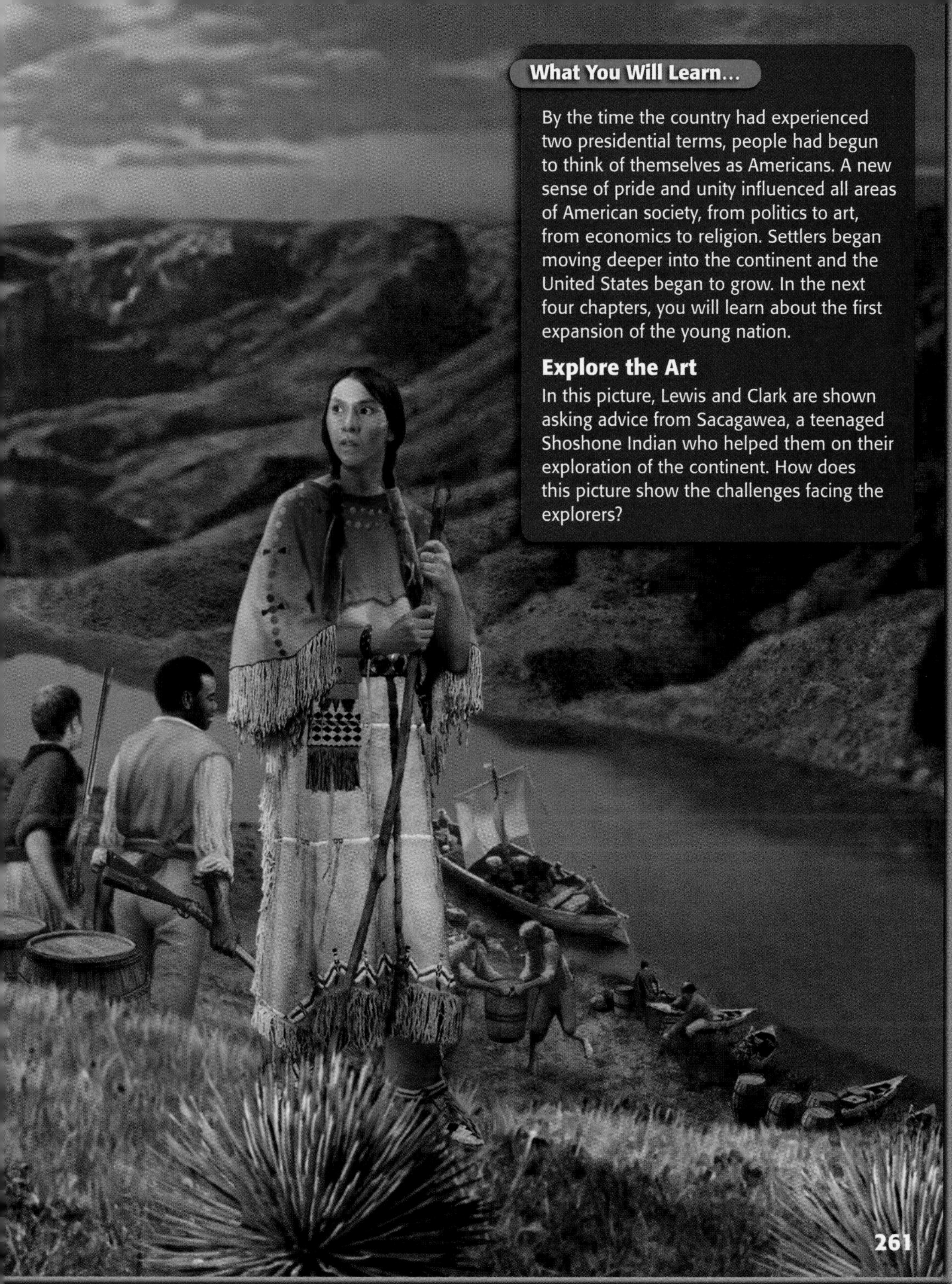

What You Will Learn...

By the time the country had experienced two presidential terms, people had begun to think of themselves as Americans. A new sense of pride and unity influenced all areas of American society, from politics to art, from economics to religion. Settlers began moving deeper into the continent and the United States began to grow. In the next four chapters, you will learn about the first expansion of the young nation.

Explore the Art

In this picture, Lewis and Clark are shown asking advice from Sacagawea, a teenaged Shoshone Indian who helped them on their exploration of the continent. How does this picture show the challenges facing the explorers?

Unit Preview

Connect to the Unit

Materials: butcher paper, drawing supplies

Activity **A Time Collage** Briefly discuss with students what the idea of national identity means. Begin by having students describe what it means to be an American. Explain to students that during the early 1800s people were just beginning to develop a sense of what it meant to be an American.

Tell students that during this unit they are going to create a linear time collage. Hang a large strip of butcher paper on the wall of the classroom. Divide the paper into seven sections and label them from 1800 to 1860. After each chapter, have students create and draw images, such as a map showing settlers' travels to the west, that apply to the topics in that chapter in appropriate places on the time line. At the end of the unit, have students discuss how their images reflect a sense of American identity.

Explore the Art

Have students examine the painting at left. Ask students to predict how the three individuals—Lewis, Clark, and Sacagawea—might have played a role in building the new nation. Then ask students to discuss how the painting expresses the optimism of the young nation.

About the Illustration

This illustration is an artist's conception based on available sources. However, historians are uncertain exactly what this scene looked like.

Democracy and Civic Education

At Level

Responsibility: Participating in the Political Process

Research Required

Background Explain that democracy expanded in the mid-1800s. More Americans gained the right to vote, and the ways in which citizens could participate in the political process expanded.

1. Discuss with students why it is important in a republic to have informed citizens who actively participate in the political process. Then discuss with students the ways in which they can participate in politics.
2. Have students choose an issue facing their school or community. During the study of this unit, have students work as a class to gather information about the issue.
3. Help students decide upon a course of action for addressing the issue. Students might write to a local or state official, organize a community awareness campaign, or form an organization to address the issue. **LS Interpersonal, Verbal/Linguistic**

Answers

Explore the Art *illustrates the rugged landscape over which they will have to travel and the limited transportation available*

Chapter 8 Planning Guide

The Jefferson Era

Chapter Overview	Reproducible Resources	Technology Resources
CHAPTER 8 **pp. 262–293** **Overview: In this chapter, students will study the presidency of Thomas Jefferson, the Louisiana Purchase, the War of 1812, and other challenges the nation faced as it grew.**	**Differentiated Instruction Teacher Management System:*** • Instructional Pacing Guides • Lesson Plans for Differentiated Instruction **Interactive Reader and Study Guide:** Chapter Summary Graphic Organizer* **Chapter Resource File:*** • Focus on Writing Activity: A Letter of Recommendation • Social Studies Skills Activity: Working in Groups to Solve Issues • Chapter Review Activity	**Power Presentations with Video CD-ROM** **Differentiated Instruction Modified Worksheets and Tests CD-ROM** **Primary Source Library CD-ROM for United States History** **Interactive Skills Tutor CD-ROM** **History's Impact: United States History Video Program (VHS/DVD):** The Impact of Expanding Frontiers* **Interactive Map:** Americas Growth to 1820
Section 1: **Jefferson Becomes President** **The Big Idea:** Thomas Jefferson's election began a new era in American government.	**Differentiated Instruction Teacher Management System:** Section 1 Lesson Plan* **Interactive Reader and Study Guide:** Section 8.1 Summary* **Chapter Resource File:*** • Vocabulary Builder Activity, Section 1 • Biography Activities: Aaron Burr; John Marshall • Primary Source: Jefferson's 1801 Inaugural Address	**Daily Bellringer Transparency 8.1*** **Quick Facts Transparency 26:** The Election of 1800* go.hrw.com **Internet Activity:** Jeffersonian Democracy
Section 2: **The Louisiana Purchase** **The Big Idea:** Under President Jefferson's leadership, the United States added the Louisiana Territory.	**Differentiated Instruction Teacher Management System:** Section 2 Lesson Plan* **Interactive Reader and Study Guide:** Section 8.2 Summary* **Chapter Resource File:*** • Vocabulary Builder Activity, Section 2 • Biography Activity: Sacagawea • History and Geography Activity: Pike Explores the Southwest	**Daily Bellringer Transparency 8.2*** **Map Transparency 32:** The Louisiana Purchase and Western Expeditions* go.hrw.com **Internet Activity:** Discovering the West **Interactive Map:** The Louisiana Purchase and Western Expeditions
Section 3: **The Coming of War** **The Big Idea:** Challenges at home and abroad led the United States to declare war on Great Britain.	**Differentiated Instruction Teacher Management System:** Section 3 Lesson Plan* **Interactive Reader and Study Guide:** Section 8.3 Summary* **Chapter Resource File:*** • Vocabulary Builder Activity, Section 3 • Biography Activity: Tecumseh • Literature Activity: *A Warrior's Speech* • Primary Source Activity: A Shawnee Leader Seeks Allies	**Daily Bellringer Transparency 8.3***
Section 4: **The War of 1812** **The Big Idea:** Great Britain and the United States went to battle in the War of 1812.	**Differentiated Instruction Teacher Management System:** Section 4 Lesson Plan* **Interactive Reader and Study Guide:** Section 8.4 Summary* **Chapter Resource File:*** • Vocabulary Builder Activity, Section 4	**Daily Bellringer Transparency 8.4*** **Map Transparency 33:** The War of 1812* **Quick Facts Transparency 27:** Analyzing the War of 1812* go.hrw.com **Internet Activity:** "Star-Spangled Banner"

SE Student Edition | Print Resource | Audio CD
TE Teacher's Edition | Transparency | CD-ROM
go.hrw.com | **LS** Learning Styles | Video
TOS Indiana Teacher One Stop | * also on Indiana Teacher One Stop

Review, Assessment, Intervention

- **Quick Facts Transparency 28:** The Jefferson Era Visual Summary*
- **Spanish Chapter Summaries Audio CD Program**
- **Progress Assessment Support System (PASS):** Chapter Tests A and B*
- **Differentiated Instruction Modified Worksheets and Tests CD-ROM:** Modified Chapter Test
- TOS **Indiana Teacher One Stop:** ExamView Test Generator (English/Spanish)
- HOAP **Holt Online Assessment Program,** in the Holt Premier Online Student Edition

---

- **PASS:** Section Quiz 8.1*
- **Online Quiz:** Section 8.1
- **Alternative Assessment Handbook**

- **PASS:** Section Quiz 8.2*
- **Online Quiz:** Section 8.2
- **Alternative Assessment Handbook**

- **PASS:** Section Quiz 8.3*
- **Online Quiz:** Section 8.3
- **Alternative Assessment Handbook**

- **PASS:** Section Quiz 8.4*
- **Online Quiz:** Section 8.4
- **Alternative Assessment Handbook**

HOLT
History's Impact
United States History Video Program (VHS/DVD)
The Impact of Expanding Frontiers
Suggested use: as a chapter introduction

Power Presentations with Video CD-ROM

Power Presentations with Video are visual presentations of each chapter's main ideas. Presentations can be customized by including Quick Facts charts, images from the text, and video clips.

DIVISION FOR PUBLIC EDUCATION
AMERICAN BAR ASSOCIATION

Developed by the Division for Public Education of the American Bar Association, these materials are part of the **Democracy and Civic Education Resources.**

- **Constitution Study Guide**
- **Supreme Court Case Studies**

Holt Online Learning

go.hrw.com
Teacher Resources
KEYWORD: SF7 TEACHER

go.hrw.com
Student Resources
KEYWORD: SF7 CH8

- Document-Based Questions
- Interactive Multimedia Activities
- Current Events
- Chapter-based Internet Activities
- and more!

Holt Interactive
Online Student Edition

Complete online support for interactivity, assessment, and reporting

- Interactive Maps and Notebook
- Standardized Test Prep
- Homework Practice and Research Activities Online

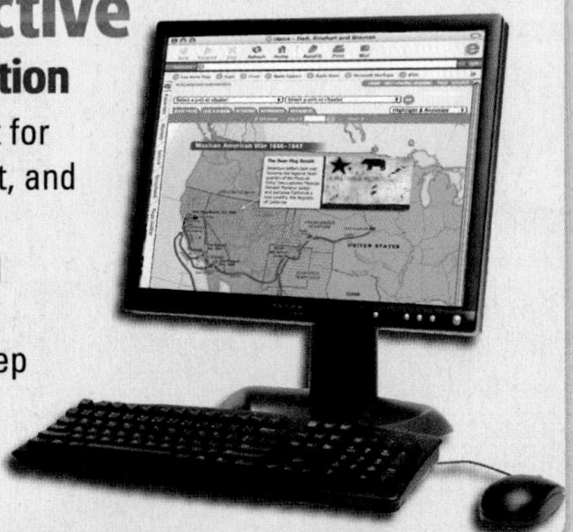

Differentiating Instruction

How do I address the needs of varied learners?

The Target Resource acts as your primary strategy for differentiated instruction.

ENGLISH-LANGUAGE LEARNERS & STRUGGLING READERS

TARGET RESOURCE

English-Language Learner Strategies and Activities

- Build Academic Vocabulary
- Develop Oral and Written Language Structures

Spanish Resources

Spanish Chapter Summaries Audio CD

Spanish Chapter Summaries Online

Teacher's One-Stop Planner:
- ExamView Test Generator, Spanish
- PuzzlePro, Spanish

Additional Resources

Differentiated Instruction Teacher Management System: Lesson Plans for Differentiated Instruction

Chapter Resources:
- Vocabulary Builder Activities
- Social Studies Skills Activity: Working in Groups to Solve Issues

Quick Facts Transparencies:
- The Election of 1800 (TR 26)
- Analyzing the War of 1812 (TR 27)
- The Jefferson Era Visual Summary (TR 28)

Student Edition on Audio CD Program

Interactive Skills Tutor CD-ROM

SPECIAL NEEDS LEARNERS

TARGET RESOURCE

Differentiated Instruction Modified Worksheets and Tests CD-ROM

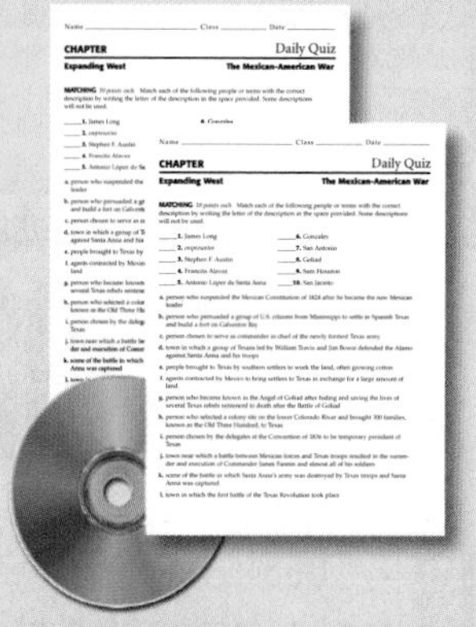

- Vocabulary Flash Cards
- Modified Vocabulary Builder Activities
- Modified Chapter Review Activity
- Modified Chapter Test

Additional Resources

Differentiated Instruction Teacher Management System: Lesson Plans for Differentiated Instruction

Interactive Reader and Study Guide

Social Studies Skills Activity: Working in Groups to Solve Issues

Student Edition on Audio CD Program

Interactive Skills Tutor CD-ROM

ADVANCED/GIFTED-AND-TALENTED STUDENTS

TARGET RESOURCE

Primary Source Library CD-ROM for United States History

The Library contains longer versions of quotations in the text, extra sources, and images. Included are point-of-view articles, journals, diaries, historical fiction, and political documents.

Additional Resources

Pre-AP Activities Guide for United States History: The Jefferson Era

Political Cartoons Activities for United States History: Cartoon 9: The Louisiana Purchase; Cartoon 8: Party Politics in the Jefferson Era

Chapter Resource File:
- Focus on Writing Activity: A Letter of Recommendation
- Literature Activity: *A Warrior's Speech*
- Primary Source Activity: Jefferson's 1801 Inaugural Address

U.S. Supreme Court Case Studies: *Marbury* v. *Madison* (1803)

Differentiated Activities in the Teacher's Edition

- Election of 1800 Symbols, p. 267
- *Marbury* v. *Madison* Graphic Organizer, p. 269
- Louisiana Purchase Time Line, p. 274
- Embargo Act of 1807 Chart, p. 280

Differentiated Activities in the Teacher's Edition

- The Journey West, p. 275

Differentiated Activities in the Teacher's Edition

- Thomas Jefferson Report Card, p. 268
- "The Star-Spangled Banner," p. 286

Teacher One Stop™

How can I manage the lesson plans and support materials for differentiated instruction?

With the Indiana Teacher One Stop, you can easily organize and print lesson plans, planning guides, and instructional materials for all learners.
The Indiana Teacher One Stop includes the following materials to help you differentiate instruction:

- Interactive Teacher's Edition
- Calendar Planner and pacing guides
- Editable lesson plans
- All reproducible ancillaries in Adobe Acrobat (PDF) format
- ExamView Test Generator (Eng & Span)
- Transparency and video previews

Professional Development

HOLT Professional Development

What teacher training resources are available to help me grow professionally?

- **In-service and staff development** as part of your Holt Social Studies product purchase
- **Quick Teacher Tutorial Lesson Presentation CD-ROM**
- Intensive tuition-based **Teacher Development Institute**
- **Convenient Holt Speaker Bureau** – face-to-face workshop options
- **PRAXIS™ Test Prep** interactive Web-based content refreshers*
- **Ask A Professional Development Expert** at http://www.hrw.com/prodev/

* PRAXIS is a trademark of Educational Testing Service (ETS).
This publication is not endorsed or approved by ETS.

• Chapter Preview •

Chapter Big Ideas

Section 1 Thomas Jefferson's election began a new era in American government.

Section 2 Under President Jefferson's leadership, the United States added the Louisiana Territory.

Section 3 Challenges at home and abroad led the United States to declare war on Great Britain.

Section 4 Great Britain and the United States went to battle in the War of 1812.

CHAPTER 8

The Jefferson Era

Indiana Standards

Social Studies Standards

8.1.8 Evaluate the significance of the presidential and congressional election of 1800 and the transfer of political authority and power to the Democratic-Republican party led by the new president, Thomas Jefferson (1801).

8.1.11 Explain the events leading up to and the significance of the Louisiana Purchase (1803) and the expedition of Lewis and Clark (1803–1806).

8.1.12 Explain the main issues, decisions, and consequences of landmark Supreme Court cases.

8.3.9 Analyze human and physical factors that have influenced migration and settlement patterns and relate them to the economic development of the United States.

go.hrw.com
Indiana
KEYWORD: SF10 IN

FOCUS ON WRITING

A Letter of Recommendation Americans love lists—the five best books of the year, the 10 best video games, the three best soccer players. As you read this chapter you will gather some information about Thomas Jefferson. Then you will write a letter to your newspaper telling why Jefferson should be on the newspaper's "Top Ten American Presidents" list.

UNITED STATES

1801 Thomas Jefferson takes office.

1803 U.S. Senate approves the Louisiana Purchase.

1800

WORLD

1802 An army of former slaves led by Toussaint-Louverture defeats a French army in Haiti.

Focus on Writing

The **Chapter Resource File** provides a Focus on Writing worksheet to help students organize and write their letters of recommendation.

CRF: Focus on Writing Activity: A Letter of Recommendation

Key to Differentiating Instruction

Below Level

Basic-level activities designed for all students encountering new material

At Level

Intermediate-level activities designed for average students

Above Level

Challenging activities designed for honors and gifted and talented students

Standard English Mastery

Activities designed to improve standard English usage

Introduce the Chapter

At Level

Focus on the Jefferson Administration

1. Explain to students that the presidential election of 1800 was very close. Have students use what they learned in the last chapter to predict what some of the main issues in the election might have been. (*Students might suggest the extent of the federal government's power, the Bank of the United States, relations with France, and the Alien and Sedition Acts.*)
2. Next, have students preview the chapter by reading the section titles and the blue headings and by looking at the images.
3. Then ask students if they can tell from this quick preview what some of the important events of the Jefferson era were. List students' responses for the class to see.
4. Conclude by having students discuss which of the events they listed would have been most significant to the development of the United States. Tell students to keep the discussion in mind as they study the chapter.
LS Verbal/Linguistic, Visual/Spatial

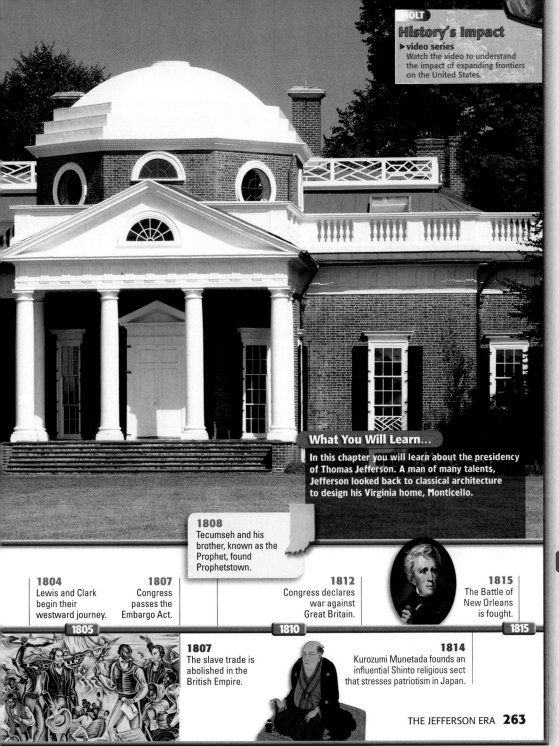

HOLT
History's Impact
▶ video series
Watch the video to understand the impact of expanding frontiers on the United States.

What You Will Learn...

In this chapter you will learn about the presidency of Thomas Jefferson. A man of many talents, Jefferson looked back to classical architecture to design his Virginia home, Monticello.

1804 Lewis and Clark begin their westward journey.

1807 Congress passes the Embargo Act.

1808 Tecumseh and his brother, known as the Prophet, found Prophetstown.

1812 Congress declares war against Great Britain.

1815 The Battle of New Orleans is fought.

1805 — 1810 — 1815

1807 The slave trade is abolished in the British Empire.

1814 Kurozumi Munetada founds an influential Shinto religious sect that stresses patriotism in Japan.

• Chapter Preview •

HOLT
History's Impact
▶ **video series**
See the Video Teacher's Guide for strategies for using the chapter video to teach about the impact of expanding frontiers on the United States.

Explore the Picture

Monticello Thomas Jefferson designed and built Monticello, his plantation home near Charlottesville, Virginia. Inside, the house provided a library for Jefferson's large collection of books as well as space for his many inventions. Outside, the grounds featured gardens where Jefferson experimented with growing new types of plants, flowers, and vegetables.

Analyzing Visuals The portion of Monticello covered by the white dome is called the Dome Room. How might Jefferson have used this room? *possible answers—for weather or astronomical observations; for observing his plantation*

go.hrw.com
Online Resources
Chapter Resources:
KEYWORD: SF7 CH8
Teacher Resources:
KEYWORD: SF7 TEACHER

Explore the Time Line

1. Who led a slave rebellion in Haiti in 1802 that defeated a French army? *Toussaint-Louverture*
2. When did the British Empire abolish the slave trade? *1807*
3. Whom did the United States go to war against during this period, and when did the war begin? *Great Britain; 1812*
4. Which event do you think led to the expansion of the United States? *U.S. Senate's approval of the Louisiana Purchase in 1803.*

Info to Know

Jefferson Thomas Jefferson had a good-humored nature. A brilliant conversationalist, he could talk just as easily about chemistry or horse racing as politics or philosophy. He loved architecture, art, and geography. He not only knew French, Greek, Italian, Latin, and Spanish but also studied some 40 Native American languages. At the same time, Jefferson struggled with a deep sense of loneliness. The death of his wife, Martha Wayles Skelton, and of five of his six children caused him untold grief.

Reading Social Studies

Understanding Themes

Two themes—geography and politics—are the focus of this chapter. Students will learn about the Louisiana Purchase and the expedition of Lewis and Clark. Help students understand the challenges that the geography of the West presented to the exploration of these lands. As students read the chapter, help them see the relationship between geography and politics during this time in American history.

Public Documents in History

Focus on Reading Have students consider the types of public documents that they have already seen or studied. The Declaration of Independence and the U.S. Constitution are two examples that students should know. They may also be familiar with state laws concerning driving or voter information bulletins that are published before an election. Point out to students that these are all examples of public documents. Guide students in a discussion of the language used in public documents. Ask students why public documents might be of use to historians.

Reading Social Studies

by Kylene Beers

Economics | **Geography** | **Politics** | Society and Culture | Science and Technology

Focus on Themes In this chapter you will learn about Thomas Jefferson's presidency. You will read what happened when Jefferson's first run to be president ended in a tie. After that, you will learn about his decision to buy Louisiana from the French, see how he encouraged the exploration of the West, and discover why, during his second term, America found itself at war with Great Britain. You will see how America's expanding **geography** and **politics** were intertwined.

Public Documents in History

Focus on Reading Historians use many types of documents to learn about the past. These documents can often be divided into two types—private and public. Private documents are those written for a person's own use, such as letters, journals, or notebooks. Public documents, on the other hand, are available for everyone to read and examine. They include such things as laws, tax codes, and treaties.

Studying Public Documents Studying public documents from the past can tell us a great deal about the politics and society of the time. However, public documents can often be confusing or difficult to understand. When you read such a document, you may want to use a list of questions like the one below to be sure you understand what you're reading.

You can often figure out the topic of a public document from the title and introduction.

Public documents often use unfamiliar words or use familiar words in unfamiliar ways. For example, the document on the next page uses the word *augmented.* Do you know what the word means in this context? If not, you should look it up.

Many public documents deal with several issues and will therefore have several main ideas.

Question Sheet for Public Documents

1. What is the topic of the document?
2. Do I understand what I'm reading?
3. Is there any vocabulary in the document that I do not understand?
4. What parts of the document should I re-read?
5. What are the main ideas and details of the document?
6. What have I learned from reading this document?

Reading and Skills Resources

Reading Support

- Interactive Reader and Study Guide
- Student Edition on Audio CD Program
- Spanish Chapter Summaries Audio CD Program

Social Studies Skills Support

- Interactive Skills Tutor CD-ROM

Vocabulary Support

- **CRF:** Vocabulary Builder Activities
- **CRF:** Chapter Review Activity
- Differentiated Instruction Modified Worksheets and Tests CD-ROM:
  - Vocabulary Flash Cards
  - Vocabulary Builder Activity
  - Chapter Review Activity

OSP Holt PuzzlePro

You Try It!

The passage below was taken from a Post Office notice from 1815. Read the passage and then answer the questions that follow.

Rates of Postage

Postmasters will take notice, that by an act of Congress, passed on the 23d instant, the several rates of postage are augmented fifty per cent; and that after the first of February next, the Rates of Postage for single Letters will be,

For any distance not exceeding 40 miles, 12 cents

Over 40 miles and not exceeding 90 miles, 15 cents

Over 90 miles and not exceeding 150 miles, 18 1/2 cents

Over 150 miles and not exceeding 300 miles, 25 1/2 cents

Over 300 miles and not exceeding 500 miles, 30 cents

Over 500 miles, 37 1/2 cents

Double letters, or those composed of two pieces of paper, double those rates.

Triple letters, or those composed of three pieces of paper, triple those rates.

Packets, or letters composed of four or more pieces of paper, and weighing one ounce or more, avoirdupois, are to be rated equal to one single letter for each quarter ounce.

After reading the document above, answer the following questions.

1. What is this document about?

2. What was the main idea or ideas of this document? What supporting details were included?

3. Look at the word *packets* in the last paragraph of the document. The word is not used here in the same way we usually use *packets* today. What does the word mean in this case? How can you tell?

4. Are there any other words in this passage with which you are unfamiliar? How might not knowing those words hinder your understanding of the passage?

Key Terms and People

Chapter 8

Section 1
John Adams *(p. 266)*
Thomas Jefferson *(p. 266)*
John Marshall *(p. 270)*
Marbury v. *Madison (p. 270)*
judicial review *(p. 270)*

Section 2
Louisiana Purchase *(p. 274)*
Meriwether Lewis *(p. 275)*
William Clark *(p. 275)*
Lewis and Clark expedition *(p. 275)*
Sacagawea *(p. 276)*
Zebulon Pike *(p. 276)*

Section 3
USS *Constitution (p. 278)*
impressment *(p. 279)*
embargo *(p. 279)*
Embargo Act *(p. 279)*
Non-Intercourse Act *(p. 280)*
Tecumseh *(p. 280)*
Battle of Tippecanoe *(p. 282)*
War Hawks *(p. 282)*
James Madison *(p. 283)*

Section 4
Oliver Hazard Perry *(p. 285)*
Battle of Lake Erie *(p. 285)*
Andrew Jackson *(p. 286)*
Treaty of Fort Jackson *(p. 286)*
Battle of New Orleans *(p. 286)*
Hartford Convention *(p. 287)*
Treaty of Ghent *(p. 287)*

Academic Vocabulary

In this chapter you will learn the following academic words:

functions *(p. 269)*
consequences *(p. 287)*

As you read Chapter 8, look for passages from other public documents. What can these documents teach you about the past?

Reading Social Studies

Key Terms and People

Preteach the key terms and people for this chapter by hosting a vocabulary game for students. Write the key terms and people for students to see. Then organize the class into teams. Read aloud definitions or descriptions and have teams take turns guessing which term identifies the description. If one team guesses incorrectly, allow the next team an opportunity to guess the answer. Assign points for each correct answer. You might want to have students keep a list of correct descriptions for each term. **LS Interpersonal, Verbal/Linguistic**

Focus on Reading

See the **Focus on Reading** questions in this chapter for more practice on this reading social studies skill.

Reading Social Studies Assessment

See the **Chapter Review** at the end of this chapter for student assessment questions related to this reading skill.

Teaching Tip

Students will often be called upon to interpret public documents. Point out to students that they should use the same techniques to analyze a public document as they do with any type of document. Have students practice reading public documents by showing them some examples, such as laws, deeds, and government proclamations. Libraries and the Internet are good places to find public documents. Encourage students to use these documents in their research.

Answers

You Try It! 1. *postage rates;* **2.** *main idea—Congress has raised postage rate; details—postage rates depend on the distance a letter will travel, letters with more than one piece of paper cost more to send, packets over one ounce are charged by the quarter ounce;* **3.** *large envelopes; they hold more than four pieces of paper and weigh more than one ounce.* **4.** *possible answers—augmented, avoirdupois; it might lead to a misinterpretation of the document.*

Preteach

Bellringer

If YOU were there . . . Use the **Daily Bellringer Transparency** to help students answer the question.

Daily Bellringer Transparency 8.1

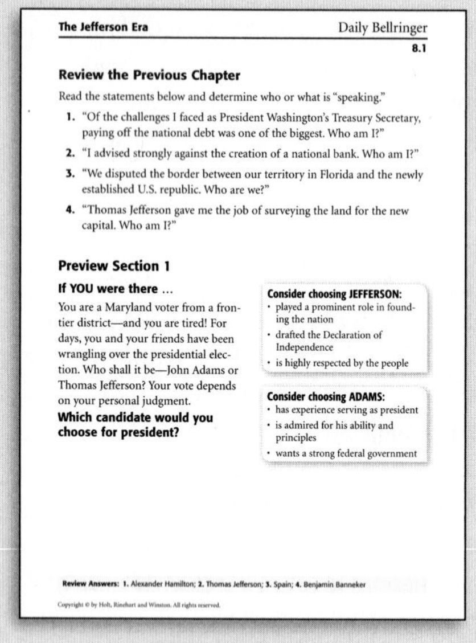

The Jefferson Era — Daily Bellringer **8.1**

Review the Previous Chapter

Read the statements below and determine who or what is "speaking."

1. "Of the challenges I faced as President Washington's Treasury Secretary, paying off the national debt was one of the biggest. Who am I?"
2. "I advised strongly against the creation of a national bank. Who am I?"
3. "We disputed the border between our territory in Florida and the newly established U.S. republic. Who are we?"
4. "Thomas Jefferson gave me the job of surveying the land for the new capital. Who am I?"

Preview Section 1

If YOU were there ...

You are a Maryland voter from a frontier district—and you are tired! For days, you and your friends have been wrangling over the presidential election. Who shall it be—John Adams or Thomas Jefferson? Your vote depends on your personal judgment.

Which candidate would you choose for president?

Consider choosing JEFFERSON:
- played a prominent role in founding the nation
- drafted the Declaration of Independence
- is highly respected by the people

Consider choosing ADAMS:
- has experience serving as president
- is admired for his ability and principles
- wants a strong federal government

Review Answers: 1. Alexander Hamilton; 2. Thomas Jefferson; 3. Spain; 4. Benjamin Banneker

Academic Vocabulary

Review with students the high-use academic term in this section.

functions uses or purposes (p. 269)

CRF: Vocabulary Builder Activity, Section 1

Taking Notes

Have students copy the graphic organizer onto their own paper and then use it to take notes on the section. This activity will prepare students for the Section Assessment, in which they will complete a graphic organizer that builds on the information using a critical-thinking skill.

Section Correlations

IN

8.1.12 Explain the main issues, decisions and consequences of landmark Supreme Court cases. **8.1.30** Formulate historical questions by analyzing primary sources and secondary sources about an issue confronting the United States during the period from 1754–1877. **8.2.1** Identify and explain essential ideas of constitutional government, which are expressed in the founding documents of the United States, including . . . Jefferson's First Inaugural Address . . . **8.2.3** Explain how and why legislative, executive and judicial powers are distributed, shared and limited in the constitutional government of the United States.

SECTION 1

Jefferson Becomes President

What You Will Learn...

Main Ideas

1. The election of 1800 marked the first peaceful transition in power from one political party to another.
2. President Jefferson's beliefs about the federal government were reflected in his policies.
3. *Marbury* v. *Madison* increased the power of the judicial branch of government.

The Big Idea

Thomas Jefferson's election began a new era in American government.

Key Terms and People

John Adams, *p. 266*
Thomas Jefferson, *p. 266*
John Marshall, *p. 270*
Marbury v. *Madison*, *p. 270*
judicial review, *p. 270*

TAKING NOTES As you read, take notes in a graphic organizer like this one. List the details of the election of 1800, Jefferson's beliefs and policies, and how the power of the judicial branch changed during his time in office.

Election of 1800	
Jefferson's Beliefs and Policies	
Power of the Judical Branch	

IN **8.1.7. 8.1.8, 8.1.9, 8.1.12, 8.1.30, 8.2.1, 8.2.3**

If YOU were there...

You are a Maryland voter from a frontier district—and you are tired! For days, you and your friends have been wrangling over the presidential election. Who shall it be—John Adams or Thomas Jefferson? Your vote depends on your personal judgment.

Which candidate would you choose for president?

BUILDING BACKGROUND John Adams had not been a popular president, but many still admired his ability and high principles. Both he and Thomas Jefferson had played major roles in winning independence and shaping the new government. Now, political differences sharply divided the two men and their supporters. In the election of 1800, voters were also divided.

The Election of 1800

In the presidential election of 1800, Federalists **John Adams** and Charles C. Pinckney ran against Democratic-Republicans **Thomas Jefferson** and Aaron Burr. Each party believed that the American republic's survival depended upon the success of their candidates. With so much at stake, the election was hotly contested.

Unlike today, candidates did not travel around giving speeches. Instead, the candidates' supporters made their arguments in letters and newspaper editorials. Adams's supporters claimed that Jefferson was a pro-French radical. Put Jefferson in office, they warned, and the violence and chaos of the French Revolution would surely follow in the United States. Plus, Federalists argued, Jefferson's interest in science and philosophy proved that he wanted to destroy organized religion.

Democratic-Republican newspapers responded that Adams wanted to crown himself king. What else, they asked, could be the purpose of the Alien and Sedition Acts? Republicans also hinted that Adams would use the newly created permanent army to limit Americans' rights.

266 CHAPTER 8

Teach the Big Idea

At Level

Jefferson Becomes President

1. **Teach** To teach the main ideas in the section, use the questions in the Direct Teach boxes.
2. **Apply** Have students list the section's key people, events, and issues. Write the list for students to see. Then ask students to imagine that they are news reporters. Have each student write a headline for each main event and issue. Model the activity by doing the first headline for students. **LS Verbal/Linguistic**
3. **Review** As you review the section, have students share their related headlines with the class.
4. **Practice/Homework** Select one headline and have each student write an article or draw a political cartoon to accompany the headline. **LS Verbal/Linguistic, Visual/Spatial**

Alternative Assessment Handbook, Rubrics 27: Political Cartoons; and 42: Writing to Inform

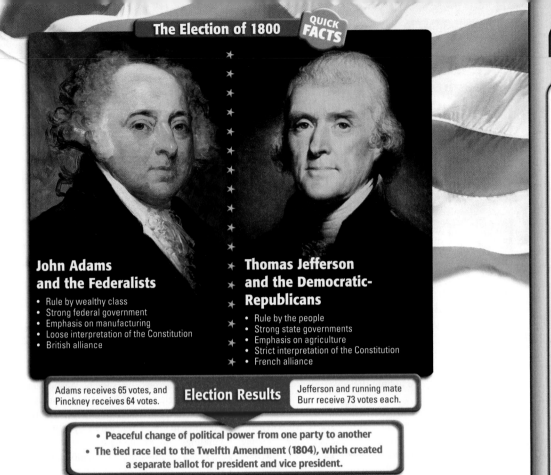

The Election of 1800 QUICK FACTS

John Adams and the Federalists

- Rule by wealthy class
- Strong federal government
- Emphasis on manufacturing
- Loose interpretation of the Constitution
- British alliance

Thomas Jefferson and the Democratic-Republicans

- Rule by the people
- Strong state governments
- Emphasis on agriculture
- Strict interpretation of the Constitution
- French alliance

Election Results

Adams receives 65 votes, and Pinckney receives 64 votes.

Jefferson and running mate Burr receive 73 votes each.

- **Peaceful change of political power from one party to another**
- **The tied race led to the Twelfth Amendment (1804), which created a separate ballot for president and vice president.**

When the election results came in, Jefferson and Burr had won 73 electoral votes each to 65 for Adams and 64 for Pinckney. The Democratic-Republicans had won the election, but the tie between Jefferson and Burr caused a problem. Under the Constitution at that time, the two candidates with the most votes became president and vice president. The decision went to the House of Representatives, as called for in the Constitution.

The House, like the electoral college, also deadlocked. Days went by as vote after vote was called, each ending in ties. Exhausted lawmakers put their heads on their desks and slept between votes. Some napped on the floor.

Jefferson finally won on the thirty-sixth vote. The election marked the first time that one party had replaced another in power in the United States.

The problems with the voting system led Congress to propose the Twelfth Amendment. This amendment created a separate ballot for president and vice president.

READING CHECK **Analyzing Information** What was significant about Jefferson's victory?

Differentiating Instruction

Below Level

English-Language Learners

1. Help students go through the Quick Facts chart above. Define any words or terms with which students are unfamiliar.
2. Then have each student create a large copy of the chart and add symbols or drawings to represent each party characteristic and election result. Model the activity to help students get started. Draw a hammer to show Federalists' emphasis on manufacturing and a sheaf of wheat to show Democratic-Republicans' emphasis on agriculture.
3. As students work, check that each one accurately understands the chart.
4. Have volunteers share some of the symbols they created with the class. **LS Visual/Spatial**

Alternative Assessment Handbook, Rubrics 3: Artwork; and 7: Charts

Quick Facts Transparency 26: The Election of 1800

Direct Teach

Main Idea

❶ The Election of 1800

The election of 1800 marked the first peaceful transition in power from one political party to another.

Identify Who were the candidates in the election, and what party did each represent? *See chart at left.*

Contrast How did the two parties' positions in the election differ? *See chart at left.*

Identify Cause and Effect Why did the election lead to the Twelfth Amendment? *because Jefferson and Burr tied; showed the need to have separate tickets for president and vice president*

Activity **Campaign Slogans** Have each student create a campaign slogan for each political party in the election of 1800.

Alternative Assessment Handbook, Rubric 34: Slogans and Banners

CRF: Biography Activity: Aaron Burr

Quick Facts Transparency 26: The Election of 1800

The Election of 1800 Have students find the Twelfth Amendment to the U.S. Constitution in their textbooks and rewrite it in their own words.

go.hrw.com

Online Resources

KEYWORD: SF7 CH8
ACTIVITY: Jeffersonian Democracy

Answers

Reading Check *The election was the first time that one party had replaced another in power in the United States.*

Analyzing the War of 1812
QUICK FACTS
Causes of the War
• Impressment of American sailors
• Interference with American shipping
• British military aid to Native Americans
Effects of the War
• Increased sense of national pride
• American manufacturing boosted
• Native American resistance weakened

Effects of the War

Before the battle of New Orleans, a group of New England Federalists gathered secretly at Hartford, Connecticut. At the **Hartford Convention**, Federalists agreed to oppose the war and send delegates to meet with Congress. Before the delegates reached Washington, however, news arrived that the war had ended. Some critics now laughed at the Federalists, and the party lost much of its political power.

Slow communications at the time meant that neither the Federalists nor Jackson knew about the **Treaty of Ghent**. The treaty, which had been signed in Belgium on December 24, 1814, ended the War of 1812.

Though each nation returned the territory it had conquered, the fighting did have several consequences. The war produced feelings of patriotism in Americans for having stood up to the mighty British. Some even called it the second war for independence. The war also broke the power of many Native American groups. Finally, a lack of goods caused by the interruption in trade boosted American manufacturing.

ACADEMIC VOCABULARY
consequences the effects of a particular event or events

READING CHECK **Analyzing Information** What were the main effects of the War of 1812?

SUMMARY AND PREVIEW The War of 1812 showed Americans that the nation would survive. In the next chapter you will see how the United States continued to grow.

Section 4 Assessment

go.hrw.com
Online Quiz
KEYWORD: SF7 HP8

Reviewing Ideas, Terms, and People

1. a. **Identify** What losses did American forces face in the early battles of the War of 1812? What victories did they win?
   b. **Make Generalizations** What role did American Indians play in the war?
2. a. **Describe** What attacks did the British lead against American forces?
   b. **Evaluate** What do you think were the two most important battles of the war? Why?
3. a. **Identify** What was the purpose of the **Hartford Convention**?
   b. **Draw Conclusions** How did the United States benefit from the War of 1812?

Critical Thinking

4. **Comparing and Contrasting** Review your notes on the battle dates. Then compare and contrast the details of the major battles during the War of 1812 in a chart like this one.

Battle	Details (Winner, Location, Importance)

FOCUS ON WRITING

5. **Organizing Your Ideas** Reorder the items on your lists from least important to most important.

Section 4 Assessment Answers

1. a. losses—Fort Detroit, failed invasions of Canada; victories—Battles of Lake Erie, Thames River, Horseshoe Bend
   b. often sided with British; Creek War
2. a. attacks at Washington, D.C., Fort McHenry and Baltimore, and New Orleans
   b. possible answer—Fort McHenry, Americans stopped the British invasion; Lake Erie, Americans regained control of Lake Erie
3. a. to organize Federalist opposition to the war
   b. increased national pride; boosted manufacturing
4. Fort Detroit—British, Detroit, Britain gained control of Lake Erie; Lake Erie—U.S., Lake Erie, Americans regained control of Lake Erie; Thames River—U.S., Thames River, broke British and Native American alliance in the Northwest; Washington, D.C.—Britain, Washington, D.C., Britain took the capitol; Fort McHenry—U.S., Baltimore, Americans stopped British invasion; New Orleans—U.S., New Orleans, last major conflict
5. Students should reorder and rank their lists.

Direct Teach

Main Idea

❸ Effects of the War

The effects of the war included prosperity and national pride.

Describe What were the terms of the Treaty of Ghent? *ended the war, returned all conquered territory, left other issues to future negotiations*

Evaluate Do you think the War of 1812 was a success from the American point of view? Explain. *possible answers—yes, for the reasons listed in Quick Facts chart at left; no, because the war did not resolve issues of British impressment*

Quick Facts Transparency 27: Analyzing the War of 1812

Review & Assess

Close

Have students discuss how the course of history might have been different had Great Britain won the War of 1812.

Review

Online Quiz, Section 8.4

Assess

SE Section 4 Assessment

PASS: Section Quiz 8.4

Alternative Assessment Handbook

Reteach/Classroom Intervention

Interactive Reader and Study Guide, Section 8.4

Interactive Skills Tutor CD-ROM

Answers

Reading Check *increased feelings of patriotism among Americans; broke power of many Native American groups; boosted American manufacturing*

History and Geography

Activity **Illustrating the Growing America** Ask students if they have ever heard the United States referred to as a young country. Point out that the United States is about 230 years old, a comparatively young nation by historical standards. Ask students to think of the United States as a developing child. In its first years, it was like an infant—13 states born along the Atlantic coast. Over time, the child began to have growth spurts—growing larger and more self-sufficient with each addition of territory. Have each student create a political cartoon or drawing that illustrates this idea of the expansion of the United States up to 1820. Have volunteers explain their cartoons or drawings to the class. **LS Visual/Spatial**

Info to Know

Population Boom The U.S. population more than doubled between 1790 and 1820, increasing from about 3.9 million to 10.1 million. The number of Americans in the West grew particularly fast during this period. In 1790 about 4 percent of the U.S. population lived west of the Appalachians. By 1820 this figure had grown significantly.

Interactive Map: America's Growth to 1820

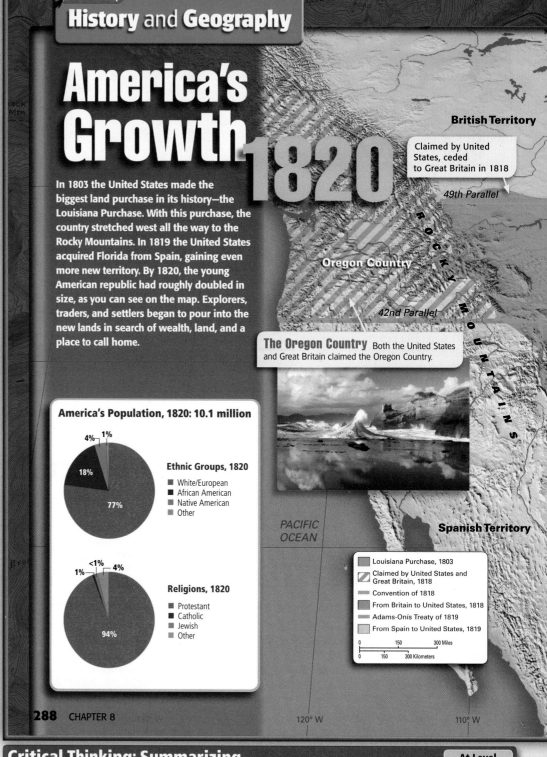

Interactive Map

History and Geography

America's Growth 1820

In 1803 the United States made the biggest land purchase in its history—the Louisiana Purchase. With this purchase, the country stretched west all the way to the Rocky Mountains. In 1819 the United States acquired Florida from Spain, gaining even more new territory. By 1820, the young American republic had roughly doubled in size, as you can see on the map. Explorers, traders, and settlers began to pour into the new lands in search of wealth, land, and a place to call home.

The Oregon Country Both the United States and Great Britain claimed the Oregon Country.

America's Population, 1820: 10.1 million

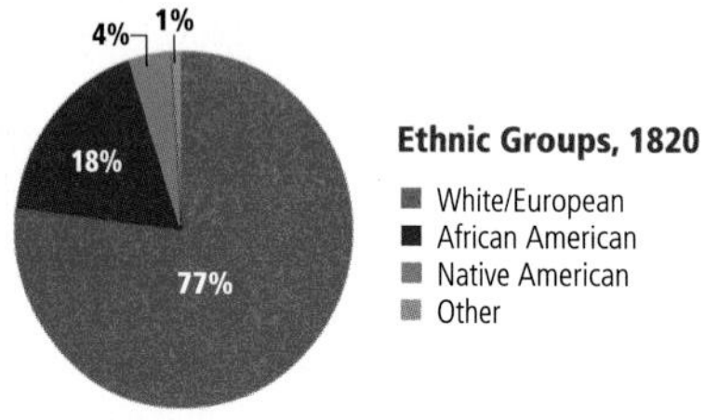

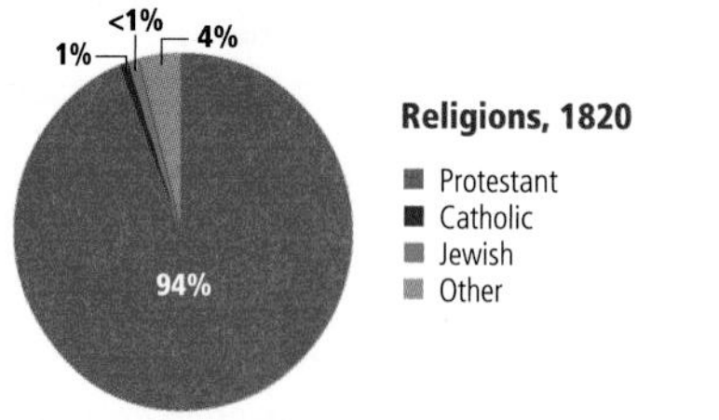

Critical Thinking: Summarizing

At Level

The Nation in 1820

1. Have volunteers read aloud the introduction and captions above. Then have students discuss the information in the feature.
2. Ask students to write a description of the United States in 1820 for someone who has never been there. Students should answer some or all of the following questions in their descriptions: What states and territories make up the United States? What major physical features does the United States include? What bodies of water form natural boundaries for the United States? What other nations have claims to lands near the United States? What is the distance from the northernmost point to the southernmost point of the United States? What is the distance from the easternmost point to the westernmost point?
3. Have volunteers present their descriptions to the class. **LS Verbal/Linguistic**

Alternative Assessment Handbook, Rubric 40: Writing to Describe

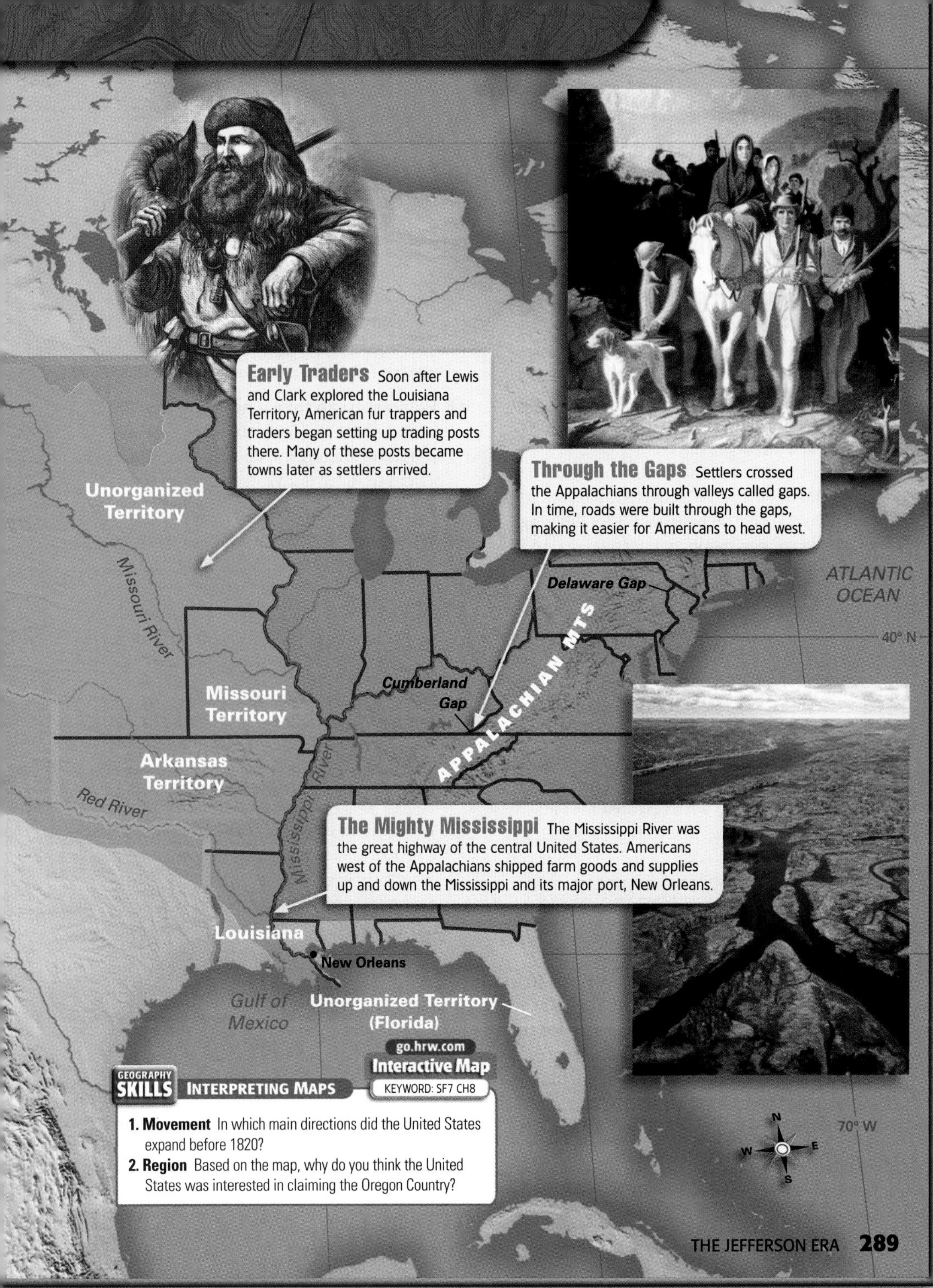
Early Traders Soon after Lewis and Clark explored the Louisiana Territory, American fur trappers and traders began setting up trading posts there. Many of these posts became towns later as settlers arrived.
Through the Gaps Settlers crossed the Appalachians through valleys called gaps. In time, roads were built through the gaps, making it easier for Americans to head west.
The Mighty Mississippi The Mississippi River was the great highway of the central United States. Americans west of the Appalachians shipped farm goods and supplies up and down the Mississippi and its major port, New Orleans.
Unorganized Territory
Missouri River
Missouri Territory
Arkansas Territory
Red River
Mississippi River
Louisiana
New Orleans
Cumberland Gap
APPALACHIAN MTS
Delaware Gap
ATLANTIC OCEAN
40° N
70° W
Gulf of Mexico
Unorganized Territory (Florida)
N
S
E
W
go.hrw.com
Interactive Map
KEYWORD: SF7 CH8

GEOGRAPHY SKILLS INTERPRETING MAPS

1. **Movement** In which main directions did the United States expand before 1820?
2. **Region** Based on the map, why do you think the United States was interested in claiming the Oregon Country?

Critical Thinking: Summarizing

At Level

Research Required

Daniel Boone Biography

Materials: *The Adventures of Colonel Daniel Boone* (optional)

1. Explain to students that Daniel Boone is one of our nation's most legendary frontiersmen and is best known for his exploration of Kentucky.
2. Have each student conduct research on Daniel Boone's life, contributions, and achievements.
3. Have students use their research to write biographical sketches of Boone, with a focus on his contributions to westward expansion and settlement.
4. **Extend** Have students locate and read part or all of *The Adventures of Colonel Daniel Boone.* Students should summarize what they read in a paragraph or short essay.
LS Verbal/Linguistic

Alternative Assessment Handbook, Rubrics 4: Biographies; and 37: Writing Assignments

History and Geography

Connect to Geography

Cumberland Gap The Cumberland Gap provided a route west for many American settlers. This gap is located near the point where the states of Kentucky, Virginia, and Tennessee now meet. Daniel Boone, who led pioneers west, blazed the Wilderness Trail through the Cumberland Gap. The main migration of settlers through the Cumberland Gap occurred between 1775 and 1810. During this period, between 200,000 and 300,000 people passed through the gap heading west. The Cumberland Gap National Historical Park now preserves part of the valley.

Connect to Math

Calculating Growth In 1790 the United States and its territories totaled 888,811 square miles. The Louisiana Purchase of 1803 added an additional 827,192 square miles of land. After the 1819 treaty negotiations with Spain, the United States gained Florida, which added another 58,560 square miles. In addition, the United States received other territories totaling 13,443 square miles.

Activity **Map Math** Have students determine the size of the United States at the end of 1803 and 1819. *(1803—1,716,003 square miles; 1819—1,788,006 square miles)* Then have students determine the percentage of the 1819 total that came from the Louisiana Purchase and from land acquired from Spain *(Louisiana Purchase—46.3 percent; from Spain—4 percent).*

Answers

Interpreting Maps 1. *mainly northwest and west; some south;* **2.** *possible answer—continued the United States westward to the Pacific Ocean and provided additional ports*

Social Studies Skills

Working in Groups to Solve Issues

Activity Discussing the Banning of Cell Phones on Campus
Ask students to imagine that they are members of the student council. The school board wants to ban the use of cell phones on campus. The student council opposes this action. Organize students into groups and assign half the members each position. Have students role play a discussion between the student council and the school board. Group members should try to find one solution to the issue and be prepared to compromise and negotiate if needed. Remind students to respect and listen to differing views and to give each member a chance to participate. Groups should select one member on each side to take notes. Each group should then write down its final solution. After students have completed the activity, have each group share its solution with the class and describe the decision-making process. Students should discuss any problems the group had and how well the group was able to compromise and listen to opposing views. **LS Interpersonal**

Alternative Assessment Handbook, Rubric 14: Group Activity

CRF: Social Studies Skills Activities, Working in Groups to Solve Issues

Social Studies Skills

Analysis | Critical Thinking | **Civic Participation** | Study

Working in Groups to Solve Issues

Define the Skill

You already know that the decision-making process is more difficult in a group than it is if just one person makes the decisions. However, group decision-making becomes an even greater challenge when controversial issues are involved.

Group members must have additional skills for the group to function effectively when conflict exists within it. These include respect for differing views, the arts of persuasion and negotiation, and an ability to compromise. A group may not be able to find solutions to controversial problems unless its members have these skills.

Learn the Skill

Some of the biggest challenges Congress faced in the early 1800s were related to the war between Great Britain and France. Some Americans supported the British, while others favored the French. Both countries hoped for American help. When the United States would not take sides, they each began interfering with U.S. ships on the open seas.

As you read in this chapter, Congress tried to solve this problem by passing the Embargo Act. That solution was controversial, however. The northern states were hard hit by the law's ban on overseas trade. Their representatives in Congress demanded a less extreme action. The result was the Non-Intercourse Act. This law was a compromise between members who wanted to lift the trade ban and those who wanted to continue it. Congress was able to solve this problem because its members were able to work around their differences.

The skills Congress needed to reach its solution are valuable ones for any group that must make decisions involving controversial issues. They include the following attitudes and behaviors.

1. **Willingness to take a position.** If an issue is controversial, it is likely that group members will have differing opinions about it. You have a right to state your views and try to persuade others that you are correct.
2. **Willingness to listen to differing views.** Every other member has the same right you do. You have a duty to listen to their views, even if you do not agree. Disrespect for those whose views differ from yours makes it more difficult for the group to reach a solution.
3. **Willingness to debate.** Debate is a form of "healthy" argument because it defends and attacks ideas instead of the people who hold them. Debating the group's differences of opinion is an important step in reaching a solution.
4. **Willingness to negotiate and compromise.** If debate does not produce agreement, a compromise may be needed. Often it is better to have a solution that members may not like, but can accept, than to have no agreement at all.

Practice the Skill

Check your understanding of the skill by answering the following questions.

1. Why would refusing to listen to other members make group decision-making more difficult?
2. Why is compromise often a better solution than forcing a decision on members who disagree?

Social Studies Skills Activity: Working in Groups to Solve Issues

Posters about How to Work in Groups

At Level

1. Ask students to imagine that they are members of a student government council. The council's discussions often lead to disagreements and arguments that seem to go nowhere and rarely result in decisions.
2. Have each student create a poster to display at council meetings. The poster should provide advice for working in groups to solve issues. Students' posters should address and elaborate upon each of the four points listed under "Learn the Skill." In addition, students' posters should explain the importance of being able to work in groups to solve issues.
3. Have volunteers share their work with the class. Select the best student posters to display in public areas of the school. **LS Verbal/Linguistic, Visual/Spatial**

Alternative Assessment Handbook, Rubric 28: Posters

Answers

Practice the Skill 1. *This refusal might lead to antagonism between members and further prevent any ability to compromise. In addition, one cannot fully present one's position without understanding others' points of view.*
2. *because a compromise gives all members something they want, instead of only certain members getting their way; leads to more group support for the final decision*

CHAPTER 8 # Chapter Review

HOLT History's Impact
▶ **video series**
Review the video to answer the closing question:
How do the background, value system, and character of the United States reflect its spirit of exploration?

Visual Summary

Use the visual summary below to help you review the main ideas of the chapter.

QUICK FACTS

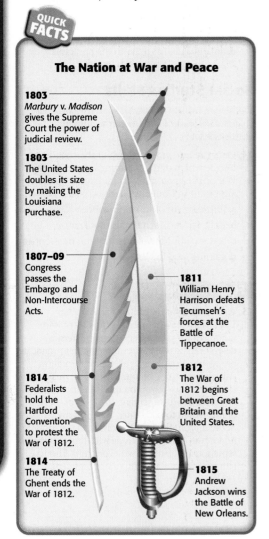

The Nation at War and Peace

1803 *Marbury* v. *Madison* gives the Supreme Court the power of judicial review.

1803 The United States doubles its size by making the Louisiana Purchase.

1807–09 Congress passes the Embargo and Non-Intercourse Acts.

1811 William Henry Harrison defeats Tecumseh's forces at the Battle of Tippecanoe.

1812 The War of 1812 begins between Great Britain and the United States.

1814 Federalists hold the Hartford Convention to protest the War of 1812.

1814 The Treaty of Ghent ends the War of 1812.

1815 Andrew Jackson wins the Battle of New Orleans.

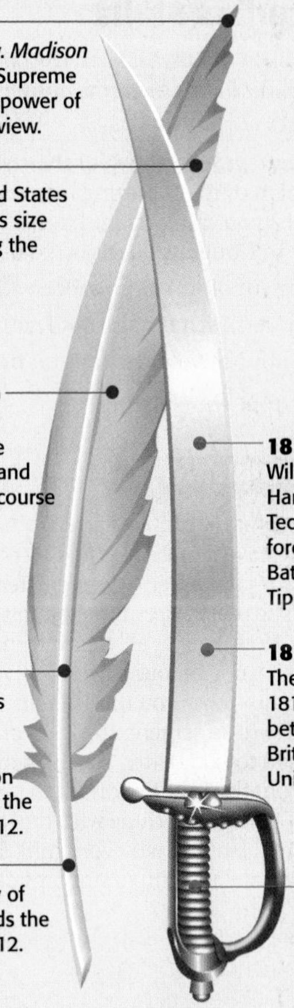

Reviewing Vocabulary, Terms, and People

Complete each sentence by filling in the blank with the correct term or person.

1. The War of 1812 ended soon after the U.S. victory over the British at the ____________.
2. After winning the election of 1800, __________ became the third president of the United States.
3. The power of the Supreme Court to declare acts of Congress unconstitutional is known as ______________.
4. After U.S. neutrality was violated, the United States issued an __________ against trade with foreign nations.
5. In 1803 Congress approved the _________ , which added former French territory in the West to the United States.

Comprehension and Critical Thinking

SECTION 1 *(Pages 266–270)*

6. a. **Recall** What were the key issues in the election of 1800?

   b. **Analyze** In what ways did *Marbury* v. *Madison* affect the power of the judicial branch?

   c. **Evaluate** Which of Jefferson's new policies do you think was most important? Why?

SECTION 2 *(Pages 272–277)*

7. a. **Describe** What was the purpose of the Lewis and Clark expedition?

   b. **Draw Conclusions** What are three ways in which the United States benefited from the Louisiana Purchase?

   c. **Evaluate** Do you think that Napoléon made a wise decision when he sold Louisiana to the United States? Explain your answer.

Answers

History's Impact

Video Series The United States has always sought new territory and knowledge; American citizens value creativity, determination, and entrepreneurialism.

Visual Summary

Review and Inquiry Have students examine the visual summary. Ask students to create flash cards for the events. Students should put the date on one side and the event on the other. Have students find five other significant dates and events to make additional flash cards. Students can quiz each other using the flash cards.

Quick Facts Transparency 28: The Jefferson Era Visual Summary

Reviewing Vocabulary, Terms, and People

1. Battle of Fort McHenry
2. Thomas Jefferson
3. judicial review
4. embargo
5. Louisiana Purchase

Comprehension and Critical Thinking

6. a. size of the national government; relations with France, civil liberties
   b. increased the power of the judicial branch in relation to the other two branches
   c. Students should identify one of Jefferson's new policies and provide reasons to support the choice.

Review and Assessment Resources

Review and Reinforce

- **SE** Chapter Review
- **CRF:** Chapter Review Activity
- Quick Facts Transparency 28: The Jefferson Era Visual Summary
- Spanish Chapter Summaries Audio CD Program
- Online Chapter Summaries in Spanish
- **OSP** Holt PuzzlePro; GameTool for ExamView
- Quiz Game CD-ROM

Assess

- **SE** Standardized Test Practice
- PASS: Chapter 8 Tests, Forms A and B
- Alternative Assessment Handbook
- **OSP** ExamView Test Generator, Chapter Test
- Differentiated Instruction Modified Worksheets and Tests CD-ROM: Chapter Test
- **HOAP** Holt Online Assessment Program (in the Premier Online Edition)

Reteach/Intervene

- Interactive Reader and Study Guide
- Differentiated Instruction Teacher Management System: Lesson Plans for Differentiated Instruction
- Differentiated Instruction Modified Worksheets and Tests CD-ROM
- Interactive Skills Tutor CD-ROM

go.hrw.com
Online Resources
Chapter Resources:
KEYWORD: SF7 CH8

Answers

7. a. to learn more about the people and land of the west; to see if there was a river route to the Pacific Ocean
b. gained a large increase in territory, new resources, land for farming and livestock, and control of New Orleans
c. possible answers—yes, he needed to focus on Europe; no, New Orleans was a major port city, and Louisiana held potential resources.

8. a. War Hawks
b. for—British impressment and violation of neutrality, British influence over frontier Indians, trade restrictions ineffective and hurting the economy; against—should renew friendly ties with Britain, cannot compete against Britain's powerful military
c. possible answer—Britain and France could trade elsewhere.

9. a. led troops to victory against the Creek at Battle of Horseshoe Bend and against the British at Battle of New Orleans
b. Washington, D.C., was the capital, and New Orleans was a major port.
c. might be seen as more of a military power; might convince others that the American experiment in democracy will survive

Reviewing Themes

10. Great Plains, Rocky Mountains, Pacific coastal region
11. The Federalist Party lost much of its political power.

Using the Internet

12. Go to the HRW Web site and enter the keyword shown to access a rubric for this activity.

KEYWORD: SF7 CH8

SECTION 3 *(Pages 278–283)*

8. **a. Identify** What group led the call for war with Great Britain?
b. Contrast What arguments were given in favor of war with Great Britain? What arguments were given against war with Britain?
c. Elaborate In your opinion, why were the Embargo Act and the Non-Intercourse Act unsuccessful?

SECTION 4 *(Pages 284–287)*

9. **a. Identify** What role did Andrew Jackson play in the War of 1812?
b. Make Inferences Why did the British want to capture the cities of Washington and New Orleans?
c. Predict In what ways might the U.S. victory over Great Britain in the war affect the status of the United States in the world?

Reviewing Themes

10. **Geography** Through what geographic regions did the Lewis and Clark expedition travel?
11. **Politics** What impact did the Hartford Convention have on American politics?

Using the Internet

go.hrw.com
KEYWORD: SF7 CH8

12. **Activity: Journal Entry** Prior to Lewis and Clark's expedition, some thought that woolly mammoths, unicorns, and seven-foot-tall beavers lived in the uncharted West. The Corps of Discovery set off to find out the truth about this uncharted land. Its members also wanted to search for a Northwest Passage that would speed commerce and bring wealth to the young nation. Enter the activity keyword. Research the Web sites and take the point of view of one of the explorers. Write a series of journal entries outlining the thoughts, feelings, discoveries, and events surrounding the journey. Include drawings of what you might have seen in the West in your journal entries.

Reading Skills

Public Documents in History *Use the Reading Skills taught in this chapter to answer the question below.*

13. Which of the following is an example of a public document?
a. the Constitution
b. the current president's journal
c. a tax return
d. an ambassador's letter to the president

Social Studies Skills

Working in Groups to Solve Issues *Use the Social Studies Skills taught in this chapter to answer the questions below.*

14. Organize into groups of two or three students. Decide which of the following reasons for the War of 1812 you think might have been most important in Congress's decision to declare war.
a. impressment of American sailors
b. trade barriers with Britain and France
c. battles with Native Americans on the frontier
d. gaining land in Canada

FOCUS ON WRITING

15. **Writing Your Letter of Recommendation** You already have a main idea and an opinion statement for your letter: Thomas Jefferson deserves to be on the list of the top-ten American presidents. Now, look at all your information and pick out three or four points—actions or character traits—that you think are the most important. Write a sentence on each of those points to add to your letter. Put the sentences in order, from the least important to the most important. Finally, conclude with one or two sentences that sum up why you think Thomas Jefferson was such an important president.

Reading Skills

13. a

Social Studies Skills

14. Group members should work together to select an answer and to supply reasons to support it.

Focus on Writing

15. **Rubric** Students' letters of recommendation should
- include at least three supporting points.
- present the points from least to most important.
- end with a summary.
- use correct grammar, punctuation, spelling, and capitalization.

CRF: Focus on Writing Activity: A Letter of Recommendation

CHAPTER 8

Standardized Test Practice

IN 8.1.8, 8.1.11, 8.1.12, 8.3.9

DIRECTIONS: Read each question and write the letter of the best response.

1 The Supreme Court's decision in the 1803 case *Marbury* v. *Madison* is an example of

A checks and balances.

B reserved powers.

C delegated powers.

D dual sovereignty.

2 Most of the fighting in the War of 1812 took place

A in Europe.

B in Canada.

C in the United States.

D at sea.

3 Why did President Jefferson agree to buy Louisiana from France?

A He wanted to learn more about the lands and peoples east of the Mississippi River.

B He believed that the United States would benefit from the purchase.

C He wanted to end the French threat in North America.

D He hoped to increase the president's constitutional powers.

4 The United States went to war with Britain in 1812 for which of the following reasons?

A to strengthen the alliance between Britain and France

B to endanger the rights of U.S. ships on the high seas

C to allow British influence among Indian groups on the frontier

D to stop trade restrictions against American merchants

5 The Lewis and Clark expedition was significant because it

A introduced the United States to valuable raw materials such as coal.

B improved America's knowledge of the West.

C led to U.S. settlement of the Southwest.

D opened trade between the United States and Native Americans in the West.

6 During the War of 1812, trade interruptions resulted in

A the repeal of the Embargo Act.

B a rise in unemployment.

C an increase in the production of cotton in the South.

D a boost to U.S. manufacturing.

7 Read the following passage from Thomas Jefferson's inaugural address and use it to answer the question below.

> "Though the will of the majority is in all cases to prevail, that will, to be rightful, must be reasonable . . . [T]he minority possess their equal rights, which equal laws must protect . . . Let us then, fellow citizens, unite with one heart and one mind . . . We have been called by different names brethren of the same principle. We are all republicans; we are all federalists."
>
> —President Thomas Jefferson, Inaugural Address, 1801

Document-Based Question **What did Jefferson mean in making this statement?**

Answers

1. A
Break Down the Question Suggest that students first eliminate the most unlikely responses and then recall what they know about the remaining options.

2. C
Break Down the Question Suggest that students first eliminate any places where fighting did not occur (in Europe) and then recall what they know about the remaining options.

3. B
Break Down the Question Point out that this question is looking for reasons for the Purchase. Students should first eliminate any options that are not reasons (D) and then rank the remaining options.

4. D
Break Down the Question Point out that this question assumes that all of the reasons except one are incorrect. Students might test each answer by asking if it is really true.

5. B
Break Down the Question Suggest that students first reject patently untrue statements (A), and then concentrate on exactly what the expedition did, not on effects that came later.

6. D
Break Down the Question Point out to students that the words *resulted in* in the question means that they need to identify an effect. Tell students that in such cases they should think about what happened after the events.

7. Jefferson was cautioning against tyranny of the majority—a situation where the rights of a minority are infringed upon by the majority.
Break Down the Question Point out to students the sentence containing the main idea of the passage—"[T]he minority possess their equal rights, which equal laws must protect."

Intervention Resources

Reproducible

- Interactive Reader and Study Guide
- Differentiated Instruction Teacher Management System: Lesson Plans for Differentiated Instruction

Technology

- Quick Facts Transparency 28: The Jefferson Era Visual Summary
- Differentiated Instruction Modified Worksheets and Tests CD-ROM
- Interactive Skills Tutor CD-ROM

Tips for Test Taking

Anticipate the Answers Read the following to students: Before you read the answer choices, answer the question yourself. Then read the choices. If the answer you gave is among the choices listed, it is probably correct!

Chapter 9 Planning Guide

A New National Identity

Chapter Overview	Reproducible Resources	Technology Resources
CHAPTER 9 **pp. 294–317** **Overview:** **In this chapter, students will analyze the development of both American foreign policy and culture.**	**Differentiated Instruction Teacher Management System:** • Instructional Pacing Guides* • Lesson Plans for Differentiated Instruction **Interactive Reader and Study Guide:** Chapter Summary Graphic Organizer* **Chapter Resource File:*** • Focus on Writing Activity: A Character Sketch • Social Studies Skills Activity: Identifying Central Issues • Chapter Review Activity	**Power Presentations with Video CD-ROM** **Differentiated Instruction Modified Worksheets and Tests CD-ROM** **Primary Source Library CD-ROM for United States History** **Interactive Skills Tutor CD-ROM** **Student Edition on Audio CD Program** **History's Impact: United States History Video Program (VHS/DVD):** The Impact of the United States on Its Neighbors*
Section 1: **American Foreign Policy** **The Big Idea:** The United States peacefully settled disputes with foreign powers.	**Differentiated Instruction Teacher Management System:** Section 1 Lesson Plan* **Interactive Reader and Study Guide:** Section 9.1 Summary* **Chapter Resource File:*** • Vocabulary Builder Activity, Section 1 • Primary Source Activity: Alexis de Tocqueville's *Democracy in America* • Primary Source Activity: John Quincy Adams's Fourth of July 1821 Address **Political Cartoons Activities for United States History,** Cartoon 10: The Monroe Doctrine*	**Daily Bellringer Transparency 9.1*** **Map Transparency 34:** U.S. Boundary Changes, 1818–1819* go.hrw.com **Internet Activity:** Revolution in Latin America
Section 2: **Nationalism and Sectionalism** **The Big Idea:** A rising sense of national unity allowed some regional differences to be set aside and national interests to be served.	**Differentiated Instruction Teacher Management System:** Section 2 Lesson Plan* **Interactive Reader and Study Guide:** Section 9.2 Summary* **Chapter Resource File:*** • Vocabulary Builder Activity, Section 2 • History and Geography Activity: The National Road **U.S. Supreme Court Case Studies:** *Gibbons* v. *Ogden* (1824)	**Daily Bellringer Transparency 9.2*** **Map Transparency 35:** U.S. Roads and Canals, 1850* **Map Transparency 36:** The Missouri Compromise, 1820* go.hrw.com **Internet Activity:** Transportation for a Nation
Section 3: **American Culture** **The Big Idea:** As the United States grew, developments in many cultural areas contributed to the creation of a new American identity.	**Differentiated Instruction Teacher Management System:** Section 3 Lesson Plan* **Interactive Reader and Study Guide:** Section 9.3 Summary* **Chapter Resource File:*** • Vocabulary Builder Activity, Section 3 • Biography Activity: Catharine Maria Sedgwick • Biography Activity: Noah Webster • Literature Activity: *The Prairie,* by James Fenimore Cooper • Biography Activity: Thomas Cole	**Daily Bellringer Transparency 9.3*** go.hrw.com **Internet Activity:** American Culture Blooms

CHAPTER 9 PLANNING GUIDE

SE Student Edition | Print Resource | Audio CD
TE Teacher's Edition | Transparency | CD-ROM
go.hrw.com | **LS** Learning Styles | Video
TOS Indiana Teacher One Stop | * also on Indiana Teacher One Stop

Review, Assessment, Intervention

- **Quick Facts Transparency 29:** A New National Identity Visual Summary*
- **Spanish Chapter Summaries Audio CD Program**
- **Progress Assessment Support System (PASS):** Chapter Tests A and B*
- **Differentiated Instruction Modified Worksheets and Tests CD-ROM:** Modified Chapter Test
- TOS **Indiana Teacher One Stop:** ExamView Test Generator (English/Spanish)
- **Alternative Assessment Handbook**
- HOAP **Holt Online Assessment Program,** in the Holt Premier Online Student Edition

- **PASS:** Section Quiz 9.1*
- **Online Quiz:** Section 9.1
- **Alternative Assessment Handbook**

- **PASS:** Section Quiz 9.2*
- **Online Quiz:** Section 9.2
- **Alternative Assessment Handbook**

- **PASS:** Section Quiz 9.3*
- **Online Quiz:** Section 9.3
- **Alternative Assessment Handbook**

HOLT
History's Impact
United States History Video Program (VHS/DVD)

The Impact of the United States on Its Neighbors
Suggested use: as a chapter introduction

Power Presentations with Video CD-ROM

Power Presentations with Video are visual presentations of each chapter's main ideas. Presentations can be customized by including Quick Facts charts, images from the text, and video clips.

DIVISION FOR PUBLIC EDUCATION
AMERICAN BAR ASSOCIATION

Developed by the Division for Public Education of the American Bar Association, these materials are part of the **Democracy and Civic Education Resources.**

- **Constitution Study Guide**
- **Supreme Court Case Studies**

Holt Online Learning

go.hrw.com
Teacher Resources
KEYWORD: SF7 TEACHER

go.hrw.com
Student Resources
KEYWORD: SF7 CH9

- Document-Based Questions
- Interactive Multimedia Activities
- Current Events
- Chapter-based Internet Activities
- and more!

Holt Interactive
Online Student Edition

Complete online support for interactivity, assessment, and reporting
- Interactive Maps and Notebook
- Standardized Test Prep
- Homework Practice and Research Activities Online

CHAPTER 9 PLANNING GUIDE

Differentiating Instruction

How do I address the needs of varied learners?

The Target Resource acts as your primary strategy for differentiated instruction.

ENGLISH-LANGUAGE LEARNERS & STRUGGLING READERS

TARGET RESOURCE

English-Language Learner Strategies and Activities

- Build Academic Vocabulary
- Develop Oral and Written Language Structures

Spanish Resources

Spanish Chapter Summaries Audio CD

Spanish Chapter Summaries Online

Teacher's One-Stop Planner:

- ExamView Test Generator, Spanish
- PuzzlePro, Spanish

Additional Resources

Differentiated Instruction Teacher Management System: Lesson Plans for Differentiated Instruction

Chapter Resources:

- Vocabulary Builder Activities
- Social Studies Skills Activity: Identifying Central Issues

Quick Facts Transparency 29: A New National Identity Visual Summary

Student Edition on Audio CD Program

Interactive Skills Tutor CD-ROM

SPECIAL NEEDS LEARNERS

TARGET RESOURCE

Differentiated Instruction Modified Worksheets and Tests CD-ROM

- Vocabulary Flash Cards
- Modified Vocabulary Builder Activities
- Modified Chapter Review Activity
- Modified Chapter Test

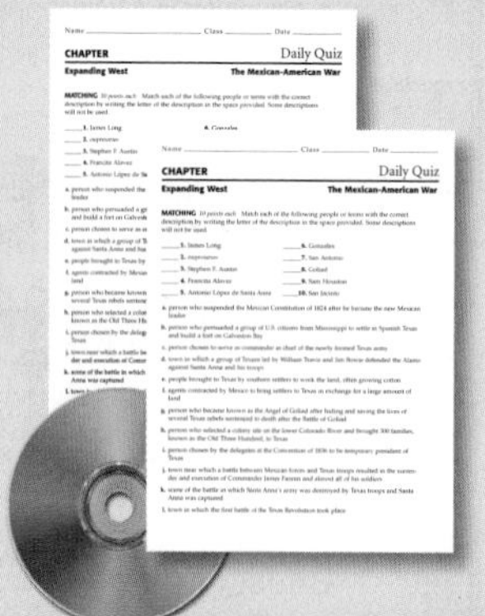

Additional Resources

Differentiated Instruction Teacher Management System: Lesson Plans for Differentiated Instruction

Interactive Reader and Study Guide

Social Studies Skills Activity: Identifying Central Issues

Student Edition on Audio CD Program

Interactive Skills Tutor CD-ROM

ADVANCED/GIFTED-AND-TALENTED STUDENTS

TARGET RESOURCE

Primary Source Library CD-ROM for United States History

The Library contains longer versions of quotations in the text, extra sources, and images. Included are point-of-view articles, journals, diaries, historical fiction, and political documents.

Additional Resources

Differentiated Instruction Teacher Management System: Lesson Plans for Differentiated Instruction

Political Cartoons Activities for United States History: Cartoon 10: The Monroe Doctrine

Chapter Resource File:

- Focus on Writing Activity: A Character Sketch
- Literature Activity: *The Prairie,* by James Fenimore Cooper
- Primary Source Activity: Alexis de Tocqueville's *Democracy in America*
- Primary Source Activity: John Quincy Adams's Fourth of July 1821 Address

Differentiated Activities in the Teacher's Edition

- Nationalism Posters, p. 303
- Group Interpretation, p. 312

Differentiated Activities in the Teacher's Edition

- Early 1800 American Writers Chart, p. 309

Differentiated Activities in the Teacher's Edition

- Erie Canal Song, p. 307
- Landscape Art and Poetry, p. 310
- Writing Historical Fiction, p. 312

Teacher One Stop™

How can I manage the lesson plans and support materials for differentiated instruction?

With the Indiana Teacher One Stop, you can easily organize and print lesson plans, planning guides, and instructional materials for all learners.

The Indiana Teacher One Stop includes the following materials to help you differentiate instruction:

- Interactive Teacher's Edition
- Calendar Planner and pacing guides
- Editable lesson plans
- All reproducible ancillaries in Adobe Acrobat (PDF) format
- ExamView Test Generator (Eng & Span)
- Transparency and video previews

Professional Development

HOLT Professional Development

What teacher training resources are available to help me grow professionally?

- **In-service and staff development** as part of your Holt Social Studies product purchase
- **Quick Teacher Tutorial Lesson Presentation CD-ROM**
- Intensive tuition-based **Teacher Development Institute**
- **Convenient Holt Speaker Bureau –** face-to-face workshop options
- **PRAXIS™ Test Prep** interactive Web-based content refreshers*
- **Ask A Professional Development Expert** at http://www.hrw.com/prodev/

* PRAXIS is a trademark of Educational Testing Service (ETS). This publication is not endorsed or approved by ETS.

Chapter Preview

Chapter Big Ideas

Section 1 The United States peacefully settled disputes with foreign powers.

Section 2 A rising sense of national unity allowed some regional differences to be set aside and national interests to be served.

Section 3 As the United States grew, developments in many cultural areas contributed to the creation of a new American identity.

Focus on Writing

The **Chapter Resource File** provides a Focus on Writing worksheet to help students organize and write their character sketches.

CRF: Focus on Writing Activity: A Character Sketch

Key to Differentiating Instruction

Below Level

Basic-level activities designed for all students encountering new material

At Level

Intermediate-level activities designed for average students

Above Level

Challenging activities designed for honors and gifted and talented students

Standard English Mastery

Activities designed to improve standard English usage

CHAPTER 9

A New National Identity

Indiana Standards

Social Studies Standards

8.1.14 Examine the international problem that led to the Monroe Doctrine (1823) and assess its consequences.

8.1.31 Obtain historical data from a variety of sources to compare and contrast examples of art, music, and literature during the nineteenth century and explain how these reflect American culture during this time period., Examine the development of the banking system in the United States.

8.4.9 Explain and evaluate examples of domstic and international interdependence throughout United States history.

go.hrw.com
Indiana
KEYWORD: SF10 IN

Focus on Writing

A Character Sketch Nations, like people, have characters. For example, a nation might be described as peaceful or aggressive, prosperous or struggling. In this chapter you'll read about the United States as a new nation with a new identity, or character. Then you'll write a paragraph describing that character.

United States

1816 James Monroe is elected president.

1815

World

1815 Napoléon returns to power in France but is defeated at the Battle of Waterloo.

Introduce the Chapter

At Level

The Character of a Country

1. Ask students to think about the character of the early United States as they have learned from their studies. Have students imagine the country as a person. How would they describe this person—young, feisty, aggressive, soft-spoken, opinionated? Write their descriptions for students to see and save the list.
2. Explain to students that they are going to learn how the United States began to be considered a major power in the North American continent. They will learn about the beginnings of U.S. foreign policy and the continued growth of the nation as it began to struggle internally with issues of slavery.
3. Have students copy the list of descriptions. At the chapter's close, discuss with students how the nation has matured. Ask students what additional qualities they would add to their list describing the nation.
LS Verbal/Linguistic

294 CHAPTER 9

HOLT

History's Impact

▶ **video series**
Watch the video to understand the impact of the United States on its neighbors.

What You Will Learn...

A modern mule team pulls a packet-boat full of passengers along the Erie Canal. Once the canal was completed, passengers and cargo could travel more easily between the Great Lakes region and the east coast. In this chapter you will learn how Americans built canals and roads to try to unite the rapidly growing young nation.

1820 The Missouri Compromise allows Maine and Missouri to become states.

1821 Mexico and Peru gain their independence from Spain.

The Granger Collection, New York

1823 The Monroe Doctrine is issued.

1824 John Quincy Adams is elected president.

1824 Liberia is founded by freed American slaves.

1825 Indianapolis becomes the capital of Indiana.

1829 The Ottoman Empire recognizes the independence of Greece.

1820 | 1825 | 1830

295

• Chapter Preview •

HOLT

History's Impact

▶ **video series**
See the Video Teacher's Guide for strategies for using the chapter video to teach about the impact of the United States on its neighbors.

Explore the Picture

The Erie Canal The Erie Canal was one of the largest projects in a boom period for canal building in the early 1800s. Canal transportation was cheaper and easier than overland transportation, but building canals was also very expensive.

Analyzing Visuals What can you tell from the photo about transporting goods by canal? *possible answers—transport larger quantities than by horse; many boats can use the same waterway; a more direct route than by land*

go.hrw.com
Online Resources
Chapter Resources:
KEYWORD: SF7 CH9
Teacher Resources:
KEYWORD: SF7 TEACHER

Explore the Time Line

1. In what year did James Monroe become president of the United States? *1816*
2. What two major U.S. events happened during Monroe's presidency? *the Missouri Compromise, the Monroe Doctrine*
3. When did Mexico and Peru gain their independence from Spain? *1821*
4. Which country was founded by freed American slaves? When? *Liberia; 1824*

Info to Know

Transportation Americans' experiences during the War of 1812 contributed to a push for better transportation following the war. When the British blockaded the U.S. coastline, American merchants and farmers were forced to rely on overland transportation to get goods to market. They found that the roads were terrible. A four-horse team pulling a wagon full of goods took 75 days to make the journey from Worcester, Massachusetts, to Charleston, South Carolina!

Reading Social Studies

Understanding Themes

Introduce the key themes of this chapter—politics and society and culture—by asking students to read the Focus on Themes section on this page. Have students pay attention to the specific issues that affected politics and society and culture in the United States. Preview for students the important political and cultural events mentioned in this chapter, such as the Missouri Compromise and the rise of Hudson River school. Then have each student draw a picture that represents one event and its related theme.

Bias and Historical Events

Focus on Reading Point out to students that letters to the editor and political cartoons commonly display bias. Provide students with a copy of a recent letter to the editor or political cartoon from a local newspaper. Have each student follow the steps listed on this page to analyze the document for bias. You may even want to provide an example of an unbiased letter so that students can compare the two. Discuss with students why recognizing bias might be important in evaluating sources for research.

Reading Social Studies

by Kylene Beers

Economics | Geography | **Politics** | **Society and Culture** | Science and Technology

Focus on Themes This chapter is titled "A New National Identity" because it explains how the United States government established relations with European powers and how Americans developed a strong sense of national pride even as they struggled with important state issues. You will learn about the Monroe Doctrine, the Missouri Compromise, the Cumberland Road project, and the rise of American music, literature, and public schools—events that changed the country's **culture** and **politics**.

Bias and Historical Events

Focus on Reading As you read this chapter, you will find that some people supported the idea of using federal dollars to create new and better roads. Others, however, did not think federal dollars should be used that way. People who can only see one side of an issue or situation may become biased, or prejudiced against the opposite view.

Recognizing Bias To understand the events and people in history, you have to be able to recognize a speaker's or writer's bias. Here are some steps you can take to do that.

"The wickedest road, I do think, the hard-heartedest road, that ever [a] wheel rumbled upon."
Frances Anne (Kemble) Butler, Journal

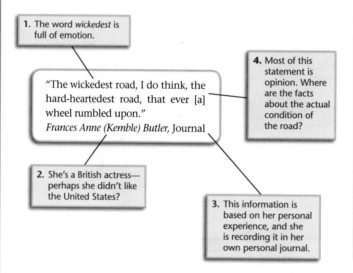

1. The word *wickedest* is full of emotion.

2. She's a British actress—perhaps she didn't like the United States?

3. This information is based on her personal experience, and she is recording it in her own personal journal.

4. Most of this statement is opinion. Where are the facts about the actual condition of the road?

Steps to Recognize Bias

1. **Look at the words and images.** Are they emotionally charged? Do they present only one side or one point of view?
2. **Look at the writer.** What's the writer's background and what does that tell you about the writer's point of view?
3. **Look at the writer's sources.** Where does the writer get his or her information? Does the writer rely on sources who only support one point of view?
4. **Look at the information.** How much is fact and how much is opinion? Remember, facts can be proven. Opinions are personal beliefs—they can easily be biased.

Reading and Skills Resources

Reading Support

- Interactive Reader and Study Guide
- Student Edition on Audio CD Program
- Spanish Chapter Summaries Audio CD Program

Social Studies Skills Support

- Interactive Skills Tutor CD-ROM

Vocabulary Support

- **CRF:** Vocabulary Builder Activities
- **CRF:** Chapter Review Activity
- Differentiated Instruction Modified Worksheets and Tests CD-ROM:
  - Vocabulary Flash Cards
  - Vocabulary Builder Activity
  - Chapter Review Activity

OSP Holt PuzzlePro

You Try It!

The following passage is from the chapter you are getting ready to read. As you read the passage, think about living during the early to mid-1800s when there were no public schools.

Architecture and Education

From Chapter 9, p. 311

Americans also embraced educational progress. Several early American political leaders expressed a belief that democracy would only succeed in a country of educated and enlightened people. But there was no general agreement on who should provide that education.

Eventually, the idea of a state-funded public school gathered support. In 1837 Massachusetts lawmakers created a state board of education. Other states followed this example, and the number of public schools slowly grew.

After you read the passage, answer the following questions.

1. You are the editor of your town's newspaper in the year 1835. You think schools should be financed by the state government rather than the federal government. You decide to write an editorial to express your opinion. Which of the phrases below would reveal your personal bias to your readers? Why? What words in each statement create bias?

- **a.** Overbearing federal government
- **b.** Protecting state interests
- **c.** Powerful federal government
- **d.** Concerned state citizens

2. If you were going to write the editorial described in question 1, how could you avoid biased statements? How do you think this might affect people's reactions to your writing?

Key Terms and People

Chapter 9

Section 1

Rush-Bagot Agreement *(p. 298)*
Convention of 1818 *(p. 298)*
James Monroe *(p. 299)*
Adams-Onís Treaty *(p. 299)*
Simon Bolívar *(p. 300)*
Monroe Doctrine *(p. 300)*

Section 2

nationalism *(p. 302)*
Henry Clay *(p. 302)*
American System *(p. 302)*
Cumberland Road *(p. 303)*
Erie Canal *(p. 303)*
Era of Good Feelings *(p. 303)*
sectionalism *(p. 304)*
Missouri Compromise *(p. 305)*
John Quincy Adams *(p. 305)*

Section 3

Washington Irving *(p. 308)*
James Fenimore Cooper *(p. 309)*
Hudson River school *(p. 310)*
Thomas Cole *(p. 310)*
George Caleb Bingham *(p. 310)*

Academic Vocabulary

Success in school is related to knowing academic vocabulary—the words that are frequently used in school assignments and discussions. In this chapter, you will learn the following academic words:

circumstances *(p. 300)*
incentive *(p. 303)*

As you read Chapter 9, study the primary source documents carefully. Do you see any examples of bias?

Reading Social Studies

Key Terms and People

Preteach the key terms and people from this chapter by having students create a three-panel flip chart FoldNote like the one below. Have students fold a piece of paper in half from top to bottom. Then have them fold the paper into thirds from side to side. Have students cut along each of the vertical fold lines to the fold in the middle of the paper. Have students label the flaps *Section 1*, *2*, and *3*, then have them write the key terms or people for that section on the outside of the flap. On the inside of the chart, have students define or describe each term. Encourage students to review these terms and people regularly.
LS Verbal/Linguistic

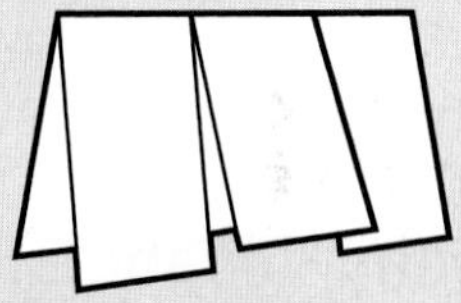

Focus on Reading

See the **Focus on Reading** questions in this chapter for more practice on this reading social studies skill.

Reading Social Studies Assessment

See the **Chapter Review** at the end of this chapter for student assessment questions related to this reading skill.

Teaching Tip

Point out to students that oftentimes bias is used in order to persuade readers to the author's point of view. Remind students to look for words that express emotion, the writer's background, and statements that express opinion rather than fact.

Answers

You Try It! 1. *a; because it slants people's opinion away from federal government; words that create bias—overbearing, protecting, powerful, and concerned;* **2.** *Students should indicate that they would present only factual information drawn from a variety of sources.*

Preteach

Bellringer

If YOU were there . . . Use the **Daily Bellringer Transparency** to help students answer the questions.

Daily Bellringer Transparency 9.1

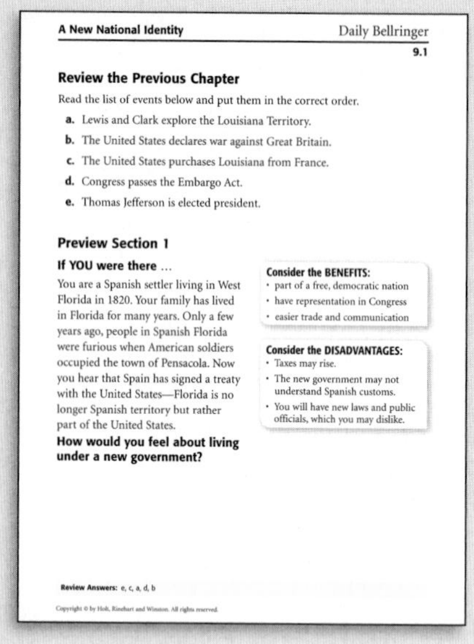

A New National Identity — Daily Bellringer **9.1**

Review the Previous Chapter

Read the list of events below and put them in the correct order.

a. Lewis and Clark explore the Louisiana Territory.
b. The United States declares war against Great Britain.
c. The United States purchases Louisiana from France.
d. Congress passes the Embargo Act.
e. Thomas Jefferson is elected president.

Preview Section 1

If YOU were there ...

You are a Spanish settler living in West Florida in 1820. Your family has lived in Florida for many years. Only a few years ago, people in Spanish Florida were furious when American soldiers occupied the town of Pensacola. Now you hear that Spain has signed a treaty with the United States—Florida is no longer Spanish territory but rather part of the United States.

How would you feel about living under a new government?

Consider the BENEFITS:
- part of a free, democratic nation
- have representation in Congress
- easier trade and communication

Consider the DISADVANTAGES:
- Taxes may rise.
- The new government may not understand Spanish customs.
- You will have new laws and public officials, which you may dislike.

Review Answers: e, c, a, d, b

Academic Vocabulary

Review with students the high-use academic term in this section.

circumstances surrounding situation (p. 300)

CRF: Vocabulary Builder Activity, Section 1

Taking Notes

Have students copy the graphic organizer onto their own paper and then use it to take notes on the section. This activity will prepare students for the Section Assessment, in which they will complete a graphic organizer that builds on the information using a critical-thinking skill.

Section Correlations

IN

8.1.14 Examine the international problem that led to the Monroe Doctrine (1823) and assess its consequences. **8.1.15** Explain the concept of Manifest Destiny and describe its impact on westward expansion of the United States. **8.2.4** Examine functions of the national government in the lives of people. **8.3.7** Using maps identify changes influenced by growth, economic development and human migration in the eighteenth and nineteenth centuries.

SECTION 1

American Foreign Policy

What You Will Learn...

Main Ideas

1. The United States and Great Britain settled their disputes over boundaries and control of waterways.
2. The United States gained Florida in an agreement with Spain.
3. With the Monroe Doctrine, the United States strengthened its relationship with Latin America.

The Big Idea

The United States peacefully settled disputes with foreign powers.

Key Terms and People

Rush-Bagot Agreement, *p. 298*
Convention of 1818, *p. 298*
James Monroe, *p. 299*
Adams-Onís Treaty, *p. 299*
Simon Bolívar, *p. 300*
Monroe Doctrine, *p. 300*

TAKING NOTES Create a chart like the one below. As you read, take notes on the foreign policy issues the United States had to deal with between 1817 and 1823.

Foreign Policy Issues
•
•
•
•
•
•
•

IN 8.1.14, 8.1.15, 8.2.4, 8.3.2, 8.3.7

If YOU were there...

You are a Spanish settler living in West Florida in 1820. Your family has lived in Florida for many years. Only a few years ago, people in Spanish Florida were furious when American soldiers occupied the town of Pensacola. Now you hear that Spain has signed a treaty with the United States—Florida is no longer Spanish territory but rather part of the United States.

How would you feel about living under a new government?

BUILDING BACKGROUND The War of 1812 left the United States stronger and more self-confident. The new nation had remained strong against a great European power. The United States then turned to diplomacy as a way to settle international issues.

Settling Disputes with Great Britain

The Treaty of Ghent had ended the War of 1812, yet there were issues left unresolved. The United States and British Canada both wanted to keep their navies and fishing rights on the Great Lakes. In the spring of 1817, the two sides compromised by establishing the **Rush-Bagot Agreement**, which limited naval power on the Great Lakes for both the United States and British Canada.

Another treaty with Britain gave the United States fishing rights off parts of the Newfoundland and Labrador coasts. This treaty, known as the **Convention of 1818**, also set the border between the United States and Canada at 49°N latitude as far west as the Rocky Mountains. Interest in the valuable fur trade in the Oregon Country was another issue resolved by this treaty. Both countries agreed to occupy the Pacific Northwest together, an agreement that would be tested in the years to come.

READING CHECK **Summarizing** What were the main disputes between the United States and Britain?

Teach the Big Idea

At Level

American Foreign Policy

1. **Teach** To teach the main ideas in the section, use the questions in the Direct Teach boxes.
2. **Apply** Explain to students that foreign policy develops as nations try to solve international problems. Create a chart with two columns and three rows for students to see. Label the columns *Dispute and How Resolved*, and *U.S. Benefits or Costs*. Label the rows *Britain, Spain,* and *Latin America*. Have each student copy and complete the chart. **LS Visual/Spatial**
3. **Review** As you review the section's main ideas, have students help you complete a master copy of the chart.
4. **Practice/Homework** Have students read, listen to, or view the daily news and take notes on current international disputes. Then have students discuss some of the disputes they listed and how countries might try to resolve them. **LS Logical/Mathematical**

Alternative Assessment Handbook, Rubric 7: Charts

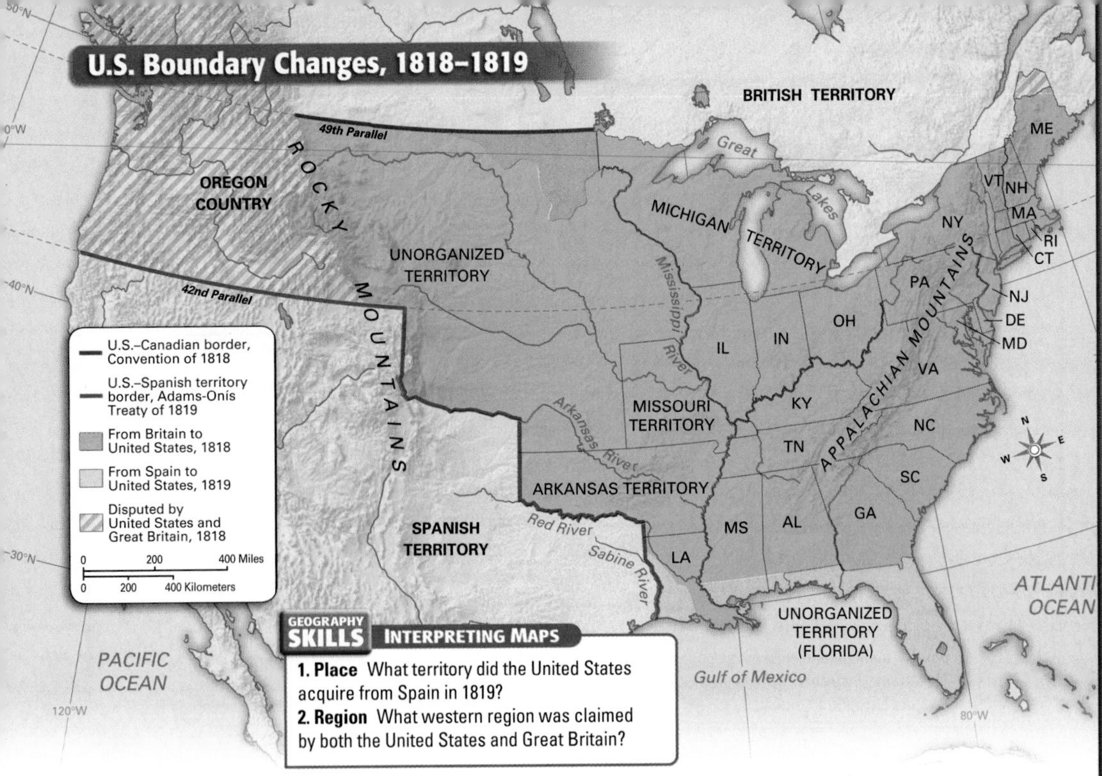

GEOGRAPHY SKILLS INTERPRETING MAPS

1. **Place** What territory did the United States acquire from Spain in 1819?
2. **Region** What western region was claimed by both the United States and Great Britain?

United States Gains Florida

The United States also had a dispute over its southern border with Spanish Florida. In 1818 Secretary of State John Quincy Adams, son of John and Abigail Adams, held talks with Spanish diplomat Luis de Onís about letting Americans settle in Florida. Meanwhile, President **James Monroe**, elected in 1816, had sent U.S. troops to secure the U.S.–Florida border. General Andrew Jackson led these soldiers.

At the same time, conflicts arose between the United States and the Seminole Indians of Florida. The Seminole often helped runaway slaves and sometimes raided U.S. settlements. In April 1818 Jackson's troops invaded Florida to capture Seminole raiders. This act began the First Seminole War. During the war Jackson took over most of Spain's important military posts. Then he overthrew the governor of Florida. He carried out these acts against Spain without receiving direct orders from President Monroe. Jackson's actions upset Spanish leaders. Most Americans, however, supported Jackson.

Jackson's presence in Florida convinced Spanish leaders to negotiate. In 1819 the two countries signed the **Adams-Onís Treaty**, which settled all border disputes between Spain and the United States. Under this treaty, Spain gave East Florida to the United States. In return, the United States gave up its claims to what is now Texas. U.S. leaders also agreed to pay up to $5 million of U.S. citizens' claims against Spain.

THE IMPACT TODAY

Florida was admitted as a U.S. state in 1845 and is now home to about 16 million people.

READING CHECK **Summarizing** How were the disagreements between the United States and Spanish Florida settled?

Direct Teach

Main Idea

❶ Settling Disputes with Great Britain

The United States and Great Britain settled their disputes over boundaries and control of waterways.

Identify Which agreement limited naval power on the Great Lakes? *Rush-Bagot Agreement of 1817*

Elaborate Why do you think the United States and Britain agreed to share the Pacific Northwest? *possible answer—The fur trade was too valuable for either country to give up the region.*

Map Transparency 34: U.S. Boundary Changes, 1818–1819

CRF: Primary Source Activity: Alexis de Tocqueville's *Democracy in America*

Main Idea

❷ United States Gains Florida

The United States gained Florida in an agreement with Spain.

Identify What country controlled Florida in 1818? *Spain*

Elaborate Why do you think most Americans supported Jackson's actions in Florida? *resented Seminole Indians helping runaway slaves and raiding settlements; wanted to expand U.S. territory*

Cross-Discipline Activity: Civics

At Level

Resolving a Problem through Compromise

1. Write the following definition of compromise for students to see:

   compromise an agreement in which each side gives up some demands

2. Work with students to come up with several school-related scenarios that could be solved through compromise.
3. Organize students into small groups and assign each group a scenario. Have each group state the issue or dispute and develop a solution that requires compromise. Each group should create a written description of its problem and solution.
4. Conclude with a group discussion on the importance of compromise as a political tool. Ask students to explain how compromise was used to solve disputes between the United States and other countries. **LS Interpersonal, Logical/Mathematical**

Alternative Assessment Handbook, Rubric 35: Solving Problems

Answers

Interpreting Maps 1. *Florida, part of Louisiana;* **2.** *Oregon Country*

Reading Check (left page) *Naval and fishing rights on the Great Lakes, location of U.S.-Canadian border, Northwest fur trade*

Reading Check *The Adams-Onís Treaty gave Florida to the United States in exchange for claims to Texas.*

Direct Teach

Main Idea

❸ Monroe Doctrine

With the Monroe Doctrine, the United States strengthened its relationship with Latin America.

Identify Cause and Effect What events in Latin America led to the Monroe Doctrine? *struggles for independence in Latin America*

Draw Conclusions Why do you think the United States chose not to issue a joint statement with Great Britain to keep European influence out of Latin America? *did not want British influence in the area, either; United States and Britain were competing for trade in the Americas.*

Make Judgments Do you think the Monroe Doctrine was a good or bad idea for U.S. foreign policy? *possible answers: good—made the United States strong in the eyes of world; bad—may have hurt the nation's relationships with European countries*

- **CRF:** Primary Source Activity: John Quincy Adams's Fourth of July 1821 Address
- Political Cartoons Activities for United States History: Cartoon 10: The Monroe Doctrine

Primary Source

The Monroe Doctrine

The Monroe Doctrine became an important U.S. policy statement. Later presidents invoked the Monroe Doctrine to build the Panama Canal and to confront the Soviet Union over missile bases it had built in Cuba.

Answers

Analyzing Primary Sources

1. *European interference in Latin America would be seen as hostile to the United States.* **2.** *The United States would not interfere with existing colonies.*

Primary Source

HISTORIC DOCUMENT

The Monroe Doctrine

President James Monroe established the foundation for U.S. foreign policy in Latin America in the Monroe Doctrine of 1823.

The occasion has been judged proper for asserting . . . that the American continents . . . are henceforth not to be considered as subjects for future colonization by any European powers . . .

The political system of the allied powers is essentially different . . . from that of America. We . . . declare that we should consider any attempt on their part to extend their system to any portion of this hemisphere as dangerous to our peace and safety . . .

> In this phrase, Monroe warns European nations against trying to influence events in the Western Hemisphere.

With the existing colonies . . . we have not interfered and shall not interfere. But with the governments who have declared their independence and maintained it, and whose independence we have . . . acknowledged, we could not view any interposition[1] for the purpose of oppressing them . . . by any European power in any other light than as the manifestation[2] of an unfriendly disposition[3] toward the United States.

> Monroe notes here the difference between existing colonies and newly independent countries.

[1] **interposition:** interference
[2] **manifestation:** evidence
[3] **disposition:** attitude

ANALYSIS SKILL ANALYZING PRIMARY SOURCES

1. What warning did President Monroe give to European powers in the Monroe Doctrine?
2. How does Monroe say the United States will treat existing European colonies?

Monroe Doctrine

Meanwhile, Spain had other problems. By the early 1820s most of the Spanish colonies in the Americas had declared independence. Revolutionary fighter **Simon Bolívar**, called the Liberator, led many of these struggles for independence. The political circumstances surrounding the revolutions reminded most American leaders of the American Revolution. As a result, they supported these struggles.

> ACADEMIC VOCABULARY
> **circumstances** surrounding situation

After Mexico broke free from Spain in 1821, President Monroe grew worried. He feared that rival European powers might try to take control of newly independent Latin American countries. He was also concerned about Russia's interest in the northwest coast of North America.

Secretary of State Adams shared President Monroe's concerns. In a Fourth of July speech before Congress, Adams said that the United States had always been friendly with European powers, and that the country did not want to be involved in wars with them. He implied that he supported the newly independent countries but said the United States would not fight their battles.

Great Britain was also interested in restraining the influence of other European nations in the Americas. This was because Britain had formed close trading ties with most of the independent Latin American countries. Britain wanted to issue a joint statement with the United States to warn the rest of Europe not to interfere in Latin America.

Instead, Secretary of State Adams and President Monroe decided to put together a document protecting American interests. The **Monroe Doctrine** was an exclusive statement of American policy warning European powers not to interfere with the Americas.

Critical Thinking: Identifying Points of View

At Level

Monroe Doctrine News Articles

1. Have students write a newspaper article about the Monroe Doctrine.
2. Students should choose whether they would like to be a reporter for a U.S. newspaper or a reporter from a country in Europe.
3. Encourage students to come up with a headline and a political cartoon, illustration, or other visual aid to accompany their newspaper articles.
4. Ask volunteers to share their articles with the class. Encourage feedback.
5. Conclude by leading a class discussion on the various points of view that Americans and others had toward the Monroe Doctrine.

LS Verbal/Linguistic, Visual/Spatial

- Alternative Assessment Handbook, Rubric 23: Newspapers

The doctrine was issued by the president on December 2, 1823, during his annual message to Congress.

The Monroe Doctrine had four basic points.

1. The United States would not interfere in the affairs of European nations.
2. The United States would recognize, and not interfere with, European colonies that already existed in North and South America.
3. The Western Hemisphere was to be off-limits to future colonization by any foreign power.
4. The United States would consider any European power's attempt to colonize or interfere with nations in the Western Hemisphere to be a hostile act.

Some Europeans strongly criticized the Monroe Doctrine, but few European countries challenged it. The doctrine has remained important to U.S. foreign policy. The United States has continued to consider Latin America within its sphere of influence—the area a nation claims some control over. At times, it has intervened in Latin American affairs when its own interests, such as national security, were at risk.

READING CHECK **Analyzing** What effect did the revolutions in Latin America have on U.S. foreign policy?

SUMMARY AND PREVIEW In this section you learned that U.S. foreign policy was characterized by both compromise and strong leadership in the years following the War of 1812. In the next section you will learn about the rising sense of national pride that developed as the United States grew and expanded.

Section 1 Assessment

go.hrw.com
Online Quiz
KEYWORD: SF7 HP9

Reviewing Ideas, Terms, and People

1. a. **Identify** What issues were settled between the United States and Great Britain in 1817 and 1818?
   b. **Make Inferences** Why would the United States and Britain agree to occupy the Pacific Northwest together?
   c. **Elaborate** Why were the **Rush-Bagot Agreement** and the **Convention of 1818** compromises?
2. a. **Recall** What problems existed between Spain and the United States?
   b. **Analyze** Why was the **Adams-Onís Treaty** important?
   c. **Evaluate** Do you think that Andrew Jackson was right to act without orders? Explain your answer.
3. a. **Describe** What did the **Monroe Doctrine** state?
   b. **Contrast** How did the Monroe Doctrine differ from Adams's Fourth of July Address?
   c. **Elaborate** What do you think the newly independent Latin American countries thought of the Monroe Doctrine?

Critical Thinking

4. **Identifying Cause and Effect** Review your notes regarding U.S. foreign policy issues. Create a new chart and, for each issue, identify the nations involved, the agreement or doctrine, and the effects.

Nations	Agreement/Doctrine	Issue	Effects

FOCUS ON WRITING

5. **Determining Relationships** One of the main ways you can learn about someone's character is by how he or she treats others. As you read this section, start a list of words and phrases that describe how the United States acted in relationships with other nations. For example, lists might include words and phrases like "willing to compromise" and "firm."

Direct Teach

Info to Know

Politics and the Monroe Doctrine The Monroe Doctrine played a role in the presidential ambitions of John Quincy Adams, who hoped to succeed Monroe in the White House. Adams knew that many Americans were suspicious of him because he desired close relations with Great Britain. When the British wanted to issue a joint declaration opposing European influence in the Americas, Adams persuaded Monroe to issue the doctrine without British involvement. Americans approved of this decision, and Adams avoided being attacked as pro-British in the 1824 election.

go.hrw.com
Online Resources
KEYWORD: SF7 CH9
ACTIVITY: Revolutions in Latin America

Review & Assess

Close

Have students work individually to write a brief summary of the major agreements and doctrines discussed in this section.

Review

Online Quiz, Section 9.1

Assess

SE Section 1 Assessment

PASS: Section Quiz 9.1

Alternative Assessment Handbook

Reteach-Classroom Intervention

Interactive Reader and Study Guide, Section 9.1

Interactive Skills Tutor CD-ROM

Section 1 Assessment Answers

1. **a.** naval and fishing rights, U.S.-Canadian border dispute, Northwest fur trade
   b. interest in the fur trade
   c. In order to gain rights, both nations accepted limits.
2. **a.** disputes over Texas and Spanish Florida
   b. settled border disputes with Spain
   c. possible answers: no—military leaders should not attack other countries without orders; yes—it forced Spain to negotiate.
3. **a.** Europe should stay out of Western Hemisphere; U.S. will not interfere in European affairs.
   b. Adams said the United States would not fight the battles of Latin American countries; Monroe Doctrine threatened force against European intervention.
   c. possible answers: good—kept Europeans from interfering; bad—gave the United States control over Latin America
4. sample answer: U.S. and British Canada; Rush-Bagot Agreement; limited both sides' naval power on Great Lakes
5. possible answers—forceful, strong, rude, protective, possessive, diplomatic

Answers

Reading Check *The United States wanted to keep European influence out of newly independent countries; created Monroe Doctrine, warning European nations not to interfere in the Western Hemisphere.*

Preteach

Bellringer

If YOU were there . . . Use the **Daily Bellringer Transparency** to help students answer the questions.

Daily Bellringer Transparency 9.2

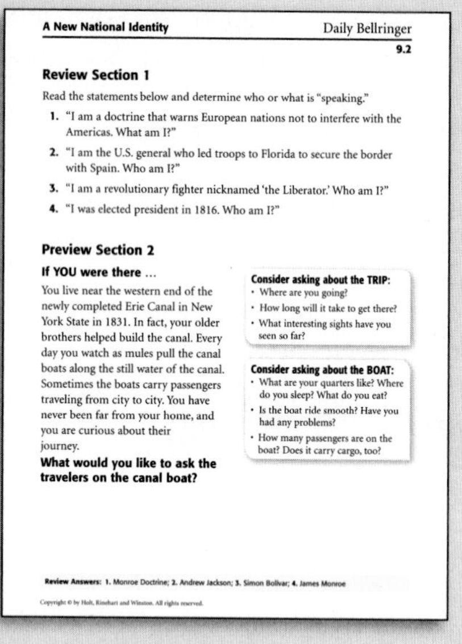

A New National Identity — Daily Bellringer 9.2

Review Section 1

Read the statements below and determine who or what is "speaking."

1. "I am a doctrine that warns European nations not to interfere with the Americas. What am I?"
2. "I am the U.S. general who led troops to Florida to secure the border with Spain. Who am I?"
3. "I am a revolutionary fighter nicknamed 'the Liberator.' Who am I?"
4. "I was elected president in 1816. Who am I?"

Preview Section 2

If YOU were there ...

You live near the western end of the newly completed Erie Canal in New York State in 1831. In fact, your older brothers helped build the canal. Every day you watch as mules pull the canal boats along the still water of the canal. Sometimes the boats carry passengers traveling from city to city. You have never been far from your home, and you are curious about their journey.

What would you like to ask the travelers on the canal boat?

Consider asking about the TRIP:
- Where are you going?
- How long will it take to get there?
- What interesting sights have you seen so far?

Consider asking about the BOAT:
- What are your quarters like? Where do you sleep? What do you eat?
- Is the boat ride smooth? Have you had any problems?
- How many passengers are on the boat? Does it carry cargo, too?

Review Answers: 1. Monroe Doctrine; 2. Andrew Jackson; 3. Simon Bolivar; 4. James Monroe

Academic Vocabulary

Review with students the high-use academic term in this section.

incentive something that leads people to follow a certain course of action (p. 303)

CRF: Vocabulary Builder Activity, Section 2

Taking Notes

Have students copy the graphic organizer onto their own paper and then use it to take notes on the section. This activity will prepare students for the Section Assessment, in which they will complete a graphic organizer that builds on the information using a critical-thinking skill.

Section Correlations

IN

8.1.10 Compare differences in ways of life in the northern and southern states, including the growth of towns and cities in the North and the growing dependence on slavery in the South. **8.1.12** Explain the main issues, decisions and consequences of landmark Supreme Court cases. **8.4.9** Explain and evaluate examples of domestic and international interdependence throughout United States history.

SECTION 2

Nationalism and Sectionalism

What You Will Learn...

Main Ideas

1. Growing nationalism led to improvements in the nation's transportation systems.
2. The Missouri Compromise settled an important regional conflict.
3. The outcome of the election of 1824 led to controversy.

The Big Idea

A rising sense of national unity allowed some regional differences to be set aside and national interests to be served.

Key Terms and People

nationalism, *p. 302*
Henry Clay, *p. 302*
American System, *p. 302*
Cumberland Road, *p. 303*
Erie Canal, *p. 303*
Era of Good Feelings, *p. 303*
sectionalism, *p. 304*
Missouri Compromise, *p. 305*
John Quincy Adams, *p. 305*

TAKING NOTES As you read, take notes on how each of the following contributed to national unity.

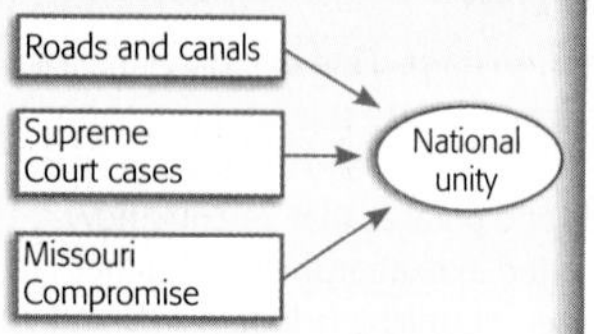

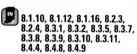

IN **8.1.10, 8.1.12, 8.1.16, 8.2.3, 8.2.4, 8.3.1, 8.3.2, 8.3.5, 8.3.7, 8.3.8, 8.3.9, 8.3.10, 8.3.11, 8.4.4, 8.4.8, 8.4.9**

If YOU were there...

You live near the western end of the newly completed Erie Canal in New York State in 1831. In fact, your older brothers helped build the canal. Every day you watch as mules pull the canal boats along the still water of the canal. Sometimes the boats carry passengers traveling from city to city. You have never been far from your home, and you are curious about their journey.

What would you like to ask the travelers on the canal boat?

BUILDING BACKGROUND Peace, prosperity, and a growing country gave Americans a sense of national unity. In practical terms, building roads and canals also helped unify the nation. They made travel easier, linking people from different regions of the country. Nevertheless, some regional conflicts continued.

Growing Nationalism

Pleased by successful negotiations with foreign powers, Americans enjoyed a rising sense of nationalism. **Nationalism** is feelings of pride and loyalty to a nation. This new national unity found a strong supporter in U.S. representative **Henry Clay** from Kentucky.

Clay believed that a strong national economy would promote national feeling and reduce regional conflicts. He developed a plan eventually known as the **American System** —a series of measures intended to make the United States economically self-sufficient. To build the economy, he pushed for a national bank that would provide a single currency, making interstate trade easier. Clay wanted the money from a protective tariff to be used to improve roads and canals. These internal improvements would unite the country.

Some members of Congress believed that the Constitution did not permit the federal government to spend money on internal improvements. Clay argued that the possible gains for the country justified federal action.

Teach the Big Idea

At Level

Nationalism and Sectionalism

1. **Teach** To teach the main ideas in the section, use the questions in the Direct Teach boxes.
2. **Apply** Organize students into three groups. Assign each group a main idea from the section. Have each group create a 10-question quiz on its topic as well as a separate answer key. Have groups exchange quizzes, complete the ones they receive, and then return the completed quizzes to their authors for grading. **LS Interpersonal, Verbal/Linguistic**
3. **Review** As you review the section, have the groups share questions and answers from their quizzes.
4. **Practice/Homework** Have each student select one quiz question to explore in a paragraph. Students should address the questions who, what, where, when, why, and how, as applicable, in their paragraphs. **LS Verbal/Linguistic**

Alternative Assessment Handbook, Rubrics 1: Acquiring Information; and 37: Writing Assignments

Roads and Canals

In the early 1800s most roads in the United States were made of dirt, making travel difficult. British actress Frances Kemble described one New York road she had struggled along during a visit in the 1830s.

> "The wickedest road, I do think, the cruellest, hard-heartedest road, that ever [a] wheel rumbled upon."
>
> —Frances Anne (Kemble) Butler, *Journal*

To improve the nation's roads, Congress agreed with Clay and invested in road building. The **Cumberland Road** was the first road built by the federal government. It ran from Cumberland, Maryland, to Wheeling, a town on the Ohio River in present-day West Virginia. Construction began in 1815. Workers had to cut a 66-foot-wide band, sometimes through forest, to make way for the road. Then they had to use shovels and pickaxes to dig a 12- to 18-inch roadbed, which they filled with crushed stone. All of the work had to be done without the benefit of today's bulldozers and steamrollers.

By 1818 the road reached Wheeling. By 1833 the National Road, as the expansion was called, stretched to Columbus, Ohio. By 1850 it reached all the way to Illinois.

Meanwhile, Americans tried to make water transportation easier by building canals. One of the largest projects was the **Erie Canal**, which ran from Albany to Buffalo, New York.

Construction of the canal began in 1817 and was completed in 1825. Using shovels, British, German, and Irish immigrants dug the entire canal by hand. The canal cost millions of dollars, but it proved to be worth the expense. The Erie Canal allowed goods and people to move between towns on Lake Erie and New York City and the east coast. Its success served as an **incentive** for a canal-building boom across the country.

Era of Good Feelings

From 1815 to 1825 the United States enjoyed the **Era of Good Feelings**, a time of peace, pride, and progress. The phrase was coined

FOCUS ON INDIANA

The path of the Cumberland Road crossed Indiana by 1839, but the road existed in various stages of completion in the state. The Wabash and Erie Canal ran through Terre Haute, linking Indiana to markets in the east.

ACADEMIC VOCABULARY

incentive something that leads people to follow a certain course of action

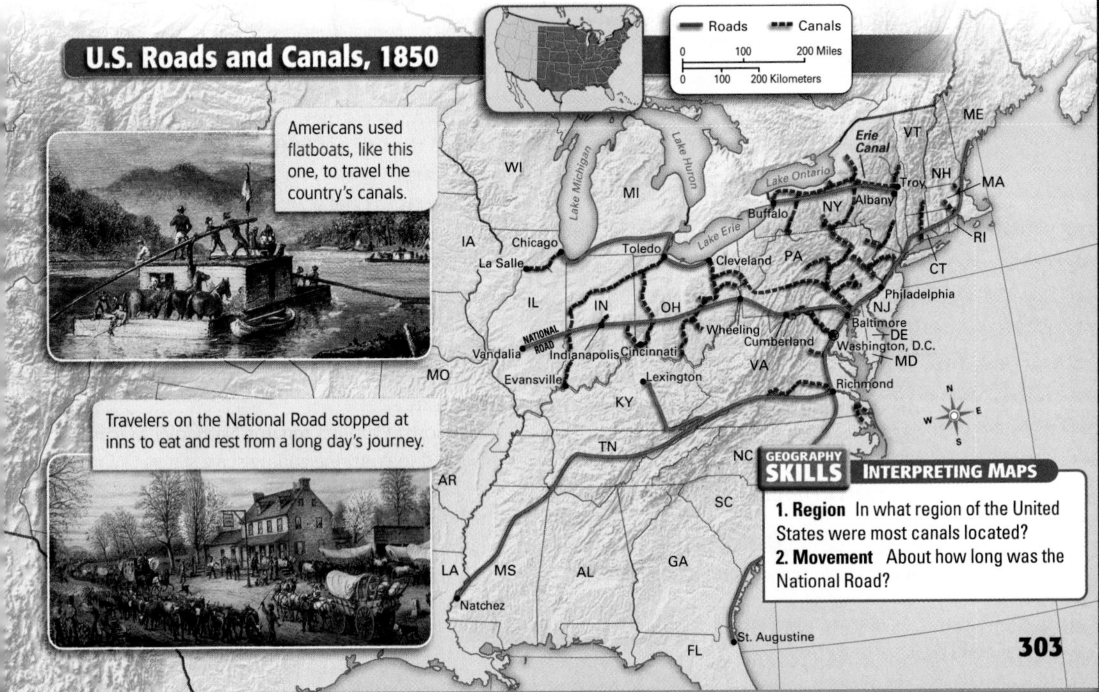

GEOGRAPHY SKILLS INTERPRETING MAPS

1. **Region** In what region of the United States were most canals located?
2. **Movement** About how long was the National Road?

Differentiating Instruction

Below Level

English-Language Learners

Prep Required

Materials: art supplies, poster board

1. Find and bring to class examples of items that promote school spirit, such as trophies; school colors; and buttons, folders, or notebooks that feature the school mascot.
2. Explain that nations also have symbols that promote national unity, such as flags, anthems, symbolic figures, slogans, and so on.
3. Ask students what symbols might have represented growing nationalism in the early 1800s. *(Students might suggest the American flag, a map of the growing country, or an image of the Erie Canal.)*
4. Have students create a Then-and-Now poster that provides a symbol for nationalism in the early 1800s and one for nationalism today. **LS Visual/Spatial**

Alternative Assessment Handbook, Rubric 28: Posters

Direct Teach

Main Idea

1 Growing Nationalism

Growing nationalism led to improvements in the nation's transportation systems.

Define What is nationalism? *feelings of pride and loyalty to a nation*

Recall What was the purpose of the American System? *to make the nation economically self-sufficient*

Evaluate How does nationalism benefit from roads and canals? *Linking goods and people helps create a unified nation and culture.*

CRF: History and Geography Activity: The National Road

Map Transparency 35: U.S. Roads and Canals, 1850

Checking for Understanding

True or False Answer each statement *T* if it is true or *F* if it is false. If false, explain why.

1. The Cumberland Road was a dirt road. *F; crushed stone*
2. The Erie Canal connected Lake Erie to the east coast. *T*
3. The Era of Good Feelings was an era of peace, pride, and progress. *T*

Focus on Indiana

IN 8.1.10

Interpret Why were internal improvements such as roads and canals important for the U.S. economy? *The speed of shipping goods was increased, thereby creating a more interdependent economy.*

go.hrw.com
Online Resources
KEYWORD: SF7 CH9
ACTIVITY: Transportation for a Nation

Answers

Interpreting Maps 1. *the Northeast* 2. *about 600 miles*

Direct Teach

Main Idea

❷ Missouri Compromise

The Missouri Compromise settled an important regional conflict.

Explain What problem did Missouri's request for statehood cause? *threatened to upset the balance of power between the free states and the slave states in the Senate*

Analyze How did the Missouri Compromise satisfy both the North and the South? *kept the number of free states and slave states equal and maintained the balance of power*

Make Judgments If you were a senator in 1820, would you have voted for or against the Missouri Compromise? Why? *possible answers: against—to prevent the spread of slavery; for—to preserve the peace between the states*

Map Transparency 36: The Missouri Compromise, 1820

History Humor

What are the three rules of diplomacy?

1. Compromise
2. Compromise
3. Compromise

The Missouri Compromise, 1820

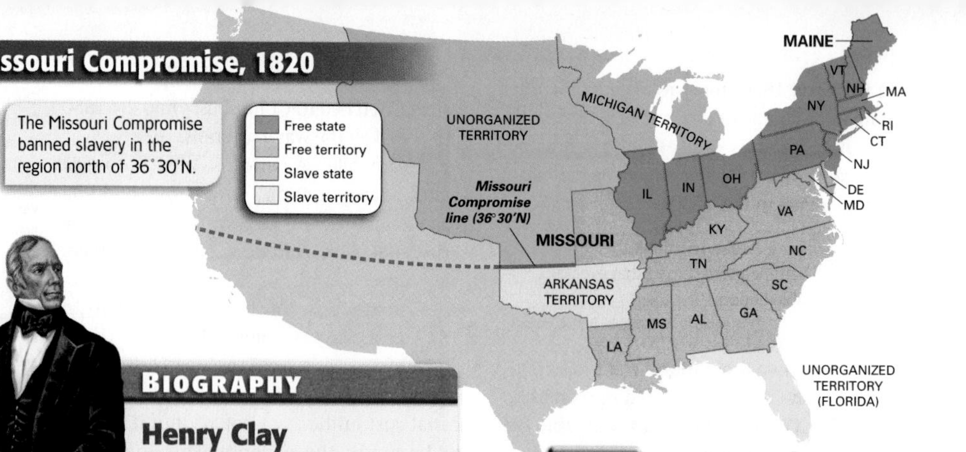

GEOGRAPHY SKILLS INTERPRETING MAPS

1. **Region** In which part of the country was slavery permitted?
2. **Human-Environment Interaction** Why did leaders choose 36° 30' as the compromise line?

BIOGRAPHY

Henry Clay

1777–1852

Known as the silver-tongued Kentuckian, Henry Clay was a gifted speaker. He became involved in local politics early in his life, and by age 29 he was appointed to the U.S. Senate. Throughout his career in the Senate, he was dedicated to preserving the Union. The Missouri Compromise and a later agreement, the Compromise of 1850, helped to ease sectional tensions, at least temporarily.

Analyzing Why did Henry Clay work for compromises between regions?

by a Boston editor in 1817 during James Monroe's visit to New England early in his presidency.

The emphasis on national unity was strengthened by two Supreme Court case decisions that reinforced the power of the federal government. In the 1819 case *McCulloch* v. *Maryland*, the Court asserted the implied powers of Congress in allowing for the creation of a national bank. In the 1824 case *Gibbons* v. *Ogden*, the Court said that the states could not interfere with the power of Congress to regulate interstate commerce.

READING CHECK **Drawing Inferences** How did new roads and canals affect the economy?

Missouri Compromise

Even during the Era of Good Feelings, disagreements between the different regions—known as **sectionalism**—threatened the Union. One such disagreement arose in 1819 when Congress considered Missouri's application to enter the Union as a slave state. At the time, the Union had 11 free states and 11 slave states. Adding a new slave state would have tipped the balance in the Senate in favor of the South.

To protect the power of the free states, the House passed a special amendment. It declared that the United States would accept Missouri as a slave state, but importing enslaved Africans into Missouri would be illegal. The amendment also set free the children of Missouri slaves. Southern politicians angrily opposed this plan.

North Carolina senator Nathaniel Macon wanted to continue adding slave states. "Why depart from the good old way, which has kept us in quiet, peace, and harmony?" he asked. Eventually, the Senate rejected the amendment. Missouri was still not a state.

Critical Thinking: Identifying Points of View

At Level

The Missouri Compromise

1. Write the following for students to see: **North—100 South—76**
2. Explain to students that these numbers show the North/South split in the House of Representatives at the time of the Missouri Compromise. While all 76 southern representatives voted to allow Missouri to enter the Union as a slave state, only 14 northerners voted for the measure.
3. Ask students how many votes were needed for a House majority *(88)* and how many the measure received *(90)*.
4. Have each student draw a copy of the map shown above. Then have students annotate the map by listing the political, economic, and social points of view in the free states and the slave states that were dividing the nation and which the Missouri Compromise addressed.
5. Ask volunteers to share the information they listed. **LS Visual/Spatial**

Alternative Assessment Handbook, Rubrics 11: Discussions; and 20: Map Creation

Answers

Interpreting Maps 1. *South;* 2. *It was Missouri's southern border, leaders may have hoped this line would maintain balance in the future.*

Biography *wanted to preserve the Union*

Reading Check *easier to transport goods across the nation*

Henry Clay convinced Congress to agree to the **Missouri Compromise**, which settled the conflict that had arisen from Missouri's application for statehood. This compromise had three main conditions:

1. Missouri would enter the Union as a slave state.
2. Maine would join the Union as a free state, keeping the number of slave and free states equal.
3. Slavery would be prohibited in any new territories or states formed north of 36°30' latitude—Missouri's southern border.

Congress passed the Missouri Compromise in 1820. Despite the success of the compromise, there were still strong disagreements between the North and South over the expansion of slavery.

READING CHECK **Drawing Conclusions** Why did Henry Clay propose the Missouri Compromise to resolve the issue of Missouri statehood?

The Election of 1824

Soon, a presidential election also brought controversy. Andrew Jackson won the most popular votes in 1824. However, he did not have enough electoral votes to win office. Under the Constitution, the House of Representatives had to choose the winner. When the House chose **John Quincy Adams** as president, Jackson's supporters claimed that Adams had made a corrupt bargain with Henry Clay. These accusations grew after Adams chose Clay to be secretary of state. The controversy weakened Adams's support.

FOCUS ON READING
How is the term **corrupt bargain** an example of semantic slanting?

READING CHECK **Drawing Inferences** Why did Adams have weak support during his presidency?

SUMMARY AND PREVIEW Strong nationalistic feeling contributed to the development of America's politics and economy. In the next section you will read about the development of a new national culture.

Section 2 Assessment

go.hrw.com
Online Quiz
KEYWORD: SF7 HP9

Reviewing Ideas, Terms, and People

1. a. **Describe** What was the **Era of Good Feelings?**
   b. **Analyze** Explain the impact the *McCulloch* v. *Maryland* and *Gibbons* v. *Ogden* decisions had on the federal government.
   c. **Predict** How would transportation improvements eventually aid the economy of the United States?
2. a. **Recall** What role did **Henry Clay** play in the debate over Missouri's statehood?
   b. **Explain** What problem did Missouri's request for statehood cause?
   c. **Elaborate** Was the **Missouri Compromise** a good solution to the debate between free states and slave states? Explain your answer.
3. a. **Identify** Who were the candidates in the presidential election of 1824? How was the winner determined?
   b. **Draw Conclusions** Why did **John Quincy Adams** lose popular support following the election of 1824?

Critical Thinking

4. **Evaluating** Review your notes on nationalism during the Era of Good Feelings. Then copy the following graphic organizer, and use it to identify how threats to nationalism were resolved by the Missouri Compromise.

FOCUS ON WRITING

5. **Judging Self-Esteem** Another way you can tell about people's characters is by how they view themselves. Are they self-confident? Do they make healthy choices? As you read this section, think of the United States as a person and jot down notes about the view the United States had of itself. Is the new nation pleased with itself? Does it feel confident or confused?

Direct Teach

Main Idea

❸ The Election of 1824

The outcome of the election of 1824 led to controversy.

Identify Who won the popular vote in 1824, and who became president? *Andrew Jackson; John Quincy Adams*

Make Inferences What evidence did Jackson's supporters have to support their claim that Adams made a corrupt bargain with Henry Clay? *Adams chose Clay to be secretary of state, which might appear to be reward for Clay's support in the House vote.*

Review & Assess

Close

Have students summarize the factors that affected nationalism and sectionalism during the Monroe administration.

Review

Online Quiz, Section 9.2

Assess

SE Section 2 Assessment

PASS: Section Quiz 9.2

Alternative Assessment Handbook

Reteach-Classroom Intervention

Interactive Reader and Study Guide, Section 9.2

Interactive Skills Tutor CD-ROM

Section 2 Assessment Answers

1. a. from 1815 to 1825, an era of peace, pride, and progress in the United States
   b. reinforced the power of the federal government
   c. made movement of goods cheaper, easier
2. a. proposed the Missouri Compromise
   b. threatened to upset Senate balance of power between free states and slave states
   c. possible answer: no—only put aside the problem, did not solve it
3. a. Andrew Jackson, John Quincy Adams; no electoral winner, so House chose winner
   b. popular vote went to Jackson; suspicion of corrupt bargain with Clay
4. possible answers—Missouri would enter Union as slave state, Maine would join Union as free state, slavery prohibited north of 36°30′ latitude
5. possible answers—Nation sees itself as confident with strong opinions, willing to work hard and take risks, proud of progress but recognizes flaws.

Answers

Focus on Reading *Negative labeling led people to feel the election was unfair and view Adams in a bad light.*

Reading Check (left) *to preserve the Union*

Reading Check (right) *did not win the popular vote; controversial appointment of Henry Clay as secretary of state*

History and Geography

Activity Erie Canal Grand Opening Flyer Lead a discussion on the Erie Canal. Have each student create a flyer advertising the opening of the canal that provides information about why canal transportation is better than other available options. Students should consider both people traveling west as well as those shipping goods.
LS Verbal/Linguistic, Visual/Spatial

Connect to Geography

The Canal Route The Erie Canal was built through the Mohawk Valley, a natural pass through the Appalachian Mountains in eastern New York. Colonists had learned this route from Native Americans. This location was chosen because no locks or aqueducts would be needed for some 80 miles.

Teaching Tip

Relate to the Familiar
Relate the height of the Erie Canal to objects with which students are familiar. Tell students to use 10 feet as the average height of a one-story building. Have students use this figure to estimate how many stories a building would need to be to equal the rise of the Erie Canal.
(60 stories)

History and Geography

The Erie Canal

In 1825 New York opened the Erie Canal, which connected Buffalo on Lake Erie to Albany on the Hudson River. With the new canal, boats and barges could travel from New York Harbor in the east to the Great Lakes region in the west. Trade boomed, new cities formed, and settlers moved farther west as the Erie Canal helped open up the Midwest region to farming and settlement.

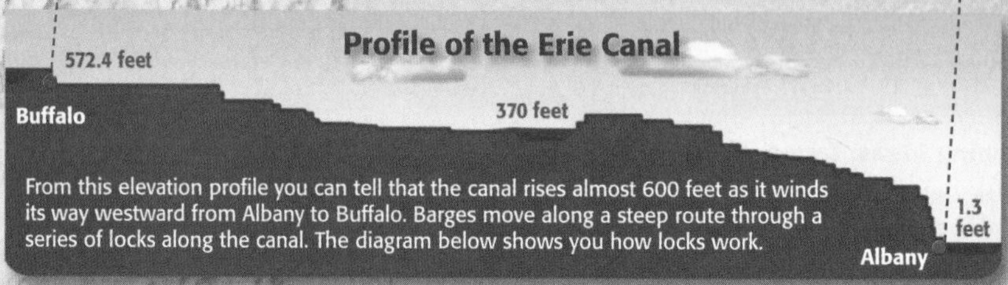

From this elevation profile you can tell that the canal rises almost 600 feet as it winds its way westward from Albany to Buffalo. Barges move along a steep route through a series of locks along the canal. The diagram below shows you how locks work.

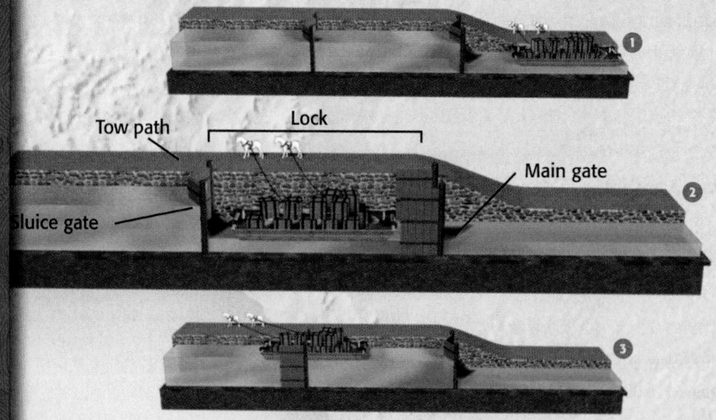

HOW Canal Locks WORK

1. The barge enters the lock through the main gate.
2. Water flows into the lock through the sluice gate to raise the boat to the next level.
3. The barge leaves the lock as mules help pull it across the water.

Critical Thinking: Comparing and Contrasting

At Level

Modern Canals

Research Required

1. Have each student conduct research on a canal in use today, such as the Panama Canal, the Suez Canal, the New York Canal System, the Sault Sainte Marie canals, the Intracoastal Waterway, or the Illinois Waterway.
2. Have each student create a chart comparing and contrasting the modern canal to the Erie Canal. Assign students specific points of comparison (such as the information listed in the Erie Canal Fast Facts on the next page) and have students provide the same information for each canal. Then have students write a summary explaining the significance of each canal.
3. Have volunteers share their charts with the class. **LS Verbal/Linguistic, Visual/Spatial**

Alternative Assessment Handbook, Rubrics 7, Charts; 9: Comparing and Contrasting; and 30: Research

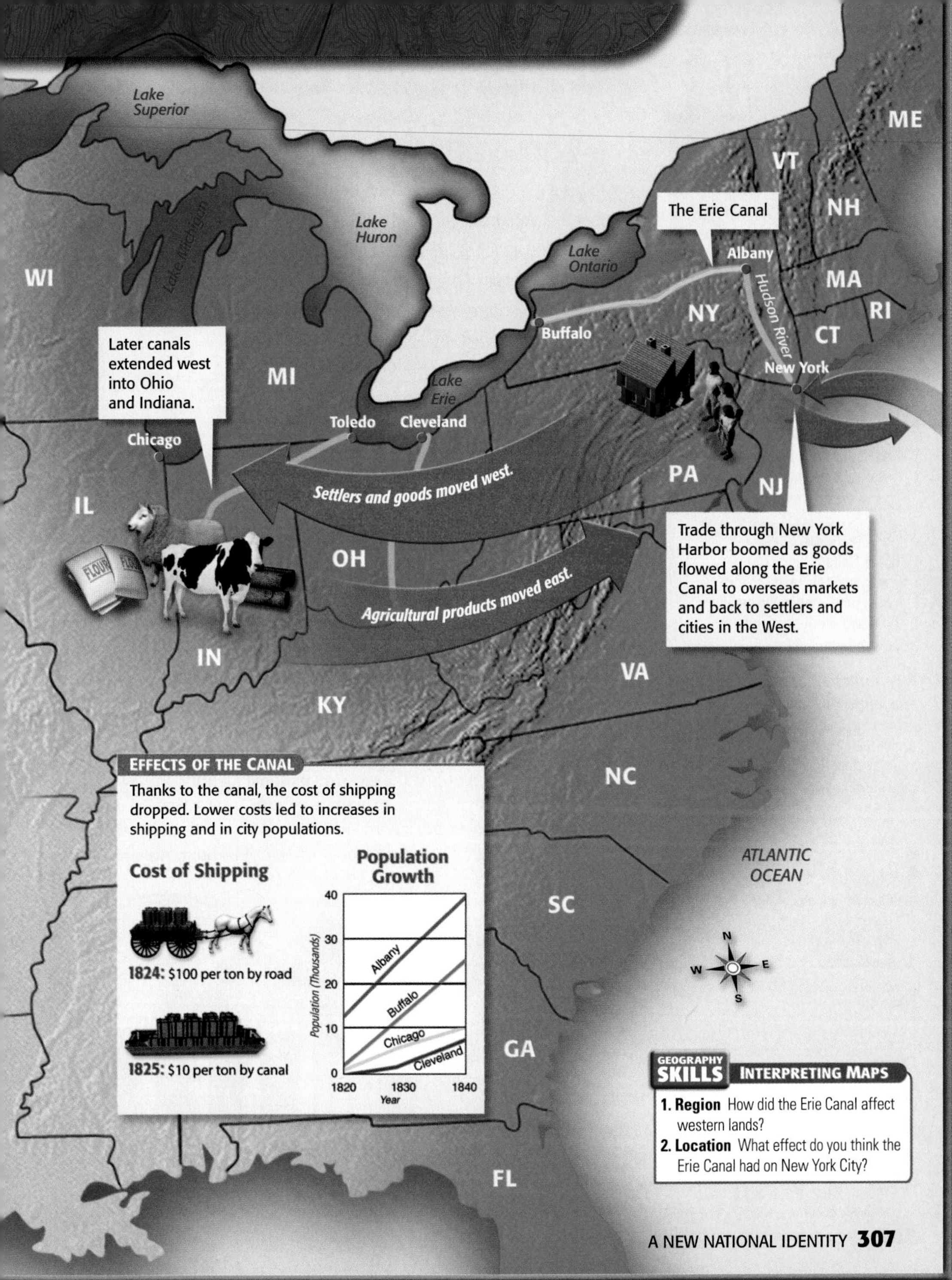

GEOGRAPHY SKILLS INTERPRETING MAPS

1. **Region** How did the Erie Canal affect western lands?
2. **Location** What effect do you think the Erie Canal had on New York City?

History and Geography

Info to Know

Erie Canal Fast Facts
opened: October 25, 1825
cost: about $7 million
endpoints: Buffalo and Albany, New York
length: 363 miles (584 km)
width: 40 feet (12 m)
towpath width: 14 feet
depth: 4 feet (1.2 m)
total number of locks: 83
total number of aqueducts: 18
nicknames: "Clinton's Folly," "Clinton's Big Ditch"

Linking to Today

Erie Canal Today Many of the Erie Canal's original 83 locks are still in use today, although the locks' sizes have been changed to accommodate larger vessels. People also use the canal towpaths for recreation, such as walking, bicycling, and even cross-country skiing.

Did you know . . .

When work began on the Erie Canal, the United States did not have a single school of engineering.

Connect to Economics

A Sound Investment Profits from the Erie Canal paid for the cost of the project within nine years of the canal's opening. The canal soon made New York the busiest port in the United States.

Did you know . . .

New York governor DeWitt Clinton was a major supporter of the Erie Canal project. Clinton's image was featured on the U.S. $1,000 bill, printed between 1869 and 1880.

Cross-Discipline Activity: Music

Above Level

Erie Canal Song

Prep Required

Materials: lyrics and recording of the song "The Erie Canal," by Thomas S. Allen, 1905

1. Distribute to students copies of the lyrics for the song "The Erie Canal." Next, play a recording of the song. Have students discuss the song's meaning and why the Erie Canal was chosen as a topic for a popular song.
2. Organize students into small groups and have each group write new lyrics to the tune of "The Erie Canal" that describe the effects and significance of the canal as described above.
3. Have each group perform its new version of "The Erie Canal" for the class.

LS Auditory/Musical, Interpersonal

Alternative Assessment Handbook, Rubrics 14: Group Activity; and 26: Poems and Songs

Answers

Interpreting Maps **1.** *It enabled trade goods to be shipped farther west, so trade boomed, new cities formed and others grew, and settlers moved farther west.* **2.** *possible answer—greatly increased the amount of goods traded through New York City and helped the city grow and prosper*

Preteach

Bellringer

If YOU were there . . . Use the Daily Bellringer Transparency to help students answer the question.

Daily Bellringer Transparency 9.3

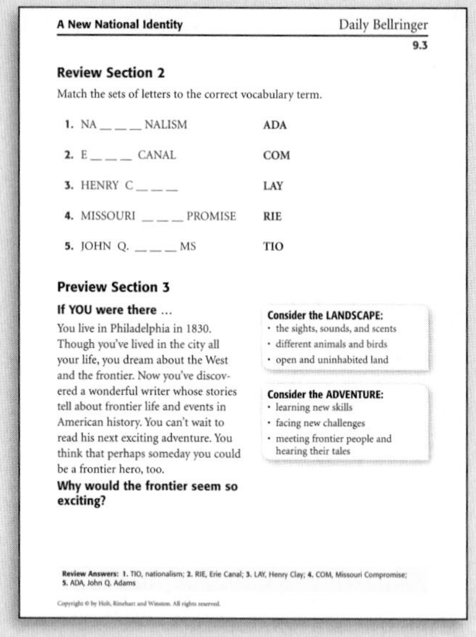

A New National Identity | Daily Bellringer 9.3

Review Section 2

Match the sets of letters to the correct vocabulary term.

1. NA _ _ _ NALISM	ADA
2. E _ _ _ CANAL	COM
3. HENRY C _ _ _	LAY
4. MISSOURI _ _ _ PROMISE	RIE
5. JOHN Q. _ _ _ MS	TIO

Preview Section 3

If YOU were there ...

You live in Philadelphia in 1830. Though you've lived in the city all your life, you dream about the West and the frontier. Now you've discovered a wonderful writer whose stories tell about frontier life and events in American history. You can't wait to read his next exciting adventure. You think that perhaps someday you could be a frontier hero, too.

Why would the frontier seem so exciting?

Consider the LANDSCAPE:
- the sights, sounds, and scents
- different animals and birds
- open and uninhabited land

Consider the ADVENTURE:
- learning new skills
- facing new challenges
- meeting frontier people and hearing their tales

Review Answers: 1. TIO, nationalism; 2. RIE, Erie Canal; 3. LAY, Henry Clay; 4. COM, Missouri Compromise; 5. ADA, John Q. Adams

Building Vocabulary

Preteach or review the following terms:

revival renewed faith (p. 310)

satire writing that uses ridicule (p. 309)

CRF: Vocabulary Builder Activity, Section 3

go.hrw.com
Online Resources
KEYWORD: SF7 CH9
ACTIVITY: American Culture Blooms

Taking Notes

Have students copy the graphic organizer onto their own paper and then use it to take notes on the section. This activity will prepare students for the Section Assessment, in which they will complete a graphic organizer that builds on the information using a critical-thinking skill.

Section Correlations IN

8.1.29 Differentiate between facts and historical interpretations recognizing that the historian's narrative reflects his or her judgment about the significance of particular facts.

SECTION 3

American Culture

What You Will Learn...

Main Ideas

1. American writers created a new style of literature.
2. A new style of art showcased the beauty of America and its people.
3. American ideals influenced other aspects of culture, including religion and music.
4. Architecture and education were affected by cultural ideals.

The Big Idea

As the United States grew, developments in many cultural areas contributed to the creation of a new American identity.

Key Terms and People

Washington Irving, *p. 308*
James Fenimore Cooper, *p. 309*
Hudson River school, *p. 310*
Thomas Cole, *p. 310*
George Caleb Bingham, *p. 310*

TAKING NOTES As you read, take notes on the new developments in American culture in the 1820s and 1830s. Write your notes in a chart like the one below.

	Characteristics
Literature	
Visual arts	
Religious music	
Architecture	
Education	

IN 8.1.14, 8.1.16, 8.1.29, 8.1.31, 8.2.4, 8.3.2, 8.3.7, 8.3.8, 8.3.11, 8.4.4

308 CHAPTER 9

If YOU were there...

You live in Philadelphia in 1830. Though you've lived in the city all your life, you dream about the West and the frontier. Now you've discovered a wonderful writer whose stories tell about frontier life and events in American history. You can't wait to read his next exciting adventure. You think that perhaps someday you could be a frontier hero, too.

Why would the frontier seem so exciting?

BUILDING BACKGROUND Until the early 1800s, Americans took most of their cultural ideas from Great Britain and Europe. But as American politics and the economy developed, so too did a new national culture. Writers and artists were inspired by American history and the American landscape.

American Writers

Like many people the world over, Americans expressed their thoughts and feelings in literature and art and sought spiritual comfort in religion and music. Developments in education and architecture also reflected the growing national identity.

One of the first American writers to gain international fame was **Washington Irving**. Born in 1783, he was named after George Washington. Irving's works often told about American

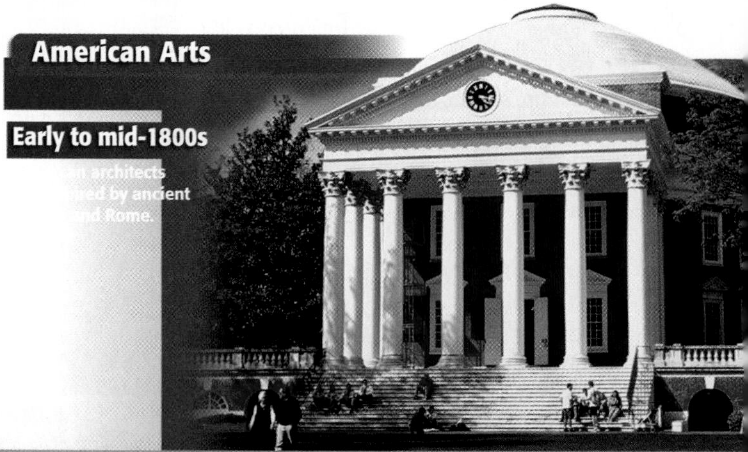

American Arts

Early to mid-1800s

Teach the Big Idea

At Level

American Culture

Materials: blank note cards

1. **Teach** To teach the main ideas in the section, use the questions in the Direct Teach boxes.
2. **Apply** Have each student create flash cards for two to three of the key people or ideas covered in the text under each of the blue headings. On the front of each card, students should label a person or idea. On the back of each card, students should provide a bulleted list of details and a one-sentence summary of how the person or idea contributed to a developing American identity. **LS Verbal/Linguistic**
3. **Review** Have students share information from their flash cards.
4. **Practice/Homework** Have students use their flash cards to create annotated time lines for the section. **LS Visual/Spatial**

Alternative Assessment Handbook, Rubric 36: Time Lines

history. Through a humorous form of writing called satire, Irving warned that Americans should learn from the past and be cautious about the future.

Irving shared this idea in one of his best-known short stories, "Rip Van Winkle." This story describes a man who falls asleep during the time of the American Revolution. He wakes up 20 years later to a society he does not recognize. Irving published this and another well-known tale, "The Legend of Sleepy Hollow," in an 1819–20 collection.

In some of his most popular works, Irving combined European influences with American settings and characters. His work served as a bridge between European literary traditions and a new type of writer who focused on authentically American characters and society.

Perhaps the best known of these new writers was **James Fenimore Cooper**. Cooper was born to a wealthy New Jersey family in 1789. Stories about the West and the Native Americans who lived on the frontier fascinated him. These subjects became the focus of his best-known works.

Cooper's first book was not very successful, but his next novel, *The Spy*, was a huge success. Published in 1821, it was an adventure story set during the American Revolution. It appealed to American readers' patriotism and desire for an exciting, action-filled story.

In 1823 Cooper published *The Pioneers*, the first of five novels featuring the heroic character Natty Bumppo. Cooper's novels told of settling the western frontier and included historical events. For example, his novel *The Last of the Mohicans* takes place during the French and Indian War. By placing fictional characters in a real historical setting, Cooper popularized a type of writing called historical fiction.

Some critics said that Cooper's characters were not interesting. They particularly criticized the women in his stories; one writer labeled them "flat as a prairie." Other authors of historical fiction, such as Catharine Maria Sedgwick, wrote about interesting heroines. Sedgwick's characters were inspired by the people of the Berkshire Hills region of Massachusetts, where she lived. Her works include *A New-England Tale* and *Hope Leslie*.

READING CHECK **Analyzing** How did American writers such as Irving and Cooper help create a new cultural identity in the United States?

A New Style of Art

The writings of Irving and Cooper inspired painters. These artists began to paint landscapes that showed the history of America and the beauty of the land. Earlier American painters had mainly painted portraits. By the

1827
John Audubon begins publishing *The Birds of America*, which is highly admired in England.

Direct Teach

Main Idea

1 American Writers

American writers created a new style of literature.

Identify What historical events did Cooper use as settings in his novels? *American Revolution, French and Indian War*

Contrast How are Cooper's works different from Sedgwick's? *Sedgwick's characters are more interesting than Cooper's; Cooper set stories on frontier, Sedgwick's in New England.*

Elaborate Why do you think Irving used his stories to caution Americans about the future? *wanted the new country to live up to its potential*

CRF: Biography Activities: Catharine Maria Sedgwick; Noah Webster

CRF: Literature Activity: *The Prairie* by James Fenimore Cooper

Info to Know

Catharine Maria Sedgwick Although she came from a wealthy family, Sedgwick's novels often criticized the wealthy and powerful. Her work reflected the more democratic values of her era. In *Hope Leslie*, for example, Sedgwick criticized the treatment that Native Americans had received from American settlers.

Differentiating Instruction

Below Level

Struggling Readers

1. Draw the graphic organizer for students to see. Omit the blue, italicized answers.
2. Have each student copy the graphic organizer and complete it by identifying significant writers of the early 1800s and describing what they wrote about. **LS Verbal/Linguistic, Visual/Spatial**

Alternative Assessment Handbook: Rubric 13: Graphic Organizers

Favorite American Writers of the Early 1800s

Writers	Subjects
Washington Irving, James Fenimore Cooper, Catharine Maria Sedgwick	*American Revolution, settlement, and the landscape*

Differentiated Instruction Resources
See page 293c for additional resources for Differentiating Instruction.

Answers

Reading Check *The characters and settings in their novels created a new vision of Americans, both at home and abroad.*

Direct Teach

Main Idea

2 A New Style of Art

A new style of art showcased the beauty of America and its people.

Recall Who was one of the founders of the Hudson River school? *Thomas Cole*

Summarize How had the style of American painting changed by the 1840s? *More artists were combining scenes of American landscapes with scenes from daily life.*

CRF: Biography Activity: Thomas Cole

Main Idea

3 Religion and Music

American ideals influenced other aspects of culture, including religion and music.

Explain What was the purpose of revival meetings? *reawakening religious faith*

Evaluate Why was a song about the Battle of New Orleans a good campaign song for Andrew Jackson? *Jackson had led American forces to a convincing victory over a larger British force at the battle.*

Focus on Indiana

8.1.19 Explain the influence of early individual social reformers and movements.

Elaborate Why was the Greek Revival style of building popular during this time period? *Because it reflected the importance that Americans placed on the Greek ideal of democracy.*

1830s the Hudson River school had emerged. The artists of the **Hudson River school** created paintings that reflected national pride and an appreciation of the American landscape. They took their name from the subject of many of their paintings—the Hudson River valley.

Landscape painter **Thomas Cole** was a founder of the Hudson River school. He had moved to the United States from Britain in 1819. He soon recognized the unique qualities of the American landscape. As his work gained fame, he encouraged other American artists to show the beauty of nature. "To walk with nature as a poet is the necessary condition of a perfect artist," Cole once said.

By the 1840s the style of American painting was changing. More artists were trying to combine images of the American landscape with scenes from people's daily lives. Painters like **George Caleb Bingham** and Alfred Jacob Miller travelled west to paint scenes of the American frontier, including trappers, traders, settlers, and Native Americans.

FOCUS ON INDIANA
The Indiana capitol building in Indianapolis was built in the Greek Revival style in the 1830s. The architect of the capitol, Alexander Davis, was the most important architect of the time and was responsible for many of the neoclassical buildings of the era.

READING CHECK **Finding Main Ideas** How did the style of American art change to reflect the American way of life in the early 1800s?

Religion and Music

Through the early and mid-1800s, several waves of religious revivalism swept the United States. During periods of revivalism, meetings were held for the purpose of reawakening religious faith. These meetings sometimes lasted for days and included large sing-alongs.

At many revival meetings people sang songs called spirituals. Spirituals are a type of folk hymn found in both white and African American folk-music traditions. This type of song developed from the practice of calling out text from the Bible. A leader would call out the text one line at a time, and the congregation would sing the words using a familiar tune. Each singer added his or her own style to the tune. The congregation of singers sang freely as inspiration led them.

While spirituals reflected the religious nature of some Americans, popular folk music of the period reflected the unique views of the growing nation in a different way. One of the most popular songs of the era was "Hunters of Kentucky," which celebrated the Battle of New Orleans. It became an anthem for the spirit of nationalism in the United States and was used successfully in Andrew Jackson's campaign for the presidency in 1828.

READING CHECK **Summarizing** How did music reflect American interests in the early to mid-1800s?

Architecture and Education

American creativity extended to the way in which people designed buildings. Before the American Revolution, most architects followed the style used in Great Britain. After the

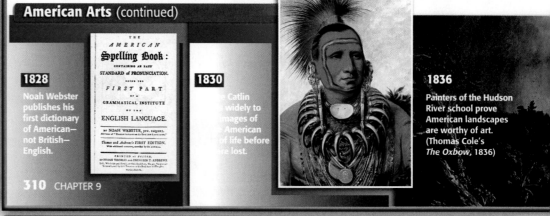

American Arts (continued)

1828
Noah Webster publishes his first dictionary of American—not British—English.

THE
AMERICAN
Spelling Book:
CONTAINING AN EASY
STANDARD of PRONUNCIATION.
BEING THE
FIRST PART
OF A
GRAMMATICAL INSTITUTE
OF THE
ENGLISH LANGUAGE.
BY NOAH WEBSTER, jun. Esquire.
Thomas and Andrews's FIRST EDITION.

1830
...e Catlin ...widely to ...mages of ...American ...f life before ...re lost.

1836
Painters of the Hudson River school prove American landscapes are worthy of art. (Thomas Cole's *The Oxbow*, 1836)

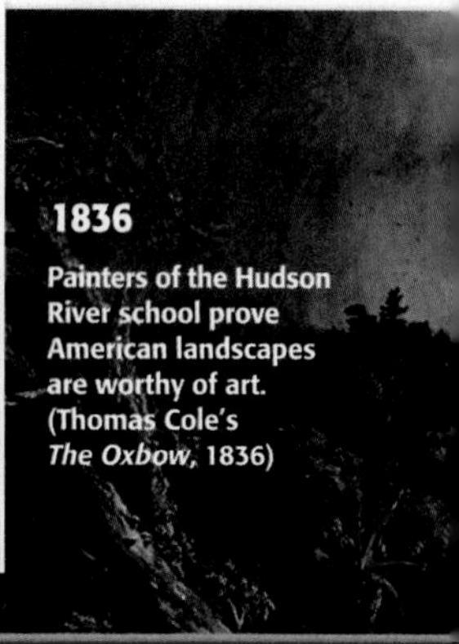

Critical Thinking: Identifying Points of View

At Level

Landscape Art and Poetry

1. Write the words *wild grandeur* for students to see. Ask students what they think the phrase means. Define *grandeur* if needed.
2. Explain that nature poet William Bryant admired painter Thomas Cole's "scenes of wild grandeur peculiar to our country." Write the quote for students to see. Ask students, based on the quotation and the paintings in this section, what qualities Bryant and Cole admired in America *(ruggedness, wild spaces, untamed nature)*.
3. Discuss with students how the American landscape has changed and how modern Americans view nature.
4. Have each student either write a poem or create a drawing or painting that conveys the student's feelings about American wilderness and nature.
5. Ask volunteers to present their works to the class. **LS Verbal/Linguistic, Visual/Spatial**

Alternative Assessment Handbook: Rubrics 3: Artwork; and 41: Writing to Express

Answers

Reading Check (left) *movement away from portraiture toward landscape painting; reflected Americans' new nationalism and pride in their country*

Reading Check (right) *spirituals—reflected emphasis on religion and revivalism; folk music—reflected spirit of nationalism*

Revolution, leaders such as Thomas Jefferson called for Americans to model their architecture after the styles used in ancient Greece and Rome. Many Americans admired the ancient civilization of Greece and the Roman Republic because they contained some of the same democratic and republican ideals as the new American nation did.

As time went by, more architects followed Jefferson's ideas. Growing American cities soon had distinctive new buildings designed in the Greek and Roman styles. These buildings were usually made of marble or other stone and featured large, stately columns.

Americans also embraced educational progress. Several early American political leaders expressed a belief that democracy would only succeed in a country of educated and enlightened people. But there was no general agreement on who should provide that education.

Eventually, the idea of a state-funded public school gathered support. In 1837 Massachusetts lawmakers created a state board of education. Other states followed this example, and the number of public schools slowly grew.

READING CHECK **Identifying Points of View** Why did some Americans call for new architectural styles and more education after the American Revolution?

ANALYSIS SKILL **ANALYZING INFORMATION**

How do these artistic developments show Americans' increasing sense of identity?

SUMMARY AND PREVIEW As the United States grew, so did a unique national identity. In Chapter 10 you will read about the changing face of American democracy.

Section 3 Assessment

go.hrw.com **Online Quiz** KEYWORD: SF7 HP9

Reviewing Ideas, Terms, and People

1. **a. Describe** What topics interested American writers in the early 1800s?
   b. Draw Conclusions Why is **Washington Irving** considered an important American writer?
2. **a. Identify** What influence did **Thomas Cole** have on American painters?
   b. Describe How did American painting styles change from the early period to the mid-1800s?
3. **a. Describe** What effect did religious revivalism have on American music?
   b. Elaborate Why do you think folk songs like "Hunters of Kentucky" were popular?
4. **a. Identify** On what historical examples did many American architects model their buildings?
   b. Predict What might be some possible results of the growing interest in education in the United States?

Critical Thinking

5. **Categorizing** Review your notes about new developments in American culture. Copy the graphic organizer below and use it to show how these cultural developments reflected a new American identity.

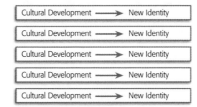

Cultural Development →	New Identity
Cultural Development →	New Identity
Cultural Development →	New Identity
Cultural Development →	New Identity
Cultural Development →	New Identity

FOCUS ON WRITING

6. **Identifying Values** You can tell much about someone's values by what that person makes. For instance, you could guess that a person who creates a collage of personal mementos for a friend's birthday is creative and values personal relationships. As you read this section, make note of what the United States created and what it valued.

Direct Teach

Main Idea

❹ Architecture and Education

Architecture and education were affected by cultural ideals.

Identify What are some features of the Greek and Roman architectural styles? *use of marble or other stone and large, stately columns*

Predict What issues do you think arose when people first proposed public education? *race, income, gender*

Review & Assess

Close

Have students summarize the many ways in which literature, art, and architecture combined to create a sense of national identity.

Review

go.hrw.com Online Quiz, Section 9.3

Assess

SE Section 3 Assessment

PASS: Section Quiz 9.3

Alternative Assessment Handbook

Reteach-Classroom Intervention

Interactive Reader and Study Guide, Section 9.3

Interactive Skills Tutor CD-ROM

Section 3 Assessment Answers

1. **a.** American history, the frontier
   b. bridge between European traditions and the new American style
2. **a.** founder of the Hudson River school; encouraged artists to concentrate on the beauty of nature
   b. from portraits, to landscapes, to landscape with scenes from daily life
3. **a.** led to the development of the spiritual form
   b. celebrated national pride
4. **a.** to show the link between American democracy and the ideals of Greece and Rome
   b. more colleges, equal rights movements
5. literature—American characteristics/settings; visual arts—pride in American landscape; religious music—faith, national pride; architecture—imitated Greece/Rome; education—growth of public schools
6. possible answers—historical fiction, landscape art, spiritual and nationalist music, Roman and Greek architecture; valued self, religion, classical ideals

Answers

Analyzing Information *Americans were looking at their own wildlife, language, people, and landscapes for inspiration.*

Reading Check *wanted architecture similar to Greece and Rome, which provided the models for the U.S. political system; thought education was good for democracy*

Literature in History

The Last of the Mohicans

As You Read As students read, have them take notes on descriptive words and phrases they find that might describe Natty Bumppo, such as *sunburnt and long-faded complexion.* Then have students draw a picture or write a summary of Bumppo's characteristics based on the words they listed. Discuss with students why Bumppo's image appealed to American readers of the period.

Meet the Writer

James Fenimore Cooper Cooper's action-packed stories illustrated two distinct ways of life. He portrayed Native American life as free and respectful of nature. On the other hand, many Europeans in his stories were rule-driven and disrespectful of the environment. Cooper's works also showed concern for individual freedoms and property rights.

Did you know . . .

Cooper's *Leatherstocking Tales* follow Natty Bumppo from a young man to old age. In the order of the hero's life, they are: *The Deerslayer* (1841), *The Last of the Mohicans* (1826), *The Pathfinder* (1840), *The Pioneers* (1823), and *The Prairie* (1827).

Literature in History

Literature of the American Frontier

from *The Last of the Mohicans*

by James Fenimore Cooper (1789–1851)

About the Reading The Last of the Mohicans *is one of five novels known as the* Leatherstocking Tales. *These novels follow the life and adventures of American pioneer Natty Bumppo (also known as Leatherstocking, Hawkeye, and the Deerslayer). Bumppo is the perfect woodsman: resourceful, honest, kind to both his friends and his enemies, but always a loner at heart.*

AS YOU READ **Try to imagine what Natty Bumppo looks like.**

On that day, two men were lingering on the banks of a small but rapid stream . . . While one of these loiterers showed the red skin and wild accoutrements of a native of the woods, the other exhibited, through the mask of his rude and nearly savage equipments, the brighter though sunburnt and long-faded complexion of one who might claim descent from a European parentage. ❶

The frame of the white man, judging by such parts as were not concealed by his clothes, was like that of one who had known hardships and exertion from his earliest youth. His person, though muscular, was rather attenuated than full; but every nerve and muscle appeared strung and indurated by unremitted exposure and toil. He wore a hunting shirt of forest green, fringed with faded yellow, and a summer cap of skins which had been shorn of their fur. He also bore a knife in a girdle of wampum, ❷ like that which confined the scanty garments of the Indian, but no tomahawk. His moccasins were ornamented after the . . . fashion of the natives, while the only part of his underdress which appeared below the hunting frock was a pair of buckskin leggings that laced at the sides, and which were gartered above the knees with the sinews of a deer. A pouch and horn completed his personal accoutrements, though a rifle of great length, which the theory of the more ingenious whites had taught them was the most dangerous of all firearms, leaned against a neighboring sapling.

GUIDED READING

WORD HELP

accoutrements dress and gear
rude crude, rough
attenuated made thin
indurated hardened
unremitted ongoing
gartered fastened
ingenious clever

❶ ***What do you learn about Natty Bumppo in the first paragraph?***

❷ A "girdle of wampum" is a belt strung with beads. Wampum were used by Native Americans for both money and decoration.

Make a list of the items Bumppo wears and carries. What does each item suggest about him?

Differentiating Instruction

Struggling Readers — Below Level

Group Interpretation Organize the class into small groups and assign each group one of the selections to interpret in the students' own words. One member of each group should record the group's descriptions and organize them into a coherent summary. Have a volunteer from each group read the summary aloud. Discuss the differences in each group's interpretation.
LS Interpersonal, Verbal/Linguistic

Advanced/Gifted and Talented — Above Level

Writing Historical Fiction Ask students to imagine that they are historical-fiction writers like Cooper. Have students use a historical event in this chapter as the basis for a short story with fictional characters. Have students either briefly describe their story ideas or write their stories. Ask for volunteers to share their ideas or stories. Then discuss how historical fiction is a useful tool in studying history. **LS Verbal/Linguistic**

Answers

Guided Reading 1. *has at least one Native American friend; likes spending time in nature; is of European descent;* **2.** *green hunting shirt (he hunts); cap of skins (he traps); a knife, a rifle, and a pouch and horn (he is resourceful and can protect himself); a girdle of wampum and moccasins (he trades or interacts with Native Americans); buckskin leggings (he travels through rough terrain)*

from *The Legend of Sleepy Hollow*

by Washington Irving (1783–1859)

About the Reading *"The Legend of Sleepy Hollow" has been called one of the first American short stories. Even though it is based on an old German folktale, its setting, a small village in the Hudson River valley, is American through and through. Irving's knack for capturing the look and the feel of the region made the story instantly popular—as did the tale's eerie central character, a horseman without a head.*

AS YOU READ **Try to picture both the ghost and the setting.**

The dominant spirit, however, that haunts this enchanted region, and seems to be commander in chief of all the powers of the air, is the apparition of a figure on horseback without a head. It is said by some to be the ghost of a Hessian trooper, ❶ whose head had been carried away by a cannon ball, in some nameless battle during the revolutionary war, and who is ever and anon seen by the country folk, hurrying along in the gloom of night, as if on the wings of the wind. His haunts are not confined to the valley, but extend at times to the adjacent roads, and especially to the vicinity of a church at no great distance. Indeed, certain of the most authentic historians of those parts, who have been careful in collecting and collating the floating facts concerning this spectre, allege, that the body of the trooper having been buried in the church yard, the ghost rides forth to the scene of battle in nightly quest of his head, ❷ and that the rushing speed with which he sometimes passes along the hollow, like a midnight blast, is owing to his being belated, and in a hurry to get back to the church yard before day break.

Such is the general purport of this legendary superstition, which has furnished materials for many a wild story in that region of shadows; and the spectre is known, at all the country firesides, by the name of The Headless Horseman of Sleepy Hollow. ❸

GUIDED READING

WORD HELP

dominant prevailing; ruling
apparition a ghostlike form that appears suddenly
collating comparing
spectre ghost
allege to firmly state
purport sense; gist

❶ A Hessian trooper is a German mercenary soldier from the American Revolution.
How and when is the horseman said to have died?

❷ ***Why does the horseman ride forth each night?***

❸ ***What is happening "at all the country firesides"? What does this suggest about how early Americans entertained themselves?***

CONNECTING LITERATURE TO HISTORY

1. **Drawing Inferences** The writing of the period reflects a new national culture and identity. What do these passages suggest about the thoughts, feelings, or lives of early Americans?
2. **Making Predictions** *The Last of the Mohicans* takes place during the French and Indian War. Whose side do you think Natty Bumppo would most likely take—that of the French and Indians, that of the English, or neither? Explain.
3. **Drawing Conclusions** Both of these stories were very popular in their time. Why do you think these stories were so popular? What is it about the stories that makes them entertaining?

Literature in History

The Legend of Sleepy Hollow

As You Read As students read, have them copy down words from the excerpt that set a spooky atmosphere, such as *spirit, haunts,* and *enchanted.* Inform students that legends and superstitions feed on common fears or traditional beliefs. Ask students for examples of superstitions they know. Then lead a discussion on why superstitions helped make *The Legend of Sleepy Hollow* so popular.

Meet the Writer

Washington Irving During his lifetime, Irving was also a lawyer, businessman, and a U.S. diplomat to England and Spain. His true passion was writing, however. He devoted himself entirely to writing in 1817. Unfavorable reviews of his *Tales of a Traveller* (1824) led him to give up writing fiction, though. He instead wrote histories and biographies until his death. His grave, fittingly, is in the Sleepy Hollow Cemetery and is now a national historic landmark.

Critical Thinking: Evaluating Information

At Level

Literary Biographical Posters

Research Required

1. Have students use the library or the Internet to conduct research on Cooper, Irving, or another writer covered in this chapter.
2. Students should write three to four questions about the selected author that they would like to answer through their research. Students should then use the questions to guide their research.
3. Have each student use the information to create a poster that shows an image of the writer, gives a short biographical description, and provides a listing of the writer's most well-known works. **LS Verbal/Linguistic**

Alternative Assessment Handbook, Rubric 28: Posters; and 30: Research

Answers

Guided Reading **1.** *A cannon ball knocked off his head during the Revolutionary War;* **2.** *to look for his head;* **3.** *People tell stories about the headless horseman; Early Americans shared stories around their fireplaces as a means of entertainment.*

Connecting Literature to History
1. *possible answer*—Mohicans *suggests that Americans viewed the frontier and those who lived there as wild and untamed.* Sleepy Hollow *suggests that Americans loved to hear and to tell imaginative stories with a basis in history;* **2.** *possible answer—French and Indian side, because he seems to have a strong relationship with the Native Americans;* **3.** *possible answers—popular because early Americans could see themselves in the stories, helped shape their national image; entertaining because stories showed the exciting and sometimes mysterious side of the New World*

Social Studies Skills

Identifying Central Issues

Activity Central Issues in the Community Write the following statement for students to see: *The school district's budget will be cut $300,000 next year.* Tell students this statement is hypothetical. Ask students to identify the most important questions and concerns that people might have in response to this news. Responses might include the following: What will the schools have to cut to lower their budgets—such as teachers, textbooks, art classes, and so on? Will classes be bigger? Will extracurricular activities be cut? Will free lunches be cut? After a brief period of discussion, ask students to identify what all these concerns have in common. Lead students to realize that the central issue involved is how will budget cuts affect educational quality and school life. To extend the activity, have students practice the skill by writing an article from their school or local newspaper. LS **Logical/Mathematical**

- Alternative Assessment Handbook, Rubric 11: Discussions
- Interactive Skills Tutor CD-ROM: Lesson 12: Identify Issues and Problems
- **CRF**: Social Studies Skills Activity: Identifying Central Issues

Answers

Practice the Skill 1. *Missouri Compromise; to discuss why he supported the Missouri Compromise and to explain his views on the issues involved;* **2.** *the issue of slavery; "that the bargain between freedom and slavery contained in the Constitution . . . is morally and politically vicious, . . . cruel and oppressive. . . ." and "If the Union must be dissolved, slavery is precisely the question upon which it ought to break."* **3.** *his comment about what might have been a bolder course of action, which might have produced a new Union of fewer states in which slavery was banned*

Social Studies Skills

Analysis | Critical Thinking | Civic Participation | Study

Identifying Central Issues

Define the Skill

The reasons for historical events are often complex and difficult to determine. An accurate understanding of them requires the ability to identify the central issues involved. A *central issue* is the main topic of concern in a discussion or dispute. In history, these issues are usually matters of public debate or concern. They generally involve political, social, moral, economic, or territorial matters.

Being able to identify central issues lets you go beyond what the participants in an event said and gain a more accurate understanding of it. The skill is also useful for understanding issues today, and for evaluating the statements of those involved.

Learn the Skill

In this chapter you learned about the dispute that arose over Missouri's admission to the Union. Yet that was not what this controversy was really about. Recognizing the central issue in this dispute helps you understand why each side fought so hard over just one state.

Use the following steps to identify central issues when you read about historical events.

1. Identify the main subject of the information.
2. Determine the nature and purpose of what you are reading. Is it a primary source or a secondary one? Why has the information been provided?
3. Find the strongest or most forceful phrases or statements in the material. These are often clues to the issues or ideas the speaker or writer thinks most central or important.
4. Determine how the information might be connected to the major events or controversies that were concerning the nation at the time.

Practice the Skill

Soon after the Missouri Compromise passed, Secretary of State John Quincy Adams wrote:

> "The impression produced upon my mind by the progress of this discussion [the dispute over Missouri] is that the bargain between freedom and slavery contained in the Constitution . . . is morally and politically vicious, . . . cruel and oppressive. . . . I have favored this Missouri Compromise, believing it to be all that can be effected [accomplished] under the present Constitution, and from an extreme unwillingness to put the Union at hazard [risk]. But perhaps it would have been a . . . bolder course to have persisted in the restriction upon Missouri till it should have terminated [ended] in a convention of the states to . . . amend the Constitution. This would have produced a new Union of thirteen or fourteen states unpolluted with slavery . . . If the Union must be dissolved, slavery is precisely the question upon which it ought to break. For the present, however, this contest [issue] is laid to sleep."

Apply the steps to identifying central issues to analyze Adams's statement and answer the following questions:

1. About what subject was Adams writing? What was his reason for making these remarks?
2. What did Adams believe was the most important issue in the dispute? What strong language does he use to indicate this?
3. What evidence suggests Adams did not think the breakup of the Union the central issue?

Social Studies Skills Activity: Identifying Central Issues — At Level

Guided and Independent Practice

1. Have volunteers read aloud the Section 1 text titled "United States Gains Florida."
2. Have students work as a class to go through the four steps listed under "Learn the Skill" to identify the central issues in this text. *(In this text, the central issues were the disagreements between the United States and Spain over American settlement and actions in Florida.)*
3. Then assign students the text in Section 1 titled "Monroe Doctrine." Have students work independently to identify the central foreign-policy issue dealt with by the doctrine. Discuss the answer as a class. *(President Monroe wanted to prevent European nations from gaining control of newly independent Latin American countries, protect American interests, and avoid wars with Europe.)* LS **Verbal/Linguistic**

- Alternative Assessment Handbook, Rubric 1: Acquiring Information

CHAPTER 9 # Chapter Review

History's Impact
▶ **video series**
Review the video to answer the closing question:
How did the Roosevelt Corollary change the Monroe Doctrine?

Visual Summary

QUICK FACTS

Use the visual summary below to help you review the main ideas of the chapter.

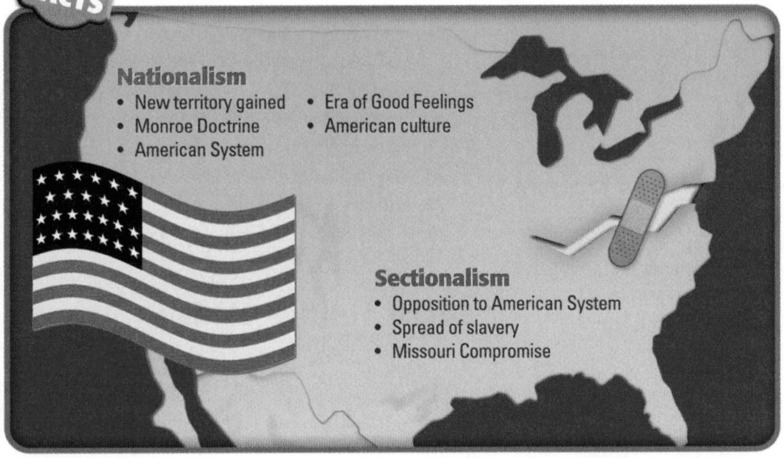

Reviewing Vocabulary, Terms, and People

Match the word in the left column with the correct definition in the right column.

1. American System
2. George Caleb Bingham
3. Simon Bolívar
4. Henry Clay
5. Erie Canal
6. Hudson River school
7. James Monroe
8. Monroe Doctrine
9. nationalism
10. Rush-Bagot Agreement

a. an agreement that limited naval power on the Great Lakes for both the United States and British Canada
b. American artist known for his focus on the American landscape and people
c. sense of pride and devotion to a nation
d. a group of American artists in the mid-1800s who focused on the American landscape
e. a leader of independence movements in Latin America, known as the Liberator
f. the plan to raise tariffs in order to finance internal improvements such as roads and canals
g. president who promoted the acquisition of Florida, closer ties to Latin America, and presided during the Era of Good Feelings
h. project that connected the Hudson River to Lake Erie and improved trade and transportation
i. representative from Kentucky who promoted improvements in transportation and the Missouri Compromise
j. U.S. declaration that any attempt by a foreign nation to establish colonies in the Americas would be viewed as a hostile act

Answers

History's Impact

Video Series The Roosevelt Corollary allowed the United States to take a more active role in maintaining stability in Latin America.

Visual Summary

Review and Inquiry Have students use the Visual Summary to review the chapter's key terms and ideas. Be sure students understand the symbolism of both the flag and the bandage in the image.

Quick Facts Transparency 29: A New National Identity Visual Summary

Reviewing Vocabulary, Terms, and People

1. f
2. b
3. e
4. i
5. h
6. d
7. g
8. j
9. c
10. a

Review and Assessment Resources

Review and Reinforce

SE Chapter Review
CRF: Chapter Review Activity
Quick Facts Transparency 29: A New National Identity Visual Summary
Spanish Chapter Summaries Audio CD Program
Online Chapter Summaries in Spanish
OSP Holt PuzzlePro; GameTool for ExamView
Quiz Game CD-ROM

Assess

SE Standardized Test Practice
PASS: Chapter 9 Tests, Forms A and B
Alternative Assessment Handbook
OSP ExamView Test Generator, Chapter Test
Differentiated Instruction Modified Worksheets and Tests CD-ROM: Chapter Test
HOAP Holt Online Assessment Program (in the Premier Online Edition)

Reteach/Intervene

Interactive Reader and Study Guide
Differentiated Instruction Teacher Management System: Lesson Plans for Differentiated Instruction
Differentiated Instruction Modified Worksheets and Tests CD-ROM
Interactive Skills Tutor CD-ROM

go.hrw.com
Online Resources
Chapter Resources:
KEYWORD: SF7 CH9

Answers

Comprehension and Critical Thinking

11. a. (1) United States would not interfere in European affairs or wars; (2) United States would recognize existing colonies in Americas; (3) Americas were off limits to future colonization; (4) United States would treat interference in Latin American countries as a threat and respond accordingly.

b. agreed to Rush-Bagot Agreement, which limited naval power on the Great Lakes, set the boundary at the 49th parallel, and shared the fur trade in the Northwest

c. possible answer: Monroe Doctrine—established the United States as the main power in the Western Hemisphere

12. a. territories gained; roads and canals built

b. northern and southern members of Congress disagreed about whether to admit Missouri to the Union as a slave state; agreed to the Missouri Compromise, which brought in Missouri as a slave state and Maine as a free state.

c. possible answer—might have weakened national unity and faith in democracy

13. a. Spirituals reflected the emphasis on religion; folk music reflected an interest in American heroes.

b. American artists and writers wanted cultural independence and a separate identity from Europe.

c. possible answer: art—prefer landscapes to portraits

Reviewing Themes

14. Success made Americans proud of their country and its leadership.

15. desire to show the country's uniqueness, rising nationalism, and improvements in education

Using the Internet

16. Go to the HRW Web site and enter the keyword shown to access a rubric for this activity.

KEYWORD: SF7 CH9

Comprehension and Critical Thinking

SECTION 1 *(Pages 298–301)*

11. a. Identify What were the four main points of the Monroe Doctrine?

b. Draw Conclusions How did the United States compromise in its disputes with British Canada?

c. Evaluate Which of the issues that the United States faced with foreign nations do you think was most important? Why?

SECTION 2 *(Pages 302–305)*

12. a. Recall What developments helped strengthen national unity in this period?

b. Analyze How was the disagreement over Missouri's statehood an example of sectionalism? How was the disagreement resolved?

c. Predict What effect might the election of 1824 have on national unity? Why?

SECTION 3 *(Pages 308–311)*

13. a. Describe How did popular music show the interests of Americans in the early 1800s?

b. Make Inferences Why do you think new American styles of art and literature emerged?

c. Elaborate Which element of American culture of the early 1800s do you find most appealing? Why?

Reviewing Themes

14. Politics How did the relations of the United States with foreign nations lead to a rise in nationalism?

15. Society and Culture What led to the creation of a uniquely American culture?

Using the Internet

go.hrw.com
KEYWORD: SF7 CH9

16. Activity: Researching In this chapter, you learned about the development of a new, creative spirit in American arts. Artists created works that featured American scenes and characters. Enter the activity keyword and research the development of American culture in art and literature. Then create a visual display.

Reading Skills

Bias and Historical Events *Use the Reading Skills taught in this chapter to answer the question about the reading selection below.*

When the House chose John Quincy Adams as president, Jackson's supporters claimed that Adams had made a corrupt bargain with Henry Clay. These accusations grew after Adams chose Clay to be secretary of state. *(p. 305)*

17. Which of the following used a biased definition, according to the above selection?

a. Andrew Jackson
b. supporters of Jackson
c. Henry Clay
d. John Quincy Adams

Social Studies Skills

Identifying Central Issues *Use the Social Studies Skills taught in this chapter to answer the question about the reading selection below.*

[Henry Clay] developed a plan that came to be known as the American System—a series of measures intended to make the United States economically self-sufficient. To build the economy, he pushed for a national bank that would provide a single currency, making interstate trade easier. Clay wanted the money from a protective tariff to be used to improve roads and canals. *(p. 302)*

18. Which of the following is the central issue addressed by the American System?

a. economic unity
b. protective tariff
c. national bank
d. improving roads and canals

FOCUS ON WRITING

19. Writing a Character Sketch Write a paragraph describing your overall impression of the nation's character. Write one sentence describing each of these aspects of the United States: its relationships with others, its feelings about itself, and its values.

Reading Skills

17. b

Social Studies Skills

18. a

Focus on Writing

19. Rubric Students' character sketches should

- start with an overall impression of the nation.
- describe the nation's relationships with others, feelings about itself, and values.
- use proper grammar, punctuation, spelling, and capitalization.

CRF: Focus on Writing Activity: A Character Sketch

CHAPTER 9 Standardized Test Practice

8.1.14, 8.1.31, 8.4.8, 8.4.9

DIRECTIONS: Read each question and write the letter of the best response.

1 Use the map below to answer the following question.

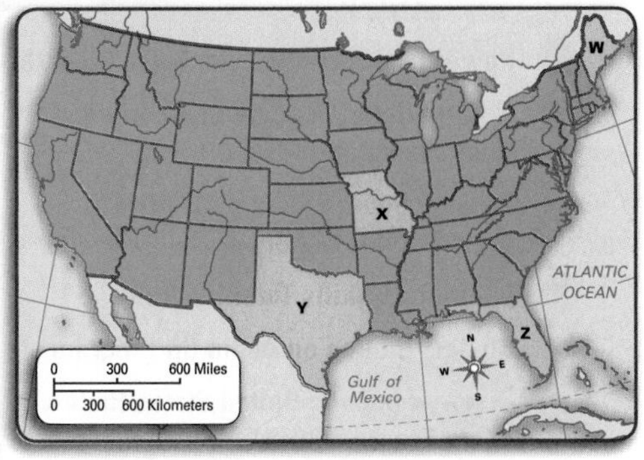

The present-day state that became part of the United States in the Adams-Onís Treaty of 1819 is shown on the map by the letter

A W.
B X.
C Y.
D Z.

2 The principle that European nations could establish no more colonies in North and South America was set forth in the

A Missouri Compromise.
B Rush-Bagot Agreement.
C Monroe Doctrine.
D Convention of 1818.

3 The Missouri Compromise had a significant effect on the United States because it

A established the present border with Canada.
B prohibited slavery north of Missouri's southern border.
C led to the expansion of roads and canals.
D settled conflicts between Native Americans in the West and the federal government.

4 Greek- and Roman-style architecture became common in the United States in the early 1800s because of

A the popularity of President George Washington, who liked the building style.
B Americans' admiration for the ideals of Greek democracy and republicanism.
C the nation's desire to build as strong a military as the Greeks and Romans had.
D Americans' great feeling of nationalism after the War of 1812.

5 Which painting would have been typical of an artist of the Hudson River school in the 1830s and 1840s?

A a portrait of a famous American
B a Native American hunting game
C a portrait of an ancient Greek or Roman lawmaker
D a scene showing America's natural beauty

6 Examine the following passage from a letter about American education and then use it to answer the question below.

> "A lady asked me one day, 'What state is Virginia in?' Another asked, 'Is Canada in Kentucky?' Another supposed that 'Joe Graphy [geography] was very hard to learn.' Such is the cause of all our mistakes in religion, morals, and politics. When we are educated we can cast off prejudice and superstition. Education improves our judgments and restrains our passions. In short, it enables us to discover what is best for our welfare."
>
> —Anne Newport Royall, adapted from *Letters from Alabama, 1817-1822*

Document-Based Question **Why might Royall and others try to make education available to more Americans? Explain.**

Answers

1. D
Break Down the Question Students need to recall information and recognize Florida on a map. Refer students who miss the question to the material "United States Gains Florida" and the map "U.S. Boundary Changes, 1818–1819" in Section 1.

2. C
Break Down the Question This question requires students to recall factual information. Students should use a process of elimination to answer the question. Refer students who miss the question to the material "Monroe Doctrine" in Section 1.

3. B
Break Down the Question This question requires students to recall cause and effect. Refer students who miss the question to the material "Missouri Compromise" in Section 2.

4. B
Break Down the Question Although A, C, and D may *seem* correct to students who do not recall the material completely, these distracters are incorrect. Refer students who miss the question to the material "Architecture and Education" in Section 3.

5. D
Break Down the Question This question requires students to recall factual information. Refer students who miss the question to the material "A New Style of Art" in Section 3.

6. possible answer—Education can keep us from making religious, moral, and political mistakes. Education helps the country.

Break Down the Question Indicate to students that the author clearly believes an educated society is a healthy society. From this it can be inferred that the author would likely have supported access to education for more Americans.

Intervention Resources

Reproducible

- Interactive Reader and Study Guide
- Differentiated Instruction Teacher Management System: Lesson Plans for Differentiated Instruction

Technology

- Quick Facts Transparency 29: A New National Identity Visual Summary
- Differentiated Instruction Modified Worksheets and Tests CD-ROM
- Interactive Skills Tutor CD-ROM

Tips for Test Taking

How Much Do I Write? If an open-ended question contains one of the following terms, then students will probably need to write several sentences to provide a complete answer.

- defend
- justify
- describe
- why
- explain
- write

Remind students that they can also provide drawings or sketches to enhance what they write.

Chapter 10 Planning Guide

The Age of Jackson

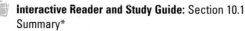

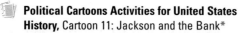

Chapter Overview	Reproducible Resources	Technology Resources
CHAPTER 10 **pp. 318–341** **Overview: In this chapter, students will study the presidency of Andrew Jackson, the increased conflict between the northern and southern states that marked his administration, and Jackson's policies toward Native Americans.**	**Differentiated Instruction Teacher Management System:*** • Instructional Pacing Guides • Lesson Plans for Differentiated Instruction **Interactive Reader and Study Guide:** Chapter Summary Graphic Organizer* **Chapter Resource File:*** • Focus on Writing Activity: An Interview • Social Studies Skills Activity: Solving Problems • Chapter Review Activity	**Power Presentations with Video CD-ROM** **Differentiated Instruction Modified Worksheets and Tests CD-ROM** **Primary Source Library CD-ROM for United States History** **Interactive Skills Tutor CD-ROM** **Student Edition on Audio CD Program** **History's Impact: United States History Video Program (VHS/DVD):** The Impact of Native American Reservations*
Section 1: **Jacksonian Democracy** **The Big Idea:** The expansion of voting rights and the election of Andrew Jackson signaled the growing power of the American people.	**Differentiated Instruction Teacher Management System:** Section 1 Lesson Plan* **Interactive Reader and Study Guide:** Section 10.1 Summary* **Chapter Resource File:*** • Vocabulary Builder Activity, Section 1	**Daily Bellringer Transparency 10.1*** go.hrw.com **Internet Activity:** Andrew Jackson
Section 2: **Jackson's Administration** **The Big Idea:** Andrew Jackson's presidency was marked by political conflicts.	**Differentiated Instruction Teacher Management System:** Section 2 Lesson Plan* **Interactive Reader and Study Guide:** Section 10.2 Summary* **Chapter Resource File:*** • Vocabulary Builder Activity, Section 2 • Biography Activities: John C. Calhoun; Daniel Webster • Primary Source Activity: President Jackson's Proclamation Regarding Nullification • Primary Source Activity: The Bank War of 1832—Two Views • Economics and History Activity: The Panic of 1837 **Political Cartoons Activities for United States History,** Cartoon 11: Jackson and the Bank* **U.S. Supreme Court Case Studies:** *McCulloch* v. *Maryland* (1819)*	**Daily Bellringer Transparency 10.2*** **Quick Facts Transparency 30:** Regions of the United States, Early 1800s* go.hrw.com **Internet Activity:** Nullification Crisis
Section 3: **Indian Removal** **The Big Idea:** President Jackson supported a policy of Indian removal.	**Differentiated Instruction Teacher Management System:** Section 3 Lesson Plan* **Interactive Reader and Study Guide:** Section 10.3 Summary* **Chapter Resource File:*** • Vocabulary Builder Activity, Section 3 • Biography Activities: Sequoya; Black Hawk • History and Geography Activity: The Seminole Wars • Literature Activity: *Surrender Speech* **U.S. Supreme Court Case Studies:** *Worcester* v. *Georgia* (1832)*	**Daily Bellringer Transparency 10.3*** **Map Transparency 37:** Second Seminole War* go.hrw.com **Internet Activity:** Indian Removal

SE Student Edition | Print Resource | Audio CD
TE Teacher's Edition | Transparency | CD-ROM
go.hrw.com | LS Learning Styles | Video
TOS Indiana Teacher One Stop | * also on Indiana Teacher One Stop

Review, Assessment, Intervention

- **Quick Facts Transparency 31:** The Age of Jackson Visual Summary*
- **Spanish Chapter Summaries Audio CD Program**
- **Progress Assessment Support System (PASS):** Chapter Tests A and B*
- **Differentiated Instruction Modified Worksheets and Tests CD-ROM:** Modified Chapter Test
- TOS **Indiana Teacher One Stop:** ExamView Test Generator (English/Spanish)
- HOAP **Holt Online Assessment Program,** in the Holt Premier Online Student Edition

- **PASS:** Section Quiz 10.1*
- **Online Quiz:** Section 10.1
- **Alternative Assessment Handbook**

- **PASS:** Section Quiz 10.2*
- **Online Quiz:** Section 10.2
- **Alternative Assessment Handbook**

- **PASS:** Section Quiz 10.3*
- **Online Quiz:** Section 10.3
- **Alternative Assessment Handbook**

HOLT
History's Impact
United States History Video Program (VHS/DVD)
The Impact of Native American Reservations
Suggested use: as a chapter introduction

Power Presentations with Video CD-ROM

Power Presentations with Video are visual presentations of each chapter's main ideas. Presentations can be customized by including Quick Facts charts, images from the text, and video clips.

DIVISION FOR PUBLIC EDUCATION
AMERICAN BAR ASSOCIATION

Developed by the Division for Public Education of the American Bar Association, these materials are part of the **Democracy and Civic Education Resources.**

- **Constitution Study Guide**
- **Supreme Court Case Studies**

Holt Online Learning

go.hrw.com
Teacher Resources
KEYWORD: SF7 TEACHER

go.hrw.com
Student Resources
KEYWORD: SF7 CH10

- Document-Based Questions
- Interactive Multimedia Activities
- Current Events
- Chapter-based Internet Activities
- and more!

Holt Interactive
Online Student Edition

Complete online support for interactivity, assessment, and reporting

- Interactive Maps and Notebook
- Standardized Test Prep
- Homework Practice and Research Activities Online

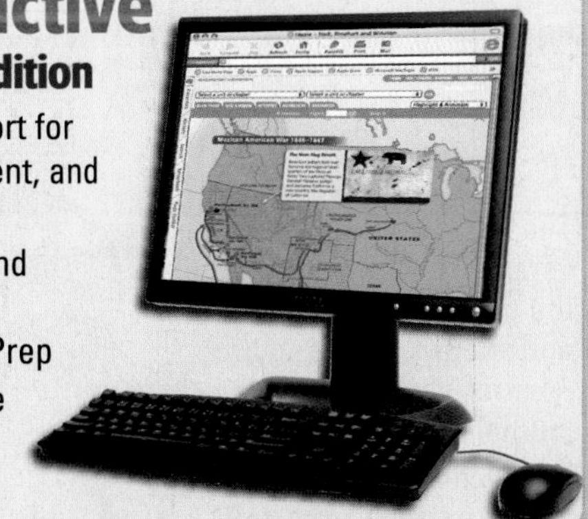

Differentiating Instruction

How do I address the needs of varied learners?

The Target Resource acts as your primary strategy for differentiated instruction.

ENGLISH-LANGUAGE LEARNERS & STRUGGLING READERS

TARGET RESOURCE

English-Language Learner Strategies and Activities

- Build Academic Vocabulary
- Develop Oral and Written Language Structures

Spanish Resources

Spanish Chapter Summaries Audio CD

Spanish Chapter Summaries Online

Teacher's One-Stop Planner:
- ExamView Test Generator, Spanish
- PuzzlePro, Spanish

Additional Resources

Differentiated Instruction Teacher Management System: Lesson Plans for Differentiated Instruction

Chapter Resources:
- Vocabulary Builder Activities
- Social Studies Skills Activity: Solving Problems

Quick Facts Transparencies:
- Regions of the United States, Early 1800s (TR 30)
- The Age of Jackson Visual Summary (TR 31)

Student Edition on Audio CD Program

Interactive Skills Tutor CD-ROM

SPECIAL NEEDS LEARNERS

TARGET RESOURCE

Differentiated Instruction Modified Worksheets and Tests CD-ROM

- Vocabulary Flash Cards
- Modified Vocabulary Builder Activities
- Modified Chapter Review Activity
- Modified Chapter Test

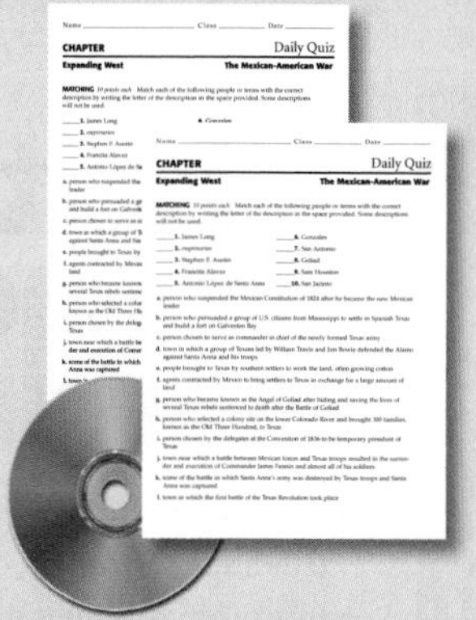

Additional Resources

Differentiated Instruction Teacher Management System: Lesson Plans for Differentiated Instruction

Interactive Reader and Study Guide

Social Studies Skills Activity: Solving Problems

Student Edition on Audio CD Program

Interactive Skills Tutor CD-ROM

ADVANCED/GIFTED-AND-TALENTED STUDENTS

TARGET RESOURCE

Primary Source Library CD-ROM for United States History

The Library contains longer versions of quotations in the text, extra sources, and images. Included are point-of-view articles, journals, diaries, historical fiction, and political documents.

Additional Resources

Differentiated Instruction Teacher Management System: Lesson Plans for Differentiated Instruction

Political Cartoons Activities for United States History: Cartoon 11: Jackson and the Bank

Internet Activites: Chapter Enrichment Links

Chapter Resource File:
- Focus on Writing Activity: An Interview
- Literature Activity: *Surrender Speech*
- Primary Source Activity: President Jackson's Proclamation Regarding Nullification
- Primary Source Activity: The Bank War of 1832

Differentiated Activities in the Teacher's Edition

- Regions of the United States Map, p. 327

Differentiated Activities in the Teacher's Edition

- Indian Removal Memorial, p. 334

Differentiated Activities in the Teacher's Edition

- Election of 1828 Political Advertisements, p. 323
- Book outline of Jackson's bank policies, p. 329
- Speech Opposing Indian Removal Act, p. 333

Teacher One Stop™

How can I manage the lesson plans and support materials for differentiated instruction?

With the Indiana Teacher One Stop, you can easily organize and print lesson plans, planning guides, and instructional materials for all learners.
The Indiana Teacher One Stop includes the following materials to help you differentiate instruction:

- Interactive Teacher's Edition
- Calendar Planner and pacing guides
- Editable lesson plans
- All reproducible ancillaries in Adobe Acrobat (PDF) format
- ExamView Test Generator (Eng & Span)
- Transparency and video previews

Professional Development

HOLT Professional Development

What teacher training resources are available to help me grow professionally?

- **In-service and staff development** as part of your Holt Social Studies product purchase
- **Quick Teacher Tutorial Lesson Presentation CD-ROM**
- Intensive tuition-based **Teacher Development Institute**
- **Convenient Holt Speaker Bureau** – face-to-face workshop options
- **PRAXIS™ Test Prep** interactive Web-based content refreshers*
- **Ask A Professional Development Expert** at http://www.hrw.com/prodev/

* PRAXIS is a trademark of Educational Testing Service (ETS).
This publication is not endorsed or approved by ETS.

• Chapter Preview •

Chapter Big Ideas

Section 1 The expansion of voting rights and the election of Andrew Jackson signaled the growing power of the American people.

Section 2 Andrew Jackson's presidency was marked by political conflicts.

Section 3 President Jackson supported a policy of Indian removal.

Focus on Writing

The **Chapter Resource File** provides a Focus on Writing worksheet to help students organize and write their interviews.

CRF: Focus on Writing Activity: An Interview

Key to Differentiating Instruction

Below Level

Basic-level activities designed for all students encountering new material

At Level

Intermediate-level activities designed for average students

Above Level

Challenging activities designed for honors and gifted and talented students

Standard English Mastery

Activities designed to improve standard English usage

CHAPTER 10

The Age of Jackson

Indiana Standards

Social Studies Standards

8.1.17 Identify the key ideas of Jacksonian democracy and explain their influence on political participation, political parties, and constitutional government.

8.3.6 Identify the agricultural regions of the United States and be able to give reasons for the type of land use and subsequent land development during different historical periods.

8.4.4 Explain the basic economic functions of the government in the economy of the United States.

8.4.8 Examine the development of the banking system in the United States.

go.hrw.com
Indiana
KEYWORD: SF10 IN

FOCUS ON WRITING

An Interview You are a reporter for a large city newspaper in the year 1837. Andrew Jackson has just left office, and you have been given the assignment of interviewing him about his presidency and his role in American politics. As you read this chapter, you will write interview questions for your interview with Jackson.

UNITED STATES

1828
Andrew Jackson is elected president.

Sequoya finishes a written language for the Cherokee.

1830

WORLD

1829
Louis Braille publishes a reading system for the blind.

Introduce the Chapter

At Level

A Controversial Character

1. Tell students that they are going to learn about the presidency of Andrew Jackson, a strong man who often found himself in disagreements with others on national issues.
2. Ask students to scan the chapter and examine the section titles, major headings, photographs, maps, and charts. Have students identify some of the controversial actions taken by Jackson. Make a list of students' responses for the class to see.
3. Explain to students that previewing a text can help them familiarize themselves with what they are about to read and make it easier to learn. Have students copy the list of topics they suggested and then jot down anything they learned about them based on their preview of the chapter. Next, have students write any questions they have about the text.
4. Tell students to add information to their lists and to answer their questions as they read the chapter. **LS Verbal/Linguistic, Visual/Spatial**

HOLT

History's Impact

▶ **video series**
Watch the video to understand the impact of Native American reservations.

What You Will Learn...

In this chapter you will learn about how President Andrew Jackson helped shape the United States. He was so influential that historians refer to his presidency as the Age of Jackson. This statue of Jackson has stood in Washington, D.C., for more than 150 years and captures the drive and spirit of the seventh president of the United States.

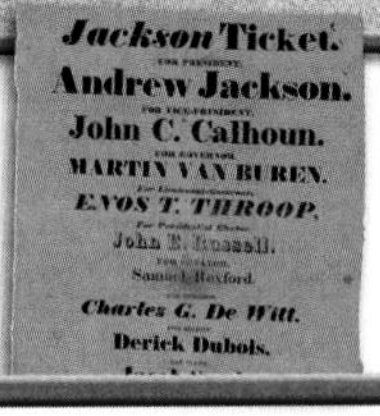

1832 Andrew Jackson vetoes the charter renewal of the national Bank of the United States.

1836 Martin Van Buren is elected president.

1838 The Trail of Tears begins when U.S. troops remove the Cherokee from Georgia.

1840 A treaty with the Miami cedes the last Native American lands in Indiana to the United States.

1835

1832 A British reform bill doubles the number of British men who can vote.

1833 Slavery is abolished in the British Empire.

1838 Dutch colonists known as Boers clash with the Zulu in southern Africa.

1839 The Opium War breaks out between Great Britain and China.

319

• Chapter Preview •

HOLT

History's Impact

▶ **video series**
See the Video Teacher's Guide for strategies for using the chapter video to teach about the impact of Native American reservations.

Explore the Picture

Statue of Andrew Jackson The statue of Andrew Jackson pictured at left stands in the center of Lafayette Park in Washington, D.C. The statue honors Jackson's leadership in the Battle of New Orleans during the War of 1812. Cast by sculptor Clark Mills, the statue was made from a bronze cannon captured during Jackson's last campaign against the Spanish in Florida. As the first equestrian statue in the United States, it is remarkable for its perfect balance, with the center of gravity based in the horse's hind feet.

Analyzing Visuals What details in the statue symbolize Jackson's drive and spirit? *possible answers—the way in which he is tipping his hat in salute; his upright mount on the rearing horse, which suggests strength and determination*

go.hrw.com
Online Resources

Chapter Resources:
KEYWORD: SF7 CH10
Teacher Resources:
KEYWORD: SF7 TEACHER

Explore the Time Line

1. In what year was Andrew Jackson elected president? *1828*
2. What did Andrew Jackson veto in 1832? *charter of the Bank of the United States*
3. What is the Trail of Tears, and when did it begin? *U.S. troops' removal of Cherokee from Georgia, which began in 1838*
4. What major contribution did Sequoya make, and when? *developed a written language for the Cherokee in 1828*

Info to Know

Jackson's Veto Power Andrew Jackson referred to the Second Bank of the United States as the "monster bank" and viewed it as a pawn of the rich and powerful in the eastern states. Jackson's 1832 veto of the charter of the Bank was only one among many vetoes he made in his quest to be a president for the poor rather than the rich.

Reading Social Studies

Understanding Themes

Introduce the main themes from this chapter—economics and politics—by asking students to explain how politics and economics might be intertwined. Help students to see that political decisions are sometimes based on economic factors. For example, northerners felt that tariffs would benefit manufacturing, therefore the federal government passed the so-called Tariff of Abominations. Ask students to think of situations in which political decisions might have an effect on economic conditions.

Drawing Conclusions about the Past

Focus on Reading Have students practice the skill of drawing conclusions. Ask students to bring in a newspaper or magazine article on a subject of interest to them. Then have each student read his or her article and select one or two paragraphs on which to make inferences. Have students write down several facts from their articles. Then have students write down two or three inferences based on those facts. Lastly, have students draw sound conclusions from their facts and inferences. Ask students to exchange papers and analyze their partner's conclusions.

Reading Social Studies

by Kylene Beers

Economics | Geography | Politics | Society and Culture | Science and Technology

Focus on Themes In this chapter you will read about the events that shaped the United States from 1828 to 1838. You will see how **political** and **economic** decisions were intertwined. For instance, you will read about the tensions between southern and northern states over tariff regulations. You will also read about the forced relocation of many Native Americans to the West. Understanding how economic issues led to political decisions will help you understand this time.

Drawing Conclusions about the Past

Focus on Reading Writers don't always tell you everything you need to know about a subject. Sometimes you need to think critically about what they have said and make your own decisions about what you've read.

Drawing Conclusions Earlier in this book, you learned how to make inferences. Sometimes when you read, you will need to make several inferences and put them together. The result is a **conclusion**, an informed judgment that you make by combining information.

Election of 1828

The 1828 campaign focused a great deal on the candidates' personalities. Jackson's campaigners described him as a war hero who had been born poor and rose to success through his own hard work.

Adams was a Harvard graduate whose father had been the second U.S. president. Jackson's supporters described Adams as being out of touch with everyday people . . . When the ballots were counted, Jackson had defeated Adams, winning a record number of popular votes. *(pp. 323–324)*

Inference: Jackson shared many qualities with American voters.

\+

Inference: Adams enjoyed many privileges that most Americans did not.

\+

Inference: Jackson easily won the election by a huge majority.

↓

Conclusion: In 1828, Americans chose a president to whom they could relate.

Reading and Skills Resources

Reading Support

- Interactive Reader and Study Guide
- Student Edition on Audio CD Program
- Spanish Chapter Summaries Audio CD Program

Social Studies Skills Support

- Interactive Skills Tutor CD-ROM

Vocabulary Support

- **CRF:** Vocabulary Builder Activities
- **CRF:** Chapter Review Activity
- Differentiated Instruction Modified Worksheets and Tests CD-ROM:
  - Vocabulary Flash Cards
  - Vocabulary Builder Activity
  - Chapter Review Activity
- **OSP** Holt PuzzlePro

You Try It!

The following passage is from the chapter you are getting ready to read. As you read the passage, look for the facts of the situation.

The Election of 1834

In 1834 a new political party formed to oppose Jackson. Its members called themselves Whigs, after an English political party that opposed the monarchy, to make the point that Jackson was using his power like a king. The Whig Party favored the idea of a weak president and a strong Congress. Unable to agree on a presidential candidate, the Whigs nominated four men to run against Vice President Martin Van Buren. With strong backing from Jackson, Van Buren won the election.

From Chapter 10, p. 330

After you read the passage, answer the following questions.

1. From this passage, what can you infer about President Jackson's popularity with the Whig Party?
2. The Whigs could not choose a single presidential candidate, so they nominated four men. Based on what you know about elections from your studies and your past experiences, how do you think this affected the votes each man received?
3. Jackson's backing helped Van Buren win the presidency. From this, what can you infer about Jackson's popularity with the American people as a whole?
4. Using the inferences you made answering questions 1 through 3, draw a conclusion about why Van Buren won the election of 1834.

As you read Chapter 10, use your personal background knowledge and experience to draw conclusions about what you are reading.

Key Terms and People

Chapter 10

Section 1
nominating conventions *(p. 323)*
Jacksonian Democracy *(p. 323)*
Democratic Party *(p. 323)*
John C. Calhoun *(p. 323)*
spoils system *(p. 324)*
Martin Van Buren *(p. 324)*
Kitchen Cabinet *(p. 324)*

Section 2
Tariff of Abominations *(p. 327)*
states' rights doctrine *(p. 328)*
nullification crisis *(p. 328)*
Daniel Webster *(p. 328)*
McCulloch v. *Maryland* *(p. 330)*
Whig Party *(p. 330)*
Panic of 1837 *(p. 331)*
William Henry Harrison *(p. 331)*

Section 3
Indian Removal Act *(p. 332)*
Indian Territory *(p. 332)*
Bureau of Indian Affairs *(p. 332)*
Sequoya *(p. 333)*
Worcester v. *Georgia* *(p. 334)*
Trail of Tears *(p. 334)*
Black Hawk *(p. 335)*
Osceola *(p. 335)*

Academic Vocabulary

Success in school is related to knowing academic vocabulary—the words that are frequently used in school assignments and discussions. In this chapter, you will learn the following academic words:

criteria *(p. 328)*
contemporary *(p. 333)*

Reading Social Studies

Key Terms and People

Preteach the key terms and people from this chapter to the class. Then have each student write a sentence for each key term. Remind students to use each term correctly. Have students rewrite their sentences, leaving blanks where the key term or person belongs. Have students exchange papers with a partner and complete the fill-in-the-blank activity.
LS Verbal/Linguistic

Focus on Reading

See the **Focus on Reading** questions in this chapter for more practice on this reading social studies skill.

Reading Social Studies Assessment

See the **Chapter Review** at the end of this chapter for student assessment questions related to this reading skill.

Teaching Tip

Remind students that there will be times when they have to draw conclusions to fill in small gaps in the text. Tell students to look carefully at the labels of questions in the textbook. When they see a label that reads *Draw Conclusions,* students should use facts from the text and their own knowledge of similar situations to draw a logical conclusion. Help students practice this skill by asking them questions that require them to draw on their own knowledge.

Answers

You Try It! 1. *Jackson was very unpopular with the Whigs because they felt he had too much power.* **2.** *It lowered the number of votes each man received.* **3.** *Jackson remained very popular and the people supported the candidate that he endorsed.* **4.** *Van Buren won the election of 1834 because the Whig Party disliked Jackson, they had too many candidates in the election, and the people supported Jackson's choice for president.*

Preteach

Bellringer

If YOU were there . . . Use the **Daily Bellringer Transparency** to help students answer the question.

Daily Bellringer Transparency 10.1

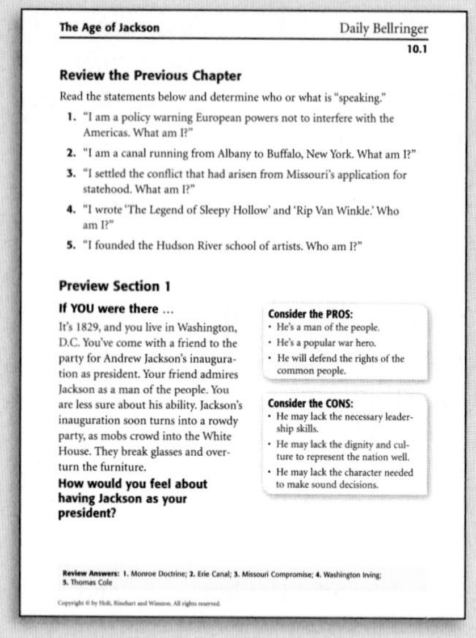

The Age of Jackson — Daily Bellringer **10.1**

Review the Previous Chapter

Read the statements below and determine who or what is "speaking."

1. "I am a policy warning European powers not to interfere with the Americas. What am I?"
2. "I am a canal running from Albany to Buffalo, New York. What am I?"
3. "I settled the conflict that had arisen from Missouri's application for statehood. What am I?"
4. "I wrote 'The Legend of Sleepy Hollow' and 'Rip Van Winkle.' Who am I?"
5. "I founded the Hudson River school of artists. Who am I?"

Preview Section 1

If YOU were there ...

It's 1829, and you live in Washington, D.C. You've come with a friend to the party for Andrew Jackson's inauguration as president. Your friend admires Jackson as a man of the people. You are less sure about his ability. Jackson's inauguration soon turns into a rowdy party, as mobs crowd into the White House. They break glasses and overturn the furniture.

How would you feel about having Jackson as your president?

Consider the PROS:
- He's a man of the people.
- He's a popular war hero.
- He will defend the rights of the common people.

Consider the CONS:
- He may lack the necessary leadership skills.
- He may lack the dignity and culture to represent the nation well.
- He may lack the character needed to make sound decisions.

Review Answers: 1. Monroe Doctrine; 2. Erie Canal; 3. Missouri Compromise; 4. Washington Irving; 5. Thomas Cole

Building Vocabulary

Preteach or review the following terms:

cabinet presidential advisors (p. 324)

inauguration a formal ceremony to place someone in office (p. 324)

spoils as used here, valued goods (p. 324)

CRF: Vocabulary Builder Activity, Section 1

Taking Notes

Have students copy the graphic organizer onto their own paper and then use it to take notes on the section. This activity will prepare students for the Section Assessment, in which they will complete a graphic organizer that builds on the information using a critical-thinking skill.

SECTION 1

Jacksonian Democracy

What You Will Learn...

Main Ideas

1. Democracy expanded in the 1820s as more Americans held the right to vote.
2. Jackson's victory in the election of 1828 marked a change in American politics.

The Big Idea

The expansion of voting rights and the election of Andrew Jackson signaled the growing power of the American people.

Key Terms and People

nominating conventions, *p. 323*
Jacksonian Democracy, *p. 323*
Democratic Party, *p. 323*
John C. Calhoun, *p. 323*
spoils system, *p. 324*
Martin Van Buren, *p. 324*
Kitchen Cabinet, *p. 324*

TAKING NOTES As you read, take notes on how an expansion of voting rights led to Andrew Jackson's election to the presidency. Write your notes in a flowchart like the one below.

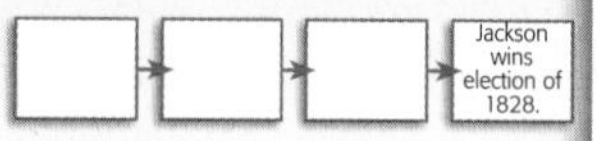

IN 8.1.17, 8.1.30, 8.2.8

If YOU were there...

It's 1829, and you live in Washington, D.C. You've come with a friend to the party for Andrew Jackson's inauguration as president. Your friend admires Jackson as a man of the people. You are less sure about his ability. Jackson's inauguration soon turns into a rowdy party, as mobs crowd into the White House. They break glasses and overturn the furniture.

How would you feel about having Jackson as your president?

BUILDING BACKGROUND In the early years of the United States, the right to vote belonged mainly to a few—free white men who owned property. As the country grew, more men were given the right to vote. This expansion of democracy led to the election of Andrew Jackson, a war hero. But not everyone approved of Jackson.

Expansion of Democracy

America in the early 1800s was changing fast. In the North, workshops run by the craftspeople who owned them were being replaced by large-scale factories owned by businesspeople and staffed by hired workers. In the South, small family farms began to give way to large cotton plantations, owned by wealthy white people and worked by enslaved African Americans. Wealth seemed to be concentrating into fewer hands. Many ordinary Americans felt left behind.

These same people also began to believe they were losing power in their government. In the late 1700s some Americans thought that government was best managed by wealthy, property-owning men. Government policies seemed targeted to help build the power of these people. The result was a growing belief that the wealthy were tightening their grip on power in the United States.

Hoping for change, small farmers, frontier settlers, and slaveholders rallied behind reform-minded Andrew Jackson, the popular hero of the War of 1812 and presidential candidate in the 1824 election. They believed Jackson would defend the rights of the common

Teach the Big Idea

At Level

Jacksonian Democracy

1. **Teach** To teach the main ideas in the section, use the questions in the Direct Teach boxes.
2. **Apply** Pair students and have each pair use the term *Jacksonian Democracy* to create an acrostic. For each letter in *Jacksonian Democracy*, students should find a key term, figure, event, or issue from the section that includes that letter. Students should then write the terms horizontally so that the letters in *Jacksonian Democracy* align vertically.
LS Interpersonal, Verbal/Linguistic
3. **Review** To review the section, have students share terms from their acrostics.
4. **Practice/Homework** Have students imagine they have just attended a Jackson inauguration party. Have each student write a journal entry about the election, the party, and the expansion of democracy.
LS Intrapersonal, Verbal/Linguistic

Alternative Assessment Handbook, Rubric 15: Journals

Section Correlations

IN

8.1.17 Identify the key ideas of Jacksonian democracy and explain their influence on political participation, political parties and constitutional government. **8.1.30** Formulate historical questions by analyzing primary sources and secondary sources about an issue confronting the United States during the period from 1754–1877. **8.2.8** Explain ways that citizens can participate in political parties, campaigns, and elections.

LINKING TO TODAY

Democracy in Action

Democracy spread in the early 1800s as more people became active in politics. Many of these people lived in the new western states. In these mostly rural areas, a political rally could be as simple as neighboring farmers meeting to talk about the issues of the day, as the farmers in the painting on the right are doing.

During the early 1800s democracy and demonstrations blossomed in the United States. The demonstrators of today owe much to the Americans of Andrew Jackson's time. Today, political rallies are a familiar sight in communities all over the country.

ANALYSIS SKILL **ANALYZING INFORMATION**

How are the people in both pictures practicing democracy?

people and the slave states. And they had been bitterly disappointed in the way Jackson had lost the 1824 election because of the decision in the House of Representatives.

During the time of Jackson's popularity, many democratic reforms were made. Some states changed their qualifications for voters to grant more white males suffrage. The revised rules, however, usually excluded free blacks from voting as they had been allowed under original state constitutions. Political parties began holding public **nominating conventions**, where party members choose the party's candidates instead of the party leaders. This period of expanding democracy in the 1820s and 1830s later became known as **Jacksonian Democracy**.

READING CHECK **Finding Main Ideas** How did voting rights change in the early 1800s?

Election of 1828

Jackson supporters were determined that their candidate would win the 1828 election. They formed the **Democratic Party** to support Jackson's candidacy. Many people who backed President Adams began calling themselves National Republicans.

The 1828 presidential contest was a rematch of the 1824 election. Once again, John Quincy Adams faced Andrew Jackson. Jackson chose **John C. Calhoun** as his vice presidential running mate.

The Campaign

The 1828 campaign focused a great deal on the candidates' personalities. Jackson's campaigners described him as a war hero who had been born poor and rose to success through his own hard work.

THE IMPACT TODAY

Just as they did in the 1820s, presidential campaigns today frequently focus on personal image—strong versus weak or government-insider versus newcomer, for example.

Direct Teach

Main Idea

1 Expansion of Democracy

Democracy expanded in the 1820s as more Americans held the right to vote.

Recall What did the revised voting rules exclude? *They excluded free blacks from voting.*

Analyze Why do historians call the expansion of voting rights during this period Jacksonian Democracy? *because Andrew Jackson was a popular politician who supported majority rule and benefited from the expansion of democracy*

Evaluate Why do you think Jackson was a popular presidential candidate? *was a popular war hero, his supporters thought he would defend the rights of common people*

Info to Know

Jacksonian Democracy In the early 1900s, historians argued that Andrew Jackson's election signaled the triumph of the common people over social elites. More recently, historians have argued that Jackson's supporters actually hoped to increase their own economic standing and to become more like the elites. Historians still agree, though, that the changes in politics in the 1820s and 1830s marked a turning point in U.S. political history.

go.hrw.com
Online Resources
KEYWORD: SF7 CH10
ACTIVITY: Andrew Jackson

Collaborative Learning

Above Level

Election of 1828 Political Advertisements

Prep Required **Research Required**

Materials: video or DVD camera, tapes, and player

1. Organize the class into large groups and assign each group either Andrew Jackson or John Quincy Adams. Have each group create a 30-second political advertisement in support of its candidate for the 1828 election.
2. Instruct the groups to assign each member a specific role, such as director, researcher, designer, writer, editor, actor, props person, or cameraperson.
3. Have each group write, act, and record its political ad. Then show the ads to the class.
4. Conclude by leading a class discussion about how the expansion in democracy in the 1820s and the 1828 campaign led to a new pattern in American political participation and power.
LS Interpersonal, Kinesthetic

Alternative Assessment Handbook, Rubrics 2: Advertisements; and 14: Group Activity

Answers

Linking to Today *They are exercising their rights to assemble and freely discuss and express ideas.*

Reading Check *Many states expanded voting rights to include more white men, but excluded free blacks from voting.*

Direct Teach

Main Idea

❷ Election of 1828

Jackson's victory in the election of 1828 marked a change in American politics.

Identify Who were the candidates in the election of 1828, and what party did each represent? *John Quincy Adams, National Republican party; Andrew Jackson, Democratic Party*

Draw Conclusions Why did Jackson's supporters view his victory as a win for the common people? *because most of his supporters were farmers and settlers, as opposed to members of the eastern elite*

Make Judgments What is your opinion of the spoils system? *possible answers: approve—an appropriate reward for hard work; disapprove—could lead to corruption*

Review & Assess

Close

Have students summarize Jacksonian Democracy.

Review

go.hrw.com Online Quiz, Section 10.1

Assess

SE Section 1 Assessment

PASS: Section Quiz 10.1

Alternative Assessment Handbook

Reteach/Classroom Intervention

Interactive Reader and Study Guide, Section 10.1

Interactive Skills Tutor CD-ROM

Answers

Analyzing Primary Sources *as "a rabble, a mob"*

Reading Check *People who were not rewarded might cause discord.*

Primary Source

LETTER

People's President

Washington resident Margaret Bayard Smith was surprised by the chaos surrounding Jackson's inauguration.

"What a scene did we witness! . . . a rabble, a mob, of boys, . . . women, children, scrambling, fighting, romping . . . Cut glass and china to the amount of several thousand dollars had been broken . . . But it was the people's day, and the people's President, and the people would rule."

—Margaret Bayard Smith, quoted in *Eyewitness to America*, edited by David Colbert

ANALYSIS SKILL ANALYZING PRIMARY SOURCES

How does the author view the people that support Jackson?

Adams was a Harvard graduate whose father had been the second U.S. president. Jackson's supporters described Adams as being out of touch with everyday people. Even a fan of Adams agreed that he was "as cold as a lump of ice." In turn, Adams's supporters said Jackson was hot tempered, crude, and ill-equipped to be president of the United States. When the ballots were counted, Jackson had defeated Adams, winning a record number of popular votes.

Jackson's Inauguration

Jackson's supporters saw his victory as a win for the common people. A crowd cheered outside the Capitol as he took his oath of office. The massive crowd followed Jackson to a huge party on the White House lawn. The few police officers on hand had difficulty controlling the partygoers.

As president, Jackson rewarded some of his supporters with government jobs. This **spoils system**—the practice of giving government jobs to political backers—comes from the saying "to the victor belong the spoils [valued goods] of the enemy."

Secretary of State **Martin Van Buren** was one of Jackson's strongest allies in his official cabinet. President Jackson also relied a great deal on his **Kitchen Cabinet**, an informal group of trusted advisers who sometimes met in the White House kitchen.

READING CHECK **Analyzing** How might the spoils system cause disputes?

SUMMARY AND PREVIEW The expansion of democracy swept Andrew Jackson into office. In the next section you will read about the increasing regional tensions that occurred during Jackson's presidency.

Section 1 Assessment

go.hrw.com **Online Quiz** KEYWORD: SF7 HP10

Reviewing Ideas, Terms, and People

1. a. **Recall** What changes did the new western states make that allowed more people to vote?
   b. **Draw Conclusions** How did **nominating conventions** allow the people more say in politics?
   c. **Predict** How might changes to the voting process brought about by **Jacksonian Democracy** affect politics in the future?
2. a. **Recall** What two new political parties faced off in the election of 1828? Which candidate did each party support?
   b. **Make Inferences** Why did **Andrew Jackson** have more popular support than did Adams?
   c. **Evaluate** Do you think the **spoils system** was an acceptable practice? Explain your answer.

Critical Thinking

3. **Identifying Effect** Review your notes on the election of Andrew Jackson to the presidency. Then use a cause-and-effect chart like this one to show the ways in which Jacksonian Democracy increased Americans' political power.

FOCUS ON WRITING

4. **Noting Significance** As you read this section, note things that made Jackson's political campaign and election significant in the history of American politics.

Section 1 Assessment Answers

1. a. loosened voting requirements to let more white men vote; nominating conventions allowed party members to choose candidates
   b. by giving people more of a say in deciding a political party's candidates
   c. possible answer—expansion in voting might lead to elected officials who represent a broader range of the common people's views
2. a. Democrats—Andrew Jackson; National Republicans—John Quincy Adams
   b. Jackson was a popular war hero and seen as a self-made man; Adams was seen as elite and out of touch with everyday people.
   c. possible answers—yes, just reward for hard work; no, could lead to corruption
3. Students' charts might include the following: expansion of voting rights; involvement of people in nominating conventions; formation of Democratic Party
4. Students should note how the expansion of voting rights and political involvement and the election of Jackson signaled the growing political power of the American people.

BIOGRAPHY

Andrew Jackson

If you were president, how would you use your powers?

When did he live? 1767–1845

Where did he live? Jackson was born in Waxhaw, a region along the border of the North and South Carolina colonies. In 1788 he moved to Nashville, Tennessee, which was still a part of North Carolina. There he built a mansion called the Hermitage. He lived in Washington as president, then retired to the Hermitage, where he died.

What did he do? Jackson had no formal education, but he taught himself law and became a successful lawyer. He became Tennessee's first representative to the U.S. Congress and also served in the Senate. Jackson became a national hero when his forces defeated the Creek and Seminole Indians. He went on to battle the British in the Battle of New Orleans during the War of 1812. Jackson was elected as the nation's seventh president in 1828 and served until 1837.

Why is he so important? Jackson's belief in a strong presidency made him both loved and hated. He vetoed as many bills as the six previous presidents together. Jackson also believed in a strong Union. When South Carolina tried to nullify, or reject, a federal tariff, he threatened to send troops into the state to force it to obey.

Identifying Cause and Effect Why did Jackson gain loyal friends and fierce enemies?

KEY EVENTS

1796–1797
Served in the U.S. House of Representatives

1797–1798
Served in the U.S. Senate

1798–1804
Served on the Tennessee Supreme Court

1821
Governor of Florida Territory

1823–1825
Served in the U.S. Senate

1829–1837
Served as president of the United States

1832
Vetoed rechartering the Second Bank of the United States. Threatened to send troops to South Carolina when it tried to nullify a federal tariff

Jackson received a scar from a British officer as a boy.

Biography

Reading Focus Question

To help students discuss the introductory question, remind them of the president's powers, such as issuing proclamations and vetoing legislation. Then instruct students as they read the biography to note the ways in which Jackson used his powers as president.

Info to Know

"Old Hickory" Jackson's belief in a strong presidency paralleled his own strong will. He received the nickname "Old Hickory" during the War of 1812 because of his reputation for being as tough as the hard wood of a hickory tree. During the war, Jackson received orders to move his troops to Mississippi. When he arrived, he was told to disband the troops. Instead, Jackson marched his troops back to Tennessee. He walked the entire way because he had given his horse to a wounded soldier.

Jackson's Legacy In his own day, Jackson was extremely popular. Since his death, however, scholars have debated his legacy. On one hand, Jackson helped broaden democracy by pushing for the expansion of voting rights for white men. On the other hand, he did little to increase equality for other groups and violated Native Americans' treaty rights and legal claims. Perhaps most controversial is Jackson's interpretation of the balance of powers. Jackson insisted that Congress consult him before considering legislation. He also rejected the principle that the Supreme Court was the final interpreter of the laws.

Critical Thinking: Evaluating Information

At Level

Overheard Dinner Conversation

1. Ask students to imagine that they are attending a dinner in honor of Andrew Jackson and his contributions to the nation. At the next table, two people are arguing the merits of Jackson's legacy. Impressed by the points they are making, students decide to jot them down.
2. Have students create notes of the imaginary discussion at the next table. The discussion should address Jackson's presidency as well as his other actions in service to the nation. One person in the discussion should argue in favor of Jackson's greatness; the other should argue against it.
3. **Extend** Have students express and defend their own points of view of Jackson and his presidency.

Alternative Assessment Handbook, Rubrics 16: Judging Information; and 37: Writing Assignments

Answers

Identifying Cause and Effect *because of his belief in a strong presidency and because of his actions as president, such as his opposition to the Bank of the United States and the forced removal of the Cherokee*

Preteach

Bellringer

If YOU were there . . . Use the **Daily Bellringer Transparency** to help students answer the question.

Daily Bellringer Transparency 10.2

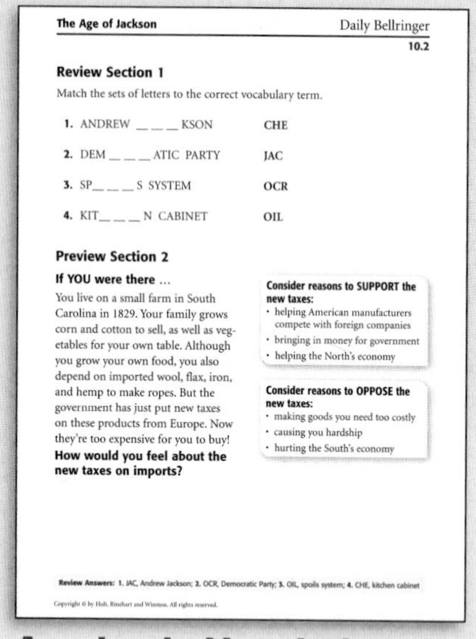

The Age of Jackson — Daily Bellringer **10.2**

Review Section 1

Match the sets of letters to the correct vocabulary term.

1.	ANDREW __ __ __ KSON	CHE
2.	DEM __ __ __ ATIC PARTY	JAC
3.	SP__ __ __ S SYSTEM	OCR
4.	KIT__ __ __ N CABINET	OIL

Preview Section 2

If YOU were there ...

You live on a small farm in South Carolina in 1829. Your family grows corn and cotton to sell, as well as vegetables for your own table. Although you grow your own food, you also depend on imported wool, flax, iron, and hemp to make ropes. But the government has just put new taxes on these products from Europe. Now they're too expensive for you to buy!

How would you feel about the new taxes on imports?

Consider reasons to SUPPORT the new taxes:
- helping American manufacturers compete with foreign companies
- bringing in money for government
- helping the North's economy

Consider reasons to OPPOSE the new taxes:
- making goods you need too costly
- causing you hardship
- hurting the South's economy

Review Answers: 1. JAC, Andrew Jackson; 2. OCR, Democratic Party; 3. OIL, spoils system; 4. CHE, kitchen cabinet

Academic Vocabulary

Review with students the high-use academic term in this section.

criteria basic requirements (p. 328)

CRF: Vocabulary Builder Activity, Section 2

Taking Notes

Have students copy the graphic organizer onto their own paper and then use it to take notes on the section. This activity will prepare students for the Section Assessment, in which they will complete a graphic organizer that builds on the information using a critical-thinking skill.

Section Correlations

IN

8.1.12 Explain the main issues, decisions and consequences of landmark Supreme Court cases. **8.1.17** Identify the key ideas of Jacksonian democracy and explain their influence on political participation, political parties and constitutional government. **8.2.10** Research and defend positions on issues in which fundamental values and principles related to the United States Constitution are in conflict, using a variety of information resources. **8.4.8** Examine the development of the banking system in the United States.

SECTION 2

Jackson's Administration

What You Will Learn...

Main Ideas

1. Regional differences grew during Jackson's presidency.
2. The rights of the states were debated amid arguments about a national tariff.
3. Jackson's attack on the Bank sparked controversy.
4. Jackson's policies led to the Panic of 1837.

The Big Idea

Andrew Jackson's presidency was marked by political conflicts.

Key Terms and People

Tariff of Abominations, *p. 327*
states' rights doctrine, *p. 328*
nullification crisis, *p. 328*
Daniel Webster, *p. 328*
McCulloch v. *Maryland*, *p. 330*
Whig Party, *p. 330*
Panic of 1837, *p. 331*
William Henry Harrison, *p. 331*

TAKING NOTES As you read, use a diagram like the one below to show the conflicts facing Andrew Jackson during his administration. Add more ovals to your organizer as necessary.

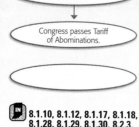

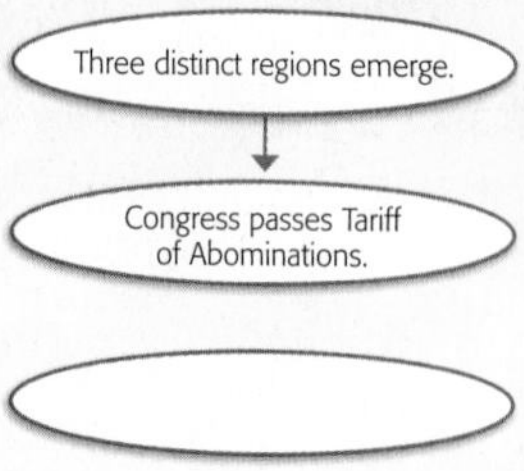

Three distinct regions emerge.
Congress passes Tariff of Abominations.

IN **8.1.10, 8.1.12, 8.1.17, 8.1.18, 8.1.28, 8.1.29, 8.1.30, 8.2.3, 8.2.10, 8.3.6, 8.4.4, 8.4.8**

If YOU were there...

You live on a small farm in South Carolina in 1829. Your family grows corn and cotton to sell, as well as vegetables for your own table. Although you grow your own food, you also depend on imported wool, flax, iron, and hemp to make ropes. But the government has just put new taxes on these products from Europe. Now they're too expensive for you to buy!

How would you feel about the new taxes on imports?

BUILDING BACKGROUND Even though Americans had a new feeling of national unity, different sections of the country still had very different interests. The industrial North competed with the agricultural South and the western frontier. As Congress favored one section over another, political differences grew.

Sectional Differences Increase

Regional differences had a major effect on Andrew Jackson's presidency. Americans' views of Jackson's policies were based on where they lived and the economy of those regions.

Three Regions Emerge

There were three main U.S. regions in the early 1800s. The North, first of all, had an economy based on trade and on manufacturing. Northerners supported tariffs because tariffs helped them compete with British factories. Northerners also opposed the federal government's sale of public land at cheap prices. Cheap land encouraged potential laborers to move from northern factory towns to the West.

The second region was the South. Its economy was based on farming. Southern farmers raised all types of crops, but the most popular were the cash crops of cotton and tobacco. Southerners sold a large portion of their crops to foreign nations.

Teach the Big Idea

At Level

Jackson's Administration

1. **Teach** To teach the main ideas in the section, use the questions in the Direct Teach boxes.
2. **Apply** For each of the section key terms and people, have students write a sentence explaining how that term or person relates to the sectional and/or political conflicts that took place during Jackson's presidency. Then have each student create a flowchart that links all the key terms and people. **LS Verbal/Linguistic, Visual/Spatial**
3. **Review** As you review the section's main ideas, have volunteers share the information they listed about each key term or person.
4. **Practice/Homework** Have each student select one of the key terms or people and write a news article about that event, issue, or person. **LS Verbal/Linguistic**

Alternative Assessment Handbook, Rubrics 7: Charts; and 42: Writing to Inform

326 CHAPTER 10

Regions of the United States, Early 1800s

QUICK FACTS

NORTH
- Economy based on manufacturing
- Support for tariffs—American goods could be sold at lower prices than could British goods

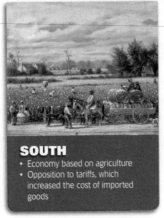

SOUTH
- Economy based on agriculture
- Opposition to tariffs, which increased the cost of imported goods

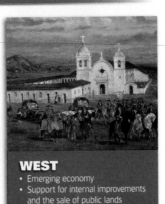

WEST
- Emerging economy
- Support for internal improvements and the sale of public lands

Southerners imported their manufactured goods. Tariffs made imported goods more expensive for southern farmers. In addition, high tariffs angered some of the South's European trading partners. These trading partners would likely raise their own tariffs in retaliation. To avoid this situation, southerners called for low tariffs.

Southerners also relied on enslaved African Americans to work the plantations. The issue of slavery would become increasingly controversial between the North and South.

In the third region, the West, the frontier economy was just emerging. Settlers favored policies that boosted their farming economy and encouraged further settlement. Western farmers grew a wide variety of crops. Their biggest priority was cheap land and internal improvements such as better roads and water transportation.

Tariff of Abominations

Tariffs became one of the first issues that President Jackson faced. In 1827, the year before Jackson's election, northern manufacturers began to demand a tariff on imported woolen goods. Northerners wanted the tariff to protect their industries from foreign competition, especially from Great Britain.

British companies were driving American ones out of business with their inexpensive manufactured goods. The tariff northerners supported, however, was so high that importing wool would be impossible. Southerners opposed the tariff, sayng it would hurt their economy.

Before Andrew Jackson took office, Congress placed a high tariff on imports. Angry southerners called it the **Tariff of Abominations**. (An abomination is a hateful thing.) Southern voters were outraged.

President John Quincy Adams signed the tariff legislation, though he did not fully support it. In early U.S. history, presidents tended to reserve veto power for legislation that they believed violated the Constitution. Signing the tariff bill meant Adams would surely be defeated in his re-election bid. The new tariff added fuel to the growing sectional differences plaguing the young nation.

READING CHECK **Summarizing** Describe the sectional economic differences in the United States during the early 1800s.

FOCUS ON INDIANA

Although Jackson won Indiana's electoral votes in 1824, 1828, and 1832, his party lost support in the state because of his economic policies. Sectional differences resulted in the state voting for Whig candidate and former Indiana Territory governor William Henry Harrison in 1836. Harrison lost the election, however.

Direct Teach

Main Idea

1 Sectional Differences Increase

Regional differences grew during Jackson's presidency.

Recall During Jackson's presidency, what was the main factor in determining whether people supported or opposed political policies? *the region where people lived*

Contrast Why were northerners and southerners at odds over tariffs? *because their economies differed; higher tariffs helped the industrial North but hurt the agricultural South*

Quick Facts Transparency 30: Regions of the United States, Early 1800s

Connect to Economics

Southerners and the Tariff Some southerners based opposition to tariffs on the "forty-bale" theory. According to this theory, a 40 percent tariff on imports made from cotton, such as clothing, would raise prices by 40 percent. This increase, in theory, would then reduce the purchase of cotton goods by 40 percent. As a result, manufacturers' demand for southern cotton would drop by 40 percent. Southerners argued that they then would lose the profit on 40 out of every 100 bales of cotton. Although the forty-bale theory was not sophisticated, it appealed to many southerners.

Analyze What are some possible weaknesses of the forty-bale theory? *possible answer—assumes that consumers will buy less when prices rise, which is not always the case with necessities, such as clothing*

Focus on Indiana

IN 8.1.17

Identify Cause and Effect Why did Jackson's political party lose power in Indiana? *People disagreed with his economic policies.*

Differentiating Instruction

Below Level

Struggling Readers

Materials: blank outline maps of the United States; colored pencils or markers

1. Give each student a blank outline map of the United States. Have students mark the nation's political borders in 1820. (Refer students to the map in the feature "History and Geography, America's Growth: 1820.")
2. Instruct students to draw caption boxes pointing roughly to the areas of the North, the South, and the West. Have students enter the information in the Quick Facts on this page into the appropriate boxes on their maps.
3. Then write three or four political issues of the period for students to see, such as tariffs, manufacturing, the sale of public lands, and internal improvements. Help students understand the views of each region toward each issue. **LS Verbal/Linguistic, Visual/Spatial**

Answers

Reading Check *See the Quick Facts at the top of the page for a summary.*

Direct Teach

Main Idea

② States' Rights Debate

The rights of the states were debated amid arguments about a national tariff.

Explain How did southerners use the states' rights doctrine to support the idea of nullification? *stated that states had the greater power and, thus, had the right to reject any federal law with which they disagreed*

Identify Points of View How did Webster and Jackson view the nullification crisis? *both opposed nullification; Webster—thought national unity was more important than states' rights; Jackson—threatened to use federal troops to enforce federal laws*

CRF: Biography Activities: John C. Calhoun; Daniel Webster

CRF: Primary Source Activity: President Jackson's Proclamation Regarding Nullification

go.hrw.com
Online Resources
KEYWORD: SF7 CH10
ACTIVITY: Nullification Crisis

Answers

Focus on Reading *that the debate further increased sectional tensions that would continue to divide the nation*

States' Rights Debate

When Andrew Jackson took office in 1829, he was forced to respond to the growing conflict over tariffs. At the core of the dispute was the question of an individual state's right to disregard a law that had been passed by the U.S. Congress.

Nullification Crisis

ACADEMIC VOCABULARY
criteria basic requirements

Early in his political career, Vice President John C. Calhoun had supported the criteria of a strong central government. But in 1828 when Congress passed the Tariff of Abominations, Calhoun joined his fellow southerners in protest. Economic depression and previous tariffs had severely damaged the economy of his home state, South Carolina. It was only beginning to recover in 1828. Some leaders in the state even spoke of leaving the Union over the issue of tariffs.

FOCUS ON READING
What conclusions can you draw about the importance of the states' rights debate after reading this section?

In response to the tariff, Calhoun drafted the *South Carolina Exposition and Protest*. It said that Congress should not favor one state or region over another. Calhoun used the *Protest* to advance the **states' rights doctrine**, which said that since the states had formed the national government, state power should be greater than federal power. He believed states had the right to nullify, or reject, any federal law they judged to be unconstitutional.

Calhoun's theory was controversial, and it drew some fierce challengers. Many of them were from the northern states that had benefited from increased tariffs. These opponents believed that the American people, not the individual states, made up the Union. Conflict between the supporters and the opponents of nullification deepened. The dispute became known as the **nullification crisis**.

Although he chose not to put his name on his *Exposition and Protest*, Calhoun did resign from the vice presidency. He was then elected to the Senate, where he continued his arguments in favor of nullification. Martin Van Buren replaced Calhoun as vice president when Jackson was re-elected president.

The Hayne-Webster Debate

The debate about states' rights began early in our nation's history. Thomas Jefferson and James Madison supported the states' power to disagree with the federal government in the Virginia and Kentucky Resolutions of 1798–99. Some of the delegates at the Hartford Convention supported states' rights. But Calhoun's theory went further. He believed that states could judge whether a law was or was not constitutional. This position put the power of the Supreme Court in question.

The issue of nullification was intensely debated on the floor of the Senate in 1830. Robert Y. Hayne, senator from South Carolina, defended states' rights. He argued that nullification gave states a way to lawfully protest federal legislation. **Daniel Webster** of Massachusetts argued that the United States was one nation, not a pact among independent states. He believed that the welfare of the nation should override that of individual states.

Jackson Responds

Although deeply opposed to nullification, Jackson was concerned about economic problems in the southern states. In 1832 he urged Congress to pass another tariff that lowered the previous rate. South Carolina thought the slight change was inadequate. The state legislature took a monumental step; it decided to test the doctrine of states' rights.

South Carolina's first action was to pass the Nullification Act, which declared the 1828 and 1832 tariffs "null, void ... [and not] binding upon this State, its officers or citizens." South Carolina threatened to withdraw from the Union if federal troops were used to collect duties. The legislature also voted to form its own army. Jackson was enraged.

The president sternly condemned nullification. Jackson declared that he would enforce the law in South Carolina. At his request, Congress passed the Force Bill,

Critical Thinking: Finding Main Ideas

At Level

Nullification Crisis Graphic Organizer

1. To help students understand the issues involved in the Nullification Crisis, draw the graphic organizer for students to see. Omit the blue, italicized answers.
2. Have each student copy the organizer and complete it by explaining the key figures, events, and issues on each side.
   LS Verbal/Linguistic, Visual/Spatial

Alternative Assessment Handbook, Rubric 13: Graphic Organizers

States' Rights
- **Southern opinion of tariffs:** *abominable*
- **States' Rights:** *state power should be greater than federal power*
- **Nullification:** *States have the right to nullify federal laws with which they disagree.*
- **John C. Calhoun:** *major proponent*

Nullification Crisis

Federal Authority
- **Daniel Webster:** *promoted national unity over states' rights*
- **President Jackson:** *opposed nullification*
- **Actions/Results:** *Jackson wanted to send troops to enforce tariffs; Congress and South Carolina compromised to lower tariffs gradually.*

approving use of the army if necessary. In light of Jackson's determined position, no other state chose to support South Carolina.

Early in 1833, Henry Clay of Kentucky had proposed a compromise that would gradually lower the tariff over several years. As Jackson's intentions became clear, both the U.S. Congress and South Carolina moved quickly to approve the compromise. The Congress would decrease the tariff, and South Carolina's leaders would enforce the law.

Despite the compromise, neither side changed its beliefs about states' rights. The argument continued for years, ending in the huge conflict known as the Civil War.

READING CHECK **Summarizing** What led to the nullification crisis, and why was it important?

Jackson Attacks the Bank

President Jackson upheld federal authority in the nullification crisis. He did not, however, always support greater federal power. For example, he opposed the Second Bank of the United States, founded by Congress in 1816.

The Second Bank of the United States was given a 20-year charter. This charter gave it the power to act exclusively as the federal government's financial agent. The Bank held federal deposits, made transfers of federal funds between states, and dealt with any payments or receipts involving the federal government. It also issued bank notes, or paper currency. Some 80 percent of the Bank was privately owned, but its operations were supervised by Congress and the president.

Many states, particularly in the South, had opposed the Bank. Small farmers believed that the Bank only helped wealthy businesspeople. Jackson also questioned the legality of the Bank. He believed it was an unconstitutional extension of the power of Congress. The states, he thought, should have the power to control the banking system.

Some states decided to take action. Maryland tried to pass a tax that would limit the

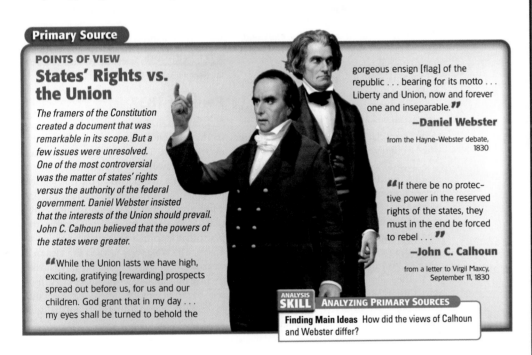

Primary Source

POINTS OF VIEW

States' Rights vs. the Union

The framers of the Constitution created a document that was remarkable in its scope. But a few issues were unresolved. One of the most controversial was the matter of states' rights versus the authority of the federal government. Daniel Webster insisted that the interests of the Union should prevail. John C. Calhoun believed that the powers of the states were greater.

"While the Union lasts we have high, exciting, gratifying [rewarding] prospects spread out before us, for us and our children. God grant that in my day . . . my eyes shall be turned to behold the gorgeous ensign [flag] of the republic . . . bearing for its motto . . . Liberty and Union, now and forever one and inseparable."

–Daniel Webster

from the Hayne-Webster debate, 1830

"If there be no protective power in the reserved rights of the states, they must in the end be forced to rebel . . ."

–John C. Calhoun

from a letter to Virgil Maxcy, September 11, 1830

ANALYSIS SKILL **ANALYZING PRIMARY SOURCES**

Finding Main Ideas How did the views of Calhoun and Webster differ?

Direct Teach

Main Idea

3 Jackson Attacks the Bank

Jackson's attack on the Bank sparked controversy.

Describe How did the state of Maryland try to take action against the Second Bank of the United States? *It passed a tax to limit the operations of the Bank's state branch and took the branch cashier, James McCulloch, to court when he refused to pay the tax.*

Identify Cause and Effect What occurred as a result of this action? *The case went to the U.S. Supreme Court, which ruled in* McCulloch v. Maryland *that the Bank was constitutional.*

Evaluate Were Jackson's actions to weaken the Bank's power effective? *His actions weakened the Bank's power and helped western expansion but also led to inflation, which hurt the economy.*

- Political Cartoons Activities for United States History, Cartoon 11: Jackson and the Bank
- **CRF:** Primary Source Activity: The Bank War of 1832—Two Views
- U.S. Supreme Court Case Studies: *McCulloch* v. *Maryland*

Differentiating Instruction

Above Level

Advanced/Gifted and Talented

1. Have each student write an outline of a chapter that might have appeared in Jackson's memoirs. The chapter should address Jackson's thoughts about the U.S. Supreme Court case *McCulloch* v. *Maryland* and the Second Bank of the United States, his actions to defeat the Bank, and how his actions affected the U.S. economy.
2. Pair students and have partners exchange outlines. Each student should then evaluate his or her partner's outline from the point of view of Jackson's publisher. Students should consider the clarity and order of the material and its publication value. Then have students revise their outlines based on the reviews.

LS Interpersonal, Verbal/Linguistic

Alternative Assessment Handbook, Rubric 42: Writing to Inform

Answers

Analyzing Primary Sources *Webster strongly supported federal power, whereas Calhoun supported the rights of the states.*

Reading Check *Southern states asserted their power to nullify tariffs, which most southerners opposed; it demonstrated the nation's growing sectionalism and division over the issue of federal versus state power.*

Direct Teach

Main Idea

4 Panic of 1837

Jackson's policies led to the Panic of 1837.

Define What was the Whig Party? *political party formed by a group of Jackson's opponents*

Explain What helped Van Buren win the election in 1836? *strong support from Jackson; division of Whig support among four candidates*

Analyze What role did the economy play in the presidential election of 1840? *The Panic of 1837 decreased support for the incumbent Van Buren, which helped Whig candidate William Henry Harrison win the election.*

CRF: Economics and History Activity: The Panic of 1837

Teaching Tip

Modernize the Symbol
The symbol of the hydra in the political cartoon at right may be unfamiliar to students. To help students understand the cartoon better, ask them to suggest images that political cartoonists today might use to portray either a difficult political problem for a president to solve or a president who is in a conflict with several political opponents.

Primary Source

POLITICAL CARTOON

Jackson against the Bank

Andrew Jackson's fight with the Bank was the subject of many political cartoons, like this one.

In this scene, Jackson is shown fighting a hydra that represents the national bank. The hydra is a mythological monster whose heads grow back when cut off. The heads of the hydra are portraits of politicians who opposed Jackson's policies.

Nicholas Biddle is at the center of the hydra. Why?
Andrew Jackson fights the hydra with a cane labeled "veto."
Why do you think the cartoonist chose this monster to represent the Bank?

ANALYSIS SKILL ANALYZING PRIMARY SOURCES

How does this image show the difficulty Jackson had politically?

Bank's operations. James McCulloch, cashier of the Bank's branch in Maryland, refused to pay this tax. The state took him to court, and the resulting case went all the way to the U.S. Supreme Court. In ***McCulloch v. Maryland***, the Court ruled that the national bank was constitutional.

Nicholas Biddle, the Bank's director, decided to push for a bill to renew the Bank's charter in 1832. Jackson campaigned for the bill's defeat. "I will kill it," he promised. True to his word, Jackson vetoed the legislation when Congress sent it to him.

Congress could not get the two-thirds majority needed to override Jackson's veto. Jackson also weakened the Bank's power by moving most of its funds to state banks. In many cases, these banks used the funds to offer easy credit terms to people buying land. While this practice helped expansion in the West, it also led to inflation.

In the summer of 1836 Jackson tried to slow this inflation. He ordered Americans to use only gold or silver—instead of paper state-bank notes—to buy government-owned land. This policy did not help the national economy as Jackson had hoped. Jackson did improve the economy by lowering the national debt. However, his policies opened the door for approaching economic troubles.

READING CHECK **Analyzing** Why did critics of the Second Bank of the United States oppose it?

Panic of 1837

Jackson was still very popular with voters in 1836. He chose not to run in 1836, however, and the Democrats nominated Vice President Martin Van Buren.

In 1834 a new political party had formed to oppose Jackson. Its members called themselves Whigs, after an English political party that opposed the monarchy, to make the point that Jackson was using his power like a king. The **Whig Party** favored the idea of a weak president and a strong Congress. Unable to agree on a candidate, the Whigs chose four men to run against Van Buren. Because of this indecision, and with backing from Jackson, Van Buren won the election.

Critical Thinking: Identifying Cause and Effect

At Level

1840 Whig Campaign Flyer

Materials: paper, colored markers, current political campaign flyer (optional)

1. Have each student create a campaign flyer supporting Whig candidate William Henry Harrison in the election of 1840.
2. Students' flyers should address the Panic of 1837, public views of Van Buren's presidency, and Harrison's background and character versus that of Van Buren's. If possible, provide students with a copy of a current political campaign advertisement to use as a model.
3. Ask for volunteers to explain their flyers to the class. Use the activity to launch a guided discussion of the causes and effects of the Panic of 1837 and the outcome of the election of 1840. **LS Intrapersonal, Visual/Spatial**

Alternative Assessment Handbook, Rubric 37: Writing Assignments

Answers

Analyzing Primary Sources *It shows that many politicians opposed Jackson's policies.*

Reading Check *Small farmers, particularly in the South, thought the Bank benefited only wealthy businesspeople; Jackson questioned the Bank's legality.*

The Supreme Court and Capitalism

CONNECT TO ECONOMICS

During the early 1800s, the Supreme Court made several rulings that helped define federal power over contracts and commerce. These rulings reinforced capitalism as the ruling economic system in the United States.

What effect did the Supreme Court have on economic development?

1810	1819		1824
Fletcher* v. *Peck State legislatures could not pass laws violating existing contracts.	***Dartmouth College* v. *Woodward*** State legislatures could not pass laws to change the charters of institutions or businesses.	***McCulloch* v. *Maryland*** States do not have the power to tax federal institutions.	***Gibbons* v. *Ogden*** Only the federal government has the power to regulate interstate and foreign commerce.

Shortly after Van Buren took office, the country experienced the **Panic of 1837**, a severe economic depression. Jackson's banking policies and his unsuccessful plan to curb inflation contributed to the panic. But people blamed Van Buren.

In 1840 the Whigs united against the weakened Van Buren to stand behind one candidate, **William Henry Harrison**, an army general. Harrison won in an electoral landslide. The Whigs had achieved their goal of winning the presidency.

READING CHECK **Identifying Cause and Effect** What contributed to the Panic of 1837, and how did it affect the 1840 election?

SUMMARY AND PREVIEW The states' rights debate dominated much of Jackson's presidency. In the next section you will learn about the removal of American Indians from the southeastern United States.

Section 2 Assessment

go.hrw.com
Online Quiz
KEYWORD: SF7 HP10

Reviewing Ideas, Terms, and People

1. **a. Recall** On what were the economies of the northern, southern, and western states based?
   b. Predict How might the sectional issues involved in the dispute over the **Tariff of Abominations** lead to future problems between North and South?
2. **a. Describe** What roles did **Daniel Webster** and John C. Calhoun play in the **nullification crisis**?
   b. Summarize What idea did supporters of the **states' rights doctrine** promote?
3. **a. Describe** What problems resulted from weakening the Bank?
   b. Draw Conclusions Why did Jackson veto the bill to renew the Second Bank of the United States?
4. **a. Recall** What caused the **Panic of 1837**?
   b. Summarize How did the **Whig Party** win the election of 1840?
   c. Elaborate Why do you think Jackson chose not to run for the presidency in 1836? Do you think he made the right decision? Why?

Critical Thinking

5. **Identifying Cause and Effect** Review your notes on the political conflicts during Jackson's administration. Then use a graphic organizer like the one below to show how some of Jackson's policies dealing with conflicts led to the Panic of 1837.

Jackson's Policies	→	Panic of 1837

FOCUS ON WRITING

6. **Identifying Important Conflicts** Stories about conflict sell newspapers. As you read this section, list important conflicts that occurred during Jackson's presidency and note the role Jackson played in creating or resolving the conflicts.

Direct Teach

Interpreting Charts

Supreme Court and Capitalism

Compare What do all four of these cases have in common? *issues of federal versus state authority*

Review & Assess

Close

Have students summarize how political and economic policies during Jackson's presidency contributed to sectional divisions in the nation.

Review

go.hrw.com Online Quiz, Section 10.2

Assess

SE Section 2 Assessment

PASS: Section Quiz 10.2

Alternative Assessment Handbook

Reteach/Classroom Intervention

Interactive Reader and Study Guide, Section 10.2

Interactive Skills Tutor CD-ROM

Section 2 Assessment Answers

1. **a.** North—trade and manufacturing, South—agriculture, West—farming and settlement
   b. possible answer—might have contributed to increased sectional divisions in Congress
2. **a.** Calhoun supported nullification and states' rights; Webster opposed nullification and supported national unity over states' rights.
   b. state power should be greater than federal
3. **a.** Smaller banks began offering easy credit terms for buying land, which led to inflation.
   b. did not think the Bank was constitutional
4. **a.** Jackson's banking policies; inflation
   b. united behind one candidate, Harrison, and emphasized his war record
   c. Students should note that Jackson's actions had angered many.
5. Jackson's policies—vetoed renewal of the national bank's charter; withdrew federal funds from the Bank and placed them in state banks; ordered purchases of government land be made in gold and silver
6. Notes should address conflicts listed above.

Answers

Connect to Economics *helped define federal power over contracts and commerce; reinforced capitalism*

Reading Check *cause—Jackson's banking policies and unsuccessful plan to curb inflation; effect—Whig Party candidate, William Henry Harrison, won the election of 1840*

Preteach

Bellringer

If YOU were there . . . Use the **Daily Bellringer Transparency** to help students answer the question.

Daily Bellringer Transparency 10.3

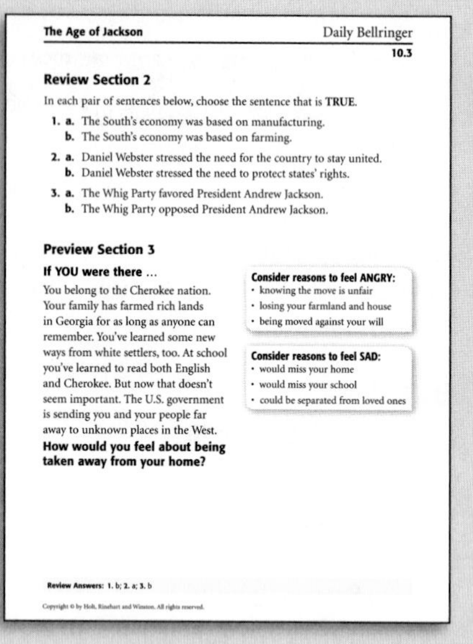

The Age of Jackson Daily Bellringer **10.3**

Review Section 2

In each pair of sentences below, choose the sentence that is **TRUE**.

1. **a.** The South's economy was based on manufacturing.
   b. The South's economy was based on farming.
2. **a.** Daniel Webster stressed the need for the country to stay united.
   b. Daniel Webster stressed the need to protect states' rights.
3. **a.** The Whig Party favored President Andrew Jackson.
   b. The Whig Party opposed President Andrew Jackson.

Preview Section 3

If YOU were there ...

You belong to the Cherokee nation. Your family has farmed rich lands in Georgia for as long as anyone can remember. You've learned some new ways from white settlers, too. At school you've learned to read both English and Cherokee. But now that doesn't seem important. The U.S. government is sending you and your people far away to unknown places in the West.

How would you feel about being taken away from your home?

Consider reasons to feel ANGRY:
- knowing the move is unfair
- losing your farmland and house
- being moved against your will

Consider reasons to feel SAD:
- would miss your home
- would miss your school
- could be separated from loved ones

Review Answers: 1. b; 2. a; 3. b

Academic Vocabulary

Review with students the high-use academic term in this section.

contemporary existing at the same time (p. 333)

CRF: Vocabulary Builder Activity, Section 3

Taking Notes

Have students copy the graphic organizer onto their own paper and then use it to take notes on the section. This activity will prepare students for the Section Assessment, in which they will complete a graphic organizer that builds on the information using a critical-thinking skill.

Section Correlations

IN

8.1.12 Explain the main issues, decisions and consequences of landmark Supreme Court cases. **8.1.17** Identify the key ideas of Jacksonian democracy and explain their influence on political participation, political parties and constitutional government. **8.1.24** Identify the influence of individuals on political and social events and movements, such as the abolition movement, the Dred Scott case, women's rights and Native American Indian removal.

SECTION 3

Indian Removal

What You Will Learn...

Main Ideas

1. The Indian Removal Act authorized the relocation of Native Americans to the West.
2. Cherokee resistance to removal led to disagreement between Jackson and the Supreme Court.
3. Other Native Americans resisted removal with force.

The Big Idea

President Jackson supported a policy of Indian removal.

Key Terms and People

Indian Removal Act, *p. 332*
Indian Territory, *p. 332*
Bureau of Indian Affairs, *p. 332*
Sequoya, *p. 333*
Worcester v. *Georgia*, *p. 334*
Trail of Tears, *p. 334*
Black Hawk, *p. 335*
Osceola, *p. 335*

TAKING NOTES As you read, use a graphic organizer like the one below to show the steps Andrew Jackson and the U.S. government took toward Indian removal.

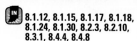

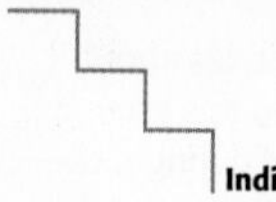

IN 8.1.12, 8.1.15, 8.1.17, 8.1.18, 8.1.24, 8.1.30, 8.2.3, 8.2.10, 8.3.1, 8.4.4, 8.4.8

If YOU were there...

You belong to the Cherokee nation. Your family has farmed rich lands in Georgia for as long as anyone can remember. You've learned some new ways from white settlers, too. At school you've learned to read both English and Cherokee. But now that doesn't seem important. The U.S. government is sending you and your people far away to unknown places in the West.

How would you feel about being taken away from your home?

BUILDING BACKGROUND President Andrew Jackson had become famous as an American Indian fighter. He had no sympathy with Native Americans' claim to the lands where they had always lived. With public support, he reversed the government's pledge to respect Indian land claims. The result was the brutal removal of the southeastern peoples to empty lands in the West.

Indian Removal Act

Native Americans had long lived in settlements stretching from Georgia to Mississippi. However, President Jackson and other political leaders wanted to open this land to settlement by American farmers. Under pressure from Jackson, Congress passed the **Indian Removal Act** in 1830, authorizing the removal of Native Americans who lived east of the Mississippi River to lands in the West.

Congress then established **Indian Territory**—U.S. land in what is now Oklahoma—and planned to move Native Americans there. Some supporters of this plan, like John C. Calhoun, argued that removal to Indian Territory would protect Indians from further conflicts with American settlers. "One of the greatest evils to which they are subject is that incessant [constant] pressure of our population," he noted. "To guard against this evil . . . there ought to be the strongest . . . assurance that the country given [to] them should be theirs." To manage Indian removal to western lands, Congress approved the creation of a new government agency, the **Bureau of Indian Affairs**.

Teach the Big Idea

At Level

Indian Removal

1. **Teach** To teach the main ideas in the section, use the questions in the Direct Teach boxes.
2. **Apply** Organize students into small groups. Assign each group one of the following: (1) Choctaw, Creek, and Chickasaw; (2) Cherokee; (3) Fox, Sauk, and Seminole. Have each group create a storyboard that uses images and captions to narrate how the policy of Indian removal affected its assigned Native American group(s). **LS Interpersonal, Visual/Spatial**
3. **Review** As you review the section, have each group explain its storyboard to the class.
4. **Practice/Homework** Have each student write a poem from the point of view of a Native American in response to the U.S. government's policy of Indian removal during this period. **LS Verbal/Linguistic**

Alternative Assessment Handbook, Rubrics 26: Poems and Songs; and 29: Presentations

Indian Removal

During the Trail of Tears, thousands of Cherokee died from disease, starvation, and harsh weather. They were forced to walk hundreds of miles to their new land in the West. Other Native Americans were also moved, with similar results.

What can you see in this painting that indicates this was a difficult journey?

The Choctaw were the first Indians sent to Indian Territory. The Mississippi legislature abolished the Choctaw government and then forced the Choctaw leaders to sign the Treaty of Dancing Rabbit Creek. This treaty gave more than 7.5 million acres of their land to the state. The Choctaw moved to Indian Territory during a disastrous winter trip. Federal officials in charge of the move did not provide enough food or supplies to the Choctaw, most of whom were on foot. About one-fourth of the Choctaw died of cold, disease, or starvation.

News of the Choctaw's hardships caused other Indians to resist removal. When the Creek resisted in 1836, federal troops moved in and captured some 14,500 of them. They led the Creek, many in chains, to Indian Territory. One Creek woman remembered the trip being filled with "the awful silence that showed the heartaches and sorrow at being taken from the homes and even separation from loved ones." The Chickasaw, who lived in upper Mississippi, negotiated a treaty for better supplies on their trip to Indian Territory. Nevertheless, many Chickasaw lives were also lost during removal.

READING CHECK **Finding Main Ideas** What major changes did President Jackson make to U.S. policy regarding Native Americans?

Cherokee Resistance

Many Cherokee had believed that they could prevent conflicts and avoid removal by adopting the contemporary culture of white people. In the early 1800s they invited missionaries to set up schools where Cherokee children learned how to read and write in English. The Cherokee developed their own government modeled after the U.S. Constitution with an election system, a bicameral council, and a court system. All of these were headed by a principal chief.

ACADEMIC VOCABULARY
contemporary existing at the same time

A Cherokee named **Sequoya** used 86 characters to represent Cherokee syllables to create a writing system for their own complex language. In 1828 the Cherokee began publishing a newspaper printed in both English and Cherokee.

The adoption of white culture did not protect the Cherokee. After gold was discovered on their land in Georgia, their treaty rights

Direct Teach

Main Idea

1 Indian Removal Act

The Indian Removal Act authorized the relocation of Native Americans to the West.

Explain Why did government officials want to relocate Native Americans in the Southeast to lands in the West? *to open the Indians' land to white settlers*

Identify Points of View Based on their actions, how do you think Native Americans viewed the Indian Removal Act? *possible answers—with outrage, fear, helplessness, desire to fight the act*

Predict How might the Southeast be different today if Native Americans had successfully resisted removal? *possible answer—Native Americans might form a larger percentage of the region's population, hold more positions of leadership, and have had a greater influence on the region.*

go.hrw.com
Online Resources
KEYWORD: SF7 CH10
ACTIVITY: Indian Removal

Critical Thinking: Supporting a Point of View

Above Level

Speech Opposing Indian Removal Act

1. Ask students to imagine that they were members of Congress during the debate over the passage of the Indian Removal Act. Have each student write and deliver a speech that a Congress member opposed to the act might have given.
2. Students' speeches should address the purpose of the act, the terms of the act, and the potential effects of the act for both Native Americans and white settlers.
3. Remind students to provide support for their points of view and to address possible arguments against their positions.
4. Have each student deliver his or her speech to the class. Conclude by having students discuss the short-and long-term effects of the Indian Removal Act. LS **Logical/Mathematical, Verbal/Linguistic**

Alternative Assessment Handbook, Rubric 24: Oral Presentations

Answers

Indian Removal *The way the people are bundled up to stay warm indicates cold weather; The expressions on people's faces and the amount of property they are moving suggests a long, hard journey.*

Reading Check *authorized the removal of Native Americans who lived east of the Mississippi River to lands to the west in Indian Territory*

Direct Teach

Main Idea

2 Cherokee Resistance

Cherokee resistance to removal led to disagreement between Jackson and the Supreme Court.

Explain Why did the adoption of white culture not protect the Cherokee from removal? *because gold was discovered on their land*

Summarize What steps did the Cherokee take to try to resist removal, and what was the result? *They sued the state, and their case went to the Supreme Court, which ruled in their favor; the state of Georgia ignored the ruling and removed them anyway; during the Trail of Tears, many Cherokee died.*

CRF: Biography Activity: Sequoya

U.S. Supreme Court Case Studies: *Worcester* v. *Georgia* (1832)

Connect to Government

Worcester* v. *Georgia The status of Indian nations in the courts remained undefined until the Supreme Court case *Worcester* v. *Georgia*. In his decision, Chief Justice John Marshall wrote that the "acts of Georgia are repugnant to the Constitution . . . [and] in direct hostility with treaties [that] . . . solemnly pledge the faith of the United States to restrain their citizens from trespassing on [Cherokee land]."

were ignored. Georgia leaders began preparing for the Cherokee's removal. When they refused to move, the Georgia militia began attacking Cherokee towns. In response, the Cherokee sued the state. They said that they were an independent nation and claimed that the government of Georgia had no legal power over their lands.

In 1832 the Supreme Court, under the leadership of Chief Justice John Marshall, agreed. In ***Worcester* v. *Georgia*** the Court ruled that the Cherokee nation was a distinct community in which the laws of Georgia had no force. The Court also stated that only the federal government, not the states, had authority over Native Americans.

THE IMPACT TODAY

Today more than 150,000 Cherokee or Cherokee descendants live in present-day Oklahoma.

Georgia, however, ignored the Court's ruling, and President Jackson took no action to make Georgia follow the ruling. "John Marshall has made his decision; now let him enforce it," Jackson supposedly said. By not enforcing the Court's decision, Jackson violated his presidential oath to uphold the laws of the land. However, most members of Congress and American citizens did not protest the ways Jackson removed Native Americans.

In the spring of 1838, U.S. troops began to remove all Cherokee to Indian Territory. A few were able to escape and hide in the mountains of North Carolina. After the Cherokee were removed, Georgia took their businesses, farms, and property.

The Cherokee's 800-mile forced march became known as the **Trail of Tears**. During the march, the Cherokee suffered from disease, hunger, and harsh weather. Almost one-fourth of the 18,000 Cherokee died on the march.

READING CHECK **Finding Main Ideas** What was the *Worcester* v. *Georgia* ruling, and what was Jackson's response?

Primary Source

PERSONAL ACCOUNTS

Trail of Tears

The Cherokee knew that they would be forced to march West, but they did not know that so many of their people would die on the way. Here are two accounts of the Trail of Tears, one written before it started and one written after, both by Cherokee who made the trip.

March 10, 1838
Beloved Martha, I have delayed writing to you so long . . . If we Cherokees are to be driven to the west by the cruel hand of oppression to seek a new home in the west, it will be impossible . . . It is thus all our rights are invaded."

—Letter from Jenny, a Cherokee girl, just before her removal

"Long time we travel on way to new land. People feel bad when they leave Old Nation. Women cry and make sad wails, Children cry and many men cry . . . but they say nothing and just put heads down and keep on go towards West. Many days pass and people die very much."

—Recollections of a survivor of the Trail of Tears

ANALYSIS SKILL **ANALYZING POINTS OF VIEW**

1. What is different about the concerns of the Cherokee before and after the Trail of Tears?
2. How do you think the survivors of the Trail of Tears felt when they reached Indian Territory?

Cross-Discipline Activity: Art

Below Level

Native American Removal Memorial

Materials: art supplies; images of memorials, such as Vietnam Veterans Memorial (optional)

1. Have students describe the main actions and events that led to the removal of Native American groups in the Southeast.
2. Then have students, working either individually or in small groups, design memorials for the many Native Americans in the Southeast who died either resisting removal or being forcibly removed. Give students choices for their memorials, such as a statue, a plaque, or a marker to set along the route of the Trail of Tears. Each student or group should write a paragraph explaining the memorial.
3. Display the memorials in the classroom.

LS Verbal/Linguistic, Visual/Spatial

Alternative Assessment Handbook, Rubric 3: Artwork

Answers

Analyzing Points of View

1. *before—author is concerned about rights, tone is angry; after—author concerned about the tragedy of the Trail of Tears.* **2.** *possible answers—exhausted, sad, angry, relieved*

Reading Check *The Supreme Court ruled that the laws of Georgia did not apply to the Cherokee nation; Jackson did not take any action to enforce the Court's ruling.*

Other Native Americans Resist

Other Native Americans decided to fight U.S. troops to avoid removal. Chief **Black Hawk**, a leader of Fox and Sauk Indians, led his people in a struggle to protect their lands in Illinois. By 1832, however, the Sauk forces were running out of food and supplies, and by 1850 they had been forced to leave.

In Florida, Seminole leaders were forced to sign a removal treaty that their followers decided to ignore. A leader named **Osceola** called upon his people to resist with force, and the Second Seminole War began. Osceola was captured and soon died in prison. His followers, however, continued to fight. Some 4,000 Seminole were removed and hundreds of others killed. Eventually, U.S. officials decided to give up the fight. Small groups of Seminole had resisted removal, and their descendants live in Florida today.

READING CHECK **Evaluating** How effective was Native American resistance to removal?

Second Seminole War

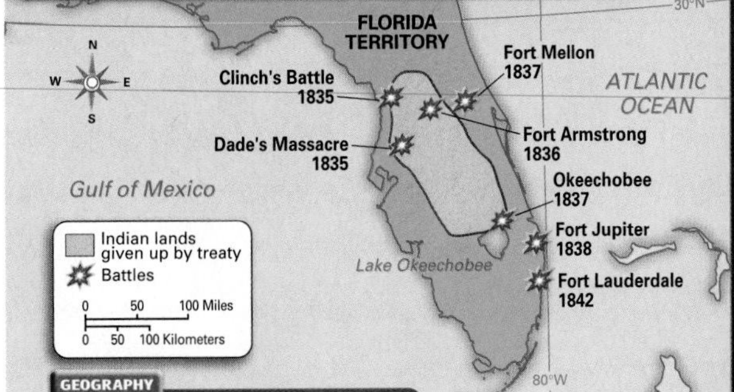

GEOGRAPHY SKILLS **INTERPRETING MAPS**

1. **Location** In what parts of Florida was the Second Seminole War fought?
2. **Place** Where was the last battle of the Second Seminole War fought?

SUMMARY AND PREVIEW President Jackson supported the removal of thousands of Native Americans from their traditional lands to the federal territory in the West. In the next chapter you will learn about the westward growth of the nation as farmers, ranchers, and other settlers moved West.

FOCUS ON INDIANA

The treaty that resulted in the Black Hawk War had been negotiated by William Henry Harrison when he was the governor of Indiana Territory.

Section 3 Assessment

go.hrw.com **Online Quiz** KEYWORD: SF7 HP10

Reviewing Ideas, Terms, and People

1. a. **Identify** What Native American groups were affected by the **Indian Removal Act**? Where were they relocated?
   b. **Explain** Why did government officials want to relocate Native Americans to the West?
   c. **Predict** What are some possible effects that the Indian Removal Act might have on Native Americans already living in the West?
2. a. **Identify** What was the **Trail of Tears**?
   b. **Analyze** Why did the state of Georgia want to relocate the Cherokee, and what did the Cherokee do in response?
   c. **Elaborate** What do you think of President Jackson's refusal to enforce the ***Worcester* v. *Georgia*** ruling?
3. a. **Describe** What led to the Second Seminole War?
   b. **Compare and Contrast** How were the Seminole and the Sauk resistance efforts similar and different?

Critical Thinking

4. **Comparing and Contrasting** Review your notes on Indian removal. Then copy the chart below and use it to identify the Native American groups and their responses to removal.

Native American Group	Response to Removal

FOCUS ON WRITING

5. **Understanding Causes and Effects** As you read, identify the causes and effects of the Jackson administration's policy of Indian relocation.

Section 3 Assessment Answers

1. a. Choctaw, Creek, Chickasaw, Cherokee, Fox, Sauk, Seminole; Indian Territory
   b. to open up more lands for settlement
   c. possible answer—conflict with newcomers, competition for resources
2. a. 800-mile forced march of the Cherokee from their lands in Georgia to Indian Territory, during which many Cherokee died
   b. why—gold had been found on their lands; Cherokee response—sued state of Georgia
   c. possible answers—His decision was unfair and possibly unconstitutional.
3. a. When Seminole leaders were forced to sign a removal treaty, other Seminole fought.
   b. similar—both resisted; different—Sauk were removed, groups of Seminole stayed
4. Choctaw and Chickasaw—sent to Indian Territory; Cherokee—adopted white culture then sued state, sent to Indian Territory; Sauk—fought, removed; Seminole—fought, ultimately successful in resistance
5. Students should indicate that the Indian removal policy led to the removal and death of many Native Americans in the Southeast.

Direct Teach

Main Idea

3 Other Native Americans Resist

Other Native Americans resisted removal with force.

Identify and Compare Who were Chief Black Hawk and Osceola, and what did they have in common? *Black Hawk—leader of Fox and Sauk Indians; Osceola—Seminole leader; both called on followers to resist removal with force*

- **CRF:** Biography Activity: Black Hawk
- **CRF:** History and Geography Activity: The Seminole Wars
- **CRF:** Literature Activity: *Surrender Speech* by Chief Black Hawk
- Map Transparency 37: Second Seminole War

Review & Assess

Close

Have students summarize the effects of Jackson's Indian removal policy.

Review

go.hrw.com Online Quiz, Section 10.3

Assess

SE Section 3 Assessment

PASS: Section Quiz 10.3

Alternative Assessment Handbook

Focus on Indiana

8.1.5 Explain the concept of Manifest Destiny and describe its impact on westward expansion of the United States.

Evaluate What role did Harrison's treaty play in the beginning of the Black Hawk War? *Black Hawk chose to fight because he did not agree with the treaty.*

Answers

Interpreting Maps **1.** *East coast and north central;* **2.** *Fort Lauderdale*

Reading Check *Overall, not effective, although some Native Americans successfully resisted removal.*

History and Geography

Activity **Analyzing Trends and Patterns** Read aloud to students the information in the feature and then lead a discussion about Indian removal and its effects. Next, have students examine the table and the map and look for trends and patterns in U.S.–Native American relations. Have volunteers identify trends and patterns. *(trends—Over time the U.S. government offered Native Americans a decreasing amount of money and then land in exchange for Indian land in treaties. The land offered amounted to removal. patterns—pattern of conflict, treaties, and removal)* To extend the activity, have each student write a short essay summarizing trends and patterns in Indian removal treaties and the effects of the treaties.
LS Verbal/Linguistic

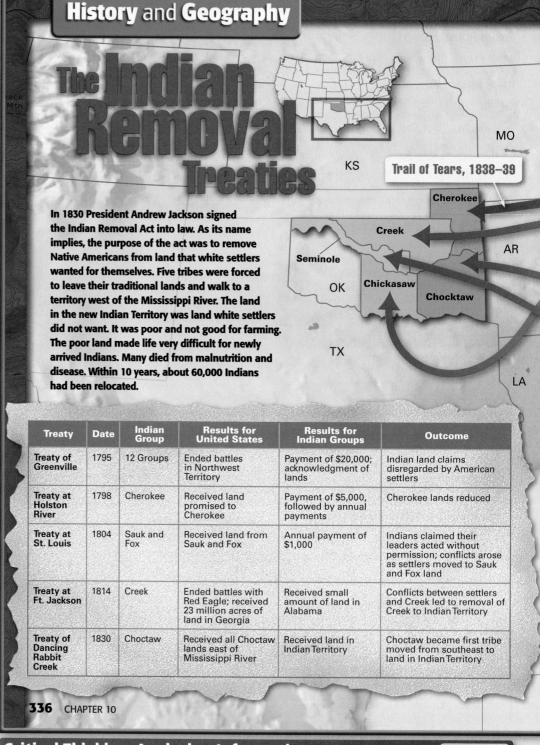

History and Geography

The Indian Removal Treaties

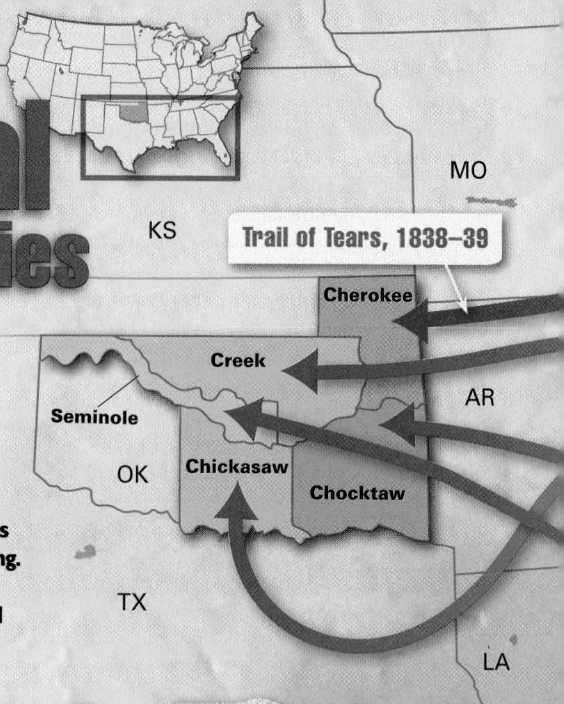

In 1830 President Andrew Jackson signed the Indian Removal Act into law. As its name implies, the purpose of the act was to remove Native Americans from land that white settlers wanted for themselves. Five tribes were forced to leave their traditional lands and walk to a territory west of the Mississippi River. The land in the new Indian Territory was land white settlers did not want. It was poor and not good for farming. The poor land made life very difficult for newly arrived Indians. Many died from malnutrition and disease. Within 10 years, about 60,000 Indians had been relocated.

Treaty	Date	Indian Group	Results for United States	Results for Indian Groups	Outcome
Treaty of Greenville	1795	12 Groups	Ended battles in Northwest Territory	Payment of $20,000; acknowledgment of lands	Indian land claims disregarded by American settlers
Treaty at Holston River	1798	Cherokee	Received land promised to Cherokee	Payment of $5,000, followed by annual payments	Cherokee lands reduced
Treaty at St. Louis	1804	Sauk and Fox	Received land from Sauk and Fox	Annual payment of $1,000	Indians claimed their leaders acted without permission; conflicts arose as settlers moved to Sauk and Fox land
Treaty at Ft. Jackson	1814	Creek	Ended battles with Red Eagle; received 23 million acres of land in Georgia	Received small amount of land in Alabama	Conflicts between settlers and Creek led to removal of Creek to Indian Territory
Treaty of Dancing Rabbit Creek	1830	Choctaw	Received all Choctaw lands east of Mississippi River	Received land in Indian Territory	Choctaw became first tribe moved from southeast to land in Indian Territory

336 CHAPTER 10

Critical Thinking: Analyzing Information

At Level

Effects of Indian Removal

Materials: 18" × 12" sheets of light-colored construction paper

1. Organize students into groups of three. Have each group select one sign maker. The other two members will serve as writers.
2. Distribute one sheet of construction paper to each group. Have the sign maker fold the paper to make two sections that are 9" × 12" and then open the sheet. Instruct students to write Indian Relocation across the top of the page and label the two columns *Effects on Native Americans' Lives* and *Effects on Settlers' Lives.*
3. Instruct the groups to discuss the ways that lives were changed by Indian removal and treaties and have writers record the group's observations in the appropriate columns.
4. Have group volunteers share some of their observations with the class. **LS Interpersonal, Verbal/Linguistic**

Alternative Assessment Handbook, Rubrics 7: Charts; and 14: Group Activity

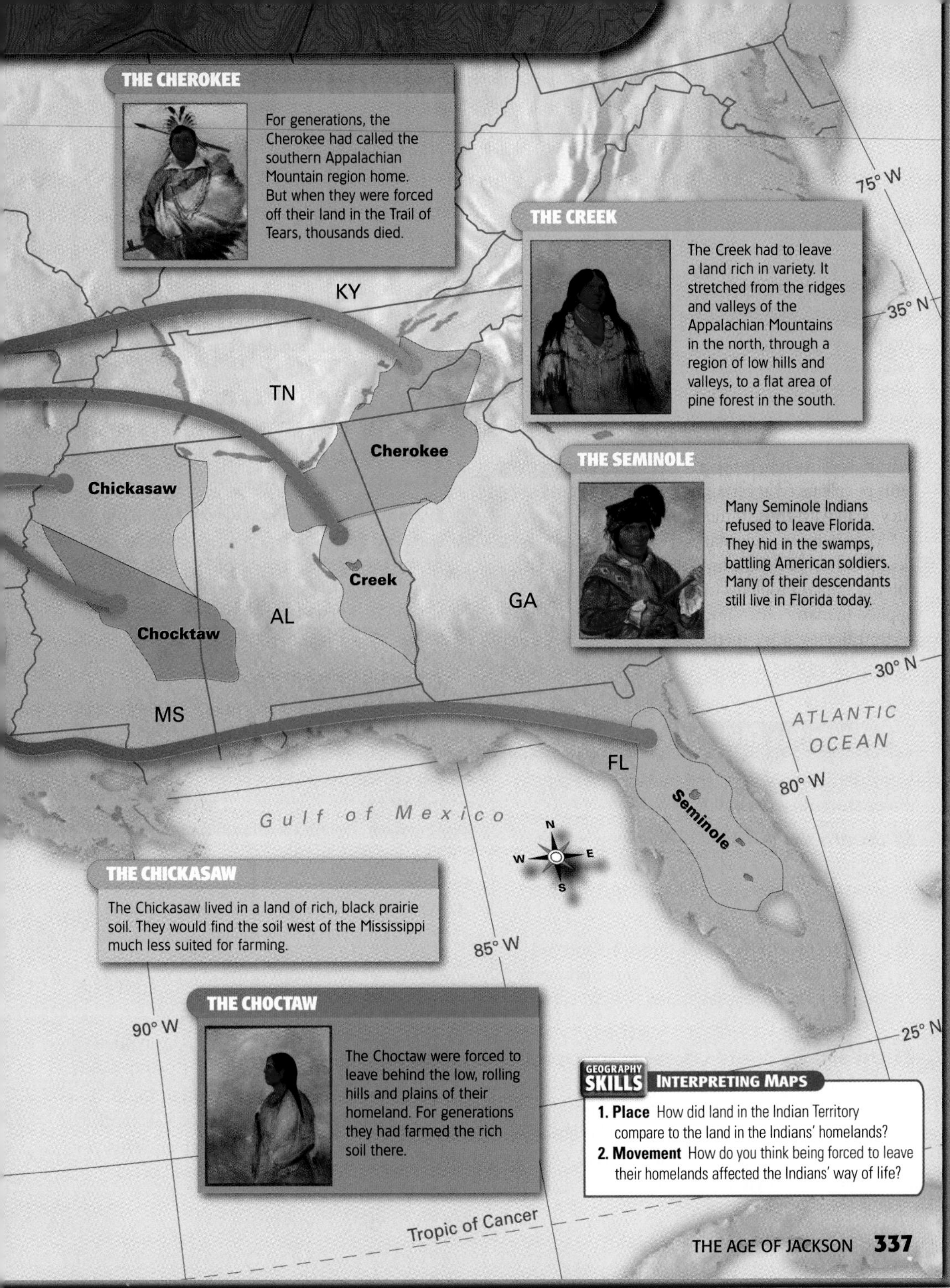

THE CHEROKEE
For generations, the Cherokee had called the southern Appalachian Mountain region home. But when they were forced off their land in the Trail of Tears, thousands died.
THE CREEK
The Creek had to leave a land rich in variety. It stretched from the ridges and valleys of the Appalachian Mountains in the north, through a region of low hills and valleys, to a flat area of pine forest in the south.
THE SEMINOLE
Many Seminole Indians refused to leave Florida. They hid in the swamps, battling American soldiers. Many of their descendants still live in Florida today.
THE CHICKASAW
The Chickasaw lived in a land of rich, black prairie soil. They would find the soil west of the Mississippi much less suited for farming.
THE CHOCTAW
The Choctaw were forced to leave behind the low, rolling hills and plains of their homeland. For generations they had farmed the rich soil there.
KY
TN
Cherokee
Chickasaw
Creek
Chocktaw
AL
GA
MS
FL
Seminole
Gulf of Mexico
ATLANTIC OCEAN
75° W
35° N
30° N
80° W
85° W
90° W
25° N
Tropic of Cancer
N
S
E
W

GEOGRAPHY SKILLS **INTERPRETING MAPS**

1. **Place** How did land in the Indian Territory compare to the land in the Indians' homelands?
2. **Movement** How do you think being forced to leave their homelands affected the Indians' way of life?

History and Geography

Linking to Today

Native American Populations A little less than half of the 2 million Native Americans in the United States today live on or near the nation's more than 250 Indian reservations. Each year the Native American population continues to grow. Of the total number of Native Americans, the majority live west of the Mississippi River, particularly in Arizona, California, Oklahoma, New Mexico, and South Dakota.

Info to Know

Native American Literacy While in the Cherokee Regiment of the U.S. Army in the early 1800s, Sequoya recognized the need for Native American literacy. Many Native Americans were unable to read military orders, send letters home, record events, or even read the treaties they signed. The creation of Talking Leaves, the Cherokee written language, had begun.

Linking to Today

The Cherokee Historians estimate that when Europeans arrived in North America, about 22,000 Cherokee lived in the present-day southeastern United States. Today the largest concentrations of Cherokee are the Eastern Band in North Carolina and the Cherokee Nation of Oklahoma. The federal government also recognizes one other Cherokee group, the United Bank of Keetoowahs, in Oklahoma. More than 50 other groups that are not recognized by the federal government also claim Cherokee heritage.

Cross-Discipline Activity: Geography

At Level

Comparing and Contrasting Regions

Research Required

1. Organize students into five groups and assign each group one of the Native American groups labeled on the map.
2. Have each group conduct research on the climate and physical geography of the assigned group's traditional homelands as well as the climate and physical geography of the area to which the group was relocated.
3. Instruct each group to create a large table comparing and contrasting the two regions. Encourage students to include images or photographs of the regions to enhance their tables. Groups should then write a summary of the differences between the two regions.
4. Have each group present its work to the class.
5. Have students discuss how geographic differences contributed to the hardships Native Americans faced when forced to relocate.

LS Interpersonal, Verbal/Linguistic

Alternative Assessment Handbook, Rubrics 7: Charts; 14: Group Activity; and 30: Research

Answers

Interpreting Maps **1.** *The land in Indian Territory was poor and not good for farming, whereas many of the relocated Indians came from areas with fertile soils, plains, and rolling hills.*
2. *possible answer—They had to adjust to a new climate and learn how to hunt differently, grow food differently, and rely on different materials for their homes and clothing.*

Social Studies Skills

Solving Problems

Activity Problem-Solving Role Play Organize students into groups to practice their problem-solving skills. Assign each group a current or hypothetical issue or problem within the school or community. Then have each group address this issue by writing an outline incorporating the steps included on this page. Groups should begin by identifying the problem and should conclude by suggesting a solution. Have a volunteer from each group present his or her group's outline to the class. Encourage other students to evaluate each group's solution. **LS Interpersonal, Logical/Mathematical**

- Alternative Assessment Handbook, Rubric 35: Solving Problems
- Interactive Skills Tutor CD-ROM: Lessons 12: Identify Issues and Problems; and 16: Identify Possible Solutions and Predict Consequences
- **CRF**: Social Studies Skills Activity, Solving Problems

Answers

Practice the Skill 1. *The South Carolina legislature passed a resolution nullifying the tariffs of 1828 and 1832 and threatened to secede if the federal government used force to try to collect the duties. This situation posed a problem because it threatened federal authority and the Union.* **2.** *passage of the 1832 tariff; passage of the 1828 tariffs and the states' rights doctrine;* **3.** *Answers will vary, but students should provide logical advantages and disadvantages for each proposed solution.* **4.** *Answers will vary, but students should exhibit an understanding of the advantages and disadvantages of using troops and provide reasons to support why another solution, if offered, would have been better.*

Social Studies Skills

Analysis | **Critical Thinking** | Civic Participation | Study

Solving Problems

Define the Skill

Problem solving is a process for finding workable solutions to difficult situations. The process involves asking questions, identifying and evaluating information, comparing and contrasting, and making judgments. Problem solving is useful in studying history because it helps you better understand problems people faced at certain points in time and how they dealt with those difficulties.

The ability to understand and evaluate how people solved problems in the past also can help in solving similar problems today. The skill can also be applied to many other kinds of difficulties besides historical ones. It is a method for thinking through almost any situation.

Learn the Skill

Using the following steps will enable you to better understand and solve problems.

1. **Identify the problem.** Ask questions of yourself and others to make sure you know exactly what the situation is and understand why it is a problem.
2. **Gather information.** Ask questions and conduct research to learn more about the problem, such as its history, what caused it, what contributes to it, and other factors.
3. **List options.** Based on the information you have gathered, identify possible options for solving the problem that you might consider. Be aware that your final solution will probably be better and easier to reach if you have as many options as possible to consider.
4. **Evaluate the options.** Weigh each option you are considering. Think of and list the advantages it has as a solution, as well as its potential disadvantages.
5. **Choose and implement a solution.** After comparing the advantages and disadvantages of each possible solution, choose the one that seems best and apply it.
6. **Evaluate the solution.** Once the solution has been tried, evaluate its effectiveness in solving the problem. This step will tell you if the solution was a good one, or if another of the possible solutions should be tried instead.

Practice the Skill

One of the most challenging situations that President Jackson faced was the nullification crisis. You can use the problem-solving skills to better understand this problem and to evaluate his solution for it. Review the information about the nullification crisis in this chapter. Then answer the questions below.

1. What was the specific problem that Jackson faced? Why was it a problem?
2. What event led to the problem? What earlier circumstances and conditions contributed to it?
3. List possible solutions to the problem that you would have considered if you had been president, along with advantages and disadvantages.
4. Jackson threatened to send troops to South Carolina to enforce federal law. Do you think his solution was the best one? Explain why, or if not, what solution would have been better.

Social Studies Skills Activity: Solving Problems

At Level

Alternate Solutions to Indian Removal

1. Have students review the text in Section 3 under the headings "Indian Removal Act" and "Cherokee Resistance."
2. Organize students into groups and ask the groups to imagine that they are members of the U.S. Congress at that time. Have each group consider a solution to the problem of American settlers wanting to move into Native American lands that does not require forcing Native Americans to move and that respects their right to their lands.
3. Each group should create a flow chart showing its responses for each of the steps listed under "Learn the Skill."
4. Have a representative from each group present his or her group's flow chart to the class. Have students evaluate each group's proposed solution and discuss possible advantages and disadvantages. **LS Interpersonal, Logical/Mathematical**

- Alternative Assessment Handbook, Rubrics 14: Group Activity; and 35: Solving Problems

CHAPTER 10 Chapter Review

HOLT
History's Impact
▶ **video series**
Review the video to answer the closing question:
How may the U.S. government's early treatment of Native Americans have contributed to the reservations' current situation?

Visual Summary

QUICK FACTS

Use the visual summary below to help you review the main ideas of the chapter.

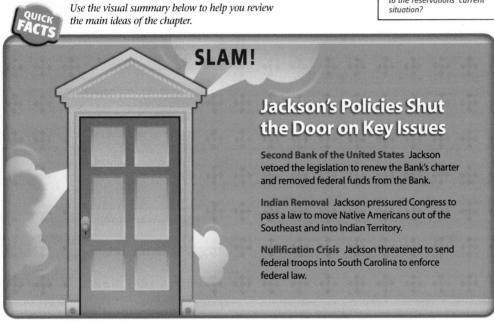

Jackson's Policies Shut the Door on Key Issues

Second Bank of the United States Jackson vetoed the legislation to renew the Bank's charter and removed federal funds from the Bank.

Indian Removal Jackson pressured Congress to pass a law to move Native Americans out of the Southeast and into Indian Territory.

Nullification Crisis Jackson threatened to send federal troops into South Carolina to enforce federal law.

Reviewing Vocabulary, Terms, and People

Complete each sentence by filling in the blank with the correct term or person.

1. In the Supreme Court case of ______________, the Court ruled that the federal government, not the states, had authority over the Cherokee.
2. President Jackson's group of advisers was known as the ____________ because of where its members met in the White House.
3. ____________ served as Andrew Jackson's vice president until he resigned due to the dispute over nullification.
4. The ____________ supported the power of the states over the federal government.
5. The practice of rewarding supporters with positions in government is known as the ______.

Comprehension and Critical Thinking

SECTION 1 *(Pages 322–324)*

6. a. **Identify** What changes took place in the early 1800s that broadened democracy in the United States?
   b. **Analyze** How was Jackson's victory in the election of 1828 a reflection of a change in American politics?
   c. **Evaluate** Do you think the changes brought about by Jacksonian Democracy went far enough in expanding democracy? Why or why not?

SECTION 2 *(Pages 326–331)*

7. a. **Describe** What conflicts troubled the Jackson administration?

Answers

History's Impact

Video Series If Native Americans hadn't been forced to relocate, their economy, health, and living conditions might be different.

Visual Summary

Review and Inquiry Ask students how the images in the Visual Summary relate to the chapter content. Ask: What is the significance of the door slammed shut? What other symbols could be used to represent some of Jackson's policies?

Quick Facts Transparency 31: The Age of Jackson Visual Summary

Reviewing Vocabulary, Terms, and People

1. *Worcester* v. *Georgia*
2. Kitchen Cabinet
3. John C. Calhoun
4. states' rights doctrine
5. spoils system

Comprehension and Critical Thinking

6. a. States expanded voting rights to enable more white men to vote; some states allowed voters to nominate electors; political parties held nominating conventions.
   b. More people had the vote, and Jackson and Calhoun received a record number of popular votes.
   c. Voting rights expanded but excluded African Americans, Native Americans, and women.

Review and Assessment Resources

Review and Reinforce

- SE Chapter Review
- **CRF:** Chapter Review Activity
- Quick Facts Transparency 31: The Age of Jackson Visual Summary
- Spanish Chapter Summaries Audio CD Program
- Online Chapter Summaries in Spanish
- OSP Holt PuzzlePro; GameTool for ExamView
- Quiz Game CD-ROM

Assess

- SE Standardized Test Practice
- PASS: Chapter 10 Tests, Forms A and B
- Alternative Assessment Handbook
- OSP ExamView Test Generator, Chapter Test
- Differentiated Instruction Modified Worksheets and Tests CD-ROM: Chapter Test
- HOAP Holt Online Assessment Program (in the Premier Online Edition)

Reteach/Intervene

- Interactive Reader and Study Guide
- Differentiated Instruction Teacher Management System: Lesson Plans for Differentiated Instruction
- Differentiated Instruction Modified Worksheets and Tests CD-ROM
- Interactive Skills Tutor CD-ROM

go.hrw.com
Online Resources
Chapter Resources:
KEYWORD: SF7 CH10

Answers

7. a. Tariff of Abominations, nullification crisis, issues connected to the Second Bank of the United States, inflation
b. led to Jackson's veto, inflation of the economy, and angered members of Congress
c. possible answer—might lead to increasing sectional divisions in the nation that could possibly threaten the unity of the nation

8. a. Cherokee who created a writing system for the Cherokee language
b. Cherokee—adopted white culture, appealed to the U.S. courts; Seminole—fought
c. possible answers—Yes, he did not personally agree with the decision; no, Jackson failed to fulfill his duties as president and to respect the power of the judiciary.

Reviewing Themes

9. Whig Party; favored a weak president

10. desire for land and wealth—Farmers wanted land, and gold was discovered on Cherokee land.

Social Studies Skills

11. a

Reading Skills

12. a

b. Draw Conclusions What were the results of the conflict over the Second Bank of the United States?

c. Predict How might sectional differences and the debate over states' rights lead to future problems for the United States?

SECTION 3 *(Pages 332–335)*

8. a. **Identify** Who was Sequoya? What important contribution did he make?

b. Contrast In what different ways did the Cherokee and the Seminole attempt to resist removal to Indian Territory?

c. Elaborate Do you agree with Jackson's refusal to enforce the *Worcester* v. *Georgia* ruling? Why or why not?

Reviewing Themes

9. **Politics** What new political party rose in opposition to President Andrew Jackson? What was the party's attitude toward the power of the president?

10. **Economics** What economic factors influenced the policy of Indian removal?

Social Studies Skills

Solving Problems *Use the Social Studies Skills taught in this chapter to answer the question about the reading selection below.*

> Northerners wanted the tariff to protect their industries from foreign competition, especially from Great Britain.
>
> British companies were driving American ones out of business because they could manufacture goods more cheaply than American businesses could . . . Southerners opposed the tariff, claiming it would hurt their economy. *(p. 327)*

11. Which of the following might be a reasonable solution to the problem discussed above?

a. passing a low tariff

b. passing a high tariff only in the South

c. Britain passing a tariff

d. selling northern and British goods for a higher price

Reading Skills

Drawing Conclusions about the Past *Use the Reading Skills taught in this chapter to answer the question about the reading selection below.*

> Native Americans had long lived in settlements stretching from Georgia to Mississippi. However, President Jackson and other political leaders wanted to open this land to settlement by American farmers. *(p. 332)*

12. Which statement below can you conclude from the passage above?

a. Farmers moved onto the Native Americans' land after removal.

b. Native Americans wanted to move from their lands.

c. Native Americans resisted removal.

d. Government officials had to use force to remove Native Americans from their land.

Using the Internet

go.hrw.com
KEYWORD: SF7 CH10

13. **Activity: Writing a newspaper** Enter the activity keyword and research Jackson's presidency. Then create a party newspaper, using the template provided, that supports or criticizes Jackson's policies. Use evidence to support your articles either in favor of or against his policies. Write from the point of view of a supporter or from the point of view of a political enemy.

Focus on Writing

14. **Writing Interview Questions** Review the notes you have taken about Jackson's political significance, the conflicts he was involved in, and the causes and effects of his policies toward Indians. Then, based on your notes, begin writing questions for your interview with Jackson. What will the readers of your newspaper want to learn more about? Write at least 10 interview questions that your readers will want answered.

Using the Internet

13. Go to the HRW Web site and enter the keyword shown to access a rubric for this activity.

KEYWORD: SF7 CH10

Focus on Writing

14. **Rubric** Students' interview questions should
- require more than a yes or no answer.
- address Jackson's campaign and election, the conflicts he was involved in, and the causes and effects of his Indian policies.
- use correct grammar, punctuation, spelling, and capitalizations.

CRF: Focus on Writing Activity: An Interview

CHAPTER 10

Standardized Test Practice

IN 8.1.17, 8.3.6, 8.4.4, 8.4.8

DIRECTIONS: Read each question and write the letter of the best response.

1 The era surrounding the presidency of Andrew Jackson is *best* known for an expansion in

A freedom of speech.
B religious toleration.
C states' rights.
D voting rights.

2 Which of the following was important to the South's economy in the 1830s?

A manufacturing
B plantation agriculture
C shipbuilding
D weaving

3 What action did the Cherokee take to resist their removal from Georgia and North Carolina to the West?

A sued the state of Georgia in the courts
B destroyed neighbors' farms and businesses
C went to war against the U.S. government
D staged a protest called the Trail of Tears

4 The debate between John C. Calhoun and Daniel Webster over states' rights was *most like* the debate between

A the Patriots and the Loyalists.
B the Antifederalists and the Federalists.
C England and France during the French and Indian War.
D the large states and the small states during the Constitutional Convention.

5 President Jackson's weakening of the Second Bank of the United States resulted in

A inflation and other economic problems.
B the nullification crisis.
C the rise of the Democratic Party.
D increasing sectionalism.

6 The ruling in the Supreme Court case of *Worcester* v. *Georgia*

A established the policy of Indian removal.
B determined that Georgia laws did not apply to the Cherokee.
C was enforced by President Andrew Jackson.
D established protective tariffs for imported goods.

7 Read the following quote from Daniel Webster's "Seventh of March" speech and use it to answer the question below.

> "The people have preserved . . . their . . . Constitution, for forty years, and have seen their happiness, prosperity, and renown grow with its growth, and strengthen with its strength . . . I have not coolly weighed the chances of preserving liberty when the bonds that unite us together shall be broken . . . [Let us not have] 'Liberty first and Union afterwards,' but . . . that other sentiment, dear to every true American heart,—Liberty and Union, now and forever, one and inseparable!"
>
> –Daniel Webster, Seventh of March Speech, 1830

Document-Based Question **How does Webster appeal to listeners to preserve the Union?**

Answers

1. D
Break Down the Question: If students have a hard time choosing between options *C* and *D*, point out that the question asks for the issue for which the era is *best* known.

2. B
Break Down the Question: Tell students to begin by eliminating items they know were unimportant to the southern economy. The remaining item will be the correct response.

3. A
Break Down the Question: This question requires students to recall factual information. Refer students who have trouble to the text titled "Cherokee Resistance" in Section 3.

4. B
Break Down the Question: This question connects to information covered in Chapter 4.

5. A
Break Down the Question: This question requires students to recall factual information. Refer students who have trouble to the text titled "Jackson Attacks the Bank" in Section 2.

6. B
Break down the Question This question requires students to recall factual information. Refer students who have trouble to the text titled "Cherokee Resistance" in Section 3.

7. Webster supports the preservation of the Union by pointing out that the citizens' happiness, prosperity, and reputation have increased during the past forty years as the United States of America has grown.

Break Down the Question: To help students identify the overall meaning of a passage, tell them to look for key repeated words or phrases. Here, point out the repetition of the idea of unity expressed through the words *unite, Union,* and *one and inseparable*. Then tell students to identify which answer is most *opposed* to unity or Union?

Intervention Resources

Reproducible

- Interactive Reader and Study Guide
- Differentiated Instruction Teacher Management System: Lesson Plans for Differentiated Instruction

Technology

- Quick Facts Transparency 31: The Age of Jackson Visual Summary
- Differentiated Instruction Modified Worksheets and Tests CD-ROM
- Interactive Skills Tutor CD-ROM

Tips for Test Taking

Significant Details Students will often be asked to recall details from a reading passage. Tell students in such situations to read the question before they read the passage. Then, as they read the passage, students should underline key details. Remind students that the correct answer will not always precisely match the wording of the passage, however.

Water Rights Water was critical in the dry West. Bitter disputes arose over who had the water rights to streams. Gold rush miners developed a simple system: whoever used the water first owned the rights to it. In other parts of the West, the community as a whole had a right to use the water source.

Manifest Destiny Supporters of manifest destiny believed it was God's will that the United States should expand and spread democracy across North America. Huge numbers of settlers headed West to tame new lands.

The Rocky Mountains The Rocky Mountains were a gigantic obstacle to settlers on their way West. Pathfinders like Lt. John C. Frémont traveled widely in the region, making maps and noting possible trails. The South Pass, through which the Oregon Trail ran, was one of the few easy ways through the great chain of mountains.

GEOGRAPHY SKILLS **INTERPRETING MAPS**

1. **Movement** Why did San Francisco grow so rapidly?
2. **Human-Environment Interaction** Why was water so important in the West?

History and Geography

MISCONCEPTION ALERT

A Salty River? A desalination plant—or a facility that takes the salt out of water—has been built near the Colorado River in Arizona. But wait, isn't the water in the Colorado River fresh water? Yes and no. Farmers spray water from the river onto fields for irrigation. Because the desert soil contains so much salt, the runoff water is salty. The desalination plant purifies the runoff water so it can be sent back into the Colorado River and reused.

Info to Know

The Mexican Cession The territory granted to the United States by the Mexican Cession had long belonged to Spain and then Mexico. By 1850, however, the Hispanic population in the region was outnumbered by settlers from the United States.

Connect to Geography

Hispanics in the Southwest According to the 2000 census, about 19.7 million Hispanic or Latino Americans lived in Arizona, California, New Mexico, and Texas. This figure is more than half the total Hispanic population of the entire United States. Nearly 3.7 million Asian Americans and some 2.25 million African Americans also live in California, making it the most diverse state in the nation.

Cross-Discipline Activity: Math

Above Level

Graphing Hispanic Populations

1. Have students use information from the U.S. Census Bureau to obtain data about the current Hispanic population in each of the states in the Southwest.
2. Have each student use the data to create a bar graph showing the percentage of each state's population that is Hispanic. Then have each student create a circle graph that shows the percentage of the nation's total Hispanic population that lives in each of the states of the Southwest. Remind students to provide a title, a legend, and a caption for each graph.
3. Ask volunteers to share their graphs with the class. **LS Visual/Spatial**

Alternative Assessment Handbook, Rubrics 7: Charts; and 30: Research

Answers

Interpreting Maps 1. *The city was located on an excellent natural port for arriving ships and during the Gold Rush, thousands of people went there.* **2.** *The West is arid, and water is needed for people, crops, and livestock.*

Social Studies Skills

Interpreting Maps: Expansion

Activity Expansion Maps Scavenger Hunt Have students go on an expansion map scavenger hunt. Give students a set amount of time to find three examples of expansion maps in their textbooks. Have students mark the pages of each map. Award the first student to find three maps a prize of some kind. Have the winning student identify the pages on which the maps are located. Then guide students in interpreting each of the three maps. Conclude by having each student write a few sentences describing in his or her own words what an expansion map is.
LS Visual/Spatial

- Alternative Assessment Handbook, Rubric 21: Map Reading
- Interactive Skills Tutor CD-ROM, Lesson 6: Interpret Maps, Graphs, Charts, Visuals, and Political Cartoons
- **CRF:** Social Studies Skills Activity, Interpreting Maps: Expansion

Social Studies Skills

Analysis | Critical Thinking | Civic Participation | **Study**

Interpreting Maps: Expansion

Define the Skill

Maps show features on Earth's surface. These can be physical features, such as mountains and rivers, or human features, such as roads and settlements. Historical maps show an area as it was in the past. Some show how a nation's boundaries changed over time. Interpreting maps can answer questions about history as well as geography.

Learn the Skill

Follow these steps to gain information from a map.

1. Read the title to determine what the map is about and the time period it covers.
2. Study the legend or key to understand what the colors or symbols on the map mean. Note the map scale, which is used to measure distances.
3. Note the map's other features. Maps often contain labels and other information in addition to what is explained in the legend or key.

Practice the Skill

Interpret the map below to answer the following questions about the expansion of the United States.

1. The addition of which territory almost doubled the size of the United States?
2. What was the smallest expansion of U.S. borders, and when did it take place?
3. According to the map, when did California become part of the United States?
4. What choice of overland routes did a traveler have for getting to California?
5. What physical obstacles does the map show such a traveler would face?

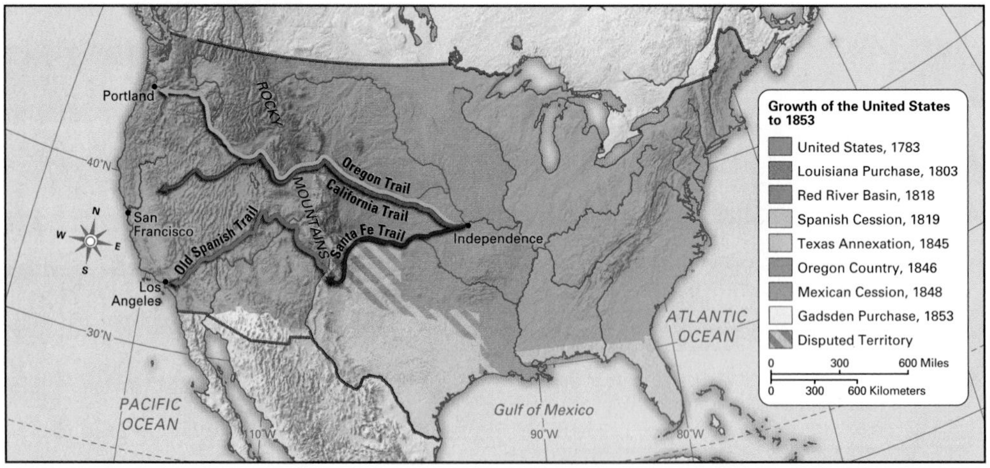

Social Studies Skills Activity: Interpreting Maps: Expansion

Interpreting Expansion Maps **At Level**

1. Display a modern political map of the United States for students to see. (One is available in the Atlas in the back of the textbook.)
2. Have students compare the map to the one shown above. Ask students to identify the states that are now located in each of the areas of expansion labeled on the map above. Use the activity to make certain students understand how to read the expansion map.
3. Then have each student write a paragraph describing the information in the map above. Tell students to be as thorough as possible.
4. Next, ask for a volunteer to read his or her description to the class. Then ask students which is easier to understand, the written description or the map. Use the question to help students understand the use of expansion maps in the study of history. **LS Visual/Spatial**

- Alternative Assessment Handbook, Rubrics 21: Map Reading

Answers

Practice the Skill 1. *Louisiana Territory;* **2.** *Gadsden Purchase in 1853;* **3.** *1848;* **4.** *California Trail, Old Spanish Trail;* **5.** *Rocky Mountains*

CHAPTER 11

Chapter Review

HOLT
History's Impact
▶ **video series**
Review the video to answer the closing question:
What does the modern success of Silicon Valley have in common with the California gold rush? How is it different?

Visual Summary

Use the visual summary below to help you review the main ideas of the chapter.

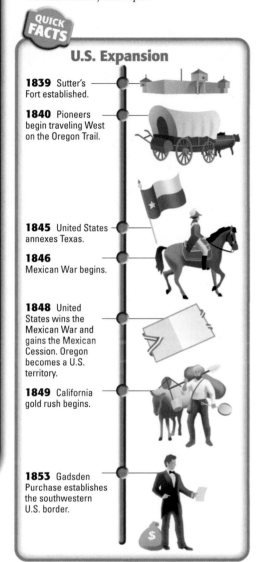

QUICK FACTS

U.S. Expansion

1839 Sutter's Fort established.

1840 Pioneers begin traveling West on the Oregon Trail.

1845 United States annexes Texas.

1846 Mexican War begins.

1848 United States wins the Mexican War and gains the Mexican Cession. Oregon becomes a U.S. territory.

1849 California gold rush begins.

1853 Gadsden Purchase establishes the southwestern U.S. border.

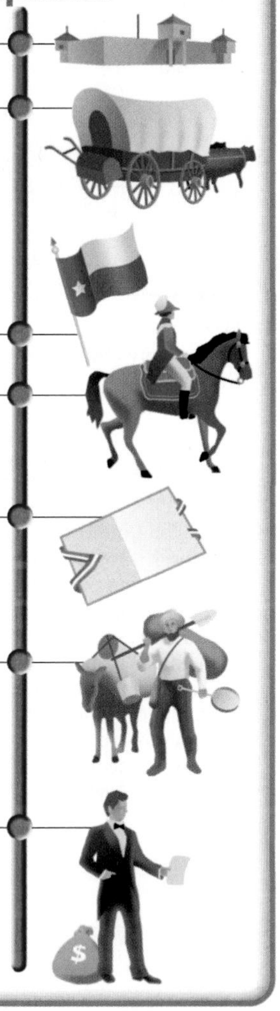

Reviewing Vocabulary, Terms, and People

Identify the correct term or person from the chapter that best fits each of the following descriptions.

1. Mexican priest who led a rebellion for independence from Spain
2. Spanish cowboys in California
3. A group of pioneers who were stranded in the Sierra Nevada Mountains and struggled to survive the winter
4. Agents hired by the Mexican government to attract settlers to Texas
5. The belief that the United States was meant to expand across the continent to the Pacific Ocean
6. Members of the Church of Jesus Christ of Latter-day Saints
7. Fur traders and trappers who lived west of the Rocky Mountains and in the Pacific Northwest
8. Mexican ruler who fought to keep Texas from gaining independence
9. Swiss immigrant who received permission from Mexico to start a colony in California
10. Western trail from Missouri to New Mexico that was an important route for trade between American and Mexican merchants

Comprehension and Critical Thinking

SECTION 1 *(Pages 346–349)*

11. a. Identify What different groups of people traveled West?

b. Draw Conclusions Why did Brigham Young move the Mormon community to Utah?

c. Predict What are some possible problems that might result from American settlement in the West?

Answers

History's Impact

Video Series People came to work in Silicon Valley to become wealthy quickly by meeting a demand; both Silicon Valley and the gold rush have given hope to people in search of the American Dream; miners relied on luck more than hard work.

Visual Summary

Review and Inquiry Have students use the visual summary to explain the causes and effects of time line events.

Quick Facts Transparency 33: Expanding West Visual Summary

Reviewing Vocabulary, Terms, and People

1. Father Miguel Hidalgo y Costilla
2. Californios
3. Donner party
4. empresarios
5. manifest destiny
6. Mormons
7. mountain men
8. Antonio López de Santa Anna
9. John Sutter
10. Santa Fe Trail

Comprehension and Critical Thinking

11. a. merchants, traders, settlers, Mormons

b. in search of religious freedom after other communities failed

c. conflict with Native Americans, slavery and statehood issues

Review and Assessment Resources

Review and Reinforce

- **SE** Chapter Review
- **CRF:** Chapter Review Activity
- Quick Facts Transparency 33: Expanding West Visual Summary
- Spanish Chapter Summaries Audio CD Program
- Online Chapter Summaries in Spanish
- **OSP** Holt PuzzlePro; GameTool for ExamView
- Quiz Game CD-ROM

Assess

- **SE** Standardized Test Practice
- PASS: Chapter 11 Tests, Forms A and B; Unit 3 Tests, Forms A and B
- Alternative Assessment Handbook
- **OSP** ExamView Test Generator, Chapter Test
- Differentiated Instruction Modified Worksheets and Tests CD-ROM: Chapter Test
- **HOAP** Holt Online Assessment Program (in the Premier Online Edition)

Reteach/Intervene

- Interactive Reader and Study Guide
- Differentiated Instruction Teacher Management System: Lesson Plans for Differentiated Instruction
- Differentiated Instruction Modified Worksheets and Tests CD-ROM
- Interactive Skills Tutor CD-ROM

go.hrw.com
Online Resources
Chapter Resources:
KEYWORD: SF7 CH11

SECTION 2 *(Pages 350–353)*

12. a. Identify Who were Stephen F. Austin and Antonio López de Santa Anna?

b. Draw Conclusions Why did settlers in Texas rebel against Mexican rule?

c. Elaborate In what ways was the Texas struggle for independence similar to that of the United States?

SECTION 3 *(Pages 354–363)*

13. a. Recall Why were some Americans opposed to the annexation of new territories?

b. Draw Conclusions What economic and cultural influences did Native Americans and Mexican Americans have on American settlers in the Mexican Cession?

c. Predict What are some possible problems the acquisition of so much territory might cause the United States?

SECTION 4 *(Pages 364–369)*

14. a. Identify What roles did women and immigrants play in the California gold rush?

b. Make Inferences Why were most gold-rush settlers young, unmarried men?

c. Predict What long-term effects might the gold rush have on California's future?

Reviewing Themes

15. Economics What role did economics play in the desire of Americans to go west?

16. Geography What were the main trails to the West, and what areas did they pass through?

Reading Skills

Vocabulary in Context *Use the Reading Skills taught in this chapter to answer the question about the reading selection below.*

> Texas politicians hoped that joining the United States would help solve the republic's financial and military problems. The Texas Congress approved annexation in June 1845. Texas became part of the United States in December. *(p. 356)*

17. Determine the definition of *annexation* using context clues.

Social Studies Skills

Interpreting Maps: Expansion *Use the Social Studies Skills taught in this chapter to answer the question about the map below.*

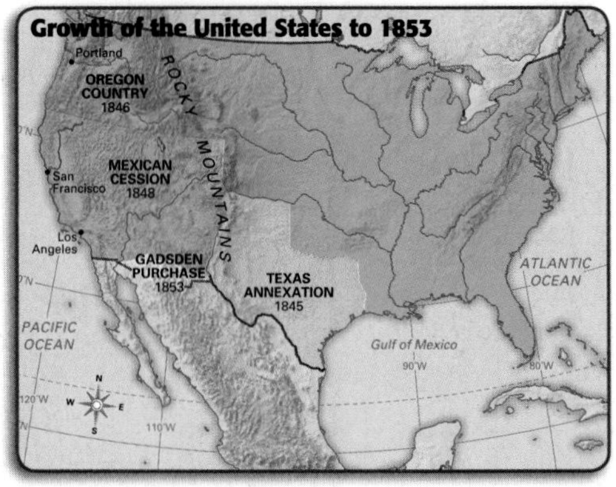

18. Place the expansions in the order in which they were acquired by the United States, according to the map.

FOCUS ON WRITING

19. Writing an Outline for a Documentary Film Look back through all your notes, and choose one topic from this chapter that you think would make a good 10-minute documentary. Your outline should be organized by scene (no more than 3 scenes), in chronological order. For each scene, give the following information: main idea of scene, costumes and images to be used, audio to be used, and length of scene. As you plan, remember that the audience will be students your own age.

Answers

12. a. Austin—empresario who founded an American colony in Mexican Texas; Santa Anna—leader of Mexico who led forces against the Texans in the Texas War for Independence

b. anger over some Mexican actions, such as banning of further American settlement and the importation of slaves; Santa Anna's suspension of Mexico's republican constitution

c. in both, the people in a colonial region fought against their mother country for protection of what they saw as their rights and liberties

13. a. concerns over the spread of slavery, balance of power between slave and free states

b. Mining, ranching, saddles, and adobe are examples of Mexican and Native American influence on American settlers.

c. problems related to governing and protecting such a large area

14. a. Both provided goods and services to miners, some opened and ran their own businesses; some immigrants mined.

b. possible answers—difficult to support and care for a family while prospecting; had few attachments to prevent them from going to California

c. continued population and economic growth, continued discrimination against Hispanics and Native Americans

Reviewing Themes

15. possible answer—Many Americans went West in the hope that they could improve their lives economically.

16. See the map titled Growth of the United States to 1853 on page 372.

Reading Skills

17. joining the United States; became part of

Social Studies Skills

18. Texas, Oregon, Mexican Cession, Gadsden Purchase

Focus on Writing

19. Rubric Students' outlines for documentary films should

- clearly introduce the main idea.
- include images.
- include narration that explains the images.
- be informative and appealing.

CRF: Focus on Writing: Outline for a Documentary Film

Standardized Test Practice

IN 8.1.15, 8.1.25, 8.3.8, 8.3.10

DIRECTIONS: Read each question and write the letter of the best response.

1 ***Use the map below to answer the following question.***

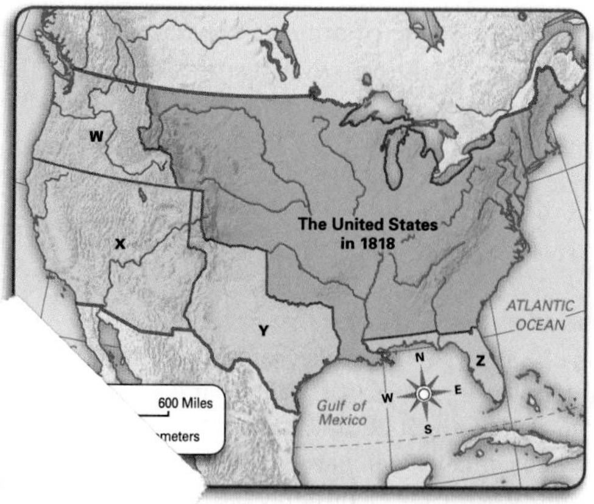

...he present-day United States ...nce claimed by Britain, Spain, and ... shown on the map by which letter?

A W

B X

C Y

D Z

2 In general, what position did Californios take toward the Mexican-American War?

A They supported the war because they wanted independence from Mexico.

B They supported the war because they wanted to become U.S. citizens.

C They opposed the war because they feared it might bring an end to slavery.

D They opposed the war because they did not want to lose control of California.

3 What was the *main* reason John Jacob Astor founded Astoria at the mouth of the Columbia River in 1811?

A Plenty of freshwater and salt-water fish were available for residents to eat.

B The soil there was rich and good for farming.

C Trappers could use the river to bring furs from the mountains to trade.

D The location offered easy protection from attacks by Native Americans or the French.

4 The *main* attraction of Texas for many Americans in the 1820s and 1830s was the

A freedom to practice the Catholic faith.

B availability of cheap or free land.

C desire to become citizens of Mexico.

D Mexican rebellion against Spain.

5 Which of the following occurred after the Mexican-American War?

A Mexican foods and festivals became more important to American culture.

B Prosperity of Mexican landowners in the Southwest increased under U.S. rule.

C Mexican Americans left the United States.

D The size of the United States was reduced.

6 Examine the following flier about cheap land available in the Dakota Territory and then use it to answer the question below.

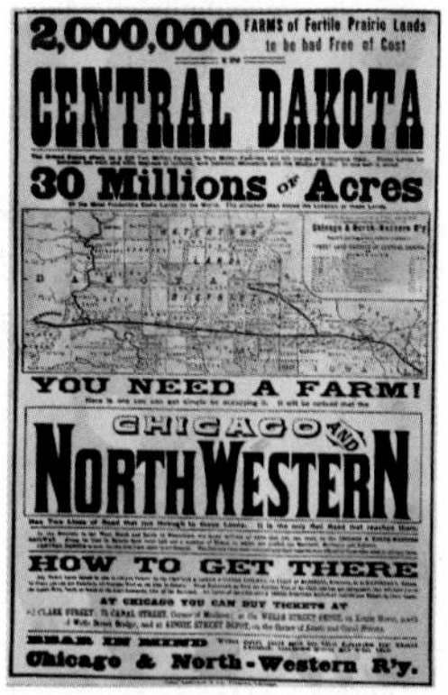

Document-Based Question **Who might have been attracted by this description of Dakota? Why?**

Answers

1. A

Break Down the Question Students need to note the lines indicating the border of each lettered region.

2. D

Break Down the Question Point out that the italicized phrase *In general* means that more than one answer may be correct and that students must choose the one that provides the best answer.

3. C

Break Down the Question Point out the italicized word *main* and explain to students that they need to identify the most *important* reason that Astor founded Astoria.

4. B

Break Down the Question This question requires students to recall factual information. Refer students who miss the question to the material "American Settlers Move to Texas" in Section 2.

5. A

Break Down the Question This question requires students to recall factual information. Refer students who miss the question to the material "American Settlement in the Mexican Cession" in Section 3.

6. possible answer—farmers, because the flyer is advertising plentiful and free land

Break Down the Question Inform students that a common advertising technique is to literally tell potential customers they have need of something. Then point out the part of the flyer claiming, "you need a farm."

Intervention Resources

Reproducible

- Interactive Reader and Study Guide
- Differentiated Instruction Teacher Management System: Lesson Plans for Differentiated Instruction

Technology

- Quick Facts Transparency 33: Expanding West Visual Summary
- Differentiated Instruction Modified Worksheets and Tests CD-ROM
- Interactive Skills Tutor CD-ROM

Tips for Test Taking

In Your Own Words Sometimes the wording of a question might be a bit different than the language students are used to using. Tell students to read the question and then restate it in their own words to make sure they understand what is being asked.

Preteach

Bellringer

Motivate Write the following for students to see: "Lissa was excited when she received her first driver's license." Ask students to brainstorm causes and effects of the event. Then have students consider the effects they listed as causes and list further effects. Help students build a cause-and-effect chain. Explain that in this workshop students will write a paper explaining causes or effects of a historical event.

SE Social Studies Skills 21: Short- and Long-term Causal Patterns

CRF The Progressive Spirit of Reform: Social Studies Skills Activity: Short- and Long-term Causal Patterns

Interactive Skills Tutor CD-ROM, Lesson 7: Identify Cause and Effect

Direct Teach

Determining Causes

Get Your Reasons Straight Remind students that not all the details they will read about as they study the War of 1812 will be causes or effects. Have students double-check the causes or effects they identified by asking one of the following questions:

- **Causes:** How did this action or situation contribute to the war?
- **Effects:** How did the war lead to this event or situation?

Organizing

How Important Is It? Explain to students that they have two choices when organizing information by importance—from least to most important, and from most to least important. Suggest that students who are organizing by order of importance make two outlines, one using each option. Then have students choose the option that works best.

Writing Workshop

Cause and Effect in History

Assignment

Write a paper explaining the causes or the effects of the War of 1812.

Historians try to make sense of an event by considering why the event happened and what resulted from it. Exploring causes and effects can provide a deeper understanding of historical events and how they are connected to one another.

1. Prewrite

Identifying Causes and Effects

A **cause** is an action or a situation that makes something else happen. What happens is called an **effect**. For example, if you stay up too late watching TV (cause), you might find yourself nodding off in class (effect). Often an event or situation will have several causes as well as several effects. In those cases, we may look at the order in which the causes or effects occurred, or we may look at their relative importance.

Researching and Organizing

For this paper, you will write about the causes or the effects of the event—the War of 1812. Gather information from the chapter in this textbook, an encyclopedia, or another source recommended by your teacher.

- Look for two or three reasons (causes) why the War of 1812 (the event or situation) occurred.
- At the same time, consider the war as a cause. Look for two or three effects of the war.

Then choose whether to write about the causes or the effects.

TIP Using a Graphic Organizer
Use a graphic organizer like this to organize your research.

Cause 1
↓
Cause 2
↓
Event or Situation
↓
Effect
↓
Effect

2. Write

You can use this framework to help you write your first draft.

A Writer's Framework

Introduction	Body	Conclusion
■ Begin with a quote or interesting fact about the event. ■ Identify the event you will discuss. [The War of 1812] ■ Identify whether you will be discussing the causes or the effects.	■ Present the causes or effects in chronological (time) order or order of importance. ■ Explain each cause or effect in its own paragraph, providing support with facts and examples.	■ Summarize your ideas about the causes or the effects of the event [the war].

Differentiating Instruction

English-Language Learners Below Level

Standard English Mastery

1. Students may not be familiar with the transitional cause-and-effect words and phrases listed in the second Tip on the next page.
2. List the words and phrases and help students define each one. Then have the class use each word or phrase in a sentence.
3. Some students may be confused by the way that placement of transitions within a sentence can vary in English. Some appear before the ideas to which they connect, and some after. Illustrate this point by having students identify the idea to which each cause-and-effect transition connects.
4. Last, have students scan the text on the War of 1812 and look for cause-and-effect transitions. Help students identify the ideas to which each one connects. **LS Verbal/Linguistic**

3. Evaluate and Revise

Evaluating

Drawing clear, logical connections is the key to writing about causes and effects. Use these questions to evaluate and revise your paper.

Evaluation Questions for an Explanation of Causes or Effects

- Does the introduction begin with an interesting quotation or fact?
- Does the introduction identify the event [the war] and the causes or events to be discussed?
- Is each cause or effect explained in its own paragraph?
- Do facts and examples help to explain each cause or effect and connect it to the event [the war]?
- Are the causes or effects organized clearly—by chronological order or order of importance?
- Does the conclusion summarize the causes or effects and their importance?

Revising

Make sure the connections between the war and its causes or effects are clear by sharing your paper with a classmate. If your classmate is confused, add background information. If he or she disagrees with your conclusions, add evidence or rethink your reasoning.

4. Proofread and Publish

Proofreading

Some transitional words and phrases need to be set off from the sentence with commas. Here are two examples:

- The Louisiana Territory was a huge region of land. *As a result,* the size of the United States almost doubled when the land was purchased.
- Jefferson wanted to know more about the land he had purchased. *Therefore,* he asked Congress to fund an expedition.

Check your paper to see if you need to add commas after or around any transitional words or phrases.

Publishing

Get together with a classmate and share causes and/or effects. Compare your lists to see whether you have identified different causes or effects. Share your findings with your class.

5. Practice and Apply

Use the steps and strategies outlined in this workshop to write your explanation of the causes or effects of the War of 1812.

TIP **Recognizing False Cause-and-Effect** In planning your essay, be careful to avoid false cause-and-effect relationships. The fact that one thing happened before or after another doesn't mean one caused the other. For example, the fact that James Madison was elected in 1808, just four years before the War of 1812, does not mean his election caused the War of 1812.

TIP **Using Transitions** Here are some transitional words and phrases that show cause or effect relationships: *because, as a result, therefore, for, since, so, consequently, for this reason.*

Reteach

Check Organization

Sort It Out Have students trade papers. In the margin next to each paragraph, have students write a word or a phrase identifying the cause or effect discussed. Have them write "divide paragraph" next to any paragraph with more than one cause or effect. Have them write "combine paragraphs" next to any paragraphs that discuss the same cause or effect and then draw an arrow linking the two paragraphs to combine.

Teaching Tip

Stay on Topic Remind students that each paragraph must have a topic sentence. In most cases, it should be the first sentence of the paragraph. Check students' papers as they write and point out any paragraphs without topic sentences.

Practice & Apply

Rubric

Students' explanations of causes or effects should

- begin with an interesting quote or fact about the War of 1812.
- clearly identify the topic.
- accurately explain the causes or effects of the War of 1812.
- provide a paragraph and support for each cause or effect.
- follow either chronological order or order of importance.
- end with a summary.
- use correct grammar, punctuation, spelling, and capitalization.

Advanced/Gifted and Talented — Above Level

1. Have students prepare their papers as if they are making a presentation to Congress either during or after the War of 1812.
2. Students writing a paper on the war's causes should present an analysis of the causes and recommend ways that war might have been avoided. Students writing a paper on the war's effects should provide solutions for addressing the negative effects. **LS Verbal/Linguistic**

Struggling Readers — Below Level

1. If students have trouble identifying cause and effect, have them practice the skill on an easier selection. Choose an applicable selection from a fifth or sixth grade history text.
2. Have students work in pairs to create a cause-and-effect chart for the selection. Tell students to look for the cause-and-effect transitions listed above to help them. Correct any student errors. **LS Logical/Mathematical**

Unit Preview

Introduce the Unit

Share the information in the chapter overviews with students.

Chapter 12 During the early 1800s the Industrial Revolution dramatically changed the way in which goods were made. Americans' lives changed as well, as many people began working in factories. These changes were coupled with dramatic advances in transportation and technology.

Chapter 13 The invention of the cotton gin created a new cash crop for the South—cotton. This crop soon dominated the southern economy. Cotton production depended heavily on slave labor. Enslaved Africans were forced to perform hard labor and suffered terrible conditions. Nonetheless, slaves developed a rich culture and a deep religious sense.

Chapter 14 In the mid 1800s, waves of immigrants led to rapid growth of cities and a rise in urban problems. Meanwhile, a number of Americans began working to reform society, improve women's rights, and end slavery. Many Americans began to look for more intense meaning in their lives through deeper religious commitment, philosophy, and Romantic art and literature.

Chapter 15 In the mid-1800s tensions between the North and the South heightened over slavery. These tensions were increased by political divisions that culminated in 1860 with the election of Abraham Lincoln. As a result, several southern states seceded from the Union.

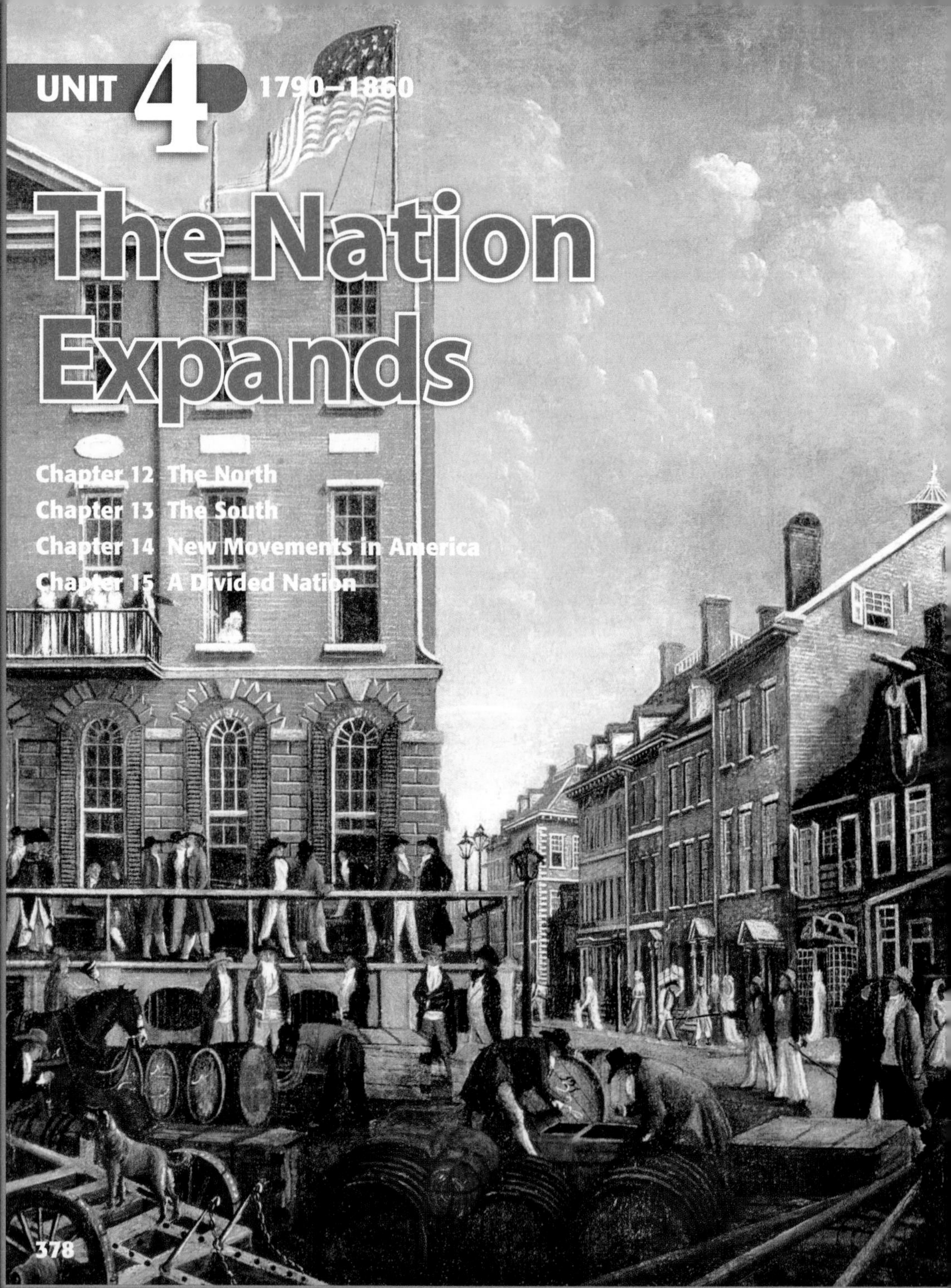

Unit Resources

Planning

- Differentiated Instruction Teacher Management System: Unit Instructional Pacing Guides
- One-Stop Planner CD-ROM with Test Generator: Calendar Planner
- Power Presentations with Video CD-ROM

Differentiating Instruction

- Differentiated Instruction Teacher Management System: Lesson Plans for Differentiated Instruction
- Pre-AP Activities Guide for United States History
- Differentiated Instruction Modified Worksheets and Tests CD-ROM

Enrichment

- **CRF The North:** Interdisciplinary Project: Using Measurements
- **CRF A Divided Nation:** Economics and History: Economic Rivalry
- Civic Participation Activities
- Primary Source Library CD-ROM
- Internet Activities: Chapter Enrichment Links

Assessment

- Progress Assessment Support System: Unit 4 Tests, Forms A and B
- OSP ExamView Test Generator: Unit Test
- HOAP Holt Online Assessment Program, in the Premier Online Student Edition
- Alternative Assessment Handbook

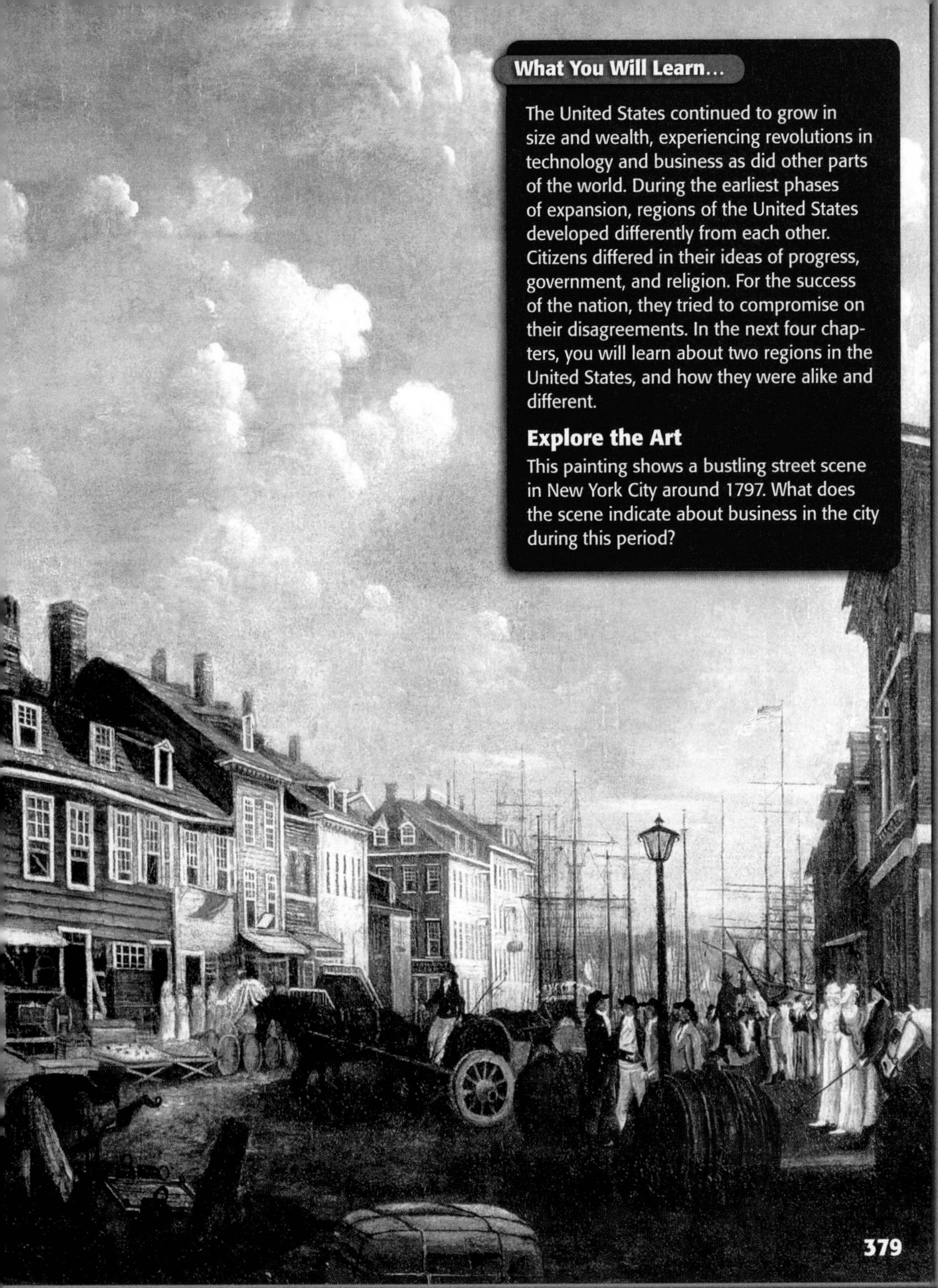

What You Will Learn...

The United States continued to grow in size and wealth, experiencing revolutions in technology and business as did other parts of the world. During the earliest phases of expansion, regions of the United States developed differently from each other. Citizens differed in their ideas of progress, government, and religion. For the success of the nation, they tried to compromise on their disagreements. In the next four chapters, you will learn about two regions in the United States, and how they were alike and different.

Explore the Art

This painting shows a bustling street scene in New York City around 1797. What does the scene indicate about business in the city during this period?

Unit Preview

Connect to the Unit

Activity Focus on Regional Differences Ask students to discuss the differences between regions of the United States today. How is the East Coast different from the West Coast? How is the Midwest different from the Southwest? After a brief discussion, point out that differences between the North and the South led to growing tensions during the first part of the 1800s.

Create a Venn diagram for students to see. Label the circles North and South. Have students use what they have learned so far to predict what some of the similarities and differences might be.
LS Verbal/Linguistic, Visual/Spatial

Explore the Art

During the early 1800s America grew at a rapid pace, and cities such as New York were a strong example of this expansion. New inventions, cheaper transportation, and more labor caused the city's economy to prosper. New York became so big that by the mid-1800s it processed more products than all other American ports combined. One result of this growth in the country's cities was slave labor, which became a bitter topic that later divided the nation.

About the Illustration

This illustration is an artist's conception based on available sources. However, historians are uncertain exactly what this scene looked like.

Democracy and Civic Education

At Level

Justice: Opposing Unjust Laws

Research Required

Background Explain that in the 1830s, some Americans began taking more organized action to try to achieve abolition, or a complete end to slavery. These Americans felt the laws that allowed slavery to exist were unjust.

1. Have students discuss what citizens should do when they think a law is unjust. What makes a law unjust? What actions can citizens take to try to change unjust laws? How can citizens work to promote justice in their local communities?
2. Organize students into groups. Have each group conduct research on actions citizens can take to oppose unjust laws.
3. Have each group use its research to create a storyboard for a televised public service announcement to educate Americans on what they can do to change unjust laws.
LS Interpersonal, Verbal/Linguistic

Alternative Assessment Handbook, Rubrics 14: Group Activity; and 29: Presentations

Civic Participation Activities Guide

Answers

Explore the Art *The scene shows large, impressive buildings, transportation vehicles, paved streets, streetlights, and large amounts of trade goods. This would seem to indicate that business in the city was thriving during this period.*

Chapter 12 Planning Guide

The North

Chapter Overview	Reproducible Resources	Technology Resources
CHAPTER 12 **pp. 380–409** **Overview: In this chapter, students will analyze the economic, cultural, physical, and social effects of technological improvements on the Northern states.**	**Differentiated Instruction Teacher Management System:*** • Instructional Pacing Guides • Lesson Plans for Differentiated Instruction **Interactive Reader and Study Guide:** Chapter Summary Graphic Organizer* **Chapter Resource File:*** • Focus on Writing Activity: Newspaper Advertisement • Social Studies Skills Activity: Personal Conviction and Bias • Chapter Review Activity	**Power Presentations with Video CD-ROM** **Differentiated Instruction Modified Worksheets and Tests CD-ROM** **Primary Source Library CD-ROM for United States History** **Interactive Skills Tutor CD-ROM** **Student Edition on Audio CD Program** **History's Impact: United States History Video Program (VHS/DVD):** The Impact of Mass Transportation*
Section 1: **The Industrial Revolution in America** **The Big Idea:** The Industrial Revolution transformed the way goods were produced in the United States.	**Differentiated Instruction Teacher Management System:** Section 1 Lesson Plan* **Interactive Reader and Study Guide:** Section 12.1 Summary* **Chapter Resource File:*** • Vocabulary Builder Activity, Section 1 • Biography Activity: Samuel Slater	**Daily Bellringer Transparency 12.1*** **Internet Activity:** Samuel Slater **Internet Activity:** Industrial Revolution
Section 2: **Changes in Working Life** **The Big Idea:** The introduction of factories changed working life for many Americans.	**Differentiated Instruction Teacher Management System:** Section 2 Lesson Plan* **Interactive Reader and Study Guide:** Section 12.2 Summary* **Chapter Resource File:*** • Vocabulary Builder Activity, Section 2 • Biography Activity: Sarah Bagley	**Daily Bellringer Transparency 12.2*** **Internet Activity:** Lowell Scrapbook
Section 3: **The Transportation Revolution** **The Big Idea:** New forms of transportation improved business, travel, and communication in the United States.	**Differentiated Instruction Teacher Management System:** Section 3 Lesson Plan* **Interactive Reader and Study Guide:** Section 12.3 Summary* **Chapter Resource File:*** • Vocabulary Builder Activity, Section 3 • Literature Activity: Mark Twain Pilots a Steamboat • History and Geography Activity: The Transportation Revolution **U.S. Supreme Court Case Studies:** *Gibbons* v. *Ogden**	**Daily Bellringer Transparency 12.3*** **Map Transparency 43:** Transportation Routes, 1850* **Interactive Map:** Transportation Routes, 1850
Section 4: **More Technological Advances** **The Big Idea:** Advances in technology led to new inventions that continued to change daily life and work.	**Differentiated Instruction Teacher Management System:** Section 4 Lesson Plan* **Interactive Reader and Study Guide:** Section 12.4 Summary* **Chapter Resource File:*** • Vocabulary Builder Activity, Section 4 • Biography Activity: John Deere • Interdisciplinary Project: Using Measurements	**Daily Bellringer Transparency 12.4***

SE Student Edition | Print Resource | Audio CD
TE Teacher's Edition | Transparency | CD-ROM
go.hrw.com | **LS** Learning Styles | Video
TOS Indiana Teacher One Stop | * also on Indiana Teacher One Stop

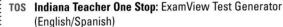

Review, Assessment, Intervention

- **Quick Facts Transparency 34:** The North Visual Summary*
- **Spanish Chapter Summaries Audio CD Program**
- **Online Chapter Summaries in Spanish**
- **Progress Assessment Support System (PASS):** Chapter Tests A and B*
- **Differentiated Instruction Modified Worksheets and Tests CD-ROM:** Modified Chapter Test
- TOS **Indiana Teacher One Stop:** ExamView Test Generator (English/Spanish)
- HOAP **Holt Online Assessment Program,** in the Holt Premier Online Student Edition

---

- **PASS:** Section Quiz 12.1*
- **Online Quiz:** Section 12.1
- **Alternative Assessment Handbook**

- **PASS:** Section Quiz 12.2*
- **Online Quiz:** Section 12.2
- **Alternative Assessment Handbook**

- **PASS:** Section Quiz 12.3*
- **Online Quiz:** Section 12.3
- **Alternative Assessment Handbook**

- **PASS:** Section Quiz 12.4*
- **Online Quiz:** Section 12.4
- **Alternative Assessment Handbook**

HOLT

History's Impact

United States History Video Program (VHS/DVD)

The Impact of Mass Transportation

Suggested use: as a chapter introduction

Power Presentations with Video CD-ROM

Power Presentations with Video are visual presentations of each chapter's main ideas. Presentations can be customized by including Quick Facts charts, images from the text, and video clips.

DIVISION FOR PUBLIC EDUCATION
AMERICAN BAR ASSOCIATION

Developed by the Division for Public Education of the American Bar Association, these materials are part of the **Democracy and Civic Education Resources.**

- **Constitution Study Guide**
- **Supreme Court Case Studies**

Holt Online Learning

go.hrw.com
Teacher Resources
KEYWORD: SF7 TEACHER

go.hrw.com
Student Resources
KEYWORD: SF7 CH12

- Document-Based Questions
- Interactive Multimedia Activities
- Current Events
- Chapter-based Internet Activities
- and more!

Holt Interactive

Online Student Edition

Complete online support for interactivity, assessment, and reporting

- Interactive Maps and Notebook
- Standardized Test Prep
- Homework Practice and Research Activities Online

Differentiating Instruction

How do I address the needs of varied learners?

The Target Resource acts as your primary strategy for differentiated instruction.

ENGLISH-LANGUAGE LEARNERS & STRUGGLING READERS

TARGET RESOURCE

English-Language Learner Strategies and Activities

- Build Academic Vocabulary
- Develop Oral and Written Language Structures

Spanish Resources

Spanish Chapter Summaries Audio CD

Spanish Chapter Summaries Online

Teacher's One-Stop Planner:

- ExamView Test Generator, Spanish
- PuzzlePro, Spanish

Additional Resources

Differentiated Instruction Teacher Management System: Lesson Plans for Differentiated Instruction

Chapter Resources:

- Vocabulary Builder Activities
- Social Studies Skills Activity: Personal Conviction and Bias

Quick Facts Transparency 34: The North Visual Summary

Student Edition on Audio CD Program

Interactive Skills Tutor CD-ROM

SPECIAL NEEDS LEARNERS

TARGET RESOURCE

Differentiated Instruction Modified Worksheets and Tests CD-ROM

- Vocabulary Flash Cards
- Modified Vocabulary Builder Activities
- Modified Chapter Review Activity
- Modified Chapter Test

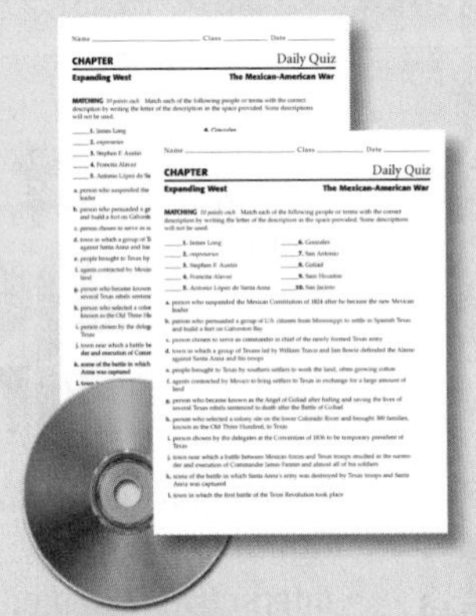

Additional Resources

Differentiated Instruction Teacher Management System: Lesson Plans for Differentiated Instruction

Interactive Reader and Study Guide

Social Studies Skills Activity: Personal Conviction and Bias

Student Edition on Audio CD Program

Interactive Skills Tutor CD-ROM

ADVANCED/GIFTED-AND-TALENTED STUDENTS

TARGET RESOURCE

Primary Source Library CD-ROM for United States History

The Library contains longer versions of quotations in the text, extra sources, and images. Included are point-of-view articles, journals, diaries, historical fiction, and political documents.

Additional Resources

Differentiated Instruction Teacher Management System: Lesson Plans for Differentiated Instruction

Political Cartoons Activities for United States History: Cartoon 14: Fears of the Railroad

Chapter Resource File:

- Focus on Writing Activity: Newspaper Advertisement
- Literature Activity: Mark Twain Pilots a Steamboat

Internet Activities: Chapter Enrichments Links

Differentiated Activities in the Teacher's Edition

- Industrial Revolution Newspaper, p. 385
- Innovations Effects Chart, p. 386
- Effects of Steamboats Headlines, p. 397
- Transportation Revolution Drawings, p. 398
- Inventions Guessing Game, p. 403

Differentiated Activities in the Teacher's Edition

- Transportation Revolution Drawings, p. 398
- Inventions Guessing Game, p. 403

Differentiated Activities in the Teacher's Edition

- Analyzing Changes in Manufacturing, p. 387
- A *Lowell Offering* Excerpt, p. 392
- Speech for Improving Mill Working Conditions, p. 394
- Baltimore and Ohio Railroad, p. 399

Teacher One Stop™

How can I manage the lesson plans and support materials for differentiated instruction?

With the Indiana Teacher One Stop, you can easily organize and print lesson plans, planning guides, and instructional materials for all learners.
The Indiana Teacher One Stop includes the following materials to help you differentiate instruction:

- Interactive Teacher's Edition
- Calendar Planner and pacing guides
- Editable lesson plans
- All reproducible ancillaries in Adobe Acrobat (PDF) format
- ExamView Test Generator (Eng & Span)
- Transparency and video previews

Professional Development

What teacher training resources are available to help me grow professionally?

- **In-service and staff development** as part of your Holt Social Studies product purchase
- **Quick Teacher Tutorial Lesson Presentation CD-ROM**
- Intensive tuition-based **Teacher Development Institute**
- **Convenient Holt Speaker Bureau** – face-to-face workshop options
- **PRAXIS™ Test Prep** interactive Web-based content refreshers*
- **Ask A Professional Development Expert** at http://www.hrw.com/prodev/

* PRAXIS is a trademark of Educational Testing Service (ETS). This publication is not endorsed or approved by ETS.

Chapter Preview

Chapter Big Ideas

Section 1 The Industrial Revolution transformed the way goods were produced in the United States.

Section 2 The introduction of factories changed working life for many Americans.

Section 3 New forms of transportation improved business, travel, and communication in the United States.

Section 4 Advances in technology led to new inventions that continued to change daily life and work.

Focus on Writing

The **Chapter Resource File** provides a Focus on Writing worksheet to help students organize and write their newspaper advertisements.

CRF: Focus on Writing Activity: Newspaper Advertisement

CHAPTER 12 The North

Indiana Standards

Social Studies Standards

8.1.10 Compare differences in ways of life in the northern and osuthern states, including the growth of towns and cities in the North and the growing dependence on slavery in the South.

8.4.5 Analyze contributions of entrepreneurs and inventors in the development of the United States economy.

8.4.6 Relate technological change and inventions to changes in labor productivity in the United States in the eighteenth and nineteenth centuries.

8.4.9 Explain and evaluate examples of domstic and international interdependence throughout United States history.

go.hrw.com
Indiana
KEYWORD: SF10 IN

Focus on Writing

Newspaper Advertisement The Industrial Revolution was a time when a great many new inventions were introduced. You work for an advertising agency, and your job is to design an advertisement for one of the inventions mentioned in this chapter. As you read, take notes on the inventions, their inventors, and how they changed life in the United States. Then choose one invention and design a newspaper advertisement to persuade readers to buy or use the invention.

UNITED STATES

1807 Robert Fulton's *Clermont* becomes the first commercially successful steamboat.

1790

WORLD

1790 The first steam-powered mill opens in Great Britain.

Key to Differentiating Instruction

Below Level
Basic-level activities designed for all students encountering new material

At Level
Intermediate-level activities designed for average students

Above Level
Challenging activities designed for honors and gifted and talented students

Standard English Mastery
Activities designed to improve standard English usage

Introduce the Chapter

At Level

Farm Versus Factory

1. Organize the students into two groups: those who work on farms and those who work in factories. You might want to show students pictures of modern-day farms and factories to get them thinking about daily activities, how hard they might have to work, where they would live, and how life differs in rural and urban areas.
2. Start a classroom discussion by asking students to complete these sentences: (a) "Working on a farm is better than working in a factory because . . . ," and (b) "Working in a factory is better than working on a farm because . . ."
3. List responses for students to see. Tell students to keep these responses in mind as they read the chapter and learn about how the Industrial Revolution changed life for Americans at home and at work. **LS Verbal/Linguistic**

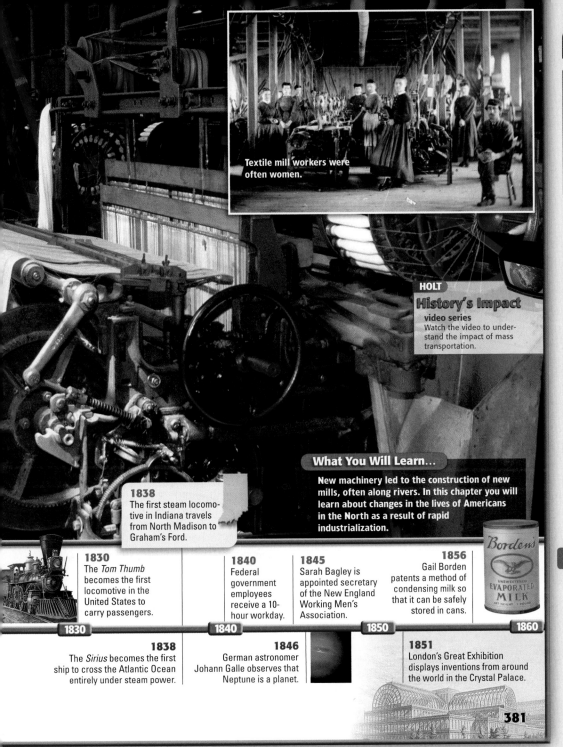

Textile mill workers were often women.

HOLT **History's Impact** video series
Watch the video to understand the impact of mass transportation.

What You Will Learn...

New machinery led to the construction of new mills, often along rivers. In this chapter you will learn about changes in the lives of Americans in the North as a result of rapid industrialization.

1838 The first steam locomotive in Indiana travels from North Madison to Graham's Ford.

1830 The *Tom Thumb* becomes the first locomotive in the United States to carry passengers.

1840 Federal government employees receive a 10-hour workday.

1845 Sarah Bagley is appointed secretary of the New England Working Men's Association.

1856 Gail Borden patents a method of condensing milk so that it can be safely stored in cans.

1830 — 1840 — 1850 — 1860

1838 The *Sirius* becomes the first ship to cross the Atlantic Ocean entirely under steam power.

1846 German astronomer Johann Galle observes that Neptune is a planet.

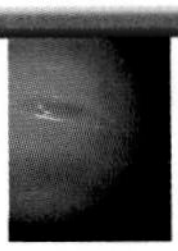

1851 London's Great Exhibition displays inventions from around the world in the Crystal Palace.

381

• Chapter Preview •

HOLT
History's Impact
▶ **video series**
See the Video Teacher's Guide for strategies for using the chapter video to teach about the impact of mass transportation.

Explore the Picture

Water-Powered Mills Textile mills built in the early 1800s relied on water for power. Flowing rivers or waterfalls turned waterwheels that powered the mill machinery inside. With developments in steam-powered machinery, factories began to shift to steam power. As a result, factories were no longer necessarily built along rivers and streams. Today, however, old mills can still be found along many streams and rivers, particularly in the Northeast.

Analyzing Visuals How do you think a textile mill, like the one shown in the picture, might change a town? *Students might suggest that it provided employment for many but also affected the environment.*

go.hrw.com
Online Resources
Chapter Resources:
KEYWORD: SF7 CH12
Teacher Resources:
KEYWORD: SF7 TEACHER

Explore the Time Line

1. When did the first steam-powered mill open in Great Britain? *1790*
2. How long after the first commercially successful steamboat in the United States was the nation's first passenger locomotive? *23 years*
3. How and when did working conditions change for government employees during this period? *Employees received a 10-hour workday in 1840.*

Info to Know

The *Sirius* Two ships competed to be the first to cross the Atlantic Ocean under steam power. The *Sirius* left England a few days before the *Great Western* but arrived in New York just a few hours before her competitor. The *Sirius* actually ran out of coal near the end of the race. The captain refused to hoist the sails and instead fed cabin doors, a spare mast, and even furniture into the furnace.

Reading Social Studies

Understanding Themes

Introduce this chapter by asking students how goods were produced in the United States prior to the 1800s. Point out to students that goods were made by hand before the Industrial Revolution introduced machines and factories to manufacturing. Ask students what types of technology would have been necessary to do this. Then ask students what sort of economic effects this faster method of producing goods might have had. Remind students to pay attention to the two themes of the chapter—science and technology and economics.

Causes and Effects in History

Focus on Reading Point out to students that causes and effects can be seen in everyday life, not just in historical events. Ask students to think of events in their lives or in their community that have a clear cause-and-effect sequence. Have each student create a cause and effect chain that has at least four links. Then have students cut their chain into separate events so that each event is on a separate piece of paper. Have students exchange papers with a partner. Then have each student try to piece together the events in the cause and effect chain. Ask students to go over the proper sequence with their partners.

Reading Social Studies

by Kylene Beers

Economics | Geography | Politics | Society and Culture | Science and Technology

Focus on Themes As you read this chapter, you will learn about how developments in **science and technology** brought about what is called the Industrial Revolution. As a result of the Industrial Revolution, you will see how American **economic** patterns changed. Next, you will read about how family life changed as more and more people went to work in factories. Finally, you will see how new methods of transportation changed where people lived and how new inventions affected daily life and work.

Causes and Effects in History

Focus on Reading Have you heard the saying, "We have to understand the past to avoid repeating it."? That is one reason we look for causes and effects in history.

Cause and Effect Chains You might say that all of history is one long chain of causes and effects. It may help you to understand the course of history better if you draw out such a chain as you read.

Since the 1790s, wars between European powers had interfered with U.S. trade. American customers were no longer able to get all the manufactured goods they were used to buying from British and European manufacturers . . . Americans began to buy the items they needed from American manufacturers instead of from foreign suppliers. As profits for American factories grew, manufacturers began to spend more money expanding their factories . . .

At the same time, many Americans began to realize that the United States had been relying too heavily on foreign goods. *(p. 389)*

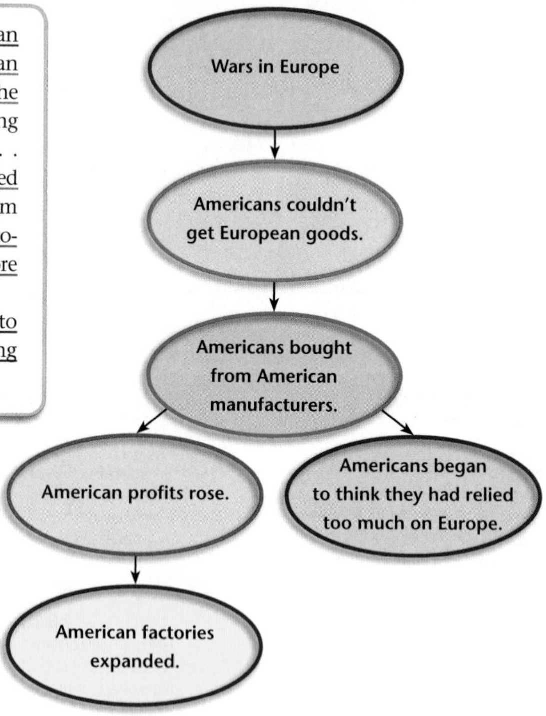

Wars in Europe
Americans couldn't get European goods.
Americans bought from American manufacturers.
American profits rose.
Americans began to think they had relied too much on Europe.
American factories expanded.

Reading and Skills Resources

Reading Support

- Interactive Reader and Study Guide
- Student Edition on Audio CD Program
- Spanish Chapter Summaries Audio CD Program

Social Studies Skills Support

- Interactive Skills Tutor CD-ROM

Vocabulary Support

- **CRF:** Vocabulary Builder Activities
- **CRF:** Chapter Review Activity
- Differentiated Instruction Modified Worksheets and Tests CD-ROM:
  - Vocabulary Flash Cards
  - Vocabulary Builder Activity
  - Chapter Review Activity

OSP Holt PuzzlePro

You Try It!

The following passage is from the chapter you are about to read. As you read each paragraph, ask yourself what is the cause and what is the effect of what is being discussed.

Workers Organize

From Chapter 12, p. 394

Factories continued to spread in the 1800s. Craftspeople, who made goods by hand, felt threatened. Factories quickly produced low-priced goods. To compete with factories, shop owners had to hire more workers and pay them less . . .

The wages of factory workers also went down as people competed for jobs. A wave of immigration in the 1840s brought people from other, poorer countries. They were willing to work for low pay. More immigrants came to the Northeast, where the mills were located, than to the South. Competition for jobs also came from people unemployed during the financial Panic of 1837.

After you have read the passage, answer the following questions.

1. What cause is being discussed in the first paragraph? What were its effects?
2. Draw a cause and effect chain that shows the events described in the first paragraph.
3. What main effect is discussed in the second paragraph? How many causes are given for it?
4. Draw a cause and effect chain that shows the events described in the second paragraph.

As you read Chapter 12, look for words that signal causes or effects. Picture these causes and effects as the links in a cause and effect chain.

Key Terms and People

Chapter 12

Section 1
Industrial Revolution *(p. 385)*
textiles *(p. 385)*
Richard Arkwright *(p. 385)*
Samuel Slater *(p. 386)*
technology *(p. 387)*
Eli Whitney *(p. 387)*
interchangeable parts *(p. 387)*
mass production *(p. 387)*

Section 2
Rhode Island system *(p. 391)*
Francis Cabot Lowell *(p. 392)*
Lowell system *(p. 392)*
trade unions *(p. 394)*
strikes *(p. 394)*
Sarah G. Bagley *(p. 395)*

Section 3
Transportation Revolution *(p. 396)*
Robert Fulton *(p. 397)*
Clermont (p. 397)
Gibbons v. *Ogden (p. 397)*
Peter Cooper *(p. 398)*

Section 4
Samuel F. B. Morse *(p. 402)*
telegraph *(p. 402)*
Morse code *(p. 403)*
John Deere *(p. 404)*
Cyrus McCormick *(p. 404)*
Isaac Singer *(p. 405)*

Academic Vocabulary

Success in school is related to knowing academic vocabulary—the words that are frequently used in school assignments and discussions. In this chapter, you will learn the following academic words:

efficient *(p. 385)*
concrete *(p. 395)*

Reading Social Studies

Key Terms and People

Read the list aloud so that students will know how to pronounce each term or name. Then organize the students into pairs and assign each pair a person or term from the list. Have each pair identify the importance of the person or term. Then have each group draw a picture that represents the significance of that term or person. Have each student present the term, description or definition, and illustration to the class. Encourage students to take notes on the presentations. **LS Verbal/Linguistic, Visual/Spatial, Interpersonal**

Focus on Reading

See the **Focus on Reading** questions in this chapter for more practice on this reading social studies skill.

Reading Social Studies Assessment

See the **Chapter Review** at the end of this chapter for student assessment questions related to this reading skill.

Teaching Tip

Students may occasionally have difficulty identifying causes and effects as they read. Point out to students that causes and effects are often signaled by certain words. Ask students what words might signal causes and effects. Help them see that words like *as, since, because,* and *motivated by* all indicate causes. Some words that signal effect are *led to, resulted in, as a result, began to, therefore,* and *then.*

Answers

You Try It! 1. *cause—factories continued to spread; effects—craftspeople felt threatened, shop owners had to compete with factories by hiring more workers, workers were paid less;* **2.** *Factories spread; craftspeople felt threatened; more workers were hired; each shop worker was paid less;* **3.** *effect—wages went down; three causes—a wave of immigration, immigrants willing to work for lower wages, and competition for jobs due to unemployment;* **4.** *causes— immigration and unemployment; effects—wages went down, immigrants willing to work for low pay, immigrants move to the Northeast.*

time, Morse put the work of other scientists together in a practical machine.

The telegraph sent pulses, or surges, of electric current through a wire. The telegraph operator tapped a bar, called a telegraph key, that controlled the length of each pulse. At the other end of the wire, these pulses were changed into clicking sounds. A short click was called a dot. A long click was called a dash. Morse's partner, Alfred Lewis Vail, developed a system known as **Morse code**—different combinations of dots and dashes that represent each letter of the alphabet. For example, *dot dot dot, dash dash dash, dot dot dot* is the distress signal called SOS. Skilled telegraph operators could send and receive many words per minute.

Several years passed before Morse was able to connect two locations with telegraph wires. Despite that achievement, people doubted his machine. Some people did not think that he was reading messages sent from miles away. They claimed that he was making lucky guesses.

Morse's break came during the 1844 Democratic National Convention in Baltimore, Maryland. A telegraph wired news of the presidential candidate's nomination to politicians in Washington. The waiting politicians responded, "Three cheers for the telegraph!" Telegraphs were soon sending and receiving information for businesses, the government, newspapers, and private citizens.

BIOGRAPHY

Samuel F. B. Morse
(1791–1872)

Like steamboat creator Robert Fulton, Samuel F. B. Morse began his career as a painter rather than as an inventor. In 1832 Morse was a widower struggling to raise his three children alone. He became interested in the idea of sending messages electrically. Morse hoped he could invent a device that would earn him enough money to support his family. Eventually, earnings from the telegraph made Morse extremely wealthy.

Drawing Conclusions What motivated Morse to invent the telegraph?

The telegraph grew with the railroad. Telegraph companies strung their wires on poles along railroads across the country. They established telegraph offices in many train stations. Thousands of miles of telegraph line were added every year in the 1850s. The first transcontinental line was finished in 1861. By the time he died in 1872, Morse was famous across the United States.

READING CHECK **Identifying Cause and Effect** What event led to the widespread use of the telegraph, and what effect did the telegraph have on cross-country communications?

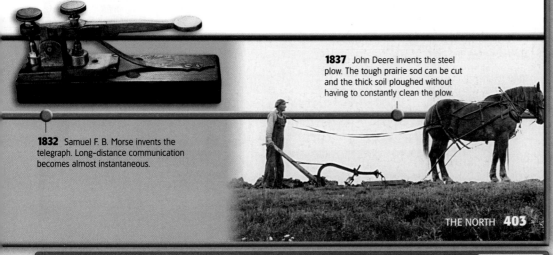

1832 Samuel F. B. Morse invents the telegraph. Long-distance communication becomes almost instantaneous.

1837 John Deere invents the steel plow. The tough prairie sod can be cut and the thick soil ploughed without having to constantly clean the plow.

Differentiating Instruction

Below Level

Struggling Readers

Prep Required

1. Give each student a sheet of paper with the name of an invention described in this section written on it.
2. Have students write brief notes or draw pictures on the reverse side of the paper to describe the invention's purpose, facts about its creation, details about how it influenced society, or its advantages over earlier devices.
3. Have volunteers read or show the clues on the back of their papers and have the rest of the class try to identify the invention.
4. Have students share and keep their papers as study aids. **LS Verbal/Linguistic, Visual/Spatial**

Alternative Assessment Handbook, Rubric 1: Acquiring Information

Direct Teach

Main Idea

1 Telegraph Speeds Communication

The telegraph made swift communication possible from coast to coast.

Describe Who invented the telegraph, and what is it? *Samuel F. B. Morse; a device that sends electric pulses through a wire to another location*

Explain How does Morse code work? *A system of dots and dashes or long and short clicks is used to represent the different letters in the alphabet.*

Evaluate What significant event occurred in 1861, and how do you think it changed the nation? *what—completion of the first transcontinental telegraph wire; effects—sped communication, made the nation seem more united, increased business productivity as a result of faster communication*

Linking to Today

Telegraphs: Hello and Goodbye

By 1866, telegraph cables had been run across the Atlantic Ocean. Cable technology of the 1870s enabled multiple uses along a single line. After Thomas Edison patented the telephone in 1876, telegraph and telephone messages shared the same lines. Despite fears that the telephone would replace the telegraph, the technology flourished for many years. Today, modern communication such as e-mail has made the telegraph obsolete.

Activity **New Technology Poster**

Have each student create a poster showing a communication device that they predict might replace the cell phone or e-mail.

Answers

Biography *wanted to earn enough money to support his family, was interested in the idea of sending messages electronically*

Reading Check *event—Democratic National Convention of 1844; effect—news and information could travel quickly over long distances*

Direct Teach

Main Idea

❷ Steam Power and New Factories

With the shift to steam power, businesses built new factories closer to cities and transportation centers.

Recall What began to replace water power in factories? *steam power*

Identify Cause and Effect How did the use of steam power change where factories were located? *Factories no longer had to be located on streams or waterfalls, so owners began to build factories near cities for better access to workers and markets.*

Main Idea

❸ Improved Farm Equipment

Improved farm equipment and other labor-saving devices made life easier for many Americans.

Recall What problem was John Deere trying to solve with his steel plow? *existing iron plows were not strong enough to plow thick soil*

Identify Cause and Effect How did Cyrus McCormick's mechanical reaper change agriculture? *enabled farmers to harvest huge fields*

CRF: Biography Activity: John Deere

Focus on Indiana

IN 8.1.27

Make Generalizations How did new technology such as Oliver's plow help the U.S. economy grow? *New technology reduced the time and effort needed to produce goods and crops.*

Answers

Reading Check (left) *Factories were built closer to cities, which led to lower wages and shipping costs, made cities industrial centers, drew immigrants and rural people, and led to urban growth.*

Reading Check (right) *advertisements, demonstrations, provided repair and spare parts departments, offered credit*

FOCUS ON INDIANA An improvement on John Deere's plow design was introduced by James Oliver in South Bend, Indiana. Oliver's "chilled plow" was made of strong iron, but the face was smooth.

Steam Power and New Factories

At the start of the Industrial Revolution, most factories ran on waterpower. In time, however, factory owners began using steam power. This shift brought major changes to the nation's industries. Water-powered factories had to be built near streams or waterfalls. In contrast, steam power allowed business owners to build factories almost anywhere. Yet the Northeast was still home to most of the nation's industry. By 1860 New England alone had as many factories as the entire South did.

Some companies decided to build their factories closer to cities and transportation centers. This provided easier access to workers, allowing businesses to lower wages. Being closer to cities also reduced shipping costs. Cities soon became the center of industrial growth. People from rural areas as well as foreign countries flocked to the cities for factory jobs.

Factory workers improved the designs of many kinds of machines. Mechanics invented tools that could cut and shape metal, stone, and wood with great precision. By the 1840s this new machinery was able to produce interchangeable parts. Within a short period of time, the growing machine-tool industry was even making customized equipment.

READING CHECK **Finding Main Ideas** What changes resulted from the shift to steam power?

Improved Farm Equipment

During the 1830s, technology began transforming the farm as well as the factory. In 1837 blacksmith **John Deere** saw that friends in Illinois had difficulty plowing thick soil with iron plows. He thought a steel blade might work better. His design for a steel plow was a success. By 1846 Deere was selling 1,000 plows per year.

In 1831 **Cyrus McCormick** developed a new harvesting machine, the mechanical reaper, which quickly and efficiently cut down wheat. He began mass producing his reapers in a Chicago factory. McCormick used new methods to encourage sales. His company advertised, gave demonstrations, and provided a repair and spare parts department. He also let customers buy on credit.

The combination of Deere's plow and McCormick's reaper allowed Midwestern farmers to plant and harvest huge crop fields. By 1860, U.S. farmers were producing more than 170 million bushels of wheat and more than 800 million bushels of corn per year.

READING CHECK **Summarizing** What marketing methods did McCormick use to help sell his farm equipment?

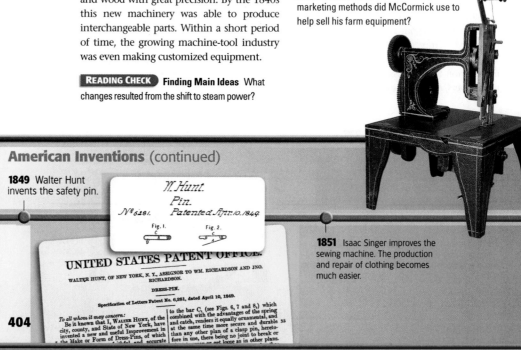

American Inventions (continued)

1849 Walter Hunt invents the safety pin.

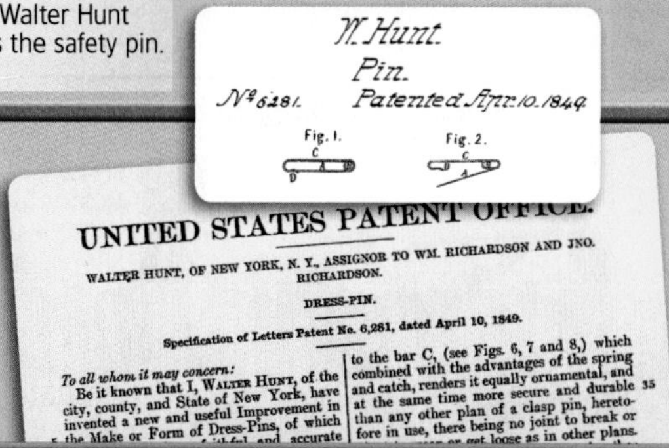
W. Hunt.
Pin.
No. 6281. Patented Apr. 10. 1849.
Fig. 1. Fig. 2.

UNITED STATES PATENT OFFICE.

WALTER HUNT, OF NEW YORK, N. Y., ASSIGNOR TO WM. RICHARDSON AND JNO. RICHARDSON.

DRESS-PIN.

Specification of Letters Patent No. 6,281, dated April 10, 1849.

To all whom it may concern:
Be it known that I, WALTER HUNT, of the city, county, and State of New York, have invented a new and useful Improvement in the Make or Form of Dress-Pins, of which ... faithful and accurate ...

to the bar C, (see Figs. 6, 7 and 8,) which combined with the advantages of the spring and catch, renders it equally ornamental, and at the same time more secure and durable than any other plan of a clasp pin, heretofore in use, there being no joint to break or ... get loose as in other plans.

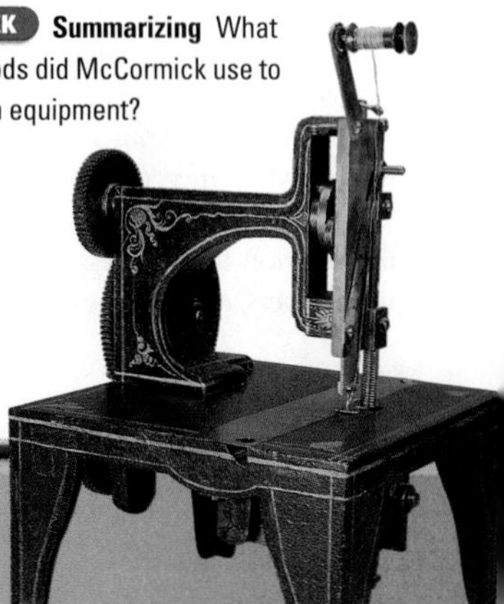

1851 Isaac Singer improves the sewing machine. The production and repair of clothing becomes much easier.

Collaborative Learning

At Level

New Technology Jingles

Materials: recordings of product jingles (optional)

1. Organize students into small groups. Assign each group one of the inventions or advances in technology mentioned in this section.
2. Have each group write a jingle promoting either the sale of the item or its use (such as the use of the telegraph service).
3. If possible, play recordings of some product jingles for students before they start working. Allow the groups to select existing tunes to use for their jingles.
4. Have each group practice its jingle and then perform it for the class. **LS Interpersonal, Verbal/Linguistic**

Alternative Assessment Handbook, Rubrics 2: Advertisements; and 26: Poems and Songs

Changing Life at Home

Many inventions of the Industrial Revolution simply made life easier. When Alexis de Tocqueville of France visited the United States in the early 1830s, he identified what he called a very American quality.

> "[Americans want] to be always making life more comfortable and convenient, to avoid trouble, and to satisfy the smallest wants [desires] without effort and almost without cost."
>
> —Alexis de Tocqueville, from *Democracy in America*

The sewing machine, first invented by Elias Howe, a factory apprentice in Lowell, Massachusetts, was one of these conveniences. **Isaac Singer** then made improvements to Howe's design. Like McCormick, Singer allowed customers to buy his machines on credit and provided service. By 1860 Singer's company was the world's largest maker of sewing machines.

Other advances improved on everyday items. In the 1830s, iceboxes cooled by large blocks of ice became available. Iceboxes stored fresh food safely for longer periods. Iron cookstoves began replacing cooking fires and stone hearths.

Companies also began to mass produce earlier inventions. This allowed many families to buy household items, such as clocks, that they could not afford in the past. For example, a clock that cost $50 in 1800 was selling for only $1.50 by the 1850s. Additional useful items created during this period include matches, introduced in the 1830s, and the safety pin, invented in 1849. All of these inventions helped make life at home more convenient for an increasing number of Americans.

THE IMPACT TODAY New inventions, such as cell phones, laptop computers, and microwave ovens, continue to make life easier and more convenient for people today.

READING CHECK **Analyzing** How did labor-saving inventions affect daily life?

SUMMARY AND PREVIEW New machines and inventions changed the way Americans lived and did business in the early 1800s. In the next section you will learn how agricultural changes affected the South.

1859 Manufactured goods become more valuable than agricultural goods in the country's economy for the first time. The United States is becoming a modern industrial nation.

ANALYSIS SKILL **READING TIME LINES**

Which two inventions improved American agriculture?

Section 4 Assessment

go.hrw.com **Online Quiz** KEYWORD: SF7 HP12

Reviewing Ideas, Terms, and People

1. a. **Describe** How did the **telegraph** work?
   b. **Predict** What impact might the telegraph have on the future of the United States?
2. a. **Describe** How did waterpowered factories differ from steam-powered factories?
   b. **Explain** How did the shift to steam power lead to the growth of cities?
3. a. **Identify** What contributions did **Cyrus McCormick** and **John Deere** make to farming?
   b. **Analyze** What effect did new inventions have on agriculture in the United States?
4. a. **Identify** What inventions improved life at home?
   b. **Evaluate** Which invention do you think had the greatest effect on the daily lives of Americans? Why?

Critical Thinking

5. **Supporting a Point of View** Review your notes on technological advances and their effects. Then create a graphic organizer like the one below that shows the top three advances you think are most important and why.

Most Important	Why

FOCUS ON WRITING

6. **Describing Technological Advances** Add notes about the inventions mentioned in this section to your chart. Think about which invention you will use for your newspaper advertisement.

Direct Teach

Main Idea

4 Changing Life at Home

New inventions changed lives in American homes.

Explain What other new inventions improved daily life for Americans? *sewing machine, icebox, iron cookstove, matches, safety pin*

Evaluate Do you think de Tocqueville's opinion of Americans is still true today? Why or why not? *possible answer—Yes, because Americans continue to create devices to improve life.*

CRF: Interdisciplinary Project: Using Measurements

Review & Assess

Close

Briefly review the ways in which new technology and inventions changed American life and business.

Review

go.hrw.com Online Quiz, Section 12.4

Assess

SE Section 4 Assessment

PASS: Section Quiz 12.4

Alternative Assessment Handbook

Reteach/Classroom Intervention

Interactive Reader and Study Guide, Section 12.4

Interactive Skills Tutor CD-ROM

Section 4 Assessment Answers

1. **a.** It sent electrical pulses through a wire, which were changed into clicking sounds that represented letters in the alphabet.
   b. more unified nation, business growth
2. **a.** Water-powered factories had to be located near running water; steam-powered factories could be built almost anywhere.
   b. Factories were built closer to cities, which drew immigrants and people from rural areas.
3. **a.** McCormick—mechanical reaper; Deere—steel plow
   b. larger harvests, ability to farm more land
4. **a.** sewing machine, icebox, iron cookstove, matches, safety pin
   b. Answers will vary but should reflect an knowledge of the effects of new inventions.
5. possible answer: Telegraph—Information could travel quickly over long distances; Steam Power—factories moved, people moved to cities, cities grew; Mass Production—more families were able to buy useful household items, such as clocks
6. Students should describe the inventions.

Answers

Reading Time Lines *steel plow, mechanical reaper*

Reading Check *People could do things faster and more easily and conveniently, had more time for leisure.*

Social Studies Skills

Personal Conviction and Bias

Activity **Bias in the News**

Materials: newspaper front and editorial pages

1. Pass out the editorial page and the front page from a local newspaper. Have students contrast the articles that appear on each page. Guide students in determining that the front-page news coverage is mainly objective reporting of facts. The editorial page likely contains many opinionated items.
2. Next, have students examine the editorials and letters to the editor. Ask students to identify any biases the writers might hold. How are these biases shaping the writers' viewpoints and opinions? See if students can find examples of stereotyping or prejudice.
3. Then assign students one editorial or letter to the editor. Have each student create a three-column chart listing the verifiable statements, or facts; the unverifiable statements, or opinions; and any examples of bias. Review students' charts as a class.

LS Verbal/Linguistic

Alternative Assessment Handbook, Rubric 7: Charts

Interactive Skills Tutor CD-ROM, Lesson 20: Evaluate Sources of Information for Authenticity, Reliability, and Bias

CRF: Social Studies Skills Activity, Personal Conviction and Bias

Social Studies Skills

Analysis | Critical Thinking | Civic Participation | Study

Personal Conviction and Bias

Define the Skill

Everyone has *convictions,* or firmly held beliefs. However, when we let our beliefs automatically slant or shape our point of view on topics, we may be showing bias. *Bias* is a fixed idea or opinion about someone or something. Some bias is based on a set of ideas about a group to which the person or thing belongs. This type of bias is called a *stereotype.* If the group is defined by race, religion, age, gender, or similar characteristics, the bias is known as *prejudice.*

Bias, stereotypes, and prejudice are not always negative in nature. They include favorable opinions too. For example, the belief that a student is good at math because that person is male is a bias that shows both stereotyping and prejudice.

We should always be on guard for the presence of personal bias. Eliminating stereotyping and prejudice is particularly important. However, even "good" biases can slant how we view, judge, and communicate information. Honest and accurate communication requires that the information and ideas we express be as free of bias as possible.

Learn the Skill

Not all beliefs are biases, even if those beliefs are strongly held. Biases are beliefs that have little or no evidence to support them. The more unreasonable a person's view is in light of facts and evidence, the more likely it is that the belief is a bias.

Another characteristic of bias is the person's reluctance to question his or her belief if it is challenged by evidence. Sometimes people stubbornly cling to views that overwhelming evidence proves wrong. This is why bias is defined as a "fixed" idea or opinion. One of the most damaging effects of bias, and a good reason for trying to avoid it, is that it can prevent us from learning new things.

The following precautions can help you to reduce the amount of bias you hold and express.

1. When discussing a topic, keep in mind beliefs and experiences in your own background that might affect how you feel about the topic.
2. Try to not mix statements of fact with statements of opinion. Clearly separate and indicate what you *know* to be true from what you *believe* to be true.
3. Avoid using emotional, positive, or negative words when communicating factual information.

Practice the Skill

In 1834 Tennessee congressman Davy Crockett visited the textile mills at Lowell, Massachusetts. Read his account of the "Lowell girls" who worked in the factory and complete the activity below.

> "Here are thousands [of young women], useful to others, . . . with the prospect before them of future comfort and respectability . . . There are more than five thousand females employed in Lowell; and when you come to see the amount of labour performed by them, in superintending [operating] the different machinery, you will be astonished."

Suppose that you were a "Lowell girl" who has just read this account of Crockett's visit. Write a letter to the editor of the *Lowell Offering* reacting to the biases and stereotypes about women that Crockett shows in his account.

Social Studies Skills Activity: Personal Conviction and Bias

Identifying Bias in Primary Sources

At Level

1. Have students review "Primary Source: Sarah G. Bagley and Workers' Rights" in Section 2 of this chapter.
2. Write the following questions for students to see. Have students work in pairs or in small groups to answer the questions.
   - What beliefs and experiences in Bagley's background might have shaped her views?
   - What opinions does she present?
   - What emotional or negative language does she use?
   - What biases and stereotypes does the passage reveal?
3. Discuss students' answers as a class. If time allows, have students compare and contrast the biases of Crockett to those of Bagley.

LS Interpersonal, Verbal/Linguistic

Alternative Assessment Handbook, Rubric 16: Judging Information

Answers

Practice the Skill *Answers will vary, but students should note that Crockett assumes that the work the women are doing makes them useful and will help ensure their respectability. He also thinks everyone will be astonished to see the amount and type of work the women are doing.*

CHAPTER 12

Chapter Review

HOLT History's Impact
▶ **video series**
Review the video to answer the closing question:
How do you think ease of travel has affected U.S. population centers?

Visual Summary

QUICK FACTS *Use the visual summary below to help you review the main ideas of the chapter.*

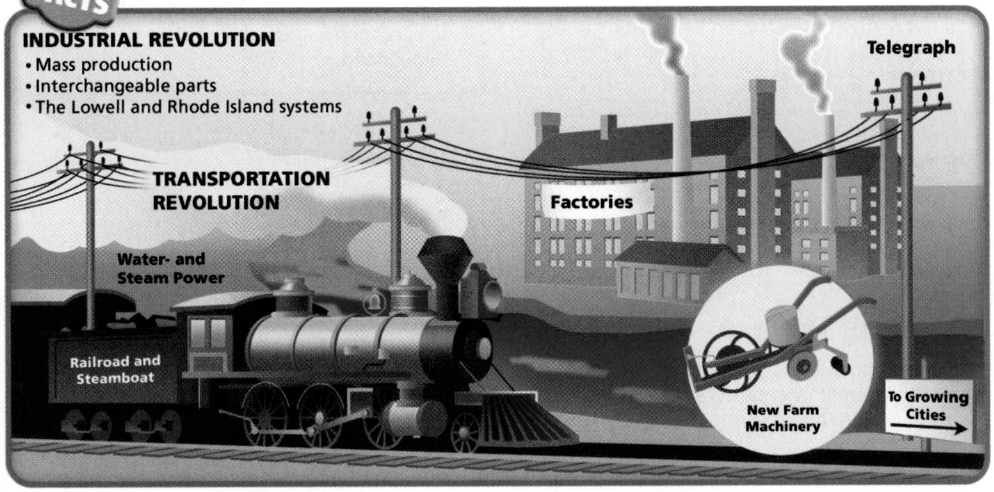

Reviewing Vocabulary, Terms, and People

Complete each sentence below by filling in the blank with the correct term or person from the chapter.

1. The system of ____________ was developed to represent letters of the alphabet when sending telegraph messages.
2. The first American woman to hold a high-ranking position in the labor movement was ________________________________.
3. The __________ was a period of rapid growth in the use of machines and manufacturing.
4. The first locomotive in the United States was built by ________________________________.
5. Workers would sometimes go on _________ to force factory owners to meet their demands for better pay and working conditions.
6. The __________ industry, which produced cloth items, was the first to use machines for manufacturing.

Comprehension and Critical Thinking

SECTION 1 *(Pages 384–389)*

7. a. Identify What ideas did Eli Whitney want to apply to the manufacture of guns?

b. Analyze How did the War of 1812 lead to a boom in manufacturing in the United States?

c. Elaborate Why do you think the Industrial Revolution began in Great Britain rather than in the United States?

SECTION 2 *(Pages 390–395)*

8. a. Describe What was mill life like?

b. Draw Conclusions How did the Rhode Island system and the Lowell system change the lives of American workers?

c. Evaluate Were reformers such as Sarah G. Bagley effective in improving labor conditions? Why?

Answers

History's Impact

Video Series It is easier to commute now, so not as many people live in the cities where they work.

Visual Summary

Review and Inquiry The inventions shown contributed to the growth of cities. Have students list the key events and people connected to each invention shown. Have students write a paragraph describing the overall effects of the Industrial Revolution.

Quick Facts Transparency 34: The North Visual Summary

Reviewing Vocabulary, Terms and People

1. Morse code
2. Sarah G. Bagley
3. Industrial Revolution
4. Peter Cooper
5. strike
6. textile

Comprehension and Critical Thinking

7. a. interchangeable parts and the use of machines powered by water
b. The War of 1812 stopped the export of many foreign goods, Americans bought American goods, manufacturing increased.
c. Great Britain had more trouble meeting the demand for goods, which led to the development of machines to improve efficiency.

Review and Assessment Resources

Review and Reinforce

- **SE** Chapter Review
- **CRF:** Chapter Review Activity
- Quick Facts Transparency 34: The North Visual Summary
- Spanish Chapter Summaries Audio CD Program
- Online Chapter Summaries in Spanish
- **OSP** Holt PuzzlePro; GameTool for ExamView
- Quiz Game CD-ROM

Assess

- **SE** Standardized Test Practice
- PASS: Chapter 12 Tests, Forms A and B
- Alternative Assessment Handbook
- **OSP** ExamView Test Generator, Chapter Test
- Differentiated Instruction Modified Worksheets and Tests CD-ROM: Chapter Test
- **HOAP** Holt Online Assessment Program (in the Premier Online Edition)

Reteach/Intervene

- Interactive Reader and Study Guide
- Differentiated Instruction Teacher Management System: Lesson Plans for Differentiated Instruction
- Differentiated Instruction Modified Worksheets and Tests CD-ROM
- Interactive Skills Tutor CD-ROM

go.hrw.com
Online Resources
Chapter Resources:
KEYWORD: SF7 CH12

Answers

8. a. monotonous work for long hours; sometimes dangerous
b. Many people, including women and children, moved to towns or cities and began working in factories instead of on farms or at home.
c. possible answers—Yes, several states passed 10-hour workday laws; no, success was limited because the courts and police supported the owners.

9. a. business and trade grew; improved travel for people
b. possible answers—They had a successful business that the country depended on for trade, travel, and transportation
c. Students' answers will vary but should reflect an understanding of the ways in which the Transportation Revolution changed the economy and life in the United States.

10. a. shifted to using steam power, which enabled factories to be built almost anywhere
b. People could communicate quickly over long distances.
c. Answers will vary, but students should consider working conditions in factories.

Reviewing Themes

11. Students might mention the water frame, the steam engine, the steamboat, the railroad, the telegraph, the mechanical reaper, the sewing machine, the icebox, or even matches or safety pins. Students should provide reasons to support their selections.

12. The Industrial Revolution created a boom in business and led to economic growth and expansion. With advances in manufacturing, agriculture, transportation, and communication, farms and businesses were able to produce more goods faster and at lower prices, and trade increased.

SECTION 3 *(Pages 396–401)*

9. a. **Describe** How were Americans affected by the introduction of steamboats?
b. **Make Inferences** How did railroad companies become some of the most powerful businesses in the country?
c. **Elaborate** What was the most important result of the Transportation Revolution? Why?

SECTION 4 *(Pages 402–405)*

10. a. **Recall** What important change took place in how factories were powered?
b. **Draw Conclusions** How did the telegraph affect communication in the United States?
c. **Evaluate** Do you think moving factories close to cities helped or hurt working life? Explain.

Reviewing Themes

11. **Science and Technology** What are the three most important inventions of the Industrial Revolution? Why?

12. **Economics** What was the overall effect of the Industrial Revolution on the U.S. economy?

Using the Internet

go.hrw.com
KEYWORD: SF7 CH12

13. **Activity: Marketing Plan** The Industrial Revolution changed the way goods were produced. New inventions created easier, faster, or completely new ways of doing things. Enter the activity keyword and research inventions made between 1790 and 1860. Then create a plan for how to sell one of the inventions. In your plan, identify the problems the invention will fix, your target audience, and how the invention should be advertised and sold.

Reading Skills

Causes and Effects in History *Use the Reading Skills taught in this chapter to answer the question about the reading selection below.*

> Many young women came to Lowell from across New England. They wanted the chance to earn money instead of working on the family farm. *(p. 392)*

14. According to the passage above, what was a cause for moving to Lowell?
a. working long hours
b. earning money
c. meeting people
d. working on a farm

Social Studies Skills

Personal Conviction and Bias *Use the Social Studies Skills taught in this chapter to answer the question about the reading selection below.*

> "Is anyone such a fool as to suppose that out of six thousand factory girls in Lowell, sixty would be there if they could help it?"
> —Sarah G. Bagley, quoted in *The Belles of New England* by William Moran

15. Do you think that Bagley's opposition to the Lowell system was unfairly biased? Why or why not?

FOCUS ON WRITING

16. **Writing Your Newspaper Advertisement** Look over your chart, and choose one invention for your advertisement. Then answer these questions to help you plan your advertisement: Who is your audience? Who will buy this invention? How will the invention benefit this audience? What words or phrases will best persuade this audience? Once you have answered these questions, design your advertisement. To draw readers' attention to your ad, include an illustration, a catchy heading, and a few lines of text.

Using the Internet

13. Go to the HRW Web site and enter the keyword shown to access a rubric for this activity.

KEYWORD: SF7 CH12

Reading Skills

14. b

Social Studies Skills

15. Answers will vary, but students should exhibit an understanding of bias and provide examples from the reading selection to support their positions.

Focus on Writing

16. **Rubric** Students' newspaper advertisements should
- briefly describe the invention.
- explain the benefits of the invention and who can use it.
- be persuasive.
- include an illustration and catchy heading that grabs readers' attentions.

CRF: Focus on Writing: Newspaper Advertisement

CHAPTER 12

Standardized Test Practice

8.1.10, 8.4.5, 8.4.6, 8.4.9

DIRECTIONS: Read each question and write the letter of the best response.

1 The first machines of the Industrial Revolution were powered by

A electricity.
B water.
C animals.
D coal.

2 The earliest important evidence of the Industrial Revolution in America was found in

A the way cotton was processed for market.
B the production of tobacco products.
C the manufacture of cloth and thread.
D the construction of the first steam railroads.

3 Which of the following was a development of the Transportation Revolution of the mid-1800s?

A automobiles
B wind-powered boats
C diesel freighters
D steam-powered trains

4 What change in technology allowed business owners to sell their goods in markets across the country?

A the Lowell system
B the growth of railroads
C the invention of the telegraph
D the Arkwright system

5 Eli Whitney's idea of interchangeable parts resulted in

A the dominance of American manufacturing.
B the beginning of the Industrial Revolution.
C a rapid expansion of railroads.
D the mass production of goods.

6 The inventions of John Deere and Cyrus McCormick

A improved communication.
B introduced two new factory labor systems.
C helped increase agricultural production in the United States.
D led to manufacturing breakthroughs in the textile industry.

7 Read the following passage written by a textile worker and use it to answer the question below.

> "The little money I could earn—one dollar a week, besides the price of my board—was needed in the family, and I must return [from home] to the mill . . . I began to reflect on life rather seriously for a girl of twelve or thirteen. What was I here for? What would I make of myself? . . . We did not forget that we were working girls . . . clearing away a few weeds from the overgrown track of independent labor for other women . . . [so that] no real odium [disrespect] could be attached to any honest toil that any self-respecting woman might undertake."
>
> —from *A New England Girlhood* by Lucy Larcom (1824–1893)

Document-Based Question **How did Larcom see the role of women changing in the workforce?**

Answers

1. B
Break Down the Question: This question requires students to place events in their correct sequence. Point out that the question focuses on the Industrial Revolution, which eliminates options A and C.

2. C
Break Down the Question: This question requires students to recall factual information. Refer students who have trouble to Section 1.

3. D
Break Down the Question: This question requires students to identify cause and effect. Tell students to begin by eliminating all the items that did not result from the Transportation Revolution of the 1800s.

4. B
Break Down the Question: This question requires students to identify cause and effect. Refer students who have trouble to Section 3.

5. D
Break Down the Question: This question requires students to recall factual information. Refer students who have trouble to Section 1.

6. C
Break Down the Question: This question requires students to recall factual information. Refer students who have trouble to Section 4.

7. Larcom saw the work she and other young girls were doing as "clearing away a few weeds from the overgrown tack of independent labor for women," indicating that she likely thought conditions in the workplace were gradually improving for women.

Break Down the Question Clearing away weeds is necessary for the overall health of a garden. Likewise, Larcom is probably suggesting that the work she engages in is necessary for the overall health of the role of women in the workplace.

Intervention Resources

Reproducible

- Interactive Reader and Study Guide
- Differentiated Instruction Teacher Management System: Lesson Plans for Differentiated Instruction

Technology

- Quick Facts Transparency 34: The North Visual Summary
- Differentiated Instruction Modified Worksheets and Tests CD-ROM
- Interactive Skills Tutor CD-ROM

Tips for Test Taking

Go With Your Gut When taking tests, a person's first impulse about an answer is many times correct. Tell students to consider carefully before changing their answers to multiple choice or true-false questions. If students do decide to change an answer, they should do so because they are confident about the change.

Chapter 13 Planning Guide

The South

Chapter Overview	Reproducible Resources	Technology Resources
CHAPTER 13 **pp. 410–433** **Overview: In this chapter, students will study the development of the South's social structure during the early 1800s.**	**Differentiated Instruction Teacher Management System:*** • Instructional Pacing Guides • Lesson Plans for Differentiated Instruction **Interactive Reader and Study Guide:** Chapter Summary Graphic Organizer* **Chapter Resource File:*** • Focus on Writing Activity: Biographical Sketch • Social Studies Skills Activity: Interpreting Graphs • Chapter Review Activity	**Power Presentations with Video CD-ROM** **Differentiated Instruction Modified Worksheets and Tests CD-ROM** **Primary Source Library CD-ROM for United States History** **Interactive Skills Tutor CD-ROM** **Student Edition on Audio CD Program** **History's Impact: United States History Video Program (VHS/DVD):** The Impact of Regional Economics*
Section 1: **Growth of the Cotton Industry** **The Big Idea:** The invention of the cotton gin made the South a one-crop economy and increased the need for slave labor.	**Differentiated Instruction Teacher Management System:** Section 1 Lesson Plan* **Interactive Reader and Study Guide:** Section 13.1 Summary* **Chapter Resource File:*** • Vocabulary Builder Activity, Section 1 • Biography Activity: Eli Whitney • History and Geography Activity: Cotton in the South	**Daily Bellringer Transparency 13.1*** **Map Transparency 44:** The Cotton Kingdom* go.hrw.com **Internet Activity:** Tredegar Iron Works
Section 2: **Southern Society** **The Big Idea:** Southern society centered around agriculture.	**Differentiated Instruction Teacher Management System:** Section 2 Lesson Plan* **Interactive Reader and Study Guide:** Section 13.2 Summary* **Chapter Resource File:*** • Vocabulary Builder Activity, Section 2 • Biography Activity: Mary Boykin Chesnut • Literature Activity: *Plantation Life before Emancipation* • Primary Source Activity: Frances Anne Kemble, *Journal of a Residence on a Georgian Plantation*	**Daily Bellringer Transparency 13.2***
Section 3: **The Slave System** **The Big Idea:** The slave system in the South produced harsh living conditions and occasional rebellions.	**Differentiated Instruction Teacher Management System:** Section 3 Lesson Plan* **Interactive Reader and Study Guide:** Section 13.3 Summary* **Chapter Resource File:*** • Vocabulary Builder Activity, Section 3 • Primary Source Activity: Jacob Stroyer, *My Life in the South* • Biography Activity: Nat Turner • Biography Activity: Denmark Vesey • Primary Source Activity: The Denmark Vesey Conspiracy	**Daily Bellringer Transparency 13.3*** **Map Transparency 45:** Nat Turner's Rebellion* go.hrw.com **Internet Activity:** Slavery and Housing go.hrw.com **Internet Activity:** Freedom Diary

SE Student Edition | Print Resource | Audio CD
TE Teacher's Edition | Transparency | CD-ROM
go.hrw.com | **LS** Learning Styles | Video
TOS Indiana Teacher One Stop | * also on Indiana Teacher One Stop

Review, Assessment, Intervention

- **Quick Facts Transparency 35:** The South Visual Summary*
- **Spanish Chapter Summaries Audio CD Program**
- **Progress Assessment Support System (PASS):** Chapter Tests A and B*
- **Differentiated Instruction Modified Worksheets and Tests CD-ROM:** Modified Chapter Test
- **Online Chapter Summaries in Spanish**
- TOS **Indiana Teacher One Stop:** ExamView Test Generator (English/Spanish)
- **Alternative Assessment Handbook**
- HOAP **Holt Online Assessment Program,** in the Holt Premier Online Student Edition

- **PASS:** Section Quiz 13.1*
- **Online Quiz:** Section 13.1
- **Alternative Assessment Handbook**

- **PASS:** Section Quiz 13.2*
- **Online Quiz:** Section 13.2
- **Alternative Assessment Handbook**

- **PASS:** Section Quiz 13.3*
- **Online Quiz:** Section 13.3
- **Alternative Assessment Handbook**

HOLT
History's Impact
United States History Video Program (VHS/DVD)
The Impact of Regional Economics
Suggested use: as a chapter introduction

Power Presentations with Video CD-ROM

Power Presentations with Video are visual presentations of each chapter's main ideas. Presentations can be customized by including Quick Facts charts, images from the text, and video clips.

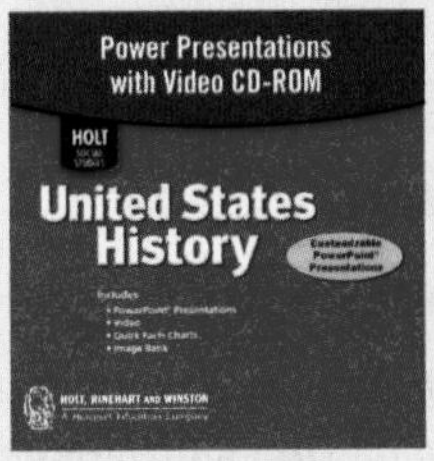

DIVISION FOR PUBLIC EDUCATION
AMERICAN BAR ASSOCIATION

Developed by the Division for Public Education of the American Bar Association, these materials are part of the **Democracy and Civic Education Resources.**

- **Constitution Study Guide**
- **Supreme Court Case Studies**

Holt Online Learning

go.hrw.com
Teacher Resources
KEYWORD: SF7 TEACHER

go.hrw.com
Student Resources
KEYWORD: SF7 CH13

- Document-Based Questions
- Interactive Multimedia Activities
- Current Events
- Chapter-based Internet Activities
- and more!

Holt Interactive
Online Student Edition

Complete online support for interactivity, assessment, and reporting

- Interactive Maps and Notebook
- Standardized Test Prep
- Homework Practice and Research Activities Online

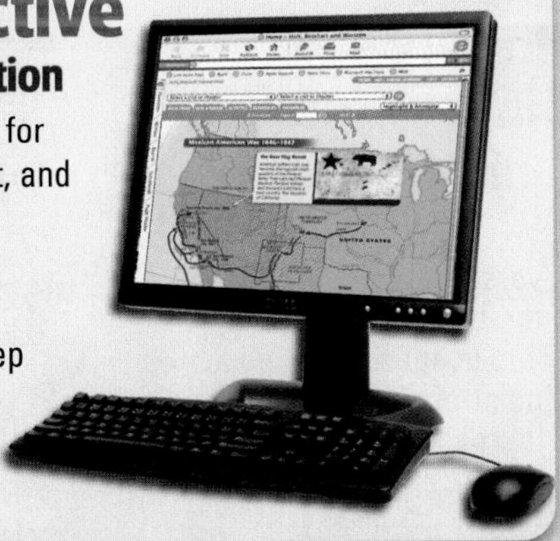

CHAPTER 13 PLANNING GUIDE

Differentiating Instruction

How do I address the needs of varied learners?

The Target Resource acts as your primary strategy for differentiated instruction.

ENGLISH-LANGUAGE LEARNERS & STRUGGLING READERS

TARGET RESOURCE

English-Language Learner Strategies and Activities

- Build Academic Vocabulary
- Develop Oral and Written Language Structures

Spanish Resources

Spanish Chapter Summaries Audio CD

Spanish Chapter Summaries Online

Teacher's One-Stop Planner:

- ExamView Test Generator, Spanish
- PuzzlePro, Spanish

Additional Resources

Differentiated Instruction Teacher Management System: Lesson Plans for Differentiated Instruction

Chapter Resources:

- Vocabulary Builder Activities
- Social Studies Skills Activity: Interpreting Graphs

Quick Facts Transparency 35: The South Visual Summary

Student Edition on Audio CD Program

Interactive Skills Tutor CD-ROM

SPECIAL NEEDS LEARNERS

TARGET RESOURCE

Differentiated Instruction Modified Worksheets and Tests CD-ROM

- Vocabulary Flash Cards
- Modified Vocabulary Builder Activities
- Modified Chapter Review Activity
- Modified Chapter Test

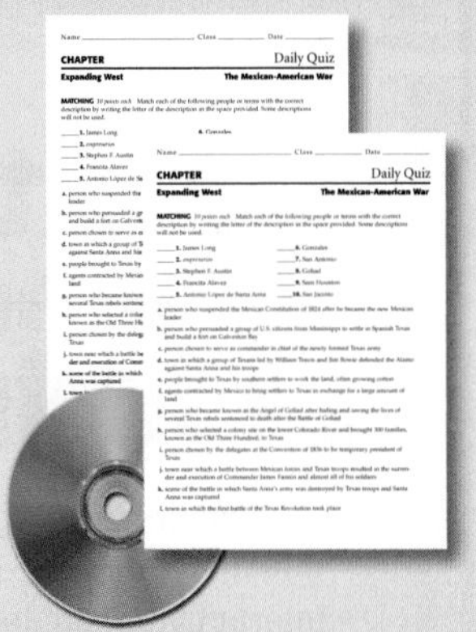

Additional Resources

Differentiated Instruction Teacher Management System: Lesson Plans for Differentiated Instruction

Interactive Reader and Study Guide

Social Studies Skills Activity: Interpreting Graphs

Student Edition on Audio CD Program

Interactive Skills Tutor CD-ROM

ADVANCED/GIFTED-AND-TALENTED STUDENTS

TARGET RESOURCE

Primary Source Library CD-ROM for United States History

The Library contains longer versions of quotations in the text, extra sources, and images. Included are point-of-view articles, journals, diaries, historical fiction, and political documents.

Additional Resources

Differentiated Instruction Teacher Management System: Lesson Plans for Differentiated Instruction

Chapter Resource File:

- Focus on Writing Activity: Biographical Sketch
- Literature Activity: Plantation Life before Emancipation
- Primary Source Activity: Frances Anne Kemble, *Journal of a Residence on a Georgian Plantation*
- Primary Source Activity: Jacob Stroyer, *My Life in the South*
- Primary Source Activity: The Denmark Vesey Conspiracy

Differentiated Activities in the Teacher's Edition

- Effects of the Cotton Boom Chart, p. 416
- Life in the Urban South Chart, p. 422
- Slave Category Identification, p. 425
- Challenges to the Slavery System Chart, p. 428

Differentiated Activities in the Teacher's Edition

- Slave Category Identification, p. 425

Differentiated Activities in the Teacher's Edition

- Dependence on Cotton Editorial, p. 418
- Slavery: An Oral History, p. 426
- Nat Turner Dialogue, p. 428

Teacher One Stop™

How can I manage the lesson plans and support materials for differentiated instruction?

With the Indiana Teacher One Stop, you can easily organize and print lesson plans, planning guides, and instructional materials for all learners.

The Indiana Teacher One Stop includes the following materials to help you differentiate instruction:

- Interactive Teacher's Edition
- Calendar Planner and pacing guides
- Editable lesson plans
- All reproducible ancillaries in Adobe Acrobat (PDF) format
- ExamView Test Generator (Eng & Span)
- Transparency and video previews

Professional Development

HOLT Professional Development

What teacher training resources are available to help me grow professionally?

- **In-service and staff development** as part of your Holt Social Studies product purchase
- **Quick Teacher Tutorial Lesson Presentation CD-ROM**
- Intensive tuition-based **Teacher Development Institute**
- **Convenient Holt Speaker Bureau** – face-to-face workshop options
- **PRAXIS™ Test Prep** interactive Web-based content refreshers*
- **Ask A Professional Development Expert** at http://www.hrw.com/prodev/

* PRAXIS is a trademark of Educational Testing Service (ETS). This publication is not endorsed or approved by ETS.

• Chapter Preview •

Chapter Big Ideas

Section 1 The invention of the cotton gin made the South a one-crop economy and increased the need for slave labor.

Section 2 Southern society centered around agriculture.

Section 3 The slave system in the South produced harsh living conditions and occasional rebellions.

Focus on Writing

The **Chapter Resource File** provides a Focus on Writing worksheet to help students organize and write their biographical sketches.

CRF: Focus on Writing Activity: Biographical Sketch

CHAPTER 13 The South

Indiana Standards

Social Studies Standards

8.1.10 Compare differences in ways of life in the northern and osuthern states, including the growth of towns and cities in the North and the growing dependence on slavery in the South.

8.3.1 Read maps to interpret symbols and determine the land forms and human features that represent physical and cultural characteristics of areas in the United States. 1 Identify ways people modified the physical environment as the United States developed and describe the impacts that resulted.

8.4.6 Relate technological change and inventions to changes in labor productivity in the United States in the eighteenth and nineteenth centuries.

8.4.9 Explain and evaluate examples of domstic and international interdependence throughout United States history.

go.hrw.com
Indiana
KEYWORD: SF10 IN

FOCUS ON WRITING

Biographical Sketch In this chapter you will learn about life in the South during the first half of the nineteenth century. Read the chapter, and then write a two-paragraph biographical sketch about a day in the life of a person living on a large cotton farm in the South. You might choose to write about a wealthy male landowner, his wife, or an enslaved man or woman working on the farm. As you read, think about what life would have been like for the different people who lived and worked on the farm. Take notes about farm life in your notebook.

UNITED STATES

1793 Eli Whitney invents the cotton gin.

1800

1794 France ends slavery in its colonies.

WORLD

410 CHAPTER 13

Introduce the Chapter

At Level

Impact of Technology

1. Tell students that in this chapter they will learn how a single invention revived the economy of the South.
2. Have students think of new technology and inventions that they have seen in their lifetime *(e.g., cell phone, DVD, GPS)*. Write the answers for students to see.
3. Then ask students how life has changed because of each new piece of technology or invention. What impact has there been on jobs, communication, and leisure, for example? Are there health or safety issues related to the new invention or technology? Can students predict other changes that might occur in their lifetime? LS **Verbal/Linguistic**

Key to Differentiating Instruction

Below Level
Basic-level activities designed for all students encountering new material

At Level
Intermediate-level activities designed for average students

Above Level
Challenging activities designed for honors and gifted and talented students

Standard English Mastery
Activities designed to improve standard English usage

HOLT

History's Impact

▶ **video series**

Watch the video to understand the impact of regional economies on the nation.

What You Will Learn...

These enslaved people were photographed on a South Carolina plantation in the year 1861. The issue of slavery would have a serious and dramatic impact on the history of the entire United States. In this chapter you will learn how the South developed an agricultural economy, and how that economy was dependent on the labor of enslaved people.

1808 A congressional ban on importing slaves into the United States takes effect.

1807 Parliament bans the slave trade in the British Empire.

1820

1831 Nat Turner's Rebellion leads to fears of further slave revolts in the South.

1835 Alexis de Tocqueville publishes *Democracy in America.*

1840

1837 Victoria is crowned queen of Great Britain.

1848 Joseph R. Anderson becomes the owner of the Tredegar Iron Works, the South's only large iron factory.

1851 Indiana voters approve a new constitution banning African Americans from moving into the state.

1860

1858 A treaty at Tianjin, China, gives Hong Kong to the United Kingdom.

• Chapter Preview •

HOLT

History's Impact

▶ **video series**

See the Video Teacher's Guide for strategies for using the chapter video to teach about the impact of regional economies on the nation.

Explore the Picture

Life on a Southern Plantation

From sunrise to sunset, enslaved Africans' lives were controlled. A ringing bell or blowing horn called workers to the fields before dawn. On cotton plantations, June was a particularly hard month because the fields had to be broken up by hand with tools. Under the glare of the hot sun, each adult slave was expected to break up a half acre of ground per day.

Analyzing Visuals What evidence can you see in the photo that life for enslaved Africans on a southern plantation was harsh? *possible answer—The people shown have no shoes; they carry hand tools; they are not smiling.*

go.hrw.com

Online Resources

Chapter Resources:
KEYWORD: SF7 CH13

Teacher Resources:
KEYWORD: SF7 TEACHER

Explore the Time Line

1. What did Eli Whitney invent in 1793? *the cotton gin*
2. In what year did the U.S. Congress ban the import of slaves into the country? *1808*
3. Which two countries limited aspects of slavery and the slave trade prior to the 1808 U.S. ban? *France and Great Britain*
4. What effect did Nat Turner's Rebellion in 1831 have? *fears of further slave revolts in the South*

Info to Know

Congressional Ban on Importing Slaves Even though the United States banned the importation of enslaved Africans in 1808, the ban did not undermine or end slavery. Planters in need of labor in Georgia and South Carolina hurried to beat the ban by importing tens of thousands of enslaved Africans before the ban took effect. The illegal smuggling of slaves continued, and the slave population increased as children—the next generation of slaves—were born into slavery.

Reading Social Studies

Understanding Themes

Two themes, economics and society and culture, are presented in this chapter about the South. Ask students to recall ways in which the economy of the South was different from that of the rest of the United States. Remind students that the South depended economically on agriculture. Then ask students to predict how the society and culture of the South might have been affected by this reliance on agriculture. Ask students to write down their predictions and to see which ones are correct as they read the chapter.

Online Research

Focus on Reading Organize the class into small groups. Have students in each group discuss their Internet use and Web sites that they find useful for conducting research. Ask groups to list what they find most valuable about those sites, such as quality of information, layout, and ease of use. Remind students that not all Web sites contain verifiable information. Ask students to list how they determine the quality of information when they are using the Internet. Have each group report its opinions to the class. Discuss the qualities of a Web site that are most important to consider when conducting research.

Reading Social Studies

by Kylene Beers

Economics | Geography | Politics | Society and Culture | Science and Technology

Focus on Themes This chapter takes you into the heart of the South from 1800 through the mid-1800s. As you read, you will discover that the South depended on cotton as its **economic** backbone, especially after the invention of the cotton gin. You will also read about the slave system in the South during this time and about the harsh living conditions slaves endured. As you will see, the South was home to a variety of **societies and cultures**.

Online Research

Focus on Reading Researching history topics on the Web can give you access to valuable information. However, just because the information is on the Web doesn't mean it is automatically valuable.

Evaluating Web Sites Before you use information you find online, you need to evaluate the site it comes from. The checklist below can help you determine if the site is worth your time.

Evaluating Web Sites

Site: ____________ **URL:** ____________ **Date of access:** ____________

Rate each item on this 1–3 scale. Then add up the total score.

	No	Some	Yes
I. Authority			
a. Authors are clearly identified by name.	1	2	3
b. Contact information is provided for authors.	1	2	3
c. Authors' qualifications are clearly stated.	1	2	3
d. Site has been updated recently.	1	2	3
II. Content			
a. Site's information is useful to your project.	1	2	3
b. Information is clear and well-organized.	1	2	3
c. Information appears to be at the right level.	1	2	3
d. Links to additional important information are provided.	1	2	3
e. Information can be verified in other sources.	1	2	3
f. Graphics are helpful, not just decorative.	1	2	3
III. Design and Technical Elements			
a. Pages are readable and easy to navigate.	1	2	3
b. Links to other sites work.	1	2	3

Total Score ____________

36–28 = very good site **27–20 = average site** **below 20 = poor site**

Reading and Skills Resources

Reading Support

- Interactive Reader and Study Guide
- Student Edition on Audio CD Program
- Spanish Chapter Summaries Audio CD Program

Social Studies Skills Support

- Interactive Skills Tutor CD-ROM

Vocabulary Support

- **CRF:** Vocabulary Builder Activities
- **CRF:** Chapter Review Activity
- Differentiated Instruction Modified Worksheets and Tests CD-ROM:
  - Vocabulary Flash Cards
  - Vocabulary Builder Activity
  - Chapter Review Activity
- **OSP** Holt PuzzlePro

You Try It!

The passage below is from the chapter you are about to read.

Cotton Becomes Profitable

From Chapter 13, pp. 414–415

Cotton had been grown in the New World for centuries, but it had not been a very profitable crop. Before cotton could be spun into thread for weaving into cloth, the seeds had to be removed from the cotton fibers.

Long-staple cotton, also called black-seed cotton, was fairly easy to process. Workers could pick the seeds from the cotton with relative ease. But long-staple cotton grew well in only a few places in the South. More common was short-staple cotton, which was also known as green-seed cotton. Removing the seeds from this cotton was difficult and time consuming. A worker could spend an entire day picking the seeds from a single pound of short-staple cotton.

After you read the passage, complete the following activity.

Suppose that after reading this passage you decide to do some research on cotton growing. You use a search engine that directs you to a site. At that site, you find the information described below. Using the evaluation criteria listed on the previous page, decide if this is a site you would recommend to others.

a. The authors of the site are listed as "Bob and Mack, good friends who enjoy working together."

b. The site was last updated on "the last time we got together."

c. The title of the site is "Cotton Pickin'." There are few headings.

d. This ten-page site includes nine pages about the authors' childhood on a cotton farm. No illustrations are included.

e. Pages are very long, but they load quickly, as there are no graphics. There is one link to a site selling cotton clothing.

Key Terms and People

Chapter 13

Section 1

cotton gin *(p. 415)*
planters *(p. 416)*
cotton belt *(p. 416)*
factors *(p. 417)*
Tredegar Iron Works *(p. 419)*

Section 2

yeomen *(p. 422)*

Section 3

folktales *(p. 427)*
spirituals *(p. 427)*
Nat Turner's Rebellion *(p. 428)*
Nat Turner *(p. 428)*

Academic Vocabulary

Success in school is related to knowing academic vocabulary—the words that are frequently used in school assignments and discussions. In this chapter, you will learn the following academic words:

primary *(p. 418)*
aspect *(p. 426)*

As you read Chapter 13, think about what topics would be interesting to research on the Web. If you do some research on the Web, remember to use the evaluation list to analyze the Web site.

Teaching Tip

Remind students of the importance of citing their sources correctly. Stress to students that as they evaluate a Web site, they should write down important information about that site. Among the items students should include in their documentation are the author or authors of a Web site, the exact URL, or address, of the site, the date they accessed the Web site, the date the site was last revised, and the name of the Web site.

Reading Social Studies

Key Terms and People

Preteach the key terms and people from this chapter by asking students what they think each term means or who each person was. Ask the class to identify the terms or people about which they know the least. Write the list of terms for the class to see. Have each student define or identify the terms or people. Then have each student draw an illustration to represent each term or person.
LS Verbal/Linguistic, Visual/Spatial

Focus on Reading

See the **Focus on Reading** questions in this chapter for more practice on this reading social studies skill.

Reading Social Studies Assessment

See the **Chapter Review** at the end of this chapter for student assessment questions related to this reading skill.

Answers

You Try It! *Students should conclude that they would not want to recommend this site to others. Students should note that, among other things, the Web site was not written by qualified authors, nor does it provide useful information about growing cotton.*

Preteach

Bellringer

If YOU were there . . . Use the **Daily Bellringer Transparency** to help students answer the question.

Daily Bellringer Transparency 13.1

The South — Daily Bellringer 13.1

Review the Previous Chapter

Read the list of events below and put them in the correct order.

- **a.** Samuel F. B. Morse perfects the telegraph.
- **b.** Robert Fulton's steamboat the *Clermont* successfully travels up the Hudson River.
- **c.** Englishman Richard Arkwright invents the water frame.
- **d.** The U.S. Supreme Court establishes precedence for the supremacy of federal law over state law in the case of *Gibbons* v. *Ogden*.
- **e.** Francis Cabot Lowell's first textile mill opens.

Preview Section 1

If YOU were there ...

You are a field-worker on a cotton farm in the South in about 1800. Your job is to separate the seeds from the cotton fibers. It is dull, tiring work because the tiny seeds are tangled in the fibers. Sometimes it takes you a whole day just to clean one pound of cotton! Now you hear that someone has invented a machine that can clean cotton 50 times faster than by hand.

How might this machine change your life?

Consider the BENEFITS:
- The job becomes less tedious.
- The machine frees you up to do other things.
- Increased production could result in personal gain.

Consider the DIFFICULTIES:
- The pace of work increases.
- The farm owner now expects you to do other things.
- Machines make competition with other farms more brutal.

Review Answers: c, b, e, d, a

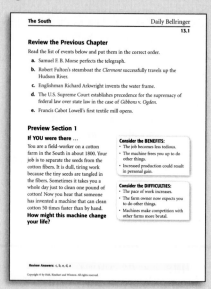

Academic Vocabulary

Review with students the high-use academic term in this section.

primary main, most important (p. 418)

CRF: Vocabulary Builder Activity, Section 1

Taking Notes

Have students copy the graphic organizer onto their own paper and then use it to take notes on the section. This activity will prepare students for the Section Assessment, in which they will complete a graphic organizer that builds on the information using a critical-thinking skill.

Section Correlations

8.1.10 Compare differences in ways of life in the northern and southern states, including the growth of towns and cities in the North and the growing dependence on slavery in the South. **8.3.6** Identify the agricultural regions of the United States and be able to give reasons for the type of land use and subsequent land development during different historical periods. **8.3.9** Analyze human and physical factors that have influenced migration and settlement patterns and relate them to the economic development of the United States.

SECTION 1

Growth of the Cotton Industry

What You Will Learn...

Main Ideas

1. The invention of the cotton gin revived the economy of the South.
2. The cotton gin created a cotton boom in which farmers grew little else.
3. Some people encouraged southerners to focus on other crops and industries.

The Big Idea

The invention of the cotton gin made the South a one-crop economy and increased the need for slave labor.

Key Terms and People

cotton gin, *p. 415*
planters, *p. 416*
cotton belt, *p. 416*
factors, *p. 417*
Tredegar Iron Works, *p. 419*

TAKING NOTES As you read, take notes on the causes of the cotton boom in the South. Record your notes in a graphic organizer like the one shown below.

○ → ○ → Cotton Boom

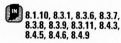

IN 8.1.10, 8.3.1, 8.3.6, 8.3.7, 8.3.8, 8.3.9, 8.3.11, 8.4.3, 8.4.5, 8.4.6, 8.4.9

If YOU were there...

You are a field-worker on a cotton farm in the South in about 1800. Your job is to separate the seeds from the cotton fibers. It is dull, tiring work because the tiny seeds are tangled in the fibers. Sometimes it takes you a whole day just to clean one pound of cotton! Now you hear that someone has invented a machine that can clean cotton 50 times faster than by hand.

How might this machine change your life?

BUILDING BACKGROUND Sectional differences had always existed between different regions of the United States. The revolutionary changes in industry and transportation deepened the differences between North and South. The South remained mainly agricultural. New technology helped the region become the Cotton Kingdom.

Reviving the South's Economy

Before the American Revolution, three crops dominated southern agriculture—tobacco, rice, and indigo. These crops, produced mostly by enslaved African Americans, played a central role in the southern economy and culture.

After the American Revolution, however, prices for tobacco, rice, and indigo dropped. When crop prices fell, the demand for and the price of slaves also went down. In an effort to protect their incomes, many farmers tried, with little success, to grow other crops that needed less labor. Soon, however, cotton would transform the southern economy and greatly increase the demand for slave labor.

Cotton Becomes Profitable

Cotton had been grown in the New World for centuries, but it had not been a very profitable crop. Before cotton could be spun into thread for weaving into cloth, the seeds had to be removed from the cotton fibers.

Teach the Big Idea

At Level

Growth of the Cotton Industry

1. **Teach** To teach the main ideas in the section, use the questions in the Direct Teach boxes.
2. **Apply** Help students understand the significance of the cotton gin to southern agriculture and the South's economy. Have students use information in the section to write a brief encyclopedia entry about the cotton gin. In their entries, have students answer the questions who, what, when, where, how, and why. **LS Verbal/Linguistic**
3. **Review** As you review the section, invite volunteers to read aloud portions of their encyclopedia entries.
4. **Practice/Homework** Ask students to imagine they are southern farm workers who spent all day removing seeds from just one pound of cotton. Have them write journal entries reacting to news of the invention of the cotton gin. **LS Verbal/Linguistic**

Alternative Assessment Handbook, Rubric 15: Journals

Cotton Gin

CONNECT TO SCIENCE AND TECHNOLOGY

Eli Whitney's cotton gin enabled workers to easily remove seeds from cotton fibers. The result was a dramatic increase in cotton production in the South.

How did the cotton gin remove seeds from cotton fibers?

1. The operator turned the crank.
2. The crank turned a roller with teeth that stripped the seeds away from the cotton fiber.
3. Brushes on a second roller lifted the seedless cotton off the teeth of the first cylinder and dropped it out of the machine.
4. A belt connected the rollers so that they would both turn when the crank was turned.

Long-staple cotton, also called black-seed cotton, was fairly easy to process. Workers could pick the seeds from the cotton with relative ease. But long-staple cotton grew well in only a few places in the South. More common was short-staple cotton, which was also known as green-seed cotton. Removing the seeds from this cotton was difficult and time consuming. A worker could spend an entire day picking the seeds from a single pound of short-staple cotton.

By the early 1790s the demand for American cotton began increasing rapidly. For instance, in Great Britain, new textile factories needed raw cotton that could be used for making cloth, and American cotton producers could not keep up with the high demand for their cotton. These producers of cotton needed a machine that could remove the seeds from the cotton more rapidly.

Eli Whitney's Cotton Gin

Northerner Eli Whitney finally patented such a machine in 1793. The year before, Whitney had visited a Georgia plantation owned by Catherine Greene where workers were using a machine that removed seeds from long-staple cotton. This machine did not work well on short-staple cotton, and Greene asked Whitney if he could improve it. By the next spring, Whitney had perfected his design for the **cotton gin**, a machine that removes seeds from short-staple cotton. ("Gin" is short for engine.) The cotton gin used a hand-cranked cylinder with wire teeth to pull cotton fibers from the seeds.

Whitney hoped to keep the design of the gin a secret, but the machine was so useful that his patent was often ignored by other manufacturers. Whitney described how his invention would improve the cotton business.

THE IMPACT TODAY

The same patent law that protected Whitney's invention of the cotton gin protects the rights of inventors today.

Collaborative Learning

At Level

Cotton Gin Marketing Campaign

1. Ask students to consider different ways they have seen one consumer good, such as a car, advertised. Explain that when a product is introduced to consumers, often a marketing campaign—made up of several different components in different media—is created.
2. Organize the class into small groups to develop a class marketing campaign to promote Eli Whitney's cotton gin. Assign each group one of the following products to create: logo and slogan, brochure, poster, and newspaper print advertisement. Encourage students to make each part of the campaign reflect how the cotton gin works and its benefits to buyers.
3. Have each group present its part of the marketing campaign and display the final products in the classroom. **LS Interpersonal, Verbal/Linguistic, Visual/Spatial**

Alternative Assessment Handbook, Rubrics 14: Group Activity; and 29: Presentations

Direct Teach

Main Idea

1 Reviving the South's Economy

The invention of the cotton gin revived the economy of the South.

Explain Why was there less demand for slave labor after the American Revolution? *Crop prices had fallen; landowners cut production or switched to crops that required less labor.*

Summarize What problem did the cotton gin solve? *the difficult and time-consuming process of removing seeds from short-staple cotton*

Predict What effect do you think the cotton gin had on the demand for slave labor? Why? *Demand increased because the cotton gin led to increased cotton farming.*

CRF: Biography Activity: Eli Whitney

Did you know . . .

How did Eli Whitney get the idea for his cotton gin? One legend claims a farm cat inspired Whitney. As the story goes, Whitney saw a farm cat try to claw at chickens. The cat waited patiently for the chickens to come near the fence. When they did, the cat quickly shot its paw through the fence, but was only able to pluck the chickens' feathers with its claws.

Answers

Science and Technology *A hand-cranked roller with wire teeth pulled cotton fibers away from the seeds.*

Direct Teach

Main Idea

❷ The Cotton Boom

The cotton gin created a cotton boom in which farmers grew little else.

Recall How did the cotton gin affect cotton production in the South? *made cotton so profitable that many southern farmers began growing cotton, and cotton production spread and increased rapidly*

Identify Cause and Effect Increased cotton production led to an economic boom in the South. What were the effects of this economic boom on the region? *attracted new settlers, built up wealth among wealthy white southerners, firmly embedded slavery in the South*

CRF: History and Geography Activity: Cotton in the South

Map Transparency 44: The Cotton Kingdom

Interpreting Maps

The Cotton Kingdom

Before and After Which states (or future states) produced cotton before 1820? *Virginia, North Carolina, South Carolina, Georgia, Alabama, Tennessee, Mississippi, Louisiana* Which grew cotton after 1820? *Missouri, Arkansas, Texas, Florida, Oklahoma (Indian Territory)*

Map Transparency 44: The Cotton Kingdom

Info to Know

Cotton Gin Patent After perfecting the cotton gin, Eli Whitney was given the sole right to make the machine in 1794. But other people were easily able to make cotton gins, and began doing so. Whitney sued planters for violating his rights, but he gained next to nothing from his legal battles.

Answers

Interpreting Charts 1. *the South;* **2.** *2.1 million bales*

Reading Check *made processing cotton easier and quicker; increased production of cotton as a cash crop; led to an economic boom*

"One man will clean ten times as much cotton as he can in any other way before known and also clean it much better than in the usual mode [method]. This machine may be turned by water or with a horse, with the greatest ease, and one man and a horse will do more than fifty men with the old machines."

—Eli Whitney, quoted in *Eli Whitney and the Birth of American Technology* by Constance McLaughlin Green

Whitney's gin revolutionized the cotton industry. **Planters**—large-scale farmers who held more than 20 slaves—built cotton gins that could process tons of cotton much faster than hand processing. A healthy crop almost guaranteed financial success because of high demand from the textile industry.

READING CHECK **Drawing Conclusions** What effects did the cotton gin have on the southern economy?

The Cotton Boom

Whitney's invention of the cotton gin made cotton so profitable that southern farmers abandoned other crops in favor of growing cotton. The removal of Native Americans opened up more land, while the development of new types of cotton plants helped spread cotton production throughout the South as far west as Texas. This area of high cotton production became known as the **cotton belt**.

Production increased rapidly—from about 2 million pounds in 1791 to roughly a billion pounds by 1860. As early as 1840, the United States was producing more than half of the cotton grown in the entire world. The economic boom attracted new settlers, built up wealth among wealthy white southerners, and firmly put in place the institution of slavery in the South.

The Cotton Kingdom

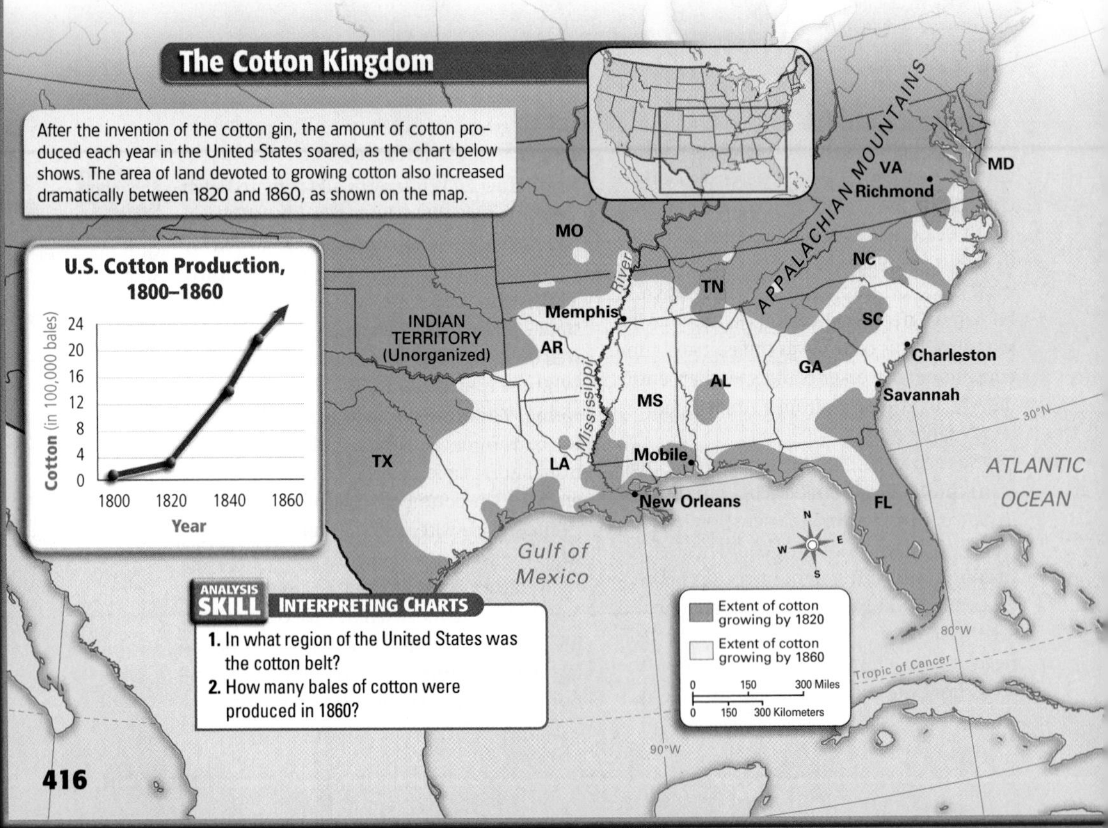

After the invention of the cotton gin, the amount of cotton produced each year in the United States soared, as the chart below shows. The area of land devoted to growing cotton also increased dramatically between 1820 and 1860, as shown on the map.

ANALYSIS SKILL **INTERPRETING CHARTS**

1. In what region of the United States was the cotton belt?
2. How many bales of cotton were produced in 1860?

Differentiating Instruction

Below Level

Struggling Readers

1. Review with students the positive and negative effects of the cotton boom.
2. Draw the chart on the right for students to see. Omit the blue, italicized answers.
3. Have students copy the chart and complete it by listing the positive and negative effects of the cotton boom on the South's economy. **LS Visual/Spatial**

Effects of Cotton Boom

Positive	Negative
• *Growth of economy* • *Build-up of wealth* • *The South became a major player in world trade.* • *Development of cotton trade* • *Growth of cotton-related industries*	• *increased reliance on one crop—cotton* • *firmly embedded the institution of slavery in the South* • *increased internal slave trade*

Cotton Belt

Cotton had many advantages as a cash crop. It cost little to market. Unlike food staples, harvested cotton could be stored for a long time. Because cotton was lighter than other staple crops, it also cost less to transport long distances.

Farmers eager to profit from growing cotton headed west to find land. Farmers also began to apply scientific methods to improve crop production. Cotton had one disadvantage as a crop—it rapidly used up the nutrients in the soil. After a few years, cotton could make the land useless for growing anything. Some agricultural scientists recommended crop rotation—changing the crop grown on a particular plot of land every few years. Different crops needed different nutrients, so crop rotation would keep the land fertile longer. Other agricultural scientists began to study soil chemistry, in an effort to keep the land rich and productive.

As the cotton belt grew, farmers continued trying to improve the crop. Agricultural scientists worked at crossbreeding short-staple cotton with other varieties. As a result, new, stronger types of cotton were soon growing throughout the cotton belt. This led to expansion of the cotton industry through the 1860s.

The cotton boom involved much more than growing and harvesting cotton. Harvested cotton had to be ginned, pressed into bales, and then shipped to market or to warehouses. Special agents helped do everything from marketing cotton to customers to insuring crops against loss or damage. Factories were built to produce items needed by cotton farmers, such as ropes to bale cotton.

Growing and harvesting cotton required many field hands. Rather than pay wages to free workers, planters began to use more slave labor. Congress had made bringing slaves into the United States illegal in 1808. However, the growing demand for slaves led to an increase in the slave trade within the United States.

Cotton Trade

In an 1858 speech before the U.S. Senate, South Carolina politician James Henry Hammond declared, "Cotton is King!" Without cotton, Hammond claimed, the global economy would fail. He believed that southern cotton was one of the most valuable resources in the world. Southern cotton was used to make cloth in England and the North. Many southerners shared Hammond's viewpoints about cotton. Southerner David Christy declared, "King cotton is a profound [learned] statesman, and knows what measures will best sustain [protect] his throne."

The cotton boom made the South a major player in world trade. Great Britain became the South's most valued foreign trading partner. Southerners also sold tons of cotton to the growing textile industry in the northeastern United States. This increased trade led to the growth of major port cities in the South, including Charleston, South Carolina; Savannah, Georgia; and New Orleans, Louisiana.

THE IMPACT TODAY

The Port of New Orleans remains a major seaport. It handles about 85 million tons of cargo annually.

In these cities, crop brokers called **factors** managed the cotton trade. Farmers sold their cotton to merchants, who then made deals with the factors. Merchants and factors also arranged loans for farmers who needed to buy supplies. They often advised farmers on how to invest profits. Once farmers got their cotton to the port cities, factors arranged for transportation aboard trading ships.

However, shipping cotton by land to port cities was very difficult in the South. The few major road projects at the time were limited to the Southeast. Most southern farmers had to ship their goods on the region's rivers. On the Ohio and Mississippi rivers, flatboats and steamboats carried cotton and other products to port. Eventually, hundreds of steamboats traveled up and down the mighty Mississippi River each day.

READING CHECK **Identifying Cause and Effect** What effect did the cotton boom have on the slave trade within the United States?

Direct Teach

Main Idea

❷ The Cotton Boom

The cotton gin created a cotton boom in which farmers grew little else.

Describe What were the advantages of cotton as a crop? *cost little to market, could be stored for a long time, cost less to transport, highly profitable*

Identify Cause and Effect What were the effects of the growing demand for labor? *an increase in the use of slave labor and of the slave trade within the United States*

Summarize What role did the region's rivers play in the cotton trade? *used to transport cotton in flatboats and steamboats to port cities*

Activity **Flowchart** Have students create a flowchart of developments in the South's economy after the invention of the cotton gin. **LS Verbal/Linguistic**

Linking to Today

Cotton Products Raw cotton is still sold to the textile industry and made into cotton goods today. Have students brainstorm a list of as many cotton products as possible that they use regularly. *(clothes, cotton balls, bed sheets and blankets, towels)*

Critical Thinking: Analyzing Information

At Level

Costs and Benefits of Cotton

1. Give students the following scenario: After the invention of the cotton gin, a southern planter is trying to decide whether to switch to growing cotton. The planter decides to create a costs-benefits chart to help make the decision.
2. Have each student create a costs-benefits chart that such a planter might have made. The chart should list the benefits and costs of making the switch to cotton. Remind students to consider the negative effects the cotton boom had on enslaved Africans in the South.
3. Ask volunteers to share information from their charts as you create a master chart. **LS Verbal/Linguistic**

Alternative Assessment Handbook, Rubric 7: Charts

Answers

Reading Check *increased the slave trade between the states*

Direct Teach

Main Idea

❸ Other Crops and Industries

Some people encouraged southerners to focus on other crops and industries.

Recall What were some other important crops in the South? *corn, rice, sweet potatoes, wheat, sugarcane, tobacco, hemp, and flax*

Explain Why were most southern factories built to serve the needs of farmers? *The South's economy centered on agriculture.*

Analyze Why did some people encourage southerners to try a variety of crops and investments? *reliance on one crop was risky; wanted to modernize and promote industry; to keep the soil healthy*

Analyzing Visuals

The South's Cotton Economy
Have students examine the image at right to answer the following:

- Where was most cotton processed? *in the South*
- Where were most of the textile mills to which sailing ships carried cotton? *northeastern United States, Great Britain*

Connect to Geography

Tobacco and the South Farmers found that healthy tobacco plants needed nutrient-rich soils. Tobacco so badly bleached the land of nutrients that after just three years, the soil required 20 years of rest before it was usable for farming again. Before farmers learned to rotate crops, they instead rotated fields, planting tobacco on fresh land until the soil's nutrients were exhausted.

The South's Cotton Economy

Eli Whitney's cotton gin began the cotton boom. Soon, the Cotton Kingdom stretched across the South. For the cotton planters to succeed, they had to get their cotton to market.

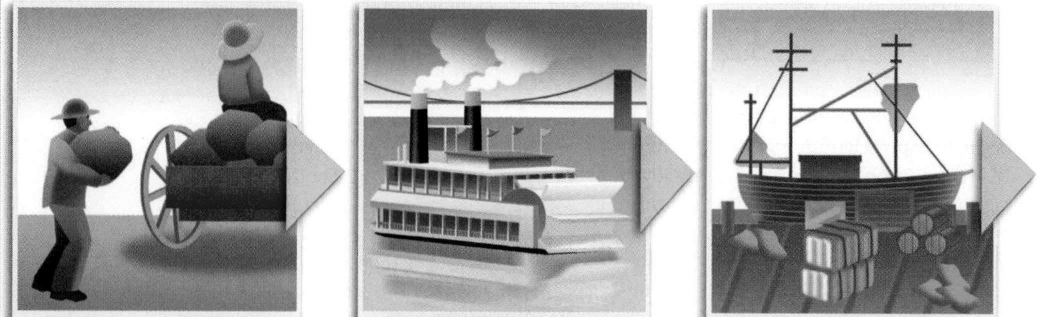

Enslaved African Americans did most of the planting, harvesting, and processing of cotton.

Cotton was shipped on river steamboats to major ports such as Charleston.

From southern ports, sailing ships carried the cotton to distant textile mills.

Other Crops and Industries

Some leaders worried that the South was depending too much on cotton. They wanted southerners to try a variety of cash crops and investments.

Food and Cash Crops

ACADEMIC VOCABULARY
primary main, most important

One such crop was corn, the **primary** southern food crop. By the late 1830s the top three corn-growing states in the nation were all in the South. The South's other successful food crops included rice, sweet potatoes, wheat, and sugarcane.

Production of tobacco, the South's first major cash crop, was very time consuming because tobacco leaves had to be cured, or dried, before they could be shipped to market. In 1839 a slave discovered a way to improve the drying process by using heat from burning charcoal. This new, faster curing process increased tobacco production.

Partly as a result of the cotton boom, hemp and flax also became major cash crops. Their fibers were used to make rope and sackcloth. Farmers used the rope and sackcloth to bundle cotton into bales.

Industry

Many of the first factories in the South were built to serve farmers' needs by processing crops such as sugarcane. In 1803 the nation's first steam-powered sawmill was built in Donaldsonville, Louisiana. This new technology enabled lumber companies to cut, sort, and clean wood quickly.

By the 1840s, entrepreneurs in Georgia began investing in cotton mills. In 1840, there were 14 cotton mills; by the mid-1850s, there were more than 50. A few mill owners followed the model established by Francis Cabot Lowell. However, most built small-scale factories on the falls of a river for waterpower. A few steam-powered mills were built in towns without enough waterpower.

Southerners such as Hinton Rowan Helper encouraged industrial growth in the South.

> "We should . . . keep pace with the progress of the age. We must expand our energies, and acquire habits of enterprise and industry; we should rouse ourselves from the couch of lassitude [laziness] and inure [set] our minds to thought and our bodies to action."
>
> — Hinton Rowan Helper, *The Impending Crisis of the South: How to Meet It*

Critical Thinking: Identifying Points of View

Above Level

Dependence on Cotton Editorial

1. Ask students to imagine themselves as one of the southern leaders who worried about over-reliance on cotton. Have each student write an editorial to support his or her position.
2. Editorials should include a position statement, present at least two strong reasons to support the position, and provide evidence (such as examples or statistics) to support each reason.
3. Remind students that some of the readers of their editorials will have different points of view on the issue. Students should try to address these people's concerns and convince them to change their positions.
4. Ask for volunteers to read their editorials aloud. **LS Verbal/Linguistic**

Alternative Assessment Handbook, Rubric 43: Writing to Persuade

A large amount of cotton was sold to textile mills in the northeastern United States.

Textile mills in Great Britain were the largest foreign buyers of southern cotton.

ANALYSIS SKILL **DRAWING CONCLUSIONS**

Why do you think cotton was so important to the South's economy?

Joseph R. Anderson followed Helper's advice. In 1848 Anderson became the owner of the **Tredegar Iron Works** in Richmond, Virginia—one of the most productive iron works in the nation. It was the only factory to produce bridge materials, cannons, steam engines, and other products.

FOCUS ON READING
What kind of Web site would you look for to learn more about the Tredegar Iron Works?

Industry, however, remained a small part of the southern economy. Southern industry faced stiff competition from the North and from England, both of which could produce many goods more cheaply. And as long as agricultural profits remained high, southern investors preferred to invest in land.

READING CHECK **Making Inferences** Why were there fewer industries in the South?

SUMMARY AND PREVIEW You have read about how southern farmers worked to improve farming methods. In the next section you will read about the structure of southern society.

Section 1 Assessment

go.hrw.com
Online Quiz
KEYWORD: SF7 HP13

Reviewing Ideas, Terms, and People

1. a. **Describe** How did the **cotton gin** make processing cotton easier?
   b. **Draw Conclusions** Why had slavery been on the decline before the invention of the cotton gin? How did slavery change as a result of the cotton gin?
   c. **Predict** How might the rise of cotton production and slavery affect Southern society?
2. a. **Identify** What areas of the United States made up the **cotton belt**?
   b. **Evaluate** Do you think the South should have paid more attention to its industrial growth? Why?
3. a. **Describe** What other crops and industries were encouraged in the South?
   b. **Make Inferences** Why were some southern leaders worried about the South's reliance on cotton?

Critical Thinking

4. **Identifying Cause and Effect** Review your notes on the causes of the cotton boom. Then add to your graphic organizer by identifying the effects of the cotton boom on the South.

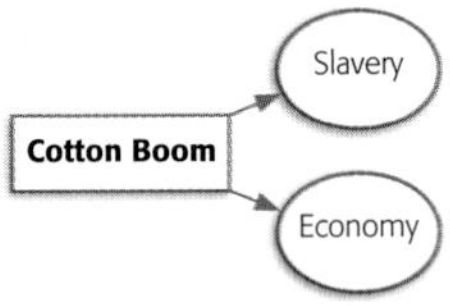

FOCUS ON WRITING

5. **Noting Life on the Cotton Farm** In your notebook, note how Whitney's gin changed life on the farm. Also note other details about cotton farming you could include in your sketch.

Section 1 Assessment Answers

1. a. much faster way to remove seeds from cotton fibers than by hand
   b. Crop prices had fallen and the demand for farm workers had declined; cotton gin led to an increase in the production of cotton, which created more demand for slave labor.
   c. possible answer—since slavery became more common, southern society would become a focal point in the fight against slavery
2. a. land stretching from Virginia to Texas
   b. possible answer—Yes, it was dangerous for the South's economy to be totally dependent on agriculture and one crop.
3. a. corn, rice, sweet potatoes, wheat, sugarcane, mills, iron works
   b. reliance on one crop was risky
4. Slavery—demand for slave labor, increase in slave trade; Economy—build-up of wealth, dependence on cotton; Population—attracted new settlers; Trade—growth of port cities
5. possible answers—more growing and harvesting of cotton; more slave labor; trade became important part of southern economy; South reliant on one crop

Direct Teach

Connect to Economics

Reliance on Cotton Have students think about some of the problems that might occur for an economy dependent on one crop. *Bad weather, labor shortages, or plague could ruin the crop and lead to a downturn in the economy.*

go.hrw.com
Online Resources
KEYWORD: SF7 CH13
ACTIVITY: Tredegar Iron Works

Review & Assess

Close

Have students describe the South's economy before and after the development of the cotton gin.

Review

Online Quiz, Section 13.1

Assess

SE Section 1 Assessment

PASS: Section Quiz 13.1

Alternative Assessment Handbook

Reteach/Classroom Intervention

Interactive Reader and Study Guide, Section 13.1

Interactive Skills Tutor CD-ROM

Answers

Drawing Conclusions *because cotton was highly profitable and was in high demand*

Focus on Reading *Internet search engines; encyclopedia sites; Richmond, Virginia, historical society sites*

Reading Check *People thought cash crops were a better investment than industry.*

Preteach

Bellringer

If YOU were there . . . Use the **Daily Bellringer Transparency** to help students answer the question.

Daily Bellringer Transparency 13.2

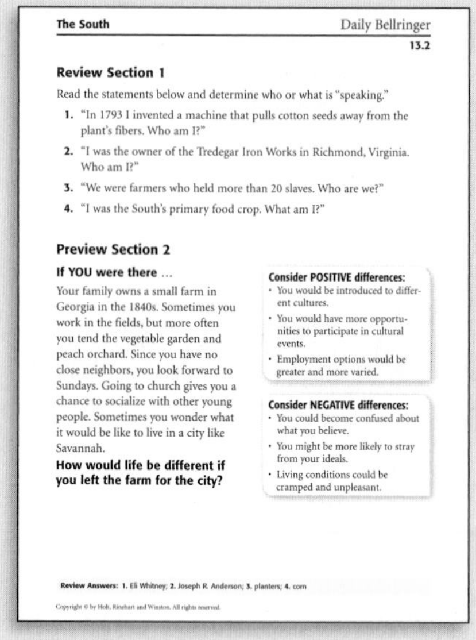
The South — Daily Bellringer 13.2

Review Section 1

Read the statements below and determine who or what is "speaking."

1. "In 1793 I invented a machine that pulls cotton seeds away from the plant's fibers. Who am I?"
2. "I was the owner of the Tredegar Iron Works in Richmond, Virginia. Who am I?"
3. "We were farmers who held more than 20 slaves. Who are we?"
4. "I was the South's primary food crop. What am I?"

Preview Section 2

If YOU were there ...

Your family owns a small farm in Georgia in the 1840s. Sometimes you work in the fields, but more often you tend the vegetable garden and peach orchard. Since you have no close neighbors, you look forward to Sundays. Going to church gives you a chance to socialize with other young people. Sometimes you wonder what it would be like to live in a city like Savannah.

How would life be different if you left the farm for the city?

Consider POSITIVE differences:
- You would be introduced to different cultures.
- You would have more opportunities to participate in cultural events.
- Employment options would be greater and more varied.

Consider NEGATIVE differences:
- You could become confused about what you believe.
- You might be more likely to stray from your ideals.
- Living conditions could be cramped and unpleasant.

Review Answers: 1. Eli Whitney; 2. Joseph R. Anderson; 3. planters; 4. corn

Building Vocabulary

Preteach or review the following terms:

descendant a person related to an individual in the past (p. 423)

discrimination unfair treatment of a person or group (p. 423)

CRF: Vocabulary Builder Activity, Section 2

Taking Notes

Have students copy the graphic organizer onto their own paper and then use it to take notes on the section. This activity will prepare students for the Section Assessment, in which they will complete a graphic organizer that builds on the information using a critical-thinking skill.

Section Correlations

8.1.26 Give examples of the changing role of women and minorities in the northern, southern, and western parts of the United States in the mid-nineteenth century, and examine possible causes for these changes.

SECTION 2

Southern Society

What You Will Learn...

Main Ideas

1. Southern society and culture consisted of four main groups.
2. Free African Americans in the South faced a great deal of discrimination.

The Big Idea

Southern society centered around agriculture.

Key Term

yeomen, *p. 422*

TAKING NOTES As you read, take notes on the different segments of southern society. Record the information you find in a graphic organizer like the one below.

Group	Life
Planters	
Yeomen	
Poor Whites	
Free African Americans	

IN 8.1.26

If YOU were there...

Your family owns a small farm in Georgia in the 1840s. Sometimes you work in the fields, but more often you tend the vegetable garden and peach orchard. Since you have no close neighbors, you look forward to Sundays. Going to church gives you a chance to socialize with other young people. Sometimes you wonder what it would be like to live in a city like Savannah.

How would life be different if you left the farm for the city?

BUILDING BACKGROUND Although the South had some industry, agriculture was the heart of the southern economy. Cotton was king. As a result, wealthy plantation families were the most prominent social class in southern society. Small farmers, however, made up the largest part of the population.

Southern Society and Culture

Popular fiction often made it seem that all white southerners had many slaves and lived on large plantations. Many fiction writers wrote about wealthy southern families who had frequent, grand parties. The ideal image of the Antebellum (before the war) South included hospitality and well-treated slaves on beautiful plantations that almost ran themselves.

This romantic view was far from the reality. During the first half of the 1800s, only about one-third of white southern families had slaves. Fewer families had plantations. Despite their small numbers, these planters had a powerful influence over the South. Many served as political leaders. They led a society made up of many different kinds of people, including yeomen farmers, poor whites, slaves, and free African Americans. Each of these segments of society contributed to the economic success of the South.

420 CHAPTER 13

Teach the Big Idea

At Level

Southern Society

1. **Teach** To teach the main ideas in the section, use the questions in the Direct Teach boxes.
2. **Apply** Ask students to fold a piece of paper into four quarters. Label each quarter with one of the following social groups in free southern society: *planters, yeomen, poor whites,* and *free African Americans.* Have students use the information in this section to fill in each section of their papers. **LS Verbal/Linguistic**
3. **Review** To review the section's main ideas, have students help you complete a master copy of the chart.
4. **Practice/Homework** Have each student write a one-sentence summary for each part of the chart. Then have students combine their sentences to create a one-paragraph summary of the chart. **LS Verbal/Linguistic**

Alternative Assessment Handbook, Rubric 7: Charts

Planters

As the wealthiest members of southern society, planters also greatly influenced the economy. Some showed off their wealth by living in beautiful mansions. Many others chose to live more simply. A visitor described wealthy planter Alexander Stephens's estate as "an old wooden house" surrounded by weeds. Some planters saved all of their money to buy more land and slaves.

Male planters were primarily concerned with raising crops and supervising slave laborers. They left the running of the plantation household to their wives. The planter's wife oversaw the raising of the children and supervised the work of all slaves within the household. Slave women typically cooked, cleaned, and helped care for the planter's children. Wives also took on the important social duties of the family. For example, many southern leaders discussed political issues at the dances and dinners hosted by their wives.

Planters often arranged their children's marriages based on business interests. Lucy Breckinridge, the daughter of a wealthy Virginia planter, was married by arrangement in 1865. Three years earlier, she had described in her journal how she dreaded the very thought of marriage. "A woman's life after she is married, unless there is an immense amount of love, is nothing but suffering and hard work." How Breckinridge's life in her own arranged marriage would have turned out cannot be known. She died of typhoid fever just months after her wedding.

History Close-up

A Southern Plantation

A typical plantation had fields as well as many buildings where different work was done. This picture shows some of the more important buildings that were a part of the plantation system.

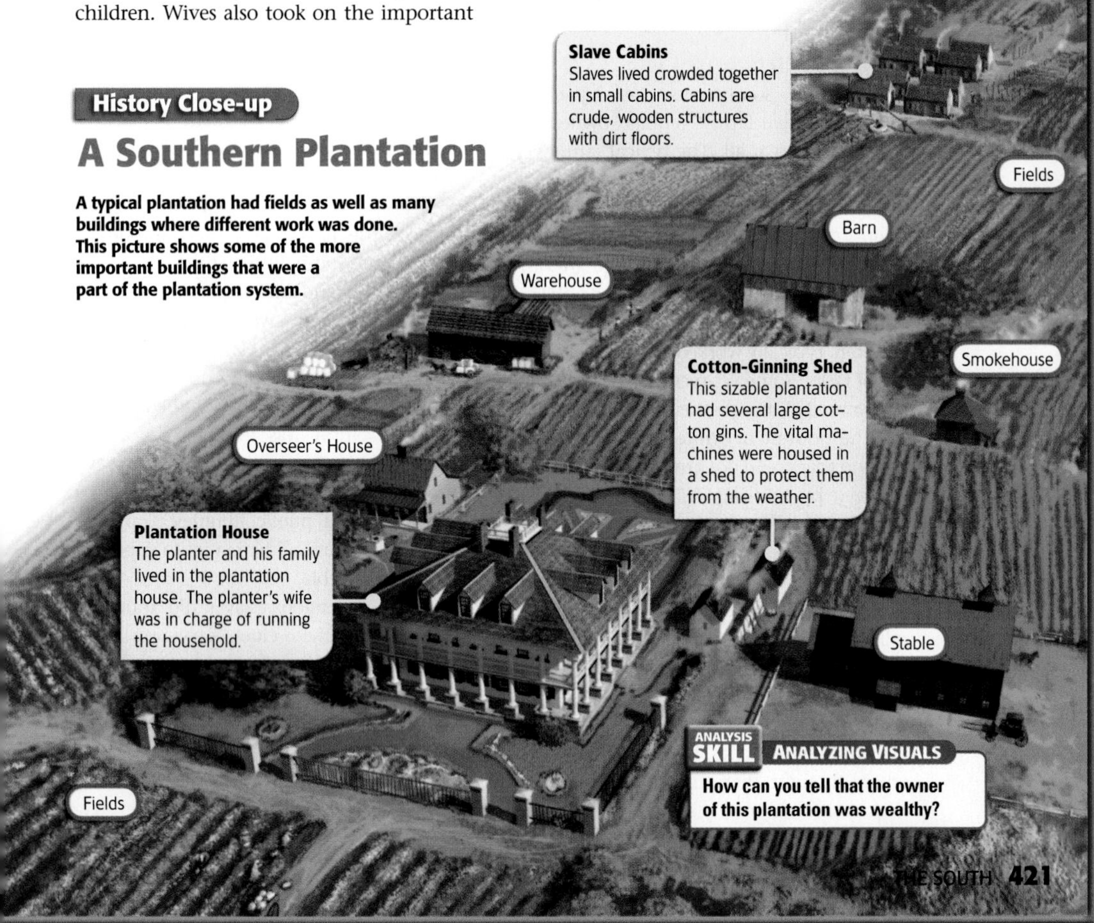

Slave Cabins
Slaves lived crowded together in small cabins. Cabins are crude, wooden structures with dirt floors.
Fields
Barn
Warehouse
Smokehouse
Cotton-Ginning Shed
This sizable plantation had several large cotton gins. The vital machines were housed in a shed to protect them from the weather.
Overseer's House
Plantation House
The planter and his family lived in the plantation house. The planter's wife was in charge of running the household.
Stable
Fields

ANALYSIS SKILL **ANALYZING VISUALS**

How can you tell that the owner of this plantation was wealthy?

Direct Teach

Main Idea

1 Southern Society and Culture

Southern society and culture consisted of four main groups.

Recall About how many white southern families had slaves in the first half of the 1800s? *one-third*

Contrast How did the social status of planters and yeomen differ? *Planters had more power and wealth than yeomen.*

Evaluate Why might some wealthy planters prefer to live simply? *possible answers—did not enjoy society life; preferred to use money to buy more land or slaves*

- **CRF:** Biography Activity: Mary Boykin Chesnut
- **CRF:** Literature Activity: R.Q. Mallard, D.D.; *Plantation Life before Emancipation*
- **CRF:** Primary Source Activity: Frances Anne Kemble, *Journal of a Residence on a Georgian Plantation*

History Close-up

A Southern Plantation *Antebellum* (Latin for "before the war") refers to the style of plantation houses such as the one shown here. This Classical Revival style was popular in the South in the 30 years prior to the Civil War. Features include a symmetrical design, pillars, gabled roofs, wrap-around balconies, and evenly spaced windows.

Collaborative Learning

At Level

The Southern News

1. Organize the class into small groups. Have each group create the front page of a southern newspaper, including a masthead, headlines, articles, advertisements, and illustrations.
2. Encourage students to direct their newspapers towards a target audience of one of the four main groups in southern society in the first half of the 1800s.
3. Have each group present its front page to the class. Then discuss with students the topics and issues of importance to southern society. **LS Interpersonal, Verbal/Linguistic**

Alternative Assessment Handbook, Rubrics 14: Group Activity; and 23: Newspapers

Answers

Analyzing Visuals *plantation house is huge, beautiful mansion; has large stable, two cotton gin sheds, many slave cabins*

Direct Teach

Main Idea

1 Southern Society and Culture

Southern society and culture consisted of four main groups.

Recall How big was the typical yeoman farm? *100 acres*

Summarize How was religion an important part of southern society? *Most white southerners shared similar religious beliefs; neighbors often visited only at church events; slaveholders used religion to defend slavery.*

Info to Know

Free African Americans in the South Free African Americans in the South were more likely to live in cities than in rural areas. By 1860, free African Americans outnumbered slaves 10 to 1 in Baltimore and 5 to 1 in Washington. On the eve of the Civil War, New Orleans was home to 10,000 free African Americans. In the cities, the discrimination that free African Americans faced could be harsh. For example, an 1832 Baltimore law stated that free African Americans were subject to the same treatment and punishment as enslaved Africans.

Free African Americans in the South

Collection of The American Numismatic Society, New York

In 1860 about 1 out of 50 African Americans in the South was free. Many worked in skilled trades, like this barber in Richmond, Virginia. In Charleston, South Carolina, a system of badges was set up to distinguish between free African Americans and slaves.

How would the work of the free African American in this picture be different from that of slaves in the South?

Yeomen and Poor Whites

Most white southerners were **yeomen**, owners of small farms. Yeomen owned few slaves or none at all. The typical farm averaged 100 acres. Yeomen took great pride in their work. In 1849 a young Georgia man wrote, "I desire above all things to be a 'Farmer.' It is the most honest, upright, and sure way of securing all the comforts of life."

Yeoman families, including women and children, typically worked long days at a variety of tasks. Some yeomen held a few slaves but worked alongside them.

The poorest of white southerners lived on land that could not grow cash crops. They survived by hunting, fishing, raising small gardens, and doing odd jobs for money.

Religion and Society

Most white southerners shared similar religious beliefs. Because of the long distances between farms, families often saw their neighbors only at church events, such as revivals or socials. Rural women often played volunteer roles in their churches. Wealthy white southerners thought that their religion justified their position in society and the institution of slavery. They argued that God created some people, like themselves, to rule others. This belief opposed many northern Christians' belief that God was against slavery.

Urban Life

Many of the largest and most important cities in the South were strung along the Atlantic coast and had begun as shipping centers. Although fewer in number, the southern cities were similar to northern cities. City governments built public water systems and provided well-maintained streets. Public education was available in a few places. Wealthy residents occasionally gave large sums of money to charities, such as orphanages and public libraries. Southern urban leaders wanted their cities to appear as modern as possible.

As on plantations, slaves did much of the work in southern cities. Slaves worked as domestic servants, in mills, in shipyards, and at skilled jobs. Many business leaders held slaves or hired them from nearby plantations.

READING CHECK **Summarizing** What different groups made up southern society?

Differentiating Instruction

Below Level

Struggling Readers

1. Draw the graphic organizer for students to see. Omit the blue, italicized answers.
2. Have each student copy the graphic organizer and complete it by identifying as many details as possible that describe southern city life.
3. Have students use their organizers to make a general statement about life in the urban South. **LS Visual/Spatial**

Alternative Assessment Handbook, Rubric 13: Graphic Organizers

Life in the Urban South

Public Services
- *Water systems*
- *Well-maintained streets*
- *Some public education*

Role of Slavery
- *Manual labor*
- *Domestic servants*
- *Hired from nearby plantations*

Answers

Free African Americans in the South *He was working of his own free will and was earning a wage.*

Reading Check *wealthy planters, yeomen, poor whites, enslaved Africans, and free African Americans*

Free African Americans and Discrimination

Although the vast majority of African Americans in the South were enslaved, more than 250,000 free African Americans lived in the region by 1860. Some were descendants of slaves who were freed after the American Revolution. Others were descendants of refugees from Toussaint L'Ouverture's Haitian Revolution in the late 1790s. Still others were former slaves who had run away, been freed by their slaveholder, or earned enough money to buy their freedom.

Free African Americans lived in both rural and urban areas. Most lived in the countryside and worked as paid laborers on plantations or farms. Free African Americans in cities often worked a variety of jobs, mostly as skilled artisans. Some, like barber William Johnson of Natchez, Mississippi, became quite successful in their businesses. Frequently, free African Americans, especially those in the cities, formed social and economic ties with one another. Churches often served as the center of their social lives.

Free African Americans faced constant discrimination from white southerners. Many governments passed laws limiting the rights of free African Americans. Most free African Americans could not vote, travel freely, or hold certain jobs. In some places, free African Americans had to have a white person represent them in any business transaction. In others, laws restricted where they were allowed to live or conduct business.

Many white southerners argued that free African Americans did not have the ability to take care of themselves, and they used this belief to justify the institution of slavery. "The status of slavery is the only one for which the African is adapted," wrote one white Mississippian. To many white southerners, the very existence of free African Americans threatened the institution of slavery.

READING CHECK **Finding Main Ideas** What challenges did free African Americans face in the South?

SUMMARY AND PREVIEW Southern society was led by rich planters but included groups of small farmers, slaves, and free African Americans as well. These groups each had their own culture. In the next section you will read about life under slavery.

Section 2 Assessment

go.hrw.com
Online Quiz
KEYWORD: SF7 HP13

Reviewing Ideas, Terms, and People

1. a. **Identify** What was the largest social group in the South? How did its members make a living?
   b. **Compare** In what ways were southern cities similar to northern cities?
   c. **Elaborate** Which southern social class do you think had the most difficult life? Why?
2. a. **Describe** What jobs were available to free African Americans in the South? Why were these jobs the only ones available?
   b. **Analyze** Why did many white southerners fear free African Americans?
   c. **Elaborate** Why do you think that discrimination against free African Americans was harsher in the South than in the North?

Critical Thinking

3. **Comparing and Contrasting** Review your notes on the different kinds of people who lived in the South. Then use a graphic organizer like the one below to identify the similarities and differences of the lives of planters, yeomen, and free African Americans.

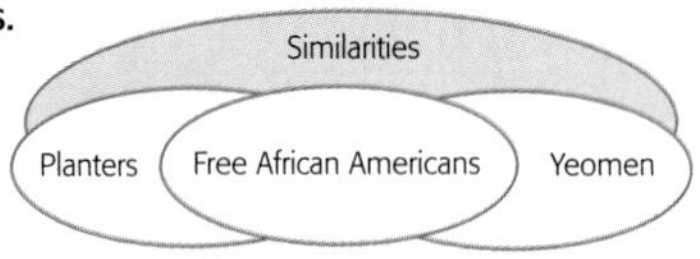

FOCUS ON WRITING

4. **Describing the Life of Cotton Farmers** In your notebook, describe the different roles played by male planters and their wives. What challenges would female planters have faced? When would the planters have had a chance to socialize?

Section 2 Assessment Answers

1. a. yeomen; owned and operated small farms
   b. both provided public services, such as water systems, streets, education
   c. enslaved Africans; no rights, hard work
2. a. (cities) skilled artisans or craftspeople, (rural) plantation or farm workers; faced discrimation and restrictive laws
   b. feared that they would start rebellions and viewed them as a threat to slavery
   c. Some southerners feared the influence free African Americans might have on slaves.
3. Planters—large plantations, wealthy, held many slaves, influential; Yeomen—small farms, few or no slaves, worked long days; Free African Americans—paid laborers, artisans; Similarities—free, agriculture important
4. Planters supervised growing of crops; wives ran plantation household. Answers will vary, but female planters might have faced challenges such as social pressure and a lack of legal rights. Planters socialized at dances and dinners organized by wives.

Direct Teach

Main Idea

2 Free African Americans and Discrimination

Free African Americans in the South faced a great deal of discrimination.

Recall What were the main types of jobs that free African Americans held in the South? *worked as paid laborers on plantations or farms, worked as skilled artisans in cities*

Summarize How had free African Americans often gained their freedom? *ancestors were freed after American Revolution, were descendants of refugees from the Haitian Revolution, bought their freedom*

Review & Assess

Close

Summarize the four main groups that made up southern society and describe the role of each group in the South's agricultural economy.

Review

Online Quiz, Section 13.2

Assess

SE Section 2 Assessment

PASS: Section Quiz 13.2

Alternative Assessment Handbook

Reteach/Classroom Intervention

Interactive Reader and Study Guide, Section 13.2

Interactive Skills Tutor CD-ROM

Answers

Reading Check *discrimination and harsh laws that limited where they could live, what work they could do, and with whom they could meet*

Preteach

Bellringer

If YOU were there . . . Use the **Daily Bellringer Transparency** to help students answer the question.

Daily Bellringer Transparency 13.3

The South — Daily Bellringer **13.3**

Review Section 2

In each pair of sentences below, choose the sentence that is TRUE.

1. a. Male planters took on the job of running the plantation household.
   b. Planter's wives took on the job of running the plantation household.
2. a. Slaves were barred from living in southern cities.
   b. Slaves did much of the work in southern cities.
3. a. Yeomen owned small farms, averaging about 100 acres.
   b. Planters owned small farms, averaging about 100 acres.

Preview Section 3

If YOU were there ...

You are a reporter for a newspaper in Philadelphia in the 1850s. You are writing a series of articles about the slave system in the South. To get background for your stories, you are planning to interview some former slaves who now live in Philadelphia. Some have bought their freedom, while others have successfully escaped from slavery.

What questions will you ask in your interviews?

Consider questions about SLAVE life:
- What were your living conditions?
- Were you allowed to be educated?
- What was the most difficult job you were given?

Consider questions about FREEDOM:
- How did you gain your freedom?
- Have you been able to find work?
- Have you found helpful people in the North?

Review Answers: 1. b; 2. b; 3. a

Academic Vocabulary

Review with students the high-use academic term in this section.

aspect part (p. 426)

CRF: Vocabulary Builder, Section 3

Taking Notes

Have students copy the graphic organizer onto their own paper and then use it to take notes on the section. This activity will prepare students for the Section Assessment, in which they will complete a graphic organizer that builds on the information using a critical-thinking skill.

Section Correlations

IN

8.1.10 Compare differences in ways of life in the northern and southern states, including the growth of towns and cities in the North and the growing dependence on slavery in the South. **8.4.3** Evaluate how the character-istics of a market economy have affected the economic and labor development of the United States. **8.4.6** Relate technolgoical change and inventions to changes in labor productivity in the United States in the eighteenth and nineteenth centuries.

SECTION 3

The Slave System

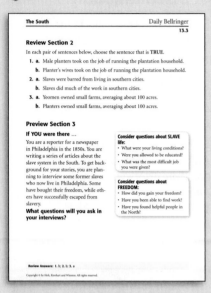

What You Will Learn...

Main Ideas

1. Slaves worked at a variety of jobs on plantations.
2. Life under slavery was difficult and dehumanizing.
3. Slave culture centered around family, community, and religion.
4. Slave uprisings led to stricter slave codes in many states.

The Big Idea

The slave system in the South produced harsh living conditions and occasional rebellions.

Key Terms and People

folktales, *p. 427*
spirituals, *p. 427*
Nat Turner's Rebellion, *p. 428*
Nat Turner, *p. 428*

TAKING NOTES As you read, take notes on the slavery system in a graphic organizer like the one shown below.

	Life as an Enslaved Person
Work	
Life	
Culture	

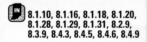

IN 8.1.10, 8.1.16, 8.1.18, 8.1.20, 8.1.28, 8.1.29, 8.1.31, 8.2.9, 8.3.9, 8.4.3, 8.4.5, 8.4.6, 8.4.9

If YOU were there...

You are a reporter for a newspaper in Philadelphia in the 1850s. You are writing a series of articles about the slave system in the South. To get background for your stories, you are planning to interview some former slaves who now live in Philadelphia. Some have bought their freedom, while others have successfully escaped from slavery.

What questions will you ask in your interviews?

BUILDING BACKGROUND While most white southern families were not slaveholders, the southern economy depended on the work of slaves. This was true not only on large plantations but also on smaller farms and in the cities. Few chances existed for enslaved African Americans to escape their hard lives.

Slaves and Work

Most enslaved African Americans lived in rural areas where they worked on farms and plantations. Enslaved people on small farms usually did a variety of jobs. On large plantations, most slaves were assigned to specific jobs, and most worked in the fields. Most slaveholders demanded that slaves work as much as possible. Supervisors known as drivers, who were sometimes slaves themselves, made sure that slaves followed orders and carried out punishments.

Working in the Field

Most plantation owners used the gang-labor system. In this system, all field hands worked on the same task at the same time. They usually worked from sunup to sundown. Former slave Harry McMillan had worked on a plantation in South Carolina. He recalled that the field hands usually did not even get a break to eat lunch. "You had to get your victuals [food] standing at your hoe," he remembered.

Men, women, and even children older than about 10 usually did the same tasks. Sickness and poor weather rarely stopped the work. "The times I hated most was picking cotton when the frost was on the bolls [seed pods]," recalled former Louisiana slave Mary Reynolds. "My hands git sore and crack open and bleed."

424 CHAPTER 13

Teach the Big Idea

At Level

The Slave System

1. **Teach** To teach the main ideas in the section, use the questions in the Direct Teach boxes.
2. **Apply** Write the Big Idea for students to see. Below it, write the following headings from the section: *Slaves and Work, Life Under Slavery, Slave Culture,* and *Slave Uprisings.*
3. **Review** As you review the section, have volunteers share important points from the text that support the Big Idea. Write the information under the appropriate headings.
4. **Practice/Homework** Ask students to imagine that they are northerners visiting the South. Have each student write a letter home describing his or her observations about the slave system. **LS Verbal/Linguistic, Visual/Spatial**

Alternative Assessment Handbook, Rubrics 7: Charts; and 25: Personal Letters

Working in the Planter's Home

Some slaves worked as butlers, cooks, or nurses in the planter's home. These slaves often had better food, clothing, and shelter than field hands did, but they often worked longer hours. They had to serve the planter's family 24 hours a day.

Working at Skilled Jobs

On larger plantations, some enslaved African Americans worked at skilled jobs, such as blacksmithing or carpentry. Sometimes planters let these slaves sell their services to other people. Often planters collected a portion of what was earned but allowed slaves to keep the rest. In this way, some skilled slaves earned enough money to buy their freedom from their slaveholders. For example, William Ellison earned his freedom in South Carolina by working for wages as a cotton gin maker. For years, he worked late at night and on Sundays. He bought his freedom with the money he earned. Eventually, he was also able to buy the freedom of his wife and daughter.

READING CHECK **Summarizing** What were some types of work done by enslaved people on plantations?

Life Under Slavery

Generally, slaveholders viewed slaves as property, not as people. Slaveholders bought and sold slaves to make a profit. The most common method of sale was at an auction. The auction itself determined whether families would be kept together or separated. Sometimes a buyer wanted a slave to fill a specific job, such as heavy laborer, carpenter, or blacksmith. The buyer might be willing to pay for the slave who could do the work, but not for that slave's family. Families would then be separated with little hope of ever getting back together.

Slave traders sometimes even kidnapped free African Americans and then sold them into slavery. For example, Solomon Northup, a free African American, was kidnapped in Washington, D.C. He spent 12 years as a slave until he finally proved his identity and gained his release.

Living Conditions

Enslaved people often endured poor living conditions. Planters housed them in dirt-floor cabins with few furnishings and often leaky roofs. The clothing given to them was usually simple and made of cheap, coarse fabric. Some slaves tried to brighten up their

A Nurse's Work

Slaveholders' children were often cared for by enslaved women. At the time, women who looked after children were called nurses. This nurse is posing with her slaveholder's child in about 1850.

As a slave, what might have happened to this woman's family?

Direct Teach

Main Idea

❶ Slaves and Work

Slaves worked at a variety of jobs on plantations.

Describe What was work in the fields like for enslaved Africans? *In all weather, adults and children older than about 10 worked from sunup to sundown often at the same tasks.*

Contrast How was life different for slaves working in the planter's home? *better food, clothing, and shelter; longer hours*

Analyze How were some skilled slaves able to buy their freedom? *saved money from selling their services to other people*

Main Idea

❷ Life Under Slavery

Life under slavery was difficult and dehumanizing.

Describe How did slaveholders generally view slaves? *as their property*

Elaborate Why did separated slave families have little hope of getting back together? *lived far apart with little chance of gaining freedom*

CRF: Primary Source Activity: Jacob Stroyer, *My Life in the South*

Linking to Today

African Craft of Ironwork Enslaved Africans brought with them from Africa the ancient craft of ironmaking. In sections of Charleston and New Orleans, you can still see elaborate wrought-iron balconies, gates, and lamp brackets created by black ironsmiths in the 1700s and 1800s.

Differentiating Instruction

Below Level

Struggling Readers

1. Create a three-column chart for students to see. Write the boldfaced headings below at the top of each column. Read aloud the italicized answers in random order and have students write them down.
   - **Agricultural Slaves:** *gang-labor; worked sunup to sundown; worked when sick; worked in poor weather*
   - **Slaves in the Home:** *butlers, cooks, nurses; better food, clothing, shelter; 24 hours a day*
   - **Skilled Slaves:** *blacksmiths, carpenters; might sell services to others; might save enough money to buy freedom*
2. Have students copy the chart and complete it by placing each answer under the appropriate heading. Then review the answers as a class.

LS Verbal/Linguistic

Alternative Assessment Handbook, Rubric 7: Charts

Answers

A Nurse's Work *possible answer—separated at a slave auction*

Reading Check *field workers, butlers, cooks, nurses, blacksmiths, carpenters*

Direct Teach

Main Idea

2 Life Under Slavery

Life under slavery was difficult and dehumanizing.

Recall How did planters encourage obedience? *more food or better living conditions; harsh punishments*

Draw Conclusions What effects do you think states' strict slave codes had on enslaved Africans' lives? *possible answer—kept slaves isolated, illiterate, and powerless*

Connect to Science

Health of Slaves Poor diet, exhaustion, unsanitary living conditions, and exposure to the outdoor elements made slaves vulnerable to many health problems and diseases, including blindness, rickets, scurvy, leprosy, tuberculosis, and pneumonia. Outbreaks of cholera and yellow fever frequently occurred as well. Poor diet and health contributed to a low life expectancy for enslaved Africans. For example, in Louisiana in 1850, an enslaved man could expect to live only 29 years, an enslaved woman only 34 years.

go.hrw.com

Online Resources

KEYWORD: SF7 CH13
ACTIVITY: Slavery and Housing

Focus on Indiana

8.1.16 Describe the ... conflicts and compromises associated with westward expansion of slavery...

Analyze Why did the Indiana government try to overturn parts of the Northwest Ordinance? *Many Indianans owned slaves and wanted slavery to be legal.*

Answers

Reading Check *harsh punishments and strict slave codes*

FOCUS ON INDIANA

Although the Northwest Ordinance declared slavery illegal in Indiana and the rest of the Northwest Territory, many residents owned slaves anyway. Many early Indianans were from the southern states, and they brought the slave system with them. The territorial government tried repeatedly to have the antislavery portion of the Northwest Ordinance suspended, but the efforts failed.

clothing by sewing on designs from discarded scraps of material. In this way, they expressed their individuality and personalized the clothing assigned to them by the planters.

Likewise, many slaves did what they could to improve their small food rations. Some planters allowed slaves to keep their own gardens for vegetables, and chickens for eggs. Other slaves were able to add a little variety to their diet by fishing or picking wild berries.

Punishment and Slave Codes

Some planters offered more food or better living conditions to encourage slaves' obedience. However, most slaveholders used punishment instead. Some would punish one slave in front of others as a warning to them all. Harry McMillan recalled some of the punishments he had witnessed.

> "The punishments were whipping, putting you in the stocks [wooden frames to lock people in] and making you wear irons and a chain at work. Then they had a collar to put round your neck with two horns, like cows' horns, so that you could not lie down ... Sometimes they dug a hole like a well with a door on top. This they called a dungeon keeping you in it two or three weeks or a month, or sometimes till you died in there."
>
> —Harry McMillan, quoted in *Major Problems in the History of the American South, Volume I*, edited by Paul D. Escott and David R. Goldfield

ACADEMIC VOCABULARY
aspect part

To further control slaves' actions, many states passed strict laws called slave codes. Some laws prohibited slaves from traveling far from their homes. Literacy laws in most southern states prohibited the education of slaves. Alabama, Virginia, and Georgia had laws that allowed the fining and whipping of anyone caught teaching enslaved people to read and write.

READING CHECK **Summarizing** How did slaveholders control slaves?

A Slave's Daily Life

Typical Daily Schedule:
3:00 a.m. Out of bed, tend animals
6:00 a.m. Prayers
7:00 a.m. Start work
12:00 p.m. Lunch
1:00 p.m. Return to work
7:00 p.m. Dinner
8:00 p.m. Return to work
11:00 p.m. Lights out

Slave Culture

Many enslaved Africans found comfort in their community and culture. They made time for social activity, even after exhausting workdays, in order to relieve the hardship of their lives.

Family and Community

Family was the most important **aspect** of slave communities, and many slaves feared separation more than they feared punishment. Josiah Henson never forgot the day that he and his family were auctioned. His mother begged the slaveholder who bought her to buy Josiah, too. The slaveholder refused, and Henson's entire family was separated. "I must have been then between five or six years old," he recalled years later. "I seem to see and hear my poor weeping mother now."

Critical Thinking: Analyzing Primary Sources

Above Level

Slavery: An Oral History

Research Required

Background: Explain to students that during the 1930s, more than 2,300 first-person narratives of former slaves were recorded and collected in *Born in Slavery: Slave Narratives from the Federal Writers' Project, 1936–1938.* This 17-volume collection is available online through the Library of Congress.

1. Ask students to conduct research on the oral histories of former slaves recorded in the slave narratives from the Federal Writers' Project.
2. Ask each student to identify one primary source that he or she finds particularly descriptive or moving in its portrayal of the slavery experience.
3. Have students take turns reading aloud their selections and invite them to share their responses. **LS Verbal/Linguistic**

Alternative Assessment Handbook, Rubric 30: Research

Hauling the Whole Week's Pickings by William Henry Brown, The Historic New Orleans Collection

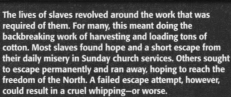

The lives of slaves revolved around the work that was required of them. For many, this meant doing the backbreaking work of harvesting and loading tons of cotton. Most slaves found hope and a short escape from their daily misery in Sunday church services. Others sought to escape permanently and ran away, hoping to reach the freedom of the North. A failed escape attempt, however, could result in a cruel whipping—or worse.

What different aspects of slavery are shown in these pictures?

Enslaved parents kept their heritage alive by passing down family histories as well as African customs and traditions. They also told **folktales**, or stories with a moral, to teach lessons about how to survive under slavery. Folktales often included a clever animal character called a trickster. The trickster—which often represented slaves—defeated a stronger animal by outwitting it. Folktales reassured slaves that they could survive by outsmarting more powerful slaveholders.

Religion

Religion also played an important part in slave culture. By the early 1800s many slaves were Christians. They came to see themselves, like the slaves in the Old Testament, as God's chosen people, much like the Hebrew slaves in ancient Egypt who had faith that they would someday live in freedom.

Some slaves sang **spirituals**, emotional Christian songs that blended African and European music, to express their religious beliefs. For example, "The Heavenly Road" reflected slaves' belief in their equality in the eyes of God.

> "Come, my brother, if you never did pray,
> I hope you pray tonight;
> For I really believe I am a child of God
> As I walk on the heavenly road."
>
> —Anonymous, quoted in *Afro-American Religious History*, edited by Milton C. Sernett

Slaves blended some aspects of their traditional African religions with those of the Christianity that the slaveholders followed. They worshipped in secret, out of sight of slaveholders. Some historians have called slave religion the invisible institution.

FOCUS ON INDIANA

Much of the art, music, and writing created by white Americans during this period depicted African Americans as unequal to whites. Some white Americans, however, chose to depict African American subjects as they would any other subject. One such painter was Winslow Homer, whose painting *At the Cabin Door* is considered a rare example of a true portrait of African American life of the time.

Cross-Discipline Activity: Music

At Level

Spirituals

Prep Required

Materials: recordings and lyrics of spirituals

1. Play several recordings of spirituals to acquaint students with the music's tones and rhythms. Distribute lyrics for students to read and study.
2. Pair students. Try to match students who enjoy music with those who enjoy creative writing. Have each pair write its own spiritual. Students might set their lyrics to an existing tune.
3. Invite pairs to perform their songs, to record and play them for the class, or to display their lyrics and musical arrangements in the classroom. **LS Auditory/Musical, Interpersonal**

Alternative Assessment Handbook, Rubric 26: Poems and Songs

Direct Teach

Main Idea

❸ Slave Culture

Slave culture centered around family, community, and religion.

Recall What did slaves fear more than physical punishment? *separation from their families*

Explain How did enslaved parents work to ensure that their children never forgot their heritage? *passed down family histories, customs, traditions*

Elaborate Why did enslaved Africans worship in secret? *possible answer—Slaveholders would not approve of mixing traditional African religions with Christianity or the focus on equality in God's eyes.*

Analyzing Visuals

A Slave's Daily Life

The collage *Hauling the Whole Week's Pickings* is one of several that artist William Henry Brown created in 1842. Brown created the collages while in Mississippi on a visit to a cotton plantation owned by the Vick family. The collages, which Brown made for the Vick family's children, portray the everyday lives of slaves on the plantation.

If you kept to the daily schedule shown, how much sleep would you get a night? *4 hours*

Info to Know

Followers of Islam Enslaved Africans from Muslim areas of West Africa brought their religion to North America. On plantations along the coasts of Georgia and South Carolina, many slaves practiced Muslim traditions.

Focus on Indiana

IN 8.1.18

Explain How was Winslow Homer's depiction of African Americans different from others of the time? *He showed them as everyday people.*

Answers

A Slave's Daily Life *work on the plantation and a religious service*

Direct Teach

Main Idea

4 Slave Uprisings

Slave uprisings led to stricter slave codes in many states.

Identify What was the most violent U.S. slave revolt? When did it occur? *Nat Turner's Rebellion; August 1831*

Elaborate How do you think slaves responded to stronger slave codes? *possible answer—increased desire to run away or revolt*

- **CRF:** Biography Activities: Nat Turner; Denmark Vesey
- **CRF:** Primary Source Activity: The Denmark Vesey Conspiracy
- Map Transparency 45: Nat Turner's Rebellion

go.hrw.com
Online Resources
KEYWORD: SF7 CH13
ACTIVITY: Freedom Diary

Answers

Analyzing Visuals **1.** *Southampton County, Virginia;* **2.** *about 68 days*

Reading Check *helped them believe that one day they would be free; helped them endure slavery; helped them see themselves as equal*

Nat Turner's Rebellion

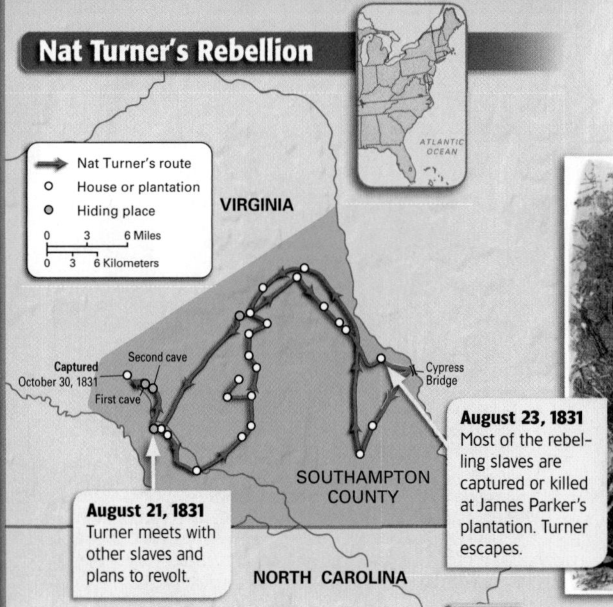

Slave Nat Turner led a revolt against white slaveholders in 1831. This is a map of his route and a depiction of his capture.

ANALYSIS SKILL **ANALYZING VISUALS**

1. **Location** Where did Nat Turner's Rebellion take place?
2. **Movement** How many days did it take to capture Nat Turner?

Seeds of Rebellion

Maintaining their own religious beliefs and practices was only one way in which enslaved people resisted slaveholders' attempts to control them completely. In small ways, slaves rebelled against the system daily. Sometimes they worked slower to protest long hours in the fields. Other times they ran away for a few days to avoid an angry slaveholder. Some slaves tried to escape permanently, but most left only for short periods, often to go and visit relatives.

Gaining freedom by escaping to the North was hard. If discovered, slaves were captured and sent back to their slaveholders, where they faced certain punishment or death. However, thousands of enslaved people succeeded in escaping.

READING CHECK **Summarizing** How did slaves' religious beliefs affect their attitudes toward slavery?

Slave Uprisings

Although violent slave revolts were relatively rare, white southerners lived in fear of them. Two planned rebellions were stopped before they began. Gabriel Prosser planned a rebellion near Richmond, Virginia, in 1800. Denmark Vesey planned one in Charleston, South Carolina, in 1822. Local authorities executed most of those involved in planning these rebellions. Though Vesey was executed as the leader of the Charleston conspiracy, several accounts written after his death by anti-slavery writers claimed he was a hero.

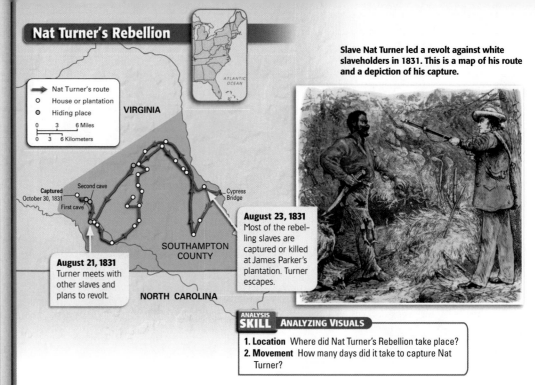

The most violent slave revolt in the country occurred in 1831 and is known as **Nat Turner's Rebellion**. **Nat Turner**, a slave from Southampton County, Virginia, believed that God had told him to end slavery. On an August night in 1831, Turner led a group of slaves in a plan to kill all of the slaveholders and their families in the county. First, they

Differentiating Instruction

English-Language Learners — Below Level

1. Copy the graphic organizer for students to see. Omit the blue, italicized answers.
2. Have each student copy the graphic organizer and complete it by listing the ways in which enslaved Africans challenged the slavery system.
3. Review the answers and then lead a discussion about why these tactics failed to end the system of slavery. **LS Visual/Spatial**

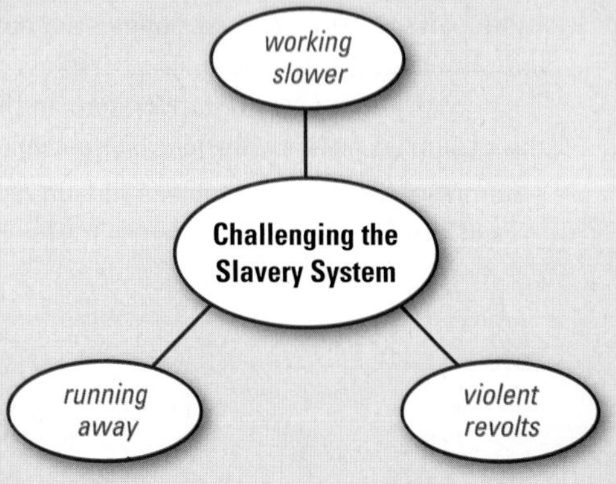

Advanced Learners/ Gifted and Talented — Above Level

Nat Turner Dialogue Have students write an imagined dialogue between Nat Turner and a fellow enslaved African. In the dialogue, Turner should persuade his fellow worker to join his rebellion. **LS Verbal/Linguistic**

- Alternative Assessment Handbook, Rubric 43: Writing to Persuade attacked the family that held Turner as a slave. Soon they had killed about 60 white people in the community.

More than 100 innocent slaves who were not part of Turner's group were killed in an attempt to stop the rebellion. Turner himself led authorities on a chase around the countryside for six weeks. He hid in caves and in the woods before he was caught and brought to trial. Before his trial, Turner made a confession. He expressed his belief that the revolt was justified and worth his death: "I am willing to suffer the fate that awaits me." Turner was executed on November 11, 1831. After the rebellion, many states strengthened their slave codes. The new codes placed stricter control on enslaved people. Despite resistance, slavery continued to spread.

READING CHECK **Finding Main Ideas** What was Nat Turner's Rebellion, and what happened as a result?

Primary Source

LETTER

Nat Turner's Rebellion

In 1831 a white southerner who had escaped the rebellion wrote a letter describing the mood of the area where Nat Turner had killed slaveholders.

"The oldest inhabitants of our county have never experienced such a distressing [terrible] time, as we have had since Sunday night last. The [slaves], about fifteen miles from this place, have massacred from 50 to 75 women and children, and some 8 or 10 men. Every house, room and corner in this place is full of women and children, driven from home, who had to take to the woods, until they could get to this place. We are worn out with fatigue [tiredness]."

The author believes no one in the county has been through a worse event.

The author says that many people went into hiding when the rebellion began.

—*Richmond Enquirer*, quoted in *The Southampton Slave Revolt of 1831* by Henry I. Tragle

ANALYSIS SKILL **ANALYZING PRIMARY SOURCES**

What emotions do you think the author of this letter was feeling?

SUMMARY AND PREVIEW Several groups of African Americans attempted to end slavery by rebellion. All of the attempts failed. In the next chapter you will read about efforts to reform American society.

Section 3 Assessment

go.hrw.com
Online Quiz
KEYWORD: SF7 HP13

Reviewing Ideas, Terms, and People

1. a. **Identify** What different types of work were done by slaves on plantations?
   b. **Elaborate** Do you think that skilled slaves had advantages over other slaves? Why or why not?
2. a. **Describe** What were living conditions like for most slaves?
   b. **Summarize** In what different ways did slaveholders encourage obedience from their slaves?
3. a. **Recall** What was the purpose of African American **folktales**?
   b. **Explain** How did slaves try to maintain a sense of community?
4. a. **Describe** What was the outcome of **Nat Turner's Rebellion**?
   b. **Elaborate** What do you think were some reasons why slaves rebelled?

Critical Thinking

5. **Evaluating** Review your notes on the slavery system. Then use a graphic organizer like the one shown below to identify the two most important reasons enslaved people challenged the system as well as how they did so.

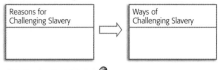

Reasons for Challenging Slavery	→	Ways of Challenging Slavery

FOCUS ON WRITING

6. **Describing the Life of Slaves** Add notes about the life of slaves to your notebook. What would it have been like to be a slave? How would it have felt to have been separated from your family?

Direct Teach

Primary Source

Reading Like a Historian

Nat Turner's Rebellion Help students practice reading the document like historians. Ask

- Who wrote this letter, and why?
- Where was this letter published?
- How is the author's account of the incident different from what you have read in this section? Why do you think the two accounts differ?

Review & Assess

Close

Have students describe in their own words the daily lives of slaves and how they responded to slavery.

Review

go.hrw.com Online Quiz, Section 13.3

Assess

SE Section 3 Assessment

PASS: Section Quiz 13.3

Alternative Assessment Handbook

Reteach/Classroom Intervention

Interactive Reader and Study Guide, Section 13.3

Interactive Skills Tutor CD-ROM

Section 3 Assessment Answers

1. a. agricultural, domestic, and skilled
   b. possible answer—yes, skilled work possibly more interesting, could have chance to buy freedom
2. a. severe work schedules and working conditions; harsh punishments; poor clothing, food, and shelter
   b. more food or improved working conditions, punishment, slave codes
3. a. to teach how to survive under slavery
   b. through religion and folktales
4. a. About 60 white people and more than 100 innocent slaves killed; Turner executed; many states strengthened slave codes
   b. hardship, injustice, lack of freedom
5. Reasons—treated as property, punishment, slave codes; Ways—work slower, try to escape, rebellion
6. possible answers: life as a slave—hard work, strict punishment, discrimination, religious faith and folktales help to cope; separated from family—anger and sadness, community becomes like family

Answers

Analyzing Primary Sources *fear, horror, exhaustion*

Reading Check *1831 slave rebellion in which 60 white people were killed; revolt failed; Turner was executed; states adopted stricter slave codes*

Social Studies Skills

Interpreting Graphs

Activity **Graphs in the Media**

Materials: copies of various graphs from magazines and newspapers

Before class, find at least one example of a bar graph, a line graph, and a circle graph in magazines or newspapers. Display each graph in turn for the class to see. Have students identify each type of graph. Then ask students to describe the information shown in the graph legend. Have students identify what each color in the graph represents. Next, ask students to identify the labels in the graph and use them to explain what information the graph is showing. To test students' understanding, ask one to two questions about each graph that require students to interpret the information in the graph and to identify relationships or trends shown.
LS Visual/Spatial

- Alternative Assessment Handbook, Rubric 7: Charts
- Interactive Skills Tutor CD-ROM, Lesson 6: Interpret Maps, Graphs, Charts, Visuals, and Political Cartoons
- **CRF:** Social Studies Skills Activity: Interpreting Graphs

Social Studies Skills

Analysis | Critical Thinking | Civic Participation | **Study**

Interpreting Graphs

Define the Skill

Graphs are drawings that classify and display data in a clear, visual format. There are three basic types of graphs. *Line graphs* and *bar graphs* plot changes in quantities over time. Bar graphs are also used to compare quantities within a category at a particular time. *Circle graphs,* also called *pie graphs,* have a similar use. The circle represents the whole of something, and the slices show what proportion of the whole is made by each part.

Being able to interpret graphs accurately lets you see and understand relationships more easily than in tables or in written explanations. This is especially true if the information is detailed or the relationships are complicated.

Learn the Skill

The following guidelines will help you interpret data that is presented as a graph.

1. Read the title to identify the subject and purpose of the graph. Note the kind of graph, remembering what each type is designed to indicate. Also note how the graph's subject relates to any printed material that accompanies it.
2. Study the graph's parts. Place close attention to the labels that define each axis. Note the units of measure. Identify the categories used. If there are different colors on bars or lines in the graph, determine what those differences mean.
3. Analyze the data in the graph. Note any increases or decreases in quantities. Look for trends, changes, and other relationships in the data.
4. Apply the information in the graph. Use the results of your analysis to draw conclusions. Ask yourself what generalizations can be made about the trends, changes, or relationships shown in the graph.

Practice the Skill

The graph below is a double-line graph. It shows both changes and relationships over time. This type of graph allows you to see how changes in one thing compare with changes in something else. Apply the guidelines to interpret the graph and answer the questions that follow.

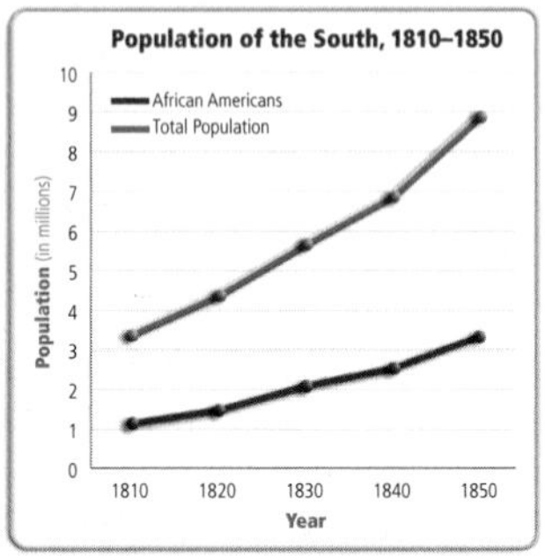

1. What is shown on each axis of this graph? What are the units of measure on each axis?
2. What do each of the lines represent?
3. What was the total population of the South in 1810? in 1850? By how much did the African American population grow during that period?
4. Was the white population or the African American population growing faster? Explain how you know.

Social Studies Skills Activity: Interpreting Graphs

At Level

Graph Quiz

1. Have students examine the graph "U.S. Cotton Production, 1800–1860" on p. 416. Have each student create a three-question quiz about the graph. Assign students the type of quiz to create, such as multiple choice, short answer, or true-false.
2. Have each student create a separate answer key for his or her quiz.
3. Then have students exchange quizzes with partners. Students should answer the quizzes they receive and return them to their authors for grading.
4. Then have each student write a few sentences summarizing the information shown in the graph. Ask for volunteers to read their summaries to the class. **LS Interpersonal, Verbal/Linguistic**

- Alternative Assessment Handbook, Rubrics 7: Charts; and 37: Writing Assignments

Answers

Practice the Skill **1.** *vertical axis—Population (in millions), in units of one million; horizontal axis—year, in 10-year increments;* **2.** *blue—African American population in the South, 1810–1850; green—total population in the South, 1810–1850;* **3.** *1810—about 3.25 million; 1850—about 8.9 million; almost 2 million;* **4.** *white population, calculated by subtracting growth of African American population from growth of total population*

CHAPTER 13 Chapter Review

HOLT History's Impact
▶ **video series**
Review the video to answer the closing question:
What could Silicon Valley learn from the economic and industrial past (and present) of the South?

Visual Summary

QUICK FACTS

Use the visual summary below to help you review the main ideas of the chapter.

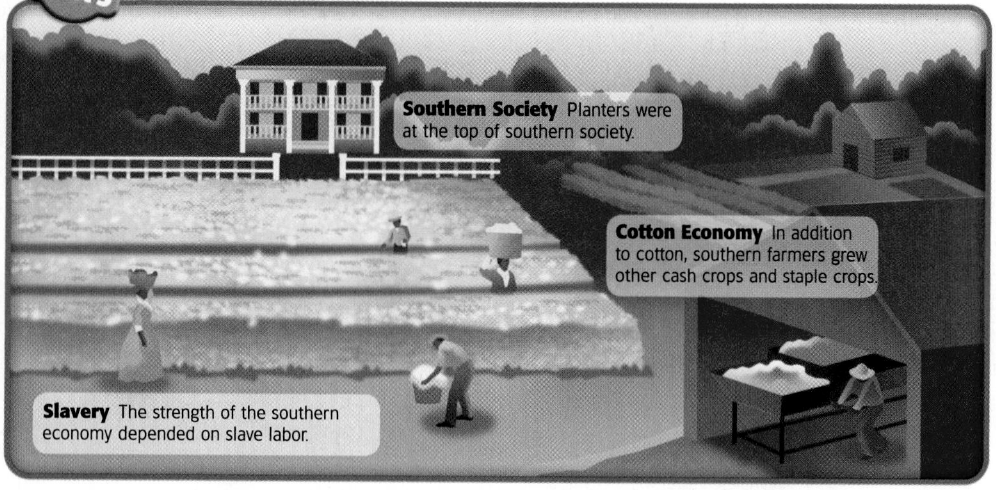

Southern Society Planters were at the top of southern society.
Cotton Economy In addition to cotton, southern farmers grew other cash crops and staple crops.
Slavery The strength of the southern economy depended on slave labor.

Reviewing Vocabulary, Terms, and People

Match the definition on the left with the correct term on the right.

1. A region of cotton-producing areas that stretched from South Carolina to Texas
2. Emotional songs that mixed African and European music and expressed religious beliefs
3. Owners of small farms who made up the largest social class in the South
4. Crop brokers who often managed the cotton trade in the South
5. Wealthy farmers and plantation owners

a. cotton belt
b. factors
c. planters
d. spirituals
e. yeomen

Comprehension and Critical Thinking

SECTION 1 *(Pages 414–419)*

6. a. Describe How did the cotton gin lead to a cotton boom in the South?

b. Analyze What were the positive and negative results of the cotton boom?

c. Evaluate Do you think that the South suffered as a result of its reliance on cotton? Why or why not?

SECTION 2 *(Pages 420–423)*

7. a. Describe What three groups made up white southern society?

b. Compare and Contrast In what ways were the lives of free African Americans and white southerners similar and different?

c. Predict What might have been the attitude of yeomen and poor white southerners toward slavery? Why?

Answers

History's Impact

Video Series Silicon Valley could expand from a strictly computer-based industry to include related, financially stable industries—just as the South moved from a cotton-dependent economy to an economy that included textiles.

Visual Summary

Review and Inquiry Ask students how the images in the Visual Summary relate to the chapter content. Have students describe what important ideas in the chapter are not part of the visual.

Quick Facts Transparency 35: The South Visual Summary

Reviewing Vocabulary, Terms, and People

1. a
2. d
3. e
4. b
5. c

Comprehension and Critical Thinking

6. a. made cotton easier to process, more cotton was planted
b. positive—created wealth, boosted southern economy; negative—increased demand for slaves, led to cotton-dependent economy
c. possible answer—yes, had nothing else to depend upon during times when cotton prices fell

Review and Assessment Resources

Review and Reinforce

- **SE** Chapter Review
- **CRF:** Chapter Review Activity
- Quick Facts Transparency 35: The South Visual Summary
- Spanish Chapter Summaries Audio CD Program
- Online Chapter Summary in Spanish
- **OSP** Holt PuzzlePro; GameTool for ExamView
- Quiz Game CD-ROM

Assess

- **SE** Standardized Test Practice
- PASS: Chapter 13 Tests, Forms A and B
- Alternative Assessment Handbook
- **OSP** ExamView Test Generator, Chapter Test
- Differentiated Instruction Modified Worksheets and Tests CD-ROM: Chapter Test
- **HOAP** Holt Online Assessment Program (in the Premier Online Edition)

Reteach/Intervene

- Interactive Reader and Study Guide
- Differentiated Instruction Teacher Management System: Lesson Plans for Differentiated Instruction
- Differentiated Instruction Modified Worksheets and Tests CD-ROM
- Interactive Skills Tutor CD-ROM

go.hrw.com
Online Resources
Chapter Resources:
KEYWORD: SF7 CH13

Answers

7. a. planters, yeomen, and poor white southerners
b. similar—both had a degree of freedom; different—African Americans suffered harsh discrimination and legal restrictions.
c. possible answers—might have felt no connection to slavery since they generally did not own slaves; might have liked it because the slaves did most of the difficult physical labor and menial tasks

8. a. work slower, run away, revolts
b. By passing down their family heritage, telling stories, and holding onto their religious beliefs, slaves could find meaning in their lives despite the arduous conditions under which they lived. Religion helped slaves hope for freedom, even if it meant waiting for the next life.
c. possible answers—greater control of slaves; more widespread encouragement of slavery; harsher life for enslaved Africans

Reading Skills

9. b

Using the Internet

10. Go to the HRW Web site and enter the keyword shown to access a rubric for this activity.

KEYWORD: SF7 CH13

Reviewing Themes

11. Planters grew wealthy, some yeomen were able to own their own land, slaves worked even harder under harsh conditions.

12. The southern economy grew, wealth built up among wealthy white southerners, the South became a major player in the world trade of cotton, a cotton trade developed, and cotton-related industries grew.

SECTION 3 *(Pages 424–429)*

8. a. **Identify** What are some small ways in which slaves tried to challenge the slave system?
b. **Make Inferences** How did religion and family help slaves cope with their lives?
c. **Predict** What could be some possible results of stronger strengthening of slave codes in the South?

Reading Skills

Online Research *Use the Reading Skills taught in this chapter to answer the question below.*

9. Which of the following would be the best Web site to find information about life in the South before the Civil War?
a. a Civil War historian's homepage
b. a collection of autobiographies written by slaves
c. a site with information about how to grow cotton
d. a collection of biographies of inventors

Using the Internet

go.hrw.com KEYWORD: SF7 CH13

10. **Activity: Writing Diary Entries** Enslaved African Americans faced harsh working and living conditions. Many tried to escape the slave system. Enter the activity keyword and research the attempts by enslaved African Americans to reach the North and the people who assisted them. Imagine you were trying to help slaves travel to freedom. Write four entries into a diary. In each entry, describe your experiences. Include thumbnail maps to trace their trip.

Reviewing Themes

11. **Society and Culture** How were the different social classes in the South affected by the cotton boom?

12. **Economics** How did the cotton boom affect the economy of the South?

Social Studies Skills

Interpreting Graphs *Use the Social Studies Skills taught in this chapter to answer the questions about the graph below.*

13. What span of time saw the largest increase in cotton production?
a. 1800 to 1820
b. 1820 to 1840
c. 1840 to 1860
d. after 1860

14. About what year did cotton production reach 1.2 million bales per year?
a. 1800
b. 1820
c. 1840
d. 1860

FOCUS ON WRITING

15. **Writing Your Biographical Sketch** Look over your notes about life on a cotton farm. Then choose an imaginary person to write about. Think about what life would have been like for this person. What might he or she have looked like? How might he or she have spoken? What might a typical day have been like? Once you have answered these questions, write two paragraphs about a day in the life of this person.

Social Studies Skills

13. b
14. c

Focus on Writing

15. **Rubric** Students' biographical sketches should
- identify the imaginary person and his or her social class.
- describe what the person does and how he or she looks.
- accurately describe a typical day in the life of a person from the selected social class.
- use precise nouns and adjectives.
- provide two paragraphs.

CRF: Focus on Writing Activity: Biographical Sketch

CHAPTER 13

Standardized Test Practice

8.1.10, 8.3.11, 8.4.6, 8.4.9

DIRECTIONS: Read each question and write the letter of the best response.

1

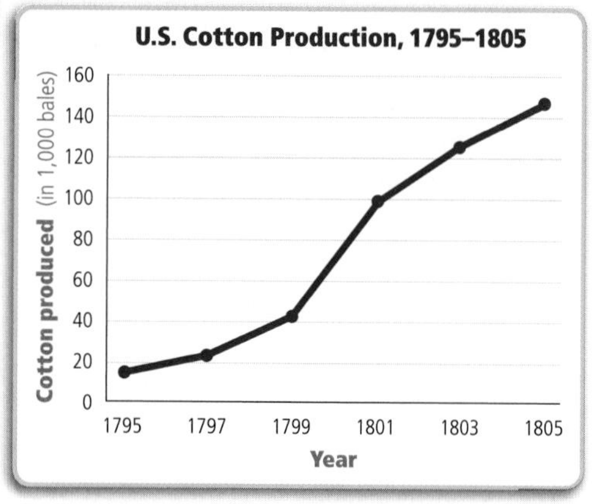

The *main* reason for the changes shown in the graph was

A the invention and use of the cotton gin.
B a decline in the number of slaves.
C the end of the international slave trade.
D a switch from food crops to cash crops.

2 Which of the following helped enslaved African Americans to endure and survive slavery?

A their work
B spirituals
C slave codes
D rebellions

3 Because some southerners feared farmers had become too reliant on cotton, they encouraged farmers to

A stop using the cotton gin.
B try growing a variety of cash crops.
C demand higher tariffs.
D introduce cotton and slavery to the West.

4 Which statement accurately describes southern society in the mid-1800s?

A Very few white southerners owned slaves.
B Few white southerners owned the land they farmed.
C Many African Americans in the South owned land.
D Most white southerners were small farmers.

5 Free African Americans in the South in the early and mid-1800s

A had the same rights and freedoms as white southerners.
B had few rights and freedoms.
C usually had escaped from slavery.
D could travel freely in their home states.

6 Examine the following passage from a northern woman's journal of her stay in Georgia and then use it to answer the question below.

> "On my return from the river I had a long and painful talk with Mr. Butler on the subject of the whipping of Teresa [a slave worn out from childbearing and field work, who asked the author to try to get her workload reduced]. Those discussions are terrible. They throw me into great distress [worry] for the slaves, whose position is completely hopeless; for myself, whose efforts on their behalf sometimes seem to me worse than useless; and for Mr. Butler, whose part in this horrible system fills me by turns with anger and pity."
>
> –Frances Anne Kemble, adapted from *Journal of a Residence on a Georgian Plantation in 1838–1839*

Document-Based Question **What might be the differences between Kemble and Butler on the question of slavery?**

Answers

1. A
Break Down the Question Students need to note the upward trend of cotton production and recall that the invention of the cotton gin in 1793 was responsible for the cotton boom.

2. B
Break Down the Question A slave's work and the slave codes that controlled a slave's life were a source of misery. Rebellions often brought on more suffering than they alleviated. Spirituals helped slaves to endure and survive.

3. B
Break Down the Question This question requires students to recall factual information. Refer students who miss this question to the material "Other Crops and Industries" in Section 1.

4. D
Break Down the Question By using the process of elimination, students who correctly recall information in the material "Southern Society and Culture" in Section 2 will realize that only *D* can be the correct answer.

5. B
Break Down the Question Refer students who miss the question to the material "Free African Americans and Discrimination" in Section 2.

6. possible answer—Butler supports slavery; Kemble opposes everything associated with slavery.
Break Down the Question Among other things, that Kemble made attempts to have the workload of a particular slave reduced, indicates her sympathy for their plight.

Intervention Resources

Reproducible

- Interactive Reader and Study Guide
- Differentiated Instruction Teacher Management System: Lesson Plans for Differentiated Instruction

Technology

- Quick Facts Transparency 35: The South Visual Summary
- Differentiated Instruction Modified Worksheets and Tests CD-ROM
- Interactive Skills Tutor CD-ROM

Tips for Test Taking

Master the Question #2 To help students answer questions testing reading comprehension, have them do the following:

- First, read the selection.
- Next, master the questions.
- Then reread the selection. The answers will be clearer with a second reading.

Remind students that tests are not meant to trick them but to test their knowledge and ability to think clearly.

Chapter 14 Planning Guide

New Movements in America

Chapter Overview	Reproducible Resources	Technology Resources
CHAPTER 14 **pp. 434–471** **Overview:** In this chapter, students will learn about the changing American society of the early 1800s.	**Differentiated Instruction Teacher Management System:*** • Instructional Pacing Guides • Lesson Plans for Differentiated Instruction **Interactive Reader and Study Guide:** Chapter Summary Graphic Organizer* **Chapter Resource File:*** • Focus on Writing Activity: Persuasive Letter • Social Studies Skills Activity: Accepting Social Responsibility • Chapter Review Activity	**Power Presentations with Video CD-ROM** **Differentiated Instruction Modified Worksheets and Tests CD-ROM** **Primary Source Library CD-ROM for United States History** **Student Edition on Audio CD Program** **History's Impact: United States History Video Program (VHS/DVD):** The Impact of Individual Rights and Beliefs*
Section 1: **Immigrants and Urban Challenges** **The Big Idea:** The population of the United States grew rapidly in the early 1800s with the arrival of millions of immigrants.	**Differentiated Instruction Teacher Management System:** Section 1 Lesson Plan* **Interactive Reader and Study Guide:** Sec. 14.1 Summary* **Chapter Resource File:*** • Vocabulary Builder Activity, Section 1	**Daily Bellringer Transparency 14.1*** **Quick Facts Transparency 36:** Push-Pull Factors of Immigration*
Section 2: **American Arts** **The Big Idea:** New movements in art and literature influenced many Americans in the early 1800s.	**Differentiated Instruction Teacher Management System:** Section 2 Lesson Plan* **Interactive Reader and Study Guide:** Sec. 14.2 Summary* **Chapter Resource File:*** • Vocabulary Builder Activity, Section 2 • Literature Activity: *Jack and Jill,* by Louisa May Alcott	**Daily Bellringer Transparency 14.2*** go.hrw.com **Internet Activity:** Transcendental Who's Who
Section 3: **Reforming Society** **The Big Idea:** Reform movements in the early 1800s affected religion, education, and society.	**Differentiated Instruction Teacher Management System:** Section 3 Lesson Plan* **Interactive Reader and Study Guide:** Sec. 14.3 Summary* **Chapter Resource File:*** • Vocabulary Builder Activity, Section 3 • Biography Activities	**Daily Bellringer Transparency 14.3*** go.hrw.com **Internet Activity:** Education Reformers
Section 4: **The Movement to End Slavery** **The Big Idea:** In the mid-1800s, debate over slavery increased as abolitionists organized to challenge slavery in the United States.	**Differentiated Instruction Teacher Management System:** Section 4 Lesson Plan* **Interactive Reader and Study Guide:** Sec. 14.4 Summary* **Chapter Resource File:*** • Vocabulary Builder Activity, Section 4 • Primary Source Activities: David Walker; Frederick Douglass • History and Geography: The Underground Railroad	**Daily Bellringer Transparency 14.4*** **Map Transparency 46:** The Underground Railroad* go.hrw.com **Internet Activity:** Abolitionists Press
Section 5: **Women's Rights** **The Big Idea:** Reformers sought to improve women's rights in American society.	**Differentiated Instruction Teacher Management System:** Section 5 Lesson Plan* **Interactive Reader and Study Guide:** Sec. 14.5 Summary* **Chapter Resource File:*** • Vocabulary Builder Activity, Section 5 • Biography Activity: Suffragettes • Primary Source Activity: Elizabeth Cady Stanton	**Daily Bellringer Transparency 14.5***

SE Student Edition | Print Resource | Audio CD
TE Teacher's Edition | Transparency | CD-ROM
go.hrw.com | **LS** Learning Styles | Video
TOS Indiana Teacher One Stop | * also on Indiana Teacher One Stop

Review, Assessment, Intervention

- **Quick Facts Transparency 37:** New Movements in America Visual Summary*
- **Spanish Chapter Summaries Audio CD Program**
- **Progress Assessment Support System (PASS):** Chapter Tests A and B*
- **Differentiated Instruction Modified Worksheets and Tests CD-ROM:** Modified Chapter Test
- TOS **Indiana Teacher One Stop:** ExamView Test Generator (English/Spanish)
- **Alternative Assessment Handbook**

- **PASS:** Section Quiz 14.1*
- **Online Quiz:** Section 14.1
- **Alternative Assessment Handbook**

- **PASS:** Section Quiz 14.2*
- **Online Quiz:** Section 14.2
- **Alternative Assessment Handbook**

- **PASS:** Section Quiz 14.3*
- **Online Quiz:** Section 14.3
- **Alternative Assessment Handbook**

- **PASS:** Section Quiz 14.4*
- **Online Quiz:** Section 14.4
- **Alternative Assessment Handbook**

- **PASS:** Section Quiz 14.5*
- **Online Quiz:** Section 14.5
- **Alternative Assessment Handbook**

HOLT
History's Impact
United States History Video Program (VHS/DVD)
The Impact of Individual Rights and Beliefs
Suggested use: as a chapter introduction

Power Presentations with Video CD-ROM

Power Presentations with Video are visual presentations of each chapter's main ideas. Presentations can be customized by including Quick Facts charts, images from the text, and video clips.

DIVISION FOR PUBLIC EDUCATION
AMERICAN BAR ASSOCIATION

Developed by the Division for Public Education of the American Bar Association, these materials are part of the **Democracy and Civic Education Resources.**

- **Constitution Study Guide**
- **Supreme Court Case Studies**

Holt Online Learning

go.hrw.com
Teacher Resources
KEYWORD: SF7 TEACHER

go.hrw.com
Student Resources
KEYWORD: SF7 CH14

- Document-Based Questions
- Interactive Multimedia Activities
- Current Events
- Chapter-based Internet Activities
- and more!

Holt Interactive
Online Student Edition

Complete online support for interactivity, assessment, and reporting

- Interactive Maps and Notebook
- Standardized Test Prep
- Homework Practice and Research Activities Online

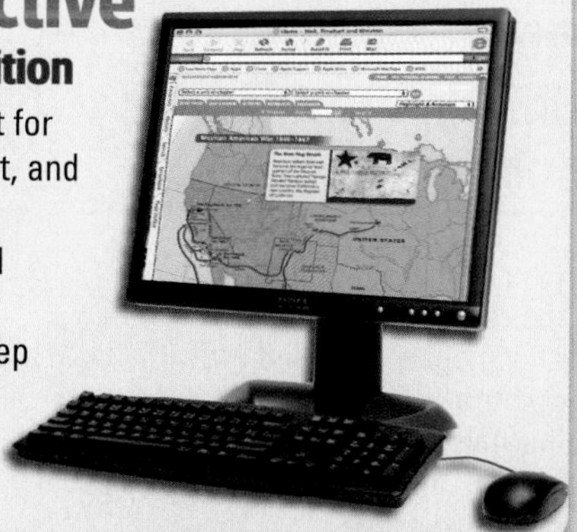

Differentiating Instruction

How do I address the needs of varied learners?

The Target Resource acts as your primary strategy for differentiated instruction.

ENGLISH-LANGUAGE LEARNERS & STRUGGLING READERS

TARGET RESOURCE

English-Language Learner Strategies and Activities

- Build Academic Vocabulary
- Develop Oral and Written Language Structures

Spanish Resources

Spanish Chapter Summaries Audio CD

Spanish Chapter Summaries Online

Teacher's One-Stop Planner:

- ExamView Test Generator, Spanish
- PuzzlePro, Spanish

Additional Resources

Differentiated Instruction Teacher Management System: Lesson Plans for Differentiated Instruction

Chapter Resource File:

- Vocabulary Builder Activities
- Social Studies Skills Activity: Accepting Social Responsibility

Quick Facts Transparencies:

- Push-Pull Factors of Immigration (TR 36)
- New Movements in America Visual Summary (TR 37)

Student Edition on Audio CD Program

Interactive Skills Tutor CD-ROM

SPECIAL NEEDS LEARNERS

TARGET RESOURCE

Differentiated Instruction Modified Worksheets and Tests CD-ROM

- Vocabulary Flash Cards
- Modified Vocabulary Builder Activities
- Modified Chapter Review Activity
- Modified Chapter Test

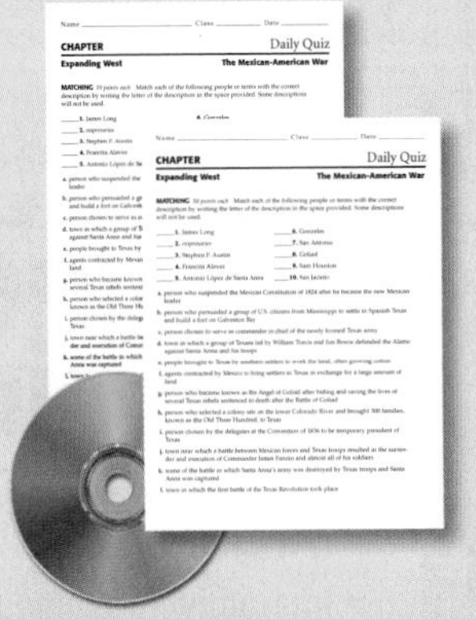

Additional Resources

Differentiated Instruction Teacher Management System: Lesson Plans for Differentiated Instruction

Interactive Reader and Study Guide

Social Studies Skills Activity: Accepting Social Responsibility

Student Edition on Audio CD Program

Interactive Skills Tutor CD-ROM

ADVANCED/GIFTED-AND-TALENTED STUDENTS

TARGET RESOURCE

Primary Source Library CD-ROM for United States History

The Library contains longer versions of quotations in the text, extra sources, and images. Included are point-of-view articles, journals, diaries, historical fiction, and political documents.

Additional Resources

Political Cartoons Activities for United States History: Cartoon 15: Temperance Reform

Chapter Resource File:

- Focus on Writing Activity: Persuasive Letter
- Literature Activity: *Jack and Jill,* by Louisa Alcott
- Primary Source Activity: David Walker, "An Appeal to the Colored Citizens of the World"
- Primary Source Activity: Frederick Douglass, "What the Black Man Wants"
- Primary Source Activity: Elizabeth Cady Stanton, Letter to Lucretia Mott, 1876

Differentiated Activities in the Teacher's Edition

- Immigrant Drawings and Captions, p. 439
- Growth of U.S. Cities Chart, p. 441
- American Romantic Movement Chart, p. 444
- Commendation Awards, p. 452
- Abolitionist Movement Chart, p. 455
- "Who Am I?" Game, p. 456
- Women's Rights Movement Chart, p. 462
- Women's Rights Collage, p. 465

Differentiated Activities in the Teacher's Edition

- "The Midnight Ride of Paul Revere" Illustration, p. 446

Differentiated Activities in the Teacher's Edition

- Mid-1850s Classified Newspaper, p. 440
- Addressing the Opposition, p. 463

Teacher One Stop™

How can I manage the lesson plans and support materials for differentiated instruction?

With the Indiana Teacher One Stop, you can easily organize and print lesson plans, planning guides, and instructional materials for all learners.
The Indiana Teacher One Stop includes the following materials to help you differentiate instruction:

- Interactive Teacher's Edition
- Calendar Planner and pacing guides
- Editable lesson plans
- All reproducible ancillaries in Adobe Acrobat (PDF) format
- ExamView Test Generator (Eng & Span)
- Transparency and video previews

Professional Development

HOLT Professional Development

What teacher training resources are available to help me grow professionally?

- **In-service and staff development** as part of your Holt Social Studies product purchase
- **Quick Teacher Tutorial Lesson Presentation CD-ROM**
- Intensive tuition-based **Teacher Development Institute**
- **Convenient Holt Speaker Bureau** – face-to-face workshop options
- **PRAXIS™ Test Prep** interactive Web-based content refreshers*
- **Ask A Professional Development Expert** at http://www.hrw.com/prodev/

* PRAXIS is a trademark of Educational Testing Service (ETS).
This publication is not endorsed or approved by ETS.

Chapter Preview

Chapter Big Ideas

Section 1 The population of the United States grew rapidly in the early 1800s with the arrival of millions of immigrants.

Section 2 New movements in art and literature influenced many Americans in the early 1800s.

Section 3 Reform movements in the early 1800s affected religion, education, and society.

Section 4 In the mid-1800s, debate over slavery increased as abolitionists organized to challenge slavery in the United States.

Section 5 Reformers sought to improve women's rights in American society.

Focus on Writing

The **Chapter Resource File** provides a Focus on Writing worksheet to help students organize and write their persuasive letters.

CRF: Focus on Writing Activity: Persuasive Letter

Key to Differentiating Instruction

Below Level

Basic-level activities designed for all students encountering new material

At Level

Intermediate-level activities designed for average students

Above Level

Challenging activities designed for honors and gifted and talented students

Standard English Mastery

Activities designed to improve standard English usage

CHAPTER 14 New Movements in America

Indiana Standards

Social Studies Standards

8.1.18 analyze different interests and points of view of individuals and groups involved in the abolitionist, feminist, and social reform movements and in sectional conflicts.

8.1.19 Explain the influence of early individual social reformers and movements.

8.1.24 Identify the influence of individuals on poltical and social events and movements, such as the abolition movement, the Dred Scott case, women's rights, and Native American Indian removal.

8.1.31 Obtain historical data from a variety of sources to compare and contrast examples of art, music, and literature during the nineteenth century and explain how these reflect American culture during this time period.

8.3.6 Identify the agricultural regions of the United States and be able to give reasons for the type of land use and subsequent land development during different historical periods.

go.hrw.com
Indiana
KEYWORD: SF10 IN

Focus on Writing

Persuasive Letter Your local newspaper is running a competition for students to answer the question, "What event or movement in history had the greatest impact on life in the United States?" This chapter tells about many important events and movements in the United States. As you read, take notes on each. Then decide which you believe has most affected life for people in the United States. Write a letter to the newspaper arguing your position.

United States

1817 Thomas Gallaudet founds a school for people who have hearing impairments.

1820

World

1824 British laws making trade unions illegal are repealed.

434 CHAPTER 14

Introduce the Chapter

At Level

Focus on Activism

1. Explain to students that Americans have developed a strong tradition of identifying social problems and creating groups and strategies to solve those problems.
2. Lead a guided discussion about activism in the United States today. Ask students to identify some activist organizations, such as Mothers Against Drunk Driving (MADD) or Habitat for Humanity. What methods do these groups use to effect change and promote their cause? What other social problems or issues exist today? What actions might students take?
3. Explain that activism, or reform, became a major trend in the United States in the early and mid-1800s. As students read the chapter, ask them to compare the issues reformers addressed in the 1800s to those activists address today. **LS Verbal/Linguistic**

Alternative Assessment Handbook, Rubric 11: Discussions

HOLT

History's Impact

▸ **video series**

Watch the video to understand the impact of individual rights and beliefs on society.

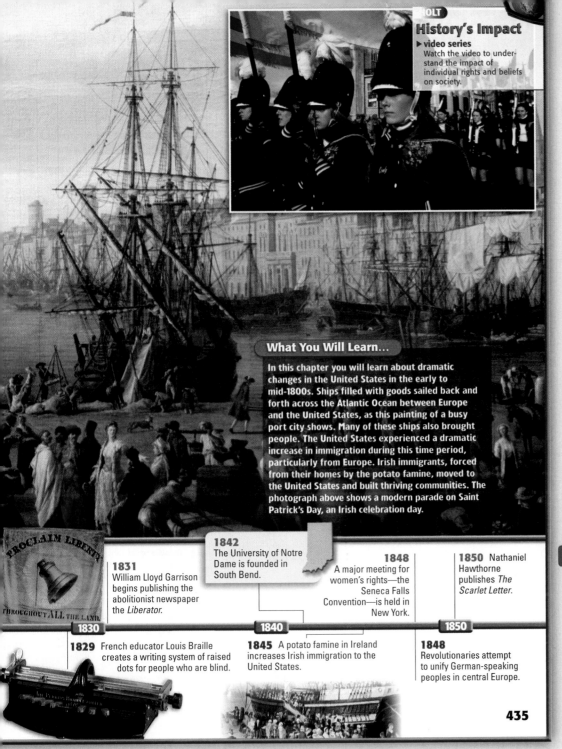

What You Will Learn...

In this chapter you will learn about dramatic changes in the United States in the early to mid-1800s. Ships filled with goods sailed back and forth across the Atlantic Ocean between Europe and the United States, as this painting of a busy port city shows. Many of these ships also brought people. The United States experienced a dramatic increase in immigration during this time period, particularly from Europe. Irish immigrants, forced from their homes by the potato famine, moved to the United States and built thriving communities. The photograph above shows a modern parade on Saint Patrick's Day, an Irish celebration day.

1829 French educator Louis Braille creates a writing system of raised dots for people who are blind.

1830

1831 William Lloyd Garrison begins publishing the abolitionist newspaper the *Liberator.*

1840

1842 The University of Notre Dame is founded in South Bend.

1845 A potato famine in Ireland increases Irish immigration to the United States.

1848 A major meeting for women's rights—the Seneca Falls Convention—is held in New York.

1848 Revolutionaries attempt to unify German-speaking peoples in central Europe.

1850

1850 Nathaniel Hawthorne publishes *The Scarlet Letter.*

435

Chapter Preview

HOLT

History's Impact

▸ **video series**

See the Video Teacher's Guide for strategies for using the chapter video regarding the impact of individual rights and beliefs on society.

Explore the Picture

Growing Immigration Between 1840 and 1860, more than 4 million immigrants came to the United States to begin new lives. The largest groups came from Ireland and Germany. Many of these immigrants entered the United States at New York Harbor. Beginning in 1855, immigrants passed through a central processing center on arrival. There, officials took down immigrants' names and provided information to try to help them.

Analyzing Visuals Based on the image, what might be some initial hardships that immigrants faced? *moving their belongings, finding their way around in a large, strange city*

go.hrw.com

Online Resources

Chapter Resources:
KEYWORD: SF7 CH14

Teacher Resources:
KEYWORD: SF7 TEACHER

Explore the Time Line

1. Who founded a school for the hearing impaired, and when? *Thomas Gallaudet, 1817*
2. In what year was a major meeting for women's rights held, and what was it called? *1848; Seneca Falls Convention*
3. What event caused an increase in Irish immigration to the United States? *potato famine in 1845*

Info to Know

Braille Writing System The Braille system of writing for the blind consists of one to six dots arranged in 63 different combinations. Over time, additional versions of Braille have been developed for math, scientific writing, and computers. More recently, the use of Braille has begun decreasing with developments in computer-voice technology.

Reading Social Studies

Understanding Themes

Introduce the main theme of this chapter to the class by discussing with students several movements that affected society and culture in the United States at this time, such as abolition, immigration, and the Second Great Awakening. Ask students how some of these issues might have been affected by the personal beliefs of some Americans. Help students to understand what effects these beliefs and society and culture had on these new movements in America.

Information and Propaganda

Focus on Reading Locate examples of each type of propaganda discussed on this page. Share those examples with the class. Then ask students to identify each type of propaganda and what information they used to determine that. Ask students to locate their own examples of propaganda by looking at magazines, Web sites, and other resources. Encourage students to share their examples with the class.

Reading Social Studies

by Kylene Beers

Economics | Geography | Politics | **Society and Culture** | Science and Technology

Focus on Themes The mid-1800s was a time of change in America. **Society and culture** changed for several reasons: thousands of immigrants arrived in America; women began to work hard for equal rights; and the North and South debated more and more over the slavery issue. Religious beliefs helped shape people's views toward abolition—the move to end slavery—and women's suffrage—the move to give women the right to vote. This chapter discusses these issues.

Information and Propaganda

Focus on Reading Where do you get information about historical events and people? One source is this textbook and others like it. You can expect the authors of your textbook to do their best to present the facts objectively and fairly. But some sources of historical information may have a totally different purpose in mind. For example, advertisements in political campaigns may contain information, but their main purpose is to persuade people to act or think in a certain way.

Recognizing Propaganda Techniques Propaganda is created to change people's opinions or get them to act in a certain way. Learn to recognize propaganda techniques, and you will be able to separate propaganda from the facts.

"People who don't support public education are greedy monsters who don't care about children!" → **Name Calling** Using loaded words, words that create strong positive or negative emotions, to make someone else's ideas seem inappropriate or wrong

"People all around the country are opening free public schools. It's obviously the right thing to do." → **Bandwagon** Encouraging people to do something because "everyone else is doing it"

"If we provide free education for all children, everyone will be able to get jobs. Poverty and unemployment will disappear." → **Oversimplification** Making a complex situation seem simple, a complex problem seem easy to solve

Reading and Skills Resources

Reading Support

- Interactive Reader and Study Guide
- Student Edition on Audio CD Program
- Spanish Chapter Summaries Audio CD Program

Social Studies Skills Support

- Interactive Skills Tutor CD-ROM

Vocabulary Support

- **CRF:** Vocabulary Builder Activities
- **CRF:** Chapter Review Activity
- Differentiated Instruction Modified Worksheets and Tests CD-ROM:
  - Vocabulary Flash Cards
  - Vocabulary Builder Activity
  - Chapter Review Activity
- OSP Holt PuzzlePro

You Try It!

The flyer below was published in 1837. Read it and then answer the questions that follow.

Flyer from 1837

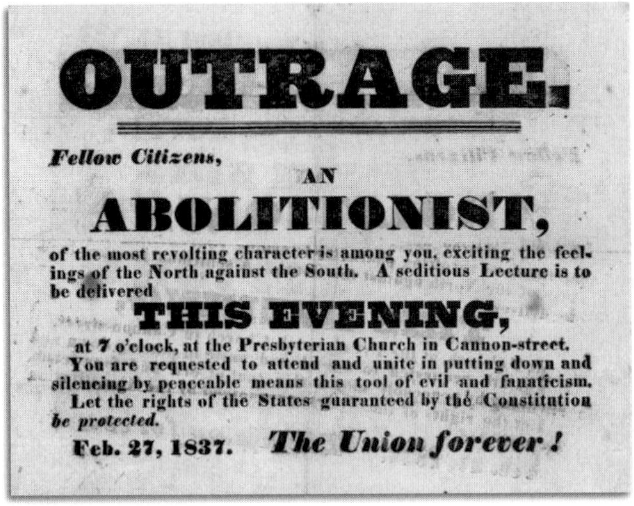

OUTRAGE.

Fellow Citizens,

AN

ABOLITIONIST,

of the most revolting character is among you, exciting the feelings of the North against the South. A seditious Lecture is to be delivered

THIS EVENING,

at 7 o'clock, at the Presbyterian Church in Cannon-street.

You are requested to attend and unite in putting down and silencing by peaceable means this tool of evil and fanaticism.

Let the rights of the States guaranteed by the Constitution *be protected.*

Feb. 27, 1837. *The Union forever!*

After studying the flyer, answer the following questions.

1. What is the purpose of this flyer?
2. Who do you think distributed this flyer?
3. Do you think this flyer is an example of propaganda? Why or why not? If you think it is propaganda, what kind is it?
4. If you were the subject of this flyer, how would you feel? How might you respond to it?

As you read Chapter 14, look carefully at all the primary sources. Do any of them include examples of propaganda?

Key Terms and People

Chapter 14

Section 1

nativists *(p. 440)*
Know-Nothing Party *(p. 440)*
middle class *(p. 440)*
tenements *(p. 442)*

Section 2

transcendentalism *(p. 443)*
Ralph Waldo Emerson *(p. 443)*
Margaret Fuller *(p. 443)*
Henry David Thoreau *(p. 443)*
utopian communities *(p. 444)*
Nathaniel Hawthorne *(p. 444)*
Edgar Allan Poe *(p. 445)*
Emily Dickinson *(p. 445)*
Henry Wadsworth Longfellow *(p. 445)*
Walt Whitman *(p. 445)*

Section 3

Second Great Awakening *(p. 448)*
Charles Grandison Finney *(p. 448)*
Lyman Beecher *(p. 448)*
temperance movement *(p. 449)*
Dorothea Dix *(p. 450)*
common-school movement *(p. 450)*
Horace Mann *(p. 450)*
Catharine Beecher *(p. 451)*
Thomas Gallaudet *(p. 451)*

Section 4

abolition *(p. 454)*
William Lloyd Garrison *(p. 455)*
American Anti-Slavery Society *(p. 455)*
Angelina and Sarah Grimké *(p. 455)*
Frederick Douglass *(p. 456)*
Sojourner Truth *(p. 456)*
Underground Railroad *(p. 456)*
Harriet Tubman *(p. 458)*

Section 5

Elizabeth Cady Stanton *(p. 464)*
Lucretia Mott *(p. 464)*
Seneca Falls Convention *(p. 464)*
Declaration of Sentiments *(p. 464)*
Lucy Stone *(p. 465)*
Susan B. Anthony *(p. 465)*

Academic Vocabulary

implicit *(p. 440)*
abstract *(p. 444)*

Reading Social Studies

Key Terms and People

Have students look over the list of key terms and people. Review with students each term that relates to a social, cultural, or reform movement *(nativism, transcendentalism, temperance, common-school movement, abolition).* Then have students preview the chapter and write a sentence about each movement and why it was important. You might wish to have students use related key terms in the same sentence. Ask for volunteers to share these sentences with the class.

Focus on Reading

See the **Focus on Reading** questions in this chapter for more practice on this reading social studies skill.

Reading Social Studies Assessment

See the **Chapter Review** at the end of this chapter for student assessment questions related to this reading skill.

Teaching Tip

Students may come across propaganda from time to time when doing research on the Internet. Ask students to carefully evaluate the Web sites they come across. Remind students of the important questions to ask to evaluate a Web site, which they learned in the previous chapter. Point out to students that occasionally they may visit a site that uses the propaganda techniques mentioned here. Ask students how propaganda Web sites might affect the validity of their research.

Answers

You Try It! 1. *possible answers—to inform supporters of slavery that an abolitionist would be delivering a lecture in their community; to encourage supporters of slavery to stop the meeting;* **2.** *possible answers—a slaveholder or opponent of abolition;* **3.** *yes, because it uses name calling to make abolition seem wrong;* **4.** *possible answer—would feel more confident than ever of the message to be delivered; would respond by giving the lecture as planned*

Preteach

Bellringer

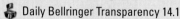

If YOU were there . . . Use the **Daily Bellringer Transparency** to help students answer the question.

Daily Bellringer Transparency 14.1

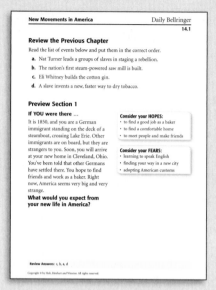

New Movements in America — Daily Bellringer **14.1**

Review the Previous Chapter

Read the list of events below and put them in the correct order.

a. Nat Turner leads a groups of slaves in staging a rebellion.
b. The nation's first steam-powered saw mill is built.
c. Eli Whitney builds the cotton gin.
d. A slave invents a new, faster way to dry tobacco.

Preview Section 1

If YOU were there ...

It is 1850, and you are a German immigrant standing on the deck of a steamboat, crossing Lake Erie. Other immigrants are on board, but they are strangers to you. Soon, you will arrive at your new home in Cleveland, Ohio. You've been told that other Germans have settled there. You hope to find friends and work as a baker. Right now, America seems very big and very strange.

What would you expect from your new life in America?

Consider your HOPES:
- to find a good job as a baker
- to find a comfortable home
- to meet people and make friends

Consider your FEARS:
- learning to speak English
- finding your way in a new city
- adopting American customs

Review Answers: c, b, a, d

Academic Vocabulary

Review with students the high-use academic term in this section:

implicit understood though not clearly put into words (p. 440)

Building Vocabulary

Preteach or review the following terms:

epidemics rapid spread of disease (p. 442)

rural in the country (p. 439)

CRF: Vocabulary Builder Activity, Section 1

Taking Notes

Have students copy the graphic organizer onto their own paper and then use it to take notes on the section. This activity will prepare students for the Section Assessment, in which they will complete a graphic organizer that builds on the information using a critical-thinking skill.

Section Correlations IN

8.1.25 Give examples of how immigration affected American culture in the decades before and after the Civil War . . .

SECTION 1

Immigrants and Urban Challenges

What You Will Learn...

Main Ideas

1. Millions of immigrants, mostly German and Irish, arrived in the United States despite anti-immigrant movements.
2. Industrialization led to the growth of cities.
3. American cities experienced urban problems due to rapid growth.

The Big Idea

The population of the United States grew rapidly in the early 1800s with the arrival of millions of immigrants.

Key Terms

nativists, *p. 440*
Know-Nothing Party, *p. 440*
middle class, *p. 440*
tenements, *p. 442*

TAKING NOTES As you read, take notes on the causes of immigration and urban growth. Record your notes in a graphic organizer like the one shown below.

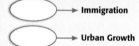

( ) → **Immigration**
( ) → **Urban Growth**

IN **8.1.10, 8.1.16, 8.1.25, 8.3.11**

If YOU were there...

It is 1850, and you are a German immigrant standing on the deck of a steamboat, crossing Lake Erie. Other immigrants are on board, but they are strangers to you. Soon, you will arrive at your new home in Cleveland, Ohio. You've been told that other Germans have settled there. You hope to find friends and work as a baker. Right now, America seems very big and very strange.

What would you expect from your new life in America?

BUILDING BACKGROUND The revolutions in industry, transportation, and technology were not the only major changes in the United States in the mid-1800s. Millions of immigrants, mostly from Europe, swelled the population. Some settled in the rich farmland of the Midwest, while others moved to cities.

Millions of Immigrants Arrive

In the mid-1800s, large numbers of immigrants crossed the Atlantic Ocean to begin new lives in the United States. More than 4 million of them settled in the United States between 1840 and 1860, most from Europe. More than 3 million of these immigrants arrived from Ireland and Germany. Many of them were fleeing economic or political troubles in their native countries.

Fleeing the Irish Potato Famine

Most immigrants from the British Isles during that period were Irish. In the mid-1840s, potato blight, a disease that causes rot in potatoes, left many families in Ireland with little food. More than a million Irish people died of starvation and disease. Even more fled to the United States.

Most Irish immigrants were very poor. Many settled in cities in Massachusetts, New Jersey, New York, and Pennsylvania. They worked at unskilled jobs in the cities or on building canals and

Teach the Big Idea

At Level

Immigrants and Urban Challenges

1. **Teach** To teach the main ideas in the section, use the questions in the Direct Teach boxes.
2. **Apply** Discuss how and why immigration to the United States increased during the mid-1800s. Then have each student create a list of questions that he or she would like to have asked an immigrant of that time period. As students read the section, have them answer as many of their questions as possible. **LS Verbal/Linguistic**
3. **Review** Have students share their questions and answers as well as some of their unanswered questions.
4. **Practice/Homework** Have each student create a five-question quiz, with answer key, for the section. Encourage students to address the causes and effects of immigration. **LS Verbal/Linguistic**

Alternative Assessment Handbook, Rubrics 6: Cause and Effect; and 37: Writing Assignments

Push-Pull Factors of Immigration

QUICK FACTS

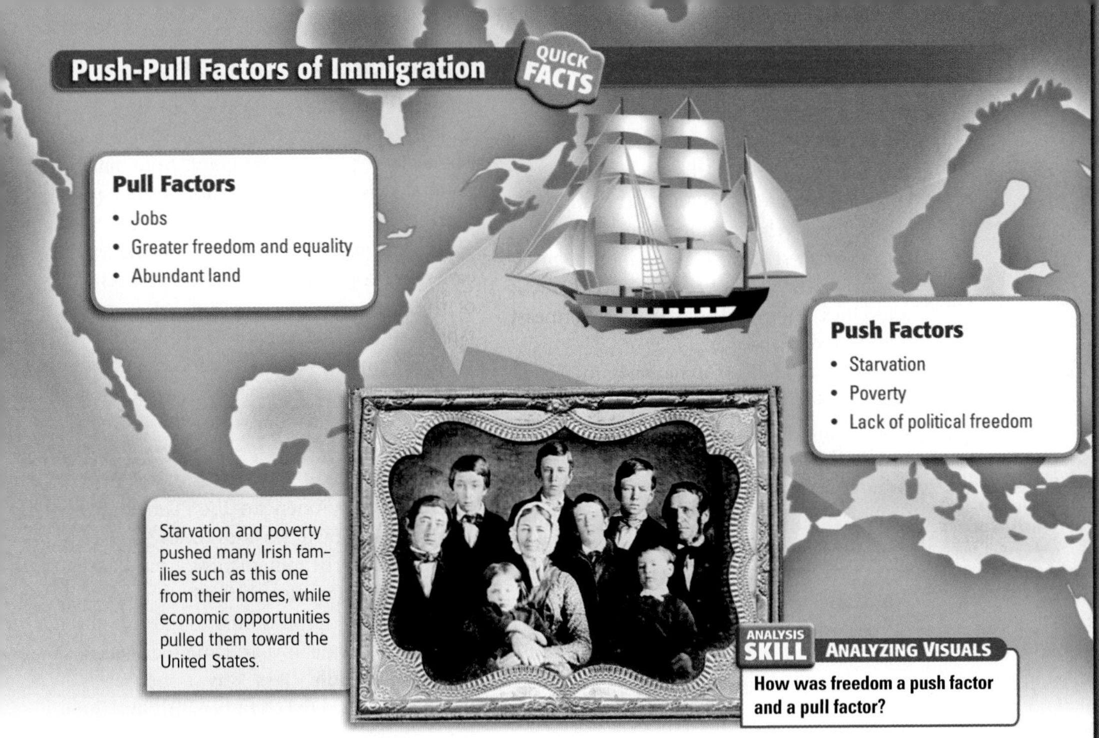

Starvation and poverty pushed many Irish families such as this one from their homes, while economic opportunities pulled them toward the United States.

ANALYSIS SKILL **ANALYZING VISUALS**

How was freedom a push factor and a pull factor?

railroads. Irish women often worked as domestic servants for wealthy families, laboring 16 or more hours per day. In 1849 a Boston health committee reported that low wages forced most Irish immigrants to live in poor housing.

Still, many immigrants enjoyed a new feeling of equality. Patrick Dunny wrote home to his family about this situation.

> "People that cuts a great dash [style] at home ... think it strange [in the United States] for the humble class of people to get as much respect as themselves."
>
> —Patrick Dunny, quoted in *Who Built America?* by Bruce Levine et al.

A Failed German Revolution

Many Germans also came to the United States during this time. In 1848 some Germans had staged a revolution against harsh rule. Some educated Germans fled to the United States to escape persecution caused by their political activities. Most German immigrants, however, were working class, and they came for economic reasons. The United States seemed to offer both greater economic opportunity and more freedom from government control. While most Irish immigrants were Catholics, German immigrant groups included Catholics, Jews, and Protestants.

German immigrants were more likely than the Irish to become farmers and live in rural areas. They moved to midwestern states where more land was available. Unlike the Irish, a high percentage of German immigrants arrived in the United States with money. Despite their funds and skills, German immigrants often were forced to take low-paying jobs. Many German immigrants worked as tailors, seamstresses, bricklayers,

THE IMPACT TODAY

Many immigrants still come to the United States today. More than 13 million entered the United States between 1990 and 2000.

Direct Teach

Main Idea

1 Millions of Immigrants Arrive

Millions of immigrants, mostly German and Irish, arrived in the United States despite anti-immigrant movements.

Recall What two groups formed the majority of immigrants to the United States during the mid-1800s? *Irish and German immigrants*

Contrast How did Irish and German immigrants tend to differ? *Irish—came to escape potato famine, starvation, disease; most poor and Catholic; most settled in cities and worked at unskilled jobs; Germans—came to escape political persecution or to pursue economic opportunity; Catholics, Protestants, and Jews; more likely to settle in Midwest and farm; many had some money*

Quick Facts Transparency 36: Push-Pull Factors of Immigration

Info to Know

German Aid Societies New immigrants faced many dangers in the United States, including scam artists, dangerous jobs, and poor housing. As a result, societies formed to help newcomers adjust to and prosper in their new country. One such group was the German Society of the City of New York. This group worked for the passage of state and federal laws to protect immigrants and achieved success despite heavy opposition. The German Society still exists today.

Differentiating Instruction

Below Level

English-Language Learners

Standard English Mastery

1. Have students examine the Quick Facts above. Discuss with students the reasons that many immigrants—particularly Irish and German immigrants—came to the United Sates in the mid-1800s.
2. Ask students to imagine that they are either Irish or German immigrants traveling to the United States in the mid-1800s. Have students, working individually or in small groups, create a series of drawings illustrating the reasons they left their homeland, their experiences on the ship, and what they hope to find in the United States.
3. Then work with students to help them write short captions for their drawings using standard English. **LS Visual/Spatial**

Alternative Assessment Handbook, Rubric 3: Artwork

Quick Facts Transparency 36: Push-Pull Factors of Immigration

Answers

Analyzing Visuals *push—left because of lack of political freedom; pull—drawn by greater U.S. freedom*

Direct Teach

Main Idea

1 Millions of Immigrants Arrive

Millions of immigrants, mostly German and Irish, arrived in the United States despite anti-immigrant movements.

Summarize How did immigration change the American labor force in the mid-1800s? *Many immigrants went to the Midwest to farm; others filled the need for cheap labor in towns and cities, especially in the Northeast.*

Identify Cause and Effect How did anti-Catholicism contribute to the creation of the Know-Nothing Party? *Nativists formed the Know-Nothing Party in part to keep Catholics out of public office.*

Main Idea

2 Rapid Growth of Cities

Industrialization led to the growth of cities.

Recall In which regions did U.S. cities grow the most during the mid-1800s? Why? *Northeast and mid-Atlantic states; contained three-quarters of the country's manufacturing jobs*

Categorize What types of jobs did the new middle class hold? *skilled workers such as master craftspeople and business owners such as merchants, manufacturers, and professionals*

servants, clerks, cabinetmakers, bakers, and food merchants.

Anti-Immigration Movements

Industrialization and the waves of people from Europe greatly changed the American labor force. While many immigrants went to the Midwest to get farmland, other immigrants filled the need for cheap labor in towns and cities. Industrial jobs in the Northeast attracted many people.

Yet a great deal of native-born Americans feared losing their jobs to immigrants who might work for lower wages. Some felt implicitly threatened by the new immigrants' cultures and religions. For example, before Catholic immigrants arrived, most Americans were Protestants. Conflicts between Catholics and Protestants in Europe caused American Protestants to mistrust Catholic immigrants. Those Americans and others who opposed immigration were called **nativists**.

ACADEMIC VOCABULARY
implicit understood though not clearly put into words

In the 1840s and 1850s some nativists became politically active. An 1844 election flyer gave Americans this warning.

FOCUS ON READING
Look carefully at the quotation to the right from an election flyer. Does it include any examples of propaganda?

> "Look at the . . . thieves and vagabonds [tramps] roaming our streets . . . monopolizing [taking] the business which properly belongs to our own native and true-born citizens."
>
> —Election flyer, quoted in *Who Built America?* by Bruce Levine et al.

In 1849 nativists founded a political organization, the **Know-Nothing Party**, that supported measures making it difficult for foreigners to become citizens or hold office. Its members wanted to keep Catholics and immigrants out of public office. They also wanted to require immigrants to live in the United States for 21 years before becoming citizens. Know-Nothing politicians had some success getting elected during the 1850s. Later, disagreements over the issue of slavery caused the party to fall apart.

READING CHECK **Understanding Cause and Effect** Why did the Know-Nothing Party try to limit the rights of immigrants?

Rapid Growth of Cities

The Industrial Revolution led to the creation of many new jobs in American cities. These city jobs drew immigrants from many nations as well as migrants from rural parts of the United States. The Transportation Revolution helped connect cities and made it easier for people to move to them. As a result of these two trends, American cities grew rapidly during the mid-1800s. Cities in the northeastern and Middle Atlantic states grew the most. By the mid-1800s, three-quarters of the country's manufacturing jobs were in these areas.

The rise of industry and the growth of cities changed American life. Those who owned their own businesses or worked in skilled jobs benefited most from those changes. The families of these merchants, manufacturers, professionals, and master craftspeople made up a growing social class. This new **middle class** was a social and economic level between the wealthy and the poor. Those in the new middle class built large, dignified homes that demonstrated their place in society.

In the growing cities, people found entertainment and an enriched cultural life. Many enjoyed visiting places such as libraries and clubs, or attending concerts or lectures. In the mid-1800s people also attended urban theaters. Favorite pastimes included bowling, boxing, and playing cards. The rules of baseball were formalized in 1845, and the game became increasingly popular.

Cities during this time were compact and crowded. Many people lived close enough to their jobs that they could walk to work. Wagons carried goods down streets paved with stones, making a noisy, busy scene. One observer noted that the professionals in New York City always had a "hurried walk."

READING CHECK **Summarizing** How did the Industrial Revolution affect life in American cities?

Collaborative Learning

Above Level

Mid-1850s Classified Newspaper

Materials: poster board, art supplies, word-processing software (optional)

1. Organize students into small groups. Ask them to imagine that they work at a classified weekly in New York City in the mid-1800s.
2. Have each group create a classified-ad page that includes ads for jobs directed at immigrants, ads for farmland for sale in the Midwest, notices for meetings of immigrant-aid societies, and notices for meetings of nativist groups and the Know-Nothing Party.
3. Groups can write their ads and then arrange them on poster board, or students might use computers to create their classified-ad pages. Display students' work around the classroom.
LS Interpersonal, Verbal/Linguistic

Alternative Assessment Handbook, Rubrics 14: Group Activity; and 23: Newspapers

Answers

Focus on Reading *yes, presents a highly biased view of immigrants*

Reading Check (left) *felt threatened by immigrants' different cultures and worried that they might lose jobs to immigrants who would work for lower wages*

Reading Check (right) *Improvements in transportation and the rise of new jobs in industry led many people to move to urban areas.*

History Close-up

New York City, Mid-1800s

In the mid-1800s, cities such as New York City lured thousands of people in search of jobs and a better life. Many city dwellers found life difficult in the crowded urban conditions.

Many city residents, particularly immigrants, lived in crowded, unsafe conditions.
Many immigrants and other poor city dwellers worked long hours in factories at dangerous jobs.
Women—and frequently children—labored all day in small rooms making clothing to be sold to the wealthy.
City streets were crowded with people buying, selling, and transporting goods.
The first floor of the building served many purposes—living quarters, kitchen, and work space. Here, garments were finished for sale.
PICKLES 1c

ANALYSIS SKILL **ANALYZING VISUALS**

How is this scene similar to one you might see in a large American city today? How is it different?

Direct Teach

History Close-up

New York City, mid-1800s

Have students examine the image and then ask them the following:

- What types of work are visible in the image? *dressmaking, market trade, hauling goods*
- What were dwellings like for many city residents? *crowded, limited furnishings, drab and unsanitary*
- Based on the image, what might be some problems that people experienced in cities in the mid-1800s? *possible answers—crowding, dirty streets from horses, poor housing and working conditions, disease as a result of crowding*

Activity Step into the Picture Ask students to imagine that they are one of the people in the image. Have them write a letter from that person's perspective to a friend who lives elsewhere describing an average day in New York City. LS **Verbal/Linguistic, Visual/Spatial**

Alternative Assessment Handbook, Rubric 40: Writing to Describe

Info to Know

Nativism Turns Violent In some cases, nativism in the mid-1800s turned violent, particularly in eastern U.S. cities. For example, in 1834 a mob burned down the Ursuline Convent outside Boston, Massachusetts. In 1844 a protest by a nativist group led to a riot in Philadelphia, Pennsylvania. Similar riots and attacks on Catholic churches occurred elsewhere.

Differentiating Instruction

Below Level

Struggling Readers

1. Discuss with students the reasons for the rapid growth of U.S. cities and the problems that developed as a result of this growth.
2. Draw the graphic organizer on the chalkboard. Omit the blue, italicized answers.
3. Have each student copy and complete the organizer. LS **Visual/Spatial**

Alternative Assessment Handbook, Rubric 13: Graphic Organizers

Growth of U.S. Cities

Reasons for Growth	Problems of Growth
• increased immigration from Europe • *Transportation Revolution connected cities.* • *Industrial Revolution created new jobs.* • *People moved to cities seeking work.*	• overcrowding • *poor, unsafe, dirty housing conditions* • *lack of public services* • *poor sanitation* • *diseases and epidemics* • *no permanent police force or firefighters*

Answers

Analyzing Visuals *similar—crowded street with people going about their work, open-air marketplace where people are buying and selling goods, people living and working in close quarters, factories; different—horses and buggies, technology, clothing*

Direct Teach

Main Idea

❸ Urban Problems

American cities experienced urban problems due to rapid growth.

Recall What urban problems developed as a result of rapid growth of cities in the mid-1800s? *overcrowding, poor and unsafe housing, lack of public services, unhealthy conditions, disease and epidemics, crime, fire danger, no permanent police force or fire protection*

Make Judgments Despite urban problems, do you think immigrants preferred life in America to that in their home countries? Why? *possible answer—yes, because life in America was still better than the conditions they left behind*

Review & Assess

Close

Have students review the causes and effects of increased U.S. immigration in the mid-1800s.

Review

Online Quiz, Section 14.1

Assess

SE Section 1 Assessment

PASS: Section Quiz 14.1

Alternative Assessment Handbook

Reteach/Classroom Intervention

Interactive Reader and Study Guide, Section 14.1

Interactive Skills Tutor CD-ROM

Urban Problems

American cities in the mid-1800s faced many challenges due to rapid growth. Because public and private transportation was limited, city residents had to live near their workplaces. In addition, there was a lack of safe housing. Many city dwellers, particularly immigrants, could afford to live only in **tenements**—poorly designed apartment buildings that housed large numbers of people. These structures were often dirty, overcrowded, and unsafe.

Public services were also poor. The majority of cities did not have clean water, public health regulations, or healthful ways to get rid of garbage and human and animal waste. Under these conditions, diseases spread easily, and epidemics were common. In 1832 and 1849, for example, New York City suffered cholera epidemics that killed thousands.

City life held other dangers. As urban areas grew, they became centers of criminal activity. Most cities—including New York, Boston, and Philadelphia—had no permanent or organized force to fight crime. Instead, they relied on volunteer night watches, which offered little protection.

Fire was another constant and serious danger in crowded cities. There was little organized fire protection. Most cities were served by volunteer fire companies. Firefighters used hand pumps and buckets to put out fires. In addition, there were not enough sanitation workers and road maintenance crews. These shortages and flaws caused health and safety problems for many city residents.

READING CHECK **Analyzing** Why did so many American cities have problems in the mid-1800s?

SUMMARY AND PREVIEW Immigrants expected a better life in America, but not all Americans welcomed newcomers. The rapid growth of cities caused many problems. In the next section you will read about how America developed its own style of art and literature.

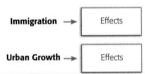

Section 1 Assessment

go.hrw.com
Online Quiz
KEYWORD: SF7 HP14

Reviewing Ideas, Terms, and People

1. a. **Identify** Who were the **nativists**?
   b. **Compare and Contrast** In what ways were Irish and German immigrants to the United States similar and different?
   c. **Predict** How might the rise of anti-immigrant groups lead to problems in the United States?
2. a. **Describe** What led to the growth of cities?
   b. **Analyze** How did the rise of industrialization and the growth of cities change American society?
3. a. **Describe** What were **tenements**?
   b. **Summarize** What problems affected American cities in the mid-1800s?
   c. **Evaluate** What do you think was the biggest problem facing cities in the United States? Why?

Critical Thinking

4. **Identifying Cause and Effect** Review your notes on the causes of immigration and urban growth. Then add the effects of each to your graphic organizer.

Immigration → Effects

Urban Growth → Effects

FOCUS ON WRITING

5. **Identifying Important Events** In your notebook, create a two-column chart. In the first column, list events described in this section. In the second column, write a description of each event and a note about how it changed life in the United States.

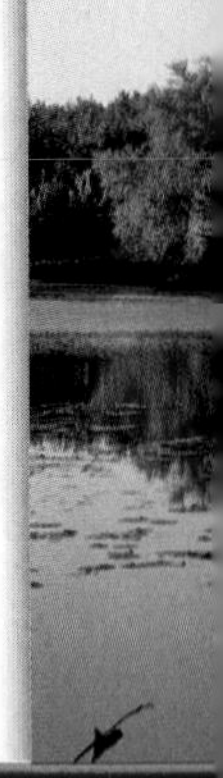

Section 1 Assessment Answers

1. **a.** Americans who opposed immigration
   b. similar—sought economic opportunity, forced to take low-paying jobs; different—reasons for coming, religions, economic status, where settled, jobs they held
   c. could lead to violence against immigrants
2. **a.** Better transportation and the Industrial Revolution led people to move to cities.
   b. A new social class, the middle class, developed; urban problems increased.
3. **a.** poorly designed apartment buildings that housed large numbers of people
   b. overcrowding, unsafe housing, lack of public services, epidemics, crime, fire danger
   c. Students should discuss one of the problems listed in the previous answer.
4. immigration—effects: rapid population and city growth, anti-immigration movements; urban growth—effects: more urban problems
5. Students should list events related to the causes and effects of increased immigration.

Answers

Reading Check *Cities did not have the necessary plans, public services, or regulations to deal with the rapid growth that was occurring.*

American Arts

SECTION 2

If YOU were there...

You are a teacher living in Massachusetts in the 1840s. Some of your neighbors have started an experimental community. They want to live more simply than present-day society allows. They hope to have time to write and think, while still sharing the work. Some people will teach, others will raise food. You think this might be an interesting place to live.

What would you ask the leaders of the community?

BUILDING BACKGROUND Great changes were taking place in American culture. The early 1800s brought a revolution in American thought. Artists, writers, and philosophers pursued their ideals and developed truly American styles.

What You Will Learn...

Main Ideas

1. Transcendentalists and utopian communities withdrew from American society.
2. American Romantic painters and writers made important contributions to art and literature.

The Big Idea

New movements in art and literature influenced many Americans in the early 1800s.

Key Terms and People

transcendentalism, *p. 443*
Ralph Waldo Emerson, *p. 443*
Margaret Fuller, *p. 443*
Henry David Thoreau, *p. 443*
utopian communities, *p. 444*
Nathaniel Hawthorne, *p. 444*
Edgar Allan Poe, *p. 445*
Emily Dickinson, *p. 445*
Henry Wadsworth Longfellow, *p. 445*
Walt Whitman, *p. 445*

TAKING NOTES Create a graphic organizer like the one shown below. Use it to take notes on the new movements in art and literature.

	Transcendentalism	Romanticism
What		
Who		

IN 8.1.19, 8.1.24, 8.1.31

Transcendentalists

Some New England writers and philosophers found spiritual wisdom in **transcendentalism**, the belief that people could transcend, or rise above, material things in life. Transcendentalists also believed that people should depend on themselves and their own insights, rather than on outside authorities. Important transcendentalists included **Ralph Waldo Emerson**, **Margaret Fuller**, and **Henry David Thoreau**.

Walden Pond, where Thoreau lived for two years

Teach the Big Idea

At Level

American Arts

1. **Teach** To teach the main ideas in the section, use the questions in the Direct Teach boxes.
2. **Apply** Have students write each of the blue headings in the section on a piece of paper. Tell students to leave space below each heading. Have students read the material under each heading and create an outline for the content under that heading.
   LS **Verbal/Linguistic**
3. **Review** To review the section, have volunteers share with the class the information they provided in their outlines.
4. **Practice/Homework** Have each student write an imaginary interview with one of the key figures covered in the section. The interview should include at least five questions and answers. LS **Verbal/Linguistic**

Alternative Assessment Handbook, Rubric 37: Writing Assignments

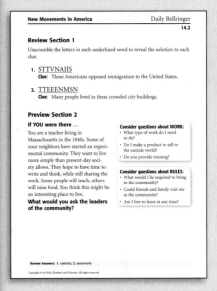

Preteach

Bellringer

If YOU were there . . . Use the **Daily Bellringer Transparency** to help students answer the question.

Daily Bellringer Transparency 14.2

New Movements in America — Daily Bellringer **14.2**

Review Section 1

Unscramble the letters in each underlined word to reveal the solution to each clue.

1. STTVNAIIS
   Clue: These Americans opposed immigration to the United States.
2. TTEEENMSN
   Clue: Many people lived in these crowded city buildings.

Preview Section 2

If YOU were there ...

You are a teacher living in Massachusetts in the 1840s. Some of your neighbors have started an experimental community. They want to live more simply than present-day society allows. They hope to have time to write and think, while still sharing the work. Some people will teach, others will raise food. You think this might be an interesting place to live.

What would you ask the leaders of the community?

Consider questions about WORK:
- What type of work do I need to do?
- Do I make a product to sell to the outside world?
- Do you provide training?

Consider questions about RULES:
- What would I be required to bring to the community?
- Could friends and family visit me at the community?
- Am I free to leave at any time?

Review Answers: 1. nativists; 2. tenements

Academic Vocabulary

Review with students the high-use academic term in this section:

abstract expressing a quality or idea without reference to an actual thing (p. 444)

Building Vocabulary

Preteach or review the following terms:

insights personal perceptions of the nature of people or things (p. 443)

self-reliance dependence on self to accomplish things and make decisions (p. 444)

transcend rise above (p. 443)

CRF: Vocabulary Builder Activity, Section 2

Taking Notes

Have students copy the graphic organizer onto their own paper and then use it to take notes on the section. This activity will prepare students for the Section Assessment, in which they will complete a graphic organizer that builds on the information using a critical-thinking skill.

Section Correlations IN

8.1.19 Explain the influence of early individual social reformers and movements.

Direct Teach

Main Idea

1 Transcendentalists

Transcendentalists and utopian communities withdrew from American society.

Define In your own words, explain transcendentalism. *possible answer—belief that people should rise above material things, depend on themselves and their own insights, and live simply in tune with nature*

Identify Who were some key transcendentalists? *Ralph Waldo Emerson, Margaret Fuller, Henry David Thoreau*

Make Judgments Do you think utopian communities are possible? Why or why not? *possible answers—yes, if people agree to work for the good of the group; no, because inherent human weaknesses will cause all attempts to fail*

Biography

Emily Dickinson (1830–1886) Emily Dickinson did not achieve fame during her lifetime. Of the more than 1,775 poems that she wrote, only 10 were published while she was alive. Not until 1955—nearly 70 years after her death—were all of her poems collected and published.

go.hrw.com

Online Resources

KEYWORD: SF7 CH14
ACTIVITY: Transcendental Who's Who

Focus on Indiana

8.1.19 Explain the influence of early individual social reformers and movements.

Define What was New Harmony? *A utopian community founded by Robert Owen.*

Answers

Reading Check *because members did not work together well enough for the groups to survive*

Art of the Romantic Movement

FOCUS ON INDIANA
George Rapp and 800 followers formed a utopian community at Harmony, Indiana, in 1814. Eleven years later Rapp and his followers left, but Robert Owen bought the town, renamed it New Harmony, and tried to make it a utopian commune.

Emerson was a popular writer and thinker who argued that Americans should disregard institutions and follow their own beliefs. "What I must do is all that concerns me, not what the people think," he wrote in an essay called "Self-Reliance." Fuller edited the famous transcendentalist publication *The Dial*. Thoreau advised even stronger self-reliance and simple living away from society in natural settings. He wrote his book *Walden* after living for two years at Walden Pond.

Some transcendentalists formed a community at Brook Farm, Massachusetts, in the 1840s. It was one of many experiments with **utopian communities**, groups of people who tried to form a perfect society. People in utopian communities pursued abstract spirituality and cooperative lifestyles. Communities sprang up in New Harmony, Oneida, and many other places. However, few communities lasted for long.

ACADEMIC VOCABULARY
abstract expressing a quality or idea without reference to an actual thing

READING CHECK **Drawing Inferences** Why did utopian communities last a short time?

American Romanticism

Ideas about the simple life and nature also inspired painters and writers in the early and mid-1800s. Some joined the Romantic movement that had begun in Europe. Romanticism involved a great interest in nature, an emphasis on individual expression, and a rejection of many established rules. These painters and writers felt that each person brings a unique view to the world. They believed in using emotion to guide their creative output. Some Romantic artists, like Thomas Cole, painted the American landscape. Their works showed the beauty and wonder of nature in the United States. Their images contrasted with the huge cities and corruption of nature that many Americans saw as typical of Europe.

Many female writers, like Ann Sophia Stephens, wrote historical fiction that was popular in the mid-1800s. New England writer **Nathaniel Hawthorne** wrote *The Scarlet Letter* during that period. One of the greatest classics of Romantic literature, it explored Puritan

Differentiating Instruction

Below Level

Struggling Readers

1. Draw the graphic organizer for students to see. Omit the blue, italicized answers.
2. Have each student copy the organizer and complete it by listing the main influences of the key people and ideas related to the American Romantic movement.
   LS Visual/Spatial

Alternative Assessment Handbook, Rubric 13: Graphic Organizers

American Romantic Movement

↓

Ideas
simple life, nature, emotion, individualism, democracy and American history

↓

Artists and Writers
artists: Thomas Cole (Hudson River school);
writers: Stephens, Hawthorne, Melville, Poe, Dickinson, Longfellow, Whitman

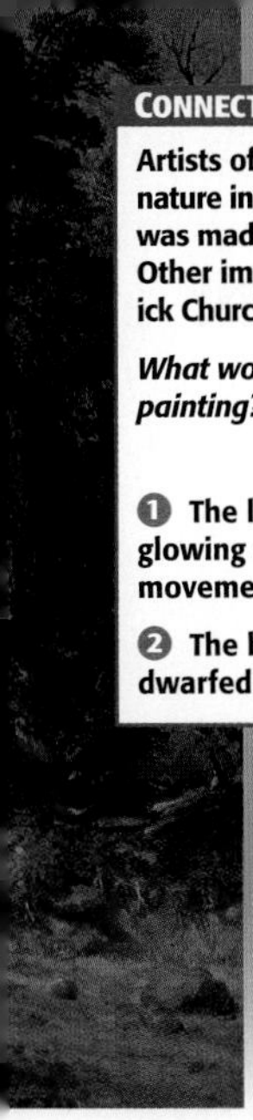

CONNECT TO THE ARTS

Artists of the Romantic movement celebrated nature in their dramatic paintings. Their work was made popular by their leader, Thomas Cole. Other important painters of the era were Frederick Church and Asher Durand.

What words would you use to describe this painting?

❶ The light in the painting has a delicate, glowing quality. Artists of the Romantic movement pioneered this technique.

❷ The human presence in this scene is dwarfed by nature but is in harmony with it.

Asher Durand's The First Harvest in the Wilderness

life in the 1600s. Hawthorne's friend Herman Melville, a writer and former sailor, wrote novels about the sea, such as *Moby-Dick* and *Billy Budd*. Many people believe that *Moby-Dick* is one of the finest American novels ever written.

American Romantic authors also wrote a great deal of poetry. The poet **Edgar Allan Poe**, also a short story writer, became famous for a haunting poem called "The Raven." Other gifted American poets included **Emily Dickinson**, **Henry Wadsworth Longfellow**, and **Walt Whitman**. Most of Dickinson's short, thoughtful poems were not published until after her death. Longfellow, the best-known poet of the mid-1800s, wrote popular story-poems, like *The Song of Hiawatha*. Whitman praised American individualism and democracy in his simple, unrhymed poetry. In his poetry collection *Leaves of Grass,* he wrote, "The United States themselves are essentially the greatest poem."

READING CHECK **Summarizing** Who were some American Romantic authors, and why were they important?

SUMMARY AND PREVIEW American Romantic artists and authors were inspired by ideas about the simple life, nature, and spirituality. In the next section you will learn about ideas that changed American society.

Section 2 Assessment

go.hrw.com
Online Quiz
KEYWORD: SF7 HP14

Reviewing Ideas, Terms, and People

1. a. **Identify** What were the main teachings of **transcendentalism**?
   b. **Summarize** What was one **utopian community** established in the United States, and what was its goal?
   c. **Elaborate** Do you agree with transcendentalists that Americans put too much emphasis on institutions and traditions? Explain your answer.
2. a. **Recall** Who were some important American authors and poets at this time?
   b. **Explain** What ideas did artists in the Romantic movement express?
   c. **Evaluate** Do you think the Romantic movement was important to American culture? Explain.

Critical Thinking

3. **Comparing and Contrasting** Review your notes on art and literature. Then copy the graphic organizer below and use it to show the similarities and differences between the two movements.

Transcendentalism | Similarities | Romanticism

FOCUS ON WRITING

4. **Describing Artistic Movements** Two artistic movements are described in this section, transcendentalism and romanticism. Write these two movements in the first column of your chart. Then in the second column, write a brief description of each and explain how writings from each either described or influenced life in the United States.

Direct Teach

Main Idea

❷ American Romanticism

American Romantic painters and writers made important contributions to art and literature.

Define What was the Romantic movement? *movement that began in Europe, drew on individual emotion and perspective, celebration of nature and simple life*

Summarize Describe Walt Whitman's poetry. *praised American individualism and democracy; simple; unrhymed*

CRF: Literature Activity: *Jack and Jill* by Louisa May Alcott

Review & Assess

Close

Have students summarize new movements in art and literature.

Review

Online Quiz, Section 14.2

Assess

SE Section 2 Assessment

PASS: Section Quiz 14.2

Alternative Assessment Handbook

Reteach/Classroom Intervention

Interactive Reader and Study Guide, Section 14.2

Interactive Skills Tutor CD-ROM

Section 2 Assessment Answers

1. **a.** the belief that people could transcend, or rise above, material things in life
   b. Brook Farm; tried to form a perfect society
   c. possible answers—Yes, America needed to focus on the individual ruggedness and natural wilderness that made it great; no, these institutions and traditions worked.
2. **a.** Ann Sophia Stephens, Nathaniel Hawthorne, Herman Melville, Edgar Allan Poe, Emily Dickinson, Henry Wadsworth Longfellow, and Walt Whitman
   b. beauty and wonder of nature, emotion, individualism, democracy, and history
   c. possible answers—Yes, the movement helped America develop an independent culture; no, the movement just copied Europe.
3. similar—focus on nature and simple life, individualism, personal insight; different—transcendentalism: philosophy; Romantics: focused more on emotion and American history
4. Students should address the ideas of each movement, described in the previous answer.

Answers

Connect to the Arts *possible answers—calm, open, beautiful, wild, panoramic, majestic*

Reading Check *See Answer 2a at left; wrote clearly American literature*

Literature in History

"The Midnight Ride of Paul Revere"

As You Read Before students read the poem, have them each write a few sentences describing what they think a hero is. Next, as students read the poem, have them list the ways in which Longfellow describes Revere as a hero. Then ask students to discuss how their descriptions of a hero compare to Longfellow's.

Connect to Literature

The Fireside Poets Henry Wadsworth Longfellow was among a group of Boston poets known as the Fireside Poets. In addition to Longfellow, the group included Oliver Wendell Holmes, James Russell Lowell, and John Greenleaf Whittier. They were called Fireside Poets because people often read their poems aloud at the fireside as family entertainment.

Meet the Writer

Henry Wadsworth Longfellow (1807–1882) A prolific poet as well as a translator of many languages, Longfellow was the most popular American poet of his time. For many Americans, he became the symbolic figure of the poet: wise, grey-bearded, and living in a world of romance. His most popular poems include *The Song of Hiawatha* (1855) and *The Courtship of Miles Standish* (1858).

Literature in History

Literature of the Young Nation: Romanticism and Realism

from "The Midnight Ride of Paul Revere"

by Henry Wadsworth Longfellow (1807–1882)

About the Reading *"The Midnight Ride of Paul Revere" was published in a book called* Tales of a Wayside Inn. *The book is a collection of poems that tell well-known stories from history and mythology. By including the story of Paul Revere with other famous stories, Longfellow helped increase the importance of Paul Revere's ride.*

AS YOU READ **Notice how Longfellow describes Revere as a hero.**

Listen my children and you shall hear
Of the midnight ride of Paul Revere,
On the eighteenth of April, in Seventy-five;
Hardly a man is now alive
Who remembers that famous day and year. ❶

He said to his friend, "If the British march
By land or sea from the town to-night,
Hang a lantern aloft in the belfry arch
Of the North Church tower as a signal light,—
One if by land, and two if by sea;
And I on the opposite shore will be,
Ready to ride and spread the alarm
Through every . . . village and farm,
For the country folk to be up and to arm." ❷
. . . .
Meanwhile, his friend, through alley and street
Wanders and watches with eager ears,
Till in the silence around him he hears
The muster of men at the barrack door,
The sound of arms, and the tramp of feet,
And the measured tread of the grenadiers,
Marching down to their boats on the shore. ❸

GUIDED READING

WORD HELP

belfry bell tower
muster gathering
barrack building where soldiers meet
grenadiers a soldier that throws grenades

❶ When the poem was written, there were still a few people alive who had lived during the Revolution.

❷ Longfellow uses poetic language to make Revere's story more dramatic.

❸ The sounds of the night are described to help the reader feel the excitement.

Differentiating Instruction

Below Level

Special Needs Learners

Materials: blank paper, colored pens or pencils, old magazines and newspapers

1. Read "The Midnight Ride of Paul Revere" aloud to the class. Discuss the meaning of the passage with students. If necessary, review the historical background. Then help students list the key events that occur in the passage.
2. Have each student create a piece of artwork that illustrates the passage. Students might choose to create a drawing, a comic strip, or a collage.
3. Instruct students to incorporate several of the key events from the passage into their artwork. In addition, each student should write a caption describing his or her artwork.
4. Display students' artwork in the classroom. **LS Visual/Spatial**

Alternative Assessment Handbook, Rubric 3: Artwork

from *Little Women*

by Louisa May Alcott (1832–1888)

About the Reading Little Women *is a novel about four sisters living in a small New England town before the Civil War. Still popular with young people today,* Little Women *describes a family much like the one Louisa May Alcott grew up in. Alcott based the main character, Jo March, on herself. Like Alcott, Jo was different from most women of her time. She was outspoken, eager for adventure, and in conflict with the role her society expected her to play.*

AS YOU READ **Try to understand how Jo is different from Aunt March.**

Jo happened to suit Aunt March, who was lame and needed an active person to wait upon her. The childless old lady had offered to adopt one of the girls when the troubles came, and was much offended because her offer was declined . . .

The old lady wouldn't speak to them for a time, but happening to meet Jo at a friend's, . . . she proposed to take her for a companion.❶ This did not suit Jo at all, but she accepted the place since nothing better appeared, and to everyone's surprise, got on remarkably well with her irascible relative . . .

I suspect that the real attraction was a large library of fine books, which was left to dust and spiders since Uncle March died . . . The dim, dusty room, with the busts staring down from the tall bookcases, the cozy chairs, the globes, and, best of all, the wilderness of books, in which she could wander where she liked, made the library a region of bliss to her . . . ❷

Jo's ambition was to do something very splendid. What it was she had no idea, as yet, but left it for time to tell her, and, meanwhile, found her greatest affliction in the fact that she couldn't read, run, and ride as much as she liked.❸ A quick temper, sharp tongue, and restless spirit were always getting her into scrapes, and her life was a series of ups and downs, which were both comic and pathetic. But the training she received at Aunt March's was just what she needed, and the thought that she was doing something to support herself made her happy in spite of the perpetual "Josy-phine!"

GUIDED READING

WORD HELP

lame disabled
irascible difficult
bliss happiness
ambition hope for the future
affliction problem
pathetic very sad
perpetual constant

❶ ***Some women kept companions to help entertain them and perform small chores. Why might Jo not want to be a companion?***

❷ ***How does Jo differ from ideas about women in the 1880s?***

❸ ***What might Jo be able to do for work in the 1800s?***

CONNECTING LITERATURE TO HISTORY

1. **Drawing Conclusions** Henry Wadsworth Longfellow was the most popular American poet of his time. How does his version of Paul Revere's ride increase the importance of the story?
2. **Comparing and Contrasting** The lives of women in the 1800s were very different from the lives of women today. How does this excerpt of *Little Women* show some similarities and differences between now and then?

Literature in History

Little Women

As You Read Tell students as they read the passage to list adjectives and phrases that describe Jo and Aunt March. Ask volunteers to share some of the items they listed. Then have students use the lists to contrast Jo and Aunt March.

Meet the Writer

Louisa May Alcott (1832–1888)

The daughter of an impractical Massachusetts philosopher, Louisa May Alcott had to work hard from childhood to support her mother and three sisters. She tried sewing, teaching in country schools, working as a domestic, and serving as a Civil War nurse before finding fame as a writer. The success of *Little Women* enabled Alcott to write in her journal, "Paid up all the debts . . . !"

Cross-Discipline Activity: Literature

At Level

Character Analysis Chart

1. Have students read the passage from *Little Women.* Then have each student create a three-column chart and label the columns *Jo, Interactions,* and *Aunt March.*
2. In the middle column, have students list each interaction between Jo and Aunt March in the passage, including inferred interactions. In the other columns, have students describe what each interaction reveals about each character.
3. Ask volunteers to share the information they listed in their charts. Have students discuss each character and how Alcott reveals their personalities.
4. Then have students discuss how the two women's characters and interactions reflect aspects of American society in the mid-1800s.

LS Verbal/Linguistic

Alternative Assessment Handbook, Rubrics 7: Charts; and 11: Discussions

Answers

Guided Reading 1. *possible answer—She is active, and the job will prevent her from running, riding, and reading as much as she would like.*
2. *Jo is outspoken, active, and ambitious at a time when women were expected to be focused on domestic concerns.*
3. *possible answers—seamstress, millworker, writer, teacher, reformer, companion, domestic*

Connecting Literature to History
1. *Longfellow's version presents Paul Revere as the lone, heroic rider who spread the news of the approaching British.*
2. *reveals that women's personalities may be much the same but that opportunities for women in the 1800s were more limited*

Preteach

Bellringer

If YOU were there . . . Use the **Daily Bellringer Transparency** to help students answer the question.

Daily Bellringer Transparency 14.3

New Movements in America — Daily Bellringer **14.3**

Review Section 2

Read the statements below and determine who or what is "speaking."

1. "One of my most famous works is the haunting poem, 'The Raven.' Who am I?"
2. "I inspired writers like Ralph Waldo Emerson and Margaret Fuller. What am I?"
3. "I lived simply, and away from society, at Walden Pond. I wrote a book describing my experiences there. Who am I?"
4. "We are groups of people who attempted to form perfect societies. Who are we?"

Preview Section 3

If YOU were there ...

You live in New York State in the 1850s. You are the oldest daughter in your family. Since childhood you have loved mathematics, which puzzles your family. Your sisters are happy learning to sew and cook and run a household. You want more. You know that there is a female seminary nearby, where you could study and learn much more. But your parents are undecided.

How might you persuade your parents to send you to the school?

Consider their CONCERNS:
- Will you be safe there?
- Will they be able to afford the school fees?
- Will you really have a chance to learn as much as you hope?

Consider PROMISES you could make:
- After graduation, you will earn a salary and repay them.
- Perhaps a chaperone could move with you to the town.
- You could share your new knowledge with others.

Review Answers: **1.** Edgar Allan Poe; **2.** transcendentalism; **3.** Henry David Thoreau; **4.** utopian communities

Building Vocabulary

Preteach or review the following terms:

conversion moving to faith or belief (p. 448)

offenders people who break a law (p. 450)

revivals emotional religious meetings (p. 448)

segregated separate (p. 452)

temperance avoidance of alcohol (p. 449)

CRF: Vocabulary Builder Activity, Section 3

Taking Notes

Have students copy the graphic organizer onto their own paper and then use it to take notes on the section. This activity will prepare students for the Section Assessment, in which they will complete a graphic organizer that builds on the information using a critical-thinking skill.

Section Correlations

IN

8.1.18 Analyze different interests and points of view of individuals and groups involved in the abolitionist, feminist and social reform movements and in sectional conflicts. **8.1.19** Explain the influence of early individual social reformers and movements. **8.1.24** Identify the influence of individuals on political and social events and movements, such as the abolition movement, the Dred Scott case, women's rights and Native American Indian removal.

SECTION 3

Reforming Society

What You Will Learn...

Main Ideas

1. The Second Great Awakening sparked interest in religion.
2. Social reformers began to speak out about temperance and prison reform.
3. Improvements in education reform affected many segments of the population.
4. Northern African American communities became involved in reform efforts.

The Big Idea

Reform movements in the early 1800s affected religion, education, and society.

Key Terms and People

Second Great Awakening, *p. 448*
Charles Grandison Finney, *p. 448*
Lyman Beecher, *p. 448*
temperance movement, *p. 449*
Dorothea Dix, *p. 450*
common-school movement, *p. 450*
Horace Mann, *p. 450*
Catharine Beecher, *p. 451*
Thomas Gallaudet, *p. 451*

TAKING NOTES Create a time line like the one shown below. As you read, list the important events of the reform movements next to the appropriate date on the time line. Some dates might have more than one event.

1817 — 1821 — 1835 — 1837 — 1841

IN 8.1.16, 8.1.18, 8.1.19, 8.1.24, 8.1.26, 8.1.31, 8.2.7

If YOU were there...

You live in New York State in the 1850s. You are the oldest daughter in your family. Since childhood you have loved mathematics, which puzzles your family. Your sisters are happy learning to sew and cook and run a household. You want more. You know that there is a female seminary nearby, where you could study and learn much more. But your parents are undecided.

How might you persuade your parents to send you to the school?

BUILDING BACKGROUND Along with changes in American culture, changes were also taking place in American society. A religious revival swept the country. Reform-minded men and women tried to improve all aspects of society, from schools to taverns. Reforms in education opened up new opportunities for young women.

Second Great Awakening

During the 1790s and early 1800s, some Americans took part in a Christian renewal movement called the **Second Great Awakening**. It swept through towns across upstate New York and through the frontier regions of Kentucky, Ohio, Tennessee, and South Carolina. By the 1820s and 1830s, this new interest in religion had spread to New England and the South.

Charles Grandison Finney was one of the most important leaders of the Second Great Awakening. After experiencing a dramatic religious conversion in 1821, Finney left his career as a lawyer and began preaching. He challenged some traditional Protestant beliefs, telling congregations that each individual was responsible for his or her own salvation. He also believed that sin was avoidable. Finney held revivals, emotional prayer meetings that lasted for days. Many people converted to Christianity during these revivals. Finney told new converts to prove their faith by doing good deeds.

Finney's style of preaching and his ideas angered some traditional ministers, like Boston's **Lyman Beecher**. Beecher wanted to prevent Finney from holding revivals in his city. "You mean to

Teach the Big Idea

At Level

Reforming Society

1. **Teach** To teach the main ideas in the section, use the questions in the Direct Teach boxes.
2. **Apply** Create a four-column chart for students to see. Title the chart *Reforming Society* and label the columns *Why, Who, What,* and *When*. Have each student copy the chart and use the information in the section to complete it. Students should list why reform was needed, key reformers, the reform efforts they made, and when these reforms occurred. **LS Verbal/Linguistic, Visual/Spatial**
3. **Review** To review, have students help you complete a master copy of the chart.
4. **Practice/Homework** Ask students to conduct research on one reformer in the section who interests them. Each student should find one fact about the reformer to share with the class. **LS Verbal/Linguistic**

Alternative Assessment Handbook, Rubrics 7: Charts; and 30: Research carry a streak of fire to Boston. If you attempt it, as the Lord liveth, I'll meet you . . . and fight every inch of the way." Despite the opposition of Beecher and other traditional ministers, Finney's appeal remained powerful. Also, the First Amendment guarantee of freedom of religion prevented the government from passing laws banning the new religious practices. Ministers were therefore free to spread their message of faith and salvation to whomever wished to listen.

Due to the efforts of Finney and his followers, church membership across the country grew a great deal during the Second Great Awakening. Many new church members were women and African Americans. The African Methodist Episcopal Church spread across the Middle Atlantic states. Although the movement had begun in the Northeast and on the frontier, the Second Great Awakening renewed some people's religious faith throughout America.

READING CHECK **Drawing Conclusions** What impact did the Second Great Awakening have on religion in America?

Social Reformers Speak Out

Renewed religious faith often led to involvement in movements to fix the problems created by urban growth. One solution was political action. For example, in 1844 New York City created the first city police force.

Members of the growing middle class, especially women, often led the efforts. Many of the women did not work outside the home and hired servants to care for their households. This gave them time to work in reform groups.

Temperance Movement

Many social reformers worked to prevent alcohol abuse. They believed that Americans drank too much. In the 1830s, on average, an American consumed seven gallons of alcohol per year. Countless Americans thought that alcohol abuse caused social problems, such as family violence, poverty, and criminal behavior.

Americans' worries about the effects of alcohol led to the growth of a **temperance movement**. This reform effort urged people to use self-discipline to stop drinking hard liquor.

FOCUS ON INDIANA

Lyman Beecher was the father of some of the most important reformers of the day. His children included Harriet Beecher Stowe, Catharine Beecher, and Henry Ward Beecher, a minister who argued for the temperance, women's suffrage, and abolitionist causes.

Reform Movements

Reform movements in America included religious meetings called revivals, where preachers urged huge crowds of people to seek salvation. The temperance movement, an effort to convince people to avoid drinking alcohol, promoted posters like the one shown here.

How might the scenes in this poster encourage people to stop drinking?

Direct Teach

Main Idea

1 Second Great Awakening

The Second Great Awakening sparked interest in religion.

Identify What areas of the United States were affected by the Second Great Awakening? *upstate New York, frontier regions of Kentucky, Ohio, Tennessee, South Carolina, New England, and the South*

CRF: Biography Activity: Charles Finney

Main Idea

2 Social Reformers Speak Out

Social reformers began to speak out about temperance and prison reform.

Explain How did the Second Great Awakening contribute to social reform? *Renewed religious faith led people to want to improve society.*

Political Cartoons Activities for United States History, Cartoon 15: Temperance Reform

Focus on Indiana

8.1.19 Explain the influence of early individual social reformers and movements.

Elaborate Why were many reformers involved in several reform movements? *Because they wanted to fix many problems of society.*

Critical Thinking: Finding Main Ideas

At Level

Second Great Awakening Magazine Cover

Materials: art supplies, heavy-stock paper

1. Lead a discussion on the Second Great Awakening and its effects on society.
2. Then ask students to imagine that they work at an early 1800s magazine that covers trends in society. Have students, working either individually or in small groups, create a cover for an edition of the magazine on the Second Great Awakening.
3. The cover should provide the name of the magazine, titles and tag lines for articles in the magazine, and one or more images. The article titles and tag lines should cover all aspects of the Second Great Awakening as well as some other issues of the day.
4. Display the covers around the classroom.
   LS Verbal/Linguistic, Visual/Spatial

Alternative Assessment Handbook, Rubric 19: Magazines

Answers

Reform Movements *by showing how temperance promotes a strong, happy family life*

Reading Check *Church membership increased, particularly among women and African Americans, and some people's religious faith increased across the nation.*

Direct Teach

Main Idea

2 Social Reformers Speak Out

Social reformers began to speak out about temperance and prison reform.

Identify How did Dorothea Dix contribute to the improvement of American society? *Dix pushed for better conditions and facilities for the mentally ill, which led to the creation of many state hospitals.*

Draw Conclusions How were reform schools an improvement over prisons? *Children were not treated as adult offenders and learned useful skills.*

Activity Civics: Responsibility Have students write short essays in response to the following question: *Do you think individuals can still make a difference in society, such as Dorothea Dix and Josiah Quincy did?* Ask volunteers to read their essays aloud to the class. LS **Verbal/Linguistic**

Alternative Assessment Handbook, Rubric 37: Writing Assignments

CRF: Biography Activity: Dorothea Dix

Connect to Science and Technology

Access to Textbooks Technological developments in the early 1800s also helped improved education. New printing techniques made producing textbooks less expensive. Textbooks became more widely distributed, and more students had access to them.

Reformers asked people to limit themselves to beer and wine in small amounts. Groups like the American Temperance Society and the American Temperance Union helped to spread the message. Minister Lyman Beecher spoke widely about the evils of alcohol. He claimed that people who drank alcohol were "neglecting the education of their families—and corrupting their morals."

Prison Reform

Another target of reform was the prison system. **Dorothea Dix** was a middle-class reformer who visited prisons throughout Massachusetts beginning in 1841. Dix reported that mentally ill people frequently were jailed with criminals. They were sometimes left in dark cells without clothes or heat and were chained to the walls and beaten. Dix spoke of what she saw to the state legislature.

THE IMPACT TODAY

McGuffey's Readers were among the first "graded" textbooks. Organizing classes by grades was a new idea that is standard practice today.

In response, the Massachusetts government built facilities for the mentally ill. Dix's work had a nationwide effect. Eventually, more than 100 state hospitals were built to give mentally ill people professional care.

Prisons also held runaway children and orphans. Some had survived only by begging or stealing, and they got the same punishment as adult criminals. Boston mayor Josiah Quincy asked that young offenders receive different punishments than adults. In the 1820s, several state and local governments founded reform schools for children who had been housed in prisons. There, children lived under strict rules and learned useful skills.

Some reformers also tried to end the overcrowding and cruel conditions in prisons. Their efforts led to the creation of houses of correction. These institutions did not use punishment alone to change behavior. They also offered prisoners education.

READING CHECK **Summarizing** How did reformers change the punishment of criminals?

Improvements in Education

Another challenge facing America in the early 1800s was poor public education. During this era, childhood was beginning to be viewed as a separate stage of life in which education was of the utmost importance in creating responsible citizens. However, many children worked in factories or on farms to help support their families. If children could read the Bible, write, and do simple math, that was often considered to be enough.

Education in the Early 1800s

The availability of education varied widely. New England had the most schools, while the South and West had the fewest. Few teachers were trained. Schoolhouses were small, and students of all ages and levels worked in one room.

McGuffey's Readers were the most popular textbooks. William Holmes McGuffey, an educator and minister, put selections from British and American literature in them as well as instruction in moral and social values.

Social background and wealth affected the quality of education. Rich families sent children to private schools or hired tutors. However, poor children had only public schools. Girls could go to school, but parents usually thought that girls needed little education and kept them home. Therefore, few girls learned to read.

Common-School Movement

People in the **common-school movement** wanted all children taught in a common place, regardless of background. **Horace Mann** was a leader of this movement.

In 1837 Mann became Massachusetts's first secretary of education. He convinced the state to double its school budget and raise teachers' salaries. He lengthened the school year and began the first school for teacher training. Mann's success set a standard for education reform throughout the country.

Critical Thinking: Solving Problems

At Level

Prisoners' Bill of Rights

1. Describe the conditions in prisons during the early 1800s. Then organize students into small groups and ask the groups to imagine that they are members of an organization involved in prison reform in the early 1800s.
2. Have each group's members discuss what they hope to achieve through reform. Students should consider living conditions in prisons, who should be placed in prisons, the privileges prisoners should be allowed, and how to deal with juvenile offenders.
3. Have each group provide its suggestions for reform in the form of a prisoners' bill of rights.
4. Write some of the suggested reforms for the class to see. Then have students compare their ideas to the actual reform efforts made in the early 1800s. LS **Verbal/Linguistic**

Alternative Assessment Handbook, Rubrics 14: Group Activity; and 37: Writing Assignments

Answers

Reading Check *provided reform schools for young offenders, and created houses of correction for adult offenders*

Women's Education

Education reform created greater opportunities for women. **Catharine Beecher** started an all-female academy in Hartford, Connecticut. The first college-level educational institution available to women was the Troy Female Seminary, opened by Emma Willard in 1821. Several other women's colleges opened during the 1830s, including Mount Holyoke College. The first medical college for women, who were barred from men's medical schools, opened in Boston in 1848.

Teaching People with Special Needs

Efforts to improve education also helped people with special needs. In 1831 Samuel Gridley Howe opened the Perkins School for the Blind in Massachusetts. Howe traveled widely, talking about teaching people with visual impairment. **Thomas Gallaudet** improved the education and lives of people with hearing impairments. He founded the first free American school for hearing-impaired people in 1817.

READING CHECK **Summarizing** What were Horace Mann's achievements?

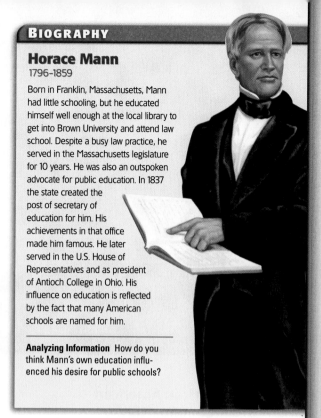

BIOGRAPHY

Horace Mann
1796–1859

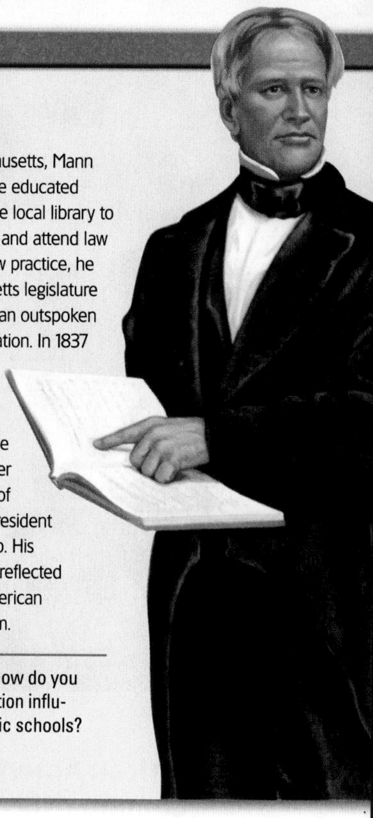

Born in Franklin, Massachusetts, Mann had little schooling, but he educated himself well enough at the local library to get into Brown University and attend law school. Despite a busy law practice, he served in the Massachusetts legislature for 10 years. He was also an outspoken advocate for public education. In 1837 the state created the post of secretary of education for him. His achievements in that office made him famous. He later served in the U.S. House of Representatives and as president of Antioch College in Ohio. His influence on education is reflected by the fact that many American schools are named for him.

Analyzing Information How do you think Mann's own education influenced his desire for public schools?

Primary Source

SPEECH

Horace Mann to the Board of Education

In a speech to the newly created Massachusetts Board of Education, Horace Mann, the board's first secretary, described the purpose of the public school system.

> "[T]here should be a free district school, sufficiently safe, and sufficiently good, for all of the children… where they may be well instructed in the rudiments [basics] of knowledge, formed to propriety of demeanor [good behavior], and imbued [filled] with the principles of duty… It is on this common platform, that a general acquaintanceship [friendship] should be formed between the children of the same neighborhood. It is here, that the affinities [qualities] of a common nature should unite them together."
>
> —Horace Mann, quoted in *The Republic and the School*, edited by Lawrence A. Cremin

Mann believed all students should receive free education.

Neighborhood children should attend school together to form a common bond.

ANALYSIS SKILL **ANALYZING PRIMARY SOURCES**

Besides knowledge, what purpose did Mann believe the public schools had?

Direct Teach

Main Idea

3 Improvements in Education

Improvements in education reform affected many segments of the population.

Recall What factors affected access to education in the early 1800s? *social background and wealth*

Summarize How did Horace Mann work to reform education? *He led the common-school movement, which called for all children to be taught in a common place, and worked to improve educational funding, training, and pay for teachers.*

Analyze Why do you think reformers wanted all children taught in a common school? *So that all students would receive the same educational experience.*

Identify Cause and Effect How did reform efforts improve access to education? *Efforts led to academies and colleges for women and schools for the blind and hearing-impaired.*

CRF: Biography Activity: Pioneers in Education: Mary Lyon and Emma Willard

go.hrw.com

Online Resources

KEYWORD: SF7 CH14
ACTIVITY: Education Reformers

Collaborative Learning

At Level

Education in Early 1800s America

Materials: butcher paper, colored markers, art supplies

1. Organize students into small groups. Have each group create an annotated time line of educational reform from 1800 to 1860.
2. The groups' time lines should cover the significant people, events, and ideas connected with the common-school movement and the expansion of educational opportunities for African Americans, women, and people with special needs.
3. Each group should provide a title for its time line and a brief caption summarizing each time line entry. Encourage students to illustrate their time lines with drawings or photographs.

LS Interpersonal, Visual/Spatial

Alternative Assessment Handbook, Rubrics 14: Group Activity; and 36: Time Lines

Answers

Biography *He did not receive much schooling but had a desire to be educated, which may have given him a desire to help other people who felt the same way.*

Analyzing Primary Sources *to provide a safe environment, teach good behavior and morals, and to form neighborhood bonds among children*

Reading Check *set a national standard for education reform; leader of common-school movement; first Massachusetts secretary of education; convinced state to increase school budget and teachers' salaries, lengthen school year; began first school for teacher training*

Direct Teach

Main Idea

4 African American Communities

Northern African American communities became involved in reform efforts.

Describe How did Quakers in Philadelphia influence opportunities for African Americans? *Quakers believed in equality and supported education for African Americans.*

Contrast How did educational opportunities for African Americans differ across the nation? *Free African Americans in the North and Midwest had some chances to attend school, but in the South laws barred most enslaved Africans from getting an education.*

Draw Conclusions How might attending college have improved African Americans' opportunities? *possible answer—They could get better jobs and learn the skills to serve as community leaders.*

Connect to Civics: Justice

School Segregation More than 100 years before the Supreme Court case *Brown* v. *the Board of Education of Topeka* (1954), another court case addressed segregation in America's schools. In 1848, Benjamin Roberts, an African American printer, sued the Boston School Committee for making his five-year-old daughter Sarah attend an all-black school. Charles Sumner and black attorney Robert Morris provided the defense in the case, but without success. In 1850 the Massachusetts Supreme Judicial Court ruled in *Sarah C. Roberts* v. *The City of Boston* that segregated schools were constitutional. The case served as a precedent, or standard, in later cases involving racial segregation, including *Plessy* v. *Ferguson* (1896).

Focus on Indiana

8.1.31

Analyze How did African American artists and writers help prove that the ideas behind slavery were wrong? *Their achievements were equal to those of other races.*

New Opportunities

FOCUS ON INDIANA

Though African Americans faced racial discrimination during the 1800s, many became successful entrepreneurs, scholars, and artists. Edmonia Lewis, a sculptor, Paul Dunbar, a poet, and Edward Bannister and Henry Ossawa Tanner, both painters, became renowned for their work. Their successes combatted the idea that African Americans were unable to produce intellectual and artistic creations that rivaled those of other races.

African American Communities

Free African Americans usually lived in segregated, or separate, communities in the North. Most of them lived in cities such as New York, Boston, and Philadelphia. Community leaders were often influenced by the Second Great Awakening and its spirit of reform.

Founded by former slave Richard Allen, the Free African Religious Society became a model for other groups that pressed for racial equality and the education of blacks. In 1816 Allen became the first bishop of the African Methodist Episcopal Church, or AME Church. This church broke away from white Methodist churches after African Americans were treated poorly in some white congregations.

Other influential African Americans of the time, such as Alexander Crummel, pushed for the creation of schools for black Americans. The New York African Free School in New York City educated hundreds of children, many of whom became brilliant scholars and important African American leaders. Philadelphia also had a long history of educating African Americans. This was largely because Philadelphia was a center of Quaker influence, and the Quakers believed strongly in equality. The city ran seven schools for African American students by the year 1800. In 1820 Boston followed Philadelphia's lead and opened a separate elementary school for African American children. The city began allowing them to attend school with whites in 1855.

African Americans rarely attended college because few colleges would accept them. In 1835 Oberlin College became the first to do so. Harvard University soon admitted African Americans, too. Several African American colleges were founded beginning in the 1840s. In 1842 the Institute for Colored Youth opened in Philadelphia. Avery College, also in Pennsylvania, was founded in 1849.

452 CHAPTER 14

Differentiating Instruction

Below Level

Struggling Readers

Prep Required

Materials: art supplies, sample certificates of commendation or awards (optional)

1. If available, show students sample certificates of commendation or awards. Explain that such items are often given to people in appreciation for their efforts or contributions.
2. Ask students to select one of the reformers mentioned in this section and to create a certificate of commendation for that person. The commendation should include the person's name, a description of the reform or problem he or she is associated with, and a summary of the person's efforts or contributions.
3. Then hold a mock award ceremony at which volunteers read aloud their certificates of commendation. **LS Verbal/Linguistic**

Alternative Assessment Handbook, Rubric 37: Writing Assignments

This photograph (left) of the 1855 class at Oberlin College shows the slow integration of African Americans into previously white colleges. Some churches also became more integrated, and preachers like the one pictured above began calling for equality between races.

Why might preachers have been particularly influential in calls for greater integration?

While free African Americans had some opportunities to attend school in the North and Midwest, few had this chance in the South. Laws in the South barred most enslaved people from getting any education, even at the primary school level. While some slaves learned to read on their own, they almost always did so in secret. Slaveholders were fearful that education and knowledge in general might encourage a spirit of revolt among enslaved African Americans.

READING CHECK **Drawing Conclusions**
Why was it difficult for African Americans to get an education in the South in the early 1800s?

SUMMARY AND PREVIEW The efforts of reformers led to improvements in many aspects of American life in the early to mid-1800s. In the next section you will learn about reform-minded people who opposed the practice of slavery.

Section 3 Assessment

go.hrw.com
Online Quiz
KEYWORD: SF7 HP14

Reviewing Ideas, Terms, and People

1. a. **Identify** What was the **Second Great Awakening**, and who was one of its leaders?
   b. **Summarize** What effects did the Second Great Awakening have on religion in the United States?
2. a. **Identify** What role did **Dorothea Dix** play in social reforms of the early 1800s?
   b. **Summarize** What different reforms helped improve the U.S. prison system?
   c. **Elaborate** How might the Second Great Awakening have led to the growth of social reform movements?
3. a. **Identify** What was the **common-school movement**, and who was one of its leaders?
   b. **Analyze** Why did reformers set out to improve education in the United States?
   c. **Evaluate** Do you think **Horace Mann**'s ideas for educational reform were good ones? Explain.
4. a. **Recall** In what cities were the first public schools for African Americans located?
   b. **Draw Conclusions** How did free African Americans benefit from educational reforms?

Critical Thinking

5. **Categorizing** Review the reform-movement events on the time line in your notes. Then use a chart like the one below to identify the leaders and accomplishments of each reform movement.

Movement	Leaders	Accomplishments
Prison and Mental Health Reform		
Temperance		
Education		

FOCUS ON WRITING

6. **Choosing Important Events** This section covers the reform of social issues such as religion, prisons, and education. Write the reforms described in your chart. Then write a note about each reform and about the important people involved in it. Think about how each one influenced life in the United States.

Section 3 Assessment Answers

1. a. Christian renewal movement; Charles Grandison Finney
   b. Church membership grew, and religious faith was renewed nationwide.
2. a. Dix pushed for facilities for the mentally ill.
   b. reform schools, houses of correction
   c. Renewed religious faith led people to want to help others and improve society.
3. a. movement to educate all children in a common place; Horace Mann
   b. poor, limited public education
   c. possible answer—yes, because they increased access to and funding for education
4. a. New York, Philadelphia, and Boston
   b. More African Americans had the chance to attend public schools and colleges.
5. Prison/Mental Health—Dix, Quincy; state hospitals, reform schools; Temperance—Beecher; reduced alcohol abuse; Education—Mann, common-school; Beecher, all-female academy; Howe and Gallaudet, special needs; Crummel, African Americans
6. See previous answer.

Direct Teach

Biography

Harriet Jacobs (1813–1897) Harriet Jacobs was born into slavery and orphaned at a young age. She learned to read from her first female slaveholder. After Jacobs escaped slavery and fled North, she wrote *Incidents in the Life of a Slave Girl.* Jacobs' emotionally charged account was a fierce indictment of slavery. On the title page, Jacobs writes, "Northerners know nothing at all about Slavery. They think it is perpetual bondage only. They have no conception of the depth of *degradation* involved in that word, *Slavery;* if they had, they would never cease their efforts until so horrible a system was overthrown." Jacobs' narrative was rediscovered during the civil rights movement of the 1960s. Many experts considered the account to be a work of fiction until scholars authenticated it in 1981.

Review & Assess

Close

Have students review the major reform movements and leading reformers covered in this section.

Review

go.hrw.com Online Quiz, Section 14.3

Assess

SE Section 3 Assessment

PASS: Section Quiz 14.3

Alternative Assessment Handbook

Reteach/Classroom Intervention

Interactive Reader and Study Guide, Section 14.3

Interactive Skills Tutor CD-ROM

Answers

New Opportunities *because they were community leaders, and many people heard them speak*

Reading Check *Southern laws barred educating most enslaved people because slaveholders feared education would lead to slave revolts.*

Preteach

Bellringer

If YOU were there . . . Use the **Daily Bellringer Transparency** to help students answer the question.

Daily Bellringer Transparency 14.4

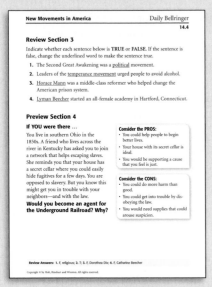

New Movements in America — Daily Bellringer **14.4**

Review Section 3

Indicate whether each sentence below is **TRUE** or **FALSE**. If the sentence is false, change the underlined word to make the sentence true.

1. The Second Great Awakening was a political movement.
2. Leaders of the temperance movement urged people to avoid alcohol.
3. Horace Mann was a middle-class reformer who helped change the American prison system.
4. Lyman Beecher started an all-female academy in Hartford, Connecticut.

Preview Section 4

If YOU were there ...

You live in southern Ohio in the 1850s. A friend who lives across the river in Kentucky has asked you to join a network that helps escaping slaves. She reminds you that your house has a secret cellar where you could easily hide fugitives for a few days. You are opposed to slavery. But you know this might get you in trouble with your neighbors—and with the law.

Would you become an agent for the Underground Railroad? Why?

Consider the PROS:
- You could help people to begin better lives.
- Your house with its secret cellar is ideal.
- You would be supporting a cause that you feel is just.

Consider the CONS:
- You could do more harm than good.
- You could get into trouble by disobeying the law.
- You would need supplies that could arouse suspicion.

Review Answers: 1. F, religious; 2. T; 3. F, Dorothea Dix; 4. F, Catharine Beecher

Building Vocabulary

Preteach or review the following terms:

emancipation freedom from slavery (p. 455)

narrative a story or account (p. 456)

obstructed blocked or hindered (p. 458)

CRF: Vocabulary Builder Activity, Section 4

Taking Notes

Have students copy the graphic organizer onto their own paper and then use it to take notes on the section. This activity will prepare students for the Section Assessment, in which they will complete a graphic organizer that builds on the information using a critical-thinking skill.

Section Correlations (IN)

8.1.16 Describe the abolition of slavery in the northern states, including the conflicts and compromises associated with westward expansion of slavery. **8.1.19** Explain the influence of early individual social reformers and movements.

SECTION 4

The Movement to End Slavery

What You Will Learn...

Main Ideas

1. Americans from a variety of backgrounds actively opposed slavery.
2. Abolitionists organized the Underground Railroad to help enslaved Africans escape.
3. Despite efforts of abolitionists, many Americans remained opposed to ending slavery.

The Big Idea

In the mid-1800s, debate over slavery increased as abolitionists organized to challenge slavery in the United States.

Key Terms and People

abolition, *p. 454*
William Lloyd Garrison, *p. 455*
American Anti-Slavery Society, *p. 455*
Angelina and Sarah Grimké, *p. 455*
Frederick Douglass, *p. 456*
Sojourner Truth, *p. 456*
Underground Railroad, *p. 456*
Harriet Tubman, *p. 458*

TAKING NOTES As you read, take notes on the different abolitionist movements that existed, the leaders of each movement, and the methods used by each group to oppose slavery. Write your notes in a chart like the one below.

Movement	Members	Methods

IN **8.1.16, 8.1.18, 8.1.19. 8.1.20, 8.1.24, 8.1.28, 8.1.31, 8.2.7**

If YOU were there...

You live in southern Ohio in the 1850s. A friend who lives across the river in Kentucky has asked you to join a network that helps escaping slaves. She reminds you that your house has a secret cellar where you could easily hide fugitives for a few days. You are opposed to slavery. But you know this might get you in trouble with your neighbors—and with the law.

Would you become an agent for the Underground Railroad? Why?

BUILDING BACKGROUND The early 1800s brought many movements for social reform in the United States. Perhaps the most important and far-reaching was the movement for the abolition of slavery. While reformers worked to end slavery, many also took risks to help slaves to escape.

Americans Oppose Slavery

Some Americans had opposed slavery since before the country was founded. Benjamin Franklin was the president of the first anti-slavery society in America, the Pennsylvania Society for Promoting the Abolition of Slavery. In the 1830s, Americans took more organized action supporting **abolition**, or a complete end to slavery.

Differences among Abolitionists

Abolitionists came from many different backgrounds and opposed slavery for various reasons. The Quakers were among the first groups to challenge slavery on religious grounds. Other religious leaders gave speeches and published pamphlets that moved many Americans to support abolition. In one of these, abolitionist Theodore Weld wrote that "everyman knows that slavery is a curse." Other abolitionists referred to the Declaration of Independence. They reminded people that the American Revolution had been fought in the name of liberty.

Teach the Big Idea

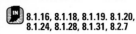

At Level

The Movement to End Slavery

1. **Teach** To teach the main ideas in the section, use the questions in the Direct Teach boxes.
2. **Apply** Have each student, working individually or in pairs, write a summary of each part of the section, indicated by the blue headings. **LS Verbal/Linguistic**
3. **Review** As you review the section, have volunteers share their summaries. Write them for the class to see and ask students to provide supporting details for each one.
4. **Practice/Homework** Ask students to imagine that they belong to an antislavery society. Have them create flyers announcing the group's next meeting, at which Harriet Tubman will be speaking. The flyers should explain the group's goals, why Americans should support abolition, and what Tubman will be talking about. **LS Verbal/Linguistic**

Alternative Assessment Handbook, Rubric 37: Writing Assignments

Antislavery reformers did not always agree on the details, however. They differed over how much equality they thought African Americans should have. Some believed that African Americans should receive the same treatment as white Americans. In contrast, other abolitionists were against full political and social equality.

Some abolitionists wanted to send freed African Americans to Africa to start new colonies. They thought that this would prevent conflicts between the races in the United States. In 1817 a minister named Robert Finley started the American Colonization Society, an organization dedicated to establishing colonies of freed slaves in Africa. Five years later, the society founded the colony of Liberia on the west coast of Africa. About 12,000 African Americans eventually settled in Liberia. However, many abolitionists who once favored colonization later opposed it. Some African Americans also opposed it. David Walker was one such person. In his 1829 essay, *Appeal to the Colored Citizens of the World*, Walker explained his opposition to colonization.

> "The greatest riches in all America have arisen from our blood and tears: and they [whites] will drive us from our property and homes, which we have earned with our blood."
>
> —David Walker, quoted in *From Slavery to Freedom* by John Hope Franklin and Alfred A. Moss Jr.

"Where there is a
human being,
I see God-given rights..."
—William Lloyd Garrison

Spreading the Abolitionist Message

Abolitionists found many ways to further their cause. Some went on speaking tours or wrote pamphlets and newspaper articles. John Greenleaf Whittier wrote abolitionist poetry and literature. **William Lloyd Garrison** published an abolitionist newspaper, the *Liberator*, beginning in 1831. In 1833 he also helped found the **American Anti-Slavery Society**. Its members wanted immediate emancipation and racial equality for African Americans. Garrison later became its president.

Both the *Liberator* and the Anti-Slavery Society relied on support from free African Americans. Society members spread antislavery literature and petitioned Congress to end federal support of slavery. In 1840 the American Anti-Slavery Society split. One group wanted immediate freedom for enslaved African Americans and a bigger role for women. The others wanted gradual emancipation and for women to play only minor roles in the movement.

Angelina and Sarah Grimké, two white southern women, were antislavery activists of the 1830s. They came from a South Carolina slaveholding family but disagreed with their parents' support of slavery. Angelina Grimké tried to recruit other white southern women in a pamphlet called *Appeal to the Christian Women of the South* in 1836.

> "I know you do not make the laws, but . . . if you really suppose you can do nothing to overthrow slavery you are greatly mistaken . . . Try to persuade your husband, father, brothers, and sons that slavery is a crime against God and man."
>
> —Angelina Grimké, quoted in *The Grimké Sisters from South Carolina*, edited by Gerda Lerner

This essay was very popular in the North. In 1839 the Grimké sisters wrote *American Slavery As It Is*. The book was one of the most important antislavery works of its time.

Direct Teach

Main Idea

1 Americans Oppose Slavery

Americans from a variety of backgrounds actively opposed slavery.

Recall What were some reasons that abolitionists opposed slavery? *for religious reasons, was morally wrong, because it went against the right to liberty for which the American Revolution had been fought*

Contrast How did some abolitionists differ in their views toward African Americans? *differed over how much equality they thought African Americans should have and whether to support colonization*

Draw Conclusions How did Angelina Grimké believe women could help bring an end to slavery? *by persuading the men in their lives that slavery was wrong*

CRF: Biography Activity: Abolitionists: Theodore Weld, Robert Purvis, and John Brown

CRF: Primary Source Activity: David Walker, "An Appeal to the Colored Citizens of the World"

World Events

British Abolitionists Many American abolitionists looked to Great Britain for examples of how to oppose slavery. The British abolitionist movement began in the 1780s and achieved success in 1807 when Britain outlawed the slave trade. In 1834 a law abolishing slavery throughout the British Empire went into effect. British antislavery efforts did not stop, however. In 1840 the British and Foreign Anti-Slavery Society held the World's Anti-Slavery Convention in London. Convention members asked the British government to pressure other countries to end slavery. In the mid-1800s, British warships began stopping slave ships and freeing any enslaved Africans they found.

Differentiating Instruction

Below Level

English-Language Learners

1. Copy the graphic organizer for students to see. Omit the blue, italicized answers.
2. Have each student copy the organizer and complete it by listing the leaders and main methods of the abolitionist movement.
3. Then have students discuss what methods reformers and activists might use today.

LS Visual/Spatial

Abolitionist Movement
movement to end slavery completely

Leaders
- *Frederick Douglass*
- *William Lloyd Garrison*
- *Angelina and Sarah Grimké*
- *Sojourner Truth*
- *Harriet Tubman*
- *and others*

Methods
- *lectures, speeches*
- *pamphlets*
- *newspapers, articles*
- *antislavery societies*
- *nonfiction books, plays, poetry, novels*
- *petitions to Congress*

Direct Teach

Main Idea

1 Americans Oppose Slavery

Americans from a variety of backgrounds actively opposed slavery.

Identify Who were some leading abolitionists? *Theodore Weld, David Walker, William Lloyd Garrison, Robert Finley, Angelina and Sarah Grimké, Frederick Douglass, Sojourner Truth, Harriet Jacobs, William Wells Brown, (discussed later, John Quincy Adams and Harriet Tubman)*

Interpret In the quotation on this page, what does Frederick Douglass mean when he says the Fourth of July is not his? *possible answer—that the freedom enjoyed and celebrated by some Americans was not available to enslaved African Americans or even fully to free African Americans*

Elaborate How did the words of former enslaved Africans, such as Frederick Douglass, serve as powerful weapons in the abolitionist movement? *provided firsthand accounts of the cruel and harsh reality of slavery*

Connect to Science

The North Star Fugitive slaves traveling by night often used the North Star to determine their route, because this star marks the general location of the North Pole.

Focus on Indiana

IN 8.1.18

Evaluate Why was Indiana an important part of the Underground Railroad? *It bordered the South and was near Canada.*

go.hrw.com
Online Resources
KEYWORD: SF7 CH14
ACTIVITY: Abolitionist Press

FOCUS ON INDIANA

Indiana became an important part of the Underground Railroad since it shared a border with the slave state of Kentucky. Although many Indianans supported slavery and worked to return escaped slaves to the South, others helped escaped slaves to reach freedom in the North or in Canada. Levi Coffin's house in Fountain City helped so many slaves escape that it was called "the Grand Central Station" of the Underground Railroad.

African American Abolitionists

Many former slaves were active in the antislavery cause. **Frederick Douglass** escaped from slavery when he was 20 and went on to become one of the most important African American leaders of the 1800s. Douglass secretly learned to read and write as a boy, despite a law against it. His public-speaking skills impressed members of the Anti-Slavery Society. In 1841 they asked him to give regular lectures.

At a Fourth of July celebration in 1852, he captured the audience's attention with his powerful voice.

> "The blessings in which you, this day, rejoice, are not enjoyed in common ... This Fourth of July is *yours*, not *mine*. You may rejoice, I must mourn."
>
> —Frederick Douglass, quoted in *From Slavery to Freedom* by John Hope Franklin and Alfred A. Moss Jr.

In addition to his many speaking tours in the United States and Europe, Douglass published a newspaper called the *North Star* and wrote several autobiographies. His autobiographies were intended to show the injustices of slavery.

Another former slave, **Sojourner Truth**, also contributed to the abolitionist cause. She claimed God had called her to travel through the United States and preach the truth about slavery and women's rights. With her deep voice and quick wit, Truth became legendary in the antislavery movement for her fiery and dramatic speeches.

Other African Americans wrote narratives about their experiences as slaves to expose the cruelties that many slaves faced. In 1861 Harriet Jacobs published *Incidents in the Life of a Slave Girl*, one of the few slave narratives by a woman. William Wells Brown wrote an antislavery play as well as a personal narrative in the form of a novel called *Clotel*.

READING CHECK **Finding Main Ideas** In what ways did African Americans participate in the abolition movement?

The Underground Railroad

By the 1830s, a loosely organized group had begun helping slaves escape from the South. Free African Americans, former slaves, and a few white abolitionists worked together. They created what became known as the **Underground Railroad**. The organization was not an actual railroad but was a network of people who arranged transportation and hiding places for fugitives, or escaped slaves.

Fugitives would travel along "freedom trails" that led them to northern states or sometimes into Canada. At no time did the Railroad have a central leadership. No one person, or group of people, was ever officially in charge. Despite the lack of any real structure, the Underground Railroad managed to achieve dramatic results.

Often wearing disguises, fugitives moved along the "railroad" at night, led by people known as conductors. Many times, the fugitives had no other guideposts but the stars. They stopped to rest during the day at "stations," often barns, attics, or other places on property owned by abolitionists known as station masters. The station masters hid and fed the fugitives.

Harriet Tubman was a courageous conductor on the Underground Railroad.

Collaborative Learning

Below Level

"Who Am I?" Game

Materials: small box from which students can draw slips of paper

1. Assign each student one of the individuals mentioned in the section. Have each student use the information in the text to write a description of the individual's contributions to the fight against slavery—without mentioning the individual's name.
2. Have students place their descriptions in a box. Then ask volunteers to pick descriptions from the box and read them aloud to the class.
3. Have other students try to identify the individuals described. Students should not answer their own descriptions.

LS **Verbal/Linguistic**

Alternative Assessment Handbook, Rubric 40: Writing to Describe

Answers

Reading Check *gave public lectures and wrote narratives, plays, and novels describing their experiences and the harsh reality of slavery*

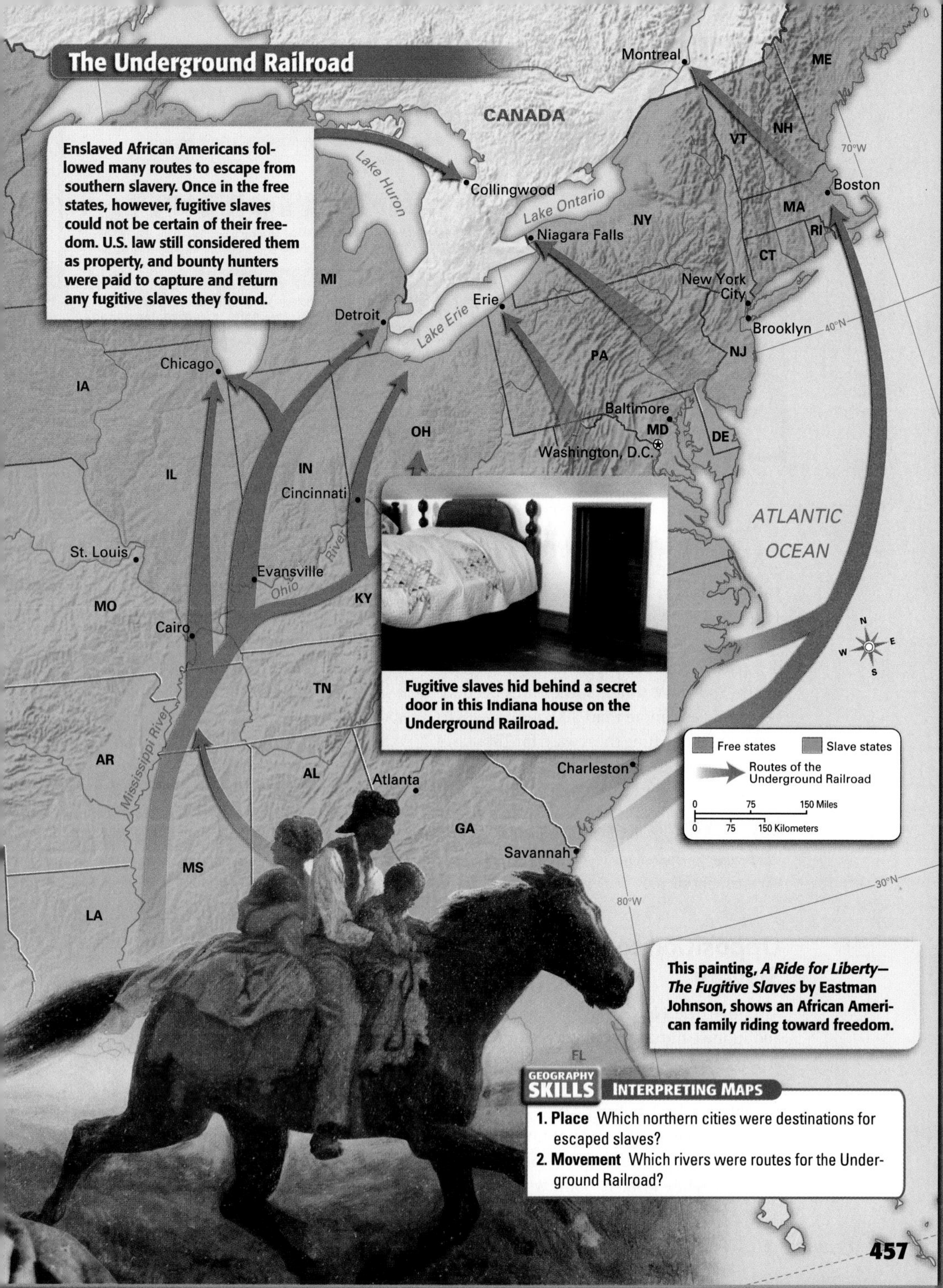

Enslaved African Americans followed many routes to escape from southern slavery. Once in the free states, however, fugitive slaves could not be certain of their freedom. U.S. law still considered them as property, and bounty hunters were paid to capture and return any fugitive slaves they found.

Fugitive slaves hid behind a secret door in this Indiana house on the Underground Railroad.

This painting, *A Ride for Liberty—The Fugitive Slaves* by Eastman Johnson, shows an African American family riding toward freedom.

GEOGRAPHY SKILLS **INTERPRETING MAPS**

1. **Place** Which northern cities were destinations for escaped slaves?
2. **Movement** Which rivers were routes for the Underground Railroad?

Critical Thinking: Making Inferences

At Level

Underground Railroad Account

1. Have students examine the above map. Ask volunteers to describe some of the main routes of fugitives on the Underground Railroad. Ask: Where were fugitives going? What geographic obstacles did they face on the way? What other risks and difficulties did fugitives and those helping them face?
2. Then ask students to imagine that they are conductors on the Underground Railroad. A fugitive they are guiding to freedom does not know how to write and has asked them to take down his or her thoughts and feelings about the experience.
3. Have each student write a series of three to five short entries describing the fugitive's experiences and his or her feelings about the freedom and new life awaiting.

LS Intrapersonal, Verbal/Linguistic

Alternative Assessment Handbook, Rubric 41: Writing to Express

Map Transparency 46: The Underground Railroad

Direct Teach

Main Idea

❷ The Underground Railroad

Abolitionists organized the Underground Railroad to help enslaved Africans escape.

Recall What was the Underground Railroad, and who was its most famous conductor? *a network of people who arranged transportation and hiding places for fugitives, or escaped slaves; Harriet Tubman*

Analyze How might the lack of a central leadership have benefited the Underground Railroad? *possible answer—might make it harder to find and stop the people in the network*

CRF: History and Geography Activity: The Underground Railroad

CRF: Primary Source Activity: Frederick Douglass, "What the Black Man Wants"

Map Transparency 46: The Underground Railroad

Info to Know

Levi Coffin House The room shown at left is in the Levi Coffin house in Newport, Indiana. This house was one of the most successful Underground Railroad stations. The house's owners, Levi and Catharine Coffin, were devout Quakers. They helped nearly 2,000 fugitives reach freedom.

Answers

Interpreting Maps **1.** *Montreal and Collingwood, Canada; Boston, MA; Niagara Falls, NY; Erie, PA; Detroit, MI; Chicago, IL;* **2.** *Mississippi and Ohio rivers*

Direct Teach

Main Idea

❸ Opposition to Ending Slavery

Despite efforts of abolitionists, many Americans remained opposed to ending slavery.

Explain What was the purpose of the gag rule in Congress? *to prevent members of Congress from discussing the many anti-slavery petitions they received*

Make Inferences How did John Quincy Adams contribute to the abolitionist movement? *He was able to get the gag rule overturned.*

Identify Cause and Effect What effect did Nat Turner's Rebellion have on southern attitudes about slavery? *Open talk about slavery ended for fear of future slave revolts.*

Did you know . . .

Most fugitives traveled by foot or in wagons with hidden compartments, but some used other means of escape. In 1849, Henry "Box" Brown escaped slavery by shipping himself in a box from Richmond, Virginia, to an antislavery office in Philadelphia, Pennsylvania. After some 27 hours in a 3-by-2-foot crate, Brown gained his freedom.

Primary Source

HANDBILL

Anti-Abolitionist Rally

Members of an anti-abolitionist group used this flyer to call people together in order to disrupt a meeting of abolitionists in 1837.

Seditious means "guilty of rebelling against lawful authority."

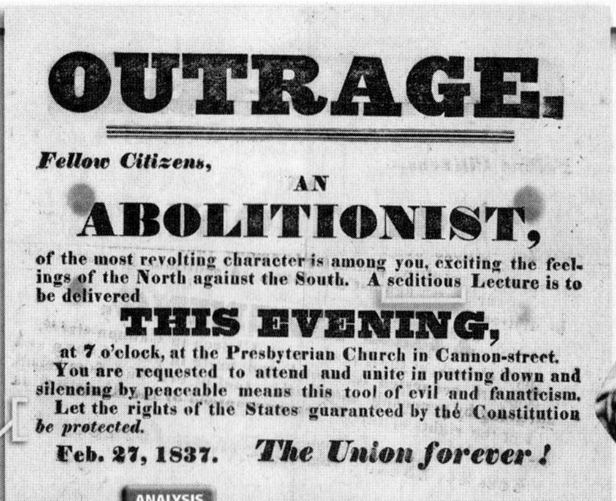
OUTRAGE.

Fellow Citizens,

AN

ABOLITIONIST,

of the most revolting character is among you, exciting the feelings of the North against the South. A seditious Lecture is to be delivered

THIS EVENING,

at 7 o'clock, at the Presbyterian Church in Cannon-street.

You are requested to attend and unite in putting down and silencing by peaceable means this tool of evil and fanaticism.

Let the rights of the States guaranteed by the Constitution *be protected.*

Feb. 27, 1837. *The Union forever!*

The group believes abolition violates the Constitution.

ANALYSIS SKILL **ANALYZING PRIMARY SOURCES**

What emotional language does this handbill use to get its message across?

The most famous and daring conductor on the Underground Railroad was **Harriet Tubman**. When Tubman escaped slavery in 1849, she left behind her family. She swore that she would return and lead her whole family to freedom in the North. Tubman returned to the South 19 times, successfully leading her family and more than 300 other slaves to freedom. At one time the reward for Tubman's capture reportedly climbed to $40,000, a huge amount of money at that time.

READING CHECK **Drawing Inferences** Why were the operations of the Underground Railroad kept secret?

Opposition to Ending Slavery

Although the North was the center of the abolitionist movement, many white northerners agreed with the South and supported slavery. Others disliked slavery but opposed equality for African Americans.

Newspaper editors and politicians warned that freed slaves would move north and take jobs from white workers. Some workers feared losing jobs to newly freed African Americans, whom they believed would accept lower wages. Abolitionist leaders were threatened with violence as some northerners joined mobs. Such a mob killed abolitionist Elijah Lovejoy in 1837 in Alton, Illinois.

The federal government also obstructed abolitionists. Between 1836 and 1844, the U.S. House of Representatives used what was called a gag rule. Congress had received thousands of antislavery petitions. Yet the gag rule forbade members of Congress from discussing them. This rule violated the First Amendment right of citizens to petition the government. But southern members of Congress did not want to debate slavery. Many northern members of Congress preferred to avoid the issue.

Eventually, representative and former president John Quincy Adams was able to get the gag rule overturned. His resolution to enact a constitutional amendment halting the expansion of slavery never passed, however.

Many white southerners saw slavery as vital to the South's economy and culture. They also felt that outsiders should not

Critical Thinking: Identifying Points of View

At Level

Report on Opposition to Abolition

1. Ask students to imagine that they are members of an antislavery society. The head of the society wants to know more about the views of people who oppose abolition, and the students have been selected to gather the information and report back.
2. Have each student create a large graphic or chart that identifies and explains both the views of northerners who oppose abolition and the views of southerners toward abolitionists and slavery.
3. In addition, each student should suggest ways that the antislavery society can address some of these views in its fight to end slavery.
4. Ask for volunteers to present their reports to the class. **LS Visual/Spatial**

Alternative Assessment Handbook, Rubrics 7: Charts; and 13: Graphic Organizers

Answers

Analyzing Primary Sources *language charged with fear and anger—"Outrage," "revolting character," "seditious Lecture," and "tool of evil and fanaticism"*

Reading Check *to make it difficult for fugitives, conductors, and station masters to be followed or captured*

Sojourner Truth was a former slave who became a leading abolitionist.

interfere with their way of life. After Nat Turner's Rebellion in 1831, when Turner led some slaves to kill slaveholders, open talk about slavery disappeared in the South. It became dangerous to voice antislavery sentiments in southern states. Abolitionists like the Grimké sisters left rather than air unpopular views to hostile neighbors. Racism, fear, and economic dependence on slavery made emancipation all but impossible in the South.

READING CHECK **Drawing Conclusions** Why did many northern workers oppose the abolition movement?

SUMMARY AND PREVIEW The issue of slavery grew more controversial in the United States during the first half of the nineteenth century. In the next section you will learn about women's rights.

Section 4 Assessment

go.hrw.com
Online Quiz
KEYWORD: SF7 HP14

Reviewing Ideas, Terms, and People

1. **a.** Identify What contributions did **William Lloyd Garrison** make to the **abolition** movement?
   b. Draw Conclusions In what ways did contributions from African Americans aid the struggle for abolition?
   c. Elaborate What do you think about the American Colonization Society's plan to return free African Americans to Liberia?
2. **a.** Describe How did the **Underground Railroad** work?
   b. Explain Why did **Harriet Tubman** first become involved with the Underground Railroad?
   c. Evaluate Do you think the Underground Railroad was a success? Why or why not?
3. **a.** Describe What action did Congress take to block abolitionists?
   b. Analyze Why did some Americans oppose equality for African Americans?
   c. Predict How might the debate over slavery lead to conflict in the future?

Critical Thinking

4. Identifying Cause and Effect Review your notes on the abolitionist movement. Then use a graphic organizer like the one below to show the reasons for opposition to the movement and the effects of that opposition.

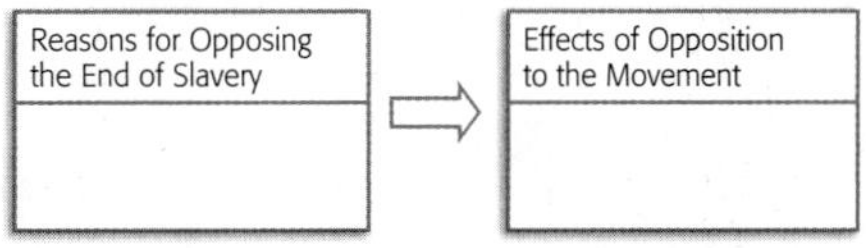

FOCUS ON WRITING

5. Describing Abolition Add notes about the abolitionist movement and its leaders to your chart. Be sure to note how abolitionists influenced life in the United States. What were they fighting for? Who opposed them, and why?

Direct Teach

Linking to Today

Human Rights Just as abolitionists fought to end slavery during the 1800s, social activists today continue to fight human rights abuses. Modern-day activists use many of the same techniques that antislavery activists did. Methods include speaking tours, petition drives, and letter-writing campaigns. The Internet also provides a powerful tool for today's activists.

Review & Assess

Close

Have students predict and discuss how the abolitionist movement might have contributed to future conflicts.

Review

Online Quiz, Section 14.4

Assess

SE Section 4 Assessment

PASS: Section Quiz 14.4

Alternative Assessment Handbook

Reteach/Classroom Intervention

Interactive Reader and Study Guide, Section 14.4

Interactive Skills Tutor CD-ROM

Section 4 Assessment Answers

1. **a.** published an antislavery newspaper; helped found American Anti-Slavery Society
   b. helped show horrors of slavery
   c. Answers will vary but should reflect an understanding of the plan.
2. **a.** Traveling at night and resting at stations during the day, conductors led fugitives north.
   b. After she escaped slavery she vowed to return and bring her family to freedom.
   c. possible answer—yes, helped many fugitives gain freedom
3. **a.** gag rule to ban talk of antislavery petitions
   b. held racist attitudes; feared losing jobs; saw slavery as vital to South's economy
   c. possible answer—by increasing divisions between groups or regions of the country
4. reasons—racist attitudes, feared losing jobs, saw slavery as vital to economy and culture; effects—became dangerous to voice antislavery opinions, made emancipation more unlikely
5. See the information in the previous answer.

Answers

Reading Check *feared that they would lose their jobs because they believed that newly freed slaves would work for lower wages*

Biography

Reading Focus Question

Have students discuss the introductory question. Ask them to consider actions they would take today as well as those they might have taken in the mid-1800s to help enslaved people. Have students list their ideas. Then as students read the biography, have them compare their ideas to the actions Douglass took to help enslaved Africans.

CRF: Primary Source Activity: Frederick Douglass, "What the Black Man Wants"

Info to Know

Douglass and His Thirst for Knowledge While living with the shipbuilder Hugh Auld, Douglass began learning to read and write after he asked Auld's wife, Lucretia, to teach him. When an excited Lucretia told her husband about the progress Douglass had made, Auld told his wife to stop teaching Douglass because it was against the law. Auld also feared that Douglass might revolt against his enslavement and gain his freedom. Douglass's thirst for knowledge was so great, however, that he found ways to continue learning. At one point, he used bread crumbs to pay for lessons. After Douglass escaped to freedom, he retained a lifelong passion for reading and writing.

Did you know . . .

In 1877, Douglass traveled to Maryland, where he visited his former slaveholder, Thomas Auld, who had beaten and starved him years before. During their meeting, Auld apologized to Douglass, and the two parted on good terms.

BIOGRAPHY

Frederick Douglass

As a freed slave, how would you help people still enslaved?

When did he live? 1817–1895

Where did he live? Frederick Douglass was born in rural Maryland. At age six he was sent to live in Baltimore, and at age 20 he escaped to New York City. For most of his life, Douglass lived in Rochester, New York, making his home into a stop along the Underground Railroad. He traveled often, giving powerful antislavery speeches to audiences throughout the North and in Europe.

What did he do? After hearing the abolitionist William Lloyd Garrison speak in 1841, Douglass began his own speaking tours about his experiences as a slave. In midlife he wrote an autobiography and started an abolitionist newspaper called the *North Star.* During the Civil War, Douglass persuaded black soldiers to fight for the North.

Why is he important? Douglass was the most famous African American in the 1800s. His personal stories and elegant speaking style helped the abolitionist movement to grow. His words remain an inspiration to this day.

Drawing Conclusions What made Frederick Douglass's speeches and writings so powerful?

KEY EVENTS

- **1817** Born a slave in Maryland
- **1837** Escapes slavery disguised as a sailor
- **1841** Begins his career as a speaker on abolition
- **1845** Writes *Narrative of the Life of Frederick Douglass*, his first autobiography
- **1847** Publishes first issue of the *North Star*
- **1863** Meets President Lincoln and becomes an adviser
- **1889** Named American consul general to Haiti
- **1895** Dies in Washington, D.C.

Frederick Douglass began publishing the *North Star*, an abolitionist newspaper, in 1847.

THE NORTH STAR.

Collaborative Learning

At Level

Legacy of Frederick Douglass Mural

Materials: butcher paper, art supplies

1. Have students list Frederick Douglass's many contributions. Write the list for students to see. Use the list to lead a discussion on Douglass's significance in his time and the lasting effects of his actions on society.
2. Then have students, working as a class or in small groups, create a mural about Frederick Douglass to display in the school. The mural should use text and images to highlight Douglass's actions and contributions in the fight against slavery. If time allows, have students conduct research to find quotations from Douglass to add to the mural. Display the completed mural in the school.

LS Interpersonal, Visual/Spatial

Alternative Assessment Handbook, Rubrics 3: Artwork; and 14: Group Activity

Answers

Drawing Conclusions *He had experienced slavery firsthand and was a charismatic speaker.*

Women's Rights

SECTION 5

If YOU were there...

You are a schoolteacher in New York State in 1848. Although you earn a small salary, you still live at home. Your father does not believe that unmarried women should live alone or look after their own money. One day in a shop, you see a poster about a public meeting to discuss women's rights. You know your father will be angry if you go to the meeting. But you are very curious.

Would you attend the meeting? Why?

BUILDING BACKGROUND Women were active in the movements to reform prisons and schools. They fought for temperance and worked for abolition. But with all their work for social change, women still lacked many rights and opportunities of their own. Throughout the 1800s, the women's rights movement gradually became stronger and more organized.

Women's Struggle for Equal Rights

Fighting for the rights of African Americans led many female abolitionists to fight for women's rights. In the mid-1800s, these women found that they had to defend their right to speak in public, particularly when a woman addressed both men and women. For example, members of the press, the clergy, and even some male abolitionists criticized the Grimké sisters. These critics thought that the sisters should not give public speeches. They did not want women to leave their traditional female roles. The Grimkés protested that women had a moral duty to lead the antislavery movement.

Early Writings for Women's Rights

In 1838 Sarah Grimké published a pamphlet arguing for equal rights for women. She titled it *Letters on the Equality of the Sexes and the Condition of Women.*

> "I ask no favors for my sex ... All I ask our brethren [brothers] is that they will take their feet from off our necks, and permit us to stand upright on that ground which God designed us to occupy."
>
> —Sarah Grimké, quoted in *The Grimké Sisters from South Carolina*, edited by Gerda Lerner

What You Will Learn...

Main Ideas

1. Influenced by the abolition movement, many women struggled to gain equal rights for themselves.
2. Calls for women's rights met opposition from men and women.
3. The Seneca Falls Convention launched the first organized women's rights movement in the United States.

The Big Idea

Reformers sought to improve women's rights in American society.

Key Terms and People

Elizabeth Cady Stanton, *p. 464*
Lucretia Mott, *p. 464*
Seneca Falls Convention, *p. 464*
Declaration of Sentiments, *p. 464*
Lucy Stone, *p. 465*
Susan B. Anthony, *p. 465*

TAKING NOTES Create a graphic organizer like the one shown below. Use it to show some of the significant events in the struggle for women's rights.

Date	Events
1838	
1848	
1851	
1860	

IN **8.1.10, 8.1.16, 8.1.18, 8.1.19, 8.1.24, 8.1.26, 8.1.28, 8.1.29, 8.1.30, 8.2.7, 8.2.9, 8.3.6, 8.3.11**

Teach the Big Idea

At Level

Women's Rights

1. **Teach** To teach the main ideas in the section, use the questions in the Direct Teach boxes.
2. **Apply** Have each student create a time line of the key events in the early women's rights movement. Above the time line, have students list the goals and leaders of the movement. Below the time line, have students list the opposition to the movement.
   LS Verbal/Linguistic, Visual/Spatial
3. **Review** Have volunteers share information from their time lines and lists. Create master versions for the class to see.
4. **Practice/Homework** Organize students into small groups and have each group write lyrics to an existing tune to create a Women's Rights Anthem for the Seneca Falls Convention. **LS Auditory/Musical, Interpersonal**

Alternative Assessment Handbook, Rubrics 26: Poems and Songs; and 36: Time Lines

Preteach

Bellringer

If YOU were there . . . Use the **Daily Bellringer Transparency** to help students answer the question.

Daily Bellringer Transparency 14.5

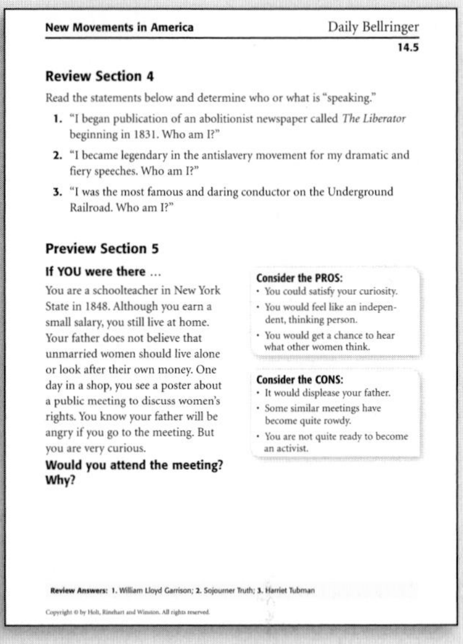

New Movements in America — Daily Bellringer 14.5

Review Section 4

Read the statements below and determine who or what is "speaking."

1. "I began publication of an abolitionist newspaper called *The Liberator* beginning in 1831. Who am I?"
2. "I became legendary in the antislavery movement for my dramatic and fiery speeches. Who am I?"
3. "I was the most famous and daring conductor on the Underground Railroad. Who am I?"

Preview Section 5

If YOU were there ...

You are a schoolteacher in New York State in 1848. Although you earn a small salary, you still live at home. Your father does not believe that unmarried women should live alone or look after their own money. One day in a shop, you see a poster about a public meeting to discuss women's rights. You know your father will be angry if you go to the meeting. But you are very curious.

Would you attend the meeting? Why?

Consider the PROS:
- You could satisfy your curiosity.
- You would feel like an independent, thinking person.
- You would get a chance to hear what other women think.

Consider the CONS:
- It would displease your father.
- Some similar meetings have become quite rowdy.
- You are not quite ready to become an activist.

Review Answers: 1. William Lloyd Garrison; 2. Sojourner Truth; 3. Harriet Tubman

Building Vocabulary

Preteach or review the following terms:

sojourner a traveler (p. 462)

suffrage right to vote (p. 463)

CRF: Vocabulary Builder Activity, Section 5

Taking Notes

Have students copy the graphic organizer onto their own paper and then use it to take notes on the section. This activity will prepare students for the Section Assessment, in which they will complete a graphic organizer that builds on the information using a critical-thinking skill.

Section Correlations

IN

8.1.19 Explain the influence of early individual social reformers and movements. **8.1.24** Identify the influence of individuals on political and social events and movements, such as the abolition movement, the Dred Scott case, women's rights and Native American Indian removal. **8.1.26** Give examples of the changing role of women and minorities in the northern, southern, and western parts of the United States in the mid-nineteenth century, and examine possible causes for these changes.

Direct Teach

Main Idea

❶ Women's Struggle for Equal Rights

Influenced by the abolition movement, many women struggled to gain equal rights for themselves.

Identify Who were some leaders in the early struggle for women's rights? *Sarah and Angelina Grimké, Margaret Fuller, Sojourner Truth*

Analyze How did the Grimké sisters' actions regarding marriage reflect their views on women's rights? *Both women disliked traditional views of marriage. Sarah chose not to marry because she thought it made her more of a slave than a wife. Angelina's marriage vows did not include the word* obey, *and her husband gave up his legal right to control her property.*

Draw Conclusions In the quotation, what message does Sojourner Truth express? *possible answer—that women are more capable than men give them credit for*

Linking to Today

Activity Changing Attitudes toward Women During this section, discuss with students the ways in which attitudes toward women have changed—and continue to change—in American society. Remind students to keep these changes in mind in particular as they study opposition to women's rights.

Sarah Grimké also argued for equal educational opportunities. She pointed out laws that negatively affected women. In addition, she demanded equal pay for equal work.

Sarah Grimké never married. She explained that the laws of the day gave a husband complete control of his wife's property. Therefore, she feared that by marrying, she would become more like a slave than a wife. Her sister, Angelina, did marry, but she refused to promise to obey her husband during their marriage ceremony. She married Theodore Weld, an abolitionist. Weld agreed to give up his legal right to control her property after they married. For the Grimkés, the abolitionist principles and women's rights principles were identical.

In 1845 the famous transcendentalist Margaret Fuller published *Woman in the Nineteenth Century.* This book used well-known sayings to explain the role of women in American society. Fuller used democratic and transcendentalist principles to stress the importance of individualism to all people, especially women. The book influenced many leaders of the women's rights movement.

Sojourner Truth

Sojourner Truth was another powerful supporter of both abolition and women's rights. She had been born into slavery in about 1797. Her birth name was Isabella Baumfree. She took the name Sojourner Truth because she felt that her mission was to be a sojourner, or traveler, and spread the truth. Though she never learned to read or write, she impressed many well-educated people. One person who thought highly of her was the author Harriet Beecher Stowe. Stowe said that she had never spoken "with anyone who had more . . . personal presence than this woman." Truth stood six feet tall and was a confident speaker.

In 1851 Truth gave a speech that is often quoted to this day.

> "That man over here says that women need to be helped into carriages and lifted over ditches, and to have the best place everywhere. Nobody ever helps me into carriages or over mud puddles, or gives me any best place . . . Look at me! I have ploughed and planted and . . . no man could head [outwork] me. And ain't I a woman?"
>
> —Sojourner Truth, quoted in *A History of Women in America* by Carol Hymowitz and Michaele Weissman

Truth, the Grimké sisters, and other supporters of the women's movement were determined to be heard.

READING CHECK Drawing Inferences Why would reformers link the issues of abolition and women's rights?

Time Line

Women's Rights

1776 Abigail Adams asks her husband, John Adams, to "remember the ladies" and their rights in the Declaration of Independence.
1848 The Seneca Falls Convention is held, and the Declaration of Sentiments is written.

Differentiating Instruction

Below Level

Struggling Readers

1. Draw the graphic organizer for students to see. Omit the blue, italicized answers.
2. Have each student copy the chart and complete it by explaining how the abolitionist movement influenced the women's rights movement. **LS Visual/Spatial**

Alternative Assessment Handbook, Rubric 13: Graphic Organizers

Abolitionist Movement

↓

Female abolitionists found they often had to defend their right to speak in public, particularly when addressing men; Fighting for others' rights led women to want to fight for their own.

↓

Women's Rights Movement

Answers

Reading Check *Female abolitionists discovered that they often had to defend their right to speak in public, and fighting for others' rights led women to want to fight for their own.*

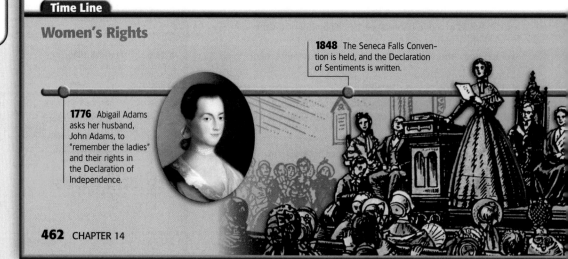

CHAPTER 15

Chapter Review

HOLT
History's Impact
▶ **video series**
Review the video to answer the closing question:
What do the Tenth Amendment and the Civil Rights Act indicate about the powers of the federal and state governments?

Visual Summary

QUICK FACTS

Use the visual summary below to help you review the main ideas of the chapter.

Differing views on slavery in the North and South gradually tore the nation apart.

Reviewing Vocabulary, Terms, and People

Identify the correct term or person from the chapter that best fits each of the following descriptions.

1. belief that voters should be given the right to decide if slavery would be permitted or banned
2. chief justice of the Supreme Court who wrote the majority opinion for the *Dred Scott* decision
3. Democratic candidate for president in 1852 who promised to enforce the Compromise of 1850 and the Fugitive Slave Act
4. a fugitive slave whose arrest led to violence between government officials and abolitionists
5. Republican candidate for the presidency in 1856 who opposed the spread of slavery in the West
6. slave who sued for freedom, claiming that by living in free territory, he had earned his freedom
7. Stephen Douglas's claim that states and territories should determine the issue of slavery through popular sovereignty

Comprehension and Critical Thinking

SECTION 1 *(Pages 476–481)*

8. a. **Describe** How did literature aid the antislavery movement?
   b. **Draw Conclusions** How did the issue of slavery promote sectionalism?
   c. **Evaluate** Do you think the Compromise of 1850 was a good solution? Explain your answer.

SECTION 2 *(Pages 483–487)*

9. a. **Identify** Who were the candidates in the presidential election of 1852, and what issues did each support?
   b. **Analyze** How did the Kansas-Nebraska Act lead to growing hostility between pro-slavery and antislavery supporters?
   c. **Elaborate** Why do you think "Bleeding Kansas" produced intense controversy between many Americans?

Answers

History's Impact

Video Series Both are examples of the federal government taking precedence over the power of individual states when states are acting against the Constitution.

Visual Summary

Review and Inquiry Have students write a paragraph about how the slavery issue gradually divided the nation until it broke apart in secession. Students should include how geographic and economic differences between the North and the South caused sectionalism.

Quick Facts Transparency 40: A Divided Nation Visual Summary

Reviewing Vocabulary, Terms, and People

1. popular sovereignty
2. Roger B. Taney
3. Franklin Pierce
4. Anthony Burns
5. John C. Frémont
6. Dred Scott
7. Kansas-Nebraska Act

Comprehension and Critical Thinking

8. a. educated people about the hardships of slavery and gained sympathy for abolitionism
   b. South's economy dependent on slave labor and North's was not; regions divided over slavery issue; encouraged leaders to promote sectional interests

Review and Assessment Resources

Review and Reinforce

- SE Chapter Review
- **CRF**: Chapter Review Activity
- Quick Facts Transparency 40: A Divided Nation Visual Summary
- Spanish Chapter Summaries Audio CD Program
- Online Chapter Summaries in Spanish
- OSP Holt PuzzlePro; GameTool for ExamView
- Quiz Game CD-ROM

Assess

- SE Standardized Test Practice
- PASS: Chapter 15 Tests, Forms A and B; Unit 4 Tests, Forms A and B
- Alternative Assessment Handbook
- OSP ExamView Test Generator, Chapter Test
- Differentiated Instruction Modified Worksheets and Tests CD-ROM: Chapter Test
- HOAP Holt Online Assessment Program (in the Premier Online Edition)

Reteach/Intervene

- Interactive Reader and Study Guide
- Differentiated Instruction Teacher Management System: Lesson Plans for Differentiated Instruction
- Differentiated Instruction Modified Worksheets and Tests CD-ROM
- Interactive Skills Tutor CD-ROM

go.hrw.com
Online Resources
Chapter Resources:
KEYWORD: SF7 CH15

Answers

c. possible answers—Yes, it prevented secession for the moment and appeased both the North and the South; no, it only postponed the resolution of the slavery issue.

9. a. Franklin Pierce—promised to honor the Compromise of 1850 and the Fugitive Slave Act; Winfield Scott—limited support of the Compromise of 1850
b. It removed the Missouri Compromise's restriction on slavery in the Kansas and Nebraska territories and let popular sovereignty decide the slavery issue.
c. because of the violence and tensions over the issue of slavery

10. a. a slave who sued for his freedom; the case declared that African Americans were not citizens and ruled that the Missouri Compromise was unconstitutional
b. The issue led to the formation of new parties and to the end of some existing parties.
c. hoped his support for the Kansas-Nebraska Act had weakened his chance for re-election

11. a. They feared more attacks like John Brown's raid, were angry over the election of 1860, and felt their economy and way of life were threatened. Lincoln tried to convince southern states to return.
b. because Lincoln had won without carrying one southern state
c. possible answers—Yes, he was fighting for justice and to free people from bondage; no, violence is never right.

Reviewing Themes

12. changed the makeup of political parties and created new ones aligned with sectional pro-slavery and antislavery views

13. electrified the nation, sparked outrage in the South, increased sectional tensions and support for abolitionism

SECTION 3 *(Pages 488–492)*

10. a. Identify Who was Dred Scott, and why was his case important?
b. Analyze How were political parties affected by the debate over slavery?
c. Elaborate Why do you think Republicans challenged Stephen Douglas's run for the Senate?

SECTION 4 *(Pages 493–497)*

11. a. Recall Why did the southern states secede, and what was the North's response?
b. Draw Conclusions Why did the results of the election of 1860 anger southerners?
c. Evaluate Do you think John Brown was right to use violence to protest slavery? Explain.

Reviewing Themes

12. Politics How did sectionalism affect American politics?

13. Society and Culture What effect did Harriet Beecher Stowe's book *Uncle Tom's Cabin* have on the debate over slavery?

Using the Internet

go.hrw.com
KEYWORD: SF7 CH15

14. Activity: Creating a Newspaper Harriet Beecher Stowe's novel and John Brown's raids were two important events that created more debate over slavery and heightened tension between sides. Enter the activity keyword and learn more about antislavery actions. Then create a newspaper with which to display your research. Remember to write from the point of view of someone from the mid-1800s.

Reading Skills

Facts, Opinions, and the Past *Use the Reading Skills taught in this chapter to answer the question about the reading selection below.*

> In 1858 John Brown tried to start an uprising. He wanted to attack the federal arsenal in Virginia and seize weapons there. He planned to arm local slaves. Brown expected to kill or take hostage white southerners who stood in his way. *(p. 493)*

15. Based on the reading selection above, which of the following statements is an opinion?
a. John Brown's raid was in 1858.
b. John Brown hated all slaveholders.
c. John Brown's raid took place in Virginia.
d. Local slaves helped John Brown.

Social Studies Skills

Assessing Primary and Secondary Sources *Use the Social Studies Skills taught in this chapter to answer the question below.*

16. Which of the following is *not* an example of a primary source used in this chapter?
a. *A People's History of the United States* by Howard Zinn
b. The Seventh of March speech by Daniel Webster
c. Abraham Lincoln's A House Divided speech
d. John Brown's last speech

FOCUS ON WRITING

17. Writing Your Autobiography Review your notes. Then write your autobiography, being sure to mention each of the events from your notes. Tell how your character heard about each event, what he or she was doing at the time, how he or she felt about the event, and how it affected him or her. What are your character's hopes and fears for the future?

Using the Internet

14. Go to the HRW Web site and enter the keyword shown to access a rubric for this activity.

KEYWORD: SF7 CH15

Reading Skills

15. b

Social Studies Skills

16. a

Focus on Writing

17. Rubric Students' autobiographies should
- explain how each of the chapter's key events affected the character.
- describe how the character learned and felt about each key event.
- describe the character's hopes and fears for the future.

CRF: Focus on Writing Activity: Writing an Autobiographical Sketch

CHAPTER 15

Standardized Test Practice

IN 8.1.16, 8.1.20, 8.3.2, 8.3.7

DIRECTIONS: Read each question and write the letter of the best response.

1 Use the map below to answer the following question.

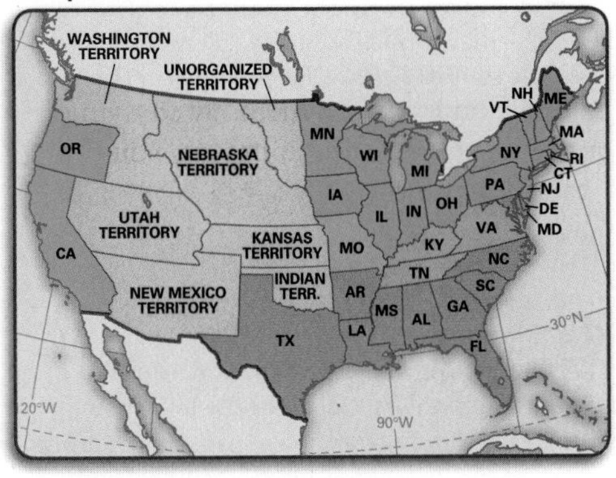

From the information in this map, you can conclude that it shows

A the provisions of the Compromise of 1850.

B the results of the election of 1860.

C the formation of the Confederacy.

D the results of the *Dred Scott* decision.

2 Which leader was responsible for settling the dispute over the expansion of slavery that arose after the Mexican War?

A David Wilmot

B Henry Clay

C Abraham Lincoln

D Jefferson Davis

3 California's admission as a free state after the Mexican War aroused controversy because

A many Californians already held slaves.

B it would upset the balance between free states and slave states.

C Mexico still claimed that California was part of Mexico's territory.

D most Californians wanted independence.

4 Widespread violence erupted in Kansas over slavery in the mid-1850s *mainly* due to

A the practice of popular sovereignty.

B the Pottawatomie Massacre.

C the Missouri Compromise.

D the threat of secession.

5 The election of 1852 led directly to which of the following?

A the Compromise of 1850

B the collapse of the Whig Party

C the collapse of the Republican Party

D the Missouri Compromise.

6 The Compromise of 1850 was *most* similar to what earlier compromise between free states and slave states?

A the Great Compromise

B the Rush-Bagot Agreement

C the Northwest Ordinance

D the Missouri Compromise

7 Examine the following passage written by a southerner before secession and then use it to answer the question below.

> "As we sat around the long table today the talk turned to the [secession] convention, so soon to meet in Tallahassee [Florida]. Father said he considered this the most important year in the history of the South. He is for secession, and he does not think that war will necessarily [certainly] follow. Brother Junius is a strong Union man, and he thinks we will certainly have war. If the South secedes, the North will fight to keep us. If we do not secede, all property rights will be taken from us and we will be forced to fight to hold our own."
>
> –Susan Bradford, adapted from *Heroines of Dixie,* edited by Katharine Jones

Document-Based Question What might be the outcome of this convention? Why?

Intervention Resources

Reproducible

- Interactive Reader and Study Guide
- Differentiated Instruction Teacher Management System: Lesson Plans for Differentiated Instruction

Technology

- Quick Facts Transparency 40 : A Divided Nation Visual Summary
- Differentiated Instruction Modified Worksheets and Tests CD-ROM
- Interactive Skills Tutor CD-ROM

Tips for Test Taking

Rely on 50/50 When students have no idea what an answer is, tell them to do the following to make an educated guess:

- Read every choice carefully.
- Eliminate the least likely choice, then the next, and so on until one answer is left.
- Watch out for distracters—choices that are true but either too broad, too narrow, or not relevant.
- If more than one choice seems correct, see if "All of the above" is an option. If none of the choices seems correct, look for "None of the above."

Answers

1. A

Break Down the Question Option B is not correct because the map does not include numbers of state electors. Option D does not make sense for a map, and Option C is incorrect because the map does not identify the seceding states.

2. B

Break Down the Question This question requires students to recall factual information. Refer students who have trouble to the text titled "Compromise of 1850" in Section 1.

3. B

Break Down the Question Explain that a question sometimes provides clues to its answer. For example, point out the phrase "admission as a free state" in this question.

4 A

Break Down the Question This question requires students to identify cause and effect. Explain that Option B is incorrect because it is an example of the violence, not a cause. Option D is an effect of the violence.

5. B

Break Down the Question This question also requires students to identify cause and effect. Refer students who have trouble to the text titled "Election of 1852" in Section 2.

6. D

Break Down the Question This question requires students to recall factual information from Chapter 9, "Missouri Compromise".

7. possible answer—Secession will probably occur, and the South will prepare for war.

Break Down the Question This question requires students to look for facts and opinions within the passage to help frame an answer.

Preteach

Bellringer

Motivate Write the words *cat* and *dog* for students to see. Ask students how the two animals are similar. Then ask students how they are different. Explain that comparing (showing how things are similar) and contrasting (showing how things are different) is one way to learn about events and people in history. Tell students that they will write a paper comparing and contrasting a historical topic.

Interactive Skills Tutor CD-ROM, Lesson 1: Compare and Contrast

Direct Teach

Writing a Thesis

Make a Point After students have selected the topic of their paper and made lists of similarities and differences, have them examine the lists. Were the two groups or events they compared mainly alike or mainly different? Did certain similarities or differences stand out as significant or influential? Have students write one sentence in answer to each question. Tell students to use the sentences as a starting point for selecting and writing a thesis.

Organizing

Once around the Block Students who use the block style to organize their papers should check that they address the same points in the same order for each topic. Have students use a different color of ink to underline each point they made about the first topic. Then have students use the same colors to underline the points they made about the second topic. The colors and order should match.

Assignment

Write a paper comparing and contrasting one of the following: (1) America before and after the Industrial Revolution, (2) the lives of free blacks in the North with the lives of free blacks in the South.

Comparing People and Events

One way to learn more about historical figures and events is to compare and contrast them. By studying how the figures or events are alike and different, you can begin to see each one more clearly.

1. Prewrite

Getting Started

"How are they alike?" "How are they different?" Jot down answers to these questions as you research the presidents or the Industrial Revolution. Group your answers into points of comparison. For example, points of comparison for the lives of free blacks might be work, education, etc. Points of comparison for the Industrial Revolution might be factories or farming.

TIP Using Graphic Organizers Venn diagrams help you focus on similarities and differences. Write details the subjects have in common in the overlapping area. Write details that make each subject different in the sections that do not overlap.

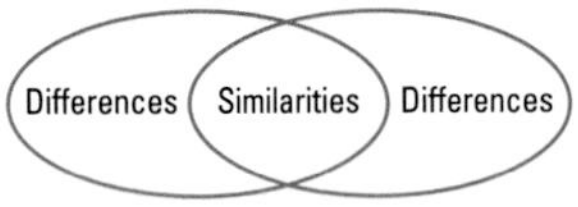

Organizing Your Information

There are two ways to organize a compare-and-contrast paper.

- **Block Style** Say everything you have to say about one subject. Then say everything you have to say about the second subject. Discuss the points of comparison in the same order for each subject.
- **Point-by-Point Style** Discuss the points of comparison one at a time. Explain how the subjects are alike and different on one point of comparison, then another, and so on. Discuss the subjects in the same order for each point of comparison.

2. Write

You can use this framework with your notes to help you write your first draft.

A Writer's Framework

Introduction	Body	Conclusion
■ Identify the two subjects and give background information to help readers understand your comparisons. ■ State your big idea, or main purpose, in comparing and contrasting them.	■ Use block or point-by-point organization. ■ Use three points of comparison. ■ Support your points with specific historical facts, details, and examples.	■ Restate your big idea. ■ Summarize the points you made. ■ Expand on your big idea, perhaps by relating it to later historical events or other historical figures.

Differentiating Instruction

Special Needs Learners — Below Level

1. Have special needs learners work in small groups to create Venn diagrams before writing.
2. Have an aide read a short part of the relevant portion of the textbook aloud. Then have the students add the information to their diagrams. Have the aide continue to read the text aloud, stopping frequently to allow students to add to their Venn diagrams. **LS Visual/Spatial**

English-Language Learners — Below Level, Standard English Mastery

1. Have English learners write the drafts for their papers in their primary language.
2. Students should then refer back to these drafts as they write their final papers in English.
3. Before students write in English, review the rules for forming comparative and superlative adjectives and adverbs. Provide guided practice as needed. **LS Verbal/Linguistic**

3. Evaluate and Revise

Evaluating

Use these questions to discover ways to improve your paper.

Evaluation Questions for a Comparison/Contrast Paper

- Do you introduce both subjects in the first paragraph?
- Do you provide relevant background information in a clear and concise manner?
- Do you state your big idea in the introduction?
- Do you include three points of comparison between the subjects?
- Do you use either the block style or point-by-point style to organize your points of comparison?
- Do you support your points of comparison with appropriate historical facts, details, and examples?
- Do you restate your big idea and summarize your points?

TIP Making Meaning Clear
One way to make relationships between ideas clear is to repeat key or similar words and phrases in your writing. For example, you can use similar wording when comparing two historical figures on the same point of comparison.

EXAMPLE
Samuel Slater filled his labor needs by hiring entire families to work in the mills. Francis Lowell filled his labor needs by hiring young, unmarried women to work in the mills.

Revising

As you reread your paper, look for sentences that start with *There was* or *There were*. Sentences beginning with *There was/There were* tend to be weak: The verbs *was* and *were* do not convey any action.

Weak

There was a decline in southern agriculture after the American Revolution.

Stronger

Southern agriculture declined after the American Revolution.

4. Proofread and Publish

Proofreading

In a research report, you may be referring to the titles of your sources of information. Check to see whether you have punctuated any titles according to these guidelines.

- Underlining (if you are writing) or italics (if you are using a computer) for books, movies, TV programs, Internet sites, and magazines or newspapers
- Quotation marks for magazine articles, newspaper articles, chapters in a book

Publishing

Share your paper with one or more classmates. After reading each other's papers, you can compare and contrast them.

5. Practice and Apply

Use the steps and strategies outlined in this workshop to write your paper comparing and contrasting two people or events.

Reteach

Providing Support

Back It Up Remind students that describing the similarities and differences for each group or period is not enough. Students must also support their descriptions with facts and examples. Have students circle each claim or point they make about each group or period in their papers. Then have students underline the support for each claim or point. If they have not provided support, have them ask themselves, "How do I know this point?" Then have students provide an answer in their papers.

Teaching Tip

Sentence Variety Tell students that comparison-contrast papers can become monotonous because they are highly structured. Explain that the papers will be more enjoyable to read if students vary their sentence structures, such as the way they start sentences. Help students rework, combine, or break sentences as needed to increase variety.

Practice & Apply

Rubric

Students' comparison-contrast papers should

- present a clear statement of the big idea, or main purpose.
- provide historical background to place the topic in context.
- use either block or point-by-point organization.
- provide three points of comparison and support for each one.
- end with a summary and a restatement of the big idea.
- use correct grammar, punctuation, spelling, and capitalization.

Struggling Readers **Below Level**

1. For students who have trouble getting words on paper, write the outline at right for them to see. Explain that the outline shows the question(s) they should answer in each part of their comparison-contrast papers.
2. Have students copy the outline and leave plenty of room to add information below each part. Then have students complete the outline by answering the questions. Encourage students to use complete sentences.

I. **Introduction:** What two things are you comparing and contrasting? What do you want to show by comparing and contrasting them?

II. **Body Paragraphs:** What is one way the two things are alike or different? How do you know? What is a second way? How do you know? What is a third way? How do you know?

III. **Conclusion:** Briefly, what have you stated in your paper? **LS Verbal/Linguistic**

Unit Preview

Introduce the Unit

Share the information in the chapter overviews with students.

Chapter 16 Soon after Lincoln's inauguration, the Civil War began, dividing the country between the North and the South. Initially, the South won several major battles. The North then turned the tide of the war with victories in both the West and the East. In April 1865 the Confederates surrendered, and the North won the war. The war resulted in terrible death and destruction but also led to the long-sought freedom of enslaved Africans.

Chapter 17 Reconstruction was a difficult and long process. The United States faced two major challenges—to reunite the country and to define the rights of African Americans. In 1865 the Thirteenth Amendment ended slavery in the United States. Additional amendments extended citizenship and other rights to African Americans. In time, however, politicians who opposed Reconstruction gained power. Southern states began passing laws limiting African Americans' civil rights. Many former slaves continued to work on plantations. Meanwhile, the South began to rebuild and develop its industry.

UNIT 5 1861–1877

The Nation Breaks Apart

Chapter 16 The Civil War
Chapter 17 Reconstruction

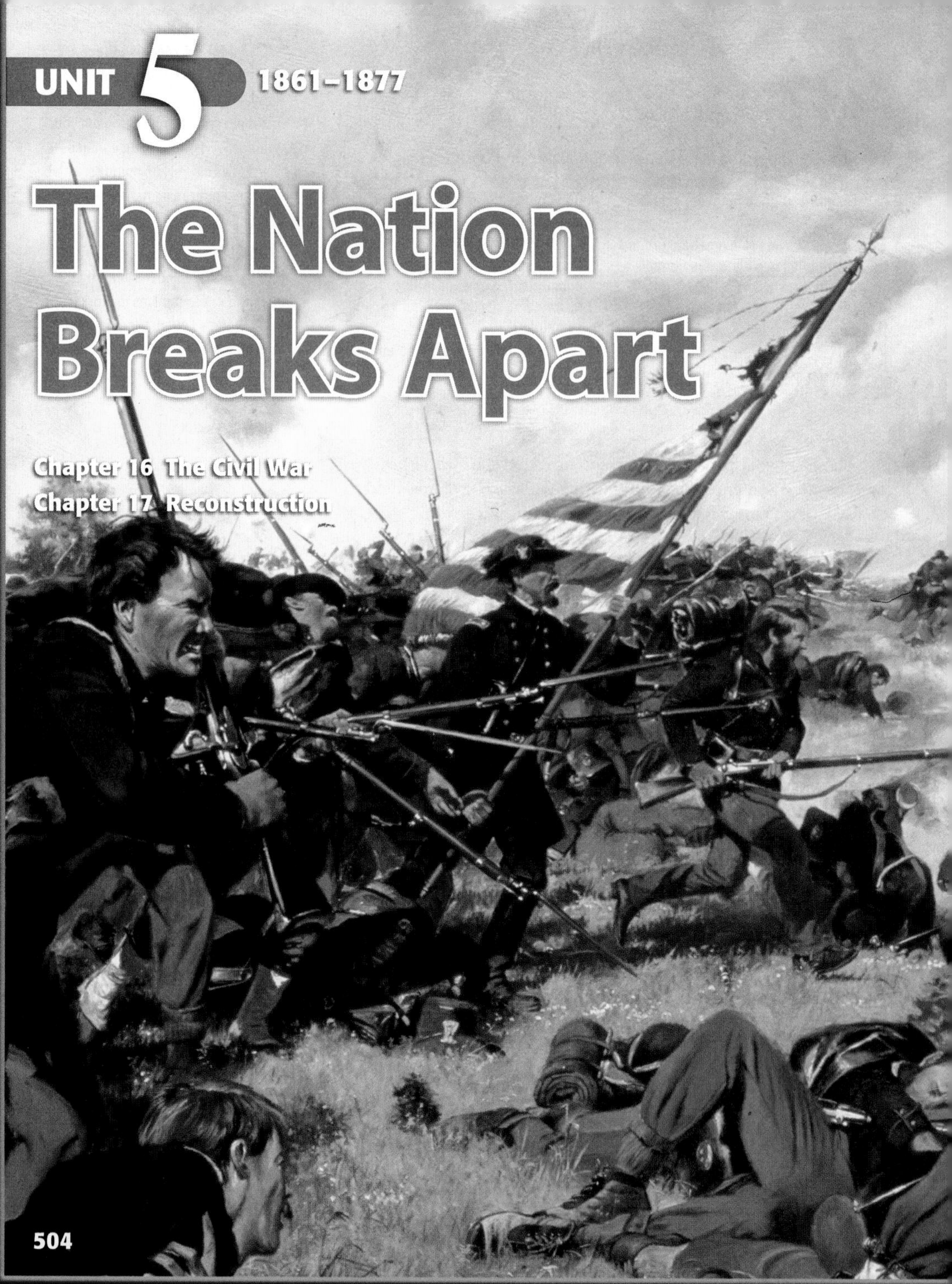

Unit Resources

Planning

- Teacher Management System: Unit Instructional Pacing Guides
- One-Stop Planner CD-ROM with Test Generator: Calendar Planner
- Power Presentations with Video CD-ROM

Differentiating Instruction

- Differentiated Instruction Teacher Management System: Lesson Plans for Differentiated Instruction
- Pre-AP Activities Guide for United States History
- Differentiated Instruction Modified Worksheets and Tests CD-ROM

Enrichment

- **CRF The Civil War:** Interdisciplinary Project: The Ironclads: The *Monitor* and the *Virginia*
- Civic Participation Activities
- Primary Source Library CD-ROM
- Internet Activities: Chapter Enrichment Links, Ch. 16 and 17

Assessment

- Progress Assessment Support System: Unit 5 Tests, Forms A and B
- OSP ExamView Test Generator: Unit Test
- HOAP Holt Online Assessment Program, (in the Premier Online Edition)
- Alternative Assessment Handbook

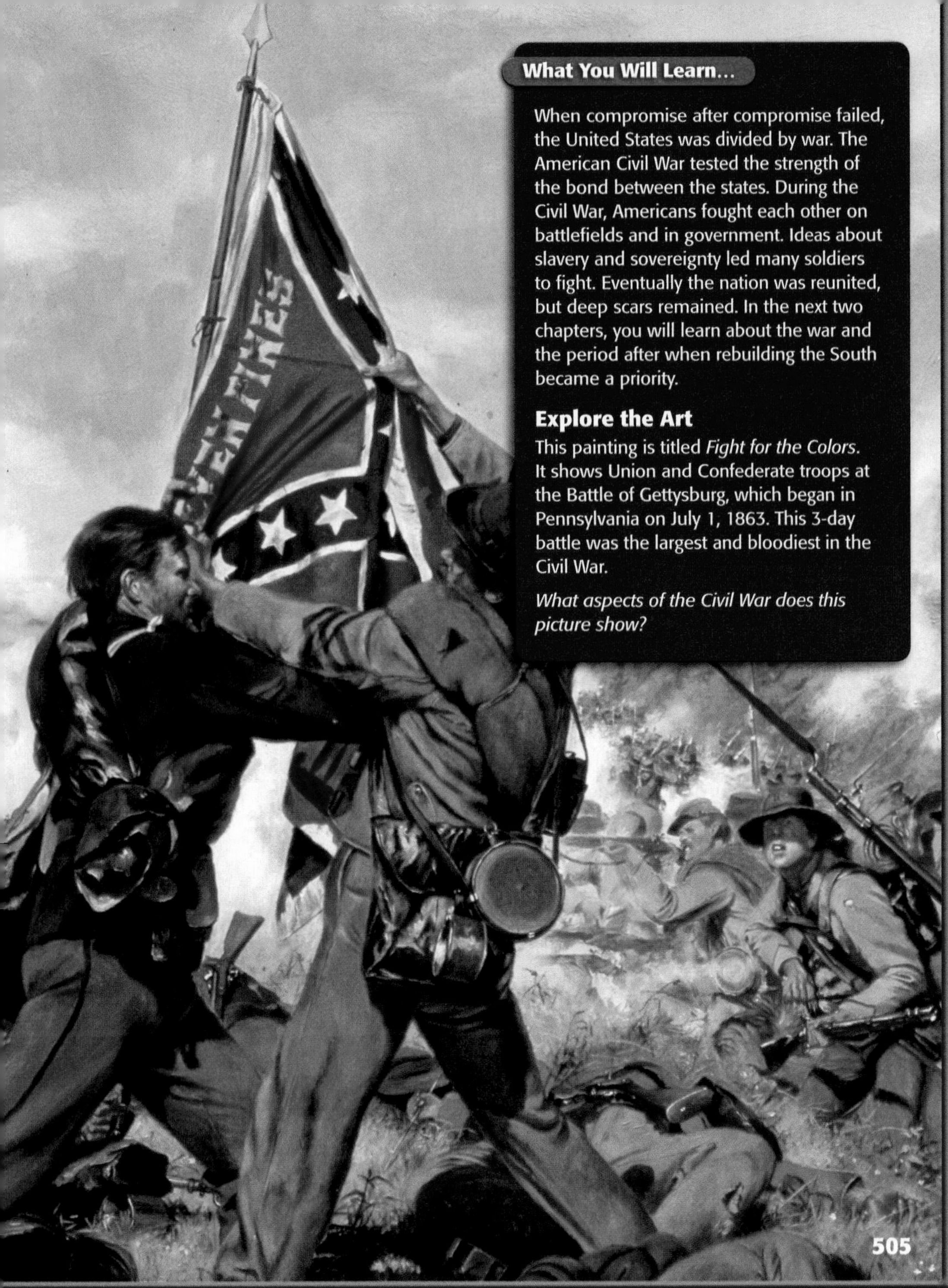

What You Will Learn...

When compromise after compromise failed, the United States was divided by war. The American Civil War tested the strength of the bond between the states. During the Civil War, Americans fought each other on battlefields and in government. Ideas about slavery and sovereignty led many soldiers to fight. Eventually the nation was reunited, but deep scars remained. In the next two chapters, you will learn about the war and the period after when rebuilding the South became a priority.

Explore the Art

This painting is titled *Fight for the Colors.* It shows Union and Confederate troops at the Battle of Gettysburg, which began in Pennsylvania on July 1, 1863. This 3-day battle was the largest and bloodiest in the Civil War.

What aspects of the Civil War does this picture show?

Unit Preview

Connect to the Unit

Activity Analyzing the Costs and Benefits of War Create a cause-and-effect chart for students to see. Ask students to consider warfare in general and to discuss some of the causes of war. Write students' ideas in the chart. Next, ask students to discuss some of the effects of war. Challenge students to consider both positive and negative effects. Add students' responses to the chart. Then have students discuss the costs and benefits of warfare. When do students think war is justified? In what situations do they think the benefits of war outweigh the costs?

Save the cause-and-effect chart. At the end of the unit, have students review the chart and then create a second chart listing the causes and effects of the Civil War, including long-term effects. Conclude by having students examine the costs and benefits of the Civil War and Reconstruction.

LS Logical/Mathematical, Visual/Spatial

Explore the Art

Not only did the Civil War have a profound effect on those who lived through it but it also shaped our nation's history as well. This painting depicts a scene from one of the war's many brutal battles involving hand-to-hand combat between Union and Confederate soldiers. The sacrifices made by the soldiers depicted here and hundreds of thousands of others like them would leave a deep mark on the country for years to come.

About the Illustration

This illustration is an artist's conception based on available sources. However, historians are uncertain exactly what this scene looked like.

Democracy and Civic Education

At Level

Justice: Equal Protection of the Laws

Research Required

Background Explain to students that the Fourteenth Amendment (1868) ensures the equal protection of laws. This protection guarantees that no person or group will be treated differently under the law from any other person or group in a similar situation unless a just and good reason exists for doing so.

1. Have students work in small groups to conduct research on how effective the equal protection clause has been over time. How have various groups used the clause to extend civil rights and to fight segregation, particularly during the 1950s and 1960s?
2. Have each group use its research to create a brochure for immigrants to inform them about their right to equal protection of the laws. The brochure should explain the concept and provide examples of how it has been used.

LS Interpersonal, Verbal/Linguistic

Alternative Assessment Handbook, Rubrics 14: Group Activity; and 37: Writing Assignments

Civic Participation Activities Guide

Answers

Explore the Art *possible answers—intense fighting and emotions; close-range, hand-to-hand combat*

Chapter 16 Planning Guide

The Civil War

Chapter Overview	Reproducible Resources	Technology Resources
CHAPTER 16 **pp. 506–547** **Overview: In this chapter, students will analyze the events of the Civil War along with the effect these events had on the lives of Americans.**	**Differentiated Instruction Teacher Management System:*** • Instructional Pacing Guides • Lesson Plans for Differentiated Instruction **Interactive Reader and Study Guide:** Chapter Summary Graphic Organizer* **Chapter Resource File:*** • Focus on Writing: Newspaper Article • Social Studies Skills: Political Cartoons • Chapter Review Activity	**Power Presentations with Video CD-ROM** **Differentiated Instruction Modified Worksheets and Tests CD-ROM** **Primary Source Library CD-ROM for United States History** **History's Impact: United States History Video Program (VHS/DVD):** The Impact of the Civil War*
Section 1: **The War Begins** **The Big Idea:** Civil War broke out between the North and the South in 1861.	**Differentiated Instruction Teacher Management System:** Section 1 Lesson Plan* **Interactive Reader and Study Guide:** Sec. 16.1 Summary* **Chapter Resource File:*** • Vocabulary Builder Activity, Section 1 • History and Geography Activity: Choosing Sides **Political Cartoons Activities for United States History,** Cartoon 17: The Folly of Secession	**Daily Bellringer Transparency 16.1*** **Map Transparency 50:** Fort Sumter * **Quick Facts Transparencies 41 and 42:** North Versus South; Resources of the North and South* go.hrw.com **Internet Activity:** Civil War Soldiers
Section 2: **The War in the East** **The Big Idea:** Confederate and Union forces faced off in Virginia and at sea.	**Differentiated Instruction Teacher Management System:** Section 2 Lesson Plan* **Interactive Reader and Study Guide:** Sec. 16.2 Summary* **Chapter Resource File:*** • Vocabulary Builder Activity, Section 2 • Interdisciplinary Project: The Ironclads	**Daily Bellringer Transparency 16.2*** **Map Transparency 51:** Battles in the East* **Map Transparency 52:** Union Blockade* **Interactive Map:** Battles in the East
Section 3: **The War in the West** **The Big Idea:** Fighting in the Civil War spread to the western United States.	**Differentiated Instruction Teacher Management System:** Section 3 Lesson Plan* **Interactive Reader and Study Guide:** Sec. 16.3 Summary* **Chapter Resource File:*** • Vocabulary Builder Activity, Section 3 • Primary Source: The Battle of Shiloh, April 1862	**Daily Bellringer Transparency 16.3*** **Map Transparency 53:** The War in the West* **Interactive Map:** The War in the West
Section 4: **Daily Life during the War** **The Big Idea:** The lives of many Americans were affected by the Civil War.	**Differentiated Instruction Teacher Management System:** Section 4 Lesson Plan* **Interactive Reader and Study Guide:** Sec. 16.4 Summary* **Chapter Resource File:*** • Vocabulary Builder Activity, Section 4 • Biography Activities: William Carney; Clara Barton • Primary Source Activity: Civil War Era Diary	**Daily Bellringer Transparency 16.4*** **Map Transparency 54:** Emancipation Proclamation* go.hrw.com **Internet Activity:** War Writers
Section 5: **The Tide of War Turns** **The Big Idea:** Union victories in 1863, 1864, and 1865 ended the Civil War.	**Differentiated Instruction Teacher Management System:** Section 5 Lesson Plan* **Interactive Reader and Study Guide:** Sec. 16.5 Summary* **Chapter Resource File:*** • Vocabulary Builder Activity, Section 5 • Biography Activity: William Tecumseh Sherman	**Daily Bellringer Transparency 16.5*** **Map Transparencies 55 and 56:** Pickett's Charge, July 3, 1863; Final Campaigns* **Quick Facts Transparency 43:** Causes and Effects of the Civil War* go.hrw.com **Internet Activity:** Gettysburg

SE Student Edition | Print Resource | Audio CD
TE Teacher's Edition | Transparency | CD-ROM
go.hrw.com | **LS** Learning Styles | Video
TOS Indiana Teacher One Stop | * also on Indiana Teacher One Stop

Review, Assessment, Intervention

- **Quick Facts Transparency 44:** The Civil War Visual Summary*
- **Progress Assessment Support System (PASS):** Chapter Tests A and B*
- **Differentiated Instruction Modified Worksheets and Tests CD-ROM:** Modified Chapter Test
- TOS **Indiana Teacher One Stop:** ExamView Test Generator (English/Spanish)
- **Alternative Assessment Handbook**

- **PASS:** Section Quiz 16.1*
- **Online Quiz:** Section 16.1
- **Alternative Assessment Handbook**

- **PASS:** Section Quiz 16.2*
- **Online Quiz:** Section 16.2
- **Alternative Assessment Handbook**

- **PASS:** Section Quiz 16.3*
- **Online Quiz:** Section 16.3
- **Alternative Assessment Handbook**

- **PASS:** Section Quiz 16.4*
- **Online Quiz:** Section 16.4
- **Alternative Assessment Handbook**

- **PASS:** Section Quiz 16.5*
- **Online Quiz:** Section 16.5
- **Alternative Assessment Handbook**

HOLT
History's Impact
United States History Video Program (VHS/DVD)
The Impact of the Civil War
Suggested use: as a chapter introduction

Power Presentations with Video CD-ROM

Power Presentations with Video are visual presentations of each chapter's main ideas. Presentations can be customized by including Quick Facts charts, images from the text, and video clips.

DIVISION FOR PUBLIC EDUCATION
AMERICAN BAR ASSOCIATION

Developed by the Division for Public Education of the American Bar Association, these materials are part of the **Democracy and Civic Education Resources.**

- **Constitution Study Guide**
- **Supreme Court Case Studies**

Holt Online Learning

go.hrw.com
Teacher Resources
KEYWORD: SF7 TEACHER

go.hrw.com
Student Resources
KEYWORD: SF7 CH16

- Document-Based Questions
- Interactive Multimedia Activities
- Current Events
- Chapter-based Internet Activities
- and more!

Holt Interactive
Online Student Edition

Complete online support for interactivity, assessment, and reporting
- Interactive Maps and Notebook
- Standardized Test Prep
- Homework Practice and Research Activities Online

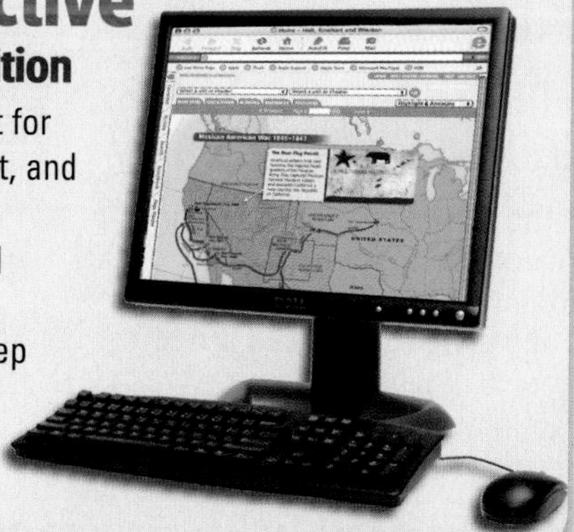

CHAPTER 16 PLANNING GUIDE

Differentiating Instruction

How do I address the needs of varied learners?

The Target Resource acts as your primary strategy for differentiated instruction.

ENGLISH-LANGUAGE LEARNERS & STRUGGLING READERS

TARGET RESOURCE

English-Language Learner Strategies and Activities

- Build Academic Vocabulary
- Develop Oral and Written Language Structures

Spanish Resources

Spanish Chapter Summaries Audio CD

Spanish Chapter Summaries Online

Teacher's One-Stop Planner:

- ExamView Test Generator, Spanish
- PuzzlePro, Spanish

Additional Resources

Differentiated Instruction Teacher Management System: Lesson Plans for Differentiated Instruction

Chapter Resources:

- Vocabulary Builder Activities
- Social Studies Skills Activity: Interpreting Political Cartoons

Quick Facts Transparencies:

- North Versus South (TR 41)
- Resources of the North and South (TR 42)
- Causes and Effects of the Civil War (TR 43)
- The Civil War Visual Summary (TR 44)

Student Edition on Audio CD Program

SPECIAL NEEDS LEARNERS

TARGET RESOURCE

Differentiated Instruction Modified Worksheets and Tests CD-ROM

- Vocabulary Flash Cards
- Modified Vocabulary Builder Activities
- Modified Chapter Review Activity
- Modified Chapter Test

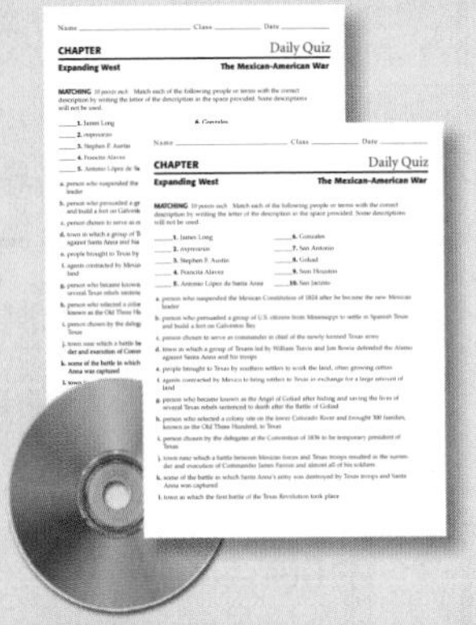

Additional Resources

Differentiated Instruction Teacher Management System: Lesson Plans for Differentiated Instruction

Interactive Reader and Study Guide

Social Studies Skills Activity: Interpreting Political Cartoons

Student Edition on Audio CD Program

ADVANCED/GIFTED-AND-TALENTED STUDENTS

TARGET RESOURCE

Primary Source Library CD-ROM for United States History

The Library contains longer versions of quotations in the text, extra sources, and images. Included are point-of-view articles, journals, diaries, historical fiction, and political documents.

Additional Resources

Differentiated Instruction Teacher Management System: Lesson Plans for Differentiated Instruction

Political Cartoons Activities for United States History: Cartoon 17: The Folly of Secession

U.S. History Document-Based Activities: Activity 5, The Civil War

Pre-AP Activities Guide for United States History: The Civil War

Chapter Resource File:

- Focus on Writing Activity: Newspaper Article
- Primary Source Activity: The Battle of Shiloh, April 1862
- Primary Source Activity: *Andersonville Diary*

Differentiated Activities in the Teacher's Edition

- 1st Battle of Bull Run Chart, p. 517
- Ironclads Cartoon, p. 520
- Understanding Words, p. 526
- African American Union Soldiers Chart, p. 530

Differentiated Activities in the Teacher's Edition

- Vicksburg Time Lines, p. 526

Differentiated Activities in the Teacher's Edition

- War Preparations Poster, p. 513
- Civil War Battle Songs, p. 519
- War Draft Debate, p. 532

Teacher One Stop™

How can I manage the lesson plans and support materials for differentiated instruction?

With the Indiana Teacher One Stop, you can easily organize and print lesson plans, planning guides, and instructional materials for all learners. The Indiana Teacher One Stop includes the following materials to help you differentiate instruction:

- Interactive Teacher's Edition
- Calendar Planner and pacing guides
- Editable lesson plans
- All reproducible ancillaries in Adobe Acrobat (PDF) format
- ExamView Test Generator (Eng & Span)
- Transparency and video previews

Professional Development

What teacher training resources are available to help me grow professionally?

- **In-service and staff development** as part of your Holt Social Studies product purchase
- **Quick Teacher Tutorial Lesson Presentation CD-ROM**
- Intensive tuition-based **Teacher Development Institute**
- **Convenient Holt Speaker Bureau** – face-to-face workshop options
- **PRAXIS™ Test Prep** interactive Web-based content refreshers*
- **Ask A Professional Development Expert** at http://www.hrw.com/prodev/

* PRAXIS is a trademark of Educational Testing Service (ETS). This publication is not endorsed or approved by ETS.

The War in the West

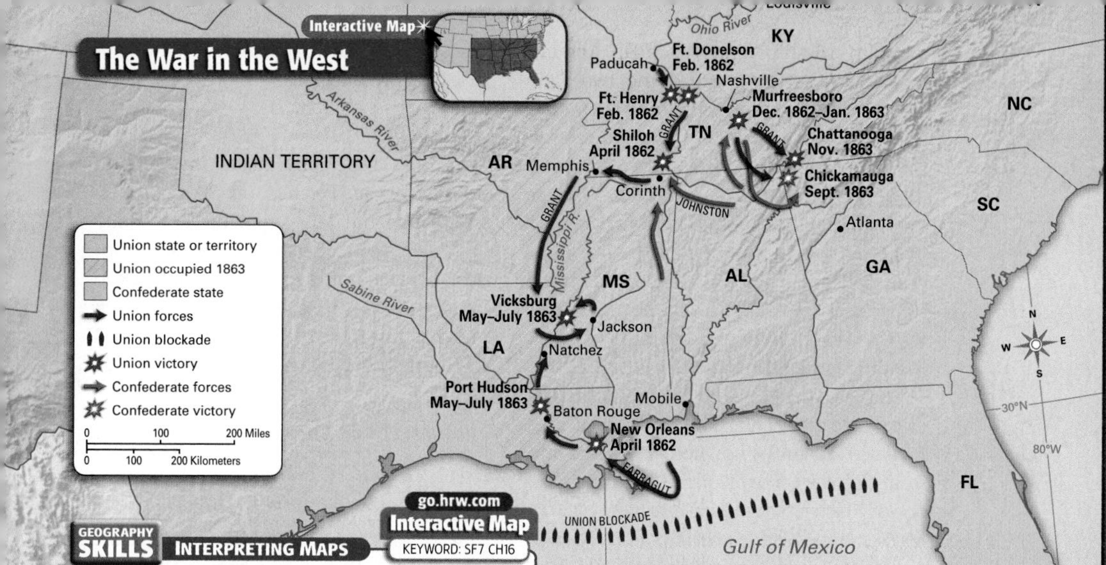

go.hrw.com
Interactive Map
KEYWORD: SF7 CH16

GEOGRAPHY SKILLS **INTERPRETING MAPS**

1. **Location** What river did Union forces fight to control?
2. **Human-Environment Interaction** Why do you think so many battles took place along rivers?

surrender can be accepted." The fort surrendered. The North gave a new name to Grant's initials: "Unconditional Surrender" Grant.

Advancing south in Tennessee, General Grant paused near Shiloh Church to await the arrival of the Army of Ohio. Grant knew that the large rebel army of General A. S. Johnston was nearby in Corinth, Mississippi, but he did not expect an attack. Instead of setting up defenses, he worked on drilling his new recruits.

In the early morning of April 6, 1862, the rebels sprang on Grant's sleepy camp. This began the **Battle of Shiloh**, in which the Union army gained greater control of the Mississippi River valley.

During the bloody two-day battle, each side gained and lost ground. Johnston was killed on the first day. The arrival of the Ohio force helped Grant regain territory and push the enemy back into Mississippi. The armies finally gave out, each with about 10,000 casualties. Both sides claimed victory, but, in fact, the victor was Grant.

The Fall of New Orleans

As Grant battled his way down the Mississippi, the Union navy prepared to blast its way upriver to meet him. The first obstacle was the port of New Orleans, the largest city in the Confederacy and the gateway to the Mississippi River.

BIOGRAPHY

David Farragut

(1801–1870)

David Farragut was born in Tennessee to a Spanish father and an American mother. At age seven Farragut was adopted by a family friend who agreed to train the young boy for the navy. Farragut received his first navy position—midshipman at large—at age nine and commanded his first vessel at 12. He spent the rest of his life in the U.S. Navy. Farragut led key attacks on the southern ports of Vicksburg and New Orleans.

Drawing Inferences How did Farragut help the war effort of the North?

Direct Teach

Main Idea

1 Union Strategy in the West

Union strategy in the West centered on control of the Mississippi River.

Explain What was the focus of the Union's western campaign? *to gain control of the Mississippi River and thereby cut off the eastern part of the South from western food production*

Analyze Why was Grant considered the victor at the Battle of Shiloh? *regained territory, pushed the Confederates back into Mississippi, gained greater control of Mississippi Valley*

CRF: Primary Source Activity: The Battle of Shiloh, April 1862

Map Transparency 53: The War in the West

Teaching Tip

Sequencing Events

Some students may have difficulty understanding the correct order of battles. For example, students might incorrectly think the Battle of Antietam took place before Shiloh because they studied Antietam first. To help students keep events in order, create a class time line.

Interactive Map: The War in the West

Critical Thinking: Summarizing

At Level

Interviews with Grant and Farragut

1. Discuss with students the main events of the war in the West. Then ask students to imagine that they are roving correspondents for a newspaper during the Civil War. Vicksburg has just surrendered, and their editor has assigned them to interview either Ulysses S. Grant or Admiral David Farragut.
2. Pair students and assign each pair either Grant or Farragut. Have each pair write at least 10 questions and answers for the interview. Questions should address the goals of the campaign in the West, the fighting in which the assigned leader has been involved, the significance of this action, and the leader's views on the progress of the war in the West.
3. Have volunteer pairs act out their interviews.
LS Interpersonal, Verbal/Linguistic

Alternative Assessment Handbook, Rubric 37: Writing Assignments

Answers

Interpreting Maps **1.** *Mississippi River;* **2.** *possible answers—both armies were vying for control of one major river, the Mississippi; both armies often traveled along rivers.*

Biography *As a strong naval commander, Farragut was able to lead the Union navy to key victories in major Confederate ports.*

Direct Teach

Main Idea

1 Union Strategy in the West

Union strategy in the West centered on control of the Mississippi River.

Explain How was Admiral Farragut able to capture New Orleans? *Unable to destroy the two forts protecting the city, he camouflaged his fleet and led a daring and successful pre-dawn dash past the forts, after which he easily took New Orleans.*

Identify Cause and Effect Why did Grant decide to starve Vicksburg into surrender? *The city's strategic geographic location on a high cliff above the Mississippi River made invasion all but impossible, and Farragut's cannons could not reach the city.*

Info to Know

The War in Indian Territory The Civil War divided Native Americans in Indian Territory. The Choctaw, Chickasaw, Cherokee, Creek, and Seminole nations split, with some supporting the Confederacy and others the Union. Some 10,000 Native Americans served with the Confederates during the war. By the war's end in 1865, an estimated 6,000 to 10,000 Native Americans had died as a result of the fighting.

With 18 ships and 700 men, Admiral **David Farragut** approached the two forts that guarded the entrance to New Orleans from the Gulf of Mexico. Unable to destroy the forts, Farragut decided to race past them.

The risky operation would take place at night. Farragut had his wooden ships wrapped in heavy chains to protect them like ironclads. Sailors slapped Mississippi mud on the ships' hulls to make them hard to see. Trees were tied to the masts to make the ships look like the forested shore.

Before dawn on April 24, 1862, the warships made their daring dash. The Confederates fired at Farragut's ships from the shore and from gunboats. They launched burning rafts, one of which scorched Farragut's own ship. But his fleet slipped by the twin forts and made it to New Orleans. The city fell on April 29.

Farragut sailed up the Mississippi River, taking Baton Rouge, Louisiana, and Natchez, Mississippi. He then approached the city of Vicksburg, Mississippi.

The Siege of Vicksburg

Vicksburg's geography made invasion all but impossible. Perched on 200-foot-high cliffs above the Mississippi River, the city could rain down firepower on enemy ships or on soldiers trying to scale the cliffs. Deep gorges surrounded the city, turning back land assaults. Nevertheless, Farragut ordered Vicksburg to surrender.

> "Mississippians don't know, and refuse to learn, how to surrender . . . If Commodore Farragut . . . can teach them, let [him] come and try."
>
> —Colonel James L. Autry, military commander of Vicksburg

Farragut's guns had trouble reaching the city above. It was up to General Grant. His solution was to starve the city into surrender.

General Grant's troops began the **Siege of Vicksburg** in mid-May 1863, cutting off the city and shelling it repeatedly. As food ran out, residents and soldiers survived by eating horses, dogs, and rats. "We are utterly cut off from the world, surrounded by a circle of fire," wrote one woman. "People do nothing

Primary Source

SPEECH

Response to Farragut

The mayor of New Orleans considered the surrender of the city to the Union navy:

> "We yield to physical force alone and maintain allegiance to the Confederate States; beyond this, a due respect for our dignity, our rights and the flag of our country does not, I think, permit us to go."
>
> **–Mayor John T. Monroe,**
> quoted in *Confederate Military History, Vol. 10*

ANALYSIS SKILL — ANALYZING PRIMARY SOURCES

How does Monroe's statement reveal his attitude about surrender?

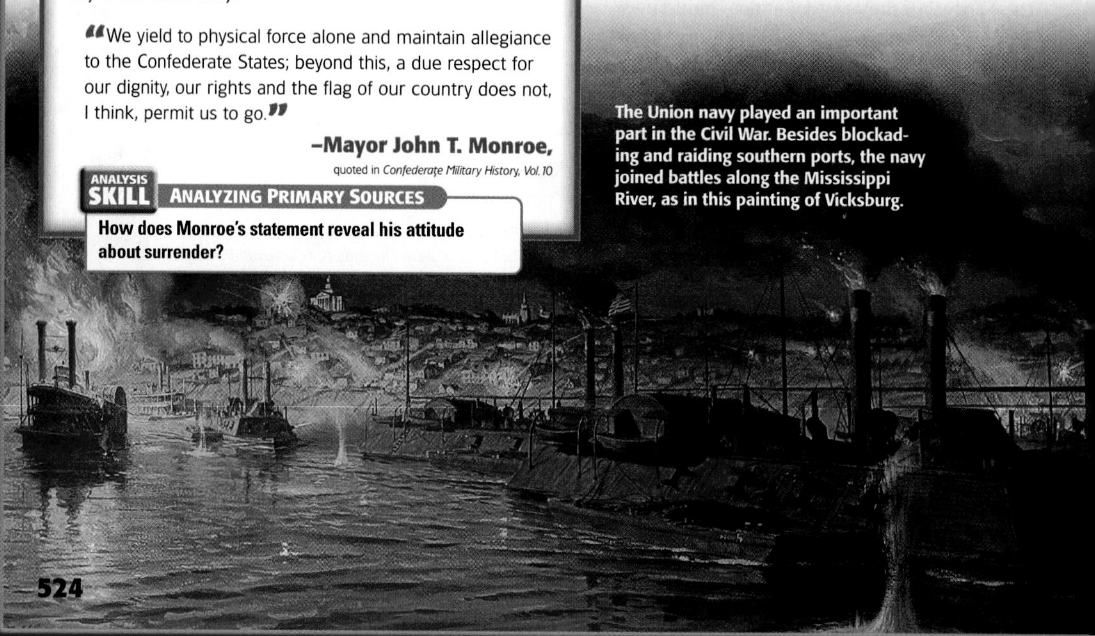

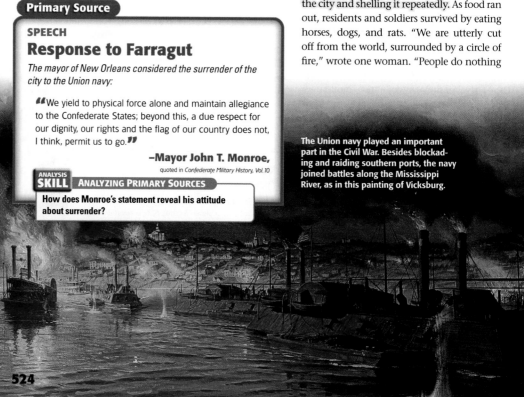

The Union navy played an important part in the Civil War. Besides blockading and raiding southern ports, the navy joined battles along the Mississippi River, as in this painting of Vicksburg.

524

Critical Thinking: Identifying Points of View

At Level

Letter from Vicksburg

1. Review with students the events of the Siege of Vicksburg. Then have students examine the History and Geography feature "The Vicksburg Strategy" that follows this section.
2. Ask students to imagine that they are either Confederate soldiers or civilians in Vicksburg during the Union siege of the city. Have each student write a letter to an imaginary friend or family member living elsewhere in the South telling them about the experience.
3. Students' letters should describe the siege, such as the constant shelling and the lack of food and supplies, their feelings about it, whether they think the city should surrender, and what the consequences of surrendering might be.
4. Have volunteers read their letters to the class.

LS Verbal/Linguistic

Alternative Assessment Handbook, Rubric 25: Personal Letters

Answers

Analyzing Primary Sources *shows that although he is surrendering he remains loyal to the South*

but eat what they can get, sleep when they can, and dodge the shells."

The Confederate soldiers were also sick and hungry. In late June a group of soldiers sent their commander a warning.

> "The army is now ripe for mutiny [rebellion], unless it can be fed. If you can't feed us, you'd better surrender us, horrible as the idea is."
>
> —Confederate soldiers at Vicksburg to General John C. Pemberton, 1863

On July 4, Pemberton surrendered. Grant immediately sent food to the soldiers and civilians. He later claimed that "the fate of the Confederacy was sealed when Vicksburg fell."

READING CHECK **Summarizing** How did the Union gain control of the Mississippi River?

Struggle for the Far West

Early on in the war, the Union halted several attempts by Confederate armies to control lands west of the Mississippi. In August 1861, a Union detachment from Colorado turned back a Confederate force at Glorieta Pass. Union volunteers also defeated rebel forces at Arizona's Pichaco Pass.

Confederate attempts to take the border state of Missouri also collapsed. Failing to seize the federal arsenal at St. Louis in mid-1861, the rebels fell back to Pea Ridge in northwest Arkansas. There, in March 1862, they attacked again, aided by some 800 Cherokee. The Indians hoped the Confederates would give them greater freedom. In addition, slavery was legal in Indian Territory, and some Native Americans who were slaveholders supported the Confederacy. Despite being outnumbered, Union forces won the Battle of Pea Ridge. The Union defense of Missouri held.

Pro-Confederate forces remained active in the region throughout the war. They attacked Union forts and raided towns in Missouri and Kansas, forcing Union commanders to keep valuable troops stationed in the area.

READING CHECK **Analyzing** What was the importance of the fighting in the Far West?

SUMMARY AND PREVIEW The North and the South continued their struggle with battles in the West. A number of key battles took place in the Western theater, and several important Union leaders emerged from these battles. One, Ulysses S. Grant, would soon become even more important to the Union army. In the next section you will learn about the lives of civilians, enslaved Africans, and soldiers during the war.

Section 3 Assessment

go.hrw.com
Online Quiz
KEYWORD: SF7 HP16

Reviewing Ideas, Terms, and People

1. a. **Identify** What role did **Ulysses S. Grant** play in the war in the West?
   b. **Explain** Why was the **Battle of Shiloh** important?
   c. **Elaborate** Do you think President Lincoln would have approved of Grant's actions in the West? Why or why not?
2. a. **Describe** How did the Union take New Orleans, and why was it an important victory?
   b. **Draw Conclusions** How were civilians affected by the **Siege of Vicksburg**?
   c. **Predict** What might be some possible results of the Union victory at Vicksburg?

Critical Thinking

3. **Identifying Cause and Effect** Review your notes on Union strategy in the West. Then copy this graphic organizer and use it to show the causes and effects of each battle.

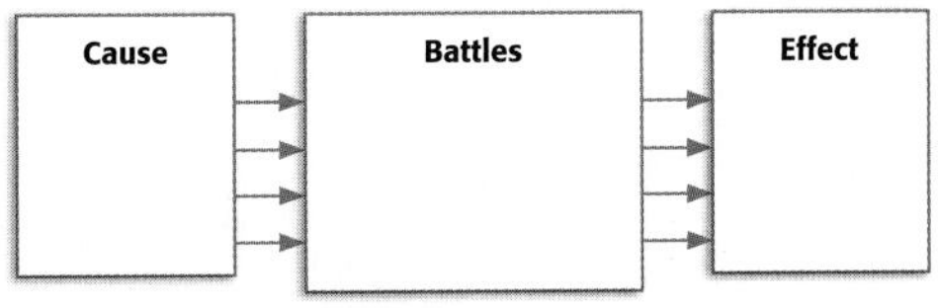

FOCUS ON WRITING

4. **Taking Notes on the War in the West** As you read this section, take notes on the fight for the Mississippi River and the Siege of Vicksburg. Be sure to answer the following questions: Who? Where? When? Why? and How?

Direct Teach

Main Idea

2 Struggle for the Far West

Confederate and Union troops struggled for dominance in the Far West.

Describe What early actions did Confederate forces take to try to control lands west of the Mississippi River? *They invaded New Mexico at Glorieta Pass, Arizona at Pichaco Pass, and Missouri at St. Louis.*

Identify Points of View Why did some Cherokee fight for the South? *They hoped the Confederates would give them greater freedom, and some Native Americans were slaveholders.*

Review & Assess

Close

Have students summarize the war in the Far West.

Review

go.hrw.com Online Quiz, Section 16.3

Assess

SE Section 3 Assessment

PASS: Section Quiz 16.3

Alternative Assessment Handbook

Reteach/Classroom Intervention

Interactive Reader and Study Guide, Section 16.3

Interactive Skills Tutor CD-ROM

Section 3 Assessment Answers

1. **a.** commander of Union forces in the West
   b. See answer to Question 3.
   c. possible answer—Yes, because Grant acted decisively, fought, and won.
2. **a.** naval night operation from the Gulf of Mexico; gained control of lower Mississippi
   b. suffered bombardment and starvation
   c. Responses should show that the victory gave the Union control of the Mississippi.
3. Shiloh—rebel surprise attack on Grant's base; increased Union control of Mississippi Valley; New Orleans—Farragut's dash past forts; Union advanced into southern territory; Vicksburg—Vicksburg's location; Union controlled Mississippi River; Pea Ridge—rebels' failure to seize federal arsenal at St. Louis; Union kept control of Missouri.
4. Students should cover Grant and Farragut and the applicable battles listed in the previous answer.

Answers

Reading Check (top) *A Union naval force took New Orleans and other cities as it moved up the river; Grant moved down the river and took Vicksburg.*

Reading Check (bottom) *The Union stopped Confederate attempts to control the area.*

History and Geography

Activity **Vicksburg Strategy Headlines** Have students read the feature. Ask a volunteer to explain why Lincoln thought Vicksburg was such an important Union target. Next, have students trace the stages in the Vicksburg strategy. Ask students to identify the geographic factors that affected Grant's decisions and actions at various points along his march. Then have students write at least one newspaper headline for each stage numbered on the map at right. Ask volunteers to read their headlines to the class. **LS Verbal/Linguistic, Visual/Spatial**

Info to Know

Grant's Supply Strategy Instead of waiting for supply wagons, Union general Ulysses S. Grant had his troops live off the land. The soldiers combed the southern countryside taking horses, oxen, farm wagons, and even carriages from area farms and plantations. Grant knew from earlier campaigns that the farms in Mississippi had plenty of food as well, and his troops raided for cattle, pigs, and other goods.

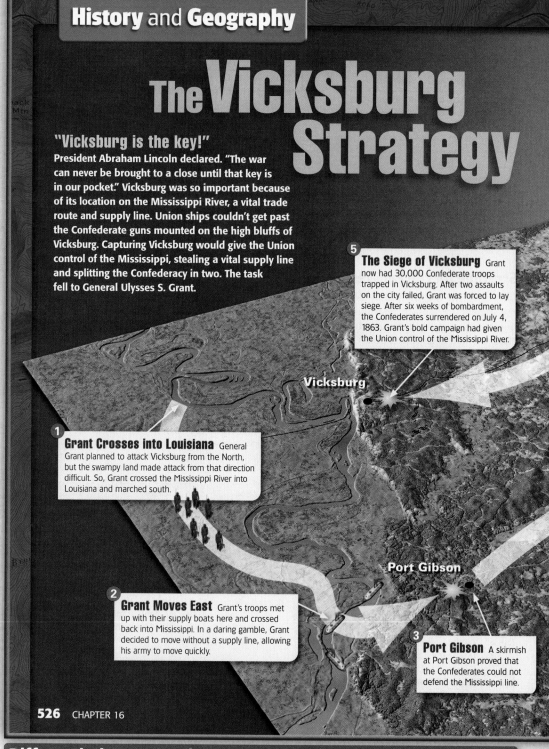

History and Geography

The Vicksburg Strategy

"Vicksburg is the key!"

President Abraham Lincoln declared. "The war can never be brought to a close until that key is in our pocket." Vicksburg was so important because of its location on the Mississippi River, a vital trade route and supply line. Union ships couldn't get past the Confederate guns mounted on the high bluffs of Vicksburg. Capturing Vicksburg would give the Union control of the Mississippi, stealing a vital supply line and splitting the Confederacy in two. The task fell to General Ulysses S. Grant.

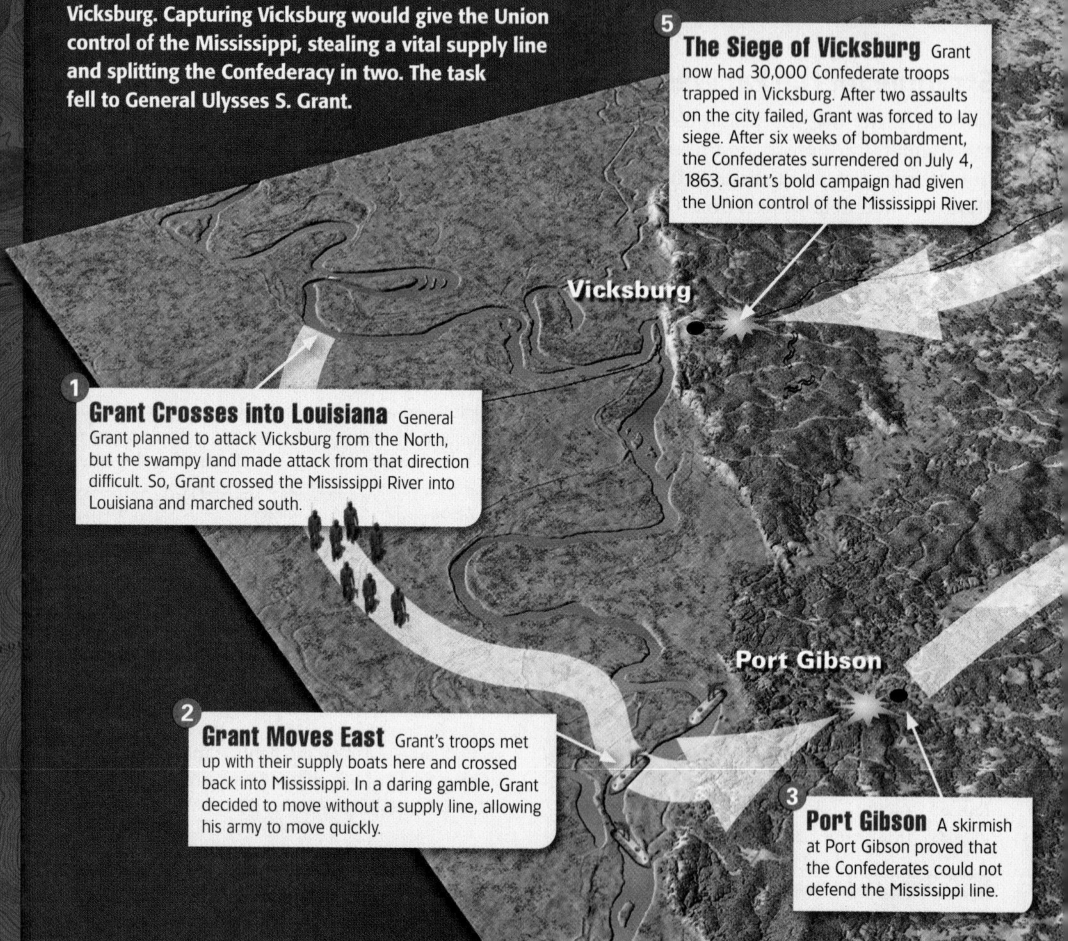

5 The Siege of Vicksburg Grant now had 30,000 Confederate troops trapped in Vicksburg. After two assaults on the city failed, Grant was forced to lay siege. After six weeks of bombardment, the Confederates surrendered on July 4, 1863. Grant's bold campaign had given the Union control of the Mississippi River.
Vicksburg
1 Grant Crosses into Louisiana General Grant planned to attack Vicksburg from the North, but the swampy land made attack from that direction difficult. So, Grant crossed the Mississippi River into Louisiana and marched south.
Port Gibson
2 Grant Moves East Grant's troops met up with their supply boats here and crossed back into Mississippi. In a daring gamble, Grant decided to move without a supply line, allowing his army to move quickly.
3 Port Gibson A skirmish at Port Gibson proved that the Confederates could not defend the Mississippi line.

Differentiating Instruction

Special Needs Learners — Below Level

1. Discuss the feature with students.
2. Have students work in pairs to create time lines of the events in the Vicksburg campaign shown above. Students should note one detail about each event. **LS Visual/Spatial**

Alternative Assessment Handbook, Rubric 36: Time Lines

English-Language Learners — Below Level

1. Have students write down each word or phrase in the feature they do not understand.
2. Organize students into mixed-ability pairs. Have partners look up the definitions of the words on their lists. Then have partners quiz each other on the words' meanings. **LS Interpersonal, Verbal/Linguistic**

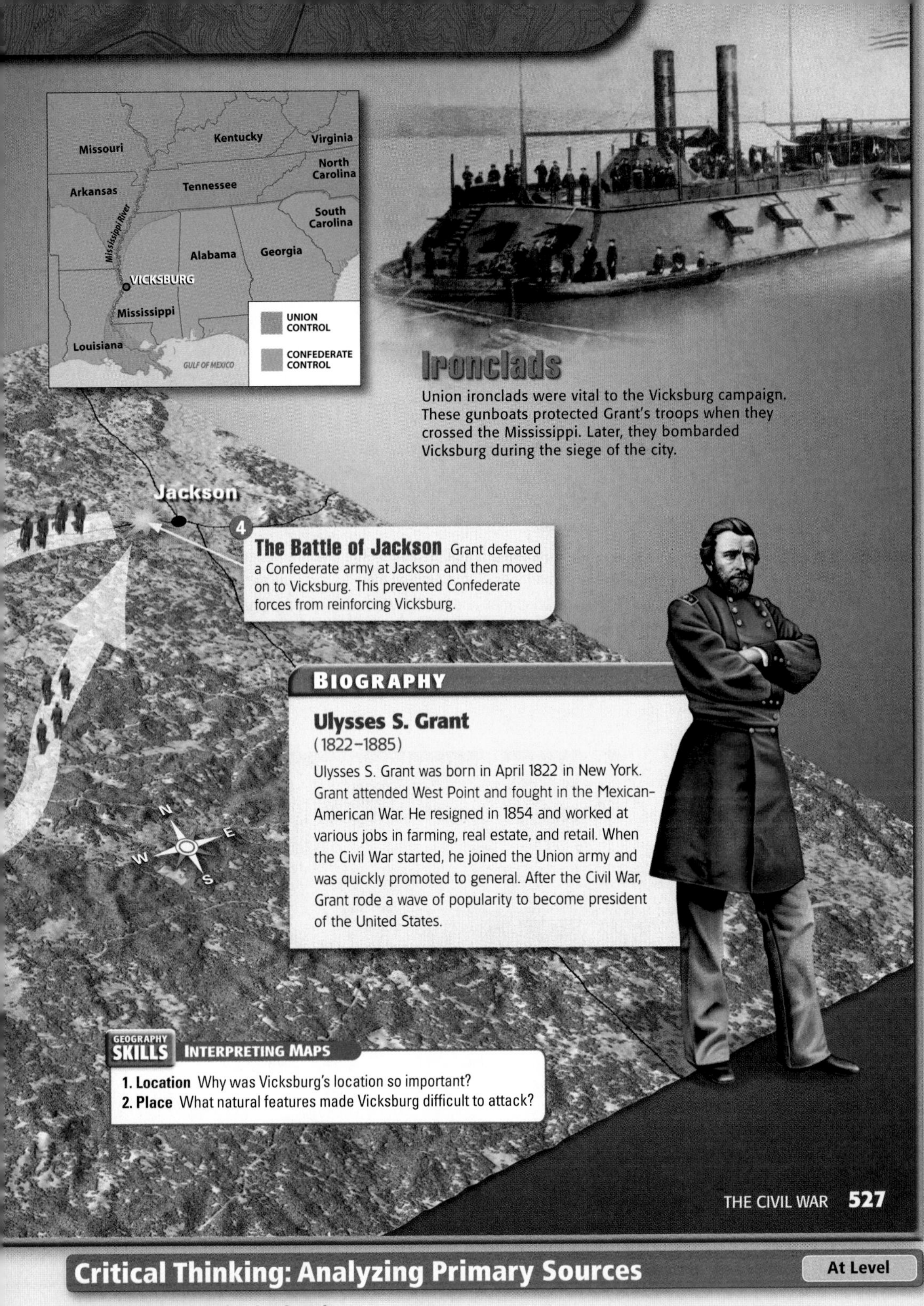

Ironclads

Union ironclads were vital to the Vicksburg campaign. These gunboats protected Grant's troops when they crossed the Mississippi. Later, they bombarded Vicksburg during the siege of the city.

The Battle of Jackson Grant defeated a Confederate army at Jackson and then moved on to Vicksburg. This prevented Confederate forces from reinforcing Vicksburg.

BIOGRAPHY

Ulysses S. Grant
(1822–1885)

Ulysses S. Grant was born in April 1822 in New York. Grant attended West Point and fought in the Mexican-American War. He resigned in 1854 and worked at various jobs in farming, real estate, and retail. When the Civil War started, he joined the Union army and was quickly promoted to general. After the Civil War, Grant rode a wave of popularity to become president of the United States.

GEOGRAPHY SKILLS INTERPRETING MAPS

1. **Location** Why was Vicksburg's location so important?
2. **Place** What natural features made Vicksburg difficult to attack?

History and Geography

Info to Know

Vicksburg Cave Homes The city of Vicksburg was built on a hill. During the Siege of Vicksburg, the city's residents burrowed a system of more than 500 caves in the side of the hill in which to take cover from the Union artillery attacks. Caves for a single family usually had one or two chambers. Some large caves could hold as many as 200 people. People furnished their caves with carpets, furniture, cook stoves, and mirrors. They also built shelves into the walls to hold candles and other belongings.

Info to Know

Terms of Surrender Although General Grant originally demanded an unconditional surrender from the Confederates at Vicksburg, his final terms were more lenient. Grant decided it would be too costly and time-consuming to take the Confederate prisoners to Union prison camps. Instead, he allowed most of the defeated soldiers to surrender their weapons and leave as prisoners on parole.

Did you know . . .

The Confederate surrender ended the Siege of Vicksburg on July 4, 1863. As a result, the city's residents did not celebrate Independence Day for more than 80 years.

Critical Thinking: Analyzing Primary Sources

At Level

The Mighty Mississippi

Background After the fall of Vicksburg, President Abraham Lincoln summed up the event's significance: "The father of waters rolls unvexed to the sea."

1. Write the above quotation from Lincoln for student to see. Discuss the expression "the father of waters" with students so that they understand that Lincoln was talking about the Mississippi River.
2. Organize the class into small groups. Have each group discuss this quotation and the importance of the Mississippi River to both the North and the South during the Civil War.
3. Then have each student write a brief essay explaining the quotation and the significance of the Siege of Vicksburg to the Civil War.

Alternative Assessment Handbook, Rubrics 14: Group Activity; and 37: Writing Assignments

Answers

Interpreting Maps **1.** *Capturing Vicksburg would give the Union control of the Mississippi River, which would cut off a vital supply line for the South and cut the Confederacy in two.* **2.** *It was located on high bluffs directly above the Mississippi, and the land to the north was swampy, which made attack from that approach difficult.*

Preteach

Bellringer

If YOU were there . . . Use the **Daily Bellringer Transparency** to help students answer the question.

Daily Bellringer Transparency 16.4

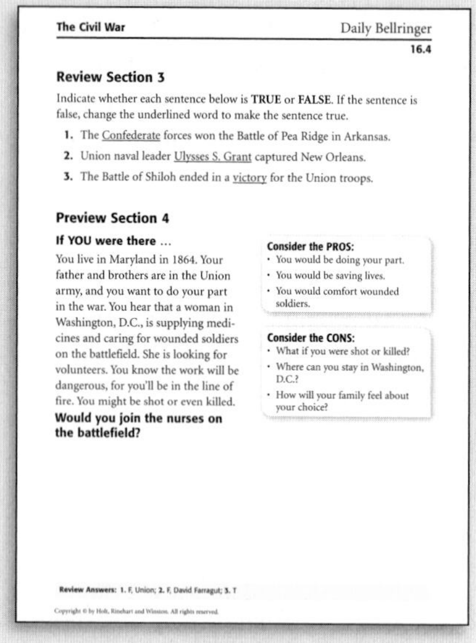

The Civil War — Daily Bellringer 16.4

Review Section 3

Indicate whether each sentence below is **TRUE** or **FALSE**. If the sentence is false, change the underlined word to make the sentence true.

1. The Confederate forces won the Battle of Pea Ridge in Arkansas.
2. Union naval leader Ulysses S. Grant captured New Orleans.
3. The Battle of Shiloh ended in a victory for the Union troops.

Preview Section 4

If YOU were there ...

You live in Maryland in 1864. Your father and brothers are in the Union army, and you want to do your part in the war. You hear that a woman in Washington, D.C., is supplying medicines and caring for wounded soldiers on the battlefield. She is looking for volunteers. You know the work will be dangerous, for you'll be in the line of fire. You might be shot or even killed.

Would you join the nurses on the battlefield?

Consider the PROS:
- You would be doing your part.
- You would be saving lives.
- You would comfort wounded soldiers.

Consider the CONS:
- What if you were shot or killed?
- Where can you stay in Washington, D.C.?
- How will your family feel about your choice?

Review Answers: 1. F, Union; 2. F, David Farragut; 3. T

Building Vocabulary

Preteach or review the following term:

abolitionist supporter of the movement to end slavery (p. 529)

CRF: Vocabulary Builder Activity, Section 4

Taking Notes

Have students copy the graphic organizer onto their own paper and then use it to take notes on the section. This activity will prepare students for the Section Assessment, in which they will complete a graphic organizer that builds on the information using a critical-thinking skill.

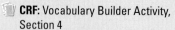

Section Correlations IN

8.1.21 Describe the importance of key events and individuals in the Civil War. **8.1.26** Give examples of the changing role of women and minorities in the northern, southern, and western parts of the United States in the mid-nineteenth century, and examine possible causes for these changes. **8.1.29** Differentiate between facts and historical interpretations recognizing that the historian's narrative reflects his or her judgment about the significance of particular facts.

SECTION 4

Daily Life during the War

What You Will Learn...

Main Ideas

1. The Emancipation Proclamation freed slaves in Confederate states.
2. African Americans participated in the war in a variety of ways.
3. President Lincoln faced opposition to the war.
4. Life was difficult for soldiers and civilians alike.

The Big Idea

The lives of many Americans were affected by the Civil War.

Key Terms and People

emancipation, *p. 529*
Emancipation Proclamation, *p. 529*
contrabands, *p. 531*
54th Massachusetts Infantry, *p. 531*
Copperheads, *p. 532*
habeas corpus, *p. 532*
Clara Barton, *p. 534*

TAKING NOTES As you read, take notes on the effects of the Civil War on the lives of African Americans, soldiers, and women and children. Write your notes in a graphic organizer like the one below.

How the Civil War affected	
African Americans	
Soldiers	
Women and children	

IN 8.1.21, 8.1.24, 8.1.26, 8.1.29, 8.1.30, 8.2.10

If YOU were there...

You live in Maryland in 1864. Your father and brothers are in the Union army, and you want to do your part in the war. You hear that a woman in Washington, D.C., is supplying medicines and caring for wounded soldiers on the battlefield. She is looking for volunteers. You know the work will be dangerous, for you'll be in the line of fire. You might be shot or even killed.

Would you join the nurses on the battlefield?

BUILDING BACKGROUND The Civil War touched almost all Americans. Some 3 million men fought in the two armies. Thousands of other men and women worked behind the lines, providing food, supplies, medical care, and other necessary services. Civilians could not escape the effects of war, as the fighting destroyed farms, homes, and cities.

Emancipation Proclamation

Teach the Big Idea

At Level

Daily Life during the War

Materials: paper, stapler

1. **Teach** To teach the main ideas in the section, use the questions in the Direct Teach boxes.
2. **Apply** Have each student take four sheets of paper and fold and staple them to create an eight-page booklet. On each left-hand page, have students write one of the section's blue headings. Below the heading, students should list the key people, events, and issues in that part of the text. Students should use the right-hand page to provide drawings, phrases, and charts that relate to the information on the left-hand page. **LS Verbal/Linguistic, Visual/Spatial**
3. **Review** As you review the section, have volunteers share the information they listed.
4. **Practice/Homework** Have students write a short summary for each part of their booklets. **LS Verbal/Linguistic**

Alternative Assessment Handbook, Rubrics 3: Artwork; and 37: Writing Assignments

Emancipation Proclamation

At the heart of the nation's bloody struggle were millions of enslaved African Americans. Abolitionists urged President Lincoln to free them.

In an 1858 speech, Lincoln declared, "There is no reason in the world why the negro is not entitled to all the natural rights numerated in the Declaration of Independence—the right to life, liberty, and the pursuit of happiness." Yet as president, Lincoln found **emancipation**, or the freeing of slaves, to be a difficult issue. He did not believe he had the constitutional power. He also worried about the effects of emancipation.

Lincoln Issues the Proclamation

Northerners had a range of opinions about abolishing slavery.

- The Democratic Party, which included many laborers, opposed emancipation. Laborers feared that freed slaves would come north and take their jobs at lower wages.
- Abolitionists argued that the war was pointless if it did not win freedom for African Americans. They warned that the Union would remain divided until the problem was resolved.
- Lincoln worried about losing support for the war. Previous wartime Confiscation Acts that had attempted to free the slaves had been unpopular in the border states.
- Others, including Secretary of War Edwin Stanton, agreed with Lincoln that the use of slave labor was helping the Confederacy make war. Therefore, as commander in chief, the president could free the slaves in all rebellious states. Freed African Americans could then be recruited into the Union army.

For several weeks in 1862, Lincoln worked intensely, thinking, writing, and rewriting. He finally wrote the **Emancipation Proclamation**, the order to free the Confederate slaves. The proclamation declared that:

> "...all persons held as slaves within any State or designated part of a State the people whereof shall then be in rebellion against the United States shall be then, thenceforward, and forever free."
>
> —Emancipation Proclamation, 1862

The Emancipation Proclamation was a military order that freed slaves only in areas

Emancipation Proclamation

GEOGRAPHY SKILLS INTERPRETING MAPS

Place In which places was slavery still legal after the Emancipation Proclamation?

The painting at left shows Lincoln and his cabinet after the signing of the Emancipation Proclamation. Above is a photo of former slaves who were freed by the proclamation.

How do you think the Emancipation Proclamation would affect the Civil War?

Direct Teach

Main Idea

❶ Emancipation Proclamation

The Emancipation Proclamation freed slaves in Confederate states.

Identify What issue lay at the heart of the Civil War? *slavery and the millions of African Americans living in bondage*

Identify Points of View Why did some northerners oppose abolishing slavery? *feared that freed slaves would work for lower wages and take jobs; feared that emancipation would weaken support for the war*

Evaluate How did Lincoln address the difficult issue of emancipation, and why did he make this choice? *He issued a military proclamation freeing all enslaved Africans in rebellious states. He did not believe he had the constitutional power to end slavery but as commander-in-chief, he believed he could take action to stop slave labor from being used to help the southern war effort.*

Map Transparency 54: Emancipation Proclamation

Info to Know

Support for Lincoln After the Emancipation Proclamation was issued, an African American congregation in Baltimore raised about $580 to buy Lincoln a Bible. The cover had a picture of Lincoln breaking off the chains of a slave working in a cotton field.

Critical Thinking: Identifying Points of View

At Level

Emancipation Proclamation

1. Have students read the Emancipation Proclamation (provided in the back of the textbook) as a class and summarize its main points. Guide the class in a discussion of the importance of the proclamation and its impact on the North and the South.
2. Ask students to identify how different groups in the North reacted to the proclamation. Encourage students to elaborate on why some northerners might have opposed it.
3. Then ask students to imagine that they live during the time of the Civil War and Lincoln has just issued the Emancipation Proclamation. Have each student write a letter to Lincoln expressing support for the proclamation and explaining how he or she thinks it will affect the war. Have volunteers read their letters to the class. **LS Verbal/Linguistic**

Alternative Assessment Handbook, Rubric 41: Writing to Express

Answers

Interpreting Maps *Missouri, Kentucky, Maryland, Delaware, Tennessee, and the southern tip of Louisiana*

Emancipation Proclamation *possible answer—might hurt the South's ability to wage war as slaves escape to Union camps; might help the northern war effort as freed slaves join the Union ranks*

Direct Teach

Main Idea

1 Emancipation Proclamation

The Emancipation Proclamation freed slaves in Confederate states.

Identify Points of View Why did some abolitionists criticize the Emancipation Proclamation? *because it did not end slavery completely or free all slaves*

Make Judgments Do you think Lincoln should have expanded the Emancipation Proclamation to free all slaves? Why or why not? *possible answers—no, because he might have lost political support and the border states might have left the Union, thereby risking the war and any chance for helping slaves; yes, because slavery is morally wrong*

Activity Celebrating Emancipation Have each student create a poem from the point of view of a freed slave celebrating the Emancipation Proclamation.

Alternative Assessment Handbook, Rubric 26: Poems and Songs

World Events

European Reactions to Emancipation
The Emancipation Proclamation drew the attention of many Europeans. Some workers from Manchester, England, wrote to President Lincoln, "We joyfully honor you . . . [for] your belief in the words of your great founders: 'All men are created free and equal.'"

Answers

Reading Check *possible answers—Abolitionists supported it, although some thought it did not go far enough; some laborers feared they would lose their jobs to freed slaves who might work for less.*

New Soldiers

NOW IN CAMP AT READVILLE!
54th REGIMENT!
AFRICAN DESCENT
Col. ROBERT G. SHAW.
Colored Men, Rally 'Round the Flag of Freedom!
BOUNTY $100!
Pay, $13 a Month!
Good Food & Clothing!
State Aid to Families!
RECRUITING OFFICE,
COR. CAMBRIDGE & NORTH RUSSELL STS.,
BOSTON.
Lieut. J. W. M. APPLETON, Recruiting Officer.

African American soldiers, such as the 54th Massachusetts Infantry and Company E of the 4th U.S. Colored Infantry, shown here, fought proudly and bravely in the Civil War. At right is a flyer used to recruit African American soldiers.

controlled by the Confederacy. In fact, the proclamation had little immediate effect. It was impossible for the federal government to enforce the proclamation in the areas where it actually applied—the states in rebellion that were not under federal control. The proclamation did not stop slavery in the border states, where the federal government would have had the power to enforce it. The words written in the Emancipation Proclamation were powerful, but the impact of the document was more symbolic than real. It defined what the Union was fighting against, and discouraged Britain from aiding the Confederacy.

Lincoln wanted to be in a strong position in the war before announcing his plan. The Battle of Antietam gave him the victory he needed. He issued the Emancipation Proclamation on September 22, 1862. The proclamation went into effect on January 1, 1863.

Reaction to the Proclamation

New Year's Eve, December 31, 1862: In "night watch" meetings at many African American churches, worshippers prayed, sang, and gave thanks. When the clocks struck midnight, millions were free. Abolitionists rejoiced. Frederick Douglass called January 1, 1863, "the great day which is to determine the destiny not only of the American Republic, but that of the American Continent."

William Lloyd Garrison was quick to note, however, that "slavery, as a system" continued to exist in the loyal slave states. Yet where slavery remained, the proclamation encouraged many enslaved Africans to escape when the Union troops came near. They flocked to the Union camps and followed them for protection. The loss of slaves crippled the South's ability to wage war.

READING CHECK **Finding Main Ideas** How did northerners view the Emancipation Proclamation?

Differentiating Instruction

Below Level

Struggling Readers

1. Review the information about African American soldiers in this section. Then draw the chart for students to see. Omit the blue, italicized answers.
2. Have each student copy the chart and complete it by listing reasons why African Americans joined the Union and some of the hardships they faced. **LS Visual/Spatial**

Alternative Assessment Handbook, Rubric 7: Charts

African American Union Soldiers

Reasons Joined	Hardships Faced
• *freedom* • *citizenship* • *honor* • *respect* • *pay*	• *if captured, often killed or sold into slavery* • *received less pay than white soldiers* • *no guarantee of gaining the rights of citizenship*

Primary Source

LETTER

June 23, 1863

Joseph E. Williams, an African American soldier and recruiter from Pennsylvania, wrote this letter describing why African Americans fought for the Union.

"We are now determined to hold every step which has been offered to us as citizens of the United States for our elevation [benefit], which represent justice, the purity, the truth, and aspiration [hope] of heaven. We must learn deeply to realize the duty, the moral and political necessity for the benefit of our race...Every consideration of honor, of interest, and of duty to God and man, requires that we should be true to our trust."

—quoted in *A Grand Army of Black Men*, edited by Edwin S. Redkey

ANALYSIS SKILL **ANALYZING PRIMARY SOURCES**

Why did Williams think being soldiers was so important for African Americans?

African Americans Participate in the War

As the war casualties climbed, the Union needed even more troops. African Americans were ready to volunteer. Not all white northerners were ready to accept them, but eventually they had to. Frederick Douglass believed that military service would help African Americans gain rights.

"Once let the black man get upon his person the brass letters, U.S.; ... and a musket on his shoulder and bullets in his pocket, and there is no power on earth which can deny that he has earned the right to citizenship."

—Frederick Douglass, quoted in *The Life and Writings of Frederick Douglass, Vol. 3*

Congress began allowing the army to sign up African American volunteers as laborers in July 1862. The War Department also gave **contrabands**, or escaped slaves, the right to join the Union army in South Carolina. Free African Americans in Louisiana and Kansas also formed their own units in the Union army. By the spring of 1863, African American army units were proving themselves in combat. They took part in a Union attack on Port Hudson, Louisiana, in May.

One unit stood out above the others. The **54th Massachusetts Infantry** consisted mostly of free African Americans. In July 1863 this regiment led a heroic charge on South Carolina's Fort Wagner. The 54th took heavy fire and suffered huge casualties in the failed operation. About half the regiment was killed, wounded, or captured. Edward L. Pierce, a correspondent for the *New York Tribune,* wrote, "The Fifty-fourth did well and nobly...They moved up as gallantly as any troops could, and with their enthusiasm they deserved a better fate." The bravery of the 54th regiment made it the most celebrated African American unit of the war.

About 180,000 African Americans served with the Union army. They received $10 a month, while white soldiers got $13. They were usually led by white officers, some from abolitionist families.

African Americans faced special horrors on the battlefield. Confederates often killed their black captives or sold them into slavery. In the 1864 election, Lincoln suggested rewarding African American soldiers by giving them the right to vote.

READING CHECK **Analyzing Information** How did African Americans support the Union?

Direct Teach

Main Idea

❷ African Americans Participate in the War

African Americans participated in the war in a variety of ways.

Identify Why did the 54th Massachusetts Infantry become the most celebrated African American unit of the Civil War? *The unit, consisting mostly of free African Americans, led a heroic charge on South Carolina's Fort Wagner and suffered heavy losses.*

Interpret How did Frederick Douglass believe that military service would help African Americans? *He believed that by serving in the military African Americans would earn the right to citizenship.*

CRF: Biography Activity: William Carney

Info to Know

African American Soldiers In July 1862, African Americans were officially allowed to join the Union army. Many men responded to the call. Although African Americans made up only 2 percent of the North's population, they made up nearly 10 percent of the Union army by the war's end.

Cross-Discipline Activity: Civics

At Level

Responsibility: Military Service

1. Discuss with students the above quotation by Frederick Douglass. Have students explain what Douglass is expressing in the statement.
2. Ask students why Douglass thought military service would prove that African Americans had earned the right to citizenship *(possible answer—because military service is a sign of good citizenship)*. Ask students if they agree with Douglass.
3. Then have students examine the primary source letter above. Have students compare and contrast the views of Douglass and Williams on military service. Help students understand that both men saw the rights and responsibilities of citizenship as connected.
4. Conclude by having students discuss why African Americans fought for the Union and why military service is an important duty of citizenship.

Alternative Assessment Handbook, Rubric 11: Discussions

Answers

Analyzing Primary Sources *He saw military service as a moral and political duty in response to the freedom African Americans had received and the gains they had made toward citizenship.*

Reading Check *served as soldiers and fought bravely for the Union*

CHAPTER 16

Standardized Test Practice

8.1.21, 8.1.29, 8.2.10

DIRECTIONS: Read each question and write the letter of the best response.

1 Use the map below to answer the following question.

The place where two major battles of the Civil War were fought is indicated on the map by which letter?

A W
B X
C Y
D Z

2 The Battle of Gettysburg was an important battle of the Civil War because

A it was an overwhelming Confederate victory.
B the Union army's advance on the Confederate capital was stopped.
C it ended Lee's hopes of advancing into northern territory.
D it enabled the Union to control the Mississippi River.

3 Overall command of Confederate forces in Virginia during most of the Civil War was held by

A Jefferson Davis.
B William Tecumseh Sherman.
C Thomas "Stonewall" Jackson.
D Robert E. Lee.

4 Which of Lincoln's speeches and writings reflected the statement that "all men are created equal"?

A the Emancipation Proclamation
B the first inaugural address (1861)
C the second inaugural address (1865)
D the Gettysburg Address

5 The tactics that Sherman used against Confederate armies in the South were based on what strategy?

A cutting off troops from their officers
B a naval blockade of southern ports
C destroying the South's resources and economy
D hit-and-run attacks on major southern cities

6 In the War of 1812 the British navy blockaded American seaports in the hope that the U.S. economy would suffer and the United States would surrender. Which Civil War strategy was similar?

A Scott's plan to destroy the southern economy
B Sherman's March to the Sea
C General Ulysses S. Grant's capture of Vicksburg
D Admiral David Farragut's defeat of New Orleans

7 Read the following quote from Grant about Lee's surrender and use it to answer the question below.

> "What General Lee's feelings were I do not know. He was a man of much dignity, without expression on his face. It was impossible to say whether he felt inwardly glad that the end had finally come, or felt sad over the result, and was too manly to show it. Whatever his feelings, they were entirely hidden from me."
>
> –Ulysses S. Grant, adapted from *Personal Memoirs of U.S. Grant, Vol. 2*

Document-Based Question **What is your opinion about what Lee might have been feeling during his surrender?**

Answers

1. D
Break Down the Question This question requires students to interpret the map and then recall factual information. Have students first try to identify the location where two battles were fought and then find the location on the map.

2. C
Break Down the Question This question requires students to identify cause and effect. Refer students who miss the question to Section 5.

3. D
Break Down the Question This question requires students to recall factual information. Suggest that students first eliminate all non-Confederate leaders (B) to narrow their choices.

4 D
Break Down the Question This question requires students to recall the main points expressed in the Gettysburg Address. Refer students who have trouble to the text in Section 5 titled "The Gettysburg Address."

5. C
Break Down the Question This question requires students to identify the main idea. Refer students who have trouble to the text in Section 5 titled "Sherman Strikes the South."

6. A
Break Down the Question This question connects to information covered in Chapter 8.

7. Answers will vary but should reflect some understanding of the character of General Lee.
Break Down the Question This question requires students to reflect on General Lee's role in the war and then, based on this assessment, to imagine what his reaction might have been to having to surrender.

Intervention Resources

Reproducible

- Interactive Reader and Study Guide
- Differentiated Instruction Teacher Management System: Lesson Plans for Differentiated Instruction

Technology

- Quick Facts Transparency 44: The Civil War Visual Summary
- Differentiated Instruction Modified Worksheets and Tests CD-ROM
- Interactive Skills Tutor CD-ROM

Tips for Test Taking

Try, Try, Try Read the following to students: Keep at it. Don't give up. This sounds obvious, so why say it? You might be surprised by how many students do give up. Remember, the last question is worth just as much as the first question, and the questions do not get harder as you go. If the question you just finished was really hard, an easier one is probably coming up soon. Take a deep breath and keep on slogging. Give it your all, all the way to the end.

Chapter 17 Planning Guide

Reconstruction

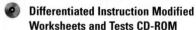

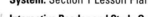

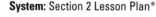

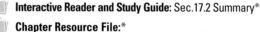

Chapter Overview	Reproducible Resources	Technology Resources
CHAPTER 17 **pp. 548–575** **Overview: In this chapter, students will learn about the challenges that faced the nation after the Civil War and the efforts made to meet those challenges.**	**Differentiated Instruction Teacher Management System:*** • Instructional Pacing Guides • Lesson Plans for Differentiated Instruction **Interactive Reader and Study Guide:** Chapter Summary Graphic Organizer* **Chapter Resource File:*** • Focus on Writing Activity: Job History • Social Studies Skills Activity: Chance, Oversight, and Error in History • Chapter Review Activity **Pre-AP Activities Guide for United States History:** Reconstruction*	**Power Presentations with Video CD-ROM** **Differentiated Instruction Modified Worksheets and Tests CD-ROM** **Primary Source Library CD-ROM for United States History** **Interactive Skills Tutor CD-ROM** **Student Edition on Audio CD Program** **History's Impact: United States History Video Program (VHS/DVD):** The Impact of the Preservation of the Union*
Section 1: **Rebuilding the South** **The Big Idea:** The nation faced many problems in rebuilding the Union.	**Differentiated Instruction Teacher Management System:** Section 1 Lesson Plan* **Interactive Reader and Study Guide:** Sec.17.1 Summary* **Chapter Resource File:*** • Vocabulary Builder Activity, Section 1 • Economics and History Activity: The Devastation of War • Biography Activity: Andrew Johnson **Political Cartoons Activities for United States History,** Cartoon 18: Lincoln Repairing the Union*	**Daily Bellringer Transparency 17.1*** go.hrw.com **Internet Activity:** Population Chart
Section 2: **The Fight over Reconstruction** **The Big Idea:** The return to power of the pre-war southern leadership led Republicans in Congress to take control of Reconstruction.	**Differentiated Instruction Teacher Management System:** Section 2 Lesson Plan* **Interactive Reader and Study Guide:** Sec.17.2 Summary* **Chapter Resource File:*** • Vocabulary Builder Activity, Section 2 • Biography Activity: Thaddeus Stevens • History and Geography Activity: The Reconstruction Acts	**Daily Bellringer Transparency 17.2*** **Map Transparency 57:** Reconstruction Military Districts* **Quick Facts Transparency 45:** The Reconstruction Amendments* go.hrw.com **Internet Activity:** Evaluate the Source
Section 3: **Reconstruction in the South** **The Big Idea:** As Reconstruction ended, African Americans faced new hurdles, and the South attempted to rebuild.	**Differentiated Instruction Teacher Management System:** Section 3 Lesson Plan* **Interactive Reader and Study Guide:** Sec.17.3 Summary* **Chapter Resource File:*** • Vocabulary Builder Activity, Section 3 • Biography Activity: Blanche K. Bruce • Primary Source Activity: Reconstruction and the Ku Klux Klan • Primary Source Activity: *Plessy* v. *Ferguson* • Literature Activity: The Jim Crow Laws **U.S. Supreme Court Case Studies:** *Plessy* v. *Ferguson* (1896)*	**Daily Bellringer Transparency 17.3*** **Map Transparency 58:** African American Representation in the South, 1870* **Quick Facts Transparency 46:** Hopes Raised and Denied* go.hrw.com **Internet Activity:** Reconstruction Poster

SE Student Edition | Print Resource | Audio CD
TE Teacher's Edition | Transparency | CD-ROM
go.hrw.com | **LS** Learning Styles | Video
TOS Indiana Teacher One Stop   * also on Indiana Teacher One Stop

Review, Assessment, Intervention

- **Quick Facts Transparency 47:** Reconstruction Visual Summary*
- **Spanish Chapter Summaries Audio CD Program**
- **Progress Assessment Support System (PASS):** Chapter Tests A and B*
- **Differentiated Instruction Modified Worksheets and Tests CD-ROM:** Modified Chapter Test
- **Online Chapter Summaries in Spanish**
- **Quiz Game CD-ROM**
- TOS **Indiana Teacher One Stop:** ExamView Test Generator (English/Spanish)
- **Alternative Assessment Handbook**
- HOAP **Holt Online Assessment Program,** in the Holt Premier Online Student Edition

---

- **PASS:** Section Quiz 17.1*
- **Online Quiz:** Section 17.1
- **Alternative Assessment Handbook**

- **PASS:** Section Quiz 17.2*
- **Online Quiz:** Section 17.2
- **Alternative Assessment Handbook**

- **PASS:** Section Quiz 17.3*
- **Online Quiz:** Section 17.3
- **Alternative Assessment Handbook**

HOLT
History's Impact
United States History Video Program (VHS/DVD)
The Impact of the Preservation of the Union
Suggested use: as a chapter introduction

Power Presentations with Video CD-ROM

Power Presentations with Video are visual presentations of each chapter's main ideas. Presentations can be customized by including Quick Facts charts, images from the text, and video clips.

DIVISION FOR PUBLIC EDUCATION
AMERICAN BAR ASSOCIATION

Developed by the Division for Public Education of the American Bar Association, these materials are part of the **Democracy and Civic Education Resources.**

- **Constitution Study Guide**
- **Supreme Court Case Studies**

Holt Online Learning

go.hrw.com
Teacher Resources
KEYWORD: SF7 TEACHER

go.hrw.com
Student Resources
KEYWORD: SF7 CH17

- Document-Based Questions
- Interactive Multimedia Activities
- Current Events
- Chapter-based Internet Activities
- and more!

Holt Interactive
Online Student Edition

Complete online support for interactivity, assessment, and reporting

- Interactive Maps and Notebook
- Standardized Test Prep
- Homework Practice and Research Activities Online

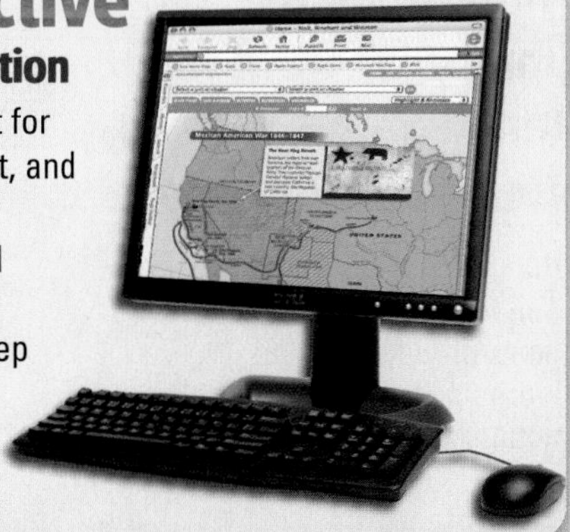

Differentiating Instruction

How do I address the needs of varied learners?

The Target Resource acts as your primary strategy for differentiated instruction.

ENGLISH-LANGUAGE LEARNERS & STRUGGLING READERS

TARGET RESOURCE

English-Language Learner Strategies and Activities

- Build Academic Vocabulary
- Develop Oral and Written Language Structures

Spanish Resources

Spanish Chapter Summaries Audio CD

Spanish Chapter Summaries Online

Teacher's One-Stop Planner:
- ExamView Test Generator, Spanish
- PuzzlePro, Spanish

Additional Resources

Differentiated Instruction Teacher Management System: Lesson Plans for Differentiated Instruction

Chapter Resources:
- Vocabulary Builder Activities
- Social Studies Skills Activity: Chance, Oversight, and Error in History

Quick Facts Transparencies:
- The Reconstruction Amendments (TR 45)
- Hopes Raised and Denied (TR 46)
- Reconstruction Visual Summary (TR 47)

Student Edition on Audio CD Program

Interactive Skills Tutor CD-ROM

SPECIAL NEEDS LEARNERS

TARGET RESOURCE

Differentiated Instruction Modified Worksheets and Tests CD-ROM

- Vocabulary Flash Cards
- Modified Vocabulary Builder Activities
- Modified Chapter Review Activity
- Modified Chapter Test

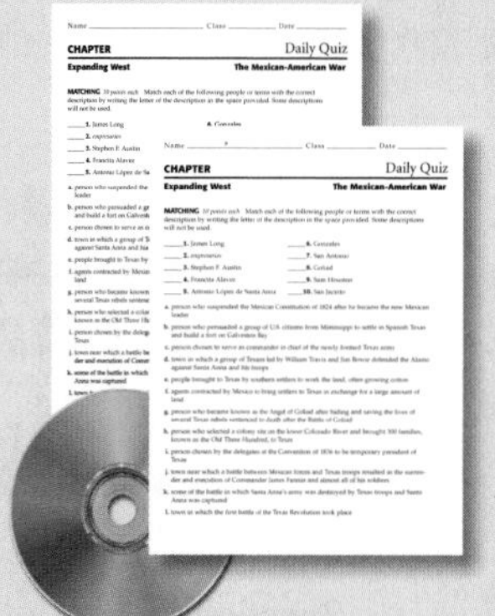

Additional Resources

Differentiated Instruction Teacher Management System: Lesson Plans for Differentiated Instruction

Interactive Reader and Study Guide

Social Studies Skills Activity: Chance, Oversight, and Error in History

Student Edition on Audio CD Program

Interactive Skills Tutor CD-ROM

ADVANCED/GIFTED-AND-TALENTED STUDENTS

TARGET RESOURCE

Primary Source Library CD-ROM for United States History

The Library contains longer versions of quotations in the text, extra sources, and images. Included are point-of-view articles, journals, diaries, historical fiction, and political documents.

Additional Resources

Differentiated Instruction Teacher Management System: Lesson Plans for Differentiated Instruction

Political Cartoons Activities for United States History: Cartoon 18: Lincoln Repairing the Union

Pre-AP Activities Guide for United States History: Reconstruction

Chapter Resource File:
- Focus on Writing Activity: Job History
- Literature Activity: The Jim Crow Laws
- Primary Source Activity: Reconstruction and the Ku Klux Klan
- Primary Source Activity: *Plessy* v. *Ferguson*

Differentiated Activities in the Teacher's Edition

- Reconstruction Acrostic, p. 559
- Letter to a Northern Newspaper, p. 569
- Southern African American Political Cartoon, p. 569

Differentiated Activities in the Teacher's Edition

- Reconstruction Plans Chart, p. 553
- Making Political Slogans, p. 565
- Cause-and-Effect Graphic Organizer, p. 566

Differentiated Activities in the Teacher's Edition

- Summary of Lincoln's 2nd Inaugural Address, p. 553
- Conducting an Impeachment Trial, p. 562
- End of Reconstruction Debate, p. 567
- Supreme Court Decisions, p. 568
- Paper on the word *Revolutionary,* p. 570

Teacher One Stop™

How can I manage the lesson plans and support materials for differentiated instruction?

With the Indiana Teacher One Stop, you can easily organize and print lesson plans, planning guides, and instructional materials for all learners.
The Indiana Teacher One Stop includes the following materials to help you differentiate instruction:

- Interactive Teacher's Edition
- Calendar Planner and pacing guides
- Editable lesson plans
- All reproducible ancillaries in Adobe Acrobat (PDF) format
- ExamView Test Generator (Eng & Span)
- Transparency and video previews

Professional Development

What teacher training resources are available to help me grow professionally?

- **In-service and staff development** as part of your Holt Social Studies product purchase
- **Quick Teacher Tutorial Lesson Presentation CD-ROM**
- Intensive tuition-based **Teacher Development Institute**
- **Convenient Holt Speaker Bureau –** face-to-face workshop options
- **PRAXIS™ Test Prep** interactive Web-based content refreshers*
- **Ask A Professional Development Expert** at http://www.hrw.com/prodev/

* PRAXIS is a trademark of Educational Testing Service (ETS).
This publication is not endorsed or approved by ETS.

Chapter Preview

Chapter Big Ideas

Section 1 The nation faced many problems in rebuilding the Union.

Section 2 The return to power of the pre-war southern leadership led Republicans in Congress to take control of Reconstruction.

Section 3 As Reconstruction ended, African Americans faced new hurdles and the South attempted to rebuild.

Focus on Writing

The **Chapter Resource File** provides a Focus on Writing worksheet to help students organize and write their job histories.

CRF: Focus on Writing Activity: Job History

Key to Differentiating Instruction

Below Level

Basic-level activities designed for all students encountering new material

At Level

Intermediate-level activities designed for average students

Above Level

Challenging activities designed for honors and gifted and talented students

Standard English Mastery

Activities designed to improve standard English usage

CHAPTER 17 1865–1877

Reconstruction

Indiana Standards

Social Studies Standards

8.1.22 Explain and evaluate the policies, practices, and consequences of Reconstruction, including the Thirteenth, Fourteenth, and Fifteenth Amendments to the Constitution.

8.1.26 Give examples of the changing role of women and minorities in the northern, southern, and western parts of the United States in the mid-nineteenth century, and examine possible causes for these changes.

8.2.3 Explain how and why legislative, executive, and judicial powers are distributed, shared, and limited in the constiutional government of the United States.

8.2.7 Explain the importance in a democratic republic of responsible participation by citizens in voluntary civil associations/nongovernmental organizations that comprise civil society.

go.hrw.com
Indiana
KEYWORD: SF10 IN

FOCUS ON WRITING

Job History When the Civil War ended, it was time to rebuild. People were ready to get back to work. But life had changed for many people and would continue to change. As you read this chapter, think about jobs people may have had during Reconstruction.

UNITED STATES

1865
Abraham Lincoln is assassinated.

1865

WORLD

1865
Black Jamaicans rebel against the wealthy planter class.

Introduce the Chapter

At Level

Focus on Rebuilding

1. Have students imagine that their town or city has been devastated by a natural disaster. For example, traffic signals do not work, hospitals and schools are closed, grocery stores have been stripped of food, and power and water plants have been destroyed.
2. Ask students to list, in order of importance, what the town should focus on rebuilding or replacing first. Ask for volunteers to share their lists with the class.
3. Explain to students that they will be learning about the efforts to rebuild and reunite the United States following the Civil War. Inform students that not only were cities and farmland destroyed but also the nation had to be put back together. Ask students to use their prior knowledge to predict what social, economic, and political issues might cause the North and South to disagree over priorities in rebuilding the nation. **LS Verbal/Linguistic**

HOLT

History's Impact

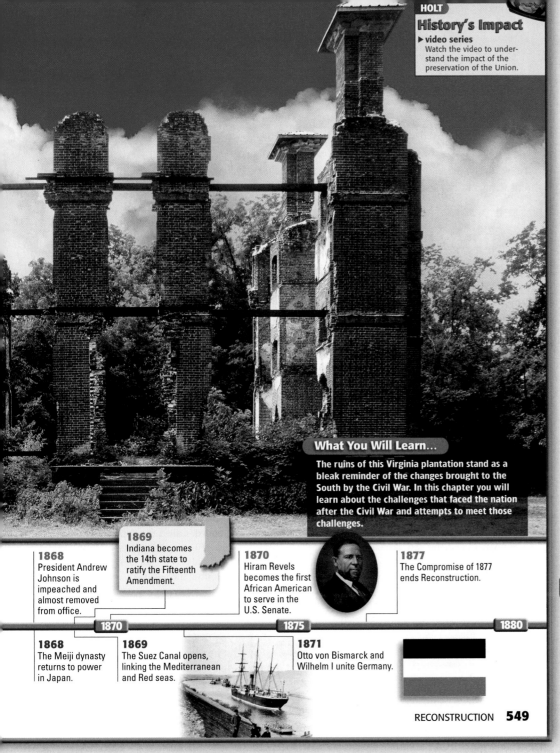

▸ **video series**
Watch the video to understand the impact of the preservation of the Union.

What You Will Learn...

The ruins of this Virginia plantation stand as a bleak reminder of the changes brought to the South by the Civil War. In this chapter you will learn about the challenges that faced the nation after the Civil War and attempts to meet those challenges.

1868 President Andrew Johnson is impeached and almost removed from office.

1869 Indiana becomes the 14th state to ratify the Fifteenth Amendment.

1870 Hiram Revels becomes the first African American to serve in the U.S. Senate.

1877 The Compromise of 1877 ends Reconstruction.

1870 — 1875 — 1880

1868 The Meiji dynasty returns to power in Japan.

1869 The Suez Canal opens, linking the Mediterranean and Red seas.

1871 Otto von Bismarck and Wilhelm I unite Germany.

• Chapter Preview •

HOLT

History's Impact

▸ **video series**
See the Video Teacher's Guide for strategies for using the chapter video to teach about the impact of the preservation of the Union.

Explore the Picture

Aftermath of War There are many ruins of plantations across the South today. Many plantations were damaged during the fighting that took place during the Civil War. Others were abandoned by their owners, who could no longer afford to run their plantations. The ruin reflected by this image shows the great challenges that faced the nation as it attempted to rebuild in the aftermath of the Civil War.

Analyzing Visuals How might the sight of abandoned or damaged plantations have affected people after the Civil War? *Wealthy southerners might have been angered or saddened by such sights. Former slaves might have felt justice had been served and seen the ruins as a symbol of the end of slavery.*

go.hrw.com

Online Resources

Chapter Resources:
KEYWORD: SF7 CH17

Teacher Resources:
KEYWORD: SF7 TEACHER

Explore the Time Line

1. In what year was President Abraham Lincoln assassinated? *1865*
2. What event occurred in Jamaica in the same year that Abraham Lincoln was assassinated? *Black Jamaicans rebelled against the planters.*
3. How many years passed between the assassination of Abraham Lincoln and the end of Reconstruction? *12 years*
4. Which president was impeached in 1868? *Andrew Johnson*

World Events

Connecting Two Seas In 1869 the Suez Canal opened, connecting the Mediterranean and Red seas. This artificial channel is just over 100 miles in length. Because the levels of both seas are relatively equal, the builders did not need to construct locks to raise or lower ships. The creation of the Suez Canal reduced the voyage from Europe to the Indian Ocean by about 5,000 miles. By 1945 the number of annual shipments through the canal peaked at 984,000. In recent years, however, traffic has dropped because more cargo is sent by other means.

Reading Social Studies

Understanding Themes

Point out to students that during Reconstruction, many political changes took place in an effort to mend the damage done by war and to grant rights to the newly-freed slaves. Ask students what political changes might have been necessary and how each change would have affected both the North and the South. What social and cultural changes might have taken place during Reconstruction? What different groups might have been affected by these changes? Help students understand the importance of these two themes.

Analyzing Historical Information

Focus on Reading Read students an article from a current, popular magazine or a short article from the local newspaper. Have students take notes as you read. Tell them to record only the relevant information from your reading. When finished, have several volunteers read their notes. Compile a list of the relevant information for all to see. Then guide students in a discussion of what was important, and what was not. Tell students that when they analyze historical information, they are using this same skill, figuring out what is important or relevant, and what is not.

Reading Social Studies

by Kylene Beers

Economics | Geography | **Politics** | **Society and Culture** | Science and Technology

Focus on Themes In this chapter you will read about the time immediately after the Civil War. You will see how the government tried to rebuild the South and will learn about how life changed for African Americans after slavery was declared illegal. You will read about the **political** conflicts that emerged as southern leadership worked to gain control of Reconstruction efforts. Throughout the chapter, you will read how the **culture** of the South changed after the War.

Analyzing Historical Information

Focus on Reading History books are full of information. As you read, you are confronted with names, dates, places, terms, and descriptions on every page. You don't want to have to deal with anything unimportant or untrue.

Identifying Relevant and Essential Information Information in a history book should be relevant to the topic you're studying. It should also be essential to understanding the topic and be verifiable. Anything else distracts from the material you are studying.

The first passage below includes several pieces of irrelevant and nonessential information. In the second, this information has been removed. Note how much easier the revised passage is to comprehend.

First Passage

President Abraham Lincoln, who was very tall, wanted to reunite the nation as quickly and painlessly as possible. He had proposed a plan for readmitting the southern states even before the war ended, which happened on a Sunday. Called the Ten Percent Plan, it offered southerners amnesty, or official pardon, for all illegal acts supporting the rebellion. Today a group called Amnesty International works to protect the rights of prisoners. Lincoln's plan certainly would have worked if it would have been implemented.

Lincoln's appearance and the day on which the war ended are not essential facts.

Amnesty International is not relevant to this topic.

There is no way to prove the accuracy of the last sentence.

Revised Passage

President Abraham Lincoln wanted to reunite the nation as quickly and painlessly as possible. He had proposed a plan for readmitting the southern states even before the war ended. Called the Ten Percent Plan, it offered southerners amnesty, or official pardon, for all illegal acts supporting the rebellion.

From Chapter 17, p. 553

Reading and Skills Resources

Reading Support

- Interactive Reader and Study Guide
- Student Edition on Audio CD Program
- Spanish Chapter Summaries Audio CD Program

Social Studies Skills Support

- Interactive Skills Tutor CD-ROM

Vocabulary Support

- **CRF:** Vocabulary Builder Activities
- **CRF:** Chapter Review Activity
- Differentiated Instruction Modified Worksheets and Tests CD-ROM:
  - Vocabulary Flash Cards
  - Vocabulary Builder Activity
  - Chapter Review Activity

OSP Holt PuzzlePro

You Try It!

The following passage is adapted from the chapter you are about to read. As you read, look for irrelevant, nonessential, or unverifiable information.

The Freedmen's Bureau

From Chapter 17, p. 556

In 1865 Congress established the Freedmen's Bureau, an agency providing relief for freedpeople and certain poor people in the South. The Bureau had a difficult job. It may have been one of the most difficult jobs ever. At its high point, about 900 agents served the entire South. All 900 people could fit into one hotel ballroom today. Bureau commissioner Oliver O. Howard eventually decided to use the Bureau's limited budget to distribute food to the poor and to provide education and legal help for freedpeople. One common food in the South at that time was salted meat. The Bureau also helped African American war veterans. Today the Department of Veterans' Affairs assists American war veterans.

After you read the passage, answer the following questions.

1. Which sentence in this passage is unverifiable and should be cut?
2. Find two sentences in this passage that are irrelevant to the discussion of the Freedmen's Bureau. What makes those sentences irrelevant?
3. Look at the last sentence of the passage. Do you think this sentence is essential to the discussion? Why or why not?

As you read Chapter 17, ask yourself what makes the information you are reading essential to a study of Reconstruction.

Key Terms and People

Chapter 17

Section 1
Reconstruction *(p. 552)*
Ten Percent Plan *(p. 553)*
Thirteenth Amendment *(p. 554)*
Freedmen's Bureau *(p. 556)*
Andrew Johnson *(p. 557)*

Section 2
Black Codes *(p. 558)*
Radical Republicans *(p. 559)*
Civil Rights Act of 1866 *(p. 560)*
Fourteenth Amendment *(p. 561)*
Reconstruction Acts *(p. 561)*
impeachment *(p. 562)*
Fifteenth Amendment *(p. 563)*

Section 3
Hiram Revels *(p. 565)*
Ku Klux Klan *(p. 566)*
Compromise of 1877 *(p. 567)*
poll tax *(p. 568)*
segregation *(p. 568)*
Jim Crow laws *(p. 568)*
Plessy v. *Ferguson* *(p. 569)*
sharecropping *(p. 569)*

Academic Vocabulary

Success in school is related to knowing academic vocabulary—the words that are frequently used in school assignments and discussions. In this chapter, you will learn the following academic words:

procedure *(p. 553)*
principle *(p. 560)*

Reading Social Studies

Key Terms and People

Introduce the key terms and people from this chapter by reviewing with the class each term and its description. Check to see that students understand the meaning of each term. Then have each student write three multiple-choice questions about terms or people from the list. Have students exchange questions with a partner and answer the questions. Have each pair review the correct answers together. **LS Verbal/Linguistic, Interpersonal**

Focus on Reading

See the **Focus on Reading** questions in this chapter for more practice on this reading social studies skill.

Reading Social Studies Assessment

See the **Chapter Review** at the end of this chapter for student assessment questions related to this reading skill.

Teaching Tip

Remind students that when there are quotes included in the text, it is important to read them and understand what the author is saying. Quotes may not necessarily include essential information; they may be reinforcing material that has already been discussed in the text. Sometimes, however, quotes by a well-known individual whose statements and beliefs were influential can be essential in analyzing historical information.

Answers

You Try It! 1. *It may have been one of the most difficult jobs ever.* **2.** *All 900 people could fit into one hotel ballroom today; One common food in the South at that time was salted meat; Today the Department of Veterans' Affairs assists American war veterans. They do not pertain to the Freedmen's Bureau.* **3.** *not essential; the paragraph is about the Freedmen's Bureau, not about current affairs*

Preteach

Bellringer

If YOU were there . . . Use the **Daily Bellringer Transparency** to help students answer the question.

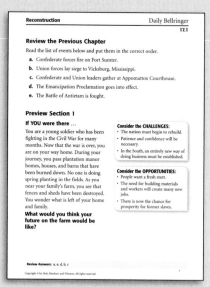

Daily Bellringer Transparency 17.1

Reconstruction — Daily Bellringer 17.1

Review the Previous Chapter

Read the list of events below and put them in the correct order.

a. Confederate forces fire on Fort Sumter.
b. Union forces lay siege to Vicksburg, Mississippi.
c. Confederate and Union leaders gather at Appomattox Courthouse.
d. The Emancipation Proclamation goes into effect.
e. The Battle of Antietam is fought.

Preview Section 1

If YOU were there ...

You are a young soldier who has been fighting in the Civil War for many months. Now that the war is over, you are on your way home. During your journey, you pass plantation manor homes, houses, and barns that have been burned down. No one is doing spring planting in the fields. As you near your family's farm, you see that fences and sheds have been destroyed. You wonder what is left of your home and family.

What would you think your future on the farm would be like?

Consider the CHALLENGES:
- The nation must begin to rebuild.
- Patience and confidence will be necessary.
- In the South, an entirely new way of doing business must be established.

Consider the OPPORTUNITIES:
- People want a fresh start.
- The need for building materials and workers will create many new jobs.
- There is now the chance for prosperity for former slaves.

Review Answers: a, e, d, b, c

Academic Vocabulary

Review with students the high-use academic term in this section.

procedure a series of steps taken to accomplish a task (p. 553)

CRF: Vocabulary Builder Activity, Section 1

Taking Notes

Have students copy the graphic organizer onto their own paper and then use it to take notes on the section. This activity will prepare students for the Section Assessment, in which they will complete a graphic organizer that builds on the information using a critical-thinking skill.

Section Correlations

IN

8.1.22 Explain and evaluate the policies, practices, and consequences of Reconstruction, including the Thirteenth, Fourteenth and Fifteenth Amendments to the Constitution.
8.1.26 Give examples of the changing role of women and minorities in the northern, southern, and western parts of the United States in the mid-nineteenth century, and examine possible causes for these changes.
8.2.7 Explain the importance in a democratic republic of responsible participation by citizens in voluntary civil associations/ nongovernmental organizations that comprise civil society.

SECTION 1

Rebuilding the South

What You Will Learn...

Main Ideas

1. President Lincoln and Congress differed in their views as Reconstruction began.
2. The end of the Civil War meant freedom for African Americans in the South.
3. President Johnson's plan began the process of Reconstruction.

The Big Idea

The nation faced many problems in rebuilding the Union.

Key Terms and People

Reconstruction, *p. 552*
Ten Percent Plan, *p. 553*
Thirteenth Amendment, *p. 554*
Freedmen's Bureau, *p. 556*
Andrew Johnson, *p. 557*

TAKING NOTES As you read, take notes on the different ways the U.S. government attempted to reconstruct the south after the Civil War. Write your notes in a graphic organizer like the one below.

Rebuilding and Reconstruction
1.
2.
3.
4.
5.
6.
7.

IN 8.1.22, 8.1.24, 8.1.26, 8.2.7

If YOU were there...

You are a young soldier who has been fighting in the Civil War for many months. Now that the war is over, you are on your way home. During your journey, you pass plantation manor homes, houses, and barns that have been burned down. No one is doing spring planting in the fields. As you near your family's farm, you see that fences and sheds have been destroyed. You wonder what is left of your home and family.

What would you think your future on the farm would be like?

BUILDING BACKGROUND When the Civil War ended, much of the South lay in ruins. Like the young soldier above, many people returned to destroyed homes and farms. Harvests of corn, cotton, rice, and other crops fell far below normal. Many farm animals had been killed or were roaming free. These were some of the challenges in restoring the nation.

Reconstruction Begins

After the Civil War ended in 1865, the U.S. government faced the problem of dealing with the defeated southern states. The challenges of **Reconstruction**, the process of readmitting the former Confederate states to the Union, lasted from 1865 to 1877.

Teach the Big Idea

At Level

Rebuilding the South

1. **Teach** To teach the main ideas in the section, use the questions in the Direct Teach boxes.
2. **Apply** Have each student examine the main ideas for this section. Then have students create as many questions for each main idea as they can. For example, for the first main idea, students might ask why President Lincoln and Congress differed in their views about Reconstruction. **LS Verbal/Linguistic**
3. **Review** Have students review the section and provide answers for each of the questions they created.
4. **Practice/Homework** Have students use their questions and answers to write a one-page summary about the effect that rebuilding the South had on American society. **LS Verbal/Linguistic**

Alternative Assessment Handbook, Rubric 1: Acquiring Information

Damaged South

Tired southern soldiers returned home to find that the world they had known before the war was gone. Cities, towns, and farms had been ruined. Because of high food prices and widespread crop failures, many southerners faced starvation. The Confederate money held by most southerners was now worthless. Banks failed, and merchants had gone bankrupt because people could not pay their debts.

Former Confederate general Braxton Bragg was one of many southerners who faced economic hardship. He found that "*all, all* was lost, except my debts." In South Carolina, Mary Boykin Chesnut wrote in her diary about the isolation she experienced after the war. "We are shut in here . . . All RR's [railroads] destroyed—bridges gone. We are cut off from the world."

Lincoln's Plan

President Abraham Lincoln wanted to reunite the nation as quickly and painlessly as possible. He had proposed a plan for readmitting the southern states even before the war ended. Called the **Ten Percent Plan**, it offered southerners amnesty, or official pardon, for all illegal acts supporting the rebellion. To receive amnesty, southerners had to do two things. They had to swear an oath of loyalty to the United States. They also had to agree that slavery was illegal. Once 10 percent of voters in a state made these pledges, they could form a new government. The state then could be readmitted to the Union.

Louisiana quickly elected a new state legislature under the Ten Percent Plan. Other southern states that had been occupied by Union troops soon followed Louisiana back into the United States.

Wade-Davis Bill

Some politicians argued that Congress, not the president, should control the southern states' return to the Union. They believed that Congress had the power to admit new states. Also, many Republican members of Congress thought the Ten Percent Plan did not go far enough. A senator from Michigan expressed their views.

> "The people of the North are not such fools as to . . . turn around and say to the traitors, 'all you have to do [to return] is . . . take an oath that henceforth you will be true to the Government.'"
>
> –Senator Jacob Howard, quoted in *Reconstruction: America's Unfinished Revolution, 1863–1877*, by Eric Foner

Two Republicans—Senator Benjamin Wade and Representative Henry Davis—had an alternative to Lincoln's plan. Following procedures of the Wade-Davis bill, a state had to meet two conditions before it could rejoin the Union. First, it had to ban slavery. Second, a majority of adult males in the state had to take the loyalty oath.

ACADEMIC VOCABULARY

procedure a series of steps taken to accomplish a task

War destroyed Richmond, Virginia, once the capital of the Confederacy.

Direct Teach

Main Idea

1 Reconstruction Begins

President Lincoln and Congress differed in their views as Reconstruction began.

Describe What problems did the South face following the Civil War? *cities, towns, and farms destroyed; high food prices; crops destroyed; Confederate money worthless; failed banks; merchants bankrupt*

Evaluate Which plan would you have supported, the Ten Percent Plan or the Wade-Davis Bill? Why? *possible answers: Ten Percent—It would reunite the nation faster and not be too harsh on the South; Wade-Davis—it would be stricter on the South.*

- **CRF:** Economics and History Activity: The Devastation of War
- Political Cartoons Activities for United States History, Cartoon 18: Lincoln Repairing the Union

Did you know . . .

Louisiana was the first Confederate state to meet the requirements of Lincoln's Ten Percent Plan. Occupied by Union military forces during the Civil War, the state held a convention in 1864 and drafted a new constitution outlawing slavery. Despite the state's having met the president's requirements for readmission to the Union, Congress refused to allow Louisiana representatives to take their seats in Washington.

Differentiating Instruction

Advanced/Gifted and Talented

Above Level | Research Required

1. Have students locate and read a copy of Abraham Lincoln's second inaugural address.
2. Have each student write a short summary of the speech, including a short explanation of Lincoln's views on Reconstruction.
3. Discuss with students their interpretations of Lincoln's ideas. **LS Verbal/Linguistic**

Special Needs Learners

Below Level

1. To help students answer the guided reading question, draw a T-chart for students to see. Label one side of the chart *Ten Percent Plan* and the other *Wade-Davis Bill.* Have each student copy and complete the chart.
2. Review with students the characteristics of each plan for Reconstruction. **LS Verbal/Linguistic**

Direct Teach

Primary Source

Reading Like a Historian

Analyzing Visuals Help students practice reading the documents like historians. Ask

- Who placed the advertisement? Why? *Saml. [Samuel] Dove; looking for family members who were separated and sold to different slaveholders*
- Why might the people on the boat be leaving Richmond? *possible answers—The city has been damaged in the war; African Americans are leaving the South now that they are free.*

Info to Know

Pocket Veto The U.S. Congress approved the Wade-Davis Bill just before adjourning in 1864. The end of the congressional session made it possible for President Lincoln to use a pocket veto to kill the measure. Usually, if a president does not sign a bill within 10 days while Congress is in session, the bill automatically becomes a law. However, if Congress is adjourned, a bill dies if the president does not sign it. A pocket veto cannot be overturned by a congressional vote.

Testing New Freedoms

aug5 Secretary.

SAML. DOVE wishes to know of the whereabouts of his mother, Areno, his sisters Maria, Neziah, and Peggy, and his brother Edmond, who were owned by Geo. Dove, of Rockingham county, Shenandoah Valley, Va. Sold in Richmond, after which Saml. and Edmond were taken to Nashville, Tenn., by Joe Mick; Areno was left at the Eagle Tavern, Richmond

Respectfully yours,
SAML. DOVE.

Utica, New York, Aug. 5, 1865–3m

U. S. CHRISTIAN COMMISSION,
NASHVILLE, TENN., July 19, 1865.

Under the Wade-Davis bill, only southerners who swore that they had never supported the Confederacy could vote or hold office. In general, the bill was much stricter than the Ten Percent Plan. Its provisions would make it harder for southern states to rejoin the Union quickly.

President Lincoln therefore refused to sign the bill into law. He thought that few southern states would agree to meet its requirements. He believed that his plan would help restore order more quickly.

READING CHECK **Contrasting** How was the Ten Percent Plan different from the Wade-Davis bill?

Freedom for African Americans

One thing Republicans agreed on was abolishing slavery. The Emancipation Proclamation had freed slaves only in areas that had not been occupied by Union forces, not in the border states. Many people feared that the federal courts might someday declare the proclamation unconstitutional.

Slavery Ends

On January 31, 1865, at President Lincoln's urging, Congress proposed the **Thirteenth Amendment**. This amendment made slavery illegal throughout the United States.

Collaborative Learning

At Level

Congressional Committees

1. Review with students the Reconstruction plans of Congress and President Lincoln. Ask students why Congress might have opposed the Ten Percent Plan and what Lincoln disliked about the Wade-Davis Bill.
2. Organize students into small groups. Ask them to imagine that they are members of Congress in 1864. Have them work in committees to write a plan that they think Lincoln would have accepted for readmitting the states. Encourage students to consider what rules they would set to ensure that ex-Confederates would support the Union and end slavery. Remind students to use standard grammar, spelling, sentence structure, and punctuation in their plans.
3. Ask groups to present their plans to the class. After all groups have presented their proposals, lead a class discussion of the pros and cons of each plan. **LS Interpersonal, Verbal/Linguistic**

Alternative Assessment Handbook, Rubrics 14: Group Activity; and 24: Oral Presentations

Answers

Reading Check *Ten Percent Plan—Ten percent of all voters in Confederate states had to pledge loyalty to the Union and accept slavery as illegal; Wade-Davis bill—A majority of voters in Confederate states had to pledge loyalty to the Union, and only southerners who had never supported the Confederacy could vote or hold office.*

The freedpeople at left have packed their household belongings and are leaving Richmond. Many people traveled in search of relatives. Others placed newspaper advertisements looking for long-lost relatives. For other freedpeople, like the couple above, freedom brought the right to marry.

In what ways did former slaves react to freedom?

The amendment was ratified and took effect on December 18, 1865. When abolitionist William Lloyd Garrison heard the news, he declared that his work was now finished. He called for the American Anti-Slavery Society to break up. Not all abolitionists agreed that their work was done, however. Frederick Douglass insisted that "slavery is not abolished until the black man has the ballot [vote]."

Freedom brought important changes to newly freed slaves. Many couples held ceremonies to legalize marriages that had not been recognized under slavery. Many freedpeople searched for relatives who had been sold away from their families years earlier. Others placed newspaper ads seeking information about their children. Many women began to work at home instead of in the fields. Still others adopted children of dead relatives to keep families together. Church members established voluntary associations and mutual-aid societies to help those in need.

Now that they could travel without a pass, many freedpeople moved from mostly white counties to places with more African Americans. Other freedpeople traveled simply to test their new freedom of movement. A South Carolina woman explained this need. "I must go, if I stay here I'll never know I'm free."

For most former slaves, freedom to travel was just the first step on a long road toward equal rights and new ways of life. Adults took new last names and began to insist on being called Mr. or Mrs. as a sign of respect, rather than by their first names or by nicknames. Freedpeople began to demand the same economic and political rights as white citizens. Henry Adams, a former slave, argued that "if I cannot do like a white man I am not free."

Forty Acres to Farm?

Many former slaves wanted their own land to farm. Near the end of the Civil War, Union general William Tecumseh Sherman had issued an order to break up plantations in coastal South Carolina and Georgia. He wanted to divide the land into 40-acre plots and give them to former slaves as compensation for their forced labor before the war.

Many white planters refused to surrender their land. Some freedpeople pointed out that it was only fair that they receive some of this land because their labor had made the plantations prosper. In the end, the U.S. government returned the land to its original owners. At this time, many freedpeople were unsure about where they would live, what kind of work they would do, and what rights they had. Freedoms that were theirs by law were difficult to enforce.

Direct Teach

Main Idea

❷ Freedom for African Americans

The end of the Civil War meant freedom for African Americans in the South.

Identify Which amendment abolished slavery? *the Thirteenth*

Explain After the Civil War, why did some African Americans feel they were not free? *They could not vote and did not have the same economic and political rights as white men did.*

Draw Inferences Why might some newly freed slaves choose to remain in the South? *possible answers—It was familiar; they had family there.*

go.hrw.com
Online Resources

KEYWORD: SF7 CH17
ACTIVITY: Population Chart

MISCONCEPTION ALERT

Resettlement Some students might assume that African Americans flocked to the North after gaining their freedom. Point out to students that in fact most freedpeople remained in the South. Many moved to southern cities and towns where African American schools and churches created a sense of community. Other freedpeople chose to remain near the plantations they had known all their lives.

Critical Thinking: Summarizing

At Level

Creating a Documentary Film

1. Review with students the effect that freedom had on many African Americans. Discuss the various changes that occurred as well as the effect those changes had on the lives of former slaves.
2. Ask students to imagine that they are documentary filmmakers living during the period of Reconstruction. Their assignment is to create a documentary about the changes African Americans experienced after the ratification of the Thirteenth Amendment.
3. Have students create storyboards for their documentaries. Remind students to consider who they would interview for the film, what scenes they would like to show, and what changes they might focus on.
4. Once the storyboards are complete, have each student write an introduction and conclusion for his or her film. LS **Verbal/Linguistic, Visual/Spatial**

Alternative Assessment Handbook, Rubric 41: Writing to Express

Answers

Testing New Freedoms *pursued new opportunities, married, looked for long-lost relatives, traveled*

Direct Teach

Main Idea

❷ Freedom for African Americans

The end of the Civil War meant freedom for African Americans in the South.

Recall What were the goals of the Freedmen's Bureau? *to distribute food to poor people, provide education and legal help for freedpeople, and assist African American war veterans*

Describe Who taught at the schools for African Americans? *mostly women who were committed to helping freedpeople*

Make Inferences How did education for African Americans benefit both black and white southerners? *possible answers—created access to better education, provided more educated workers*

Linking to Today

Howard University Howard University was named for Oliver O. Howard, the head of the Freedmen's Bureau. The university opened in May 1867 in response to the move to provide more educational opportunities for freedpeople. The original goal of the school was "training for preachers and teachers." From the beginning, Howard University was open to men and women of all races. Today Howard University has expanded to include schools of law, dentistry, medicine, education, social work, business, and more.

Answers

Helping the Freedpeople *See the bulleted list above the question.*

Reading Check *It helped establish schools and several colleges in the South.*

Freedmen's Bureau

In 1865 Congress established the **Freedmen's Bureau**, an agency providing relief for freedpeople and certain poor people in the South. The Bureau had a difficult job. At its high point, about 900 agents served the entire South. Bureau commissioner Oliver O. Howard eventually decided to use the Bureau's limited budget to distribute food to the poor and to provide education and legal help for freedpeople. The Bureau also helped African American war veterans.

The Freedmen's Bureau played an important role in establishing more schools in the South. Laws against educating slaves meant that most freedpeople had never learned to read or write. Before the war ended, however, northern groups, such as the American Missionary Association, began providing books and teachers to African Americans. The teachers were mostly women who were committed to helping freedpeople. One teacher said of her students, "I never before saw children so eager to learn . . . It is wonderful how [they] . . . can have so great a desire for knowledge, and such a capacity for attaining [reaching] it."

After the war, some freedpeople organized their own education efforts. For example, Freedmen's Bureau agents found that some African Americans had opened schools in abandoned buildings. Many white southerners continued to believe that African Americans should not be educated. Despite opposition, by 1869 more than 150,000 African American students were attending more than 3,000 schools. The Freedmen's Bureau also helped establish a number of universities for African Americans, including Howard and Fisk universities.

Students quickly filled the new classrooms. Working adults attended classes in the evening. African Americans hoped that education would help them to understand and protect their rights and to enable them to find better jobs. Both black and white southerners benefited from the effort to provide greater access to education in the South.

READING CHECK **Analyzing** How did the Freedmen's Bureau help reform education in the South?

Helping the Freedpeople

Congress created the Freedmen's Bureau to help freedpeople and poor southerners recover from the Civil War. The Bureau assisted people by:

- **providing supplies and medical services**
- **establishing schools**
- **supervising contracts between freedpeople and employers**
- **taking care of lands abandoned or captured during the war**

What role did the Freedmen's Bureau play during Reconstruction?

556

Critical Thinking: Supporting a Point of View

At Level

Writing a Proposal

1. Review with students the goals and accomplishments of the Freedmen's Bureau. Then ask students to imagine that they are serving on a committee working to promote the contributions of the Freedmen's Bureau.
2. Organize students into pairs. Ask each pair to select some method of honoring and promoting the accomplishments of the Freedmen's Bureau. Examples might include a commemorative postage stamp, a statue or historical marker, or even a national holiday. Have students develop the specifics for their plans.
3. Have each pair of students write a proposal that explains why the Freedmen's Bureau deserves an honor and what the memorial would be like. Encourage students to create an image of the memorial, if applicable.
4. Have volunteers share their proposals with the class. **LS Interpersonal, Visual/Spatial**

Alternative Assessment Handbook, Rubric 43: Writing to Persuade

President Johnson's Reconstruction Plan

While the Freedmen's Bureau was helping African Americans, the issue of how the South would politically rejoin the Union remained unresolved. Soon, however, a tragic event ended Lincoln's dream of peacefully reuniting the country.

A New President

On the evening of April 14, 1865, President Lincoln and his wife attended a play at Ford's Theater in Washington, D.C. During the play, John Wilkes Booth, a southerner who opposed Lincoln's policies, sneaked into the president's theater box and shot him. Lincoln was rushed to a boardinghouse across the street, where he died early the next morning. Vice President **Andrew Johnson** was sworn into office quickly. Reconstruction had now become his responsibility. He would have to win the trust of a nation shocked at its leader's death.

Johnson's plan for bringing southern states back into the Union was similar to Lincoln's plan. However, he decided that wealthy southerners and former Confederate officials would need a presidential pardon to receive amnesty. Johnson shocked Radical Republicans by eventually pardoning more than 7,000 people by 1866.

New State Governments

Johnson was a Democrat whom Republicans had put on the ticket in 1864 to appeal to the border states. A former slaveholder, he was a stubborn man who would soon face a hostile Congress.

Johnson offered a mild program for setting up new southern state governments. First, he appointed a temporary governor for each state. Then he required that the states revise their constitutions. Next, voters elected state and federal representatives. The new state government had to declare that secession was illegal. It also had to ratify the Thirteenth Amendment and refuse to pay Confederate debts.

By the end of 1865, all the southern states except Texas had created new governments. Johnson approved them all and declared that the United States was restored. Newly elected representatives came to Washington from each reconstructed southern state. However, Republicans complained that many new representatives had been leaders of the Confederacy. Congress therefore refused to readmit the southern states into the Union. Clearly, the nation was still divided.

READING CHECK **Summarizing** What was President Johnson's plan for Reconstruction?

SUMMARY AND PREVIEW In this section you learned about early plans for Reconstruction. In the next section, you will learn that disagreements about Reconstruction became so serious that the president was almost removed from office.

Section 1 Assessment

go.hrw.com
Online Quiz
KEYWORD: SF7 HP17

Reviewing Ideas, Terms, and People

1. **a. Identify** What does **Reconstruction** mean?
   b. Summarize What was President Lincoln's plan for Reconstruction?
2. **a. Recall** What is the **Thirteenth Amendment**?
   b. Elaborate In your opinion, what was the most important accomplishment of the **Freedmen's Bureau**? Explain.
3. **a. Recall** Why was President Lincoln killed?
   b. Analyze Why did some Americans oppose President Johnson's Reconstruction plan?

Critical Thinking

4. **Summarizing** Review your notes on Reconstruction. Then copy the graphic organizer below and use it to show how African Americans were affected by the end of the war.

FOCUS ON WRITING

5. **Considering Historical Context** Many people planned to continue doing what they had done before the war. Others planned to start a new life. How do you think events and conditions you just read about might have affected their plans?

Direct Teach

Main Idea

❸ President Johnson's Reconstruction Plan

President Johnson's plan began the process of Reconstruction.

Explain After President Johnson approved the new governments of the southern states, Republicans complained. Why? *complained that many of the new southern representatives had been Confederate leaders and that Johnson's plan was too lenient on the South*

CRF: Biography Activity: Andrew Johnson

Review & Assess

Close

Have students write a short paragraph that summarizes the section.

Review

Online Quiz, Section 17.1

Assess

SE Section 1 Assessment

PASS: Section Quiz 17.1

Alternative Assessment Handbook

Reteach/Classroom Intervention

Interactive Reader and Study Guide, Section 17.1

Interactive Skills Tutor CD-ROM

Section 1 Assessment Answers

1. **a.** the process of reuniting and rebuilding the nation after the Civil War
   b. offer amnesty if people swore loyalty to the U.S. and agreed that slavery was illegal; a state could be readmitted once 10 percent of the state's voters had done this
2. **a.** a constitutional amendment that made slavery illegal in the United States
   b. possible answer—creating more educational opportunities in the South; creating a better educated workforce
3. **a.** Booth opposed Lincoln's policies.
   b. New representatives from the South had been Confederate leaders.
4. family members could search for each other; women worked in the home; families could stay together; traveled; took new names; began demanding same rights as white people
5. Aftermath of war made it impossible for some to resume former life; others gained new opportunities.

Answers

Reading Check *Johnson wanted southern states to revise their constitutions, elect new representatives, declare secession illegal, and ratify the Thirteenth Amendment.*

Preteach

Bellringer

If YOU were there . . . Use the **Daily Bellringer Transparency** to help students answer the question.

Daily Bellringer Transparency 17.2

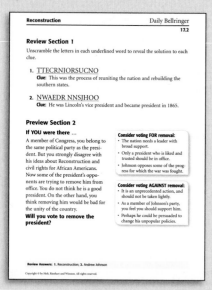

Reconstruction — Daily Bellringer **17.2**

Review Section 1

Unscramble the letters in each underlined word to reveal the solution to each clue.

1. TTECRNIORSUCNO
   Clue: This was the process of reuniting the nation and rebuilding the southern states.
2. NWAEDR NNSJHOO
   Clue: He was Lincoln's vice president and became president in 1865.

Preview Section 2

If YOU were there ...

A member of Congress, you belong to the same political party as the president. But you strongly disagree with his ideas about Reconstruction and civil rights for African Americans. Now some of the president's opponents are trying to remove him from office. You do not think he is a good president. On the other hand, you think removing him would be bad for the unity of the country.

Will you vote to remove the president?

Consider voting FOR removal:
- The nation needs a leader with broad support.
- Only a president who is liked and trusted should be in office.
- Johnson opposes some of the progress for which the war was fought.

Consider voting AGAINST removal:
- It is an unprecedented action, and should not be taken lightly.
- As a member of Johnson's party, you feel you should support him.
- Perhaps he could be persuaded to change his unpopular policies.

Review Answers: 1. Reconstruction; 2. Andrew Johnson

Academic Vocabulary

Review with students the high-use academic term in this section.

principle basic belief, rule, or law (p. 560)

Building Vocabulary

Preteach or review the following term:

moderate one who holds views that are not extreme or excessive (p. 559)

CRF: Vocabulary Builder Activity, Section 2

Taking Notes

Have students copy the graphic organizer onto their own paper and then use it to take notes on the section. This activity will prepare students for the Section Assessment, in which they will complete a graphic organizer that builds on the information using a critical-thinking skill.

Section Correlations

IN

8.1.22 Explain and evaluate the policies, practices, and consequences of Reconstruction, including the Thirteenth, Fourteenth and Fifteenth Amendments to the Constitution.
8.1.24 Identify the influence of individuals on political and social events and movements, such as the abolition movement, the Dred Scott case, women's rights and Native American Indian removal.

SECTION 2

The Fight over Reconstruction

What You Will Learn...

Main Ideas

1. Black Codes led to opposition to President Johnson's plan for Reconstruction.
2. The Fourteenth Amendment ensured citizenship for African Americans.
3. Radical Republicans in Congress took charge of Reconstruction.
4. The Fifteenth Amendment gave African Americans the right to vote.

The Big Idea

The return to power of the pre-war southern leadership led Republicans in Congress to take control of Reconstruction.

Key Terms and People

Black Codes, *p. 558*
Radical Republicans, *p. 559*
Civil Rights Act of 1866, *p. 560*
Fourteenth Amendment, *p. 561*
Reconstruction Acts, *p. 561*
impeachment, *p. 562*
Fifteenth Amendment, *p. 563*

TAKING NOTES As you read, take notes on how Republicans in Congress took over Reconstruction and how they changed Reconstruction policies. Write your notes in a graphic organizer like the one below.

Issues that Concerned Republicans	Changes by the Republican Congress

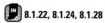

IN 8.1.22, 8.1.24, 8.1.28

If YOU were there...

A member of Congress, you belong to the same political party as the president. But you strongly disagree with his ideas about Reconstruction and civil rights for African Americans. Now some of the president's opponents are trying to remove him from office. You do not think he is a good president. On the other hand, you think removing him would be bad for the unity of the country.

Will you vote to remove the president?

BUILDING BACKGROUND Americans were bitterly divided about what should happen in the South during Reconstruction. They disagreed about ending racial inequality and guaranteeing civil rights for African Americans. These conflicts split political parties. They led to showdowns between Congress and the president. Political fights even threatened the president's job.

Opposition to President Johnson

In 1866 Congress continued to debate the rules for restoring the Union. Meanwhile, new state legislatures approved by President Johnson had already begun passing laws to deny African Americans' civil rights. "This is a white man's government, and intended for white men only," declared Governor Benjamin F. Perry of South Carolina.

Black Codes

Soon, every southern state passed **Black Codes**, or laws that greatly limited the freedom of African Americans. They required African Americans to sign work contracts, creating working conditions similar to those under slavery. In most southern states, any African Americans who could not prove they were employed could be arrested. Their punishment might be one year of work without pay. African Americans were also prevented from owning guns. In addition, they were not allowed to rent property except in cities.

The Black Codes alarmed many Americans. As one Civil War veteran asked, "If you call this freedom, what do you call slavery?"

Teach the Big Idea

At Level

The Fight over Reconstruction

1. **Teach** To teach the main ideas in the section, use the questions in the Direct Teach boxes.
2. **Apply** Draw a four-column chart for students to see. Label the columns *Opposition to President Johnson, Fourteenth Amendment, Congress Takes Control,* and *Fifteenth Amendment.* Have each student make a copy of the chart and complete it by listing the section's main ideas and events in the appropriate column. **LS Verbal/Linguistic**
3. **Review** To review the section's main ideas, have students help you complete the master copy of the chart.
4. **Practice/Homework** For each column in the chart, have students write one to three sentences summarizing the information they identified. **LS Verbal/Linguistic**

Alternative Assessment Handbook, Rubric 7: Charts

African Americans organized to oppose the codes. One group sent a petition to officials in South Carolina.

> "We simply ask . . . that the same laws which govern *white men* shall govern *black men* . . . that, in short, we be dealt with as others are—in equity [equality] and justice."
>
> —Petition from an African American convention held in South Carolina, quoted in *There Is a River: The Black Struggle for Freedom in America* by Vincent Harding

Radical Republicans

The Black Codes angered many Republicans. They thought the South was returning to its old ways. Most Republicans were moderates who wanted the South to have loyal state governments. They also believed that African Americans should have rights as citizens. They hoped that the government would not have to force the South to follow federal laws.

Radical Republicans, on the other hand, took a harsher stance. They wanted the federal government to force change in the South. Like the moderates, they thought the Black Codes were cruel and unjust. The Radicals, however, wanted the federal government to be much more involved in Reconstruction. They feared that too many southern leaders remained loyal to the former Confederacy and would not enforce the new laws. Thaddeus Stevens

Primary Source

POLITICAL CARTOON

Supporting Radical Republican Ideas

Republicans were outraged to see former Confederates return to power as leaders of the Democratic Party. This 1868 political cartoon shows former Confederates Raphael Semmes and Nathan Bedford Forrest. Semmes was a Confederate admiral who had captured 62 Union merchant ships during the Civil War. Forrest was a cavalry officer known for brutality who later founded the Ku Klux Klan.

How do the actions of the people in these illustrations support the artist's point of view?

How do events in the background of these illustrations support the artist's point of view?

ANALYSIS SKILL **ANALYZING PRIMARY SOURCES**

Why do you think that the men are shown in their Confederate uniforms?

Direct Teach

Main Idea

1 Opposition to President Johnson

Black Codes led to opposition to President Johnson's plan for Reconstruction.

Describe In what ways did Black Codes limit the freedom of African Americans? *by requiring them to sign work contracts and to have a job or be subject to arrest, and by forbidding the ownership of guns and the rental of property in cities*

Explain What were Radical Republicans' goals for Reconstruction? *They wanted the federal government to be much more involved and the South to change much more before returning to the Union.*

Primary Source

Reading Like a Historian

Supporting Radical Republican Ideas Help students practice reading the political cartoon like historians. Ask

- What is the point of view expressed in the political cartoon?
- Does the cartoon appear to be objective about the subject matter? What indicates that?

Differentiating Instruction

Below Level

English-Language Learners

1. Organize students into mixed-ability pairs. Have each pair review the information on opposition to President Johnson's Reconstruction plan.
2. Explain to students that an acrostic is a type of poem in which the first letter from each line spells out a word. Have students create an acrostic for one of the key terms or people discussed under this heading. Each acrostic should reflect the views or concepts associated with the key term or person. You may want to model an example for the class by using a person or idea from the previous section for your acrostic.
3. As students work on their acrostics, they might require assistance thinking of words to fit in their poem. Help students or refer them to a thesaurus. **LS Verbal/Linguistic**

Alternative Assessment Handbook, Rubric 26: Poems and Songs

Answers

Analyzing Primary Sources *possible answers—to show that they are still Confederates at heart; to show that the Confederacy condoned their actions*

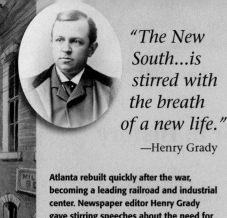

"The New South...is stirred with the breath of a new life."

—Henry Grady

Atlanta rebuilt quickly after the war, becoming a leading railroad and industrial center. Newspaper editor Henry Grady gave stirring speeches about the need for industry in the South. He became one of the best-known spokesmen of the "New South."

Why might Grady point to Atlanta as a model for economic change?

Southern Mill Life

Work in the cotton mills appealed to farm families who had trouble making ends meet. As one mill worker explained, "It was a necessity to move and get a job, rather than depend on the farm." Recruiters sent out by the mills promised good wages and steady work.

Entire families often worked in the same cotton mill. Mills employed large numbers of women and children. Many children started working at about the age of 12. Some children started working at an even earlier age. Women did most of the spinning and were valued workers. However, few women had the opportunity to advance within the company.

Many mill workers were proud of the skills they used, but they did not enjoy their work. One unhappy worker described it as "the same thing over and over again . . . The more you do, the more they want done." Workers often labored 12 hours a day, six days a week. Cotton dust and lint filled the air, causing asthma and an illness known as brown-lung disease. Fast-moving machinery caused injuries and even deaths. Despite the long hours and dangerous working conditions, wages remained low. However, mill work did offer an alternative to farming.

READING CHECK **Finding Main Ideas** What did southern business leaders hope industry would do?

SUMMARY AND PREVIEW In this section you learned about the end of Reconstruction. In the next chapter you will learn about America's continued westward expansion.

Section 3 Assessment

go.hrw.com
Online Quiz
KEYWORD: SF7 HP17

Reviewing Ideas, Terms, and People

1. a. **Identify** Who were some prominent African American leaders during Reconstruction?
   b. **Evaluate** What do you think was the most important change made by Reconstruction state governments? Explain your answer.
2. a. **Recall** For what reasons did some local governments not stop the **Ku Klux Klan**?
   b. **Draw Conclusions** How did the Ku Klux Klan's use of terror interfere with elections in the South?
3. a. **Recall** How did Reconstruction come to an end?
   b. **Explain** What was the relationship between **Jim Crow laws** and **segregation**?
4. a. **Identify** Who was Henry Grady, and why was he important?
   b. **Predict** What are some possible results of the rise of the "New South"?

Critical Thinking

5. **Identifying Causes and Effects** Review your notes on Reconstruction governments. Then copy the graphic organizer below and use it to show why Reconstruction ended, as well as the results of its end.

Causes → **Effect/Cause** End of Reconstruction → **Effects**

WRITING JOURNAL

6. **Relating Historical Change to Individual Choice** Despite the difficulties of Reconstruction, the Freedmen's Bureau and plans to bring industry to the "New South" did create new jobs. What might have led people to leave their jobs for new ones?

Direct Teach

Checking for Understanding

True or False Answer each statement *T* if it is true or *F* if it is false. If the statement is false, explain why.

1. Reconstruction was led by Democrats in Congress. *F; led by Republicans*
2. Several competing plans were proposed for Reconstruction. *T*
3. As more African Americans took public office in the South, resistance to Reconstruction decreased among white southerners. *F; it increased*

Review & Assess

Close

Ask students to write a short description of life in the South after the end of Reconstruction.

Review

go.hrw.com Online Quiz, Section 17.3

Assess

SE Section 3 Assessment

PASS: Section Quiz 17.3

Alternative Assessment Handbook

Reteach/Classroom Intervention

Interactive Reader and Study Guide, Section 17.3

Interactive Skills Tutor CD-ROM

Section 3 Assessment Answers

1. **a.** Hiram Revels and Blanche K. Bruce
   b. possible answers: education—led to a better-educated workforce; transportation—improved the economy
2. **a.** They were either afraid of or sympathized with them.
   b. They attacked voters and public officials, preventing some people from voting.
3. **a.** Republicans began to abandon Reconstruction due to other problems, and the disputed election of 1876 led to a compromise officially ending Reconstruction.
   b. Jim Crow laws were segregation laws.
4. **a.** a leader of the New South movement
   b. possible answer—Discrimination against African Americans might continue.
5. Causes—violence of Ku Klux Klan; Democrats gained control of southern states; former Confederates allowed to serve in public offices; Republicans lost power in the North; economic hardships; Effects—African Americans' rights restricted; sharecropping system; rise of southern industry
6. mill jobs, desire to escape sharecropping

Answers

The New South *It rebuilt quickly, becoming a railroad and industrial center in the South.*

Reading Check *strengthen the southern economy and create a New South*

Social Studies Skills

Chance, Oversight, and Error in History

Activity Make it Personal Ask students if they think differently about chance, oversight, and error after learning about the critical ways in which they can shape history. After a brief discussion, ask volunteers to share examples of when chance, oversight, or error shaped events in their lives. Then challenge students to identify examples in which chance, oversight, or error have shaped recent national or world events. Correct students' interpretations where necessary. Use the discussion to make certain that students understand the differences among error, chance, and oversight and how they can affect historical events. **LS Intrapersonal, Verbal/Linguistic**

- Alternative Assessment Handbook, Rubric 11: Discussions
- **CRF:** Social Studies Skills Activity: Chance, Oversight, and Error in History

Social Studies Skills

Analysis | Critical Thinking | Civic Participation | Study

Chance, Oversight, and Error in History

Understand the Skill

Sometimes, history can seem very routine. One event leads to others which, in turn, lead to still others. You learn to look for cause-and-effect relationships among events. You learn how point of view and bias can influence decisions and actions. These approaches to the study of history imply that the events of the past are orderly and predictable.

In fact, many of the events of the past *are* orderly and predictable! They may seem even more so since they're over and done with, and we know how things turned out. Yet, predictable patterns of behavior *do* exist throughout history. Recognizing them is one of the great values and rewards of studying the past. As the philosopher George Santayana once famously said, "Those who cannot remember the past are condemned to repeat it."

At its most basic level, however, history is people, and people are "human." They make mistakes. Unexpected things happen to them, both good things and bad. This is the unpredictable element of history. The current phrase "stuff happens" is just as true of the past as it is today. Mistakes, oversights, and just plain "dumb luck" have shaped the course of history—and have helped to make the study of it so exciting.

Learn the Skill

California merchant John Sutter decided to build a sawmill along a nearby American river in 1848. He planned to sell the lumber it produced to settlers who were moving into the area. Sutter put James W. Marshall to work building the mill. To install the large water wheel that would power the saw, Marshall first had to deepen the river bed next to the mill. During his digging, he noticed some shiny bits of yellow metal in the water. The result of this accidental find was the California gold rush, which sent thousands of Americans to California, and speeded settlement of the West.

In 1863 the army of Confederate General Robert E. Lee invaded Maryland. The Civil War had been going well for the South. Lee hoped a southern victory on Union soil would convince the British to aid the South in the war. However, a Confederate officer forgot his cigars as his unit left its camp in the Maryland countryside. Wrapped around the cigars was a copy of Lee's battle plans. When a Union soldier came upon the abandoned camp, he spotted the cigars. This chance discovery enabled the Union army to defeat Lee at the Battle of Antietam. The Union victory helped keep the British out of the war. More importantly, it allowed President Lincoln to issue the Emancipation Proclamation and begin the process of ending slavery in the United States.

Practice the Skill

In April 1865 President Lincoln was assassinated while attending the theater in Washington, D.C. Bodyguard John Parker was stationed outside the door of the president's box. However, Parker left his post to find a seat from which he could watch the play. This allowed the killer to enter the box and shoot the unprotected president.

Write an essay about how this chance event altered the course of history. How might Reconstruction, North–South relations, and African Americans' struggle for equality have been different had Lincoln lived?

Answers

Practice the Skill *Essays will vary, but students may speculate that Reconstruction might have been less bitter had Lincoln lived. His strength, experience, and popularity—particularly as compared to that of Andrew Johnson—might have kept the Radical Republicans from gaining control over Reconstruction. This change might have resulted in a Reconstruction plan that stressed unity and forgiveness more and, thus, might have resulted in less bitterness and resentment on the part of the South toward the North.*

Social Studies Skills Activity: Chance, Oversight, and Error in History

Analyzing Previous Chapters — At Level

1. Organize students into small groups and assign each group a chapter that they have studied recently.
2. Have each group scan the chapter and look for events where chance, oversight, or error played a role in influencing the course of history.
3. Each group should make a list of the instances it finds and write a brief explanation of the way in which chance, oversight, or error shaped history in that instance.
4. Have each group share its findings with the class. Correct students' interpretations where necessary. Then conclude by having students predict how the course of history might have changed if some of the instances they mentioned had turned out differently. **LS Interpersonal, Verbal/Linguistic**

- Alternative Assessment Handbook, Rubric 14: Group Activity

CHAPTER 17

Chapter Review

HOLT
History's Impact
▶ **video series**
Review the video to answer the closing question:
Name three ways the Thirteenth, Fourteenth, and Fifteenth Amendments are related.

Visual Summary

QUICK FACTS

Use the visual summary below to help you review the main ideas of the chapter.

Reform During Reconstruction, the Freedmen's Bureau opened schools for former slaves and performed other services to help the poorest southerners.

Dispute Differing ideas about how to govern the South led to conflicts between African Americans and white southerners, as well as between Republicans and Democrats.

Division After the Compromise of 1877 ended Reconstruction, segregation laws were enacted by southern governments and upheld by the U.S. Supreme Court.

Reviewing Vocabulary, Terms, and People

Complete each sentence by filling in the blank with the correct term or person from the chapter.

1. _______________ were laws that allowed racial segregation in public places.
2. The Radical Republicans were led by _______, a member of Congress from Pennsylvania.
3. The period from 1865 to 1877 that focused on reuniting the nation is known as _______.
4. Following the Civil War, many African Americans in the South made a living by participating in the __________ system.
5. After opposing Congress, Andrew Johnson became the first president to face _____ proceedings.
6. The _____ Amendment made slavery in the United States illegal.
7. In 1870 ________ became the first African American to serve in the U.S. Senate.

Comprehension and Critical Thinking

SECTION 1 *(Pages 552–557)*

8. a. **Describe** How did the lives of African Americans change after the Civil War?
   b. **Compare and Contrast** How was President Johnson's Reconstruction plan similar and different from President Lincoln's Ten Percent Plan?
   c. **Evaluate** Which of the three Reconstruction plans that were originally proposed do you think would have been the most successful? Why?

SECTION 2 *(Pages 558–563)*

9. a. **Identify** Who were the Radical Republicans, and how did they change Reconstruction?
   b. **Analyze** How did the debate over the Fourteenth Amendment affect the election of 1866?
   c. **Elaborate** Do you think Congress was right to impeach President Andrew Johnson? Explain.

Answers

History's Impact

Video Series all passed in about five years; tried to give African Americans the rights owed to them; once the Thirteenth Amendment outlawed slavery, freed African Americans were recognized as citizens and given right to vote

Visual Summary

Review and Inquiry Have students use the visual summary to explain the results of Reconstruction.

Quick Facts Transparency 47: Reconstruction Visual Summary

Reviewing Vocabulary, Terms, and People

1. Jim Crow laws
2. Thaddeus Stevens
3. Reconstruction
4. sharecropping
5. impeachment
6. Thirteenth
7. Hiram Revels

Comprehension and Critical Thinking

8. a. could move about freely, legalize marriages, search for relatives
   b. similar—granted amnesty, recognized that slavery is illegal; different—Johnson's plan required a temporary governor, declaration that secession was illegal, and refusal to pay Confederate debts; Lincoln's plan required oath of loyalty from 10 percent of state's voters

Review and Assessment Resources

Review and Reinforce

- SE Chapter Review
- **CRF:** Chapter Review Activity
- Quick Facts Transparency 47: Reconstruction Visual Summary
- Spanish Chapter Summaries Audio CD Program
- Online Chapter Summaries in Spanish
- OSP Holt PuzzlePro; GameTool for ExamView
- Quiz Game CD-ROM

Assess

- SE Standardized Test Practice
- PASS: Chapter 17 Tests, Forms A and B; Unit 5 Tests, Forms A and B
- Alternative Assessment Handbook
- OSP ExamView Test Generator, Chapter Test
- Differentiated Instruction Modified Worksheets and Tests CD-ROM: Chapter Test
- HOAP Holt Online Assessment Program (in the Premier Online Edition)

Reteach/Intervene

- Interactive Reader and Study Guide
- Differentiated Instruction Teacher Management System: Lesson Plans for Differentiated Instruction
- Differentiated Instruction Modified Worksheets and Tests CD-ROM
- Interactive Skills Tutor CD-ROM

go.hrw.com
Online Resources
Chapter Resources:
KEYWORD: SF7 CH17

Answers

c. Students should indicate why the plan they chose would have been more successful than the others.

9. a. Republicans who wanted the federal government to be much more involved in Reconstruction; they took control of Reconstruction away from President Johnson
b. Debate over civil rights for African Americans became the key issue of the election of 1866 and even led to riots.
c. possible answers: yes—He defied the law by firing Edwin Stanton without their approval; no—Congress did not have the power to limit the president.

10. a. They tried to help the South recover from the war by establishing public schools, hospitals, and prisons; passing laws prohibiting discrimination against African Americans; and aiding the construction of railroads, bridges, and public buildings.
b. They worked to limit the rights of African Americans, reduce the size of state governments, eliminate social programs, and prevent African Americans from voting.
c. Answers will vary, but students should support their answers with specific examples.

Reviewing Themes

11. The key political struggle was between Republicans, who supported rights for African Americans and strict guidelines for readmitting southern states, and Democrats, who favored leniency toward southern states and limited freedoms for African Americans.

12. The rights of African Americans were severely limited by poll taxes, Jim Crow laws, and the separate-but-equal doctrine. Many southerners were negatively affected by the sharecropping system and poor working conditions in mills.

SECTION 3 *(Pages 564–571)*

10. a. Describe What reforms did Reconstruction governments in the South support?

b. Draw Conclusions In what ways did southern governments attempt to reverse the accomplishments of Reconstruction?

c. Evaluate Do you think the South was successful or unsuccessful in its rebuilding efforts? Explain your answer.

Reviewing Themes

11. Politics Explain the political struggles that took place during Reconstruction.

12. Society and Culture How were the lives of ordinary southerners affected in the years after Reconstruction?

Using the Internet

go.hrw.com
KEYWORD: SF7 CH17

13. Activity: Drawing Conclusions A challenge for anyone trying to understand Reconstruction is drawing conclusions from primary and secondary sources from the time period. This activity will help you see how complex this can be. Enter the activity keyword, and then rate the credibility of the sources provided. Make sure you explain whether the source is a primary or secondary source, whether or not you think the source is credible, and the reasons for your thoughts.

Reading Skills

Analyzing Historical Information *Use the Reading Skills taught in this chapter to answer the question about the reading selection below.*

> Radical Republicans, on the other hand, took a harsher stance. They wanted the Federal government to force change in the South. Like the moderates, they thought the Black Codes were cruel and unjust. *(p. 559)*

14. Which of the following is relevant information for the passage above?

a. Thaddeus Stevens was a Radical Republican.
b. Andrew Johnson was a Democrat.
c. Radical Republicans wanted the federal government to make major changes in the South.
d. Radical Republicans were eventually removed from power.

Social Studies Skills

Chance, Oversight, and Error in History *Use the Social Studies Skills taught in this chapter to answer the question about the reading selection below.*

> Johnson's speaking tour was a disaster. It did little to win votes for the Democratic Party. Johnson even got into arguments with people in the audiences of some of his speaking engagements. *(p. 561)*

15. Which of the following is an example of chance, oversight, or error that affected history?

a. Johnson got into arguments with audiences.
b. The tour was a disaster.
c. The tour did not win votes.
d. Johnson spoke for the Democratic Party.

FOCUS ON WRITING

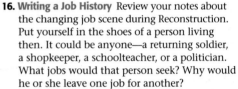

16. Writing a Job History Review your notes about the changing job scene during Reconstruction. Put yourself in the shoes of a person living then. It could be anyone—a returning soldier, a shopkeeper, a schoolteacher, or a politician. What jobs would that person seek? Why would he or she leave one job for another?

Write a brief job history for that person during Reconstruction. Include at least four jobs. Make each job description two to four sentences long. End each one with a sentence or two about why the person left that job. Add one sentence explaining why he or she took the next job. Be sure to include specific historical details.

Using the Internet

13. Go to the HRW Web site and enter the keyword shown to access a rubric for this activity.

KEYWORD: SF7 CH17

Reading Skills

14. a

Social Studies Skills

15. d

Focus on Writing

16. Rubric Students' job histories should
- include at least four job descriptions.
- end each description with an explanation of why the person left.
- explain why the person took each job.
- include specific historical details.

CRF: Focus on Writing Activity: Job History

CHAPTER 17

Standardized Test Practice

IN 8.1.22, 8.1.26, 8.2.3, 8.2.7

DIRECTIONS: Read each question and write the letter of the best response.

1 Use the map below to answer the following question.

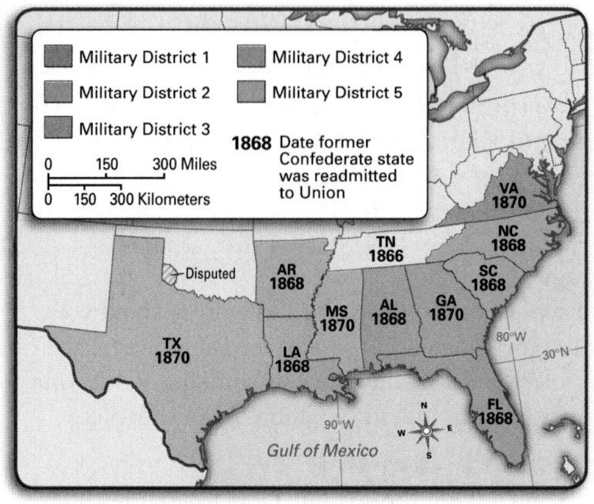

Which military district contained the largest number of states?

A Military District 2

B Military District 3

C Military District 4

D Military District 5

2 What can you infer from the map information?

A South Carolina was difficult to reconstruct.

B The largest number of troops was in Military District 1.

C Military District 5 was the last district to end Reconstruction.

D Tennessee was readmitted to the Union before the other southern states.

3 The quickest approach to reuniting the nation was proposed by the

A Ten Percent Plan.

B Wade-Davis Bill.

C Civil Rights Act of 1866.

D Compromise of 1877.

4 What development convinced Republicans in Congress to take control of Reconstruction from the president?

A President Abraham Lincoln was assassinated by a southern sympathizer.

B President Andrew Johnson vetoed the Wade-Davis bill.

C Southern states began passing Black Codes to restrict African Americans' freedoms.

D White southern women refused to support the Fifteenth Amendment.

5 Which of the following limited opportunities for African Americans in the South after Reconstruction ended?

A Ten Percent plan

B Radical Republicans

C Jim Crow laws

D carpetbaggers

6 Examine the following passage from a northern schoolteacher's letter home and then use it to answer the question.

> "Wishing to work where there was the most need—there are so many places where nothing has been done for the freedmen, and where they are sorely persecuted—we came here. A schoolhouse built by the soldiers had just been destroyed by the citizens. The feeling is intensely bitter against anything northern. The affairs of the [Freedmen's] Bureau have been very much mismanaged in Columbus, and our government has been disgraced by the troops who were stationed here."
>
> –Sarah Chase, from *Dear Ones at Home*

Document-Based Question What were some of the problems facing the Freedmen's Bureau in the South?

Answers

1. B

Break Down the Question: Students should note that District 3 has three states, more than any other district.

2. D

Break Down the Question: Point out to students that answer choices A, B, and C cannot be inferred from the map, but D can.

3. A

Break Down the Question: This question requires students to recall factual information from Section 1.

4. C

Break Down the Question: This question requires students to recall factual information from Section 2.

5. C

Break Down the Question: Point out that the Ten Percent plan applied to former confederate states, not African Americans. The Radical Republicans helped, rather than limited, African Americans.

6. The bureau had to deal with freedpeople suffering persecution, destruction of property, intense anti-northern feelings, and mismanagement.

Break Down the Question: The writer mentions intensely bitter feelings, destruction of a school house, and the misbehavior of Union soldiers.

Intervention Resources

Reproducible

- Interactive Reader and Study Guide
- Differentiated Instruction Teacher Management System: Differentiated Instruction Lesson Plans

Technology

- Quick Facts Transparency 47: Reconstruction Visual Summary
- Differentiated Instruction Modified Worksheets and Tests CD-ROM
- Interactive Skills Tutor CD-ROM

Tips for Test Taking

Find the Main Idea Tell students that the main goal of a reading comprehension section is to test their understanding of a reading passage. Have students keep these suggestions in mind when they read a selection on a test:

- Read the passage once to get a general overview of the topic.
- If you don't understand the passage at first, keep reading. Try to find the main idea.
- Then read the questions so that you know what to look for when you reread the passage.

Preteach

Bellringer

Motivate Ask students to think about topics related to the Civil War that interested them. What Civil War topics would students like to know more about? What questions do students have about these topics? Write the questions for students to see. Then tell students that in this workshop they will answer a similar question by conducting research and writing an informative report.

Direct Teach

Finding Historical Information

Ask an Expert Another source students might consult is an expert on their topic. Students might arrange an interview with an expert or attend a presentation that he or she is giving. If students plan to interview a person, they should write out several questions in advance and leave space after each question for taking notes. If students wish to record an interview, remind them to ask the person's permission in advance.

Taking Notes

Keep It Relevant Tell students that when they are not sure whether to take notes on a piece of information, they should ask themselves, "Does this information help answer my research question?" If the answer is yes, they should include the information in their notes. If the answer is no, they should not.

Assignment
Collect information and write an informative report on a topic related to the Civil War.

A Social Studies Report

All research begins with a question. Why did the North win the Civil War? Why did Abraham Lincoln choose Ulysses S. Grant? In a research report, you find answers to questions like these and share what you learn with your reader.

TIP **Narrowing the Task** The key to a successful research report is picking a topic that is broad enough that you can find information, but narrow enough that you can cover it in detail. To narrow a subject, focus on one aspect of the larger subject. Then think about whether that one aspect can be broken down into smaller parts. Here's an example of how to narrow a topic:
Too Broad: Civil War Leaders
Less Broad: Civil War Generals
Narrower: Robert E. Lee's Role in the Civil War

1. Prewrite

Choosing a Subject

Since you will spend a lot of time researching and writing about your topic, pick one that interests you. First, think of several topics related to the Civil War. Narrow your list to one topic by thinking about what interests you and where you can find information about the topic.

Developing a Research Question

A guiding question related to your topic will help focus your research. For example, here is a research question for the topic "Robert E. Lee's Role in the Civil War": *How did Lee's decision to turn down the leadership of the Union army affect the Civil War?* The answer to this question becomes the thesis, or the big idea of your report.

Finding Historical Information

Use at least three sources of historical information besides your textbook. Good sources include

- books, maps, magazines, newspapers
- television programs, movies, Internet sites, CD-ROMs.

For each source, write down the kinds of information shown below. When taking notes, put a circled number next to each source.

Encyclopedia article
① "Title of Article." Name of Encyclopedia. Edition or year published.
Book
② Author. Title. City of Publication: Publisher, year published.
Magazine or newspaper article
③ Author. "Title of Article." Publication name. Date: page number(s).
Internet site
④ Author (if known). "Document title." Web site. Date of electronic publication. Date information was accessed <url>.

Differentiating Instruction

Struggling Readers — Below Level

1. When doing research, students need to learn to evaluate each source quickly to determine its usefulness. As guided practice, write the list of fictional sources at right for students to see. Have students identify which of the sources they think would be most helpful for an informative report on Ulysses S. Grant.
2. Have students use the following scale to rate each source: 4 = extremely useful; 3 = useful; 2 = might be useful; 1 = not useful.

- *Ulysses S. Grant: A Biography* (book)
- *The Life and Times of Lincoln* (book)
- "Grant's Military Campaigns" (historical journal article)
- "Interactive History of the Civil War" (university Web site)
- "My General Grant Page" (personal Web site)

LS Verbal/Linguistic

Taking Notes

As you read the source material, take thorough notes on facts, statistics, comparisons, and quotations. Take special care to spell names correctly and to record dates and facts accurately. If you use a direct quotation from a source, copy it word for word and enclose it in quotation marks. Along with each note, include the number of its source and its page number.

Organizing Your Ideas and Information

Informative research reports are usually organized in one of these ways:

- Chronological order (the order in which events occurred)
- Order of importance
- Causes (actions or situations that make something else happen) and effects (what happened as a result of something else).

Use one of these orders to organize your notes in an outline. Here is a partial outline for a paper on Robert E. Lee.

The Thesis/Big Idea: Robert E. Lee's decision to decline the leadership of the Union army had serious consequences for the path of the Civil War.

I. Lee's Military Expertise
   A. Achievements at the U.S. Military Academy
   B. Achievements during the Mexican War
II. Lee's Personality and Character
   A. Intelligence and strength
   B. Honesty and fairness
   C. Daring and courage
III. Lee's Military Victories
   A. Battle of Fredericksburg
   B. Battle of Chancellorsville

TIP Seeing Different Viewpoints Consult a variety of sources, including those with different points of view on the topic. Reading sources with different opinions will give you a more complete picture of your subject. For example, reading articles about Robert E. Lee written by a southern writer as well as a northern writer may give you a more balanced view of Lee.

TIP Recording Others' Ideas You will be taking three types of notes.
Paraphrases Restatements of all the ideas in your own words.
Summaries Brief restatements of only the most important parts.
Direct quotations The writer's exact words inside quotation marks.

2. Write

You can use this framework to help you write your first draft.

A Writer's Framework

Introduction	Body	Conclusion
■ Start with a quote or an interesting historical detail to grab your reader's attention. ■ State the main idea of your report. ■ Provide any historical background readers need to understand your main idea.	■ Present your information under at least three main ideas, using logical order. ■ Write at least one paragraph for each of these main ideas. ■ Add supporting details, facts, or examples to each paragraph.	■ Restate your main idea, using slightly different words. ■ Include a general comment about your topic. ■ You might comment on how the historical information in your report relates to later historical events.

Direct Teach

Writing Introductions

First Things Last Tell students that they will probably be able to write a stronger introduction after they have drafted the body of the paper. Have students begin by writing their thesis statement. They should then start a new paragraph to begin the body of the report. After they have drafted the body, have students reread the report and then write the introduction. Have students ask themselves the following questions before they write the introduction:

- How can I grab my readers' attention?
- How can I set the scene for what I am about to discuss in the rest of my report?
- How can I make my readers want to read more?

Writing the Body

The Right Fit Explain to students that if they are having trouble making their reports flow, they may need to reconsider the kind of organization they chose. Tell students to scan their papers for transitions and other words that determine the logical relationship of the information. For example, words such as *because, therefore,* and *so* indicate a cause-and-effect relationship. Words such as *first, next, then,* and *after* indicate a chronological relationship. Words such as *primarily, main,* and *major* indicate a relationship based on importance. Students should make sure they are using the organization that best matches what they are trying to say. If not, students should create a new outline with a different organization and then use the outline to revise their drafts.

Advanced/Gifted and Talented — Above Level

1. Challenge students to choose a research topic about which there is some disagreement or controversy. Students should then address in their reports the complexity of their topics, the reasons for controversy, and the discrepancies in the available information.
2. Check students' topics to make sure you approve before students begin their research. **LS Verbal/Linguistic**

Special Needs Learners — Below Level

1. Assign all special education students one topic.
2. Have an aide take the students as a group to the library to assist with research. The aide should instruct students in the use of card catalogs, computer catalogs, and library media centers.
3. The aide should then help the students select and find sources. **LS Verbal/Linguistic**

Direct Teach

Studying a Model

Identify Organization Lead a class discussion to identify the type of organization used in the model research paper. Write the three types of organization for students to see. Have students consider each type of organization in turn.

- **Chronological order:** Point out that although the first body paragraph describes Lee's education and the last discusses his actions during the war, the middle body paragraph discusses his personality, which does not fit a chronological scheme.
- **Cause and effect:** Point out that while the thesis states a cause and effect (Lee's decision strengthened the South and likely lengthened the war), the supporting points are not related by cause and effect.
- **Order of importance:** Students should conclude that the model is organized by order of importance.

Then discuss whether the most important main ideas are provided first or last *(last, because Lee's actual performance in the field is the strongest evidence).*

Technology Tip

Using Technology to Provide Visual Aids Students may want to include maps, charts, diagrams, or illustrations in their papers. Explain that many word-processing programs include drawing tools or provide ways to import graphics from other computer programs. Encourage students who want to include visual aids to find out more about the graphic tools available.

Studying a Model

Here is a model of a research report. Study it to see how one student developed a paper. The first and the concluding paragraphs are shown in full. The paragraphs in the body of the paper are summarized.

INTRODUCTORY PARAGRAPH

Attention grabber

Statement of thesis

"I cannot raise my hand against my birthplace, my home, my children." With these words, Robert E. Lee changed the course of the Civil War. Abraham Lincoln had turned to Lee as his first choice for commander of the Union army. However, Lee turned Lincoln down, choosing instead to side with his home state of Virginia and take command of the Confederate army. Lee's decision to turn Lincoln down weakened the North and strengthened the Confederates, turning what might have been an easy victory for the North into a long, costly war.

BODY PARAGRAPHS

In the first part of the body, the student points out that Lee graduated from the U.S. Military Academy at West Point, served in the Mexican War, and was a member of the Union army. She goes on to explain that he would have been a strong leader for the North, and his absence made the North weaker.

In the middle of the report, the writer discusses Lee's personality and character. She includes information about the strength of character he showed while in the military academy and while leading the Confederate army. She discusses and gives examples of his intelligence, his daring, his courage, and his honesty.

In the last part of the body of the report, the student provides examples of Lee leading the outnumbered Confederate army to a series of victories. The student provides details of the battles of Fredericksburg and Chancellorsville and explains how a lesser general than Lee may have lost both battles.

CONCLUDING PARAGRAPH

Summary of main points

Restatement of big idea

Lee's brilliant and resourceful leadership bedeviled a series of Union generals. He won battles that most generals would have lost. If Lee had used these skills to lead the larger and more powerful Union army, the Civil War might have ended in months instead of years.

Cross-Discipline Activity: Math

At Level

Research Guided Practice

1. Send students to the library on an information scavenger hunt. Tell them their task is to find out how much the Civil War cost in lives and money. The monetary cost might include both the costs of maintaining the armies and the property losses suffered by civilians. The first student to find the information from a credible source wins.
2. Ask students to use their textbooks to calculate how many months, weeks, and days the Civil War lasted.
3. As a class, divide the monetary and human costs of the war by its length to determine the costs per month, week, and day. Explain to students that the actual costs were not incurred evenly throughout the period, so the numbers produced by the class are averages, not actual figures.
4. Use the findings to discuss the effects of war on soldiers, civilians, property, economies, and the environment. LS **Logical/Mathematical, Verbal/Linguistic**

3. Evaluate and Revise

Evaluating and Revising Your Draft

Evaluate your first draft by carefully reading it twice. Ask the questions below to decide which parts of your first draft should be revised.

Evaluation Questions for an Informative Report

- Does the introduction attract the readers' interest and state the big idea/thesis of your report?
- Does the body of your report have at least three paragraphs that develop your big idea? Is the main idea in each paragraph clearly stated?
- Have you included enough information to support each of your main ideas? Are all facts, details, and examples accurate? Are all of them clearly related to the main ideas they support?
- Is the report clearly organized? Does it use chronological order, order of importance, or cause and effect?
- Does the conclusion restate the big idea of your report? Does it end with a general comment about the importance or significance of your topic?
- Have you included at least three sources in your bibliography? Have you included all the sources you used and not any you did not use?

TIP **Organizing Your Time** By creating a schedule and following it, you can avoid that panicky moment when the due date is near and you haven't even started your research. To create your schedule and manage your time, include these six steps.

1 Develop a question and research your topic (10% of your total time).
2 Research and take notes (25%).
3 Write your main idea statement and create an outline (15%).
4 Write a first draft (25%).
5 Evaluate and revise your first draft (15%).
6 Proofread and publish your report (10%).

4. Proofread and Publish

Proofreading

To improve your report before sharing it, check the following:

- The spelling and capitalization of all proper names for people, places, things, and events.
- Punctuation marks around any direct quotation.
- Your list of sources (Works Cited or Bibliography) against a guide to writing research papers. Make sure you follow the examples in the guide when punctuating and capitalizing your source listings.

Publishing

Choose one or more of these ideas to publish your report.

- Share your report with your classmates by turning it into an informative speech.
- Submit your report to an online discussion group that focuses on the Civil War and ask for feedback.
- With your classmates, create a magazine that includes reports on several different topics or post the reports on your school Web site.

5. Practice and Apply

Use the steps and strategies outlined in this workshop to research and write an informative report on the Civil War.

Collaborative Learning

At Level

Peer Editing

Standard English Mastery

1. Divide students into groups of four.
2. One student will pretend to be an author submitting his or her work to a scholarly journal. The other three students will pretend to be the editorial board of the journal. The first board member will examine the report to see if it meets the journal's standards for grammar, usage, and mechanics. The second board member will determine whether the content of the report is coherent and interesting enough to publish. The third board member will decide whether the report meets professional standards for factual accuracy based on the provided documentation and Bibliography or Works Cited.
3. The report will be "accepted" only if all board members agree that it meets the journal's standards. Have students trade roles until all four reports have been reviewed.

LS Interpersonal, Verbal/Linguistic

Reteach

Proofreading

Shift into Reverse

Standard English Mastery Tell students that one reason it is difficult for people to proofread their own work is that they are too familiar with it. Since they know what they meant to say, it can be difficult for them to realize when their words do not convey their ideas. One way to counteract this familiarity is to proofread backwards. First, have students start at the end of the paper and look at each word in reverse order to make sure every word is used and spelled correctly. Then have students start at the end of the paper and read each sentence in reverse order to make sure every sentence is grammatically correct and written in standard English.

Practice & Apply

Integrating Facts, Details, and Examples

Go with the Flow Some students may become bogged down in details. Direct these students to write a first draft without worrying about including specific facts, details, or examples. Next, instruct students to put a letter next to each fact, detail, or example in their notes. Then have students write each letter next to the paragraph in their drafts where they want to insert the information.

Rubric

Students' reports should

- start with an interesting quote or historical detail.
- provide a clear thesis statement.
- present at least three main points about the chosen topic.
- provide at least one paragraph for each main point.
- provide supporting details, facts, and examples for each main point.
- end with a summary and a general comment about the topic.
- use correct grammar, punctuation, spelling, and capitalization.

Unit Preview

Introduce the Unit

Share the information in the chapter overviews with students.

Chapter 18 Continued westward expansion brought economic change and conflict. Mining, ranching, and railroads changed the economy of the West. Offers of free land encouraged farmers to settle in the Great Plains. At the same time, more conflicts broke out between white settlers and Native Americans.

Chapter 19 The Second Industrial Revolution led to new sources of power and to advances in transportation and communications. New forms of business organization also emerged, and more workers joined labor unions.

Chapter 20 In the late 1800s a new wave of immigration brought many people to America. The journey was often difficult, as was adjusting to a new life upon arrival. This new wave of immigrants led to the growth of American cities. New technology and ideas helped cities change and adapt to this rapid growth. Though problems still remained, people worked hard to improve the quality of life in American cities.

UNIT 6 1850–1914

A Growing America

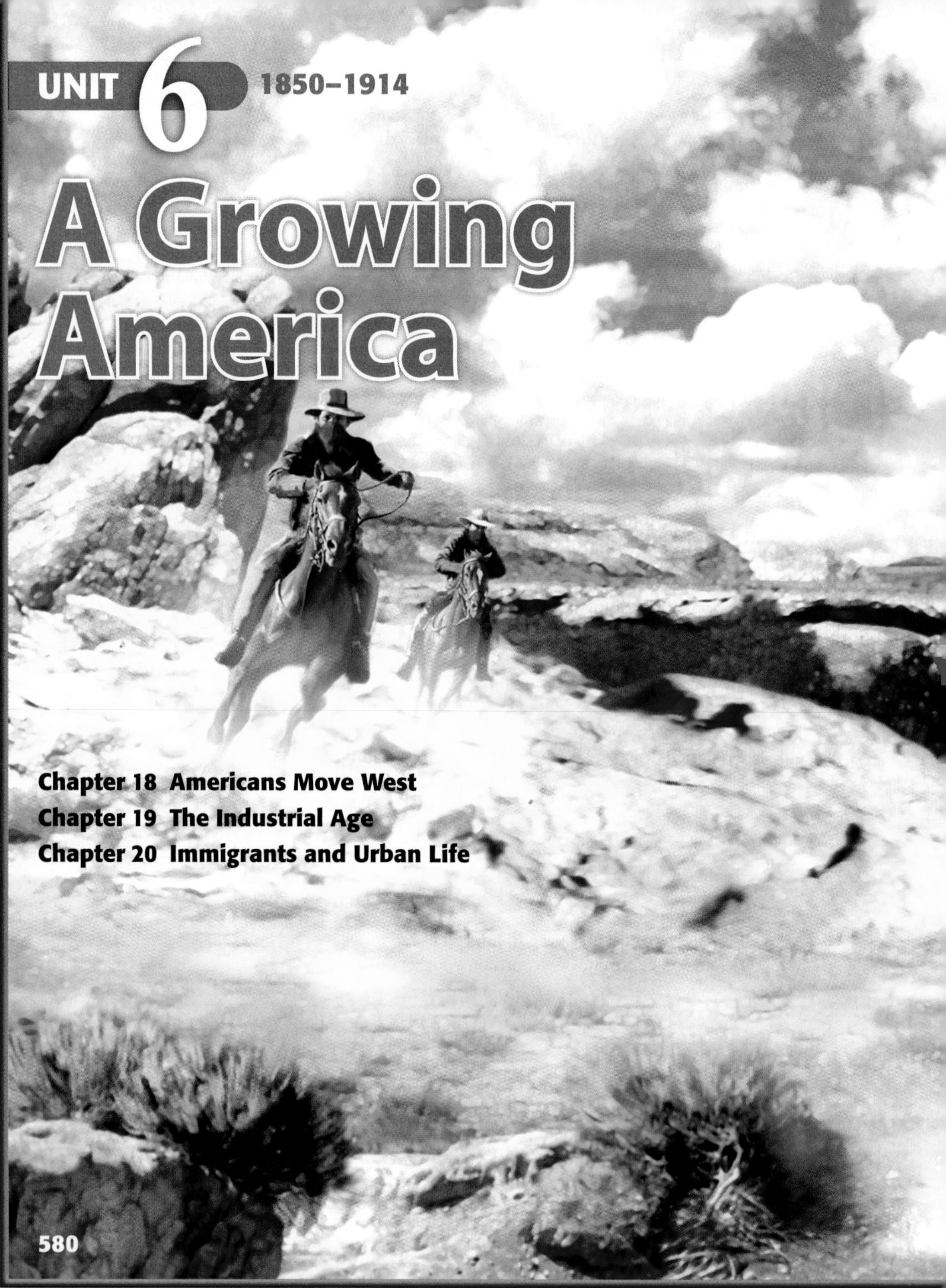

Chapter 18 Americans Move West
Chapter 19 The Industrial Age
Chapter 20 Immigrants and Urban Life

580

Unit Resources

Planning

- Differentiated Instruction Teacher Management System: Unit Instructional Pacing Guides
- One-Stop Planner CD-ROM with Test Generator: Calendar Planner
- Power Presentations with Video CD-ROM

Differentiating Instruction

- Differentiated Instruction Teacher Management System: Lesson Plans for Differentiated Instruction
- Pre-AP Activities Guide for United States History
- Differentiated Instruction Modified Worksheets and Tests CD-ROM

Enrichment

- **CRF The Industrial Age:** Economics and History: Monopolies and Trusts
- **CRF The Industrial Age:** Interdisciplinary Project: Technology Time Line
- Civic Participation Activities Guide
- Primary Source Library CD-ROM

Assessment

- Progress Assessment Support System: Unit 6 Tests, Forms A and B
- **OSP** ExamView Test Generator: Benchmark Test
- **HOAP** Holt Online Assessment Program (in the Premier Online Edition)
- Alternative Assessment Handbook

What You Will Learn...

After the American Civil War, the United States began a process of building a new economy and political structure. Events in the rest of the world began affecting the nation more noticeably.

During this period of expansion, the U.S. population spread across the continent. New immigrants and new technology began to change life in many parts of the country, especially in cities. In the next three chapters, you will learn about changes in the United States that helped the country increase its size, wealth, and power.

Explore the Art

In this picture, a teenage Buffalo Bill Cody flees from bandits on his Pony Express route. How does this picture show the importance of communication in the expansion of the United States?

Unit Preview

Connect to the Unit

Activity Visual Chapter Preview

Have students write down each of the chapter titles on a sheet of paper. Share the information in the chapter overviews with the class. Then have students scan the headings, images, maps, and charts in each chapter in this unit. Have students use the visual preview to write five questions that they have about each chapter. At the end of the unit, discuss students' questions and answers.
LS Verbal/Linguistic, Visual/Spatial

Explore the Art

William "Buffalo Bill" Cody went to work for a wagon freight company as a mounted messenger at age 11. He was 14 when he began delivering U.S. mail for the Pony Express. Cody was one of many teens who rode for the Pony Express, which advertised for "skinny, expert riders willing to risk death daily." Cody went on to become a buffalo hunter, U.S. Army scout, Indian fighter, and later the host of his own Wild West show.

About the Illustration

This illustration is an artist's conception based on available sources. However, historians are uncertain exactly what this scene looked like.

Democracy and Civic Education

At Level

Authority: Evolving Understandings

1. Organize students into small groups. Assign to each group one of the following topics: the colonies become the United States, the United States acquires the Louisana territory, Southern states are readmitted to the Union.
2. Have each group brainstorm the ways in which their topic necessitated a change in the ways people perceived authority in their lives.
3. Ask questions to get students thinking in the right direction. What did it mean for the individual colonies to agree to become united? How might it have affected the formerly French citizens of Louisiana to suddenly become Americans? What accommodations did both North and South have to make to reunify following the Civil War?
4. Allow groups some time to generate ideas, making sure that each has assigned a note taker. Then have each group share their ideas with the class. **LS Interpersonal, Verbal/Linguistic**

Answers

Explore the Art *possible answer—The dangerous conditions under which the mail is being delivered indicates the importance of mail delivery and the difficulties people faced to communicate.*

Chapter 18 Planning Guide

Americans Move West

Chapter Overview	Reproducible Resources	Technology Resources
CHAPTER 18 **pp. 582–609** **Overview: In this chapter, students will analyze the increased migration of Americans westward across the continent, along with the conflicts this migration caused.**	**Differentiated Instruction Teacher Management System:*** • Instructional Pacing Guides • Lesson Plans for Differentiated Instruction **Interactive Reader and Study Guide:*** Chapter Summary Graphic Organizer **Chapter Resource File*** • Focus on Writing Activity: A Letter • Social Studies Skills Activity: Migration Maps • Chapter Review Activity	**Student Edition on Audio CD Program** **Differentiated Instruction Modified Worksheets and Tests CD-ROM** **Interactive Skills Tutor CD-ROM** **Primary Source Library CD-ROM for United States History** **Power Presentations with Video CD-ROM** **History's Impact: United States History Video Program (VHS/DVD):** The Impact of the West on American Culture*
Section 1: **Miners, Ranchers, and Railroads** **The Big Idea:** As more settlers moved West, mining, ranching, and railroads soon transformed the western landscape.	**Differentiated Instruction Teacher Management System:*** Section 1 Lesson Plan **Interactive Reader and Study Guide:*** Section 1 Summary **Chapter Resource File*** • Vocabulary Builder, Section 1 • Biography Activity: Nat Love • Literature Activity: *A Letter From a Pony Express Rider* by Lucius Lodosky Hickock • Primary Source Activity: E. C. Abbott's Memoirs of Cowhands and Cattle Drives **Political Cartoons Activities for United States History,** Cartoon 19: Transcontinental Railroad*	**Daily Bellringer Transparency 18.1** **Quick Facts Transparency 48:** Causes and Effects of Westward Expansion* **Map Transparency 59:** Routes West, 1870* **Quick Facts Transparency 49:** Effects of the Transcontinental Railroad* go.hrw.com **Internet Activity:** Myth, Legend, or Reality?
Section 2: **Wars for the West** **The Big Idea:** Native Americans and the U.S. government came into conflict over land in the West.	**Differentiated Instruction Teacher Management System:*** Section 2 Lesson Plan **Interactive Reader and Study Guide:*** Section 2 Summary **Chapter Resource File*** • Vocabulary Builder, Section 2 • Biography Activity: George Armstrong Custer • Biography Activity: Sarah Winnemucca • History and Geography Activity: Conflicts with Native Americans • Primary Source Activity: Battle of the Little Bighorn	**Daily Bellringer Transparency 18.2** **Map Transparency 60:** Native American Land Loss in the West, 1850–1890* **Interactive Map:** Native American Land Loss in the West, 1850–1890 go.hrw.com **Internet Activity:** Geronimo Diary
Section 3: **Farming and Populism** **The Big Idea:** Settlers on the Great Plains created new communities and unique political groups.	**Differentiated Instruction Teacher Management System:*** Section 3 Lesson Plan **Interactive Reader and Study Guide:*** Section 3 Summary **Chapter Resource File*** • Vocabulary Builder, Section 3 • Biography Activity: Laura Ingalls Wilder **Political Cartoons Activities for United States History,** Cartoon 20: Farmers Face Hard Times*	**Daily Bellringer Transparency 18.3** go.hrw.com **Internet Activity:** Chapter Enrichment; The Homestead Act of 1862

SE Student Edition | Print Resource | Audio CD
TE Teachers Edition | Transparency | CD-ROM
go.hrw.com | Learning Styles | Video
TOS Indiana Teacher One Stop | * also on Indiana Teacher One Stop

HOLT
History's Impact
United States History Video Program (VHS/DVD)
The Impact of the West on American Culture
Suggested use: as a chapter introduction

Review, Assessment, Intervention

- **Quick Facts Transparency 50:** Americans Move West Visual Summary*
- **Spanish Chapter Summaries Audio CD Program**
- **Differentiated Instruction Modified Worksheets and Tests CD-ROM:** Modified Chapter Test
- **Progress Assessment Support System (PASS):** Chapter Tests A and B*
- TOS **Indiana Teacher One Stop:** ExamView Test Generator (English/Spanish)
- **Alternative Assessment Handbook**
- HOAP **Holt Online Assessment Program:** in the Holt Premier Online Student Edition

- **PASS:** Section Quiz 18.1*
- **Online Quiz:** Section 18.1
- **Alternative Assessment Handbook**

- **PASS:** Section Quiz 18.2*
- **Online Quiz:** Section 18.2
- **Alternative Assessment Handbook**

- **PASS:** Section Quiz 18.3*
- **Online Quiz:** Section 18.3
- **Alternative Assessment Handbook**

Power Presentations with Video CD-ROM

Power Presentations with Video are visual presentations of each chapter's main ideas. Presentations can be customized by including Quick Facts charts, images from the text, and video clips.

DIVISION FOR PUBLIC EDUCATION
AMERICAN BAR ASSOCIATION

Developed by the Division for Public Education of the American Bar Association. These materials are part of the **Democracy and Civic Education Resources.**

- **Constitution Study Guide**
- **Supreme Court Case Studies**

Holt Online Learning

go.hrw.com
Teacher Resources
KEYWORD: SF7 TEACHER

go.hrw.com
Student Resources
KEYWORD: SF7 CH18

- Document-Based Questions
- Interactive Multimedia Activities
- Current Events
- Chapter-based Internet Activities
- and more!

Holt Interactive
Online Student Edition

Complete online support for interactivity, assessment, and reporting

- Interactive Maps and Notebook
- Standardized Test Prep
- Homework Practice and Research Activities Online

CHAPTER 18 PLANNING GUIDE

Differentiating Instruction

How do I address the needs of varied learners?

The Target Resource acts as your primary strategy for differentiated instruction.

ENGLISH-LANGUAGE LEARNERS & STRUGGLING READERS

TARGET RESOURCE

English-Language Learner Strategies and Activities

- Build Academic Vocabulary
- Develop Oral and Written Language Structures

Spanish Resources

Spanish Chapter Summaries Audio CD

Spanish Chapter Summaries Online

Teacher's One-Stop Planner:

- ExamView Test Generator, Spanish
- PuzzlePro, Spanish

Additional Resources

Differentiated Instruction Teacher Management System: Lesson Plans for Differentiated Instruction

Chapter Resources:

- Vocabulary Builder Activities
- Social Studies Skills Activity: Migration Maps

Quick Facts Transparencies:

- Causes and Effects of Westward Expansion (TR 48)
- Effects of the Transcontinental Railroad (TR 49)
- Americans Move West Visual Summary (TR 50)

Student Edition on Audio CD Program

Interactive Skills Tutor CD-ROM

SPECIAL NEEDS LEARNERS

TARGET RESOURCE

Differentiated Instruction Modified Worksheets and Tests CD-ROM

- Vocabulary Flash Cards
- Modified Vocabulary Builder Activities
- Modified Chapter Review Activity
- Modified Chapter Test

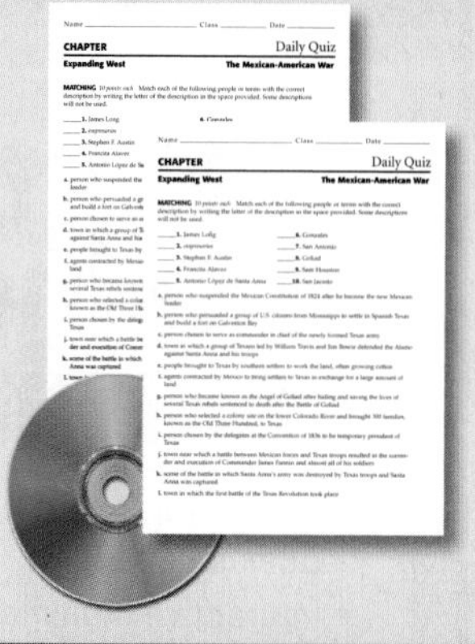

Additional Resources

Differentiated Instruction Teacher Management System: Lesson Plans for Differentiated Instruction

Interactive Reader and Study Guide

Social Studies Skills Activity: Migration Maps

Student Edition on Audio CD Program

Interactive Skills Tutor CD-ROM

ADVANCED/GIFTED-AND-TALENTED STUDENTS

TARGET RESOURCE

Primary Source Library CD-ROM for United States History

The Library contains longer versions of quotations in the text, extra sources, and images. Included are point-of-view articles, journals, diaries, historical fiction, and political documents.

Additional Resources

Political Cartoons Activities for United States History: Cartoon 19: Transcontinental Railroad; Cartoon 20: Farmers Face Hard Times

Differentiated Instruction Teacher Management System: Lesson Plans for Differentiated Instruction

Chapter Resource File:

- Focus on Writing Activity: A Letter
- Primary Source Activity: The Battle of Little Bighorn
- Primary Source Activity: E.C. Abbot's Memoirs of Cowhands and Cattle Drives

U.S. History Document-Based Activities: Activity 6, Westward Expansion

Differentiated Activities in the Teacher's Edition

- Map of a Boomtown, p. 588
- Miners, Cowboys, and Rail Workers, p. 590
- Reasons for Moving to the Great Plains, p. 601

Differentiated Activities in the Teacher's Edition

- Cattle Kingdom Comic Books, p. 589
- Plains Indians Museum Exhibit, p. 594
- Daily Life on the Plains Mural, p. 602

Differentiated Activities in the Teacher's Edition

- Mining Mock Trial, p. 587
- 1896 Presidential Debate, p. 604

Teacher One Stop™

How can I manage the lesson plans and support materials for differentiated instruction?

With the Indiana Teacher One Stop, you can easily organize and print lesson plans, planning guides, and instructional materials for all learners.
The Indiana Teacher One Stop includes the following materials to help you differentiate instruction:

- Interactive Teacher's Edition
- Calendar Planner and pacing guides
- Editable lesson plans
- All reproducible ancillaries in Adobe Acrobat (PDF) format
- ExamView Test Generator (Eng & Span)
- Transparency and video previews

Professional Development

HOLT Professional Development

What teacher training resources are available to help me grow professionally?

- **In-service and staff development** as part of your Holt Social Studies product purchase
- **Quick Teacher Tutorial Lesson Presentation CD-ROM**
- Intensive tuition-based **Teacher Development Institute**
- **Convenient Holt Speaker Bureau** – face-to-face workshop options
- **PRAXIS™ Test Prep** interactive Web-based content refreshers*
- **Ask A Professional Development Expert** at http://www.hrw.com/prodev/

* PRAXIS is a trademark of Educational Testing Service (ETS).
This publication is not endorsed or approved by ETS.

CHAPTER 18

Standardized Test Practice

8.1.23, 8.1.24, 8.2.4, 8.4.7, 8.4.8

DIRECTIONS: Read each question and write the letter of the best response.

1

- Government ownership of railroads
- Free and unlimited coinage of silver
- An eight-hour day for industrial workers
- Strict limits on foreign immigration
- Election of officials who will help farmers

Which of the following intended to accomplish the changes listed above in American society?

A the Morrill Act
B the Populist Party
C the National Grange
D the Homestead Act

2 The goal of many reformers who wanted to help Native Americans in the late 1800s was to

A get Indians to adopt the ways of white people.
B return to Indians all the land that had been taken from them.
C relocate all the nations to create an American Indian state in Oklahoma.
D negotiate treaties to bring peace to the frontier.

3 What played the *most* important part in the growth of the West's population and economy between 1865 and 1900?

A the mining industry
B the Cattle Kingdom
C the Populist Party
D the railroad

4 In general, the policy of the United States government toward Native Americans in the West was to

A send the army to track them down and engage them in battle.
B move them onto reservations and open their homelands to white settlers.
C kill all the buffalo so that they could not continue their traditional way of life.
D drive them into Canada or Mexico to settle.

5 The biggest problem facing western farmers in the late 1800s was

A a scarcity of good, cheap land to farm.
B their lack of organization to achieve change.
C overproduction and low crop prices.
D the threat of attacks by Native Americans.

6 Read the following speech from Comanche chief Ten Bears and use it to answer the question below.

> "You said that you wanted to put us upon a reservation, to build us houses and make us medicine lodges [places of religious practice]. I do not want them. I was born upon the prairie, where the wind blew free and there was nothing to break the light of the sun. I was born where there were no enclosures and where everything drew a free breath. I want to die there and not within walls."
>
> —Ten Bears, quoted in *Eyewitnesses and Others*

Document-Based Question **Why does Ten Bears not want to move to a reservation?**

Answers

1. B
Break Down the Question Students need to recall the platform for the Populist Party and recognize that the distracter answers are too limited.

2. A
Break Down the Question Students must remember who the reformers were and what their goals were.

3. D
Break Down the Question Point out that the word *most* means that more than one answer may be correct and that students must choose the one that provides the best answer.

4. B
Break Down the Question Point out that the phrase *in general* means that more than one answer may be correct and that students must choose the one that provides the best answer.

5. C
Break Down the Question The word *biggest* indicates that more than one answer may be correct, but students must choose the answer that was the biggest problem during the indicated time.

6. possible answer—Ten Bears does not want to move onto a reservation because conditions there would not be like where he was born.

Break Down the Question Students should recognize that Ten Bears very clearly explains his reasons for not wanting to move onto a reservation following his statement, "I do not want them."

Intervention Resources

Reproducible

- Interactive Reader and Study Guide
- Differentiated Instruction Teacher Management System: Lesson Plans for Differentiated Instruction

Technology

- Quick Facts Transparency 50: Americans Move West Visual Summary
- Differentiated Instruction Modified Worksheets and Tests CD-ROM
- Interactive Skills Tutor CD-ROM

Tips for Test Taking

Search for Skips and Smudges Read the following tip to students. To avoid losing points on machine-graded tests, make sure you

- did not skip any answers,
- provided only one answer per question,
- made your marks dark enough, and
- kept all marks neatly within the lines.

Then erase all smudges and stray pencil marks on your answer sheet. Cleanly erase those places where you changed your mind. Check everything. You are the only person who can!

Chapter 19 Planning Guide

The Industrial Age

Chapter Overview	Reproducible Resources	Technology Resources
CHAPTER 19 **pp. 610–631** **Overview: In this chapter, students will learn about how the United States became an industrial power in the late 1800s.**	**Differentiated Instruction Teacher Management System:*** • Instructional Pacing Guide • Lesson Plans for Differentiated Instruction **Interactive Reader and Study Guide:*** Chapter Summary Graphic Organizer **Chapter Resource File*** • Focus on Writing Activity: A Business Plan • Social Studies Skills Activity: Analyzing Costs and Benefits • Chapter Review Activity **Pre-AP Activities Guide for United States History:*** An Industrial Nation	**Student Edition on Audio CD Program** **Interactive Skills Tutor CD-ROM** **Differentiated Instruction Modified Worksheets and Tests CD-ROM** **Primary Source Library CD-ROM for United States History** **Power Presentations with Video CD-ROM** **History's Impact: United States History Video Program (VHS/DVD):** The Impact of the United States as the World's Most Powerful Industrial Nation*
Section 1: **The Second Industrial Revolution** **The Big Idea:** The Second Industrial Revolution led to new sources of power and advances in transportation and communication.	**Differentiated Instruction Teacher Management System:*** Section 1 Lesson Plan **Interactive Reader and Study Guide:*** Section 1 Summary **Chapter Resource File*** • Vocabulary Builder, Section 1 • Biography Activity: Inventors (T.A. Edison, A. Bell) • Biography Activity: Orville and Wilbur Wright • Interdisciplinary Project: Technology Time Line	**Daily Bellringer Transparency 19.1** **Quick Facts Transparency 51:** Factors Affecting Industrial Growth* **Internet Activity:** Technology Time Line
Section 2: **Big Business** **The Big Idea:** The growth of big business in the late 1800s led to the creation of monopolies.	**Differentiated Instruction Teacher Management System:*** Section 2 Lesson Plan **Interactive Reader and Study Guide:*** Section 2 Summary **Chapter Resource File*** • Vocabulary Builder, Section 2 • Biography Activity: Leland Stanford • Economics and History Activity: Monopolies and Trusts • Literature Activity: "The Lords of Industry" H.D. Lloyd	**Daily Bellringer Transparency 19.2**
Section 3: **Industrial Workers** **The Big Idea:** Changes in the workplace led to a rise in labor unions and workers' strikes.	**Differentiated Instruction Teacher Management System:*** Section 3 Lesson Plan **Interactive Reader and Study Guide:*** Section 3 Summary **Chapter Resource File*** • Vocabulary Builder, Section 3 • Biography Activity: Mother Jones • History and Geography Activity: Pullman's Company Town • Primary Source Activity: Samuel Gompers • Primary Source Activity: In Support of the Coal Miners	**Daily Bellringer Transparency 19.3** **Map Transparency 61:** Major Labor Strikes, Late 1800s* **Interactive Map:** Major Labor Strikes, Late 1800s **Internet Activity:** Life of a Steelworker **Internet Activity:** Recognizing Mother Jones

SE Student Edition | Print Resource | Audio CD
TE Teachers Edition | Transparency | CD-ROM
go.hrw.com | **LS** Learning Styles | Video
TOS Indiana Teacher One Stop | * also on Indiana Teacher One Stop

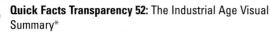

Review, Assessment, Intervention

- **Quick Facts Transparency 52:** The Industrial Age Visual Summary*
- **Spanish Chapter Summaries Audio CD Program**
- **Online Chapter Summaries in Spanish**
- **Progress Assessment Support System (PASS):** Chapter Tests A and B*
- **Differentiated Instruction Modified Worksheets and Tests CD-ROM:** Modified Chapter Test
- TOS **Indiana Teacher One Stop:** ExamView Test Generator (English/Spanish)
- HOAP **Holt Online Assessment Program,** in the Holt Premier Online Student Edition

- **PASS:** Section Quiz 19.1*
- **Online Quiz:** Section 19.1
- **Alternative Assessment Handbook**

- **PASS:** Section Quiz 19.2*
- **Online Quiz:** Section 19.2
- **Alternative Assessment Handbook**

- **PASS:** Section Quiz 19.3*
- **Online Quiz:** Section 19.3
- **Alternative Assessment Handbook**

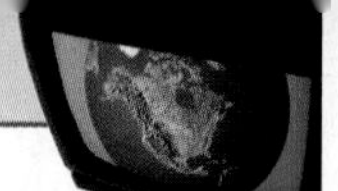

HOLT
History's Impact
United States History Video Program (VHS/DVD)

The Impact of the United States as the World's Most Powerful Industrial Nation

Suggested use: as a chapter introduction

Power Presentations with Video CD-ROM

Power Presentations with Video are visual presentations of each chapter's main ideas. Presentations can be customized by including Quick Facts charts, images from the text, and video clips.

DIVISION FOR PUBLIC EDUCATION
AMERICAN BAR ASSOCIATION

Developed by the Division for Public Education of the American Bar Association. These materials are part of the **Democracy and Civic Education Resources.**

- **Constitution Study Guide**
- **Supreme Court Case Studies**

Holt Online Learning

go.hrw.com
Teacher Resources
KEYWORD: SF7 TEACHER

go.hrw.com
Student Resources
KEYWORD: SF7 CH19

- Document-Based Questions
- Interactive Multimedia Activities
- Current Events
- Chapter-based Internet Activities
- and more!

Holt Interactive
Online Student Edition

Complete online support for interactivity, assessment, and reporting

- Interactive Maps and Notebook
- Standardized Test Prep
- Homework Practice and Research Activities Online

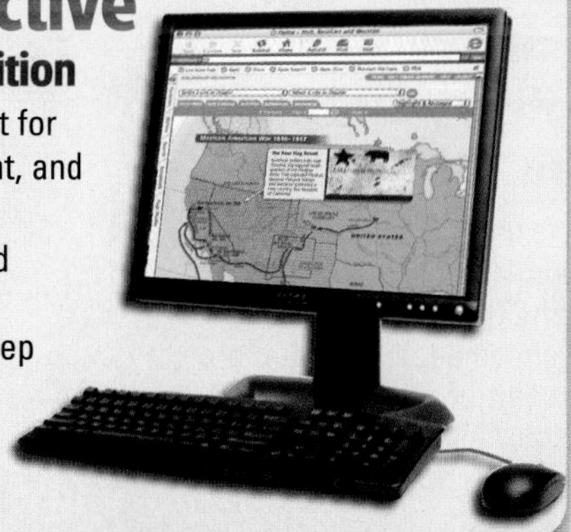

Differentiating Instruction

How do I address the needs of varied learners?

The Target Resource acts as your primary strategy for differentiated instruction.

ENGLISH-LANGUAGE LEARNERS & STRUGGLING READERS

TARGET RESOURCE

English-Language Learner Strategies and Activities

- Build Academic Vocabulary
- Develop Oral and Written Language Structures

Spanish Resources

Spanish Chapter Summaries Audio CD

Spanish Chapter Summaries Online

Teacher's One-Stop Planner:
- ExamView Test Generator, Spanish
- PuzzlePro, Spanish

Additional Resources

Differentiated Instruction Teacher Management System: Lesson Plans for Differentiated Instruction

Chapter Resources:
- Vocabulary Builder Activities
- Social Studies Skills Activity: Analyzing Costs and Benefits

Quick Facts Transparencies:
- Factors Affecting Industrial Growth (TR 51)
- The Industrial Age Visual Summary (TR 52)

Student Edition on Audio CD Program

Interactive Skills Tutor CD-ROM

SPECIAL NEEDS LEARNERS

TARGET RESOURCE

Differentiated Instruction Modified Worksheets and Tests CD-ROM

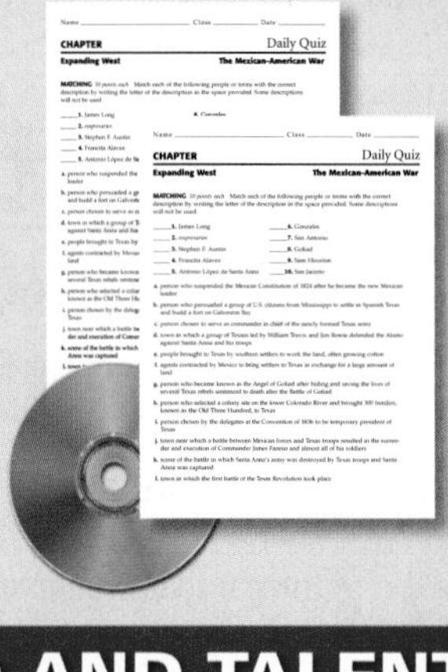

- Vocabulary Flash Cards
- Modified Vocabulary Builder Activities
- Modified Chapter Review Activity
- Modified Chapter Test

Additional Resources

Differentiated Instruction Teacher Management System: Lesson Plans for Differentiated Instruction

Interactive Reader and Study Guide

Social Studies Skills Activity: Analyzing Costs and Benefits

Student Edition on Audio CD Program

Interactive Skills Tutor CD-ROM

ADVANCED/GIFTED-AND-TALENTED STUDENTS

TARGET RESOURCE

Primary Source Library CD-ROM for United States History

The Library contains longer versions of quotations in the text, extra sources, and images. Included are point-of-view articles, journals, diaries, historical fiction, and political documents.

Additional Resources

Differentiated Instruction Teacher Management System: Lesson Plans for Differentiated Instruction

Pre-AP Activities Guide for United States History: An Industrial Nation

Chapter Resource File:
- Focus on Writing Activity: A Business Plan
- Primary Source Activity: Samuel Gomper's Testimony
- Primary Source Activity: In Support of the Coal Miners
- Interdisciplinary Projects: Technology Time Line; A Primer Lesson

Differentiated Activities in the Teacher's Edition
- Advances in Uses of Oil and Electricity, p. 617

Differentiated Activities in the Teacher's Edition
- Interventions Science Fair, p. 616

Differentiated Activities in the Teacher's Edition
- Studying the Stock Market, p. 620
- Major Labor Strikes, p. 626

Teacher One Stop™

How can I manage the lesson plans and support materials for differentiated instruction?

With the Indiana Teacher One Stop, you can easily organize and print lesson plans, planning guides, and instructional materials for all learners.
The Indiana Teacher One Stop includes the following materials to help you differentiate instruction:

- Interactive Teacher's Edition
- Calendar Planner and pacing guides
- Editable lesson plans
- All reproducible ancillaries in Adobe Acrobat (PDF) format
- ExamView Test Generator (Eng & Span)
- Transparency and video previews

Professional Development

HOLT Professional Development

What teacher training resources are available to help me grow professionally?

- **In-service and staff development** as part of your Holt Social Studies product purchase
- **Quick Teacher Tutorial Lesson Presentation CD-ROM**
- Intensive tuition-based **Teacher Development Institute**
- **Convenient Holt Speaker Bureau** – face-to-face workshop options
- **PRAXIS™ Test Prep** interactive Web-based content refreshers*
- **Ask A Professional Development Expert** at http://www.hrw.com/prodev/

* PRAXIS is a trademark of Educational Testing Service (ETS).
This publication is not endorsed or approved by ETS.

• Chapter Preview •

Chapter Big Ideas

Section 1 The Second Industrial Revolution led to new sources of power and advances in transportation and communication.

Section 2 The growth of big business in the late 1800s led to the creation of monopolies.

Section 3 Changes in the workplace led to a rise in labor unions and workers' strikes.

Focus on Writing

The **Chapter Resource File** provides a Focus on Writing worksheet to help students organize and create their memos.

CRF: Focus on Writing Activity: A Business Plan

Key to Differentiating Instruction

Below Level

Basic-level activities designed for all students encountering new material

At Level

Intermediate-level activities designed for average students

Above Level

Challenging activities designed for honors and gifted and talented students

Standard English Mastery

Activities designed to improve standard English usage

CHAPTER 19

The Industrial Age

IN Indiana Standards

Social Studies Standards

8.1.27 Give examples of scientific and technolgoical developments that changed cultural life in the nineteenth-century United States, such as the use of photography, growth in the use of the telegraph, the completion of the transcontinental railroad, and, the invention of the telephone.

8.4.3 Evaluate how the characteristics of a market economy have affected the economic and labor development of the United States.

8.4.5 Analyze contributions of entrepreneurs and inventors in the development of the United States economy.

8.4.6 Relate technological change and inventions to changes in labor productivity in the United States in the eighteenth and nineteenth centuries.

go.hrw.com
Indiana
KEYWORD: SF10 IN

FOCUS ON WRITING

A Business Plan You are an inventor in the late 1800s, and you want to start a business to sell your new inventions. Write a business plan for investors that will encourage them to lend you money to start your business. As you read this chapter, gather information about the new business practices that you can use to run your business. Then write your plan. Include information about what you will sell, how you will make it, and how you can avoid conflicts with the workers who make your product.

UNITED STATES

1879 Thomas Edison invents the first lightbulb.

1870

1876 German engineer Nikolaus A. Otto perfects a gasoline-powered engine.

WORLD

610 CHAPTER 19

Introduce the Chapter

At Level

Focus on Industry and Technology

1. Discuss with students how industrialization has changed life in the United States. Explain that before goods were mass produced, they were made by hand.
2. Have students create a chart with two columns. In the first column, have them list technological innovations we may take for granted, such as electricity, the telephone, etc. In the second column, have students explain how these technologies, and the way they are produced, have affected American society. For instance, e-mail and cell phones have improved communication.
3. Discuss the list with the class, then review some of the changes brought on by increased industrialization and the rise of big business in the late 1800s. Ask students to identify why workers joined unions in the late 1800s, and what might attract them to join unions today. **LS Verbal/Linguistic**

History's Impact

▶ **video series**

Watch the video to understand the impact of the United States as the world's most powerful industrial nation.

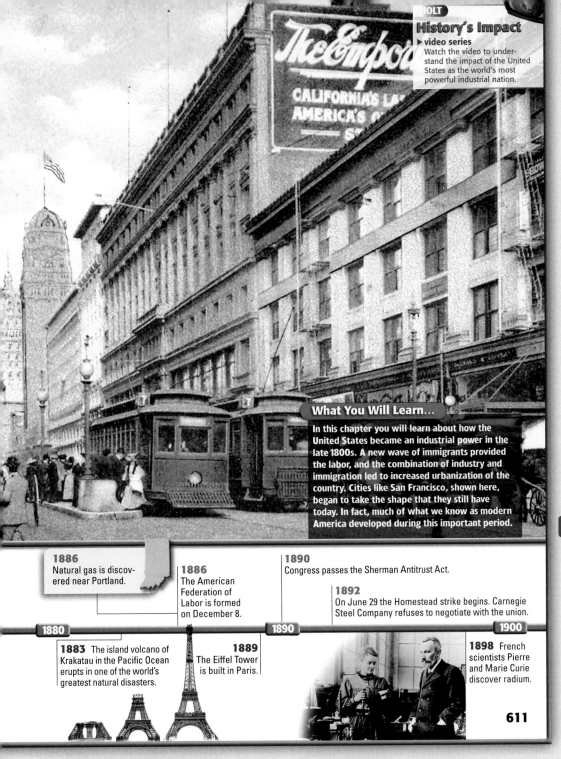

What You Will Learn...

In this chapter you will learn about how the United States became an industrial power in the late 1800s. A new wave of immigrants provided the labor, and the combination of industry and immigration led to increased urbanization of the country. Cities like San Francisco, shown here, began to take the shape that they still have today. In fact, much of what we know as modern America developed during this important period.

1880 — **1890** — **1900**

1883 The island volcano of Krakatau in the Pacific Ocean erupts in one of the world's greatest natural disasters.

1886 Natural gas is discovered near Portland.

1886 The American Federation of Labor is formed on December 8.

1889 The Eiffel Tower is built in Paris.

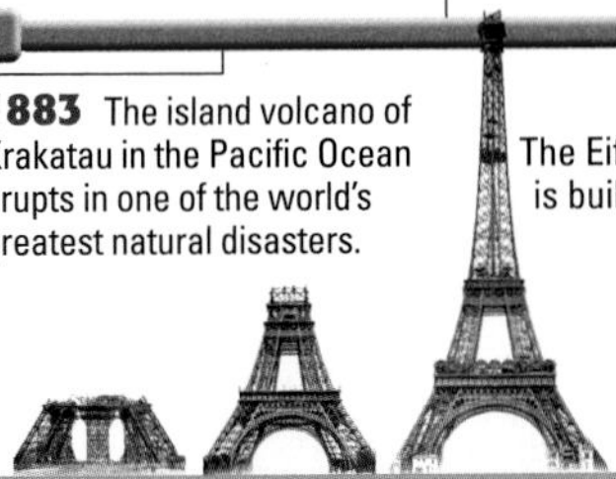

1890 Congress passes the Sherman Antitrust Act.

1892 On June 29 the Homestead strike begins. Carnegie Steel Company refuses to negotiate with the union.

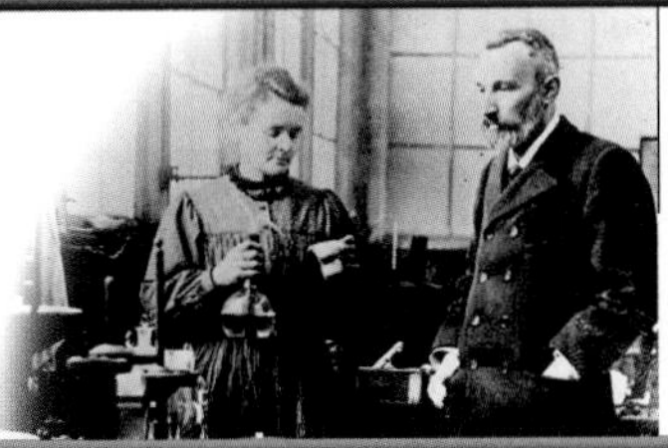

1898 French scientists Pierre and Marie Curie discover radium.

• Chapter Preview •

History's Impact

▶ **video series**

See the Video Teacher's Guide for strategies for using the chapter video to study the impact of the United States as the world's most powerful industrial nation.

Explore the Picture

San Francisco In the late 1800s inventions and improvements made urban life much easier. This photo of Market Street in San Francisco, California, shows many elements of urban life at the turn-of-the-century. From cable cars to department stores and skyscrapers, San Francisco epitomized an industrialized, urban center.

Analyzing Visuals Have students examine the image and identify at least three modern inventions shown in the picture. *Answers may include tall buildings, a department store, electric trolleys, and streetlights.*

go.hrw.com

Online Resources

Chapter Resources:
KEYWORD: SF7 CH19
Teacher Resources:
KEYWORD: SF7 TEACHER

Explore the Time Line

1. How many years passed from the formation of the American Federation of Labor to the Homestead Strike? *about 5 years*
2. In what year did Pierre and Marie Curie discover radium? *1898*
3. Which two inventions listed on the time line would have a major impact on the development of city life? *gasoline-powered engines and the electric light bulb*
4. What two inventions took place in the 1870s? *the invention of a gasoline-powered engine and the invention of the first lightbulb*

Info to Know

The Eiffel Tower The Eiffel Tower was built in honor of the 100th anniversary of the French Revolution. To prepare for the International Exhibition of Paris of 1889, a competition was held to design a monument for the event. Bridge designer and engineer Gustave Eiffel's plan was the winning design for the Exhibition. The structure took 300 steel workers and about two years to build. Until 1930, it was the world's tallest man-made structure, standing at over 1,050 feet.

Reading Social Studies

Understanding Themes

Tell students that they will be learning about the economic and social changes that resulted from the Second Industrial Revolution and the rise of powerful corporations. Ask students to predict what types of inventions and new ideas might have resulted from this period. Point out to students that the light bulb, the telephone, automobiles, and the use of petroleum all originated at this time. Then ask students to discuss what effects inventions like these might have had on the economy and on society and culture during the Second Industrial Revolution.

Organization of Facts and Information

Focus on Reading Organize the class into four groups. Ask each group to imagine that they are preparing a weather report for a television news station. Assign each group one of the four patterns of organization listed on this page. Then, have each group write and deliver a report on some aspect of the weather for its newscast. In their presentations, students must also create a graphic organizer that matches the pattern they were assigned. The graphic organizer should contain the information they are presenting. When the groups have finished their presentations, use the graphic organizers to review the patterns of organization.

Reading Social Studies

by Kylene Beers

Economics | Geography | Politics | **Society and Culture** | Science and Technology

Focus on Themes In this chapter, you will read about the advancements in transportation and communication made during what is called the Second Industrial Revolution. You will learn about the rise of powerful corporations. You will also read about the workers who organized in the late 1800s and will see what happened as unions began demanding better treatment for workers. Throughout the chapter, you will see how **society** was affected by the changing **economy**.

Organization of Facts and Information

Focus on Reading How are clothes organized in a department store? How are files arranged in a file cabinet? Clear organization helps us find the product we need, and it also helps us find facts and information.

Understanding Structural Patterns Writers use structural patterns to organize information in sentences or paragraphs. What's a structural pattern? It's simply a way of organizing information. Learning to recognize those patterns will make it easier for you to read and understand social studies texts.

Patterns of Organization

Pattern	Clue Words	Graphic Organizer
Cause-effect shows how one thing leads to another.	as a result, therefore, because, this led to	Cause → Effect, Effect → Effect
Chronological order shows the sequence of events or actions.	after, before, first, then, not long after, finally	First → Next → Last
Comparison-contrast points out similarities and/or differences.	although, but, however, on the other hand, similarly, also	Differences / Similarities
Listing presents information in categories such as size, location, or importance.	also, most important, for example, in fact	Category • Fact • Fact • Fact

To use text structure to improve your understanding, follow these steps:

1. Look for the main idea of the passage you are reading.
2. Then look for clues that signal a specific pattern.
3. Look for other important ideas and think about how the ideas connect. Is there any obvious pattern?
4. Use a graphic organizer to map the relationships among the facts and details.

Reading and Skills Resources

Reading Support

- Interactive Reader and Study Guide
- Student Edition on Audio CD
- Spanish Chapter Summaries Audio CD Program

Social Studies Skills Support

- Interactive Skills Tutor CD-ROM

Vocabulary Support

- **CRF:** Vocabulary Builder Activities
- **CRF:** Chapter Review Activity
- Differentiated Instruction Modified Worksheets and Tests CD-ROM:
  - Vocabulary Flash Cards
  - Vocabulary Builder Activity
  - Chapter Review Activity

OSP Holt PuzzlePro

You Try It!

The following passages are from the chapter you are about to read. As you read each set of sentences, ask yourself what structural pattern the writer used to organize the information.

Recognizing Structural Patterns

(A) Great advances in communication technologies took place in the late 1800s. By 1861, telegraph wires connected the East and West coasts. Five years later, a telegraph cable on the floor of the Atlantic Ocean connected the United States and Great Britain. *(p. 617)*

(B) Many business leaders justified their business methods through their belief in social Darwinism . . . Other business leaders, however, believed that the rich had a duty to aid the poor. *(p. 621)*

(C) During the late 1800s, several factors led to a decline in the quality of working conditions. Machines run by unskilled workers were eliminating the jobs of many skilled craftspeople. These low-paid workers could be replaced easily. *(p. 624)*

After you read the passages, answer the questions below:

1. Reread passage A. What structural pattern did the writer use to organize this information? How can you tell?
2. Reread passage B. What structural pattern did the writer use to organize this information? How can you tell? Why do you think the writer chose this pattern?
3. Reread passage C. What structural pattern did the writer use to organize this information? How can you tell? Why do you think the writer chose this pattern?

As you read Chapter 19, think about the organization of the ideas. Ask yourself why the writer chose to organize the information in this way.

Key Terms and People

Chapter 19

Section 1

Second Industrial Revolution *(p. 615)*
Bessemer process *(p. 615)*
Thomas Edison *(p. 616)*
patents *(p. 616)*
Alexander Graham Bell *(p. 617)*
Henry Ford *(p. 617)*
Wilbur and Orville Wright *(p. 618)*

Section 2

corporations *(p. 619)*
Andrew Carnegie *(p. 620)*
vertical integration *(p. 620)*
John D. Rockefeller *(p. 620)*
horizontal integration *(p. 621)*
trust *(p. 621)*
Leland Stanford *(p. 621)*
social Darwinism *(p. 621)*
monopoly *(p. 622)*
Sherman Antitrust Act *(p. 622)*

Section 3

Frederick W. Taylor *(p. 624)*
Knights of Labor *(p. 625)*
Terence V. Powderly *(p. 625)*
American Federation of Labor *(p. 625)*
Samuel Gompers *(p. 625)*
collective bargaining *(p. 626)*
Mary Harris Jones *(p. 626)*
Haymarket Riot *(p. 626)*
Homestead strike *(p. 627)*
Pullman strike *(p. 627)*

Academic Vocabulary

In this chapter, you will learn the following academic words:

implement *(p. 617)*
acquire *(p. 620)*

Reading Social Studies

Key Terms and People

Preteach the key terms and people in this chapter by having students create a Four-Corner FoldNote. Tell students to label the four sides *People*, *Events*, *Things*, and *Ideas*. As you read each word, have students repeat it after you. Then have students write that word on the correct section of the FoldNote. Discuss any terms that students do not recognize.

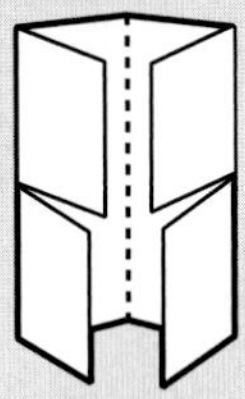

Focus on Reading

See the **Focus on Reading** questions in this chapter for more practice on this reading social studies skill.

Reading Social Studies Assessment

See the **Chapter Review** at the end of this chapter for student assessment questions related to this reading skill.

Teaching Tip

Understanding the structural patterns of texts not only helps writers who are organizing text, but it also helps students to understand what they are reading. Stress the importance of learning this skill as a way for students to better understand not only textbooks, but any material they read. Remind students that before they write an essay or prepare a presentation for class, they should take time to think about the organizational pattern that works best for the information they are trying to present.

Answers

You Try It! 1. *chronological; the writer lists dates and time periods in chronological order.* **2.** *comparison-contrast; it describes one view, and then presents an opposing view.*
3. *cause-effect; words like* therefore *and* as a result*; because the writer wanted to demonstrate how the increased use of machines led to deteriorating conditions in the workplace*

Preteach

Bellringer

If YOU were there . . . Use the **Daily Bellringer Transparency** to help students answer the question.

Daily Bellringer Transparency 19.1

The Industrial Age — Daily Bellringer **19.1**

Review the Previous Chapter

Read the list of events below and put them in the correct order.

a. The Battle of the Little Bighorn takes place in Montana.
b. The Interstate Commerce Act is passed by Congress.
c. The Pony Express begins delivering messages by horseback.
d. Railroads from the East and the West are joined.
e. California is admitted into the Union as a state.

Preview Section 1

If YOU were there ...

You live in a small town but are visiting an aunt in the city in the 1890s. You are amazed when your aunt pushes a button on the wall to turn on electric lights. At home you still use kerosene lamps. You hear a clatter outside and see an electric streetcar traveling down the street. You are shocked when a telephone rings, and your aunt speaks to someone miles away!

Which of these inventions would you find most amazing?

Consider the benefits of ELECTRICITY:
- comes right to the home
- eliminates the need for kerosene, a flammable liquid with a bad odor
- powers industries and homes

Consider the benefits of the TELEPHONE:
- spreads news quickly
- helps handle emergencies
- brings people closer together

Review Answers: e, c, d, a, b

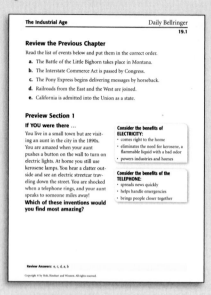

Academic Vocabulary

Review with students the high-use academic term in this section.

implement to put in place (p. 617)

CRF: Vocabulary Builder Activity, Section 1

Taking Notes

Have students copy the graphic organizer onto their own paper and then use it to take notes on the section. This activity will prepare students for the Section Assessment, in which they will complete a graphic organizer that builds on the information using a critical-thinking skill.

Section Correlations

IN

8.1.27 Give examples of scientific and technological developments that changed cultural life in the nineteenth-century United States, such as the use of photography, growth in the use of the telegraph, the completion of the transcontinental railroad, and the invention of the telephone. **8.4.3** Evaluate how the characteristics of a market economy have affected the economic and labor development of the United States. **8.4.5** Analyze contributions of entrepreneurs and inventors in the development of the United States economy.

SECTION 1

The Second Industrial Revolution

What You Will Learn...

Main Ideas

1. Breakthroughs in steel processing led to a boom in railroad construction.
2. Advances in the use of oil and electricity improved communications and transportation.
3. A rush of inventions changed Americans' lives.

The Big Idea

The Second Industrial Revolution led to new sources of power and advances in transportation and communication.

Key Terms and People

Second Industrial Revolution, *p. 615*
Bessemer process, *p. 615*
Thomas Edison, *p. 616*
patents, *p. 616*
Alexander Graham Bell, *p. 617*
Henry Ford, *p. 617*
Wilbur and Orville Wright, *p. 618*

TAKING NOTES As you read this section, take notes on the inventors of the Second Industrial Revolution. Organize your notes in a table like the one below.

Inventor

IN **8.1.27, 8.3.6, 8.3.8, 8.4.1, 8.4.3, 8.4.5**

If YOU were there...

You live in a small town but are visiting an aunt in the city in the 1890s. You are amazed when your aunt pushes a button on the wall to turn on electric lights. At home you still use kerosene lamps. You hear a clatter outside and see an electric streetcar traveling down the street. You are shocked when a telephone rings, and your aunt speaks to someone miles away!

Which of these inventions would you find most amazing?

BUILDING BACKGROUND The first Industrial Revolution in America began in the early 1800s. It changed the way products were made, from handwork to machines. It moved the workplace from cottages to factories. Later, it brought advances in transportation and communication. The Second Industrial Revolution built on these changes, introducing new technology and new sources of power.

Teach the Big Idea

At Level

The Second Industrial Revolution

1. **Teach** To teach the main ideas in the section, use the questions in the Direct Teach boxes.
2. **Apply** Give students a blank outline map of the United States. As they read this section, have students use their maps to locate and identify the places discussed in the section. Students should also create a key or legend identifying the reason the place is important. For example, oil was first pumped in Titusville, Pennsylvania, and Thomas Edison's research was done in Menlo Park, New Jersey. **LS Visual/Spatial**
3. **Review** Have students work in groups to share and compare their maps.
4. **Practice/Homework** Have students select an event from their maps that they feel had a great effect on daily life. Have them write essays explaining and defending their choices. **LS Verbal/Linguistic**

Alternative Assessment Handbook, Rubrics 20: Map Creation; and 37: Writing Assignments

Breakthroughs in Steel Processing

Technological advances were important to the **Second Industrial Revolution**, a period of rapid growth in U.S. manufacturing in the late 1800s. By the mid-1890s, the United States had become the world's industrial leader.

The Steel Industry

Some of the most important advances in technology happened in the steel industry. Steel is iron that has been made stronger by heat and the addition of other metals. In the mid-1850s Henry Bessemer invented the **Bessemer process**, a way to manufacture steel quickly and cheaply by blasting hot air through melted iron to quickly remove impurities. Before, turning several tons of iron ore into steel took a day or more. The Bessemer process took only 10 to 20 minutes.

The Bessemer process helped increase steel production. U.S. mills had produced 77,000 tons of steel in 1870. By 1879 production had risen to more than 1 million tons in one year.

Riding the Rails

As steel dropped in price, so did the cost of building railroads. Companies built thousands of miles of new steel track. The design of elegant passenger and sleeping cars improved passenger service. Manufacturers and farmers sent products to market faster than ever by rail in newly invented refrigerated shipping cars. Cities where major rail lines crossed, such as Chicago, grew rapidly. Railroads also increased western growth by offering free tickets to settlers. Finally, as rail travel and shipping increased, railroads and related industries began employing more people.

QUICK FACTS

Factors Affecting Industrial Growth

- Greater ability to use natural resources
- A growing population
- Transportation advances
- Rising immigration
- Inventions and innovations
- Increasing business investment
- Government policies assisting business, such as protective tariffs

READING CHECK **Identifying Cause and Effect** How did steel processing change in the 1850s, and how did this affect the United States?

Homestead Steel Mill

Steel mills like this one in Homestead, Pennsylvania, were the center of the new steel industry that led to advancements in rail travel. Workers used the Bessemer process to make steel more quickly.

How do you think mills like this one affected the surrounding area?

615

Direct Teach

Main Idea

1 Breakthroughs in Steel Processing

Breakthroughs in steel processing led to a boom in railroad construction.

Describe How did the Bessemer process change the steel industry? *It made changing iron ore into steel much faster than before, which led to an increase in steel production.*

Analyze How did the Bessemer process affect industry in the United States? *It helped increase steel production, which caused steel prices to drop. Lower steel prices led to more railroads and increased shipping.*

Quick Facts Transparency 51: Factors Affecting Industrial Growth

Connect to Science

The Bessemer Process Two men—American William Kelly and Englishman Henry Bessemer—simultaneously developed ideas for improving steel manufacturing. Kelly and Bessemer both discovered that forcing air into molten iron would generate intense heat. Oxygen from this blast of air would react with impurities in the iron, making it possible to remove the impurities, thereby creating a higher-quality steel. Bessemer actually built the converter that made possible the process bearing his name. The Bessemer process was first used in the United States in November 1864, in a factory in Wyandotte, Michigan.

Critical Thinking: Identifying Cause and Effect

At Level

Cause and Effect Posters

1. Review with students the information about breakthroughs in steel processing. Ask students to identify the important breakthrough and the results it had.
2. Write the following for students to see: *U.S. steel production increases.* Then have students identify the causes of the rise in steel production, as well as its effects.
3. Have each student create a cause and effect poster that illustrates the causes of the rise in U.S. steel production and the effects of this rise. Remind students that there may be more than one result. Encourage students to make their posters visually appealing.
4. Ask volunteers to share their posters with the class. **LS Visual/Spatial**

Alternative Assessment Handbook, Rubrics 6: Cause and Effect; and 28: Posters

Answers

Homestead Steel Mill *possible answers—provided jobs, created pollution*

Reading Check *The Bessemer process made the production of steel faster and cheaper and increased steel production in the United States, which in turn benefited other industries.*

Direct Teach

Main Idea

2 Use of Oil and Electricity

Advances in the use of oil and electricity improved communications and transportation.

Recall What were some of the uses of kerosene? *cooking, heating, and lighting*

Analyze What problem did Thomas Edison face regarding the use of electricity, and how did he solve it? *Few homes or businesses could get electricity; he built a power plant.*

Draw Conclusions What effect did competition have on the use of electricity? *Westinghouse and Edison competed to build improved power systems, which led to the rapid spread of electricity in the United States.*

CRF: Biography Activity: Inventors

Focus on Indiana

8.1.27 Give examples of scientific and technological developments that changed cultural life in the nineteenth-century United States, such as the use of photography, growth in the use of the telegraph, the completion of the transcontinental railroad, and the invention of the telephone.

Evaluate What effect do you think the discovery of natural gas in Indiana had on the state? *The state economy became more industrial.*

go.hrw.com
Online Resources
KEYWORD: SF7 CH19
ACTIVITY: Technology Time Line

Answers

Focus on Reading *It starts with the words* "As demand grew," *which are common cause and effect signal words.*

Time Line

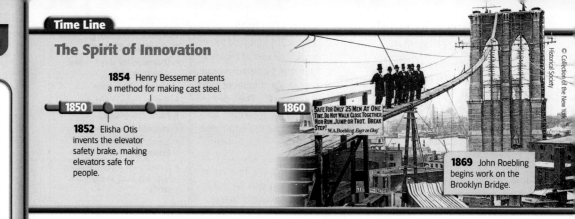

The Spirit of Innovation

1850

1852 Elisha Otis invents the elevator safety brake, making elevators safe for people.

1854 Henry Bessemer patents a method for making cast steel.

1860

SAFE FOR ONLY 25 MEN AT ONE TIME. DO NOT WALK CLOSE TOGETHER NOR RUN, JUMP, OR TROT. BREAK STEP!
W.A.Roebling Eng'r in Chief

1869 John Roebling begins work on the Brooklyn Bridge.

© Collection of the New York Historical Society

FOCUS ON INDIANA

Natural gas also helped fuel the steel industry and light cities and homes. The Trenton Field in western Indiana, discovered in 1886, was the largest know field of natural gas at the time. Natural gas wells in the region contributed to the rise of a "gas belt" in the state, but overuse of the field resulted in diminishing output by the early 1900s.

FOCUS ON READING

How does this paragraph show the cause and effect structure?

Use of Oil and Electricity

The Second Industrial Revolution was characterized by dramatic developments in the use and distribution of oil and electricity. These power sources fueled other changes.

Oil as a Power Source

An important technological breakthrough in the late 1800s was the use of petroleum, or oil, as a power source. People had known about oil for many years but had discovered few ways to use it. However, in the 1850s, chemists invented a way to convert crude, or unprocessed, oil into a fuel called kerosene. Kerosene could be used for cooking, heating, and lighting. Suddenly there was a demand for oil.

As demand grew, people began searching for a reliable source for oil. In 1859 Edwin L. Drake proved that it was possible to pump crude oil from the ground. Soon, wildcatters, or oil prospectors, drilled for oil in Ohio, Pennsylvania, and West Virginia. Oil became a big business as these states began producing millions of barrels per year. Oil companies built refineries to turn the crude oil into finished products like kerosene. One oil company supervisor referred to oil workers as "men who are supplying light for the world."

Electricity Spreads

In addition to kerosene, electricity became a critical source of light and power during the Second Industrial Revolution. The possible uses of electricity interested inventors like **Thomas Edison**. His research center in Menlo Park, New Jersey, was called an invention factory. Edison explained his practical approach to science.

> "I do not regard myself as a pure scientist, as so many persons have insisted that I am. I do not search for the laws of nature ... for the purpose of learning truth. I am only a professional inventor ... with the object [goal] of inventing that which will have commercial utility [use]."
>
> —Thomas Edison, quoted in *American Made*, by Harold C. Livesay

Edison eventually held more than 1,000 **patents**, exclusive rights to make or sell inventions. Patents allowed inventors to protect their inventions from being manufactured by others.

In 1878 Edison announced that he would soon invent a practical electric light. By the end of 1879 Edison and his team of inventors had created the electric lightbulb. The public was excited. However, Edison had a problem. At the time, few homes or businesses could get electricity. Edison therefore built a power plant that began supplying electricity to dozens of New York City buildings in

Cross-Discipline Activity: Science

At Level

Inventions Science Fair

Research Required

1. Review with students the advances that took place in the late 1800s as a result of the Second Industrial Revolution. Discuss with students advancements that have had a major effect on their world, such as electricity.
2. Tell students that they will research one of the inventions discussed in this section and create a science fair exhibit that explains how the invention or process works. Assign students to small groups and have each group research an invention.
3. Have students use their research to create a poster that explains how the idea or process works, what it is used for, and what effect it has had on the world.
4. Conduct a class science fair and have each group present their exhibit to the class.

LS Visual/Spatial, Verbal/Linguistic, Interpersonal

Alternative Assessment Handbook, Rubrics 28: Posters; and 29: Presentations

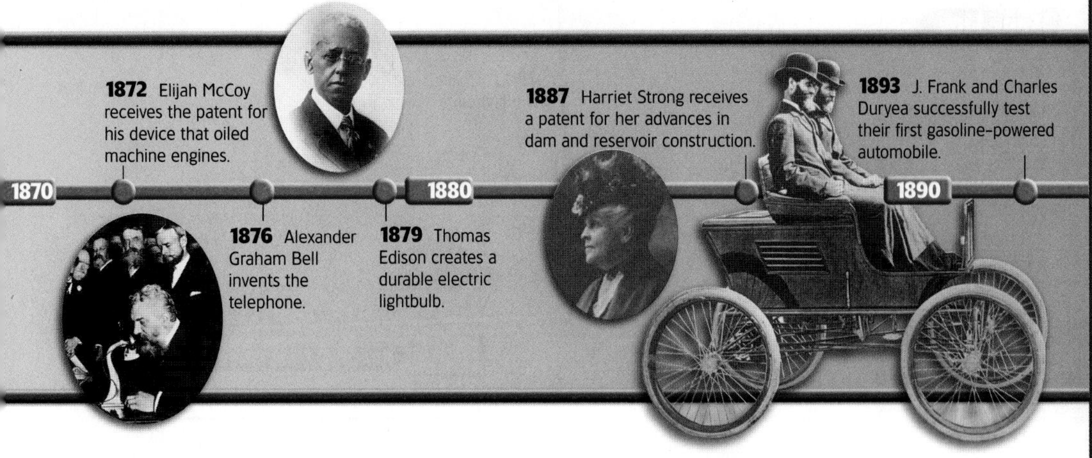

1872 Elijah McCoy receives the patent for his device that oiled machine engines.
1876 Alexander Graham Bell invents the telephone.
1879 Thomas Edison creates a durable electric lightbulb.
1887 Harriet Strong receives a patent for her advances in dam and reservoir construction.
1893 J. Frank and Charles Duryea successfully test their first gasoline-powered automobile.
1870
1880
1890

September 1882. The *New York Times* reported that with electric lighting in the newspaper offices, "it seemed almost like writing by daylight." However, Edison's equipment could not send electricity over long distances. As a result, his power company, Edison Electric, provided electricity mainly to central cities.

In the late 1880s, George Westinghouse built a power system that could send electricity across many miles. As Edison and Westinghouse competed, the use of electricity spread rapidly in the nation's cities. After a while, electricity soon lit homes and businesses and powered city factories. Electricity also was used to power streetcars in cities across the nation.

READING CHECK **Drawing Conclusions** Why did people begin to pump oil from the ground?

Rush of Inventions

In the late 1800s, inventors focused on finding solutions to practical problems. Communication and transportation took the lead.

Advances in Communication

Great advances in communication technologies took place in the late 1800s. By 1861, telegraph wires connected the East and West coasts. Five years later, a telegraph cable on the floor of the Atlantic Ocean connected the United States and Great Britain.

However, the telegraph carried only written messages and was difficult for untrained people to use. These problems were solved in March 1876, when inventor **Alexander Graham Bell** patented the telephone. Bell was a Scottish-born speech teacher who studied the science of sound. He called the telephone a "talking telegraph."

Telephone companies raced to lay thousands of miles of phone lines. By 1880 there were about 55,000 telephones in the United States, and by 1900 there were almost 1.5 million.

Automobiles and Planes

In 1876 a German engineer invented an engine powered by gasoline, another fuel made from oil. In 1893 Charles and J. Frank Duryea used a gasoline engine to build the first practical motorcar in the United States. By the early 1900s, thousands of cars were being built in the United States.

At first, only the wealthy could buy these early cars. **Henry Ford** introduced the Model T in 1908. Ford was the first to implement the moving assembly line in manufacturing, a process that greatly reduced the cost of building a product, thus making cars more affordable.

THE IMPACT TODAY

AT&T Corporation is a direct descendant of Bell's original company. AT&T pioneered the use of telephone cables across the oceans, satellite communications, and a radar system for the U.S. Defense Department.

ACADEMIC VOCABULARY

implement to put in place

Differentiating Instruction

Below Level

English-Language Learners

Standard English Mastery

1. Organize students into mixed-ability pairs. Then have each pair review the information on the advances in the use of oil and electricity.
2. Ask each pair to select two events that played a role in the use of oil and electricity. Then have each pair work together to write a newspaper headline for that event. Remind students that newspaper headlines should catch the readers' attention and give some information about the event. Encourage students to look at actual newspaper headlines before writing their own.
3. Ask students to read their headlines to the class. Then have each pair of students select one of their headlines and write the entire newspaper article. Remind students to write their articles using standard English.

LS Verbal/Linguistic, Interpersonal

Alternative Assessment Handbook, Rubric 23: Newspapers

Direct Teach

Main Idea

3 Rush of Inventions

A rush of inventions changed Americans' lives.

Recall What advances were made in communication and transportation? *the telegraph connected the United States and Britain, the telephone was invented, automobiles were invented and became more affordable, and the first piloted flight in a gas-powered airplane was made*

Analyze How did telephones improve communication? *They allowed people to communicate by voice over long distances.*

Making Inferences How do you think telephones and automobiles changed the lives of people who used them? *They made life easier because people could communicate over long-distances and travel from place to place quickly.*

CRF: Biography Activity: Orville and Wilbur Wright

CRF: Interdisciplinary Project: Technology Time Line

Info to Know

Telephone Companies At first, the telephone was considered so unusual that Western Union called it a toy and refused to buy the rights from Alexander Graham Bell. However, the potential of the telephone quickly became apparent, and many companies tried to start their own phone services. In 1879 the Bell Telephone Company successfully sued Western Union after it started the American Speaking Telephone Company. Bell himself faced 587 lawsuits contesting his exclusive patent on the telephone. Bell won every case, including 13 that went all the way to the Supreme Court.

Answers

Reading Check *As people developed uses for oil, they began to search for more reliable sources for the substance. Edwin L. Drake proved it was possible to pump crude oil from the ground.*

Direct Teach

Teaching Tip

To help students remember the inventors and inventions discussed in this section, have them create jingles in which they include the name of each inventor and invention. Suggest that students use a familiar melody as the basis of their jingle. Ask volunteers to share their jingles with the class. Then have the class vote on their favorite jingle.

Review & Assess

Close

Review with students the major inventions and processes discussed in the section.

Review

go.hrw.com Online Quiz, Section 19.1

Assess

SE Section 1 Assessment

PASS: Section Quiz 19.1

Alternative Assessment Handbook

Reteach/Classroom Intervention

Interactive Reader and Study Guide, Section 19.1

Interactive Skills Tutor CD-ROM

Time Line

The Spirit of Innovation

1893 George Ferris displays the first Ferris wheel at the World's Columbian Exposition in Chicago.

1900

1903 Orville Wright makes the first flight in a motorized airplane.

ANALYSIS SKILL READING TIME LINES

When was the telephone invented?

New engine technology helped make another breakthrough in transportation possible—air flight. Brothers **Wilbur and Orville Wright** built a lightweight airplane that used a small, gas-powered engine. In Kitty Hawk, North Carolina, Orville Wright made the first piloted flight in a gas-powered plane on December 17, 1903. This invention would change the way that many Americans traveled in the future and would increase the demand for oil production.

READING CHECK **Comparing** What new inventions excited the public in the 1800s, and how were they used?

SUMMARY AND PREVIEW The Second Industrial Revolution led to advances in energy sources, communication, and transportation. In the next section you will learn about the growth of big business.

Section 1 Assessment

go.hrw.com **Online Quiz** KEYWORD: SF7 HP19

Reviewing Ideas, Terms, and People

1. a. **Describe** What was the **Bessemer process**?
   b. **Summarize** How did improvements to railroads affect the economy and transportation in the United States?
   c. **Elaborate** What do you think was the most important effect of the Bessemer process? Why?
2. a. **Identify** What is kerosene, and for what could it be used?
   b. **Explain** What problem did **Thomas Edison** face regarding the use of electricity, and how did he solve it?
3. a. **Recall** What contribution did **Wilbur and Orville Wright** make to transportation?
   b. **Draw Conclusions** How did **Alexander Graham Bell**'s invention improve life in the United States?
   c. **Elaborate** Why do you think there was a rush of inventions in the late 1800s?

Critical Thinking

4. **Analyzing** Look over your notes on inventors. Use them to complete a table like the one below about inventors and their inventions.

Inventor	Invention

FOCUS ON WRITING

5. **Information on a Product** In your notes, list what kinds of new products became available at this time. What do you think would be a good thing to make and sell during the late 1800s?

Section 1 Assessment Answers

1. **a.** a process of making steel quickly and cheaply by blasting air through melted iron
   b. It led to faster transportation and increased employment.
   c. possible answer—Steel production increased, causing steel prices to drop and lowering the cost of building railroads.
2. **a.** a fuel made from petroleum; cooking, heating, and home lighting
   b. Few locations could receive electricity; he built a power plant to supply electricity to New York City buildings.
3. **a.** They built a gas-powered airplane.
   b. It allowed for faster communication.
   c. possible answer—People were inspired by other inventions.
4. Edison—electric lighting, inexpensive form of lighting; Wright Brothers—gas-powered airplane, improved transportation; Bell—telephone, improved communication; Bessemer—Bessemer process, improved steel production
5. new products—light bulb, telephone, automobile; product ideas—electrical appliances, gas-powered products

Answers

Reading Time Lines *1876*

Reading Check *airplanes for flying; electricity for power; telegraphs and telephones for communicating; automobiles for transportation*

Big Business

SECTION 2

If YOU were there...

It is 1895, and your town is home to a large corporation. The company's founder and owner, a wealthy man, lives in a mansion on a hill. He is a fair employer but not especially generous. Many townspeople work in his factory. You and other town leaders feel that he should contribute more to local charities and community organizations.

How could this business leader help the town more?

BUILDING BACKGROUND Advanced technology along with the use of oil and electric power helped American businesses grow. Soon the shape of the American economy changed. Some companies grew so large that they began to dominate entire industries.

Dominance of Big Business

In the late 1800s many entrepreneurs formed their businesses as **corporations**, or businesses that sell portions of ownership called stock shares. The leaders of these corporations were some of the most widely respected members of American society in the late 1800s. Political leaders praised prosperous businesspeople as examples of American hard work, talent, and success.

New sales techniques like those taught by John H. Patterson helped change business practices.

What You Will Learn...

Main Ideas

1. The rise of corporations and powerful business leaders led to the dominance of big business in the United States.
2. People and the government began to question the methods of big business.

The Big Idea

The growth of big business in the late 1800s led to the creation of monopolies.

Key Terms and People

corporations, *p. 619*
Andrew Carnegie, *p. 620*
vertical integration, *p. 620*
John D. Rockefeller, *p. 620*
horizontal integration, *p. 621*
trust, *p. 621*
Leland Stanford, *p. 621*
social Darwinism, *p. 621*
monopoly, *p. 622*
Sherman Antitrust Act, *p. 622*

TAKING NOTES As you read this section, take notes on the new business practices you learn about. Keep them organized in a chart like the one below.

New Business Practice

IN 8.2.4, 8.4.2, 8.4.3, 8.4.4, 8.4.5

Preteach

Bellringer

If YOU were there . . . Use the **Daily Bellringer Transparency** to help students answer the question.

Daily Bellringer Transparency 19.2

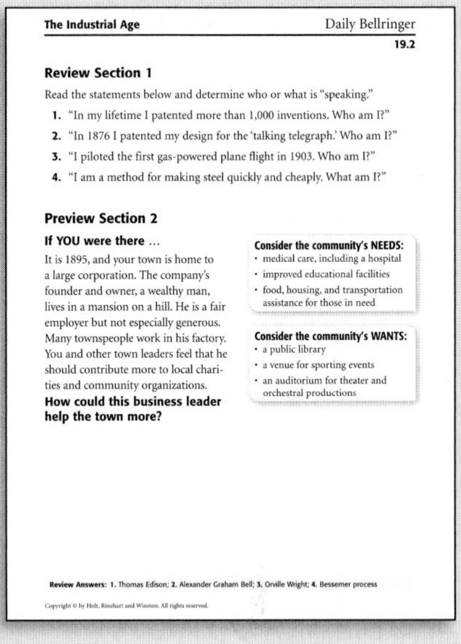

The Industrial Age — Daily Bellringer 19.2

Review Section 1

Read the statements below and determine who or what is "speaking."

1. "In my lifetime I patented more than 1,000 inventions. Who am I?"
2. "In 1876 I patented my design for the 'talking telegraph.' Who am I?"
3. "I piloted the first gas-powered plane flight in 1903. Who am I?"
4. "I am a method for making steel quickly and cheaply. What am I?"

Preview Section 2

If YOU were there ...

It is 1895, and your town is home to a large corporation. The company's founder and owner, a wealthy man, lives in a mansion on a hill. He is a fair employer but not especially generous. Many townspeople work in his factory. You and other town leaders feel that he should contribute more to local charities and community organizations.

How could this business leader help the town more?

Consider the community's NEEDS:
- medical care, including a hospital
- improved educational facilities
- food, housing, and transportation assistance for those in need

Consider the community's WANTS:
- a public library
- a venue for sporting events
- an auditorium for theater and orchestral productions

Review Answers: 1. Thomas Edison; 2. Alexander Graham Bell; 3. Orville Wright; 4. Bessemer process

Academic Vocabulary

Review with students the high-use academic term in this section:

acquire to get (p. 620)

CRF: Vocabulary Builder Activity, Section 2

Taking Notes

Have students copy the graphic organizer onto their own paper and then use it to take notes on the section. This activity will prepare students for the Section Assessment, in which they will complete a graphic organizer that builds on the information using a critical-thinking skill.

Teach the Big Idea

At Level

Big Business

1. **Teach** To teach the main ideas in the section, use the questions in the Direct Teach boxes.
2. **Apply** Have students create an outline of this section. Ask students to use the same headings and subheadings as used in the section. Then have students identify three or four specific details to support each heading or subheading. Remind students to include bolded terms or people in their outlines.
   LS Verbal/Linguistic
3. **Review** Organize the class into small groups. Have students in each group compare and contrast their outlines as a review of the section.
4. **Practice/Homework** Have students use their outlines to write a one-page summary of the section. Remind students to write the summary in their own words.
   LS Verbal/Linguistic

Alternative Assessment Handbook, Rubric 37: Writing Assignments

Section Correlations

IN

8.2.4 Examine functions of the national government in the lives of people. **8.4.2** Illustrate elements of the three types of economic systems, using cases from United States history. **8.4.3** Evaluate how the characteristics of a market economy have affected the economic and labor development of the United States. **8.4.4** Explain the basic economic functions of the government in the economy of the United States. **8.4.5** Analyze contributions of entrepreneurs and inventors in the development of the United States economy.

Direct Teach

Main Idea

1 Dominance of Big Business

The rise of corporations and powerful business leaders led to the dominance of big businesses in the United States.

Describe What role do stockholders play in corporations? *Individuals invest money through the purchase of stock. This money enables corporations to engage in business, and hopefully, generate profit, of which stockholders are entitled to a portion.*

Explain Why are corporations advantageous for stockholders? *They can only lose the money they have invested and they are free to sell stock to whomever they want.*

Elaborate Why do you think Andrew Carnegie was one of the most admired businesspeople of his time? *possible answer—due to his great success in the steel industry.*

CRF: Biography Activity: Leland Stanford

Info to Know

New York Stock Exchange One of the world's largest stock markets, the New York Stock Exchange (NYSE) was founded in New York City in 1792. A meeting of some 24 New York stockbrokers under a buttonwood tree on Wall Street led to the Buttonwood Agreement, which established the Exchange. The first listed company was the Bank of New York. Today, the NYSE lists stocks for some 2,800 companies.

Focus on Indiana

IN 8.4.5 Analyze contributions of entrepreneurs and inventors in the development of the United States economy.

Identify Who was Madame CJ Walker? *She owned a hair-care product company and was the first African American woman millionaire.*

Answers

The Rise of Investing *They wanted to share in the profits of the corporation.*

FOCUS ON INDIANA

One of the most successful businesses of the late 1800s was the Madame CJ Walker Manufacturing Company. The company was one of the only providers of hair care products for African Americans. It was started by Sarah Breedlove and her husband C.J. Walker in 1906, and by 1914 Madame Walker had become the first African American woman millionaire.

ACADEMIC VOCABULARY

acquire to get

Corporations Generate Wealth

Successful corporations reward not only the people who found them but also investors who hold stock. Stockholders in a corporation typically get a percentage of profits based on the amount of stock they own. Although stockholders actually own the corporation, they do not run its day-to-day business. Instead, they elect a board of directors that chooses the corporation's main leaders, such as the president.

Corporations provided several important advantages over earlier business forms. Stockholders in a corporation are not responsible for business debts. If a corporation fails financially, the stockholders lose only the money that they invested. Stockholders are also usually free to sell their stock to whomever they want, whenever they want. As a result, corporations encouraged more investment in businesses. By 1900 more than 100 million shares per year were being traded on the New York Stock Exchange.

Business Leaders

Countless business leaders became wealthy, powerful, and famous because of the business boom. **Andrew Carnegie** was one of the most admired businesspeople of the time. Born in Scotland, Carnegie came to the United States as a poor immigrant. As a teenager he took a job with a railroad company and quickly worked his way up to the position of railroad superintendent.

In 1873 he focused his efforts on steelmaking. Carnegie expanded his business by buying out competitors when steel prices were low. By 1901 Carnegie's mills were producing more steel than all of Great Britain's mills combined. Carnegie's businesses succeeded largely through **vertical integration**, or ownership of businesses involved in each step of a manufacturing process. For example, to lower production costs, Carnegie acquired the iron ore mines, coalfields, and railroads needed to supply and support his steel mills.

John D. Rockefeller was also successful in consolidating, or combining, businesses. By age 21, while a partner in a wholesale business, he decided to start an oil-refining company. In only 10 years Rockefeller's Standard Oil Company was the country's largest oil refiner. Like Carnegie, Rockefeller used ver-

The Rise of Investing

Investors purchased stock in corporations in record numbers in the late 1800s. They received stock certificates, like the one shown here, to document their part ownership in corporations. Corporations used the money raised by selling stocks to expand. Standard Oil Company financed the building of this refinery in Richmond, California, by selling stock.

Why did investors buy stock?

Cross-Discipline Activity: Economics

Above Level

Studying the Stock Market

Research Required

1. Review with students the advantages of corporations and the way in which corporations function. Tell students that stock is traded in several major stock markets, including the New York Stock Exchange and the NASDAQ in the United States.
2. Have each student choose a company that was in existence during the late 1800s and track the stock of that company. Companies might include U.S. Steel, Western Union, or Ford Motor Company. Discuss the symbols used by corporations and how to find symbols for companies they will track.
3. Have students track the value of stock for the companies they selected for a set period of time. Then have students create a line graph that depicts changes in value over this period.
4. Have students display their line graph for the class to see. **LS Visual/Spatial, Verbal/Linguistic**

Alternative Assessment Handbook, Rubric 1: Acquiring Information

Primary Source

POLITICAL CARTOON

Trusts

The wealth and size of trusts such as Standard Oil made many Americans fear the influence of business leaders over government.

What do you think the smokestacks on the Capitol building represent?

What does the position of the White House suggest?

ANALYSIS SKILL **ANALYZING PRIMARY SOURCES**

How does the cartoonist show Rockefeller's power?

tical integration. For example, the company controlled most of the pipelines it used.

Rockefeller's company also developed **horizontal integration**, or owning all businesses in a certain field. By 1880 Rockefeller's companies controlled about 90 percent of the oil refining business in the United States. Rockefeller also formed a **trust**, a legal arrangement grouping together a number of companies under a single board of directors. To earn more money, trusts often tried to get rid of competition and to control production.

Leland Stanford was another important business leader of the late 1800s. He made a fortune selling equipment to miners. While governor of California, he became one of the founders of the state's Central Pacific railroad. Stanford also founded Stanford University.

Late in life, Stanford argued that industries should be owned and managed cooperatively by workers. He believed this would be the fulfillment of democracy.

READING CHECK **Comparing and Contrasting** Why did Andrew Carnegie use vertical integration?

Questioning the Methods of Big Business

By the late 1800s, people and the government were becoming uncomfortable with child labor, low wages, and poor working conditions. They began to view big business as a problem.

Social Darwinism

Many business leaders justified their business methods through their belief in **social Darwinism**, a view of society based on scientist Charles Darwin's theory of natural selection. Social Darwinists thought that Darwin's "survival of the fittest" theory decided which human beings would succeed in business and in life in general.

Other business leaders, however, believed that the rich had a duty to aid the poor. These leaders tried to help the less fortunate through philanthropy, or giving money to charities. Carnegie, Rockefeller, Stanford, and other business leaders gave away large sums. Carnegie gave away more than $350 million to charities, about $60 million of which went to

Direct Teach

Main Idea

❷ Questioning the Methods of Big Business

People and the government began to question the methods of big business.

Define What is social Darwinism? *the view that Darwin's "survival of the fittest" theory determines who would succeed in business and in life*

Make Inferences Why did some business leaders give money to charity? *They felt that the rich had a duty to aid the poor.*

CRF: Literature Activity: Henry Demarest Lloyd, "The Lords of Industry"

Info to Know

Big Business and Philanthropy

American industrialists were well-known for their philanthropy to important causes. John D. Rockefeller, head of Standard Oil, established foundations for medical research and education. Steel magnate Andrew Carnegie gave generously to universities, public libraries, and cultural institutions, including the well-known Carnegie Hall theater in New York City. California's Stanford University was founded by a grant from railroad tycoon Leland Stanford in honor of his son, and only child, who died of typhoid fever.

Critical Thinking: Supporting a Point of View

At Level

Big Business Panel Discussion

1. Review the meaning of social Darwinism and how it was interpreted and viewed during the Second Industrial Revolution. Ask students what problems might have caused people to question the practices of big business. How did business leaders respond to the criticism?
2. Organize the class into three groups, one representing business leaders, one representing workers, and one representing government. Tell the students that they will stage a panel discussion about the methods of big business. Ask each group to write a short opening statement that explains their stance on the methods of big business. Then have students write questions to ask during the discussion.
3. On the day of the panel discussion, select several students to serve as moderators and on the panel. Have the other students serve as audience members who ask questions of the panel. **LS Verbal/Linguistic, Interpersonal**

Alternative Assessment Handbook, Rubric 10: Debates

Answers

Analyzing Primary Sources *by making him much larger and putting the White House in his hands*

Reading Check *to increase control and profits and lower production costs*

Direct Teach

Main Idea

❷ Questioning the Methods of Big Business

People and the government began to question the methods of big business.

Explain Why did critics oppose the practices of big business? *They believed big business used unfair practices like driving smaller competitors out of business and creating monopolies.*

Evaluate Was the Sherman Antitrust Act successful in curbing the power of wealthy trusts? Why? *No, because it did not legally define a trust and was too difficult to enforce.*

CRF: Economics and History Activity: Monopolies and Trusts

Review & Assess

Close

Have students write a short summary of this section as a review.

Review

go.hrw.com Online Quiz, Section 19.2

Assess

SE Section 2 Assessment

PASS: Section Quiz 19.2

Alternative Assessment Handbook

Reteach/Classroom Intervention

Interactive Reader and Study Guide, Section 19.2

Interactive Skills Tutor CD-ROM

Answers

Reading Check *Voters were concerned about the political power of trusts and wanted the government to control monopolies and trusts.*

fund public libraries to expand access to books. By the late 1800s, various charities had received millions of dollars from philanthropists.

The Antitrust Movement

Critics of big business said that many business leaders earned their fortunes through unfair business practices. These criticisms grew stronger in the 1880s as corporations became more powerful. Large corporations often used their size and strength to drive smaller competitors out of business. Carnegie and Rockefeller, for example, pressured railroads to charge their companies lower shipping rates. Powerful trusts also arranged to sell goods and services below market value. Smaller competitors went out of business trying to match those prices. Then the trusts raised prices again.

Some people became concerned when a trust gained a **monopoly**, or total ownership of a product or service. Critics argued that monopolies reduced necessary competition. They believed competition in a free market economy kept prices low and the quality of goods and services high.

Some Americans also worried about the political power of wealthy trusts. Many citizens and small businesses wanted the government to help control monopolies and trusts. People who favored trusts responded that trusts were more efficient and gave the consumer dependable products or services.

Many members of Congress favored big business. However, elected officials could not ignore the concerns of voters. In July 1890 Congress passed the **Sherman Antitrust Act**, a law that made it illegal to create monopolies or trusts that restrained trade. It stated that any "attempt to monopolize . . . any part of the trade or commerce among the several States" was a crime. However, the act did not clearly define a trust in legal terms. The antitrust laws were therefore difficult to enforce. Corporations and trusts kept growing in size and power.

READING CHECK **Analyzing** How did concerns about trusts lead to the Sherman Antitrust Act?

SUMMARY AND PREVIEW In the late 1800s some corporations became monopolies that dominated industries such as oil. In the next section you will learn about how industrial workers organized to improve working conditions.

Section 2 Assessment

go.hrw.com Online Quiz KEYWORD: SF7 HP19

Reviewing Ideas, Terms, and People

1. a. **Identify** What are **horizontal** and **vertical integration**?
   b. **Explain** What are the benefits of investing in **corporations**?
   c. **Evaluate** What do you think about the business methods of **Carnegie**, **Rockefeller**, and **Stanford**?
2. a. **Describe** What is **social Darwinism**?
   b. **Summarize** What concerns did critics of big business have regarding **trusts**?
   c. **Evaluate** Was the **Sherman Antitrust Act** successful? Why or why not?

Critical Thinking

3. **Contrasting** Look back over your notes about new business practices. Find examples of the new business practices. Use them to complete a graphic organizer like the one below.

New Practices	Example

FOCUS ON WRITING

4. **Gathering Information on Business** Look back over your notes and determine what new practices helped businesses expand during this time. Which practices could you use to start your business? Where would you try to sell your product?

Section 2 Assessment Answers

1. **a.** horizontal—owning all businesses in a certain field; vertical—ownership of businesses involved in each step of manufacturing
   b. Stockholders receive a share of profits, and are not responsible for business debts.
   c. Answers should show an understanding of the impact made by each business leader.
2. **a.** a view of society based on Charles Darwin's theory of natural selection; the fittest would succeed in business and in life in general.
   b. they used unfair business practices to drive competitors out of the marketplace
   c. not successful; it did not clearly define a trust and was difficult to enforce
3. vertical integration—Carnegie's acquisition of businesses to supply and support his steel mills; horizontal integration—Rockefeller's ownership of 90% of the U.S. oil refining industry; corporations and trusts—Rockefeller's Standard Oil Company
4. new practices—development of corporations and trusts, vertical/horizontal integration, new sales techniques

BIOGRAPHY

Andrew Carnegie, John D. Rockefeller, and Leland Stanford

How would you go about building an industry?

Andrew Carnegie (1835–1919) Born in Scotland, Carnegie rose to become a multibillionaire in the steel industry. He brought new technologies to his steel mills and made them extremely efficient. In 1901 he sold Carnegie Steel Company for $250 billion, making him the richest man in the world.

John D. Rockefeller (1839–1937) Rockefeller got his start in the oil business in Cleveland, Ohio. Rockefeller's Standard Oil Company quickly bought out its competitors throughout the United States. To better control oil production and delivery, Rockefeller also bought railroad rights, terminals, and pipelines.

Leland Stanford (1825–1893) Leland Stanford was born to a New York farming family that sent him to excellent private schools. After practicing law in Wisconsin, he made his career in California. Stanford was instrumental in building the western section of the transcontinental railroad. He then plunged into politics, serving one term as governor. His political connections helped him obtain huge state land grants and other benefits for his railroad companies. As president of Central Pacific and Southern Pacific, he oversaw the laying of thousands of miles of track throughout the West.

Why are they so important? Carnegie, Rockefeller, and Stanford helped make America the world's greatest industrial power by the end of the 1800s. They built giant industries that made goods cheaply by keeping workers' wages low. They also engaged in ruthless business practices to defeat their competition and create monopolies. The Sherman Antitrust Act was passed in reaction to the Standard Oil monopoly. Later in life, all three men became philanthropists, people devoted to charity work. Rockefeller's philanthropies gave out $500 million in his lifetime. Carnegie spent $350 million, funding educational grants, concert halls, and nearly 3,000 public libraries. Stanford founded Stanford University in 1884.

Finding Main Ideas
Why are these three men important figures in U.S. history?

Critical Thinking: Summarizing

At Level

Writing Eulogies

1. Review with students the biographies of John D. Rockefeller, Andrew Carnegie, and Leland Stanford.
2. Ask each student to imagine that he or she has been selected to give the eulogy at the funeral of one of these famous American business leaders. Ask students to select which man they will eulogize.
3. Remind students that family members, trusted friends, and advisors will be in attendance. Ask students to consider what they will say in a eulogy. Then have each student write a one-page eulogy evaluating the life and achievements of the person selected.
4. Ask volunteers to deliver their eulogy to the class. LS **Verbal/Linguistic**

Alternative Assessment Handbook, Rubric 37: Writing Assignments

Biography

Reading Focus Question

Ask students to consider how they might go about building a multibillion dollar industry. Have students consider what it would take to build an industry. Examples might include investors, political connections, and ambition. Ask students how people might feel about a businessperson who is able to build an industry from the ground up.

Info to Know

Standard Oil Trust In the late 1800s and early 1900s John D. Rockefeller's oil trust controlled virtually all oil production, processing, and transportation in the United States. In 1892 the Ohio Supreme Court forced Rockefeller to dissolve the trust, although it continued to operate until 1911 when the trust was finally forced to break apart. Today, former Standard Oil companies still remain, but as independent companies, among them are ExxonMobil, Chevron, and Amoco.

Did you know . . .

Andrew Carnegie's first job was as a bobbin boy at a cotton factory in Pennsylvania, where he made about $1.20 a week. Fifty-two years later, at the age of 64, Carnegie sold his Carnegie Steel Company for $480 million.

Answers

Finding Main Ideas *They each built companies that made millions of dollars, introduced new business practices or technologies, and made many charitable contributions.*

Preteach

Bellringer

If YOU were there . . . Use the **Daily Bellringer Transparency** to help students answer the question.

Daily Bellringer Transparency 19.3

The Industrial Age — Daily Bellringer **19.3**

Review Section 2

Unscramble the letters in each underlined word to reveal the solution to each clue.

1. NRADWE RNGEAIEC
   Clue: He was a business leader in the steel industry.
2. PRTCOSNROOAI
   Clue: These are businesses that sell portions of ownership called shares.
3. STTUR
   Clue: This legal arrangement grouped together several companies under one board of directors.

Preview Section 3

If YOU were there ...

You run a button machine in a clothing factory in the 1890s. You work from 7:00 in the morning until 6:00 at night, every day except Sunday. Your only break is fifteen minutes for lunch. Now you hear about a movement to start a workers' union to bargain with your employer. Union members will ask for an eight-hour workday. But you think your employer might fire you if you join.

Would you join the union?

Consider the PROS:
- potential for shorter work hours
- potential for better pay
- potential for better working conditions

Consider the CONS:
- risk of being fired
- risk that the union won't win
- risk of getting swept up into something beyond your control

Review Answers: 1. Andrew Carnegie; 2. corporations; 3. trust

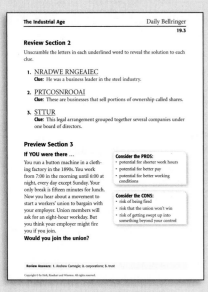

Building Vocabulary

Preteach or review the following terms:

conspiracy an agreement among two or more people to perform an illegal act (p. 627)

specialization the act of concentrating on a specific activity (p. 624)

strike a temporary stoppage of work by employees (p. 626)

CRF: Vocabulary Builder Activity, Section 3

Taking Notes

Have students copy the graphic organizer onto their own paper and then use it to take notes on the section. This activity will prepare students for the Section Assessment, in which they will complete a graphic organizer that builds on the information using a critical-thinking skill.

Section Correlations

IN

8.4.3 Evaluate how the characteristics of a market economy have affected the economic and labor development of the United States. **8.4.6** Relate technolgoical change and inventions to changes in labor productivity in the United States in the eighteenth and neneteenth centuries.

SECTION 3

Industrial Workers

What You Will Learn...

Main Ideas

1. The desire to maximize profits and become more efficient led to poor working conditions.
2. Workers began to organize and demand improvements in working conditions and pay.
3. Labor strikes often turned violent and failed to accomplish their goals.

The Big Idea

Changes in the workplace led to a rise in labor unions and workers' strikes.

Key Terms and People

Frederick W. Taylor, *p. 624*
Knights of Labor, *p. 625*
Terence V. Powderly, *p. 625*
American Federation of Labor, *p. 625*
Samuel Gompers, *p. 625*
collective bargaining, *p. 626*
Mary Harris Jones, *p. 626*
Haymarket Riot, *p. 626*
Homestead strike, *p. 627*
Pullman strike, *p. 627*

TAKING NOTES As you read this section, take notes about the problems workers faced in the new economy. Organize your notes in a chart like the one below.

Problems of Workers

IN 8.1.27, 8.3.1, 8.4.3, 8.4.5, 8.4.6

If YOU were there...

You run a button machine in a clothing factory in the 1890s. You work from 7:00 in the morning until 6:00 at night, every day except Sunday. Your only break is 15 minutes for lunch. Now you hear about a movement to start a workers' union to bargain with your employer. Union members will ask for an eight-hour workday. But you think your employer might fire you if you join.

Would you join the union?

BUILDING BACKGROUND The rise of corporations and the establishment of monopolies gave big business a great deal of power. An antitrust movement arose to try to limit the power of trusts. Workers themselves began to organize and take action against bad working conditions and other problems.

Maximizing Profits and Efficiency

During the late 1800s, several factors led to a decline in the quality of working conditions. Machines run by unskilled workers were eliminating the jobs of many skilled craftspeople. These low-paid workers could be replaced easily. Factories began to focus on specialization, or workers repeating a single step again and again. Specialization brought costs down and caused production to rise. But it also made workers tired, bored, and more likely to be injured. Specialization allowed for Henry Ford's idea of a moving assembly line to speed production. Ford's use of the moving assembly line allowed automobiles to be made more quickly and cheaply. Automobiles soon became available to a wider segment of the population than ever before.

In 1909 **Frederick W. Taylor**, an efficiency engineer, published a popular book called *The Principles of Scientific Management.* He encouraged managers to view workers as interchangeable parts of the production process. In factories, managers influenced by Taylor paid less attention to working conditions. Injuries increased, and as conditions grew worse, workers looked for ways to bring about change.

READING CHECK **Identifying Cause and Effect** Why did companies begin to use scientific management, and how did it affect workers?

Teach the Big Idea

At Level

Industrial Workers

1. **Teach** To teach the main ideas in the section, use the questions in the Direct Teach boxes.
2. **Apply** Organize the class into two groups. Assign one group to represent labor unions and workers and the other to represent the management of a large company. Ask students to imagine that their company has been operating on a ten-hour workday for many years, which has been highly profitable. Now, the labor union wants to cut the workers' hours to eight per day. Ask each group to develop points in support of its position, then stage a mock debate to argue for its cause. **LS Interpersonal**
3. **Review** As you review the section, ask students to discuss labor and management views of labor issues.
4. **Practice/Homework** Ask each student to list the pros and cons of labor unions. **LS Verbal/Linguistic**

Alternative Assessment Handbook, Rubrics 10: Debates; and 37: Writing Assignments

Poor Working Conditions

Small, crowded rooms. Stuffy air. Unsafe workplaces. Long hours. Low pay. No job security. These were the facts of working life for millions of Americans during the Second Industrial Revolution.

How did workers respond to these conditions?

Workers Organize

Workers formed labor unions to get better wages and working conditions for all workers in a factory or industry. The first national labor union, the **Knights of Labor**, was founded in the 1870s. It pushed for an eight-hour workday, equal pay for equal work, and an end to child labor. Union members also wanted the government to regulate trusts. Unlike most unions at the time, the Knights included both skilled and unskilled workers. The Knights of Labor was originally organized much like a secret society. In 1879 **Terence V. Powderly** became leader of the Knights. He ended all secrecy, creating the first truly national labor union in the United States.

Another early labor union was the **American Federation of Labor (AFL)**, led by **Samuel Gompers**. Unlike the Knights, the American Federation of Labor organized individual national unions, such as the mine-workers' and steelworkers' unions. The AFL

BIOGRAPHY

Samuel Gompers
1850–1924

Samuel Gompers was a Jewish immigrant born in London. He came to the United States with his parents in 1863 at age 13. He worked as a cigar maker and joined a local union, eventually becoming its president. The Cigarmakers Union was reorganized and later joined the American Federation of Labor. Gompers became the AFL's first president and remained so, except for the year 1895, until his death. He campaigned for basic trade-union rights, such as the right to picket and to organize boycotts and strikes. His efforts on behalf of workers helped organized labor to gain respect.

Summarizing How did Samuel Gompers help the labor-union movement?

Direct Teach

Main Idea

❶ Maximizing Profits and Efficiency

The desire to maximize profits and become more efficient led to poor working conditions.

Recall Why did factories focus on specialization? *It brought down costs and increased production.*

Explain How did machines lead to a decrease in jobs? *Skilled craftspeople were no longer needed, and a single machine could replace several workers.*

Main Idea

❷ Workers Organize

Workers began to organize and demand improvements in working conditions and pay.

Recall What were two important labor unions in the late 1800s? *the Knights of Labor and the American Federation of Labor*

Make Inferences Why did collective bargaining give workers a greater chance of success? *because laborers worked together to convince employers to meet their demands*

CRF: Biography Activity: Mother Jones

CRF: Primary Source Activity: Samuel Gompers, Testimony before Congress

go.hrw.com
Online Resources
KEYWORD: SF7 CH19
ACTIVITY: Life of a Steelworker

Critical Thinking: Supporting a Point of View — At Level

Expressing Workers' Views

1. Review with students the decline in the quality of working conditions that many factories experienced in the late 1800s. Ask students to discuss what effect these poor conditions might have had on the workers. Remind students that many workers responded by organizing labor unions to represent the demands of workers.
2. Have students make a list of complaints that workers may have had about their working conditions and steps that labor unions might have taken to correct these problems.
3. Have students create speeches, songs, or poems that express these ideas. For example a song might tell of poor working conditions and encourage workers to join a union. Remind students that they must include both complaints of workers and the goals of labor unions.
4. Ask volunteers to share their speeches, songs, or poems with the class. LS **Verbal/Linguistic, Auditory/Musical**

Alternative Assessment Handbook, Rubrics 24: Oral Presentations; and 26: Poems and Songs

Answers

Reading Check (previous page) *to help increase efficiency; working conditions grew worse, injuries increased, and workers looked for ways to bring about change*

Poor Working Conditions *formed labor unions to get better wages and working conditions*

Biography *campaigned for basic trade union rights*

Direct Teach

Main Idea

3 Labor Strikes

Labor strikes often turned violent and failed to accomplish their goals.

Recall What were union members protesting during the Homestead Strike? *a plan to buy new machinery and cut jobs*

Analyze Did the Haymarket Riot help or hurt the labor movement? *possible answer—hurt, because it resulted in a decline in Knights of Labor membership*

Make Judgments Do you think strikes are an effective and appropriate way to handle labor disputes? Explain. *Answers will vary, but students should use examples from the text to support their answer.*

- **CRF:** History and Geography Activity: Pullman's Company Town
- **CRF:** Primary Source Activity: In Support of the Coal Miners
- Map Transparency 61: Major Labor Strikes, Late 1800s

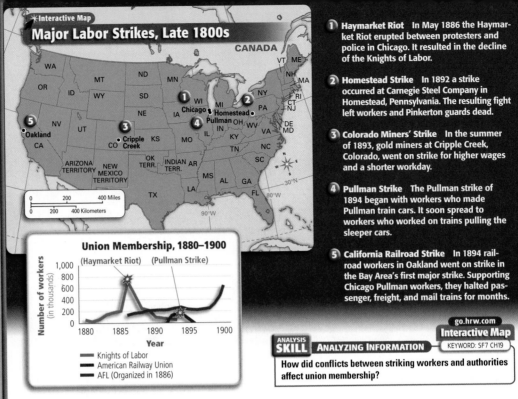

Interactive Map: Major Labor Strikes, Late 1800s

go.hrw.com
Online Resources
KEYWORD: SF7 CH19
ACTIVITY: Recognizing Mother Jones

Interactive Map

Major Labor Strikes, Late 1800s

1 **Haymarket Riot** In May 1886 the Haymarket Riot erupted between protesters and police in Chicago. It resulted in the decline of the Knights of Labor.

2 **Homestead Strike** In 1892 a strike occurred at Carnegie Steel Company in Homestead, Pennsylvania. The resulting fight left workers and Pinkerton guards dead.

3 **Colorado Miners' Strike** In the summer of 1893, gold miners at Cripple Creek, Colorado, went on strike for higher wages and a shorter workday.

4 **Pullman Strike** The Pullman strike of 1894 began with workers who made Pullman train cars. It soon spread to workers who worked on trains pulling the sleeper cars.

5 **California Railroad Strike** In 1894 railroad workers in Oakland went on strike in the Bay Area's first major strike. Supporting Chicago Pullman workers, they halted passenger, freight, and mail trains for months.

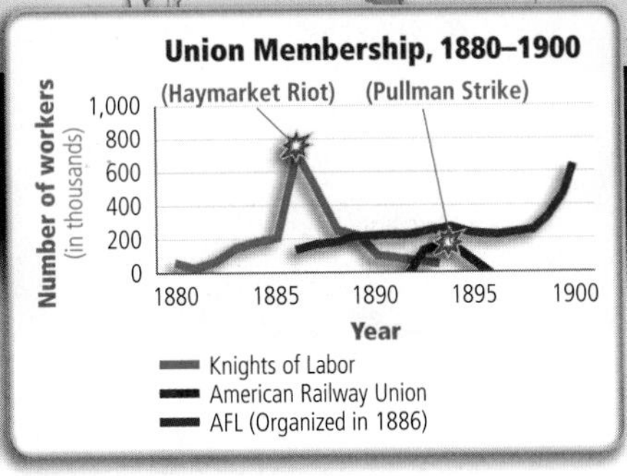

go.hrw.com
Interactive Map
KEYWORD: SF7 CH19

ANALYSIS SKILL ANALYZING INFORMATION

How did conflicts between striking workers and authorities affect union membership?

also limited its membership to skilled workers. This gave the union great bargaining power but left out most workers. The AFL tried to get better wages, hours, and working conditions for laborers. By 1890 the AFL's membership was larger than that of the Knights. With **collective bargaining**—all workers acting collectively, or together—workers had a much greater chance of success in negotiating with management. Most employers opposed collective bargaining. One company president said, "I shall never give in. I would rather go out of business."

THE IMPACT TODAY

In 1955 the AFL merged with the Congress of Industrial Organizations to become the AFL-CIO. Today the organization has more than 10 million members.

Many women took active roles in unions. For example, **Mary Harris Jones**, an Irish immigrant, worked for better conditions for miners. A fiery speaker, she organized strikes and helped educate workers.

READING CHECK **Contrasting** How did the Knights of Labor and the AFL differ?

Labor Strikes

By the late 1800s, other unions were gaining strength. Major workers' strikes swept the country and included miners in Colorado, steel workers in Pennsylvania, and railroad workers in Illinois and California. The first major labor strike began in 1886 in Chicago.

In May 1886, thousands of union members in Chicago went on strike because they wanted an eight-hour workday. Two strikers were killed in a fight with police. The next night, workers met at Haymarket Square to protest the killings. In what became known as the **Haymarket Riot**, someone threw a bomb that wounded many police officers and killed eight. The police fired into the crowd, killing several people and wounding 100 others.

Differentiating Instruction

Above Level

Advanced/Gifted and Talented

Research Required

1. Review with students the major labor strikes discussed above. Discuss the causes and results of these strikes.
2. Ask each student to select one of the major labor strikes from the map above and use the library, Internet, or other resources to research information about that strike. Students should identify the cause of the strike, how the strike was settled, and the results of the strike.
3. Have students write a newspaper or magazine article about the strike and its results. If possible, have students include quotations from the sources they researched.
4. Ask volunteers to read their article aloud to the class.

Alternative Assessment Handbook, Rubrics 23: Newspapers; and 30: Research

Answers

Analyzing Information *often resulted in a decline in Union membership*

Reading Check *Knights of Labor—had both skilled and unskilled workers; AFL—had skilled workers, was organized into individual unions, and was larger than the Knights of Labor*

Eight people, some of whom were not at the riot, were arrested and convicted of conspiracy. One of them had a Knights of Labor membership card. Though Knights leadership had not supported the strike, several local chapters had. Membership in the Knights fell quickly.

Sometimes, business owners succeeded in breaking up unions. In 1892 a violent strike called the **Homestead strike** took place at Andrew Carnegie's Homestead steel factory in Pennsylvania. Union members there protested a plan to buy new machinery and cut jobs. The company refused to negotiate with the union and locked workers out of the plant, hiring strike breakers to perform their jobs. The workers responded by seizing control of the plant. Gunfire erupted on July 6, when Pinkerton detectives hired by the company tried to enter the plant. A fierce battle raged for 14 hours, leaving 16 people dead. The governor called out the state militia to restore order. Continuing for four more months, the union was eventually defeated.

Another major strike happened at George Pullman's Pullman Palace Car Company in the company town of Pullman, Illinois. Most of the company workers lived there, paying high rents. During a financial depression that began in 1893, Pullman laid off about half of the workers and cut pay for those that were left, without lowering their rents. On May 11, 1894, workers began the **Pullman strike**, which stopped traffic on many railroad lines until federal courts ordered the workers to return to their jobs. President Grover Cleveland sent federal troops to Chicago to stop the strike. Such defeats seriously damaged the labor movement for years.

READING CHECK **Analyzing** What were the effects of early major strikes on workers?

SUMMARY AND PREVIEW Workers formed unions to fight for better conditions and to keep their jobs. In the next section, you will learn about a new wave of immigrants in the late 1800s.

Section 3 Assessment

go.hrw.com
Online Quiz
KEYWORD: SF7 HP19

Reviewing Ideas, Terms, and People

1. a. **Recall** Why did conditions in factories begin to decline?
   b. **Draw Conclusions** How were workers affected by specialization and scientific management?
   c. **Evaluate** Do you think scientific management made businesses more successful? Explain.
2. a. **Identify** What role did **Mary Harris Jones** play in the labor movement?
   b. **Analyze** Why did workers demand **collective bargaining**, and why did business owners oppose it?
   c. **Elaborate** Do you think the demands made by labor unions were reasonable? Explain your answer.
3. a. **Describe** What major labor strikes took place in the late 1800s?
   b. **Evaluate** Do you think President Cleveland was right to use federal troops to end the **Pullman strike**? Explain.

Critical Thinking

4. **Analyzing** Review your notes about the problems workers faced. Use them to complete a table like the one below about how workers tried to solve the problems they faced.

Problem	Solution

FOCUS ON WRITING

5. **Taking Notes on Working Conditions** In your notebook, list some reasons why industrial workers were unhappy with working conditions. Can you think of ways to run your business so that you can avoid the problem of strikes?

Direct Teach

Info to Know

Labor Day Labor unions in the late 1800s organized the first Labor Day celebrations in the United States. Union leaders Peter J. McGuire and Matthew Maguire first suggested the idea of a celebration to honor American workers. The first observance of American laborers took place in September 1882 with a parade in New York City. Two years later, the Knights of Labor pushed to make the first Monday in September an annual celebration of Labor Day. Shortly after the Pullman strike in 1894, Congress officially made Labor Day a national holiday.

Review & Assess

Close

Review with students the hardships industrial workers faced, the steps they took to try to address those problems, and the consequences of their efforts.

Review

Online Quiz, Section 19.3

Assess

SE Section 3 Assessment

PASS: Section Quiz 19.3

Alternative Assessment Handbook

Reteach/Classroom Intervention

Interactive Reader and Study Guide, Section 19.3

Interactive Skills Tutor CD-ROM

Section 3 Assessment Answers

1. **a.** Scientific management encouraged managers to pay less attention to working conditions.
   b. specialization—workers became tired, bored, and likely to be injured; scientific management—working conditions declined
   c. possible answers—yes, they became more efficient; no, workers were unhappy
2. **a.** organized strikes, gave speeches, and educated workers
   b. Workers would have a better chance of success with collective bargaining, but employers did not want to give in to unions.
   c. Students' answers will vary, but should support their stance with specific details.
3. **a.** Haymarket Riot, Homestead Strike, and Pullman Strike
   b. Students' answers should indicate why President Cleveland used federal troops.
4. problems—jobs eliminated by machines, specialization, scientific management; solutions—formed labor unions, bargained collectively, organized labor strikes
5. Responses will vary but should address ways to avoid conflict with workers.

Answers

Reading Check *Strikes that turned violent did not benefit workers; companies received help from the government to end strikes.*

Social Studies Skills

Analyzing Costs and Benefits

Activity Cost-Benefit Analysis in the News Find a newspaper article about a current event in which students might be interested (an election, trial, arrest, environmental concern, and so on). The event and the article's coverage of it should provide students with enough information to determine costs and benefits. Provide each student with a photocopy of the article. Create a costs-benefits chart for students to see. Model the activity by listing one cost and one benefit. Then have students complete the chart independently. Review students' answers as a class. Encourage discussion of any effects that some students see as benefits and other students see as costs.

LS Logical/Mathematical

Alternative Assessment Handbook, Rubric 7: Charts

CRF: Social Studies Skills Activity: Analyzing Costs and Benefits

Social Studies Skills

Analysis | Critical Thinking | Civic Participation | Study

Analyzing Costs and Benefits

Define the Skill

Everything you do has both costs and benefits connected to it. *Benefits* are things that you gain from something. *Costs* are what you give up to obtain benefits. For example, if you buy a video game, the benefits of your action include the game itself and the enjoyment of playing it. The most clear cost is what you pay for the game. However, there are other costs that do not involve money. One is the time you spend playing the game. This is a cost because you give up something else, such as doing your homework or watching a TV show, when you choose to play the game.

The ability to analyze costs and benefits is a valuable life skill as well as a useful tool in the study of history. Weighing an action's benefits against its costs can help you decide whether or not to take it.

Learn the Skill

Analyzing the costs and benefits of historical events will help you to better understand and evaluate them. Follow these guidelines to do a cost-benefit analysis of an action or decision in history.

1. First determine what the action or decision was trying to accomplish. This step is needed in order to determine which of its effects were benefits and which were costs.
2. Then look for the positive or successful results of the action or decision. These are its benefits.
3. Consider the negative or unsuccessful effects of the action or decision. Also think about what positive things would have happened if it had *not* occurred. All these things are its costs.
4. Making a chart of the costs and benefits can be useful. By comparing the list of benefits to the list of costs you can better understand the action or decision and evaluate it.

For example, you learned in Chapter 19 about the Second Industrial Revolution and its effects on the American economy. A cost-benefit analysis of the changes in American businesses might produce a chart like this one:

Benefits	Costs
New inventions made life easier. Communication became easier with new technologies. Efficient management reduced costs of products. Workers began to organize for better conditions.	New business methods ran smaller companies out of business. Workers received lower wages. Strikes resulted in violence and deaths.

Based on this chart, one might conclude that the Second Industrial Revolution was beneficial to the nation's economy.

Practice the Skill

Among the changes that occurred in the early 1900s was an increase in specialization and efficiency in the workplace. Use information from the chapter and the guidelines above to do a cost-benefit analysis of this development. Then write a paragraph explaining whether or not it was a wise one.

Social Studies Skills Activity: Analyzing Costs and Benefits

Big Business Costs-and-Benefits Chart

At Level

1. Lead a brief review of Section 2, which covers the growth of big business.
2. Ask students to create costs-and-benefits charts for the growth of big business. Break down the topic and assign students either corporations, horizontal and vertical integration, trusts, or government antitrust measures.
3. Have volunteers share their answers as you complete master charts for the class to see. Then have students use the activity to analyze government policy in dealing with big business. **LS Logical/Mathematical**
4. **Extend** Have each student write a short essay analyzing government policies toward trusts based on the cost-benefit analysis.

Alternative Assessment Handbook, Rubrics 7: Charts; and 37: Writing Assignments

Answers

Practice the Skill *possible benefits—increased production, lower costs of production, greater use of machines, less need for skilled workers, greater control over workers and the workplace; possible costs—lower pay, loss of worker freedom, worsening working conditions; factors that might be listed as benefits or costs—rise of labor unions; Students' final analyses should provide a valid interpretation of the cost-benefit analysis provided.*

CHAPTER 19

Chapter Review

HOLT
History's Impact
▶ **video series**
Review the video to answer the closing question:
What advantages and disadvantages did the assembly line create? Do you think assembly lines still exist today?

Visual Summary

QUICK FACTS

Use the visual summary below to help you review the main ideas of the chapter.

Inventions
- Bessemer process
- Lightbulb
- Automobile

Big Business
- Growth of corporations
- Wealthy business owners
- Antitrust movements

Labor Movement
- Knights of Labor
- American Federation of Labor
- Haymarket Riot
- Homestead Strike

Reviewing Vocabulary, Terms, and People

Identify the descriptions below with the correct term or person from the chapter.

1. Labor organization that represented both skilled and unskilled laborers and was the first national labor union in the United States
2. Inventor who patented the telephone in 1876
3. A way of making steel quickly and cheaply by blasting hot air through melted iron to quickly remove waste
4. A system of business in which one company owns businesses in each step of the manufacturing process
5. Powerful business leader who helped to found the Central Pacific Railroad
6. Union speaker who worked to better the lives of mine workers
7. A method of negotiating for better wages or working conditions in which all workers act together to ensure a better chance for success

Comprehension and Critical Thinking

SECTION 1 *(Pages 614–618)*

8. a. Identify What was the Second Industrial Revolution?

b. Draw Conclusions Why were advances in transportation and communication important to the Second Industrial Revolution?

c. Elaborate Which invention do you think had the greatest effect on people's lives in the late 1800s? Explain your answer.

SECTION 2 *(Pages 619–622)*

9. a. Recall What criticisms were made of business leaders and trusts?

b. Analyze How did the rise of corporations and powerful business leaders lead to the growth of big business?

c. Evaluate Do you think the growth of big business helped or hurt ordinary Americans? Explain your answer.

Answers

History's Impact

Video Series Advantage: products made quickly and consistently; Disadvantage: poor working conditions; possible answer: They are still used efficiently today, but workers' rights are better protected.

Visual Summary

Review and Inquiry Have students identify the effects of the Second Industrial Revolution.

Quick Facts Transparency 52: The Industrial Age Visual Summary

Reviewing Vocabulary, Terms, and People

1. Knights of Labor
2. Alexander Graham Bell
3. Bessemer process
4. vertical integration
5. Leland Stanford
6. Mary Harris Jones
7. collective bargaining

Comprehension and Critical Thinking

8. a. a time in the late 1800s of rapid growth in U.S. manufacturing
b. The telephone, cars, and planes improved U.S. production.
c. Students should show effects of the invention on people's lives.

Review and Assessment Resources

Review and Reinforce

SE Chapter Review
CRF: Chapter Review Activity
Quick Facts Transparency 52: The Industrial Age Visual Summary
Spanish Chapter Summaries Audio CD Program
Online Chapter Summaries in Spanish
OSP Holt PuzzlePro; GameTool for ExamView
Quiz Game CD-ROM

Assess

SE Standardized Test Practice
PASS: Chapter 19 Tests, Forms A and B
Alternative Assessment Handbook
OSP ExamView Test Generator, Chapter Test
Differentiated Instruction Modified Worksheets and Tests CD-ROM: Chapter Test
HOAP Holt Online Assessment Program (in the Premier Online Edition)

Reteach/Intervene

Interactive Reader and Study Guide
Differentiated Instruction Teacher Management System: Lesson Plans for Differentiated Instruction
Differentiated Instruction Modified Worksheets and Tests CD-ROM
Interactive Skills Tutor CD-ROM

go.hrw.com
Online Resources
Chapter Resources:
KEYWORD: SF7 CH19

Answers

9. a. They earned money through unfair business practices and used their size and strength to drive smaller competitors out of business.
b. They used practices like vertical integration and trusts to dominate entire industries, create monopolies, and drive competitors out of business.
c. possible answers: helped—it led to important advances like oil and steel production and provided more jobs; hurt—it led to the creation of trusts which created higher prices and drove small competitors out of business

10. a. Scientific management led many managers to pay less attention to working conditions, machines replaced skilled workers with unskilled workers, and specialization made employees tired, bored, and more likely to be injured.
b. Labor unions represented large numbers of workers and could use collective bargaining to negotiate with business owners, while individuals had no such influence.
c. possible answer—They hurt the labor movement because many unions declined in membership as a result of labor strikes.

Reviewing Themes

11. led to monopolies and trusts, which drove competition out of business and forced prices to rise

12. Workers and their families benefited from higher incomes. Management had to learn to negotiate with organized labor. Strikes became more common and were sometimes dangerous.

SECTION 3 *(Pages 624–627)*

10. a. Recall What led to poor working conditions in factories during the Second Industrial Revolution?
b. Make Inferences Why did labor unions have a better chance of improving working conditions than laborers did on their own?
c. Evaluate Did the strikes of the 1880s and 1890s hurt or help the labor movement in the long run? Explain your answer.

Reviewing Themes

11. Economics How did the rise of big business affect consumers in the United States?

12. Society and Culture What changes in society were brought about by the organization of labor?

Using the Internet

go.hrw.com
KEYWORD: SF7 CH19

13. Activity: Creating a Time Line Technology in some sense has been part of human history since we began to write history. All tools are, in a sense, technology. In this chapter you read about new scientific discoveries that had positive and negative effects. Enter the activity keyword. Then choose one technological innovation mentioned in the chapter and trace its development to the present day. Create an illustrated time line to present your research.

Reading Skills

Organization of Facts and Information *Use the Reading Skills taught in this chapter to answer the question about the reading selection below.*

> Corporations provided several important advantages over earlier business forms. Stockholders in a corporation are not responsible for business debts. If a corporation fails financially, the stockholders lose only the money that they invested. Stockholders are also usually free to sell their stock to whomever they want, whenever they want. *(p. 620)*

14. By which structural pattern is the above passage organized?
a. Listing
b. Cause-effect
c. Chronological order
d. Comparison-contrast

Social Studies Skills

Analyzing Costs and Benefits *Use the Social Studies Skills taught in this chapter to answer the question below.*

15. Write two costs and two benefits of the Pullman strike from the point of view of the workers who participated.

FOCUS ON WRITING

16. Writing Your Business Plan Collect your notes and determine a good product to sell during the late 1800s. Decide which business practices you would use and which you would not. Write two to three paragraphs in which you explain why your product would sell, which business practices you can use to make your product, and how to avoid conflicts with workers. Remember to explain to the investors why your plan will work.

Using the Internet

13. Go to the HRW Web site and enter the keyword shown to access a rubric for this activity.

KEYWORD: SF7 CH19

Reading Skills

14. b

Social Studies Skills

15. possible answers: costs—they could lose their jobs, they could get injured or arrested; benefits—higher wages, shorter working hours, improved working conditions

Focus on Writing

16. Rubric Students' business plans should:
- present a good product to sell in the late 1800s.
- illustrate which business practices to use and which to not use.
- explain to investors why the plan will work.
- be two to three paragraphs in length.
- include correct spelling, punctuation, and grammer.

CHAPTER 19

Standardized Test Practice

8.1.27, 8.4.3, 8.4.5, 8.4.6

DIRECTIONS: Read each question and write the letter of the best response. Use the map below to answer question 1.

1

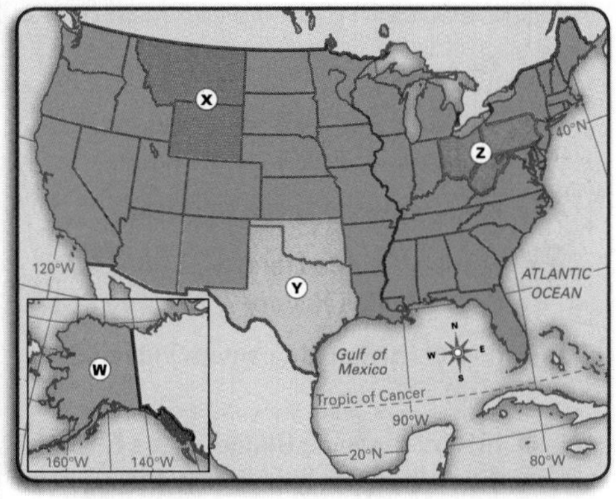

Which area on the map provided the petroleum for the oil-refining industry that arose in the United States in the mid- to late 1800s?

A the area labeled W
B the area labeled X
C the area labeled Y
D the area labeled Z

2 **The person *most* responsible for making the steel industry a big business in the United States is**

A John D. Rockefeller.
B Andrew Carnegie.
C Henry Bessemer.
D Leland Stanford.

3 **The exclusive right to make or sell an invention or product is called**

A a corporation.
B a patent.
C vertical integration.
D a trust.

4 **The development of corporations in America was helped by**

A suburbs.
B vertical integration.
C the Sherman Antitrust Act.
D social Darwinism.

5 **Which of the following was an inventor of the late 1800s?**

A Andrew Carnegie
B Thomas Edison
C Leland Stanford
D John D. Rockefeller

6 **One cause of labor strikes in the late 1800s was that workers sought**

A shorter workdays.
B vertical integration.
C social Darwinism.
D lower wages.

7 **Read the following excerpt from the 1889 book *Recent Economic Changes* and use it to answer the question below.**

> "Machinery is now recognized as essential to cheap production. Nobody can produce effectively and economically without it, and what was formerly known as domestic manfacture is now almost obsolete. But machinery is one of the most expensive of all products, and its extensive purchase and use require an amount of capital far beyond the capacity [ability] of the ordinary individual to furnish."
>
> —David Wells, quoted in *Voices of the American Past*

Document-Based Question **How might the large amounts of money needed for machinery affect the future of business?**

Answers

1. D
Break Down the Question Students should recall from Section 1 that prospectors drilled for oil in Ohio, Pennsylvania and West Virginia.

2. B
Break Down the Question Point out to students that the question asks who made steel a big business, not who improved steel technology.

3. B
Break Down the Question This questions requires students to recall definitions of key terms from Section 2.

4. B
Break Down the Question Students should recall from Section 2 that vertical integration was a business strategy that helped corporations consolidate their power.

5. B
Break Down the Question This question requires students to recall factual information from the chapter.

6. A
Break Down the Question Students should recall from Section 2 that Carnegie, Stanford, and Bell were leaders of corporations. Edison, from Section 1, was the only inventor.

7. possible answer: Small businesses will likely be even less competitive. Only businesses with the necessary connections to obtain large amounts of startup money will be able to enter the market.
Break Down the Question This question requires students to make inferences based on information presented in the chapter.

Intervention Resources

Reproducible

- Interactive Reader and Study Guide
- Differentiated Instruction Teacher Management System: Lesson Plans for Differentiated Instruction

Technology

- Quick Facts Transparency 52: The Industrial Age Visual Summary
- Differentiated Instruction Modified Worksheets and Tests CD-ROM
- Interactive Skills Tutor CD-ROM

Tips for Test Taking

I'm Stuck! Read the following to students: If you come across a question that stumps you, don't get frustrated or worried. First master the question to make sure you understand what is being asked and then work through many of the strategies you have previously learned. If you are still stuck, circle the question and go on to others. Come back to the problem question later. What if you still have no idea? Practice the 50/50 strategy and then take your best educated guess.

Chapter 20 Planning Guide

Immigrants and Urban Life

Chapter Overview	Reproducible Resources	Technology Resources
CHAPTER 20 **pp. 632–655** **Overview: In this chapter, students will learn about the changes in American society and culture brought about by an increase in immigration.**	**Differentiated Instruction Teacher Management System:*** • Instructional Pacing Guides • Lesson Plans for Differentiated Instruction **Interactive Reader and Study Guide:** Chapter Summary Graphic Organizer* **Chapter Resource File:*** • Focus on Writing Activity: A Memo • Social Studies Skills Activity: Making Comparisons • Chapter Review Activity	**Student Edition on Audio CD Program** **Differentiated Instruction Modified Worksheets and Tests CD-ROM** **Interactive Skills Tutor CD-ROM** **Primary Source Library CD-ROM for United States History** **Power Presentations with Video CD-ROM** **History's Impact: United States History Video Program (VHS/DVD):** The Impact of Immigrants on the United States*
Section 1: **A New Wave of Immigration** **The Big Idea:** A new wave of immigration in the late 1800s brought large numbers of immigrants to the United States.	**Differentiated Instruction Teacher Management System:** Section 1 Lesson Plan* **Interactive Reader and Study Guide:** Section 20.1 Summary* **Chapter Resource File:*** • Vocabulary Builder Activity, Section 1 • History and Geography: Patterns of Immigration • Primary Source Activity: Immigrant's First-Person Account	**Daily Bellringer Transparency:** Section 20.1* go.hrw.com **Internet Activity:** Asian Immigrant Experience
Section 2: **The Growth of Cities** **The Big Idea:** American cities experienced dramatic expansion and change in the late 1800s.	**Differentiated Instruction Teacher Management System:** Section 2 Lesson Plan* **Interactive Reader and Study Guide:** Section 20.2 Summary* **Chapter Resource File:*** • Vocabulary Builder Activity, Section 2 • Biography Activity: Joseph Pulitzer • Primary Source Activity: Handbill Recruiting Railroad Workers	**Daily Bellringer Transparency:** Section 20.2* go.hrw.com **Internet Activity:** Columbian Exposition
Section 3: **City Life** **The Big Idea:** The rapid growth of cities in the late 1800s created both challenges and opportunities.	**Differentiated Instruction Teacher Management System:** Section 3 Lesson Plan* **Interactive Reader and Study Guide:** Section 3 Summary* **Chapter Resource File:*** • Vocabulary Builder Activity, Section 3 • Biography Activity: Alice Hamilton • Literature Activity: *The Jungle* by Upton Sinclair • Primary Source: Photo of Immigrant's Home **Political Cartoons Activities for United States History,** Cartoon 21: Urban Life and Tenements*	**Daily Bellringer Transparency:** Section 20.3* **Quick Facts Transparency 53:** Tenement Life*

SE Student Edition | Print Resource | Audio CD
TE Teacher's Edition | Transparency | CD-ROM
go.hrw.com | **LS** Learning Styles | Video
TOS Indiana Teacher One Stop | * also on Indiana Teacher One Stop

Review, Assessment, Intervention

- **Quick Facts Transparency 54:** Immigrants and Urban Life Visual Summary*
- **Spanish Chapter Summaries Audio CD Program**
- **Online Chapter Summaries in Spanish**
- **Quiz Game CD-ROM**
- **Progress Assessment Support System (PASS):** Chapter Tests A and B*
- **Differentiated Instruction Modified Worksheets and Tests CD-ROM:** Modified Chapter Test
- TOS **Indiana Teacher One Stop:** ExamView Test Generator (English/Spanish)
- **Alternative Assessment Handbook**
- HOAP **Holt Online Assessment Program,** in the Holt Premier Online Student Edition

---

- **PASS:** Section Quiz 20.1*
- **Online Quiz:** Section 20.1
- **Alternative Assessment Handbook**

- **PASS:** Section Quiz 20.2*
- **Online Quiz:** Section 20.2
- **Alternative Assessment Handbook**

- **PASS:** Section Quiz 20.3*
- **Online Quiz:** Section 20.3
- **Alternative Assessment Handbook**

HOLT
History's Impact
United States History Video Program (VHS/DVD)
The Impact of Immigrants on the United States
Suggested use: as a chapter introduction

Power Presentations with Video CD-ROM

Power Presentations with Video are visual presentations of each chapter's main ideas. Presentations can be customized by including Quick Facts charts, images from the text, and video clips.

DIVISION FOR PUBLIC EDUCATION
AMERICAN BAR ASSOCIATION

Developed by the Division for Public Education of the American Bar Association, these materials are part of the **Democracy and Civic Education Resources.**

- **Constitution Study Guide**
- **Supreme Court Case Studies**

Holt Online Learning

go.hrw.com
Teacher Resources
KEYWORD: SF7 TEACHER

go.hrw.com
Student Resources
KEYWORD: SF7 CH20

- Document-Based Questions
- Interactive Multimedia Activities
- Current Events
- Chapter-based Internet Activities
- and more!

Holt Interactive
Online Student Edition

Complete online support for interactivity, assessment, and reporting

- Interactive Maps and Notebook
- Standardized Test Prep
- Homework Practice and Research Activities Online

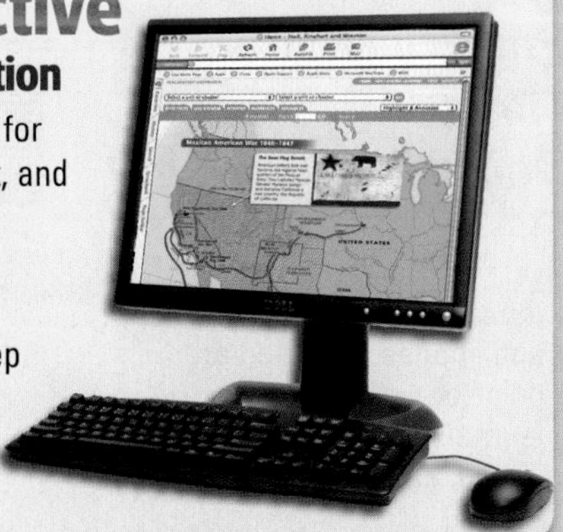

Differentiating Instruction

How do I address the needs of varied learners?

The Target Resource acts as your primary strategy for differentiated instruction.

ENGLISH-LANGUAGE LEARNERS & STRUGGLING READERS

TARGET RESOURCE

English-Language Learner Strategies and Activities

- Build Academic Vocabulary
- Develop Oral and Written Language Structures

Spanish Resources

Spanish Chapter Summaries Audio CD

Spanish Chapter Summaries Online

Teacher's One-Stop Planner:

- ExamView Test Generator, Spanish
- PuzzlePro, Spanish

Additional Resources

Differentiated Instruction Teacher Management System: Lesson Plans for Differentiated Instruction

Chapter Resources:

- Vocabulary Builder Activities
- Social Studies Skills Activity: Making Comparisons

Quick Facts Transparencies:

- Tenement Life (TR 53)
- Immigrants and Urban Life Visual Summary (TR 54)

Student Edition on Audio CD Program

Interactive Skills Tutor CD-ROM

SPECIAL NEEDS LEARNERS

TARGET RESOURCE

Differentiated Instruction Modified Worksheets and Tests CD-ROM

- Vocabulary Flash Cards
- Modified Vocabulary Builder Activities
- Modified Chapter Review Activity
- Modified Chapter Test

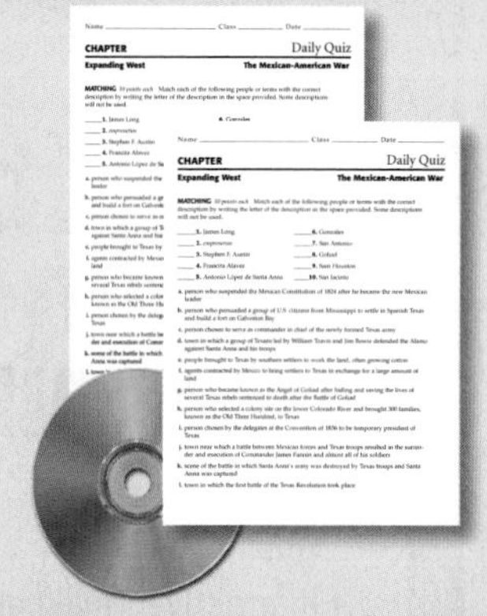

Additional Resources

Differentiated Instruction Teacher Management System: Lesson Plans for Differentiated Instruction

Interactive Reader and Study Guide

Social Studies Skills Activity: Making Comparisons

Student Edition on Audio CD Program

Interactive Skills Tutor CD-ROM

ADVANCED/GIFTED-AND-TALENTED STUDENTS

TARGET RESOURCE

Primary Source Library CD-ROM for United States History

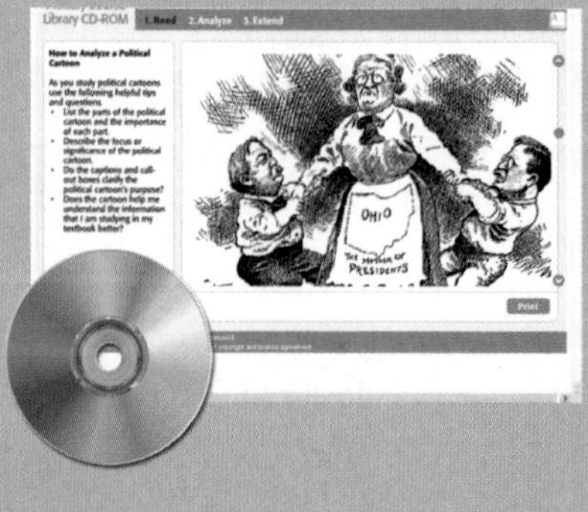

The Library contains longer versions of quotations in the text, extra sources, and images. Included are point-of-view articles, journals, diaries, historical fiction, and political documents.

Additional Resources

Differentiated Instruction Teacher Management System: Lesson Plans for Differentiated Instruction

Political Cartoons Activities for United States History, Cartoon 21: Urban Life and Tenements

Chapter Resource File:

- Focus on Writing Activity: A Memo
- Primary Source Activities: Immigrant's First-Person Account; Handbill Recruiting Railroad Workers; Photo of Immigrant's Home
- Literature Activity: *The Jungle* by Upton Sinclair

Internet Activities: Chapter Enrichment Links

Differentiated Activities in the Teacher's Edition

- Reformers Graphic Organizers, p. 648

Differentiated Activities in the Teacher's Edition

- Immigrant Posters, p. 637

Differentiated Activities in the Teacher's Edition

- Chinese Immigrant Letters, p. 640

Teacher One Stop™

How can I manage the lesson plans and support materials for differentiated instruction?

With the Indiana Teacher One Stop, you can easily organize and print lesson plans, planning guides, and instructional materials for all learners.
The Indiana Teacher One Stop includes the following materials to help you differentiate instruction:

- Interactive Teacher's Edition
- Calendar Planner and pacing guides
- Editable lesson plans
- All reproducible ancillaries in Adobe Acrobat (PDF) format
- ExamView Test Generator (Eng & Span)
- Transparency and video previews

Professional Development

HOLT Professional Development

What teacher training resources are available to help me grow professionally?

- **In-service and staff development** as part of your Holt Social Studies product purchase
- **Quick Teacher Tutorial Lesson Presentation CD-ROM**
- Intensive tuition-based **Teacher Development Institute**
- **Convenient Holt Speaker Bureau** – face-to-face workshop options
- **PRAXIS™ Test Prep** interactive Web-based content refreshers*
- **Ask A Professional Development Expert** at http://www.hrw.com/prodev/

* PRAXIS is a trademark of Educational Testing Service (ETS).
This publication is not endorsed or approved by ETS.

Chapter Preview

Chapter Big Ideas

Section 1 A new wave of immigration in the late 1800s brought large numbers of immigrants to the United States.

Section 2 American cities experienced dramatic expansion and change in the late 1800s.

Section 3 The rapid growth of cities in the late 1800s created both challenges and opportunities.

Focus on Writing

The Chapter Resource File provides a Focus on Writing worksheet to help students create their memos.

CRF: Focus on Writing Activity: A Memo

Key to Differentiating Instruction

Below Level

Basic-level activities designed for all students encountering new material

At Level

Intermediate-level activities designed for average students

Above Level

Challenging activities designed for honors and gifted and talented students

Standard English Mastery

Activities designed to improve standard English usage

APTER 20

Immigrants and Urban Life

Indiana Standards

Social Studies Standards

8.1.25 Give examples of how immigration affected American culture in the decades before and after the Civil War, including growth of industrialism in the North; religious differences; tensions between middle-class and working-lcass people, particularly in the Northeast; and intensification of cultural differences between the North and the South.

8.3.9 Analyze human and physical factors that have influenced migration and settlement patterns and relate them to the economic development of the United States.

8.4.5 Analyze contributions of entrepreneurs and inventors in the development of the United States economy.

go.hrw.com
Indiana
KEYWORD: SF10 IN

Focus on Writing

A Memo You are a writer at a television network, and you have an idea for a TV drama series set in the late 1800s. Draft a memo telling your boss about your story idea. As you read this chapter, gather information about the people, places, and events of this time period. Tell about the cast of characters, the setting, and the basic plot of your series.

United States

1873 Olmsted designs the U.S. Capitol grounds.

1876 The Centennial Exposition opens in Philadelphia.

1870

World

1878 Electric streetlights are introduced in London.

Introduce the Chapter

At Level

Focus on Immigration

1. Write two headings for students to see: *Reasons to Leave Home,* and *Reasons to Immigrate to the United States.* Ask students why people might leave the countries where they were born and move to America. What continues to attract people to move to the United States today? Direct the students to copy the headings and write reasons under the appropriate heading as they read the chapter.
2. Discuss the contributions immigrants have made to American life and culture.
3. Tell students that in this chapter they will learn that many people wanted to move to the United States to improve their lives. Have students consider how our country's cities and culture developed as they read the chapter.

LS Verbal/Linguistic

Alternative Assessment Handbook, Rubric 7: Charts

HOLT

History's Impact

▶ **video series**

Watch the video to understand the impact of immigrants on the United States.

What You Will Learn...

Millions of immigrants from Europe came through Ellis Island, shown here. They came in search of jobs, freedom, and better lives for their families. Most settled in New York, Chicago, and other growing cities. American cities began to take the shape they still have today. In this chapter you will learn about the wave of immigration that changed the United States in the late 1800s and early 1900s.

1886 Workers complete the Statue of Liberty.

1889 Jane Addams founds Hull House in Chicago.

1893 The Ferris Wheel is introduced at the 1893 Columbian Exposition in Chicago.

1906 The United States Steel Corporation founds the town of Gary, Indiana.

1880 | 1890 | 1900 | 1910

1886 Impressionists' exhibit opens in Paris.

1891 Construction begins on Russia's Trans-Siberian Railroad.

1901 The first Nobel Prizes are awarded in Stockholm, Sweden.

Chapter Preview

HOLT

History's Impact

▶ **video series**

See the Video Teacher's Guide for strategies to use the chapter video to teach about the impact of immigrants on the United States.

Explore the Picture

Analyzing Visuals Notice the tags worn by many of the people in the photograph as they arrive on Ellis Island. Why might they have needed labels as they went through the immigration process? *Most of the new immigrants did not yet speak English, and most of the Americans working with the immigrants spoke only English.*

Travel Options In the 1900s people had only one choice if they wanted to travel across an ocean. They had to travel by ship, and a voyage from Bristol, England to New York could take between one to two weeks. How do most travelers cross the Atlantic Ocean today? *by airliner* How long does this voyage take today? *one half day*

go.hrw.com

Online Resources

Chapter Resources:
KEYWORD: SF7 CH20

Teacher Resources:
KEYWORD: SF7 TEACHER

Explore the Time Line

1. What art exhibit opened in Paris in 1886? *The Impressionists' exhibit*
2. When did workers complete the Statue of Liberty? *1886*
3. Where were the first Nobel Prizes awarded? *Stockholm, Sweden*
4. Where and when were the two Expositions shown on the time line held? *Philadelphia, 1876; Chicago, 1893*

Info to Know

The Nobel Prize and You Have you ever had an X-ray? Maybe it was for a broken bone, or just getting your teeth checked at the dentist's office. The 1901 Nobel Prize in Physics was awarded to a physicist from Germany. His name was Wilhelm Conrad Roentgen, and he discovered X-rays in 1895. Now, over one hundred years later, medical images have advanced and use various types of radiant energy.

Reading Social Studies

Understanding Themes

The main themes of this chapter are economics, and society and culture. To focus on these ideas, ask students if they have ever travelled somewhere entirely new to them, even if just for a weekend. Ask them to recall the things they had to adjust to (different language or dialect, food, customs, currency, etc.). Next, have students write three things that they think new immigrants had to adjust to in America. As students read this chapter, they can see if any of their ideas were mentioned.

Understanding Historical Fact versus Historical Fiction

Focus on Reading Bring in several newspaper articles from a daily newspaper. Remind students that in math classes, they have probably seen theories proven as fact. Ask how this is done. *(by performing a mathematical operation to test the theory)* Suggest to students that for every math theory that has been proven as fact, there are countless others that have been disproven. Organize students into groups of three or four. Have them discuss the various ways that theories or statements can be proven or disproven. *(research, interviews)* Distribute the newspaper articles to students. Have students practice how to distinguish fact from fiction by determining how the details in the article they were given can be verified.

Reading Social Studies

by Kylene Beers

Economics | Geography | Politics | Society and Culture | Science and Technology

Focus on Themes In this chapter, you will read about the changes in **society and culture** in the late 1800s. Among these changes was an increase in immigration. New immigrants to America found a society full of **economic** opportunities and hardships. Immigration and technology combined to change the way of life in cities.

Understanding Historical Fact versus Historical Fiction

Focus on Reading When you read a book like *The Red Badge of Courage* or see a movie about World War II, do you ever wonder how much is fiction and how much is fact?

Distinguishing Fact from Fiction Historical fiction gives readers a chance to meet real historical people and real historical events in the framework of a made-up story. Some of what you read in historical fiction could be verified in an encyclopedia, but other parts existed only in the author's mind until he or she put it on paper. As a good reader of history, you should know the difference between facts, which can be proved or verified, and fiction.

Notice how one reader determined which details could be verified or proved.

That was a <u>*woman filling her pail by the hydrant*</u> you just bumped against. The <u>*sinks are in the hallway,*</u> that all the tenants may have access—and all be poisoned alike by their summer stenches. Hear the pump squeak! It is the lullaby of tenement house babes. In summer, when <u>*a thousand thirsty throats pant for a cooling drink in this block,*</u> it is worked in vain ...

— From *How the Other Half Lives*, by Jacob Riis

The woman filling her pail isn't a fact I can check. He's just using her as an example of what women did.

We could probably check city records to see whether the buildings really had sinks in the hallways.

The writer is generalizing here. We probably can't prove 1,000 thirsty throats. We could find out whether the city's water pumps actually went dry in the summer. That's verifiable.

Reading and Skills Resources

Reading Support

- Interactive Reader and Study Guide
- Student Edition on Audio CD Program
- Spanish Chapter Summaries Audio CD Program

Social Studies Skills Support

- Interactive Skills Tutor CD-ROM

Vocabulary Support

- **CRF:** Vocabulary Builder Activities
- **CRF:** Chapter Review Activity
- Differentiated Instruction Modified Worksheets and Tests CD-ROM:
  - Vocabulary Flash Cards
  - Vocabulary Builder Activity
  - Chapter Review Activity

OSP Holt PuzzlePro

You Try It!

The following passage is from *Bread Givers* by Anzia Yezierska, a young immigrant to New York. After you read it, answer the questions below.

> Mashah [Anzia's sister] came home with stories that in rich people's homes they had silver knives and forks, separate, for each person. And new-ironed tablecloths and napkins every time they ate on them. And rich people had marble bathtubs in their own houses, with running hot and cold water all day and night long so they could take a bath any time they felt like it, instead of having to stand on a line before the public bath-house, as we had to do when we wanted a bath for the holidays. But these millionaire things were so far over our heads that they were like fairy tales.
>
> That time when Mashah had work hemming towels in an uptown house, she came home with another new-rich idea, another money-spending thing, which she said she had to have. She told us that by those Americans, everybody in the family had a toothbrush and a separate towel for himself.
>
> —Anzia Yezierska, *Bread Givers*

1. Which facts from the paragraph above can be confirmed?
2. What sources might you check to confirm some of these facts?
3. List two things from the passage that could not be confirmed.
4. Why are these two things not able to be confirmed?

As you read Chapter 20, notice which facts you could easily confirm.

Key Terms and People

Chapter 20

Section 1

old immigrants *(p. 636)*
new immigrants *(p. 636)*
steerage *(p. 637)*
benevolent societies *(p. 639)*
tenements *(p. 639)*
sweatshops *(p. 640)*
Chinese Exclusion Act *(p. 641)*

Section 2

mass transit *(p. 644)*
suburbs *(p. 644)*
mass culture *(p. 644)*
Joseph Pulitzer *(p. 645)*
William Randolph Hearst *(p. 645)*
department stores *(p. 645)*
Frederick Law Olmsted *(p. 645)*

Section 3

Jacob Riis *(p. 646)*
settlement houses *(p. 648)*
Jane Addams *(p. 648)*
Hull House *(p. 648)*
Florence Kelley *(p. 648)*

Academic Vocabulary

advocate *(p. 641)*
factor *(p. 643)*

Reading Social Studies

Key Terms and People

To introduce students to the key terms and people in this chapter, first have them write each of the following headings at the top of four pieces of notebook paper: *Section 1, Section 2, Section 3,* and *Academic Vocabulary.* Have students write the key terms and people on the appropriate page and then define or describe each one. Encourage students to see how many definitions they can remember as they read each section. **LS Verbal/Linguistic**

Focus on Reading

See the **Focus on Reading** questions in this chapter for more practice on this reading social studies skill.

Reading Social Studies Assessment

See the **Chapter Review** at the end of this chapter for student assessment questions related to this reading skill.

Teaching Tip

Many books and movies that students have experienced are historical fiction. Explain to students that it is easy to be fooled into believing a character is real, particularly if the book or movie was done well. Tell students to make a habit of watching for the words "based on" in the introduction or credits to discover whether or not the story is real or just realistic.

Answers

You Try It! 1. *whether Anzia Yezierska existed and had a sister named Mashah; whether it was common for the rich to have the luxuries Mashah describes* **2.** *immigration records, genealogical records; historical society records, museums, memoirs* **3.** *that Mashah ever said the things Anzia attributes to her; that everybody in American families had their own toothbrush and towel* **4.** *there likely are no recordings of Mashah having said these things; there is no way to verify that all Americans had these items*

Preteach

Bellringer

If YOU were there... Use the **Daily Bellringer Transparency** for this section to help students answer the question.

Daily Bellringer Transparency, 20.1

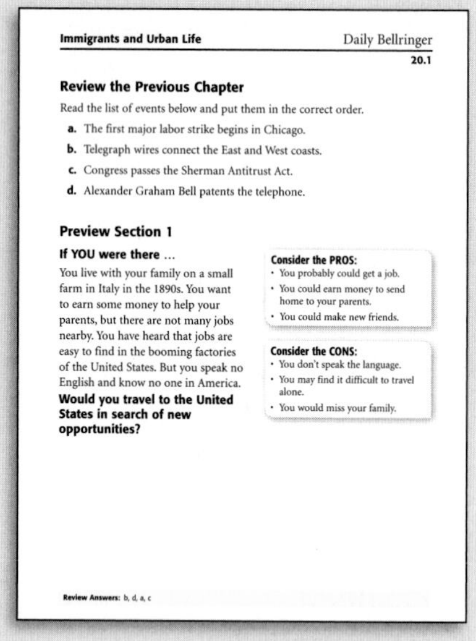
Immigrants and Urban Life | Daily Bellringer **20.1**

Review the Previous Chapter

Read the list of events below and put them in the correct order.

a. The first major labor strike begins in Chicago.
b. Telegraph wires connect the East and West coasts.
c. Congress passes the Sherman Antitrust Act.
d. Alexander Graham Bell patents the telephone.

Preview Section 1

If YOU were there ...

You live with your family on a small farm in Italy in the 1890s. You want to earn some money to help your parents, but there are not many jobs nearby. You have heard that jobs are easy to find in the booming factories of the United States. But you speak no English and know no one in America.

Would you travel to the United States in search of new opportunities?

Consider the PROS:
- You probably could get a job.
- You could earn money to send home to your parents.
- You could make new friends.

Consider the CONS:
- You don't speak the language.
- You may find it difficult to travel alone.
- You would miss your family.

Review Answers: b, d, a, c

Academic Vocabulary

Review with students the high-use academic term in this section.

advocate to plead in favor of (p. 641)

CRF: Vocabulary Builder Activity, Section 1

Taking Notes

Have students copy the graphic organizer onto their own paper and then use it to take notes on the section. This activity will prepare students for the Section Assessment, in which they will complete a graphic organizer that builds on the information using a critical-thinking skill.

Section Correlations

IN

8.1.25 Give examples of how immigration affected American culture in the decades before and after the Civil War, including growth of industrial sites in the North; religious differences; tensions between middle-class and working-class people, particularly in the Northeast; and intensification of cultural differences between the North and the South. **8.3.7** Using maps identify changes influenced by growth, economic development and human migration in the eighteenth and nineteenth centuries.

SECTION 1

A New Wave of Immigration

What You Will Learn...

Main Ideas

1. U.S. immigration patterns changed during the late 1800s as new immigrants arrived from Europe, Asia, and Mexico.
2. Immigrants worked hard to adjust to life in the United States.
3. Some Americans opposed immigration and worked to restrict it.

The Big Idea

A new wave of immigration in the late 1800s brought large numbers of immigrants to the United States.

Key Terms and People

old immigrants, *p. 636*
new immigrants, *p. 636*
steerage, *p. 637*
benevolent societies, *p. 639*
tenements, *p. 639*
sweatshops, *p. 640*
Chinese Exclusion Act, *p. 641*

TAKING NOTES As you read, look for information about new immigrants' lives in the United States. Take notes on the benefits and challenges immigrants found. Use a diagram like the one below.

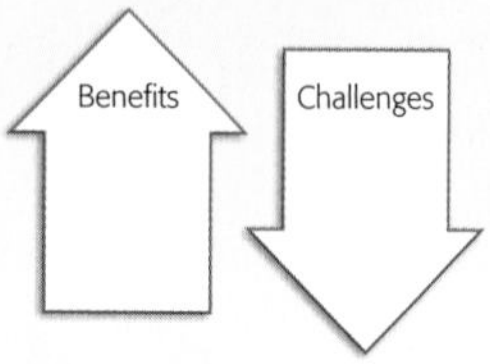

IN 8.1.25, 8.3.7, 8.3.9

If YOU were there...

You live with your family on a small farm in Italy in the 1890s. You want to earn some money to help your parents, but there are not many jobs nearby. You have heard that jobs are easy to find in the booming factories of the United States. But you speak no English and know no one in America.

Would you travel to the United States in search of new opportunities?

BUILDING BACKGROUND From its beginnings, America has attracted people from many parts of the world. They came for many reasons, including land, religious freedom, and the chance to start new lives. In the late 1800s, jobs created by the rapid growth of the U.S. economy drew millions of new immigrants.

Changing Patterns of Immigration

Millions of immigrants came to the United States from northern Europe in the mid-1800s. They came mainly from Great Britain, Germany, Ireland, and the countries of Scandinavia. Except for the Irish, who were Roman Catholics, most were Protestants. Many were skilled workers. Others settled in rural areas and became farmers. By the late 1800s immigrants from northern Europe were known as **old immigrants**. A newer and larger wave of immigration—from different parts of the world—was arriving in the United States.

New Immigrants

During the 1880s more than 5 million immigrants arrived in the United States—about the same number of people as had arrived during the six decades from 1800 to 1860 combined. The majority of these **new immigrants** were from southern and eastern Europe. Thousands of Czechs, Greeks, Hungarians, Italians, Poles, Russians, and Slovaks came to the United States to find new opportunities and better lives. A young woman from Russia spoke for many of her

Teach the Big Idea

At Level

A New Wave of Immigration

1. **Teach** To teach the main ideas in the section, use the questions in the Direct Teach boxes.
2. **Apply** Instruct students to fold a sheet of paper lengthwise. Have them title the chart *New Arrivals,* then label the left column *Country of Origin,* and the right column *Processing Center.* Tell students to write entries under each heading as they read this section. **LS Verbal/Linguistic**
3. **Review** Let students share their completed charts with the class. Make sure all three ports of entry are listed (*Ellis Island, New York; Angel Island, California; El Paso, Texas*), and point out the wide appeal of the United States that inspired people to move so far from their own homelands.
4. **Practice/Homework** Have students draw a simple outline map with arrows to indicate the flow of immigrants from foreign countries to the United States. **LS Visual/Spatial**

Alternative Assessment Handbook, Rubrics 7: Charts; and 20: Map Creation fellow immigrants when she said she hoped "for all manner of miracles in a strange, wonderful land!"

New immigrants came from many different cultural and religious backgrounds. They included Orthodox Christians, Roman Catholics, and Jews. Some were escaping political or religious persecution. They were eager for the job opportunities created by the U.S. industrial boom of the late 1800s.

Arriving in a New Land

Immigrants usually faced a difficult journey by ship to America. Most traveled in **steerage**—an area below a ship's deck where steering mechanisms were located. Steerage tickets were inexpensive, but the cabins were hot, cramped, and foul-smelling. Many passengers were seasick for the entire journey. Some even died of diseases contracted along the way.

Once in the United States, new arrivals were processed through government-run immigration centers. The busiest center on the East Coast was Ellis Island, which opened in New York Harbor in 1892. The first immigrant processed through Ellis Island was Annie Moore Schayer, a 14 year old from Ireland. Over the next 40 years, millions of European immigrants came through Ellis Island.

At immigration centers officials interviewed and examined immigrants to decide whether to let them enter the country. People with contagious diseases or legal problems could be turned away. "There was this terrible anxiety that one of us might be rejected," remembered one immigrant traveling with his family. "And if one of us was, what would the rest of the family do?" This rarely happened, however. Less than 2 percent of the people who arrived at Ellis Island were not allowed into the country.

On the West Coast, many Chinese immigrants entered the United States through Angel Island, which opened near San Francisco in 1910. Because laws limited immigration from China, only people whose fathers were U.S. citizens were allowed into the country. Chinese immigrants were often kept at Angel Island for weeks or months while officials investigated their families.

Mexican immigrants also came to the United States in large numbers in the late 1800s. The main processing center for immigrants from Mexico was in El Paso, Texas. Most settled in the Southwest. They found work in construction, steel mills, and mines, and on large commercial farms.

READING CHECK **Contrasting** How was the experience of immigrants at Ellis Island different from that of immigrants at Angel Island?

Primary Source

AUTOBIOGRAPHY

An Immigrant's Story

Mary Antin and her family were Jewish. They moved from Russia to Boston in the 1890s to find religious freedom. Here, Antin writes about their journey.

For sixteen days the ship was our world ... [It] pitched and rolled so that people were thrown from their berths [beds] ... All this while the seasickness lasted. Then came happy hours on deck, with fugitive sunshine, birds atop the crested waves, band music and dancing and fun ... And so suffering, fearing, brooding [worrying], rejoicing, we crept nearer and nearer to the coveted [wished for] shore, until, on a glorious May morning, six weeks after our departure from Polotzk our eyes beheld the Promised Land [the United States].

—Mary Antin, *The Promised Land*

What do you think *fugitive* means here?

Antin describes a mix of emotions.

ANALYSIS SKILL **ANALYZING PRIMARY SOURCES**

Why do you think Antin was both "fearing" and "rejoicing" during her trip?

THE IMPACT TODAY

Almost half of all Americans today are related to someone who passed through Ellis Island. Visitors can now research their family origins at the Ellis Island Immigration Museum.

Direct Teach

Main Idea

❶ Changing Patterns of Immigration

U.S. immigration patterns changed during the late 1800s as new immigrants arrived from Europe, Asia, and Mexico.

Identify What areas of Europe did old immigrants come from? *northern Europe* Where did new immigrants come from? *southern and eastern Europe, Asia, and Mexico*

Making Predictions Some people imagined that their lives in the United States would be ideal. Once they arrived, how do you think their opinion might have changed? *They realized that opportunities were available, but it would take hard work to reach their goals.*

Make Judgments What kind of character would people need to face the hardships of immigration? *should be brave, determined, ambitious, hard working*

Info to Know

Fuel for Growth Between 1870 and 1900 the United States became the world leader in industrial development. Though the nation used its wealth of natural resources to produce steel, timber, packaged meat products, coal, and refined metals, it couldn't have achieved such a stunning increase in production without immigrant workers.

Differentiating Instruction

Below Level

Special Needs Learners

Materials: 11" x 18" construction paper

1. Remind the class that during the 1880s, over 5 million people came to live in the United States. Ask students to imagine what it would be like for an immigrant to pass through an immigration processing center. *(crowded, busy, frightening)*
2. Tell students they will create a poster to be displayed inside an immigration processing center welcoming immigrants. The poster can show either the opportunities immigrants might find in their new home or friendly American people welcoming newcomers to the United States.
3. Remind students that their posters must communicate a message without words because new immigrants often did not speak English.
4. Ask volunteers to share their posters with the class. Then lead a class discussion about the posters and how students communicated their ideas. **LS Visual/Spatial**

Alternative Assessment Handbook, Rubric 28: Posters

Answers

Analyzing Primary Sources *She probably feared being rejected at Ellis Island, not knowing where the family would live or how they would earn money. She likely rejoiced because she was getting off the ship and seeing America for the first time.*

Reading Check *Less than two percent of Ellis Island immigrants were turned away, but only Chinese immigrants whose fathers were U.S. citizens were allowed into the country. Chinese immigrants were often detained at Angel Island for weeks or months.*

Direct Teach

Main Idea

❷ Adjusting to a New Life

Immigrants worked hard to adjust to life in the United States.

Explain Tell why people might want to move into neighborhoods with others from the same country. *They could hear and speak their own language, eat familiar foods, and keep their customs.*

Predict How might loaning money to immigrants have helped the economy? *allowed people to set up new businesses, which provided jobs for others*

Activity Make a Packing List An immigrant was allowed to bring only one small suitcase about the size of a backpack to America. Ask students to imagine that they are moving to the United States. Give students a few minutes to list what they would have brought with them. Organize students into small groups and have them create a new list of what they would choose to bring as an immigrant family.

CRF: History and Geography Activity, Patterns of Immigration

Teaching Tip

Using Prior Experience Remind students of the Oregon Trail pioneers they have studied. These people also traveled as families and could only take limited items with them. Ask: What is the difference between what immigrants and families moving West could pack? *(Wagons could carry more.)*

Answers

Focus on Reading *look for online or text sources about immigration*

Coming to America

In this photo, Japanese men and Chinese women leave the detention center on Angel Island in San Francisco Bay. Angel Island was the processing center for many immigrants from Asia.

Augustin and Maria Lozano and their two children are shown after moving from Mexico to California. Many Mexican immigrants moved into the Southwest.

Adjusting to a New Life

Once they entered the United States, immigrants began the hard work of adjusting to life in a new country. They needed to find homes and jobs. They had to learn a new language and get used to new customs. This was all part of building a new life.

Immigrant Neighborhoods

Focus on Reading
How could you verify the facts in this paragraph?

Many immigrants moved into neighborhoods with others from the same country. In these neighborhoods, they could speak their native language and eat foods that reminded them of home. Immigrants could also practice the customs that their families had passed down from generation to generation. An Italian immigrant remembered that in his new neighborhood, "cheeses from Italy, sausage, salamis were all hanging in the window."

In their newly adopted neighborhoods, many immigrant groups published newspapers in their own languages. They founded schools, clubs, and places of worship to help preserve their customs. In New York City, for example, Jewish immigrants founded a theater that gave performances in Yiddish—the language spoken by Jews from central and eastern Europe.

Immigrants often opened local shops and small neighborhood banks. Business owners helped new arrivals by offering credit and giving small loans. Such aid was important for newcomers because there were few commercial banks in immigrant neighborhoods. In 1904 Italian immigrant Amadeo Peter Giannini started the Bank of Italy in San Francisco. This bank later grew and became the Bank of America.

Critical Thinking: Predicting

At Level

The Effect of Sudden Population Growth

1. Copy this sentence from the text for students to see: "During the 1880s more than 5 million immigrants arrived in the United States—about the same number of people as had arrived during the six decades from 1800 to 1860 combined."
2. Ask students to name the basic needs of new immigrants. *(food, shelter, clothing, employment)*
3. Ask students to predict the challenges there might be for the neighborhoods where so many immigrants came to live. *(lack of housing, sanitation, transportation)*
4. What could city leaders do to solve the problems caused by this sudden growth? Instruct students to write down their suggestions to help city leaders deal with these new problems. Then have students save their ideas to compare with what they will learn later in this chapter. **LS Verbal/Linguistic**

Alternative Assessment Handbook, Rubric 35: Solving Problems

Swedish immigrant Swan August Swanson followed his father to Wisconsin to help with the family farm. Like many new Americans, he married within the immigrant community.

The son of Italian immigrants, Amadeo Peter Giannini founded the Bank of Italy in San Francisco in 1904. Due to his guidance and perseverance, it became the largest privately owned bank in the world.

Shifting Patterns of Immigration

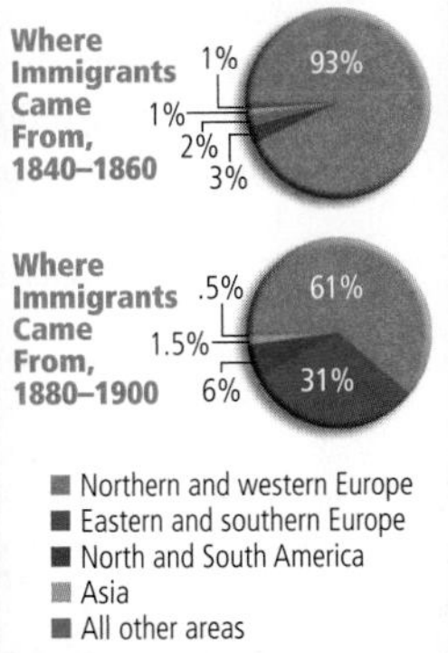

During the late 1800s the places people came from began to change. The charts above show the percentages of people who moved from different places. The total number of immigrants reached a peak in the 1880s, when about 5 million people came to the United States.

By how much did the percentage of immigrants from northern and western Europe change from 1840 to 1900?

Some immigrant communities formed **benevolent societies**. These aid organizations offered immigrants help in cases of sickness, unemployment, or death. At that time, few national government agencies provided such aid.

Even with neighborhood support, however, immigrants often found city life difficult. Many immigrants lived in **tenements**—poorly built, overcrowded apartment buildings. One young woman in New York City described the difference between her hopes and reality in the new land:

> "[I dreamed] of the golden stairs leading to the top of the American palace where father was supposed to live. [I] went 'home' to . . . an ugly old tenement in the heart of the Lower East Side. There were stairs to climb but they were not golden."
>
> – Miriam Shomer Zusner, *Yesterday: A Memoir of a Russian Jewish Family*

Immigrants worked hard to adjust to their new country. Children often learned American customs more quickly than their parents. In public schools immigrant children learned English from McGuffey's Readers—illustrated textbooks that taught reading and writing.

Finding Work

Many new immigrants had worked on farms in their homelands. Few could afford to buy land in the United States, however. Instead, they found jobs in cities, where most of the country's manufacturing took place.

Having come from rural areas, few new immigrants were skilled in modern manufacturing or industrial work. They often had no choice but to take low-paying, unskilled jobs in garment factories, steel mills, or construction. Long hours were common.

Direct Teach

Recall What were some of the types of work new immigrants did for their employers? *low-paying, unskilled jobs in factories, mills, and construction*

CRF: Primary Source Activity, Handbill Recruiting Railroad Workers

Interpreting Graphs Use the pie charts on this page to answer the following:

1. Where did the majority of immigrants come from between 1840 and 1860? between 1880 and 1900? *northern and western Europe in both periods*
2. What percent came from eastern and southern Europe between 1840 and 1860? between 1880 and 1900? *3%; 31%*

Did you know . . .

A.P. Giannini was on the board of directors of a bank in an Italian neighborhood in the late 1800s. When he found that local banks would not make small loans, he resigned and opened the "little fellows bank" in 1904. By making loans as small as $25, he allowed working-class consumers to enjoy the benefits of bank loans.

Checking for Understanding

True or False Answer each statement *T* if it is true or *F* if it is false. If false, explain why.

1. Benevolent societies helped immigrant families with unemployment. *T*
2. Parents found it easier to adjust to their new country than their children. *F; Children often learned American customs more quickly than their parents.*
3. Most new immigrants arrived with modern industrial skills. *F; Few new immigrants were skilled in modern manufacturing or industrial work.*

Collaborative Learning

At Level

Defining Workers' Needs

1. Tell students: Imagine you are members of The Everyman Group, an imaginary benevolent society of the 1880s.
2. Ask students to name the types of help new immigrants might have needed. *(jobs, housing, food, childcare, health care)*
3. Organize students into groups of two or three. Have each group create a Booklet that shows new immigrants what kinds of help The Everyman Group offers. Students should use the example on page 635 to create their booklets.
4. Allow time for each group to present their booklet and explain its message.

LS Interpersonal, Visual/Spatial

Alternative Assessment Handbook, Rubric 14: Group Activity

Answers

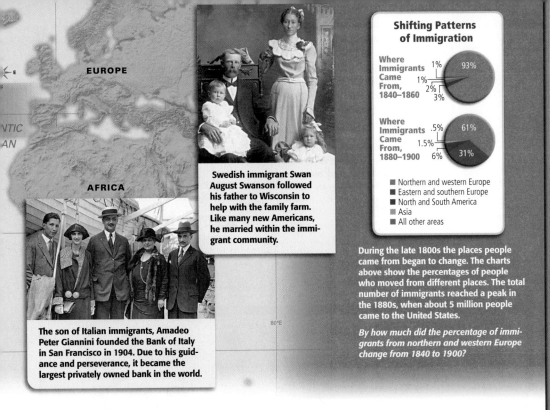

Shifting Patterns of Immigration
32 percent

Direct Teach

Main Idea

❷ Adjusting to a New LIfe

Immigrants worked hard to adjust to life in the United States.

Describe What kinds of businesses did immigrants open? *laundries, barbershops, street vending carts*

Analyze How do the Asian Americans pictured on the right appear different from those on the left? *Those on the right have adopted American dress and culture.*

Make Inferences Why do you think new immigrants often opened the same types of businesses as earlier immigrants from the same country had opened? *possible answer— They knew it was likely to succeed.*

Evaluate How might you feel about your job if you worked as a thread trimmer in a shirtwaist factory? *Possible answers may include dissatisfaction with the low pay and boredom because of the monotonous tasks.*

CRF: Primary Source Activity: Immigrant's First-Person Account

go.hrw.com
Online Resources
KEYWORD: SF7 CH20
ACTIVITY: Asian Immigrant Experience

Not all industrial labor took place in large factories. Some immigrants worked for little pay in small shops or mills located in their own neighborhoods. Often associated with the clothing industry, these workplaces were called **sweatshops** because of long hours and hot, unhealthy working conditions. One young immigrant worker remembered:

> "When the shirtwaists were finished at the machine ... we were given scissors to cut the threads off. It wasn't heavy work, but it was monotonous [boring], because you did the same thing from seven-thirty in the morning till nine at night."
>
> – Pauline Newman, quoted in *American Mosaic: The Immigrant Experience in the Words of Those Who Lived It,* by Joan Morrison and Charlotte Fox Zabusky

Immigrants with skills that were in demand sometimes found work outside factories and sweatshops. For example, some immigrants worked as bakers, carpenters, masons, or skilled machinists. Others saved or borrowed money to open small businesses such as laundries, barbershops, or street vending carts. New immigrants often opened the same types of businesses in which other immigrants from the same country were already succeeding. They worked hard for long hours to become successful themselves.

READING CHECK **Summarizing** How did new immigrants help themselves and others to try to make successful lives in the United States?

LINKING TO TODAY

Asian Americans Today

Today, more than 12 million people in the United States are of Asian origin. They account for nearly 5 percent of the U.S. population—or about 1 in 20 Americans. Asian Americans trace their roots to various countries, including China, India, the Philippines, and, like this family, Vietnam. Most Asian Americans live in the West. California has by far the largest Asian American population of any state.

ANALYSIS SKILL **ANALYZING INFORMATION**

Why have so many people moved to the United States?

Differentiating Instruction

Above Level

Advanced/Gifted and Talented

Research Required

1. Explain that the immigrant people from China, who passed though Angel Island, called their new land "Gold Mountain." They were the only immigrants whose numbers were limited by law.
2. Have students conduct research to determine how Chinese immigrants' work transformed the entire nation. Students should include the Chinese Exclusion Act in their research.
3. Have each student use their discoveries in a letter to a fictitious U.S. Congressman from 1912. Letters should persuade the congressman to reconsider the value of Chinese immigrants' contributions to the developing nation and to vote against the Chinese Exclusion Act. **LS Verbal/Linguistic**

Alternative Assessment Handbook, Rubric 43: Writing to Persuade

Answers

Linking to Today *possible answers— economic opportunity, freedom, escape from oppression*

Reading Check *They published newspapers and founded schools, clubs, and places of worship; opened local shops and small neighborhood banks; and formed benevolent societies.*

Opposition to Immigration

Some Americans welcomed new immigrants. Many business leaders, for example, wanted immigrant workers who were willing to work for low pay. In general, however, anti-immigrant feelings grew along with the rise in immigration in the late 1800s. Some labor unions opposed immigration because their members believed immigrants would take jobs away from native-born Americans.

Other Americans called nativists also feared that too many new immigrants were being allowed into the country. Many nativists held racial and ethnic prejudices. They thought that the new immigrants would not learn American customs, which might harm American society.

Some nativists were violent toward immigrants. Others advocated laws to stop or limit immigration. For example, in 1880 about 105,000 Chinese immigrants lived in the United States. Two years later, Congress passed the **Chinese Exclusion Act**, banning Chinese people from immigrating to the United States for 10 years. This law marked the first time a nationality was banned from entering the country. Although the law violated treaties with China, Congress continued to renew the law for decades to come. In 1892 another law was passed restricting convicts, immigrants with certain diseases, and those likely to need public assistance from entering the country.

Despite such opposition immigrants continued to arrive in large numbers. They worked for low pay in factories and built buildings, highways, and railroads. Their labor helped power the continuing industrial growth of the late 1800s and early 1900s. Although they did not always achieve their dreams as quickly as they had hoped, most immigrants were still confident about the future for themselves and their families in the United States. A Russian immigrant named Abraham Hyman expressed this idea, saying, "Your feeling is that a better time is coming, if not for yourself, for your families, for your children."

ACADEMIC VOCABULARY
advocate to plead in favor of

READING CHECK **Analyzing** Why did nativists oppose immigration?

SUMMARY AND PREVIEW Immigrants helped build the nation's economy and cities, but they met resistance from some native-born Americans. In the next section you will learn about what life was like in urban America.

Section 1 Assessment

go.hrw.com
Online Quiz
KEYWORD: SF7 HP20

Reviewing Ideas, Terms, and People

1. a. **Identify** What was Ellis Island?
   b. **Contrast** What differences existed between the **old immigrants** and the **new immigrants**?
2. a. **Identify** What job opportunities were available to new immigrants?
   b. **Summarize** How did immigrants attempt to adapt to their new lives in the United States?
   c. **Elaborate** Why do you think many immigrants tolerated difficult living and working conditions?
3. a. **Recall** What was the purpose of the **Chinese Exclusion Act**?
   b. **Explain** Why did some labor unions oppose immigration?
   c. **Predict** How might the growing opposition to immigration lead to problems in the United States?

Critical Thinking

4. **Categorizing** Review your notes on the benefits and challenges new U.S. immigrants faced. Then use the following graphic organizer to categorize the challenges into different areas of life.

FOCUS ON WRITING

5. **Writing about Immigrants and Their Lives** Make a list of potential characters for your TV series, and be sure to include new immigrants. Take notes about what life was like for them.

Direct Teach

Main Idea

③ Opposition to Immigration

Some Americans opposed immigration and worked to restrict it.

Identify During which time period was there great industrial growth in the United States? *the late 1800s and early 1900s*

Evaluate In what ways did the new wave of immigrants contribute to the development of America? *They built buildings, highways, and railroads, and their labor helped industrial growth.*

Review & Assess

Close

Review the obstacles and opposition that immigrants overcame, as well as their contribution to industrial development in the United States.

Review

Online Quiz, Section 20.1

Assess

SE Section 1 Assessment
PASS: Section Quiz 20.1
Alternative Assessment Handbook

Reteach/Classroom Intervention

Interactive Reader and Study Guide, Section 20.1
Interactive Skills Tutor CD-ROM

Section 1 Assessment Answers

1. **a.** N.Y. immigration processing center
   b. old—from northern Europe; new—from southern and eastern Europe and Mexico
2. **a.** unskilled jobs in garment or steel factories or construction, opened small businesses
   b. learned English, lived with immigrants from the same country, encouraged children to adopt American customs, founded places of worship, schools, and benevolent societies
   c. It was an improvement over life in their native lands; they believed hard work would lead to success.
3. **a.** 10-year ban on Chinese immigration
   b. fear that immigrants would take away jobs from native-born Americans
   c. possible answers—increasing polarization, social tension, possibility of violence
4. education—did not speak English, often no formal education; culture—different customs and religions; work—took low-paying jobs; living conditions—poorly built tenements
5. Students should have immigrants in their list of characters and include a description of what their lives were like.

Answers

Reading Check *They feared new immigrants would not learn American customs, which might harm American society.*

Preteach

Bellringer

If YOU were there... Use the **Daily Bellringer Transparency** for this section to help students answer the question.

Daily Bellringer Transparency, 20.2

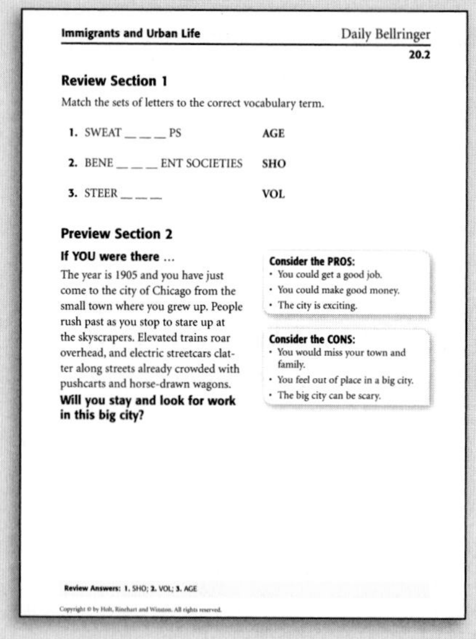
Immigrants and Urban Life — Daily Bellringer **20.2**

Review Section 1

Match the sets of letters to the correct vocabulary term.

1. SWEAT _ _ _ PS	AGE
2. BENE _ _ _ ENT SOCIETIES	SHO
3. STEER _ _ _	VOL

Preview Section 2

If YOU were there ...

The year is 1905 and you have just come to the city of Chicago from the small town where you grew up. People rush past as you stop to stare up at the skyscrapers. Elevated trains roar overhead, and electric streetcars clatter along streets already crowded with pushcarts and horse-drawn wagons.

Will you stay and look for work in this big city?

Consider the PROS:
- You could get a good job.
- You could make good money.
- The city is exciting.

Consider the CONS:
- You would miss your town and family.
- You feel out of place in a big city.
- The big city can be scary.

Review Answers: 1. SHO; 2. VOL; 3. AGE

Academic Vocabulary

Review with students the high-use academic term in this section.

factor cause (p. 643)

CRF: Vocabulary Builder Activity, Section 2

Taking Notes

Have students copy the graphic organizer onto their own paper and then use it to take notes on the section. This activity will prepare students for the Section Assessment, in which they will complete a graphic organizer that builds on the information using a critical-thinking skill.

Section Correlations

IN

8.3.7 Using maps identify changes influenced by growth, economic development and human migration in the eighteenth and nineteenth centuries. **8.3.9** Analyze human and physical factors that have influenced migration and settlement patterns and relate them to the economic development of the United States. **8.3.11** Identify ways people modified the physical environment as the United States developed and describe the impacts that resulted.

SECTION 2

The Growth of Cities

What You Will Learn...

Main Ideas

1. Both immigrants and native-born Americans moved to growing urban areas in record numbers in the late 1800s and early 1900s.
2. New technology and ideas helped cities change and adapt to rapid population growth.

The Big Idea

American cities experienced dramatic expansion and change in the late 1800s.

Key Terms and People

mass transit, *p. 644*
suburbs, *p. 644*
mass culture, *p. 644*
Joseph Pulitzer, *p. 645*
William Randolph Hearst, *p. 645*
department stores, *p. 645*
Frederick Law Olmsted, *p. 645*

TAKING NOTES As you read, take notes on the causes of the growth of cities.

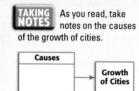

Causes	→	Growth of Cities

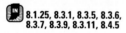

IN 8.1.25, 8.3.1, 8.3.5, 8.3.6, 8.3.7, 8.3.9, 8.3.11, 8.4.5

If YOU were there...

The year is 1905 and you have just come to the city of Chicago from the small town where you grew up. People rush past as you stop to stare up at the skyscrapers. Elevated trains roar overhead, and electric streetcars clatter along streets already crowded with pushcarts and horse-drawn wagons.

Will you stay and look for work in this big city?

BUILDING BACKGROUND Industrial growth and a new wave of immigration swelled the populations of American cities in the late 1800s. Cities changed quickly to accommodate so many new people, offering urban residents excitement and new kinds of entertainment.

Growth of Urban Areas

In 1850 New York City was the only U.S. city with a population of more than 500,000. By 1900 New York City, Chicago, Philadelphia, St. Louis, Boston, and Baltimore all had more than half a million residents. More than 35 U.S. cities had populations greater than 100,000. About 40 percent of Americans now lived in urban areas.

As you have read, new immigrants were responsible for a lot of this urban growth. So were families from rural areas in the United States. As farm equipment replaced workers in the countryside, large numbers of rural residents moved to the cities in search of work. African Americans from the rural South also began moving to northern cities in the 1890s. They hoped to escape discrimination and find better educational and economic opportunities. Cities such as Chicago; Cleveland, Ohio; Detroit, Michigan; and New York saw large increases in their African American populations during the late 1800s and early 1900s.

Perhaps the most dramatic example of urban growth was the rise of Chicago. The city's population exploded from 30,000 in 1850 to 1.7 million in 1900. Chicago passed St. Louis as the

Teach the Big Idea

At Level

The Growth of Cities

Materials: U.S. outline maps for each student

1. **Teach** To teach the main ideas in the section, use the questions in the Direct Teach boxes.
2. **Apply** Tell students that after 1850 certain U.S. cities grew quickly. Have students find the six cities listed on this page that grew to over half a million people by 1900. *New York City, Chicago, Philadelphia, St. Louis, Boston, Baltimore.* Have students find these cities on a U.S. map and label the cities' locations on their maps. LS **Visual/Spatial**
3. **Review** Discuss each city's location and what factors may have influenced population growth. *ports—New York City, Boston, Baltimore; on railroad lines—all listed cities; on major rivers—New York City, Philadelphia, St. Louis* LS **Visual/Spatial**
4. **Practice/Homework** Have students color their maps and add illustrations or symbols.

Alternative Assessment Handbook, Rubrics 12: Drawing Conclusions; and 21: Map Reading

Primary Source

POSTCARD

Chicago, 1900

Postcards like this one were one way people shared the experience of visiting or living in a big city like Chicago. This scene shows a bustling street corner at which modern transportation like streetcars mingle with horse-drawn carts.

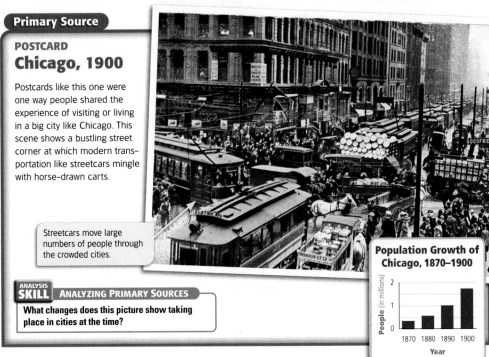

Streetcars move large numbers of people through the crowded cities.

Population Growth of Chicago, 1870–1900

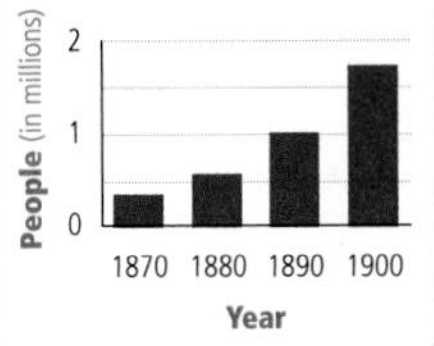

ANALYSIS SKILL ANALYZING PRIMARY SOURCES

What changes does this picture show taking place in cities at the time?

biggest city in the Midwest. Along with the large numbers of African Americans moving to the city, many of Chicago's new residents were immigrants from southern and eastern Europe. In 1900 immigrants and their children made up three quarters of Chicago's population.

Chicago's location was another **factor** in its rapid growth. Many of the new railroad lines connecting the East and West coasts ran through Chicago. This put Chicago at the heart of the nation's trade in lumber, grain, and meat. Thousands of new Chicago residents found work in the city's huge slaughterhouses and meatpacking plants. Here, meat from the West and Midwest was packed into refrigerated train cars and shipped to the growing cities of the East, where it could be sold in shops to customers.

READING CHECK **Identifying Cause and Effect** What factors led to massive population growth in urban areas during the late 1800s and early 1900s?

Changing Cities

American cities such as Chicago were ill-prepared for the rapid urban growth of the late 1800s and early 1900s. Where was everyone going to live? How were people going to get from home to work on crowded city streets? Several new technologies helped cities meet these challenges. These technologies forever changed the look and function of U.S. cities.

ACADEMIC VOCABULARY
factor cause

Building Skyscrapers

With so many people moving to urban areas, cities quickly ran out of building space in downtown areas. One solution would be to build taller buildings. Typical city buildings in the mid-1800s were only five stories tall, but taller structures were impossible to construct because the building materials available were either too weak or too heavy.

This changed with the rise of the American steel industry in the late 1800s.

Direct Teach

Main Idea

❶ Growth of Urban Areas

Both immigrants and native-born Americans moved to growing urban areas in record numbers in the late 1800s and early 1900s.

Explain What system put Chicago at the heart of the nation's trade in lumber, grain, and meat? *the railroad system*

Cause and Effect Railroad lines intersected in Chicago, bringing new workers to growing industries. What industry employed many new residents in Chicago? *Thousands of new residents found work in slaughterhouses and meatpacking plants.*

Predict How might Chicago's population growth eventually change the look of the city? *more and taller buildings, more traffic, crowded housing*

Did you know . . .

At the age of 12, Thomas Edison began working for the railroads. Later he became an apprentice telegrapher. His severe hearing loss inspired him to make new equipment, sparking his career as one of the most important inventors of his time.

go.hrw.com
Online Resources
KEYWORD: SF7 CH20
ACTIVITY: Columbian Exposition

Cross-Discipline Activity: Science

At Level

How'd They Do That?

1. Tell students that the Edison Electric Light Company began supplying electricity to New York City in 1882. This changed people's lives in many ways. For example, they had used gas and oil lamps for light, which caused many fires. After electrification, New Yorkers used electric lamps with light bulbs.
2. Have students create a Three-Panel Flip Chart as shown on page 635.
3. On each of the three top flaps, have them sketch or write the name of an electrical item in common use today. Under each flap, have them sketch or write how they think the task done by the electric appliance was done before electrification.
4. As students complete their flip charts, have them exchange their charts and try to guess what is under each flap. Above-level students can create more than one Flip Note.

LS Interpersonal, Visual/Spatial

Alternative Assessment Handbook, Rubric 9: Comparing and Contrasting

Answers

Analyzing Primary Sources *mass transportation, taller buildings, crowded streets, industrialization*

Reading Check *the arrival of new immigrants, farm equipment replaced workers, poverty and discrimination in the South, the location of cities along major rail routes*

Direct Teach

Main Idea

❷ Changing Cities

New technology and ideas helped cities change and adapt to rapid population growth.

Recall What building material allowed architects to build taller buildings? *steel*

Evaluate Would you rather have lived in the city or in a suburb in the 1880s? *possible answer—city: good job and cultural opportunities; suburb: less crowded, quieter, cleaner*

CRF: Biography Activity: Joseph Pulitzer

Connect to Geography

Human/Environment Interaction Have students look at the trails designed by Olmsted in Central Park. Ask: Why aren't the trails straight like the roads around the park? *People are not in a hurry. It is more interesting to discover new sights around curves.*

Checking for Understanding

Select the best answer for each of the following:

1. What did the increased production of steel make possible?
   a. It employed more sweatshop workers.
   b. *It allowed architects to build skyscrapers.*
   c. It increased production of automobiles.
2. Which of Elisha Otis's inventions were important in making skyscrapers practical?
   a. elevated trains
   b. moveable type
   c. *the safety elevator*

THE IMPACT TODAY

Skyscrapers today use much of the same technology that was developed in the late 1800s—steel skeletons and elevators. Chicago's Sears Tower, with 110 stories, is one of the tallest buildings in the world.

Mills began producing tons of strong and inexpensive steel. Soon, architects such as Louis Sullivan of Chicago began designing multistory buildings called skyscrapers. Architects used steel beams to make sturdy frames that could support the weight of tall buildings. This allowed builders to use limited city space more efficiently.

The safety elevator, patented by Elisha Otis in the 1850s, helped make skyscrapers practical. Previous elevators had been unsafe because they would crash to the ground if the elevator cable snapped. Otis's safety elevator included a device to hold the elevator in place if the cable broke.

Getting Around

Taller buildings made it possible for more people to live and work in city centers. This increased the need for **mass transit**, or public transportation designed to move many people. By the late 1860s New York City had elevated trains running on tracks above the streets. Chicago followed in the 1890s.

Some cities built underground railroads, known as subways. In 1897 the first subway in the United States opened in Boston. In 1904 the first line of the New York City subway system began operation. Cable cars and electric trolleys also became common. These streetcars cheaply and quickly carried people in the cities to and from work.

Many Americans who could afford it moved to **suburbs**, residential neighborhoods outside of downtown areas that had begun springing up before the Civil War. Mass transit networks made such moves possible. People could live in the suburbs and take trolleys, subways, or trains into the cities.

New Ideas

In the late 1800s the United States also began to develop forms of **mass culture**, or leisure and cultural activities shared by many people. One factor contributing to mass culture was a boom in publishing. The invention of the Linotype, an automatic typesetting machine, greatly reduced the time and cost of printing. In 1850

Frederick Law Olmsted

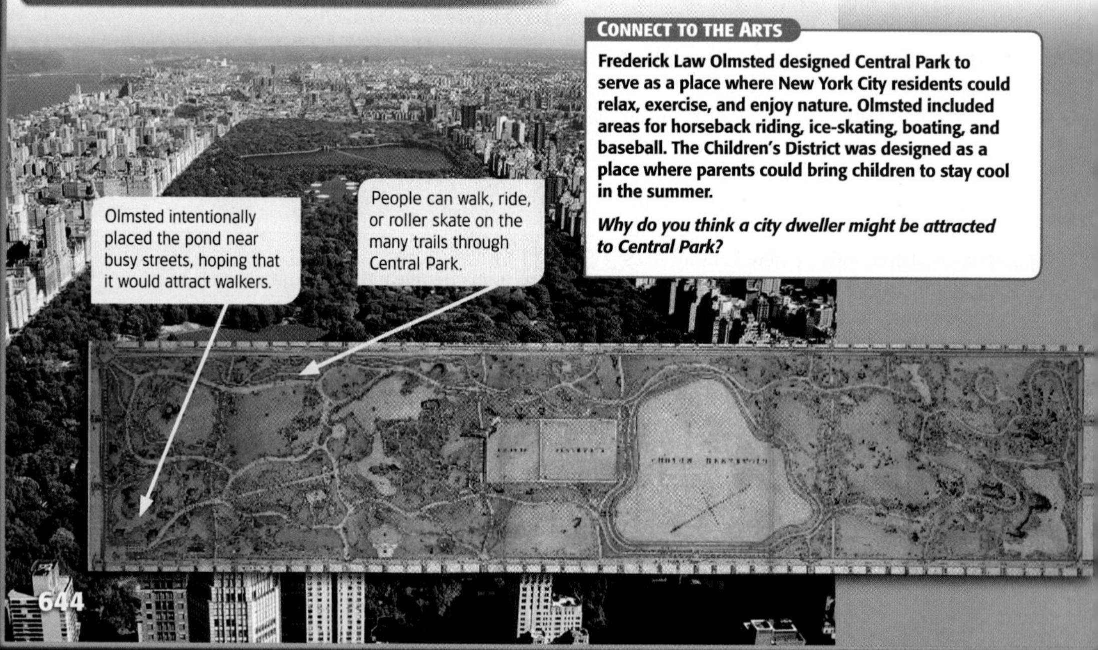

Olmsted intentionally placed the pond near busy streets, hoping that it would attract walkers.
People can walk, ride, or roller skate on the many trails through Central Park.
644

CONNECT TO THE ARTS

Frederick Law Olmsted designed Central Park to serve as a place where New York City residents could relax, exercise, and enjoy nature. Olmsted included areas for horseback riding, ice-skating, boating, and baseball. The Children's District was designed as a place where parents could bring children to stay cool in the summer.

Why do you think a city dweller might be attracted to Central Park?

Cross-Discipline Activity: Geography

At Level

Design a Park

Materials: 11" × 18" construction paper

1. Ask students to imagine they have been asked to design a park for their neighborhood. Have them imagine they are flying over the parkland.
2. Ask students what they hope to see in the parks they are designing *(possible answers—trees, playgrounds, baseball diamonds, trails, people, dogs)*. Have students name different types of activities that people would enjoy doing there *(possible answers—playing, walking, hiking, skateboarding, picnicking)*.
3. Distribute the construction paper. Using Olmsted's Central Park design as a model, have students design and name their own parks.
4. Ask students to display their designs as they complete them. **LS Visual/Spatial, Kinesthetic**

Alternative Assessment Handbook, Rubrics 3: Artwork; and 20: Map Creation

Answers

Connect to the Arts *allows a city dweller to exercise and enjoy nature without traveling far from home*

there were fewer than 300 daily newspapers in the country. Because of the use of Linotype machines, by 1900 there were more than 2,000 newspapers.

Big cities often had many newspapers, so publishers had to compete for readers. In 1896 **Joseph Pulitzer** added a color comic to his *New York World* newspaper. More people started buying Pulitzer's paper. **William Randolph Hearst**, publisher of the *New York Journal*, saw that comics helped sell newspapers. So he added a color comic strip to the *Journal*. Soon, newspapers across the country were adding comic strips.

Mass culture affected how people shopped as well. Giant retail shops, or **department stores**, appeared in some cities during the late 1800s. One of the earliest was Marshall Field in Chicago, which offered low prices and large quantities of products. It also was the first department store to offer its customers a restaurant where they could eat while shopping. Newspaper advertising was used to bring in customers. The public was also attracted by fancy window displays.

World fairs were another example of mass culture. Fairs brought merchants together, which sometimes resulted in new ideas and products. At the 1904 St. Louis World's Fair, for example, a Syrian food vendor began making cones for a nearby ice cream vendor who had run out of dishes. Ice cream cones became popular throughout the country.

The demand for public entertainment also led to the creation of amusement parks, such as New York's Coney Island. The inexpensive entry tickets made Coney Island a favorite destination for children and families. For a nickel, visitors could ride a new invention called the Switchback Railway—the country's first roller coaster.

As cities grew, people became aware of the need for open public space. Landscape architect **Frederick Law Olmsted** became nationally famous. He designed Central Park in New York City, as well as many state and national parks. Some of his other well-known projects include Prospect Park in Brooklyn, New York, and the U.S. Capitol grounds, which he worked on between 1874 and 1895.

READING CHECK **Summarizing** What forms of mass culture were available in urban areas?

SUMMARY AND PREVIEW Immigration and new technology helped cities grow in the late 1800s. In the next section you will learn about some of the problems caused by rapid urban growth.

Section 2 Assessment

go.hrw.com
Online Quiz
KEYWORD: SF7 HP20

Reviewing Ideas, Terms, and People

1. a. **Identify** What groups of people began moving to cities in the late 1800s?
   b. **Explain** Why did African Americans begin to move to northern cities in the 1890s?
   c. **Predict** Do you think cities such as Chicago continued to grow in the 1900s? Why or why not?
2. a. **Define** What is **mass transit**? What made mass transit necessary?
   b. **Explain** How did new inventions make it possible for people to build skyscrapers?
   c. **Evaluate** Which improvement to urban living do you think had the greatest impact on people's lives? Explain your answer.

Critical Thinking

3. **Identifying Cause and Effect** Review your notes on the causes for the growth of cities. Then copy the following graphic organizer and use it to identify the effects of city growth. You may need to add more circles.

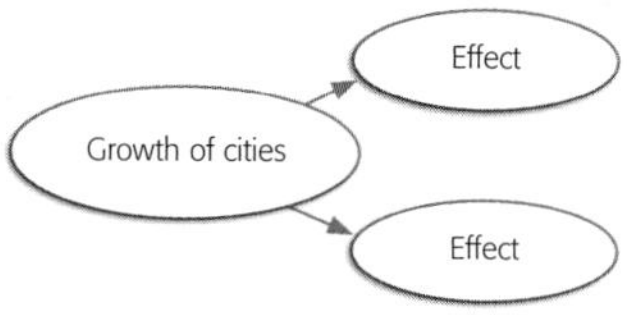

FOCUS ON WRITING

4. **Describing Setting** A city like those you have read about could serve as the setting of your TV series. How could you describe the city?

Direct Teach

Main Idea

❷ Changing Cities

New technology and ideas helped cities change and adapt to rapid population growth.

Identify Name two newspaper publishers who used color comics to attract more readers. *Joseph Pulitzer and William Randolph Hearst*

Evaluate How would the Marshall Field department store have attracted the business of eighth graders? Justify your choice. *possible answers—low prices, large quantities of products, restaurant, newspaper advertising, fancy window displays; Answers should include a reason for the choice.*

Review & Assess

Close

Ask students to refer to their notes and review with them the reasons for the rapid growth of American cities in the late 1800s. Discuss the challenges and developments which resulted from population growth.

Review

go.hrw.com Online Quiz, Section 20.2

Assess

SE Section 2 Assessment

PASS: Section Quiz 20.2

Alternative Assessment Handbook

Reteach/Classroom Intervention

Interactive Reader and Study Guide, Section 20.2

Interactive Skills Tutor CD-ROM

Section 2 Assessment Answers

1. **a.** new immigrants, families from rural areas in the United States, African Americans from the rural South
   b. to escape discrimination and find better educational and economic opportunities
   c. yes, skyscrapers and mass transit allowed more people to live in and near the city
2. **a.** public transportation designed to move many people; people who lived in the suburbs needed to get to work
   b. Steel beams supported tall buildings, safety elevator made tall buildings practical
   c. possible answers—mass transit, newspapers, department stores, or parks; Students must explain how the improvement they chose improved people's lives.
3. possible effects—more workers for industrial growth, development of skyscrapers, publishing boom, development of mass transit, development of mass culture
4. Answers should include a description of bustling city life with tall buildings, crowded streets, and busy shops.

Answers

Reading Check *newspapers, department stores, fairs, amusement parks, public parks*

Preteach

Bellringer

If YOU were there... Use the **Daily Bellringer Transparency** for this section to help students answer the question.

Daily Bellringer Transparency, 20.3

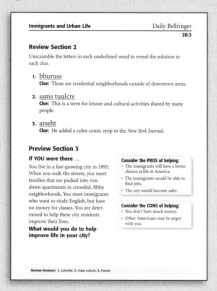

Immigrants and Urban Life — Daily Bellringer **20.3**

Review Section 2

Unscramble the letters in each underlined word to reveal the solution to each clue.

1. bburuss
   Clue: These are residential neighborhoods outside of downtown areas.
2. sams tuulcre
   Clue: This is a term for leisure and cultural activities shared by many people.
3. arseht
   Clue: He added a color comic strip to the *New York Journal.*

Preview Section 3

If YOU were there ...

You live in a fast-growing city in 1895. When you walk the streets, you meet families that are packed into run-down apartments in crowded, filthy neighborhoods. You meet immigrants who want to study English, but have no money for classes. You are determined to help these city residents improve their lives.

What would you do to help improve life in your city?

Consider the PROS of helping:
- The immigrants will have a better chance at life in America.
- The immigrants would be able to find jobs.
- The city would become safer.

Consider the CONS of helping:
- You don't have much money.
- Other Americans may be angry with you.

Review Answers: 1. suburbs; 2. mass culture; 3. Hearst

Building Vocabulary

Preteach or review the following terms:

charity an institution engaged in relief for the poor (p. 648)

sanitation the promotion of hygiene and prevention of disease (p. 646)

CRF: Vocabulary Builder Activity, Section 3

Taking Notes

Have students copy the graphic organizer onto their own paper and then use it to take notes on the section. This activity will prepare students for the Section Assessment, in which they will complete a graphic organizer that builds on the information using a critical-thinking skill.

Section Correlations IN

8.1.25 Give examples of how immigration affected American culture in the decades before and after the Civil War, including growth of industrial sites in the North; religious differences; tensions between middle-class and working-class people, particularly in the Northeast; and intensification of cultural differences between the North and the South.

SECTION 3

City Life

What You Will Learn...

Main Ideas

1. Crowded urban areas faced a variety of social problems.
2. People worked to improve the quality of life in U.S. cities.

The Big Idea

The rapid growth of cities in the late 1800s created both challenges and opportunities.

Key Terms and People

Jacob Riis, *p. 646*
settlement houses, *p. 648*
Jane Addams, *p. 648*
Hull House, *p. 648*
Florence Kelley, *p. 648*

TAKING NOTES As you read, take notes on problems facing city residents. You can organize your notes in a table like this one.

Urban Problems

IN 8.1.25, 8.3.8, 8.3.9, 8.3.11

If YOU were there...

You live in a fast-growing city in 1895. When you walk the streets, you meet families that are packed into run-down apartments in crowded, filthy neighborhoods. You meet immigrants who want to study English but have no money for classes. You are determined to help these city residents improve their lives.

What would you do to help improve life in your city?

BUILDING BACKGROUND Despite the new public parks, skyscrapers, and mass transit systems, many cities were not ready for the rapid population growth that began taking place in the late 1800s. Overcrowding and poor living conditions forced people to search for solutions to these problems.

Urban Problems

In the late 1800s and early 1900s, shortages of affordable housing forced many poor families to squeeze into tiny tenement apartments, which were frequently unsafe and unsanitary. Journalist and photographer **Jacob Riis** became famous for exposing the horrible conditions in New York City tenements. Riis wrote about one typical tenement family:

> "There were nine in the family: husband, wife, an aged grandmother, and six children ... All nine lived in two rooms, one about ten feet square that served as parlor, bedroom, and eating-room, the other a small hall-room made into a kitchen."
>
> — Jacob Riis, *How the Other Half Lives*

This kind of overcrowding caused sanitation problems. Most cities did not have a good system for collecting trash, so garbage often piled up outside apartment buildings. An article in the *New York Tribune* described the garbage in front of one tenement as a "mass of air poisoning, death-breeding filth, reeking in the fierce sunshine."

Unsafe conditions were also common in tenements. Before 1900 most cities did not have laws requiring landlords to fix their tenements or to maintain safety standards. A fire on one floor could easily spread, and fire escapes were often blocked or broken.

Teach the Big Idea

At Level

City Life

1. **Teach** To teach the main ideas in the section, use the questions in the Direct Teach boxes.
2. **Apply** One of the ways people improved city life was by starting charitable organizations, which had to determine what problems needed their attention. Have students list the needs they think such a group might address. *(education, food, employment, childcare)*
3. **Review** Have students write a sentence for each listed problem, telling how a charity might help solve the problem.
4. **Practice/Homework** Instruct students to create a jingle to advertise a fictitious charitable organization. Give an example such as: "When your children need care, just make us aware. Smith House, Baltimore." Have volunteers share their slogans with the class.
   LS Auditory/Musical, Verbal/Linguistic

Alternative Assessment Handbook, Rubric 2: Advertisements

Tenement Life QUICK FACTS

Causes
- Overcrowding
- Unsafe buildings
- Unsanitary conditions
- Scarce running water
- Poor ventilation

Effects
- Diseases such as tuberculosis and cholera
- High child death rates
- Fire
- Crime

Tenement rooms had few or no windows to let in fresh air and sunshine. Comfort was also scarce, with so many people crowded into such small spaces. Running water and indoor plumbing were also scarce. So was clean water—cities often dumped garbage into local rivers that were used for drinking water.

Disease-causing bacteria grew easily in these conditions. Diseases such as cholera, typhoid, influenza, and tuberculosis spread quickly in crowded neighborhoods. Children were the most vulnerable to these diseases. For example, babies born in Chicago in 1870 had only a 50 percent chance of living to the age of five.

Air pollution was also a serious problem in many growing cities. This was a time when many business leaders were building huge oil refineries, steel mills, and other factories. The steel mills of Andrew Carnegie, for example, helped make Pittsburgh the nation's steel-making center in the late 1800s. Steel mills brought jobs and wealth to Pittsburgh, but they also caused some of the nation's worst air pollution. "Every street appears to end in a huge, black cloud," said one writer. "Pittsburgh is smoke, smoke, smoke—everywhere smoke." The air was so polluted at times that the city had to turn on outdoor lighting during the day.

THE IMPACT TODAY
Like many industrial cities, Pittsburgh has made great progress in cleaning its air and water. Today, Pittsburgh is ranked as one of the cleanest American cities.

The work of many city governments slowly helped to lessen some of these urban problems. By the late 1800s new sewage and water purification systems improved city sanitation. Many major cities also were hiring full-time firefighters and police officers. Police officers in cities were typically placed in one neighborhood. They knew the local residents and were frequently involved in local activities. They could spot local problems and, in many cases, provide help to immigrants.

READING CHECK **Summarizing** What challenges did many city residents face in the late 1800s?

Direct Teach

Main Idea

1 Urban Problems

Crowded urban areas faced a variety of social problems.

Recall Name four diseases caused by poor sanitation. *cholera, typhoid, influenza, tuberculosis*

Make Inferences If a family living in Chicago had six babies during the 1870s, how many of them could they expect to live past age five? *3 (50%)*

Develop What kinds of problems did growing city governments in the late 1800s face, and which problems did they try to fix first? *Possible answer—Public health, safety, and fire prevention services are usually the most critical and therefore the problems that are first addressed.*

Activity Appreciation Poster Have each student write or draw an expression of thanks to workers at a local government service agency such as the fire department, police department, or recreation and parks service. Collect and glue them to a large sheet of construction paper and enlist students and parents to deliver them.

LS Verbal/Linguistic, Visual/Spatial

- Alternative Assessment Handbook, Rubrics 3: Artwork; and 25: Personal Letters
- Political Cartoons Activities for United States History, Cartoon 21: Urban Life and Tenements
- **CRF:** Biography Activity: Alice Hamilton; Primary Source Activity: Photo of Immigrant Home
- Quick Facts Transparency 53: Tenement Life

Cross-Discipline Activity: Drama

At Level

Improving Tenement Life

1. Tell students they are going to write a short play. In the first scene, a tenement family of the 1880s will talk to another family about their problems and needs. In the second scene, the play must demonstrate how charities and city agencies, over a period of time, helped improve the lives of the families.
2. Organize students into small groups and allow them time to work together.
3. Set aside class time for each group to perform its play.
4. Encourage students to perform their plays for another class or for a parent group.

LS Interpersonal, Kinesthetic, Verbal/Linguistic

- Alternative Assessment Handbook, Rubrics 14: Group Activity; and 33: Skits and Reader's Theater

Answers

Reading Check *shortages of affordable housing, unsafe and unsanitary conditions, air pollution*

Direct Teach

Main Idea

❷ Improving City Life

People worked to improve the quality of life in U.S. cities.

Explain What was the purpose of *How the Other Half Lives? to show conditions in tenement housing*

Analyze How did Florence Kelley help reform working conditions? *convinced lawmakers to limit women's working hours and prevent child labor*

Elaborate How might the 1893 Illinois labor law have changed the lives of children? *would become healthier because they had time to eat and rest; would have more time for education and play*

Info to Know

Where Is Sue? In 1893 Chicago citizens donated money for a museum to house collections displayed at the World's Columbian Exhibition that year. They named it the Field Museum after American merchant, Marshall Field. Today it houses over 19 million artifacts, including Sue, the largest and most complete *Tyrannosaurus Rex* fossil ever found.

Focus on Indiana

8.1.25 Interpret How did settlement houses try to help immigrants? *They tried to help immigrants learn American language and culture.*

Answers

Hull House *staff provided day care, club meetings, classes, plays, sports; worked to pass a law to prevent child labor*

FOCUS ON INDIANA

Many immigrants came to Indiana from eastern and southern Europe to work in the steel mills and other heavy industries there. Groups in cities such as Indianapolis and Gary founded settlement houses that helped immigrants adjust to life in the United States.

Improving City Life

Jacob Riis hoped his book *How the Other Half Lives* would shock many Americans—and it did. A reformer named Lawrence Veiller helped lead the effort to improve conditions in tenements. Describing the effects of tenement living on children, he wrote:

> "A child living its early years in dark rooms, without sunlight or fresh air, does not grow up to be a normal, healthy person ... It is not of such material that strong nations are made."
>
> –Lawrence Veiller, quoted in *Readings in American History, Vol. 2*

Veiller worked with an organization called the Charity Organization Society (COS) to get changes made to New York laws. In 1900 he and the COS sponsored an exhibit of photographs and maps graphically showing the conditions of New York tenements. More than 10,000 people visited the exhibit, and they were shocked by what they saw. The work of Veiller and the COS helped to get the 1901 New York State Tenement House Act passed. This law required new buildings to have better ventilation and running water. The act became a model for housing reform in other states.

Because there was little government aid available in the 1800s, private organizations generally took on the task of helping the urban poor. Some individuals set up **settlement houses**, or neighborhood centers in poor areas that offered education, recreation, and social activities.

Settlement houses were staffed by professionals and volunteers. Many were educated women who came from wealthy families. In 1886 Charles B. Stover and Stanton Coit established the first settlement house in the United States. It was called Neighborhood Guild and was located on the Lower East Side in New York City. In 1889 **Jane Addams** and Ellen Gates Starr moved into a run-down building in a poor Chicago neighborhood and turned it into **Hull House**, the most famous settlement house of the period.

The Hull House staff focused on the needs of immigrant families, and by 1893 Hull House was serving 2,000 people a week. It provided services such as English classes, day care, and cooking and sewing classes. Children and adults came to take part in club meetings, art classes, plays, and sports.

Jane Addams and the staff at Hull House also worked for reforms. They studied the problems facing immigrants and poor city dwellers, then searched for ways to improve conditions. **Florence Kelley** was one important reformer at Hull House. She visited sweatshops and wrote about the problems there. Her work helped convince lawmakers to take action. Illinois passed a law in 1893 to limit working hours for women and to prevent child labor.

Kelley became the state's chief factory inspector and helped enforce the law. Although she believed more reforms were needed, she did report some improvements:

Hull House

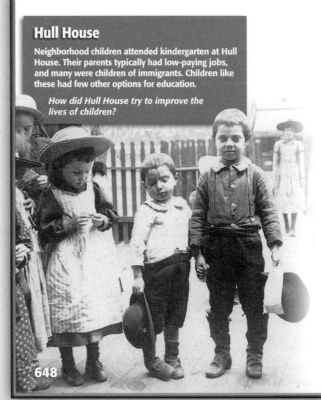

Neighborhood children attended kindergarten at Hull House. Their parents typically had low-paying jobs, and many were children of immigrants. Children like these had few other options for education.

How did Hull House try to improve the lives of children?

Differentiating Instruction

Below Level

Struggling Readers

1. Draw the graphic organizer for students to see. Omit the answers in blue.
2. Explain each category to students and ask them to name a person for each category. Note: Jane Addams appears in both categories. Have students copy the graphic organizer and use information from their texts to complete the missing names. Review the answers with the class. **LS Visual/Spatial**

Alternative Assessment Handbook, Rubric 13: Graphic Organizers

Reformers of Big City Troubles

Living Conditions	Working Conditions
a. Jacob Riis	*a. Florence Kelley*
b. Lawrence Veiller	*b. Alzina P. Stevens*
c. Charles B. Stover	*c. Jane Addams*
d. Stanton Coit	
e. Jane Addams	
f. Ellen Gates Starr	

“Previous to the passage of the factory law of 1893, it was the rule of [a candy] factory to work the children ... from 7 A.M. to 9 P.M., with twenty minutes for lunch, and no supper, a working week of eighty-two hours ... Since the enactment of the factory law, their working week has consisted of six days of eight hours each, a reduction of thirty-four hours a week.”

– Florence Kelley and Alzina P. Stevens, from *Hull House Maps and Papers*

As Hull House gained recognition, the settlement house movement spread to other cities. Most settlement houses continued to provide programs and services for city dwellers through the early 1900s. Some, such as Germantown Settlement in Pennsylvania, remain active today.

READING CHECK **Drawing Conclusions** How did Hull House help improve city life?

SUMMARY AND PREVIEW Reformers in the late 1800s worked to solve urban problems. In the next chapter you will learn how Progressives pushed for further reforms.

BIOGRAPHY

Jane Addams

1860–1935

Jane Addams was born in Cedarville, Illinois. Like many upper-class women of the era, she received a college education but found few jobs open to her. In 1888, on a visit to England with classmate Ellen Gates Starr, she visited a London settlement house. On their return to the United States, Addams and Starr opened a settlement house in Chicago. They started a kindergarten and a public playground. Addams also became involved in housing safety and sanitation issues, factory inspection, and immigrants' rights. In 1931 she shared the Nobel Peace Prize for her work with the Women's International League for Peace and Freedom.

Summarizing How did Jane Addams try to improve the lives of workers?

Section 3 Assessment

go.hrw.com
Online Quiz
KEYWORD: SF7 HP20

Reviewing Ideas, Terms, and People

1. a. **Describe** What were conditions like in tenements?
   b. **Summarize** What problems resulted from the rapid growth of cities?
   c. **Draw Conclusions** Why do you think people lived in tenements?
2. a. **Define** What is a **settlement house**?
   b. **Explain** How did settlement houses help city dwellers?
   c. **Evaluate** Do you think settlement houses were successful? Why or why not?

Critical Thinking

3. **Categorizing** Review your notes on urban problems. Then copy the chart to the right onto your own sheet of paper and use it to identify the responses to those problems.

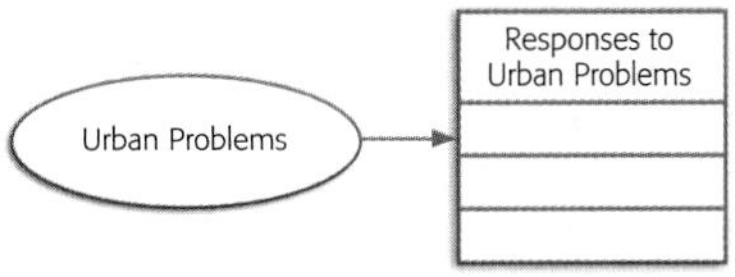

FOCUS ON WRITING

4. **Writing about Urban Problems** Finding solutions to problems is an important part of the plot of many stories. Take notes on scenes you could include in your TV series in which characters deal with the problems of urban life.

• Review & Assess •

Close

Ask students to name problems poor city dwellers faced in the 1880s and how their needs were met.

Review

go.hrw.com Online Quiz, Section 20.3

Assess

SE Section 3 Assessment

PASS: Section Quiz 20.3

Alternative Assessment Handbook

Reteach/Classroom Intervention

Interactive Reader and Study Guide, Section 20.3

Interactive Skills Tutor CD-ROM

Section 3 Assessment Answers

1. **a.** overcrowded, unsanitary, dangerous
   b. overcrowding, sanitation and safety problems, crime, pollution
   c. Tenements were the only affordable housing, and factory jobs were nearby.
2. **a.** a neighborhood center in a poor area that offers education, recreation, and social activities
   b. They provided classes in English, cooking, sewing, and day care.
   c. possible answer—They helped so many people so effectively that some remain active today.
3. new sewage system, new water purification system, full-time city firefighters and police
4. Scenes described should include a problem of urban life as well as its solution.

Answers

Biography *Addams opened a settlement house and became involved in housing, safety and sanitation issues, factory inspection, and immigrants' rights.*

Reading Check *by providing programs and services for city dwellers*

Social Studies Skills

Making Comparisons

Activity **Influential People Essays**

Tell students that in studying history, it is often useful to compare leaders of nations. These leaders can shape events and their responses often affect how others perceive their nation when they are in power. It is much the same with influential friends and family members. Have students choose two people who are important in their lives and identify how they are alike or different. Have students think about the influence these people have had on their character and the decisions they make. For example, one friend may encourage another to try out for a certain sport or pursue a certain career. Ask students to write an essay comparing these people and describing their effects on the student's life. Students should use specific details or examples and make a concluding statement. Remind students that their subjects may read their writing.
LS Verbal/Linguistic, Intrapersonal, Interpersonal

- Alternative Assessment Handbook, Rubrics 9: Comparing and Contrasting; 12: Drawing Conclusions; and 37: Writing Assignments
- Interactive Skills Tutor CD-ROM, Lessons 1: Compare and Contrast; and 15: Make Inferences and Draw Conclusions
- **CRF:** Social Studies Skills Activity: Making Comparisons

Answers

Practice the Skill **1.** *Students' responses should include two people, events, or ideas, and indicate their historical importance.* **2.** *Writing should compare and contrast two specific choices.*

Social Studies Skills

Analysis | **Critical Thinking** | Civic Participation | Study

Making Comparisons

Define the Skill

Understanding similarities is important when studying history. Comparing two or more people, things, events, or ideas highlights the similarities between them. Making comparisons can help clarify larger historical issues. This is true when comparing different time periods or when comparing different things from the same time period. Making comparisons is important in identifying historical connections.

Learn the Skill

When you encounter similar people, things, events, or ideas in history, use the following guidelines to make comparisons.

1. Identify who or what you are going to compare.
2. Look for similarities between them. Find examples of what makes them alike. Note any differences as well.
3. Use comparison words such as "like," "both," and "similar" to point out similarities.

In this chapter, you have learned about several reformers, including Lawrence Veiller and Florence Kelley. Veiller helped lead the effort to improve conditions in tenements. Kelley was a reformer who worked at Hull House.

Lawrence Veiller and Florence Kelley were alike in many ways. Although Veiller focused on tenements and Kelley concentrated on factory work, both were concerned with problems that affected children. Both did research about their issues. Both then wrote about the poor conditions they found.

Both Veiller and Kelley worked successfully for laws that would improve those conditions. Kelley's work helped convince Illinois lawmakers to pass a law to limit child labor. Similarly, Veiller helped to get the 1901 New York State Tenement House Act passed.

Practice the Skill

Review the chapter to find two people, things, events, or ideas that are similar. Then apply the guidelines to answer the following questions.

1. Which people, events, or ideas will you compare? Why is each of them important?
2. How are they alike? How are they different?

Social Studies Skills Activity: Making Comparisons

At Level

Comparing Influential People or Events

1. Tell students that they will now have an opportunity to challenge their classmates.
2. Organize students into groups by the things, people, events, or ideas they chose to compare in Practice the Skill above. Have students in each group secretly share their answers with one another and highlight the similarities, differences, and reasons for their importance in history.
3. Ask one group at a time to challenge the other groups by stating the two items chosen. Have students in the group ask the other groups to come up with the same or similar responses they have highlighted.
4. When each group has had an opportunity to challenge the other groups, remind students to look for such pairings as they continue their study of history. **LS Verbal/Linguistic, Interpersonal**

- Alternative Assessment Handbook, Rubrics 9: Comparing and Contrasting; and 12: Drawing Conclusions

CHAPTER 20

Chapter Review

HOLT
History's Impact
▸ **video series**
Review the video to answer the closing question:
Why do you think the United States had stricter immigration regulations for Asian immigrants?

Visual Summary

QUICK FACTS

Use the visual summary below to help you review the main ideas of the chapter.

People Arrived
- New immigrants, mostly from southern and eastern Europe
- Came for new opportunities and better lives
- Mostly found jobs in cities
- Faced opposition from some Americans

Cities Grew
- Massive urban growth
- New technologies emerged—skyscrapers and mass transit
- New urban culture

Problems Developed
- Overcrowded tenements
- Unsanitary conditions

Reviewing Vocabulary, Terms, and People

Identify the descriptions below with the correct term or person from the chapter.

1. Public transportation systems built to move many people and ease traffic in crowded cities
2. Founded Hull House with Ellen Gates Starr in 1889
3. Organizations created by immigrants to help each other in times of sickness, unemployment, or other troubles
4. Law banning Chinese people from moving to the United States
5. Neighborhood centers in poor urban areas that offered education, recreation, and social activities
6. Landscape architect who designed New York City's Central Park
7. Small shops or mills where immigrants worked for long hours in hot, unhealthy conditions

Comprehension and Critical Thinking

SECTION 1 *(Pages 636–641)*

8. a. Identify From what parts of the world did the wave of new immigrants come?

b. Analyze In what ways did immigration patterns in the United States change in the late 1800s?

c. Elaborate In your opinion, were the difficulties that immigrants faced worth the benefits of life in the United States? Explain.

SECTION 2 *(Pages 642–645)*

9. a. Recall Why did U.S. cities experience such rapid growth in the late 1800s?

b. Analyze How did new technologies help cities deal with population growth?

c. Elaborate Would you have preferred to live in a city or in a suburb? Why?

Answers

History's Impact

Video Series The United States had a history of predominantly European settlers, so Asian immigrants may have seemed unfamiliar to Americans during the first major waves of immigration.

Visual Summary

Review and Inquiry Have students examine the visual summary. Ask them to imagine what the lives of people in the picture will be like when they reach the city. Have them write one or two paragraphs describing this family's new way of life in the city.

Quick Facts Transparency 54, Immigrants and Urban Life Visual Summary

Reviewing Vocabulary, Terms, and People

1. mass transit
2. Jane Addams
3. benevolent societies
4. Chinese Exclusion Act
5. settlement houses
6. Frederick Law Olmsted
7. sweatshops

Comprehension and Critical Thinking

8. a. southern and eastern Europe, China, Mexico

b. different cultural and religious backgrounds

Review and Assessment Resources

Review and Reinforce

SE Chapter Review

CRF: Chapter Review Activity

Quick Facts Transparency 54, Immigrants and Urban Life Visual Summary

Spanish Chapter Summaries Audio CD Program

Online Chapter Summaries in Spanish

OSP Holt PuzzlePro, GameTool for ExamView

Quiz Game CD-ROM

Assess

SE Standardized Test Practice

PASS: Chapter 20 Tests, Forms A and B; Unit 6 Test, Forms A and B

Alternative Assessment Handbook

OSP ExamView Test Generator, Chapter Test

Differentiated Instruction Modified Worksheets and Tests CD-ROM: Chapter Test

HOAP Holt Online Assessment Program (in the Premier Online Edition)

Reteach/Intervene

Interactive Reader and Study Guide

Differentiated Instruction Teacher Management System: Lesson Plans for Differentiated Instruction

Differentiated Instruction Modified Worksheets and Tests CD-ROM

Interactive Skills Tutor CD-ROM

go.hrw.com
Online Resources
Chapter Resources:
KEYWORD: SF7 CH20

Answers

c. possible answer— The benefits were probably worth the difficulties immigrants faced because they were confident things would improve in the future. They could find jobs, and they did not have to face political or religious persecution.

9. a. industrial growth, immigration, advances in farm equipment replacing workers, African Americans moving away from the South
b. Steel beams and safety elevators helped engineers construct taller buildings to house more people.
c. either of the following: suburbs—more fresh air, less crowded; city—closer to work, more cultural opportunities

10. a. overcrowded, unsafe, unsanitary
b. The cities did not have enough housing, water, sewage, trash, or transportation services for so many people.
c. The settlement house movement grew because there were so many new immigrants who needed the services they offered, such as English classes and day care.

Reviewing Themes

11. Immigrants often worked in factories and built buildings, highways, and railroads. Their labor helped contribute to the growth and development of cities and to the nation's economy.

12. City dwellers' lives were improved by mass culture. There were more newspapers to read, department stores, new foods, city and national parks, amusement parks, and fairs to enjoy.

Reading Skills

13. facts—name of the department store, its location, types of products and prices; verification—check advertisements in the Chicago newspapers of the 1880s

SECTION 3 *(Pages 646–649)*

10. a. Recall What were conditions like in tenements in the late 1800s?
b. Make Inferences Why did rapid population growth cause problems in cities?
c. Elaborate Why do you think the settlement house movement grew in the late 1800s and early 1900s?

Reviewing Themes

11. Economics What role did economics play in the growth of cities?

12. Society and Culture How did the lives of city dwellers change with the rise of mass culture?

Reading Skills

Understanding Historical Fact versus Historical Fiction *Use the Reading Skills taught in this chapter to answer the question about the reading selection below.*

> Mass culture affected how people shopped as well. Giant retail shops, or department stores, appeared in some cities during the late 1800s. One of the earliest was Marshall Field in Chicago, which offered low prices and large quantities of products. It also was the first department store to offer its customers a restaurant where they could eat while shopping. Newspaper advertising was used to bring in customers. The public was also attracted by fancy window displays. *(p. 645)*

13. Which facts above can be verified? Where would you look to verify them?

Social Studies Skills

Making Comparisons *Use the Social Studies Skills taught in this chapter to answer the question below.*

14. Choose two reforms that were discussed in this chapter. Make a comparison between the two.

Using the Internet

go.hrw.com
KEYWORD: SF7 CH20

15. Activity: Investigating Culture Mass culture developed in the late 1800s and early 1900s as a result of new and broader forms of communication taking root. Enter the activity keyword and explore some of the early influences on mass culture. Then research the ways in which modern culture is influenced by the media, the Internet, and other forms of mass communication. How does today's society experience mass culture? Create a visual display or computer-based presentation that compares mass culture then and now.

FOCUS ON WRITING

16. Writing Your Memo Look back over your notes about the people, places, and events of the late 1800s. Decide which of these you will include in your television drama series. Then draft a one- to two-paragraph memo to your boss describing the series. Remember to describe the basic plot, setting, and characters.

Social Studies Skills

14. Possible answer: Benevolent societies and settlement houses were two reform strategies. Both were formed to help immigrants adapt to a new way of life in America. Both helped people find housing and employment and worked for needed improvements whenever possible.

Using the Internet

15. Go to the HRW Web site and enter the keyword shown to access a rubric for this activity.

KEYWORD: SF7 CH20

Focus on Writing

16. Rubric Students' memos should:
- describe series' plot, characters, and setting
- include correct spelling, punctuation, and grammar

CRF: Focus on Writing: A Memo

won the right to vote in Wyoming. Colorado, Idaho, and Utah followed.

Carrie Chapman Catt became president of the NAWSA in 1900. Catt mobilized more than 1 million volunteers for the movement. She argued that women should have a voice in creating laws that affected them. "We women demand an equal voice," she said. "We shall accept nothing less."

Some women believed that NAWSA did not go far enough. In 1913 **Alice Paul** founded what would become the National Woman's Party (NWP). The NWP used parades, public demonstrations, picketing, hunger strikes, and other means to draw attention to the suffrage cause. Paul even organized picketing in front of the White House. Paul and other NWP leaders were jailed for their actions.

Suffragists finally succeeded in gaining the vote. In 1919 the U.S. Congress passed the **Nineteenth Amendment**, granting American women the right to vote. The Nineteenth Amendment was ratified by the states the following year, making it law.

READING CHECK **Analyzing** How did reformers draw attention to the temperance and women's suffrage movements?

African Americans Challenge Discrimination

White reformers often overlooked issues such as racial discrimination and segregation. African American reformers took the lead in addressing these problems.

One of the most important African American leaders was **Booker T. Washington**. Born into slavery, he became a respected educator while in his twenties. Washington's strategy was not to fight discrimination directly. Instead, he encouraged African Americans to improve their educational and economic well-being. This, he believed, would eventually lead to the end of discrimination.

Other African Americans spoke out more directly against discrimination. Journalist **Ida B. Wells** wrote articles about the unequal education available to African American children. In her Memphis newspaper *Free Speech,* Wells also drew attention to the lynching of African Americans. During lynchings people were murdered by mobs instead of receiving a trial after being accused of a crime, or even for breaking social codes. More than 3,000 African Americans were lynched between 1885 and 1915.

Although death threats forced Wells to move to the North, she continued campaigning against lynching. In 1900 she wrote:

> "Our country's national crime is *lynching* ... In fact, for all kinds of offenses—and, for no offenses—from murders to misdemeanors, men and women are put to death without judge or jury."
>
> —Ida B. Wells, from her article "Lynch Law in America"

FOCUS ON INDIANA

Booker T. Washington founded the Tuskegee Institute in Tuskegee, Alabama, to help educate African Americans. One famous professor there, George Washington Carver, urged southern farmers to grow crops such as peanuts and sweet potatoes instead of cotton.

1920

August 18, 1920 Tennessee becomes the thirty-sixth state to ratify the Nineteenth Amendment.

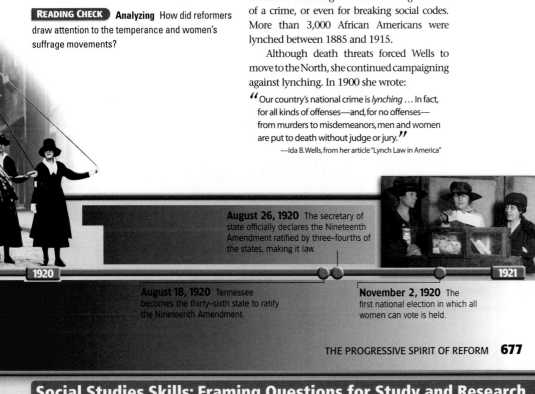

August 26, 1920 The secretary of state officially declares the Nineteenth Amendment ratified by three-fourths of the states, making it law.

November 2, 1920 The first national election in which all women can vote is held.

1921

Direct Teach

Main Idea

1 Women Fight for Temperance and Voting Rights

Women fought for temperance and the right to vote.

Identify Name the four states that allowed women to vote in the 1890s. *Wyoming, Colorado, Idaho, and Utah*

Sequence In what years were the two suffragist organizations founded? *NAWSA—1890; NWP—1913*

Main Idea

2 African Americans Challenge Discrimination

African American reformers challenged discrimination and called for equality.

Recall Name two issues which were often overlooked by white reformers. *racial discrimination and segregation*

Explain What was Booker T. Washington's strategy to end racial discrimination? *to improve educational and economic wellbeing of African Americans*

CRF: Biography Activity W.E.B. Du Bois

Info to Know

Unequal Rights In the 1880s a system of segregationist laws separated blacks and whites and restricted African American rights. For example, one Alabama law prohibited blacks and whites from playing checkers together.

Focus on Indiana

IN 8.4.5

Analyze Why might George Washington Carver urge farmers to grow crops besides cotton? *Because cotton depleted the soil.*

Social Studies Skills: Framing Questions for Study and Research

Interview with a Historical Figure

At Level

1. Have students review the text and choose a historical figure mentioned in this chapter whom they would like to interview.
2. Have students make a list of questions to ask their chosen person. Students should frame questions based on information in the text.
3. Review students' questions and help them revise their questions if necessary.
4. Organize students into pairs. Have students in each pair take turns asking each other their questions. The person answering should pretend to be that historical figure and base his or her answers on information from the text.

LS Verbal/Linguistic

Alternative Assessment Handbook, Rubrics 1: Acquiring Information; 14: Group Activity; and 30: Research

Answers

Reading Check *They used parades, public demonstrations, picketing, and hunger strikes.*

Direct Teach

Main Idea

❷ African Americans Challenge Discrimination

African American reformers challenged discrimination and called for equality.

Identify Which organization fought discrimination in the courts? *the NAACP*

Compare What organization helped African Americans the way settlement houses helped new immigrants? *the National Urban League*

Interpret How did "grandfather clauses" discriminate against African Americans? *Most African Americans' grandfathers had been enslaved and could not vote.*

Evaluate Which approach do you think is more effective in fighting discrimination, self-improvement or using the courts? Why? *possible answers: self-improvement—better for the individual; using the courts—helps more people*

Did you know . . .

W.E.B. Du Bois earned a bachelor's degree from Harvard University in 1890. In 1969 the school proposed the creation of the W.E.B. Du Bois Institute for African and African American Research, which awards fellowships to scholars in African and African American studies. Ironically, Du Bois once hinted at feeling like an outsider at the prestigious college when he said, "I was in Harvard but not of it."

Like Wells, **W. E. B. Du Bois** took a direct approach to fighting racial injustice. Born in Massachusetts, Du Bois was a college graduate who earned a doctorate from Harvard University. As part of his research, he studied and publicized cases of racial prejudice. Du Bois believed that African Americans should protest unjust treatment and demand equal rights.

In 1909 Du Bois and other reformers founded the **National Association for the Advancement of Colored People** (NAACP), an organization that called for economic and educational equality for African Americans. The NAACP attacked discrimination by using the courts. In 1915 it won the important case of *Guinn* v. *United States,* which made grandfather clauses illegal. These laws were used in the South to keep African Americans from voting. Grandfather clauses imposed strict qualifications on voters unless their grandfathers had been allowed to vote. Many white voters met this requirement and were therefore automatically permitted to vote in elections. However, most African Americans' grandfathers had been enslaved and could not vote.

THE IMPACT TODAY
Today the NAACP claims around 2,200 adult branches and 1,700 branches for young people.

Another important organization, the National Urban League, was formed in 1911 by Dr. George Edmund Haynes. This organization aided many African Americans moving from the South by helping them find jobs and housing in northern cities. The League addressed many of the same problems faced by other Progressives, such as health, sanitation, and education.

READING CHECK **Finding Main Ideas** What was the purpose of the NAACP?

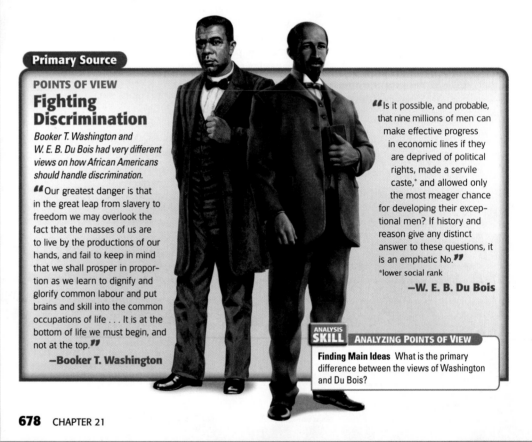

Primary Source

POINTS OF VIEW

Fighting Discrimination

Booker T. Washington and W. E. B. Du Bois had very different views on how African Americans should handle discrimination.

"Our greatest danger is that in the great leap from slavery to freedom we may overlook the fact that the masses of us are to live by the productions of our hands, and fail to keep in mind that we shall prosper in proportion as we learn to dignify and glorify common labour and put brains and skill into the common occupations of life . . . It is at the bottom of life we must begin, and not at the top."

—Booker T. Washington

"Is it possible, and probable, that nine millions of men can make effective progress in economic lines if they are deprived of political rights, made a servile caste,* and allowed only the most meager chance for developing their exceptional men? If history and reason give any distinct answer to these questions, it is an emphatic No."

*lower social rank

—W. E. B. Du Bois

ANALYSIS SKILL **ANALYZING POINTS OF VIEW**

Finding Main Ideas What is the primary difference between the views of Washington and Du Bois?

Differentiating Instruction

Above Level

Advanced/Gifted and Talented

1. The language we use when we speak differs from the language we use when we write. Remind students that both Washington and Du Bois were well-educated men and that their writings are sophisticated and written in the style of their time.
2. Have students copy the statements of each man on separate sheets of lined paper.
3. Next, have students reword these statements using today's language and writing style. Students should break up the ideas into shorter sentences for better comprehension. Tell students to write their new wordings in pencil, below each original version.
4. Ask volunteers to share their statements, in the fashion of an orator, with the class. Guide students in a discussion of the two distinct points of view presented. Were the ideas in the student rewrites as emphatic as they were in the original? **LS Verbal/Linguistic**

Alternative Assessment Handbook, Rubrics 24: Oral Presentation; and 37: Writing Assignments

Answers

Finding Main Ideas *Washington—felt self-improvement in education and economic well-being would eventually lead to the end of discrimination; Du Bois—believed African Americans should strongly protest unjust treatment and demand equal rights*

Reading Check *The NAACP called for economic and educational equality for African Americans.*

Failures of Reform

Other minority groups felt left behind by the Progressive movement. Although some reformers tried to aid such groups, the aim of many was to encourage other ethnicities to adopt the ways of European society. The Society of American Indians, formed in 1911, was one such attempt. Started by Native American doctors Carlos Montezuma and Charles Eastman, the society believed that integration into white society would end Native American poverty. Many Native Americans, however, wanted to preserve their traditional culture. They resisted the movement toward adopting white culture.

Immigrant groups from non-European countries also formed groups to help support their members. Chinese immigrants, for example, organized neighborhood associations in the communities in which they lived. District associations, cultural groups, churches, and temples provided public services that white reformers ignored. Such groups provided the money for building San Francisco's Chinese hospital in 1925. Chinese immigration dropped, however, due in part to anti-Chinese riots that occurred in some western towns and cities.

While fewer Chinese immigrants came to the United States, the number of Mexican immigrants increased. The northern and southern borders between the United States and its neighbors were fairly easy to cross in this period. Many Mexican immigrants moved to the South and Southwest, where they became an important part of the societies and economies of these regions. Many Mexican immigrants found jobs in the mining and railroad industries. Others began farms or became migrant workers. Progressive labor laws and factory reforms did nothing to improve the poor living and working conditions of migrant farm workers.

READING CHECK **Summarizing** What were the limitations of progressive reforms?

SUMMARY AND PREVIEW Many U.S. citizens worked for progressive reforms. In the next section you will read about presidents who also worked for progressive goals.

Section 3 Assessment

go.hrw.com
Online Quiz
KEYWORD: SF7 HP21

Reviewing Ideas, Terms, and People

1. a. **Identify** What did the **Eighteenth** and **Nineteenth Amendments** accomplish?
   b. **Summarize** How did **Alice Paul** and the National Woman's Party try to draw attention to the issue of women's suffrage?
2. a. **Identify** What role did **Ida B. Wells** play in reform efforts for African Americans?
   b. **Contrast** How did **Booker T. Washington** differ from other African American leaders?
   c. **Evaluate** Do you think the **National Association for the Advancement of Colored People** was successful in fighting discrimination? Explain.
3. a. **Describe** What discrimination did Chinese Americans face?
   b. **Summarize** How were some minority groups overlooked by the Progressive movement?

Critical Thinking

4. **Analyzing** Review your notes on Progressives' causes. Then copy the diagram shown and use it to identify the progressive reforms introduced by the temperance movement, the women's suffrage movement, and African Americans.

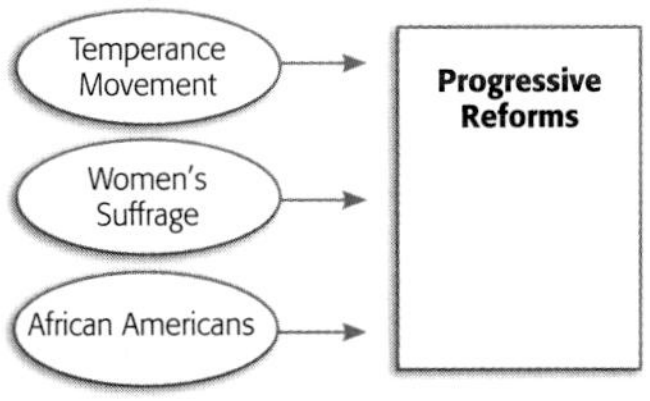

FOCUS ON SPEAKING

5. **Addressing the Rights of Women and Minorities** Review this section's material on education for women, women's suffrage, temperance, racial discrimination, and segregation. As a politician, what promises would you make regarding these issues? Think about how you would make your ideas acceptable to the American public. Would you be willing to compromise your ideals?

Direct Teach

Main Idea

❸ Failures of Reform

Progressive reforms failed to benefit all minorities.

Explain Why did many Native Americans resist adopting white culture? *They wanted to preserve their traditional culture.*

Identify Cause and Effect What caused Chinese immigrants to form their own communities? *They wanted to support each other and protect themselves.*

Predict What are some possible ways American life would have been affected if progressive reforms had helped migrant farm workers? *possible answer—Farm workers might have had better pay and health benefits; food might have cost more.*

Review & Assess

Close

Review with students the problems faced by members of minority groups and how reforms made in the early 1900s were effective for some, but not for others.

Review

go.hrw.com Online Quiz, Section 21.3

Assess

SE Section 3 Assessment

PASS: Section Quiz 21.3

Alternative Assessment Handbook

Reteach/Classroom Intervention

Interactive Reader and Study Guide, Section 21.3

Interactive Skills Tutor CD-ROM

Section 3 Assessment Answers

1. **a.** Eighteenth—banned U.S. production, sale, and transportation of alcoholic beverages; Nineteenth—granted women the right to vote
   b. used parades, public demonstrations, picketing, and hunger strikes
2. **a.** wrote articles about the unequal education available to African American children and the lynching of African Americans
   b. believed that African Americans should improve their own educational and economic wellbeing, gradually ending discrimination
   c. possible answer—Yes: NAACP fought in courts, made "grandfather clauses" illegal
3. **a.** anti-Chinese riots
   b. Non-European immigrant groups were overlooked by Progressive reformers.
4. Progressive Reforms: Temperance Movement—Eighteenth Amendment; Women's Suffrage—Nineteenth Amendment; African Americans—*Guinn* v. *United States*
5. Students' campaign promises should address women's suffrage, temperance, and racial discrimination and segregation.

Answers

Reading Check *could not provide many public services; living and working conditions not improved; some cultures not preserved*

Preteach

Bellringer

If YOU were there . . . Use the **Daily Bellringer Transparency** to help students answer the question.

Daily Bellringer Transparency, 21.4

The Progressive Spirit of Reform — Daily Bellringer **21.4**

Review Section 3

In each of the following pairs of sentences, choose the sentence that is **TRUE**.

1. **a.** Women fought for temperance and the right to vote.
   b. Women fought for the rights of Mexican immigrants.
2. **a.** The Nineteenth Amendment gave African Americans the right to vote.
   b. The Nineteenth Amendment gave women the right to vote.
3. **a.** Many white reformers helped African Americans in their fight against racial discrimination.
   b. African Americans like Booker T. Washington led the fight against racial discrimination and segregation.
4. **a.** The Progressive movement failed many other minority groups.
   b. Minority groups were a focus of the Progressive movement.

Preview Section 4

If YOU were there ...

It is 1912 and you're voting in your first presidential election. This election is unusual—there are three major candidates. One is the popular former president Theodore Roosevelt, who is running as a third-party candidate. He thinks the Republican candidate will not make enough progressive reforms. But the Democratic candidate is a progressive reformer, too.

How will you decide which candidate to support?

Consider reasons to vote FOR Theodore Roosevelt:
- He has experience.
- He was a good president.
- He supports needed reforms.

Consider reasons to vote AGAINST Theodore Roosevelt:
- Other candidates are progressive.
- Other candidates have new ideas.
- Other candidates offer change.

Review Answers: 1. a; 2. b; 3. b; 4. a

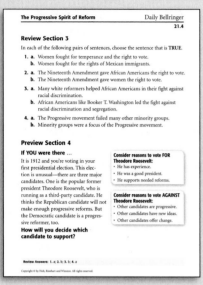

Academic Vocabulary

Review with students the high-use academic term in this section.

various of many types (p. 682)

CRF: Vocabulary Builder Activity, Section 4

Taking Notes

Have students copy the graphic organizer onto their own paper and then use it to take notes on the section. This activity will prepare students for the Section Assessment, in which they will complete a graphic organizer that builds on the information using a critical-thinking skill.

Section Correlations

IN

8.3.8 Gather information on ways people changed the physical environment of the United States in the nineteenth century using primary sources and secondary sources including digitized photo collections and historic maps. **8.3.11** Identify ways people modified the physical environment as the United States developed and describe the impacts that resulted. **8.4.4** Explain the basic economic functions of the government in the economy of the United States.

SECTION 4

The Progressive Presidents

What You Will Learn...

Main Ideas

1. Theodore Roosevelt's progressive reforms tried to balance the interests of business, consumers, and laborers.
2. William Howard Taft angered Progressives with his cautious reforms, while Woodrow Wilson enacted far-reaching banking and antitrust reforms.

The Big Idea

American presidents in the early 1900s did a great deal to promote progressive reforms.

Key Terms and People

Theodore Roosevelt, *p. 680*
Pure Food and Drug Act, *p. 681*
conservation, *p. 681*
William Howard Taft, *p. 682*
Progressive Party, *p. 682*
Woodrow Wilson, *p. 682*
Sixteenth Amendment, *p. 683*

TAKING NOTES As you read, take notes on the achievements of each of the progressive presidents. Use a table like the one below to organize your notes.

Roosevelt	Taft	Wilson

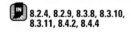

IN 8.2.4, 8.2.9, 8.3.8, 8.3.10, 8.3.11, 8.4.2, 8.4.4

680 CHAPTER 21

If YOU were there...

It is 1912 and you're voting in your first presidential election. This election is unusual—there are three major candidates. One is the popular former president Theodore Roosevelt, who is running as a third-party candidate. He thinks the Republican candidate will not make enough progressive reforms. But the Democratic candidate is a progressive reformer too.

How will you decide which candidate to support?

BUILDING BACKGROUND Political corruption was one early target of the progressive reformers. Some politicians who joined them believed that government—local, state, and national—should play an active role in improving society and people's lives.

Roosevelt's Progressive Reforms

During a summer tour after his second inauguration in 1901, President William McKinley met a friendly crowd in Buffalo, New York. Suddenly, anarchist Leon Czolgosz stepped forward and shot the president. A little more than a week later, McKinley died. Vice President **Theodore Roosevelt** took office.

Roosevelt's Square Deal

Roosevelt believed that the interests of businesspeople, laborers, and consumers should be balanced for the public good. He called this policy the Square Deal. He put the policy to the test in 1902 when faced by a coal miners' strike. Roosevelt knew the strike might leave the country without heating fuel for the coming winter. He threatened to take over the mines unless managers and strikers agreed to arbitration—a formal process to settle disputes. He felt this was the only fair way to protect Americans.

> "The labor unions shall have a square deal, and the corporations shall have a square deal, and in addition all private citizens shall have a square deal."
>
> —President Theodore Roosevelt, quoted in *The Presidency of Theodore Roosevelt*, by Lewis L. Gould

Teach the Big Idea

At Level

The Progressive Presidents

1. **Teach** To teach the main ideas in the section, use the questions in the Direct Teach boxes.
2. **Apply** Ask students to imagine they are advisors to President Theodore Roosevelt. Railroad engineers are threatening to strike. Ask students to explain the effect such a strike would have on business and industry. *Businesses would run out of products to sell, and industries would be unable to produce goods without raw materials.*
3. **Review** Organize students into groups of four to six. Have them discuss and list what they would advise the president to do.
4. **Practice/Homework** Instruct students to compose letters to President Roosevelt, advising him how best to resolve this issue. **LS Verbal/Linguistic**

Alternative Assessment Handbook, Rubrics 14: Group Activity; and 43: Writing to Persuade

The National Park System

In 1872 Yellowstone National Park, located mostly in Wyoming, became the first national park in the United States—and the world. Today there are 55 national parks in the United States. They are managed by the National Park Service (NPS), an agency of the federal government established in 1916. The National Park Service administers almost 84 million acres (133,000 square miles) of land.

President Theodore Roosevelt and conservationist John Muir in Yosemite National Park in California

Cathedral Rocks, Yosemite National Park

Regulating Big Business

Roosevelt made regulating big business a top goal of his administration. Muckrakers helped build support for this regulation. The public was shocked, for instance, after reading Upton Sinclair's description of the meatpacking industry in *The Jungle*. Roosevelt opened an investigation and later convinced Congress to pass a meat inspection law.

In 1906 Congress passed the **Pure Food and Drug Act**. This law prohibited the manufacture, sale, and transport of mislabeled or contaminated food and drugs. Roosevelt also was the first president to successfully use the 1890 Sherman Antitrust Act to break up a monopoly. He persuaded Congress to regulate railroad shipping rates. The public largely supported this expansion of federal regulatory powers.

Conservation

Roosevelt's love of the outdoors inspired him to join other Progressives in supporting **conservation**, or the protection of nature and its resources. Roosevelt was the first president to consider conservation an important national priority.

People believed in conservation for various reasons. Preservationists such as John Muir thought that nature should be left untouched so that people could enjoy its beauty:

> "Thousands of tired, nerve-shaken, over-civilized people are beginning to find out that going to the mountains is going home; that wildness is a necessity; and that mountain parks and reservations are useful not only as fountains of timber and irrigating rivers, but as fountains of life."
>
> —John Muir, *Our National Parks*

Other conservationists wanted to make sure the nation used its natural resources efficiently. Gifford Pinchot, the first head of the newly created Forest Service, valued forests for the resources they provided to build "prosperous homes." The disagreement between the two ideals of conservation eventually widened.

While Roosevelt was in office, the Forest Service gained control of nearly 150 million acres of public land. Roosevelt doubled the number of national parks, created 18 national monuments, and started 51 bird sanctuaries.

READING CHECK **Summarizing** What reforms did Roosevelt support?

Direct Teach

Main Idea

1 Roosevelt's Progressive Reforms

Theodore Roosevelt's progressive reforms tried to balance the interests of business, consumers, and laborers.

Recall What did the Square Deal policy do for the public good? *balanced the interests of businesspeople, laborers, and consumers*

Make Generalizations In what way does the Pure Food and Drug Act protect citizens? *protects us from buying contaminated food and drugs*

Evaluate What do you think about Roosevelt's accomplishments in conservation? *possible answer—He did well because he preserved land for public enjoyment, protected forests as natural resources, and made refuges for wildlife.*

MISCONCEPTION ALERT

Which Roosevelt? Theodore Roosevelt is often confused with his distant relative, Franklin Delano Roosevelt. A Republican, "Teddy" was President of the United States from 1901 to 1909 and was a well-known outdoorsman. However, Democrat "FDR" served later as president, from 1933 to 1945.

go.hrw.com
Online Resources
KEYWORD: SF7 CH21
ACTIVITY: Tammany Hall

Cross-Discipline Activity: Geography

At Level

Conservation Charts

Research Required

Materials: U.S. wall map, poster paper

1. Tell students they will learn how much land is conserved in our nation today. They will search all the states in the union to learn the names of national parks, forests, and wetlands.
2. Have students create a chart with three columns labeled *State; National Park, Forest, or Wetland;* and *Acres.* Assign one or two states to each student. Have them find the names and locations of the national parks, forests, and wetlands and their area in acres.
3. Choose one or two students to record and display the results using a computer spreadsheet or several sheets of poster paper with the same labels. Ask another volunteer to keep a running total of the acreage.
4. Discuss the results with the class, noting which states have the most land designated for conservation. **LS Visual/Spatial**

Alternative Assessment Handbook, Rubrics 7, Charts; and 30: Research

Answers

Reading Check *regulating big business and conservation*

Direct Teach

Main Idea

❷ Reforms of Taft and Wilson

William Howard Taft angered Progressives with his cautious reforms, while Woodrow Wilson enacted far-reaching banking and antitrust reforms.

Explain To what was Wilson referring when he used the term, "human cost"? *terrible conditions under which many working-class Americans lived*

Sequence Describe the sequence of events leading up to and including the election of Wilson. *1908—Taft elected; 1909—Taft signed Payne-Aldrich Tariff; 1912—Taft won Republican nomination; Roosevelt furious with Taft so decides to run for president; Taft and Roosevelt split the Republican vote; Wilson wins*

Map Transparency 62: The Election of 1912

Checking for Understanding

True or False Answer each statement *T* if it is true or *F* if it is false. If false, explain why.

1. Taft favored socialism and opposed business regulation. *F; Taft favored business regulation and opposed socialism.*
2. Progressives were not satisfied with Taft's efforts to reform and regulate big business. *T*
3. Industrial achievement was Wilson's main goal. *F; Passing reform legislation was Wilson's top goal.*
4. Wilson received two electoral votes from California. *T*

Reforms of Taft and Wilson

Theodore Roosevelt hoped that his secretary of war, **William Howard Taft**, would take his place as president in 1908. Like Roosevelt, Taft favored business regulation and opposed socialism. With Roosevelt's assistance, Taft defeated William Jennings Bryan in the election of 1908.

Taft Angers Progressives

Despite their friendship, Roosevelt and Taft held different ideas about how a president should act. Taft thought Roosevelt had claimed more power than a president was constitutionally allowed.

As president, therefore, Taft chose to move cautiously toward reform and regulation. This upset Roosevelt and various Progressives, who supported stricter regulation of big business. Although Taft's administration started twice as many antitrust lawsuits as Roosevelt's had, Progressives were not satisfied.

ACADEMIC VOCABULARY
various of many types

Taft angered Progressives further by signing the Payne-Aldrich Tariff of 1909. This tariff reduced some rates on imported goods, but it raised others. Progressives wanted all tariffs to be lowered, in order to lower prices for consumers.

Furious with Taft, Roosevelt decided to run for president again in 1912. After Taft won the Republican nomination, Roosevelt and his followers formed the **Progressive Party**. It was nicknamed the Bull Moose Party because Roosevelt said he was "as strong as a bull moose." The split between Taft and Roosevelt divided the Republican vote, and Democratic candidate **Woodrow Wilson** won the electoral vote by a wide margin.

Wilson's Reforms

In his inaugural address, Wilson spoke of the terrible social conditions under which many working-class Americans lived. "We have been proud of our industrial achievements," he said, "but we have not hitherto [yet] stopped thoughtfully enough to count the human cost." Passing reform legislation was Wilson's top goal. He pushed for two measures soon after taking office: tariff revision and banking reform.

Wilson backed the Underwood Tariff Act of 1913, which lowered tariffs. The act also introduced a version of the modern

The Election of 1912

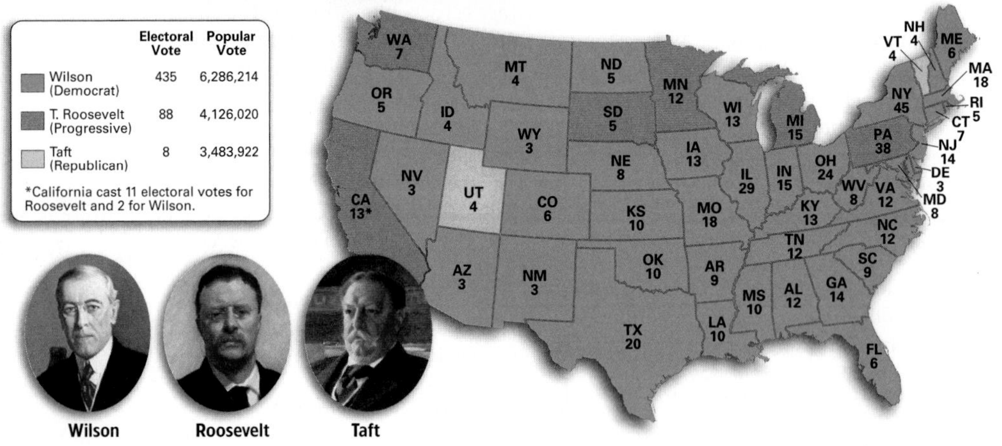

	Electoral Vote	Popular Vote
Wilson (Democrat)	435	6,286,214
T. Roosevelt (Progressive)	88	4,126,020
Taft (Republican)	8	3,483,922

*California cast 11 electoral votes for Roosevelt and 2 for Wilson.

Differentiating Instruction

Below Level

Struggling Readers

Materials: poster board, colored pencils, markers

1. To help students understand this chapter, have them refer to the notes they have been taking on the reforms made by presidents Roosevelt, Taft, and Wilson. Tell them our nation grew vigorously during this time.
2. Have students review the text and make a list of the reforms made by each president mentioned in this chapter. Next, have students choose one of the presidents and create a poster illustrating the reforms made during his presidency.
3. As students work, check to make sure they are finding all the reforms made by each president.
4. When students have completed their posters, ask volunteers to share and explain their posters with the class. **LS Visual/Spatial, Verbal/Linguistic**

Alternative Assessment Handbook, Rubrics 3: Artwork; and 28 Posters

The Progressive Amendments, 1909–1920

QUICK FACTS

Number	Description	Proposed by Congress	Ratified by States
16th	Federal income tax	1909	1913
17th	Senators elected by people rather than state legislatures	1912	1913
18th	Manufacture, sale, and transport of alcohol prohibited	1917	1919
19th	Women's suffrage	1919	1920

income tax. The new tax was made possible in 1913 by the ratification of the **Sixteenth Amendment**. This amendment allows the federal government to impose direct taxes on citizens' incomes.

President Wilson next addressed banking reform with the 1913 Federal Reserve Act. This law created a national banking system called the Federal Reserve to regulate the economy.

Wilson also pushed for laws to regulate big business. The Clayton Antitrust Act of 1914 strengthened federal laws against monopolies. The Federal Trade Commission, created in 1914, had the power to investigate and punish unfair trade practices. Wilson's success in guiding reform programs through Congress helped him to win re-election in 1916.

READING CHECK **Analyzing** Why did Wilson win the election of 1912?

SUMMARY AND PREVIEW The progressive presidents tried to change American society for the better. In the next chapter you will learn how they also helped the United States become a world power.

Section 4 Assessment

go.hrw.com **Online Quiz** KEYWORD: SF7 HP21

Reviewing Ideas, Terms, and People

1. a. **Describe** How did **Theodore Roosevelt** support progressive reforms?
   b. **Analyze** Why did many Americans support **conservation**?
   c. **Evaluate** Do you think Roosevelt's reforms benefited the nation? Why or why not?
2. a. **Identify** What was the **Progressive Party**? Why was it created?
   b. **Compare and Contrast** How were the administrations of **William Howard Taft** and Roosevelt similar, and how were they different?
   c. **Evaluate** Which president do you think had the biggest influence on progressive reform—Roosevelt, Taft, or **Woodrow Wilson**? Explain your choice.

Critical Thinking

3. **Comparing and Contrasting** Review your notes on the progressive presidents. Then copy the diagram below and use it to compare and contrast the reforms of the progressive presidents.

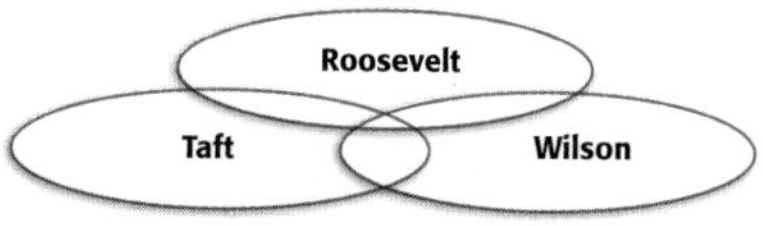

FOCUS ON SPEAKING

4. **The Ideas of Roosevelt, Taft, and Wilson** Do you agree or disagree with Presidents Roosevelt, Taft, and Wilson? Take notes on any of their ideas that you would include in your campaign promises.

Section 4 Assessment Answers

1. **a.** investigation of meatpacking industry led to Pure Food and Drug Act; used Sherman Anti-Trust Act to break up a monopoly
   b. so people could enjoy nature's beauty; use natural resources efficiently
   c. yes, His reforms helped balance the interests of businesspeople, laborers, and consumers
2. **a.** a political party that promoted stricter regulation of big business; to allow Roosevelt to run for President
   b. Sample answer: Similar—favored business regulation and opposed socialism; Taft—moved toward reform and regulation; Roosevelt—supported stricter business regulation
   c. Possible answer—Roosevelt, because he expanded federal regulatory powers over big business and supported conservation
3. Sample answer: Roosevelt—regulated big business, enacted reforms, supported conservation; Taft—cautious about using expanded federal regulatory powers; Wilson—passed reform legislation, helped regulate tariffs
4. Notes should include possible progressive campaign promises by Roosevelt, Taft, or Wilson.

Direct Teach

Main Idea

2 Reforms of Taft and Wilson

William Howard Taft angered Progressives with his cautious reforms, while Woodrow Wilson enacted far-reaching banking and antitrust reforms.

Recall What allowed the modern income tax to go into effect? *the Sixteenth Amendment*

Explain What power does the Federal Trade Commission have? *It can investigate and punish unfair trade practices.*

Quick Facts Transparency 57: The Progressive Amendments, 1909–1920

Review & Assess

Close

Review with students the way American presidents of the early 1900s promoted progressive reform.

Review

go.hrw.com Online Quiz, Section 21.4

Assess

SE Section 4 Assessment

PASS: Section Quiz 21.4

Alternative Assessment Handbook

Reteach/Classroom Intervention

Interactive Reader and Study Guide, Section 21.4

Interactive Skills Tutor CD-ROM

Answers

Reading Check *Taft and Roosevelt divided the Republican vote allowing Wilson to win the electoral vote by a large margin.*

Social Studies Skills

Short- and Long-term Causal Relationships

Activity Effects of Moving Chart Write the headings *Short-term* and *Long-term* on a large sheet of butcher paper. Tell students that causal relationships can be found in the lives of families who move to a new town. Ask students to suggest what short-term effects a move might cause, say within the first month or two. Provide markers and ask volunteers to write effects on the chart. Then ask students to suggest long-term effects that a move might have after a couple of years. Have students add these to the chart. Remind students that with historical events, long-term effects may appear even after many decades.
LS Verbal/Linguistic, Visual/Spatial

- Alternative Assessment Handbook, Rubrics 6: Cause and Effect; and 7: Charts
- Interactive Skills Tutor CD-ROM: Lesson 7: Identify Cause and Effect
- **CRF:** Social Studies Skills Activity: Short- and Long-term Causal Patterns

Social Studies Skills

Analysis | Critical Thinking | Civic Participation | Study

Short- and Long-term Causal Relationships

Define the Skill

Most historical events are the result of other events. When something happens as a result of other things that occur, it is an effect of those things. Some events take place soon after the things that cause them. Such events are called *short-term effects*. In contrast, *long-term effects* can occur years, decades, or even hundreds of years after the events that caused them. Being able to recognize short-term and long-term cause-and-effect relationships will help you to better understand historical events.

Learn the Skill

Clue words can sometimes reveal a cause-and-effect relationship between events. Often, however, such language clues may not be present. Therefore, when you study history, you should always look for other clues that might explain why an action or event occurred.

Short-term effects are usually fairly easy to identify. In historical writing they are often closely linked to the event that caused them. For example, consider this passage from Chapter 21.

> "Some Progressives worked to change state and local governments in order to reduce the power of political machines. In many places, reformers replaced corrupt ballots that listed only one party's candidates with government-prepared ballots that listed all candidates. Under pressure from reformers, many states adopted secret ballots, giving every voter a private vote."

This passage contains no clue words. Yet it is clear that cause-and-effect relationships exist. The power of political machines created corrupt voting practices. Reformers wanted to change this. One effect of this situation was the government-prepared ballot, and another was the secret ballot.

Recognizing long-term causal relationships is often more difficult. Since long-term effects take place well after the event that caused them, they may not be discussed at the same time as their cause. This is why you should always question why an event occurred as you learn about it. For example, in 1971 Congress passed the first federal law to protect the health and safety of all workers. This law was a long-term result of efforts begun years earlier by the progressives you read about in this chapter.

Many long-term effects result from major forces running through history that make things happen. They include economics, science and technology, expansion, conflict and cooperation among people, cultural clashes and differences, and moral and religious issues. Ask yourself if one of these forces is involved in the event being studied. If so, the event may have long-term effects that you should be on the lookout for when studying later events.

Practice and Apply the Skill

Review the information in Chapter 21 and answer these questions to practice recognizing short- and long-term causal relationships.

1. All packaged food today must have its contents listed on the container. This requirement is a long-term effect of what progressive reform?
2. Write a paragraph explaining the effects of the muckrakers on the news media today.

Social Studies Activity: Short- and Long-term Causal Relationships

Finding Causal Relationships

Research Required | **At Level**

1. Tell students that some of the most important improvements of the Progressive Era were accomplished by people fighting against what they saw as harmful or unfair. Tell students that they will conduct research to discover the effects of early reforms on today's society.
2. Organize students into groups of three. Assign each group one of the following subjects for study: workers' rights, women's suffrage, and African Americans' civil rights.
3. Tell students to look for causal relationships between the issues presented in this chapter and those that occurred later in the development of our nation.
4. If time permits, allow students who were assigned the same subject to compare findings.
LS Verbal/Linguistic

- Alternative Assessment Handbook, Rubrics 6: Cause and Effect; 14: Group Activity; and 30: Research

Answers

1. *the 1906 Pure Food and Drug Act*
2. *Students' paragraphs will vary but should explain realistic long-term effects of the muckrakers on the news media today.*

CHAPTER 21

Chapter Review

HOLT **History's Impact**
▶ **video series**
Review the video to answer the closing question:
How did the rights of women in individual states play a role in the women's suffrage movement?

Visual Summary

QUICK FACTS

Use the visual summary below to help you review the main ideas of the chapter.

Progressives hoped to improve society through reform. Their goals included

- Temperance
- Women's suffrage
- Big business regulation
- Conservation
- Tariff and banking reform

Reviewing Vocabulary, Terms, and People

Complete each sentence by filling in the blank with the correct term or person from the chapter.

1. Some Americans supported a _________ system, which proposed government ownership of the country's means of production.
2. Republican _________ began a program to reform state politics in Wisconsin.
3. The _________ granted women in the United States the right to vote.
4. The _________ prohibited the manufacture, sale, and transport of mislabeled or contaminated food and drugs.
5. During the Gilded Age, _________ often dominated local politics and used corruption to get their candidates elected.
6. _________ were journalists who wrote about troubling issues such as child labor, tenement housing, and political corruption.

Comprehension and Critical Thinking

SECTION 1 *(Pages 662–667)*

7. a. Describe What tactics did bosses and political machines use to gain control of local governments?

b. Analyze What changes did Progressives make to city life?

c. Elaborate Which progressive reform do you think had the greatest effect on Americans?

SECTION 2 *(Pages 670–674)*

8. a. Identify What reforms were made to improve working conditions, and who was affected by these reforms?

b. Contrast What are the differences between capitalism and socialism?

c. Elaborate If you were a business owner, would you have supported the progressive workplace reforms? Explain your answer.

Answers

History's Impact

Video Series Several states, including Wyoming and Montana, granted women the right to vote years before the federal government passed an amendment to the Constitution. States followed their own course of action, regardless of the lack of attention by the federal government.

Visual Summary

Review and Inquiry Discuss the summary with students. Ask them to identify what each figure in the picture represents. What reforms can be applied to each figure? Ask volunteers to respond.

Quick Facts Transparency 58: The Progressive Spirit of Reform Visual Summary

Reviewing Vocabulary, Terms, and People

1. socialist
2. Robert M. La Follette
3. Nineteenth Amendment
4. Pure Food and Drug Act
5. political machines
6. muckrakers

Comprehension and Critical Thinking

7. a. stuffed ballot boxes, bribed vote counters, traded favors for votes, intimidated voters
b. improved education, housing, and sanitation
c. education reform; more people were educated and taught to think, not just memorize facts

Review and Assessment Resources

Review and Reinforce

- SE Chapter Review
- **CRF:** Chapter Review Activity
- Quick Facts Transparency 58: The Progressive Spirit of Reform Visual Summary
- Spanish Chapter Summaries Audio CD Program
- go.hrw.com Online Chapter Summaries in Spanish
- OSP Holt PuzzlePro, GameTool for ExamView
- Quiz Game CD-ROM

Assess

- SE Standardized Test Practice
- PASS: Chapter 21 Tests, Forms A and B
- Alternative Assessment Handbook
- OSP ExamView Test Generator, Chapter Test
- Differentiated Instruction Modified Worksheets and Tests CD-ROM: Chapter Test
- HOAP Holt Online Assessment Program (in the Premier Online Edition)

Reteach/Intervene

- Interactive Reader and Study Guide
- Differentiated Instruction Teacher Management System: Lesson Plans for Differentiated Instruction
- Differentiated Instruction Modified Worksheets and Tests CD-ROM
- Interactive Skills Tutor CD-ROM

go.hrw.com
Online Resources
Chapter Resources:
KEYWORD: SF7 CH21

Answers

8. a. minimum wage law—all workers; child labor laws—school-aged children; workers' compensation laws—workers injured on the job and their families; limits on working hours—women and children
b. capitalism—private business runs most industries and competition determines the price of goods; socialism—government owns and operates a country's means of production
c. possible answer—No; I would not want to pay higher wages to my workers or pay them when they aren't working.

9. a. Native Americans, non-European immigrant groups such as Chinese and Mexican immigrants
b. Their efforts led to the passage of the Eighteenth (temperance) and Nineteenth (women's suffrage) Amendments.
c. possible answer—No; I think laws are needed to protect people from discrimination and segregation because it is too hard for some individuals to improve their education and economic well-being on their own.

10. a. He did not act strongly enough to regulate big business.
b. They all wanted to regulate big business and improve the lives of working-class Americans without harming the industrial achievements of the nation.
c. possible answer— I would have supported Wilson's tariff, banking, income tax, and antitrust reforms. They would help keep the prices of products down, keep our nation's economy steady, and keep big businesses from getting too much power.

Reviewing Themes

11. Political machines controlled who was elected to office and traded favors for votes.

12. Younger children not permitted to work outside the home got the opportunity to rest, play, and be educated. Older working children had limited working hours and better wages.

SECTION 3 *(Pages 675–679)*

9. a. **Recall** What minority groups were overlooked by progressive reform efforts?
b. **Analyze** How did women's involvement in the Progressive movement lead to constitutional change?
c. **Elaborate** Do you agree with Booker T. Washington's approach to improving life for African Americans? Explain your answer.

SECTION 4 *(Pages 680–683)*

10. a. **Describe** How did William Howard Taft disappoint Progressives?
b. **Compare** In what ways were the reforms of Presidents Roosevelt, Taft, and Wilson similar?
c. **Elaborate** Would you have supported Wilson's progressive reforms? Explain your answer.

Reviewing Themes

11. **Politics** What role did political machines play in local politics during the Gilded Age?

12. **Society and Culture** How were children affected by the movement for workplace reforms?

Reading Skills

Evaluating Sources *Use the Reading Skills taught in this chapter to answer the question about the reading selection below.*

> The next day Rose went to town [Chicago] alone. The wind had veered [turned] to the south, the dust blew, and the whole terrifying panorama [view] of life in the street seemed some way blurred together, and forms of men and animals were like figures in tapestry. The grind and clang and clatter and hiss and howl of the traffic was all about her . . .
>
> —Hamlin Garland, from his novel *Rose of Dutcher's Coolly*, 1895

13. Is this a good source for understanding the experiences of Chicago in the late 1800s? Why or why not?

Social Studies Skills

Short- and Long-Term Causal Relationships *Use the Social Studies Skills taught in this chapter to answer the question about the reading selection below.*

> Despite their friendship, Roosevelt and Taft held different ideas about how a president should act. Taft thought Roosevelt had claimed more power than a president was constitutionally allowed.
>
> As president, therefore, Taft chose to move cautiously toward reform and regulation.
> *(p. 682)*

14. According to the passage above, what was a long-term cause of Taft's cautious reforms?

Using the Internet

go.hrw.com
KEYWORD: SF7 CH21

15. **Activity: Researching Progressives** Rapid industrial and urban growth in America in the late 1800s resulted in a number of problems. Progressives worked to address these issues in many ways, including efforts to clean up political corruption, improve working conditions, and enact social reforms. Enter the activity keyword and explore the lives of some of the leaders of the Progressive movement. Then write a profile of a Progressive leader that outlines his or her life and impact on American reform.

FOCUS ON SPEAKING

16. **Share Your Campaign Promises** Review your notes about possible campaign promises. Which promises will be most helpful in getting you elected? Look at your promises to see whether they focus on issues important to voters. Then write a speech including your campaign promises that you can deliver to your class.

Reading Skills

13. The passage is from a novel, which is not a factual account. But the language in the passage captures the busy nature of Chicago.

Social Studies Skills

14. Taft was concerned about presidents who might claim more power than they are allowed by the Constitution.

Using the Internet

15. Go to the HRW Web site and enter the keyword shown to access a rubric for this activity.

KEYWORD: SF7 CH21

Focus on Speaking

16. Students' speeches should include campaign promises which will appeal to most voters and which reflect the issues of the Progressive Movement. A rubric for this activity is provided in the Chapter Resource File: Focus on Speaking Activity: Campaign Promises.

CHAPTER 21

Standardized Test Practice

IN 8.2.9, 8.4.2, 8.4.4, 8.4.5

DIRECTIONS: Read each question and write the letter of the best response.

1

The people in this photograph would probably have been *most* interested in which of the following reforms?

A secret ballots
B the Pure Food and Drug Act
C child labor laws
D elimination of political machines

2 One direct result of immigration and urban growth was the rise of

A political machines.
B the civil-service system.
C the spoils system.
D primary elections.

3 What was the *main* idea behind the creation of the civil-service system in the late 1800s?

A Government jobs should be awarded to people who support the party in power.
B Government workers should be required to support the elected officials who hire them.
C Government employees should be qualified to do the jobs for which they were hired.
D Government jobs should not be filled with employees who serve in those jobs for life.

4 The Nineteenth Amendment to the Constitution increased democracy in the United States by

A granting women the right to vote.
B allowing the people of each state to elect their senators.
C establishing direct primary elections.
D enabling voters to remove elected officials from office before the end of their terms.

5 Earlier in the book you learned how Frederick Douglass wrote and spoke against slavery and unfair treatment of African Americans. What later reformer also spoke out for equal rights for African Americans?

A John Dewey
B W. E. B. Du Bois
C William Howard Taft
D Upton Sinclair

6 Read the following excerpt from an interview with a boss at Tammany Hall and use it to answer the question below.

> There's only one way to hold a district: you must study human nature and act accordin' . . . To learn real human nature you have to go among the people, see them and be seen. I know every man, woman, and child in the Fifteenth District, except them that's been born this summer—and I know some of them, too. I know what they like and what they don't like, what they are strong at and what they are weak in, and I reach them by approachin' at the right side.
>
> —George Washington Plunkitt, quoted in *Eyewitnesses and Others*

Document-Based Question How did Plunkitt say he kept his position in the political machine?

Answers

1. C
Break Down the Question Tell students to read the question closely. The key word is *most*.

2. A
Break Down the Question This question requires students to connect the immigrants' needs to the political machines who helped them. Refer students to "Political Machines" in Section 1.

3. C
Break Down the Question Tell students to focus on the beginnings, or creation of the civil-service system. Direct students having difficulty with this question to "Cleaning Up Political Corruption" in Section 1.

4. A
Break Down the Question This question requires students to recall one of four amendments presented in this chapter. Answers C and D can be eliminated as they do not refer to amendments.

5. B
Break Down the Question This question requires students to identify which of the four men, who all appear in this chapter, was concerned with African American rights. Students who miss this may be referred to "African Americans Challenge Discrimination" in Section 3.

6. Plunkitt retained his political power by going out among the people of his district, getting to know them, and using this knowledge to decide his approach

Breaking Down the Question
Document-based questions are best approached by reading the question first, then the passage. It often helps to read and consider each sentence by itself, especially with dialect.

Intervention Resources

Reproducible

- Interactive Reader and Study Guide
- Differentiated Instruction Teacher Management System: Lesson Plans for Differentiated Instruction

Technology

- Quick Facts Transparency 58: The Progressive Spirit of Reform Visual Summary
- Differentiated Instruction Modified Worksheets and Tests CD-ROM
- Interactive Skills Tutor CD-ROM

Tips for Test Taking

Listen in Your Mind's Ear When they answer questions about a reading selection such as Question 6, have students keep these suggestions in mind:

- First, read the question carefully so you are sure you understand what is being asked.
- When you notice that a selection is written in dialect, imagine you are hearing it in your mind.
- Restate the text in Standard English. Then, reread the selection and focus on finding the answer.

Chapter 22 Planning Guide

America as a World Power

Chapter Overview	Reproducible Resources	Technology Resources
CHAPTER 22 **pp. 688–715** **Overview:** **Students will learn how the United States rose to become a global power in the late 1800s and early 1900s.**	**Differentiated Instruction Teacher Management System:*** • Instructional Pacing Guides • Lesson Plans for Differentiated Instruction **Interactive Reader and Study Guide:** Chapter Summary Graphic Organizer* **Chapter Resource File:*** • Focus on Writing Activity: A List of Pros and Cons • Social Studies Skills Activity: Continuity and Change in History • Chapter Review Activity	**Student Edition on Audio CD Program** **Differentiated Instruction Modified Worksheets and Tests CD-ROM** **Interactive Skills Tutor CD-ROM** **Primary Source Library CD-ROM for United States History** **Power Presentations with Video CD-ROM** **History's Impact: United States History Video Program (VHS/DVD):** The Impact of the United States as a World Power*
Section 1: **The United States Gains Overseas Territories** **The Big Idea:** In the last half of the 1800s, the United States joined the race for control of overseas territories.	**Differentiated Instruction Teacher Management System:** Section 1 Lesson Plan* **Interactive Reader and Study Guide:** Section 22.1 Summary* **Chapter Resource File:*** • Vocabulary Builder Activity, Section 1 • Literature Activity: *The Story of Seward's Folly* • Primary Source Activity: *Hawaii's Story by Hawaii's Queen* by Liliuokalani	**Daily Bellringer Transparency:** Section 22.1* **Map Transparency 63:** U.S. Territories in the Pacific, 1856–1899*
Section 2: **The Spanish-American War** **The Big Idea:** The United States expanded into new parts of the world as a result of the Spanish-American War.	**Differentiated Instruction Teacher Management System:** Section 2 Lesson Plan* **Interactive Reader and Study Guide:** Section 22.2 Summary* **Chapter Resource File:*** • Vocabulary Builder Activity, Section 2 • Biography Activity: Douglas MacArthur • Primary Source Activity: The Spanish-American War Volunteer	**Daily Bellringer Transparency:** Section 22.2* **Map Transparency 64:** War in the Philippines* **Map Transparency 65:** War in the Caribbean* **Internet Activity:** Yellow Fever
Section 3: **The United States and Latin America** **The Big Idea:** The United States expanded its role in Latin America in the early 1900s.	**Differentiated Instruction Teacher Management System:** Section 3 Lesson Plan* **Interactive Reader and Study Guide:** Section 22.3 Summary* **Chapter Resource File:*** • Vocabulary Builder Activity, Section 3 • History and Geography Activity: Territories in Latin America • Biography Activity: George Washington Goethals **Political Cartoons Activities for United States History,** Cartoon 24: Roosevelt and the Panama Canal*	**Daily Bellringer Transparency:** Section 22.3* **Map Transparency 66:** The Panama Canal* **Map Transparency 67:** The United States in Latin America* **Quick Facts Transparency 59:** U.S. Foreign Policy* **Internet Activity:** Mexican Revolution Mural **Interactive Maps:** The Panama Canal; The United States in Latin America

SE Student Edition | Print Resource | Audio CD
TE Teacher's Edition | Transparency | CD-ROM
go.hrw.com | **LS** Learning Styles | Video
TOS Indiana Teacher One Stop | * also on Indiana Teacher One Stop

Review, Assessment, Intervention

- **Quick Facts Transparency 60:** America as a World Power Visual Summary*
- **Spanish Chapter Summaries Audio CD Program**
- **Online Chapter Summaries in Spanish**
- **Quiz Game CD-ROM**
- **Progress Assessment Support System (PASS):** Chapter Tests A and B*
- **Differentiated Instruction Modified Worksheets and Tests CD-ROM:** Modified Chapter Test
- TOS **Indiana Teacher One Stop:** ExamView Test Generator (English/Spanish)
- **Alternative Assessment Handbook**
- HOAP **Holt Online Assessment Program,** in the Holt Premier Online Student Edition

- **PASS:** Section Quiz 22.1*
- **Online Quiz:** Section 22.1
- **Alternative Assessment Handbook**

- **PASS:** Section Quiz 22.2*
- **Online Quiz:** Section 22.2
- **Alternative Assessment Handbook**

- **PASS:** Section Quiz 22.3*
- **Online Quiz:** Section 22.3
- **Alternative Assessment Handbook**

HOLT
History's Impact
United States History Video Program (VHS/DVD)
The Impact of the United States as a World Power
Suggested use: as a chapter introduction

Power Presentations with Video CD-ROM

Power Presentations with Video are visual presentations of each chapter's main ideas. Presentations can be customized by including Quick Facts charts, images from the text, and video clips.

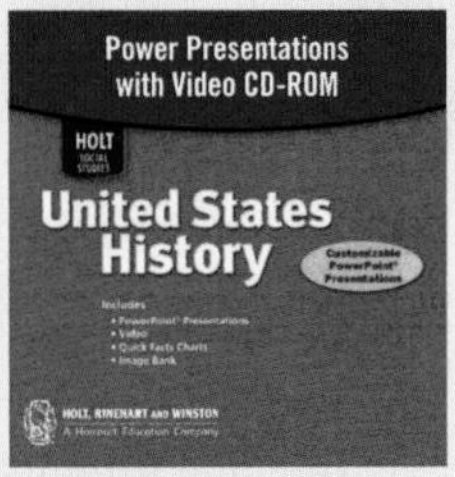

DIVISION FOR PUBLIC EDUCATION
AMERICAN BAR ASSOCIATION

Developed by the Division for Public Education of the American Bar Association, these materials are part of the **Democracy and Civic Education Resources.**

- **Constitution Study Guide**
- **Supreme Court Case Studies**

Holt Online Learning

go.hrw.com
Teacher Resources
KEYWORD: SF7 TEACHER

go.hrw.com
Student Resources
KEYWORD: SF7 CH22

- Document-Based Questions
- Interactive Multimedia Activities
- Current Events
- Chapter-based Internet Activities
- and more!

Holt Interactive
Online Student Edition

Complete online support for interactivity, assessment, and reporting

- Interactive Maps and Notebook
- Standardized Test Prep
- Homework Practice and Research Activities Online

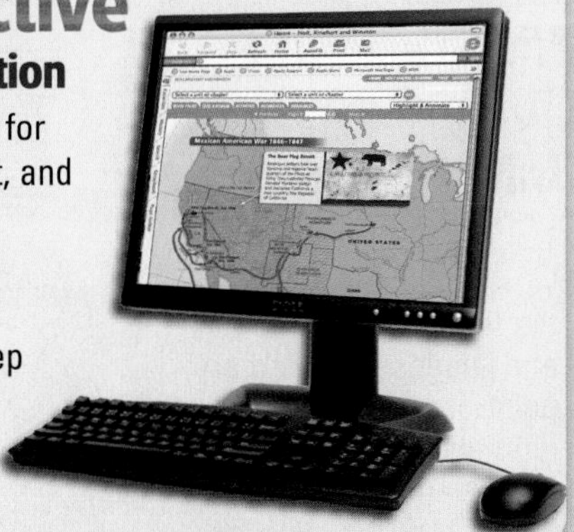

Differentiating Instruction

How do I address the needs of varied learners?

The Target Resource acts as your primary strategy for differentiated instruction.

ENGLISH-LANGUAGE LEARNERS & STRUGGLING READERS

TARGET RESOURCE

English-Language Learner Strategies and Activities

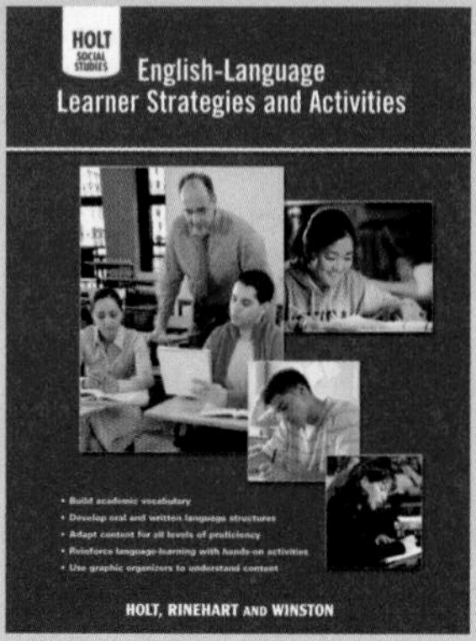

- Build Academic Vocabulary
- Develop Oral and Written Language Structures

Spanish Resources

Spanish Chapter Summaries Audio CD

Spanish Chapter Summaries Online

Teacher's One-Stop Planner:

- ExamView Test Generator, Spanish
- PuzzlePro, Spanish

Additional Resources

Differentiated Instruction Teacher Management System: Lesson Plans for Differentiated Instruction

Chapter Resources:

- Vocabulary Builder Activities
- Social Studies Skills Activity: Continuity and Change in History

Quick Facts Transparencies:

- U.S. Foreign Policy (TR 59)
- America as a World Power Visual Summary (TR 60)

Student Edition on Audio CD Program

Interactive Skills Tutor CD-ROM

SPECIAL NEEDS LEARNERS

TARGET RESOURCE

Differentiated Instruction Modified Worksheets and Tests CD-ROM

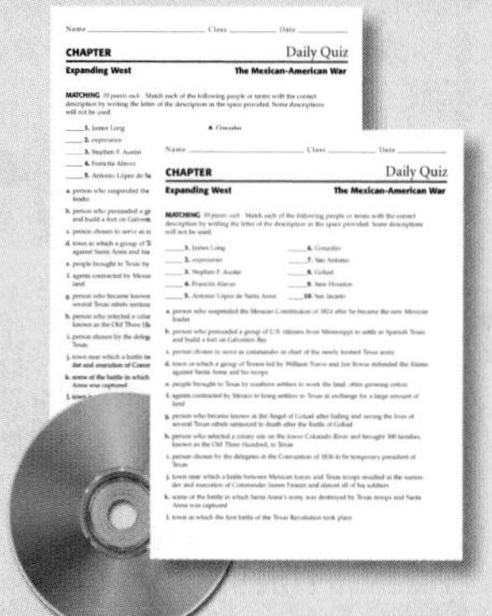

- Vocabulary Flash Cards
- Modified Vocabulary Builder Activities
- Modified Chapter Review Activity
- Modified Chapter Test

Additional Resources

Differentiated Instruction Teacher Management System: Lesson Plans for Differentiated Instruction

Interactive Reader and Study Guide

Social Studies Skills Activity: Continuity and Change in History

Student Edition on Audio CD Program

Interactive Skills Tutor CD-ROM

ADVANCED/GIFTED-AND-TALENTED STUDENTS

TARGET RESOURCE

Primary Source Library CD-ROM for United States History

The Library contains longer versions of quotations in the text, extra sources, and images. Included are point-of-view articles, journals, diaries, historical fiction, and political documents.

Additional Resources

Differentiated Instruction Teacher Management System: Lesson Plans for Differentiated Instruction

Political Cartoons Activities for United States History, Cartoon 24: Roosevelt and the Panama Canal

Chapter Resource File:

- Focus on Writing Activity: A List of Pros and Cons
- Primary Source Activities: *Hawaii's Story by Hawaii's Queen* by Liliuokalani; The Spanish-American War Volunteer
- Literature Activity: *The Story of Seward's Folly*

Differentiated Activities in the Teacher's Edition

- Mapping a Route Across the Pacific, p.693

Differentiated Activities in the Teacher's Edition

- Spanish-American War Events, p. 698
- Personnel Posters, p. 705

Differentiated Activities in the Teacher's Edition

- Rough Rider Skits, p. 699
- Letters to the Editor, p. 701
- Lending and Owing Chart, p. 707
- America's Global Influence Posters, p. 711

Teacher One Stop™

How can I manage the lesson plans and support materials for differentiated instruction?

With the Indiana Teacher One Stop, you can easily organize and print lesson plans, planning guides, and instructional materials for all learners.

The Indiana Teacher One Stop includes the following materials to help you differentiate instruction:

- Interactive Teacher's Edition
- Calendar Planner and pacing guides
- Editable lesson plans
- All reproducible ancillaries in Adobe Acrobat (PDF) format
- ExamView Test Generator (Eng & Span)
- Transparency and video previews

Professional Development

HOLT Professional Development

What teacher training resources are available to help me grow professionally?

- **In-service and staff development** as part of your Holt Social Studies product purchase
- **Quick Teacher Tutorial Lesson Presentation CD-ROM**
- Intensive tuition-based **Teacher Development Institute**
- **Convenient Holt Speaker Bureau** – face-to-face workshop options
- **PRAXIS™ Test Prep** interactive Web-based content refreshers*
- **Ask A Professional Development Expert** at http://www.hrw.com/prodev/

* PRAXIS is a trademark of Educational Testing Service (ETS). This publication is not endorsed or approved by ETS.

• Chapter Preview •

Chapter Big Ideas

Section 1 In the last half of the 1800s, the United States joined the race for control of overseas territories.

Section 2 The United States expanded into new parts of the world as a result of the Spanish-American War.

Section 3 The United States expanded its role in Latin America in the early 1900s.

Focus on Writing

The **Chapter Resource File** provides a Focus on Writing worksheet to help students create their lists of pros and cons.

CRF: Focus on Writing Activity: A List of Pros and Cons

Key to Differentiating Instruction

Below Level

Basic-level activities designed for all students encountering new material

At Level

Intermediate-level activities designed for average students

Above Level

Challenging activities designed for honors and gifted and talented students

Standard English Mastery

Activities designed to improve standard English usage

CHAPTER 22 1867–1920

America as a World Power

Indiana Standards

Social Studies Standards

8.3.9 Analyze human and physical factors that have influenced migration and settlement patterns and relate them to the economic development of the United States.

8.4.2 Illustrate elements of the three types of economic systems, using cases from United States history.

8.4.10 Examine the importance of borrowing and lending (the use of credit) in the United States and list the advantages and disadvantages of using credit.

go.hrw.com
Indiana
KEYWORD: SF10 IN

FOCUS ON WRITING

A List of Pros and Cons In the last half of the 1800s, the United States became more involved in international affairs. As you read this chapter, you will analyze the nation's new role and use the results of your analysis to guide U.S. policy in the future. In order to analyze the advantages and disadvantages of an aggressive foreign policy, you will need to create a list of the pros and cons of U.S. involvement with other nations in the late 1800s and early 1900s. As you create your list, note which items are facts and which are opinions—either yours or someone else's.

UNITED STATES

1867 The United States buys Alaska.

1867

WORLD

1868 Japan begins a time of modernization known as the Meiji Restoration.

Introduce the Chapter

At Level

Focus on U.S. Influence

1. Tell students that in this chapter they will learn how Americans dramatically changed their relationship with the rest of the world during the late 1800s and early 1900s.
2. Using the maps in the chapter, have students make a list of all U.S. Territories, Possessions, and Protectorates. *Alaska, American Samoa, Cuba, Dominican Republic, Guam, Haiti, Hawaii, Howland Is., Johnston Is., Midway Is., Nicaragua, Panama, the Philippine Islands, Puerto Rico,* and *Wake Is.*
3. Review each map with students, emphasizing how wide the United States' sphere of influence became during this period.
4. Tell students that in this chapter they will learn that the United States grew from an isolated country to a great power with influence all over the world.
LS Visual/Spatial, Verbal/Linguistic

Alternative Assessment Handbook, Rubric 21: Map Reading

HOLT

History's Impact

▶ **video series**
Watch the video to understand the impact of the United States as a world power.

What You Will Learn...

In this chapter you will learn about how the United States became a global power in the late 1800s and early 1900s. Through a combination of economic strength, military might, and aggressive foreign policy, America made its presence known in many parts of the world. One such place was Panama, where the United States built the Panama Canal, shown here. The United States has remained a powerful force on the international stage to this day.

1898 Within 24 hours of the call for troops, Indiana becomes the first state to fulfill a request for volunteers to fight in the Spanish-American War.

1890 Congress passes the McKinley Tariff, which gives a subsidy to U.S. sugar producers.

1898 The United States wins the Spanish-American War, gaining the Philippine Islands and Puerto Rico.

1914 The Panama Canal officially opens.

1880 | 1890 | 1900 | 1910 | 1920

1885 The Indian National Congress is formed in British-controlled India.

1895 Cubans rebel against Spanish rule.

1900 The Boxer Rebellion erupts in China.

1903 Panama declares itself an independent nation.

1910 The Mexican Revolution begins.

• Chapter Preview •

HOLT

History's Impact

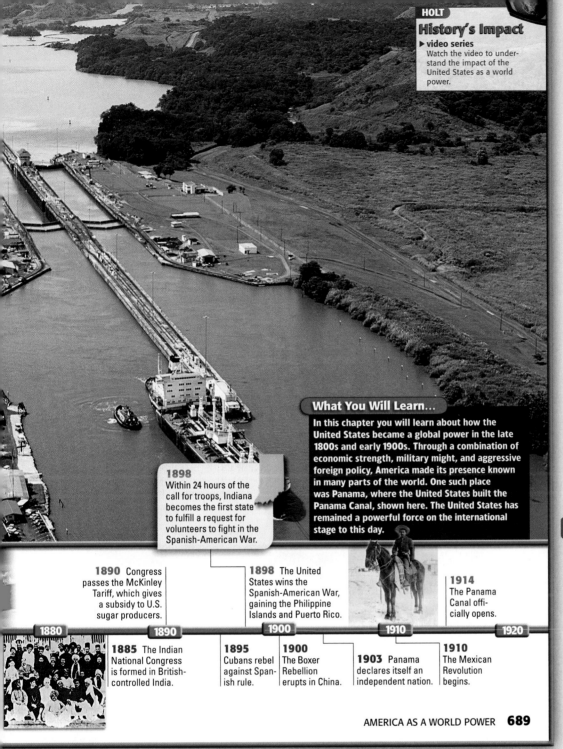

▶ **video series**
See the Video Teacher's Guide for strategies for using the chapter video to help students understand the impact of the United States as a world power.

Explore the Picture

Connecting Two Oceans Take a moment to look over this photograph. Notice how the geography seems perfect for canal building. The Europeans who explored the area saw the great value of this land bridge. As long ago as the 17th century, Panama was a significant part of world commerce.

Analyzing Visuals Remember that this land was undeveloped prior to the canal project. What do you see that might indicate Panamanians have benefited from the canal? *Roads and buildings show that people are employed there.*

go.hrw.com
Online Resources
Chapter Resources:
KEYWORD: SF7 CH22
Teacher Resources:
KEYWORD: SF7 TEACHER

Explore the Time Line

1. What land purchase did Secretary of State Seward make for the United States in 1867? *Alaska*
2. When was the Indian National Congress formed? *1885*
3. What did the United States gain at the end of the Spanish-American War in 1898? *the Philippine Islands and Puerto Rico*
4. When did the Mexican Revolution begin? *1910*

Info to Know

The Indian National Congress India was governed by the British Empire for many years. The Indian people wanted to govern themselves. They formed the Indian National Congress which began the process of self-government by urging limited democratic reforms. In 1905 the INC called for self-government. Mohandas Ghandi devised a strategy of non-violent resistance, adopted in 1920. Independence was finally gained in 1947. Today many Indians still speak English, and the style of their military uniforms still reflects India's years under British rule.

Reading Social Studies

Understanding Themes

The main themes of this chapter, geography and politics, involve the incorporation of new territories and the use of economic and military strengths that characterize the United States to this day. To focus on these themes, ask students which two states most recently joined the union. *Alaska and Hawaii* Ask them why they think the United States would value those locations as new territory. As students read through the chapter, help them notice the advantages of those locations, as well as those of other areas in which the United States became involved between 1867 and 1920.

Comparing Historical Texts

Focus on Reading In language arts, students have probably written persuasive essays. Ask students why someone who reads a persuasive essay would need to know something about the writer. *It would help them understand the bias of the author.* Ask students why it might be important to include more than one viewpoint in research. *Sometimes there is unexpected information presented by the other side; students' research will be more accurate and balanced as a result.*

Reading Social Studies

by Kylene Beers

Economics | **Geography** | **Politics** | Society and Culture | Science and Technology

Focus on Themes In this chapter, you will learn about how the physical **geography** of the United States changed as it acquired overseas territories. You will also read about how national and international **politics** affected foreign policy and brought new responsibilities to the government of the United States.

Comparing Historical Texts

Focus on Reading A good way to learn what people in the past thought is to read what they wrote. However, most documents will only tell you one side of the story. By comparing writings by different people, you can learn a great deal about various sides of a historical issue or debate.

Comparing Texts When you compare historical texts, you should consider two things: who wrote the documents and what the documents were meant to achieve. To do this, you need to find the writers' main point or points.

Document 1

"We have cherished the policy of non-interference with affairs of foreign governments wisely inaugurated [begun] by Washington, keeping ourselves free from entanglement, either as allies or foes, content to leave undisturbed with them the settlement of their own domestic concerns."

–President William McKinley, First Inaugural Address, 1897

Document 2

"Therefore, Mr. President, here is a war with terrible characteristics flagrant [obvious] at our very doors [in Cuba]. We have the power to bring it to an end. I believe that the whole American people would welcome steps in that direction."

–Senator Henry Cabot Lodge, Speech in Congress, 1896

Document 1	Document 2
Writer	
President William McKinley	Senator Henry Cabot Lodge
Main point	
The United States should not involve itself in the affairs of other countries.	The United States should go to war in Cuba.
Both Sides of the Issue	
Americans were torn over the war in Cuba. Some thought the United States should remain uninvolved as it always had. Others thought it was time for a change in foreign policy.	

Reading and Skills Resources

Reading Support

- Interactive Reader and Study Guide
- Student Edition on Audio CD Program
- Spanish Chapter Summaries Audio CD Program

Social Studies Skills Support

- Interactive Skills Tutor CD-ROM

Vocabulary Support

- **CRF:** Vocabulary Builder Activities
- **CRF:** Chapter Review Activity
- Differentiated Instruction Modified Worksheets and Tests CD-ROM:
  - Vocabulary Flash Cards
  - Vocabulary Builder Activity
  - Chapter Review Activity
- **OSP** Holt PuzzlePro

You Try It!

Read the following passages, both taken from presidential addresses to Congress. As you read, look for the main point each president makes in his address.

Foreign Policy

In treating of our foreign policy and of the attitude that this great Nation should assume in the world at large, it is absolutely necessary to consider the Army and the Navy, and the Congress, through which the thought of the Nation finds its expression, should keep ever vividly in mind the fundamental fact that it is impossible to treat our foreign policy, whether this policy takes shape in the effort to secure justice for others or justice for ourselves, save as conditioned upon the attitude we are willing to take toward our Army, and especially toward our Navy.

—President Theodore Roosevelt, Message to Congress, 1904

The diplomacy of the present administration has sought to respond to modern ideas of commercial intercourse [involvement]. This policy has been characterized as substituting dollars for bullets. It is one that appeals alike to idealistic humanitarian sentiments [feelings], to the dictates [rules] of sound policy and strategy, and to legitimate [make real] commercial aims.

—President William Howard Taft, Message to Congress, 1912

After you read the passages, answer the following questions.

1. What was the main point Roosevelt made in his address?

2. What was the main point Taft made in his address?

3. How can a comparison of Roosevelt's and Taft's addresses to Congress help you understand the issues that shaped U.S. foreign policy in the early 1900s?

Key Terms and People

Chapter 22

Section 1
imperialism *(p. 692)*
isolationism *(p. 693)*
William H. Seward *(p. 693)*
Liliuokalani *(p. 694)*
spheres of influence *(p. 695)*
Open Door Policy *(p. 695)*
Boxer Rebellion *(p. 695)*

Section 2
yellow journalism *(p. 697)*
Teller Amendment *(p. 698)*
Emilio Aguinaldo *(p. 699)*
Anti-Imperialist League *(p. 700)*
Platt Amendment *(p. 701)*

Section 3
Panama Canal *(p. 705)*
Roosevelt Corollary *(p. 707)*
dollar diplomacy *(p. 708)*
Mexican Revolution *(p. 708)*
John J. Pershing *(p. 709)*
Francisco "Pancho" Villa *(p. 709)*

Academic Vocabulary
In this chapter, you will learn the following academic words:

process *(p. 695)*
role *(p. 707)*

As you read Chapter 22, organize your notes to help you point out the similarities and differences among events or policies.

Reading Social Studies

Key Terms and People

To introduce students to the key terms and people in this chapter, have students make a three-column chart with the section headings at the top of each column. Tell students to record important facts in each column for people and titles of things as they read through the chapter. Next, review the non-capitalized terms in all three sections plus the Academic Vocabulary. Tell students to note the meaning of each term you review in the appropriate column. **LS Visual/Spatial**

Focus on Reading

See the **Focus on Reading** questions in this chapter for more practice on this reading social studies skill.

Reading Social Studies Assessment

See the **Chapter Review** at the end of this chapter for student assessment questions related to this reading skill.

Teaching Tip

The controversial issues in student's lives at this age have progressed from schoolyard disagreements to the limits their parents set on them—from hairstyles to curfews. No matter what the controversy, remind students that both sides must be listened to and understood before a fair decision can be made. Getting viewpoints from both sides of an issue is not only fair, but wise.

Answers

You Try It! 1. *The United States' dealings with foreign nations should be determined by whether or not we are willing to commit our military to support the cause.* **2.** *The dollars for bullets plan is a sound strategy that will promote commercial interests.* **3.** *Each president had a different approach to foreign policy, so reading both addresses shows how policy changed to promote the interests of the nation.*

America Then and Now

In the years since 1914, the United States has faced many difficult challenges that have drawn citizens together. The terrorist attacks of September 11, 2001, are one of the latest of these challenges. Since 2001, a War on Terror has been ongoing as the United States tries to effectively end the threat of terrorism around the world. Parts of this War on Terror have been a military action in Afghanistan and Operation Iraqi Freedom.

Terrorism in Iraq and other foreign countries continues to be a danger to all citizens. Kidnappings and bombings threaten peace efforts across the world. In late 2008 attacks on luxury hotels in Mumbai, India, left more than 150 people dead. Concerns about the nuclear programs of Iran and North Korea also shape the international relationships of the United States.

In the final years of President Bush's second term of office, his approval rating dropped dramatically. One contributing factor to this decline was criticism of the federal government's response to the disaster left by Hurricane Katrina, which hit New Orleans and the Gulf Coast in 2005. During the 2008 presidential campaign, both Democrats and Republicans made historic choices for their candidates. Democrat Barack Obama, a U.S. senator from Illinois, became the first African American presidential nominee of a major party, while Republican Sarah Palin, governor of Alaska, became the second woman to gain a major-party nomination for vice president. The campaign focused on issues such as the war in Iraq, health care, and repairing the economy. Obama won, the first African American to be elected president of the United States.

The terrorist attacks of September 11, 2001, marked the beginning of a new challenge in American history—the war against terrorism.

Cities such as St. Louis, shown here, are part of America's past, present, and future. Once a small town known as the Gateway to the West, St. Louis has grown into a large and modern American city.

Economics Handbook

What Is Economics?

Economics may sound dull, but it touches almost every part of your life. Here are some examples of the kinds of economic choices you may have made yourself:

- Which pair of shoes to buy—the ones on sale or the ones you really like, which cost much more
- Whether to continue saving your money for the DVD player you want or use some of it now to go to a movie
- Whether to give some money to a fundraiser for a new park or to housing for the homeless

As these examples show, we can think of economics as a study of choices. These choices are the ones people make to satisfy their needs or their desires.

Glossary of Economic Terms

Here are some of the words we use to talk about economics:

ECONOMIC SYSTEMS

Countries have developed different economic systems to help them make choices, such as what goods and services to produce, how to produce them, and for whom to produce them. The most common economic systems in the world are market economies and mixed economies.

capitalism See market economy.

command economy an economic system in which the central government makes all economic decisions, such as in the countries of Cuba and North Korea

communism a political system in which the government owns all property and runs a command economy

free enterprise a system in which businesses operate with little government involvement, such as in a country with a market economy

market economy an economic system based on private ownership, free trade, and competition; the government has little to say about what, how, or for whom goods and services are produced; examples include Germany and the United States

mixed economy an economy that is a combination of command, market, and traditional economies

traditional economy an economy in which production is based on customs and tradition, and in which people often grow their own food, make their own goods, and use barter to trade

THE ECONOMY AND MONEY

People, businesses, and countries obtain the items they need and want through economic activities such as producing, selling, and buying goods or services. Countries differ in the amount of economic activity that they have and in the strength of their economies.

consumer a person who buys goods or services for personal use

consumer good a finished product sold to consumers for personal or home use

corporation a business in which a group of owners share in the profits and losses

currency paper or coins that a country uses for its money supply

demand the amount of goods and services that consumers are willing and able to buy at a given time

depression a severe drop in overall business activity over a long period of time

developed countries countries with strong economies and a high quality of life; often have high per capita GDPs and high levels of industrialization and technology

developing countries countries with less productive economies and a lower quality of life; often have less industrialization and technology

economic development the level of a country's economic activity, growth, and quality of life

economy the structure of economic life in a country

goods objects or materials that humans can purchase to satisfy their wants and needs

gross domestic product (GDP) total market value of all goods and services produced in a country in a given year; *per capita GDP* is the average value of goods and services produced per person in a country in a given year

industrialization the process of using machinery for all major forms of production

inflation an increase in overall prices

investment the purchase of something with the expectation that it will gain in value; usually property, stocks, etc.

money any item, usually coins or paper currency, that is used in payment for goods or services

producer a person or group that makes goods or provides services to satisfy consumers' wants and needs

productivity the amount of goods or services that a worker or workers can produce within a given amount of time

profit the gain or excess made by selling goods or services over their costs

purchasing power the amount of income that people have available to spend on goods and services

services any activities that are performed for a fee

standard of living how well people are living; determined by the amount of goods and services they can afford

stock a share of ownership in a corporation

supply the amount of goods and services that are available at a given time

INTERNATIONAL TRADE

Countries trade with each other to obtain resources, goods, and services. Growing global trade has helped lead to the development of a global economy.

balance of trade the difference between the value of a country's exports and imports

barter the exchange of one good or service for another

black market the illegal buying and selling of goods, often at high prices

comparative advantage the ability of a company or country to produce something at a lower cost than other companies or countries

competition rivalry between businesses selling similar goods or services; a condition that often leads to lower prices or improved products

e-commerce the electronic trading of goods and services, such as over the Internet

exports goods or services that a country sells and sends to other countries

free trade trade among nations that is not affected by financial or legal barriers; trade without barriers

imports goods or services that a country brings in or purchases from another country

interdependence a relationship between countries in which they rely on one another for resources, goods, or services

market the trade of goods and services

market clearing price the price of a good or service at which supply equals demand

one-crop economy an economy that is dominated by the production of a single product

opportunity cost the value of the next-best alternative that is sacrificed when choosing to consume or produce another good or service

scarcity a condition of limited resources and unlimited wants by people

specialization a focus on only one or two aspects of production in order to produce a product more quickly and cheaply; for example, one worker washes the wheels of the car, another cleans the interior, and another washes the body

trade barriers financial or legal limitations to trade; prevention of free trade

trade-offs the goods or services sacrificed in order to consume or produce another good or service

underground economy illegal economic activities and unreported legal economic activities

PERSONAL ECONOMICS

Individuals make personal choices in how they manage and use their money to satisfy their needs and desires. Individuals have the choice to spend, save, or invest their money. Individuals can also borrow money or buy goods and services on credit.

budget a plan listing the expenses and income of an individual or organization

credit a system that allows consumers to pay for goods and services over time

debt an amount of money that is owed

financial institutions businesses that keep and invest people's money and loan money to people; include banks and credit unions

income a gain of money that comes typically from labor or capital

interest the money that a borrower pays to a lender in return for a loan

loan money given on the condition that it will be paid back, often with interest

savings money or income that is not used to purchase goods or services

tax a required payment to a local, state, or national government; different kinds of taxes include sales taxes, income taxes, and property taxes

wage the payment a worker receives for his or her labor

RESOURCES

People and businesses need resources—such as land, labor, and money—to produce goods and services.

capital generally refers to wealth, in particular wealth that can be used to finance the production of goods or services

human capital sometimes used to refer to human skills and education that affect the production of goods and services in a company or country

labor force all people who are legally old enough to work and are either working or looking for work

natural resource any material in nature that people use and value

nonrenewable resource a resource that cannot be replaced naturally, such as coal or petroleum

raw material a natural resource used to make a product or good

renewable resource a resource that Earth replaces naturally, such as water, soil, and trees

ORGANIZATIONS

Countries have formed many organizations to promote economic cooperation, growth, and trade. These organizations are important in today's global economy.

European Union (EU) an organization that promotes political and economic cooperation in Europe

International Monetary Fund (IMF) a UN agency that promotes international cooperation and stability in trade and the exchange of countries' currencies

Organization of Economic Cooperation and Development (OECD) an organization of countries that promotes democracy and market economies

United Nations (UN) an organization of countries that promotes peace and security around the globe

World Bank a UN agency that provides loans to countries for development and recovery

World Trade Organization (WTO) an international organization dealing with trade between nations

Economic Handbook Review

Reviewing Vocabulary and Terms

On a separate sheet of paper, fill in the blanks in the following sentences:

ECONOMIC SYSTEMS

1. A. Businesses are able to operate with little government involvement in a ________ system.

B. In a ________, a central government makes all economic decisions.

C. ________ is a political system in which the government owns all property and runs a command economy.

D. Economies that combine elements of command, market, and traditional economies are called ________.

E. ________ is another name for a market economy.

THE ECONOMY AND MONEY

2. A. ________ are objects or materials that humans can buy to satisfy their needs and wants.

B. A ________ is any activity that is performed for a fee.

C. A person who buys goods or services is a ________.

D. The amount of goods and services that consumers are willing and able to buy at any given time is known as ________.

E. The total value of all the goods and services produced in the United States in one year is its ________.

INTERNATIONAL TRADE

3. A. If we have an unlimited demand for a natural resource, such as oil, and there is only so much oil in the ground, we have a condition called ________.

B. Goods or services that a country sells to other countries are ________.

C. Rivalry between producers that provide the same good or service is called ________.

D. If a country is able to produce a good or service at a lower cost than other countries, it is said to have a ________.

E. Trade among nations that is not limited by legal or economic barriers is called ________.

PERSONAL ECONOMICS

4. A. A ________ is a required payment to a local, state, or national government.

B. The money we do not spend on goods or services is our ________.

C. You can use ________ to pay for goods and services over time.

D. The payment that a worker receives for his or her labor is called a ________.

E. Individuals and companies use ________ to plan and manage their expenses and their income.

RESOURCES

5. A. Diamonds and gold are examples of ________, which are any materials in nature that people use and value.

B. The ________ consists of all people who are legally able to work and are working or looking for work.

C. Wealth that can be used to finance the production of goods and services is called ________.

D. Oil is an example of a ________, which is a resource that cannot be replaced naturally.

E. Water, soil, and trees are examples of ________, which are resources that Earth replaces naturally.

ORGANIZATIONS

6. A. Many European countries have joined the ________ to help promote political and economic cooperation across Europe.

B. The ________ consists of many agencies that promote peace and security around the world.

C. The ________ is a UN agency that provides loans to countries to help them develop their economies.

D. The ________ is a UN agency that helps protect the stability of countries' currencies.

E. Many democratic countries promote market economies through their membership in the ________.

Activities

1. With a partner, compare prices in two grocery stores. Create a chart showing the price of five items in the two stores. Also, figure the average price of the items in each store. How do you think the fact that the stores are near each other affects prices? How might prices be different if one store went out of business? How might the prices be different or similar if the United States had a command economy? Present what you have learned about prices and competition to your class.
2. With a group, choose five countries from a unit region to research. Look up the per capita GDP and the life expectancy rates for each of these countries in the regional atlas. Then use your textbook, go to your library, or use the Internet to research the literacy rate and the number of TVs per 1,000 people for each of these countries. Organize this information in a five-column chart like the one shown here. Study the information to see if you can find any patterns. Write a brief paragraph explaining what you have learned about the five countries.

Region				
Country	Per Capita GDP (U.S. $)	Life Expectancy at Birth	Literacy Rate	TVs per 1,000 People

3. Work with a partner to identify some of the types of currency used in Europe. Then imagine that you are the owners of a business in the United States. You have created a new product that you want to sell in Europe, but people there do not use the same currency as you do. To sell your product, you will need to be able to exchange one type of currency for another. Search the Internet or look in a newspaper to find a list of currency exchange rates. If your product sells for 1,000 dollars, what should the cost be in euros? In British pounds? In Russian rubles? In Norwegian kroner?

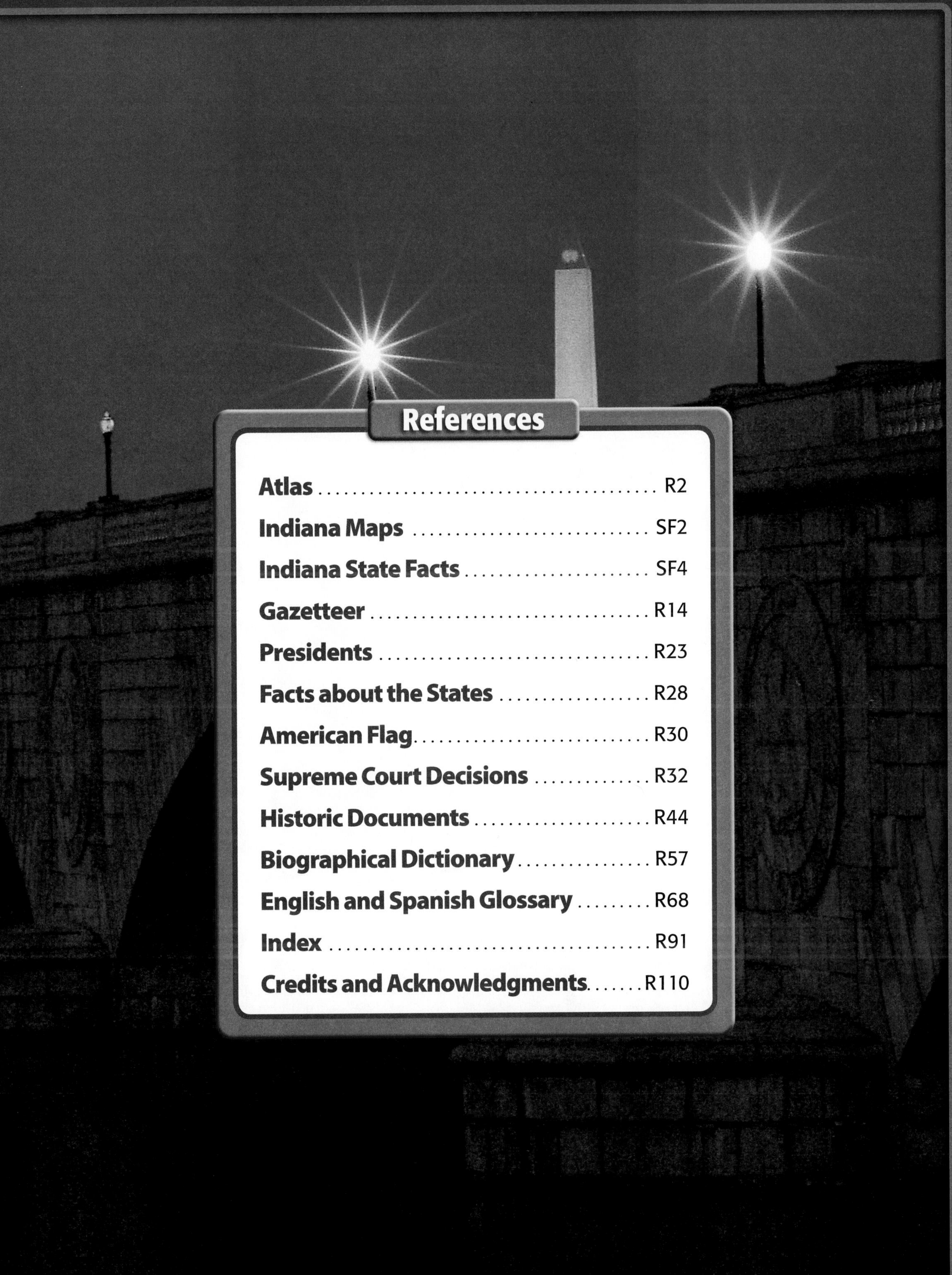

References

The United States of America: Political

CANADA
MEXICO
PACIFIC OCEAN
WASHINGTON
OREGON
CALIFORNIA
NEVADA
IDAHO
MONTANA
WYOMING
UTAH
COLORADO
ARIZONA
NEW MEXICO
NORTH DAKO
SOUTH DAKOT
NEBRASKA
KANS
OKLAHO
TEXAS
Puget Sound
Franklin D. Roosevelt Lake
Seattle
Tacoma
Olympia
Spokane
Pend Oreille
Flathead Lake
Portland
Columbia River
Salem
Eugene
Great Falls
Helena
Missouri River
Fort Peck Lake
Yellowstone River
Billings
Lake Sakakawea
Bismarck
Lake Oahe
Pierre
Rapid City
Boise
Sun Valley
Snake River
Pocatello
Yellowstone Lake
Cheyenne
Goose Lake
Cape Mendocino
Shasta Lake
Sacramento River
Pyramid Lake
Reno
Carson City
Lake Tahoe
Berkeley
Oakland
San Francisco
San Francisco Bay
Sacramento
San Joaquin River
San Jose
Monterey Bay
Fresno
Great Salt Lake
Ogden
Salt Lake City
Utah Lake
Provo
Green River
Platte River
Boulder
Vail
Denver
Aspen
Colorado Springs
Pueblo
Arkansas River
Lake Powell
Las Vegas
Lake Mead
Colorado River
Santa Barbara
Ventura
Los Angeles
Long Beach
Riverside
Anaheim
Palm Springs
Santa Ana
Salton Sea
San Diego
Channel Islands
Flagstaff
Phoenix
Gila River
Casa Grande
Tucson
Taos
Santa Fe
Albuquerque
Las Cruces
El Paso
Canadian River
Amarillo
Oklahoma
Law
Lubbock
Brazos River
Abilene
Fort W
Midland
Odessa
Pecos River
Colorado River
Rio Grande
Amistad Reservoir
San Antonio
Aust
Corpus Chri
Laredo
Gulf of California
45°N
40°N
35°N
30°N
125°W
120°W
To understand the relative locations of Alaska and Hawaii, as well as the vast distances separating them from the rest of the United States, see the world map.
HAWAII
Kauai
Niihau
Oahu
Honolulu
Molokai
Maui
Lanai
Kahoolawe
Hilo
Hawaii
PACIFIC OCEAN
22°N
19°N
155°W
160°W
0 75 150 Miles
0 75 150 Kilometers
Projection: Mercator
ARCTIC OCEAN
RUSSIA
Bering Strait
Arctic Circle
Nome
Yukon River
Fairbanks
ALASKA
CANADA
St. Lawrence Island
St. Matthew Island
Nunivak Island
Bering Sea
Attu Island
Anchorage
Valdez
Skagway
Gulf of Alaska
Kodiak Island
Juneau
Alexander Archipelago
PACIFIC OCEAN
0 250 500 Miles
0 250 500 Kilometers
Projection: Albers Equal Area
55°N
50°N
170°E
180°
170°W
160°W
150°W
140°W

CANADA
MINNESOTA
WISCONSIN
MICHIGAN
IOWA
MISSOURI
ILLINOIS
INDIANA
OHIO
KENTUCKY
TENNESSEE
ARKANSAS
MISSISSIPPI
ALABAMA
GEORGIA
LOUISIANA
FLORIDA
SOUTH CAROLINA
NORTH CAROLINA
VIRGINIA
WEST VIRGINIA
PENNSYLVANIA
NEW YORK
VT
NH
MAINE
MA
CT
RI
NJ
DE
MD
ATLANTIC OCEAN
Gulf of Mexico
THE BAHAMAS
Lake Superior
Lake Michigan
Lake Huron
Lake Ontario
Lake Erie
Lake Champlain
St. Lawrence River
Hudson R.
Connecticut R.
Susquehanna River
Mississippi River
Missouri River
Minnesota River
Red River
Illinois River
Ohio River
Savannah River
Chattahoochee R.
Lake of the Ozarks
Lake Barkley
Kentucky Lake
Keystone Lake
Lake Texoma
Toledo Bend Reservoir
Lake Okeechobee
Chesapeake Bay
Delaware Bay
Long Island Sound
Long Island
Cape Cod
Cape Hatteras
Cape Canaveral
Cape Sable
Sea Islands
Chandeleur Islands
Florida Keys
Straits of Florida
Grand Forks
Fargo
Duluth
Superior
Marquette
Sault Ste. Marie
Minneapolis
St. Paul
Green Bay
Madison
Milwaukee
Sioux Falls
Sioux City
Cedar Rapids
Davenport
Des Moines
Rockford
Chicago
Gary
South Bend
Fort Wayne
Peoria
Springfield
Indianapolis
Kansas City
Jefferson City
St. Louis
East St. Louis
Springfield
Louisville
Evansville
Frankfort
Lexington
Grand Rapids
Lansing
Saginaw
Detroit
Ann Arbor
Toledo
Cleveland
Youngstown
Akron
Columbus
Dayton
Cincinnati
Charleston
Buffalo
Rochester
Syracuse
Albany
Burlington
Montpelier
Augusta
Portland
Concord
Manchester
Boston
Worcester
Springfield
Providence
Hartford
New Haven
Bridgeport
Yonkers
Jersey City
Newark
New York City
Trenton
Allentown
Harrisburg
Philadelphia
Camden
Pittsburgh
Atlantic City
Dover
Baltimore
Annapolis
Washington, D.C.
Richmond
Newport News
Norfolk
Virginia Beach
Winston-Salem
Greensboro
Durham
Raleigh
Knoxville
Asheville
Charlotte
Nashville
Chattanooga
Memphis
Tulsa
Fayetteville
Little Rock
Pine Bluff
Greenville
Columbia
Charleston
Huntsville
Birmingham
Atlanta
Macon
Columbus
Savannah
Meridian
Montgomery
Vicksburg
Jackson
Shreveport
Dallas
Waco
Beaumont
Houston
Galveston
Baton Rouge
New Orleans
Biloxi
Mobile
Pensacola
Tallahassee
Jacksonville
Gainesville
Orlando
Tampa
St. Petersburg
Fort Myers
Fort Lauderdale
Miami
National capital
State capitals
Other cities
0 100 200 Miles
0 100 200 Kilometers
Projection: Albers Equal Area
N
S
E
W
40°N
35°N
30°N
25°N
70°W
75°W
80°W
85°W
90°W
95°W

The United States of America: Physical

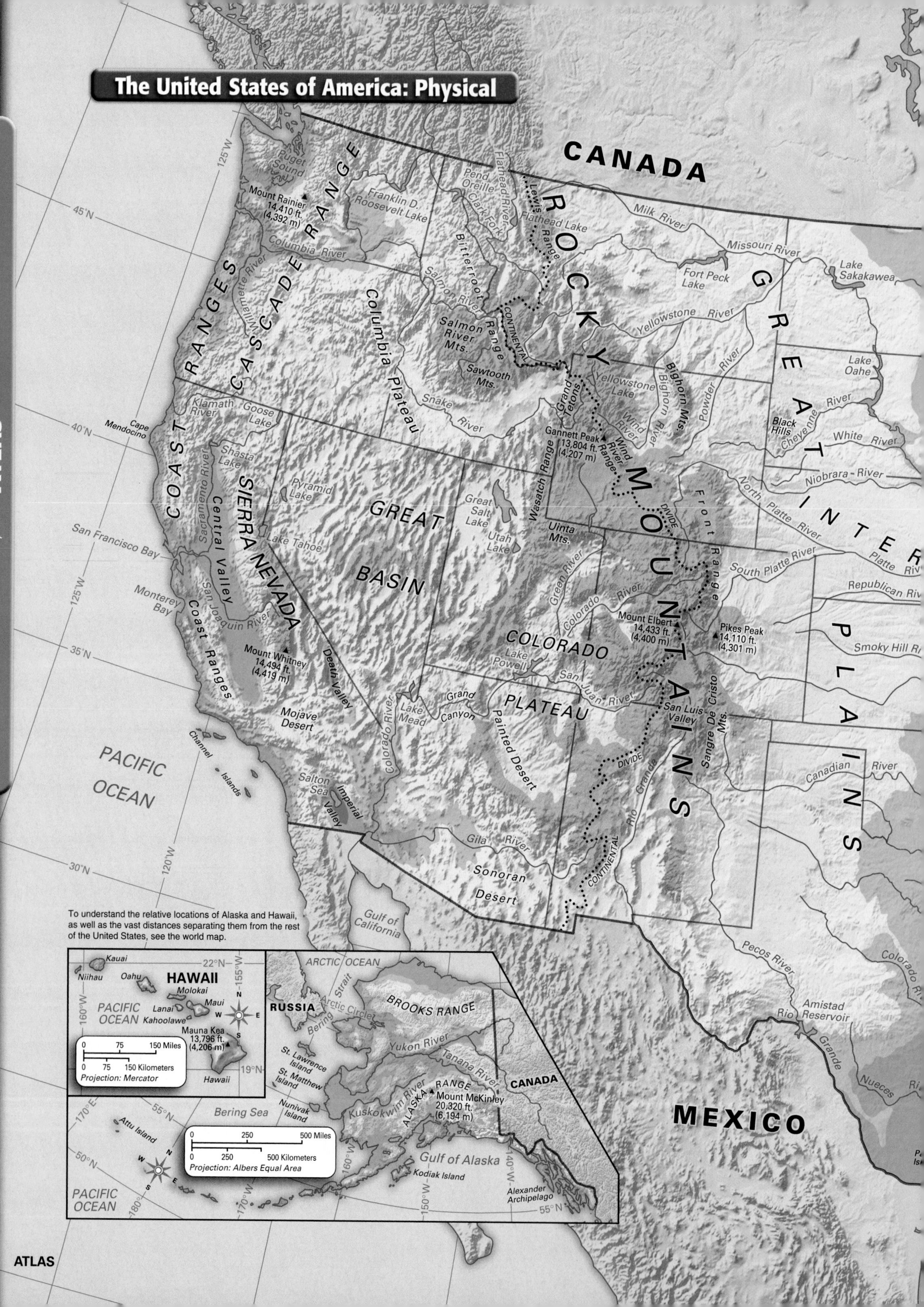
CANADA
MEXICO
PACIFIC OCEAN
Puget Sound
Mount Rainier 14,410 ft. (4,392 m)
CASCADE RANGE
COAST RANGES
Franklin D. Roosevelt Lake
Columbia River
Willamette River
Columbia Plateau
Pend Oreille
Clark Fork
Flathead River
Flathead Lake
Lewis Range
Bitterroot Range
Salmon River
Salmon River Mts.
Sawtooth Mts.
Snake River
ROCKY MOUNTAINS
CONTINENTAL DIVIDE
Milk River
Missouri River
Fort Peck Lake
Lake Sakakawea
Yellowstone River
Yellowstone Lake
Grand Tetons
Wind River
Wind River Range
Bighorn River
Bighorn Mts.
Powder River
Lake Oahe
Black Hills
Cheyenne River
White River
Niobrara River
North Platte River
Platte River
South Platte River
Republican River
Smoky Hill River
GREAT PLAINS
INTERIOR PLAINS
Gannett Peak 13,804 ft. (4,207 m)
Klamath River
Goose Lake
Cape Mendocino
Shasta Lake
Sacramento River
Central Valley
SIERRA NEVADA
Pyramid Lake
Lake Tahoe
GREAT BASIN
Great Salt Lake
Utah Lake
Wasatch Range
Uinta Mts.
Green River
Colorado River
Front Range
Mount Elbert 14,433 ft. (4,400 m)
Pikes Peak 14,110 ft. (4,301 m)
San Francisco Bay
Monterey Bay
San Joaquin River
Coast Ranges
Mount Whitney 14,494 ft. (4,419 m)
Death Valley
COLORADO PLATEAU
Lake Powell
San Juan River
Lake Mead
Grand Canyon
Painted Desert
San Luis Valley
Sangre De Cristo Mts.
Mojave Desert
Channel Islands
Salton Sea
Imperial Valley
Rio Grande
Canadian River
Gila River
Sonoran Desert
Gulf of California
Pecos River
Amistad Reservoir
Nueces River
45°N
40°N
35°N
30°N
125°W
120°W
To understand the relative locations of Alaska and Hawaii, as well as the vast distances separating them from the rest of the United States, see the world map.
HAWAII
Kauai
Niihau
Oahu
Molokai
Maui
Lanai
Kahoolawe
PACIFIC OCEAN
Mauna Kea 13,796 ft. (4,206 m)
Hawaii
22°N
19°N
155°W
160°W
0 75 150 Miles
0 75 150 Kilometers
Projection: Mercator
ARCTIC OCEAN
RUSSIA
Bering Strait
Arctic Circle
BROOKS RANGE
Yukon River
Tanana River
St. Lawrence Island
St. Matthew Island
Nunivak Island
Bering Sea
Kuskokwim River
ALASKA RANGE
Mount McKinley 20,320 ft. (6,194 m)
CANADA
Attu Island
Gulf of Alaska
Kodiak Island
Alexander Archipelago
PACIFIC OCEAN
0 250 500 Miles
0 250 500 Kilometers
Projection: Albers Equal Area
55°N
50°N
170°E
180°
170°W
160°W
150°W
140°W

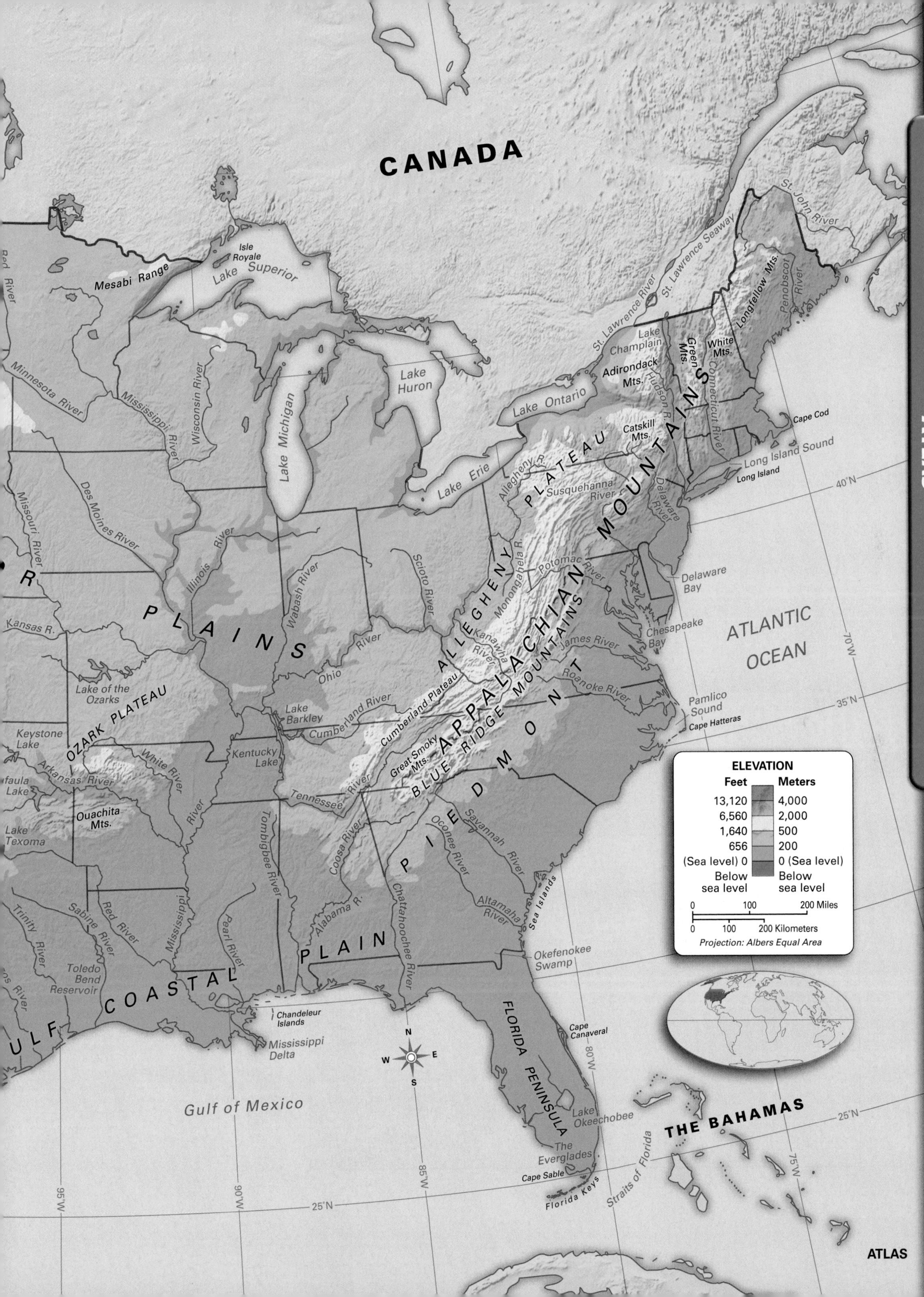
CANADA
Isle Royale
Lake Superior
Mesabi Range
Red River
Minnesota River
Mississippi River
Wisconsin River
Lake Michigan
Lake Huron
Lake Ontario
Lake Erie
St. Lawrence River
St. Lawrence Seaway
St. John River
Penobscot River
Longfellow Mts.
White Mts.
Green Mts.
Lake Champlain
Adirondack Mts.
Hudson R.
Connecticut River
Catskill Mts.
Cape Cod
Long Island Sound
Long Island
40°N
PLATEAU
Allegheny R.
Susquehanna River
Delaware River
MOUNTAINS
Missouri River
Des Moines River
Illinois River
Wabash River
Scioto River
Monongahela R.
ALLEGHENY
Potomac River
Delaware Bay
ATLANTIC OCEAN
Chesapeake Bay
James River
Kanawha River
Ohio River
PLAINS
Kansas R.
Lake of the Ozarks
OZARK PLATEAU
Keystone Lake
Arkansas River
White River
Lake Barkley
Cumberland River
Cumberland Plateau
APPALACHIAN
BLUE RIDGE MOUNTAINS
Great Smoky Mts.
PIEDMONT
Roanoke River
Pamlico Sound
Cape Hatteras
35°N
70°W
Kentucky Lake
Tennessee River
Ouachita Mts.
Lake Texoma
Tombigbee River
Coosa River
Oconee River
Savannah River
Alabama R.
Chattahoochee River
Altamaha River
Sea Islands
Trinity River
Sabine River
Red River
Mississippi River
Pearl River
Toledo Bend Reservoir
GULF COASTAL PLAIN
Okefenokee Swamp
Chandeleur Islands
Mississippi Delta
FLORIDA PENINSULA
Cape Canaveral
N
E
S
W
Gulf of Mexico
Lake Okeechobee
The Everglades
Cape Sable
Florida Keys
Straits of Florida
THE BAHAMAS
25°N
95°W
90°W
85°W
80°W
75°W
ELEVATION
Feet
Meters
13,120
6,560
1,640
656
(Sea level) 0
Below sea level
4,000
2,000
500
200
0 (Sea level)
Below sea level
0
100
200 Miles
0
100
200 Kilometers
Projection: Albers Equal Area

World: Political

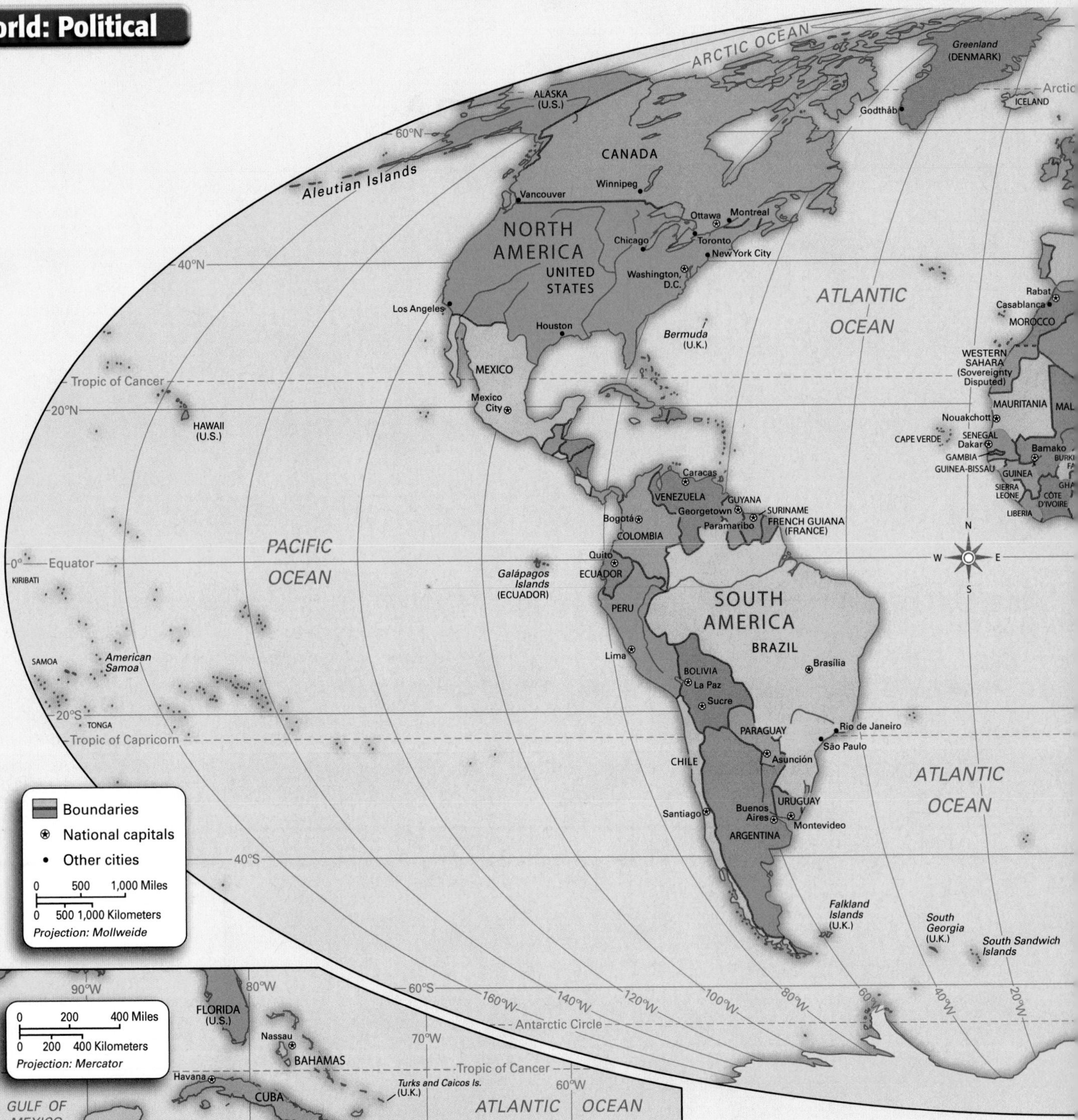

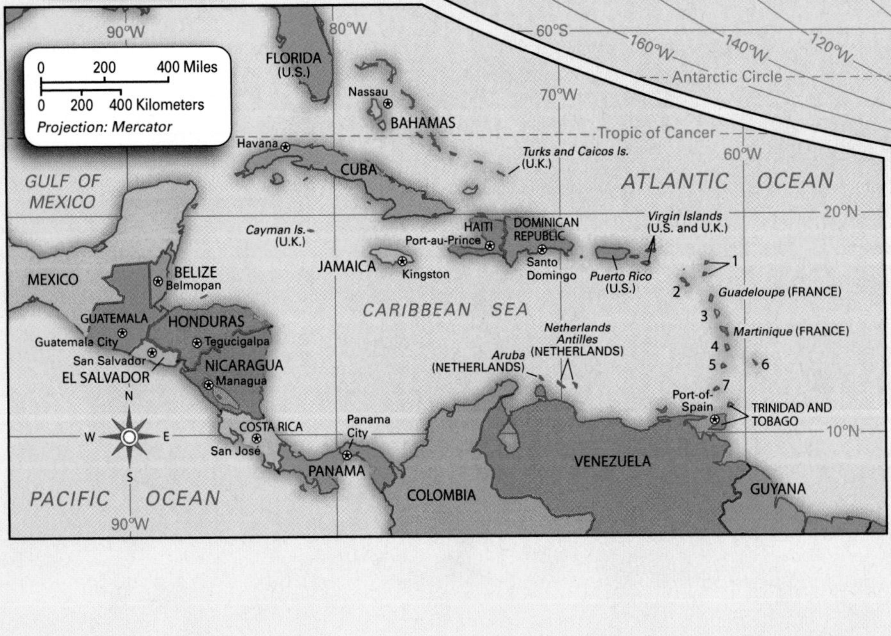

COUNTRY	CAPITAL
1 Antigua and Barbuda	St. Johns
2 St. Kitts and Nevis	Basseterre
3 Dominica	Roseau
4 St. Lucia	Castries
5 St. Vincent and the Grenadines	Kingstown
6 Barbados	Bridgetown
7 Grenada	St. George's

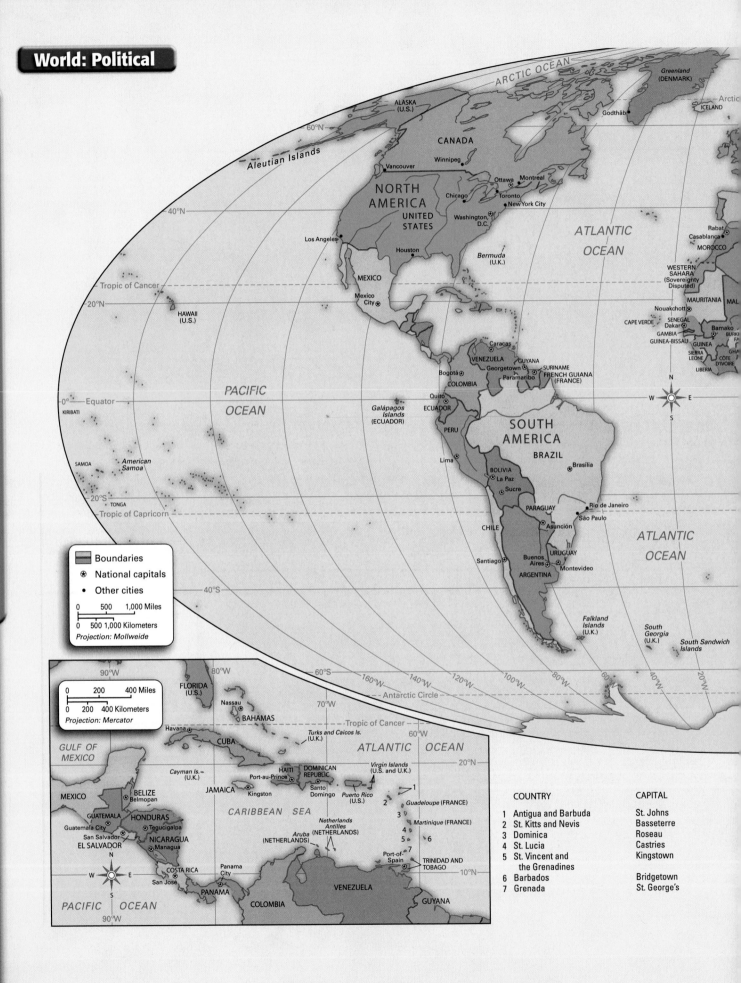

COUNTRY		CAPITAL
1	Czech Republic	Prague
2	Slovakia	Bratislava
3	Slovenia	Ljubljana
4	Croatia	Zagreb
5	Bosnia and Herzegovina	Sarajevo
6	Macedonia	Skopje
7	Serbia	Belgrade
8	Montenegro	Podgorica
9	Lithuania	Vilnius
10	Latvia	Riga
11	Estonia	Tallinn
12	Kosovo	Pristina

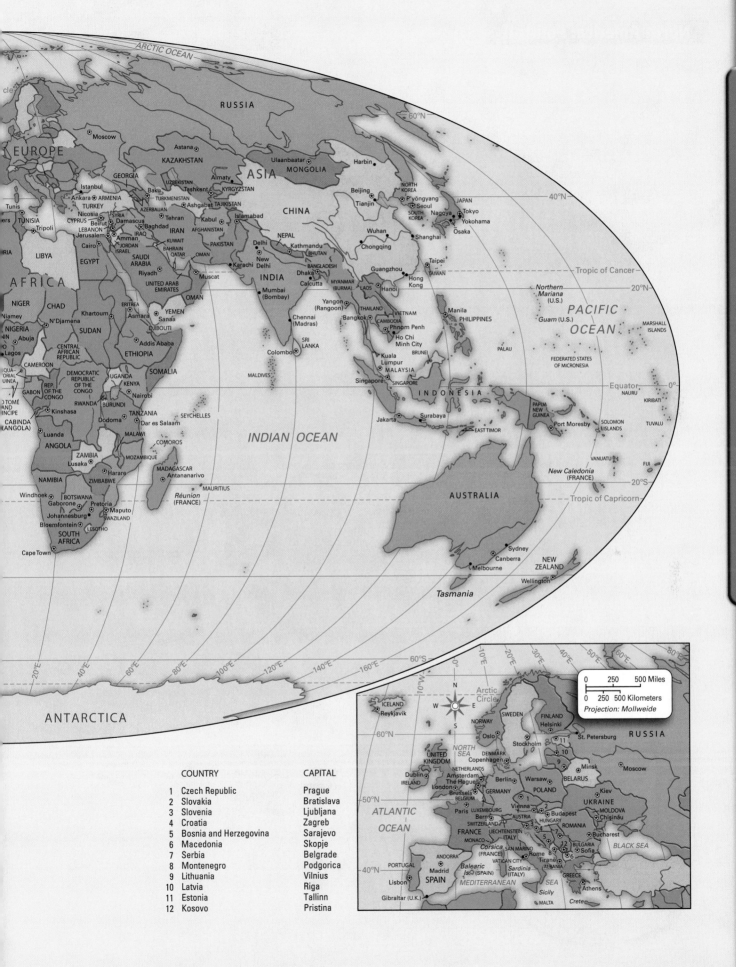

North America: Political

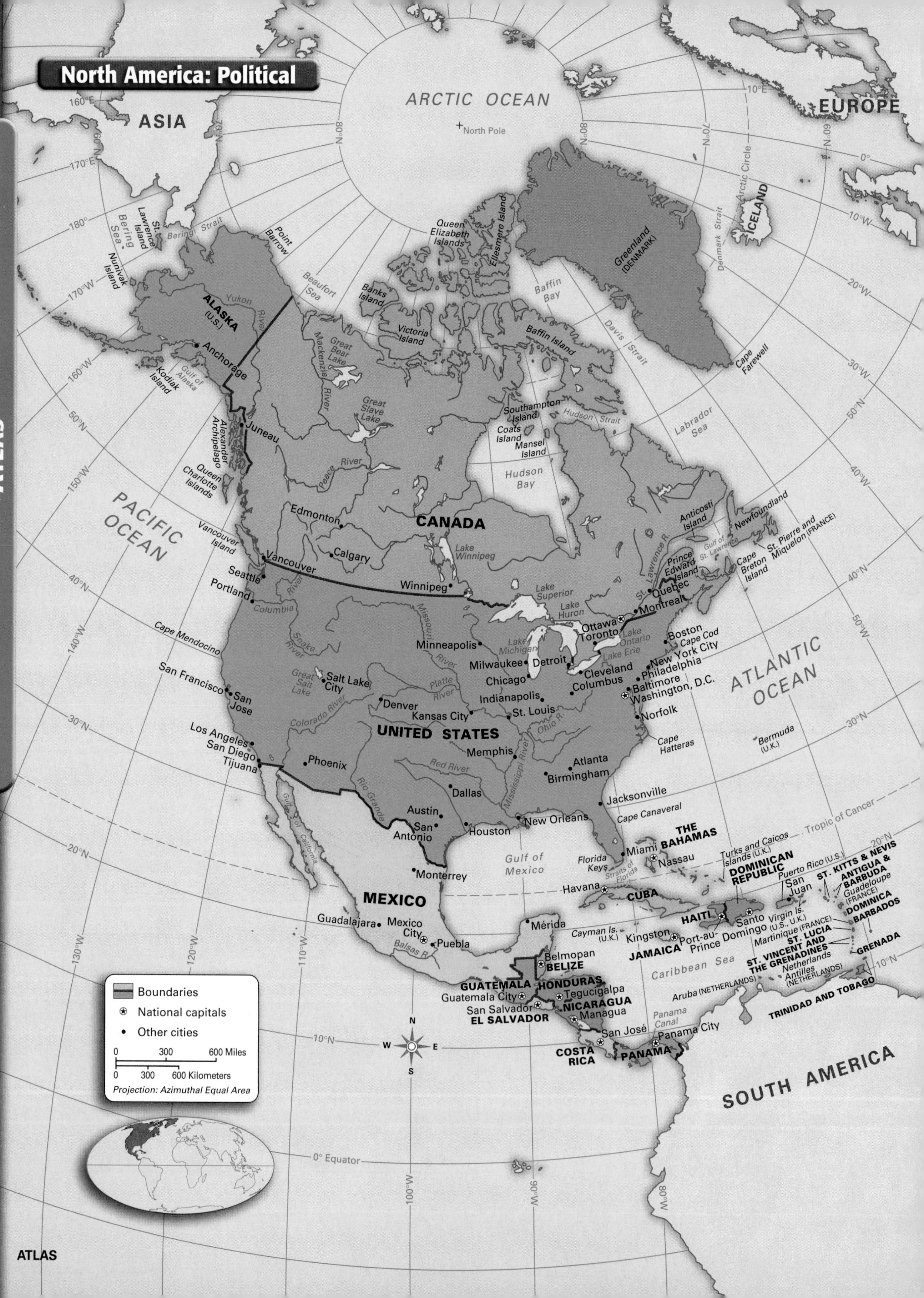
ARCTIC OCEAN
North Pole
ASIA
EUROPE
PACIFIC OCEAN
ATLANTIC OCEAN
SOUTH AMERICA
CANADA
UNITED STATES
MEXICO
ALASKA (U.S.)
Greenland (DENMARK)
ICELAND
Bering Sea
Bering Strait
St. Lawrence Island
Nunivak Island
Point Barrow
Beaufort Sea
Yukon River
Anchorage
Kodiak Island
Gulf of Alaska
Juneau
Alexander Archipelago
Queen Charlotte Islands
Vancouver Island
Banks Island
Victoria Island
Queen Elizabeth Islands
Ellesmere Island
Baffin Bay
Baffin Island
Davis Strait
Denmark Strait
Arctic Circle
Cape Farewell
Labrador Sea
Hudson Strait
Southampton Island
Coats Island
Mansel Island
Hudson Bay
Mackenzie River
Great Bear Lake
Great Slave Lake
Peace River
Edmonton
Calgary
Vancouver
Seattle
Portland
Columbia River
Snake River
Lake Winnipeg
Winnipeg
Missouri River
Lake Superior
Lake Huron
Lake Michigan
Lake Ontario
Lake Erie
Ottawa
Toronto
Montreal
Quebec
St. Lawrence R.
Anticosti Island
Gulf of St. Lawrence
Prince Edward Island
Cape Breton Island
Newfoundland
St. Pierre and Miquelon (FRANCE)
Cape Mendocino
San Francisco
San Jose
Great Salt Lake
Salt Lake City
Platte River
Denver
Kansas City
Minneapolis
Milwaukee
Detroit
Chicago
Cleveland
Columbus
Indianapolis
St. Louis
Ohio R.
Boston
Cape Cod
New York City
Philadelphia
Baltimore
Washington, D.C.
Norfolk
Cape Hatteras
Bermuda (U.K.)
Colorado River
Los Angeles
San Diego
Tijuana
Phoenix
Memphis
Mississippi River
Atlanta
Birmingham
Red River
Rio Grande
Dallas
Austin
San Antonio
Houston
New Orleans
Jacksonville
Cape Canaveral
Tropic of Cancer
Gulf of California
Monterrey
Gulf of Mexico
Florida Keys
Straits of Florida
Miami
THE BAHAMAS
Nassau
Turks and Caicos Islands (U.K.)
DOMINICAN REPUBLIC
Puerto Rico (U.S.)
San Juan
ST. KITTS & NEVIS
ANTIGUA & BARBUDA
Guadeloupe (FRANCE)
DOMINICA
BARBADOS
Havana
CUBA
HAITI
Santo Domingo
Port-au-Prince
Virgin Is. (U.S., U.K.)
Martinique (FRANCE)
ST. LUCIA
ST. VINCENT AND THE GRENADINES
GRENADA
Netherlands Antilles (NETHERLANDS)
Aruba (NETHERLANDS)
TRINIDAD AND TOBAGO
Cayman Is. (U.K.)
Kingston
JAMAICA
Caribbean Sea
Mérida
Guadalajara
Mexico City
Puebla
Balsas R.
Belmopan
BELIZE
GUATEMALA
Guatemala City
HONDURAS
Tegucigalpa
San Salvador
EL SALVADOR
NICARAGUA
Managua
San José
COSTA RICA
Panama Canal
Panama City
PANAMA
Boundaries
National capitals
Other cities
0 300 600 Miles
0 300 600 Kilometers
Projection: Azimuthal Equal Area
N
S
E
W
0° Equator
10°N
20°N
30°N
40°N
50°N
100°W
90°W
80°W
110°W
120°W
130°W
140°W
150°W
160°W
170°W
180°
170°E
160°E

South America: Political

CENTRAL AMERICA
Caribbean Sea
Barranquilla
Cartagena
Caracas
Lake Maracaibo
VENEZUELA
Orinoco River
Georgetown
Paramaribo
Cayenne
GUYANA
SURINAME
FRENCH GUIANA (FRANCE)
ATLANTIC OCEAN
Medellín
Bogotá
COLOMBIA
Cali
Malpelo Island (COLOMBIA)
Río Negro
Quito
ECUADOR
Guayaquil
Galápagos Islands (ECUADOR)
Equator
Amazon River
Belém
PERU
BRAZIL
Marañón River
Ucayali River
Trujillo
Recife
Callao
Lima
São Francisco River
Salvador
Brasília
Lake Titicaca
La Paz
Arequipa
PACIFIC OCEAN
Lake Poopó
BOLIVIA
Sucre
Paraguay River
Belo Horizonte
PARAGUAY
Campinas
São Paulo
Rio de Janeiro
Asunción
Curitiba
Tropic of Capricorn
San Ambrosio Island (CHILE)
San Félix Island (CHILE)
CHILE
Paraná River
Uruguay River
Pôrto Alegre
Córdoba
Juan Fernández Islands (CHILE)
Valparaíso
Santiago
Rosario
URUGUAY
Buenos Aires
Montevideo
Río de la Plata
ATLANTIC OCEAN
ARGENTINA
Boundaries
National capitals
Other cities
0 250 500 Miles
0 250 500 Kilometers
Projection: Azimuthal Equal Area
Strait of Magellan
Falkland Islands (U.K.)
Tierra del Fuego
South Georgia Island (U.K.)
N
S
E
W
20°N
10°N
0°
10°S
20°S
30°S
40°S
50°S
90°W
80°W
70°W
60°W
50°W
40°W
30°W
20°W

Europe: Political

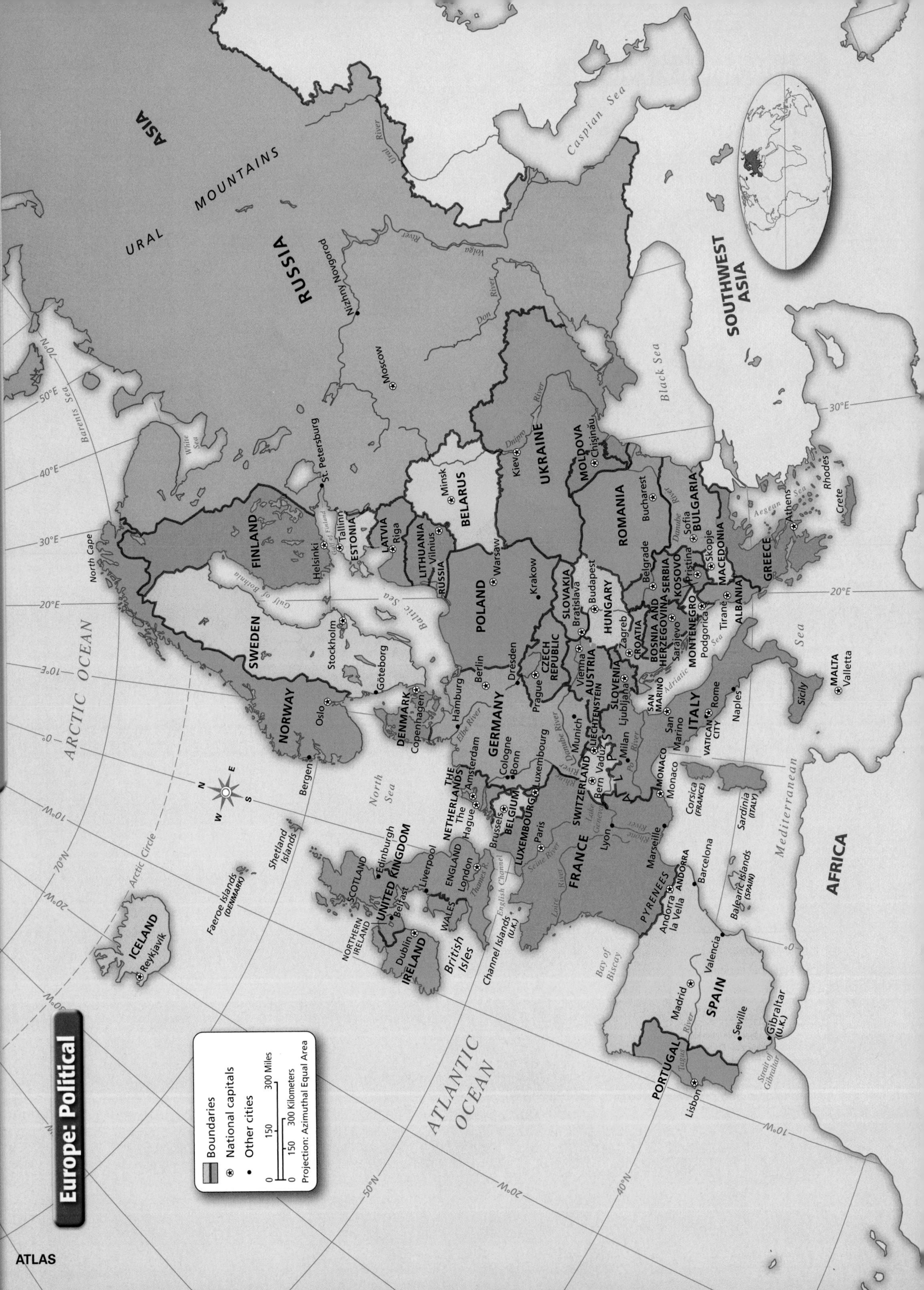

Asia: Political

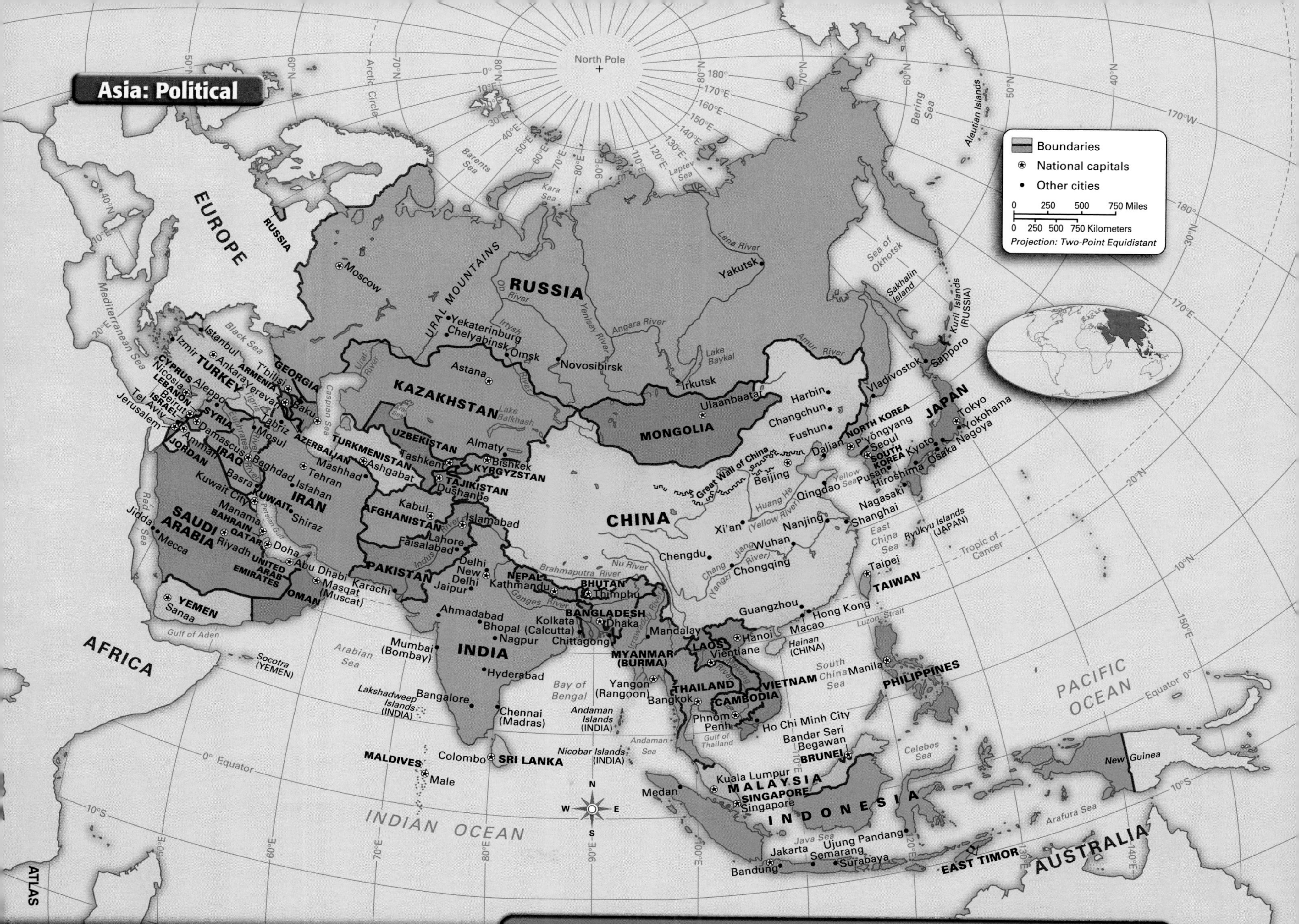
Boundaries
National capitals
Other cities
0 250 500 750 Miles
0 250 500 750 Kilometers
Projection: Two-Point Equidistant
North Pole
EUROPE
RUSSIA
AFRICA
Mediterranean Sea
Black Sea
Caspian Sea
Red Sea
Persian Gulf
Gulf of Aden
Arabian Sea
Bay of Bengal
Andaman Sea
Gulf of Thailand
South China Sea
East China Sea
Yellow Sea
Sea of Okhotsk
Bering Sea
Barents Sea
Kara Sea
Laptev Sea
Celebes Sea
Java Sea
Arafura Sea
PACIFIC OCEAN
INDIAN OCEAN
URAL MOUNTAINS
Ob River
Irtysh River
Yenisey River
Angara River
Lena River
Amur River
Ural River
Lake Baykal
Lake Balkhash
Aral Sea
Tigris River
Euphrates River
Indus River
Ganges River
Brahmaputra River
Nu River
Irrawaddy River
Mekong River
Huang He (Yellow River)
Chang Jiang (Yangzi River)
Great Wall of China
Aleutian Islands
Kuril Islands (RUSSIA)
Sakhalin Island
Ryukyu Islands (JAPAN)
Hainan (CHINA)
Socotra (YEMEN)
Lakshadweep Islands (INDIA)
Andaman Islands (INDIA)
Nicobar Islands (INDIA)
New Guinea
Luzon Strait
Arctic Circle
Tropic of Cancer
0° Equator
Moscow
Yekaterinburg
Chelyabinsk
Omsk
Novosibirsk
Irkutsk
Yakutsk
Vladivostok
Sapporo
KAZAKHSTAN
Astana
Almaty
UZBEKISTAN
Tashkent
TURKMENISTAN
Ashgabat
KYRGYZSTAN
Bishkek
TAJIKISTAN
Dushanbe
AFGHANISTAN
Kabul
PAKISTAN
Islamabad
Lahore
Faisalabad
Karachi
GEORGIA
T'bilisi
ARMENIA
Yerevan
AZERBAIJAN
Baku
TURKEY
Istanbul
Ankara
Izmir
CYPRUS
Nicosia
SYRIA
Aleppo
Damascus
LEBANON
Beirut
ISRAEL
Tel Aviv
Jerusalem
JORDAN
Amman
IRAQ
Mosul
Baghdad
Basra
IRAN
Tabriz
Tehran
Mashhad
Isfahan
Shiraz
KUWAIT
Kuwait City
BAHRAIN
Manama
QATAR
Doha
SAUDI ARABIA
Riyadh
Jidda
Mecca
UNITED ARAB EMIRATES
Abu Dhabi
OMAN
Masqat (Muscat)
YEMEN
Sanaa
INDIA
New Delhi
Delhi
Jaipur
Ahmadabad
Bhopal
Nagpur
Mumbai (Bombay)
Hyderabad
Bangalore
Chennai (Madras)
Kolkata (Calcutta)
NEPAL
Kathmandu
BHUTAN
Thimphu
BANGLADESH
Dhaka
Chittagong
SRI LANKA
Colombo
MALDIVES
Male
MONGOLIA
Ulaanbaatar
CHINA
Harbin
Changchun
Fushun
Dalian
Beijing
Qingdao
Xi'an
Nanjing
Shanghai
Wuhan
Chengdu
Chongqing
Guangzhou
Hong Kong
Macao
NORTH KOREA
P'yŏngyang
SOUTH KOREA
Seoul
Pusan
JAPAN
Tokyo
Yokohama
Kyoto
Osaka
Nagoya
Hiroshima
Nagasaki
TAIWAN
Taipei
MYANMAR (BURMA)
Mandalay
Yangon (Rangoon)
THAILAND
Bangkok
LAOS
Vientiane
VIETNAM
Hanoi
Ho Chi Minh City
CAMBODIA
Phnom Penh
PHILIPPINES
Manila
MALAYSIA
Kuala Lumpur
SINGAPORE
Singapore
BRUNEI
Bandar Seri Begawan
INDONESIA
Medan
Jakarta
Bandung
Semarang
Surabaya
Ujung Pandang
EAST TIMOR
AUSTRALIA
N
E
S
W

Africa: Political

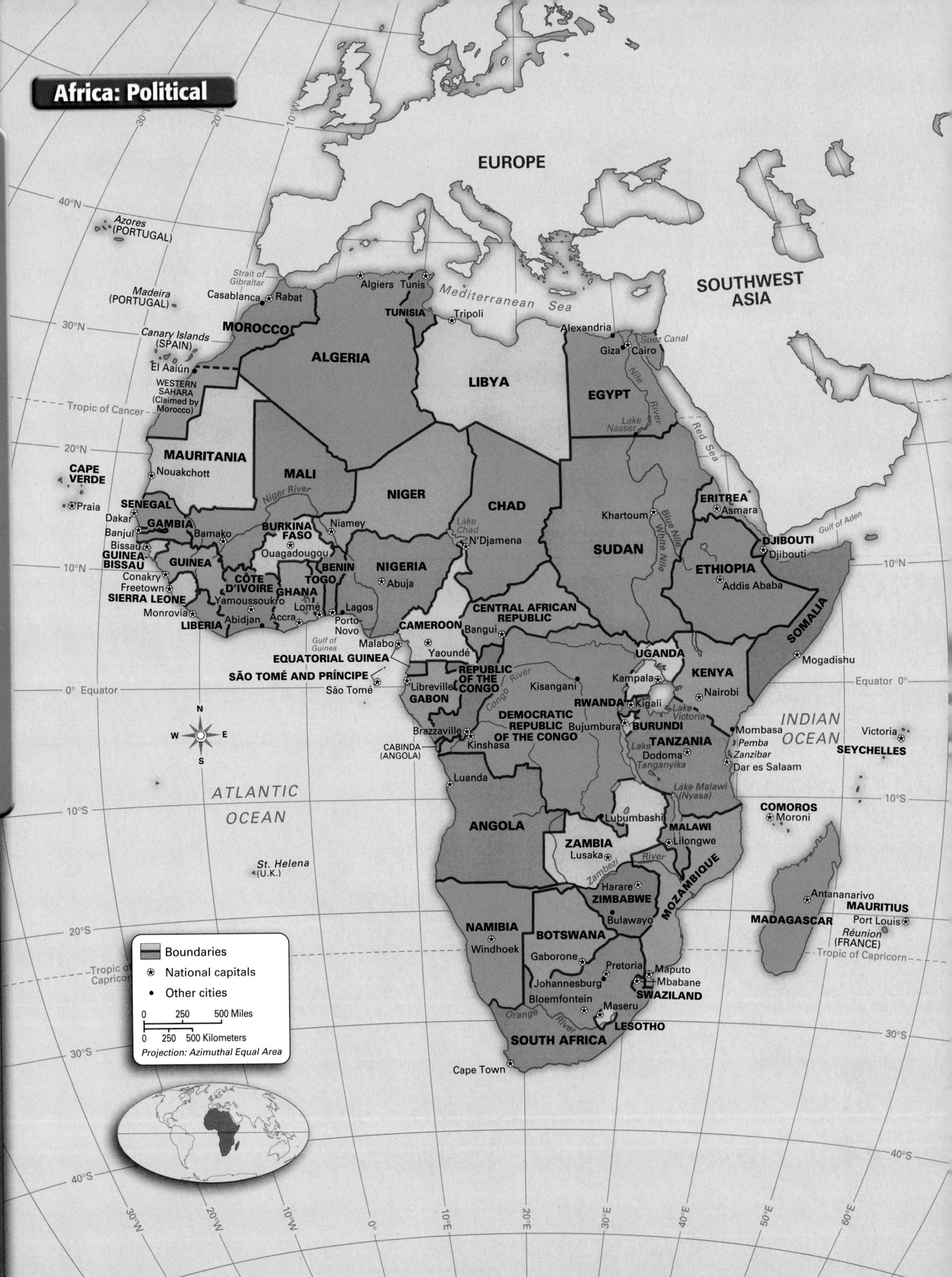
EUROPE
SOUTHWEST ASIA
Azores (PORTUGAL)
Madeira (PORTUGAL)
Canary Islands (SPAIN)
Strait of Gibraltar
Mediterranean Sea
Suez Canal
Red Sea
Gulf of Aden
Nile River
Lake Nasser
Blue Nile
White Nile
Lake Chad
Niger River
Congo River
Lake Victoria
Lake Tanganyika
Lake Malawi (Nyasa)
Zambezi River
Orange River
Gulf of Guinea
ATLANTIC OCEAN
INDIAN OCEAN
St. Helena (U.K.)
Tropic of Cancer
Tropic of Capricorn
Equator 0°
40°N
30°N
20°N
10°N
10°S
20°S
30°S
40°S
30°W
20°W
10°W
0°
10°E
20°E
30°E
40°E
50°E
60°E
N
S
E
W
MOROCCO
Casablanca
Rabat
ALGERIA
Algiers
TUNISIA
Tunis
LIBYA
Tripoli
EGYPT
Alexandria
Giza
Cairo
El Aaiún
WESTERN SAHARA (Claimed by Morocco)
MAURITANIA
Nouakchott
CAPE VERDE
Praia
MALI
Bamako
NIGER
Niamey
CHAD
N'Djamena
SUDAN
Khartoum
ERITREA
Asmara
DJIBOUTI
Djibouti
ETHIOPIA
Addis Ababa
SOMALIA
Mogadishu
SENEGAL
Dakar
GAMBIA
Banjul
GUINEA-BISSAU
Bissau
GUINEA
Conakry
SIERRA LEONE
Freetown
LIBERIA
Monrovia
CÔTE D'IVOIRE
Yamoussoukro
Abidjan
BURKINA FASO
Ouagadougou
GHANA
Accra
TOGO
Lomé
BENIN
Porto-Novo
NIGERIA
Abuja
Lagos
CAMEROON
Yaoundé
CENTRAL AFRICAN REPUBLIC
Bangui
EQUATORIAL GUINEA
Malabo
SÃO TOMÉ AND PRÍNCIPE
São Tomé
GABON
Libreville
REPUBLIC OF THE CONGO
Brazzaville
DEMOCRATIC REPUBLIC OF THE CONGO
Kinshasa
Kisangani
Lubumbashi
CABINDA (ANGOLA)
UGANDA
Kampala
KENYA
Nairobi
Mombasa
RWANDA
Kigali
BURUNDI
Bujumbura
TANZANIA
Dodoma
Dar es Salaam
Pemba
Zanzibar
SEYCHELLES
Victoria
COMOROS
Moroni
ANGOLA
Luanda
ZAMBIA
Lusaka
MALAWI
Lilongwe
MOZAMBIQUE
Maputo
ZIMBABWE
Harare
Bulawayo
NAMIBIA
Windhoek
BOTSWANA
Gaborone
SOUTH AFRICA
Pretoria
Johannesburg
Bloemfontein
Cape Town
SWAZILAND
Mbabane
LESOTHO
Maseru
MADAGASCAR
Antananarivo
MAURITIUS
Port Louis
Réunion (FRANCE)
Boundaries
National capitals
Other cities
0 250 500 Miles
0 250 500 Kilometers
Projection: Azimuthal Equal Area

Australia and New Zealand: Political

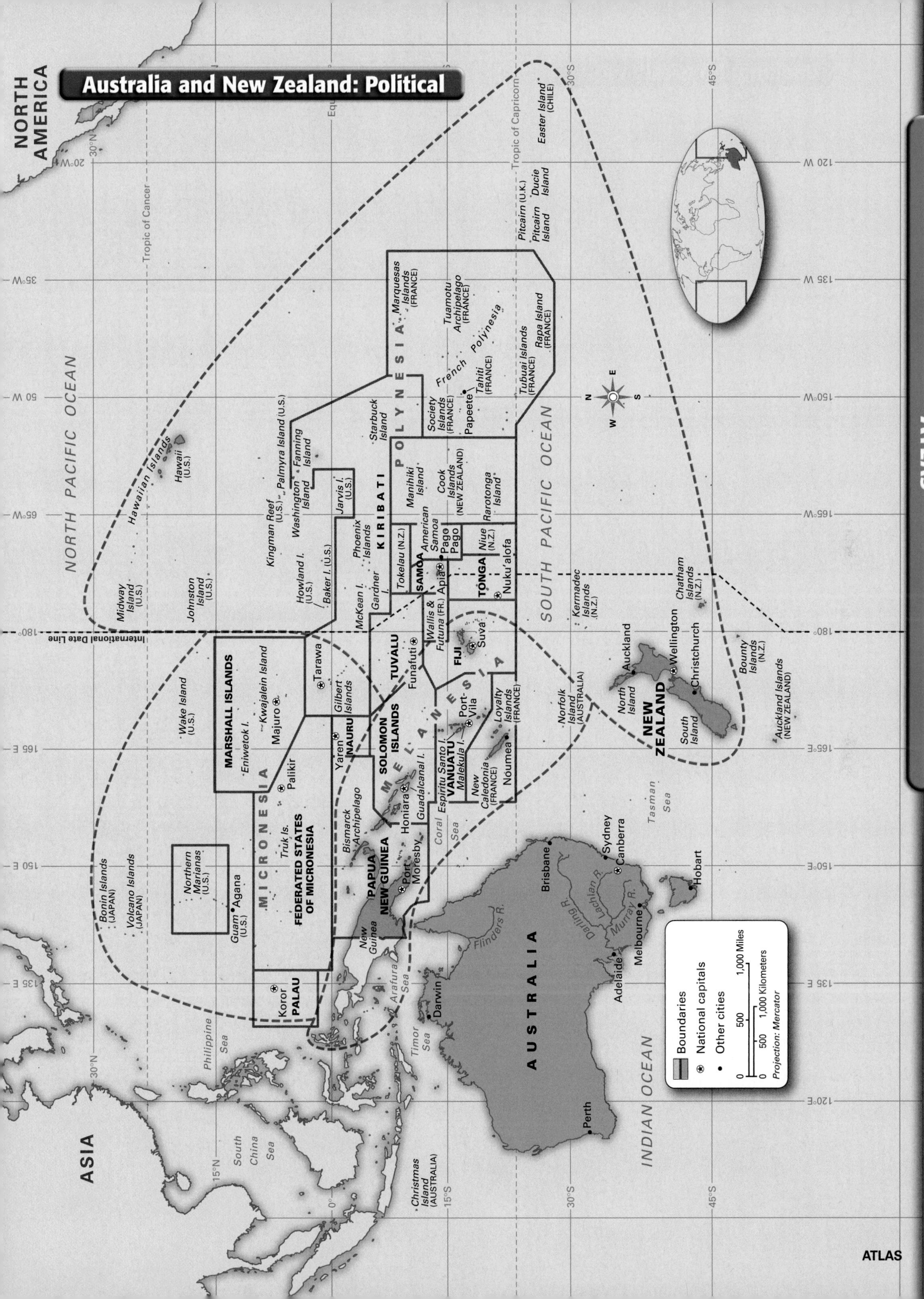

NORTH AMERICA
ASIA
AUSTRALIA
NEW ZEALAND
NORTH PACIFIC OCEAN
SOUTH PACIFIC OCEAN
INDIAN OCEAN
MICRONESIA
MELANESIA
POLYNESIA
PALAU
Koror
FEDERATED STATES OF MICRONESIA
Palikir
Truk Is.
MARSHALL ISLANDS
Majuro
Eniwetok I.
Kwajalein Island
Wake Island (U.S.)
Northern Marianas (U.S.)
Guam (U.S.)
Agana
Bonin Islands (JAPAN)
Volcano Islands (JAPAN)
Midway Island (U.S.)
Johnston Island (U.S.)
Hawaiian Islands
Hawaii (U.S.)
Kingman Reef (U.S.)
Palmyra Island (U.S.)
Washington Island
Fanning Island
Jarvis I. (U.S.)
Howland I. (U.S.)
Baker I. (U.S.)
McKean I.
Gardner I.
Phoenix Islands
KIRIBATI
Tarawa
Gilbert Islands
NAURU
Yaren
TUVALU
Funafuti
SOLOMON ISLANDS
Honiara
Guadalcanal I.
PAPUA NEW GUINEA
Port Moresby
New Guinea
Bismarck Archipelago
VANUATU
Port-Vila
Espiritu Santo I.
Malekula I.
New Caledonia (FRANCE)
Noumea
Loyalty Islands (FRANCE)
FIJI
Suva
Wallis & Futuna (FR.)
Tokelau (N.Z.)
SAMOA
Apia
American Samoa
Pago Pago
TONGA
Nuku'alofa
Niue (N.Z.)
Rarotonga Island
Cook Islands (NEW ZEALAND)
Manihiki Island
Starbuck Island
Society Islands (FRANCE)
Papeete
Tahiti (FRANCE)
French Polynesia
Tuamotu Archipelago (FRANCE)
Marquesas Islands (FRANCE)
Tubuai Islands (FRANCE)
Rapa Island (FRANCE)
Pitcairn (U.K.)
Pitcairn Island
Ducie Island
Easter Island (CHILE)
Kermadec Islands (N.Z.)
Chatham Islands (N.Z.)
Bounty Islands (N.Z.)
Auckland Islands (NEW ZEALAND)
Norfolk Island (AUSTRALIA)
North Island
South Island
Auckland
Wellington
Christchurch
Tasman Sea
Coral Sea
Arafura Sea
Timor Sea
Philippine Sea
South China Sea
Christmas Island (AUSTRALIA)
Darwin
Perth
Adelaide
Melbourne
Canberra
Sydney
Brisbane
Hobart
Flinders R.
Darling R.
Lachlan R.
Murray R.
International Date Line
Tropic of Cancer
Tropic of Capricorn
Equator
Boundaries
National capitals
Other cities
0 500 1,000 Miles
0 500 1,000 Kilometers
Projection: Mercator
N
E
S
W

Plessy v. *Ferguson* (1896)

Significance This case upheld the constitutionality of racial segregation by ruling that separate facilities for different races were legal as long as those facilities were equal to one another. This case provided a legal justification for racial segregation for nearly 60 years until it was overturned by *Brown* v. *Board of Education* in 1954.

Background An 1890 Louisiana law required that all railway companies in the state use "separate-but-equal" railcars for white and African American passengers. A group of citizens in New Orleans banded together to challenge the law and chose Homer Plessy to test the law in 1892. Plessy took a seat in a whites-only coach, and when he refused to move, he was arrested. Plessy eventually sought review by the U.S. Supreme Court, claiming that the Louisiana law violated his Fourteenth Amendment right to equal protection.

Decision This case was decided on May 18, 1896, by a vote of 7 to 1. Justice Henry Billings Brown spoke for the Court, which upheld the constitutionality of the Louisiana law that segregated railcars. Justice John M. Harlan dissented, arguing that the Constitution should not be interpreted in ways that recognize class or racial distinctions.

Northern Securities Co. v. *United States* (1904)

Significance In this ruling the Court declared that the federal government had the right to break up companies if their formation was illegal, whether or not dissolving the company would have a harmful impact on the business community.

Background The Northern Securities Company held stock in several major railroads. Although President Theodore Roosevelt claimed the company was a trust and therefore illegal under the Sherman Antitrust Act, some disagreed that the idea of trusts extended into the realm of owning stocks.

Decision In a 5-to-4 decision, the Court ruled that the formation of the company was illegal, and that the federal government had the power to disband it. Writing for the majority, Justice John Marshall Harlan said, "every corporation created by a state is necessarily subject to the supreme law of the land," meaning the federal government.

Lochner v. *New York* (1905)

Significance This decision established the Supreme Court's role in overseeing state regulations. For more than 30 years, Lochner was often used as a precedent in striking down state laws such as minimum-wage laws, child labor laws, and regulations placed on the banking and transportation industries.

Background In 1895 the state of New York passed a labor law limiting bakers to working no more than 10 hours per day or 60 hours per week. The purpose of the law was to protect the health of bakers, who worked in hot and damp conditions and breathed in large quantities of flour dust. In 1902 Joseph Lochner, the owner of a small bakery in New York, claimed that the state law violated his Fourteenth Amendment rights by unfairly depriving him of the liberty to make contracts with employees. This case went to the U.S. Supreme Court.

Decision This case was decided on April 17, 1905, by a vote of 5 to 4 in favor of Lochner. The Supreme Court judged that the Fourteenth Amendment protected the right to sell and buy labor, and that any state law restricting that right was unconstitutional. The Court rejected the argument that the limited workday and workweek were necessary to protect the health of bakery workers.

Muller v. *Oregon* (1908)

Significance A landmark for cases involving social reform, this decision established the Court's recognition of social and economic conditions (in this case, women's health) as a factor in making laws.

Background In 1903 Oregon passed a law limiting workdays to 10 hours for female workers in laundries and factories. In 1905 Curt Muller's Grand Laundry was found guilty of breaking this law. Muller appealed, claiming that the state law violated his freedom of contract (the Supreme Court had upheld a similar claim that year in *Lochner* v. *New York*). When this case came to the Court, the National Consumers' League hired lawyer Louis D. Brandeis to present Oregon's argument. Brandeis argued that the Court had already defended the state's police power to protect its citizens' health, safety, and welfare.

Decision This case was decided on February 24, 1908, by a vote of 9 to 0 upholding the Oregon law. The Court agreed that women's well-being was in the state's public interest and that the 10-hour law was a valid way to protect their well-being.

Schechter Poultry Corporation v. *United States* (1935)

Significance This ruling declared that the United States could not regulate businesses that operated only within one state. It dealt a severe blow to President Franklin Roosevelt's New Deal.

Background In an attempt to lessen the effects of the Great Depression, Roosevelt encouraged Congress to pass a Recovery Act that set a minimum wage and restricted working hours. The Schechter Poultry Corporation, which operated only within New York City, maintained that the federal government did not have a constitutional right to regulate its businesses practices.

Decision In a unanimous decision, the Court upheld the Schechter Corporation's claim. Chief Justice Charles Evans Hughes wrote the opinion, which stated that the transactions in the case—wages, salaries, and working hours—were a local concern outside of the scope of federal regulation.

Korematsu v. *United States* (1944)

Significance This case addressed the question of whether government action that treats a racial group differently from other people violates the Equal Protection Clause of the Fourteenth Amendment. The ruling in the case held that distinctions based on race are "inherently suspect," and that laws and rules based on race must withstand "strict scrutiny" by the courts. The Court still applies the "strict scrutiny" standard today to cases involving race and other groups.

Background When the United States declared war on Japan in 1941, about 112,000 Japanese Americans lived on the West Coast. About 70,000 of these Japanese Americans were citizens. In 1942 the U.S. military was afraid that these people could not be trusted in wartime. They ordered most of the Japanese Americans to move to special camps far from their homes. Fred Korematsu, a Japanese American and an American citizen, did not go to the camps as ordered. He stayed in California and was arrested. He was sent to a camp in Utah. Korematsu then sued, claiming that the government acted illegally when it sent people of Japanese descent to camps.

Decision By a 6-to-3 margin, the Supreme Court said the orders moving the Japanese-Americans into the camps were constitutional. Justice Hugo Black wrote the opinion for the Court. He said that the unusual demands of wartime security justified the orders. However, he made it clear that distinctions based on race are "inherently suspect," and that laws based on race must withstand "strict scrutiny" by the courts. Justice Robert H. Jackson dissented; he wrote that Korematsu was "convicted of an act not commonly a crime ... being present in the state [where] he is a citizen, near where he was born, and where all his life he has lived." Justice Frank Murphy, another dissenter, said the military order was based on racial prejudice.

Brown v. *Board of Education* (1954)

Significance This ruling reversed the Supreme Court's earlier position on segregation set by *Plessy* v. *Ferguson* (1896). The decision also inspired Congress and the federal courts to help carry out further civil rights reforms for African Americans.

Background Beginning in the 1930s, the National Association for the Advancement of Colored People (NAACP) began using the courts to challenge racial segregation in public education. In 1952 the NAACP took a number of school segregation cases to the Supreme Court. These included the Brown family's suit against the school board of Topeka, Kansas, over its "separate-but-equal" policy.

Decision This case was decided on May 17, 1954, by a vote of 9 to 0. Chief Justice Earl Warren spoke for the unanimous Court, which ruled that segregation in public education created inequality. The Court held that racial segregation in public schools was by nature unequal, even if the school facilities were equal. The Court noted that such segregation created feelings of inferiority that could not be undone. Therefore, enforced separation of the races in public education is unconstitutional.

Watkins v. *United States* (1957)

Significance The decision limited the inquiry powers of Congress. It was expected not to engage in law enforcement (an executive function), nor to act as a trial agency (a judicial function), but to inquire only as far as was necessary for the functioning of Congress.

Background Watkins was a labor union officer who appeared before the House Un-American Activities Committee during the 1950s Red Scare. Although he was willing to answer personal questions about himself and others whom he knew to be members of the Communist Party, he would not answer questions about past members of the Communist Party. He was therefore held in contempt of Congress.

Decision In a vote of 6 to 1 handed down on June 17, 1957, the Court threw out the charge of contempt against Watkins. Congress, it said, did not have the right to invade the private lives of individuals.

Mapp v. *Ohio* (1961)

Significance In this ruling the Court declared that evidence discovered in the process of an illegal search could not be used in state courts.

Background While searching for a bombing suspect, police found evidence of a separate crime in the house of Dollree Mapp. The police did not have permission to enter the home, nor did they have a search warrant. Upon conviction for the separate crime, Mapp appealed her case to the Supreme Court.

Decision In a 5-to-3 decision, the Court stated that convictions based on illegally obtained evidence must be overturned. Justice Tom Clark wrote for the majority, "all evidence obtained by searches and seizures in violation of the Constitution is ... inadmissible in a state court."

Baker v. *Carr* (1962)

Significance Through this decision, the Court ruled that the judiciary branch may involve itself in hearing cases about political matters.

Background Voters from Tennessee sued their state in federal court, arguing that the way the state drew the boundary lines between representative districts created unequal representation within the legislature, and therefore unequal protection under the laws of the state. Tennessee argued that the federal court did not have the jurisdiction to hear the case.

Decision By a 6-to-2 margin, the Court decided that the federal court did have the right to hear the case and that the voters had the right to sue over the issue. Writing for the majority, Justice William Brennan said that the voters "are entitled to a trial and a decision" on whether they were denied equal protection.

Engel v. *Vitale* (1962)

Significance This case deals with the specific issue of organized prayer in schools and the broader issue of the proper relationship between government and religion under the First Amendment. The question in the case was whether a state violates the First Amendment when it composes a prayer that students must say at the beginning of each school day.

Background The state of New York recommended that public schools in the state begin the day by having students recite a prayer written by the state government. A group of parents sued to stop the official prayer, saying that it was contrary to their beliefs and their children's beliefs. They believed the law was unconstitutional because it "established" (officially supported) religion. Though students were permitted to remain silent, the parents claimed that there would always be pressure on students to pray.

Decision By a 6-to-1 margin (two justices did not take part in the case), the Court agreed with the parents. It struck down the state law. Justice Hugo Black wrote for the decision for the majority. He pointed out that the prayer was clearly religious. He said that under the First Amendment, "it is no part of the business of government to compose official prayers for any group of American people to recite as part of a religious program carried on by government." Black, referring to Jefferson and Madison, said "These men knew that the First Amendment, which tried to put an end to governmental control of religion and prayer, was not written to destroy either."

Gideon v. *Wainwright* (1963)

Significance This ruling was one of several key Supreme Court decisions establishing free legal help for those who cannot otherwise afford representation in court.

Background Clarence Earl Gideon was accused of robbery in Florida. Gideon could not afford a lawyer for his trial, and the judge refused to supply him with one for free. Gideon tried to defend himself and was found guilty. He eventually appealed to the U.S. Supreme Court, claiming that the lower court's denial of a court-appointed lawyer violated his Sixth and Fourteenth Amendment rights.

Decision This case was decided on March 18, 1963, by a vote of 9 to 0 in favor of Gideon. The Court agreed that the Sixth Amendment (which protects a citizen's right to have a lawyer for his or her defense) applied to the states because it fell under the due process clause of the Fourteenth Amendment. Thus, the states are required to provide legal aid to those defendants in criminal cases who cannot afford to pay for legal representation.

Heart of Atlanta Motel v. *United States* (1964)

Significance This ruling upheld the public accommodations clause of the Civil Rights Act of 1964. It enforced the right of African Americans to receive access to the same accommodations as whites and gave Congress judicial backing for passing more civil rights legislation.

Background The owner of the Heart of Atlanta Motel routinely discriminated against African Americans. He claimed that his business was not an interstate business and therefore not subject to regulation by congressional acts.

Decision In a unanimous decision, the Court declared that as a business that served people from across state boundaries, the Heart of Atlanta Motel was in fact an interstate business and that, therefore, congressional acts did apply.

Miranda v. *Arizona* (1966)

Significance This decision ruled that an accused person's Fifth Amendment rights begin at the time of arrest. The ruling caused controversy because it made the questioning of suspects and collecting evidence more difficult for law enforcement officers.

Background In 1963 Ernesto Miranda was arrested in Arizona for a kidnapping. Miranda signed a confession and was later found guilty of the crime. The arresting police officers, however, admitted that they had not told Miranda of his right to talk with an attorney before his confession. Miranda appealed his conviction on the grounds that by not informing him of his legal rights the police had violated his Fifth Amendment right against self-incrimination.

Decision This case was decided on June 13, 1966, by a vote of 5 to 4. Chief Justice Earl Warren spoke for the Court, which ruled in Miranda's favor. The Court decided that an accused person must be given four warnings after being taken into police custody: (1) the suspect has the right to remain silent, (2) anything the suspect says can and will be used against him or her, (3) the suspect has the right to consult with an attorney and to have an attorney present during questioning, and (4) if the suspect cannot afford a lawyer, one will be provided before questioning begins.

Tinker v. *Des Moines Independent Community School District* (1969)

Significance This ruling established the extent to which American public school students can take part in political protests in their schools. The question the case raised is whether, under the First Amendment, school officials can prohibit students from wearing armbands to symbolize political protest.

Background Students in Des Moines, Iowa, decided to wear black armbands to protest the Vietnam War. Two days before the protest, the school board created a new policy. The policy stated that any student who wore an armband to school and refused to remove it would be suspended. Three students wore armbands and were suspended. They said that their First Amendment right to freedom of speech had been violated. In 1969 the United States Supreme Court decided their case.

The Decision By a 7-to-2 margin, the Court agreed with the students. Justice Abe Fortas wrote the decision for the majority. He said that students do not "shed their constitutional rights to freedom of speech ... at the schoolhouse gate." Fortas admitted that school officials had the right to set rules. However, their rules must be consistent with the First Amendment. In this case, Des Moines school officials thought their rule was justified. They feared that the protest would disrupt learning. Fortas's opinion held that wearing an armband symbolizing political protest was a form of speech called symbolic speech. Symbolic speech is conduct that expresses an idea. Symbolic speech is protected in the same manner as the spoken word. Fortas wrote that student symbolic speech could be punished only if it disrupts the learning process. Fortas also noted that school officials allowed other political symbols, such as campaign buttons, to be worn in school.

Reed v. *Reed* (1971)

Significance This ruling was the first in a century of Fourteenth Amendment decisions to say that gender discrimination violated the equal protection clause. This case was later used to strike down other statutes that discriminated against women.

Background Cecil and Sally Reed were separated. When their son died without a will, the law gave preference to Cecil to be appointed the administrator of the son's estate. Sally sued Cecil for the right to administer the estate, challenging the gender preference in the law.

Decision This case was decided on November 22, 1971, by a vote of 7 to 0. Chief Justice Warren Burger spoke for the unanimous Supreme Court. Although the Court had upheld laws based on gender preference in the past, in this case it reversed its position. The Court declared that gender discrimination violated the equal protection clause of the Fourteenth Amendment and therefore could not be the basis for a law.

New York Times v. *United States* (1971)

Significance In this ruling the Court dismissed the idea of "prior restraint," or attempting to stop an action before it happens, by the government as unconstitutional. The ruling allowed the *New York Times* to continue publishing documents that were critical of the government's handling of the Vietnam War.

Background The *New York Times* began publishing a series of papers called the Pentagon Papers that were critical of the government. The government attempted to stop publication of the papers with a court order, citing national security. Because of the national importance of the case, the Supreme Court agreed to hear the case quickly.

Decision In a 6-to-3 decision, the Court declared that the government could not stop publication of the Pentagon Papers. Although the government did have the right to stop publication if it could prove the danger to national security, the Court said that in this case the government had not met the burden of proof.

Roe v. *Wade* (1973)

Significance This ruling made abortions available to women during their first trimester of pregnancy, even when their health was not in danger.

Background The case was brought in the name of Jane Roe against the restrictive abortion laws of Texas. Until this case, states had widely varying laws about the availability of abortions, some restricting them altogether.

Decision With a 7 to 2 decision, the Court said that elective abortions must be available to any woman in her first three months of pregnancy. Because of the variety of moral opinions about when life begins, the court ruled that a fetus does not have the same rights as an infant.

United States v. *Nixon* (1974)

Significance This ruling forced President Nixon to turn over tapes of White House conversations to the congressional committee investigating his wrongdoing in the Watergate breakin. Nixon resigned shortly after.

Background Nixon had been secretly taping every conversation that took place in the Oval Office. After the president was implicated in the cover-up of the Watergate Hotel break in, Congress wanted to hear these tapes. Nixon refused to hand them over, claiming "executive privilege" to keep some information secret.

Decision In a unanimous decision, the Court ruled that Nixon must turn the tapes over to the prosecution as requested. Writing for the court, Chief Justice Warren Burger stated that finding the truth requires that courts have all the evidence they need, even if it includes presidential communication.

New Jersey v. *TLO* (1985)

Significance In this ruling, the Court declared that searches of juveniles on school grounds are not subject to the same standards of "reasonableness" and "probable cause" that protect other citizens.

Background T. L. O. was a fourteen year old who was caught smoking in the girls' bathroom of her school. A principal at the school questioned the girl and searched her purse, finding marijuana and other drug paraphernalia.

Decision In a 7 to 2 decision, the Court ruled that the suspension of the rules of "reasonable" search and seizure as defined by the Fourth Amendment and later court rulings applied only to school officials and not to law enforcement officers.

Texas v. *Johnson* (1989)

Significance This ruling answered the question of whether the First Amendment protects burning the U.S. flag as a form of symbolic speech. It deals with the limits of symbolic speech. This case is particularly important because it involves burning the flag, one of our national symbols.

Background At the 1984 Republican National Convention in Texas, Gregory Lee Johnson doused a U.S. flag with kerosene. He did this during a demonstration, as a form of protest. Johnson was convicted of violating a Texas law that made it a crime to desecrate [treat disrespectfully] the national flag. He was sentenced to one year in prison and fined $2,000. The Texas Court of Criminal Appeals reversed the conviction because, it said, Johnson's burning of the flag was a form of symbolic speech protected by the First Amendment. Texas then appealed to the U.S. Supreme Court.

Decision The Court ruled for Johnson, five to four. Justice William Brennan wrote for the majority. He said that Johnson was within his constitutional rights when he burned the U.S. flag in protest. As in Tinker v. Des Moines Independent Community School District (1969), the Court looked at the First Amendment and "symbolic speech." Brennan concluded that Johnson's burning the flag was a form of symbolic speech—like the students wearing armbands in Des Moines—is protected by the First Amendment. According to Brennan, "Government may not prohibit the expression of an idea [because it is] offensive." Chief Justice Rehnquist dissented. He said the flag is "the visible symbol embodying our Nation. It does not represent the views of any particular political party, and it does not represent any particular political philosophy. The flag is not simply another 'idea' or 'point of view' competing for recognition in the marketplace of ideas." Since this decision, several amendments banning flag burning have been proposed in Congress, but so far all have failed.

Cruzan v. *Director, Missouri Department of Health* (1990)

Significance This ruling helped define who may refuse medical treatment. Although the issue is still undecided, this case began a series of efforts to provide legislative and judicial guidelines for the "right to die."

Background The parents of comatose patient Nancy Cruzan wanted to remove her life support system. The Department of Health ruled that Cruzan had not previously made clear her desire to refuse medical treatment in the event of brain damage.

Decision By a 5-to-4 margin, the Court ruled that Cruzan's parents could not remove her from life support because she had not clearly expressed her desires previously. Writing for the majority, Chief Justice William Rehnquist stated that it was Nancy's demand to be removed from life support, not her parents' wishes, that the state must respect in such cases.

Planned Parenthood of Southeastern Pennsylvania, et al. v. *Casey* (1992)

Significance In this ruling the Court upheld its decision in *Roe* v. *Wade* of the right to elective abortion, but allowed the state of Pennsylvania to impose restrictions of notification and consent upon minors.

Background In 1988 and 1989, Pennsylvania revised its laws to require that, to receive an abortion, minors must receive consent from a parent, and married women must notify their husbands. The laws were challenged by several abortion clinics and physicians.

Decision In a 5-to-4 decision, the Court upheld its previous ruling of *Roe* v. *Wade* that women have the right to an abortion in the first trimester of pregnancy, but provided that a state may require that minors have the consent of one parent 24 hours before the procedure. The Court struck down the part of the Pennsylvania laws that required married women to notify their husbands, saying that it could be an "undue burden" upon women.

Vernonia School District v. *Acton* (1995)

Significance This ruling allowed random drug testing of minors on school property as a safety measure.

Background James Acton, a student athlete in the Vernonia School District, refused to participate in drug testing, stating that the policy invaded his right to privacy and was an illegal search and seizure.

Decision In a 6-to-3 decision, the Court ruled that while on school property, students are subject to greater control of personal rights than are free adults. Furthermore, concern over the safety of minors under governmental supervision outweighs the minimal intrusion into a student's privacy.

Bush v. *Gore* (2000)

Significance In this ruling, the question before the court was whether ballots that could not be read by voting machines should be recounted by hand. The broader issues were whether the Supreme Court can overrule state court decisions on state laws, and whether an appointed judiciary can affect the result of democratic elections.

Background The 2000 presidential election between Democrat Al Gore and Republican George Bush was very close. Ultimately, the outcome would be determined by votes in the state of Florida. People in Florida voted by punching a hole in a ballot card. The votes were counted by a machine that detected these holes. According to that count, Bush won the state of Florida by a few hundred votes. Florida's Election Commission declared that Bush had won Florida. However, about 60,000 ballots were not counted because the machines could not detect a hole in the ballot. Gore argued in the Florida Supreme Court that these votes should be recounted by hand. The Florida Supreme Court ordered counties to recount all those votes. Bush appealed to the United States Supreme Court, which issued an order to stop the recounts while it made a decision.

The Decision On December 12, 2000, the Supreme Court voted 5 to 4 to end the hand recount of votes ordered by the Florida Supreme Court. The majority said that the Florida Supreme Court had ordered a recount without setting standards for what was a valid vote. Different vote-counters might use different standards. The Court said that this inconsistency meant that votes were treated arbitrarily—based on a person's choice rather than on standards. This arbitrariness, said the Court, violated the due process clause and the equal protection clause of the Constitution. Also, the justices said that Florida law required the vote count to be finalized by December 12. The justices said that rules for recounts could not be made by that date, so they ordered election officials to stop recounting votes.

Gratz v. *Bollinger* and *Grutter* v. *Bollinger* (2003)

Significance These cases considered whether a university violates the Constitution by using race as a factor for admitting students to its undergraduate school and its law school. The ruling affects use of affirmative action programs in higher education. The decisions gave colleges guidelines as to what is permitted and what is not. The decisions were limited to higher education and may not apply to other affirmative action programs such as those for applying for a job or for a government contract.

Background Jennifer Gratz and Barbara Grutter are both white. They challenged the University of Michigan's affirmative action admissions policies. Gratz said that the university violated the Constitution by considering race as a factor in its undergraduate admissions programs. Grutter claimed that the University of Michigan Law School did so.

Decisions In Gratz, the Court ruled 6 to 3 that the undergraduate program—which gave each minority applicant an automatic 20 points toward admission—was unconstitutional. Chief Justice William Rehnquist's opinion held that the policy violated the equal protection clause because it did not consider each applicant individually. "The ... automatic distribution of 20 points has the effect of making 'the factor of race ... decisive' for virtually every minimally qualified underrepresented minority applicant." The result was different when the Court turned to the affirmative action policy of Michigan's Law School, however, which used race as one factor for admission. In Grutter, by a 5-to-4 margin, the Court held that this policy did not violate the equal protection clause. Justice Sandra Day O'Connor wrote for the majority. "Truly individualized consideration demands that race be used in a flexible, nonmechanical way ... Universities can ... consider race or ethnicity ... as a 'plus' factor [when individually considering] each and every applicant." Thus, the law school's policy was constitutional.

United States v. *American Library Association* (2003)

Significance This case deals with the constitutionality of a federal law called the Children's Internet Protection Act (CIPA). The law was designed to protect children from being exposed to pornographic Web sites while using computers in public libraries. The question before the court was this: Does a public library violate the First Amendment by installing Internet filtering software on its public computers?

Background CIPA applies to public libraries that accept federal money to help pay for Internet access. These libraries must install filtering software to block pornographic images. Some library associations sued to block these filtering requirements. They argued that by linking money and filters, the law required public libraries to violate the First Amendment's guarantees of free speech. The libraries argued that filters block some nonpornographic sites along with pornographic ones. That, they said, violates library patrons' First Amendment rights. CIPA does allow anyone to ask a librarian to unblock a specific Web site. It also allows adults to ask that the filter be turned off altogether. But, the libraries argued, people using the library would find these remedies embarrassing and impractical.

Decision In this case, Chief Justice William Rehnquist authored a plurality opinion. He explained that the law does not require any library to accept federal money. A library can choose to do without federal money. If the library makes that choice, it does not have to install Internet filters. And Rehnquist did not think that filtering software's tendency to overblock nonpornographic sites was a constitutional problem. Adult patrons could simply ask a librarian to unblock a blocked site or could have the filter disabled entirely.

The Dissents Justice John Paul Stevens viewed CIPA "as a blunt nationwide restraint on adult access to an enormous amount of valuable" and often constitutionally protected speech. Justice David Souter noted that he would have joined the plurality if the First Amendment interests raised in this case were those of children rather than those of adults.

Hamdi v. *Rumsfeld* and *Rasul* v. *Bush* (2004)

Significance These cases addressed the balance between the government's powers to fight terrorism and the Constitution's promise of due process. Each case raised a slightly different question:

1. Can the government hold American citizens for an indefinite period as "enemy combatants" and not permit them access to American courts, and

2. Do foreigners captured overseas and jailed at Guantánamo Bay, Cuba, have the right to take their cases to American courts to decide if they are being held legally?

Background In *Hamdi* v. *Rumsfeld*, Yaser Hamdi, an American citizen, was captured in Afghanistan in 2001. The U.S. military said Hamdi was an enemy combatant and claimed that "it has the authority to hold ... enemy combatants captured on the battlefield ... to prevent them from returning to the battle." Hamdi's attorney said that Hamdi deserved the due process rights that other Americans have, including a hearing in court to argue that he was not an enemy combatant.

The prisoners in *Rasul* v. *Bush* also claimed they were wrongly imprisoned. They wanted a court hearing, but Guantánamo Bay Naval Base is on Cuban soil. Cuba leases the base to the United States. In an earlier case, the Court had ruled that "if an alien is outside the country's sovereign territory, then ... the alien is not permitted access to the courts of the United States to enforce the Constitution."

Decision In *Hamdi*, the Court ruled 6 to 3 that Hamdi had a right to a hearing. Justice Sandra Day O'Connor wrote that the Court has "made clear that a state of war is not a blank check for the president when it comes to the rights of the nation's citizens." The government decided not to prosecute Hamdi. In *Rasul*, also decided 6 to 3, Justice John Paul Stevens wrote that the prisoners had been held for more than two years in territory under U.S. control. Thus, even though the prisoners are not on U.S. soil, they can ask U.S. courts if their detention is legal. The *Rasul* cases were still pending when this book was printed.

Historic Documents

Magna Carta

England's King John angered many people with high taxes. In 1215 a group of English nobles joined the archbishop of Canterbury to force the king to agree to sign Magna Carta. This document stated that the king was subject to the rule of law, just as other citizens of England were. It also presented the ideas of a fair and speedy trial and due process of law. These principles are still a part of the U.S. Bill of Rights.

1. In the first place have granted to God, and by this our present charter confirmed for us and our heirs for ever that the English church shall be free, and shall have its rights undiminished and its liberties unimpaired . . . We have also granted to all free men of our kingdom, for ourselves and our heirs for ever, all the liberties written below, to be had and held by them and their heirs of us and our heirs.
2. If any of our earls or barons or others holding of us in chief by knight service dies, and at his death his heir be of full age and owe relief he shall have his inheritance on payment of the old relief, namely the heir or heirs of an earl 100 for a whole earl's barony, the heir or heirs of a baron 100 for a whole barony, the heir or heirs of a knight 100s, at most, for a whole knight's fee; and he who owes less shall give less according to the ancient usage of fiefs.
3. If, however, the heir of any such be under age and a ward, he shall have his inheritance when he comes of age without paying relief and without making fine.

40. To no one will we sell, to no one will we refuse or delay right or justice.
41. All merchants shall be able to go out of and come into England safely and securely and stay and travel throughout England, as well by land as by water, for buying and selling by the ancient and right customs free from all evil tolls, except in time of war and if they are of the land that is at war with us . . .
42. It shall be lawful in future for anyone, without prejudicing the allegiance due to us, to leave our kingdom and return safely and securely by land and water, save, in the public interest, for a short period in time of war—except for those imprisoned or outlawed in accordance with the law of the kingdom and natives of a land that is at war with us and merchants (who shall be treated as aforesaid).

62. And we have fully remitted and pardoned to everyone all the ill–will, indignation and rancour that have arisen between us and our men, clergy and laity, from the time of the quarrel. Furthermore, we have fully remitted to all, clergy and laity, and as far as pertains to us have completely forgiven, all trespasses occasioned by the same quarrel between Easter in the sixteenth year of our reign and the restoration of peace. And, besides, we have caused to be made for them letters testimonial patent of the lord Stephen archbishop of Canterbury, of the lord Henry archbishop of Dublin and of the aforementioned bishops and of master Pandulf about this security and the aforementioned concessions.
63. An oath, moreover, has been taken, as well on our part as on the part of the barons, that all these things aforesaid shall be observed in good faith and without evil disposition. Witness the above–mentioned and many others. Given by our hand in the meadow which is called Runnymede between Windsor and Staines on the fifteenth day of June, in the seventeenth year of our reign.

From "English Bill of Rights." Britannica Online. Vers. 99.1. 1994–1999.

The Mayflower Compact

In November 1620, the Pilgrim leaders aboard the Mayflower *drafted the Mayflower Compact. This was the first document in the English colonies to establish guidelines for self-government. This excerpt from the Mayflower Compact describes the principles of the Pilgrim colony's government.*

The Mayflower Compact

We whose names are underwritten, the loyal subjects of our dread Sovereign Lord King James, by the Grace of God of Great Britain, France and Ireland, King, Defender of the Faith, etc.

Having undertaken, for the Glory of God and advancement of the Christian Faith and Honour of our King and Country, a Voyage to plant the First Colony in the Northern Parts of Virginia, do by these presents solemnly and mutually in the presence of God and one of another, Covenant and Combine ourselves together into a Civil Body Politic, for our better ordering and preservation and furtherance of the ends aforesaid; and by virtue hereof to enact, constitute and frame such just and equal Laws, Ordinances, Acts, Constitutions and Offices, from time to time, as shall be thought most meet and convenient for the general good of the Colony, unto which we promise all due submission and obedience. In witness whereof we have hereunder subscribed our names at Cape Cod, the 11th of November, in the year of the reign of our Sovereign Lord King James, of England, France and Ireland the eighteenth, and of Scotland the fifty-fourth. Anno Domini 1620.

From William Bradford, *Of Plymouth Plantation, 1620–1647* (Samuel Eliot Morison, ed., 1952), 75–76.

Fundamental Orders of Connecticut

In January 1639, settlers in Connecticut led by Thomas Hooker drew up the Fundamental Orders of Connecticut—America's first written constitution. It is essentially a compact among the settlers and a body of laws.

Forasmuch as it hath pleased the All-mighty God by the wise disposition of his divyne pruvidence so to Order and dispose of things that we the Inhabitants and Residents of Windsor, Harteford and Wethersfield are now cohabiting and dwelling in and uppon the River of Conectecotte and the Lands thereunto adioyneing; As also in our Civell Affaires to be guided and governed according to such Lawes, Rules, Orders and decrees as shall be made, ordered & decreed, as followeth:—

1. It is Ordered . . . that there shall be yerely two generall Assemblies or Courts, the one the second thursday in Aprill, the other the second thursday in September, following; the first shall be called the Courte of Election, wherein shall be yerely Chosen . . . soe many Magestrats and other publike Officers as shall be found requisitte: which choise shall be made by all that are admitted freemen and have taken the Oath of Fidelity, and doe cohabitte within this Jurisdiction, (having beene admitted Inhabitants by the major part of the Towne wherein they live,) or the major parte of such as shall be then present . . .

From F. N. Thorpe, ed., *Federal and State Constitutions,* vol. 1 (1909), 519.

The English Bill of Rights

In 1689, after the Glorious Revolution, Parliament passed the English Bill of Rights, which ensured that Parliament would have supreme power over the monarchy. The bill also protected the rights of English citizens.

Whereas the late King James the Second, by the assistance of divers evil counsellors, judges and ministers employed by him, did endeavour to subvert and extirpate the Protestant religion and the laws and liberties of this kingdom;

By assuming and exercising a power of dispensing with and suspending of laws and the execution of laws without consent of Parliament;

By committing and prosecuting divers worthy prelates for humbly petitioning to be excused from concurring to the said assumed power;

By issuing and causing to be executed a commission under the great seal for erecting a court called the Court of Commissioners for Ecclesiastical Causes;

By levying money for and to the use of the Crown by pretence of prerogative for other time and in other manner than the same was granted by Parliament;

By raising and keeping a standing army within this kingdom in time of peace without consent of Parliament, and quartering soldiers contrary to law; . . .

By violating the freedom of election of members to serve in Parliament;

By prosecutions in the Court of King's Bench for matters and causes cognizable only in Parliament, and by divers other arbitrary and illegal courses;

And whereas of late years partial corrupt and unqualified persons have been returned and served on juries in trials, and particularly divers jurors in trials for high treason which were not freeholders;

And excessive bail hath been required of persons committed in criminal cases to elude the benefit of the laws made for the liberty of the subjects;

And excessive fines have been imposed;

And illegal and cruel punishments inflicted;

And several grants and promises made of fines and forfeitures before any conviction or judgment against the persons upon whom the same were to be levied;

All which are utterly and directly contrary to the known laws and statutes and freedom of this realm; ...

That the pretended power of suspending of laws or the execution of laws by regal authority without consent of Parliament is illegal;

That the pretended power of dispensing with laws or the execution of laws by regal authority, as it hath been assumed and exercised of late, is illegal;

That the commission for erecting the late Court of Commissioners for Ecclesiastical Causes, and all other commissions and courts of like nature, are illegal and pernicious;

That levying money for or to the use of the Crown by pretence of prerogative, without grant of Parliament, for longer time, or in other manner than the same is or shall be granted, is illegal;

That it is the right of the subjects to petition the king, and all commitments and prosecutions for such petitioning are illegal;

That the raising or keeping a standing army within the kingdom in time of peace, unless it be with consent of Parliament, is against law;

That the subjects which are Protestants may have arms for their defence suitable to their conditions and as allowed by law;

That election of members of Parliament ought to be free;

That the freedom of speech and debates or proceedings in Parliament ought not to be impeached or questioned in any court or place out of Parliament;

(continued next page)

That excessive bail ought not to be required, nor excessive fines imposed, nor cruel and unusual punishments inflicted;

That jurors ought to be duly impanelled and returned, and jurors which pass upon men in trials for high treason ought to be freeholders;

That all grants and promises of fines and forfeitures of particular persons before conviction are illegal and void;

And that for redress of all grievances, and for the amending, strengthening and preserving of the laws, Parliaments ought to be held frequently.

Articles of Confederation

After winning the Revolutionary War in 1777, the newly formed United States of America created a government under the Articles of Confederation. This government allowed the states to have more power than the central government, a situation that would lead to problems later.

Articles of Confederation and perpetual Union between the states of New Hampshire, Massachusetts-bay Rhode Island and Providence Plantations, Connecticut, New York, New Jersey, Pennsylvania, Delaware, Maryland, Virginia, North Carolina, South Carolina and Georgia.

I.
The Stile of this Confederacy shall be
"The United States of America".

II.
Each state retains its sovereignty, freedom, and independence, and every power, jurisdiction, and right, which is not by this Confederation expressly delegated to the United States, in Congress assembled.

III.
The said States hereby severally enter into a firm league of friendship with each other, for their common defense, the security of their liberties, and their mutual and general welfare, binding themselves to assist each other, against all force offered to, or attacks made upon them, or any of them, on account of religion, sovereignty, trade, or any other pretense whatever.

VI.
No State, without the consent of the United States in Congress assembled, shall send any embassy to, or receive any embassy from, or enter into any conference, agreement, alliance or treaty with any King, Prince or State; nor shall any person holding any office of profit or trust under the United States, or any of them, accept any present, emolument, office or title of any kind whatever from any King, Prince or foreign State; nor shall the United States in Congress assembled, or any of them, grant any title of nobility.

VIII.
All charges of war, and all other expenses that shall be incurred for the common defense or general welfare, and allowed by the United States in Congress assembled, shall be defrayed out of a common treasury, which shall be supplied by the several States in proportion to the value of all land within each State, granted or surveyed for any person, as such land and the buildings and improvements thereon shall be estimated according to such mode as the United States in Congress assembled, shall from time to time direct and appoint.

The taxes for paying that proportion shall be laid and levied by the authority and direction of the legislatures of the several States within the time agreed upon by the United States in Congress assembled.

Federalist Paper No. 51

In 1788 the newly written Constitution faced opponents who believed it gave too much power to the federal government. James Madison, Alexander Hamilton, and John Jay wrote, anonymously, a collection of essays that became known as the Federalist Papers. The following essay, written by James Madison, outlines reasons why the division of power written into the Constitution would keep the government from harming citizens.

In order to lay a due foundation for that separate and distinct exercise of the different powers of government, which to a certain extent is admitted on all hands to be essential to the preservation of liberty, it is evident that each department should have a will of its own; and consequently should be so constituted that the members of each should have as little agency as possible in the appointment of the members of the others. Were this principle rigorously adhered to, it would require that all the appointments for the supreme executive, legislative, and judiciary magistracies should be drawn from the same fountain of authority, the people, through channels having no communication whatever with one another. Perhaps such a plan of constructing the several departments would be less difficult in practice than it may in contemplation appear. Some difficulties, however, and some additional expense would attend the execution of it. Some deviations, therefore, from the principle must be admitted. In the constitution of the judiciary department in particular, it might be inexpedient to insist rigorously on the principle: first, because peculiar qualifications being essential in the members, the primary consideration ought to be to select that mode of choice which best secures these qualifications; secondly, because the permanent tenure by which the appointments are held in that department, must soon destroy all sense of dependence on the authority conferring them.

Washington's Farewell Address

In 1796 at the end of his second term as president, George Washington wrote his farewell address with the help of Alexander Hamilton and James Madison. In it he spoke of the dangers facing the young nation. He warned against the dangers of political parties and sectionalism, and he advised the nation against permanent alliances with other nations.

In contemplating the causes, which may disturb our Union, it occurs as matter of serious concern, that any ground should have been furnished for characterizing parties by geographical discriminations-Northern and Southern-Atlantic and Western . . .

No alliances, however strict, between the parts can be an adequate substitute; they must inevitably experience the infractions and interruptions which all alliances in all times have experienced . . .

The great rule of conduct for us, in regard to foreign nations, is, in extending our commercial relations, to have with them as little political connexion as possible. So far as we have already formed engagements, let them be fulfilled with perfect good faith. Here let us stop.

From *Annals of Congress,* 4th Congress, pp. 2869–2880. American Memory. Library of Congress. 1999.

Monroe Doctrine

In 1823 President James Monroe proclaimed the Monroe Doctrine. Designed to end European influence in the Western Hemisphere, it became a cornerstone of U.S. foreign policy.

With the existing colonies or dependencies of any European power we have not interfered and shall not interfere. But with the governments who have declared their independence and maintained it, and whose independence we have, on great consideration and on just principles, acknowledged, we could not view any interposition for the purpose of oppressing them, or controlling in any other manner their destiny, by any European power in any other light than as the manifestation of an unfriendly disposition toward the United States. . . .

Our policy in regard to Europe, which was adopted at an early stage of the wars which have so long agitated that quarter of the globe, nevertheless remains the same, which is not to interfere in the internal concerns of any of its powers; to consider the government de facto as the legitimate government for us; to cultivate friendly relations with it, and to preserve those relations by a frank, firm, and manly policy, meeting in all instances the just claims of every power, submitting to injuries from none.

From "The Monroe Doctrine" by James Monroe. Reprinted in *The Annals of America: Volume 5, 1821–1832.* Copyright © 1976 by Encyclopaedia Britannica.

Seneca Falls Declaration of Sentiments

One of the first documents to express the desire for equal rights for women is the Declaration of Sentiments, issued in 1848 at the Seneca Falls Convention in Seneca Falls, New York. Led by Elizabeth Cady Stanton and Lucretia Mott, the delegates adopted a set of resolutions modeled on the Declaration of Independence.

When, in the course of human events, it becomes necessary for one portion of the family of man to assume among the people of the earth a position different from that which they have hitherto occupied, but one to which the laws of nature and of nature's God entitle them, a decent respect to the opinions of mankind requires that they should declare the causes that impel them to such a course.

We hold these truths to be self–evident: that all men and women are created equal; that they are endowed by their Creator with certain inalienable rights; that among these are life, liberty, and the pursuit of happiness; that to secure these rights governments are instituted, deriving their just powers from the consent of the governed. Whenever any form of government becomes destructive of these ends, it is the right of those who suffer from it to refuse allegiance to it, and to insist upon the institution of a new government, laying its foundation on such principles, and organizing its powers in such form, as to them shall seem most likely to effect their safety and happiness.

From "Seneca Falls Declaration on Women's Rights." Reprinted in *The Annals of America: Volume 7, 1841–1849.* Copyright © 1976 by Encyclopaedia Britannica.

Pontiac (c.1720–1769) Ottawa chief who united the Great Lakes' Indians to try to halt the advance of European settlements, he attacked British forts in a rebellion known as Pontiac's Rebellion; he eventually surrendered in 1766. (p. 97)

Powderly, Terence V. (1849–1924) American labor leader for the Knights of Labor, he removed the secrecy originally surrounding the organization, leading to its becoming the first truly national American labor union. (p. 625)

Pulitzer, Joseph (1847–1911) American journalist and newspaper publisher, he established the Pulitzer Prize for public service and advancement of education. (p. 645)

R

Revels, Hiram (1822–1901) American clergyman, educator, and politician, he became the first African American in the U.S. Senate. (p. 565)

Riis, Jacob (1849–1914) Photographer and journalist who took shocking pictures of the lives of poverty-stricken immigrants, sweatshop workers, and tenement dwellers. These photos were published in *How the Other Half Lives.* (p. 646)

Rochambeau, Comte de (1725–1807) French soldier who commanded the French troops in the American Revolutionary War. He was with General George Washington at the Battle of Yorktown. (p. 137)

Rockefeller, John D. (1839–1937) American industrialist and philanthropist, he made a fortune in the oil business and used vertical and horizontal integration to establish a monopoly on the steel business. (p. 620)

Roosevelt, Theodore (1858–1919) Twenty-sixth president of the United States after William McKinley was assassinated, he organized the first volunteer cavalry regiment known as the Rough Riders who fought in Cuba during the Spanish-American War. As President, he acquired the Panama Canal Zone, and announced the Roosevelt Corollary, making the United States the defender of the Western Hemisphere. (p. 680)

S

Sacagawea (sak-uh-juh-WEE-uh) (1786?–1812) Shoshone woman who, along with her French fur-trapper husband, accompanied and aided Lewis and Clark on their expedition. (p. 276)

Santa Anna, Antonio López de (1794–1876) Mexican general and politician, he was president of Mexico and became a dictator. He fought in the Texas Revolution and seized the Alamo but was defeated and captured by Sam Houston at San Jacinto. (p. 351)

Scott, Dred (1795?–1858) Enslaved African who filed suit for his freedom stating that his time living in a free state made him a free man; the Supreme Court ruling known as the Dred Scott decision upheld slavery and found the Missouri Compromise unconstitutional. (p. 489)

Scott, Winfield (1786–1866) American general, he served as commander in the Mexican War and used a two-part strategy against the South in the Civil War; he wanted to destroy the South's economy with a naval blockade and gain control of the Mississippi River. (p. 513)

Sequoya (between 1760 and 1770–1843) American Indian scholar and craftsman, he created a writing system for the Cherokee language and taught literacy to many Cherokee. (p. 333)

Seward, William H. (1801–1872) Secretary of state under Abraham Lincoln, he also was responsible for the purchase of Alaska from Russia. (p. 693)

Shays, Daniel (1747?–1825) Revolutionary War officer who led Shays's Rebellion, an uprising of farmers in western Massachusetts that shut down the courts so that farmers would not lose their farms for tax debts. He was defeated and condemned to death, but pardoned. (p. 161)

Sherman, William Tecumseh (1820–1891) American Union army officer, his famous March to the Sea captured Atlanta, Georgia, marking an important turning point in the war. (p. 541)

Singer, Isaac (1811–1875) American inventor; he patented an improved sewing machine and by 1860, was the largest manufacturer of sewing machines in the country. (p. 405)

BIOGRAPHICAL DICTIONARY

Sitting Bull (c.1831–1890) American Indian leader who became the head chief of the entire Sioux nation, he encouraged other Sioux leaders to resist government demands to buy lands on the Black Hills reservations. (p. 596)

Slater, Samuel (1768–1835) English industrialist who brought a design for a textile mill to America, he is considered the founder of the American cotton industry. (p. 386)

Smith, John (c.1580–1631) English colonist to the Americas who helped found the Jamestown Colony and encouraged settlers to work harder and build better housing. (p. 73)

Socrates (c. 470–399 BC) Greek philosopher and teacher who wanted to make people question their own beliefs and think for themselves. (p. 22)

Squanto (?–1622) Patuxet Indian who was captured and enslaved in Spain but later escaped to England and then America; he taught the Pilgrims native farming methods and helped them establish relations with the Wampanoag, the Indians at the feast later known as Thanksgiving. (p. 79)

Stanford, Leland (1824–1893) American railroad builder and politician, he established the California Central Pacific Railroad and founded Stanford University. (p. 621)

Stanton, Elizabeth Cady (1815–1902) American woman suffrage leader, she organized the Seneca Falls Convention with Lucretia Mott. The convention was the first organized meeting for women's rights in the United States, which launched the suffrage movement. (p. 464)

Steuben, Baron Friedrich von (1730–1794) Prussian soldier who helped train American forces at Valley Forge during the American Revolutionary War. (p. 131)

Stone, Lucy (1818–1893) American woman suffragist, she was a well-known and accomplished antislavery speaker who supported the women's rights movement. (p. 465)

Stowe, Harriet Beecher (1811–1896) American author and daughter of Lyman Beecher, she was an abolitionist and author of the famous antislavery novel, *Uncle Tom's Cabin.* (p. 481)

Stuyvesant (STY-vi-suhnt), Peter (c.1610–1672) Director general of the Dutch New Netherland colony, he was forced to surrender New Netherland to the English. (p. 85)

Sumner, Charles (1811–1874) A Senator from Massachusetts, he was attacked by Preston Brooks with a cane over the issue of slavery. (p. 487)

Sutter, John (1803–1880) American pioneer who built Sutter's Fort, a trading post on the California frontier; gold was discovered leading to the California gold rush. (p. 365)

T

Taft, William Howard (1857–1930) Twenty-seventh president of the United States, he angered progressives by moving cautiously toward reforms and by supporting the Payne–Aldrich Tariff, which did not lower tariffs very much. He lost Roosevelt's support and was defeated for a second term. (p. 682)

Taney (TAW-nee), Roger B. (1777–1864) U.S. Supreme Court Chief Justice he wrote the majority opinion in the Dred Scott decision, stating that African Americans were not citizens and that the Missouri Compromise was unconstitutional. (p. 490)

Taylor, Frederick W. (1856–1915) American efficiency engineer, he introduced the manufacturing system known as scientific management that viewed workers as mechanical parts of the production process, not as human beings. (p. 624)

Tecumseh (1768–1813) Shawnee chief who attempted to form an Indian confederation to resist white settlement in the Northwest Territory. (p. 280)

Thoreau, Henry David (1817–1862) American writer and transcendentalist philosopher, he studied nature and published a magazine article, "Civil Disobedience," as well as his famous book, Walden Pond. (p. 443)

Truth, Sojourner (c.1797–1883) American evangelist and reformer, she was born an enslaved African but was later freed and became a speaker for abolition and women's suffrage. (p. 456)

Tubman, Harriet (c.1820–1913) American abolitionist who escaped slavery and assisted other enslaved Africans to escape; she is the most famous Underground Railroad conductor and is known as the Moses of her people. (p. 458)

Turner, Nat (1800–1831) American slave leader, he claimed that divine inspiration had led him to end the slavery system. Called Nat Turner's Rebellion, the slave revolt was the most violent one in U.S. history; he was tried, convicted, and executed. (p. 428)

Tweed, William Marcy (1823–1878) New York city politician known for his control of the corrupt political machine called the Tammany Ring. (p. 663)

V

Vallejo, Mariano Guadalupe (1808–1890) Californio leader who urged equal rights for Mexicans living in California after the state was captured in the Mexican-American War. (p. 357)

Van Buren, Martin (1782–1862) American politician and secretary of state under Andrew Jackson, he later became the eighth president of the United States. (p. 324)

Villa, Francisco "Pancho" (1878–1923) Mexican bandit and revolutionary leader, he led revolts against Carranza and Huerta. He was pursued by the U.S. but evaded General Pershing. (p. 709)

W

Washington, Booker T. (1856–1915) African American educator and civil rights leader, he was born into slavery and later became head of the Tuskegee Institute for career training for African Americans. He was an advocate for conservative social change. (p. 677)

Washington, George (1732–1799) Revolutionary War hero and Patriot leader, he served as a representative to the Continental Congresses, commanded the Continental Army, and was unanimously elected to two terms as president of the United States. (pp. 114, 234)

Washington, Martha (1731–1802) Wife of George Washington, she was the first First Lady. (p. 234)

Webster, Daniel (1782–1852) American lawyer and statesman, he spoke out against nullification and states' rights, believing that the country should stay unified. (p. 328)

Wells, Ida B. (1862–1931) African American journalist and anti-lynching activist, she was part owner and editor of the Memphis Free Speech. (p. 677)

Whitman, Walt (1819–1892) American poet, he gained recognition abroad and later at home for unrhymed works of poetry praising the United States, Americans, democracy, and individualism. (p. 445)

Whitney, Eli (1765–1825) American inventor whose cotton gin changed cotton harvesting procedures and enabled large increases in cotton production; he introduced the technology of mass production through the development of interchangeable parts in gun-making. (p. 387)

Willard, Frances (1839–1898) American reformer who helped found the Women's Christian Temperance Union and was also active in the Women's suffrage movement. (p. 676)

Winnemucca, Sarah (1844–1891) Paiute Indian reformer, she was an activist for Indian rights and lectured specifically about the problems of the reservation system. (p. 598)

Winthrop, John (1588–1649) Leader of the Massachusetts Bay Colony who led Puritan colonists to Massachusetts to establish an ideal Christian community; he later became the colony's first governor. (p. 80)

Wright, Orville (1871–1948) and **Wilbur** (1867–1912) American pioneers of aviation, they went from experiments with kites and gliders to piloting the first successful gas-powered airplane flight and later founded the American Wright Company to manufacture airplanes. (p. 618)

Y

Young, Brigham (1801–1877) American religious leader who headed the Mormon Church after the murder of Joseph Smith, he moved the community to Utah, leading thousands along what came to be known as the Mormon Trail to the main settlement at Salt Lake City. (p. 349)

English and Spanish Glossary

MARK	AS IN	RESPELLING	EXAMPLE
a	alphabet	a	*AL-fuh-bet
ā	Asia	ay	AY-zhuh
ä	cart, top	ah	KAHRT, TAHP
e	let, ten	e	LET, TEN
ē	even, leaf	ee	EE-vuhn, LEEF
i	it, tip, British	i	IT, TIP, BRIT-ish
ī	site, buy, Ohio	y	SYT, BY, oh-HY-oh
	iris	eye	EYE-ris
k	card	k	KAHRD
ō	over, rainbow	oh	OH-vuhr, RAYN-boh
u̇	book, wood	ooh	BOOHK, WOOHD
ȯ	all, orchid	aw	AWL, AWR-kid
ȯi	foil, coin	oy	FOYL, KOYN
au̇	out	ow	OWT
ə	cup, butter	uh	KUHP, BUHT-uhr
ü	rule, food	oo	ROOL, FOOD
yü	few	yoo	FYOO
zh	vision	zh	VIZH-uhn

*A syllable printed in small capital letters receives heavier emphasis than the other syllable(s) in a word.

Phonetic Respelling and Pronunciation Guide

Many of the key terms in this textbook have been respelled to help you pronounce them. The letter combinations used in the respelling throughout the narrative are explained in the following phonetic respelling and pronunciation guide. The guide is adapted from *Merriam-Webster's Collegiate Dictionary, 11th Edition; Merriam-Webster's Geographical Dictionary;* and *Merriam-Webster's Biographical Dictionary.*

A

abolition an end to slavery (p. 454)
abolición fin de la esclavitud (pág. 454)

Adams-Onís Treaty (1819) an agreement in which Spain gave East Florida to the United States (p. 299)
Tratado de Adams y Onís (1819) acuerdo en el que España le dio el territorio del este de Florida a Estados Unidos (pág. 299)

African Diaspora the population of displaced Africans and their descendants around the world (p. 60)
diáspora africana población de africanos desplazados y sus descendientes en todo el mundo (pág. 60)

Alamo Spanish mission in San Antonio, Texas, that was the site of a famous battle of the Texas Revolution in 1836 (p. 352)
El Álamo misión española en San Antonio, Texas; escenario de una famosa batalla durante la Revolución Texana de 1836 (pág. 352)

Alien and Sedition Acts (1798) laws passed by a Federalist-dominated Congress aimed at protecting the government from treasonous ideas, actions, and people (p. 253)
Leyes de No Intervención Extranjera y Sedición (1798) leyes aprobadas por un Congreso mayormente federalista para proteger al gobierno de la influencia de ideas, acciones y personas desleales (pág. 253)

amendment official change, correction, or addition to a law or constitution (p. 173)
enmienda cambio, corrección o adición oficial a una ley o constitución (pág. 173)

American Anti-Slavery Society an organization started by William Lloyd Garrison whose members wanted immediate emancipation and racial equality for African Americans (p. 455)
Sociedad Americana contra la Esclavitud organización fundada por William Lloyd Garrison cuyos miembros pedían la emancipación inmediata y la igualdad racial de los afroamericanos (pág. 455)

American Federation of Labor (AFL) an organization that united skilled workers into national unions for specific industries (p. 625)
Federación Americana del Trabajo (AFL, por sus siglas en inglés) organización que unió a obreros especializados en sindicatos nacionales para industrias específicas (pág. 625)

American System Henry Clay's plan for raising tariffs to pay for internal improvements such as better roads and canals (p. 302)
Sistema Estadounidense plan de alza de aranceles creado por Henry Clay para hacer mejoras internas como la reparación de caminos y canales (pág. 302)

Antifederalists people who opposed ratification of the Constitution (p. 170)

antifederalistas personas que se oponían a la aprobación de la Constitución (pág. 170)

Anti-Imperialist League a group of citizens opposed to imperialism, and, specifically, to the peace treaty that gave the United States control of Cuba, Guam, Puerto Rico, and the Philippines (p. 700)
Liga Antiimperialista grupo de ciudadanos que se oponían al imperialismo y, más específicamente, al tratado de paz que daba a Estados Unidos el control de Cuba, Guam, Puerto Rico y Filipinas (pág. 700)

Appomattox Courthouse the location where General Robert E. Lee was forced to surrender, thus ending the Civil War (p. 542)
Appomattox Courthouse poblado de Virginia donde el general Robert E. Lee fue obligado a rendirse, dando fin a la Guerra Civil (pág. 542)

Articles of Confederation (1777) the document that created the first central government for the United States; was replaced by the Constitution in 1789 (p. 154)
Artículos de Confederación (1777) documento que creó el primer gobierno central en Estados Unidos; fue reemplazado por la Constitución en 1789 (pág. 154)

astrolabe a device that enabled navigators to learn their ship's location by charting the position of the stars (p. 40)
astrolabio aparato que permitía a los navegantes saber la ubicación de su barco al trazar la posición de las estrellas (pág. 40)

B

Bacon's Rebellion (1676) an atttack led by Nathaniel Bacon against American Indians and the colonial government in Virginia (p. 74)
Rebelión de Bacon (1676) ataque encabezado por Nathaniel Bacon contra los indígenas norteamericanos y el gobierno colonial en Virginia (pág. 74)

Bank of the United States a national bank chartered by Congress in 1791 to provide security for the U.S. economy (p. 242)
Banco de Estados Unidos banco nacional formado por el Congreso en 1791 para dar seguridad a la economía de Estados Unidos (pág. 242)

Battle of Antietam (1862) a Union victory in the Civil War that marked the bloodiest single-day battle in U.S. military history (p. 519)
batalla de Antietam (1862) victoria del ejército de la Unión durante la Guerra Civil en la batalla de un solo día más sangrienta de la historia militar de Estados Unidos (pág. 519)

Battle of Bunker Hill (1775) a Revolutionary War battle in Boston that demonstrated that the colonists could fight well against the British army (p. 115)
batalla de Bunker Hill (1775) batalla de la Guerra de Independencia estadounidense en Boston; en ésta se demostró que los colonos podían luchar bien contra el ejército británico (pág. 115)

Battle of Fallen Timbers (1794) a battle between U.S. troops and an American Indian confederation that ended Indian efforts to halt white settlement in the Northwest Territory (p. 247)
batalla de Fallen Timbers (1794) batalla entre las tropas estadounidenses y una confederación de indígenas norteamericanos que puso fin a los intentos de los indígenas para detener la emigración de personas de raza blanca al Territorio del Noroeste (pág. 247)

Battle of Gettysburg (1863) a Union Civil War victory that turned the tide against the Confederates at Gettysburg, Pennsylvania (p. 537)
batalla de Gettysburg (1863) victoria del ejército de la Unión durante la Guerra Civil que cambió el curso de la guerra en contra de los confederados en Gettysburg, Pensilvania (pág. 537)

Battle of Lake Erie (1813) U.S. victory in the War of 1812, led by Oliver Hazard Perry; broke Britain's control of Lake Erie (p. 285)
batalla del lago Erie (1813) victoria en la Guerra de 1812 en la que el ejército estadounidense, comandado por Oliver Hazard Perry, puso fin al control británico del lago Erie (pág. 285)

Battle of New Orleans (1815) the greatest U.S. victory in the War of 1812; actually took place two weeks after a peace treaty had been signed ending the war (p. 286)
batalla de Nueva Orleáns (1815) la mayor victoria del ejército estadounidense en la Guerra de 1812; tuvo lugar dos semanas después de la firma de un tratado de paz en el que se declaraba el final de la guerra (pág. 286)

Battle of San Jacinto (1836) the final battle of the Texas Revolution; resulted in the defeat of the Mexican army and independence for Texas (p. 352)
batalla de San Jacinto (1836) batalla final de la Revolución Texana en la que el ejército mexicano fue derrotado y Texas obtuvo su independencia (pág. 352)

Battle of Saratoga (1777) a Revolutionary War battle in New York that resulted in a major defeat of British troops; marked the Patriots' greatest victory up to that point in the war (p. 130)
batalla de Saratoga (1777) batalla de la Guerra de Independencia estadounidense que tuvo lugar en Nueva York y en la que las fuerzas británicas sufrieron una de sus mayores derrotas; los patriotas obtuvieron su mayor victoria hasta ese momento (pág. 130)

Battle of Shiloh (1862) a Civil War battle in Tennessee in which the Union army gained greater control over the Mississippi River valley (p. 523)
batalla de Shiloh (1862) batalla de la Guerra Civil en Tennessee en la que el ejército de la Unión adquirió mayor control sobre el valle del río Mississippi (pág. 523)

Battle of the Little Big Horn (1876) "Custer's Last Stand"; battle between U.S. soldiers, led by George Armstrong Custer, and Sioux warriors, led by Crazy Horse and Sitting Bull, that resulted in the worst defeat for the U.S. Army in the West (p. 596)
batalla de Little Big Horn (1876) última batalla del general Custer; esta batalla entre las tropas de George Armstrong Custer y los guerreros siux al mando de Caballo Loco y Toro Sentado produjo la mayor derrota del ejército estadounidense en el Oeste (pág. 596)

Battle of Tippecanoe (1811) U.S. victory over an Indian confederation that wanted to stop white settlement in the Northwest Territory; increased tensions between Great Britain and the United States (p. 282)
batalla de Tippecanoe (1811) victoria del ejército estadounidense sobre la confederación indígena que intentaba evitar el establecimiento de poblaciones de blancos en el Territorio del Noroeste; esta batalla aumentó las hostilidades entre Gran Bretaña y Estados Unidos (pág. 282)

Battle of Trenton (1776) a Revolutionary War battle in New Jersey in which Patriot forces captured more than 900 Hessian troops (p. 129)
batalla de Trenton (1776) batalla de la Guerra de Independencia estadounidense que tuvo lugar en Nueva Jersey; en esta batalla las fuerzas de los patriotas capturaron a más de 900 soldados hessianos (pág. 129)

Battle of Yorktown (1781) the last major battle of the Revolutionary War; site of British general Charles Cornwallis's surrender to the Patriots in Virginia (p. 137)
batalla de Yorktown (1781) la última batalla importante de la Guerra de Independencia estadounidense; lugar donde se rindió el general británico Charles Cornwallis ante los patriotas en Virginia (pág. 137)

Bear Flag Revolt (1846) a revolt against Mexico by American settlers in California who declared the territory an independent republic (p. 358)
Revuelta de Bear Flag (1846) rebelión iniciada por colonos estadounidenses en contra de México para declarar al territorio de California una república independiente (pág. 358)

benevolent society an aid organization formed by immigrant communities (p. 639)
sociedad de beneficencia organización de ayuda formada por comunidades de inmigrantes (pág. 639)

Berbers a group of people from northern Africa (p. 16)
bereberes grupo de habitantes del norte de África (pág. 16)

Bering Land Bridge a strip of land connecting Alaska with Russia that emerged from underwater around 38,000 BC (p. 6)
Puente de Tierra de Bering franja de tierra que conecta Alaska con Rusia y que surgió del agua alrededor del año 38,000 a.C. (pág. 6)

Bessemer process a process developed in the 1850s that led to faster, cheaper steel production (p. 615)
proceso de Bessemer proceso de producción de acero más económico y rápido, desarrollado en la década de 1850 (pág. 615)

Bill of Rights the first 10 amendments to the Constitution; ratified in 1791 (p. 173)
Declaración de Derechos primeras 10 enmiendas a la Constitución; aprobada en 1791 (pág. 173)

Black Codes laws passed in the southern states during Reconstruction that greatly limited the freedom and rights of African Americans (p. 558)
códigos de negros decretos aprobados en los estados sureños en la época de la Reconstrucción que limitaron en gran medida la libertad y los derechos de los afroamericanos (pág. 558)

Black Death a series of plagues that killed about 25 million people in Europe starting in 1347 (p. 25)
Peste Negra serie de plagas que mataron a unos 25 millones de personas en Europa a partir de 1347 (pág. 25)

bond a certificate that represents money the government has borrowed from private citizens (p. 238)
bono certificado que representa dinero que el gobierno toma prestado de los ciudadanos (pág. 238)

boomtown a Western community that grew quickly because of the mining boom and often disappeared when the boom ended (p. 588)
pueblo de rápido crecimiento comunidad del Oeste que se desarrolló con gran rapidez debido a la fiebre del oro, pero que desapareció cuando la fiebre terminó (pág. 588)

border states Delaware, Kentucky, Maryland, and Missouri; slave states that lay between the North and the South and did not join the Confederacy during the Civil War (p. 512)
estados fronterizos Delaware, Kentucky, Maryland y Missouri; estados esclavistas ubicados entre el Norte y el Sur y que no se unieron a la Confederación durante la Guerra Civil (pág. 512)

Boston Massacre (1770) an incident in which British soldiers fired into a crowd of colonists, killing five people (p. 101)
masacre de Boston (1770) incidente en el que los soldados británicos le dispararon a una multitud de colonos, dando muerte a cinco personas (pág. 101)

Boston Tea Party (1773) a protest against the Tea Act in which a group of colonists boarded British tea ships and dumped more than 340 chests of tea into Boston Harbor (p. 102)
Motín del Té de Boston (1773) protesta en contra de la Ley del Té en la que un grupo de colonos abordó barcos británicos que transportaban té y arrojó al mar alrededor de 340 baúles de té en el puerto de Boston (pág. 102)

Boxer Rebellion (1900) a siege of a foreign settlement in Beijing by Chinese nationalists who were angry at foreign involvement in China (p. 695)
rebelión de los boxers (1900) asedio a un asentamiento extranjero en Beijing por parte de un grupo de nacionalistas chinos que estaban enojados por la participación extranjera en China (pág. 695)

buffalo soldiers African American soldiers who served in the cavalry during the wars for the west (p. 596)
soldados búfalo soldados afroamericanos que sirvieron en la caballería durante las guerras del oeste (pág. 596)

Bureau of Indian Affairs a government agency created in the 1800s to oversee federal policy toward Native Americans (p. 332)
Oficina de Asuntos Indígenas agencia creada por el gobierno en el siglo XIX para supervisar las políticas federales en cuanto a los indígenas norteamericanos (pág. 332)

C

Californios Spanish colonists in California in the 1800s (p. 357)
californios colonos españoles que vivían en California en el siglo XIX (pág. 357)

capitalism an economic system in which private businesses run most industries (p. 674)
capitalismo sistema económico en el que las empresas privadas controlan la mayoría de las industrias (pág. 674)

caravels ships that used triangular sails to sail against the wind, and had rudders to improve steering (p. 40)
carabelas barcos con velas triangulares usadas para navegar contra el viento y que tenían timones para mejorar la dirección (pág. 40)

cattle drive a long journey on which cowboys herded cattle to northern markets or better grazing lands (p. 589)
arreo de ganado viaje largo en el que los vaqueros arreaban ganado para llevarlo a los mercados del Norte o a mejores pastos (pág. 589)

Cattle Kingdom an area of the Great Plains on which many ranchers raised cattle in the late 1800s (p. 589)
Reino del Ganado área de las Grandes Planicies en la que muchos rancheros criaban ganado a finales de siglo XIX (pág. 589)

charter an official document that gives a person the right to establish a colony (p. 54)
carta de constitución documento oficial que da a una persona el derecho de establecer una colonia (pág. 54)

checks and balances a system established by the Constitution that prevents any branch of government from becoming too powerful (p. 167)
equilibrio de poderes sistema establecido por la Constitución para evitar que cualquier poder del gobierno adquiera demasiada autoridad (pág. 167)

Chinese Exclusion Act (1882) a law passed by Congress that banned Chinese from immigrating to the United States for 10 years (p. 641)
Ley de Exclusión de Chinos (1882) ley aprobada por el Congreso que prohibió la inmigración de chinos a Estados Unidos por 10 años (pág. 641)

Chisholm Trail a trail that ran from San Antonio, Texas, to Abilene, Kansas, established by Jesse Chisholm in the late 1860s for cattle drives (p. 589)
Camino de Chisholm camino creado por Jesse Chisholm a finales de la década de 1860 que iba desde San Antonio, Texas hasta Abilene, Kansas, para arreos de ganado (pág. 589)

circumnavigate to travel all the way around the globe (p. 44)
circunnavegar darle la vuelta al planeta (pág. 44)

Civil Rights Act of 1866 a law that gave African Americans legal rights equal to those of white Americans (p. 560)
Ley de Derechos Civiles de 1866 ley que dio a los afroamericanos los mismos derechos legales que tenían los estadounidenses blancos (pág. 560)

Clermont the first full-sized U.S. commercial steamboat; developed by Robert Fulton and tested in 1807 (p. 397)
Clermont primer barco comercial de vapor de gran tamaño, diseñado por Robert Fulton y probado en 1807 (pág. 397)

collective bargaining a technique used by labor unions in which workers act collectively to change working conditions or wages (p. 626)
negociación colectiva método empleado por los sindicatos en el que los trabajadores actúan colectivamente para cambiar las condiciones laborales o los salarios (pág. 626)

Columbian Exchange the transfer of plants, animals, and diseases between the Americas and Europe, Asia, and Africa (p. 45)
intercambio colombino intercambio de plantas, animales y enfermedades entre las Américas y Europa, Asia y África (pág. 45)

Committees of Correspondence committees created by the Massachusetts House of Representatives in the 1760s to help towns and colonies share information about resisting British laws (p. 99)
comités de correspondencia comités creados por la Cámara de Representantes de Massachusetts en la década de 1760 para que los pueblos y colonias compartieran información sobra la resistencia a las leyes británicas (pág. 99)

common-school movement a social reform effort that began in the mid-1800s and promoted the idea of having all children educated in a common place regardless of social class or background (p. 450) movimiento de escuelas comunes reforma social iniciada a mediados del siglo XIX para fomentar la idea de que todos los niños debían recibir educación en un mismo lugar sin importar su origen o clase social (pág. 450)

Common Sense (1776) a pamphlet written by Thomas Paine that criticized monarchies and convinced many American colonists of the need to break away from Britain (p. 118)
Sentido común (1776) folleto escrito por Thomas Paine en el que criticaba a las monarquías y convenció a muchos colonos norteamericanos de la necesidad de independizarse de Gran Bretaña (pág. 118)

Compromise of 1850 Henry Clay's proposed agreement that allowed California to enter the Union as a free state and divided the rest of the Mexican Cession into two territories where slavery would be decided by popular sovereignty (p. 479)
Compromiso de 1850 acuerdo propuesto por Henry Clay en que se permitía a California entrar en la Unión como estado libre y se proponía la división del resto del territorio de la Cesión Mexicana en dos partes donde la esclavitud sería reglamentada por soberanía popular (pág. 479)

Compromise of 1877 an agreement to settle the disputed presidential election of 1876; Democrats agreed to accept Republican Rutherford B. Hayes as president in return for the removal of federal troops from the South (p. 567)
Compromiso de 1877 acuerdo en el que se resolvieron las disputadas elecciones presidenciales de 1876; los demócratas aceptaron al republicano Rutherford B. Hayes como presidente a cambio del retiro de las tropas federales del Sur (pág. 567)

Comstock Lode Nevada gold and silver mine discovered by Henry Comstock in 1859 (p. 587)
veta de Comstock mina de oro y plata descubierta en Nevada por Henry Comstock en 1859 (pág. 587)

Confederate States of America the nation formed by the southern states when they seceded from the Union; also known as the Confederacy (p.497)
Estados Confederados de América nación formada por los estados del Sur cuando se separaron de la Unión; también conocida como Confederación (pág. 497)

conquistador a Spanish soldier and explorer who led military expeditions in the Americas and captured land for Spain (p. 46)
conquistador soldado y explorador español que encabezó expediciones militares en América y capturó territorios en nombre de España (pág. 46)

conservation the planned management of natural resources to prevent their destruction (p. 681)
conservación administración planificada de los recursos naturales para evitar su destrucción (pág. 681)

constitution a set of basic principles that determines the powers and duties of a government (p. 153)
constitución conjunto de principios básicos que determina los poderes y las obligaciones de un gobierno (pág. 153)

Constitutional Convention (1787) a meeting held in Philadelphia at which delegates from the states wrote the Constitution (p. 164)
Convención Constitucional (1787) reunión en Filadelfia en la que delegados de los estados redactaron la Constitución (pág. 164)

Constitutional Union Party a political party formed in 1860 by a group of northerners and southerners who supported the Union, its laws, and the Constitution (p. 495)
Partido Constitucional por la Unión partido político formado en 1860 por habitantes del Norte y del Sur en apoyo de la Unión, sus leyes y la Constitución (pág. 495)

Continental Army the army created by the Second Continental Congress in 1775 to defend the American colonies from Britain (p. 114)
Ejército Continental ejército creado por el Segundo Congreso Continental en 1775 para defender a las colonias norteamericanas del dominio británico (pág. 114)

contraband an escaped slave who joined the Union army during the Civil War (p. 531)
contrabando esclavo que escapó y se unió al ejército de la Unión durante la Guerra Civil (pág. 531)

Convention of 1818 an agreement between the United States and Great Britain that settled fishing rights and established new North American borders (p. 298)
Convención de 1818 acuerdo entre Estados Unidos y Gran Bretaña para definir los derechos de pesca y establecer las nuevas fronteras norteamericanas (pág. 298)

Copperheads a group of northern Democrats who opposed abolition and sympathized with the South during the Civil War (p. 532)
copperheads grupo de demócratas del Norte que se oponían a la abolición de la esclavitud y simpatizaban con las creencias sureñas durante la Guerra Civil (pág. 532)

corporation a business that sells portions of ownership called stock shares (p. 619)
corporación compañía que vende algunas partes en forma de acciones (pág. 619)

cotton belt a region stretching from South Carolina to east Texas where most U.S. cotton was produced during the mid-1800s (p. 416)
región algodonera zona que se extendía desde Carolina del Sur hasta el este de Texas, en la que se producía la mayor parte del algodón cosechado en Estados Unidos a mediados del siglo XIX (pág. 416)

cotton diplomacy Confederate efforts to use the importance of southern cotton to Britain's textile industry to persuade the British to support the Confederacy in the Civil War (p. 513)

diplomacia del algodón esfuerzos de la Confederación por aprovechar la importancia del algodón del Sur en la industria textil británica para convencer a Gran Bretaña de apoyar a la Confederación en la Guerra Civil (pág. 513)

cotton gin a machine invented by Eli Whitney in 1793 to remove seeds from short-staple cotton; revolutionized the cotton industry (p. 415)
desmotadora de algodón máquina inventada por Eli Whitney en 1793 para separar las fibras de algodón de las semillas; revolucionó la industria del algodón (pág. 415)

culture the common values and traditions of a society, such as language, government, and family relationships (p. 7)
cultura valores y tradiciones comunes de una sociedad, como el lenguaje, la forma de gobierno y las relaciones familiares (pág. 7)

Cumberland Road the first federal road project, construction of which began in 1815; ran from Cumberland, Maryland, to present-day Wheeling, West Virginia (p. 303)
camino de Cumberland primer proyecto federal de construcción de carreteras, iniciado en 1815 para crear un camino entre Cumberland, Maryland y el poblado que actualmente lleva el nombre de Wheeling, en Virginia Occidental (pág. 303)

D

Dawes General Allotment Act (1887) legislation passed by Congress that split up Indian reservation lands among individual Indians and promised them citizenship (p. 598)
Ley de Adjudicación General de Dawes (1887) ley aprobada por el Congreso que dividía el terreno de las reservas indígenas entre sus habitantes y les prometía la ciudadanía (pág. 598)

Declaration of Independence (1776) the document written to declare the colonies free from British rule (p. 119)
Declaración de Independencia (1776) documento redactado para declarar la independencia de las colonias del dominio británico (pág. 119)

Declaration of Sentiments (1848) a statement written and signed by women's rights supporters at the Seneca Falls Convention; detailed their beliefs about social injustice against women (p. 464)
Declaración de Sentimientos (1848) declaración redactada y firmada por partidarios de los derechos de la mujer durante la Convención de Seneca Falls; se describía con detalle su punto de vista sobre las injusticias sociales que afectaban a las mujeres (pág. 464)

deflation a decrease in money supply and overall lower prices (p. 604)
deflación reducción de la disponibilidad del dinero y baja general en los precios (pág. 604)

democracy a government in which people rule themselves (p. 23)
democracia gobierno en el que el pueblo se gobierna a sí mismo (pág. 23)

Democratic Party a political party formed by supporters of Andrew Jackson after the presidential election of 1824 (p. 323)
Partido Demócrata partido político formado por partidarios de Andrew Jackson después de las elecciones presidenciales de 1824 (pág. 323)

Democratic-Republican Party a political party founded in the 1790s by Thomas Jefferson, James Madison, and other leaders who wanted to preserve the power of the state governments and promote agriculture (p. 250)
Partido Demócrata Republicano partido político formado en la década de 1790 por Thomas Jefferson, James Madison y otros líderes políticos para preservar el poder de los gobiernos estatales y promover la agricultura (pág. 250)

department store giant retail shop (p. 645)
tiendas por departamentos grandes comercios de venta al público (pág. 645)

deport to send an immigrant back to his or her country of origin (p. 222)
deportar enviar a un inmigrante de regreso a su país de origen (pág. 222)

depression a steep drop in economic activity combined with rising unemployment (p. 161)
depresión bajón considerable en la actividad económica, combinado con un alza en el desempleo (pág. 161)

Donner party a group of western travelers who were stranded in the Sierra Nevada during the winter of 1846-47; only 45 of the party's 87 members survived (p. 365)
grupo Donner grupo de viajeros del Oeste perdidos en la Sierra Nevada durante el invierno de 1846-47; sólo 45 de los 87 viajeros sobrevivieron (pág. 365)

double jeopardy the act of trying a person twice for the same crime (p. 218)
doble proceso acto de juzgar a una persona dos veces por el mismo delito (pág. 218)

draft a system of required service in the armed forces (p. 223)
conscripción sistema de servicio obligatorio en las fuerzas armadas (pág. 223)

dry farming a method of farming used by Plains farmers in the 1890s that shifted focus from water-dependent crops to more hardy crops (p. 601)

agricultura de secano método de cultivo que usaban los agricultores de las Planicies en la década de 1890 que provocó un cambio de los cultivos que dependían del agua a otros más resistentes (pág. 601)

due process the fair application of the law (p. 218)
debido proceso aplicación justa de la ley (pág. 218)

E

Eighteenth Amendment (1919) a constitutional amendment that outlawed the production and sale of alcoholic beverages in the United States; repealed in 1933 (p. 676)
Decimoctava Enmienda (1919) enmienda constitucional que prohibió la producción y venta de bebidas alcohólicas en Estados Unidos; revocada en 1933 (pág. 676)

electoral college a group of people selected from each of the states to cast votes in presidential elections (p. 234)
colegio electoral grupo de personas seleccionado en cada estado para votar en las elecciones presidenciales (pág. 234)

emancipation freeing of the slaves (p. 529)
emancipación liberación de los esclavos (pág. 529)

Emancipation Proclamation (1862) an order issued by President Abraham Lincoln freeing the slaves in areas rebelling against the Union; took effect January 1, 1863 (p. 529)
Proclamación de Emancipación (1862) orden emitida por el presidente Abraham Lincoln para liberar a los esclavos en las áreas que se rebelaban contra la Unión; entró en vigor el primero de enero de 1863 (pág. 529)

embargo the banning of trade with a country (p. 279)
embargo prohibición del comercio con un país (pág. 279)

Embargo Act (1807) a law that prohibited American merchants from trading with other countries (p. 279)
Ley de Embargo (1807) ley que prohibía a los comerciantes norteamericanos comerciar con otros países (pág. 279)

eminent domain the government's power to take personal property to benefit the public (p. 218)
derecho de expropiación poder otorgado al gobierno para tomar propiedades personales en beneficio del público (pág. 218)

empresarios agents who were contracted by the Mexican republic to bring settlers to Texas in the early 1800s (p. 350)
empresarios agentes contratados por la República Mexicana para traer pobladores a Texas a principios del siglo XIX (pág. 350)

encomienda system a system in Spanish America that gave settlers the right to tax local Indians or to demand their labor in exchange for protecting them and converting them to Christianity (p. 50)
sistema de encomienda sistema adoptado en la América española que permitía a los colonos cobrar impuestos a los indígenas o exigirles trabajo a cambio de su protección y de convertirlos al cristianismo (pág. 50)

English Bill of Rights (1689) a shift of political power from the British monarchy to Parliament (p. 91)
Declaración de Derechos inglesa (1689) cambio del poder político de la monarquía británica al Parlamento inglés (pág. 91)

Enlightenment the Age of Reason; movement that began in Europe in the 1700s as people began examining the natural world, society, and government (p. 95)
Ilustración Era de la Razón; movimiento iniciado en Europa en el siglo XVIII cuando las personas empezaron a examinar la naturaleza, la sociedad y el gobierno (pág. 95)

environment the climate and landscape that surrounds living things (p. 7)
medio ambiente clima y paisaje donde habitan seres vivos (pág. 7)

Era of Good Feelings a period of peace, pride, and progress for the United States from 1815 to 1825 (p. 303)
Era de los Buenos Sentimientos período de paz, orgullo y progreso en Estados Unidos de 1815 a 1825 (pág. 303)

Erie Canal the canal that runs from Albany to Buffalo, New York; completed in 1825 (p. 303)
canal de Erie canal que va de Albany a Buffalo, Nueva York; completado en 1825 (pág. 303)

executive branch the division of the federal government that includes the president and the administrative departments; enforces the nation's laws (p. 167)
poder ejecutivo división del gobierno federal que incluye al presidente y a los departamentos administrativos; hace cumplir las leyes de la nación (pág. 167)

executive orders nonlegislative directives issued by the U.S. president in certain circumstances; executive orders have the force of congressional law (p. 185)
órdenes ejecutivas órdenes no legislativas dictadas por el presidente de Estados Unidos en circunstancias específicas; tienen la misma validez que las leyes del Congreso (pág. 185)

Exodusters African Americans who settled western lands in the late 1800s (p. 601)
Exodusters afroamericanos que se establecieron en el Oeste a finales del siglo XIX (pág. 601)

F

factor a crop broker who managed the trade between southern planters and their customers (p. 417)
agente agrícola persona que administraba el comercio entre las plantaciones del Sur y sus clientes (pág. 417)

federal system a system that divided powers between the states and the federal government (p. 182)
sistema federal sistema en el que se distribuye el poder entre los estados y el gobierno federal (pág. 182)

federalism U.S. system of government in which power is distributed between a central government and individual states (p. 167)
federalismo sistema de gobierno de Estados Unidos en el que el poder se divide entre una autoridad central y estados individuales (pág. 167)

Federalist Papers a series of essays that defended and explained the Constitution and tried to reassure Americans that the states would not be overpowered by the proposed national government (p. 171)
Federalist Papers serie de ensayos que defendían y explicaban la Constitución para convencer a los estadounidenses de que el gobierno nacional propuesto no tendría más poder que los estados (pág. 171)

Federalist Party a political party created in the 1790s and influenced by Alexander Hamilton that wanted to strengthen the federal government and promote industry and trade (p. 250)
Partido Federalista partido político creado en la década de 1790 e influenciado por las ideas de Alexander Hamilton para fortalecer al gobierno federal y fomentar la industria y el comercio (pág. 250)

Federalists people who supported ratification of the Constitution (p. 170)
federalistas personas que apoyaban la ratificación de la Constitución (pág. 170)

Fifteenth Amendment (1870) a constitutional amendment that gave African American men the right to vote (p. 563)
Decimoquinta Enmienda (1870) enmienda constitucional que daba a los hombres afroamericanos el derecho al voto (pág. 563)

54th Massachusetts Infantry African American Civil War regiment that captured Fort Wagner in South Carolina (p. 531)
54to Batallón de Infantería de Massachusetts regimiento afroamericano de la Guerra Civil que tomó el fuerte Wagner en Carolina del Sur (pág. 531)

First Battle of Bull Run (1861) the first major battle of the Civil War, resulting in a Confederate victory; showed that the Civil War would not be won easily (p. 517)
primera batalla de Bull Run (1861) primera batalla importante de la Guerra Civil, en la cual ganó el ejército confederado; demostró que la guerra no se ganaría fácilmente (pág. 517)

First Continental Congress (1774) a meeting of colonial delegates in Philadelphia to decide how to respond to the closing of Boston Harbor, increased taxes, and abuses of authority by the British government; delegates petitioned King George III, listing the freedoms they believed colonists should enjoy (p. 112)
Primer Congreso Continental (1774) reunión de delegados de las colonias en Filadelfia para decidir cómo responder al cierre del puerto de Boston, al alza de impuestos y a los abusos de la autoridad por parte del gobierno británico; los delegados hicieron peticiones al rey Jorge III, enumerando los derechos que consideraban justos para los colonos (pág. 112)

folktale a story that often provides a moral lesson (p. 427)
cuento popular narración que con frecuencia ofrece una moraleja (pág. 427)

Fort Sumter a federal outpost in Charleston, South Carolina, that was attacked by the Confederates in April 1861, sparking the Civil War (p. 511)
fuerte Sumter puesto de avanzada federal en Charleston, Carolina del Sur, cuyo ataque por parte de los confederados en abril de 1861 dio origen a la Guerra Civil (pág. 511)

forty-niner a gold-seeker who moved to California during the gold rush (p. 365)
del cuarenta y nueve buscador de oro que se mudó a California durante la fiebre del oro (pág. 365)

Fourteenth Amendment (1866) a constitutional amendment giving full rights of citizenship to all people born or naturalized in the United States, except for American Indians (p. 561)
Decimocuarta Enmienda (1866) enmienda constitucional que otorgaba derechos totales de ciudadanía a todas las personas nacidas en Estados Unidos o naturalizadas estadounidenses, con excepción de los indígenas americanos (pág. 561)

Freedmen's Bureau an agency established by Congress in 1865 to help poor people throughout the South (p. 556)
Oficina de Esclavos Libertos oficina creada por el Congreso en 1865 para ayudar a los pobres del Sur del país (pág. 556)

Freeport Doctrine (1858) a statement made by Stephen Douglas during the Lincoln-Douglas debates that pointed out how people could use popular sovereignty to determine if their state or territory should permit slavery (p. 492)
Doctrina de Freeport (1858) declaración hecha por Stephen Douglas durante los debates Lincoln-Douglas que señalaba que el pueblo podía usar la soberanía popular para decidir si su estado o territorio debía permitir la esclavitud (pág. 492)

Free-Soil Party a political party formed in 1848 by antislavery northerners who left the Whig and Democratic parties because neither addressed the slavery issue (p. 477)
Partido Tierra Libre partido político formado en 1848 por abolicionistas de los estados del Norte que habían abandonado el Partido Whig y el Partido Demócrata porque ninguno de los dos partidos tenía una postura sobre la esclavitud (pág. 477)

French Revolution French rebellion that began in 1789 in which the French people overthrew the monarchy and made their country a republic (p. 243)
Revolución Francesa rebelión francesa iniciada en 1789 en la que la población francesa derrocó a la monarquía y convirtió el país en una república (pág. 243)

frontier an undeveloped area (p. 586)
frontera área que no está siendo utilizada por el ser humano (pág. 586)

Fugitive Slave Act (1850) a law that made it a crime to help runaway slaves; allowed for the arrest of escaped slaves in areas where slavery was illegal, and required their return to slaveholders (p. 479)
Ley de Esclavos Fugitivos (1850) ley que hacía que ayudar a un esclavo a escapar de su amo fuera un delito; permitía la captura de esclavos fugitivos en zonas donde la esclavitud era ilegal para devolverlos a sus dueños (pág. 479)

G

Gadsden Purchase (1853) U.S. purchase of land from Mexico that included the southern parts of presentday Arizona and New Mexico (p. 361)
Compra de Gadsden (1853) compra por parte del gobierno de Estados Unidos de territorio mexicano que incluía la región ocupada actualmente por el sur de Arizona y Nuevo México (pág. 361)

Gettysburg Address (1863) a speech given by Abraham Lincoln in which he praised the bravery of Union soldiers and renewed his commitment to winning the Civil War (p. 540)
Discurso de Gettysburg (1863) discurso de Abraham Lincoln en el que alababa la valentía de las tropas de la Unión y renovaba su compromiso de triunfar en la Guerra Civil (pág. 540)

Ghost Dance a religious movement among Native Americans that spread across the Plains in the 1880s (p. 598)
Danza de los Espíritus movimiento religioso de los indígenas norteamericanos que se extendió por la región de las Planicies en la década de 1880 (pág. 598)

Gibbons* v. *Ogden (1824) a Supreme Court ruling that reinforced the federal government's authority over the states (p. 397)
Gibbons* contra *Ogden (1824) decisión de la Corte Suprema que reforzó la autoridad del gobierno federal sobre los estados (pág. 397)

Great Awakening a religious movement that became widespread in the American colonies in the 1730s and 1740s (p. 94)
Gran Despertar movimiento religioso que tuvo gran popularidad en las colonias norteamericanas en las décadas de 1730 y 1740 (pág. 94)

Great Compromise (1787) an agreement worked out at the Constitutional Convention establishing that a state's population would determine representation in the lower house of the legislature, while each state would have equal representation in the upper house of the legislature (p. 165)
Gran Compromiso (1787) acuerdo redactado durante la Convención Constitucional en el que se establece que la población de un estado debe determinar su representación en la cámara baja de la asamblea legislativa y que cada estado debe tener igual representación en la cámara alta de la asamblea. (pág. 165)

H

habeas corpus the constitutional protection against unlawful imprisonment (p. 532)
hábeas corpus protección constitucional contra el encarcelamiento ilegal (pág. 532)

hajj a pilgrimage to Mecca made by devout Muslims (p. 18)
hajj peregrinación a La Meca realizada por los musulmanes devotos (pág. 18)

Hartford Convention (1815) a meeting of Federalists at Hartford, Connecticut, to protest the War of 1812 (p. 287)
Convención de Hartford (1815) reunión de federalistas en Hartford, Connecticut, para protestar por la Guerra de 1812 (pág. 287)

Haymarket Riot a riot that broke out at Haymarket Square in Chicago over the deaths of two strikers (p. 626)
Revuelta de Haymarket revuelta que se originó en la Plaza Haymarket de Chicago por la muerte de dos huelguistas (pág. 626)

Homestead Act (1862) a law passed by Congress to encourage settlement in the West by giving government-owned land to small farmers (p. 600)
Ley de Colonización de Tierras (1862) ley aprobada por el Congreso para fomentar la colonización del Oeste mediante la cesión de tierras del gobierno a pequeños agricultores (pág. 600)

Homestead strike (1892) a labor-union strike at Andrew Carnegie's Homestead Steel factory in Pennsylvania that erupted in violence between strikers and private detectives (p. 627)
huelga de Homestead (1892) huelga sindical en la fábrica de acero Homestead de Andrew Carnegie en Pensilvania, que produjo violencia entre huelguistas y detectives privados (pág. 627)

horizontal integration owning all the businesses in a certain field (p. 621)
integración horizontal posesión de todas las empresas en un campo específico (pág. 621)

Hudson River school a group of American artists in the mid-1800s whose paintings focused on the American landscape (p. 310)
Escuela del Río Hudson grupo de artistas estadounidenses de mediados del siglo XIX que pintaban diversos paisajes del territorio estadounidense (pág. 310)

Hull House a settlement house founded by Jane Addams and Ellen Gates Starr in 1889 (p. 648)
Casa Hull casa de asistencia a la comunidad fundada por Jane Addams y Ellen Gates Starr en 1889 (pág. 648)

hunter-gatherer a person who hunts animals and gathers wild plants to provide for his or her needs (p. 6)
cazador y recolector persona que caza animales y recolecta plantas para satisfacer sus necesidades (pág. 6)

I

immigrant a person who moves to another country after leaving his or her homeland (p. 78)
inmigrante persona que abandona su país para establecerse en un país diferente (pág. 78)

immune having a natural resistance to disease (p. 58)
inmune la condición de tener resistencia natural contra la enfermedad (pág. 58)

impeach to bring charges against a public official (p. 184)
someter a juicio político presentar cargos en contra de un funcionario público (pág. 184)

impeachment the process used by a legislative body to bring charges of wrongdoing against a public official (p. 562)
juicio político proceso por el cual un cuerpo legislativo presenta cargos en contra de un funcionario público (pág. 562)

imperialism the practice of extending a nation's power by gaining territories for a colonial empire (p. 692)
imperialismo práctica en la que una nación amplía su poder adquiriendo territorios para un imperio colonial (pág. 692)

impressment the practice of forcing people to serve in the army or navy; led to increased tensions between Great Britain and the United States in the early 1800s (p. 279)
leva práctica que obligaba a las personas a servir en el ejército o la marina; aumentó las fricciones entre Gran Bretaña y Estados Unidos a principios del siglo XIX (pág. 279)

indentured servant a colonist who received free passage to North America in exchange for working without pay for a certain number of years (p. 74)
sirviente por contrato colono que recibía un pasaje gratuito a América del Norte a cambio de trabajar sin salario por varios años (pág. 74)

Indian Removal Act (1830) a congressional act that authorized the removal of Native Americans who lived east of the Mississippi River (p. 332)
Ley de Expulsión de Indígenas (1830) ley del Congreso que autorizaba la expulsión de los indígenas norteamericanos que vivían al este del río Mississippi (pág. 332)

Indian Territory an area covering most of present-day Oklahoma to which most Native Americans in the Southeast were forced to move in the 1830s (p. 332)
Territorio Indígena área que abarcaba la mayor parte del actual estado de Oklahoma a la que la mayoría de las tribus indígenas del sureste fueron obligadas a trasladarse durante la década de 1830 (pág. 332)

indict to formally accuse (p. 218)
acusar presentar cargos formales en contra de alguien (pág. 218)

Industrial Revolution a period of rapid growth in the use of machines in manufacturing and production that began in the mid-1700s (p. 385)
Revolución Industrial período de rápido desarrollo debido al uso de maquinaria en la fabricación y producción; comenzó a mediados del siglo XVIII (pág. 385)

Industrial Workers of the World (IWW) a union founded in 1905 by socialists and union leaders that included workers not welcomed in the AFL (p. 674)
Trabajadores Industriales del Mundo (IWW, por sus siglas en inglés) sindicato fundado en 1905 por socialistas y líderes sindicales que incluía a los trabajadores que no admitía la Federación Americana del Trabajo (pág. 674)

inflation increased prices for goods and services combined with the reduced value of money (p. 161)
inflación subida en los precios de los bienes al mismo tiempo que se reduce al valor del dinero (pág. 161)

initiative a method of allowing voters to propose a new law if enough signatures are collected on a petition (p. 666)
iniciativa método que permite a los votantes proponer una nueva ley si consiguen suficientes firmas para una petición (pág. 666)

interchangeable parts a process developed by Eli Whitney in the 1790s that called for making each part of a machine exactly the same (p. 387)
piezas intercambiables proceso desarrollado por Eli Whitney en la década de 1790 para que todas las piezas de una máquina fueran exactamente iguales (pág. 387)

interest group a group of people who share common interests for political action (p. 224)
grupo de interés grupo de personas que comparten intereses comunes en iniciativas políticas (pág. 224)

interstate commerce trade between two or more states (p. 160)
comercio interestatal intercambio comercial entre dos o más estados (pág. 160)

Intolerable Acts (1774) laws passed by Parliament to punish the colonists for the Boston Tea Party and to tighten government control of the colonies (p. 102)
Leyes Intolerables (1774) serie de leyes aprobadas por el Parlamento para castigar a los colonos que participaron en el Motín del Té de Boston y para aumentar su control sobre las colonias (pág. 102)

ironclad a warship that is heavily armored with iron (p. 520)
acorazado buque de guerra fuertemente protegido con hierro (pág. 520)

Iroquois League a political confederation of five northeastern Native American nations of the Seneca, Oneida, Mohawk, Cayuga, and Onondaga that made decisions concerning war and peace (p. 14)
Liga de Iroqueses confederación política formada por cinco naciones indígenas del noreste de Estados Unidos (los senecas, los oneidas, los mohawks, los cayugas y los onondagas) para tomar decisiones relacionadas con asuntos de guerra y paz (pág. 14)

isolationism a national policy of avoiding involvement in other countries' affairs (p. 693)
aislacionismo política nacional de evitar involucrarse en los asuntos de otras naciones (pág. 693)

J

Jacksonian Democracy an expansion of voting rights during the popular Andrew Jackson administration (p. 323)
democracia jacksoniana ampliación del derecho al voto durante el popular gobierno del presidente Andrew Jackson (pág. 323)

Jamestown the first colony in the United States; set up in 1607 along the James River in Virginia (p. 72)
Jamestown primera colonia en territorio estadounidense; fundada en 1607 a orillas del río James en Virginia (pág. 72)

Jay's Treaty (1794) an agreement negotiated by John Jay to work out problems between Britain and the United States over northwestern lands, British seizure of U.S. ships, and U.S. debts owed to the British (p. 245)
Tratado de Jay (1794) acuerdo negociado por John Jay para resolver los problemas entre Gran Bretaña y Estados Unidos por los territorios del noroeste, la confiscación británica de barcos estadounidenses, y las deudas que los estadounidenses les debían a los británicos (pág. 245)

Jim Crow law a law that enforced segregation in the southern states (p. 568)
ley de Jim Crow ley que imponía la segregación en los estados del Sur (pág. 568)

John Brown's raid (1859) an incident in which abolitionist John Brown and 21 other men captured a federal arsenal in Harpers Ferry, Virginia, in hope of starting a slave rebellion (p. 493)
ataque de John Brown (1859) incidente en el que el abolicionista John Brown y otros 21 hombres capturaron un arsenal federal en Harpers Ferry, Virginia, con la esperanza de iniciar una rebelión de esclavos (pág. 493)

joint-stock company a business formed by a group of people who jointly make an investment and share in the profits and losses (p. 27)
sociedad por acciones negocio formado por un grupo de personas que hacen una inversión juntos y comparten las ganancias y las pérdidas (pág. 27)

judicial branch the division of the federal government that is made up of the national courts; interprets laws, punishes criminals, and settles disputes between states (p. 167)
poder judicial división del gobierno federal formada por las cortes nacionales; interpreta las leyes, castiga a los delincuentes y resuelve las disputas entre estados (pág. 167)

judicial review the Supreme Court's power to declare acts of Congress unconstitutional (p. 270)
recurso de inconstitucionalidad poder de la Corte Suprema para declarar inconstitucionales las leyes del Congreso (pág. 270)

Judiciary Act of 1789 legislation passed by Congress that created the federal court system (p. 236)
Ley de Judicatura de 1789 ley aprobada por el Congreso para crear el sistema federal de cortes (pág. 236)

K

Kansas-Nebraska Act (1854) a law that allowed voters in Kansas and Nebraska to choose whether to allow slavery (p. 485)
Ley de Kansas y Nebraska (1854) ley que permitía a los votantes de Kansas y Nebraska decidir si permitían la esclavitud (pág. 485)

Kentucky and Virginia Resolutions (1798–1799) Republican documents that argued that the Alien and Sedition Acts were unconstitutional (p. 253)
Resoluciones de Kentucky y Virginia (1798–1799) documentos republicanos que argumentaban que las Leyes de No Intervención Extranjera y Sedición eran inconstitucionales (pág. 253)

Kitchen Cabinet President Andrew Jackson's group of informal advisers; so called because they often met in the White House kitchen (p. 324)
gabinete de la cocina grupo informal de consejeros del presidente Andrew Jackson; llamado así porque solían reunirse en la cocina de la Casa Blanca (pág. 324)

kivas underground ceremonial chambers at the center of Anasazi communities (p. 11)
kivas cámaras ceremoniales subterráneas en el centro de las comunidades anasazi (pág. 11)

knights warriors who fought on horseback in return for land from nobles (p. 24)
caballeros guerreros que luchaban a caballo a cambio de tierras de los nobles (pág. 24)

Knights of Labor secret society that became the first truly national labor union in the United States (p. 625)
Caballeros del Trabajo sociedad secreta que se convirtió en el primer sindicato verdaderamente nacional en Estados Unidos (pág. 625)

Know-Nothing Party a political organization founded in 1849 by nativists who supported measures making it difficult for foreigners to become citizens and to hold office (p. 440)
Partido de los Ignorantes organización política fundada en 1849 por un grupo de nativistas; apoyaba medidas que dificultaban que los extranjeros obtuvieran la ciudadanía y que tuvieran cargos públicos (pág. 440)

Ku Klux Klan a secret society created by white southerners in 1866 that used terror and violence to keep African Americans from obtaining their civil rights (p. 566)
Ku Klux Klan sociedad secreta creada en 1866 por blancos del Sur que usaba el terror y la violencia para impedir que los afroamericanos obtuvieran derechos civiles (pág. 566)

L

Land Ordinance of 1785 legislation passed by Congress authorizing surveys and the division of public lands in the western region of the country (p. 155)
Ordenanza de Territorios de 1785 legislación aprobada por el Congreso en la que se autorizaban las mediciones de terreno y la división de territorios públicos en el oeste del país (pág. 155)

legislative branch the division of the government that proposes bills and passes them into laws (p. 167)
poder legislativo división del gobierno que propone proyectos de ley y los aprueba para convertirlos en leyes (pág. 167)

Lewis and Clark expedition an expedition led by Meriwether Lewis and William Clark that began in 1804 to explore the Louisiana Purchase (p. 275)
expedición de Lewis y Clark expedición encabezada por Meriwether Lewis y William Clark que empezó en 1804 para explorar la Compra de Luisiana (pág. 275)

Lincoln-Douglas debates a series of debates between Republican Abraham Lincoln and Democrat Stephen Douglas during the 1858 U.S. Senate campaign in Illinois (p. 491)
debates Lincoln-Douglas serie de debates entre el republicano Abraham Lincoln y el demócrata Stephen Douglas durante la campaña de 1858 para el Senado estadounidense en Illinois (pág. 491)

Line of Demarcation boundary between Spanish and Portuguese territories in the New World (p. 44)
Línea de Demarcación límite entre los territorios españoles y portugueses en el Nuevo Mundo (pág. 44)

Long Walk (1864) a 300-mile march made by Navajo captives to a reservation in Bosque Redondo, New Mexico, that led to the deaths of hundreds of Navajo (p. 597)
Larga Marcha (1864) caminata de 300 millas que hizo un grupo de prisioneros navajos hasta una reserva indígena en Bosque Redondo, Nuevo México, en la que murieron cientos de ellos (pág. 597)

loose construction a way of interpreting the Constitution that allows the federal government to take actions that the Constitution does not specifically forbid it from taking (p. 242)
interpretación flexible interpretación de la Constitución que permite al gobierno federal tomar acciones que la Constitución no prohíbe de manera específica (pág. 242)

Louisiana Purchase (1803) the purchase of French land between the Mississippi River and the Rocky Mountains that doubled the size of the United States (p. 274)

Compra de Luisiana (1803) adquisición del territorio francés localizado entre el río Mississippi y las montañas Rocallosas que duplicó el tamaño de Estados Unidos (pág. 274)

Lowell system the use of waterpowered textile mills that employed young, unmarried women in the 1800s (p. 392)
sistema de Lowell uso de molinos de agua en la industria textil, dando empleo a muchas mujeres jóvenes solteras en el siglo XIX (pág. 392)

Loyalists colonists who sided with Britain in the American Revolution (p. 119)
leales colonos que apoyaron la causa británica durante la Guerra de Independencia estadounidense (pág. 119)

M

Magna Carta (1215) a charter of liberties agreed to by King John of England, it made the king obey the same laws as citizens (p. 152)
Carta Magna (1215) carta de libertades firmada por el rey Juan de Inglaterra que decía que el rey debía obedecer las mismas leyes que los ciudadanos (pág. 152)

majority rule the idea that policies are decided by the greatest number of people (p. 216)
gobierno de la mayoría idea de que las políticas se adoptan según lo que decida el mayor número de personas (pág. 216)

manifest destiny a belief shared by many Americans in the mid-1800s that the United States should expand across the continent to the Pacific Ocean (p. 354)
destino manifiesto creencia de muchos ciudadanos estadounidenses a mediados del siglo XIX de que Estados Unidos debía expandirse por todo el continente hasta el océano Pacífico (pág. 354)

Marbury* v. *Madison (1803) U.S. Supreme Court case that established the principle of judicial review (p. 270)
Marbury contra *Madison* (1803) caso de la Corte Suprema de Estados Unidos que estableció recurso de inconstitucionalidad (pág. 270)

Massacre at Wounded Knee (1890) the U.S. Army's killing of approximately 150 Sioux at Wounded Knee Creek in South Dakota; ended U.S-Indian wars on the Plains (p. 597)
masacre de Wounded Knee (1890) matanza de aproximadamente 150 indios siux en Wounded Knee Creek, Dakota del Sur; dio por terminadas las guerras entre estadounidenses e indígenas en las Planicies (pág. 597)

mass culture leisure and cultural activities shared by many people (p. 644)
cultura de masas actividades culturales y del tiempo libre que les gustan a muchas personas (pág. 644)

mass production the efficient production of large numbers of identical goods (p. 387)
producción en masa producción eficiente de grandes cantidades de productos idénticos (pág. 387)

mass transit public transportation (p. 644)
transporte colectivo transporte público (pág. 644)

matrilineal related to ancestry traced through the maternal, or mother's, line (p. 14)
materno basado en linaje seguido por línea materna, o de la madre (pág. 14)

Mayflower Compact (1620) a document written by the Pilgrims establishing themselves as a political society and setting guidelines for self-government (p. 79)
Pacto del Mayflower (1620) documento redactado por los peregrinos en el que se establecían como sociedad política y establecían principios para gobernarse a sí mismos (pág. 79)

McCulloch* v. *Maryland (1819) U.S. Supreme Court case that declared the Second Bank of the United States was constitutional and that Maryland could not interfere with it (p. 330)
McCulloch contra *Maryland* (1819) caso de la Corte Suprema de Estados Unidos que declaraba que el Segundo Banco de la Nación era constitucional y que Maryland no podía intervenir en sus operaciones (pág. 330)

mercenaries hired foreign soldiers (p. 128)
mercenario s soldados extranjeros a sueldo (pág. 128)

Mexican Revolution a revolution led by Francisco Madero in 1910 that eventually forced the Mexican dictator Díaz to resign (p. 708)
Revolución Mexicana revolución iniciada en 1910 por Francisco Madero, que finalmente obligó al dictador mexicano Díaz a renunciar (pág. 708)

middle class the social and economic level between the wealthy and the poor (p. 440)
clase media nivel social y económico ubicado entre la clase rica y la clase pobre (pág. 440)

Middle Passage a voyage that brought enslaved Africans across the Atlantic Ocean to North America and the West Indies (p. 59)
Viaje Intermedio viaje a través del océano Atlántico para transportar esclavos africanos a América del Norte y a las Antillas (pág. 59)

migration the movement of people from one region to another (p. 6)
migración movimiento de personas de una región a otra (pág. 6)

minutemen American colonial militia members ready to fight at a minute's notice (p. 114)
minutemen milicanos norteamericanos en la época colonial que estaban preparados para combatir en cualquier momento si la situación lo requería (pág. 114)

Missouri Compromise (1820) an agreement proposed by Henry Clay that allowed Missouri to enter the Union as a slave state and Maine to enter as a free state and outlawed slavery in any territories or states north of 36°30´ latitude (p. 305)
Compromiso de Missouri (1820) acuerdo propuesto por Henry Clay en el que se aceptaba a Missouri en la Unión como estado esclavista y a Maine como estado libre, además de prohibir la esclavitud en los territorios o estados al norte del paralelo 36°30´ (pág. 305)

monopoly a complete control over the entire supply of goods or a service in a particular market (p. 622)
monopolio control absoluto de toda la oferta de bienes o de un servicio en un mercado en particular (pág. 622)

Monroe Doctrine (1823) President James Monroe's statement forbidding further colonization in the Americas and declaring that any attempt by a foreign country to colonize would be considered an act of hostility (p. 300)
Doctrina Monroe (1823) declaración hecha por el presidente James Monroe en la que se prohibía la colonización adicional de las Américas y se declaraba que cualquier intento de colonización por parte de otro país se consideraría un acto hostil (pág. 300)

Mormon a member of the Church of Jesus Christ of Latter-day Saints (p. 349)
mormón miembro de la Iglesia de Jesucristo de los Santos de los Últimos Días (pág. 349)

Morrill Act (1862) a federal law passed by Congress that gave land to western states to encourage them to build colleges (p. 600)
Ley de Morrill (1862) ley federal aprobada por el Congreso que otorgaba tierras a los estados del Oeste para fomentar la construcción de universidades (pág. 600)

Morse code a system developed by Alfred Lewis Vail for the telegraph that used a certain combination of dots and dashes to represent each letter of the alphabet (p. 403)
clave Morse sistema desarrollado por Alfred Lewis Vail para el telégrafo en el que una combinación de puntos y rayas representa cada letra del alfabeto (pág. 403)

mosques buildings used for Muslim prayer (p. 19)
mezquitas casas de oración musulmanas (pág. 19)

mountain men men hired by eastern companies to trap animals for fur in the Rocky Mountains and other western regions of the United States (p. 346)
montañeses hombres contratados por compañías del este para atrapar animales y obtener sus pieles en las montañas Rocallosas y en otras regiones del oeste de Estados Unidos (pág. 346)

muckrakers a term coined for journalists who "raked up" and exposed corruption and problems of society (p. 664)
muckrakers término acuñado para nombrar a los periodistas que se dedicaban a investigar y exponer la corrupción y los problemas de la sociedad (pág. 664)

N

National American Woman Suffrage Association (NAWSA) an organization founded by Elizabeth Cady Stanton and Susan B. Anthony in 1890 to obtain women's right to vote (p. 676)
Asociación Nacional Americana para el Sufragio Femenino (NAWSA, por sus siglas en inglés) organización fundada en 1890 por Elizabeth Cady Stanton y Susan B. Anthony para obtener el derecho al voto de las mujeres (pág. 676)

National Association for the Advancement of Colored People (NAACP) an organization founded in 1909 by W. E. B. Du Bois and other reformers to bring attention to racial inequality (p. 678)
Asociación Nacional para el Progreso de la Gente de Color (NAACP, por sus siglas en inglés) organización fundada en 1909 por W. E. B. Du Bois y otros reformadores para llamar la atención sobre la desigualdad racial (pág. 678)

national debt the total amount of money owed by a country to its lenders (p. 238)
deuda pública cantidad total de dinero que un país debe a quienes se lo prestaron (pág. 238)

National Grange a social and educational organization for farmers (p. 603)
National Grange organización social y educativa para los agricultores (pág. 603)

nationalism a sense of pride and devotion to a nation (p. 302)
nacionalismo sentimiento de orgullo y lealtad a una nación (pág. 302)

nativists U.S. citizens who opposed immigration because they were suspicious of immigrants and feared losing jobs to them (p. 440)
nativistas ciudadanos estadounidenses que se oponían a la inmigración porque sospechaban de los inmigrantes y temían que se apropiaran de sus empleos (pág. 440)

Nat Turner's Rebellion (1831) a rebellion in which Nat Turner led a group of slaves in Virginia in an unsuccessful attempt to overthrow and kill planter families (p. 428)
Rebelión de Nat Turner (1831) rebelión de un grupo de esclavos encabezados por Nat Turner en Virginia en un intento frustrado de derrocar y asesinar familias que eran dueñas de plantaciones (pág. 428)

naturalized citizen a person born in another country who has been granted citizenship in the United States (p. 222)
ciudadano naturalizado persona nacida en otro país que ha obtenido la ciudadanía estadounidense (pág. 222)

Neutrality Proclamation (1793) a statement made by President George Washington that the United States would not side with any of the nations at war in Europe following the French Revolution (p. 244)
Proclamación de Neutralidad (1793) declaración en la que el presidente George Washington anunció que Estados Unidos no sería aliado de ninguna de las naciones europeas en guerra después de la Revolución Francesa (pág. 244)

new immigrant a term often used for an immigrant who arrived in the United States beginning in the 1880s (p. 636)
nuevo inmigrante término empleado a menudo para referirse a los inmigrantes que llegaron a Estados Unidos a partir de la década de 1880 (pág. 636)

New Jersey Plan a proposal to create a unicameral legislature with equal representation of states rather than representation by population; rejected at the Constitutional Convention (p. 165)
Plan de Nueva Jersey propuesta para la creación de un gobierno de una cámara con la misma representación para cada estado sin importar el tamaño de su población; fue rechazada en la Convención Constitucional (pág. 165)

Nineteenth Amendment (1920) a constitutional amendment that gave women the vote (p. 677)
Decimonovena Enmienda (1920) enmienda constitucional que dio a la mujer el derecho al voto (pág. 677)

nominating conventions a meeting at which a political party selects its presidential and vice presidential candidate; first held in the 1820s (p. 323)
convenciones de nominación reunión en la que un partido político elige a sus candidatos a la presidencia y la vicepresidencia; se realizaron por primera vez en la década de 1820 (pág. 323)

Non-Intercourse Act (1809) a law that replaced the Embargo Act and restored trade with all nations except Britain, France, and their colonies (p. 280)
Ley de No Interacción (1809) ley que reemplazaba a la Ley de Embargo, restableciendo el comercio con todas las naciones, excepto Gran Bretaña, Francia y sus colonias (pág. 280)

Northwest Ordinance of 1787 legislation passed by Congress to establish a political structure for the Northwest Territory and create a system for the admission of new states (p. 155)
Ordenanza del Noroeste de 1787 legislación aprobada por el Congreso para establecer una estructura política en el Territorio del Noroeste y crear un proceso de admisión de nuevos estados (pág. 155)

Northwest Passage a nonexistent path through North America that early explorers searched for that would allow ships to sail from the Atlantic to the Pacific Ocean (p. 54)
Paso del Noroeste ruta inexistente buscada por muchos exploradores a lo largo de América del Norte para cruzar en barco del océano Atlántico al océano Pacífico (pág. 54)

Northwest Territory lands including present-day Illinois, Indiana, Michigan, Ohio, and Wisconsin; organized by the Northwest Ordinance of 1787 (p. 155)
Territorio del Noroeste región que incluía los actuales estados de Illinois, Indiana, Michigan, Ohio y Wisconsin; creado por la Ordenanza del Noroeste de 1787 (pág. 155)

nullification crisis a dispute led by John C. Calhoun that said that states could ignore federal laws if they believed those laws violated the Constitution (p. 328)
crisis de anulación controversia iniciada por John C. Calhoun que decía que los estados no tenían que hacer caso a las leyes federales si consideraban que desobedecían la Constitución (pág. 328)

O

old immigrant a term often used for an immigrant who arrived in the United States before the 1880s (p. 636)
antiguo inmigrante término empleado con frecuencia para referirse a los inmigrantes que llegaron a Estados Unidos antes de la década de 1880 (pág. 636)

Open Door Policy a policy established by the United States in 1899 to promote equal access for all nations to trade in China (p. 695)
política de puertas abiertas política establecida por Estados Unidos en 1899 para promover el acceso igualitario de todas las naciones al comercio con China (pág. 695)

Oregon Trail a 2,000-mile trail stretching through the Great Plains from western Missouri to the Oregon Territory (p. 348)
Camino de Oregón ruta de 2,000 millas que cruzaba las Grandes Planicies desde el oeste de Missouri hasta el Territorio de Oregón (pág. 348)

P

Paleo-Indians the first Americans who crossed from Asia into North America sometime between 38,000 and 10,000 BC (p. 6)
paleoindígenas primeros habitantes de América que cruzaron de Asia a América del Norte entre 38,000 y 10,000 a. C. (pág. 6)

Panama Canal an artificial waterway across the Isthmus of Panama; completed by the United States in 1914 (p. 705)
canal de Panamá canal artificial que atraviesa el istmo de Panamá; Estados Unidos completó su construcción en 1914 (pág. 705)

Panic of 1837 a financial crisis in the United States that led to an economic depression (p. 331)
Pánico de 1837 crisis financiera en Estados Unidos que provocó una depresión económica (pág. 331)

pardon freedom from punishment (p. 185)
indulto liberación de un castigo (pág. 185)

patent an exclusive right to make or sell an invention (p. 616)
patente derecho exclusivo para fabricar o vender un invento (pág. 616)

Patriots American colonists who fought for independence from Great Britain during the Revolutionary War (p. 113)
patriotas colonos norteamericanos que lucharon para independizarse de Gran Bretaña durante la Guerra de Independencia estadounidense (pág. 113)

petition to make a formal request of the government (p. 217)
peticionar hacer una solicitud formal al gobierno (pág. 217)

Pickett's Charge (1863) a failed Confederate attack during the Civil War led by General George Pickett at the Battle of Gettysburg (p. 539)
ataque de Pickett (1863) ataque fallido del ejército confederado, al mando del general George Pickett, en la batalla de Gettysburg durante la Guerra Civil (pág. 539)

Pilgrim a member of a Puritan Separatist sect that left England in the early 1600s to settle in the Americas (p. 78)
peregrino miembro de una secta separatista puritana que se fue de Inglaterra a principios del siglo XVII para establecerse en América (pág. 78)

Pinckney's Treaty (1795) an agreement between the United States and Spain that changed Florida's border and made it easier for American ships to use the port of New Orleans (p. 245)
Tratado de Pinckney (1795) acuerdo entre Estados Unidos y España que modificó los límites de Florida y facilitó a los barcos estadounidenses el uso del puerto de Nueva Orleáns (pág. 245)

placer miner a person who mines for gold by using pans or other devices to wash gold nuggets out of loose rock and gravel (p. 366)
buscador de oro con batea persona que busca oro con bateas u otros aparatos similares para lavar las pepitas de oro y separarlas de las piedras y la gravilla (pág. 366)

plantation a large farm that usually specialized in growing one kind of crop for profit (p. 50)
plantación gran finca que por lo general se especializaba en un cultivo específico para obtener ganancias (pág. 50)

planter a large-scale farmer who held more than 20 slaves (p. 416)
hacendado agricultor a gran escala que tenía más de 20 esclavos (pág. 416)

Platt Amendment a part of the Cuban constitution drafted under the supervision of the United States that limited Cuba's right to make treaties, gave the U.S. the right to intervene in Cuban affairs, and required Cuba to sell or lease land to the U.S (p. 701)
Enmienda Platt parte de la constitución cubana redactada bajo la supervisión de Estados Unidos que limitaba el derecho de Cuba a firmar tratados, le daba a Estados Unidos el derecho de intervenir en los asuntos cubanos y le exigía a Cuba vender o arrendar tierras a Estados Unidos (pág. 701)

Plessy* v. *Ferguson (1896) U.S. Supreme Court case that established the "separate-but-equal" doctrine for public facilities (p. 569)
Plessy contra Ferguson (1896) caso en el que la Corte Suprema de Estados Unidos estableció la doctrina de "separados pero iguales" en los lugares públicos (pág. 569)

political action committee (PAC) an organization that collects money to distribute to candidates who support the same issues as the contributors (p. 224)
comité de acción política (PAC, por sus siglas en inglés) organización que recolecta dinero para distribuirlo a los candidatos que apoyen los mismos asuntos que los contribuyentes (pág. 224)

political machine a powerful organization that influenced city and county politics in the late 1800s (p. 662)
maquinaria política organización poderosa que influía en la política municipal y del condado a finales del siglo XIX (pág. 662)

political party a group of people who organize to help elect government officials and influence government policies (p. 250)
partido político grupo de personas que se organiza para facilitar la elección de los funcionarios del gobierno e influye en las políticas del gobierno (pág. 250)

poll tax a special tax that a person had to pay in order to vote (p. 568)
impuesto electoral impuesto especial que tenía que pagar una persona para poder votar (pág. 568)

Pony Express a system of messengers that carried mail between relay stations on a route 2,000-miles long in 1860 and 1861 (p. 590)
Pony Express sistema de mensajeros que llevaban el correo entre estaciones de relevo a lo largo de una ruta de 2,000 millas en 1860 y 1861 (pág. 590)

ENGLISH AND SPANISH GLOSSARY

popular sovereignty the idea that political authority belongs to the people (p. 167, 476)
soberanía popular idea de que la autoridad política pertenece al pueblo (pág. 167, 476)

Populist Party a political party formed in 1892 that supported free coinage of silver, work reforms, immigration restrictions, and government ownership of railroads and telegraph and telephone systems (p. 604)
Partido Populista partido político formado en 1892 que apoyaba la libre producción de monedas de plata, reformas laborales y restricciones de la inmigración, además de asignar al gobierno la propiedad de los sistemas ferroviario, telegráfico y telefónico (pág. 604)

Pottawatomie Massacre (1856) an incident in which abolitionist John Brown and seven other men murdered pro-slavery Kansans (p. 487)
masacre de Pottawatomie (1856) incidente en el que el abolicionista John Brown y siete hombres más asesinaron a habitantes esclavistas de Kansas (pág. 487)

precedent an action or decision that later serves as an example (p. 235)
precedente acción o decisión que más tarde sirve de ejemplo (pág. 235)

privateer a private ship authorized by a nation to attack its enemies (p. 244)
corsario barco privado autorizado por una nación para atacar a sus enemigos (pág. 244)

Progressives a group of reformers who worked to improve social and political problems in the late 1800s (p. 664)
progresistas grupo de reformistas que trabajaron para resolver problemas sociales y políticos a finales del siglo XIX (pág. 664)

Progressive Party a short-lived political party that attempted to institute social reforms (p. 682)
Partido Progresista partido político de poca duración que intentó establecer reformas sociales (pág. 682)

prospect to search for gold (p. 366)
prospectar buscar oro (pág. 366)

Protestant Reformation a religious movement begun by Martin Luther and others in 1517 to reform the Catholic Church (p. 53)
Reforma Protestante movimiento religioso iniciado por Martín Lutero y otros en 1517 para reformar la Iglesia católica (pág. 53)

Protestants reformers who protested certain practices of the Catholic Church (p. 53)
protestantes reformistas que protestaban por ciertas prácticas de la Iglesia católica (pág. 53)

pueblos above ground houses made of a heavy clay called adobe that were built by Native Americans of the southwestern United States (p. 11)
pueblos casas de arcilla gruesa, llamada adobe, construidas más arriba de la superficie por indígenas del suroeste de Estados Unidos (pág. 11)

Pullman strike (1894) a railroad strike that ended when President Grover Cleveland sent in federal troops (p. 627)
huelga de Pullman (1894) huelga del ferrocarril que terminó cuando el presidente Grover Cleveland envió a tropas federales (pág. 627)

Pure Food and Drug Act (1906) a law that set regulatory standards for industries involved in preparing food (p. 681)
Ley de Alimentos y Medicamentos Puros (1906) ley que estableció normas regulatorias para las industrias de preparación de productos alimenticios (pág. 681)

Puritans Protestants who wanted to reform the Church of England (p. 78)
puritanos protestantes que querían reformar la Iglesia anglicana (pág. 78)

Q

Quakers Society of Friends; Protestant sect founded in 1640s in England whose members believed that salvation was available to all people (p. 86)
cuáqueros Sociedad de Amigos; secta protestante fundada en la década de 1640 en Inglaterra cuyos miembros creían que la salvación estaba al alcance de todos (pág. 86)

R

Radical Republicans members of Congress who felt that southern states needed to make great social changes before they could be readmitted to the Union (p. 559)
republicanos radicales miembros del Congreso convencidos de que los estados del Sur necesitaban hacer grandes cambios sociales antes de volver a ser admitidos en la Unión (pág. 559)

ratification an official approval (p. 154)
ratificación aprobación formal (pág. 154)

reason clear and ordered thinking; Greek philosopher Aristotle believed it was the basis of a good life (p. 22)
razón ideas claras y ordenadas; el filósofo griego Aristóteles pensaba que la razón era la base de una vida buena (pág. 22)

recall a vote to remove an official from office (p. 666)
destitución votación para sacar a un funcionario de su cargo (pág. 666)

Reconstruction (1865–1877) the period following the Civil War during which the U.S. government worked to reunite the nation and to rebuild the southern states (p. 552)
Reconstrucción (1865–1877) período posterior a la Guerra Civil en el que el gobierno de Estados Unidos trabajó por reunificar de la nación y reconstruir los estados del Sur (pág. 552)

Reconstruction Acts (1867–1868) the laws that put the southern states under U.S. military control and required them to draft new constitutions upholding the Fourteenth Amendment (p. 561)
Leyes de Reconstrucción (1867–1868) leyes que declaraban a los estados del Sur territorio sujeto al control militar estadounidense y los obligaban a reformar sus constituciones de manera que defendieran la Decimocuarta Enmienda (pág. 561)

Redcoats British soldiers who fought against the colonists in the American Revolution; so called because of their bright red uniforms (p. 114)
casacas rojas soldados británicos que lucharon contra los colonos en la Guerra de Independencia estadounidense, llamados así por el color rojo fuerte de sus uniformes (pág. 114)

referendum a procedure that allows voters to approve or reject a law already proposed or passed by government (p. 666)
referéndum proceso que permite a los votantes aprobar o rechazar una ley previamente propuesta o aprobada por el gobierno (pág. 666)

Republican Party a political party formed in the 1850s to stop the spread of slavery in the West (p. 488)
Partido Republicano partido político formado en la década de 1850 para detener la expansión de la esclavitud en el Oeste (pág. 488)

reservations federal lands set aside for American Indians (p. 595)
reservas territorios federales reservados para los indígenas norteamericanos (pág. 595)

Rhode Island system a system developed by Samuel Slater in the mid-1800s in which whole families were hired as textile workers and factory was divided into simple tasks (p. 391)
sistema de Rhode Island sistema desarrollado por Samuel Slater a mediados del siglo XIX mediante el cual se contrataba a familias completas para trabajar en la industria textil y en el que el trabajo de las fábricas estaba dividido en tareas sencillas (pág. 391)

Rush-Bagot Agreement (1817) an agreement that limited naval power on the Great Lakes for both the United States and British Canada (p. 298)
Acuerdo de Rush-Bagot (1817) acuerdo que limitaba el poder naval de Estados Unidos y la Canadá británica en los Grandes Lagos (pág. 298)

S

Santa Fe Trail an important trade trail west from Independence, Missouri, to Santa Fe, New Mexico (p. 349)
Camino de Santa Fe importante ruta comercial que va desde Independence, Missouri, hasta Santa Fe, Nuevo México (pág. 349)

search warrant a judge's order authorizing the search of a person's home or property to look for evidence of a crime (p. 218)
orden de registro orden de un juez que permite registrar el hogar y las pertenencias de una persona en busca de pruebas de un delito (pág. 218)

secede to formally withdraw from the Union (p. 478)
separarse salirse formalmente de la Unión (pág. 478)

Second Battle of Bull Run (1862) a Civil War battle in which the Confederate army forced most of the Union army out of Virginia (p. 518)
segunda batalla de Bull Run (1862) batalla de la Guerra Civil en la que el ejército confederado obligó a gran parte del ejército de la Unión a abandonar Virginia (pág. 518)

Second Continental Congress (1775) a meeting of colonial delegates in Philadelphia to decide how to react to fighting at Lexington and Concord (p. 114)
Segundo Congreso Continental (1775) reunión de delegados coloniales en Filadelfia para decidir cómo reaccionar ante la lucha en Lexington y Concord (pág. 114)

Second Great Awakening a period of religious evangelism that began in the 1790s and became widespread in the United States by the 1830s (p. 448)
Segundo Gran Despertar período de evangelización religiosa iniciado en la década de 1790 que se extendió por Estados Unidos para la década de 1830 (pág. 448)

Second Industrial Revolution a period of rapid growth in manufacturing and industry in the late 1800s (p. 615)
Segunda Revolución Industrial período de gran crecimiento en la manufactura y en la industria a finales del siglo XIX (pág. 615)

sectionalism a devotion to the interests of one geographic region over the interests of the country as a whole (p. 304, 477)
regionalismo lealtad a los intereses de una región geográfica más que a los del país entero (págs 304, 477)

segregation the forced separation of people of different races in public places (p. 568)
segregación separación obligada de personas de diferentes razas en lugares públicos (pág. 568)

Seneca Falls Convention (1848) the first national women's rights convention at which the Declaration of Sentiments was written (p. 464)
Convención de Seneca Falls (1848) primera convención nacional a favor de los derechos de la mujer, en la cual se redactó la Declaración de Sentimientos (pág. 464)

settlement houses neighborhood centers staffed by professionals and volunteers for education, recreation, and social activities in poor areas (p. 648)
organizaciones de servicio a la comunidad centros comunitarios atendidos por profesionales y voluntarios para ofrecer educación, recreación y actividades sociales en zonas pobres (pág. 648)

Seven Days' Battles (1862) a series of Civil War battles in which Confederate army successes forced the Union army to retreat from Richmond, Virginia, the Confederate capital (p. 518)
batallas de los Siete Días (1862) serie de batallas de la Guerra Civil en las que las victorias del ejército confederado obligaron a las tropas de la Unión a retirarse de Richmond, Virginia, la capital confederada (pág. 518)

Seventeenth Amendment (1913) a constitutional amendment allowing American voters to directly elect U.S. senators (p. 666)
Decimoséptima Enmienda (1913) enmienda constitucional que permite a los votantes estadounidenses elegir directamente a los senadores de Estados Unidos (pág. 666)

sharecropping a system used on southern farms after the Civil War in which farmers worked land owned by someone else in return for a small portion of the crops (p. 569)
cultivo de aparceros sistema usado en las granjas sureñas después de la Guerra Civil en el que los agricultores trabajaban las tierras de otra persona a cambio de una pequeña porción de la cosecha (pág. 569)

Shays's Rebellion (1786-87) an uprising of Massachusetts's farmers, led by Daniel Shays, to protest high taxes, heavy debt, and farm foreclosures (p. 161)
Rebelión de Shays (1786-87) rebelión de agricultores de Massachusetts, encabezados por Daniel Shays, para protestar por los altos impuestos, las grandes deudas y el embargo de las granjas (pág. 161)

Sherman Antitrust Act (1890) a law that made it illegal to create monopolies or trusts that restrained free trade (p. 622)
Ley Antimonopolio de Sherman (1890) ley que prohibía la creación de monopolios o consorcios que restringieran el libre comercio (pág. 622)

Siege of Vicksburg (1863) the Union army's six-week blockade of Vicksburg that led the city to surrender during the Civil War (p. 524)
Sitio de Vicksburg (1863) bloqueo de seis semanas realizado por el ejército de la Unión en Vicksburg para forzar la rendición de esa ciudad durante la Guerra Civil (pág. 524)

Sixteenth Amendment (1913) an amendment to the Constitution that allows personal income to be taxed (p. 683)
Decimosexta Enmienda (1913) enmienda constitucional que permite los impuestos sobre los ingresos personales (pág. 683)

slave codes laws passed in the colonies to control slaves (p. 77)
códigos de esclavos leyes aprobadas por las colonias para controlar a los esclavos (pág. 77)

social Darwinism a view of society based on Charles Darwin's scientific theory of natural selection (p. 621)
darwinismo social visión de la sociedad basada en la teoría científica de la selección natural de Charles Darwin (pág. 621)

socialism economic system in which the government owns and operates a country's means of production (p. 674)
socialismo sistema económico en el que el gobierno controla y maneja los medios de producción de un país (pág. 674)

sodbusters the name given to Plains farmers who worked hard to break up the region's tough sod (p. 601)
sodbusters nombre dado a los agricultores de las Planicies que se esforzaron mucho para trabajar el duro terreno de la región (pág. 601)

Spanish Armada a large Spanish fleet defeated by England in 1588 (p. 53)
Armada española gran flota española derrotada por las tropas de Inglaterra en 1588 (pág. 53)

speculator an investor who buys items at low prices in hope that their values will rise (p. 239)
especulador inversionista que compra artículos a precios bajos con la esperanza de que su valor aumente (pág. 239)

sphere of influence an area where foreign countries control trade or natural resources of another nation or area (p. 695)
esfera de influencia nación o lugar cuyos recursos naturales y comercio son controlados por otro país (pág. 695)

spirituals emotional Christian songs sung by enslaved people in the South that mixed African and European elements and usually expressed slaves' religious beliefs (p. 427)
espirituales canciones religiosas emotivas cantadas por los esclavos del Sur que combinaban elementos de origen africano y europeo y solían expresar sus creencias religiosas (pág. 427)

spoils system a politicians' practice of giving government jobs to his or her supporters (p. 324)
tráfico de influencias práctica de los políticos de ofrecer empleos a las personas que los apoyan (pág. 324)

Stamp Act of 1765 a law passed by Parliament that raised tax money by requiring colonists to pay for an official stamp whenever they bought paper items such as newspapers, licenses, and legal documents (p. 100)
Ley del Sello de 1765 ley aprobada por el Parlamento para recaudar impuestos en la que se obligaba a los colonos a pagar un sello oficial cada vez que compraran artículos de papel, como periódicos, licencias y documentos legales (pág. 100)

staple crop a crop that is continuously in demand (p. 87)
cultivo básico cultivo de demanda constante (pág. 87)

states' rights doctrine the belief that the power of the states should be greater than the power of the federal government (p. 328)
doctrina de los derechos estatales creencia de que el poder de los estados debe ser mayor que el del gobierno federal (pág. 328)

steerage the area on a ship in the lower levels where the steering mechanisms were located and where cramped quarters were provided for people who could only afford cheap passage (p. 637)
tercera clase nivel inferior un barco en el que se encontraban los mecanismos del timón y se ofrecían habitaciones reducidas para las personas que sólo podían comprar un pasaje barato (pág. 637)

strict construction a way of interpreting the Constitution that allows the federal government to take only those actions the Constitution specifically says it can take (p. 242)
interpretación estricta interpretación de la Constitución que sólo permite al gobierno federal hacer las acciones mencionadas específicamente en ella (pág. 242)

strike the refusal of workers to perform their jobs until employers meet their demands (p. 394)
huelga negativa de los empleados a trabajar hasta que sus empleadores satisfagan sus demandas (pág. 394)

suburb a neighborhood outside of a downtown area (p. 644)
suburbio vecindario en las afueras de una ciudad (pág. 644)

suffrage voting rights (p. 153)
sufragio derecho al voto (pág. 153)

sweatshops hot, stuffy workshops in which workers prepare materials for low wages (p. 640)
fábricas explotadoras talleres calurosos y con el aire cargado en los cuales los trabajadores preparan materiales por salarios reducidos (pág. 640)

T

tariff a tax on imports or exports (p. 159)
arancel impuesto pagado por las importaciones o exportaciones (pág. 159)

Tariff of Abominations (1828) the nickname given to a tariff by southerners who opposed it (p. 327)
Arancel de Abominaciones (1828) sobrenombre dado a un arancel por los habitantes del Sur que se oponían a éste (pág. 327)

Tea Act (1773) a law passed by Parliament allowing the British East India Company to sell its low-cost tea directly to the colonies, undermining colonial tea merchants; led to the Boston Tea Party (p. 102)
Ley del Té (1773) ley aprobada por el Parlamento británico que le permitía a la British East India Company vender té a bajo costo a las colonias directamente, afectando a los comerciantes de té coloniales; dio origen al Motín del Té de Boston (pág. 102)

technology the tools used to produce goods or to do work (p. 387)
tecnología herramientas utilizadas para producir bienes o realizar un trabajo (pág. 387)

teepees cone-shaped shelters made of buffalo skins used by Native Americans in the Plains region (p. 14)
tipis viviendas en forma de cono hechas de piel de búfalo que usaban los indígenas norteamericanos en la región de las Planicies (pág. 14)

telegraph a machine perfected by Samuel F. B. Morse in 1832 that uses pulses of electric current to send messages across long distances through wires (p. 402)
telégrafo máquina perfeccionada por Samuel F. B. Morse en 1832 que emplea impulsos eléctricos transmitidos por cables para enviar mensajes a grandes distancias (pág. 402)

Teller Amendment (1898) a congressional resolution stating that the U.S. had no interest in taking control of Cuba (p. 698)
Enmienda Teller (1898) resolución del Congreso en la que Estados Unidos declaró que no tenía intención de tomar el control de Cuba (pág. 698)

temperance movement a social reform effort begun in the mid-1800s to encourage people to drink less alcohol (p. 449)
movimiento de abstinencia movimiento de reforma social iniciado a mediados del siglo XIX para promover el que las personas bebieran menos alcohol (pág. 449)

tenements poorly built, overcrowded housing where many immigrants lived (p. 442)
casas de vecindad viviendas mal construidas y llenas de gente donde vivían muchos inmigrantes (pág. 442)

Ten Percent Plan President Abraham Lincoln's plan for Reconstruction; once 10 percent of voters in a former Confederate state took a U.S. loyalty oath, they could form a new state government and be readmitted to the Union (p. 553)
Plan del Diez por Ciento plan de Reconstrucción del presidente Abraham Lincoln; si el 10 por ciento de los votantes de un estado que había sido confederado juraba lealtad a la nación, podían formar un nuevo gobierno y ser readmitidos en la Unión (pág. 553)

textile cloth (p. 385)
textil tela (pág. 385)

Thirteenth Amendment (1865) a constitutional amendment that outlawed slavery (p. 554)
Decimotercera Enmienda (1865) enmienda constitucional que prohibió la esclavitud (pág. 554)

Three-Fifths Compromise (1787) an agreement worked out at the Constitutional Convention stating that only three-fifths of the slaves in a state would count when determining a state's population for representation in the lower house of Congress (p. 166)
Compromiso de las Tres Quintas Partes (1787) acuerdo negociado durante la Convención Constitucional en el que se estableció que solamente tres quintas de los esclavos en un estado contrarían para al determinar la representación de ese estado en la cámara baja del Congreso (pág. 166)

Toleration Act of 1649 a Maryland law that made restricting the religious rights of Christians a crime; the first law guaranteeing religious freedom to be passed in America (p. 75)
Ley de Tolerancia de 1649 ley de Maryland que calificaba como delito la restricción de los derechos religiosos de los cristianos; fue la primera ley que garantizó la libertad religiosa en América (pág. 75)

total war a type of war in which an army destroys its opponent's ability to fight by targeting civilian and economic as well as military resources (p. 542)
guerra total tipo de guerra en la que un ejército destruye la capacidad de lucha de su oponente mediante ataques a la población civil y a la economía así como a los recursos militares (pág. 542)

totems images of ancestors or animal spirits; often carved onto tall, wooden poles by Native American peoples of the Pacific Northwest (p. 12)
tótems imágenes de antepasados o espíritus de animales; a menudo talladas en altos troncos de madera por los indígenas americanos de la costa noroeste del Pacífico (pág. 12)

town meeting a political meeting at which people make decisions on local issues; used primarily in New England (p. 91)
reunión del pueblo reunión política en la que las personas toman decisiones sobre temas locales; se usan principalmente en Nueva Inglaterra (pág. 91)

trade unions workers' organizations that try to improve working conditions (p. 394)
sindicatos organizaciones de trabajadores que intentan mejorar sus condiciones laborales (pág. 394)

Trail of Tears (1838-39) an 800-mile forced march made by the Cherokee from their homeland in Georgia to Indian Territory; resulted in the deaths of almost one fourth of the Cherokee people (p. 334)
Ruta de las Lágrimas (1838-39) marcha forzada de 800 millas que hicieron los cheroquíes desde su territorio natal en Georgia hasta el Territorio Indígena, y en la que perdió la vida casi una cuarta parte del pueblo cheroquí (pág. 334)

transcendentalism the idea that people could rise above the material things in life; a popular movement among New England writers and thinkers in the mid-1800s (p. 443)
trascendentalismo creencia de que las personas podían prescindir de los objetos materiales en la vida; movimiento popular entre los escritores y pensadores de Nueva Inglaterra a mediados del siglo XIX (pág. 443)

transcontinental railroad a railroad system that crossed the continental United States; construction began in 1863 (p. 590)
tren transcontinental línea ferroviaria que cruzaba Estados Unidos de un extremo a otro; su construcción se inició en 1863 (pág. 590)

Transportation Revolution the rapid growth in the speed and convenience of transportation (p. 396)
Revolución del Transporte rápido desarrollo de la velocidad y comodidad de los medios de transporte (pág. 396)

Treaty of Fort Jackson (1814) a treaty signed after the U.S. victory at the Battle of Horseshoe Bend; the Creek were forced to give up 23 million acres of their land (p. 286)
Tratado del Fuerte Jackson (1814) tratado que se firmó tras la victoria de Estados Unidos en la batalla de Horseshoe Bend; los indígenas creek se vieron obligados a ceder 23 millones de acres de su territorio (pág. 286)

Treaty of Fort Laramie (1851) a treaty signed in Wyoming by the United States and northern Plains nations (p. 594)
Tratado del Fuerte Laramie (1851) tratado firmado en Wyoming por Estados Unidos y las naciones indígenas de las Planicies del norte (pág. 594)

Treaty of Ghent (1814) a treaty signed by the United States and Britain ending the War of 1812 (p. 287)
Tratado de Gante (1814) tratado firmado por Estados Unidos y Gran Bretaña para dar fin a la Guerra de 1812 (pág. 287)

Treaty of Greenville (1795) an agreement between Native American confederation leaders and the U.S. government that gave the United States Indian lands in the Northwest Territory and guaranteed that U.S. citizens could safely travel through the region (p. 247)
Tratado de Greenville (1795) acuerdo entre los líderes de la confederación de indígenas norteamericanos y el gobierno estadounidense que otorgó a Estados Unidos tierras indígenas en el Territorio del Noroeste y garantizó la seguridad a los ciudadanos estadounidenses que viajaran por la región (pág. 247)

Treaty of Guadalupe Hidalgo (1848) a treaty that ended the Mexican-American War and gave the United States much of Mexico's northern territory (p. 361)
Tratado de Guadalupe Hidalgo (1848) tratado que daba por terminada la Guerra contra México y daba a Estados Unidos gran parte del norte del territorio mexicano (pág. 361)

Treaty of Medicine Lodge (1867) an agreement between the U.S. government and southern Plains Indians in which the Indians agreed to move onto reservations (p. 595)
Tratado de Medicine Lodge (1867) acuerdo entre el gobierno de Estados Unidos y los indígenas de las Planicies del sur en el que los indígenas aceptaron irse a las reservas (pág. 595)

Treaty of Paris of 1783 a peace agreement that officially ended the Revolutionary War and established British recognition of the independence of the United States (p. 139)
Tratado de París de 1783 acuerdo de paz que oficialmente dio por terminada la Guerra de Independencia estadounidense y en el que Gran Bretaña reconocía la independencia de Estados Unidos (pág. 139)

Treaty of Tordesillas (1494) a treaty between Spain and Portugal that moved the Line of Demarcation (p. 44)
Tratado de Tordesillas (1494) tratado entre España y Portugal que modificó la Línea de Demarcación (pág. 44)

Tredegar Iron Works a large iron factory that operated in Richmond, Virginia, in the early to mid-1800s (p. 419)
Tredegar Iron Works gran fábrica de acero que operaba a mediados del siglo XIX en Richmond, Virginia (pág. 419)

Triangle Shirtwaist Fire a factory fire that killed 146 workers trapped in the building; led to new safety standard laws (p. 673)
incendio de Triangle Shirtwaist incendio de una fábrica en el que murieron 146 trabajadores atrapados en el edificio; este suceso obligó a crear nuevas leyes de seguridad (pág. 673)

triangular trade trading networks in which goods and slaves moved among England, the American colonies, and Africa (p. 93)
comercio triangular redes comerciales en las que los bienes y los esclavos se intercambiaban entre Inglaterra, las colonias americanas y África (pág. 93)

trust a number of companies legally grouped under a single board of directors (p. 621)
consorcio varias compañías agrupadas legalmente bajo el mando de una sola junta directiva (pág. 621)

U

Uncle Tom's Cabin (1852) an antislavery novel written by Harriet Beecher Stowe that showed northerners the violent reality of slavery and drew many people to the abolitionists' cause (p. 481)
La cabaña del tío Tom (1852) novela abolicionista escrita por Harriet Beecher Stowe que mostró a los habitantes del norte del país la violenta realidad de la esclavitud e hizo que muchos se unieran a la causa abolicionista (pág. 481)

Underground Railroad a network of people who helped thousands of enslaved people escape to the North by providing transportation and hiding places (p. 456)
Tren Clandestino red de personas que ayudó a miles de esclavos a escapar al Norte ofreciéndoles transporte y lugares para esconderse (pág. 456)

USS *Constitution* a large warship (p. 278)
USS *Constitution* gran buque de guerra (pág. 278)

utopian communities places where people worked to establish a perfect society; such communities were popular in the United States during the late 1700s and early to mid-1800s (p. 444)
comunidades utópicas lugares en los que un grupo de personas trabajaba para establecer una sociedad perfecta; se popularizaron en Estados Unidos a finales del siglo XVIII y principios y mediados del XIX (pág. 444)

V

vaqueros Mexican cowboys in the West who tended cattle and horses (p. 357)
vaqueros arrieros mexicanos que vivían en el Oeste y se ganaban la vida ocupándose del ganado y los caballos (pág. 357)

vertical integration the business practice of owning all of the businesses involved in each step of a manufacturing process (p. 620)
integración vertical práctica empresarial de poseer todas las empresas que participan en cada paso de un proceso de manufactura (pág. 620)

veto to cancel a law (p. 184)
vetar cancelar una ley (pág. 184)

Virginia Plan (1787) the plan for government proposed at the Constitutional Convention in which the national government would have supreme power and a legislative branch would have two houses with representation determined by state population (p. 164)
Plan de Virginia (1787) plan de gobierno propuesto en la Convención Constitucional por el que el gobierno nacional tendría poder supremo y habría un poder legislativo con dos cámaras en las que la representación de cada estado sería determinada por su población (pág. 164)

Virginia Statute for Religious Freedom (1786) a document that gave people in Virginia freedom of worship and prohibited tax money from being used to fund churches (p. 153)
Estatuto de Virginia para la Libertad Religiosa (1786) documento que reconocía a los habitantes de Virginia la libertad de culto y prohibía utilizar los impuestos para financiar iglesias (pág. 153)

W

War Hawks members of Congress who wanted to declare war against Britain after the Battle of Tippecanoe (p. 282)
halcones de guerra miembros del Congreso que querían declarar la guerra a Gran Bretaña tras la batalla de Tippecanoe (pág. 282)

Whig Party a political party formed in 1834 by opponents of Andrew Jackson and who supported a strong legislature (p. 330)
Partido Whig partido político formado en 1834 por oponentes de Andrew Jackson que apoyaba una asamblea legislativa con mucha autoridad (pág. 330)

Whiskey Rebellion (1794) a protest of small farmers in Pennsylvania against new taxes on whiskey (p. 247)
Rebelión del Whisky (1794) protesta de pequeños agricultores de Pensilvania contra los nuevos impuestos sobre el whisky (pág. 247)

Wilderness Campaign (1864) a series of battles between Union and Confederate forces in northern and central Virginia that delayed the Union capture of Richmond (p. 540)
Campaña de Wilderness (1864) serie de batallas entre la Unión y los confederados en el norte y el centro de Virginia que retrasaron la captura de Richmond por parte de la Unión (pág. 540)

Wilmot Proviso (1846) a proposal to outlaw slavery in the territory added to the United States by the Mexican Cession; passed in the House of Representatives but was defeated in the Senate (p. 476)
Condición de Wilmot (1846) propuesta de prohibir la esclavitud en el territorio anexado a Estados Unidos por la Cesión Mexicana; aprobada por la Cámara de Representantes, pero rechazada por el Senado (pág. 476)

Worcester* v. *Georgia (1832) the Supreme Court ruling that stated that the Cherokee nation was a distinct territory over which only the federal government had authority; ignored by both President Andrew Jackson and the state of Georgia (p. 334)
Worcester* contra *Georgia (1832) decisión de la Corte Suprema que establecía que la nación cheroquí era un territorio distinto sobre el que sólo el gobierno federal tenía autoridad; fue ignorada por el presidente Andrew Jackson y por el estado de Georgia (pág. 334)

X

XYZ affair (1797) an incident in which French agents attempted to get a bribe and loans from U.S. diplomats in exchange for an agreement that French privateers would no longer attack American ships; it led to an undeclared naval war between the two countries (p. 252)
incidente XYZ (1797) incidente en el que funcionarios franceses intentaron obtener sobornos y préstamos de diplomáticos estadounidenses a cambio de un acuerdo por el cual sus corsarios no atacarían más a los barcos estadounidenses; provocó una guerra no declarada entre las fuerzas navales de ambas naciones (pág. 252)

Y

yellow journalism the reporting of exaggerated stories in newspapers to increase sales (p. 697)
prensa amarillista publicación de noticias exageradas en los periódicos para aumentar las ventas (pág. 697)

yeomen owners of small farms (p. 422)
pequeños terratenientes dueños de granjas pequeñas (pág. 422)

Index

KEY TO INDEX

c = chart	*p* = photo
f = feature	*m* = map
R = Reference	

A

B

D

E

H

K

L

M

N

INDEX

O

P

S

T

U

V

W

X

Y

Z

Credits and Acknowledgments

For permission to reproduce copyrighted material, grateful acknowledgment is made to the following sources:

Norwegian-American Historical Association: From quote by Gro Svendsen from *Frontier Mother: The Letters of Gro Svendsen,* translated and edited by Pauline Farseth and Theodore C. Blegen. Copyright © 1950 Norwegian-American Historical Association.

Sources Cited:

Quote by an Aztec messenger from *The Broken Spears: The Aztec Account of the Conquest of Mexico,* Expanded and Updated Edition, edited by Miguel León-Portilla. Published by Beacon Press, Boston, 1992.

From *Yesterday: A Memoir of a Russian Jewish Family* by Miriam Shomer Zunser, edited by Emily Wortis Leider. Published by HarperCollins Publishers, New York, 1978.

Quote by a Hungarian immigrant from *This Was America* by Oscar Handlin. Published by Harvard University Press, Cambridge, Mass., 1949.

Illustration and Photo Credits

Front Cover: © Wolfgang Kaehler/CORBIS.

Front Matter: Page ii (l) Seth Joel/HRW; (r) Michael Denora/HRW Photo; v (b), Mary Evans Picture Library; v (t), The Field Museum of Natural History, Neg. A108557-c, Photo by Ron Testa;; vi (l), © Dennis Degnan/CORBIS; vi (r), American Antiquarian Society; vii, © David Butow/CORBIS; viii, © 1993 Mickey Osterreischer/Black Star/ stockphoto.com; ix (l) (Art Reference) © Board of Trustees, National Gallery of Art, Washington; (r) The Hermitage, Home of Andrew Jackson; xi, National Museum of American History, Smithsonian Institution, Washington, DC. Photo by Kim Neilson, #83-2953; xiii, Nebraska State Historical Society, Photograph Collections; xv, The Granger Collection, New York; xvi (art ref) PRC Archive; xx, © Collection of the New-York Historical Society, [neg. 41800]; xxv, Picture Research Consultants & Archives; H2, ©Bettmann/CORBIS; H4, Laurie Platt Winfrey/Woodfin Camp &Associates; H6, Superstock; H7, The Granger Collection, New York; H8, Library of Congress, H9, The Granger Collection, New York; H25 (t) © Daily News Pix; (l) © Randy Wells/CORBIS; (cr) © Robert Maass/CORBIS; (b) © Glen Allison/Getty Images.

Unit 1: 00-01 © Burstein Collection/Corbis. **Chapter 1:** Pages 2-3 (t)© Annie Griffiths/CORBIS; 2 (br) The Art Archive/National Anthropological Museum Mexico/Dagli Orti; 3 (bc) ©Yoshio Tomii/SuperStock, (br) ©Rabatti - Domingie/akg-images; 7 (t) Smithsonian Institution, Washington, DC. Photograph by Chip Clark # 90-14563, (c) PRC Archive, (b) Getty Images; 11 © David Muench/CORBIS; 13 (tr) From the Collection of Gilcrease Museum, Tulsa, 13 (bl) © 2000 The Art Institute of Chicago (detail), (tl) Ohio Historical Society; 14 (tl) Marilyn Wynn/Nativestock Pictures, 14 (tr) The Granger Collection, New York; 17 (tl) Carol Beckwith & Angela Fisher/HAGA/The Image Works, Inc., 17 (tl) © John Elk III Photography; 19 (bc) Reuters/Corbis, (br) AFP/Getty Images; 21 (br) The Granger Collection, New York; 23 (b) Ben Mangor/SuperStock; 24 (bc) © Archivo Iconografico, S.A./CORBIS, (bl) ©Christopher Groenhout/Lonely Planet Images; 25 (bl) © Bettmann/CORBIS, (br) ©G K & Vikki Hart/PhotoDisc, (bc) The Granger Collection, New York. **Chapter 2:** Pages 34-35 (all) © Rebecca Marvil/Index Stock Imagery, Inc.; 34 (b) National Maritime Museum; 35 (cl) SuperStock, (c) Tate Gallery, London/Art Resource, NY, (bl) Fundacion Miguel Mujica Gallo, Museo do Oro del Peru, (bc) G. Tortoli/Ancient Art & Architecture Collection, Ltd., (br) Victoria & Albert Museum, London/Art Resource, NY, (cr) David Muench/Corbis; 40 (bkgd) © Royalty Free/CORBIS; 44 SuperStock; 47 (br) © Scott Nelson/Getty Images; 49 The Granger Collection, New York; 51 (cr) PRC Archive; 52 (bl) Saint Bride Printing Library; 53 (bl) AKG-Images, (br) Mary Evans Picture Library; 54 (t) Tate Gallery, London/Art Resource, NY; 59 (br) Copyright The New York Public Library / Art Resource, NY; 60 (tr) **Chapter 3:** Pages 68-69 (t) Ted Curtin for Plimoth Plantation, (c) Courtesy of the Pilgrim Society, Plymouth, Massachusetts; 68 (bl) © David Ball/CORBIS; 69 (br) © Culver Pictures, Inc., (bl) © SuperStock, (cr) Courtesy of the Burton Historical Collection, Detroit Public Library; 75 (t) Colonial Williamsburg Foundation; 82 (t) Art Reference: PRC Archive; 85 (b) © SuperStock; 86 (bl) Art Reference: Historical Society of Pennsylvania; 88 (l) SuperStock, (t) NASA, (b) © SuperStock, Inc./SuperStock; 93 (r) Art Reference: Royal Albert Memorial Museum, Exeter, Devon, UK/Bridgeman Art Library, (l) Private Collection/www.bridgeman.co.uk; 94 (t) National Portrait Library, London/Bridgeman Art Library; 97 (tr) Art Reference: Courtesy of the Burton Historical Collection, Detroit Public Library; 99 (t) Virginia Historical Society; 101 (t) Peter Newark's American Pictures; 102 (tr) Courtesy of the Massachusetts Historical Society, (tl) © Hulton-Deutsch Collection/CORBIS; 103 (tl) © Bettmann/CORBIS, (tr) American Antiquarian Society. **Chapter 4:** Pages 108-109 (t) © James Lemass/Index Stock Imagery; 108 (cl) The Granger Collection, New York; 109 (br) © Christie's Images, (cr) North Wind Picture Archives; 113 (b) © Concord Museum/Photograph by Chip Fanelli, (t) The Granger Collection, New York; 117 (br) © Robert Llewellyn/SuperStock; 119 (br) The Granger Collection, New York, (bl) © 2003-2005 clipart.com; 120 (t) © Bettmann/CORBIS; 123 (br) The Granger Collection, New York; 127 (l) #1921.101, ©Collection of The New-York Historical Society, (r) ©Collection of The New-York Historical Society, neg. 31665; 128-129 (t) © SuperStock; 130 (r) Chateau de Versailles, France/Giraudon/ Bridgeman Art Library, (l) Saratoga National Historic Park; 131 (r) Hotel Galvez, Galveston, Texas, (l) Falmouth Art Gallery, Cornwall, UK/The Bridgeman Art Library; 132 © SuperStock, Inc. / SuperStock; 136 (t) The Granger Collection, New York; 138 The Granger Collection, New York.

Unit 2. Chapter 5: Pages 148-149 (t) © 2009 Jay Mallin; 148 (b) Library of Congress/PRC Archive; 149 (br) © Andrea Jemolo/CORBIS, (bl) © Nik Wheeler/CORBIS, (c) Collection of the American Numismatic Society, New York; 153 The Granger Collection, New York; 156 (t) © Bettmann/CORBIS, (b) © Bettmann/CORBIS; 157 (t) © Bettmann/CORBIS, (c) © Michael Nicholson/CORBIS , (br) © Archivo Iconografico, S.A./CORBIS; 160-161 (b) The Granger Collection, New York; 163 © Dennis Degnan/CORBIS; 164 (t) Hall of Representatives, Washington, DC/ Bridgeman Art Library, (bl) Independence National Historical Park , (bc) Stock MontageStrock, (br) Portrait by Robert S. Susan, Collection of the Supreme Court of the United States; 166 (l) South Carolina Legal History Collection, (r) City of Bristol Museum and Art Gallery/Bridgeman Art Library; 167 © Alex Wong/Getty Images; 169 (br) American Antiquarian Society; 171 (r) © Bettmann/CORBIS, (l) Stock Montage, Inc., (bkgd) © Alan Schein Photography/CORBIS. **Chapter 6:** Pages 178-179 (t) Sam Dudgeon/HRW Photo; 179 (b) © Bettmannn/CORBIS, (cl) PRC Archive, (cr) © Tony Freeman/PhotoEdit; 185 Getty Images; 187 (bc) National Archives (NARA), (br) National Archives/PRC Archive; 192 (br) Dennis Cook/AP/Wide World Photos; 192-193 (bc) © Mark Wilson/Getty Images, (t) © Miles Ertman/Masterfile; 193 (br) © Brooks Kraft/CORBIS; 194 © Royalty-Free/CORBIS; 204 (bl) © Yang Liu/CORBIS, (bc) Norm Detlaff, Las Cruces Sun-News/AP/Wide World Photos; 205 (bl) ©Alex Webb/Magnum Photos, (bc) © David Young-Wolff/PhotoEdit, (br) © Bettmann/CORBIS; © Royalty-Free/CORBIS; 209 (t) Library of Congress/PRC Archive; 211 (tr) Library of Congress; 213 (l) © Bettmann/CORBIS, (r) © Oscar White/CORBIS; 214 (tr) ©1978 Matt Herron/TakeStock, (tc) Texas State Library & Archives Commission, (tl) Dr. Hector P. Garcia Papers, Special Collections & Archives, Texas A&M University-Corpus Christi, Bell Library; 217 (b) © Daily News Pix; 219 © Spencer Grant/PhotoEdit; 220-221 (b) © Ariel Skelley/CORBIS; 223 (t) © David Butow/CORBIS; 224 (tl) ©James Pickerell/The Image Works, (tr) © Brownie Harris/CORBIS; 225 (l) © Ariel Skelly/CORBIS, (c) Janet Knott/The Boston Globe. Republished with permission of The Globe Newspaper Company, Inc., (r) © Jeff Greenberg/PhotoEdit. **Chapter 7:** Pages 230 (b) © Christie's Images; 231 (bl) Giraudon/Art Resource, NY ,(r) Art Resource, NY; 235 (r) Library of Congress/PRC Archive; 237 (inset) © Collection of The New-York Historical Society, 31907.32; 240 (b) © Joseph Sohm; Chromosohm, Inc./CORBIS, (c) Photo ©2004 Roger Foley; 241 (r) Stock Montage/Getty Images, (l) Stock Montage, Inc.; 243 (b) Réunion des Musées Nationaux/Art Resource, NY; 244 (l) Chicago Historical Society, (r) Library of Congress/PRC Archive, (c) Chicago Historical Society, #i35980aa; 245 (l) HRW Photo Research Library; 246 Courtesy Ohio Historical Society; 248 © Museum of the City of New York/CORBIS; 251 (tl) ©The New York Historical Society, New York, NY/ Bridgeman Art Library, (tc) The Art Archive/Chateau de Biernacourt/Dagli Orti, (bl) Independence National Historical Park Collection, (bc) The Henry Luce III Center for the Study of American Culture/SuperStock, (tr) ©The New-York Historical Society, New York, NY/Bridgeman Art Library, (br) National Portrait Gallery, Smithsonian Institution, Washington, DC/Art Resource, NY; 252 Library of Congress/PRC Archive.

Unit 3. Chapter 8: Pages 262 (b) The Granger Collection, New York; 262-263 (t) Superstock; 263 (cl) Benninghoff Collection of the American Revolution, (cr) Portrait of the

Founder, Munetada Kurozumi. Image courtesy of Kurozumikyo Shinto, (cr) Library of Congress, LC-USZC4-6466; 267 (l) The Art Archive/Chateau de Blernacourt/Dagli Orti, (r) © Bettmann/CORBIS, (bkgd) © Alan Schein Photography/CORBIS; 269 (b) Getty Images; 270 Washington and Lee University; 275 (r) © Jeff Vanuga/CORBIS, (l) © Joseph Sohm/Chromosohm, Inc./CORBIS; 280 (l) The Mariners Museum, (r) North Wind Picture Archives; 281 (t) North Wind Picture Archives, (br) © 1993 Mickey Osterreischer/ Black Star, (bl) The Granger Collection, New York; 282 (r) National Portrait Gallery, Smithsonian Institution; gift of Mrs. Herbert Lee Pratt, Jr, (l) ©The Field Museum, Neg #A93851.1c, Chicago; 286 (inset) © New-York Historical Society/ Bridgeman Art Library, (b) © Bettmann/CORBIS; 288 (c) © Craig Tuttle/CORBIS; 289 (tl) © Bettmann/ CORBIS, (b) © Tom Bean/Getty Images, (tr) © SuperStock. **Chapter 9:** Pages 294 (tl) National Portrait Gallery, Smithsonian Institution, Washington, DC/Art Resource, NY; 294-295 (t) © Lee Snider/Photo Images/ CORBIS; 295 (bl) Courtesy PRC Archive, (c) Library of Congress #LC-USZC4-5801, (br) The Granger Collection, New York; 302 (t) © Bettmann/CORBIS, (b) Maryland Historical Society, Baltimore, Maryland; 308 © Andre Jenny/Alamy Photos; 309 Library of Congress/PRC Archive; 310 (c) Smithsonian American Art Museum, Washington DC/Art Resource, NYSmithsonian American Art Museum, Washington DC/Art Resource, NY, (l) American Antiquarian Society; 311 (r) © Francis G. Mayer/CORBIS. **Chapter 10:** Pages 318 (b) The Granger Collection, New York; 318-319 (t) Detroit Publishing Company Collection, from Birth of A Century, KEA Publishing Services Ltd.; 319 (cl) Janice L. and David J. Frent Collection of Political Americana, (bl) The Stapleton Collection, UK/ Bridgeman Art Library, (cr) National Portrait Gallery, Smithsonian Institution/Art Resource, NY, (br) The Art Archive; 323 (r) R.W. Norton Art Gallery, Shreveport, LA. Used by permission., (l) David Young-Wolff/PhotoEdit; 325 (br) The Hermitage, Home of Andrew Jackson; 327 (l) American Museum of Textile History, (c) Christie's Images/ Bridgeman Art Library, (r) The Fine Arts Museum of San Francisco, Gift of Eleanor Martin, 37566; 330 The Granger Collection, New York; 333 © SuperStock, Inc. / SuperStock; 337 (tl) Smithsonian American Art Museum, Washington, DC /Art Resource, NY, (tr) Smithsonian American Art Museum, Washington, DC/Art Resource, NY, (cr) Smithsonian American Art Museum, Washington, DC /Art Resource, NY, (b) Smithsonian American Art Museum, Washington, DC /Art Resource, NY. **Chapter 11:** Pages 342-343 (t) Seaver Center for Western History Research, Natural History Museum of Los Angeles County; 343 (cr) © The Oakland Museum, The City of Oakland, (br) Library of Congress, LC-USZC4-1307/PRC Archive, (cl) Panhandle-Plains Historical Museum, Research Center, Canyon, Texas; 347 (c) © Bettmann/CORBIS; 348 (t) Used by permission, Utah State Historical Society, all rights reserved.; 351 (tl) Institute of Texan Cultures, University of Texas at San Antonio (colorized), (tr) Courtesy Texas General Land Office, HRW Photo by Peter Van Steen; 352 (b) Jack Lewis/TxDOT, (bl) The Center For American History, University of Texas at Austin; 355 (t) Library of Congress/PRC Archive; 356 (b) James Walker, Vaqueros in a Horse Corral, 1877, #0126.1480, From the Collection of Gilcrease Museum, Tulsa, Oklahoma.; 357 (t) Society of California Pioneers; 360-361 (t) Texas State Library and Archives Commission; 362 (t) J. Griffiths Smith/TxDOT; 365 (br) Collection of Matthew Isenburg, (bl) Collection of Matthew Isenburg; 366 (t) Courtesy of the California History Room, California State Library, Sacramento, California; 367 (tl) Seaver Center for Western History Research; 369 (t) Library of Congress. #LC-USZC4-7421; 370 (c) © George F. Mobley/Getty Images; 371 (t) © Bettmann/CORBIS, (b) © Lester Lefkowitz/ CORBIS , (c) © SuperStock, Inc./SuperStock; 375 (br) The Granger Collection, New York.

Unit 4: 378-379 Tontine Coffee House, c. 1797 (oil on linen), Guy Francis (1760–1820)/© New York Historical Society, New York, USA/Bridgeman Art Library. **Chapter 12:** Pages 380-381 (c) © Marilyn Root/Index Stock Imagery, Inc.; 380 (b) Fenimore Art Museum, Cooperstown, New York/Photo by Richard Walker; 381 (bl) NASA, (cr) © Southeast Museum, (cl) PRC Archive, (br) © CORBIS; 386 (l) Samuel Finley Breese Morse, Eli Whitney (1765-1825), Yale University Art Gallery. Gift of George Hoadley, B.A. 1801., (r) Museum of Connecticut History; 387 (l) Museum of Connecticut History, (r) New Haven Colony Historical Society; 388 © Bob Krist/CORBIS; 391 Rhode Island Historical Society; 392 Jack Naylor Collection; 397 Library of Congress, Detroit Publishing Company Collection, #LC-D401-19395; 402 Museum of Connecticut History; 403 (bl) Smithsonian Institution, Washington, DC (Photograph by Charles Phillips), (br) Courtesy John Deere & Company Archives; 404 (r) National Museum of American History, Smithsonian Institution, Washington, DC (#89-6626), (c) U.S. Patent Office, (l) U.S. Patent Office; Pate. **Chapter 13:** Pages 410 (b) National Museum of American History, Smithsonian Institution, Washington, DC. Photo by Kim Neilson, #83-2953; 410-411 (t) Penn School Papers, Southern Historical Collection, University of North Carolina at Chapel Hill, Wilson Library, #P.3615/0824(A); 411 (c) Library of Congress, (b) © Hulton-Deutsch Collection/CORBIS; 422 (tl) The Valentine Museum, (tr) Collection of the American Numismatic Society, New York; 425 The J. Paul Getty Museum, Los Angeles; 426-427 (t) Hauling the Whole Week's Picking by WIlliam Henry Brown, The Historic New Orleans Collection; 427 (tr) South Carolina Historical Society; 428 (tr) North Wind Picture Archives; 432 Sam Dudgeon/HRW. **Chapter 14:** Pages 434-435 (t) The Metropolitan Museum of Art, Gift of I.N. Phelps Stokes, Edward S. Hawes, Alice Mary Hawes, Marion Augusta Hawes, 1937.[37.14.22]. All rights reserved, The Metropolitan Museum of Art.; 435 (cl) Courtesy of the Massachusetts Historical Society, (cr) PRC Archive, (bl) Photo © David Modica, courtesy American Printing House for the Blind Museum, (br) Peter Newark's American Pictures; 437 Library of Congress; 439 (c) Wiliam B. Becker Collection/American Museum of Photography; 443 © Royalty-Free/CORBIS; 444 Brooklyn Museum of Art, Gift of the Brooklyn Institute of Arts and Sciences/ Bridgeman Art Library; 449 (inset) Hulton Archive/Getty Images, (b) The Granger Collection, New York; 452 Courtesy of Oberlin Archives; 453 Museum of Art, Rhode Island School of Design. Gift of Lucy T. Aldrich; 455 (t) Trustees of the Boston Public Library; 456 Library of Congress; 457 (t) Courtesy of the Levi Coffin House Association and Waynet, (b) Courtesy of The Brooklyn Museum of Art [40.59]; 458 Library of Congress; 459 Courtesy of the Massachusetts Historical Society; 460 (r) Library of Congress, Manuscript Division; 462 (l) Courtesy of the Massachusetts Historical Society, (r) The Granger Collection, New York; 463 (l) Courtesy of the Susan B. Anthony House, Rochester, NY, (r) Library of Congress/ PRC Archive; 465 Stock Montage, Inc.; 466 © Bettmann/CORBIS; 467 (r) © 1973 Historical Documents Co. Harcourt Photo by Maria Paraskevas.; 470 Sam Dudgeon/HRW; 471 © CORBIS. **Chapter 15:** Pages 472-473 (t) © Dave G. Houser; 473 (bl) The Art Archive/Private Collection/Dagli Orti, (br) India Office Library & Records, The British Library, (cr) Chicago Historical Society, (cl) PRC Archive; 478 (b) PRC Archive; 480 (t) The J. Paul Getty Museum, Los Angeles.; 483 (b) Library of Congress, LC-USZ62-92043; 486 (b) Kansas State Historical Society, Topeka, Kansas; 487 (t) The Granger Collection, New York; 489 (b) Missouri Historical Society, (cl) Getty Images; 491 (tr) Library of Congress/PRC Archive; 492 (t) The Museum of American Political Life, University of Hartford, West Hartford, CT.; 494 (t) Ohio Historical Society; 496 (b) Boston Athenaeum.

Unit 5 Chapter 16: Pages 506 (b) Confederate Museum, United Daughters of the Confederacy; 506-507 (t) Library of Congress, Brady Civil War Photo Collection, #LC-B8171-7514; 507 (b) Chicago Historical Society, # i26736aa, (cl) © SuperStock, (cr) © SuperStock; 518-519 (b) National Park Service; 519 (br) Library of Congress/PRC Archive; 520 (t) Library of Congress/ PRC Archive; 524 (b) © 1989, The Greenwich Workshop, Inc., Reproduced with the permission of the Greenwich Workshop, Inc., Shelton, CT; 528 (b) SuperStock; 529 (b) South Carolina Historical Society; 530 (inset) Courtesy of the Massachusetts Historical Society, (t) Library of Congress; 532 (b) © Bettmann/CORBIS; 533 (t) National Museum of American History, Smithsonian Institution, Washington, DC (ID#84-9312), (b) © REUTERS/Kai Pfaffenbach/CORBIS; 534 (t) American Antiquarian Society; 543 (t) © SuperStock; 544 The Granger Collection, New York, (b). **Chapter 17:** Pages 548 (b) © Kean Collection/Getty Images; 548-549 (t) © Paul Rocheleau; 549 (bl) © Michael Maslan Historic Photographs/CORBIS, (cr) Herbert F. Johnson Museum of Art, Cornell University, (cl) The Granger Collection, New York; 552-553 (b) National Archives (NARA); 554 (inset) Chicago Historical Society; 554-555 (t) Library of Congress; 555 (t) University of Texas at El Paso Library, Special Collections Department, Ada Tharp Photograph Collection.; 556 (b) © William Gladstone Collection; 559 (b) Library of Congress, #LC-USZ62-43958; 560 (l) Library of Congress, (r) © CORBIS; 562 (b) North Wind Picture Archives; 565 (t) Library of Congress, (b) Library of Congress; 566 (r) The Granger Collection, New York, (l) Tennessee State Museum Collection. Photography by June Dorman; 568 (t) Getty Images; 570 (t) Courtesy of The Charleston Renaissance Gallery, Robert M. Hicklin, Jr. Inc., Charleston, South Carolina; 571 © Bettmann/CORBIS.

Unit 6. Chapter 18: Pages 582-583 © James L. Amos/CORBIS; 582 (b) Courtesy Wells Fargo Bank; 583 (bl) The Art Archive / Musée d'Orsay Paris/ Dagli Orti, (cl) Southern Pacific Lines/PRC Archive, (cr) © CORBIS, (br) The Granger Collection, New York; 587 (tr) © Collection of the New-York Historical Society, [neg. 41800]; 588 (l) Denver Public Library, Western History Collection; 588-589 (r) Nebraska State Historical Society, Photograph

Unit 6. Chapter 18: Pages 582-583 © James L. Amos/CORBIS; 582 (b) Courtesy Wells Fargo Bank; 583 (bl) The Art Archive / Musée d'Orsay Paris/ Dagli Orti, (cl) Southern Pacific Lines/PRC Archive, (cr) © CORBIS, (br) The Granger Collection, New York; 587 (tr) © Collection of the New-York Historical Society, [neg. 41800]; 588 (l) Denver Public Library, Western History Collection; 588-589 (r) Nebraska State Historical Society, Photograph Collections; 589 (inset) Bob Boze Bell, True West Magazine; 590 (inset) © James L. Amos/CORBIS; 591 Union Pacific Historical Collection; 592 (t) The Granger Collection, New York; 592-593 (b) SuperStock; 595 (t) George Lane/AP/Wide World Photos; 596 (t) © Bettmann/CORBIS; 597 (t) Western History Division, National Museum of American History/Smithsonian Institution, Washington, DC; 598 The Granger Collection, New York; 599 (l) (art Reference) all LOC -no credit needed, (r); 601 (b) Western History Collections, University of Oklahoma; 602 (bl) Library of Congress, (tr) Elias Carr Papers, East Carolina Manuscript Collection, J.Y. Joyner Library, East Carolina University, Greenville, NC. Photo by Dewane Frutiger., (br) Nebraska State Historical Society; 603 (l) Culver Pictures; 604 (art reference) LOC/ PRC No credit needed; 605 (t) © CORBIS; 608 (bl) Sam Dudgeon/HRW. **Chapter 19:** Pages 610-611 (t) PRC Archive; 611 (bl) © Bettmann/CORBIS, (br) Archives Larousse, Paris, France/ Bridgeman Art Library, (c) George Meany Memorial Archives; 614-615 (b) Library of Congress; 616 (r) [neg. #40578] ©Collection of The New-York Historical Society, (l) Whittier Museum; 617 (l) Property of AT&T Archives. Printed with permission of AT&T., (r) © Hulton Archive/Getty Images; 618 (l) © CORBIS, (r) Library of Congress/PRC Archive; 619 (b) Montgomery County Historical Society; 620 (b) © CORBIS, (inset) Courtesy of the Rockefeller Archive Center; 621 (t) [#71880T] © Collection of The New-York Historical Society; 623 (l) (Art Reference) AP/Wide World Photos & © Bettmann/CORBIS, (c) (Art Reference) AP/ Wide World Photos, (r) (Art Reference) Photo courtesy Union Pacific Historical Collection; 625 (b) (Art Reference) © Bettmann/CORBIS, (t) Brown Brothers. **Chapter 20:** Pages 632-633 © Bettmann/CORBIS; 633 (cl) © Joseph Sohm, Chromosohm, Inc./CORBIS, (cr) © CORBIS, (br) © Ted Spiegel/CORBIS; 637 (t) PictureHistory/NewsCom; 638 (cr) Shades of L.A. Archives/Los Angeles Public Library, (cl) National Archives, #90-G-152-2038; 639 (tc) Col. Ernest Swanson Papers, Swenson Swedish Immigration Research Center, Augustana College, Rock Island, IL, (cl) © CORBIS; 640 (bl) Library of Congress, Arnold Genthe Collections, #LC-G403-T01-0363, (br) Library of Congress, Arnold Genthe Collections, #LC-G403-T01-0363; 643 (t) Lake County (IL) Museum /Curt Teich Postcard Archives; 644 (bc) New York State Historical Association, (br) © David Bell/CORBIS; 647 The Granger Collection, New York; 648 Jane Addams Memorial Collection (JAMC neg 227), Special Collections, University Library, University of Illinois at Chicago.

Unit 7: 656-657 Courtesy of the U.S. Naval Academy Museum. **Chapter 21:** 658-659 (t) Elizabeth Cady Stanton Trust; 659 (cl, cr) Janice L. and David J. Frent Collection of Political Americana, (b) The Granger Collection, New York; 663 (t) The Granger Collection, New York; 664 (tl) PRC Archive, (tr) PRC Archive, (cl) PRC Archive, (cr) PRC Archive, (bl) PRC Archive, (br) PRC Archive; 665 (t) © Bettmann/CORBIS; 668 (t) Barnes & Noble, Inc.; 669 (t) Library of Congress/PRC Archive; 671 (b) National Archives/PRC Archive; 673 (t) Courtesy of Steve Latham; 676 (b) © Bettmann/CORBIS; 677 (b) Library of Congress; 681 (tc) Leroy Radanovich/Yosemite Museum, (tl) © W. Perry Conway/CORBIS; 682 (br) White House Collection, copyright White House Historical Association, (bl) White House Collection, copyright White House Historical Association, (bc) White House Collection, copyright White House Historical Association; 687 (t) Library of Congress. **Chapter 22:** Pages 688 (b) © Charles Sleicher; 688-689 (t) © Bettmann/CORBIS; 689 (bl) Press Information Bureau of India, (c) Denver Public Library, Western History Collection; 694 (c) © Douglas Peebles/CORBIS; 695 National Portrait Gallery, Smithsonian Institution/Art Resource, NY; 696 Trustees of the British Museum; 698 (b) © Bettmann/CORBIS, (c) PRC Archive; 700 (tr) Library of Congress; 701 (bl) © Richard Cohen/CORBIS; 703 (br) © CORBIS; 704-705 (b) Library of Congress; 707 The Granger Collection, New York; 708 (inset) © Bettmann/CORBIS; 710 (b) © Bettmann/CORBIS, (c) © Bettmann/CORBIS; 711 (tr, b) © Bettmann/CORBIS. R0-R1 (bkgd) © Royalty-free/CORBIS; R23 –R27 White House Historical Association (White House Collection); R27 (bc) The White House, photo by Eric Draper; (br), © Pete Souza. R30 © Getty Images; R31, The Granger Collection, New York; R33 (t) © Tom Brakefi eld/Digital Vision/Getty Images.

Staff Credits. The people who contributed to ***Holt McDougal Social Studies: United States History, Beginnings to 1914*** are listed below. They represent editorial, design, intellectual property resources, production, emedia, and permissions.

Lissa B. Anderson, Charles Becker, Ed Blake, Gillian Brody, Erin Cornett, Michelle Dike, Mescal Evler, Leanna Ford, Bob Fullilove, Rhonda Haynes, Wilonda Ieans, Cathy Jenevein, Shannon Johnston, Cathy Kuhles, Debbie Lofland, Bob McClellan, Joe Melomo, Richard Metzger, Mercedes Newman, Holly Norman, Nathan O'Neal, Karl Pallmeyer, Shelly Ramos, Gene Rumann, Kay Selke, Ken Shepardson, Michele Shukers, Chris Smith, Jeannie Taylor, Joni Wackwitz, Ken Whiteside, Nadyne Wood